COMPETITION LAW

Online Resource Centre

www.oxfordtextbooks.co.uk/orc/whish6e/

This edition is accompanied by an **Online Resource Centre** offering a range of resources to support teaching and learning.

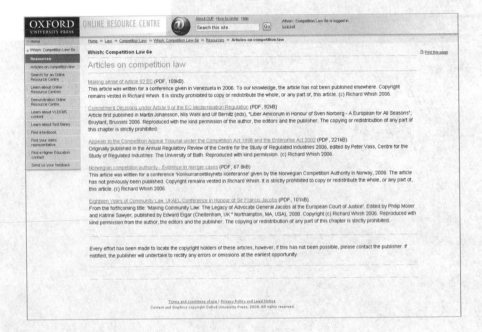

- Articles written by the author
- Chapters from the book
- Updates to the law post-publication

Please visit **www.oxfordtextbooks.co.uk/orc/whish6e/** to find the resources and enter the following details for access to the articles:

Username: whish6e

Password: new_material

COMPETITION LAW

Sixth Edition

RICHARD WHISH

BA BCL (OXON)

Professor of Law at King's College London

OXFORD
UNIVERSITY PRESS

OXFORD

UNIVERSITY PRESS

Great Clarendon Street, Oxford OX2 6DP

Oxford University Press is a department of the University of Oxford.
It furthers the University's objective of excellence in research, scholarship,
and education by publishing worldwide in

Oxford New York

Auckland Cape Town Dar es Salaam Hong Kong Karachi
Kuala Lumpur Madrid Melbourne Mexico City Nairobi
New Delhi Shanghai Taipei Toronto

With offices in

Argentina Austria Brazil Chile Czech Republic France Greece
Guatemala Hungary Italy Japan Poland Portugal Singapore
South Korea Switzerland Thailand Turkey Ukraine Vietnam

Oxford is a registered trade mark of Oxford University Press
in the UK and in certain other countries

Published in the United States
by Oxford University Press Inc., New York

British Library Cataloguing in Publication Data

Data available

Library of Congress Cataloging in Publication Data
Whish, Richard.
Competition law / Richard Whish.—6th ed.
p. cm.
Includes bibliographical references and index.
ISBN 978-0-19-928938-7
1. Restraint of trade—Great Britain.   2. Antitrust law—
Great Britain.   3. Restraint of trade—European Union countries.
4. Antitrust law—European Union countries.   I. Title.
KD2212.W48 2008
343.41'0721—dc22   2008028893

Typeset by Newgen Imaging Systems (P) Ltd., Chennai, India
Printed in Great Britain
on acid-free paper by
Ashford Colour Press Ltd, Gosport, Hampshire

ISBN 978-0-19-928938-7

1 3 5 7 9 10 8 6 4 2

Preface to the sixth edition

So much has changed since I completed the fifth edition of this book in 2003 that I have felt, at times, as though I have had to write a completely new one. I see that I made the same comment in the preface to the fourth edition in 2001: such is the rate of development of competition law over the last decade. 2004 was, of course, a hugely important year for the EU generally, with the accession of ten new Member States; and for competition law specifically, with the entry into force of the new Merger Regulation, the Modernisation Regulation, and the Technology Transfer Regulation. Each of those Regulations led to the publication of important guidelines. Indeed it has struck me forcefully, while preparing this edition, how much 'soft' competition law there now is to complement the hard provisions of the Treaty, Community Regulations, and domestic legislation: for example there is now a complete set of guidance on all aspects of merger control, both in the EU and the UK; and there are complex guidelines at both levels on matters such as the determination of the level of fines and the possibility of immunity or reduced fines for whistleblowing and cooperation. In this edition I have attempted to hack my way through the thickets of guidance in order to illuminate what appear to be the more important points, and to direct the reader to places where answers not found in my own text might be found; in the interest of keeping the word-count under control (this edition is roughly speaking the same length as the fifth) I have tended not to cite the jurisprudence on which many of the various guidelines are based, but the reader should be aware that they do contain extensive cross-references to relevant judgments of the Community courts.

The EU Modernisation Regulation led to many changes in UK law and to the revision of most of the guidance that had been issued by the OFT in the early years of the Competition Act 1998. In addition to all these changes there has been a significant amount of new case law since 2003, both at the EU level and the domestic level; and the provisions of the Enterprise Act 2002 on market investigations and mergers, which entered into force only months before the publication of the fifth edition, have now been extensively applied in practice. Only one area of competition law – the treatment of unilateral conduct under Article 82 EC – has been free from 'reform' in the last few years; however a huge amount of time and effort has been expended, in particular prompted by DG COMP's *Discussion Paper on the application of Article 82 EC to exclusionary abuses* of December 2005, in the quest to understand precisely what is meant by an abuse of a dominant position and to develop principled, administrable rules for its enforcement. At the time of writing – April 2008 – it is still not clear what the Commission intends to do next with its review of Article 82. It seems less and less likely that it will publish draft Guidelines; but it may perhaps make a statement as to the principles that it will apply when deciding which cases to investigate under Article 82. I have attempted to capture some of the debate about what, if anything, is 'wrong' with Article 82, in particular in chapter 5 of this edition; in later chapters, in particular chapters 17 and 18 on non-pricing and pricing abuses, I have attempted to explain in some detail what the current law on abusive behaviour is and to highlight some of the criticisms of it (without necessarily agreeing with them).

I was tempted to write this edition on the assumption that the Reform Treaty, agreed in Lisbon in October 2007, will be ratified and enter into force fairly soon after publication. This would have meant, for example, that references to the European Community would have been replaced by the European Union, that the Court of First Instance would be referred to as the General Court, and that the discussion of Articles 3 and 4 of the Treaty would have been deleted. However recollection of the results of the French and Dutch referenda in 2005 rejecting the Constitutional Treaty caused me to conclude that such an assumption would be unwise. Instead, chapter 2 of this edition contains a brief discussion of the implications for competition policy if the Treaty becomes law. Readers should be aware that the Lisbon Treaty will result in a renumbering of the Articles of the EC Treaty: in particular Articles 81 and 82 EC will become Articles 101 and 102 of the Treaty on the Functioning of the Union (the 'TFU').

The text of the sixth edition is written with a cut-off point of 12 March 2008, although I was able to make a few amendments subsequent to that date before the book went into production; and a few minor updates will be possible at the stage of proof-correction.

As with previous editions of this book I have had the benefit of many comments and corrections from friends in the competition policy village: these include Carole Begent, Philip Collins, Charles Dhanowa, John Fingleton, Leo Flynn, Peter Freeman, Daniel Gordon, Dorte Hoeg-Nielsen, Jonathan May, Sarah Northam, Simon Priddis, Hannah Priest, Simon Pritchard, Martin Stanley, Chris Townley, Simon Williams, and Rob Williamson. I thank all of them warmly for their generosity. I am also very grateful to OUP, who have been remarkably understanding about my pleas for more time to finish the task: ideally this edition would have been ready two years ago, but for a variety of reasons this proved not to be possible. Their patient understanding has been greatly appreciated.

There are three people to whom I owe particular gratitude. Wouter Wils of the Legal Service of the Commission has offered innumerable insightful comments on various aspects of the text, which I have been able to improve enormously as a result. I am delighted that he has become a visiting professor at King's College London; we have benefited already from several visits by him, and look forward to many more in the future. David Bailey, who was my research assistant at the time of producing the fifth edition of this book but who is now a referendaire at the Competition Appeal Tribunal and a colleague of mine at King's, has generously spent a huge amount of time reading and commenting on the text, and has helped me to improve it immeasurably. Finally I have had terrific support from my current research assistant, Dimitris Mourkas, who has worked tirelessly and uncomplainingly – even when it seemed that there would never be light at the end of the tunnel – and with great accuracy and intelligence over a long period to help me to complete the task. Thanks also are due to the Centre of European Law at King's for the financial support that made the assistance of Dimitris possible.

As for many years past, Anil Sinanan has striven hard, at all times, to distract me from the strain of competition law with the strains of Bollywood: the theme song from *Om Shanti Om* has been good for stimulation, but without compare to *Jaage Hain* from *Guru* for inspiration.

Richard Whish
Marshfield, April 2008

Contents

17 Abuse of dominance (1): non-pricing practices   672

18 Abuse of dominance (2): pricing practices   706

19 The relationship between intellectual property rights and competition law   756

Table of statutes

Table of statutory instruments

Table of EC legislation

Decisions

Table of treaties and conventions

EC Treaty (Treaty of Rome) 1957
NB *For the main provisions of Articles 81 and 82 please refer to the index and in particular*
Restrictive agreements [Art 81]; 'Legal exceptions' [Art 81(3)]; Abuse of dominant position [Art 82]

Table of competition commission reports

Table of OFT reports, decisions and publications

Table of cases

G

I

U

W

Y

Decisions of the European Court of Justice are listed below numerically. These decisions are also included in the preceding alphabetical list.

List of abbreviations

AAC	Average Avoidable Cost
Am Ec Rev	American Economic Review
ATC	Average Total Cost
AVC	Average Variable Cost
Bell J Ec	Bell Journal of Economics
CA 1980	Competition Act 1980
CA 1998	Competition Act 1998
CAT	UK Competition Appeal Tribunal
CC	UK Competition Commission
CDDA	UK Company Directors Disqualification Act 1986
CDO	Competition Disqualification Order
CFI	Court of First Instance
CML Rev	Common Market Law Review
CMLR	Common Market Law Reports
CompAR	Competition Appeal Reports
CWP	Concurrency Working Party
DBERR	Department of Business, Enterprise and Regulatory Reform
DG COMP	Directorate General of the Commission for Competition Policy
DoJ	US Department of Justice
DTI	Department of Trade and Industry
EA 2002	Enterprise Act 2002
Ec J	Economic Journal
ECJ	European Court of Justice
ECLR	European Competition Law Review
ECMR	European Community Merger Regulation
ECOSOC	Economic and Social Committee
ECN	European Competition Network
ECR	European Court Reports
ECSC	European Coal and Steel Community
EEA	European Economic Area
EFTA	European Free Trade Association
EIPR	European Intellectual Property Review
EL Rev	European Law Review
ESA	EFTA Surveillance Authority
ETSI	European Telecommunication Standards Institute
EWCA	England and Wales Court of Appeal
EWHC	England and Wales High Court
FRAND	Fair, Reasonable and Non-discriminatory
FSA	Financial Services Authority
FTC	US Federal Trade Commission
GISC	General Insurance Standards Council
HHI	Herfindahl-Hirschman Index

ICN	International Competition Network
ICPAC	International Competition Policy Advisory Committee
J Ind Ec	Journal of Industrial Economics
J L Ec	Journal of Law and Economics
J Pol Ec	Journal of Political Economics
LRIC	Long-run Incremental Cost
NCAs	National Competition Authorities
OECD	Organisation for Economic Cooperation and Development
OFCOM	Office of Communications
OFGEM	Office of Gas and Electricity Markets
OFT	Office of Fair Trading
OFTEL	Office of Telecommunications
OFWAT	Office of Water Services
OJ	Official Journal of the European Communities
ORR	Office of Rail Regulation
PACE	UK Police and Criminal Evidence Act 1984
PRS	Performing Rights Society
Qu J Ec	Quebec Journal of Economics
RAND	Reasonable and Non-discriminatory
Rev Ec Stud	Review of Economic Studies
RPI	Retail Price Index
SFO	Serious Fraud Office
SIEC	Significant Impediment to Effective Competition
SLC	Substantial Lessening of Competition
SMEs	Small and Medium-sized Enterprises
SSNIP	Small but Significant Non-transitory Increase in Price
SWIFT	Society for Worldwide International Financial Telecommunications
UKCLR	United Kingdom Competition Law Reports
UNCTAD	United Nations Conference on Trade and Development
WTO	World Trade Organisation

1

Competition policy and economics

CHAPTER CONTENTS

1. INTRODUCTION

As a general proposition competition law consists of rules that are intended to protect the process of competition in order to maximise consumer welfare. Competition law has grown at a phenomenal rate in recent years in response to the enormous changes in political thinking and economic behaviour that have taken place around the world. There are now more than 100 systems of competition law in the world; several others are in contemplation. Competition laws will be found in all continents and in all types of economies – large, small, continental, island, advanced, developing, industrial, trading, agricultural, liberal, and post-communist. In 2008 competition laws will enter into force both in China and in India, potentially bringing the benefits of competitive markets to an additional two and a half billion citizens of the world[1]. Quite apart from the geographical growth of competition law, it is now applied to many economic activities that once were regarded as natural monopolies or the preserve of the state: telecommunications, energy, transport, broadcasting and postal services, to name a few obvious examples, have become the subject of competition law scrutiny. Other sectors, such as the liberal professions, sport and the media, are also within the scope of the subject.

A central concern of competition policy is that a firm or firms with market power are able, in various ways, to harm consumer welfare, for example by reducing output, raising prices, degrading the quality of products on the market, suppressing innovation and depriving consumers of choice. These concerns cannot be expressed in a codified table of rules capable of precise application in the way, for example, that laws on taxation or

---

[1] A helpful way of accessing the competition laws of the world is through the website of the International Bar Association's Global Competition Forum, at www.globalcompetitionforum.org; other useful sources are the websites of the International Competition Network, www.internationalcompetitionnetwork.org; the OECD, www.oecd.org; and UNCTAD, www.unctad.org.

the relationship of landlord and tenant can. The analysis of competition issues invariably requires an assessment of market power, and such an assessment cannot be conducted without an understanding of the economic concepts involved. The same is true of the types of behaviour – for example cartelisation, predatory pricing, discrimination, mergers – with which competition law is concerned. Competition lawyers must understand economic concepts, and competition economists must understand legal processes. It is common practice today – and much to be welcomed – that competition lawyers attend courses on economics and vice versa. Complex cases require both legal and economic input. A (possibly apocryphal) story is that a competition lawyer once remarked at a competition law conference that, in his view, in any competition law case the lawyer should be in the driving seat; and that a competition economist readily agreed, since he always preferred to have a chauffeur. To the extent that this suggests that there is inevitably a conflict between lawyers and economists it is, hopefully, outdated: it is better to think of the two as co-pilots of an aeroplane, each understanding the contribution to be made by the other.

In the early days of competition law in the European Community the role of economics was not particularly strongly emphasised. Competition law developed in a fairly formalistic manner, and there were many more 'rules' of a legalistic nature than is the case today. The position – from the middle of the 1990s onwards – has changed dramatically, not least as a result of eminent economists being appointed to some of the most influential positions in institutions entrusted with the application of competition law[2]. An attempt will be made throughout this book to place the competition law of the EC and the UK in its economic context.

This chapter will begin with a brief description of the types of behaviour that competition law is concerned with. It will then attempt to explain why competition policy is considered to be so important to modern economies based on the market mechanism: first it will explore the theory of competition itself and then the various functions that a system of competition law might be expected to fulfil. The chapter will then introduce two key economic concepts – market definition and, more importantly, market power – that are of fundamental importance to understanding competition policy, and that are central to all competition analysis in practice. The chapter will conclude with a table of market share figures that have significance in the application of EC and UK competition law, while reminding the reader that market shares are only ever a proxy for market power and can never be determinative of market power in themselves.

2. OVERVIEW OF THE PRACTICES CONTROLLED BY COMPETITION LAW

Systems of competition law are concerned with practices that are harmful to the competitive process. In particular competition law is concerned with:

- **Anti-competitive agreements**: agreements that have as their object or effect the restriction of competition are unlawful. In particular agreements between competitors, for example to

---

[2] Obvious examples are the appointment of Mario Monti as European Commissioner for Competition, Sir Derek Morris as Chairman of the UK Competition Commission and Sir John Vickers as Chairman and Chief Executive of the UK Office of Fair Trading.

fix prices, to share markets or to restrict output – often referred to as horizontal agreements – are severely punished, and in some systems of law can even lead to the imprisonment of the individuals responsible for them. Agreements between firms at different levels of the market – known as vertical agreements – may also be struck down when they could be harmful to competition: an example would be where a supplier of goods instructs its retailers not to resell them at less than a certain price, a practice often referred to as resale price maintenance. As a general proposition, vertical agreements are much less likely to harm competition than horizontal ones.

- **Abusive behaviour**: abusive behaviour by a monopolist, or by a dominant firm with substantial market power which enables it to behave as if it were a monopolist, can also be condemned by competition law. An example would be where a dominant firm reduces its prices to less than cost in order to drive a competitor out of the market or to deter a competitor from entering the market so that it can subsequently charge higher prices, a phenomenon known as predatory pricing.

- **Mergers**: many systems of competition law enable a competition authority to investigate mergers between firms that could be harmful to the competitive process: clearly if one competitor were to acquire its main competitor the possibility exists that consumers would be deprived of choice and may have to pay higher prices. Many systems of competition law provide that certain mergers cannot be completed until the approval of the relevant competition authority has been obtained.

- **Public restrictions of competition**: the State is often responsible for restrictions and distortions of competition, for example as a result of legislative measures, regulations, licensing rules or the provision of subsidies. Some systems of competition law give a role to competition authorities to scrutinise 'public' restrictions of competition and to play a 'competition advocacy' role by commenting on, and even recommending the removal of, such restrictions.

3. THE THEORY OF COMPETITION

Competition means a struggle or contention for superiority, and in the commercial world this means a striving for the custom and business of people in the market place: the UK Competition Commission has described competition as 'a process of rivalry between firms…seeking to win customers' business over time'[3]. The ideological struggle between capitalism and communism was a dominant feature of the twentieth century. Many countries had the greatest suspicion of competitive markets and saw, instead, benefits in state planning and management of the economy. However enormous changes took place as the millennium approached, leading to widespread demonopolisation, liberalisation and privatisation. These phenomena, coupled with rapid technological changes and the opening up of international trade, unleashed unprecedentedly powerful economic forces. These changes impact upon individuals and societies in different ways, and sometimes the effects can be uncomfortable. Underlying them, however, is a growing consensus that, on the whole, markets deliver better outcomes than state planning; and central to the idea of a market is the process of competition.

---

[3] See *Merger References: Competition Commission Guidelines* (June 2003, CC 2), para 1.20 and the companion *Market Investigation References: Competition Commission Guidelines* (June 2003, CC 3), para 1.16, available at www.competition-commission.org.uk.

The important issue therefore is to determine the effect which competition can have on economic performance. To understand this one must first turn to economic theory and consider what would happen in conditions of perfect competition and compare the outcome with what happens under monopoly, recognising as one does so that a theoretical analysis of perfect competition does not adequately explain business behaviour in the 'real' world.

(A) The benefits of perfect competition

At its simplest – and it is sensible in considering competition law and policy not to lose sight of the simple propositions – the benefits of competition are lower prices, better products, wider choice and greater efficiency than would obtain under conditions of monopoly. According to neo-classical economic theory, social welfare is maximised in conditions of perfect competition[4]. For this purpose 'social welfare' is not a vague generalised concept, but instead has a more specific meaning: that allocative and productive efficiency will be achieved; the combined effect of allocative and productive efficiency is that society's wealth overall is maximised. Consumer welfare, which is specifically concerned with gains to consumers as opposed to society at large, is also maximised in perfect competition[5]. A related benefit of competition is that it will have the dynamic effect of stimulating innovation as competitors strive to produce new and better products for consumers: this is a particularly important feature of high technology markets.

(i) Allocative efficiency

Under perfect competition economic resources are allocated between different goods and services in such a way that it is not possible to make anyone better off without making someone else worse off; consumer surplus – the net gain to a consumer when buying a product – is at its largest. Goods and services are allocated between consumers according to the price they are prepared to pay, and price never rises above the marginal cost[6] of

---

[4] See Asch *Industrial Organization and Antitrust Policy* (Wiley, revised ed, 1983), ch 1; Scherer and Ross *Industrial Market Structure and Economic Performance* (Houghton Mifflin, 3rd ed, 1990), chs 1 and 2; Lipsey and Chrystal *Principles of Economics* (Oxford University Press, 11th ed, 2007), ch 7; on industrial economics and competition generally see Tirole *The Theory of Industrial Organization* (MIT Press, 1988); Hay and Morris *Industrial Economics: Theory and Evidence* (Oxford University Press, 1991); Peeperkorn and Mehta 'The Economics of Competition', ch 1 in Faull and Nikpay *The EC Law of Competition* (Oxford University Press, 2nd ed, 2007); Bishop and Walker *The Economics of EC Competition Law* (Sweet & Maxwell, 2nd ed, 2002), ch 2; Sullivan and Harrison *Understanding Antitrust and Its Economic Implications* (LexisNexis, 4th ed, 2003); Hylton *Antitrust Law: Economic Theory and Common Law Evolution* (Cambridge University Press, 2003); Motta *Competition Policy: Theory and Practice* (Cambridge University Press, 2004); Carlton and Perloff *Modern Industrial Organisation* (Addison Wesley, 4th ed, 2005); Van den Bergh and Camesasca *European Competition Law and Economics: A Comparative Perspective* (Sweet & Maxwell, 2006); on the psychology of competition from the business manager's perspective, see Porter *Competitive Strategy: Techniques for Analyzing Industries and Competitors* (Macmillan, 1998). Readers may find helpful, in coping with the terminology of the economics of competition law, the *Glossary of Industrial Organisation, Economics and Competition Law* (OECD, 1993); Black *Oxford Dictionary of Economics* (Oxford University Press, 3rd ed, 2003); and the European Commission's *Glossary of Terms used in Competition related matters*, available at www.europa.eu.int/comm/competition/general_info/glossary_en.html.

[5] See *Bishop and Walker*, paras 2.22–2.26.

[6] That is to say, the cost of producing an additional unit of output.

production (cost for this purpose including a sufficient profit margin to have encouraged the producer to invest his capital in the industry in the first place, but no more).

The achievement of allocative efficiency, as this phenomenon is known[7], can be shown analytically on the economist's model[8]. Allocative efficiency is achieved under perfect competition because the producer, assuming he is acting rationally and has a desire to maximise his profits, will expand his production for as long as it is privately profitable to do so. As long as he can earn more by producing one extra unit of whatever he produces than it costs to make it, he will presumably do so. Only when the cost of a further unit (the 'marginal cost') exceeds the price he would obtain for it (the 'marginal revenue') will he cease to expand production. Where competition is perfect, a reduction in a producer's own output cannot affect the market price and so there is no reason to limit it; the producer will therefore increase output to the point at which marginal cost and marginal revenue (the net addition to revenue of selling the last unit) coincide. This means that allocative efficiency is achieved, as consumers can obtain the amounts of goods or services they require at the price they are prepared to pay: resources are allocated precisely according to their wishes. A monopolist however can restrict output and increase his own marginal revenue as a consequence of doing so[9].

(ii) Productive efficiency

Apart from allocative efficiency many economists consider that under perfect competition goods and services will be produced at the lowest cost possible, which means that as little of society's wealth is expended in the production process as necessary. Monopolists, free from the constraints of competition, may be high cost producers. Thus competition is said to be conducive to productive efficiency. Productive efficiency is achieved because a producer is unable to sell above cost (if he did his customers would immediately desert him) and he will not of course sell below it (because then he would make no profit). If a producer were to charge above cost, other competitors would move into the market in the hope of profitable activity[10]. They would attempt to produce on a more efficient basis so that they could earn a greater profit. In the long run the tendency will be to force producers to incur the lowest cost possible in order to be able to earn any profit at all. Eventually an equilibrium will be reached where price and the average cost of producing goods necessarily coincide. This in turn means that price will never rise above cost. If on the other hand price were to fall below cost, there would be an exit of capital from the industry and, as output would therefore decrease, price would be restored to the competitive level.

(iii) Dynamic efficiency

A further benefit of competition, which cannot be proved scientifically, is that producers will constantly innovate and develop new products as part of the continual battle of striving for consumers' business. Thus competition may have the desirable dynamic effect of stimulating important technological research and development. This assumption has been questioned. Some argue that only monopolists enjoy the wealth to

---

[7] Allocative efficiency is also sometimes referred to as 'Pareto efficiency'.

[8] *Scherer and Ross*, pp 19ff; *Lipsey and Chrystal*, pp 153–155.   [9] See pp 6–7 below.

[10] As will be seen, determining what is meant by 'cost' is, in itself, often a complex matter in competition law: see ch 18, pp 707–708.

innovate and carry out expensive research[11]. Schumpeter was a champion of the notion that the motivation to innovate was the prospect of monopoly profits and that, even if existing monopolists earned such profits in the short term, outsiders would in due course enter the market and displace them[12]. A 'perennial gale of creative destruction' would be sufficient to protect the public interest, so that short-term monopoly power need not cause concern. Empirical research tends to suggest that neither monopolists nor fierce competitors have a superior track record in this respect, but it would seem clear that the assertion that only monopolists can innovate is incorrect[13].

It is important to acknowledge that in certain industries, particularly where technology is sophisticated and expensive, one firm may, for a period of time, enjoy very high market shares; however, in due course, a competitor may be able to enter that market with superior technology and replace the incumbent firm. In cases such as this, high market shares over a period of time may exaggerate the market power of the firm that is currently the market leader, but vulnerable to dynamic entry.

(B) The harmful effects of monopoly

The theoretical model just outlined suggests that in perfect competition any producer will be able to sell his product on the market only at the price which the market is prepared to bear. The producer is a price-taker, with no capacity to affect the price by his own unilateral action. The consumer is sovereign. The reason why the producer cannot affect the price is that any change in his own individual output will have only a negligible effect on the aggregate output of the market as a whole, and it is aggregate output that determines price through the 'law' of supply and demand.

Under conditions of monopoly the position is very different[14]. The monopolist is in a position to affect the market price. Since he is responsible for all the output, and since it is aggregate output that determines price through the relationship of supply to demand, he will be able either to increase price by reducing the volume of his own production or to reduce sales by increasing price: the latter occurs in the case of highly branded products which are sold at a high price, such as luxury perfumes. Furthermore, again assuming a motive to maximise profits, the monopolist will see that he will be able to earn the largest profit if he refrains from expanding his production to the maximum possible. The result will be that output is lower than would be the case under perfect competition and that therefore consumers will be deprived of goods and services that they would have been prepared to pay for at the competitive market price. There is therefore allocative inefficiency in this situation: society's resources are not distributed in the most efficient way possible. The inefficiency is accentuated by the fact that consumers, deprived of the monopolised product they would have bought, will spend their money on products which they wanted less. The economy to this extent is performing below its potential. The extent of this allocative inefficiency is sometimes referred to as the 'deadweight loss' attributable to monopoly; the loss itself is known as the 'social welfare cost of monopoly'.

The objection to monopoly does not stop there. There is also the problem that productive efficiency may be lower because the monopolist is not constrained by competitive forces to reduce costs to the lowest possible level. Instead the firm becomes 'X-inefficient'.

---

[11] Galbraith *American Capitalism: The Concept of Countervailing Power* (Houghton Mifflin, 1952).
[12] *Capitalism, Socialism and Democracy* (Taylor & Francis Books, 1976).
[13] *Scherer and Ross*, ch 17. [14] See *Scherer and Ross*, ch 2; *Lipsey and Chrystal*, ch 8.

This term, first used by Liebenstein[15], refers to a situation in which resources are used to make the right product, but less productively than they might be: management spends too much time on the golf-course, outdated industrial processes are maintained and a general slackness pervades the organisation of the firm. Furthermore the monopolist may not feel the need to innovate, because he does not experience the constant pressure to go on attracting custom by offering better, more advanced, products. Thus it has been said that the greatest benefit of being a monopolist is the quiet life he is able to enjoy. However it is important to bear in mind that inefficient managers of a business may be affected by pressures other than those of competition. In particular their position may be undermined by uninvited takeover bids on stock exchanges from investors who consider that more efficient use could be made of the firm's assets[16]. Competition may be felt in capital as well as product markets.

A final objection to the monopolist is that, since he can charge a higher price than in conditions of competition (he is a price-maker), wealth is transferred from the hapless consumer to him. This may be particularly true where he is able to discriminate between customers, charging some more than others: however it is important to recognise that price discrimination in some circumstances may be welfare-enhancing, or at least neutral in terms of social welfare[17]. While it is not the function of competition authorities themselves to determine how society's wealth should be distributed, it is manifestly a legitimate matter for Governments to take an interest in economic equity, and it may be that one of the ways in which policy is expressed on this issue is through competition law[18].

Thus runs the theory of perfect competition and monopoly. It indicates that there is much to be said for the 'invisible hand' of competition which magically and surreptitiously orders society's resources in an optimal way, as opposed to the lumbering inefficiency of monopoly. However, we must now turn from the models used in the economist's laboratory to the more haphazard ways of commercial life before rendering a final verdict on the desirability of competition.

(C) Questioning the theory of perfect competition

(i) The model of perfect competition is based on assumptions unlikely to be observed in practice

The first point which must be made about the theory of perfect competition is that it is only a theory; the conditions necessary for perfect competition are extremely unlikely to be observed in practice. Perfect competition requires that on any particular market there is a very large number of buyers and sellers, all producing identical (or 'homogeneous') products; consumers have perfect information about market conditions; resources can flow freely from one area of economic activity to another: there are no 'barriers to entry' which might prevent the emergence of new competition, and there are no 'barriers to exit' which might hinder firms wishing to leave the industry[19]. Of

[15] 'Allocative Efficiency vs X-Efficiency' (1966) 56 Am Ec Rev 392–415.
[16] See eg Hall 'Control Type and the Market for Corporate Control in Large US Corporations' (1977) 25 J Ind Ec 259–273; this issue is discussed further in ch 20, p 804.
[17] See *Lipsey and Chrystal*, pp 166–169; on abusive pricing by dominant firms generally see ch 18.
[18] See pp 19–23 below on the various functions of competition law.
[19] See pp 42–43 below for further discussion of barriers to entry and exit.

course a market structure satisfying all these conditions is unlikely, if not impossible: we are simply at this stage considering theory, and the theory is based upon a number of assumptions.

Between the polar market structures, of perfect competition on the one hand and monopoly on the other, there are many intermediate positions. Many firms sell products which are slightly differentiated from those of their rivals or command some degree of consumer loyalty, so that there will not be the homogeneity required for perfect competition. This means that an increase in price will not necessarily result in a substantial loss of business. It is unlikely that a customer will have such complete information of the market that he will immediately know that a lower price is available elsewhere for the product he requires, yet the theory of perfect competition depends on perfect information being available to consumers. This is why legislation sometimes requires that adequate information must be made available to consumers about prices, terms and conditions[20]. There are often barriers to entry and exit to and from markets; this is particularly so where a firm that enters a market incurs 'sunk costs', that is to say costs that cannot be recovered when it ceases to operate in the future.

Just as perfect competition is unlikely to be experienced in practice, monopoly in its purest form is also rare. There are few products where one firm is responsible for the entire output: normally this happens only where the state confers a monopoly, for example to deliver letters[21]. Most economic operators have some competitors; and even a true monopolist may hoist prices so high that customers cease to buy: demand is not infinitely inelastic[22]. In practice, most cases involve not a monopolist, in the etymological sense of one firm selling all the products on a particular market. Rather, competition law concerns itself with firms that have a dominant position, which in competition law terms is equated with significant market power. The economic concept of market power is key to understanding and applying competition law. A definition suggested by the UK Competition Commission is that market power 'may be described as the ability to raise price consistently and profitably above competitive levels (or where a buyer has market power, the ability to obtain prices lower than their competitive levels)'[23]. When assessing whether a firm or firms have market power it is normal to begin by defining the relevant product and geographical markets; then the competitive constraints upon firms both from within and from outside those markets are considered. These issues are considered further in section 5 of this chapter.

(ii) Other problems with the theory of perfect competition

Apart from the fact that perfect competition and pure monopoly are inherently unlikely, there are other problems with the theory itself. It depends on the notion that all businessmen are rational and that they always attempt to maximise profits, but this is not necessarily the case. Directors of a company may not think that earning large profits for their shareholders is the most important consideration they face: they may be

---

[20] This is a possible remedy under UK law following a market or merger investigation: see Enterprise Act 2002, Sch 8, paras 15–19; the CC has imposed remedies requiring the provision of clearer information to consumers on a number of occasions: see ch 11, pp 464–468.

[21] See ch 23, pp 977–978 on the 'reserved area' permitted under EC law in the postal sector.

[22] Demand is inelastic when an increase in price does not produce a large change in the level of demand; it is elastic when demand falls swiftly if prices are raised.

[23] See *Merger References: Competition Commission Guidelines* (June 2003, CC 2), para 1.24, available at www.competition-commission.org.uk.

more interested to see the size of their business empire grow or to indulge themselves in the quiet life that monopolists may enjoy[24].

A further problem with the theory of perfect competition is that its assertion that costs are kept to an absolute minimum is not necessarily correct. It is true that the private costs of the producer will be kept low, but that says nothing about the social costs or 'externalities' which arise for society at large from, for example, the air pollution that a factory causes, or the severed limbs that must be paid for because cheap machinery is used which does not include satisfactory safeguards against injury. It has been argued that competition law should not concern itself with these social costs[25], and perhaps it is true that this is a matter best left to specific legislation on issues such as conservation, the environment and health and safety at work; also it would be wrong to suppose that monopolists do not themselves produce social costs. However it is reasonable to be at least sceptical of the argument that in perfect competition the costs of society overall will inevitably be kept at a minimal level. Lastly, there is the difficulty with the theory of perfect competition that it is based on a static model of economic behaviour which may fail to account for the dynamic nature of markets and the way in which they operate over a period of time. Firms such as Xerox and IBM, that may have dominated their industries at a particular time in history, nevertheless have found themselves to be engulfed subsequently by competitive forces in the market; it remains to be seen whether the same fate might befall Microsoft. Schumpeter's gale of perennial destruction may affect even the most powerful economic operators.

Given these doubts it might be wondered whether pursuit of an unattainable ideal of perfect competition is worthwhile at all. Indeed some theoreticians have asserted that it might be positively harmful to aspire to a 'second-best solution' in which something similar to, but falling short of, perfect competition is achieved[26]. A second-best solution may actually compound allocative inefficiency and harm consumer welfare, as one distortion in the market inevitably affects performance in other parts of the economy. Where competition is imperfect and monopoly exists, attacking individual vulnerable monopolies while leaving other ones intact might simply exacerbate the pre-existing allocative inefficiency. One should guard against the assumption that tinkering with individual sectors of the economy will necessarily improve performance in the economy as a whole.

Apart from the issue of 'second-best', there is the further problem that if perfect competition cannot be attained, some alternative model is needed to explain how imperfect markets work or should work. In particular it will be necessary to decide how monopolists or dominant firms should be treated, and an adequate theory will be needed to deal with oligopoly, a common industrial phenomenon which exists where a few firms between them supply most of the products within the relevant market without any of them having a clear ascendancy over the others. Some economists would argue that, as the most common market form is oligopoly, competition policy ought to be designed around an analytical model of this phenomenon rather than the theory of perfect competition[27].

[24] *Scherer and Ross*, pp 44–46; see also *Bishop and Walker*, p 16, n 13.
[25] Bork *The Antitrust Paradox* (The Free Press, 1993), pp 114–115.
[26] Lipsey and Lancaster 'The General Theory of Second Best' (1956–57) 24 Rev Ec Stud 11–32; see also *Scherer and Ross*, pp 33–38 and *Asch*, pp 97–100.
[27] On tacit collusion, oligopoly and parallel behaviour see ch 14.

(D) Questioning competition itself

The comments just made question various aspects of the theory of perfect competition. A second line of enquiry considers whether competition is so obviously beneficial anyway. There are some arguments that suggest that competition may not yield the best outcome for society.

(i) Economies of scale and scope and natural monopolies

The first relates to economies of scale, scope and the phenomenon of 'natural monopoly'[28]. In some industries products can be produced very cheaply and the market for them may be large, so that there is no difficulty in each producer expanding output to the point at which marginal cost and marginal revenue intersect and disposing of the entire amount. In reality this is often not the case. In some markets there may be significant economies of scale, meaning that the average cost per unit of output decreases with the increase in the scale of the outputs produced; economies of scope occur where it is cheaper to produce two products together than to produce them separately. In some markets a profit can be made only by a firm supplying at least one quarter or one third of total output; it may even be that the 'minimum efficient scale' of operation is achieved only by a firm with a market share exceeding 50 per cent, so that monopoly may be seen to be a natural market condition[29]. Similarly, economies of scope may be essential to profitable behaviour. Natural monopoly means a situation in which any amount of output is always produced more cheaply by a single firm: the cost of production is lowest when one firm serves the entire market. Natural monopoly is an economic phenomenon, to be contrasted with statutory monopoly, where the right to exclude rivals from the market is derived from law. Where natural monopoly exists, it is inappropriate to attempt to achieve a level of competition which would destroy the efficiency that this entails. This problem may be exacerbated where the 'natural monopolist' is also required to perform a 'universal service obligation', such as the daily delivery of letters to all postal addresses at a uniform price; performance of such an obligation may not be profitable in normal market conditions, so that the state may confer a statutory monopoly on the undertaking entrusted with the task in question. The lawfulness under EC and UK competition law of 'special or exclusive rights' conferred by the state is one of the more complex issues to be considered in this book[30].

Where the minimum efficient scale is very large in relation to total output, a separate question arises as to how that industry can be made to operate in a way that is beneficial to society as a whole. It may be that public ownership is a solution, or that a system of regulation should be introduced while leaving the producer or producers in the private sector[31]. A further possibility is that firms should be allowed to bid for a franchise to run the industry in question for a set period of time, at the end of which there will be a further round of bidding. In other words there will be periodic competition to run the industry, although no actual competition within it during the period of the

---

[28] *Lipsey and Chrystal*, pp 291–293; *Scherer and Ross*, pp 97–141.
[29] See Schmalensee *The Control of Natural Monopolies* (Lexington, 1979); Sharkey *The Theory of Natural Monopoly* (Cambridge University Press, 1982).
[30] See ch 6, pp 220–242 and ch 9, p 345.   [31] See ch 23, pp 970–972.

franchise[32]: this happens in the UK, for example, when companies bid for television or rail franchises or to run the national lottery. The 100 per cent share of the market that a firm might have after it has won the bid does not accurately reflect its market power if it was subject to effective competition when making its bid[33].

(ii) Network effects and two-sided markets[34]

(A) Network effects Certain markets are characterised by 'network effects'. A network effect arises where the value of a product increases with the number of other customers consuming the same product. A simple example of a direct network effect is a telecommunications network. Suppose that Telcom has one hundred subscribers to its network; suppose further that it is impossible for the users of Telcom's network to communicate with subscribers to competing networks. If a new consumer subscribes to the Telcom system the 100 original subscribers can now make contact with an additional person, without having incurred any additional cost themselves: for this reason the benefit to those subscribers is sometimes described as a network externality. In the same way users of a particular computer software system will benefit as more people use the same system, since it becomes possible to share documents, images and music with more people. Where this occurs computer programmers will increasingly write new software that is compatible with the system, so that the system becomes even more valuable to the consumers that use it.

(B) Two-sided markets[35] In the simple example given above of subscribers joining a telecommunications network, the value of the network increased because of the number of consumers joining it: the network effect was a result of an increase in demand. However there are some markets, often referred to as 'two-sided markets', where two or more groups of customers are catered for, and where a network effect arises as more consumers join one or the other side of the market. A simple example is a newspaper. A newspaper publisher sells advertising space; it also supplies newspapers to citizens, sometimes at a cover price and sometimes free of charge. The publisher's ability to sell advertising space increases according to the number of citizens expected to read the newspaper. Exactly the same is true of commercial television stations: advertising slots during the soccer World Cup final will be hugely expensive because of the opportunity that exists to advertise products to a large number of people. The same phenomenon can be seen at play in the case of credit cards: the more merchants that accept a particular

---

[32] See Demsetz 'Why Regulate Utilities?' (1968) 11 J L Ec 55–66; for criticism of the idea of franchise bidding see Williamson 'Franchise Bidding for Natural Monopolies in General and with respect to CATV' (1976) 7 Bell J Ec 73–104.

[33] For further discussion of so-called 'bidding markets' see p 40 below.

[34] See OFT Economic Discussion Paper 3 (OFT 377) *Innovation and Competition Policy* (Charles River Associates, March 2002), paras 1.6–1.8; *Merger References: Competition Commission Guidelines* (June 2003, CC 2), para 3.13; see further Salop and Romaine 'Preserving Monopoly: Economic Analysis, Legal Standards, and Microsoft' (1999) 7 George Mason Law Review 617; Cass and Hylton 'Preserving Competition: Economic Analysis, Legal Standards and Microsoft' (1999) 8 George Mason Law Review 1; Posner 'Antitrust in the New Economy' (2001) 68 Antitrust Law Journal 925; and the contributions at a symposium on two-sided markets, specifically concerned with payment cards, at (2006) 73 Antitrust Law Journal 571ff; see also the series of essays in (2007) 3(1) Competition Policy International 147ff.

[35] For discussion of two-sided markets see the series of essays in (2007) 3(1) Competition Policy International 147ff.

card, the more consumers will use that card; and the more consumers that use that card, the more merchants will accept it.

(C) Network effects and competition policy Network effects may have positive effects on competition, since consumers become better off as a product becomes more popular. The increased utility of a telecommunications network is of value both to the operator and to the subscribers. In the two-sided case of a successful credit card system, merchants, the card issuer and consumers benefit. However network effects also give rise to the possibility of one firm dominating a market, in particular because there may be 'tipping effects' where all the customers in a particular market decide to opt for the product of one firm or for one particular technology. Many years ago, when video cassettes and video recorders were first introduced to the market, there were two competing technologies, Betamax and VHS; many people considered that the Betamax technology was superior, and yet the market tipped in favour of VHS. In the same way the market can be seen to have tipped in favour of Microsoft's Windows operating system[36]. If tipping does take place, or if it is a likely consequence of a merger, a question for competition policy is to determine how the issue should be addressed. Various possibilities exist, including remedies in merger cases[37] and the possibility that third parties should be allowed to have access to the product of the successful firm in whose favour the tipping has occurred: however, mandatory access to the successful products of innovative firms risks chilling the investment that created the product in the first place[38].

A specific point about two-sided markets is that pricing practices that, at first sight, appear to be anti-competitive might have an objective justification in their specific context. For example in the case of free-to-air television the broadcaster, in one sense, could be seen to be acting in a predatory manner by supplying a service at below the cost of production, which would be abusive if it was in a dominant position; but in a two-sided market this analysis may be wrong if the free-to-air broadcasting is paid for by the sale of advertising; the same is true of the 'free' newspapers that are now so prevalent, for example, in London and other major cities.

(iii) Particular sectors

As well as the complexity of introducing competition into markets that might be regarded as natural monopolies, it is possible that social or political value-judgments may lead to the conclusion that competition is inappropriate in particular economic sectors. Agriculture is an obvious example. Legislatures have tended to the view that agriculture possesses special features entitling it to protection from the potentially ruthless effects of the competitive system. An obvious illustration of this is the Common Agricultural Policy of the EC[39]. Similarly it might be thought inappropriate (or politically impossible) to expose the labour market to the full discipline of the competitive

[36] The Commission discussed tipping effects in *Microsoft*, Commission decision of 24 March 2004, paras 448–472.

[37] See eg Case M 1069 *WorldCom/MCI* , decision of 8 July 1998; the Commission subsequently prohibited the merger in Case M 1741 *MCIWorldCom/Sprint*, decision of 28 June 2000 where it had network concerns, but this decision was annulled on appeal, Case T-310/00 *MCI Inc v Commission* [2004] ECR II-3253, [2004] 5 CMLR 1274.

[38] See in particular ch 17, pp 691–699 on the so-called 'essential facilities' doctrine.

[39] On the (non-)application of EC competition law to the agricultural sector see ch 23, pp 957–961; leading texts on the common agricultural policy are cited at p 957.

process; this point is demonstrated by the judgment of the European Court of Justice in *Albany International BV v Stichting Begrijfspensioenfonds Textielindustrie*[40] which concluded that collective bargaining between organisations representing employers and employees is outside Article 81 EC. Systems of competition law have often shown a tendency to refrain from insisting that the liberal professions should have to sully their hands with anything as offensive as price competition or advertising, although the European Commission has taken a stricter line in recent years[41]; however the ECJ has held that restrictive rules that are proportionate and ancillary to a regulatory system that protects a legitimate public interest fall outside Article 81(1) EC[42]. The European Court of Justice in 2006 established that the competition rules are capable of application to sport[43], overturning a judgment of the CFI to the contrary[44].

(iv) Beneficial restrictions of competition

Another line of argument is that in some circumstances restrictions of competition can have beneficial results. This may manifest itself in various ways. One example is the suggestion that firms which are forced to pare costs to the minimum because of the pressures of competition will skimp on safety checks. This argument is particularly pertinent in the transport sector, where fears are sometimes expressed that safety considerations may be subordinated to the profit motive: an example would be where airlines compete fiercely on price. It may be that specific safety legislation can be used to overcome this anxiety; and monopolists seeking to enlarge their profits may show the same disregard for safety considerations as competing firms, a charge levelled against Railtrack (since replaced by Network Rail) in the UK following a series of serious rail accidents in the late 1990s and 2000. Safety was an important issue in the debate in the UK as to whether National Traffic Control Services, responsible for the control of air navigation, should be privatised, provision for which was made in sections 41 to 65 of the Transport Act 2000.

Another possibly beneficial restriction of competition could arise where two or more firms, by acting in concert and restricting competition between themselves, are able to develop new products or to produce goods or services on a more efficient scale: the benefit to the public at large may be considerable; both Article 81(3) EC and section 9 of the UK Competition Act 1998 recognise that, in some cases, agreements may be tolerated which, though restrictive of competition, produce beneficial effects[45]. A further example of the same point is that a producer might impose restrictions on his distributors in order to ensure that they promote his products in the most effective way possible; although this might diminish competition in his own goods (intra-brand competition), the net effect may be to enhance the competitive edge of them as against those produced by his competitors (inter-brand competition)[46]. These examples suggest that a blanket prohibition of agreements that restrict competition would deprive the public of substantial advantages.

---

[40] Case C-67/96 [1999] ECR I-5751, [2000] 4 CMLR 446; see ch 3, p 90.   [41] See ch 3, pp 89–90.

[42] Case C-309/99 *Wouters v Algemene Raad van de Nederlandse Orde van Advocaten* [2002] ECR I-1577, [2002] 4 CMLR 913: see ch 3, pp 126–130.

[43] Case C-519/04 P *David Meca-Medina v Commission* [2006] ECR I-6991, [2006] 5 CMLR 1023; see ch 3, pp 130–131.

[44] Case T-313/02 *David Meca-Medina v Commission* [2004] ECR II-3291, [2004] 3 CMLR 1314.

[45] On horizontal cooperation agreements generally see ch 15.

[46] On vertical agreements generally see ch 16.

(v) Ethical and other objections

A more fundamental objection to competition might be that it is considered in some sense to be inherently objectionable. The very notion of a process of rivalry whereby firms strive for superiority may be considered ethically unsound. One argument (now largely discredited) is that 'cut-throat' competition means that firms are forced to charge ever lower prices until in the end the vicious cycle leads them to charge below marginal cost in order to keep custom at all; the inevitable effect of this will be insolvency. The prevailing attitude in much of UK industry during the first half of the twentieth century was that competition was 'harmful' and even destructive and it was this entrenched feeling that led to the adoption of a pragmatic and non-doctrinaire system of control in 1948[47]. It was not until the Competition Act 1998 – 50 years later – that the UK finally adopted legislation that gave the Office of Fair Trading effective powers to unearth and penalise pernicious cartels[48]. Economically the argument that competition is a cut-throat business that leads to insolvency is implausible, but industrialists do use it.

Another argument is that competition should be arrested where industries enter cyclical recessions – or even long-term decline – in order that they do not disappear altogether[49]. Again competition might be thought undesirable because of its wasteful effects. The consumer may be incapable of purchasing a tin of baked beans in one supermarket because of the agonising fear that at the other end of town a competitor is offering them more cheaply. He will waste his time (a social cost) and money 'shopping around': such an argument once commended itself to the (now abolished) Restrictive Practices Court in the UK[50]. Meanwhile competitors will be wasting their own money by paying advertising agencies to think up more expensive and elaborate campaigns to promote their products[51]. A commentator on the petrochemicals industry has argued that conventional competition leads to chronic waste in which everyone loses, and that attention should be focused not on the supposed evils of cartelisation but rather on the freedom for firms to *exit* from an industry if and when they see the opportunity to operate more profitably on another market[52].

(vi) Industrial policy

One practical objection to promoting competition is that it may be considered to be inimical to the general thrust of industrial policy. Admittedly the suggestion has been made that, in conditions of perfect competition, firms will innovate in order to keep or attract new custom. However Governments often encourage firms to collaborate where this would lead to economies of scale or to more effective research and development; and they may adopt a policy of promoting 'national champions' which will be effective as competitors in international markets[53]. There are certainly circumstances in which the innovator, the entrepreneur and the risk-taker may require some immunity

---

[47] See Allen *Monopoly and Restrictive Practices* (George Allen & Unwin, 1968).

[48] On these powers see ch 10, pp 385–393 and 400–404.

[49] *Scherer and Ross*, pp 294–306; see also ch 15, pp 600–601 on restructuring agreements.

[50] See *Re Black Bolt and Nut Association of Great Britain's Agreement* (1960) LR 2 RP 50, [1960] 3 All ER 122.

[51] *Scherer and Ross*, pp 404–407.

[52] Bower *When Markets Quake: The Management Challenge of Restructuring Industry* (Harvard Business School, 1986).

[53] This can be an important issue in some merger cases: see ch 20, p 803.

from competition if they are to indulge in expensive technological projects. This is recognised in the law of intellectual property rights which provides an incentive to firms to innovate by preventing the appropriation of commercial ideas which they have developed[54]. A patentee in the UK is given the exclusive right for 20 years to exploit the subject-matter of his patent[55]. A similar incentive and/or reward is given to the owners of copyright, registered designs and analogous rights[56]. This is a recognition of the fact that in some circumstances competition suppresses innovation and an indication of the vacuity of relentlessly pursuing the ideal of perfect competition. The relationship between competition law and the law of intellectual property is a fascinating one, in particular the apparent tension between on the one hand the desire to keep markets open and free from monopoly and on the other the need to encourage innovation precisely by granting monopoly rights; in fact, however, this tension is more apparent than real[57]. These issues will be considered in chapter 19.

(vii) Competitions are there to be won

The last point which should be made in this brief survey of objections to competition is that the competitive process contains an inevitable paradox. Some competitors win. By being the most innovative, the most responsive to customers' wishes, and by producing goods or services in the most efficient way possible, one firm may succeed in seeing off its rivals. It would be strange, and indeed harmful, if that firm could then be condemned for being a monopolist. As Judge Learned Hand opined in *US v Aluminum Co of America*[58]:

[A] single producer may be the survivor out of a group of active companies, merely by virtue of his superior skill, foresight and industry...The successful competitor, having been urged to compete, must not be turned upon when he wins.

(E) Empirical evidence

A separate issue is whether there is any empirical evidence to support, or indeed to contradict, the case for competition and, if so, what the evidence can tell us. It is notoriously difficult to measure such things as allocative efficiency or the extent to which innovation is attributable to the pressure of competition upon individual firms. Economists have often suggested that there is some direct causal relationship between industrial structure, the conduct of firms on the market and the quality of their economic performance[59]: this is often referred to as the 'structure-conduct-performance paradigm'. A monopolistic structure can be expected to lead to a restriction of output and a loss of economic efficiency: a natural consequence of this view would be that competition law should be watchful for any acts or omissions that could be harmful to the structure of the market, and in particular for conduct that could foreclose access to it and mergers that lead to fewer players. Others argue that this schematic presentation is too simplistic. In particular it is said to be unsound because it is uni-directional and

---

[54] See generally Cornish and Llewellyn *Intellectual Property Law* (Sweet & Maxwell, 6th ed, 2007); see also speech by Vickers 'Competition Policy and Innovation' 27 June 2001, available at www.oft.gov.uk.
[55] Patents Act 1977, s 25.   [56] Copyright, Designs and Patents Act 1988, ss 12–15, 191, 216, 269.
[57] See ch 19, pp 758–759.   [58] 148 F 2d 416 (2nd Cir 1945).
[59] This schematic model of industrial behaviour was first suggested by Mason 'Price and Production Policies of Large-Scale Enterprise' (1939) 29 Am Ec Rev Supplement 61–74; see *Scherer and Ross*, chs 3 and 4.

fails to indicate the extent to which performance itself can influence structure and conduct[60]. Good performance, for example, may in itself affect structure by attracting new entrants into an industry.

Other economists have attempted to measure the extent to which monopoly results in allocative inefficiency and leads to a deadweight loss to society[61]. There are of course formidable difficulties associated with this type of exercise, and many of the studies that have been published have been criticised for their methodology. Scherer and Ross devote a chapter of their book to this problem[62] and point out that there has been a dramatic expansion in the range and intensity of empirical research into industrial organisation in recent years. Their conclusion is that, despite the theoretical problems of such research, important relationships do exist between market structure and performance, and that the research should continue[63]. These issues are considered further in an Economic Discussion Paper, published by the OFT in June 2002, which contains literature reviews looking in turn at the deadweight welfare loss attributable to monopoly, at competition and efficiency and at price fixing and cartels[64]. More prosaically it might be added that, even if there are difficulties in measuring scientifically the harmful effects of monopoly in liberalised market economies, the economic performance of the Soviet Union and its neighbours in the second half of the twentieth century suggests that the effects of state planning and monopoly can be pernicious.

(F) Workable competition

The discussion so far has presented a model of perfect competition, but has acknowledged that it is based upon a set of assumptions that are unlikely to be observed in practice; it has also been pointed out that there are some arguments that can be made against competition, although some of them are less convincing than others. If perfect competition is unattainable, the question arises whether there is an alternative economic model to which it would be reasonable to aspire. Some economists have been prepared to settle for a more prosaic theory of 'workable competition'[65]. They recognise the limitations of the theory of perfect competition, but nonetheless consider that it is worthwhile seeking the best competitive arrangement that is practically attainable. Quite what workable competition should consist of has caused theoretical difficulties[66]; however a workably competitive structure might be expected to have a beneficial effect on conduct and performance, and therefore be worth striving for and maintaining.

[60]   Phillips 'Structure, Conduct and Performance – and Performance, Conduct and Structure' in Markham and Papanek (eds) *Industrial Organization and Economic Development* (1970); Sutton *Sunk Costs and Market Structure: Price Competition, Advertising and the Evolution of Concentration* (MIT Press, 1991).

[61]   Weiss 'Concentration-Profit Relationship' in *Industrial Concentration: the New Learning* (eds Goldschmid and others, 1974); Gribbin *Postwar Revival of Competition as Industrial Policy*; Cowling and Mueller 'The Social Costs of Monopoly Power' (1978) 88 Ec J 724–748, criticised by Littlechild at (1981) 91 Ec J 348–363.

[62]   *Industrial Market Structure and Economic Performance*, ch 11.   [63]   Ibid, p 447.

[64]   OFT Economic Discussion Paper 4 (OFT 386) *The development of targets for consumer savings arising from competition policy* (Davies and Majumdar, June 2002), available at www.oft.gov.uk.

[65]   Clark 'Toward a Concept of Workable Competition' (1940) 30 Am Ec Rev 241–256; Sosnick 'A Critique of Concepts of Workable Competition' (1958) 72 Qu J Ec 380–423 (a general review of the literature); see also *Scherer and Ross* pp 52–55.

[66]   See Asch *Industrial Organization and Antitrust Policy* (Wiley, revised ed, 1983), pp 100–104.

(G) Contestable markets

In recent years some economists have advanced a theory of 'contestable markets' upon which competition law might be based[67]. According to this theory, firms will be forced to ensure an optimal allocation of resources provided that the market on which they operate is 'contestable', that is to say provided that it is possible for firms to enter the market without incurring sunk costs[68] and to leave it without loss. While this theory aims to have general applicability, it has been particularly significant in discussion of the deregulation of industries in the US. In a perfectly contestable market, entry into an industry is free and exit is costless. The emphasis on exit is important as firms should be able to leave an industry without incurring a loss if and when opportunities to profit within it disappear. A perfectly *contestable* market need not be perfectly *competitive*: perfect competition requires an infinite number of sellers on a market; in a perfectly contestable market an economically efficient outcome can be achieved even where there are only a few competitors, since there is always the possibility of 'hit and run' entry into the market. Even an industry in which only one or two firms are operating may be perfectly contestable where there are no impediments to entry or exit, so that intervention by the competition authorities is unnecessary. The theory shifts the focus of competition policy, as it is more sanguine about markets on which few firms operate than the 'traditional' model of perfect competition; having said this, it is questionable whether the theory of contestability really adds a great deal to traditional thinking on industrial economics or whether it simply involves a difference of emphasis.

As far as the specific issue of deregulation is concerned, the theory of contestability suggests, for example, that the existence within the air transport sector of only a few airlines need not have adverse economic effects provided that the conditions for entry and exit to and from the market are not disadvantageous. It is not clear how significant the theory of contestable markets is likely to be in the formulation of EC and UK competition policy, other than in the particular area of deregulation. In the UK Competition Commission's investigation of *CHC Helicopter Corpn/Helicopter Services Group ASA*[69] the Commission cleared a merger that would create a duopoly in helicopter services where the market was found to be contestable. The European Commission was less impressed by contestable market theory in *Far East Trade Tariff Charges and Surcharges Agreement (FETTCSA)*[70].

(H) Effective competition

On some occasions, legal provisions and regulators use the expression 'effective competition'. For example it is found in Article 2(3) of the European Community Merger Regulation ('the ECMR'), as part of the test for determining when a merger is incompatible with the common market: 'effective competition' must not be significantly impeded. In the UK the Office of Telecommunications (now the Office of Communications) published

---

[67] See Baumol, Panzar and Willig *Contestable Markets and the Theory of Industry Structure* (Harcourt Brace Jovanovich, revised ed, 1988); Bailey 'Contestability and the Design of Regulatory and Antitrust Policy' (1981) 71 Am Ec Rev 178–183.

[68] See p 8 above.

[69] Cm 4556 (2000); for comment see Oldale 'Contestability: The Competition Commission Decision on North Sea Helicopter Services' (2000) 21 ECLR 345.

[70] OJ [2000] L 268/1, [2000] 5 CMLR 1011, para 119.

a strategy statement in January 2000, one of the objectives of which would be to achieve 'effective competition in all main UK telecoms markets'[71]. The UK Utilities Act 2000 provides that the Gas and Electricity Markets Authority should have, as one of its tasks, the promotion of effective competition in the gas and electricity sectors[72]. The idea of effective competition does not appear to be the product of any particular theory or model of competition – perfect, workable, contestable or any other. Indeed, given the number of theories and assumptions already discussed in this chapter, and the many others not discussed, the idea of effective competition, free from theoretical baggage, may have much to commend it. Effective competition does connote the idea, however, that firms should be subject to a reasonable degree of competitive constraint, from actual and potential competitors and from customers, and that the role of a competition authority is to see that such constraints are present on the market[73].

(I) Conclusion

What can perhaps be concluded at the end of this discussion is that, despite the range of different theories and the difficulties associated with them, competition does possess sufficient properties to lead to a strong policy choice in its favour. Competitive markets seem, on the whole, to deliver better outcomes than monopolistic ones, and there are demonstrable benefits for consumers[74]. The UK Government, in its White Paper *Productivity and Enterprise: A World Class Competition Regime*[75], stated that:

Vigorous competition between firms is the lifeblood of strong and effective markets. Competition helps consumers get a good deal. It encourages firms to innovate by reducing slack, putting downward pressure on costs and providing incentives for the efficient organisation of production[76].

This is why competition policy has been so widely embraced in recent years; there is probably a greater global consensus on the desirability of competition and free markets today than at any time in the history of human economic behaviour. In particular monopoly does seem to lead to a restriction in output and higher prices; there is a greater incentive to achieve productive efficiency in a competitive market; the suggestion that only monopolists can innovate is unsound; and competition provides the consumer with a greater degree of choice. Furthermore, in markets such as electronic communications, energy and transport competition has been introduced where once there was little, if any, and this seems to have produced significant benefits for consumers.

   It may be helpful to summarise the benefits that are expected to be derived from effective competition:

* Competition promotes allocative and productive efficiency
* Competition leads to lower prices for consumers
* Competition means that firms will be innovative in order to win business: innovation and dynamic efficiency mean that there will be better products available on the market
* Where there is effective competition, consumers have a choice as to the products that they buy.

   [71] *OFTEL strategy statement: Achieving the best deal for telecoms consumers*, January 2000, available at www.oftel.gov.uk/publications/about_oftel/strat100.htm.
   [72] Utilities Act 2000, ss 9 and 13, amending the Gas Act 1986 and the Electricity Act 1989 respectively.
   [73] For further discussion see *Bishop and Walker*, ch 2, 'Effective Competition'.
   [74] See speech by Vickers 'Competition is for Consumers' 21 February 2002, available at www.oft.gov.uk.
   [75] Cm 5233 (2001).   [76] Ibid, para 1.1.

4. THE FUNCTION OF COMPETITION LAW

(A) Goals of competition law

In recent years many competition authorities have stressed the central importance of consumer welfare when applying competition law. A very clear statement to this effect can be found in a speech of the current European Commissioner for competition policy, Neelie Kroes, given in London in October 2005:

Consumer welfare is now well established as the standard the Commission applies when assessing mergers and infringements of the Treaty rules on cartels and monopolies. Our aim is simple: to protect competition in the market as a means of enhancing consumer welfare and ensuring an efficient allocation of resources.[77]

However it would be reasonable to point out that, although the consumer welfare standard is currently in the ascendancy, many different policy objectives have been pursued in the name of competition law over the years; some of these were not rooted in notions of consumer welfare in the technical sense at all, and some were plainly inimical to the pursuit of allocative and productive efficiency. The result has sometimes been inconsistency and contradiction, but it is as well for the reader to be aware of this before coming to the law itself. Historically there has not been one single, unifying, policy that bound the development of EC and UK law together. In particular competition policy does not exist in a vacuum: it is an expression of the current values and aims of society and is as susceptible to change as political thinking generally. Because views and insights shift over a period of time, competition law is infused with tension. Different systems of competition law reflect different concerns, an important point when comparing the laws of the US, the EC and the UK[78]. As already noted, competition law has now been adopted in at least 100 countries, whose economies and economic development may be very different from one another. It is impossible to suppose that each system will have identical concerns[79]. The debate at the time of the negotiation of the Lisbon Treaty of 2007 demonstrated that some Member States are less enthusiastic about the process of competition than others[80].

(i) Consumer protection

Several different objectives other than the maximisation of consumer welfare in the technical sense can be ascribed to competition law. The first is that its essential purpose should be to protect the interests of consumers, not by protecting the competitive process itself, but by taking direct action against offending undertakings, for example by requiring dominant firms to reduce their prices. It is of course correct in principle that competition law should be regarded as having a 'consumer protection' function: ultimately the process of competition itself is intended to deliver benefits to consumers. However the possibility exists that competition law might be invoked in a more 'populist' manner; this appeared to happen in the UK in 1998 and 1999, at a time when the

---

[77] SPEECH/05/512 of 15 September 2005, available at www.ec/europa/eu.

[78] On the differences between the policies of competition law in the US and the EC see eg Jebsen and Stevens 'Assumptions, Goals and Dominant Undertakings; the Regulation of Competition under Article [82] of the European Union' (1996) 64 Antitrust Law Journal 443.

[79] See Fox 'The Kaleidoscope of Antitrust and its Significance in the World Economy: Respecting Differences' [2001] Fordham Corporate Law Institute (ed Hawk), 597.

[80] See ch 2, pp 50–51.

Government wished to be seen to be doing something about so-called 'rip-off Britain', where Ministers suggested that excessive prices were being charged by both monopolists and non-monopolists[81]. A problem with using competition law to assume direct control over prices, however, is that competition authorities are ill-placed to determine what price a competitive market would set for particular goods or services, and indeed by fixing a price they may further distort the competitive fabric of the market. The UK Competition Commission declined to recommend price control following its report in 2000 on *Supermarkets*[82] where it found that, in general, the market was working well for consumers and that such intervention would be disproportionate and unduly regulatory. Populist measures taken to have electoral appeal may ultimately be more harmful than the high prices themselves.

Similarly the consumer may be harmed – or at least consider himself to be harmed – where a producer insists that all his goods should be sold by dealers at maintained prices, or that dealers should provide a combined package of goods plus after-sales service. Here the consumer's choice is restricted by the producer's decision. Competition law may proscribe resale price maintenance or tie-in sales for this reason, although there are those who argue that this intervention is undesirable: the producer is restricting intra-brand competition, but inter-brand competition may be enhanced as a result[83]. The obsession with protecting the consumer can also be considered short-sighted since, in the longer run, the producer might choose to abandon the market altogether rather than comply with an unreasonable competition law; short-term benefits will then be outweighed by long-term harm to consumer welfare[84].

(ii) Redistribution

A second possible objective of competition law might be the dispersal of economic power and the redistribution of wealth: the promotion of economic equity rather than economic efficiency. Aggregations of resources in the hands of monopolists, multinational corporations or conglomerates could be considered a threat to the very notion of democracy, individual freedom of choice and economic opportunity. This argument was influential in the US for many years at a time when there was a fundamental mistrust of big business. President Roosevelt warned Congress in 1938 that:

The liberty of a democracy is not safe if the people tolerate the growth of a private power to a point where it becomes stronger than the democratic state itself...Among us today a concentration of private power without equal in history is growing[85].

It was under the US antitrust laws that the world's largest corporation at the time, AT&T, was dismembered. Some critics of the action brought by the Department of Justice against Microsoft were concerned that it amounted to an attack on a spectacularly successful business[86], while others welcomed the attempt to restrain its undoubted economic muscle[87].

---

[81] See ch 18, pp 716–718 on the control of exploitative pricing practices under UK law.

[82] Cm 4842 (2000).   [83] See in particular ch 16 on vertical agreements.

[84] This is one of Bork's most pressing arguments in The Antitrust Paradox (The Free Press, 1993).

[85] 83 Cong Rec 5992 (1938).

[86] For a highly critical view of the Microsoft case generally see McKenzie *Antitrust on Trial: How the Microsoft Case Is Reframing the Rules of Competition* (Perseus Publishing, 2nd ed, 2001).

[87] See 'Now Bust Microsoft's Trust' *The Economist* 13 November 1999; 'Bill Rockefeller?' *The Economist* 29 April 2000.

(iii) Protecting competitors

Linked to the argument that competition law should be concerned with redistribution is the view that competition law should be applied in such a way as to protect small firms against more powerful rivals: the competition authorities should hold the ring and ensure that the 'small guy' is given a fair chance to succeed. To put the point another way, there are some who consider that competition law should be concerned with competitors as well as the process of competition. This idea has at times had a strong appeal in the US, in particular during the period when Chief Justice Warren led the Supreme Court. However it has to be appreciated that the arrest of the Darwinian struggle, in which the most efficient succeed and the weak disappear, for the purpose of protecting small business can run directly counter to the idea of consumer welfare in the technical economic sense. It may be that competition law is used to preserve the inefficient and to stunt the performance of the efficient. In the US the 'Chicago School' of economists has been particularly scathing of the 'uncritical sentimentality' in favour of the small competitor, and in the 1980s, in particular, US law developed in a noticeably less sentimental way[88]. To the Chicago School, the essential question in an antitrust case should be whether the conduct under investigation could lead to consumers paying higher prices, and whether those prices could be sustained against the forces of competition; antitrust intervention to protect competitors from their more efficient rivals is harmful to social and consumer welfare. Even firms with high market shares are subject to competitive constraints provided that barriers to entry and exit are low, so that intervention on the part of the regulator is usually uncalled for.

There seems to be little doubt that EC competition law has, in some cases, been applied with competitors in mind: this is particularly noticeable in some decisions under Article 82, and some commentators have traced this phenomenon back to the influence of the so-called 'Freiburg School' of ordoliberalism[89]. Scholars of the Freiburg School, which originated in Germany in the 1930s, saw the free market as a necessary ingredient in a liberal economy, but not as sufficient in itself. The problems of Weimar and Nazi Germany were attributable in part to the inability of the legal system to control and, if necessary, to disperse private economic power. An economic constitution was necessary to constrain the economic power of firms, but without giving Government unrestrained control over their behaviour: public power could be just as pernicious as private. Legal rules could be put in place which would achieve both of these aims. It is not surprising that the beneficiaries of such thinking would be small and medium-sized firms, the very opposite of the monopolists and cartels feared by the members of the Freiburg School. There is no doubt that ordoliberal thinking had a direct influence on the leading figures involved in the establishment of the three European Communities in the 1950s[90]. This may have led to decisions and judgments in which the

[88] See Fox 'The New American Competition Policy – from Anti-Trust to Pro-Efficiency' (1981) 2 ECLR 439 where the author traces the change in the policy of the Supreme Court from judgments such as *Brown Shoe Co v US* 370 US 294 (1962) to the position in *Continental TV Inc v GTE Sylvania Inc* 433 US 36 (1977); Fox 'What's Harm to Competition? Exclusionary Practices and Anticompetitive Effect' (2002) 70 Antitrust Law Journal 371; Kolasky 'North Atlantic Competition Policy: Converging Toward What?' 17 May 2002, available at www.usdoj.gov/atr/public/speeches/11153.htm.

[89] See Gerber *Law and Competition in Twentieth Century Europe: Protecting Prometheus* (Clarendon Press Oxford, 1998), ch VII; see also Gerber 'Constitutionalising the Economy: German Neo-liberalism, Competition Law and the New Europe' (1994) 42 American Journal of Comparative Law 25.

[90] See *Gerber*, pp 263–265; ch IX.

law was applied to protect competitors rather than the process of competition, although it may be that the role of ordoliberalism in competition law cases has been exaggerated: some commentators assert that economic efficiency was a key goal of competition policy from the outset[91]. However, without questioning the appropriateness of decisions taken in the early years of the Communities, it can be questioned whether it is appropriate in the new millennium to maintain this approach: there is much to be said for applying competition rules to achieve economic efficiency rather than economic equity. The two ideas sit awkwardly together: indeed they may flatly contradict one another, since an efficient undertaking will inevitably be able to defeat less efficient competitors, whose position in the market ought not to be underwritten by a competition authority on the basis of political preference or, as Bork might say, sentimentality. This is an issue that will be considered further in later chapters, and in particular in chapters 5, 17, and 18 on abusive practices on the part of dominant firms.

(iv) Other issues

In some cases, particularly involving mergers, the relevant authorities might find that other issues require attention: whether they can be taken into account will depend on the applicable law[92]. For example, unemployment and regional policy are issues which arise in the analysis of mergers and cooperation agreements; the ability of competition to dampen price-inflation may be considered to be important; merger controls may be used to prevent foreign takeovers of domestic companies; and there have been situations in which a competition authority may have been concerned with the problem of inequality of bargaining power between the parties to an agreement[93].

(v) The single market imperative

Lastly, we must consider two more issues of particular significance. One is that competition policy in the context of the EC fulfils an additional but quite different function from those just described (although EC law may be applied with them in mind as well). This is that competition law plays a hugely important part in the overriding goal of achieving single market integration[94]. The very idea of the single market is that internal barriers to trade within the Community should be dismantled and that goods, services, workers and capital should have complete freedom of movement. Firms should be able to outgrow their national markets and operate on a more efficient, transnational, scale throughout the Community. The accession of ten new Member States on 1 May 2004 and two more on January 2007, and the possibility of further accessions in the future, means that the single market imperative will continue to have an influential role in competition law enforcement for many years to come. Competition law has both a negative and a positive role to play in the integration of the single market. The negative one is that it can prevent measures which attempt to maintain the isolation of one domestic

---

[91] See Akman 'Searching for the long-lost soul of Article 82 EC' (*Centre for Competition Policy Working Paper 07-5*), available at www.ccp.uea.ac.uk.

[92] On the relevant tests to be applied to mergers under EC and UK law see respectively ch 21, pp 849–871 and ch 22, pp 921–928.

[93] The European Commission's block exemption for the distribution of motor cars seems, in part, to be influenced by the desire to 'protect' the car dealer from the supplier: see ch 16, pp 663–666.

[94] See Ehlermann 'The Contribution of EC Competition Policy to the Single Market' (1992) 29 CML Rev 257; the Commission's XXIXth *Report on Competition Policy* (1999), point 3.

market from another: for example national cartels, export bans and market-sharing will be seriously punished[95]. A fine of €102 million was imposed in *Volkswagen*[96] where Volkswagen sought to prevent exports of its cars from Italy to Germany and Austria. At the time this was the largest fine to have been imposed in relation to a so-called 'vertical agreement', between firms operating at different levels of the market, for an infringement of Article 81(1) EC; however this was exceeded by the fines of €167.8 million imposed in *Nintendo*[97], where Nintendo was found to have taken action to prevent exports of game consoles and related products from the UK to the Netherlands and Germany[98].

The positive role is that competition law can be moulded in such a way as to encourage trade between Member States, partly by 'levelling the playing fields of Europe' as one contemporary catchphrase puts it, and partly by facilitating cross-border transactions and integration. Horizontal collaboration between firms in different Member States may be permitted in some circumstances[99]; and a producer in one Member State can be permitted to appoint an exclusive distributor in another and so penetrate a market which individually he could not have done[100]. Unification of the single market is an obsession of the Community authorities; this has meant that decisions have sometimes been taken prohibiting behaviour which a competition authority elsewhere, unconcerned with single market considerations, would not have reached. Faced with a conflict between the narrow interests of a particular firm and the broader problem of integrating the market, the tendency has been to subordinate the former to the latter.

(B) Who decides?

A further issue that should be mentioned is that competition law may not be so much about any particular policy – for example the promotion of consumer welfare or protection of the weak – but about who actually should make decisions about the way in which business should be conducted. The great ideological debate of the twentieth century was between capitalism and communism: whether to have a market or not. For the most part that debate has been concluded in favour of the market mechanism. But competition law and policy by their very nature envisage that there may be situations in which some control of economic behaviour in the market-place may be necessary in order to achieve a desirable outcome. To some the market, and the vast rewards it brings to successful operators, remains an object of suspicion; to others, the spectre of the state as regulator is more alarming. These matters have been eloquently discussed by Amato[101]:

It is a fact that within liberal society itself one of the key divisions of political identity (and hence identification) is between these two sides: the side that fears private power more, and in order to

---

[95] See ch 7 pp 272–278 on the powers of the European Commission to impose fines for infringements of Articles 81 and 82.
[96] OJ [1998] L 124/60, [1998] 5 CMLR 33: on appeal the fine was reduced to €90 million, Case T-62/98 *Volkswagen v Commission* [2000] ECR II-2707, [2000] 5 CMLR 853; the case was upheld on appeal to the ECJ, Case C-338/00 P *Volkswagen v Commission* [2003] ECR I-9189, [2004] 4 CMLR 351.
[97] OJ [2003] L 255/33, [2004] 4 CMLR 421, on appeal Case T-13/03 *Nintendo v Commission*, not yet decided.
[98] It is conceivable that the single market imperative, at least in the pharmaceutical sector, may be less tenacious than was once the case: see the discussion of the *Glaxo* cases in ch 3, pp 121–122.
[99] See generally ch 15.   [100] See generally ch 16.
[101] Amato *Antitrust and the Bounds of Power: The Dilemma of Liberal Democracy in the History of the Market* (Hart Publishing, 1997), p 4.

fight it is ready to give more room to the power of government; and the side that fears the expansion of government more, and is therefore more prepared to tolerate private power.

In Europe there seems little doubt that, notwithstanding the demonopolisation and liberalisation of economic behaviour and the promotion of free enterprise that occurred in the late twentieth century, there remains a scepticism about the market, and that this results in 'active' enforcement of the competition rules by the European Commission and by the national competition authorities[102].

In the European Community there has been a fair degree of dirigism in the way that the Commission has developed its policy. For example, historically it has taken a wide view of the circumstances in which competition is restricted for the purposes of Article 81(1), but has then given block exemption under Article 81(3) to certain types of agreements which satisfy criteria, specified by it, in various regulations[103]. The legal adviser is highly likely to advise a client to comply with these criteria, whether suitable or not, because of the administrative and juridical advantages of doing so. In this case the invisible hand of competition is replaced by the much more visible hand of the Commission and, specifically, DG COMP, the Directorate of the Commission responsible for competition matters[104]. This in turn raises an additional, complex, issue: if there are to be competition authorities to decide on what is and what is not acceptable business behaviour, what type of institution should be asked to make these decisions (a court, a commission, an individual?); how should individuals be appointed to those institutions (by ministerial appointment, by election, by open competition?); and how should those institutions themselves be controlled (by judicial review, or by an appellate court?). Here we leave law and economics and move into the world of political science which, though fascinating, is beyond the scope of this book[105].

(C) Competition advocacy and public restrictions of competition

A final point about the function of competition law is that competition authorities can usefully be given a different task, which is to scrutinise legislation that will bring about, or is responsible for, a distortion of competition in the economy. The reality is that states and international regulatory authorities are capable of harming the competitive process at least as seriously as private economic operators on the market itself, for example by granting legal monopolies to undertakings, by limiting in other ways the number of competitors in the market, or by establishing unduly restrictive rules and regulations. Some competition authorities are specifically mandated to scrutinise legislation that will distort competition[106]. Some developing countries might more usefully deploy

---

[102]   See Gerber *Law and Competition in Twentieth Century Europe* (Clarendon Press Oxford, 1998), pp 421ff.

[103]   The Commission's 'new style' regulations, of which Regulation 2790/99 is the first, are less formalistic, and therefore less dirigiste, than their predecessors: see ch 4, pp 166–167.

[104]   See further ch 2, pp 53–55 on the role of the Commission in EC competition law and policy.

[105]   On these issues see generally Doern and Wilks (eds) *Comparative Competition Policy: National Institutions in a Global Market* (Clarendon Press Oxford, 1996) and, in particular, chs 1 and 2; Cini and McGowan *Competition Policy in the European Union* (Macmillan, 1998); Craig *Administrative Law* (Sweet & Maxwell, 5th ed, 2003), ch 11.

[106]   See eg s 21(1)(k) of the South African Competition Act 1998, which requires the Competition Commission to 'review legislation and public regulations and report to the Minister concerning any provision that permits uncompetitive behaviour'; and s 49(1) of the Indian Competition Act 2002 which provides that the Indian Competition Commission can review legislation, but only if a reference is made to it by either the Central or the State governments.

their resources on this issue rather than adopting their own competition rules[107]. In the UK the Office of Fair Trading, acting under section 7 of the Enterprise Act 2002, can bring to the attention of Ministers laws or proposed laws that could be harmful to competition[108]. The International Competition Network (an association of various national competition authorities), through the work originally of its competition advocacy working group and now of its competition policy implementation group, is seeking to develop best practices in promoting competition law and policy[109].

5. MARKET DEFINITION AND MARKET POWER

This section will discuss the issues of market definition and market power. As has been noted already competition law is concerned, above all, with the problems that occur where one or more firms possess, or will possess after a merger, market power: market power presents undertakings with the possibility of limiting output, raising price and depriving consumers of choice, which are clearly inimical to consumer welfare[110]. There are numerous ways in which this key concern – the exercise of market power – is manifested, by implication if not expressly, in EC and UK competition law. For example there are rules that firms should not enter into agreements to restrict competition (Article 81 EC; Chapter I prohibition, Competition Act 1998): however any such restriction must be appreciable, and there are various '*de minimis*' exceptions where the parties lack market power[111]; block exemption is not available to parties to agreements where the parties' market share exceeds a certain threshold[112]; firms should not abuse a dominant position (Article 82 EC; Chapter II prohibition, Competition Act 1998); concentrations can be prohibited under the ECMR that would create or strengthen a dominant position as a result of which competition would be significantly impeded; mergers can be prohibited under UK law that would substantially lessen competition (Part 3 of the Enterprise Act 2002); 'market investigations' can be conducted by the Competition Commission where features of a market could have an adverse effect on competition (Part 4 of the Enterprise Act). Other variants can be found[113]. Each of these provisions reflects a concern about the abuse or potential abuse of market power. Throughout this

---

[107] Rodriguez and Coate 'Competition Policy in Transition Economies: the Role of Competition Advocacy' (1997) 23 Brooklyn Journal of International Law 365.

[108] On the functions of the OFT see ch 2, pp 65–66.

[109] See www.internationalcompetitionnetwork.org/advocacy.html. and www.internationalcompetition-network.org/index.php/en/library/working-group/16; see also Emberger 'How to strengthen competition advocacy through competition screening' *Competition Policy Newsletter* Spring 2006, 28.

[110] See Landes and Posner 'Market power in antitrust cases' (1981) 94 Harvard Law Review 937; Vickers 'Market power in competition cases' [2006] European Competition Journal 3.

[111] See eg ch 3, pp 137–142.

[112] See eg Article 3 of Regulation 2790/99, OJ [1999] L 336/21, [2000] 4 CMLR 398 on vertical agreements: 30 per cent market share cap; Article 4 of Regulation 2658/2000, OJ [2000] L 304/3, [2001] 4 CMLR 800 on specialisation agreements: 20 per cent market share cap; Article 4 of Regulation 2659/2000, OJ [2000] L 304/7, [2001] 4 CMLR 808 on research and development agreements: 25 per cent market share cap; and Article 3 of Regulation 772/2004, OJ [2004] L 123/11 on technology transfer agreements: 20 per cent market share cap in the case of horizontal agreements and 30 per cent cap in the case of vertical agreements.

[113] For example in the electronic communications sector regulatory obligations can be imposed upon firms that have 'significant market power', which has the same meaning for this purpose as 'dominance' under Article 82 EC: see ch 23, pp 972–973.

book and throughout competition law and practice generally, therefore, two key issues recur: first, the definition of the relevant product and geographic (and sometimes the temporal) markets in relation to which market power may be found to exist; secondly, and more importantly, the identification of market power itself.

(A) Market definition

Pure monopoly is rare, but a firm or firms collectively may have sufficient power over the market to enjoy some of the benefits available to the true monopolist. If the notion of 'power over the market' is key to analysing competition issues, it becomes immediately obvious that it is necessary to understand what is meant by 'the market' or, as will be explained below, the 'relevant market' for this purpose. The concept is an economic one, and in many cases it may be necessary for lawyers to engage the services of economists to assist in the proper delineation of the market, as highly sophisticated economic and econometric analysis is sometimes called for.

In recent years the 'science' of market definition has evolved considerably. There are numerous sources of information on how to define markets. Of particular importance in Europe is the European Commission's *Notice on the Definition of the Relevant Market for the Purposes of Community Competition Law*[114] which adopts the so-called 'hypothetical monopolist' test (also known as the 'SSNIP test') for defining markets. This Notice provides a conceptual framework within which to think of market definition, and then explains some of the techniques that may be deployed when defining markets. The Commission's Notice adopts the approach taken by the antitrust authorities in the US in the analysis of horizontal mergers[115]; the OFT in the UK has adopted a guideline which adopts a similar approach to that of the Commission[116]. Other competition authorities also apply the hypothetical monopolist test[117].

Paragraph 2 of the Commission's Notice explains why market definition is important:

Market definition is a tool to identify and define the boundaries of competition between firms. It serves to establish the framework within which competition policy is applied by the Commission. The main purpose of market definition is to identify in a systematic way the competitive constraints that the undertakings involved face. The objective of defining a market in both its product and geographic dimension is to identify those actual competitors of the undertakings involved that are capable of constraining those undertakings' behaviour and of preventing them from behaving independently of effective competitive pressure.

This paragraph contains a number of important points. First, market definition is not an end in itself[118]. Rather it is an analytical tool that assists in determining the competitive constraints upon undertakings: market definition provides a framework

---

[114] OJ [1997] C 372/5, [1998] 4 CMLR 177; the Notice can be accessed on the Commission's website at www.europa.eu.int/comm/competition/mergers/legislation/mergmrkt.html; see further Baker and Wu 'Applying the Market Definition Guidelines of the European Commission' (1998) 19 ECLR 273; *Bishop and Walker*, ch 3; for a discussion of the position prior to the adoption of the Notice see Kauper 'The Problem of Market Definition under EC Competition Law' [1996] Fordham Corporate Law Institute (ed Hawk), ch 13.

[115] See p 30 below.

[116] *Market Definition* OFT Guideline 403, December 2004, available at www.oft.gov.uk.

[117] See eg the *Merger Guidelines* of the Australian Competition and Consumer Commission, available at www.accc.gov.au; the *Mergers and Acquisitions Guidelines* of the New Zealand Commerce Commission, available at www.comcom.govt.nz; and the *Merger Enforcement Guidelines* of the Canadian Competition Bureau, available at www.competitionbureau.gc.ca.

[118] For an interesting discussion of the limits of market definition see Carlton 'Market Definition: Use and Abuse' (2007) 3(1) Competition Policy International 3.

within which to assess the critical question of whether a firm or firms possess market power. Second, both the product and geographic dimensions of markets must be analysed. Third, market definition enables the competitive constraints only from *actual* competitors to be identified: it tells us nothing about *potential* competitors. However, as paragraph 13 of the Notice points out, there are three main sources of competitive constraint upon undertakings: demand substitutability, supply substitutability and potential competition. As will be explained below, demand substitutability is the essence of market definition. In some, albeit fairly narrow, circumstances supply substitutability may also be part of the market definition; however normally supply substitutability lies outside market definition and is an issue of potential competition. It is also necessary, when assessing a supplier's market power, to take into account any countervailing power on the buyer's side of the market. It is very important to understand that factors such as potential entry and buyer power are relevant, since this means that a particular share of a market cannot, in itself, indicate that a firm has market power; an undertaking with 100 per cent of the widget market would not have market power if there are numerous potential competitors and no barriers to entry into the market. Lawyers must not be seduced by numbers when determining whether a firm has market power; market shares, of course, are helpful; indeed there are circumstances in which they are very important: a share of 50 per cent or more of a market creates a legal presumption of dominance in a case under Article 82[119], and a market share of 30 per cent or more will prevent the application of the block exemption in Regulation 2790/99 on vertical agreements[120]. However, calculating an undertaking's market share is only one step in determining whether it has market power.

(B) Circumstances in which it is necessary to define the relevant market

The foregoing discussion may be rendered less abstract by considering the circumstances in EC and UK competition law in which it may be necessary to define the relevant market.

(i) EC competition law

- Under Article 81(1), when considering whether an agreement has the effect of restricting competition[121].

- Under Article 81(1), when considering whether an agreement *appreciably* restricts competition; in particular there are market share tests in the *Notice on Agreements of Minor Importance*: a horizontal agreement, that is one between competitors, will usually be *de minimis* where the parties' market share is 10 per cent or less, and a vertical agreement, that is one between undertakings operating at different levels of the market, will usually be *de minimis* where their market share is 15 per cent or less[122].

- Under the Commission's guidelines on the application of Article 81(1) to horizontal cooperation agreements, where further market share thresholds will be found[123].

- Under Article 81(3)(b), when considering whether an agreement would substantially eliminate competition[124].

---

[119] See ch 5, p 117.   [120] See ch 16, pp 650–652.
[121] See eg Case C-234/89 *Delimitis v Henninger Bräu* [1991] ECR I-935, [1992] 5 CMLR 210.
[122] OJ [2001] C 368/13, [2002] 4 CMLR 699, para 7.   [123] See ch 15, p 580.
[124] See ch 4, pp 159–160.

- Under numerous block exemptions containing market share tests, for example Regulation 2790/99 on vertical agreements[125], Regulation 2658/2000 on specialisation agreements[126] and Regulation 2659/2000 on research and development agreements[127].
- Under Article 82, when considering whether an undertaking has abused a dominant position[128].
- Under the ECMR when determining whether a merger would create or strengthen a dominant position[129].

(ii) UK law

- When applying the Chapter I and Chapter II prohibitions of the Competition Act, which are based on the provisions in Articles 81 and 82[130].
- When determining the level of a penalty under the Competition Act[131].
- When scrutinising mergers under Part 3 of the Enterprise Act 2002[132].
- When conducting 'market investigations' under Part 4 of the Enterprise Act 2002[133].

Market definition, therefore, plays an important part in much competition law analysis. The table at the end of this chapter captures some of the important market share thresholds that may be relevant to competition law analysis.

(C) The relevant product market

The ECJ, when it heard its first appeal on the application of Article 82 in *Europemballage Corpn and Continental Can Co Inc v Commission*[134], held that when identifying a dominant position the delimitation of the relevant product market was of crucial importance. This has been repeated by the ECJ on numerous occasions[135]. In *Continental Can Co Inc*[136] it was the Commission's failure to define the relevant product market that caused the ECJ to quash its decision. The Commission had held that Continental Can and its subsidiary SLW had a dominant position in three different product markets – cans for meat, cans for fish and metal tops – without giving a satisfactory explanation of why these markets were separate from one another or from the market for cans and containers generally. The ECJ in effect insisted that the Commission should define the relevant product market and support its definition in a reasoned decision.

(i) The legal test

The judgments of the ECJ show that the definition of the market is essentially a matter of interchangeability. Where goods or services can be regarded as interchangeable, they are within the same product market. In *Continental Can* the ECJ enjoined the Commission, for the purpose of delimiting the market, to investigate:

[those] characteristics of the products in question by virtue of which they are particularly apt to satisfy an inelastic need and are only to a limited extent interchangeable with other products[137].

---

[125] See ch 16, pp 650–652.   [126] See ch 15, p 591.   [127] See ch 15, p 586.
[128] See ch 5, pp 175–179.   [129] See ch 21, pp 850–851.   [130] See ch 9, generally.
[131] *Guidance as to the Appropriate Amount of a Penalty* (OFT Guideline 423), para 2.3.
[132] See ch 22, pp 921–922.   [133] See ch 11, pp 452–459.
[134] Case 6/72 [1973] ECR 215, [1973] CMLR 199, para 32.
[135] See eg Case 27/76 *United Brands v Commission* [1978] ECR 207, [1978] 1 CMLR 429, para 10.
[136] JO [1972] L 7/25, [1972] CMLR D11.   [137] Case 6/72 [1973] ECR 215, [1973] CMLR 199, para 32.

Similarly in *United Brands v Commission*, where the applicant was arguing that bananas were in the same market as other fruit, the ECJ said that this issue depended on whether the banana could be:

singled out by such special features distinguishing it from other fruits that it is only to a limited extent interchangeable with them and is only exposed to their competition in a way that is hardly perceptible[138].

(ii) Measuring interchangeability

Conceptually, the idea that a relevant market consists of goods or services that are inter-changeable with one another is simple enough. In practice, however, the measurement of interchangeability can give rise to considerable problems for a variety of reasons: for example there may be no data available on the issue, or the data that exist may be unre-liable, incomplete or deficient in some other way. A further problem is that, in many cases, the data will be open to (at least) two interpretations. It is often the case therefore that market definition is extremely difficult.

(iii) Commission Notice on the Definition of the Relevant Market for the Purposes of Community Competition Law[139]

Useful guidance on market definition is provided by the Commission's Notice. The introduction of the European Community Merger Regulation in 1990 had, as an inevit-able consequence, that the Commission was called upon to define markets in a far larger number of situations than previously. Whereas it may have had to deal with complaints under Article 82, say, 20 times a year in the 1980s, by the 1990s it was having to deal with 100 or more notifications under the ECMR each year, and it now receives at least 300 notifications a year: indeed in 2007 the number reached 402[140]. Furthermore, whereas an Article 82 case would normally require the definition of just one market – the one in which the dominant firm was alleged to have abused its position – a case under the ECMR might be quite different, since the merging parties might conduct business in a number of different markets giving rise to competition considerations[141]. This necessar-ily meant that the Commission was called upon to develop more systematic methods for defining the market, although it remains the case that a fair amount of subjective assessment is involved in this difficult process.

(iv) Demand-side substitutability

As mentioned above, the Commission explains at paragraph 13 of the Notice that firms are subject to three main competitive constraints: demand substitutability, supply sub-stitutability and potential competition. It continues that, for the purpose of market definition, it is demand substitutability that is of the greatest significance; supply sub-stitutability may be relevant to market definition in certain special circumstances, but normally this is a matter to be examined when determining whether there is market power; potential competition in the market is always a matter of market power rather than market definition.

---

[138] Case 27/76 [1978] ECR 207, [1978] 1 CMLR 429, para 22.   [139] OJ [1997] C 372/5, [1998] 4 CMLR 177.
[140] See www.ec.europa.eu/comm/competition/mergers/statistics.pdf.
[141] Case COMP/M 2547 *Bayer Crop Science/Aventis* concerned a merger in which there were no fewer than 130 affected markets.

Paragraph 14 of the Notice states that the assessment of demand substitution entails a determination of the range of products which are viewed as substitutes by the consumer. It proposes a test whereby it becomes possible to determine whether particular products are within the same market. The so-called 'SSNIP' test, first deployed by the Department of Justice and the Federal Trade Commission under US competition law when analysing horizontal mergers[142], works as follows: suppose that a producer of a product – for example a widget – were to introduce a Small but Significant Non-transitory Increase in Price. In those circumstances, would enough customers be inclined to switch their purchases to other makes of widgets, or indeed even to blodgets, to make the price rise unprofitable? If the answer is yes, this would suggest that the market is at least as wide as widgets generally and includes blodgets as well. The same test can be applied to the delineation of the geographic market: if the price of widgets were to be raised in France by a small but significant amount, would customers switch to suppliers in Germany? If a firm could raise its price by a significant amount and retain its customers, this would mean that the market would be worth monopolising: prices could be raised profitably, since there would be no competitive constraint. For this reason, the SSNIP test is also – and more catchily – referred to sometimes as the 'hypothetical monopolist test'. The hypothetical monopolist test is given formal expression in paragraph 17 of the Commission's Notice, where it states that:

The question to be asked is whether the parties' customers would switch to readily available substitutes or to suppliers located elsewhere in response to a hypothetical small (in the range 5 per cent to 10 per cent) but permanent relative price increase in the products and areas being considered. If substitution were enough to make the price increase unprofitable because of the resulting loss of sales, additional substitutes and areas are included in the relevant market.

This formulation of the test takes the 'range' of 5 per cent to 10 per cent to indicate 'significance' within the SSNIP formula[143].

(v) The 'Cellophane Fallacy'

It is necessary to enter a word of caution on the hypothetical monopolist test when applied to abuse of dominance cases. A monopolist may already be charging a monopoly price: if it were to raise its price further, its customers may cease to buy from it at all. In this situation the monopolist's 'own-price elasticity' – the extent to which consumers switch from its products in response to a price rise – is high. If a SSNIP test is applied in these circumstances between the monopolised product and another one, this might suggest a high degree of substitutability, since consumers are already at the point where they will cease to buy from the monopolist; the test therefore would exaggerate the breadth of the market by the inclusion of false substitutes. This error was committed by the US Supreme Court in *United States v EI du Pont de Nemour and Co*[144] in a case concerning packaging materials, including cellophane, since when it has been known as the 'Cellophane Fallacy'.

---

[142] *Horizontal Merger Guidelines* (issued in 1992 and revised in 1997), available at www.usdoj.gov/atr/public/guidelines/horiz_book/hmg1.html; the SSNIP test is not used in the US for the purpose of market definition in cartel and monopolisation cases under ss 1 and 2 Sherman Act 1890.

[143] In the UK the Competition Commission has said that it will postulate a price rise of 5 per cent when applying the hypothetical monopolist test: see *Merger References: Competition Commission Guidelines* (June 2003, CC 2), para 2.8; *Market Investigation References: Competition Commission Guidelines* (June 2003, CC 3), para 2.8, available at www.competition-commission.org.uk.

[144] 351 US 377 (1956).

In the US the SSNIP test was devised in the context of merger cases, and is usually applied only in relation to them. In the European Commission's Notice, it states in the first paragraph that it is to be used for cases under Articles 81, 82 and the ECMR; the Cellophane Fallacy is briefly acknowledged at paragraph 19 of the Notice, where it says that in cases under Article 82 'the fact that the prevailing price might already have been substantially increased will be taken into account'. In DG COMP's *Discussion Paper on the application of Article 82 of the Treaty to exclusionary abuses*[145] the Commission acknowledges that the SSNIP text needs to be particularly carefully considered in Article 82 cases, and that it is necessary in such cases to rely on a variety of methods for checking the robustness of alternative market definitions[146]. The *Discussion Paper* specifically notes that the SSNIP test should be applied to competitive prices, but that in Article 82 cases the prevailing price may not be competitive[147]. It suggests that, in Article 82 cases, it may be appropriate to examine the characteristics and intended use of the products in question and whether they are capable of satisfying an inelastic consumer need[148]; and adds that it may be helpful to compare the prices of particular products across different regions: it may be that a firm charges higher prices where it has higher market shares, and this could provide an insight into market definition[149].

In the UK the OFT's Guideline on *Market Definition* notes the problem of the Cellophane Fallacy, and states that the possibility that market conditions are distorted by the presence of market power will be accounted for 'when all the evidence on market definition is weighed in the round'[150]. The OFT's decisions in *Aberdeen Journals II*[151] and *BSkyB*[152] both acknowledged the problem of the Cellophane Fallacy in defining the relevant markets in circumstances where competition may already have been distorted; in each case the OFT concluded that it was necessary to find alternative ways of determining whether the firms under consideration had market power and/or were guilty of abuse; in *BSkyB* the OFT looked at the physical characteristics of premium sports pay-TV channels and consumers' underlying preferences and, in *Aberdeen Journals II*, it looked at the conduct and statements of the allegedly dominant firm. In the appeal against the latter decision the Competition Appeal Tribunal specifically stated that, in a case concerning an alleged abuse of a dominant position, the market to be taken into consideration means the market that would exist in normal competitive conditions, disregarding any distortive effects that the conduct of the dominant firm has itself created[153].

(vi) Supply-side substitutability

In most cases interchangeability will be determined by examining the market from the customer's perspective. However it is helpful in some situations to consider the degree of substitutability on the supply side of the market. Suppose that A is a producer of widgets and that B is a producer of blodgets: if it is a very simple matter for B to change

---

[145] December 2005, available at www.ec.europa.eu/comm/competition/antitrust/art82/discpaper 2005.
[146] Ibid, para 13.   [147] Ibid, para 15.   [148] Ibid, para 18.   [149] Ibid, para 19.
[150] *Market Definition*, OFT 403, December 2004, paras 5.4–5.6; see also OFT Economic Discussion Paper 2, OFT 342, *The Role of Market Definition in Monopoly and Dominance Inquiries* (National Economic Research Associates, July 2001); *Merger References: Competition Commission* Guidelines (June 2003, CC 2), paras 2.9–2.10 and the companion *Market Investigation References: Competition Commission Guidelines* (June 2003, CC 3), paras 2.9–2.10, available at www.competition-commission.org.uk.
[151] *Aberdeen Journals (remitted case)*, 25 September 2002, paras 94–99, available at www.oft.gov.uk.
[152] *BSkyB investigation*, 30 January 2003, paras 88–97, available at www.oft.gov.uk.
[153] Case No 1009/1/1/02 *Aberdeen Journals Ltd v Office of Fair Trading* [2003] CAT 11, para 276.

its production process and to produce widgets, this might suggest that widgets and blodgets are part of the same market, even though consumers on the demand-side of the market might not regard widgets and blodgets as substitutable. Dicta of the ECJ in *Continental Can v Commission*[154] indicate that the supply side of the market should be considered for the purpose of defining the market. Among its criticisms of the decision[155], the ECJ said that the Commission should have made clear why it considered that producers of other types of containers would not be able to adapt their production to compete with Continental Can. The Commission has specifically addressed the issue of supply-side substitutability in some subsequent decisions[156]. A good example is *Tetra Pak 1 (BTG Licence)*[157], where it took into account the fact that producers of milk-packaging machines could not readily adapt their production to make aseptic packaging machines and cartons in arriving at its market definition.

In paragraphs 20 to 23 of the *Notice on Market Definition* the Commission explains the circumstances in which it considers that supply-side substitutability is relevant to market definition[158]. At paragraph 20 the Commission says that where suppliers are able to switch production to other products and to market them 'in the short term' without incurring significant additional costs or risks in response to small and permanent changes in relative prices, then the market may be broadened to include the products that those suppliers are already producing. A footnote to paragraph 20 suggests that the short term means 'such a period that does not entail a significant adjustment of existing tangible and intangible assets'. A practical example is given in paragraph 22 of a company producing a particular grade of paper: if it could change easily to producing other grades of paper, they should all be included in the market definition. However, where supply substitution is more complex than this, it should be regarded as a matter of determining market power rather than establishing the market[159].

While it may seem unimportant whether the issue of supply-side substitution is dealt with at the stage of market definition or of market power, where competition law deploys a market share test, as for example in Article 3 of Regulation 2790/99[160], the possibility of broadening the market definition through the inclusion of supply-side substitutes may have a crucial effect on the outcome of a particular case.

(vii) Evidence relied on to define relevant markets

The SSNIP test establishes a conceptual framework within which markets should be defined. In practice, however, the critical issue is to know what evidence can be adduced to determine the scope of the relevant market. If the world were composed of an infinite number of market research organisations devoted to asking SSNIP-like questions

[154] Case 6/72 [1973] ECR 215, [1973] CMLR 199, paras 32ff.

[155] *Continental Can Co Inc* JO [1972] L7/25, [1972] CMLR D11.

[156] See eg *Eurofix-Bauco v Hilti* OJ [1988] L 65/19, [1989] 4 CMLR 677, para 55, upheld on appeal to the CFI Case T-30/89 *Hilti AG v Commission* [1991] ECR II-1439, [1992] 4 CMLR 16 and on appeal to the ECJ Case C-53/92 P [1994] ECR I-667, [1994] 4 CMLR 614.

[157] OJ [1988] L 272/27, [1988] 4 CMLR 47, upheld on appeal to the CFI Case T-51/89 *Tetra Pak Rausing SA v Commission* [1990] ECR II-309, [1991] 4 CMLR 334.

[158] See also *Market Investigations: Competition Commission Guidelines* (June 2003, CC 3), paras 2.20–2.23 and fn 33 to para 3.45, recognising the difficulty of distinguishing potential entry from supply-side substitution; the *Guidelines* are available at www.competition-commission.org.uk.

[159] It is interesting to note that, in US antitrust practice, supply-side substitution is generally taken into account at the stage of determining market power rather than defining the relevant market.

[160] OJ [1999] L 336/21, [2000] 4 CMLR 398; on market definition under this block exemption, see the Commission's *Guidelines on Vertical Restraints*, OJ [2000] C 291/1, [2000] 5 CMLR 1074, Section V, paras 78–90.

of customers and consumers, market definition would be truly scientific. But of course the world is not so composed, and a variety of techniques, some of considerable sophistication, are deployed by economists and econometrists in order to seek solutions. The Commission's Notice, from paragraph 25 onwards[161], considers some of the evidence that may be available, but it quite correctly says that tests that may be suitable in one industry may be wholly inappropriate in another. A moment's reflection shows that this must be so: for example, the demand-substitutability of one alcoholic beverage for another in the ordinary citizen's mind is likely to be tested by different criteria than an airline choosing whether to purchase aeroplanes from Boeing or Airbus. In *Aberdeen Journals Ltd v Office of Fair Trading*[162] the Competition Appeal Tribunal in the UK has said that there is no 'hierarchy' of evidence on issues such as market definition that would require, for example, objective economic evidence to be given greater weight than subjective evidence such as the statements or conduct of the parties[163].

(viii) Examples of evidence that may be used in defining the relevant product market

As far as definition of the product market is concerned the *Notice* suggests that the following evidence may be available.

(A) Evidence of substitution in the recent past There may recently have been an event – such as a price increase or a 'shock', perhaps a failure of the Brazilian coffee crop due to a late frost – giving rise to direct evidence of the consequences that this had for consumers' consumption (perhaps a large increase in the drinking of tea).

(B) Quantitative tests Various econometric and statistical tests have been devised which attempt to estimate own-price elasticities and cross-price elasticities for the demand of a product, based on the similarity of price movements over time, the causality between price series and the similarity of price levels and/or their convergence. Own-price elasticities measure the extent to which demand for a product changes in response to a change in its price. Cross-price elasticities measure the extent to which demand for a product changes in response to a change in the price of some other product. Own-price elasticities provide more information about the market power that an undertaking possesses than cross-price elasticities; however cross-price elasticities help more with market definition, since they provide evidence on substitutability.

(C) Views of customers and competitors The Commission will contact customers and competitors in a case that involves market definition, and will, where appropriate, specifically ask them to answer the SSNIP question. This happens routinely, for example, when it seeks to delineate markets under the ECMR.

(D) Marketing studies and consumer surveys The Commission will look at marketing studies as a useful provider of information about the market, although it specifically states in paragraph 41 of the *Notice* that it will scrutinise 'with utmost care' the methodology

---

[161] See also *Bishop and Walker*, chs 7–15, which considers techniques that may be relevant to market definition; also OFT Research Paper 17 (OFT 266) *Quantitative techniques in competition analysis* (LECG Ltd, October 1999): this can be obtained from the OFT's website at www.oft.gov.uk.

[162] Case No 1009/1/1/02 *Aberdeen Journals Ltd v Office of Fair Trading* [2003] CAT 11.

[163] Ibid, para 127.

followed in consumer surveys carried out *ad hoc* by the undertakings involved in merger cases or cases under Articles 81 and 82. Its concern is that the selection of questions in the survey may be deliberately made in order to achieve a favourable outcome.

(E) Barriers and costs associated with switching demand to potential substitutes There may be a number of barriers and/or costs that result in two apparent demand substitutes not belonging to one single product market. The Commission deals with these in paragraph 42 of the Notice, and gives as examples regulatory barriers, other forms of State intervention, constraints occurring in downstream markets, the need to incur capital investment and other factors. The OFT has published an Economic Discussion Paper that specifically considers the issue of switching costs[164].

(F) Different categories of customers and price discrimination At paragraph 43 the Commission states that the extent of the product market might be narrowed where there exist distinct groups of customers for a particular product: the market for one group may be narrower than for the other, if it is possible to identify which group an individual belongs to at the moment of selling the relevant products and there is no possibility of trade between the two categories of customer.

(ix) A word of caution on the Notice

It is important to point out a few words of caution about the *Notice on Market Definition*. The problem of the Cellophane Fallacy has already been mentioned[165]. There are three other points about the Notice.

First, it is 'only' a Commission Notice: it does not have the force of law, and ought not to be treated as a legislative instrument.

A second point about the Notice is that, no matter how well it explains the SSNIP test and the evidence that may be used when applying it, the fact remains that in some sectors actual price data about substitutability may not be available: the information that can be captured varies hugely from one sector to another, and in some cases one will be thrown back on fairly subjective assessments of the market for want of hard, scientific evidence. In this situation it may be necessary to predict the likely effect of an SSNIP on customers by looking at various factors such as the physical characteristics of the products concerned or their intended use. In some cases it may not be possible to apply the SSNIP test at all. An example is the Commission's decision in *British Interactive Broadcasting*[166]: there the Commission stated that it could not delineate the markets for interactive broadcasting services by applying a SSNIP test since no data were available in relation to a product that had yet to be launched. In several broadcasting cases the fact that public-sector broadcasting is available 'free-to-air' to end users meant that an SSNIP test was inapplicable[167]. Clearly this is always likely to be a problem in relation to products introduced into the 'new' economy[168].

---

[164] OFT Economic Discussion Paper 5 (OFT 655) *Switching Costs* (National Economic Research Associates, April 2003).

[165] See pp 30–31 above.   [166] OJ [1999] L 312/1, [2000] 4 CMLR 901.

[167] See eg Case M 553 *RTL/Veronica/Endemol* OJ [1996] L 134/32, upheld on appeal Case T-221/95 *Endemol Entertainment Holding BV v Commission* [1999] ECR II-1299, [1999] 5 CMLR 611.

[168] On the issue of market definition in cases involving e-commerce see OFT Economic Discussion Paper 1, OFT 308, *E-commerce and its implications for competition policy* (Frontier Economics Group, August 2000), ch 4.

A third point about the Notice is that there are by now very many cases – in particular under the ECMR – in which the Commission has been called upon to define the market. With more than 3,500 mergers having been notified to the Commission under the ECMR, there are few sectors in which it has not been called upon to analyse relevant markets. As a consequence of this there is a very considerable 'decisional practice' of the Commission in which it has opined – from cars, buses and trucks to pharmaceuticals and agrochemicals, from banking and insurance services to international aviation and deep-sea drilling[169]. Not unnaturally, an undertaking in need of guidance on the Commission's likely response to a matter of market definition will wish to find out what it has had to say in the past in actual decisions; however the caveat should be entered that the CFI has established that the market must always be defined in any particular case by reference to the facts prevailing at the time and not by reference to precedents[170].

(x) Spare parts and the aftermarket[171]

There are numerous sectors in which a consumer of one product – for example a car – will need to purchase at a later date complementary products such as spare parts. The same can be true where a customer has to buy 'consumables', such as cartridges to be used in a laser printer, or maintenance services. In such cases one issue is to determine how the relevant product market should be defined. If there is a separate market for the complementary product, it may be that an undertaking that has no power over the 'primary' market may nevertheless be dominant in the 'secondary' one. An illustration is *Hugin v Commission*[172], where the ECJ upheld the Commission's finding that Hugin was dominant in the market for spare parts for its own cash machines. Liptons, a firm which serviced Hugin's machines, could not use spare parts produced by anyone else for this purpose because Hugin would have been able to prevent this by relying on its rights under the UK Design Copyright Act 1968. Therefore, although for other purposes it might be true to say that there is a market for spare parts generally, in this case, given the use to which Liptons intended to put them, the market had to be more narrowly defined. Liptons was 'locked in', as it was dependent on Hugin, and this justified a narrow market definition. This case, and the judgments of the ECJ in *AB Volvo v Erik Veng*[173] and *CICRA v Régie Nationale des Usines Renault*[174], establish that spare parts can form

---

[169] See ch 21, pp 821–822 on how to access the Commission's decisions under the ECMR.

[170] In Joined Cases T-125/97 etc *Coca-Cola v Commission* [2000] ECR II-1733, [2000] 5 CMLR 467, para 82, the CFI stated that in the course of any decision applying Article 82, 'the Commission must define the relevant market again and make a fresh analysis of the conditions of competition which will not necessarily be based on the same considerations as those underlying the previous finding of a dominant position'; examples of how market definitions can change over a period of time are afforded by cross-channel ferry services between the UK and continental Europe, where the Channel Tunnel has altered the market: see *The Peninsular and Oriental Steam Navigation Corpn and Stena Line AB* Cm 4030 (1998); and the market for betting shops in the UK: see *Ladbroke Group plc and The Coral Betting Business* Cm 4030 (1998); in the UK the OFT, pursuant to the *Coca-Cola* judgment, conducted a fresh market analysis in its BSkyB decision, 17 December 2002, paras 29 ff, available at www.oft.gov.uk; see also *Market Definition*, OFT 403, December 2004, paras 5.7–5.9.

[171] See Bishop and Walker, paras 6.45–6.53; this issue often arises in cases concerning alleged 'tie-in transactions', as to which see ch 17, pp 679–687.

[172] Case 22/78 [1979] ECR 1869, [1979] 3 CMLR 345; the Commission's decision was quashed in this case as it had failed to establish the necessary effect on inter-state trade.

[173] Case 238/87 [1988] ECR 6211, [1989] 4 CMLR 122.

[174] Case 53/87 [1988] ECR 6039, [1990] 4 CMLR 265.

a market separate from the products for which they are needed. Likewise consumables, such as nails for use with nail-guns[175] and cartons for use with filling-machines[176], have been held to be a separate market from the product with which they are used.

However, as a matter of economics, it would be wrong to conclude that the primary and secondary markets are necessarily always discrete. It may be that a consumer, when deciding to purchase the primary product, will also take into account the price of the secondary products that will be needed in the future: this is sometimes referred to as 'whole life costing'. Where this occurs high prices in the secondary market may act as a competitive constraint when the purchaser is making his initial decision as to which primary product to purchase. It is an empirical question whether there is a separate aftermarket. The Commission has stated that it regards the issue as one that needs to be examined on a case-by-case basis[177], and that it will look at all important factors such as the price and life-time of the primary product, the transparency of the prices for the secondary product and the proportion of the price of the secondary product to the value of the primary one. In its investigation of *Kyocera/Pelikan*[178] the Commission concluded that Kyocera was not dominant in the market for toner cartridges for printers, since consumers took the price of cartridges into account when deciding which printer to buy; the Commission came to the opposite view in the later case of *Digital*[179]. In the UK both OFTEL (now OFCOM) and the OFT have reached similar conclusions[180], and the OFT's guideline on *Market Definition* adopts the same approach[181].

(xi) Procurement markets

In some cases the business behaviour under scrutiny is that of buyers rather than sellers. For example where supermarkets merge[182], or where their procurement policies are under investigation[183], the market must be defined from the demand rather than the supply side of the market. In the case of an exclusive supply obligation, as that term is used in Regulation 2790/99 on vertical restraints, Article 3(b) requires that the market be defined from the demand side[184].

---

[175] Case T-30/89 *Hilti AG v Commission* [1990] ECR II-163, [1992] 4 CMLR 16, upheld on appeal Case 53/92 P *Hilti AG v Commission* [1994] ECR I-667, [1994] 4 CMLR 614.

[176] *Tetra Pak II* OJ [1992] L 72/1, [1992] 4 CMLR 551, upheld on appeal to the CFI Case T-83/91 *Tetra Pak International SA v Commission* [1994] ECR II-755, [1997] 4 CMLR 726, and on appeal to the ECJ Case C-333/94 P *Tetra Pak International SA v Commission* [1996] ECR I-5951, [1997] 4 CMLR 662.

[177] XXVth *Report on Competition Policy* (1995), point 86; see also the *Notice on Market Definition* (p 29, n 139 above), para 56; the *Guidelines on Vertical Restraints* (p 32, n 160 above), para 86; DG COMP's *Discussion paper on the application of Article 82 of the Treaty to exclusionary abuses* paras 243–265.

[178] XXVth *Report on Competition Policy* (1995), point 87.

[179] Commission's XXVIIth *Report on Competition Policy* (1997), pp 153–154; see Andrews 'Aftermarket Power in the Computer Services Market: The Digital Undertaking' (1998) 19 ECLR 176.

[180] See OFTEL Decision, *Swan Solutions Ltd/Avaya ECS Ltd*, 6 April 2001 and OFT Decision, *ICL/Synstar*, 26 July 2001; both decisions are available on the OFT's website: www.oft.gov.uk.

[181] OFT 403, December 2004, paras 6.1–6.7.

[182] See eg Case M 1221 *Rewe/Meinl* OJ [1999] L 274/1, [2000] 5 CMLR 256.

[183] See the report of the UK Competition Commission on *Supermarkets* Cm 4842 (2000).

[184] See ch 16, p 651.

(xii) Innovation markets[185]

In the US a 'market for innovation', separate from products already on the market, has been found in some cases involving high technology industries[186]. The Commission's decision in *Shell/Montecatini*[187] suggested that it would be prepared to define a market for innovation, although in other cases it has made use of the more conventional idea of 'potential competition' to deal with the situation[188]. The Commission's *Guidelines on Horizontal Cooperation Agreements*[189] provide some guidance on this issue.

(D) The relevant geographic market

It is also necessary, when determining whether a firm or firms have market power, that the relevant geographic market should be defined. The definition of the geographic market may have a decisive impact on the outcome of a case, as in the *Volvo/Scania* decision under the ECMR: the Commission's conclusion that there were national, rather than pan-European, markets for trucks and buses led to an outright prohibition of that merger[190]. Some products can be supplied without difficulty throughout the Community or even the world. In other cases there may be technical, legal or practical reasons why a product can be supplied only within a narrower area. The delineation of the geographic market helps to indicate which other firms impose a competitive constraint on the one(s) under investigation. The cost of transporting products is an important factor: some goods are so expensive to transport in relation to their value that it would not be economic to attempt to sell them on distant markets. Another factor might be legal controls which make it impossible for an undertaking in one Member State to export goods or services to another. This problem may be dealt with by the Commission bringing proceedings against the Member State to prevent restrictions on the free movement of goods (under Articles 28 to 30) or of services (under Articles 49 to 55). With the completion of the internal market, there should be fewer claims that fiscal, technical and legal barriers to inter-state trade exist.

(i) *United Brands v Commission*

That the geographic market should be identified is clear from the ECJ's judgment in *United Brands v Commission*[191]. It said that the opportunities for competition under Article 82 must be considered:

with reference to a clearly defined geographic area in which [the product] is marketed and where the conditions are sufficiently homogeneous for the effect of the economic power of the undertaking concerned to be able to be evaluated.

---

[185] See Rapp 'The Misapplication of the Innovative Market Approach to Merger Analysis' (1995) 64 Antitrust Law Journal 19.

[186] See eg *United States v Flow International Corpn* 6 Trade Reg Rep (CCH) ¶ 45,094; US Department of Justice and Federal Trade Commission *Antitrust Guidelines for the Licensing of Intellectual Property* available at www.usdoj.gov/atr/public/guidelines/ipguide.htm.

[187] OJ [1994] L 332/48.

[188] See Temple Lang 'European Community Antitrust Law: Innovation Markets and High Technology Industries' [1996] Fordham Corporate Law Institute (ed Hawk), ch 23; Landman 'Innovation Markets in Europe' (1998) 19 ECLR 21; OFT Economic Discussion Paper 3 (OFT 377) *Innovation and Competition Policy* (Charles River Associates, March 2002), Annex B.

[189] OJ [2001] C 3/2, [2001] 4 CMLR 819, paras 51–53.   [190] See ch 21, p 893.

[191] Case 27/76 [1978] ECR 207, [1978] 1 CMLR 429, paras 10–11.

In that case the Commission had excluded the UK, France and Italy from the geographic market since in those countries special arrangements existed as to the importing and marketing of bananas. United Brands argued that, even so, the Commission had drawn the geographic market too widely, since competitive conditions varied between the remaining six Member States[192]; the ECJ however concluded that the Commission had drawn it correctly. The significance of the geographic market in determining dominance was emphasised by the ECJ in *Alsatel v Novasam SA*[193]. There the ECJ held that the facts before it failed to establish that a particular region in France rather than France generally constituted the geographic market, so that the claim that Novasam had a dominant position failed in the absence of evidence of power over the wider, national, market.

(ii) The Commission's *Notice on Market Definition*

The Commission provides helpful guidance on the definition of the geographic market in its *Notice on Market Definition*[194]. At paragraph 28, it says that its approach can be summarised as follows:

it will take a preliminary view of the scope of the geographic market on the basis of broad indications as to the distribution of market shares between the parties and their competitors, as well as a preliminary analysis of pricing and price differences at national and Community or EEA level. This initial view is used basically as a working hypothesis to focus the Commission's enquiries for the purposes of arriving at a precise geographic market definition.

In the following paragraph the Commission says that it will then explore any particular configuration of prices or market shares in order to test whether they really do say something about the possibility of demand substitution between one market and another: for example it will consider the importance of national or local preferences, current patterns of purchases of customers and product differentiation. This survey is to be conducted within the context of the SSNIP test outlined above, the difference being that, in the case of geographic market definition, the question is whether, faced with an increase in price, consumers located in a particular area would switch their purchases to suppliers further away. Further relevant factors are set out in paragraphs 30 and 31 of the Notice, and at paragraph 32 the Commission points out that it will take into account the continuing process of market integration in defining the market, the assumption here being that, over time, the single market should become more of a reality, with the result that the geographic market should have a tendency to get wider. There is no reason in principle why the relevant geographic market should not extend to the entire world, and there have been decisions in which this has been so[195].

(iii) Examples of evidence that may be used in defining the relevant geographic market

As far as definition of the geographic market is concerned, the Commission suggests that the following evidence may be available.

---

[192] This decision was reached before the accession of Greece, Spain and Portugal etc.
[193] Case 247/86 [1988] ECR 5987, [1990] 4 CMLR 434.   [194] See p 29, n 139 above.
[195] For example the Commission found global markets for top-level internet connectivity in Case M.1069 *WorldCom/MCI* OJ [1999] L 116/1, [1999] 5 CMLR 876, para 82 and Case M.1741 *MCI WorldCom/Sprint*, decision of 28 June 2000, para 97, available at www.europa.eu.int/comm/competition/mergers/cases.

(A) Past evidence of diversion of orders to other areas It may be that direct evidence is available of changes in prices between areas and consequent reactions by customers. The Commission points out that care may be needed in comparing prices where there have been exchange rate movements, where taxation levels are different and where there is significant product differentiation between one area and another.

(B) Basic demand characteristics The scope of the geographic market may be determined by matters such as national preferences or preferences for national brands, language, culture and life style, and the need for a local presence.

(C) Views of customers and competitors As in the case of defining the product market, the Commission will take the views of customers and competitors into account when determining the scope of the geographic market.

(D) Current geographic pattern of purchases The Commission will examine where customers currently purchase goods or supplies. If they already purchase across the Community, this would indicate a Community-wide market.

(E) Trade flows/patterns of shipments Information on trade flows may be helpful in determining the geographic market, provided that the trade statistics are sufficiently detailed for the products in question.

(F) Barriers and switching costs associated with the diversion of orders to companies located in other areas Barriers that isolate national markets, transport costs and transport restrictions may all contribute to the isolation of national markets.

(E) The temporal market

It may also be necessary to consider the temporal quality of the market[196]. Competitive conditions may vary from season to season, for example because of the variation of weather conditions or of consumer habits. A firm may find itself exposed to competition at one point in a year but effectively free from it at another. In this situation it may be that its behaviour may be controlled under Article 82 during the part of the year in which it can be shown to be dominant.

The issue arose in *United Brands v Commission*[197]. There was evidence in that case which suggested that the cross-elasticity of demand for bananas fluctuated from season to season. When other fruit was plentiful in summer, demand for bananas dropped: this suggests that the Commission might have considered that there were two seasonal markets, and that United Brands had no market power over the summer months. The Commission however identified just the one temporal market and held that UBC was dominant within it. On appeal the ECJ declined to deal with this issue. In *ABG*[198] on the other hand the Commission did define the temporal market for oil more narrowly by limiting it to the period of crisis which followed the decision of OPEC to increase dramatically the price of oil in the early 1970s. The Commission held that during the

---

[196] The temporal market is discussed briefly in the OFT guideline on *Market Definition*, OFT 403, December 2004, paras 5.1–5.3.

[197] Case 27/76 [1978] ECR 207, [1978] 1 CMLR 429.   [198] OJ [1977] L 117/1, [1977] 2 CMLR D1.

crisis companies had a special responsibility to supply existing customers on a fair and equitable basis; the ECJ quashed the Commission's decision on the issue of abuse, but not on the definition of the market[199].

(F) Market power

A crucial issue in competition assessment is whether a firm or firms have or will have market power. As has been stressed, market definition provides a framework within which to carry out this assessment: however market definition is not an end in itself. Three issues are relevant to an assessment of market power: market shares and the concentration level of the market; barriers to expansion and entry; and buyer power. It requires only a moment's reflection to realise that market share figures cannot provide any insights into the potential competition of firms; nor as to the strength of any buyer power in the market. This is why market share figures are, at best, a proxy for market power without being determinative in themselves.

The Commission has not published a notice on the assessment of market power, as it has in the case of the *Notice on Market Definition*. However DG COMP's *Discussion Paper on the application of Article 82 of the Treaty to exclusionary abuses*[200] contains some invaluable insights into its thinking; and in the UK the OFT has published a helpful document on the topic[201].

(i) Market shares and market concentration

(A) Market shares Market shares provide a useful first indication of the competitive importance of firms that are active on a market: where one firm has a high market share compared with other players on the market this is an indication of dominance, provided that it has been held for some time[202]. The Commission usually looks at current market shares in its competitive analysis, although in some cases it may look at the historical position, particularly in markets where orders are 'large and lumpy': for example, a firm that builds power stations or hydro-electric dams will not receive many orders, but those that it does receive will be very substantial[203]. Markets of this kind are sometimes referred to as 'bidding markets', where market share figures may provide little insight into market power: in cases of this kind an auction may be arranged, so that undertakings compete *for* the market rather than *in* the market[204]. A market share of more than 50 per cent may indicate dominance where rivals hold a much smaller share of the market[205]. However market power cannot be determined on the basis of market share figures alone[206].

---

[199] Case 77/77 *BP v Commission* [1978] ECR 1513, [1978] 3 CMLR 174.

[200] December 2005, available at ww.ec.europa.eu/comm/competition/antitrust/art82/discpaper2005.

[201] *Assessment on market power*, OFT 415, December 2004.

[202] See 'DG COMP's' *Discussion Paper on exclusionary abuses*, para 29.   [203] Ibid, para 30.

[204] A helpful discussion of the types of auction that may be held and the decisional practice in the EU and the UK can be found in Szilági Pál 'Bidding Markets and Competition Law in the European Union and the United Kingdom' (2008) 29 ECLR 16 and (2008) 29 ECLR 89.

[205] *Discussion Paper on exclusionary abuses*, para 31; note that the ECJ in Case C-62/86 *AKZO v Commission* [1991] ECR I-3359, [1993] 5 CMLR 215, held that there is a rebuttable presumption of dominance where a firm has a market share of 50 per cent or more.

[206] *Discussion Paper on exclusionary abuses*, para 32.

(B) Market concentration and the Herfindahl-Hirschman Index In some cases the Commission uses market share figures in order to determine how concentrated the market is, or how concentrated it will be following a merger or the entry into force, for example, of a cooperation agreement. Competition concerns may be greater as the market becomes more concentrated. One way of determining the level of concentration in the market is to use the so-called 'Herfindahl-Hirschman Index' ('the HHI')[207]. This sums up the squares of the individual market shares of all the competitors in a market: the higher the total, the more concentrated the market. The concentration level will be low where the total is below 1,000; moderate if between 1,000 and 1,800; and high where it is above 1,800. This is a relatively simple way of calculating market concentration, and its effectiveness is demonstrated by the following three examples:

Example 1

In the widget industry there are 15 competitors: 5 of them each has a market share in the region of 10 per cent, and 10 of them each has a market share in the region of 5 per cent

$$HHI = 5 \times 10^2 + 10 \times 5^2 = 500 + 250 = 750$$

The market concentration is low

Example 2

In the blodget industry there are 8 competitors: 2 of them each has a market share in the region of 20 per cent, and 6 of them each has a market share in the region of 10 per cent

$$HHI = 2 \times 20^2 + 6 \times 10^2 = 800 + 600 = 1400$$

The market concentration is moderate

Example 3

In the sprocket industry there are 4 competitors: 2 of them each has a market share in the region of 30 per cent and the other 2 each has a market share in the region of 20 per cent

$$HHI = 2 \times 30^2 + 2 \times 20^2 = 1800 + 800 = 2600$$

The market concentration is high

The same approach can be used to work out the consequences for the concentration of the market of any of the competitors merging or entering into an agreement with one another. For example if, in Example 2, the two firms with 20 per cent were to merge, the HHI after the agreement would be:

$$40^2 + 6 \times 10^2 = 1600 + 600 = 2200$$

The market concentration will have moved from moderate to high. The difference in the pre- and post-merger concentration levels – that is to say the increase of 800 from 1400 to 2200, is referred to as the 'Delta', represented by the symbol Δ.

---

[207] See *Guidelines on the applicability of Article 81 to horizontal co-operation agreements* [2001] OJ C 3/2, para 29 and *Guidelines on the assessment of horizontal mergers* [2004] OJ C 31/5, para 16.

If however, in Example 2, two of the firms with 10 per cent had entered into an agreement with one another, the HHI after the agreement would be:

$$2 \times 20^2 + 1 \times 20^2 + 4 \times 10^2 = 800 + 400 + 400 = 1600$$

The market concentration will remain moderate, and the Delta would be merely 200.

Thus, the HHI demonstrates arithmetically the difference between the two situations, indicating that greater caution should be exercised by a competition authority in relation to the former than the latter case.

The Commission also suggests, in paragraph 29 of its *Horizontal Cooperation Agreement Guidelines*, that, in determining the concentration level of the market, another possible indicator is the leading firm concentration ratio. For example the three-firm concentration ratio is the sum of the market shares of the leading three competitors in a market, and is depicted as 'CR3'; 'CR4' would indicate the outcome of the same exercise in relation to the leading four firms[208].

(ii) Barriers to expansion and entry

Where barriers to expansion by firms already in the market or barriers to entry by firms outside it are low, the fact that one firm has a very high market share may not be indicative of significant market power[209]. The Commission in unlikely to consider that barriers are high in an industry that has experienced frequent and successful examples of entry[210]. The Commission considers that barriers to expansion and entry are factors that make entry impossible or unprofitable while permitting established undertakings to charge prices above the competitive level[211]. DG COMP's *Discussion Paper* lists various factors that can give rise to barriers to expansion or entry[212]:

- **Legal barriers**: legislation may limit the number of market participants, for example by limiting the number of firms that can be granted licences to carry on a certain activity, granting special or exclusive rights or conferring intellectual property rights that can be used to prevent other firms from entering the market

- **Capacity constraints**: it may not be possible to expand capacity without incurring substantial sunk costs

- **Economies of scale and scope**: where there are substantial economies of scale or scope expansion or entry may be costly and risky

- **Absolute cost advantages**: firms that have preferential access to essential facilities, natural resources, innovation and R&D, intellectual property rights, and capital may enjoy significant cost advantages over other firms

- **Privileged access to supply**: for example a vertically-integrated firm may enjoy advantages over rivals if it enjoys control over vital inputs

- **A highly-developed distribution and sales network**: it may be difficult for rivals to match a well-established distribution system

- **The established position of the incumbent firms on the market**: it may be difficult for a firm to challenge the experience or reputation of a firm already established in the market

---

[208] See *Guidelines on the applicability of Article 81 to horizontal co-operation agreements* [2001] OJ C3/2.

[209] See DG COMP's *Discussion Paper on exclusionary abuses*, para 34.   [210] Ibid, para 36.

[211] Ibid, para 38.   [212] Ibid, para 40.

- **Other strategic barriers to expansion or entry**: other factors may make it expensive for customers to switch from established firms to a new one, for example where an incumbent firm enjoys network effects[213].

(iii) Buyer power

It is possible that the market position of buyers may constrain the behaviour of suppliers. This would be the position when, in the event of an increase in selling prices, buyers are able to encourage existing firms to expand their output or potential firms to enter the market[214].

(iv) Summary

The discussion above has explained the key features involved in the determination of whether a firm or firms have market power. In particular it was explained that:

- **Market definition** is an important part of the analysis of market power, but it is not an end in itself and is simply one stage in the overall process
- **Market shares** provide us with important information about the state of existing competition within the market, but they cannot, in themselves, be determinative, since they tell us nothing about barriers to expansion and entry, nor about buyer power
- **Barriers to expansion and entry** are important, since they provide us with information about the existence of potential competition, something which cannot be captured by a market share figure, precisely because the competition is potential only
- **Buyer power** is also an important part of the analysis of market power.

(G) A final reflection on market shares

It has been said several times in this chapter that market share does not, in itself, determine whether an undertaking possesses market power; assessing market power is not and cannot be reduced simply to numbers. This having been said, however, it is interesting to consider the large range of situations in which EC and UK competition law require competition lawyers and their clients to consider market share figures for the purpose of deciding how to handle a particular case. This arises partly from numerous pieces of legislation, both hard and soft, which contain a market share threshold; and partly from case law which has attributed significance to particular market share figures. The following table sets out a series of market share thresholds that should be embedded in the mind of in-house counsel to *DoItAll*, a diversified conglomerate company conducting business in the EU. The list is not exhaustive, and was compiled in a more light-hearted mood than the rest of this chapter: it does nevertheless reveal how influential market share figures can be in analysing competition law cases in the EC and the UK.

---

[213] See pp 11–12 above on network effects.
[214] *Discussion Paper on exclusionary abuses*, para 41.

1.1 Table of market share thresholds

0%	With a market share of 0% even the most zealous of competition authorities is unlikely to take action against you
	With a market share of less than 5% your agreements are unlikely to have an effect on trade between Member States provided that certain other criteria are satisfied[1]
5%	At 5% or more your agreements with undertakings that are not actual or potential competitors may significantly contribute to any 'cumulative' foreclosure effect of parallel networks of similar agreements[2]
	Agreements with undertakings that concern imports and exports have been found to have an effect on trade between Member States where your market share is around the 5% level[3]
	When notifying mergers under the EC Merger Regulation you will be required to provide information about competitors that have more than 5% of the relevant geographic market[4]
10%	At 10% or more your agreements with actual or potential competitors are no longer *de minimis* under the European Commission's *Notice on Agreements of Minor Importance*[5]
	It is unlikely that your group purchasing agreements[6] or your commercialisation[7] agreements infringe Article 81(1) where your market share is below 15%
15%	At 15% or more your agreements with undertakings that are not actual or potential competitors are no longer *de minimis* under the *Notice on Agreements of Minor Importance*[8]
	Under the EC Merger Regulation, in the case of horizontal mergers, markets in which your market share exceeds 15% are 'affected markets', necessitating the provision of substantial information on Form CO to DG COMP[9]
	With more than 15% of the market you are no longer eligible to take advantage of the 'simplified procedure' for certain horizontal mergers under the EC Merger Regulation[10]
20%	At 20% or more block exemption for certain co-insurance agreements ceases to be available[11]; some marginal relief is provided up to a market share cap of 22%[12] and even, exceptionally, beyond 22%[13]
	Block exemption ceases to be provided for specialisation agreements under Regulation 2658/2000 where the parties' market share exceeds 20%[14]; some marginal relief is available up to a market share cap of 25%[15]
	Block exemption ceases to be available for technology transfer agreements between competing undertakings where their combined market share exceeds 20%[16]

25%	At 25% or more block exemption ceases to be available for research and development agreements under Regulation 2659/2000[17]; some marginal relief is provided up to a market share cap of 30%[18] and even, exceptionally, beyond 30%[19]
	At 25% or more block exemption for certain co-reinsurance, as opposed to co-insurance, agreements ceases to be available[20]; some marginal relief is provided up to a threshold of 27%[21] and even, for a limited period, beyond 27%[22]
	Under the EC Merger Regulation at 25% you cease to benefit from a presumption that your merger will not significantly impede effective competition[23]
	Under the EC Merger Regulation you do not benefit from the simplified procedure in the case of vertical mergers where your market share exceeds 25%[24]
	Under the EC Merger Regulation, in the case of vertical mergers, markets in which your market share exceeds 25% are affected markets[25]
	Under UK law you could be referred to the Competition Commission under the merger provisions of the Enterprise Act 2002[26] where you supply or are supplied with 25% or more of the goods or services of a certain description
	With a market share of less than 25% it is unlikely that the exclusion of agreements leading to mergers from the Chapter I prohibition of the Competition Act 1998 would be withdrawn[27]
	Where a merger leads to a market share of less than 25% the Competition Commission in the UK is unlikely to find a substantial lessening of competition, although this cannot be ruled out[28]
30%	At 30% your agreements with undertakings that are not actual or potential competitors cease to benefit from the EC block exemption for vertical agreements[29], although there is some marginal relief up to 35%[30]
	Your liner consortia agreements run into problems under Commission Regulation 823/2000 if operated within a liner conference[31], with some marginal relief of up to 10% (that is to say up to a market share of 33%)
	Block exemption ceases to be available for technology transfer agreements between non-competing undertakings where their combined market share exceeds 30%
	At less than 30% your non-horizontal mergers are unlikely to give rise to any problems under the EC Merger Regulation; and there is no presumption against them where your market share is more than 30%[32]
35%	At 35% your liner consortia agreements run into problems, even if operated outside a liner conference[33]; there is some marginal relief of up to 10% of 35%, so be careful as you approach 38.5%.

40%	You may be dominant under Article 82 with a market share of 40% or more (there has been only one finding by the European Commission of dominance under Article 82 below 40%)[34]; if you are dominant, you have a special responsibility not to hinder competition[35]
	If your market share is below 40% the OFT considers it 'unlikely' that you are dominant[36]
	There is unlikely to be a cumulative foreclosure effect arising from your single branding agreements where all the companies at the retail level have market shares below 30% and the total tied market share is less than 40%[37]
45%	
50%	There is a legal presumption that, with 50% or more of the market, you have a dominant position[38]; this presumption applies in the case of collective dominance as well as single-firm dominance[39]
	With 50% or more of the relevant market you can no longer take advantage of the opposition procedure for certain shipping consortia[40]
	Where the market share of the 5 largest suppliers in a market is below 50% there is unlikely to be a single or cumulative anti-competitive effect arising from a single branding agreement[41]
	There is unlikely to be such an effect where the share of the market covered by selective distribution systems is less that 50%[42]
55%	
60%	
65%	
70%	
75%	
80%	At 80% you may now be approaching a position of 'super-dominance', where you have a particularly special responsibility not to indulge in abusive behaviour[43]
85%	
90%	At 90% you are approaching 'quasi-monopoly'[44]
95%	
100%	At 100% you are a monopolist.

[1] *Guidelines on the effect on trade concept*, OJ [2004] C 101/81, para 52.
[2] OJ [2001] C 368/13, [2002] 4 CMLR 699, para 8; OFT Guidance *Agreements and concerted practices*, OFT 401, December 2004, para 2.16.
[3] *Guidelines on the effect on trade concept*, OJ [2004] C 101/81, para 46.
[4] Regulation 802/2004, OJ [2004] L 133/1, section 7.3.

5 OJ [2001] C 368/13, [2002] 4 CMLR 699, para 7; OFT Guidance *Agreements and concerted practices*, OFT 401, December 2004, para 2.16.
6 Commission's *Guidelines on Horizontal Co-operation Agreements* OJ [2001] C3/2, [2001] 4 CMLR 819, para 130.
7 OJ [2001] C 3/2, [2001] 4 CMLR 819, para 149.
8 OJ [2001] C 368/13, [2002] 4 CMLR 699, para 7; OFT Guidance *Agreements and concerted practices*, OFT 401, December 2004, para 2.16.
9 See ch 21, p 850.
10 Ibid, p 845.
11 Regulation 358/2003 OJ [2003] L 53/8, [2003] 4 CMLR 734, Article 7(2)(a).
12 Ibid, Article 7(4).
13 Ibid, Article 7(5).
14 Regulation 2658/2000, OJ [2000] L 304/3, [2001] 4 CMLR 800, Article 7(4).
15 Ibid, Article 6.
16 Regulation 772/2004, OJ [2004] L 123/11, Article 3(1).
17 Regulation 2659/2000, OJ [2000] L 304/7, [2001] 4 CMLR 808, Article 4.
18 Ibid, Article 6(2).
19 Ibid, Article 6(3).
20 Regulation 358/2003 OJ [2003] L 53/8, [2003] 4 CMLR 734, Article 7(2)(b).
21 Ibid, Article 7(7).
22 Ibid, Article 7(8).
23 Regulation 139/2004, OJ [2004] L 24/1, Recital 32.
24 Ch 21, p 845.
25 Ibid, p 850.
26 See ch 22, pp 911–912.
27 OFT Guidance *Mergers – substantive assessment guidance*, OFT 516, May 2003.
28 CC Guidance *Merger references: Competition Commission Guidelines*, CC 2, June 2003, para 3.4.
29 Regulation 2790/99, Article 3.
30 Regulation 2790/99, Article 9(2)(c).
31 Regulation 823/2000 OJ [2000] L 100/24, [2000] 5 CMLR 92, as amended by Regulation 611/2005, OJ [2005] L 101/10, Article 6(1).
32 *Guidelines on the assessment of non-horizontal mergers*, para 25.
33 Regulation 823/2000.
34 See *Virgin/British Airways* OJ [2000] L 30/1, [2000] 4 CMLR 999: dominance at 39.7% of the market, upheld on appeal Case T-219/99 *British Airways v Commission* [2003] ECR II-5917.
35 On the special responsibility of dominant firms see ch 5, pp 183–184.
36 OFT Guidance *Abuse of a dominant position*, OFT 402, December 2004, para 4.18 and *Assessment of market power*, OFT 415, para 2.12.
37 Commission's *Guidelines on Vertical Restraints* (p 32, n 160), para 149.
38 See Case-62/86 *AKZO Chemie v Commission* [1991] ECR I-3359, [1993] 5 CMLR 215, para 60.
39 Case T-191/98 *Atlantic Container Line AB v Commission* [2003] ECR II-3275, paras 931–932.
40 Article 7(1) of Regulation 823/2000.
41 Commission's *Guidelines on Vertical Restraint*, para 143.
42 Ibid, para 189.
43 See ch 5, pp 184–186.
44 Ibid, p 184.

Overview of EC and UK competition law

CHAPTER CONTENTS

1. INTRODUCTION

This chapter will provide a brief overview of EC and UK competition law and the relevant institutions; it will also explain the relationship between EC competition law and the domestic competition laws of the Member States, in particular in the light of Article 3 of Regulation 1/2003[1] ('the Modernisation Regulation'). The rules of the European Economic Area are briefly referred to, and the trend on the part of Member States to adopt domestic competition rules modelled on those in the EC Treaty is noted. Three diagrams at the end of the chapter explain the institutional structure of EC and UK competition law.

---

[1] Council Regulation 1/2003 on the implementation of the rules on competition laid down in Articles 81 and 82 of the Treaty OJ [2003] L 1/1, available at www.ec.europa.eu/comm/competition/antitrust/legislation/regulations.html.

2. EC LAW

(A) The Rome Treaty

The Rome Treaty of 1957[2] established what is now known as the European Community[3]. There are currently 27 Member States[4]. The 'Reform Treaty' that was signed in Lisbon in December 2007, if it enters into force, will rename the European Community as the European Union[5]. The Rome Treaty, as renumbered by the Amsterdam Treaty of 1997, consists of 314 Articles. It is a complex document which has generated a considerable body of jurisprudence[6]. Much of EC law is concerned with the elimination of obstacles to the free movement of goods, services, persons and capital; the removal of these obstacles in itself promotes competition within the Community. Initiatives such as the establishment of a public procurement regime[7], the creation of the Euro[8] and the 'Lisbon Strategy'[9] with its emphasis on promoting knowledge and innovation for economic growth also contribute substantially to greater competition within the European economy. However, quite apart from this 'macro' effect on competition, the Treaty also contains specific competition rules that apply to undertakings and to the Member States themselves.

(i) The competition chapter in the Treaty

EC competition law is contained in Chapter 1 of Part III of the EC Treaty, which consists of Articles 81 to 89. It is necessary to read these provisions in conjunction with the principles of the Treaty laid down in its early Articles. Of particular significance are Articles 2 and 3. The former provides that:

The Community shall have as its task, by establishing a common market and an economic and monetary union and by implementing the common policies or activities referred to in Articles 3

---

[2] The Treaty of Paris of 1951 had earlier established a special regime for coal and steel which contained provisions dealing specifically with competition; this Treaty expired on 23 July 2002: it is discussed briefly in ch 23, p 961.

[3] The original name 'European Economic Community' was replaced by its current title by the Maastricht Treaty 1992, primarily to reflect the move away from a purely economic Community to one with a stronger political emphasis; following the Maastricht and Amsterdam Treaties, the EC constitutes one of three 'pillars' of the European Union, the other two, Police and Judicial Cooperation in Criminal Matters and Common Foreign and Security Policy, being of an inter-Governmental nature, more akin to conventional international treaties.

[4] As to the position of territories such as the Isle of Man and Gibraltar under Community Law see Murray *EU & Member State Territories – The Special Relationship under Community Law* (Palladian Law Publishing, 2004).

[5] See pp 50–51 below.

[6] For comprehensive analysis of EC law in general see Wyatt and Dashwood's *European Union Law* (Sweet & Maxwell, 5th ed, 2006, eds Arnull, Dashwood, Dougan, Ross, Spaventa and Wyatt); Chalmers, Hadjiemmanuil, Monti and Tomkins *European Union Law* (Cambridge University Press, 2006); Craig and De Búrca *EU Law: Texts, Cases and Materials* (Oxford University Press, 4th ed, 2007).

[7] On public procurement see Bovis *EC Public Procurement: Case Law and Regulation* (Oxford University Press, 2005); Arrowsmith *The Law of Public and Utilities Procurement* (Sweet & Maxwell, 2nd ed, 2005); Trepte *Public Procurement in the EU* (Oxford University Press, 2007).

[8] On the Euro see Herdegen 'Price Stability and Budgetary Restraints in Economic and Monetary Union: the Law as Guardian of Economic Wisdom' (1998) 35 CML Rev 9; Louis 'A Legal and Institutional Approach for Building a Monetary Union' (1998) 35 CML Rev 33; Swann *The Economics of Europe* (Penguin Books, 9th ed, 2000), ch 7; see further p 52 below.

[9] See www.ec.europa.eu/growthandjobs; see also *A Pro-active Competition Policy for a Competitive Europe* COM(2004)293 final, available at www.ec.europa.eu/comm/competition/publications/proactive/en.pdf.

and 4, to promote throughout the Community a harmonious, balanced and sustainable development of economic activities, a high level of employment and of social protection, equality between
men and women, sustainable and non-inflationary growth, a high degree of competitiveness and
convergence of economic performance, a high level of protection and improvement of the quality of the environment, the raising of the standard of living and quality of life, and economic and
social cohesion and solidarity among Member States.

Article 3 sets out certain activities of the Community intended to help the achievement
of the task laid down in Article 2; paragraph (g) of Article 3(1)[10] specifically refers to:

a system ensuring that competition in the internal market is not distorted.

Furthermore Article 4 provides that the activities of the Member States and the
Community shall be conducted in accordance with the principle of an open market
economy with free competition[11]. These references to competition in the constitution
of the EC have a significant effect on the decisions and judgments of the European
Commission ('the Commission'), the Court of First Instance and the European
Court of Justice ('the CFI' and 'the ECJ' respectively or, collectively, 'the Community
Courts'), which have often interpreted the specific competition rules teleologically
from the starting point of Articles 2 and 3(1)(g)[12]. Within Chapter 1 of Part III of the
Treaty Article 81(1) prohibits agreements, decisions by associations of undertakings
and concerted practices that have as their object or effect the restriction of competition[13], although this prohibition may be declared inapplicable where the conditions in
Article 81(3) are satisfied[14]. Article 82 prohibits the abuse by an undertaking or undertakings of a dominant position[15]. Article 86(1) imposes obligations on Member States in
relation to the Treaty generally and the competition rules specifically, while Article 86(2)
concerns the application of the competition rules to public undertakings and private
undertakings to which a Member State entrusts particular responsibilities[16]. Articles 87
to 89 prohibit state aid to undertakings by Member States which might distort competition in the common market[17]. An important additional instrument of EC competition
law is the EC Merger Regulation ('the ECMR') which applies to concentrations between
undertakings that have a Community dimension[18].

(ii) The Reform Treaty of December 2007

A European Constitution was signed in 2003 but was never ratified, and has since
been abandoned[19]. Instead the Member States adopted the so-called 'Reform Treaty' in
Lisbon in December 2007[20]. The intention is that the Reform Treaty should be ratified

[10] Note that the Reform Treaty of 2007, if it is ratified and enters into force, will repeal Article 3(1) of the
EC Treaty.
[11] Note that under the Reform Treaty of 2007 Article 4 will become Article 97b.
[12] For examples of teleological interpretation of the competition rules see Cases C-68/94 and 30/95
France v Commission [1998] ECR I-1375, [1998] 4 CMLR 829, paras 169–178 and Case T-102/96 *Gencor v
Commission* [1999] ECR II-753, [1999] 4 CMLR 971, paras 148–158.
[13] On Article 81(1) see ch 3.   [14] On Article 81(3) see ch 4.   [15] On Article 82 see chs 5, 17 and 18.
[16] On Article 86 see ch 6, pp 220–244.   [17] Articles 87–89 are briefly discussed in ch 6, pp 244–245.
[18] Regulation 139/2004 OJ [2004] L 24/1, available at www.ec.europa.eu/comm/competition/mergers/
legislation/legislation.html.
[19] The text of this 'Treaty establishing a Constitution for Europe' can be accessed at www.european-
convention.eu.int or at OJ [2004] C 310/1.
[20] The text of this 'Treaty of Lisbon amending the Treaty on European Union and the Treaty establishing
the European Community' can be accessed at OJ [2007] C 306/1.

in time for elections to the European Parliament in 2009, although it cannot be guaranteed that this will occur. If and when the Reform Treaty is ratified and enters into force the Rome Treaty will be renamed the Treaty on the Functioning of the European Union ('the TFU'), and the word 'Community' will be replaced throughout by the word 'Union'. It follows that, in future, references would be to EU competition law, not to EC competition law. The Reform Treaty also provides that all references to the common market will in future be replaced by the expression 'internal market'. The Court of First Instance will be known in future as the General Court. Articles 81 and 82 EC will become Articles 101 and 102 TFU.

The non-ratified Constitution listed as one of the EU's objectives the achievement of a highly competitive social market economy. However the reference to competition as a separate objective was not included in the Reform Treaty; indeed the Reform Treaty, if it enters into force, will repeal Article 3(1)(g) of the EC Treaty that establishes as one of the activities of the Community the achievement of a system of undistorted competition. The Reform Treaty would instead amend the Treaty on European Union with a simple statement, in a revised Article 3(3), that 'The Union shall establish an internal market'. However a Protocol on the Internal Market and Competition is annexed to the Treaty, and it states clearly that the internal market provided for in Article 2 includes a system ensuring that competition is not distorted.

As the Reform Treaty was being negotiated, concerns were expressed that the removal of the reference to competition as an objective in the draft Constitution meant that the significance of competition policy was being downgraded. However this is unconvincing as a matter of law given that the establishment of an internal market is reaffirmed as one of the objectives of the Union and that the Protocol on the Internal Market and Competition, which has the same force as a Treaty provision, emphasises the importance of undistorted competition as a feature of the single market[21]. This point was made by a speech of Commissioner Kroes of 8 November 2007, in which she said that 'The Protocol maintains in full force the competition rules which have served European citizens so well for fifty years'[22]. This is not to say that the contribution that competition policy should play in the life of the European Union may not be questioned at a political level at some point in the future: it was noted in chapter 1 that competition policy can change over time. However the Reform Treaty would not appear to change the legal status of competition policy.

(iii) The single market imperative

As mentioned in chapter 1[23], it is important to stress that EC competition law is applied by the Commission and the Community Courts very much with the issue of single market integration in mind. Agreements and conduct which might have the effect of dividing the territory of one Member State from another will be closely scrutinised and may be severely punished. The existence of 'single market' competition rules as well as 'conventional' competition rules is a unique feature of Community competition law. The fact that ten further countries acceded to the European Union on 1 May 2004 and two more on 1 January 2007, together with the possibility of future accessions, for example by some of the Balkan states and Turkey, means that single market

---

[21] See to similar effect the statement of Commissioner Kroes of 23 June 2007, MEMO/07/250.
[22] Available at www.ec.europa.eu/comm/competition/speeches/index_2007.html.
[23] See ch 1, pp 22–23.

integration is likely[24] to remain a key feature of competition policy[25]. The Commissioner for Competition Policy made a powerful speech extolling the benefits of the single market, and the dangers of a renaissance of national protectionism within the EU, at St Gallen on 11 May 2007[26].

(iv) Economic and monetary union

The creation of the Euro has an important influence on competition within the Community. As explained in chapter 1 the competitive process depends, amongst other things, on consumers having adequate information to enable them to make rational choices[27]. Price comparisons are difficult when the same goods and services are sold in different, variable currencies; the problem is compounded by the cost of exchanging money. The Euro brings a transparency to price information that fundamentally transforms the position, and has a considerable impact on the way in which business is conducted. The Commission has stressed the significance of the Euro for competition policy on a number of occasions[28].

(v) The modernisation of Community competition law

During the course of the 1990s it became apparent that many aspects of Community competition law were in need of modernisation; in particular the law on vertical agreements, on horizontal cooperation agreements and on the obtaining of individual exemptions under Article 81(3) of the Treaty were perceived by many people, including Commission officials, to be in need of radical reform. Proposals for reform were set out by the Director General of Competition in an address to the 25th Annual Conference of the Fordham Corporate Law Institute in New York in October 1998[29], and the modernisation programme gathered pace in 1999 and 2000[30]. The adoption of Regulation 2790/99 radically changed the application of Article 81(3) to vertical agreements[31], and a transformation of the Commission's approach to horizontal cooperation agreements was completed at the end of 2000[32]. The law and practice of the ECMR has been considerably reformed in recent years[33]. Even more radically, with effect from 1 May 2004 the way in which Articles 81 and 82 are applied in practice was fundamentally changed as a result of the entry into force of the Modernisation

---

[24] Note however the judgment of the CFI in Case T-168/01 *GlaxoSmithKline Services v Commission* [2006] ECR II-2969, [2006] 5 CMLR 29 and the Opinion of AG Jacobs in Case C-53/03 *Syfait and Others v GlaxoSmithKline and Others* [2005] ECR I-4609, [2005] 5 CMLR 1, suggesting the possibility of a less strict approach to the issue of the single market, at least in relation to parallel trade in pharmaceutical products within the EU: see ch 3, pp 121–122; note that both the Commission and GSK have appealed against the CFI judgment of 2006: see Cases C-501/06 P and C-513/06 P, not yet decided.

[25] For details of the progress of talks on enlargement of the Community see ec.europa.eu/enlargement/key_documents/reports_nov_2006_en.htm.

[26] Available at www.ec.europa.eu/comm/competition/speeches/index_speeches_by_the_commissioner.html.

[27] See ch 1, p 7.

[28] See eg the Commission's XXVIIth *Report on Competition Policy* (1997), pp 7–8 and XXVIIIth *Report on Competition Policy* (1998), pp 24–25.

[29] Schaub 'EC Competition System – Proposals for Reform' [1998] Fordham Corporate Law Institute (ed Hawk), ch 9; see also Ehlermann 'The Modernisation of EC Antitrust Policy: A Legal and Cultural Revolution' (2000) 37 CML Rev 537.

[30] See the Commission's XXIXth *Report on Competition Policy* (1999), points 8–42.

[31] See ch 16, pp 639–662.   [32] See ch 15, pp 581–592.   [33] See ch 21 generally.

Regulation[34]; in particular this Regulation abolished the system of notifying agreements to the Commission for individual exemption under Article 81(3), and removed the Commission's monopoly over the application of that provision to individual agreements[35]. There is no question that these are major changes in the direction of competition law and policy in the Community.

(B) Institutions[36]

(i) Council of the European Union

The supreme legislative body of the European Community is the Council of the European Union, often referred to as the Council of Ministers[37]. The Council is not involved in competition policy on a regular basis. However, acting under powers conferred by Articles 83 and 308 EC, the Council has adopted several major pieces of legislation, including the ECMR; it has delegated important powers to the Commission through regulations to enforce the competition rules in the Treaty, in particular Regulation 17 of 1962[38], replaced with effect from 1 May 2004 by the Modernisation Regulation[39]; and it has given the Commission power to grant block exemptions in respect of certain agreements caught by Article 81(1) but which satisfy the criteria of Article 81(3)[40].

(ii) European Commission

The European Commission in Brussels is at the core of Community competition policy[41] and is responsible for fact-finding, taking action against infringements of the law, imposing penalties, adopting block exemption regulations, conducting sectoral inquiries, investigating mergers and state aids, and for developing policy and legislative initiatives. The Commission is also involved in the international aspects of competition policy, including cooperation with competition authorities in jurisdictions such as the US, Canada and Japan[42]. One of the 27 Commissioners takes special responsibility for competition matters; this is regarded as one of the most important portfolios within the Commission, and confers upon the incumbent a high public profile. Certain decisions can be taken by the Commissioner for Competition rather than by the College of Commissioners. There are two Hearing Officers, directly responsible to the Commissioner, who are responsible for ensuring that the rights of the defence are respected in proceedings under Articles 81 and 82 and the ECMR and that draft decisions of the Commission take due account of the relevant facts[43].

DG COMP (formerly known as DG IV) is the Directorate of the Commission specifically responsible for competition policy. DG COMP's website is an invaluable source

---

[34] See n 1 above; the Modernisation Regulation is discussed at pp 75–78 below, and further in ch 4, pp 162–164 and in ch 7 generally.

[35] The system of block exemptions continues: see ch 4, pp 164–169.

[36] The institutional structure of EC and UK law is set out in diagrammatic form at the end of this chapter: see pp 78–80 below.

[37] The Council renamed itself the Council of the European Union in 1993 (see OJ [1993] L 281/18).

[38] OJ [1962] 13/204, OJ [1959–62] spec ed 87.

[39] On the Commission's powers of enforcement see ch 7.   [40] See ch 4, pp 165–166.

[41] See Case C-344/98 *Masterfoods Ltd v HB Ice Cream Ltd* [2001] ECR I-11369, [2001] 4 CMLR 449, para 46.

[42] On the international dimension of competition policy see ch 12.

[43] On the role of the Hearing Officers see ch 7, p 279.

of material. From the index page it is possible to navigate to a series of policy areas, including antitrust (that is to say Articles 81 and 82, though there is a specific area for cartels), mergers, state aid, liberalisation, and international matters[44]. Within each policy area there is a 'What's new' section as well as relevant legislation, draft legislation, and details of current and decided cases; there is also useful statistical information. The website also leads to information about specific sectors such as agriculture, consumer goods, energy and financial services. There is information about the Commissioner for Competition Policy, the composition of DG COMP and the European Competition Network, which consists of the Commission and the 27 national competition authorities of the Member States who are jointly responsible for the enforcement of Articles 81 and 82[45]. Press Releases about competition policy matters can be accessed through the website, as can speeches of the Commissioner and officials of DG COMP, policy documents and the Competition Policy Newsletter, which is published three times a year; there is also a helpful *Glossary of Terms used in Competition related matters*[46]. It is easy to follow the progress of public consultations – for example on Article 82 EC and on private enforcement of the competition rules – through the website, and forthcoming Commission events of relevance to competition policy are announced there.

The Commission publishes an *Annual Management Plan* in which it sets out its key objectives for the year ahead[47]. The Commission's *Annual Report on Competition Policy* provides essential information on matters of both policy and enforcement, as well as a statistical review of DG COMP's activities[48]. In 2004 the Commission published a booklet *EC competition policy and the consumer* with the intention of creating an awareness and interest in the general public in competition policy[49]. DG COMP's website also has links to other important sites, including those of the Community Courts and the national competition authorities.

DG COMP has a Director General and three Deputy Directors General; they have responsibility for operations, mergers and antitrust and state aid respectively. There is also a Chief Competition Economist who reports directly to the Director General. DG COMP is divided into nine administrative units. Directorate A is responsible for policy and strategic support, including the European Competition Network, and for international relations. Directorates B to F are the operational units, each with responsibility for particular sectors, which conduct cases under Articles 81 and 82 and the ECMR, other than cartel cases, from start to finish; they also deal with state aid cases. Directorate G is exclusively concerned with cartels, the detection and eradication of which is a major priority of the Commission[50]. Directorate H is responsible for cohesion and enforcement issues arising in relation to state aid. Directorate R is responsible for the registry and for strategic planning and resources. DG COMP also has a Consumer Liaison Officer. Formal decisions of DG COMP must be vetted by the Legal Service of the Commission, with which it works closely. The Legal Service represents

---

[44] See www.ec.europa.eu/comm/competition/index_en.html.
[45] See ch 7, pp 283–284; note that, in the UK, the sectoral regulators such as OFCOM and GEMA are also empowered to apply Articles 81 and 82 EC; see pp 68–69 below.
[46] See www.europa.eu.int/comm/competition/general_info/glossary_en.html.
[47] See www.ec.europa.eu/dgs/competition/index_en.htm.
[48] This can be found at www.ec.europa.eu/comm/competition/annual_reports.
[49] This can be found at www.ec.europa.eu/comm/competition/consumers/index_en.html.
[50] On cartels see ch 13 generally.

the Commission in proceedings before the Community Courts[51]. An organigramme showing the composition of DG COMP can be accessed on its website[52].

(iii) Court of First Instance[53]

In general actions against the Commission in competition cases (including cases on state aid) are brought in the first instance before the CFI[54]. Member States' actions used to be taken to the ECJ as happened, for example, in the case of *France v Commission*[55], an important judgment which established, amongst other things, that the ECMR was capable of application to collective dominance[56]; however since the Nice Treaty all actions for annulment of Commission decisions, including those brought by Member States, are taken to the CFI. It can happen that substantially similar matters are before both the CFI and the ECJ simultaneously, in which case it is likely that the CFI will suspend its proceedings pending the judgment of the ECJ: this happened, for example, in the case of the 'Irish ice-cream war', where the CFI stayed the appeal of Van den Bergh Foods Ltd against the Commission's decision finding infringements of Articles 81 and 82[57] pending the outcome of the Article 234 reference in the case of *Masterfoods Ltd v HB Ice Cream Ltd*[58].

The website of the CFI (and of the ECJ) is an invaluable source of material where, for example, recent judgments of the Courts, opinions of the Advocates General of the ECJ and information about pending cases can be found; there is also an Annual Report and a bibliography listing literature on the case law of the Community Courts[59]. The rules of the CFI were amended in December 2000 to provide for the possibility of a 'fast-track' or 'expedited' procedure for appeals in certain cases[60]; the expedited procedure in Article 76(a) of the amended rules has been used in several cases under the ECMR[61] and against a commitment decision adopted by the Commission under Article 9 of the Modernisation Regulation[62].

(iv) European Court of Justice[63]

The ECJ hears appeals from the CFI on points of law only. The ECJ has been strict about what is meant by an appeal on a point of law, and it will not get drawn into factual

---

[51] For details of the Legal Service see www.ec.europa.eu/dgs/legal_service/index_en.htm.

[52] See www.ec.europa.eu/dgs/competition/directory/organ_en.pdf.

[53] See the *Codified version of the Rules of Procedure of the CFI* OJ [2003] C 19 3/41, [2003] 3 CMLR 25; on the CFI see Kerse and Khan *EC Antitrust Procedure* (Sweet & Maxwell, 5th ed, 2005), paras 1.58–1.60; the CFI's (and the ECJ's) website is www.curia.europa.eu/en/instit/txtdocfr/index.htm; note that under the Reform Treaty the Court of First Instance will be renamed the 'General Court'.

[54] On the types of action that can be brought see ch 7, pp 285–289.

[55] Cases C-68/94 and 30/95 [1998] ECR I-1375, [1998] 4 CMLR 829; on collective dominance see ch 14, pp 556–567 and ch 21, pp 852–853.

[56] See further ch 21, pp 852–853.

[57] *Masterfoods Ltd and Valley Ice Cream (Ireland) Ltd v Van den Bergh Foods Ltd (formerly HB Ice Cream Ltd)* OJ [1998] L 246/1, [1998] 5 CMLR 530, on appeal Case T-65/98 *Van den Bergh Foods v Commission* [2003] ECR II-4653, [2004] 4 CMLR 14; the final Order disposing of this issue was made by the ECJ in 2006: Case C-552/03 P, [2006] ECR I-9091, [2006] 5 CMLR 1494.

[58] Case C-344/98 [2000] ECR I-11369, [2001] 4 CMLR 449.

[59] See www.curia.europa.eu/en/instit/presentationfr/index_cje.htm.

[60] OJ [2000] L 322/4; the expedited procedure came into force on 1 February 2001.

[61] See ch 21, p 882–883.   [62] See ch 7, pp 256–257.

[63] See the *Codified version of the Rules of Procedure of the ECJ* OJ [2001] C 34/1, [2001] 3 CMLR 383; on the ECJ see Kerse and Khan (n 53 above), paras 1.55–1.57; Arnull *The European Union and its Court of*

disputes[64]. The ECJ also deals with points of law referred to it by national courts under Article 234 EC[65]. As mentioned above, the ECJ's website contains much useful material. The ECJ is assisted by an Advocate General, drawn from a panel of eight, who delivers an opinion on each case that comes before it[66]. Although not binding, this opinion is frequently followed by the ECJ, and is often more cogent than the judgment of the ECJ itself which may be delphic, particularly where it represents a compromise between the judges (no dissenting judgments are given by the ECJ). Anyone interested in competition law is strongly recommended to read the opinions of the Advocates General in competition cases, which are frequently of very high quality and contain a large amount of invaluable research material.

The ECJ and (to a lesser extent) the CFI are sometimes over-stretched, and there can be considerable delays in some cases. The ECJ published a document in May 1999 setting out proposals to deal with some of the problems it experiences[67]. The Treaty of Nice[68] made provision for some changes to the structure of the Community Courts; in particular judicial panels may be created to deal with specific types of case[69]. There has been a debate within the UK as to whether a specialist competition court should be established below the level of the CFI; the House of Lords Select Committee on the European Union published a report recommending against this idea, preferring instead an improvement in the procedures of the CFI and a reduction in its workload[70].

(v) Advisory Committee on Restrictive Practices and Dominant Positions

The Advisory Committee on Restrictive Practices and Dominant Positions consists of officials from the national competition authorities of the Member States[71]. They attend

---

Justice (Oxford EC Law Library, 1999); Neville Brown and Kennedy *The Court of Justice of the European Communities* (Sweet & Maxwell, 5th ed, 2000); Lasok *The European Court of Justice: Practice and Procedure* (Butterworths, 3rd ed, 2003); Arnull *The European Union and its Court of Justice* (Oxford University Press, 2nd ed, 2006).

[64] See eg Case C-7/95 P *John Deere v Commission* [1998] ECR I-3111, [1998] 5 CMLR 311, paras 17–22; Case C-551/03 P *General Motors BV v Commission* [2006] ECR I-3173, [2006] 5 CMLR 1, paras 50–51.

[65] On the Article 234 reference procedure see Anderson *References to the European Court* (Sweet & Maxwell, 1995); *Kerse and Khan* (n 53 above) para 1.57; Collins *European Community Law in the United Kingdom* (Butterworths, 5th ed, 2003); Hartley *The Foundations of European Community Law* (Oxford University Press, 5th ed, 2003), ch 9.

[66] The InterGovernmental Conference held in Lisbon in October 2007 declared that the number of Advocates General may be increased to 11: see www.consilium.europa.eu/uedocs/cmsUpload/ds00866.en07.pdf.

[67] Press Release 36/99, 28 May 1999; see also the discussion paper of the President of the ECJ 'The Future of the Judicial System of the European Union', which can be found at www.curia.europa.eu/en/instit/txtdocfr/autrestxts/ave.pdf; also 'The EC Court of Justice and the Institutional Reform of the European Union' (April 2000), which can be found at www.curia.europa.eu/en/instit/txtdocfr/autrestxts/rod.pdf; see Vesterdorf 'The Community Court System Ten Years from Now and Beyond: Challenges and Possibilities' (2003) 28 ELRev 303.

[68] OJ [2001] C 80/1.

[69] Article 2(26) of the Nice Treaty makes provision for amendment of Article 220 of the EC Treaty.

[70] See 15th Report, Session 2006–2007, HL Paper 75, available at www.publications.parliament.uk; the UK Government's Response agreed with the Committee: see www.parliament.uk/documents/upload/govrespeucomp.pdf.

[71] Provision is made for this Committee by Article 14 of the Modernisation Regulation: it was formerly provided for by Article 10(4) of Regulation 17; on this Committee see ch 7, p 264.

oral hearings, consider draft decisions of the Commission and comment on them; they also discuss draft legislation and the development of policy generally. This Committee also deals with certain matters in the maritime and air transport sectors and in relation to the insurance sector[72].

(vi) Advisory Committee on Concentrations

The Advisory Committee on Concentrations consists of officials from the national competition authorities of the Member States; they attend oral hearings and must be consulted on draft decisions of the Commission under the ECMR[73].

(vii) National courts

National courts are increasingly asked to apply the EC competition rules, which are directly applicable and may be invoked by natural and legal persons (both as defendant and as claimant)[74]. The Commission maintains on its website a database of judgments given by the courts of the Member States on the application of Articles 81 and 82 EC in the original language arranged in a chronological order[75]. An Association of European Competition Law Judges has been established aimed at bringing together members of the judiciary of the Member States.

(viii) Parliament and ECOSOC

The European Parliament – in particular its Standing Committee on Economic and Monetary Matters – and the Economic and Social Committee, 'ECOSOC', are consulted on matters of competition policy and may be influential, for example, in the legislative process or in persuading the Commission to take action in relation to a particular issue.

(C) European Economic Area

On 21 October 1991 the EC and its Member States and the Member States of the European Free Trade Association ('EFTA') signed an Agreement to establish the European Economic Area ('the EEA')[76]; it consists of the Member States of the EC[77], Norway, Iceland and Liechtenstein. The referendum in Switzerland on joining the EEA led to a 'no' vote, so that that signatory country remains outside. The EEA Agreement entered into force in 1994. It includes rules on competition which follow closely the EC Treaty and the ECMR. Article 81 on agreements appears as Article 53 of the EEA Agreement; Article 82 on the abuse of a dominant position is mirrored in Article 54; the

---

[72] See the Modernisation Regulation, Articles 38, 41 and 42.

[73] See Council Regulation 139/2004, Article 19(3)-(7); on this Committee see ch 21, pp 885–886.

[74] On the position of national courts see ch 8 generally.

[75] See ec.europa.eu/comm/competition/antitrust/national_courts/index_en.html.

[76] OJ [1994] L 1/1; the agreement entered into force on 1 January 1994; see Stragier 'The Competition Rules of the EEA Agreement and Their Implementation' (1993) 14 ECLR 30; Diem 'EEA Competition Law' (1994) 15 ECLR 263; see Blanchet, Piiponen and Wetman-Clément *The Agreement on the European Economic Area (EEA)* (Clarendon, 1999); Forman 'The EEA Agreement Five Years On: Dynamic Homogeneity In Practice and Its Implementation by the Two EEA Courts' (1999) 36 CML Rev 751; Blanco *EC Competition Procedure* (Oxford University Press, 2nd ed, 2006), ch 28; Broberg *The European Commission's Jurisdiction to Scrutinise Mergers* (Kluwer International, 3rd ed, 2006), ch 7.

[77] The EEA Agreement has yet to enter into force with Bulgaria and Romania.

ECMR is reflected in Article 57; and Article 86 on public undertakings and Article 87 on state aids appear as Articles 59 and 61 of the Agreement respectively.

The EEA Agreement and its associated texts establish a 'twin pillar' approach to jurisdiction: there are two authorities responsible for competition policy, the European Commission and the EFTA Surveillance Authority ('the ESA')[78], but any particular case will be investigated by only one of them. Article 108 of the EEA Agreement established the ESA; it mirrors the European Commission and is vested with similar powers. The ESA is subject to review by the EFTA Court of Justice[79], which sits in Luxembourg. Article 55 of the Agreement provides that the European Commission or the ESA shall ensure the application of Articles 53 and 54; Article 56 of the Agreement deals with the attribution of jurisdiction between these two bodies in cases caught by these Articles; Article 57 provides for the division of competence in respect of mergers.

An important principle of the EEA Agreement is that there should be cooperation between the European Commission and the ESA, in order to develop and maintain uniform surveillance throughout the European Economic Area and in order to promote a homogeneous implementation, application, and interpretation of the provisions of the Agreement. Article 58 requires the authorities to cooperate, in accordance with specific provisions contained in Protocol 23 (dealing with restrictive practices and the abuse of market power) and Protocol 24 (dealing with mergers). Similarly Article 106 of the Agreement establishes a system for the exchange of information between the two courts with a view to achieving a uniform interpretation of its terms.

(D) Modelling of domestic competition law on Articles 81 and 82[80]

The Member States of the European Community and the EEA now have systems of competition law modelled to a greater or lesser extent upon Articles 81 and 82[81]. An easy way of accessing the websites, and the national laws, of the national competition authorities is through a hyperlink provided by DG COMP[82]. Another simple way of doing so is through the website of the Global Competition Forum[83].

The so-called 'Europe Agreements' between the European Community and the countries of central and eastern Europe were part of the framework for implementation of the accession process towards full membership of the Community. Since the accessions of

---

[78] The website of the ESA is www.eftasurv.int.

[79] The EFTA States signed an *Agreement on the Establishment of a Surveillance Authority and a Court of Justice* on 2 May 1992: it is reproduced in (1992) 15 Commercial Laws of Europe, Part 10; the ECJ delivered two Advisory Opinions on these arrangements: Opinion 1/91 [1991] ECR I-6079, [1992] 1 CMLR 245; and Opinion 1/92 [1992] ECR I-2821, [1992] 2 CMLR 217. The website of the EFTA Court is www.eftacourt.lu.

[80] See generally Gerber *Law and Competition in Twentieth Century Europe: Protecting Prometheus* (Clarendon Press Oxford, 1998), ch X; Maher 'Alignment of Competition Laws in the European Community' (1996) 16 Oxford Yearbook of European Law 223; *European Competition Laws: A Guide to the EC and its Member States* (Matthew Bender, 2002, ed Fine); Geradin and Henry 'Competition Law in the new Member States: Where do we come from? Where do we go?' in *Modernisation and Enlargement: Two Major Challenges for EC Competition Law*, GCLC First Annual Conference, 2005, available at www.papers.ssrn.com; *A Practical Guide to National Competition Rules Across Europe* (Kluwer, 2008).

[81] For some sceptical comments on the alignment of the domestic competition laws of the Member States see Ullrich 'Harmonisation within the European Union' (1996) 17 ECLR 178.

[82] www.ec.europa.eu/comm/competition/nca/index_en.html.

[83] www.globalcompetitionforum.org/europe.htm.

many of those countries in 2004 and 2006 there are no remaining Europe Agreements[84]. There are also moves towards the establishment of a 'Euro-Mediterranean Economic Area', with the result that countries on the Mediterranean coast from Algeria to Turkey will be parties to Euro-Mediterranean (Association) Agreements containing provisions based on the Community competition rules[85].

3. UK LAW

The Competition Act 1998 and the Enterprise Act 2002 fundamentally changed both the substantive provisions and the institutional architecture of the domestic competition law of the UK; in the course of this reform a raft of old legislation – in particular the competition provisions in the Fair Trading Act 1973, the Restrictive Trade Practices Act 1976, the Resale Prices Act 1976 and the Competition Act 1980[86] – were swept away. A further key piece of legislation is the Competition Act 1998 and Other Enactments (Amendment) Regulations 2004[87] which brought UK law into conformity with the principles of the EC Modernisation Regulation.

(A) Competition Act 1998

The Competition Act 1998 received the Royal Assent on 9 November 1998; the main provisions entered into force on 1 March 2000. The Act contains two prohibitions. The so-called 'Chapter I prohibition' is modelled on Article 81 EC, and forbids agreements, decisions by associations of undertakings and concerted practices that have as their object or effect the restriction of competition[88]. The Chapter II prohibition in the Competition Act is modelled on Article 82 EC and forbids the abuse of a dominant position[89]. The Act gives to the Office of Fair Trading ('the OFT') wide powers to obtain information, to carry out on-the-spot investigations, to adopt decisions and to impose penalties on

---

[84] See www.ec.europa.eu/enlargement/glossary/terms/europe-agreement_en.htm; Bulgaria and Romania acceded to the Community in 2006 so that the reference there to Europe Agreements with those two countries is now otiose. It is possible in principle for agreements between the Community and third countries to have direct effect: see Case 104/81 *Hauptzollamt Mainz v Kupferburg* [1982] ECR 3641, [1983] 1 CMLR 1; Case C-192/89 *Sevince v Staatssecretaris van Justitie* [1990] ECR I-3461, [1992] 2 CMLR 57 and Wyatt and Dashwood's *European Union Law*, pp 104–109; however there has yet to be a judgment on whether the competition rules in the Europe Agreements themselves have direct effect; on one occasion the Commission required amendments to Chanel's distribution agreements to remove restrictions on exports to countries with which the Community had negotiated 'Free Trade Agreements', but this was done by agreement and without a reasoned decision on the part of the Commission: *Chanel* OJ [1994] C 334/11, [1995] 4 CMLR 108.

[85] See www.ec.europa.eu/external_relations/euromed/free_trade_area.htm; Hakura 'The Extension of EC Competition Law to the Mediterranean Region' (1998) 19 ECLR 204; Geradin and Petit 'Competition Policy and the Euro-Mediterranean Partnership' (2003) 8 European Foreign Affairs Review 153; Geradin *Competition Law and Regional Integration: An Analysis of the Southern Mediterranean Countries* (The World Bank, 2004).

[86] Section 11 of the Competition Act, which provides for 'efficiency audits' of public-sector bodies, remains in force but has not been used for many years.

[87] SI 2004/1261.   [88] See ch 9, pp 327–353.   [89] See ch 9, pp 353–362.

undertakings[90]. In relation to certain sectors such as electronic communications and energy the powers of the OFT are shared concurrently with the relevant regulator, such as the Office of Communications or the Gas and Electricity Markets Authority[91]. As 'public authorities' the bodies invested with powers to enforce the Competition Act are obliged under section 6 of the Human Rights Act 1998 (which received the Royal Assent on the same day as the Competition Act) to construe the legislation in a manner that is compatible with the European Convention for the Protection of Human Rights and Fundamental Freedoms of 1950. In competition law the right to a fair trial (Article 6 of the Convention), the right to respect for private life (Article 8) and the right to peaceful enjoyment of possessions (Article 1 of the First Protocol) are of particular significance[92]. Section 60 of the Competition Act contains provisions designed to maintain consistency between the application of EC and domestic competition law; however this is subject to limitations, in particular with the result that judgments of the Community Courts motivated by single market considerations will not necessarily be followed in the UK[93].

(B) Enterprise Act 2002

The Enterprise Act 2002 received the Royal Assent on 7 November 2002; the main provisions entered into force on 20 June 2003. The Enterprise Act is a major piece of legislation that amends domestic competition law in a number of ways[94].

First, the Act effected a number of reforms to the institutional architecture of the domestic system. It abolished the office of Director General of Fair Trading[95] and created a new corporate body, the Office of Fair Trading[96]: the OFT has a variety of functions under the Competition Act and the Enterprise Act, including those formerly exercised by the Director General of Fair Trading[97]. The Act conferred on the Competition Commission ('the CC') decision-making powers, including the making of final decisions, in relation to merger and market investigations[98]. The Act created a new institution, the Competition Appeal Tribunal ('the CAT'), that has appellate and judicial review functions in relation to decisions of the OFT, the sectoral regulators, the Secretary of State and the CC[99]. The Act also diminished substantially the powers of the Secretary of State to make decisions in competition law cases, particularly in relation to mergers[100].

Second, the Act contained new provisions for the investigation of mergers and markets, replacing the merger and monopoly provisions formerly contained in the Fair Trading Act 1973[101]. Third, the Enterprise Act supplemented and reinforced the Competition Act 1998 in various ways, in particular by introducing a new and separate criminal 'cartel offence' which, on indictment, can lead to the imprisonment of

---

[90] On the enforcement powers under the 1998 Act see ch 10.   [91] On concurrency see ch 10, pp 424–426.
[92] See further ch 10, pp 391–392.   [93] See ch 9, pp 362–367.
[94] A summary of the main provisions in the Enterprise Act can be found in an OFT publication *Overview of the Enterprise Act: the competition and consumer provisions*, OFT 518, June 2003; it is available on the OFT's website, www.oft.gov.uk; see also Graham 'The Enterprise Act 2002 and Competition Law' (2004) 67 MLR, 273.
[95] Enterprise Act 2002, s 2(2).   [96] Ibid, s 1(1).
[97] Ibid, s 2(1); the functions of the OFT are described at pp 65–66 below.
[98] See further pp 69–71 below and ch 22 (merger investigations) and ch 11 (market investigations).
[99] See further pp 72–73 below; note that, prior to the Enterprise Act, the Competition Act 1998 had created a Competition Commission Appeals Tribunal within the Competition Commission: its functions were transferred by the 2002 Act to the Competition Appeal Tribunal.
[100] See further ch 22, pp 951–954.
[101] See further ch 22 (merger investigations) and ch 11 (market investigations).

individuals for up to five years and/or a fine of an unlimited amount[102]; by providing for company director disqualification for directors who knew or ought to have known of competition law infringements committed by their companies[103]; and by enhancing the possibility of third parties, including consumer groups, obtaining remedies against anti-competitive behaviour[104].

(C) Changes to domestic law as a result of the EC Modernisation Regulation

The adoption of the EC Modernisation Regulation required or made desirable a number of changes to the Competition Act 1998. Section 209 of the Enterprise Act 2002, in conjunction with section 2(2) of the European Communities Act 1972, gave the Secretary of State power, by statutory instrument, to make such modifications as may be appropriate for the purpose of eliminating or reducing any differences between the Competition Act and EC competition law. The Competition Act 1998 and Other Enactments (Amendment) Regulations 2004[105] effected a number of changes to the Competition Act and to various other enactments pursuant to the Modernisation Regulation; in particular they repealed the provisions in the Competition Act on the notification to the OFT of agreements and/or conduct for guidance and/or a decision. The OFT published guidance in December 2004 on the implications of the Modernisation Regulation[106]; at the same time it reissued most of the Competition Act guidelines that had originally been published in 2000 in order to reflect the changes in law and practice flowing from the Modernisation Regulation. The *OFT's Rules* were also amended in 2004[107]; and the exclusion of vertical agreements from the Chapter I prohibition of the Competition Act was repealed in order to bring domestic law into line with EC law[108].

(D) Institutions[109]

Competition law in the UK assigns roles to the Secretary of State for Business, Enterprise and Regulatory Reform (formerly the Secretary of State for Trade and Industry), the Lord Chancellor, the OFT, the Serious Fraud Office (or, in Scotland, the Lord Advocate), the sectoral regulators, the CC, the CAT and to the civil and criminal courts. The competition authorities are also subject to Parliamentary scrutiny, for example by the Treasury Committee, the Business Enterprise and Regulatory Reform Committee and the Public Accounts Committee of the House of Commons and the European Committee of the House of Lords.

(i) Secretary of State and the Department for Business, Enterprise and Regulatory Reform

The Secretary of State for Business, Enterprise and Regulatory Reform has various functions under the Competition Act 1998 and the Enterprise Act 2002. In the exercise of

---

[102] See ch 10, pp 400–414.   [103] See ch 10, pp 422–423.   [104] See ch 8, pp 299–309.   [105] SI 2004/1261.

[106] *Modernisation*, OFT 442, December 2004.

[107] Competition Act 1998 (Office of Fair Trading's Rules) Order 2004, SI 2004/2751.

[108] Competition Act 1998 (Land Agreements Exclusion and Revocation) Order 2004, SI 2004/1260, Art 2.

[109] The institutional structure of EC and UK law is set out in diagrammatic form at the end of this chapter: see pp 78–80 below.

these functions he is assisted by a Parliamentary Under-Secretary of State for Trade and Consumer Affairs whose portfolio includes competition issues. Within the Department for Business, Enterprise and Regulatory Reform (formerly the Department of Trade and Industry) there is a Consumer and Competition Policy Directorate: it has a Director and is organised into four branches focussing on different policy areas, for example Competition, Regulation and Markets (Branch CCP 2) and Economics, Mergers and Sponsorship (Branch CCP 3). The Directorate's website provides information and guidance on aspects of competition law and policy, including public consultations[110].

(A) *Appointments* The Secretary of State for Business, Enterprise and Regulatory Reform makes most of the senior appointments in competition law, for example of the chairman and other members of the Board of the OFT[111]; the members of the CAT[112]; the Registrar of the CAT[113]; the 'appointed members' of the Competition Service within the CAT[114]; the Chairman, Deputy Chairmen and members of the CC[115]; and members of the Competition Commission Council[116]. The Secretary of State can also designate consumer bodies for the purpose of the 'super-complaint' procedure introduced by the Enterprise Act 2002[117].

(B) *Amendment of legislation, the adoption of delegated legislation and the making or approval of guidance* The Secretary of State is given various powers to amend primary legislation, to adopt delegated legislation and to make or approve rules under the Competition Act 1998 and the Enterprise Act 2002. For example under the Competition Act the Secretary of State has power to amend (and has amended) Schedules 1 and 3[118]; to adopt block exemptions from the Chapter I prohibition[119]; to make provision for the determination of turnover for the purpose of setting the level of penalties[120]; to approve the guidance of the OFT as to the appropriate amount of penalties under the Chapter I and Chapter II prohibitions and Articles 81 and 82 EC[121]; to determine the criteria for conferring limited immunity on 'small agreements' and 'conduct of minor significance'[122]; to vary the application of the Competition Act to vertical and land agreements[123]; to approve the procedural rules of the OFT[124]; to make regulations on the concurrent application of the Competition Act by the OFT and the sectoral regulators[125]; and to amend the list of appealable decisions in section 46 of the Act[126]. The

---

[110] The website will be found at www.berr.gov.uk. [111] Enterprise Act 2002, s 1 and Sch 1, para 1.
[112] Ibid, s 12(2)(c); note that the President of the Tribunal and the members of the panel of chairmen are appointed by the Lord Chancellor upon the recommendation of the Judicial Appointments Commission: ibid, s 12(2)(a) and (b).
[113] Ibid, s 12(3). [114] Ibid, Sch 3, para 1(2). [115] Ibid, Sch 7, para 3 (Chairman) and para 2 (members).
[116] Ibid, Sch 7, para 5(2). [117] Enterprise Act 2002, s 11(5); see further ch 11, pp 442–445.
[118] Competition Act 1998, s 3(2), s 19(2) (Sch 1, dealing with mergers and concentrations) and s 3(3), s 19(3) (Sch 3, dealing with general exclusions): see ch 9, pp 341–347 and p 362 respectively.
[119] Ibid, ss 6–8: see ch 9, pp 352–353. [120] Ibid, s 36(8): see ch 10, p 401.
[121] Ibid, s 38(4): see ch 10, pp 401–403.
[122] Ibid, s 39 (small agreements) and s 40 (conduct of minor significance): see ch 10, p 404.
[123] Ibid, s 50: see ch 9, pp 348–350 and ch 16, pp 668–669. [124] Ibid, s 51.
[125] Ibid, s 54(4)–(5); see also Enterprise Act 2002, s 204, which creates a power for the Secretary of State to make regulations in relation to concurrency functions as to company director disqualification: for a discussion of the rules on concurrency see ch 10, pp 424–426.
[126] See the Competition Act 1998 (Notification of Excluded Agreements and Appealable Decisions) Regulations 2000, SI 2000/263, Art 10.

Secretary of State also has power under paragraph 7 of Schedule 3 of the Competition Act to order that the Chapter I and Chapter II prohibitions do not apply to particular agreements or conduct where there are exceptional and compelling reasons of public policy for doing so[127].

Under the Enterprise Act the Secretary of State has power to make rules or to amend primary legislation in relation to a variety of matters: these include the procedural rules of the CAT[128]; the determination of turnover for the purpose of domestic merger control[129]; the maximum penalties that the Competition Commission can impose for procedural infringements[130]; the payment of fees for merger investigations[131]; for the alteration of the 'share of supply' test applicable to merger cases[132]; and for shortening the period within which merger inquiries should be completed[133]. The Act also enables the Secretary of State to extend the 'super-complaint' system to complaints made to sectoral regulators[134] and to designate consumer bodies for the purposes of bringing claims under section 47B of the Competition Act[135]; to modify Schedule 8 to the Act, which sets out the provisions that can be contained in enforcement orders[136]; and to make such modifications to the Competition Act 1998 as are appropriate for the purpose of eliminating or reducing any differences between that Act and EC law as a result of the Modernisation Regulation[137].

(C) Receipt of reports The Secretary of State receives Annual Reports from the OFT[138] and from the CC[139].

(D) Involvement in individual cases The Secretary of State has little involvement in individual competition cases. Prior to the Enterprise Act 2002 the Secretary of State had an important role in merger and monopoly investigations. However the provisions of the Enterprise Act confer upon the CC the final decision-making role in relation to merger and market investigations[140]. The Secretary of State retains powers in relation to such investigations only in strictly limited circumstances[141]; one such case was *BSkyB/ITV*[142].

(ii) The Lord Chancellor

The Lord Chancellor is responsible for appointing the President of the CAT and the panel of chairmen, pursuant to a recommendation from the Judicial Appointments Commission[143]. He is also given power to make provision for civil courts in England and Wales to transfer to the CAT cases based on an infringement decision of the European Commission or of the OFT or sectoral regulators under Articles 81 and/or 82 EC or the Chapter I and II prohibitions in the Competition Act[144]. There is also provision to

---

[127] See ch 9, pp 346–347.   [128] Enterprise Act 2002, s 15 and Sch 4, Part 2; see pp 69–70 below.
[129] Ibid; see ch 22, pp 910–911.   [130] Ibid, s 111(4); see ch 22, p 937.   [131] Ibid, s 121; see ch 22, p 917.
[132] Ibid, s 123; see ch 22, pp 911–912.   [133] Ibid, s 40(8).   [134] Ibid, s 205; on super-complaints, see ch 10.
[135] Ibid, s 19; see ch 8, p 308.   [136] Ibid, s 206; see ch 22, pp 934–936.
[137] Ibid, s 209; see further p 61 above.   [138] Ibid, s 4; see p 65 below.
[139] Competition Act 1998, Sch 7, para 12A, inserted by Enterprise Act 2002, s 186; see p 70 below.
[140] See ch 22, pp 918–921 (merger investigations) and ch 11, pp 452–459 (market investigations).
[141] Ibid, explaining ss 42–68, s 132, ss 139–153 and Sch 7 Enterprise Act 2002.
[142] See ch 22, p 953.
[143] Enterprise Act 2002, s 12(2)(a) and (b) and Sch 2, para 1; the Judicial Appointments Commission was established by the Constitutional Reform Act 2005.
[144] Ibid, s 16(1)–(4).

make rules for the receipt of cases by the civil courts that are transferred to them by the CAT[145]. As of 12 March 2008 these powers had not been exercised.

(iii) The OFT

(A) Establishment of the OFT The OFT is established by section 1 of the Enterprise Act 2002. Section 1 of the Fair Trading Act 1973 had established the office of Director General of Fair Trading, and many of the most important functions in competition law were carried out in the name of the individual appointed by the Secretary of State to this position. Similarly in the regulated sectors individuals, such as the Director General of Telecommunications and the Director General of Gas Supply, were given a wide variety of responsibilities[146]. However there was a growing acceptance that it was not appropriate that such significant powers should be invested in an individual office-holder as opposed to a group of people. The Enterprise Act therefore created a corporate entity known as the Office of Fair Trading ('the OFT')[147], and abolished the office of Director General of Fair Trading[148]; his functions were transferred to the OFT[149]. The Board of the OFT consists of a (non-executive) Chairman and no fewer than four other members, appointed by the Secretary of State[150]. The Secretary of State must also appoint a Chief Executive of the OFT, who may or may not be a member of the OFT Board[151]; since 2005 the Chief Executive may not be the same person as the Chairman[152]. On 12 March 2008 there were 10 members of the Board, of whom three (the Chief Executive and two executive directors) were executive members and seven non-executive[153]. The Rules of Procedure of the Board of the OFT are available on its website, and minutes of its meetings will also be found there[154]. The Board is responsible for the strategic direction, priorities, plans and performance of the OFT, including the adoption of the Annual Plan[155]. It also makes the decision whether to institute market studies or to make market investigation references to the CC; other operational decisions are delegated by the Board to the executive of the OFT.

Many of the decisions of the OFT under the Competition Act can be appealed on the merits to the CAT[156]. In cases where the OFT's behaviour is not subject to the scrutiny of the CAT it may, nevertheless, be subject to judicial review by the Administrative Court of the Queen's Bench Division. Decisions under the Enterprise Act 2002 in relation to mergers and market investigations are subject to judicial review by the Competition Appeal Tribunal[157].

(B) The staff of the OFT The Chief Executive of the OFT is responsible for the day-to-day running of the organisation. There are two further Executive Directors who sit on the Board of the OFT, one responsible for Policy and Strategy and the other for Markets and Projects. The Policy and Strategy groups lead policy and strategy across the consumer and competition functions of the OFT; the General Counsel's office and the Chief Economist's office sit within the Policy and Strategy area of the OFT.

---

[145] Ibid, s 16(5); on s 16 see further ch 8, p 300.   [146] See further pp 68–69 below.
[147] Enterprise Act 2002, s 1(1).   [148] Ibid, s 2(2).
[149] Ibid, s 2(1); the transfer took place on 1 April 2003.   [150] Ibid, Sch 1(1).   [151] Ibid, Sch 1(5)(1).
[152] Ibid, Sch 1(5)(2).   [153] Details of the members of the OFT Board are available at www.oft.gov.uk.
[154] See www.oft.gov.uk.   [155] See p 65 below.   [156] See ch 10, pp 426–436.
[157] See ch 11, pp 463–464 and ch 22, pp 937–938.

Operational matters such as the investigation of mergers and possible infringements of the Competition Act are handled by staff who work in the Markets and Projects area of the OFT; its project and enforcement work is conducted in three market groupings covering goods, services and infrastructure supported by dedicated merger and cartel teams[158]. The total number of permanent staff of the OFT at 31 March 2007 was 649[159].

(C) Annual plan and annual report The OFT is required, following a public consultation, to publish an annual plan containing a statement of its main objectives and priorities for the year; both the annual plan and the consultation document must be laid before Parliament[160]. The most recent annual plan was published in March 2008 setting out the main objectives, the first of which is to deliver 'high-impact outcomes', that is to say to focus on areas of work that will have the highest impact and the greatest effect[161]. The OFT must also make an annual report to the Secretary of State containing an assessment of the extent to which the objectives and priorities set out in the Annual Plan have been met and a summary of significant decisions, investigations and other activities in the year[162]. The report must be laid before Parliament and must be published[163]. The report for 2006–2007 was published in July 2007[164].

(D) Functions of the OFT The OFT has stated that its mission is to make markets work well for consumers[165]. In order to achieve this end the OFT's activities are to enforce the competition and consumer protection rules, to investigate how well markets are working and to explain and improve public awareness and understanding. The general functions, as opposed to the enforcement functions, of the OFT include obtaining, compiling and keeping under review information relating to the exercise of its functions; making the public aware of ways in which competition may benefit consumers and the economy; providing information and advice to Ministers; and promoting good consumer practice[166].

The OFT has numerous consumer protection responsibilities under a variety of legal provisions, including:

- the Consumer Credit Act 1974
- the Estate Agents Act 1979
- the Consumer Protection (Cancellation of Contracts concluded away from Business Premises) Regulations 1987[167]
- the Control of Misleading Advertisements Regulations 1988[168]
- the Consumer Credit (Advertisements) Regulations 1989[169]
- the Package Travel, Package Holidays and Package Tours Regulations 1992[170]
- the Timeshare Regulations 1997[171]
- the Unfair Terms in Consumer Contracts Regulations 1999[172]
- the Consumer Protection (Distance Selling) Regulations 2000[173]

---

[158] See the *Annual Report and Resource Accounts 2006–2007*, HC 532, p 19.   [159] Ibid, p 68.
[160] Enterprise Act 2002, s 3.   [161] *Annual Plan 2008–09*, HC 374, available at www.oft.gov.uk.
[162] Enterprise Act 2002, s 4(1) and (2).   [163] Ibid, s 4(3).
[164] *Annual Report and Resource Accounts 2006–2007*, HC 532.   [165] Ibid, p 14.
[166] Enterprise Act 2002, ss 5–8.   [167] SI 1987/2117.   [168] SI 1988/915.   [169] SI 1989/1125.
[170] SI 1992/3288.   [171] SI 1997/1081.   [172] SI 1999/2083.   [173] SI 2000/2334.

- the Stop Now Orders (EC Directive) Regulations 2001[174]
- the Consumer Protection Cooperation Regulation[175]
- the Consumer Credit Act 2006
- the Consumers, Estate Agents and Redress Act 2007.

Further functions have followed as a result of the Unfair Commercial Practices Directive, which was implemented in the UK in May 2008[175a]. The OFT manages Consumer Direct, a national telephone and online consumer advice scheme; and it also provides a national voice for, and strategic leadership to, local Trading Standards Services. The OFT also has functions under the Money Laundering Regulations 2007[176].

The competition and consumer protection functions of the OFT are legally distinct. However in practice they are closely related since they are used collectively by the OFT with the aim of ensuring that markets work well for consumers. As far as competition law is concerned the OFT has considerable powers under the Competition Act 1998: it plays the principal role in enforcing the Chapter I and Chapter II prohibitions, and has significant powers to obtain information, enter premises to conduct investigations, make interim and final decisions and impose financial penalties; it also has the power, by virtue of the EC Modernisation Regulation in conjunction with Article 3 of the Competition Act 1998 and Other Enactments (Amendment) Regulations 2004[177], to enforce Articles 81 and 82 EC[178]. The OFT has an important role in relation to merger and market investigations under the Enterprise Act 2002[179], and works with the Serious Fraud Office in the case of a prosecution for commission of the 'cartel offence' under that Act[180]. The OFT has specific responsibilities in relation to competition as a result of provisions in the Courts and Legal Services Act 1990, the Law Reform (Miscellaneous Provisions) (Scotland) Act 1990, the Water Industry Act 1991, the Financial Services and Markets Act 2000[181], the Transport Act 2000, the Transport (Scotland) Act 2001 and the Legal Services Act 2007. The OFT also has a duty to keep under review undertakings given as a result of investigations conducted under the monopoly and merger provisions of the now-repealed Fair Trading Act 1973[182]. The OFT liaises on competition matters with the European Commission in Brussels and is a member of the European Competition Network that brings together the Commission and the national competition authorities of the Member States pursuant to the Modernisation Regulation[183]. The OFT attends meetings on competition policy on behalf of the UK at the Organisation for Economic Co-operation and Development and the United Nations Conference on Trade and Development, and is an active participant in the International Competition Network[184].

(E) Rules Section 51 and Schedule 9 of the Competition Act 1998 make provision for the adoption of procedural rules by the OFT, which require the approval of the Secretary of

---

[174] SI 2001/1422.
[175] EC Regulation 2006/2004; see also the Enterprise Act 2002 (Amendment) Regulations, SI 2006/3363 and the Enterprise Act 202 (Part 8 Community Infringements Specified UK Laws) Order 2006, SI 2006/3372.
[175a] SI 2008/1277.
[176] SI 2007/2157. [177] SI 2004/1261. [178] See ch 10 generally.
[179] See ch 22, pp 902–917 (merger investigations) and ch 11, pp 452–456 (market investigations).
[180] On the cartel offence see ch 10, pp 415–422. [181] See ch 9, p 344.
[182] See further ch 11, pp 468–469 and ch 22, p 936. [183] See ch 7, pp 283–284.
[184] On the work of these bodies see ch 12, pp 490–492.

State[185]; the Competition Act 1998 (Office of Fair Trading's Rules) were adopted under this provision in 2004[186].

(F) Publications, information, guidance etc The OFT is required by sections 6 and 7 of the Enterprise Act 2002 to provide information to the public and to Ministers. The OFT's website is a vital source of information on UK competition law and includes, among other things, a Public Register of its decisions and the decisions of the sectoral regulators under the Competition Act and the OFT's decisions under the Enterprise Act, the numerous guidelines on these Acts, Press Releases, the Annual Plan and the Annual Report of the OFT, consultations, speeches and articles and details of litigation in the UK courts involving competition law issues[187].

The OFT has published a number of research papers on important issues in competition policy, for example on market definition, barriers to entry and exit and predatory behaviour, which are available on its website. The first of a new series of economic discussion papers, on *E-commerce and its Implications for Competition Policy*[188] was published in August 2000; this was followed by:

- *The Role of Market Definition in Monopoly and Dominance Inquiries*[189]
- *Innovation and Competition Policy*[190]
- *The Development of Targets for Consumer Savings arising from Competition Policy*[191]
- *Switching costs*[192]
- *Assessing Profitability in Competition Policy Analysis*[193]
- *Predicting Cartels*[194]
- *Selective Price Cuts and Fidelity Rebates*[195]
- *Research into the costs of inappropriate intervention/non-intervention under Article 82*[196]
- *The competitive effects of buyer groups*[197]
- *Productivity and competition*[198]
- *Competition in markets with commission rates*[199]
- *Economic analysis of markets characterized by bidding processes*[200]
- *The deterrent effect of competition enforcement*[201].

The OFT's Economic Discussion Paper Series is available on the OFT website[202].

The OFT has increasingly sought to carry out an evaluation of its work, both as a matter of external accountability, so that it can attempt to demonstrate that it provides value for money to the taxpayers that pay for it, and as a matter of internal management, in order to test whether it is prioritising its work effectively. The OFT has agreed to a performance target of delivering benefits to consumers worth more than five times the organisation's spending on competition enforcement[203]. In September 2007 the OFT launched a consultation on the way in which it calculates the direct financial benefits

---

[185] Competition Act 1998, s 51(5).
[186] SI 2004/2751, replacing the earlier rules in SI 2000/293.
[187] See www.oft.gov.uk. [188] OFT 327. [189] OFT 342, July 2001. [190] OFT 377, March 2002.
[191] OFT 386, June 2002. [192] OFT 655, April 2003. [193] OFT 657, July 2003. [194] OFT 773, March 2005.
[195] OFT 804, July 2005. [196] OFT 864, September 2006. [197] OFT 863, January 2007.
[198] OFT 887, January 2007. [199] OFT 889, January 2007. [200] OFT 923, May 2007.
[201] OFT 962, November 2007. [202] See www.oft.gov.uk/advice_and_resources/publications.
[203] OFT 962, November 2007, p 71.

to consumers of its work[204]. The OFT has estimated that it saved consumers on average £126 million per year in the years from 2004 to 2007 as a result of its work in enforcing the Competition Act, reviewing mergers and taking action under its consumer powers against scams[205].

The OFT has published guidance explaining how it deals with requests for information under the Freedom of Information Act 2000[206].

(iv) Serious Fraud Office

Section 188 of the Enterprise Act 2002 introduced a criminal cartel offence for individuals responsible for 'hard-core' cartels[207]. Serious penalties – of up to five years in prison – can be imposed upon those found guilty of this offence. Prosecutions may be brought by or with the consent of the OFT[208]; however cases will usually be prosecuted by the Serious Fraud Office[209], working in close liaison with the OFT[210]. In Scotland the prosecution of the criminal offence is the responsibility of the Lord Advocate. Quite apart from the criminal cartel offence, there are some rare circumstances in which some cartel agreements might be illegal under the common law criminal offence of conspiracy to defraud; the Serious Fraud Office is the prosecutor for this offence as well[211].

(v) Sectoral regulators

Various industries in the UK are subject to specific regulatory control, in particular utilities such as telecommunications and water. Originally the regulatory powers were vested in individuals such as the Director General of Telecommunications and the Director General of Water Services. Just as the position of Director General of Fair Trading has been superseded by the creation of an OFT Board, so too the individual regulators have been replaced by corporate boards, each supported by an office: these are the Gas and Electricity Markets Authority (supported by OFGEM)[212], the Office of Communications (OFCOM)[213], the Water Services Regulation Authority (OFWAT)[214], the Office of Rail Regulation (the ORR)[215], and the Northern Ireland Authority for Energy Regulation (NIAER)[216]. These sectoral regulators have concurrent power to enforce the Competition Act 1998, and Articles 81 and 82 EC, with the OFT; and the Civil Aviation Authority also has competition law functions[217]. Arrangements are in place for coordination of the performance of the concurrent functions under the Act[218]. Appeals against 'appealable decisions' of the sectoral regulators in the exercise of their Competition Act powers lie to the CAT[219]; references in relation to the licensing

---

[204]   Available at www.oft.gov.uk.
[205]   See *Positive Impact 06/07*, OFT 928, July 2007, available at www.oft.gov.uk/about/benefits/evaluation/ publications.
[206]   *Freedom of Information Act 2000 publication scheme*, OFT 622, January 2005, available at www.oft. gov.uk/advice_and_resources/publications/corporate/general/oft622.
[207]   See ch 10, pp 415–422 below.   [208]   Enterprise Act 2002, s 190(2)(b).
[209]   The website of the SFO is www.sfo.gov.uk.   [210]   Enterprise Act 2002, s 190(1); see ch 10, pp 418–419.
[211]   See ch 10, pp 423–424.   [212]   Utilities Act 2000, s 1.   [213]   Office of Communications Act 2002, s 1.
[214]   Water Act 2003, s 34.   [215]   Railway and Transport Safety Act 2003, s 15.
[216]   See The Energy Order 2003, SI 2003/419, s 3.
[217]   See Airports Act 1986, s 41, which deals with anti-competitive practices at regulated airports, and Chapter V of the Transport Act 2000, which gives the CAA concurrent powers to enforce the Chapter I and II prohibitions in relation to air traffic services; further details of these powers can be found at www.caa.co.uk.
[218]   On concurrency see ch 10, pp 424–426.
[219]   On the meaning of appealable decisions see ch 10, pp 427–431.

functions of the sectoral regulators[220] and market investigations may be made to the CC[221]. Super-complaints may be made to the sectoral regulators under the provisions set out in section 11 of the Enterprise Act 2002[222]. A report of the House of Lords Select Committee on Regulators recommended in November 2007 that the utility regulators should work to ensure that cases most likely to establish useful precedents are brought to the Competition Commission[223].

The OFT also works closely with the Financial Services Authority across a range of matters; the OFT and the FSA have published a Joint Action Plan explaining their efforts to work more closely together[224].

(vi) Competition Commission

(A) Establishment of the Competition Commission The CC is an independent public body which was established by section 45(1) of the Competition Act 1998 and came into existence on 1 April 1999. Section 45(3) of the Act dissolved the Monopolies and Mergers Commission, which had been in existence under various names since 1948, and transferred its functions to the new Commission[225]. Schedule 7 of the Competition Act, as amended by Schedule 11 of the Enterprise Act 2002, makes detailed provision in relation to the CC. It has a Chairman and three Deputy Chairmen. The Chairman is appointed on a full-time basis, as may be the Deputy Chairmen.

At the end of March 2007 there were 46 'reporting panel' members of the CC[226]. Members are appointed by the Secretary of State, following an open competition, for a single period of eight years; all members (other than the Chairman and some of the Deputy Chairmen) are part-time. They are appointed for their diversity of background, individual experience and ability, not as representatives of particular organisations, interests or political parties. In each case referred to the CC a group will be appointed to conduct the investigation[227]. The Chairman appoints between three to six members to serve on an inquiry group[228]. In 2006/07 most of the investigations completed were conducted by groups of four or five[229]. There is a utilities panel from which the Chairman must appoint at least one member when conducting an investigation concerned with the regulation of the water, electricity or gas sectors or an energy code modification appeal. There is also a newspaper panel and a Communications Act panel. The Chairman of the CC has published *Guidance to Groups* on the procedures to be

---

[220] On licence modification references see ch 23, p 971.   [221] Enterprise Act 2002, Sch 9, Part 2.

[222] The Enterprise Act 2002 (Super-complaints to Regulators) Order 2003, SI 2003/1368; on super-complaints, see ch 11, pp 442–445.

[223] *UK Economic Regulators*, November 2007, para 6.26, available at www.parliament.uk/parliamentary_committees/lordsregulators.cfm.

[224] See www.oft.gov.uk/oft_at_work/partnership_working/financial_services.

[225] For an account of the work of the Monopolies and Mergers Commission in the 50 years from 1948 to 1998 see Wilks *In the Public Interest: Competition Policy and the Monopolies and Mergers Commission* (Manchester University Press, 1999).

[226] See the CC's *Annual Report and Accounts 2006/2007*, pp 75–81.

[227] Provision is made for this by the Competition Act 1998, Sch 7, Part II, as amended by the Enterprise Act 2002, Sch 11, paras 10–12.

[228] Competition Act 1998, Sch 7, para 15(2).

[229] Details of the groups will be found in the short discussions of each investigation in the CC's *Annual Report and Accounts*.

adopted when conducting inquiries[230]: the *Guidance* must be read in conjunction with the *Competition Commission Rules of Procedure*[231].

The CC has a Council through which some of its functions, such as the appointment of staff and the keeping of accounts, must be performed; the Council consists of the Chairman, the Deputy Chairmen, such other members as the Secretary of State may appoint[232] and the Chief Executive (referred to in the legislation as the Secretary) of the CC[233]. Management of the CC and its policy development are taken forward through four key groups, an Operations Board, an Analysis Group, a Procedures and Practices Group and a Remedies Standing Group which oversees implementation of any remedial action required by the CC following an inquiry; each of the four groups reports to the Competition Commission Council.

The CC is subject to judicial review by the CAT under provisions contained in the Enterprise Act 2002[234]; it is also subject to judicial review by the Administrative Court of the Queen's Bench Division of the High Court.

(B) The staff of the CC The most senior member of staff of the CC is the chief executive, referred to in the legislation as the Secretary, who is a member of the Competition Commission Council. At the end of March 2007 the CC had a permanent staff of 165 officials, including administrators and specialists such as accountants, economists, business advisors and lawyers[235].

(C) Corporate plan and annual report The CC publishes its Corporate Plan on its website; it is required to make an Annual Report to the Secretary of State[236].

(D) Functions of the CC The CC has no power to conduct investigations on its own initiative. Rather it conducts market investigations under the Enterprise Act 2002 referred to it by either the OFT, one of the sectoral regulators or the Secretary of State and merger inquiries referred to it by the OFT or the Secretary of State. The CC can be asked to conduct 'efficiency audits' of public sector bodies under the Competition Act 1980: this provision has not been used for many years[237].

The CC has various regulatory functions in relation to privatised utilities as a result of provisions in:

- the Airports Act 1986[238] and the Airports (Northern Ireland) Order 1994
- the Gas Act 1986 and the Gas (Northern Ireland) Order 1996
- the Electricity Act 1989 and the Electricity (Northern Ireland) Order 1992

---

[230] CC 6, March 2006, available at www.competition-commission.org.uk. [231] CC 1, March 2006.
[232] At the end of January 2008 the Council had two non-executive members.
[233] Competition Act 1998, Sch 7, para 5(3), as amended by Enterprise Act 2002, Sch 11, para 4 and Sch 26.
[234] See further pp 72–73 below and ch 11, pp 463–464 (market investigations) and ch 22, pp 937–938 (merger investigations) respectively.
[235] See the *Annual Report and Accounts 2006–2007*, p 44.
[236] Competition Act 1998, Sch 7, para 12A, inserted by the Enterprise Act 2002, s 186.
[237] On efficiency audits see *Halsbury's Laws of England*, Vol 47, (4th ed reissue, 2001), paras 143–145.
[238] The Civil Aviation Authority asked the CC to commence a quinquennial review of airport charges at Heathrow and Gatwick Airports in March 2007 which ended in September 2007; this investigation must not be confused with the market investigation reference of *BAA Airports* under the Enterprise Act 2002, as to which see www.competition-commission.org.uk/inquiries/ref2007/airports/index.htm.

- the Water Industry Act 1991 and the Water Services (Scotland) Act 2005 (Consequential Provisions and Modifications) Order 2005
- the Railways Act 1993
- the Postal Services Act 2000
- the Transport Act 2000
- the Communications Act 2003.

The CC has not been called upon to exercise these regulatory functions (other than the mandatory quinquennial review of airport charges) for a considerable time, a matter that is of some concern to it[239]. The CC has a role under the Financial Services and Markets Act 2000 to ensure that the rules and practices of the Financial Services Authority do not impede competition. It also has a role under the Legal Services Act 2007 in relation to possible distortions on competition arising from regulatory rules applicable to the legal profession. The CC also conducts appeals in respect of modifications to the codes covering the energy industry by virtue of sections 173 to 177 of the Energy Act 2004[240]. The CC dealt with its first case under these provisions in 2007, allowing an appeal by E.ON UK Ltd against a decision of the Gas and Electricity Markets Authority[241].

The CC is not a designated competition authority for the purposes of Article 35 of the EC Modernisation Regulation, with the result that it does not have the power to enforce Articles 81 and 82 EC[242]. The CC participates in the activities of the OECD, UNCTAD and the ICN.

(E) Rules Schedule 7A of the Competition Act, inserted by Schedule 12 of the Enterprise Act 2002, makes provision for the adoption of procedural rules for the conduct of merger and market references by the CC. The current *Competition Commission Rules of Procedure* were adopted in March 2006 and are available on its website[243]. The CC has also published a series of guidance documents describing its approach to, and procedures for, merger and market investigations[244] and on several other matters, including *General Advice and Information*[245], a *Statement of Policy on Penalties*[246] and *Guidance on Disclosure of Information in Merger and Market Inquiries*[247].

(F) Publications, information, guidance etc The CC has a website that contains a wide variety of information, for example on current inquiries, completed inquiries, press releases, evaluation reports and occasional papers, speeches, texts from the CC's lectures series, the *Annual Report and Accounts*, the Corporate Plan and the way in which the CC is organised[248]. The CC has estimated that customers would have paid an extra £322 million for goods and services but for the decisions it took during the period from 1 April 2006 to 31 March 2007[249].

---

[239] See the *Annual Report and Accounts 2006–2007*, p 6.

[240] See further the *Energy Modification Rules*, CC 10, July 2005, available at www.competition-commission.org.uk.

[241] See www.competition-commission.org.uk/appeals/energy/completed_cases.htm.

[242] See Art 3 of the Competition Act 1998 and Other Enactments (Amendment) Regulations 2004, SI 2004/1261 which designates the OFT and the sectoral regulators for this purpose.

[243] CC 1, March 2006, available at www.competition-commission.org.uk.

[244] CC 2 and CC 3, June 2003.   [245] CC 4, March 2004.

[246] CC 5, June 2003.   [247] CC 7, July 2003.

[248] The website of the CC is www.competition-commission.org.uk.

[249] See the *Annual Report and Accounts 2006–2007*, HC 603 2007, p 7.

(vii) Competition Appeal Tribunal

(A) Establishment of the CAT The CAT is established by section 12(1) of the Enterprise Act 2002[250]. It consists of a President[251], a panel of Chairmen appointed by the Lord Chancellor following a recommendation from the Judicial Appointments Commission[252] (the judges of the Chancery Division of the High Court have been appointed to this panel), and a panel of ordinary members appointed by the Secretary of State[253]. Cases are heard by a Tribunal of three persons, chaired by the President or one person from the panel of Chairmen. Interim matters can be dealt with either by the President or, in the case of urgency, by one of the Chairmen sitting alone. The CAT has a Registrar, also appointed by the Secretary of State[254]. Schedule 2 of the Enterprise Act contains provisions on such matters as eligibility for appointment as President or chairman of the Tribunal. Section 14 of the Act and Part I of Schedule 4 deal with the constitution of the Tribunal. Section 13 and Schedule 3 establish the Competition Service, the purpose of which is to fund and provide support services to the Tribunal[255]. The CAT's website provides details of decided and pending cases, and all of its judgments will be found there[256]. The CAT may sit outside London[257]. The CAT publishes an Annual Review and Accounts[258]. On 31 January 2008 the CAT had a staff of 16, including the Registrar and three referendaires.

(B) Functions of the CAT The CAT, which is an independent judicial body, has four functions under the Enterprise Act[259]; it also has some functions in relation to regulatory matters (see below). The first function under the Enterprise Act is to hear appeals from 'appealable decisions' of the OFT and the sectoral regulators under the Competition Act 1998 and Articles 81 and 82 EC[260]. Appeals on a point of law or as to the amount of a penalty lie from decisions of the CAT with permission to the Court of Appeal in England and Wales, to the Court of Session in Scotland and to the Court of Appeal of Northern Ireland in Northern Ireland[261]. From the Court of Appeal a further appeal may be taken, with permission, to the House of Lords. It is also possible for the CAT to refer a matter of Community law to the ECJ[262]. The second function of the CAT is to hear monetary claims arising from infringement decisions made by the UK competition authorities or the European Commission under the Competition Act or

---

[250] The Competition Act 1998 had established, within the CC, appeal tribunals which could hear appeals under that Act; these tribunals have been abolished, and the Competition Appeal Tribunal inherited their functions on 1 April 2003; s 21 and Sch 5 of the Enterprise Act amend various provisions of the Competition Act 1998 in relation to proceedings of the Tribunal.

[251] Enterprise Act 2002, s 12(2)(a).   [252] Ibid, s 12(2)(b).   [253] Ibid, s 12(2)(c).   [254] Ibid, s 12(3).

[255] Ibid, s 13(2).   [256] The website of the CAT is www.catribunal.org.uk.

[257] See the Competition Appeal Tribunal Rules 2003, SI 2003/1372, rule 18; the CAT has sat in Belfast, in the *BetterCare* case and in Edinburgh in the *Aberdeen Journals* and *Claymore* cases: for details of these cases see the CAT's website.

[258] Available at www.catribunal.org.uk.

[259] A fifth function, to hear appeals against decisions of the OFT under the EC Competition Law (Articles 84 and 85) Enforcement Regulations 2001, SI 2001/2916, ended when those regulations were revoked by SI 2007/1846, Art 2.

[260] On appealable decisions see ch 10, pp 427–431; it is also possible that an action for judicial review of the OFT and sectoral regulators may be brought before the Administrative Court: ibid, p 427.

[261] Competition Act 1998, s 49: see *The Competition Appeal Tribunal Rules 2003*, SI 2003/1372, rules 58 and 59 and ch 10, pp 435–436.

[262] See *The Competition Appeal Tribunal Rules 2003*, SI 2003/1372, rule 60 and ch 10, p 437.

the EC Treaty[263]. The third function is to deal with applications for review of decisions of the OFT, the Secretary of State or other Minister or the CC in relation to mergers[264] and market investigations[265]. The fourth function of the CAT under the Enterprise Act is to hear appeals against penalties imposed by the CC for failure to comply with notices requiring the attendance of witnesses or the production of documents in the course of a market or merger investigation[266].

The Communications Act 2003 provides that the CAT will hear appeals on the merits against certain decisions taken by the OFT, OFCOM or the Secretary of State (as the case may be) under its provisions; in certain circumstances under this legislation, where issues of price control arise, the CAT must make a reference to the CC before disposing of the case[267]. The CAT has also been given certain functions under the Electricity (Single Wholesale Market)(Northern Ireland) Order 2007[268] and the Mobile Roaming (European Communities) Regulations 2007[269].

Provision is made by section 16 of the Enterprise Act 2002 for the Lord Chancellor to adopt regulations enabling the transfer of cases between the civil courts and the CAT for it to determine whether there has been an infringement of Article 81 and/or 82 EC or of the Chapter I and II prohibitions in the Competition Act. These provisions had not been activated as at 12 March 2008.

(C) Rules Section 15 of the Enterprise Act 2002 and Part 2 of Schedule 4 provide for the Secretary of State to make rules with respect to proceedings before the CAT. The Competition Appeal Tribunal Rules 2003[270] entered into force in June 2003. The 2003 rules have been amended by the Competition Appeal Tribunal (Amendment and Communications Act Appeals) Rules 2004[271]. Following an Introduction in Part I, Part II of the 2003 Rules deals with appeals to the CAT under the Competition Act[272]; Part III is concerned with proceedings under the Enterprise Act, that is appeals against penalties in merger and market investigations[273] and reviews of merger and market investigation references[274]. Part IV of the Rules deals with claims for damages under section 47A and 47B of the Competition Act[275], and Part V contains provisions on matters such as hearings, confidentiality, decisions of the CAT, appeals to the Court of Appeal and Article 234 references to the ECJ[276]. The CAT published a *Guide to Proceedings* in October 2005 which provides practical guidance for parties and their legal representatives as to its procedures in relation to all cases which it is competent to entertain and which has the status of a Practice Direction under Rules 68(2) of the 2003 Rules. Dissenting judgments are possible: the only time that this had occurred by 12 March 2008 was in the case of *Makers UK Ltd v OFT* where one member of the CAT dissented on the level of the penalty in that case[277].

[263] See ch 8, pp 307–309.   [264] Enterprise Act 2002, s 120: see ch 22, pp 937–938.

[265] Enterprise Act 2002, s 179: see ch 11, pp 463–464.   [266] See further ch 11, p 463 and ch 22, p 937.

[267] Communications Act 2003, s 193 and Rule 3 of the Competition Appeal Tribunal (Amendment and Communications Act Appeals) Rules 2004, SI 2004/2068; see Case 1083/3/3/07 *Hutchison 3G UK Ltd v OFCOM: Ruling on the formulation of the preliminary issue* [2007] CAT 26.

[268] SI 2007/913.   [269] SI 2007/1933.

[270] SI 2003/1372; rule 70 of these Rules repeals the earlier Competition Commission Appeal Tribunal Rules 2000, SI 2000/261, except that Rule 69 provides that they continue to govern proceedings commenced prior to the coming into force of the new rules.

[271] SI 2004/2068.   [272] On appeals under the Competition Act see ch 10, pp 426–436.

[273] See ch 11, p 463 and ch 22, p 937.

[274] See ch 22, pp 937–938 (mergers) and ch 11, pp 463–464 (market investigations).

[275] See ch 8, pp 307–309.   [276] On Article 234 references see ch 10, pp 436–438.

[277] Case 1061/1/1/06 [2007] CAT 11, [2007] CompAR 699.

(viii) Civil courts

Where a warrant is required to enter premises under section 28, section 28A or section 62A of the Competition Act 1998, this must be obtained from a judge of the High Court[278]. The High Court may also issue warrants to enter premises in relation to investigations under the EC competition rules[279].

Actions may be brought in the High Court where there are infringements of Articles 81 and 82 of the EC Treaty or the Chapter I and II prohibitions[280]; such actions are usually brought in the Chancery Division, but sometimes may be dealt with by the Commercial Court[281]. Where the OFT or the CAT has already found such an infringement its decisions are binding in proceedings before the ordinary courts[282]. As noted above, the Enterprise Act makes provision for the Lord Chancellor to adopt regulations for the transfer of cases to and from the CAT.

(ix) Criminal courts

The Competition Act 1998 and the Enterprise Act 2002 create a number of criminal offences. Most notably, the Enterprise Act establishes the 'cartel offence', the commission of which could attract a prison sentence of up to five years as well as a fine[283]. The cartel offence is described in detail in chapter 10[284], as is the possibility that some cartel behaviour may, in exceptional circumstances, be criminal at common law as a conspiracy to defraud[285]. Under the Competition Act various criminal offences may also be committed where investigations are obstructed, documents are destroyed or falsified or where false or misleading information is provided[286]. It is also a criminal offence to obstruct investigations conducted under the EC competition rules[287].

4. THE RELATIONSHIP BETWEEN EC COMPETITION LAW AND NATIONAL COMPETITION LAWS

(A) Introduction

All the Member States of the EC have systems of competition law, in large part modelled upon Articles 81 and 82. Some Member States require that domestic law should be interpreted consistently with the EC rules, thereby reinforcing the alignment of Community and domestic law[288]. It follows that many cases will have the same outcome whether they are investigated under EC or under domestic law: for example,

---

[278] Competition Act 1998, s 28(1) and s 59; in Scotland the relevant court is the Court of Session: ibid.

[279] Ibid, ss 62 and 63.

[280] On the enforcement of Articles 81 and 82 EC and the Competition Act in the civil courts see ch 8 generally.

[281] *Practice Direction – Competition Law – Claims Relating to the Application of Articles 81 and 82 of the EC Treaty and Chapters I and II of Part I of the Competition Act 1998*, available at www.justice.gov.uk/civil/procrules_fin/contents/practice_directions/competitionlaw_pd.htm.

[282] Enterprise Act 2002, s 20 which inserts a new s 58A into the Competition Act 1998.

[283] Enterprise Act 2002, s 190.   [284] See ch 10, pp 415–422.   [285] Ibid, pp 423–424.

[286] Competition Act 1998, ss 42–44, ss 65L–65N and s 72: see ch 10, pp 392–393.

[287] Competition Act 1998, s 65.

[288] Section 60 of the UK Competition Act 1998 is an example of this: see ch 9, pp 362–367.

a horizontal price-fixing agreement would infringe Article 81(1), and would normally also be caught by any domestic system of competition law in the Community unless, for example, it occurred in a sector which was not subject to the domestic rules. Even though there is a high degree of convergence between EC and domestic competition law, nevertheless the possibility remains that there could be different outcomes depending on which system of law is applied. In some cases domestic law may be more generous than EC law; in other cases the possibility exists that domestic law could have a stricter effect than EC law.

Much thought has gone into the issue of conflicts between EC and domestic competition law over the years[289]. The starting point is that Community law takes precedence over national law, so that where a clash occurs it is the former which must be applied[290]: in *Walt Wilhelm v Bundeskartellamt*[291] the ECJ ruled that conflicts between the rules of the Community and national rules on cartels must be resolved by applying the principle that Community law takes precedence. However the *Walt Wilhelm* judgment did not provide answers to all the situations that could arise: for example, could a Member State prohibit an agreement that the Commission had individually exempted, or which benefited from a Community block exemption[292]? These matters are now dealt with by Article 3 of the Modernisation Regulation.

(B) The Modernisation Regulation[293]

Under the regime introduced by the Modernisation Regulation[294] the Commission shares the competence to apply Articles 81 and 82 with national competition authorities ('NCAs') and national courts; of course NCAs and national courts can also apply domestic law. Member States are required by Article 35 of the Regulation to designate the authorities responsible for the application of Articles 81 and 82: in the UK the

---

[289] See eg Market 'Some Legal and Administrative Problems of the Co-existence of Community and National Competition Law in the EC' (1974) 11 CML Rev 92; Stockmann 'EC Competition Law and Member State Competition Laws' [1987] Fordham Corporate Law Institute (ed Hawk), pp 265–300; Bellamy and Child *European Community Law of Competition* (Sweet & Maxwell, 5th ed, 2001, ed Roth), paras 10–074 to 10–080; Whish *Competition Law* (Butterworths, 4th ed, 2001), pp 322–329; Goyder *EC Competition Law* (Oxford EC Law Library, 4th ed, 2003), pp 440–445; Kerse and Khan *EC Antitrust Procedure* (Sweet & Maxwell, 5th ed, 2005), para 5.56.

[290] See Case 6/64 *Costa v ENEL* [1964] ECR 585, [1964] CMLR 425; Case 106/77 *Amministrazione delle Finanze dello Stato v Simmenthal* [1978] ECR 629, [1978] 3 CMLR 263; Case C-213/89 *R v Secretary of State for Transport, ex p Factortame (No 2)* [1991] 1 AC 603, [1990] 3 CMLR 1; Case C-221/89 *R v Secretary of State for Transport, ex p Factortame Ltd (No 3)* [1991] ECR I-3905, [1991] 3 CMLR 589; note also that national competition authorities have an obligation to disapply national law that involves an infringement of EC competition law: Case Case C-198/01 *Consorzio Industrie Fiammiferi* [2003] ECR I-8055, [2003] 5 CMLR 829, discussed in Case 1024/2/3/04 *Floe Telecom Ltd (in administration) v OFCOM* [2006] CAT 17, paras 317–348.

[291] Case 14/68 [1969] ECR 1, [1969] CMLR 100.

[292] The ECJ declined to give an answer to this question in Case C-70/93 *Bayerische Motoren Werke AG v ALD Auto-Leasing* [1995] ECR I-3439, [1996] 4 CMLR 478 and Case C-266/93 *Bundeskartellamt v Volkswagen ACT and VAG Leasing GmbH* [1995] ECR I-3477, [1996] 4 CMLR 478, since it concluded that the agreements under consideration in those cases were not covered by the block exemption for motor car distribution in force at that time.

[293] For further discussion of Art 3 of the Modernisation Regulation see Faull and Nikpay *The EC Law of Competition* (Oxford University Press, 2nd ed, 2007), paras 2.28–2.73; O'Neill and Saunders *UK Competition Procedure* (Oxford University Press, 2007), paras 3.08–3.93; see also the OFT's guidance *Modernisation* (OFT 442, December 2004), paras 4.1–4.30.

[294] See n 1 above.

OFT and the sectoral regulators have been designated as NCAs[295]. Recitals 8 and 9 and Article 3 of the Regulation deal with the relationship between Articles 81 and 82 and national competition laws.

(i) Obligation to apply Articles 81 and 82

Recital 8 states that, in order to ensure the effective enforcement of Community competition law, it is necessary to oblige NCAs and national courts, where they apply national competition law to agreements or practices, to also apply Articles 81 or 82 where those provisions are applicable. Article 3(1) therefore provides that, where NCAs or national courts apply national competition law to agreements, decisions by associations of undertakings or concerted practices that may affect trade between Member States, they shall also apply Article 81; similarly they must apply Article 82 to any abuse prohibited by that provision. It is the concept of 'trade between Member States' that triggers the obligation to apply Articles 81 and 82, which is why the Commission published guidance on it in 2004[296]. The OFT's view is that the prosecution of *individuals* for commission of the cartel offence contained in section 188 of the Enterprise Act 2002 does *not* trigger the obligation to apply Article 81, since Article 81 is aimed at the anti-competitive agreements of *undertakings* rather than individuals[297]. The position is not free from doubt, however[298]. The cartel offence is certainly part of national competition law, and it is intended to deter anti-competitive agreements; it is aimed at individuals because fines on undertakings appear not to prevent them from entering into cartels. In practice the reality is that the OFT, when proceeding against individuals under the Enterprise Act, would probably also conduct an investigation against the undertakings involved in the cartel under domestic and/or EC law[299]: whether it would be doing so as a result of an obligation arising from Article 3(1) may be a merely academic question. However if the OFT were to proceed purely under the Enterprise Act the question could arise whether it was 'acting under Article 81 or Article 82 of the Treaty' for the purposes of Article 11(3) of the Modernisation Regulation; if it was so doing the Commission would have power under Article 11(6), by commencing its own proceedings, to relieve the OFT of the power to proceed.

In certain circumstances the use by sectoral regulators of their regulatory powers might amount to the application of national competition law, with the consequence that the obligation to apply Articles 81 and 82 EC would arise in the event that the agreement or behaviour in question had an effect on trade between Member States[300].

(ii) Conflicts: Article 81

Recital 8 of the Modernisation Regulation states that it is necessary to create a 'level playing field' for agreements within the internal market. What this means is that, if an agreement is not prohibited under EC competition law, it should not be possible for an NCA or national court to apply stricter national competition law to it; this may

---

[295] Competition Act 1998 and Other Enactments (Amendment) Regulations 2004, SI 2004/1261, Art 3.

[296] *Guidelines on the effect on trade concept contained in Articles 81 and 82 of the Treaty*, OJ [2004] C 101/81; the *Guidelines* are discussed in ch 3, pp 142–146.

[297] See the OFT's guidance *Modernisation*, OFT 442, December 2004, paras 4.21–4.22; see also Dekeyser's comments during a roundtable discussion at [2004] Fordham Corporate Law Institute (ed Hawk), pp 734–735.

[298] See eg Wils *Principles of European Antitrust Enforcement* (Hart Publishing, 2005), paras 153–157 and Wils 'Is Criminalization of EC Competition Law the Answer?' (2005) 28(2) World Competition 117, pp 130–133.

[299] *Modernisation*, OFT 442, December 2004, paras 4.23–4.27.   [300] Ibid, paras 4.28–4.30.

be termed a 'convergence rule'[301]. Article 3(2) therefore provides that the application of national competition law may not lead to the prohibition of agreements, decisions by associations of undertakings or concerted practices which may affect trade between Member States but which do not restrict competition within the meaning of Article 81(1) or which fulfil the conditions of Article 81(3) or which are covered by a block exemption. In terms of UK law it follows that, in so far as agreements affect trade between Member States but do not infringe Article 81(1) or do satisfy the criteria set out in Article 81(3), it would not be possible to take action against them under the market investigation provisions of the Enterprise Act 2002[302].

(iii) Conflicts: Article 82

The position in relation to Article 82 is different, since the Modernisation Regulation does not demand convergence in relation to unilateral behaviour. Recital 8 of the Regulation states that Member States should not be precluded from adopting and applying on their territory stricter national competition laws which prohibit or impose sanctions on unilateral conduct. Article 3(2) therefore makes provision to this effect. An example of a stricter national law on unilateral behaviour would be one that is intended to protect economically dependent undertakings: several Member States have laws to this effect[303]. In terms of UK law it follows from Article 3(2) that it would be possible to take action under the market investigation provisions of the Enterprise Act 2002 against unilateral behaviour, such as refusal to supply or the imposition of unfair prices or other trading conditions, to stricter effect than the position under Article 82[304]. In so far as legislation such as the UK Gas Act 1986 or Electricity Act 1989 provides for the imposition of *ex ante* regulatory controls on the unilateral behaviour of regulated undertakings, and in so far as those controls could be regarded as provisions of competition law, Article 3(2) would allow them to be applied to achieve a stricter outcome than under Article 82. In the event that they were intended to protect some other legitimate interest than the protection of competition they could be applied by virtue of Article 3(3) (below).

(iv) Protection of 'other legitimate interests'

Recital 9 of the Modernisation Regulation states that its provisions should not preclude Member States from applying national legislation that protects legitimate interests other than the protection of competition on the market, provided that such legislation is compatible with the general principles and other provisions of Community law[305]. Article 3(3) therefore provides that the Regulation does not preclude the application of provisions of national law that 'predominantly pursue an objective different from that pursued by Articles 81 and 82 of the Treaty'. Recital 9 of the Regulation says that Articles 81 and 82 EC have as their objective 'the protection of competition on the market', which provides a benchmark against which to measure whether a particular national provision pursues an objective different from the EC competition rules. The

---

[301] See the Commission's *Guidelines on the application of Article 81(3) of the Treaty*, OJ [2004] C 101/8, para 14; Faull and Nikpay, para 2.30.

[302] See further ch 11, p 455.

[303] See eg in France Code of Commercial Law Book IV Article L 420–2 and in Germany Act Against Restrictions of Competition 1958 Article 20(2).

[304] See further ch 11, p 455.

[305] See, to similar effect, Article 21(4) of the ECMR, discussed in ch 21, pp 839–843.

recital specifically says that a Member State could apply legislation intended to combat unfair trading practices, for example a law that prevents the imposition on customers of terms and conditions that are unjustified, disproportionate or without consideration.

There may be situations in which it will be unclear whether a particular national provision is predominantly concerned with matters other than the protection of competition. Certain regulatory rules – for example requiring the provision of a universal service or the protection of vulnerable consumers – clearly pursue objectives other than the protection of competition and so could be applied by virtue of Article 3(3)[306]. Consumer laws which provide protection against, for example, unfair contract terms, misleading advertising or sharp selling practices would also seem to pursue a predominantly different objective from Articles 81 and 82 EC. However a national rule that was dependent, for example, on a prior finding of market dominance or significant market power would look more like a rule whose concern was the protection of competition. In that case the derogation provided by Article 3(3) would not be applicable, so that the position would be governed by Article 3(2): a stricter national rule in relation to agreements could not be applied, but a stricter rule on unilateral behaviour could be.

In *Days Medical Aids Ltd v Pihsiang*[307] the High Court in England and Wales suggested that the common law doctrine of restraint of trade could not be said predominantly to pursue an objective different from Articles 81 and 82 EC, with the result that it could not be applied to invalidate an agreement that did not infringe Article 81.

5. THE INSTITUTIONAL STRUCTURE OF EC AND UK COMPETITION LAW

The following diagrams set out the institutional architecture of EC and UK competition law.

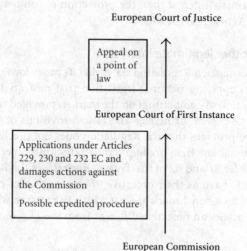

Fig. 2.1 Articles 81 and 82 EC; EC Merger Regulation

---

[306] See further the OFT's guidance *Concurrent application to regulated industries*, OFT 405, December 2004, para 4.7.

[307] [2004] EuLR 477, [2004] ECC 297 (QBD).

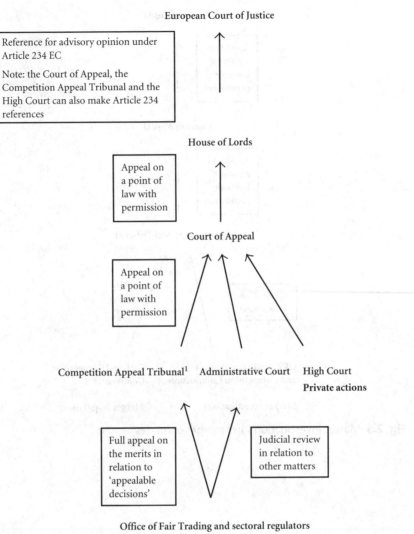

Fig. 2.2 Articles 81 and 82 EC; Competition Act 1998, Chapter I and II Prohibitions

[1] The Competition Appeal Tribunal also has an original jurisdiction in relation to 'follow-on' actions for damages under sections 47A and 47B of the Competition Act 1998.

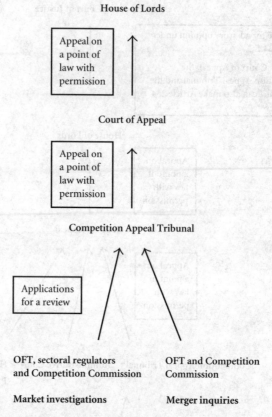

Fig. 2.3 Market investigations and merger enquiries

3

Article 81(1)[1]

CHAPTER CONTENTS

1. INTRODUCTION

This chapter is concerned with Article 81(1) EC which prohibits agreements, decisions by associations of undertakings and concerted practices that are restrictive of competition. Article 81(1) may be declared inapplicable where the criteria set out in Article 81(3) are satisfied: the provisions of Article 81(3) are considered in chapter 4. An agreement which is prohibited by Article 81(1) and which does not satisfy Article 81(3) is stated to be automatically void by virtue of Article 81(2)[2]. The full text of Article 81 is as follows:

1. The following shall be prohibited as incompatible with the common market: all agreements between undertakings, decisions by associations of undertakings and concerted practices which may affect trade between Member States and which have as their object or effect the prevention, restriction or distortion of competition within the common market, and in particular those which:
   (a) directly or indirectly fix purchase or selling prices or any other trading conditions;
   (b) limit or control production, markets, technical development, or investment;
   (c) share markets or sources of supply;
   (d) apply dissimilar conditions to equivalent transactions with other trading parties, thereby placing them at a competitive disadvantage;

---

[1] For further reading on Article 81(1) readers are referred to Faull and Nikpay *The EC Law of Competition* (2nd ed, 2007), ch 2, paras 3.01–3.392; Bellamy & Child *European Community Law of Competition* (eds Roth and Rose, Oxford University Press, 6th ed, 2008) ch 3.

[2] See ch 8, pp 309–317 on the implications of the sanction of voidness in Article 81(2).

(e) make the conclusion of contracts subject to the acceptance by other parties of supplementary obligations which, by their nature or according to commercial usage, have no
connection with the subject of such contracts.

2. Any agreements or decisions prohibited pursuant to this Article shall be automatically void.

3. The provisions of paragraph 1 may, however, be declared inapplicable in the case of:
   – any agreement or category of agreements between undertakings;
   – any decision or category of decisions by associations of undertakings;
   – any concerted practice or category of concerted practices;
   which contributes to improving the production or distribution of goods or to promoting
   technical or economic progress, while allowing consumers a fair share of the resulting benefit, and which does not:
   (a) impose on the undertakings concerned restrictions which are not indispensable to the
   attainment of these objectives;
   (b) afford such undertakings the possibility of eliminating competition in respect of a substantial part of the products in question.

Many aspects of the basic prohibition in Article 81(1) require elaboration. First, the
meaning of 'undertakings' and then the terms 'agreements', 'decisions' and 'concerted
practices' will be explained. The fourth section of this chapter will consider what is
meant by agreements that 'have as their object or effect the prevention, restriction or
distortion of competition'. The fifth section deals with the *de minimis* doctrine. Section 5
explains the requirement of an effect on trade between Member States. The chapter concludes with a checklist of agreements that, for a variety of reasons, normally will fall
outside Article 81(1).

2. UNDERTAKINGS[3]

Four issues must be considered in respect of this term: first, its basic definition for the
purpose of Articles 81 and 82[4]; second, whether two or more legal persons form a single
economic entity – and therefore comprise one undertaking – and the significance of
such a finding; third, whether two or more entities may be treated as one undertaking
where there is a corporate reorganisation; and fourth which undertaking is liable for an
infringement of competition law when one business is sold to another.

(A) Basic definition

The Treaty does not define an 'undertaking'[5]. However it is a critically important
term, since only agreements *between undertakings* are caught by Article 81; similarly,
Article 82 applies only to abuses committed by dominant *undertakings*. The term has
been given extensive consideration by the Community Courts and the Commission.
It can be particularly problematic where agreements are entered into by organs of the

---

[3] For a particularly interesting discussion of this expression see Odudu 'The meaning of undertaking
within Article 81 EC' in *The Boundaries of EC Competition Law: The Scope of Article 81* (Oxford University
Press, 2006).

[4] The term undertaking has the same meaning under Article 82, and this section discusses cases decided
under both Article 81 and Article 82.

[5] Article 80 of the former ECSC Treaty and Article 80 of the Euratom Treaty do contain definitions of an
undertaking for their respective purposes.

Member States (for example public authorities, municipalities, communes, the health service) or by entities entrusted by the Member States with regulatory or other functions. The question that arises is whether such agreements can be challenged under Article 81; similarly it is important to know whether the conduct of such an entity can be challenged under Article 82. A separate question, considered in chapter 6, is whether Member States themselves may be liable for the anti-competitive behaviour of such entities.

The ECJ held in *Höfner and Elser v Macrotron GmbH*[6] that:

the concept of an undertaking encompasses every entity engaged in an economic activity regardless of the legal status of the entity and the way in which it is financed.

In *Pavlov*[7] the ECJ added that:

It has also been consistently held that any activity consisting in offering goods or services on a given market is an economic activity.

In *Wouters v Algemene Raad van de Nederlandsche Orde van Advocaten*[8] the ECJ said that the competition rules in the Treaty:

do not apply to activity which, by its nature, its aim and the rules to which it is subject does not belong to the sphere of economic activity...or which is connected with the exercise of the powers of a public authority.

These statements are a helpful starting point in understanding the meaning of the term undertaking and will be considered in the text that follows.

(i) Need to adopt a functional approach

It is important to understand at the outset that the same legal entity may be acting as an undertaking when it carries on one activity but not when it is carrying on another. A 'functional approach' must be adopted when determining whether an entity, when engaged in a particular activity, is doing so as an undertaking for the purpose of the competition rules[9]. As the CFI said in *SELEX Sistemi Integrati SpA v Commission*[10]:

the various activities of an entity must be considered individually and the treatment of some of them as powers of a public authority does not mean that it must be concluded that the other activities are not economic[11].

Thus, for example, a local authority in the UK may (a) have powers to adopt bye-laws specifying where cars can and cannot park and (b) own land which it operates commercially as a car park. When performing function (a) the authority would, in the language of *Wouters*, be exercising the powers of a public authority and therefore would not be acting as an undertaking; the behaviour in (b), however, would be economic, and

---

[6] Case C-41/90 [1991] ECR I-1979, [1993] 4 CMLR 306, para 21.

[7] Cases C-180/98 etc [2000] ECR I-6451, [2001] 4 CMLR 30, para 75.

[8] Case C-309/99 [2002] ECR I-1577, [2002] 4 CMLR 913, para 57.

[9] On this point see the Opinion of Advocate General Jacobs in Cases C-67/96 etc *Albany International BV v SBT* [1999] ECR I-5751, [2000] 4 CMLR 446, para 207; this Opinion contains an invaluable discussion of the meaning of undertakings in Article 81(1).

[10] Case T-155/04 [2006] ECR II-4797, [2007] 4 CMLR 372; this case is on appeal to the ECJ, Case C-113/07 P, not yet decided.

[11] Ibid, para 54; see also Case T-128/98 *Aéroports de Paris v Commission* [2000] ECR II-3929, [2001] 4 CMLR 1376, paras 108 and 109, upheld on appeal Case C-82/01 P *Aéroports de Paris v Commission* [2002] ECR I-9297, [2003] 4 CMLR 609, paras 68–83.

therefore that of an undertaking[12]. In *SELEX* itself the CFI held that some of Eurocontrol's functions – for example setting technical standards, procuring prototypes and managing intellectual property rights – were not economic activities[13]; however the CFI also concluded that the provision of technical assistance to national administrations – for example drafting contract documents of public tenders – could be separated from its other functions[14], and that this service amounted to economic activity[15].

(ii) 'Engaged in an economic activity'

The sentence quoted from the *Höfner and Elser* judgment states that every entity engaged in economic activity does so as an undertaking: it is the idea of economic activity, therefore, that needs to be explored.

(A) 'Offering goods or services on a given market is an economic activity' It was noted above that the ECJ stated in *Pavlov* that activity consisting in offering goods or services on a market is an economic activity. The Commission held in *Spanish Courier Services*[16] that the Spanish Post Office, in so far as it was providing services on the market, was acting as an undertaking; in *Höfner and Elser v Macrotron*[17] the ECJ reached the same conclusion in respect of the German Federal Employment Office. In *Ambulanz Glöckner v Landkreis Südwestpfalz*[18] the ECJ held that medical aid organisations providing ambulance services for remuneration were acting as undertakings for the purpose of the competition rules[19]. In SELEX *Sistemi Integrati SpA v Commission*[20] the CFI concluded that Eurocontrol's activity of setting technical standards for its founding States did not amount to the provision of goods or services on a market[21], but that the provision of technical services did[22]. A legal entity that acts as a 'secretary' to a cartel can be an undertaking, even though it does not itself produce the goods or services that are cartelised[23].

(B) No need for a profit-motive or economic purpose The fact that an organisation lacks a profit-motive[24] or does not have an economic purpose[25] does not, in itself, mean that an activity is not economic. On this basis the Commission held in *Distribution of Package Tours During the 1990 World Cup*[26] that FIFA, the body responsible for the 1990 Football World Cup in Italy, as well as the Italian football association and the

---

[12] See eg *Eco-Emballages* OJ [2001] L 233/37, [2001] 5 CMLR 1096, para 70: French local authorities were acting as undertakings when entering into contracts in relation to the collection of household waste.
[13] See below.   [14] Case T-155/04, [2006] ECR II-4797, [2007] 4 CMLR 372, para 86.
[15] Ibid, para 92.   [16] OJ [1990] L 233/19, [1991] 4 CMLR 560.
[17] Case C-41/90 [1991] ECR I-1979, [1993] 4 CMLR 306.
[18] Case C-475/99 [2001] ECR I-8089, [2002] 4 CMLR 726.
[19] Ibid, paras 19–22.
[20] Case T-155/04 [2006] ECR II-4797, [2007] 4 CMLR 372; this case is on appeal to the ECJ, Case C-113/07 P, not yet decided.
[21] Case T-155/04 [2006] ECR II-4797, [2007] 4 CMLR 372, paras 61–62.   [22] Ibid, paras 89–92.
[23] *Organic peroxides*, Commission decision of 10 December 2003, paras 331–249; this finding is on appeal to the CFI, Case T-99/04 *AC Treuhand v Commission*, not yet decided.
[24] See eg Cases 209/78 etc *Van Landewyck v Commission* [1980] ECR 3125, [1981] 3 CMLR 134, para 88; *P & I Clubs* OJ [1985] L 376/2, [1989] 4 CMLR 178; *P & I Clubs* OJ [1999] L 125/12, [1999] 5 CMLR 646; Case C-244/94 *Fédération Française des Sociétés d'Assurance* [1995] ECR I-4013, [1996] 4 CMLR 536, para 21; Cases C-67/96 etc *Albany International BV v SBT* [1999] ECR I-5751, [2000] 4 CMLR 446, para 85.
[25] Case 155/73 *Italy v Sacchi* [1974] ECR 409, [1974] 2 CMLR 177, paras 13–14.
[26] OJ [1992] L 326/31, [1994] 5 CMLR 253, para 43.

local organising committee, were undertakings subject to Article 81[27]. In *Piau*[28] the CFI held that the practice of football by football clubs is an economic activity[29], and that national associations that group the clubs together are associations of undertakings; the position does not alter because the national associations group amateur clubs alongside professional ones[30]. The CFI also held in this case that FIFA was an association of undertakings[31].

(C) 'Regardless of the legal status of the entity and the way in which it is financed' The ECJ in *Höfner and Elser* held that an assessment of whether an entity was acting as an undertaking was to be determined 'regardless of the legal status of the entity and the way in which it is financed'. An entity can be found to be acting as an undertaking only as a result of the activity it is engaged in; its legal form is irrelevant. Companies and partnerships of course can qualify as undertakings, but so too can other entities such as agricultural cooperatives[32], P and I clubs[33] and trade associations: it follows that agreements between trade associations may themselves be caught by Article 81(1)[34]. Natural persons have often been held to qualify as undertakings[35], although an individual acting as an employee would not be[36]; nor would an individual purchasing goods or services as an end user/consumer, since that behaviour is not economic[37].

Public authorities, such as the Federal Employment Office in *Höfner* or the Autonomous Administration of State Monopolies in the *Banchero*[38] case, have been held to be engaged in activities of an economic nature with regard to employment procurement and the offering of goods and services on the market for manufactured tobacco respectively. State-owned corporations may act as undertakings[39], as may

---

[27] Ibid, paras 44–57; see similarly *UEFA's Broadcasting Regulations* OJ [2001] L 171/12, [2001] 5 CMLR 654, para 47.

[28] Case T-193/02 [2005] ECR I-209, [2005] 5 CMLR 42.   [29] Ibid, para 69.   [30] Ibid, para 70.

[31] Ibid, para 72.

[32] See eg Case 61/80 *Coöperative Stremsel-en Kleurselfabriek v Commission* [1981] ECR 851, [1982] 1 CMLR 240; *MELDOC* OJ [1986] L 348/50, [1989] 4 CMLR 853.

[33] *P & I Clubs* OJ [1985] L 376/2, [1989] 4 CMLR 178; *P & I Clubs* OJ [1999] L 125/12, [1999] 5 CMLR 646, paras 50–51.

[34] See eg Case 71/74 *FRUBO v Commission* [1975] ECR 563, [1975] 2 CMLR 123; Case 96/82 *IAZ International Belgium NV v Commission* [1983] ECR 3369, [1984] 3 CMLR 276; *Algemene Schippersvereniging v ANTIB* OJ [1985] L 219/35, [1988] 4 CMLR 698, upheld on appeal Case 272/85 *ANTIB v Commission* [1987] ECR 2201, [1988] 4 CMLR 677.

[35] See eg *AOIP v Beyrard* OJ [1976] L 6/8, [1976] 1 CMLR D14 where a patent licence between an individual and a company was held to fall within Article 81(1); *Reuter/BASF* OJ [1976] L 254/40, [1976] 2 CMLR D44; *RAI v UNITEL* OJ [1978] L 157/39, [1978] 3 CMLR 306 where opera singers were undertakings; *Vaessen BV v Moris* OJ [1979] L 19/32, [1979] 1 CMLR 511; Case 35/83 *BAT v Commission* [1985] ECR 363, [1985] 2 CMLR 470; Case 42/84 *Remia BV and Verenigde Bedrijven Nutricia NV v Commission* [1985] ECR 2545, [1987] 1 CMLR 1; *Breeders' Rights: Roses* OJ [1985] L 369/9, [1988] 4 CMLR 193: *French Beef* OJ [2003] L 209/12, paras 104–108, upheld on appeal Cases T-217/03 and T-245/03 *FNCBV v Commission*, [2006] ECR II-4987, on appeal Cases C-101/07 P and C-110/07 P, not yet decided; Case C-172/03 *Wolfgang Heiser v Finanzamt Innsbruck* [2005] ECR I-1627, [2005] 2 CMLR 402, a case on state aid in which a self-employed dentist was held to be acting as an undertaking.

[36] See pp 90–91 below.

[37] On this point see Cases C-180/98 etc *Pavel Pavlov v Stichting Pensioenfonds Medische Specialisten* [2000] ECR I-6451, [2001] 4 CMLR 30, paras 78–81.

[38] Case C-387/93 [1995] ECR I-4663, [1996] 1 CMLR 829, para 50.

[39] See eg Case 155/73 *Sacchi* [1974] ECR 409, [1974] 2 CMLR 177; Case 41/83 *Italy v Commission* [1985] ECR 873, [1985] 2 CMLR 368.

bodies entrusted by the state with particular tasks[40] and quasi-Governmental bodies which carry on economic activities[41]. Aéroports de Paris, responsible for the planning, administration and development of civil air transport installations in Paris, the Portuguese Airports Authority, ANA, and the Finnish Civil Aviation Administration were all found by the Commission to constitute undertakings[42]. In *Aluminium Products*[43] foreign trade organisations in eastern European countries were regarded as undertakings, even though they had no existence separate from the state under their domestic law: claims of sovereign immunity should be confined to acts which are those of Government and not of trade. The same point was made by the Commission in its decision in *Amministrazione Autonoma dei Monopoli di Stato*[44].

(iii) Activities that are not economic

Activities provided on the basis of 'solidarity' are not economic; nor is the exercise of public power. Procurement pursuant to a non-economic activity is not economic.

(A) Solidarity[45] There have been several cases in which the question has arisen whether entities providing social protection, for example social security, pensions, health insurance or health care, did so as undertakings. The case law makes a distinction between situations in which such protection is provided in a market context on the one hand, or on the basis of so-called 'solidarity' on the other. Solidarity was defined by Advocate General Fennelly in *Sodemare v Regione Lombardia*[46] as 'the inherently uncommercial act of involuntary subsidisation of one social group by another'[47]. Where social protection is provided on the basis of solidarity, it is not provided by an undertaking.

In *Poucet v Assurances Générales de France*[48] the ECJ concluded that French regional social security offices administering sickness and maternity insurance schemes to self-employed persons were not acting as undertakings, but it reached the opposite conclusion in relation to a differently-constituted scheme in *Fédération Française des Sociétés d'Assurance*[49]. The difference between the cases was that in *Poucet* the benefits payable were identical for all recipients, contributions were proportionate to income, the pension rights were not proportionate to the contributions made and schemes that were in surplus helped to finance those which had financial difficulties; the schemes were based on the principle of solidarity. In the *Fédération Française* case, on the other hand, the benefits payable depended on the amount of the contributions paid by recipients and the financial results of the investments made by the managing organisation. Thus

[40] Such bodies have a limited dispensation from the competition rules by virtue of Article 86(2) of the Treaty: see ch 6, pp 233–239.

[41] Case 258/78 *Nungesser KG v Commission* [1982] ECR 2015, [1983] 1 CMLR 278.

[42] See respectively *Alpha Flight Services/Aéroports de Paris* OJ [1998] L 230/10, [1998] 5 CMLR 611, paras 49–55, upheld on appeal Case T-128/98 [2000] ECR II-3929, [2001] 4 CMLR 1376, paras 120–126 and by the ECJ in Case C-82/01 P [2002] ECR I-9297, [2003] 4 CMLR 609, paras 78–82; *Portuguese Airports* OJ [1999] L 69/31, [1999] 5 CMLR 103, para 12, upheld on appeal Case C-163/99 *Portugal v Commission* [2001] ECR I-2613; *Ilmailulaitos/Luftfartsverket* OJ [1999] L 69/24, [1999] 5 CMLR 90, paras 21–23.

[43] OJ [1985] L 92/1, [1987] 3 CMLR 813: see XIVth *Report on Competition Policy* (1984), point 57; see similarly *Re Colombian Coffee* OJ [1982] L 360/31, [1983] 1 CMLR 703.

[44] OJ [1998] L 252/47, [1998] 5 CMLR 786, para 21.

[45] See Winterstein 'Nailing the Jellyfish: Social Security and Competition Law' (1999) 20 ECLR 324.

[46] Case C-70/95 [1997] ECR I-3395, [1997] 3 CMLR 591.

[47] [1997] ECR I-3395, [1997] 3 CMLR 591, para 29.   [48] Cases C-159/91 and 160/91 [1993] ECR I-637.

[49] Case C-244/94 [1995] ECR I-4013, [1996] 4 CMLR 536.

the manager of the scheme was carrying on an economic activity in competition with life assurance companies. In *Albany International BV v Stichting Bedrijfspensioenfonds Textielindustrie*[50] the ECJ held that the pension fund in that case was acting as an undertaking, since it was carrying on an economic activity: its function was to make investments, the result of which determined the amount of benefits that the fund could pay to its members[51]; as such, this fund was different from the one in *Poucet*[52].

In *Cisal di Battistello Venanzio & C Sas v INAIL*[53] the ECJ held that INAIL, entrusted by law with management of a scheme providing insurance against accidents at work, was not acting as an undertaking for the purposes of the competition rules because it fulfilled an exclusively social function based on the principle of solidarity. Similarly in *AOK Bundesverband*[54] the ECJ held that German sickness funds were involved in the management of the social security system, fulfilling an exclusively social function founded on the principle of solidarity. It followed that they were not acting as undertakings.

(B) Activities connected with the exercise of the powers of a public authority are not economic Although it is clear that state-owned corporations or public authorities may qualify as undertakings when engaged in economic activity, the *Wouters* judgment says they would not do so when their behavior 'is connected with the exercise of the powers of a public authority'[55]. In *Corinne Bodson v Pompes Funèbres des Régions Libérées SA*[56] a French law entrusted the performance of funeral services to local communes; many of the communes in turn awarded concessions to provide those services to private undertakings. The ECJ held that Article 81 did not apply to 'contracts for concessions concluded between communes *acting in their capacity as public authorities* and undertakings entrusted with the provision of a public service' (emphasis added)[57]. An entity acts in the exercise of official authority where the activity in question is 'a task in the public interest which forms part of the essential functions of the State' and where that activity 'is connected by its nature, its aim and the rules to which it is subject with the exercise of powers ... which are typically those of a public authority'[58]. For the same reason, in *SAT Fluggesellschaft v Eurocontrol*[59] the ECJ concluded that Eurocontrol was not acting as an undertaking when it created and collected route charges from users of air navigation services on behalf of the States that had created it[60]. In *Calì e Figli*[61] the ECJ held that a private company engaged in anti-pollution surveillance in Genoa harbour would not be acting as an undertaking when discharging that particular responsibility, since this was a task in the public interest, forming part of one of the essential functions

---

[50] Cases C-67/96 etc [1999] ECR I-5751, [2000] 4 CMLR 446: for commentary on this case see Gyselen (2000) 37 CML Rev 425; see also Cases C-180/98 etc *Pavel Pavlov v Stichting Pensioenfonds Medische Specialisten* [2000] ECR I-6451, [2001] 4 CMLR 30, paras 102–119.

[51] Ibid, paras 71–87.   [52] See p 86, n 48 above.

[53] Case C-218/00 [2002] ECR I-691, [2002] 4 CMLR 833.

[54] Cases C-264/01 etc [2004] ECR I-2493; see also, under Article 87 EC on state aid, Cases C-266/04 *Casino France* [2005] ECR I-9481, paras 45–55.

[55] See, to the same effect, Case C-343/95 *Calì e Figli* [1997] ECR I-1547, [1997] 5 CMLR 484, paras 16–17.

[56] Case 30/87 [1988] ECR 2479, [1989] 4 CMLR 984.   [57] Ibid, para 18.

[58] Case C-343/95 *Calì e Figli* [1997] ECR I-1547, [1997] 5 CMLR 484, para 23.

[59] Case C-364/92 [1994] ECR I-43, [1994] 5 CMLR 208.

[60] A similar conclusion had earlier been reached by the Commercial Court in London in *Irish Aerospace (Belgium) NV v European Organisation for the Safety of Air Navigation* [1992] 1 Lloyd's Rep 383.

[61] Case C-343/95 [1997] ECR I-1547, [1997] 5 CMLR 484.

of the State in protecting the maritime environment: this judgment is of particular interest as the public duty was being carried out by a private body.

(C) Procurement that is ancillary to a non-economic activity is not economic In *FENIN v Commission*[62] a complaint was made to the Commission that 26 public bodies in Spain responsible for the operation of the Spanish national health system were abusing their dominant buyer power by delaying unreasonably the payment of invoices. The Commission rejected the complaint on the basis that the public bodies were not acting as undertakings. FENIN, an association representing most undertakings marketing medical goods and equipment used in Spanish hospitals, appealed to the CFI. The CFI dismissed the appeal. Its reasoning was that, when providing health care to citizens, the public bodies did so on the basis of solidarity: that behaviour therefore was not economic. The CFI then held that the activity of purchasing goods should not be dissociated from the purpose to which they would be put. Since the provision of health care was not economic, the ancillary behaviour of procurement for that purpose was not economic either[63]. This judgment was upheld on appeal to the ECJ[64]. The CFI's judgment did not say what the position would be where a health organisation purchasing goods uses them partly for the provision of state-sponsored health care on the basis of solidarity, but also charges certain patients, for example tourists from overseas, according to market principles: as the point had not been raised in the original complaint to the Commission, the CFI held that it did not need to adjudicate upon it[65].

The reasoning in *FENIN* has since been applied in *SELEX Sistemi Integrati SpA v Commission*[66]. SELEX had made a complaint to the Commission that Eurocontrol (the European Organisation for the Safety of Air Navigation), an international organisation established by a number of European States responsible, among other things, for the establishment of technical standardisation for air navigation, was guilty of abusing its dominant position. The Commission rejected the complaint as Eurocontrol was not acting as an undertaking. The CFI agreed with the Commission's position on appeal, holding that Eurocontrol did not provide technical standardisation services to a market, but simply to the States in their capacity as air traffic control authorities[67]. The CFI then held that, in so far as Eurocontrol procured prototypes necessary for producing technical standards, this should not be dissociated from the non-economic purpose to which they would be put[68]; therefore Eurocontrol did not purchase as an undertaking. The CFI explicitly applied the *FENIN* judgment, saying that the reasoning in that case was equally applicable to the facts in the *SELEX* case[69]. A similar conclusion was reached in relation to the management of intellectual property rights, which were ancillary to Eurocontrol's non-economic activity in setting standards[70].

[62] Case T-319/99 [2003] ECR II-357, [2003] 5 CMLR 34; it is interesting to compare this judgment with that of the UK Competition Appeal Tribunal in Case No 1006/2/1/01 *BetterCare Group Ltd v Director General of Fair Trading* [2002] CAT 7, [2002] Comp AR 299, a judgment which preceded that in *FENIN* and which came to a different view in relation to the procurement activities of the Health Trust in that case: see ch 9, pp 329–330.

[63] Ibid, paras 35–36.

[64] Case C-205/03 P [2006] ECR I-6295, [2006] 5 CMLR 559, paras 25–26; Advocate General Maduro's Opinion in this case contains an extensive review of the law and literature on the issues raised.

[65] Case T-319/99 [2003] ECR II-357, [2003] 5 CMLR 34, paras 41–44.

[66] Case T-155/04 [2006] ECR II-4797, [2007] 4 CMLR 372; this case is on appeal to the ECJ, Case C-113/07 P, not yet decided.

[67] Ibid, paras 61–62. [68] Ibid, para 65. [69] Ibid, paras 66–68. [70] Ibid, para 77.

(iv) The professions[71]

Members of the liberal professions can be undertakings for the purpose of the competition rules. In *Commission v Italy*[72] the ECJ held that customs agents in Italy, who offer for payment services consisting of the carrying out of customs formalities in relation to the import, export and transit of goods, were undertakings; it rejected the Italian Government's argument that the fact that the activity of customs agents is intellectual and requires authorisation and compliance with conditions meant that they were not undertakings. The ECJ further held that the National Council of Customs Agents was an association of undertakings, relying on *BNIC v Clair*[73] for the proposition that its public law nature did not remove it from the application of Article 81[74]. In *Coapi*[75] the Commission concluded that industrial property agents were undertakings, notwithstanding that they were members of a regulated profession, that their services were of an intellectual, technical or specialised nature, and that they provided services on a personal and direct basis. A similar conclusion was reached in *EPI code of conduct*[76] in relation to professional representatives before the European Patent Office. Self-employed medical specialists have been held to be undertakings[77], including when they are making contributions to their own supplementary pension scheme[78]. It is clear that it is possible that a Member State might be found to have breached the competition rules by delegating to a professional association the power to fix prices[79]; and that the professional association itself might be liable for actually doing so[80]. Registered members of the Dutch Bar have been held to be undertakings for the purposes of the competition rules[81].

The Commission has taken a close interest in (the lack of) competition in the liberal professions in recent years. It commissioned research into the state of competition in six professions – lawyers, notaries, accountants, architects, engineers, and pharmacists – which found many restrictive rules affecting matters such as prices, advertising and business structures; subsequently the Commission published two reports, urging all

---

[71] See *European Competition Law Annual: The Relationship Between Competition Law and the Liberal Professions* (eds Ehlermann and Atanasiu, Hart Publishing, 2006).

[72] Case C-35/96 [1998] ECR I-3851, [1998] 5 CMLR 889; see similarly Case T-513/93 *CNSD v Commission* [2000] ECR II-1807, [2000] 5 CMLR 614, upholding the Commission's decision in *CNSD* OJ [1993] L 203/27, [1995] 5 CMLR 889.

[73] Case 123/83 [1985] ECR 391, [1985] 2 CMLR 430.

[74] Case C-35/96 [1998] ECR I-3851, [1998] 5 CMLR 889, para 40; see similarly Case T-513/93 *CNSD v Commission* [2000] ECR II-1807, [2000] 5 CMLR 614; Cases C-180/98 etc *Pavel Pavlov v Stichting Pensioenfonds Medische Specialisten* [2000] ECR I-6451, [2001] 4 CMLR 30, paras 85–89.

[75] OJ [1995] L 122/37, [1995] 5 CMLR 468.

[76] OJ [1999] L 106/14, [1999] 5 CMLR 540, partially annulled on appeal to the CFI Case T-144/99 *Institut des Mandataires Agréés v Commission* [2001] ECR II-1087, [2001] 5 CMLR 77.

[77] Cases C-180/98 etc *Pavel Pavlov v Stichting Pensioenfonds Medische Specialisten* [2000] ECR I-6451, [2001] 4 CMLR 30, para 77.

[78] Ibid, paras 78–82; the Commission, intervening, had argued that, when making such contributions, the specialists were acting as consumers rather than as undertakings.

[79] See ch 6, pp 214–220.

[80] *Coapi* OJ [1995] L 122/37, [1995] 5 CMLR 468, paras 44–48; Case T-513/93 *CNSD v Commission* [2000] ECR II-1807, [2000] 5 CMLR 614, para 73.

[81] Case C-309/99 *Wouters v Algemene Raad van de Nederlandse Orde van Advocaten* [2002] ECR I-1577, [2002] 4 CMLR 913, paras 45–49; see also the Opinion of Advocate General Léger on members of the Italian Bar in Case C-35/99 *Arduino* [2002] ECR I-1529, [2002] 4 CMLR 866, paras 46–50.

interest groups to make a joint effort to reform or eliminate restrictive rules that lack justification[82]. The Commission also imposed a fine of €100,000 on the Belgian Architects Association in 2004 for publishing a scale of recommended minimum fees which prevented architects from determining their fees independently of their competitors[83]. It published a study on competition in the market for conveyancing services in January of 2008[84]. The Commission works closely with the national competition authorities in promoting pro-competitive reform of professional services: anti-competitive behaviour in this sector is more naturally dealt with at national than Commission level, since typically it is national associations that adopt and enforce the rules and regulations. In October 2006 the Commission published on its website an *Overview of National Competition Authorities' Advocacy and Enforcement Activities in the Area of Professional Services*[85].

(v) Employees and trades unions

In *Jean Claude Becu*[86] the ECJ held that workers are, for the duration of their employment relationship, incorporated into the undertakings that employ them and thus form part of an economic unit with them; as such they do not constitute undertakings within the meaning of Community competition law[87]. Nor should the dock workers in that case, taken collectively, be regarded as constituting an undertaking[88]. However an ex-employee who carries on an independent business would be[89].

In the *Albany* case[90] the ECJ was concerned with a case where organisations representing employers and employees collectively agreed to set up a single pension fund responsible for managing a supplementary pension scheme and requested the public authorities to make affiliation to the fund compulsory. One of the issues in the case was whether an agreement between such organisations was an agreement between undertakings. The ECJ's answer was that it was not. The Treaty's activities include not only the adoption of a competition policy, but also a policy in the social sphere: this is stated in Article 3(1)(j) and revealed, for example, in Article 137, the purpose of which is to promote close cooperation between Member States in the social field, particularly in matters relating to the right of association and collective bargaining between employers and workers. The ECJ's view was that the social objectives pursued by collective agreements would be seriously undermined if they were subject to Article 81 of the Treaty and that therefore they fall outside it[91]. However the same exclusion does not apply in relation to a decision taken by members of the liberal professions, since it is not concluded in the context of collective bargaining between employers and employees[92]. In *Norwegian*

---

[82] The materials referred to in the text can be accessed at www.ec.europa.eu/comm/competition/sectors/professional_services/overview_en.html.

[83] Commission decision of 24 June 2004 OJ [2005] L 4/10.

[84] Commission Press Release IP/08/101, 29 January 2008.

[85] Available at www.ec.europa.eu/comm/competition/ecn/reference_paper/pdf.

[86] Case C-22/98 [1999] ECR I-5665, [2001] 4 CMLR 968.

[87] [1999] ECR I-5665, [2001] 4 CMLR 968, para 26.   [88] Ibid, para 27.

[89] See eg *Reuter/BASF* OJ [1976] L 254/40, [1976] 2 CMLR D44.   [90] See p 87, n 50 above.

[91] Ibid, para 59; for critical comment see Van den Bergh and Camesasca 'Irreconcilable Principles? The Court of Justice Exempts Collective Labour Agreements from the Wrath of Antitrust' (2000) 25 EL Rev 492; Boni and Manzini 'National Social Legislation and EC Antitrust Law' (2001) 24 World Competition 239; see also Case C-222/98 *Van der Woude v Stichting Beatrixoord* [2000] ECR I-7111, [2001] 4 CMLR 93.

[92] Cases C-180/98 etc *Pavel Pavlov v Stichting Pensioenfonds Medische Specialisten* [2000] ECR I-6451, [2001] 4 CMLR 30, paras 67–70.

Federation of Trade Unions v Norwegian Association of Local and Regional Authorities[93] the EFTA Court took a similar view of collective labour agreements under Article 53 of the EEA Agreement, but noted that provisions in such agreements which pursue objectives extraneous to that of improving conditions of work and employment could amount to an infringement[94].

In *FNCBV v Commission*[95] the CFI rejected an argument that the application of Article 81 to agreements between associations of farmers to fix prices and to prevent imports of beef into France restricted the freedom of trade union activity[96].

(B) The 'single economic entity' doctrine

Article 81(1) does not apply to agreements between two or more legal persons that form a single economic entity: collectively they comprise a single undertaking. The most obvious example of this is an agreement between a parent and a subsidiary company, though the relationship between a principal and agent and between a contractor and sub-contractor is analogous.

(i) Parent and subsidiary

(A) The basic rule Firms within the same corporate group can enter into legally enforce-able contracts with one another. However such an agreement will not fall within Article 81 if the relationship between them is so close that economically they form a single economic entity, that is to say that they 'consist of a unitary organisation of personal, tangible and intangible elements, which pursue a specific economic aim on a long-term basis, and can contribute to the commission of an infringement of the kind referred to in [Article 81 EC]'.[97] Where this is the case the agreement is regarded as the internal allocation of functions within a corporate group rather than a restrictive agreement between independent undertakings. In *Béguelin Import v GL Import Export*[98] the ECJ held that Article 81 would not apply to an agreement between a parent and its subsidiary 'which, although having separate legal personality, enjoys no economic independ-ence'. In *Corinne Bodson v Pompes Funèbres des Régions Libérées SA*[99] the ECJ held that Article 81 would not apply if the undertakings 'form an economic unit within which the subsidiary has no real freedom to determine its course of action on the market, and if the agreements or practices are concerned merely with the internal allocation of tasks as between the undertakings'[100]. A logical consequence of this doctrine is that, when counting the number of undertakings that are party to an agreement for the purpose of

---

[93] Case E-8/00 [2002] 5 CMLR 160, paras 33–46.   [94] [2002] 5 CMLR 160, paras 33–46, paras 47–59.

[95] Cases T-217/03 and T-245/03 [2006] ECR II-4987, on appeal Cases C-101/07 P and C-110/07 P not yet decided.

[96] Ibid, paras 97–103.

[97] See Case T-112/05 *Akzo Nobel NV v Commission* [2007] ECR II-000, paras 57–58.

[98] Case 22/71 [1971] ECR 949, [1972] CMLR 81; see also Case 15/74 *Centrafarm BV v Sterling Drug Inc* [1974] ECR 1147, [1974] 2 CMLR 480 and Cases T-68/89 etc *Società Italiano Vetro v Commission* [1992] ECR II-1403, [1992] 5 CMLR 302, para 357; the Commission reached a similar conclusion in *Re Christiani and Nielsen NV* JO [1969] L 165/12, [1969] CMLR D36 and in *Re Kodak* JO [1970] L 147/24, [1970] CMLR D19; see also *TFI/France 2 and France 3*, Commission's XXIXth *Report on Competition Policy* (1999) p 167.

[99] Case 30/87 [1988] ECR 2479, [1989] 4 CMLR 984.

[100] [1988] ECR 2479, [1989] 4 CMLR 984, para 19.

applying one of the block exemptions, the legal and natural persons that form a single economic entity are counted as one[101].

(B) The Viho *judgment* The issue was revisited in *Viho v Commission*[102]. Parker Pen had established an integrated distribution system for Germany, France, Belgium, Spain and the Netherlands, where it used subsidiary companies for the distribution of its products. The Commission concluded that Article 81 had no application to this allocation of tasks within the Parker Pen group. This finding was challenged by a third party, Viho, which had been trying to obtain supplies of Parker Pen's products and which considered that the agreements between Parker Pen and its subsidiaries infringed Article 81. The CFI and the ECJ upheld the decision of the Commission, that Article 81 had no application. At paragraph 15 of its judgment the ECJ noted that Parker Pen held 100 per cent of the shares in the subsidiary companies, it directed their sales and marketing activities and it controlled sales, targets, gross margins, sales costs, cash flow and stocks:

Parker and its subsidiaries thus form a single economic unit within which the subsidiaries do not enjoy real autonomy in determining their course of action in the market, but carry out the instructions issued to them by the parent company controlling them[103].

The ECJ went on to say that in those circumstances the fact that Parker Pen could divide national markets between its subsidiaries was outside Article 81, although it pointed out that such unilateral conduct could fall foul of Article 82 where the requirements for its application were satisfied[104].

(C) The test of control The crucial question, therefore, is whether parties to an agreement are independent in their decision-making or whether one has sufficient control over the other that the latter does not enjoy 'real autonomy' in determining its course of action on the market. For these purposes it is necessary to examine various factors such as the shareholding that a parent company has in its subsidiary, the composition of the board of directors, the extent to which the parent influences the policy of or issues instructions to the subsidiary and similar matters[105]. Where a parent owns the totality, or almost the totality, of the shares of a subsidiary, the presumption will be that it controls the subsidiary's affairs; the presumption can be rebutted, the burden being on the party wishing to do so, by showing that the parent company was not in a position to exert a decisive influence on its subsidiary's commercial policy or that the subsidiary

---

[101] Case 170/83 *Hydrotherm Gerätebau v Andreoli* [1984] ECR 2999, [1985] 3 CMLR 224; this is relevant, for example, under Regulation 2790/99, which requires that, for the block exemption to apply, there must not be two undertakings to a vertical agreement operating at the same level of the market: see ch 16, p 649; and under Regulation 772/2004 on technology transfer agreements, which confers block exemption only on bilateral agreements: see ch 19, pp 773–774.

[102] Case T-102/92 [1995] ECR II-17, [1995] 4 CMLR 299, upheld by the ECJ in Case C-73/95 P [1996] ECR I-5457, [1997] 4 CMLR 419: in his Opinion Advocate General Lenz discusses the case law on the economic entity doctrine ('an inconsistent picture') at paras 48–73; see also Case T-198/98 *Micro Leader Business v Commission* [1999] ECR II-3989, [2000] 4 CMLR 886, para 38 (agreements within the Microsoft group not subject to Article 81); on the similar position in US law see *Copperweld Corpn v Independence Tube Corpn* 467 US 752 (1984).

[103] Case C-73/95 P [1996] ECR I-5457, [1997] 4 CMLR 419, para 16.

[104] [1996] ECR I-5457, [1997] 4 CMLR 419, para 17; as to the possible application of Article 82 see *Interbrew* XXVIth *Report on Competition Policy* (1996), pp 139–140.

[105] See also Case 107/82 *AEG-Telefunken v Commission* [1983] ECR 3151, [1984] 3 CMLR 325, paras 47–53.

was autonomous[106]. In *Akzo Nobel NV v Commission*[107] the CFI held that Akzo had failed to rebut the presumption that it exercised decisive influence over subsidiaries in which it held 100 per cent of the share capital[108].

What is not clear is whether a minority shareholder might be held to have sufficient control to negate autonomy on the part of the subsidiary. Clearly the presumption discussed in the previous paragraph would not apply, since that arises where a parent owns the totality, or almost the totality, of the shares of the subsidiary. Under Article 3(2) of the EC Merger Regulation ('the ECMR') a minority shareholder that would have the 'possibility of exercising decisive influence' over the affairs of another undertaking would have sufficient control for there to be a concentration[109]. The case law has yet to explain whether the notion of control in the ECMR should be applied to the 'single economic entity' doctrine under Article 81(1), or whether the notions of control differ as between these two provisions. There are arguments for the adoption of a consistent approach[110]; however the notion of control under the ECMR includes negative control, and it may be that Article 81 requires positive rather than negative control.

(D) Decisions where the economic entity doctrine did not apply In *Ijsselcentrale*[111] the Commission rejected the argument that four Dutch electricity generating companies and the joint venture that they controlled formed a single economic entity, and that therefore Article 81 did not apply to agreements between them. The fact that the generators formed part of an indivisible system of public electricity supply did not mean that they were one unit, for they were separate legal persons, not controlled by a single natural or legal person, and were able to determine their own conduct independently. In *Gosmé/Martell-DMP*[112] DMP was a joint subsidiary of Martell and Piper-Hiedsieck. Each parent held 50 per cent of the capital of DMP and the voting rights; half of the supervisory board members represented Martell shareholders and half Piper-Hiedsieck shareholders; DMP distributed brands not belonging to its parent companies; Martell and Piper-Hiedsieck products were invoiced to wholesalers on the same document; DMP had its own sales force and it alone concluded the contracts of sale with buying syndicates in France. In these circumstances the Commission concluded that Martell and DMP were independent undertakings, so that an agreement between them to identify and prevent parallel exports infringed Article 81 and attracted fines of €300,000 in the case of Martell and €50,000 in the case of DMP[113].

---

[106] See to similar effect Cases T-71/03 etc *Tokai Carbon Co Ltd v Commission* [2005] ECR II-10, [2005] 5 CMLR 489, paras 59–60 and the judgments cited therein.

[107] Case T-112/05 [2007] ECR II-000.

[108] Ibid, paras 57–85; see also the Commission's decisions in *Raw Tobacco Spain*, Commission decision of 20 October 2004, paras 371–400, on appeal to the CFI Case T-29/05 *Deltafina v Commission*, not yet decided; and *Raw Tobacco Italy*, Commission decision of 20 Ocotber 2005, paras 325–351, on appeal to the CFI Case T-11/06 *Romana Tobacchi v Commission*, not yet decided.

[109] See ch 21 pp 824–825; note the more formalistic test of control for the purpose of calculating the turnover of 'undertakings concerned' in Article 5(4) of the ECMR: pp 830–831.

[110] See Wils 'The Undertaking as Subject of EC Competition Law and the Imputation of Infringements to Natural or Legal Persons' (2000) 25 EL Rev 99, pp 104–108.

[111] OJ [1991] L 28/32, [1992] 5 CMLR 154, paras 22–24.

[112] OJ [1991] L 185/23, [1992] 5 CMLR 586, para 30.

[113] Note, however, the CFI's judgment in Case T-314/01 *Coöperatieve Verkoop- en Productievereniging van Aardappelmeel en Derivaten Avebe BA* [2006] ECR II-3085, [2007] 4 CMLR 9, where the CFI held that the

If a subsidiary becomes independent of its parent, for example by being sold off, an agreement between the two companies could be caught by Article 81 once the parent–subsidiary relationship ends. In *Austin Rover/Unipart*[114] the relationship between those undertakings following the privatisation of British Leyland and the selling off of Unipart was investigated by the Commission under Article 81, but was found to satisfy the criteria of Article 81(3).

(E) Concluding comments on the economic entity doctrine Various points should be noted. First, although an agreement between connected firms may not infringe Article 81, the manipulation of a subsidiary company by a parent might mean that the competition rules are broken in other ways; for example a parent might order its subsidiaries to impose export bans on their distributors: the agreements containing such restrictions could themselves infringe Article 81[115]. Second, the economic entity doctrine means that a parent company can be liable for the activities of its subsidiaries: the Commission has frequently addressed infringement decisions to both a parent and its subsidiary, each of which is then jointly and severally liable for the infringement[116]; the parents of a joint venture can also be the addressees of a decision where their joint venture has infringed Article 81[117]. Third, where a parent and a subsidiary (or subsidiaries) form a single economic entity, the maximum fine permitted by Article 23(2) of Regulation 1/2003 of 10 per cent of an undertaking's worldwide turnover refers to the entire group's turnover, not just the turnover of the entity that actually committed the infringement: clearly this means that the maximum fine that can be imposed – for example where the subsidiary is part of a large conglomerate group – may be vastly greater than would otherwise be the case[118]. Fourth, it may be that an action for damages can be brought either against a parent of a subsidiary company, or against a subsidiary of a parent company, and that this can have significant implications for jurisdictional issues in civil litigation, potentially increasing the range of countries in which the action may be brought[119]. Fifth, from the competition authority's point of view, it is desirable to attribute responsibility for infringements of the competition rules to the highest possible entity within a corporate group, and if possible to the holding company, not least in the hope that the board of directors of the holding company will then take responsibility for eradicating anti-competitive behaviour from the entire corporate group. Sixth, the economic entity doctrine means that a parent company might find that any fine imposed upon it could be significantly increased on the basis of recidivism because of previous infringements by any subsidiary within the economic entity[120].

parents of a joint venture were responsible for its participation in a cartel and could therefore be fined: see in particular paras 135–142.

[114] OJ [1988] L 45/34, [1988] 4 CMLR 513.   [115] See eg *Re Kodak* JO [1970] L 147/24, [1970] CMLR D 19.

[116] See eg Case T-65/89 *BPB Industries plc v Commission* [1993] ECR II-389, [1993] 5 CMLR 32, paras 148–155; Case T-77/92 *Parker Pen Ltd v Commission* [1994] ECR II-549, [1995] 5 CMLR 435; Case T-354/94 *Stora v Commission* [1998] ECR II-2111, para 79; *Greek Ferry Services Cartel* OJ [1999] L 109/24, [1999] 5 CMLR 47, para 138, upheld on appeal Cases T-56/99 etc *Marlines SA v Commission* [2003] ECR II-5225, [2005] 5 CMLR 1761; *Amino Acids* OJ [2001] L 152/24, [2001] 5 CMLR 322, paras 439–441.

[117] Case T-314/01 *Coöperatieve Verkoop- en Productievereniging van Aardappelmeel en Derivaten Avebe BA* [2006] ECR II-3085, [2007] 4 CMLR 9.

[118] See Case T-112/05 *Akzo Nobel NV v Commission* [2007] ECR II-000, paras 90–91.

[119] See *Provimi Ltd v Aventis Animal Nutrition SA* [2003] EWHC 961 (Comm), [2003] All ER (D) 59 (May), a case arising out of the *Vitamins Cartel*, paras 31–36; see further ch 8, p 301.

[120] On the significance of recidivism to the level of fines see ch 7, p 274.

A seventh point is that the Commission can carry out a surprise inspection of a legal entity that is part of an economic unit even though the alleged infringement of the competition rules was the responsibility of another part of it[121]. The next point is that a subsidiary may be fined for action which it takes in disobedience to the instructions of its parent[122]. Lastly, the immunity of agreements from Article 81 is in a sense a double-edged weapon: the Community Courts and the Commission have held that EC law can be applied to a parent company not present within the Community because of the conduct of its subsidiaries carried on there[123].

(ii) Principal and agent

In some cases the relationship between a principal and agent will be dealt with in a similar way, with the result that Article 81 will not be applicable: this issue is dealt with in chapter 16[124].

(iii) Contractor and sub-contractor

Agreements between a contractor and a sub-contractor may also fall outside Article 81 because of the close relationship between them; this issue is also dealt with in chapter 16[125].

(C) Undertakings related by succession

Separate legal entities may be treated as one and the same undertaking where there is a corporate reorganisation in which one entity succeeds another: the liabilities of the latter may be attributed to the former[126]. In *Compagnie Royale Asturienne des Mines SA and Rheinzink GmbH v Commission*[127] the ECJ held that:

a change in the legal form and name of an undertaking does not create a new undertaking free of liability for the anticompetitive behaviour of its predecessor when, from an economic point of view, the two are identical.

In *PVC*[128] the Commission held that it is a matter of Community law whether one undertaking can be liable for the past conduct of another: changes in organisation under national company law are not decisive. In order to decide whether there is 'undertaking

---

[121] Case T-66/99 *Minoan Lines v Commission* [2003] ECR II-5515, [2005] 5 CMLR 1597.

[122] Case 32/78 *BMW Belgium SA v Commission* [1979] ECR 2435, [1980] 1 CMLR 370.

[123] See Case 48/69 *ICI v Commission* [1972] ECR 619, [1972] CMLR 557; Case 6/72 *Europemballage Corpn and Continental Can Co Inc v Commission* [1973] ECR 215, [1973] CMLR 199; see ch 12 on extra-territoriality generally.

[124] See ch 16, pp 609–612 and, in particular, the Commission's *Guidelines on Vertical Restraints* OJ [2000] 5 291/1, [2000] 5 CMLR 1176, paras 12–20.

[125] See ch 16, pp 666–667 and, in particular, the Commission's *Notice on Sub-contracting Agreements* OJ [1979] C 1/2, [1979] 1 CMLR 264.

[126] See Garzaniti and Scassellati-Sforzolini 'Liability of Successor Undertakings for Infringements of EC Competition Law Committed Prior to Corporate Reorganisations' (1995) 16 ECLR 348; Dyekjær-Hansen and Hoegh 'Succession for Competition Law Infringements with Special Reference to Due Diligence and Warranty Claims' (2003) 24 ECLR 203; Chandler 'Successor Liability for Competition Law Infringements and How to Avoid It' (2006) 5 Competition Law Journal 63.

[127] Cases 29, 30/83 [1984] ECR 1679, [1985] 1 CMLR 688, para 9; see also Case T-134/94 *NMH Stahlwerke GmbH v Commission* [1999] ECR II-239, [1997] 5 CMLR 227, paras 122–141; Case C-297/98 P *SCA Holdings Ltd v Commission* [2000] ECR I-10101, [2001] 4 CMLR 413, paras 23–32; Cases C-204/00 etc *Aalborg Portland v Commission* [2004] ECR I-123, para 59.

[128] OJ [1989] L 74/1, [1990] 4 CMLR 345, para 42.

identity', the expression used by the Commission in the *PVC* decision, the determining factor 'is whether there is a functional and economic continuity between the original infringer and the undertaking into which it was merged'[129]. It repeated this formulation in the second *PVC* decision[130]. In *All Weather Sports Benelux BV v Commission*[131] the CFI held that the Commission must adequately explain its reasoning when it imposes a fine on a successor to the entity that committed the infringement.

In *Autoritá Garante della Concurrenza e del Mercato v Ente tabacchi italiani – ETI SpA*[132] the Amministrazione autonoma del monopoli di Stato ('AAMS') was an organ of the Italian state that had responsibility for managing the tobacco monopoly in that country. In 1999 its activities were transferred by law to a newly-created public body, Ente tabacchi italiani ('ETI'). ETI was subsequently transformed into a public company and was then privatised, coming under the control of British American Tobacco plc. The Italian competition authority adopted a decision that the Philip Morris group of companies had implemented a cartel in Italy in conjunction with AAMS and, subsequently, with ETI. A fine of €20 million was imposed on ETI. In its decision the Italian competition authority attributed AAMS's conduct prior to 1999 to ETI. An Italian court held that it was wrong to have done so; on appeal the Italian Council of State referred the matter to the ECJ under Article 234 EC. The ECJ held that it was legitimate for the Italian competition authority to have imposed the fine on ETI: AAMS and ETI were answerable to the same public authority, and the same unlawful conduct was carried out first by AAMS and then by its successor, ETI; the Court applied the reasoning of the *Rheinzink* case, and said that it made no difference that the activity transferred to ETI occurred not as a result of individuals but through the action of the legislature preparing ETI for privatisation[133].

(D) Liability for competition law infringements when one business is sold to another

An important question arises where one undertaking commits an infringement of the competition rules, but then sells the business that was responsible for the infringement to a third party. Clearly the purchaser will need to know whether it bears the risk of a future fine in the event of a competition authority adopting a decision. The basic rule is that, if the undertaking that was responsible for the business is still in existence, it remains liable for the infringement rather than the acquirer[134]. For example in *Zinc Phosphate*[135] the Commission decided that, where an undertaking commits an infringement of Article 81 and then disposes of the assets that were the vehicle of the infringement and withdraws from the market, it will still be held responsible if it is still in existence[136]. However the liability may pass to a successor where the corporate entity

---

[129] OJ [1989] L 74/1, [1990] 4 CMLR 345, para 43; see similarly *LdPE* OJ [1989] L 74/21, paras 49–54; other decisions of the Commission dealing with this point are *Peroxygen Products* OJ [1985] L 35/1, [1985] 1 CMLR 481, *Polypropylene* OJ [1986] L 230/1, [1988] 4 CMLR 347 and *Welded Steel Mesh* OJ [1989] L 260/1, [1991] 4 CMLR 13, para 194.

[130] OJ [1994] L 239/14, paras 14–43.

[131] Case T-38/92 [1994] ECR II-211, [1995] 4 CMLR 43, paras 26–36.

[132] Case C-280/06 [2007] ECR I-000.   [133] Ibid, paras 38–52.

[134] See eg Case C-279/98 P *Cascades v Commission* [2000] ECR I-9693, para 78.[135] OJ [2003] L 153/1.

[136] Ibid, para 238, relying, *inter alia*, on Case T-80/89 *BASF v Commission* [1995] ECR II-729.

which committed the violation has ceased to exist in law after the infringement was committed[137].

3. AGREEMENTS, DECISIONS AND CONCERTED PRACTICES

The policy of Article 81 is to prohibit cooperation between independent undertakings which prevents, restricts or distorts competition: in particular it is concerned with the eradication of cartels and 'hard-core' restrictions of competition. Chapter 13 will examine this subject in detail. The application of Article 81(1) is not limited to legally enforceable agreements: this would make evasion of the law simple. Article 81 applies also to cooperation achieved through the decisions of trade associations and to more informal understandings, known as concerted practices. The Chapter I prohibition in the UK Competition Act 1998 has the same scope[138]. A broad interpretation has been given to each of the terms 'agreement', 'decision' and 'concerted practice'. A difficult issue is whether parallel behaviour by firms in an oligopolistic industry is attributable to an agreement or concerted practice between them, in which case Article 81(1) would be applicable; or whether it is a natural effect of the structure of the market, in which case a different competition law response might be needed. Chapter 14 will consider the issue of oligopoly, tacit collusion and so-called 'collective dominance' under Article 82 and the Chapter II prohibition in the Competition Act. In several decisions, particularly in the context of distribution systems, conduct which appeared to be unilateral has been held to be sufficiently consensual to fall within Article 81(1), although the Commission has lost some of these cases on appeal[139].

(A) Agreements

(i) Examples of agreements

A legally enforceable contract of course qualifies as an agreement, including a compromise of litigation such as a trade mark delimitation agreement[140] or the settlement of a patent action[141]. 'Gentleman's agreements'[142] and simple understandings[143] have been

---

[137] Case C-49/92 *Commission v Anic Partecipazioni SpA* ECR [1999] ECR I-4125, [2001] 4 CMLR 602, para 145.

[138] See ch 9, pp 331–335.   [139] See pp 107–113 below.

[140] See eg *Re Penney's Trade Mark* OJ [1978] L 60/19, [1978] 2 CMLR 100; *Re Toltecs and Dorcet* OJ [1982] L 379/19, [1983] 1 CMLR 412, upheld on appeal Case 35/83 *BAT v Commission* [1985] ECR 363, [1985] 2 CMLR 470; it is not entirely clear what effect embodiment of the compromise in an order of a national court has on the applicability of Article 81(1): see Case 258/78 *LC Nungesser KG v Commission* [1982] ECR 2015, [1983] 1 CMLR 278, paras 80–91, where the ECJ was delphic on this issue; the tenor of the ECJ's judgment in *BAT v Commission* would suggest that the agreement would be caught even where sanctioned by a national court. On trade mark delimitation agreements, see further ch 19, pp 785–786.

[141] See eg Case 65/86 *Bayer v Süllhofer* [1988] ECR 5249, [1990] 4 CMLR 182.

[142] Case 41/69 *ACF Chemiefarma NV v Commission* [1970] ECR 661, [1970] CMLR 43.

[143] *Re Stichting Sigarettenindustrie Agreements* OJ [1982] L 232/1, [1982] 3 CMLR 702 (an 'understanding' between trade associations held to be an agreement); *National Panasonic* OJ [1982] L 354/28, [1983] 1 CMLR 497, where there was no formal agreement between Panasonic and its dealers, but the Commission still held that there was an agreement as opposed to a concerted practice between them; *Viho/Toshiba* OJ [1991]

held to be agreements, though neither is legally binding; there is no requirement that an agreement should be supported by enforcement procedures[144]. A 'protocol' which reflects a genuine concurrence of will between the parties constitutes an agreement within the meaning of Article 81(1)[145]. Connected agreements may be treated as a single one[146]. An agreement may be oral[147]. The Commission will treat the contractual terms and conditions in a standard-form contract as an agreement within Article 81(1)[148]. An agreement which has expired by effluxion of time but the effects of which continue to be felt can be caught by Article 81(1)[149]. The constitution of a trade association qualifies as an agreement within Article 81[150]. An agreement entered into by a trade association might be construed as an agreement on the part of its members[151]. An agreement to create a European Economic Interest Grouping, or the byelaws establishing it, may be caught by Article 81(1)[152]. There may be 'inchoate understandings and conditional or partial agreement' during a bargaining process sufficient to amount to an agreement in the sense of Article 81(1)[153]. Guidelines issued by one person that are adhered to by another can amount to an agreement[154]; and circulars and warnings sent by a manufacturer to its dealers may be treated as part of the general agreement that exists between them, although the Commission lost a case of this kind in the *Volkswagen* case[155]. The fact that formal agreement has not been reached on all matters does not preclude a finding of an agreement[156], and there can be an agreement or concerted practice notwithstanding the fact that only one of the participants at a meeting reveals its intentions[157]. Undertakings cannot justify infringement of the rules on competition by claiming that they were forced into an agreement by the conduct of other traders[158]. Where an agreement is entered into unwillingly, this may be significant in influencing the

L 287/39, [1992] 5 CMLR 180, where the Commission found an understanding between Toshiba's German subsidiary and certain distributors that an export prohibition should apply, even though the standard distribution agreements had been amended to remove an export prohibition clause.

[144] *Soda-ash/Solvay, CFK* OJ [1991] L 152/16, [1994] 4 CMLR 645, para 11; *PVC* OJ [1994] L 239/14, para 30.

[145] *HOV SVZ/MCN* [1994] OJ L 104/34, para 46.

[146] *ENI/Montedison* OJ [1987] L 5/13, [1988] 4 CMLR 444.

[147] Case 28/77 *Tepea v Commission* [1978] ECR 1391, [1978] 3 CMLR 392; Cases T-25/95 etc *Cimenteries CBR SA v Commission* [2000] ECR II-491, [2000] 5 CMLR 204, para 2341.

[148] *Putz v Kawasaki Motors (UK) Ltd* OJ [1979] 1 16/9, [1979] 1 CMLR 448; *Sandoz* OJ [1987] L 222/28, [1989] 4 CMLR 628, upheld on appeal Case 277/87 *Sandoz Prodotti Farmaceutici SpA v Commission* [1990] ECR I-45.

[149] Case T-7/89 *SA Hercules NV v Commission* [1991] ECR II-1711, [1992] 4 CMLR 84, para 257; Case 51/75 *EMI Records Ltd v CBS UK Ltd* [1976] ECR 811, pp 848–849, [1976] 2 CMLR 235, p 267; Case T-48/98 *Acerinox v Commission* [2001] ECR II-3859, para 63.

[150] *Re Nuovo CEGAM* OJ [1984] L 99/29, [1984] 2 CMLR 484.

[151] Cases 209/78 etc *Heintz Van Landewyck v Commission* [1980] ECR 3125, [1981] 3 CMLR 134.

[152] *Orphe* Commission's XXth *Report on Competition Policy* (1990), point 102; *Tepar* [1991] 4 CMLR 860; *Twinning Programme Engineering Group* OJ [1992] C 148/8, [1992] 5 CMLR 93.

[153] *Pre-Insulated Pipe Cartel* OJ [1999] L 24/1, [1999] 4 CMLR 402, para 133, substantially upheld on appeal Cases T-9/99 etc *HFB Holding v Commission* [2002] ECR II-1487, [2002] 5 CMLR 571.

[154] *Anheuser-Busch Incorporated/Scottish & Newcastle* OJ [2000] L 49/37, [2000] 5 CMLR 75, para 26.

[155] See p 112 below.

[156] *Pre-Insulated Pipe Cartel* OJ [1999] L 24/1, [1999] 4 CMLR 402, para 134.

[157] Cases T-202/98 etc *Tate & Lyle v Commission* [2001] ECR II-2035, [2001] 5 CMLR 859, para 54.

[158] Case 16/61 *Modena v High Authority* [1962] ECR 289, [1962] CMLR 221; *Musique Diffusion Française v Commission* [1983] ECR 1825, [1983] 3 CMLR 221, paras 90 and 100; Cases T-25/95 etc *Cimenteries CBR SA v Commission* [2000] ECR II-491, [2000] 5 CMLR 204, para 2557.

Commission to mitigate a fine[159], not to impose a fine[160] or not to institute proceedings at all. The Commission may abstain from fining parties which had no input in the drafting of the agreements into which they have entered[161].

(ii) Complex cartels

Many cartels are complex and of long duration. Over a period of time some firms may be more active than others in the running of a cartel; some may 'drop out' for a while but subsequently re-enter; others may attend meetings or communicate in other ways in order to be kept informed, without necessarily intending to fall in line with the agreed plan; there may be few occasions on which all the members of a cartel actually meet or behave precisely in concert with one another. This presents a problem for a competition authority: where the shape and active membership of a cartel changes over a period of time, must the authority prove a series of discrete agreements or concerted practices, and identify each of the parties to each of those agreements and concerted practices? This would require a considerable amount of evidence and impose a very high burden on the competition authority. It might also mean that it would not be possible to impose fines in relation to 'old' agreements and concerted practices, in relation to which infringement proceedings had become time-barred[162]: precisely this issue arose, for example, in *BASF AG v Commission*[163], an appeal in the *Choline Chloride* case. The Commission, upheld by the Community Courts, has addressed these problems in two ways: first, by developing the idea that it is not necessary to characterise infringements of Article 81(1) specifically as an agreement on the one hand or a concerted practice on the other; and secondly by establishing the concept of a 'single overall agreement' for which all members of a cartel bear responsibility, irrespective of their precise involvement from day to day[164].

(A) Agreement 'and/or' concerted practice The Commission has stated that agreements and concerted practices are conceptually distinct[165]. However Advocate General Reischl has said that there is little point in defining the exact point at which agreement ends and concerted practice begins[166]. It may be that, in a particular case, linguistically it is more natural to use one term than the other, but legally nothing turns on the distinction: the important distinction is between collusive and non-collusive

[159] *Hasselblad* OJ [1982] L 161/18, [1982] 2 CMLR 233; *Wood Pulp* OJ [1985] L 85/1, [1985] 3 CMLR 474, para 131.
[160] *Burns Tractors Ltd v Sperry New Holland* OJ [1985] L 376/21, [1988] 4 CMLR 306; *Fisher-Price/Quaker Oats Ltd—Toyco* OJ [1988] L 49/19, [1989] 4 CMLR 553.
[161] *Viho/Toshiba* OJ [1991] OJ L 287/39, [1992] 5 CMLR 180, para 26; guidance on the Commission's fining policy can be found in two Commission notices, one on the level of fines and the other on leniency: they are discussed in ch 7, pp 272–278.
[162] Under Article 26 of Regulation 1/2003 (the 'Modernisation Regulation') OJ [2003] L 1/1, [2003] 4 CMLR 551, which replaces Regulation 2988/74, the Commission cannot impose fines in relation to an infringement that ended five years or more before it initiated proceedings: see Kerse and Khan *EC Antitrust Procedure* (Sweet & Maxwell, 5th ed, 2005), paras 7.82–7.85.
[163] Cases T-101/05 and T-111/05 [2007] ECR II-000, paras 132–223.
[164] See generally Joshua 'Attitudes to Anti-Trust Enforcement in the EU and US: Dodging the Traffic Warden, or Respecting the Law' [1995] Fordham Corporate Law Institute (ed Hawk), 85.
[165] See *Polypropylene* OJ [1986] L 230/1, [1988] 4 CMLR 347, para 86.
[166] See Cases 209/78 etc *Van Landewyck v Commission* [1980] ECR 3125, p 3310, [1981] 3 CMLR 134, p 185.

behaviour[167]. In the PVC[168] decision the Commission reached the conclusion that the parties to the cartel had participated in an agreement 'and/or' a concerted practice. On appeal to the CFI Enichem argued that the Commission was not entitled to have made this 'joint classification', which would be lawful only if it could prove the existence of both an agreement and a concerted practice. In its judgment the CFI rejected this argument and upheld the Commission[169]. It held that:

In the context of a complex infringement which involves many producers seeking over a number of years to regulate the market between them the Commission cannot be expected to classify the infringement precisely, for each undertaking and for any given moment, as in any event both those forms of infringement are covered by Article [81] of the Treaty[170].

The CFI went on to say that joint classification was permissible where the infringement includes elements both of an agreement and of a concerted practice, without the Commission having to prove that there was both an agreement and a concerted practice throughout the period of the infringement. This approach has been confirmed by the ECJ in *Commission v ANIC*[171] and in *Asnef-Equifax*[172], where, in the case of cooperation between competitors in the form of an indirect exchange of information, it concluded that there was no need to characterise the cooperation at issue specifically as a concerted practice, an agreement or a decision of an association of undertakings.

The Commission has adopted a joint classification approach in a number of decisions, for example *British Sugar*[173], *Cartonboard*[174] and *Pre-Insulated Pipe Cartel*[175]. As one former Commission official has put it: the search should not be for an agreement on the one hand or a concerted practice on the other; rather for a 'partnership for unlawful purposes with all the possible disagreements about methods that may occur in such a venture without affecting the cohesion of the shared purpose and design'[176].

(B) The concept of a 'single, overall agreement' In a series of decisions from the mid-1980s the Commission has developed the concept of a 'single, overall agreement' for which undertakings bear responsibility, even though they may not be involved in its

---

[167] *Polypropylene* OJ [1986] L 230/1, [1988] 4 CMLR 347, para 87, substantially upheld on appeal Case T-7/89 *SA Hercules NV v Commission* [1991] ECR II-1711, [1992] 4 CMLR 84, upheld on appeal to the ECJ Case C-51/92 P *Hercules Chemicals v Commission* [1999] ECR I-4235, [1999] 5 CMLR 976; *Soda-ash/Solvay, ICI* OJ [1991] L 152/1, [1994] 4 CMLR 645, para 55.

[168] OJ [1994] L 239/14, paras 30–31; this decision was taken by the Commission after its earlier decision, OJ [1989] L 74/1, had been annulled by the ECJ for infringement of essential procedural requirements: Cases C-137/92 P etc *Commission v BASF* [1994] ECR I-2555.

[169] Cases T-305/94 etc *NV Limburgse Vinyl Maatschappij v Commission* [1999] ECR II-931, [1999] 5 CMLR 303, paras 695–699; the CFI had noted the possibility of a joint classification in its earlier judgments in the *Polypropylene* case: see eg Case T-1/89 *Rhone-Poulenc v Commission* [1991] ECR II-867, paras 125–127 and Case T-8/89 Rev *DSM v Commission* [1991] ECR II-1833, paras 234–235.

[170] Cases T-305/94 etc *NV Limburgse Vinyl Maatschappij v Commission* [1999] ECR II-931, [1999] 5 CMLR 303, para 696.

[171] Case C-49/92 [1999] ECR I-4125, paras 132 and 133: for critical comment on the ECJ's judgment in *ANIC* see Wessely (2001) 38 CML Rev 739, 762–764; see also Case T-62/98 *Volkswagen AG v Commission* [2000] ECR II-2707, [2000] 5 CMLR 853, para 237

[172] Case C-238/05 [2006] ECR I-11125, [2007] 4 CMLR 224, para 32.

[173] OJ [1999] L 76/1, [1999] 4 CMLR 1316, para 70.   [174] OJ [1994] L 243/1, [1994] 5 CMLR 547, para 128.

[175] OJ [1999] L 24/1, [1999] 5 CMLR 402, paras 131–132.

[176] Joshua 'Attitudes to Anti-Trust Enforcement in the EU and US: Dodging the Traffic Warden, or Respecting the Law?' [1995] Fordham Corporate Law Institute (ed Hawk), 85.

operation on a day-to-day or a continuing basis. For example in *Polypropylene*[177] the Commission investigated a complex cartel agreement in the petrochemicals sector involving 15 firms over many years. It held that the detailed arrangements whereby the cartel operated were all part of a single, overall agreement: this agreement was oral, not legally binding, and there were no sanctions for its enforcement. Having established that there was a single agreement, the Commission concluded that all 15 firms were guilty of infringing Article 81, even though some had not attended every meeting of the cartel and had not been involved in every aspect of its decision-making: participation in the overall agreement was sufficient to establish guilt. Furthermore, the fact that some members of the cartel had reservations about whether to participate – or indeed intended to cheat by deviating from the agreed conduct – did not mean that they were not party to an agreement. The Commission reached similar conclusions in other cases, for example *PVC*[178], *LdPE*[179], in its second decision on *PVC*[180], in *Amino Acids*[181] and in *Dutch Bitumen*[182].

The CFI has confirmed the concept of a 'single overall agreement'[183]. In the appeal against the second *PVC* decision the CFI upheld the Commission's view that an undertaking can be held responsible for an overall cartel, even though it participated in only one or some of its constituent elements, 'if it is shown that it knew, or must have known, that the collusion in which it participated ... was part of an overall plan intended to distort competition and that the overall plan included all the constituent elements of the cartel'[184]. However the CFI has also said, in the *Cement* cases, that where there are numerous bilateral and multilateral agreements between a large number of undertakings, it cannot be *presumed* from this that they form part of a single, overall agreement: it is necessary for the Commission to prove that this is the case[185]. In *BASF v Commission*[186] the CFI annulled a Commission finding of a single overall agreement: the global and the European cartels were separate from one another, and the Commission was time-barred from imposing a fine in respect of the global cartel, which had ended in 1994[187].

In *Tréfileurope v Commission*[188], one of the appeals in the *Welded Steel Mesh* case, the CFI held that the fact that an undertaking does not abide by the outcome of meetings which have a manifestly anti-competitive purpose does not relieve it of full responsibility for its participation in the cartel, if it has not publicly distanced itself from what was agreed in the meetings[189]. This has been repeated on numerous occasions, for example in *BPB de Eendracht NV v Commission*[190], an appeal in the *Cartonboard* case, and in the *Cement* cases[191]: the reason for this rule is that, having participated

---

[177] OJ [1986] L 230/1, [1988] 4 CMLR 347.   [178] OJ [1989] L 74/1, [1990] 4 CMLR 345.

[179] OJ [1989] L 74/21, [1990] 4 CMLR 382, paras 49–54.   [180] OJ [1994] L 239/14, paras 30–31.

[181] OJ [2001] L 152/24, [2001] 5 CMLR 322, paras 237–238.

[182] Commission decision of 13 December 2006, paras 138–141.

[183] See Case T-1/89 *Rhône Poulenc v Commission* [1991] ECR II-867, para 126.

[184] Cases T-305/94 etc *NV Limburgse Vinyl Maatschappij v Commission* [1999] ECR II-931, [1999] 5 CMLR 303, para 773.

[185] Cases T-25/95 etc *Cimenteries CBR SA v Commission* [2000] ECR II-491, [2000] 5 CMLR 204, paras 4027, 4060, 4109 and 4112.

[186] Cases T-101/05 and T-111/05 [2007] ECR II-000.   [187] Ibid, paras 157–210.

[188] Case T-141/89 [1995] ECR II-791, para 85.

[189] See Bailey 'Publicly distancing oneself from a cartel', (2008) 32 World Competition 177.

[190] Case T-311/94 [1998] ECR II-1129, para 203.

[191] Cases T-25/95 etc *Cimenteries CBR SA v Commission* [2000] ECR II-491, [2000] 5 CMLR 204, paras 1353, 1389 and 3199.

in the meeting without publicly distancing itself from what was discussed, the undertaking has given the other participants to believe that it subscribed to what was decided there and that it would comply with it[192]. The Commission repeated the point in *Amino Acids*[193]. In *Steel Beams*[194] the CFI held that attendance by an undertaking at meetings involving anti-competitive activities suffices to establish its participation in those activities in the absence of proof capable of establishing the contrary[195]. In *Westfalen Gassen Nederland BV*[196], an appeal in the *Industrial and medical gases* case, the CFI said that the notion of 'public distancing' as a means of excluding liability must be interpreted narrowly[197]; the Court did not go so far as to say that, in order to do so, the undertaking concerned should have blown the whistle to a competition authority, but it did suggest that, at the least, it should have written to its competitors and to the secretary of the trade association responsible for the meetings held in that case to say that it did not wish to be considered to be a member of the cartel nor to participate in meetings that were a cover for unlawful concerted action[198].

The cumulative effect of these judgments is clearly beneficial to the Commission in its anti-cartel policy, since the Community Courts seem to have deliberately refrained from construing the expressions 'agreement' and 'concerted practice' in a legalistic or formalistic manner: what emerges, essentially, is that any contact between competitors that touches upon business behaviour such as pricing, markets, customers and volume of output is risky in the extreme.

(B) Decisions by associations of undertakings

Coordination between independent undertakings may be achieved through the medium of a trade association. A trade association may have a particularly important role where the cartel consists of a large number of firms, in which case compliance with the rules of the cartel needs to be monitored: where only a few firms collude, it is relatively easy for each firm to monitor what the others are doing[199]. The possibility that trade associations may play a part in cartel activity is explicitly recognised in Article 81(1) by the proscription of 'decisions by associations of undertakings' that could restrict competition. The application of Article 81(1) to decisions means that the trade association itself may be held liable and be fined[200]; where the Commission intends to impose a fine on the association as well as, or in addition to, its members, this must be made clear in the statement of objections[201]. In *FNCBV v Commission*[202] the CFI upheld a decision of the Commission in which it had held that, as farm operators, farmers and breeders were

---

[192]   See eg Cases C-403/04 P *Sumitomo Metal Industries Ltd v Commission* [2007] ECR I-729, [2007] 4 CMLR 650, para 48.

[193]   OJ [2001] L 152/24, [2001] 5 CMLR 322, para 221.

[194]   Cases T-141/94 etc *Thyssen Stahl v Commission* [1999] ECR II-347, [1999] 4 CMLR 810.

[195]   Ibid, applying Case T-14/89 *Montedipe v Commission* [1992] ECR II-1155, [1993] 4 CMLR 110; see similarly Cases T-202/98 etc *Tate & Lyle v Commission* [2001] ECR II-2035, [2001] 5 CMLR 859, paras 64–65 and Case T-48/98 *Acerinox v Commission* [2001] ECR II-3859, paras 29–46.

[196]   Case T-302/02 [2006] ECR II-4567, [2007] 4 CMLR 334.   [197]   Ibid, para 103.   [198]   Ibid.

[199]   See ch 14, pp 545–552 on tacit collusion in oligopolistic markets.

[200]   See eg *AROW v BNIC* OJ [1982] L 379/1, [1983] 2 CMLR 240 where BNIC was fined €160,000; *Fenex* OJ [1996] L 181/28, [1996] 5 CMLR 332 where Fenex was fined €1,000; *Belgian Architects Association* Commission decision of 24 June 2004 OJ [2005] L 4/10, where the association was fined €100,000.

[201]   Cases T-25/95 etc *Cimenteries CBR SA v Commission* [2000] ECR II-491, [2000] 5 CMLR 204, para 485.

[202]   Cases T-217/03 and T-245/03 [2006] ECR II-4987.

engaged in economic activities, they were acting as undertakings; and that it followed that their trade unions and the federations that grouped those unions together were associations of undertakings. The federations, rather than the individual undertakings, were fined in this case[203]: the CFI reduced the fines slightly.

It has been held that the constitution of a trade association is itself a decision[204], as well as regulations governing the operation of an association[205]. An agreement entered into by an association might also be a decision. A recommendation made by an association has been held to amount to a decision: the fact that the recommendation is not binding upon its members does not prevent the application of Article 81(1)[206]. In such cases it is necessary to consider whether members in the past have tended to comply with recommendations that have been made, and whether compliance with the recommendation would have a significant influence on competition within the relevant market. In *IAZ International Belgium NV v Commission*[207] an association of water-supply undertakings recommended its members not to connect dishwashing machines to the mains system which did not have a conformity label supplied by a Belgian association of producers of such equipment. The ECJ confirmed the Commission's view that this recommendation, though not binding, could restrict competition, since its effect was to discriminate against appliances produced elsewhere in the EC.

A decision does not acquire immunity because it is subsequently approved and extended in scope by a public authority[208], nor does a trade association fall outside Article 81(1) because it is given statutory functions or because its members are appointed by the Government[209]. The ECJ has specifically stated that the public law status of a national body (for example an association of customs agents) does not preclude the application of Article 81[210]. In *Wouters v Algemene Raad van de Nederlandsche Orde van Advocaten*[211] the ECJ held that the General Council of the Dutch Bar was an association

[203] Note that the association is obliged to ask for contributions from its members in the event that the association is insolvent: Article 23(4) of the Modernisation Regulation.

[204] See eg *Re ASPA* JO [1970] L 148/9, [1970] CMLR D25; *National Sulphuric Acid Association* OJ [1980] L 260/24, [1980] 3 CMLR 429.

[205] *Publishers' Association – Net Book Agreements* OJ [1989] L 22/12, [1989] 4 CMLR 825, upheld on appeal Case T-66/89 *Publishers' Association v Commission (No 2)* [1992] ECR II-1995, [1992] 5 CMLR 120, partially annulled on appeal to the ECJ in Case C-360/92 P *Publishers' Association v Commission* [1995] ECR I-23, [1995] 5 CMLR 33; *Sippa* OJ [1991] L 60/19; *Coapi* OJ [1995] L 122/37, [1995] 5 CMLR 468, para 34; *Nederlandse Federatieve Vereniging voor de Grootlandel op Elektrotechnisch Gebied and Technische Unie (FEG and TU)* OJ [2000] L 39/1, [2000] 4 CMLR 1208, para 95; *Visa International* OJ [2001] L 293/24, [2002] 4 CMLR 168, para 53; *Visa International – Multilateral Interchange Fee* OJ [2002] L 318/17, [2003] 4 CMLR 283, para 55.

[206] Case 8/72 *Vereeniging van Cementhandelaren v Commission* [1972] ECR 977, [1973] CMLR 7; Case 71/74 *FRUBO v Commission* [1975] ECR 563; [1975] 2 CMLR 123; Cases 209/78 etc *Van Landewyck v Commission* [1980] ECR 3125, [1981] 3 CMLR 134; Case 45/85 *VDS v Commission* [1987] ECR 405, [1988] 4 CMLR 264, para 32; see also *Distribution of railway tickets by travel agents* OJ [1992] L 366/47, paras 62–69, partially annulled on appeal Case T-14/93 *UIC v Commission* [1995] ECR II-1503, [1996] 5 CMLR 40; *Fenex* OJ [1996] L 181/28, [1996] 5 CMLR 332, paras 32–42.

[207] Cases 96/82 etc [1983] ECR 3369, [1984] 3 CMLR 276.

[208] *AROW v BNIC* OJ [1982] L 379/1, [1983] 2 CMLR 240; *Coapi* OJ [1995] L 122/37, [1995] 5 CMLR 468, para 32.

[209] Ibid and *Pabst and Richarz KG v BNIA* OJ [1976] L 231/24, [1976] 2 CMLR D63.

[210] Case C-35/96 *Commission v Italy* [1998] ECR I-3851, [1998] 5 CMLR 889, para 40; Cases C-180/98; C-184/98 *Pavel Pavlov v Stichting Pensioenfonds Medische Specialisten* [2000] ECR I-6451, [2001] 4 CMLR 30, para 85.

[211] Case C-309/99 [2002] ECR I-1577, [2002] 4 CMLR 913; the Opinion of Advocate General Leger deals with the meaning of 'association of undertakings' at length: see paras 56–87.

of undertakings, and rejected the argument that this was not so in so far as it was exercising its regulatory functions; the position might have been different if a majority of the members of the Council had been appointed by the State, rather than by members of the profession, and if the State had specified the public interest criteria to be taken into account by the Council[212]. Just as a 'functional' approach should be taken to the concept of an undertaking[213], so too it may be that a body can qualify as an association of undertakings when carrying out some of its tasks, but not when performing others (for example regulatory supervision on behalf of the State)[214].

A trade association does not have to have a commercial or economic activity of its own to be subject to Article 81(1)[215]; it follows that Article 81(1) may be applicable to the *decisions* of a trade association, even if it does not apply to its *agreements* because the association does not enter into the agreements as an undertaking[216]. Where an association is an undertaking, an agreement between it and other undertakings may be caught by Article 81(1)[217]. Article 81(1) also applies to decisions by associations of trade associations[218].

(C) Concerted practices

The inclusion of concerted practices within Article 81 means that conduct which is not attributable to an agreement or a decision may nevertheless amount to an infringement. While it can readily be appreciated that loose, informal understandings to limit competition must be prevented as well as agreements, it is difficult both to define the type or degree of coordination within the mischief of the law and to apply that rule to the facts of any given case. In particular there is the problem that parties to a cartel may do all they can to destroy incriminating evidence of meetings, e-mails, faxes and correspondence, in which case the temptation of the competition authority may be to infer the existence of an agreement or concerted practice from circumstantial evidence such as parallel conduct on the market. This can be dangerous, for it may be that firms act in parallel not because of an agreement or concerted practice, but because their individual appreciation of market conditions tells them that a failure to match a rival's strategy could be damaging or even disastrous. The application of the law in this area is complex, and competition authorities must proceed with care in order to distinguish covert cartels from rational and innocent parallel commercial activities. The problem of parallel behaviour in oligopolistic markets will be examined in chapter 14.

---

[212] Case C-309/99 [2002] ECR I-1577, [2002] 4 CMLR 913, paras 50–71.   [213] See pp 83–84 above.

[214] On this point see the Opinion of Advocate General Jacobs in Cases C-67/96 etc *Albany International BV v SBT* [1999] ECR I-5751, [2000] 4 CMLR 446, para 214 and Case C-309/99 *Wouters* [2002] ECR I-1577, [2002] 4 CMLR 913, para 64.

[215] Cases T-25/95 etc *Cimenteries CBR SA v Commission* [2000] ECR II-491, [2000] 5 CMLR 204, para 1320 citing many earlier judgments of the ECJ and CFI to similar effect.

[216] See the Opinion of Advocate General Slynn in Case 123/85 *BNIC v Clair* [1985] ECR 391, p 396, [1985] 2 CMLR 430, p 442.

[217] Cases T-25/95 etc *Cimenteries CBR SA v Commission* [2000] ECR II-491, [2000] 5 CMLR 204, paras 1325 and 2622.

[218] See eg *Cematex* JO [1971] L 227/26, [1973] CMLR D135 and *Milchförderungsfonds* OJ [1985] L 35/35, [1985] 3 CMLR 101.

It is necessary to consider first the legal meaning of a concerted practice; secondly the question of whether a concerted practice must have been put into effect for Article 81(1) to have been infringed; and lastly the burden of proof in such cases.

(i) Meaning of concerted practice[219]

ICI v Commission[220] (usually referred to as the *Dyestuffs* case) was the first important case on concerted practices to come before the ECJ. The Commission had fined several producers of dyestuffs which it considered had been guilty of price fixing through concerted practices[221]. The Commission's decision relied upon various pieces of evidence, including the similarity of the rate and timing of price increases and of instructions sent out by parent companies to their subsidiaries and the fact that there had been informal contact between the firms concerned. The ECJ upheld the Commission's decision. It said that the object of bringing concerted practices within Article 81 was to prohibit:

a form of coordination between undertakings which, without having reached the stage where an agreement properly so-called has been concluded, knowingly substitutes practical cooperation between them for the risks of competition[222].

In *Suiker Unie v Commission*[223] (the *Sugar Cartel* case) the ECJ elaborated upon this test. The Commission had held[224] that various sugar producers had taken part in concerted practices to protect the position of two Dutch producers on their domestic market. The producers denied this as they had not worked out a plan to this effect. The ECJ held that it was not necessary to prove that there was an actual plan. Article 81 strictly precluded:

any direct or indirect contact between such operators, the object or effect whereof is either to influence the conduct on the market of an actual or potential competitor or to disclose to such a competitor the course of conduct which they themselves have decided to adopt or contemplate adopting on the market[225].

These two cases provide the legal test of what constitutes a concerted practice for the purpose of Article 81: there must be a mental consensus whereby practical cooperation is *knowingly* substituted for competition; however the consensus need not be achieved verbally, and can come about by direct or indirect contact between the parties. In *Züchner v Bayerische Vereinsbank AG*[226] the ECJ quoted both of these extracts when repeating the test of a concerted practice. In *Wood Pulp*[227] Advocate General Darmon noted at paragraphs 170 to 175 of his Opinion that the concept of a concerted practice implies the existence of reciprocal contact. However, this reciprocity can be quite easily established. In the *Cement* appeals[228] the CFI found that Lafarge was party to a

---

[219] For stimulating discussion of the complexity of the notion of a concerted practice see Black 'Communication and Obligation in Arrangements and Concerted Practices' (1992) 13 ECLR 200; Black 'Concerted Practices, Joint Action and Reliance' (2003) 24 ECLR 219; Odudu *The Boundaries of EC Competition Law* (Oxford University Press, 2006), pp 71–91.

[220] Cases 48/69 etc [1972] ECR 619, [1972] CMLR 557.

[221] *Re Aniline Dyes Cartel* JO [1969] L 195/11, [1969] CMLR D23.

[222] [1972] ECR 619, [1972] CMLR 557, para 64.

[223] Cases 40/73 etc [1975] ECR 1663, [1976] 1 CMLR 295.

[224] *Re European Sugar Cartel* OJ [1973] L 140/17, [1973] CMLR D65.

[225] [1975] ECR 1663, p 1942, [1976] 1 CMLR 295, p 425.

[226] Case 172/80 [1981] ECR 2021, [1982] 1 CMLR 313.

[227] Cases 89/85 etc *A Ahlström Oy v Commission* [1993] ECR I-1307, [1993] 4 CMLR 407.

[228] Cases T-25/95 etc *Cimenteries CBR SA v Commission* [2000] ECR II-491, [2000] 5 CMLR 204.

concerted practice when it received information at a meeting about the future conduct of a competitor: it could not argue that it was merely the passive recipient of such information[229]. In the same case the CFI stated that a concerted practice does not require a formal undertaking to have been given as to future behaviour[230].

In *Polypropylene*[231], *PVC*[232] and *LdPE*[233] the Commission stressed that a concerted practice did not require proof of a plan, and it is notable that in *LdPE* BP, Monsanto and Shell were held to be parties to a concerted practice even though they were on the 'periphery' of the cartel[234]. In *Soda-ash/Solvay*[235] the Commission pointed out that it would be unlikely, given the well-known legal risks under Article 81(1), that one would find a written record of an illegal resolution; it said that:

There are many forms and degrees of collusion and it does not require the making of a formal agreement. An infringement of Article 81 may well exist where the parties have not even spelled out an agreement in terms but each infers commitment from the other on the basis of conduct[236].

(ii) Must a concerted practice have been put into effect?

The judgment of the ECJ in the *Polypropylene*[237] cases deals with the question of whether a concerted practice must have been put into effect in order for there to be an infringement of Article 81. If the answer to this is yes it would follow, for example, that if competitors were 'merely' to meet or to exchange information, without actually producing any effects on the market by doing so, this would not amount to a concerted practice; the Commission would therefore have to prove there to be an agreement, the object or effect of which is to restrict competition. The Commission has been keen not to allow there to be legalistic distinctions between the treatment of agreements and concerted practices in Article 81(1), and has received the support of the Community Courts in this endeavour[238]. The ECJ held in *Hüls*, one of the *Polypropylene* cases, that 'a concerted practice ... is caught by Article 81(1) EC, even in the absence of anti-competitive effects on the market'[239]; however, in the *Cement* cases the CFI said that there would be no infringement if the parties can prove to the contrary[240]. In reaching its conclusion in *Hüls* the ECJ stated that, as established by its own case law[241], Article 81(1) requires that each economic operator must determine its policy on the market independently. At paragraph 161 the ECJ acknowledged that the concept of a concerted practice implies

[229] [2000] ECR II-491, [2000] 5 CMLR 204, para 1849.   [230] Ibid, para 1852.
[231] OJ [1986] L 230/1, [1988] 4 CMLR 347.   [232] OJ [1989] L 74/1, [1990] 4 CMLR 345.
[233] OJ [1989] L 74/21, [1990] 4 CMLR 382, paras 49–54.   [234] Ibid, para 41.   [235] OJ [1991] L 152/1.
[236] Ibid, para 59.
[237] Cases C-51/92 P etc *Hercules Chemicals NV v Commission* [1999] ECR I-4235, [1999] 5 CMLR 976: for critical comment see Wessely (2001) 38 CML Rev 739, 751–762; see also the Opinion of Advocate General Stix-Hackl given on 26 September 2002 in Case C-194/99 P *Thyssen Stahl AG v Commission* [2003] ECR I-10821 at fn 57, suggesting that the ECJ's formulation in *Polypropylene* may have been 'excessively broad'.
[238] See pp 99–102 above on complex cartels.
[239] Case C-199/92 P etc *Hüls AG v Commission* [1999] ECR I-4287, [1999] 5 CMLR 1016, para 163; see similarly the CFI in Cases T-141/94 etc *Thyssen Stahl v Commission* [1999] ECR II-347, [1999] 4 CMLR 810, paras 269–272, dealing in this case with former Article 65(1) ECSC.
[240] Cases T-25/95 etc *Cimenteries CBR SA v Commission* [2000] ECR II-491, [2000] 5 CMLR 204, para 1865.
[241] Cases 40/73 etc *Suiker Unie v Commission* [1975] ECR 1663, [1976] 1 CMLR 295, para 73; Case 172/80 *Züchner v Bayerische Vereinsbank AG* [1981] ECR 2021, [1982] 1 CMLR 313, para 13; Cases 89/85 etc *Ahlström v Commission* [1993] ECR I-1307, [1993] 4 CMLR 407, para 63; Case C-7/95 P *John Deere v Commission* [1998] ECR I-3111, [1998] 5 CMLR 311, para 86.

that there will be common conduct on the market, but added that there must be a presumption that, by making contact with one another, such conduct will follow: the ECJ appears to be saying that, because of this presumption, the Commission does not have to go further and actually prove those effects[242]. At paragraph 164 the ECJ specifically stated that a concerted practice may have an anti-competitive *object*, thus harnessing the words of Article 81(1) itself (agreements and concerted practices *the object or effect of which*…) in support of the proposition that the concerted practice does not need to have produced effects on the market. In *British Sugar*[243] the Commission specifically concluded that there can be a concerted practice in the absence of an actual effect on the market.

(iii) The burden of proof

An important issue, having established the legal definition of what constitutes a concerted practice, is to consider who bears the burden of proof. It is clear that the burden is on the Commission to establish that there has been a concerted practice; the Community Courts have annulled decisions where they were unhappy about the evidence on which the Commission relied[244]. In particular, the ECJ's judgment in *Compagnie Royale Asturienne des Mines SA and Rheinzink GmbH v Commission*[245] established that, whereas parallel behaviour can be circumstantial evidence of a concerted practice, it cannot be conclusive where there are other explanations of what has taken place[246]. In that case the Commission had concluded that the simultaneous cessation of deliveries to a Belgian customer, Schlitz, by CRAM and Rheinzink of Germany was attributable to a concerted practice to protect the German market. The ECJ held that there was a possible alternative explanation of the refusal to supply, which was that Schlitz had been failing to settle its accounts on the due date; as the Commission had not dealt with this possible explanation of the conduct in question its decision should be quashed.

(D) 'Unilateral' conduct and Article 81(1) in vertical cases

The scheme of the EC competition rules is that Article 81 applies to conduct by two or more undertakings which is consensual and that Article 82 applies to unilateral action by a dominant firm. It follows that unilateral conduct by a firm that is not dominant is not caught at all, which is why in some cases fairly outlandish claims of dominance have been made[247]. In a number of vertical cases the Commission has held that conduct which at first sight appeared to be unilateral fell within Article 81(1) as an agreement or

---

[242] The Commission relied on this point in *Zinc Phosphate* OJ [2003] L 153/1, para 202.

[243] *British Sugar plc, Tate & Lyle plc, Napier Brown & Co Ltd, James Budgett Sugars Ltd* OJ [1999] L 76/1, [1999] 4 CMLR 1316, paras 95ff, substantially upheld on appeal Cases T-202/98 etc *Tate & Lyle v Commission* [2001] ECR II-2035, [2001] 5 CMLR 859.

[244] See eg Case 40/73 *Suiker Unie v Commission* [1975] ECR 1663, [1976] 1 CMLR 295; Cases 29/83 and 30/83 *Compagnie Royale Asturienne des Mines SA and Rheinzink GmbH v Commission* [1984] ECR 1679, [1985] 1 CMLR 688; and Cases T-68/89 etc *Società Italiano Vetro v Commission* [1992] ECR II-1403, [1992] 5 CMLR 302, in each of which the Community Courts quashed some or all of the findings of concerted practices.

[245] Cases 29/83 and 30/83 [1984] ECR 1679, [1985] 1 CMLR 688.

[246] See Commission's XIVth *Report on Competition Policy* (1984), point 126.

[247] See eg Case 75/84 *Metro v Commission (No 2)* [1986] ECR 3021, [1987] 1 CMLR 118, paras 79–92; Case 210/81 *Demo-Studio Schmidt v Commission* [1983] ECR 3045, [1984] 1 CMLR 63.

a concerted practice; these were cases in which the Commission was concerned either that exports from one Member State to another were being inhibited or that resale prices were being maintained. Several of these decisions were upheld on appeal by the Community Courts; however in a number of cases, beginning with *Bayer AG/Adalat*[248] in 1996, findings of the Commission that there were agreements between a supplier and its distributors have been annulled on appeal[249].

(i)   *AEG Telefunken v Commission; Ford v Commission*

Two judgments of the ECJ in the 1980s provide an important starting point when considering this issue. In *AEG-Telefunken v Commission*[250] the ECJ rejected a claim that refusals to supply retail outlets which were objectively suitable to handle AEG's goods were unilateral acts falling outside Article 81(1). The ECJ held that the refusals arose out of the contractual relationship between AEG and the established distributors within its selective distribution system and their mutual acceptance, tacit or express, of AEG's intention to exclude from the network distributors who, though qualified technically, were not prepared to adhere to its policy of maintaining a high level of prices and excluding modern channels of distribution[251]. The frequency of AEG's refusals to supply precluded the possibility that they were isolated cases not forming part of systematic conduct[252]. The *AEG* case suggested that it may be relatively easy to infer an agreement and/or concerted practice between the participants in a selective distribution system who have a strong mutual interest in excluding firms willing to undercut the prevailing retail price[253].

In *Ford v Commission*[254] the ECJ held that a refusal by Ford's German subsidiary to supply right-hand drive cars to German distributors was attributable to the contractual relationship between them; at the time right-hand drive cars were sold in Germany to British military forces stationed there: they could then bring them back to the UK, having bought them in Germany at prices considerably below those in the UK. The *Ford* judgment appeared to be a considerable extension of *AEG*. In *AEG* there was an obvious community of interest between participants in the selective distribution system in excluding discounters. In *Ford*, however, the German distributors with whom Ford had entered into contracts did not themselves benefit from the refusal to supply right-hand drive cars: the beneficiaries of this policy were distributors in the UK, who would be shielded from cheaper parallel imports. In *Ford* the 'unilateral' act held to be attributable to the agreements between the supplier and its distributors was not an act for the benefit of those very distributors. However, the main issue in *Ford* was not whether there were agreements between Ford and its German distributors: of course there were. Rather the issue with which the ECJ was concerned was whether the agreements, as implemented in practice, satisfied the criteria of Article 81(3), and the ECJ

---

[248]   OJ [1996] L 201/1, [1996] 5 CMLR 416.   [249]   See pp 111–112 below.

[250]   Case 107/82 [1983] ECR 3151, [1984] 3 CMLR 325.

[251]   On selective distribution systems see ch 16, pp 630–635.   [252]   Ibid, paras 31–39.

[253]   Note also the two UK cases, *Football Replica Kit* and *Toys*, in which it was found that there could be a multilateral agreement between a supplier and its distributors, having both horizontal and vertical characteristics, that comes about as a result of contact between each distributor and the supplier, though without necessarily there being any contact between the distributors themselves (a so-called 'hub and spoke' arrangement in which the supplier is the hub and the vertical agreement with each distributor are spokes): see ch 9, pp 331–333.

[254]   Cases 25/84 and 26/84 [1985] ECR 2725, [1985] 3 CMLR 528.

decided that they did not[255]. This is how the ECJ distinguished the *Ford* judgment in its 2004 judgment in the *Bayer* case[256], and is an important limiting principle.

(ii) Subsequent cases prior to *Bayer*

In a number of decisions after *AEG* and *Ford* the Commission successfully applied Article 81(1) to apparently unilateral conduct. In *Sandoz*[257] it held that, where there was no written record of agreements between a producer and its distributors, unilateral measures, including placing the words 'export prohibited' on all invoices, were attributable to the continuing commercial relationship between the parties and were within Article 81(1). On appeal the ECJ upheld the Commission's decision[258]. In *Vichy*[259] the Commission specifically applied paragraph 12 of the *Sandoz* judgment, and its decision finding an agreement was upheld on appeal[260]. In *Tipp-Ex*[261] the Commission applied the ECJ's judgments in *AEG* and *Ford*, holding that there was an infringement of Article 81 consisting of agreements between Tipp-Ex and its authorised dealers regarding the mutual protection of territories; again the Commission's decision was upheld on appeal[262]. In *Konica*[263] the Commission held that the sending of a circular to its distributors requiring them not to export Konica film from the UK to Germany was an offer by Konica, and that by complying with the circular the distributors had accepted it, with the result that there was an agreement or at least a concerted practice within Article 81; there was no appeal in this case. In *Bayo-n-ox*[264] goods were supplied at a special price, on condition that customers use them for their own requirements: they could not resell them; this stipulation was contained in circulars sent by the supplier to the customers. The Commission said that by accepting the products at the special price the customers had tacitly agreed to abide by the 'own requirements' condition. The Commission has said that the fact that a customer is acting contrary to its own best interests in agreeing to its supplier's terms does not mean that it is not party to a prohibited agreement under Article 81(1)[265]. In *Volkswagen AG v Commission*[266] the CFI rejected Volkswagen's argument that it had acted unilaterally as opposed to by agreement with its distributors to restrict parallel trade from Italy to Germany and Austria[267]. These cases clearly demonstrated the considerable risks borne by suppliers that attempt to control the resale activities of their distributors; however the *Bayer* case discussed in the next section demonstrated that the notion of an agreement in Article 81(1) is not infinitely elastic, and that the Commission will be successful on appeal before the Community Courts only where it can adduce convincing evidence of a meeting of minds between a supplier and its distributor(s).

---

[255] Ibid, para 12.   [256] See pp 110–111 below.   [257] OJ [1987] L 222/28, [1989] 4 CMLR 628.

[258] Case C-277/87 *Sandoz Prodotti Farmaceutici SpA v Commission* [1990] ECR I-45.

[259] OJ [1991] L 75/57.   [260] Case T-19/91 *Vichy v Commission* [1992] ECR II-415.

[261] OJ [1987] L 222/1, [1989] 4 CMLR 425.

[262] Case C-279/87 *Tipp-ex GmbH v Commission* [1990] ECR I-261.

[263] OJ [1988] L 78/34, [1988] 4 CMLR 848.

[264] OJ [1990] L 21/71, [1990] 4 CMLR 930; see also *Bayer Dental* OJ [1990] L 351/46, [1992] 4 CMLR 61.

[265] See eg *Gosmé/Martell-DMP* OJ [1991] L 185/23, [1992] 5 CMLR 586.

[266] Case T-62/98 [2000] ECR II-2707, [2000] 5 CMLR 853, upheld on appeal to the ECJ Case C-338/00 P *Volkswagen AG v Commission* [2003] ECR I-9189, [2004] 4 CMLR 351, paras 60–69.

[267] Ibid, paras 236–239.

(iii) *Bayer v Commission*

In *Bayer AG/Adalat*[268] the Commission adopted a decision that Bayer and its wholesalers were parties to an agreement to restrict parallel trade in a pharmaceutical product, Adalat, from France and Spain to the UK. On this occasion, however, the CFI annulled the decision since, in its view, the Commission had failed to prove the existence of an agreement[269]; an appeal by the Commission and a parallel importer to the ECJ to reverse the CFI's judgment failed[270].

In order to prevent its French and Spanish wholesalers from supplying to parallel exporters to the UK, and thereby to protect its UK pricing strategy, Bayer had reduced the volume of its supplies of Adalat to France and Spain. An important feature of the case was that wholesalers in France and Spain were required to maintain sufficient stocks to enable them to supply local pharmacies with their requirements for drugs: clearly this meant that, if Bayer assessed the level of domestic demand correctly, it could limit the volumes of Adalat supplied to the point where there would be none available for export. Prices for pharmaceuticals in France and Spain were as much as 40 per cent lower than in the UK, so that the market was ripe for parallel trade. The Commission concluded that a tacit agreement existed between Bayer and its wholesalers not to export to the UK that was contrary to Article 81(1): in its view the agreement was evidenced by the fact that the wholesalers had ceased to supply the UK in response to Bayer's tactic of reducing supplies. It has to be said that this would appear to be counter-intuitive, given that the wholesalers had tried every means possible to defy Bayer and to obtain extra supplies for the purpose of exporting to the UK: there was no 'common interest' in this case between Bayer and its wholesalers, whose respective needs were diametrically opposed. To put the point another way, this case was certainly not like *AEG*; if anything it was like *Ford*, where the beneficiary of Ford's restriction of supplies was not the German distributors deprived of suppliers, but the UK distributors protected from parallel trade. Bayer did not deny that it had reduced the quantities delivered to France and Spain, but it argued that it had acted unilaterally rather than pursuant to an agreement.

On appeal the CFI held that there was no agreement and annulled the Commission's decision. After stressing that Article 81(1) applies only to conduct that is coordinated bilaterally or multilaterally[271], the Court reviewed the case law and stated that the concept of an agreement:

> centres around the existence of a concurrence of wills between at least two parties, the form in which it is manifested being unimportant so long as it constitutes the faithful expression of the parties' intention[272].

The CFI acknowledged that there could be an agreement where one person tacitly acquiesces in practices and measures adopted by another[273]; however it concluded that

---

[268] OJ [1996] L 201/1, [1996] 5 CMLR 416; for criticism of the Commission's decision see Kon and Schoeffer 'Parallel Imports of Pharmaceutical Products: a New Realism or Back to Basics?' (1997) 22 EL Rev 123; Lidgard 'Unilateral Refusal to Supply: an Agreement in Disguise?' (1997) 18 ECLR 352; Jakobsen and Broberg 'The Concept of Agreement in Article 81(1) EC: On the Manufacturer's Right to Prevent Parallel Trade within the European Community' (2002) 23 ECLR 127.

[269] Case T-41/96 [2000] ECR II-3383, [2001] 4 CMLR 176.

[270] Cases C-2/01 P and C-3/01 P *Bundesverband der Arzneimittel-Importeure eV v Bayer* AG [2004] ECR I-23, [2004] 4 CMLR 653.

[271] Case T-41/96 [2000] ECR II-3383, [2001] CMLR 176, para 64.

[272] [2000] ECR II-3383, [2001] 4 CMLR 176, para 69.   [273] Ibid, para 71.

the Commission had failed both to demonstrate that Bayer had intended to impose an export ban[274] and to prove that the wholesalers had intended to adhere to a policy on the part of Bayer to reduce parallel imports[275]. The CFI was satisfied that earlier judgments, including *Sandoz*, *Tipp-Ex* and *AEG*, were distinguishable[276]. It also rejected the argument that the wholesalers, by maintaining their commercial relations with Bayer after the reduction of supplies, could thereby be held to have agreed with it to restrain exports[277]. The CFI was not prepared to extend the scope of Article 81(1), acknowledging the importance of 'free enterprise' when applying the competition rules[278].

The Commission and a parallel importer appealed to the ECJ, which upheld the CFI's judgment[279]. At paragraph 88 of its judgment the ECJ held that:

The mere fact that the unilateral policy of quotas implemented by Bayer, combined with the national requirements on the wholesalers to offer a full product range, produces the same effect as an export ban does not mean either that the manufacturer imposed such a ban or that there was an agreement prohibited by Article 81(1) of the Treaty.

The ECJ noted that the Commission's analysis risked confusing the respective roles of Articles 81 and 82[280], and that the *AEG* and *Ford* cases were distinguishable[281].

The importance of the judgments of the CFI and ECJ in *Bayer* cannot be overstated. Had the Commission's decision been upheld, the notion that an agreement for the purpose of Article 81(1) requires consensus between the parties would have been virtually eliminated; while this would have given the Commission greater control over restrictions of parallel trade within the Community, it would have done so at the expense of the integrity of the competition rules, which clearly apprehend unilateral behaviour only where a firm has a dominant position in the sense of Article 82.

(iii) Judgments since *Bayer v Commission* annulling Commission findings of an agreement

There have been several cases since *Bayer* in which decisions of the Commission that vertical agreements existed between a supplier and its distributors have been annulled on appeal. For example in *JCB* the Commission imposed fines on JCB for various infringements of Article 81, including for entering into agreements with distributors to fix discounts and resale prices[282]. On appeal the CFI annulled the Commission's decision on this point: it was true that JCB had recommended prices to its distributors, and that the prices that it charged to them would influence their own resale prices; however this was not sufficient in itself to show that there was an agreement between JCB and the distributors[283]. In *General Motors Nederland BV v Commission*[284] the CFI heard an appeal from a Commission decision, *Opel Nederland BV*[285], in which it had imposed

---

[274] Ibid, paras 78–110.   [275] Ibid, paras 111–157.   [276] Ibid, paras 158–171.

[277] Ibid, paras 172–182.   [278] Ibid, para 180.

[279] Cases C-2/01 P and C-3/01 P *Bundesverband der Arzneimittel-Importeure eV v Bayer AG*; the Court of Appeal in the UK applied the ECJ's judgment in *Bayer* in *Unipart Group Ltd v O2 (UK) Ltd* [2004] EWCA 1034, [2004] UKCLR 1453, in deciding that Unipart was not the victim of a margin squeeze imposed upon it by a co-contractor, O2: since O2 was not dominant Unipart could not proceed against it on the basis of Article 82 and therefore tried to argue that the margin squeeze arose from its contractual relationship with O2.

[280] Ibid, para 101.   [281] Ibid, paras 107–108.   [282] OJ [2002] L 69/1, [2002] 4 CMLR 148, paras 138–149.

[283] Case T 67/01 *JCB Service v Commission* [2004] ECR II-49, [2004] 4 CMLR 1346, paras 121–133.

[284] Case T-368/00 [2003] ECR II-4491, [2004] 4 CMLR 1302.

[285] OJ [2001] L 59/1, [2001] 4 CMLR 1441.

fines of €43 million on Opel, a subsidiary of General Motors. The CFI annulled one of the Commission's findings: the Commission had argued that Opel's policy was to limit the number of cars that would be supplied to its Dutch dealers in order to prevent exports, and that this policy had been communicated to the dealers and agreed to by them; the CFI held that there was no direct proof in the decision that there had been any such communication, and even less that that measure had entered into the contractual relations between Opel and its dealers[286]. As a consequence the fine was reduced from €43 million to €35 million. A separate point in this case – that a bonus system that the dealers had undoubtedly agreed to had as its object the restriction of competition – is discussed below[287].

In a second decision involving Volkswagen[288] the Commission fined that company €30.96 million for agreeing to fix prices with its distributors for the VW Passat car. Volkswagen had sent circulars and letters to its distributors urging them not to sell the Passat at discounted prices. In the Commission's view the objectives set out in these circulars or letters became integral parts of the dealership agreement that the distributors had entered into; relying on cases such as *AEG* and others on selective distribution systems[289] the Commission argued that, within a selective distribution system, calls by a supplier such as Volkswagen of the type set out in the circulars and letters became part of the contractual relationship, without the need to prove any acquiescence on the part of the distributors. The CFI rejected the Commission's arguments and annulled the decision in *Volkswagen v Commission*[290]: the CFI did not accept the Commission's analysis of the case law on selective distribution, especially given that this would mean that the distributors, who had signed perfectly lawful dealership agreements in the first place, would be taken to have agreed to subsequent calls from Volkswagen that would make the implementation of the agreements illegal. On appeal the ECJ set aside the judgment of the CFI[291] in so far as it had suggested that a lawful clause in an agreement could never authorise a call contrary to Article 81[292]; nevertheless the ECJ still reached the same substantive conclusion, that the Commission had failed to establish an agreement[293].

Similar issues are pending before the Commission in appeals against the Commission's decisions in *Nintendo*[294] and in *SEP et autres/Peugeot SA*[295].

(iv) Comment

Clearly the judgments in the previous section in which Commission findings of agreements in vertical relationships were annulled mean that it must be particularly careful to adduce evidence that there exists 'a concurrence of wills between at least two parties', in the words of the CFI's judgment in *Bayer*. However it would be dangerous for suppliers, wishing to suppress exports or to maintain resale prices, to suppose that this case

---

[286] Ibid, paras 78–89.   [287] See p 122 below.

[288] *Volkswagen* OJ [2001] L 262/14, [2001] 5 CMLR 1309, paras 61–69.

[289] See the cases cited in paras 18 and 19 of the CFI's judgment.

[290] Case T-208/01 *Volkswagen v Commission* [2003] ECR I-5141, [2004] 4 CMLR 727, paras 30–68.

[291] Case C-74/04 P *Commission v Volkswagen* [2006] ECR I-6585.

[292] Ibid, paras 43–44.   [293] Ibid, para 54.

[294] OJ [2003] L 255/33, on appeal Case T-13/03 *Nintendo v Commission*, not yet decided.

[295] Commission decision of 5 October 2005, on appeal Case T-450/05 *Automobiles Peugeot and Peugeot Nederland v Commission*, not yet decided.

law means that this is something that can be achieved without risk. In so far as they can achieve their intended purpose on a purely unilateral basis, *Bayer* shows that Article 81 can be avoided. However it should be stressed that, in that case, if it were not for the stock-holding obligations to supply French and Spanish pharmacies with Adalat, the wholesalers in question could have decided to sell all the Adalat that they acquired to parallel traders: in other words Bayer's unilateral reduction of suppliers was not enough, in itself, to staunch the parallel trade. In the *General Motors* case the Commission lost on the point about Opel's export policy because it had failed to show that the policy had been communicated to its distributors or that they had reacted to a policy known to them: if one reverses the facts – suppose that Opel had communicated the policy and the distributors had changed their behaviour accordingly – there would have been an agreement. As far as *Volkswagen* is concerned, the Commission appears to have argued its case in much too legalistic a manner, basing itself on the terms of the standard-form dealership agreement and the inferences to be drawn from it. Had the Commission argued that the distributors knew of Volkswagen's intentions and altered their pricing practices accordingly, it might have succeeded. These cases are highly fact-specific, and it would be wrong for suppliers and their distributors to draw too comforting a conclusion from the Commission's succession of defeats.

4. **THE OBJECT OR EFFECT OF PREVENTING, RESTRICTING OR DISTORTING COMPETITION**

Article 81(1) prohibits agreements that have as their object or effect the prevention, restriction or distortion of competition[296]. It contains an illustrative list of agreements that may be caught such as price fixing and market sharing, but this is insufficient in itself to explain the numerous intricacies involved in understanding how this provision works. Judgments of the CFI and, at the top of the hierarchy, the ECJ contain the most authoritative statements of the law, and some of the best analyses will be found in Opinions of the Advocates General; the Commission's decisions, Notices and Guidelines provide important insights of its views on the application of Article 81(1), as do its *Annual Report on Competition Policy* and the quarterly *Competition Policy Newsletter*[297].

The application of Article 81(1) to agreements, in particular by the Commission, was for many years controversial. In essence the complaint of many commentators was that Article 81(1) was applied too broadly, catching many agreements that were not detrimental to competition at all[298]. Agreements that are caught by Article 81(1) are void

---

[296] In the text that follows the term 'restriction' of competition is taken to include the prevention and distortion of competition.

[297] All of these materials are available on DG COMP's website at www.europa.eu.int/comm/competition/publications/cpn.

[298] See eg Bright 'EU Competition Policy: Rules, Objectives and Deregulation' (1996) 16 Oxford Journal of Legal Studies 535; there is a considerable amount of academic literature criticising the 'over'-application of Article 81(1): see eg Joliet *The Rule of Reason in Antitrust Law; American, German and Common Market Laws in Comparative Perspective* (1967), pp 77–106, 117 to the end; Korah 'The Rise and Fall of Provisional Validity' (1981) 3 NJILB 320; Schechter 'The Rule of Reason in European Competition Law' [1982(2)] Legal Issues in European Integration 1; Forrester and Norall 'The Laicization of Community Law: Self-help and the Rule of

and unenforceable[299], and may attract a fine, unless they satisfy the criteria set out in Article 81(3). Under Regulation 17[300], which conferred upon the Commission the power to enforce Articles 81 and 82, only it could grant a so-called 'individual exemption' to an agreement under Article 81(3); individual exemptions were rarely given, and the procedure for obtaining one was time-consuming, costly and cumbersome. A consequence was that many firms would ensure that they satisfied the terms of one of the 'block exemptions' under Article 81(3) in order to be certain that their agreements were legally enforceable[301]; where no block exemption was available firms that did not notify their agreements to the Commission for an individual exemption ran the risk of voidness and fines. An obvious solution proposed by critics of this situation was that Article 81(1) should be applied to fewer agreements: only those agreements that posed a real threat to competition should be caught in the net of competition law; others should not be ensnared by the competition rules at all.

These criticisms were loud and persistent throughout the 1980s and 1990s. However it is important to note that the advent of Regulation 1/2003[302] ('the Modernisation Regulation') in May 2004 has changed this position significantly. Under this Regulation the Commission no longer enjoys a 'monopoly' over individual exemptions under Article 81(3) – indeed there is no longer any such thing as an individual exemption; and the procedure of notifying agreements to the Commission for such an exemption has been abolished[303]. Instead the Commission now shares with national courts and national competition authorities ('NCAs') the power to make decisions on the application of Article 81 in its entirety. It follows that it is no longer necessary to argue that an agreement falls outside Article 81(1) for the procedural reason that it is not block exempted and has not been notified to the Commission for an individual exemption. Since the Modernisation Regulation it is always possible to argue that an agreement that is restrictive of competition under Article 81(1) satisfies the terms of Article 81(3), whether a case is being decided by the Commission, a national court or an NCA: there is no longer a procedural tail to wag the substantive dog[304]. Coupled with the introduction of the Modernisation Regulation is the undoubted fact that the Commission, for many years, has taken a more realistic approach both to Article 81(1) and Article 81(3), in particular to ensure that Article 81 as a whole is applied in accordance with sound economic principles. The Commission today takes a much narrower view of what is meant by a restriction of competition for the purpose of Article 81(1); and it also has a narrower approach to the circumstances in which Article 81(3) is satisfied[305]. In the post-Modernisation Regulation world the precise sphere of application of Article 81(1) on the one hand and Article 81(3) on the other does not have the significance that it did in the days of notification for individual exemption[306]; today the real question is whether an agreement infringes Article 81 as a whole.

Reason' (1984) 21 CML Rev 11; Korah 'EEC Competition Policy – Legal Form or Economic Efficiency' (1986) 39 CLP 85; Venit 'Pronuptia: Ancillary Restraints or Unholy Alliances?' (1986) 11 EL Rev 213; Holley 'EEC Competition Practice; a Thirty-Year Retrospective' in [1992] Fordham Corp L Inst (ed Hawk), 669, p 689.

[299] See further ch 8, pp 309–317.   [300] JO 204/62, OJ (Special Edition 1959–62) p 57.
[301] On block exemptions see ch 4, pp 164–169.   [302] OJ [2003] L 1/1, [2003] 4 CMLR 551.
[303] See ch 4, pp 162–163.
[304] See Wils *Principles of European Antitrust Enforcement* (Hart Publishing, 2005), para 35.
[305] See ch 4, pp 152–157 for a discussion of the 'narrow' and the 'broad' interpretations of Article 81(3).
[306] Note however that the burden of proof rests with different persons under Article 81(1) and Article 81(3): see ch 4, pp 149–150.

(A) Three preliminary comments

The text that follows will examine the meaning of agreements having as their 'object or effect' the prevention, restriction or distortion of competition. However, a few preliminary comments may be helpful.

First, there are many judgments of the Community Courts that demonstrate that a contractual restriction does not necessarily result in a restriction of competition[307]. It is essential to understand this key point: the concept of a restriction of competition is an economic one, and as a general proposition economic analysis is needed to determine whether an agreement could have an anti-competitive effect. A relatively small class of agreements are considered by law to have as their object the restriction of competition[308]; in the case of all other agreements anti-competitive effects must be demonstrated for there to be an infringement of Article 81(1)[309].

Second, in several judgments the Community Courts have made clear that the Commission must adequately demonstrate that an agreement is restrictive of competition, and that they will not simply 'rubber-stamp' its analysis: a particularly good example is *European Night Services v Commission*[310], where the CFI exposed the thorough inadequacy of the Commission's reasoning in its decision in that case[311].

Third, the CFI has said that in a case under Article 81(1) the definition of the market is relevant at the stage of determining whether there has been an impairment of competition or an effect on trade between Member States; it is not something that must be undertaken as a preliminary matter, as in the case of Article 82 where it is a necessary precondition to a finding of abuse[312].

(B) Horizontal and vertical agreements

One point is absolutely clear: Article 81 is capable of application both to horizontal agreements (between undertakings at the same level of the market) and to vertical agreements (between undertakings at different levels of the market). It was at one time thought that Article 81 might have no application at all to vertical agreements, but that idea was firmly contradicted by the ECJ's judgment in *Consten and Grundig v Commission*[313]; it remains the case that undertakings must carry out a careful assessment of whether their vertical agreements are compliant with the law. However major changes have taken place in relation to vertical agreements, in particular the adoption of a block exemption in December 1999 which entered into force on 1 June 2000 and which takes a fairly permissive approach[314]. The application of Article 81 to vertical agreements will be considered in detail in chapter 16.

---

[307] See the cases discussed at pp 124–126 below.   [308] See pp 119–122.

[309] See pp 122–134 below.   [310] Cases T-374/94 etc [1998] ECR II-3141, [1998] 5 CMLR 718.

[311] *European Night Services Ltd* OJ [1994] L 259/20, [1995] 5 CMLR 76.

[312] Case T-29/92 *SPO v Commission* [1995] ECR II-289, para 75; Cases T-25/95 etc *Cimenteries CBR SA v Commission* [2000] ECR II-491, [2000] 5 CMLR 204, para 833; Case T-62/98 *Volkswagen AG v Commission* [2000] ECR II-2707, [2000] 5 CMLR 853, paras 230–232; Case T-213/00 *CMA CGM v Commission* [2003] ECR II-913, [2003] 5 CMLR 268, para 206.

[313] Cases 56 and 58/64 [1966] ECR 299, [1966] CMLR 418.

[314] Regulation 2790/99 OJ [1999] L 336/21, [2000] 4 CMLR 398.

(C) The 'object or effect' of preventing, restricting or distorting competition

Article 81(1) prohibits agreements 'which have as their *object or effect* the prevention, restriction or distortion of competition' (emphasis added). It is important to understand the significance of the words 'object or effect' in Article 81(1).

(i) 'Object or effect' to be read disjunctively

It is clear that these are alternative, and not cumulative, requirements for a finding of an infringement of Article 81(1). In *Société Technique Minière v Maschinenbau Ulm*[315] the ECJ stated that the words were to be read disjunctively, so that it is first necessary to consider what the object of an agreement is; only if it is not clear that the object of an agreement is to harm competition is it necessary to consider whether it might have the effect of doing so.

(ii) 'Object'[316]

There are some types of agreement the anti-competitiveness of which can be determined simply from their object; the word 'object' in this context means not the subjective intention of the parties when entering into the agreement, but the objective meaning and purpose of the agreement considered in the economic context in which it is to be applied[317]. Where an agreement has as its object the restriction of competition, it is unnecessary to prove that the agreement would have an anti-competitive effect in order to find an infringement of Article 81(1). This was repeated by the ECJ two weeks after the *Société Technique Minière* judgment in *Consten and Grundig v Commission*[318]; in *VdS v Commission*[319] the ECJ again stated that if the object of an agreement is to restrict competition, there is no need for the Commission also to show that it might have an anti-competitive effect. The Community Courts have frequently reaffirmed the position[320], and have confirmed that a concerted practice can have the object of restricting competition as well as an agreement[321]. The Commission has also stated the same thing on a number of occasions; for example it said in its *TACA*[322] decision in 1998:

There is no need to wait to observe the concrete effects of an agreement once it appears that it has as its object the prevention, restriction or distortion of competition[323].

---

[315] Case 56/65 [1966] ECR 235, p 249, [1966] CMLR 357, p 375.

[316] The Commission discusses agreements that restrict competition by object at paras 20–23 of its *Guidelines on the application of Article 81(3) of the Treaty*, OJ [2004] C 101/8.

[317] Cases 29/83 and 30/83 *Compagnie Royale Asturienne des Mines SA and Rheinzinc GmbH v Commission* [1984] ECR 1679, [1985] 1 CMLR 688, paras 25–26; Case C-277/87 *Sandoz Prodotti Farmaceutici v Commission* [1990] ECR I-45; Case T-148/89 *Tréfilunion v Commission* [1995] ECR II-1063, para 79; Case C-551/03 *General Motors v Commission* [2006] ECR II-3173, [2006] 5 CMLR 4491, paras 77–78; on the relevance of subjective intention see Odudu 'Interpreting Article 81(1): Object as Subjective Intention' (2001) 26 EL Rev 60 and Odudu 'Interpreting Article 81(1): the Object Requirement Revisited' (2001) 26 EL Rev 379.

[318] Cases 56 and 58/64 [1966] ECR 299, p 342, [1966] CMLR 418, p 473.

[319] Case 45/85 [1987] ECR 405, [1988] 4 CMLR 264, para 39.

[320] See eg Cases T-25/95 *Cimenteries CBR SA v Commission* [2000] ECR II-491, [2000] 5 CMLR 204, paras 837, 1531 and 2589; Case T-202/98 etc *Tate & Lyle v Commission* [2001] ECR II-2035, [2001] 5 CMLR 859, paras 72–74.

[321] See eg Case C-199/92 P etc *Hüls AG v Commission* [1999] ECR I-4287, [1999] 5 CMLR 1016, para 164.

[322] OJ [1999] L 95/1, [1999] 4 CMLR 1415.

[323] [1999] 4 CMLR 1415, para 381; see similarly *FETTCSA* OJ [2000] L 268/1, [2000] 5 CMLR 1011, para 135, substantially upheld on appeal to the CFI, Case T-213/00 *CMA v Commission* [2003] ECR II-913, [2003] 5 CMLR 268, para 183; *Amino Acids* OJ [2001] L 152/24, [2001] 5 CMLR 322, para 230.

The classification of an agreement as having as its object the restriction of competition means that the parties, for example to a hard-core price-fixing agreement, cannot argue that the fixing of prices does not restrict competition: the Community Courts have decided, on the basis of the wording of the Treaty and subsequent experience acquired through case law, that it does; it follows that the parties to a price-fixing agreement who wish to assert that it could produce efficiency-enhancing effects can do so only by proving that it satisfies the criteria of Article 81(3), the burden of proof being on them to prove that this is so[324]. It will be readily understood that, from a competition authority's point of view, the fact that it does not need to demonstrate that hard-core price-fixing agreements produce adverse economic effects relieves it of some of the burden that would otherwise rest upon it. In cartel cases it can be difficult to prove that an agreement exists; to have to also demonstrate empirically, for example, that the agreement has led to or would lead to higher prices could impose a strain on its resources.

The fact that there is no need to prove, in the case of an agreement that has as its object the restriction of competition, that the agreement has an anti-competitive effect does not mean that there is no quantitative component to Article 81(1) analysis at all. There is a rule that any restriction of competition must be *appreciable*: even a restriction of competition by object could fall outside Article 81(1) if its likely impact on the market is minimal[325]. As a jurisdictional matter, an agreement is caught by Article 81(1) only if it has an *appreciable* effect on trade between Member States: again, therefore, some quantitative analysis may be required before determining that Article 81(1) is infringed, although it is important to understand that, given that all the Member States have domestic laws similar to Article 81, the fact that Article 81 is not applicable may be of little significance, assuming that NCAs are effective in applying their own laws. The requirement of an effect on trade between Member States is discussed below[326]. A further point is that the likely effect that an agreement may have on the market is relevant to the gravity of the infringement and therefore to the amount of any fine[327].

The ECJ has held that, if an agreement is one that has as its object the restriction of competition, it is irrelevant that it was not in the commercial interest of some of the participants.[328]

(iii) 'Effect'[329]

Where an agreement does not have as its object the restriction of competition, it is necessary to demonstrate that it would have a restrictive effect; this is a much more onerous task for the Commission or the person wishing to establish an infringement

---

[324] See ch 4 generally on Article 81(3), including the burden of proof and the nature of the evidence required to succeed in showing that that provision is satisfied.

[325] For discussion of this rule see pp 137–142 below.

[326] See pp 137–142 below on the so-called *de minimis* doctrine and pp 142–146 below on the requirement of an effect on trade between Member States.

[327] See eg *Amino Acids* OJ [2001] L 154/24, [2001] 5 CMLR 322, paras 261–298; see further ch 7, p 274.

[328] See eg Cases C-403/04 P *Sumitomo Metal Industries Ltd v Commission* [2007] ECR I-729, [2007] 4 CMLR 650, paras 45–46.

[329] The Commission discusses agreements that restrict competition by effect at paras 24–27 of its *Guidelines on the application of Article 81(3) of the Treaty*, OJ [2004] C 101/8.

of Article 81(1). The position was stated clearly by the CFI in *European Night Services v Commission*[330]:

> it must be borne in mind that in assessing an agreement under Article [81(1)] of the Treaty, account should be taken of the actual conditions in which it functions, in particular the economic context in which the undertakings operate, the products or services covered by the agreement and the actual structure of the market concerned... *unless it is an agreement containing obvious restrictions of competition such as price-fixing, market-sharing or the control of outlets*.... In the latter case, such restrictions may be weighed against their claimed pro-competitive effects only in the context of Article [81(3)] of the Treaty, with a view to granting an exemption from the prohibition in Article [81(1)] (emphasis added).

(iv) Comment on the 'object or effect' distinction

Clearly it is important to know which agreements can be classified as having as their object the restriction of competition since in such cases it is not necessary to prove that anti-competitive effects would follow.

It may be helpful to think of the position in terms of two boxes, as follows:

OBJECT	EFFECT
Agreements that have as their object the restriction of competition	Agreements that have as their effect the restriction of competition

Article 81(1), as interpreted by the Community Courts, allocates particularly pernicious types of agreement that are overwhelmingly likely to harm consumer welfare to the object box, with the consequences just described. This is done as a matter of policy: certain agreements are so clearly inimical to the objectives of the Community that they can be permitted only where they can be shown to satisfy the requirements of Article 81(3). In all other cases, however, the lawfulness of an agreement under Article 81(1) must be tested according to its anti-competitive effects and this, as we shall see, requires a wide-ranging analysis of the market[331].

There is clearly an analogy here with the position under section 1 of the Sherman Act 1890 in the US, which characterises some agreements as *per se* infringements of the Act, whereas others are subject to so-called 'rule of reason' analysis[332]. Where there is a *per se* infringement, it is not open to the parties to the agreement to argue that it does not restrict competition: it belongs to a category of agreement that has, by law, been found to be restrictive of competition. However, there is an important difference in EC law in that, even if an agreement has as its object the restriction of competition, that is to say that it infringes Article 81(1) *per se*, the parties can still argue that the agreement satisfies the terms of Article 81(3). This possibility does not exist in US law, since there is no equivalent of Article 81(3) in that system. For this reason a judgment such as that of the US Supreme Court in *Leegin*[333], in which that Court determined that minimum resale price maintenance should be analysed under a rule of reason standard, rather than being subjected to a *per se* rule, brings US law into alignment with that of the

---

[330] Cases T-374/94 etc [1998] ECR II-3141, [1998] 5 CMLR 718, para 136.   [331] See pp 122–134 below.

[332] For an interesting discussion of this topic see Black 'Per Se Rules and Rules of Reason: What Are They?' (1997) 18 ECLR 145; this article contains extensive citation of the literature on the position under US law; see also Jones 'Analysis of agreements under US and EC antitrust law – Convergence or divergence?' (2006) 51 Antitrust Bulletin 691.

[333] *Leegin Creative Leather Products Inc v PSKS Inc* 551 US _ (2007).

EC: it has always been possible for an undertaking to argue that resale price maintenance satisfies Article 81(3), even though it is classified as having as its object the restriction of competition for the purpose of Article 81(1). Paragraph 46 of the Commission's
Guidelines on the application of Article 81(3) of the Treaty[334] cites the CFI's judgment
in *Matra Hachette v Commission*[335], which established that there is no type of agreement that, on *a priori* grounds, can be said to be incapable of satisfying the criteria of
Article 81(3): even agreements that restrict competition by object can do so, provided
that probative evidence in support of efficiency gains can be adduced.

(D) Agreements that have as their object the prevention, restriction or distortion of competition

In *European Night Services v Commission*[336] the CFI referred to agreements 'containing
obvious restrictions of competition such as price-fixing, market-sharing or the control
of outlets'; without using the terminology used in this chapter, it seems clear that the
CFI considered that agreements of this nature should be allocated to the 'object' box.

(i) Price fixing

Price fixing is specifically cited as an example of an anti-competitive agreement in
Article 81(1)(a) of the Treaty, and it is unsurprising that it is characterised as having
as its object the restriction of competition, whether horizontal[337] or vertical[338]. The
exchange of information about current and future prices is also regarded as having as
its object the restriction of competition[339], although other information exchanges are
likely to require effects analysis[340].

(ii) Market sharing, quotas, collective exclusive dealing

Market-sharing agreements are specifically mentioned in Article 81(1)(c), and again
their treatment as restrictive by object is to be expected, in particular because they are
likely to be harmful to the single market[341].

The CFI did not refer in *European Night Services* to agreements to limit output when
discussing 'obvious' restrictions of competition, but they must also be allocated to the
object box on the basis that they clearly restrict competition, and they are specifically
referred to in Article 81(1)(b) of the Treaty; analogous agreements, for example to limit
sales, must also be included[342].

The Commission has characterised collective exclusive dealing as restricting competition by object[343].

---

[334] OJ [2004] C 101/8.   [335] Case T-17/93 [1994] ECR II-595.

[336] See Cases T-374/94 etc [1998] ECR II-3141, [1998] 5 CMLR 718.

[337] See ch 13, pp 505–513.   [338] See ch 16, pp 653–654.

[339] See eg Cases T-25/95 etc *Cimenteries CBR SA v Commission* [2000] ECR II-491, [2000] 5 CMLR 204,
para 1531.

[340] See eg Case C-238/05 *Asnef-Equifax v Asociación de Usuarios de Servcicios Bancarios (Ausbanc)* [2006]
ECR I-11125, [2007] 4 CMLR 224; information agreements are discussed in ch 13, pp 523–532.

[341] See ch 13, pp 513–519.   [342] See ch 13, pp 535–538.

[343] See eg *Nederlandse Federative Vereniging voor de Grootlandel op Elektrotechnisch Gebied and
Technische Unie (FEG and TU)* OJ [2000] L 39/1, [2000] 4 CMLR 1208, para 105, and the further examples
given in footnote 120 of that decision; the Commission's decision was upheld on appeal, Cases T-5&6/00
[2003] ECR II-5761, [2004] 5 CMLR 962.

(iii) Controlling outlets; export bans

The CFI in *European Night Services* referred to agreements to control outlets as containing obvious restrictions of competition; the control of outlets is not specifically referred
to in Article 81(1), but the CFI presumably had in mind the imposition on distributors
of export bans from one Member State to another, which have consistently been found
to have as their object the restriction of competition: nothing could be more obviously
inimical to the goal of market integration than restrictions of this kind, although the
judgment of the CFI in the *GlaxoSmithKline* case has somewhat muddied this apparently simple point[344]. An example of the Community Courts' attitude to export bans is
to be found in the judgment of the CFI in *BASF v Commission*[345], in which it dismissed
two appeals against the Commission's finding that such bans in distribution agreements infringed Article 81(1), and in doing so confirmed its strict approach to such
provisions:

It is settled case law that, by its nature, a clause designed to prevent a buyer from reselling or
exporting goods he has bought is liable to partition the markets and consequently to affect trade
between Member States. The CFI finds that that agreement, *by virtue of its object*, constitutes a
restriction on competition prohibited by Article 81(1) EC (emphasis added).

Following the order of the text above, it seems that the contents of the 'object' box can
be depicted as follows:

The object box[346]

Horizontal agreements:

- to fix prices
- to exchange current or future price information
- to share markets
- to limit output
- to limit sales
- for collective exclusive dealing

Vertical agreements:

- to fix minimum resale prices
- to impose export bans

(iv) Refinement of the range of agreements within the object box

An important qualification must be made. This presentation of the position slightly
oversimplifies the law. For example in *Visa International – Multilateral Interchange Fee*[347]

[344] See pp 121–122 below.
[345] Cases T-175/95 and T-176/95 [1999] ECR II-1581, [2000] 4 CMLR 33; see similarly Case T-176/95
Accinauto SA v Commission [1999] ECR II-1635, [2000] 4 CMLR 67.
[346] It will be seen that the contents of the object box correspond to a large extent with the provisions that
are black-listed in Article 4(a) and 4(b) of Regulation 2790/99 on vertical agreements (ch 16, pp 653–656),
Article 5 of Regulation 2658/00 on specialisation agreements (ch 15, p 592) and Article 5 of Regulation
2659/00 on research and development agreements (ch 15, p 586).
[347] OJ [2002] L 318/17, [2003] 4 CMLR 283.

participants in the Visa system agreed on the level of the 'multilateral interchange fee' that 'acquiring banks' (which act for merchants) pay to 'issuing banks' (which issue Visa cards to consumers) for each transaction with a Visa card; the Commission concluded that this did restrict the freedom of banks to decide their own pricing policies[348], but that this did not amount to a restriction of competition by object[349], but by effect[350]; the Commission decided that the agreement satisfied the criteria of Article 81(3)[351]. In *MasterCard*[352] the Commission left open the question of whether the interchange fee restricted by object since it considered that it clearly had an anti-competitive effect[353]. Similarly there have been a few occasions on which the ECJ has concluded that an export ban, in the context of a specific type of agreement, did not have as its object the restriction of competition. An example can be found in *Erauw-Jacquery Sprl v La Hesbignonne Société Coopérative*[354], where the ECJ held that a provision preventing a licensee from exporting so-called 'basic' seeds protected by plant breeders' rights could fall outside Article 81(1) where it was necessary to protect the right of the licensor to select his licensees. In *Javico v Yves St Laurent*[355], where an export ban was imposed on distributors in Russia and the Ukraine, the ECJ held that:

In the case of agreements of this kind stipulations of the type mentioned in the question must be construed not as being intended to exclude parallel imports and marketing of the contractual product within the Community but as being designed to enable the producer to penetrate a market outside the Community by supplying a sufficient quantity of contractual products to that market. That interpretation is supported by the fact that, in the agreements at issue, the prohibition of selling outside the contractual territory also covers other non-member countries[356].

Having concluded that the agreement in *Javico* did not have as its object the restriction of competition, the ECJ went on to consider whether it might have this effect.

The *Javico* judgment is easy to understand, given that the export ban was not imposed on a distributor within the EU, but rather concerned exports from Russia and the Ukraine. A more surprising judgment was *GlaxoSmithKline v Commission*[357] where the CFI held that an indirect export ban imposed on Spanish distributors of pharmaceutical products, which the Commission had held restricted competition by object[358], did not do so; the specific and unusual conditions in which pharmaceutical products are bought and sold led the CFI to this conclusion[359]. However the CFI went on to conclude that the indirect export ban did restrict competition by effect[360]. The Commission has appealed this point to the ECJ, no doubt in the hope that the ECJ will reimpose the

---

[348] Ibid, paras 64–66.   [349] Ibid, para 69.

[350] Ibid, para 68.   [351] Ibid, paras 74–110; see further ch 13, p 512.

[352] Commission decision of 19 December 2007.   [353] Ibid, paras 401–407.

[354] Case 27/87 [1988] ECR 1919, [1988] 4 CMLR 576; see similarly the Commission's decision in *Sicasov* OJ [1999] L 4/27, [1999] 4 CMLR 192, paras 53–61.

[355] Case C-306/96 [1998] ECR I-1983, [1998] 5 CMLR 172.   [356] Ibid, para 19.

[357] Case T-168/01 *GlaxoSmithKline Services v Commission* [2006] ECR II-2969, [2006] 5 CMLR 1623, on appeal Cases C-501/06 P *GlaxoSmithKline Services v Commission*, not yet decided, and C-513/06 P *Commission v GlaxoSmithKline Services*, not yet decided; for comment on the CFI judgment see Junod 'An End to Parallel Imports of Medicines? Comments on the Judgment of the Court of First Instance in *GlaxoWellcome*' (2007) 30(2) World Competition 291; Korah 'Judgment of the Court of First Instance in GlaxoSmithKline' (2007) 6 Competition Law Journal 101.

[358] Commission decision of 8 May 2001, OJ [2001] L 301/1.

[359] Case T-168/01 *GlaxoSmithKline Services v Commission* [2006] ECR II-2969, [2006] 5 CMLR 1623, paras 114–147.

[360] Ibid, paras 148–192.

'orthodox' view that direct and indirect export bans restrict competition by object; such analysis leaves the parties to the agreement free to argue that the agreement produces economic efficiencies cognisable under Article 81(3). The CFI's judgment was clearly influenced by the particular economics of the pharmaceutical industry[361]: in *General Motors BV v Commission*, which concerned an indirect ban on exports of cars from the Netherlands, neither the CFI[362] nor the ECJ[363] had any doubt that the agreements were restrictive by object; the ECJ specifically said that, where an agreement has an anti-competitive object, it does not cease to be characterised as such because it had an alternative, lawful, purpose[364].

Cases such as *Visa International*, *Erauw-Jacquery*, *Javico* and *GlaxoSmithKline* indicate that the broad headings used in the object box above may require refinement from time to time to exclude from the 'object' category some types of agreements that are not so obviously restrictive of competition as others. The size and content of the object box is capable of change over a period of time, as the Community Courts are called on to consider, or perhaps to reconsider, the restrictive nature of particular types of agreements. This process of categorisation and recategorisation is natural and to be expected, and has a parallel in the US where the courts are from time to time called upon to determine whether a particular type of agreement should be tested according to a *per se* or a rule of reason standard[365]. However the fact that such a process takes place does not call into question the underlying 'object or effect' distinction contained in Article 81(1).

(E) Agreements that have as their effect the prevention, restriction or distortion of competition

(i) Extensive analysis of an agreement in its market context is required to determine its effect[366]

Where it is not possible to say that the object of an agreement is to restrict competition, it is necessary to conduct an extensive analysis of its effect on the market before it can

---

[361] For a discussion of the specific issues in the pharmaceutical industry see Rey and Venit 'Parallel trade and pharmaceuticals: a policy in search of itself' (2004) 29 ELR 153; Holmes 'Competition, Trade and Regulation – The Application of the EC Competition Rules to the Pharmaceutical Industry' (2005) 4 Competition Law Journal 48; see also the discussion of the *Syfait* case under Article 82 in ch 17, p 700.

[362] Case T-368/00 [2003] ECR II-4491, [2004] 4 CMLR 1362; see in particular paras 97–106.

[363] Case C-551/03 P [2006] ECR I-3173, [2006] 5 CMLR 9; see in particular paras 64–80

[364] Case C-551/03 P [2006] ECR I-3173, [2006] 5 CMLR 9, para 64; the same point was made by the CFI in Cases T-49/02 etc *Brasserie Nationale SA v Commission* [2005] ECR II-3033, [2006] 4 CMLR 266, para 85.

[365] In the US see *Continental TV v GTE Sylvania* 433 US 36 (1977), where the Supreme Court overruled an earlier judgment, *US v Arnold Schwinn & Co* 388 US 365 (1967), that had subjected non-price vertical restraints to a *per se* rule; *National Society of Professional Engineers v US* 435 US 679 (1978), where a trade association's rules prohibiting competitive bidding by members were tested under the rule of reason rather than a *per se* rule; *Broadcast Music Inc v CBS* 441 US 1 (1979), where the rule of reason was applied to the rules of a copyright collecting society: the Supreme Court accepted that the agreement was a price fixing agreement 'in the literal sense', but concluded that it was not a 'naked restraint', but instead enabled copyright owners to market their product more efficiently; *State Oil Co v Khan* 522 US 3 (1997), where the Supreme Court held that maximum resale price maintenance should be tested under the rule of reason and not a *per se* standard; and *Leegin Creative Leather Products, Inc v PSKS, Inc* 551 US _ (2007) where the Supreme Court decided that agreements on *minimum* resale prices should be transferred from *per se* to rule of reason analysis.

[366] On the issue of anti-competitive effect see Odudu 'Interpreting Article 81(1): Demonstrating Restrictive Effect' (2001) 26 EL Rev 261 and Odudu 'A New Economic Approach to Article 81(1)?' (2001) 26 EL Rev 100.

be found to infringe Article 81(1). This has been stressed by the Community Courts on a number of occasions. For example, in *Brasserie de Haecht v Wilkin*[367] the ECJ said that:

it would be pointless to consider an agreement, decision or practice by reason of its effect if those effects were to be taken distinct from the market in which they are seen to operate, and could only be examined apart from the body of effects, whether convergent or not, surrounding their implementation. Thus in order to examine whether it is caught by Article [81(1)] an agreement cannot be examined in isolation from the above context, that is, from the factual or legal circumstances causing it to prevent, restrict or distort competition. The existence of similar contracts may be taken into consideration for this objective to the extent to which the general body of contracts of this type is capable of restricting the freedom of trade[368].

An important case which demonstrates the depth of analysis required in determining whether an agreement has the effect of restricting competition is *Delimitis v Henninger Bräu AG*[369]. There the ECJ considered a provision in an agreement between a brewery and a licensee of a public house owned by the brewery, whereby the licensee was required to purchase a minimum amount of beer each year. The litigation in the German courts concerned the refusal by the brewery, on termination, to return the full deposit to the licensee that he had paid when entering into the agreement: the brewery had deducted sums that it considered it was entitled to. The licensee claimed that the agreement was void and unenforceable under Article 81; an appeal court in Germany referred the case to the ECJ under Article 234 EC. The ECJ said that beer supply agreements of the type under consideration do not have as their object the restriction of competition[370]. Instead it stressed that the agreement had to be considered in the context in which it occurred[371]. To begin with it was necessary to define the relevant product and geographic markets[372]: these were defined as the sale of beer in licensed premises (as opposed to beer sold in retail outlets) in Germany. Having defined the markets, the Court then said that it was necessary to determine whether access to the market was impeded: could a new competitor enter the market, for example by buying an existing brewery together with its network of sales outlets or by opening new public houses[373]? If the answer was that access to the market was impeded, it was necessary to ask whether the agreements entered into by Henninger Bräu contributed to that foreclosure effect, for example because of their number and duration[374]. Only if the answer to both of these questions was yes could it be held that Article 81(1) was infringed. The analysis suggested in this case was specific to the issues raised by beer supply agreements, and is not necessarily the same to be deployed, for example, to restrictive covenants taken on

---

[367] Case 23/67 [1967] ECR 407, [1968] CMLR 26.

[368] Case 23/67 [1967] ECR 407, p 415, [1968] CMLR 26, p 40; see similarly Cases C-7/95 P and C-8/95 P *John Deere v Commission* [1998] ECR I-3111, [1998] 5 CMLR 311, paras 76 and 91 respectively and Cases C-215/96 and C-216/96 *Carlo Bagnsaco v BPN* [1999] ECR I-135, [1999] 4 CMLR 624, para 33.

[369] Case C-234/89 [1991] ECR I-935, [1992] 5 CMLR 210, para 13; see Korah 'The Judgment in *Delimitis*: A Milestone Towards a Realistic Assessment of the Effects of an Agreement – or a Damp Squib' (1992) 14 EIPR 167; there is a longer version in (1998) 8 Tulane European and Civil Law Forum 17; Lasok 'Assessing the Economic Consequences of Restrictive Agreements: A Comment on the Delimitis Case' (1991) 12 ECLR 194; see similarly Case C-214/99 *Neste Markkinointi Oy v Yötuuli* [2000] ECR I-11121, [2001] 4 CMLR 993; Case T-65/98 *Van den Bergh Foods Ltd v Commission* [2003] ECR II-4653, [2004] 4 CMLR 14, paras 75–119.

[370] [1991] ECR I-935, [1992] 5 CMLR 210, para 13.   [371] Ibid, para 14.

[372] Ibid, paras 16–18; on market definition see ch 1, pp 26–40.

[373] [1991] ECR I-935, [1992] 5 CMLR 210, paras 19–23.

[374] [1991] ECR I-935, [1992] 5 CMLR 210, paras 24–27.

the sale of a business[375] or to the rules of a group purchasing association[376]. However the important point about the judgment is its requirement that a full analysis of the agreement in its market context must be carried out before it is possible to determine whether its effect is to restrict competition.

Useful guidance on analysing the anti-competitive effect of an agreement can be found in the Commission's *Guidelines on the application of Article 81(3) of the Treaty*[377].

(ii) The need to establish a 'counter-factual'

In determining whether an agreement has a restrictive effect on competition, it is necessary to consider what the position would have been in the absence of the agreement[378]: by comparing the two situations it should be possible to form a view as to whether the agreement could restrict competition. The need to examine the 'counter-factual' was stressed by the CFI in *O2 (Germany) GmbH & Co, OHG v Commission*[379], where it annulled a Commission decision[380] finding that a roaming agreement in the mobile telephony sector had the effect of restricting competition: the Commission had failed to show what the position would have been in the absence of the agreement, or that the agreement could have restrictive effects on competition[381].

(iii) Cases in which agreements containing contractual restrictions were found not to have anti-competitive effects

The point was made earlier that a contractual restriction does not necessarily result in a restriction of competition[382]. There have been many judgments in which the Community Courts have concluded that agreements containing contractual restrictions did not have the effect of restricting competition. Several of these cases were Article 234 references, where one party was trying to avoid a contractual restriction freely entered into by invoking Article 81(2) of the Treaty – which says that agreements that infringe Article 81 are void – in litigation in a national court.

The first case of note was as long ago as 1966: in *Société Technique Minière v Maschinenbau Ulm*[383] the ECJ said that a term conferring exclusivity on a distributor might not infringe Article 81(1) where this seemed to be 'really necessary for the penetration of a new area by an undertaking'. Two weeks later, the ECJ in *Consten and Grundig v Commission*[384] reached the conclusion that an agreement conferring absolute territorial protection on a distributor had as its object the restriction of competition and did not satisfy the criteria of Article 81(3). These two judgments are highly instructive. *Société Technique Minière* shows that simply granting exclusive rights to a territory, without export bans, may not infringe Article 81(1) at all: it is an empirical question whether such an agreement, assessed in its market context, has a restrictive effect;

---

[375] On agreements of this kind see *Remia BV and Verenidge Bedrijven and Nutricia v Commission*, p 125 below.

[376] On agreements of this kind see *Gøttrup-Klim Grovvareforeninger v Dansk Landburgs Grovvareselskab AmbA*, pp 125–126 below.

[377] OJ [2004] C 101/97, paras 24–27.

[378] See Case 56/65 *Société Technique Minière* [1966] ECR 235, pp 249–250.

[379] Case T-328/03 [2006] ECR II-1231, [2006] 5 CMLR 258.

[380] *T-Mobile Deutschland/O2 Germany: Network Sharing Rahmenvertrag* OJ [2004] L 75/32.

[381] See in particular paras 65–117 of the CFI's judgment.   [382] See p 115 above.

[383] Case 56/65 [1966] ECR 235, p 250, [1966] CMLR 357, p 375.

[384] Cases 56 and 58/64 [1966] ECR 299, [1966] CMLR 418.

Consten and Grundig, however, shows that where an agreement goes further, imposing export bans and preventing the possibility of parallel trade, it is considered by law to have as its object the restriction of competition. There is no better illustration of the impact of the 'single market imperative'[385] than this.

In *Metro SB–Grossmärkte v Commission*[386] the ECJ held that restrictive provisions in a selective distribution system may fall outside Article 81(1) where they satisfy objective, qualitative criteria and are applied in a non-discriminatory manner[387]. In *LC Nungesser KG v Commission*[388] the ECJ held that an open exclusive licence of plant breeders' rights would not infringe Article 81(1) where, on the facts of the case, the licensee would not have risked investing in the production of maize seeds at all without some immunity from intra-brand competition[389]. In *Coditel v Ciné Vog Films SA (No 2)*[390] the ECJ held that an exclusive copyright licence to exhibit a film in a Member State would not neces-sarily infringe Article 81(1), even where this might prevent transmission of that film by cable broadcasting from a neighbouring Member State, where this was necessary to protect the investment of the licensee. Restrictive covenants may fall outside Article 81(1), provided that they are duly limited in time, space and subject-matter; in other words that they satisfy the principle of proportionality. This was established by the Commission in *Reuter/BASF*[391], and confirmed by the ECJ in *Remia BV and Verenidge Bedrijven and Nutricia v Commission*[392]; there the Court recognised that, in order to effect the sale of a business together with its associated goodwill, it may be necessary that the vendor should be restricted from competing with the purchaser; in the absence of such a covenant it may not be possible to sell the business at all. In *Métropole télévi-sion v Commission*[393] the CFI held that an ancillary restriction is one that is 'directly related and necessary to the implementation of a main operation'[394], and said that this is a 'relatively abstract' matter that does not require a full market analysis[395]. The *Remia* doctrine allows the purchaser of a business to be protected from its vendor: it does not apply in the reverse situation[396].

In *Pronuptia de Paris v Schillgalis*[397] the ECJ held that many restrictive provisions in franchising agreements designed to protect the intellectual property rights of the franchisor and to maintain the common identity of the franchise system fall outside Article 81(1). In *Erauw-Jacquery Sprl v La Hesbignonne Société Coopérative*[398] the ECJ held that a provision preventing a licensee from exporting basic seeds protected by plant breeders' rights could fall outside Article 81(1) where it was necessary to protect the right of the licensor to select his licensees. In *Gøttrup-Klim Grovvareforeninger v*

---

[385] See ch 1, pp 22–23 and ch 2, pp 51–52. [386] Case 26/76 [1977] ECR 1875, [1978] 2 CMLR 1.

[387] See ch 16, pp 630–635. [388] Case 258/78 [1982] ECR 2015, [1983] 1 CMLR 278.

[389] See ch 19, pp 764–765. [390] Case 262/81 [1982] ECR 3381, [1983] 1 CMLR 49.

[391] OJ [1976] L 254/40, [1976] 2 CMLR D44. [392] Case 42/84 [1985] ECR 2545, [1987] 1 CMLR 1.

[393] Case T-112/99 [2001] ECR II-2459, [2001] 5 CMLR 1236.

[394] [2001] ECR II-2459, [2001] 5 CMLR 1236, para 104, citing the Commission's *Notice on Ancillary Restraints* OJ [1990] C 203/5, which has since been replaced by the *Notice on restrictions directly related and necessary to concentrations* OJ [2005] C 56/24; ancillary restraints are discussed further in the context of the EC Merger Regulation: see ch 21, pp 870–871.

[395] [2001] ECR II-2459, [2001] 5 CMLR 1236, para 109; on ancillary restraints under Article 81 see the Commission's *Guidelines on the application of Article 81(3) of the Treaty*, OJ [2004] C 101/8, paras 28–31.

[396] *Quantel International-Continuum/Quantel SA* OJ [1992] L 235/9, [1993] 5 CMLR 497, para 42.

[397] Case 161/84 [1986] ECR 353, [1986] 1 CMLR 414.

[398] Case 27/87 [1988] ECR 1919, [1988] 4 CMLR 576, see similarly the Commission's decision in *Sicasov* OJ [1999] L 4/27, [1999] 4 CMLR 192, para 53–61.

Dansk Landburgs Grovvareselskab AmbA[399] the ECJ held that a provision in the statutes of a cooperative purchasing association, forbidding its members from participating in other forms of organised cooperation which were in direct competition with it, did not necessarily restrict competition, and may even have beneficial effects on competition[400]; it was necessary to consider the effect of the provision on the market, and it would not be caught by Article 81(1) if it was restricted to what was necessary to ensure that the cooperative could function properly and maintain its contractual power in relation to the suppliers with which it had to deal[401]. The ECJ subsequently applied *Gøttrup-Klim* in *Dijkstra v Friesland Coöperatie BA*[402] and in *Luttikhuis v Verenigde Coöperatieve Melkindustrie Coberco BA*[403]; so did the Commission in *P and I Clubs*[404].

(iv) Commercial ancillarity

These judgments of the Community Courts show that, when considering whether an agreement has the effect of restricting competition, it is possible to argue successfully that restrictions which are necessary to enable the parties to an agreement to achieve a legitimate commercial purpose fall outside Article 81(1): the legitimate purposes under consideration were of various kinds: for example the penetration of a new market, the sale of a business, and the successful establishment of a group purchasing association. An idea that unifies these judgments is that the restrictions found to fall outside Article 81(1) were ancillary to a legitimate commercial operation, and the expression 'commercial ancillarity' might be helpful in understanding that group of cases[405]; they can be distinguished from the judgment of the ECJ in *Wouters*, discussed in the next section, which recognises the idea of 'regulatory ancillarity'.

(v) Regulatory ancillarity: the judgment of the ECJ in *Wouters*

In the cases discussed in the previous section the ECJ concluded that restrictions in agreements fell outside Article 81(1) where they were necessary to facilitate a commercial activity. In *Wouters v Algemene Raad van de Nederlandsche Orde van Advocaten*[406] the ECJ dealt with a rather different situation. In that case Mr Wouters challenged a rule adopted by the Dutch Bar Council which prohibited lawyers in the Netherlands from entering into partnership with non-lawyers: Mr Wouters wished to practise as a lawyer in a firm of accountants. A number of questions were referred to the ECJ as to the compatibility of such a rule with EC competition law. In its judgment the Court, consisting of 13 judges, stated that a prohibition of multi-disciplinary partnerships 'is liable to

---

[399] Case C-250/92 [1994] ECR I-5641, [1996] 4 CMLR 191.   [400] Ibid, para 34.

[401] Ibid, paras 35–45.   [402] Cases 319/93 etc [1995] ECR I-4471, [1996] 5 CMLR 178.

[403] Case C-399/93 [1995] ECR I-4515, [1996] 5 CMLR 178, paras 14 and 18.

[404] OJ [1999] L 125/12, [1999] 5 CMLR 646, para 66 ff.

[405] The term 'commercial ancillarity' is used here to connote a broader concept than the narrowly-focused 'ancillary restraints doctrine' considered in the *Métropole* judgment discussed above and in ch 21 at pp 870–871.

[406] Case C-309/99 [2002] ECR I-1577, [2002] 4 CMLR 913; for comment on this case see Vossestein (2002) 39 CML Rev 841; Monti 'Article 81 EC and Public Policy' (2002) 39 CML Rev 1057; O'Loughlin 'EC Competition Rules and Free Movement Rules: An Examination of the Parallels and their Furtherance by the ECJ *Wouters* Decision' (2003) 24 ECLR 62; Loozen 'Professional ethics and restraints of competition' (2006) 31 EL Rev 28; see also the judgment of the High Court in Ireland that the Medical Council of Ireland was not subject to competition law when making and applying professional rules in *Hemat v The Medical Council*, [2006] IEHC 187; the case is noted by Ahern at (2007) 28 ECLR 366.

limit production and technical development within the meaning of Article [81(1)(b)] of the Treaty'[407]; it also considered that the rule had an effect on trade between Member States[408]. However, at paragraph 97 of its judgment the Court stated:

However, not every agreement between undertakings or any decision of an association of under-takings which restricts the freedom of action of the parties or of one of them necessarily falls within the prohibition laid down in Article [81(1)] of the Treaty. For the purposes of application of that provision to a particular case, account must first of all be taken of the overall context in which the decision of the association of undertakings was taken or produces its effects. More particularly, account must be taken of its objectives, which are here connected with the need to make rules relating to organisation, qualifications, professional ethics, supervision and liability, in order to ensure that the ultimate consumers of legal services and the sound administration of justice are provided with the necessary guarantees in relation to integrity and experience...It has then to be considered whether the consequential effects restrictive of competition are inherent in the pursuit of those objectives[409].

This is a most interesting, and controversial, judgment. The early part of the judgment reads as though the Court would conclude that Article 81(1) was infringed, whereas from paragraph 97 onwards it explains why Article 81(1) would not be infringed if the rule in question could 'reasonably be considered to be necessary in order to ensure the proper practice of the legal profession, as it is organised in [the Netherlands]'[410]. The judgment means that, in certain cases, it is possible to balance *non-competition* object-ives against a restriction of competition, and to conclude that the former outweigh the latter, with the consequence that there is no infringement of Article 81(1). The Court does not make findings of fact in an Article 234 reference; rather it gives a preliminary ruling which the domestic court must apply to the case before it. However, it is clear that the judgment provides a basis on which the Dutch court could decide that the rule in question did not infringe Article 81(1). It also would seem from paragraphs 107 and 108 of the *Wouters* judgment that the ECJ was disinclined to interfere with the Bar Council's assessment of the need for, and content of, the rules in question; the position should be contrasted with Article 81(3), where the burden of proof rests on the undertaking(s) defending the agreement and where the Commission insists on convincing evidence of economic efficiencies[411].

Numerous questions arise from the judgment in *Wouters*. First, why did the ECJ decide that Article 81(1) was not applicable? Secondly, how does this judgment fit with those discussed in section (iii) above? Thirdly, how broad is the rule in *Wouters*? Finally, could the Court have decided the case in a different way, but still have come to the conclusion that the rule in question did not infringe Article 81?

(A) Why was Article 81(1) not applicable? On the first point, the ECJ must have felt that it was appropriate to establish that 'reasonable' regulatory rules fall outside Article 81(1): the fact that this judgment was delivered soon after the debacle of the collapse of Enron, apparently in part due to ineffective regulation of accountancy firms, may have con-tributed to the sympathetic treatment of the particular rule in question. Furthermore, it is possible that the Court was deliberately trying to reach a similar outcome under Article 81 to that which would have been achieved under Article 49 of the EC Treaty had

---

[407] [2002] ECR I-1577, [2002] 4 CMLR 913, para 90; see also paras 86 and 94.   [408] Ibid, para 95.

[409] To similar effect see Case T-144/99 *Institut des Mandataires Agréés v Commission* [2001] ECR II-1087, [2001] 5 CMLR 77, para 78.

[410] [2001] ECR I-1577, [2002] 4 CMLR 913, para 107.   [411] See ch 4, pp 149–150.

the case been argued under the provisions on the free movement of services. It might have been the case that the rule in question had been adopted by the Dutch Government itself, if the regulatory regime for the legal profession in the Netherlands had been different: in that case the rule could not have been challenged under Article 81(1), but might have been under Article 49. Under that provision a Member State may adopt rules which restrict the free movement of services to the extent that they are necessary to achieve a legitimate public interest[412]; the judgment in *Wouters* effectively applies the same reasoning to a case in which the regulatory function was not carried out by a Member State, and so was not susceptible to challenge under Article 49, but by a private body empowered by the State to adopt regulatory rules, subject to control, if at all, under the competition rules[413].

(B) The relationship between the judgment in Wouters *and earlier case law of the Community Courts* On the second point, the judgment in *Wouters* does have a conceptual similarity to the cases discussed in section (iii) above, in that they all are concerned with the idea of ancillarity: restrictions on conduct, even ones that, in a colloquial sense, appear to restrict competition, do not infringe Article 81(1) where they are ancillary to some other legitimate purpose. What is of interest about *Wouters*, however, is that the restriction in that case was not necessary for the execution of a commercial transaction or the achievement of a commercial outcome on the market; instead it was ancillary to a regulatory function 'to ensure that the ultimate consumers of legal services and the sound administration of justice are provided with the necessary guarantees in relation to integrity and experience'[414]. This seems to be a different application of the concept of ancillarity from that in the earlier case law: the *Wouters* case is concerned with what could be described as 'regulatory' ancillarity, whereas earlier judgments were concerned with 'commercial ancillarity'; perhaps the use of these two terms would be useful in, first, demonstrating a continuity with the earlier case law, through the common use of the idea of ancillarity, while also capturing the difference between the two situations, by distinguishing commercial and regulatory cases.

(C) How broad is the rule in Wouters? On the third point, that is the breadth of the rule in *Wouters*, there is nothing in the judgment itself that expressly limits its application to so-called 'deontological' (that is to say professional ethical) rules for the regulation of the legal profession, nor to the liberal professions generally. The ECJ's judgment in *Meca-Medina v Commission*[415] confirms that the *Wouters* doctrine can apply to other

---

[412] See eg Case 33/74 *Van Binsbergen v Bestuur Van de Bedrijfsvereniging voor de Metaalnijverheid* [1974] ECR 1299, [1975] 1 CMLR 298, para 14.

[413] The Court cited Case 107/83 *Klopp* [1984] ECR 2971, para 17 and Case C-3/95 *Reisebüro Broede* [1996] ECR I-6511, para 37, cases on Article 49 EC, in para 99 of its judgment in *Wouters*: in these cases it had held that, in the absence of specific Community rules in the field, each Member State is in principle free to regulate the exercise of the legal profession in its territory; on the point discussed in the text see Monti 'Article 81 EC and Public Policy' (2002) 39 CML Rev 1057, in particular at pp 1086–1090, and Mortelmans 'Towards Convergence in the Application of the Rules on Free Movement and on Competition?' (2001) 38 CML Rev 613; see also O'Loughlin 'EC Competition Rules and Free Movement Rules: An Examination of the Parallels and their Furtherance by the ECJ *Wouters* Decision' (2003) 24 ECLR 62.

[414] Case C-309/99 *Wouters v Algemene Raad van de Nederlandsche Orde van Advocaten* [2002] ECR I-1577, [2002] 4 CMLR 913, para 97.

[415] Case C-519/04 P [2006] ECR I-6991, [2006] 5 CMLR 1023; see Weatherill 'Anti-doping revisited – the demise of the rule of "purely sporting interest"?' (2006) 27 ECLR 645.

regulatory rules. In *Meca-Medina* the Commission rejected a complaint by two swim-
mers that the anti-doping rules of the International Swimming Federation, for which
the International Olympic Committee was ultimately responsible, infringed Article 81.
The ECJ concluded that the Commission was entitled to decide that the rules had a legitimate objective: to combat doping in order for competitive sport to be conducted fairly,
including the need to safeguard equal chances for athletes, athletes' health, the integrity
and objectivity of competitive sport and ethical values in sport[416]; the Court went on to
decide that the restrictions of competition inherent in the rules were proportionate[417].
The *Meca-Medina* judgment justifies the way in which the Commission had dismissed,
in June 2002, a complaint by ENIC plc against rules of UEFA, the body responsible for
the Champions League football tournament, which restricted the ownership of shares
in more than one football team competing in the Champions League. The Commission
expressly stated that the rules in question were necessary to protect the integrity of the
tournament and were therefore, pursuant to *Wouters*, outside Article 81(1)[418]: spectators
would not be confident that the results of football matches were genuine if the same
person controlled opposing teams[419]. An important case pending before the ECJ should
shed further light on the scope of the *Wouters* judgment, in which the right of national
football associations to insist on their nationals being made available by their clubs for
international matches without compensation is being tested[420].

In the *Wouters* case the rules under scrutiny undoubtedly had a public law character: Dutch legislation provided for the regulation of the legal profession, albeit that
the rule-making function belonged to a private law association of undertakings. In
Meca-Medina the International Olympic Committee was responsible for the regulatory system: the IOC is a creature of public international law, which may explain the
ECJ's willingness to apply the *Wouters* doctrine in that case. An intriguing question
for the future is whether *Wouters* could be extended yet further, to a purely private
regulatory system where there is no public component at all. Many sporting organisations have a purely private law character, such as the Football Association in the UK:
the ECJ may be prepared to extend the *Wouters* case to such bodies. However other
cases are less easy to predict: for example, suppose that firms in a particular sector were
to adopt rules for the protection of the environment on their own initiative, without
any encouragement by the kind cognisable under Article 81(3): it remains to be seen
whether *Wouters* could be invoked in such a case. In *Hilti v Commission*[421] the CFI said
that, where there is a public authority with powers, for example, in relation to product
safety, it is not for private undertakings to take private initiatives to eliminate products
that they consider to be unsafe[422].

(D) Could the ECJ in Wouters *have reached the same conclusion by a different route?* On
the fourth point, it is interesting to consider whether the ECJ could have reached the
conclusion that there was no infringement of the competition rules in *Wouters* by some
other route than the one it adopted. Perhaps the most obvious alternative solution
would have been to hold that the rules did infringe Article 81(1) – as noted, the Court

---

[416] Case C-519/04 P [2006] ECR I-6991, [2006] 5 CMLR 1023, paras 42–45.   [417] Ibid, paras 47–56.

[418] Commission Press Release IP/02/942, 27 June 2002.

[419] See further pp 130–131 below on the application of Article 81 to sporting rules.

[420] Case C-243/06 *SA Sporting du Pays de Charleroi and Groupement des Clubs de football européens* (usually referred to as the *Oulmers* case), not yet decided.

[421] Case T-30/89 [1991] ECR II-1439, [1992] 4 CMLR 16.   [422] Ibid, para 118.

did say that the prohibition on multi-disciplinary partnerships was liable to limit production and technical development within the meaning of Article 81(1)(b) – but that
they satisfied the terms of Article 81(3)[423]. However this approach was not available in
Wouters since, at the relevant time, a decision under Article 81(3) could be made only
by the Commission pursuant to a notification under Article 4 of Regulation 17 and
no notification had been made. It was not open to the ECJ to apply the provisions of
Article 86(2) EC, since the Bar Council itself was not an entrusted undertaking[424]. The
Court could have concluded that there was no effect on trade between Member States,
so that Article 81(1) did not apply, thereby in effect referring the matter back to The
Netherlands for the application of Dutch competition law; however it expressly held
that trade between Member States was affected[425].

(vi) The application of Article 81(1) to sporting rules[426]

This discussion of the *Wouters* judgment provides an opportunity for a brief diversion, to discuss the application of Article 81(1) to sporting rules. All sports have rules:
footballers, with the exception of goalkeepers, cannot handle the ball; boxers must not
hit 'below the belt'; javelin throwers should not throw the javelin at other javelin throwers. These are 'the rules of the game', and self-evidently do not infringe Article 81(1).
Similarly, all sports have disciplinary rules: violent conduct can lead to suspension;
taking prohibited drugs may lead to bans. Again, football clubs that belong to one
league will be prohibited from belonging to another one. A conundrum for EC competition law has been to determine whether, and if so when, sporting rules might infringe
Article 81 or 82. It is clear that some rules could have restrictive effects on competition
in the market, for example where they go beyond 'the rules of the game' and instead
distort competition in neighbouring broadcasting markets[427].

   In the *Meca-Medina* case discussed above, the CFI had held that a sporting rule
that 'has nothing to do with any economic consideration'[428] falls entirely outside
Articles 81 and 82. On appeal the ECJ held that this was an error of law on the CFI's
part and therefore set the judgment aside[429]. The ECJ's approach is clearly preferable to
that of the CFI: the CFI's judgment would mean that sporting rules could not be scru-

---

   [423] On this point see Case No. 1003/2/1/01 *Institute of Independent Insurance Brokers v Director General
of Fair Trading* [2001] CAT 4, [2001] CompAR 62, paras 168–178, in which the UK Competition Appeal
Tribunal considered that the regulatory rules of the General Insurance Standards Council infringed s 2 of
the Competition Act 1998 (the domestic equivalent of Article 81(1)), and should have been examined under
ss 4 and 9 of that Act (the equivalent of Article 81(3)): see further ch 9, pp 335–336.
   [424] See ch 6, pp 233–239 on the derogation from the application of Articles 81 and 82 provided by
Article 86(2).
   [425] Case C-309/99 [2002] ECR I-1577, [2002] 4 CMLR 913, para 95.
   [426] For a general discussion of EC law and sport see Weatherill ' "Fair Play Please": Recent Developments
in the Application of EC law to Sport' (2003) 40 CML Rev 51; Van den Bogaert and Vermeersch 'Sport and
the EC Treaty: a Tale of Uneasy Bedfellows?' (2006) 31 ECLR 821; Szyszcak 'Competition and sport' (2007)
32 ELRev 95; Kienapfel and Stein 'The application of Articles 81 and 82 EC in the sport sector' *Competition
Policy Newsletter*, Number 3, 2007, 6; the Opinion of Advocate General Kokott in Case C-49/07 *MOTOE*,
6 March 2008; note also the Commission's *Declaration on Sport*, annexed to the final act of the Treaty of
Amsterdam, OJ [1997] C 340/136. For the position in the US see *National Collegiate Athletic Association v
Board of Regents of University of Oklahoma* 468 US 85 (1984).
   [427] On the joint selling of sporting rights see ch 13, p 509.
   [428] Case T-313/02 [2004] ECR II-3291, [2004] 3 CMLR 1314, para 47.
   [429] Case C-519/04 P [2006] ECR I-6991, [2006] 5 CMLR 1023, paras 33 and 34.

tinised at all under the competition provisions, whereas the ECJ's means that they can be tested for anti-competitive effects, albeit that they might be permissible by virtue of the *Wouters* doctrine.

(vii) Have the Community Courts embraced the 'rule of reason'?

As mentioned above, critics of Article 81(1) complain that it is applied to too many agreements; they argue for the application of a 'rule of reason', which would result in fewer agreements being caught. The judgments that have just been discussed raise the question of whether the Community Courts have adopted a rule of reason under Article 81(1). Discussion of the rule of reason under Article 81(1) is often very imprecise. It is sometimes used as little more than a slogan by opponents of the judgments of the Courts and, in particular, decisions of the Commission. In so far as the call for a rule of reason is a request for good rather than bad, or reasonable rather than unreasonable, judgments and decisions, noone could disagree with it. However, if proponents of the rule of reason mean that US jurisprudence on the rule of reason under the Sherman Act 1890 should be incorporated into EC competition law, this seems to be misplaced: EC law is different in many ways from US law, not least in that it has the 'bifurcation' of Article 81(1) and Article 81(3), which does not exist in the Sherman Act, and that it is concerned with the promotion of a single market as well as with 'conventional' competition law concerns[430].

(A) The rule of reason in US law In US law the rule of reason has a particular meaning. In *Continental TV Inc v GTE Sylvania* the Supreme Court defined the rule of reason as calling for a case-by-case evaluation 'that is, the factfinder weighs all the circumstances of a case in deciding whether a restrictive practice should be prohibited as imposing an unreasonable restraint on competition'[431]. In particular this means that, when determining whether an agreement restrains trade in the sense of section 1 of the Sherman Act, it is necessary to balance the agreement's pro- and anti-competitive effects; where the latter outweigh the former, the agreement will be unlawful. However US and EC competition law are materially different in numerous respects, and terminology should not be imported from US law that could blur this significant fact[432]. The fact that the ECJ has handed down reasonable judgments does not mean that it has adopted the rule of reason in the sense in which that expression is used in the US. Various commentators have argued against incorporation into EC law of a rule of reason modelled upon US experience[433]. In its *White Paper on Modernisation*[434] the Commission said that it did not see the adoption of the rule of reason as a solution to the problems of enforcement and procedure that it had identified. In particular, it said that it would 'be paradoxical to

---

[430] See ch 1, pp 22–23 and ch 2, pp 51–52.

[431] US 36, 49 (1977); see also *National Collegiate Athletic Association v Board of Regents of University of Oklahoma* 468 US 85 (1984); *California Dental Association v Federal Trade Commission* 526 US 756 (1999); for discussion of the rule of reason in US law see Areeda and Hovenkamp *Antitrust Law* Vol VII, ch 15 (2nd ed, 2003); Hovenkamp *Federal Antitrust Policy: The Law of Competition and its Practice* (West Publishing Company, 2nd ed, 2000), paras 6.4, 11.1, 11.2 and 11.6.

[432] See Whish and Sufrin 'Article [81] and the Rule of Reason' (1987) 7 Ox YEL 1.

[433] *Whish and Sufrin* (1987) 7 Ox YEL 1; Waelbroeck 'Vertical Agreements: is the Commission Right not to Follow the US Policy?' (1985) 25 Swiss Rev ICL; Schröter 'Antitrust Analysis and Article [81(1)] and (3)' [1987] Fordham Corp L Inst (ed Hawk), ch 27; Caspari (formerly Director General of DG COMP at the Commission) [1987] Fordham Corp L Inst (ed Hawk), p 361.

[434] OJ [1999] C 132/1, [1999] 5 CMLR 208.

cast aside Article [81(3)] when that provision in fact contains all the elements of a "rule of reason"' and that the adoption of the rule of reason under Article 81(1) would 'run the risk of diverting Article [81(3)] from its purpose, which is to provide a legal framework for the economic assessment of restrictive practices and not to allow application of the competition rules to be set aside because of political considerations'[435].

(B) The judgment of the CFI in Métropole In *Métropole Télévision v Commission*[436] the CFI expressly rejected the suggestion that a rule of reason existed under Article 81(1). Six television companies in France had established a joint venture, Télévision par Satellite ('TPS'), to devise, develop and broadcast digital pay-TV services in French in Europe: TPS would be a competitor to the dominant pay-TV company, Canal+. The parties notified a number of agreements to the Commission. In 1999 the Commission adopted a decision that the creation of TPS was not caught by Article 81(1); however it concluded that a non-competition clause, preventing the parents of TPS from becoming involved in other digital pay-TV satellite companies, could be cleared (that is, found not to infringe Article 81(1)) for a period of three years; and that clauses giving TPS rights of pre-emption in relation to certain channels and services offered by its parents and exclusive rights to other channels infringed Article 81(1) but could be exempted under Article 81(3) for three years. Four of the shareholders in TPS applied to the CFI requesting that the Commission's decision should be annulled. They argued that the Commission should have applied the rule of reason, according to which 'an anti-competitive practice falls outside Article [81(1)] of the Treaty if it has more positive than negative effects on competition on a given market'[437]; in particular the clauses in the agreements giving TPS rights of pre-emption and exclusivity would enable it to enter the market dominated by Canal+, and therefore would 'favour' new competition[438]. Several well-known judgments of the ECJ and CFI were cited in support of this version of the rule of reason[439]. What is of interest is the explicit way in which the CFI's judgment rejected the applicants' argument:

72. According to the applicants, as a consequence of the existence of a rule of reason in Community competition law, when Article [81(1)] of the Treaty is applied it is necessary to weigh the pro and anti-competitive effects of an agreement in order to determine whether it is caught by the prohibition laid down in that article. It should, however, be observed, first of all, that contrary to the applicant's assertions the existence of such a rule has not, as such, been confirmed by the Community courts. Quite the contrary, in various judgments the Court of Justice and the Court of First Instance have been at pains to indicate that the existence of a rule of reason in Community competition law is doubtful[440].

The CFI went on to say that the pro- and anti-competitive aspects of a restriction of competition should be weighed at the stage of considering whether an agreement satisfies the terms of Article 81(3)[441]: in the CFI's view:

Article [81(3)] would lose much of its effectiveness if such an examination had to be carried out already under Article [81(1)] of the Treaty[442].

---

[435] OJ [1999] C 132/1, [1999] 5 CMLR 208, para 57.
[436] Case T-112/99 [2001] ECR II-2459, [2001] 5 CMLR 1236: for comment on this case see Manzini 'The European Rule of Reason – Crossing the Sea of Doubt' (2002) 23 ECLR 392.
[437] Case T-112/99 [2001] ECR II-2459 [2001] 5 CMLR 1236, para 68.   [438] Ibid, para 69.
[439] Ibid, paras 68 and 70, referring, *inter alia*, to Case 258/78 *Nungesser and Eisele v Commission (Maize Seeds)* [1982] ECR 2015; Case 262/81 *Coditel v Ciné Vog Films* [1982] ECR 3381 and Cases T-374/94 etc *European Night Services v Commission* [1998] ECR II-3141.
[440] Case T-112/99 [2001] ECR II-2459 [2001] 5 CMLR 1236, para 72.
[441] [2001] ECR II-2459 [2001] 5 CMLR 1236, para 74.   [442] Ibid, para 74.

The CFI acknowledged that in various judgments the Community Courts have been 'more flexible' in their interpretation of Article 81(1), but concluded that this did not mean that they had adopted the 'rule of reason' in the sense argued for by the applicants[443]. Rather, the more flexible judgments of the Courts demonstrate that they are not willing to find a restriction 'wholly abstractly'; instead a full market analysis is required[444]. The CFI came to the same conclusion in *Van den Bergh Foods Ltd v Commission*[445] and in *O2 (Germany) GmbH & Co, OHG v Commission*[446]. The Commission cites the *Métropole* judgment in paragraph 11 of its *Guidelines on the application of Article 81(3) of the Treaty* in support of its proposition that '[t]he balancing of anti-competitive and pro-competitive effects is conducted exclusively within the framework laid down by Article 81(3)'[447].

(C) Comment In the author's view the judgment in *Métropole* was correct to reject the US-style rule of reason in Article 81(1). Of course, the Commission and the Courts should be 'reasonable' when applying Article 81(1), but that does not mean that they should import the method of analysis adopted in the quite different context of the Sherman Act. An interesting question is whether the judgment of the ECJ in *Wouters* should be read as importing a rule of reason under Article 81(1)[448]. The doctrine of regulatory ancillarity in that case provides for a balancing of any restriction of competition against the reasonableness of regulatory rules adopted for non-competition reasons; as such, it appears to this author that the *Wouters* judgment does not apply a US-style rule of reason, and it is preferable not to use this expression in order to explain it[449].

(viii) Actual and potential competition

In deciding whether Article 81 is infringed the Commission and the Community Courts will not limit their consideration to whether existing competition will be restricted by the agreement; they will also take into account the possibility that an agreement might affect potential competition in a particular market. Following criticism of its overly interventionist approach in the 1980s the Commission shifted its perception of 'potential competition' under Article 81(1), and it now adopts a more realistic view of the expression so that fewer agreements are caught than previously[450]. The CFI in *European Night Services v Commission*[451] rejected in its entirety a finding of the Commission that the establishment of the joint venture European Night

---

[443] Ibid, paras 75–76.   [444] Ibid, para 76.

[445] Case T-65/98 [2003] ECR II-4653, [2004] 4 CMLR 14, para 106.

[446] Case T-328/03 [2006] ECR II-1231, [2006] 5 CMLR 258, para 69; for discussion of this case see Marquis 'O2(Germany) v Commission and the exotic mysteries of Article 81(1) EC' (2007) 21 ELR 29.

[447] OJ [2004] C 101/8.

[448] See Korah 'Rule of reason: apparent inconsistency in the case law under Article 81' (2002) 1 Competition Law Insight 24.

[449] An alternative would be to refer to the rule in *Wouters* as a 'European style rule of reason': see Monti 'Article 81 EC and Public Policy' (2002) 39 CML Rev 1057.

[450] See eg *Konsortium ECR 900* OJ [1990] L 228/31, [1992] 4 CMLR 54; *Elopak/Metal Box—Odin* OJ [1990] L 209/15, [1991] 4 CMLR 832; Commission's *Guidance on Horizontal Cooperation Agreements* OJ [2001] C 3/2, [2001] 4 CMLR 819, para 9 and footnotes 8 and 9; see further ch 15, p 576.

[451] Cases T-374/94 etc [1998] ECR II-3141, [1998] 5 CMLR 718.

Services Ltd could restrict actual or potential competition between its parents: the Court considered this to be:

a hypothesis unsupported by any evidence or any analysis of the structure of the relevant market from which it might be concluded that it represented a real, concrete possibility[452].

However, the Commission would be erring in law if it were to disregard altogether the impact of an agreement on potential competition[453].

(ix) Joint ventures

Article 81(1) does not apply to full-function joint ventures, which are dealt with under the provisions on merger control: this is explained in chapter 21[454].

(F) Article 86(2)

Article 86(2) precludes the application of the competition rules to undertakings in so far as compliance with them would obstruct them in the performance of a task entrusted to them by a Member State. This subject is dealt with in chapter 6[455].

(G) State compulsion

The competition rules do not apply to undertakings in so far as they are compelled by law to behave in a particular way. The 'state compulsion' defence has been raised on numerous occasions, but has always failed. In *Wood Pulp*[456] the Commission concluded that the defence was not available to parties to an agreement within the US Webb–Pomerene Act 1918, which allows US exporters to form cartels, as that Act merely authorises cartels, but does not compel firms to enter into them. In *ENI/Montedison*[457] the parties to a restructuring agreement in the thermoplastics sector claimed that there was no infringement of Article 81(1) as they were acting under directives from the Italian Government as set out in its 'Chemical Plan'. The Commission rejected this: the role of Government planning in this case was not so large as to absolve the parties of responsibility for their agreements. In *Aluminium Products*[458] parties to a cartel agreement in the aluminium industry argued that their conduct was known of and encouraged by the UK Government. The Commission held that there was no compulsion by the Government, nor indeed did there appear to be any legislative mechanism whereby there could be such compulsion. The fact of approval and encouragement did not in itself override the free will of the undertakings in question to make their own commercial decisions.

In *SSI*[459] Dutch cigarette producers argued that they had entered into various agreements because, at meetings with Government representatives, the Government had explained its objectives which included the raising of substantial tax revenue; the undertakings had merely fallen in line with what they considered the Government expected

---

[452] [1998] ECR II-3141, [1998] 5 CMLR 718, paras 139–147.

[453] See Case C-504/93 *Tiercé-Ladbroke v Commission* [1997] ECR II-923, [1997] 5 CMLR 309, where the CFI annulled a Commission decision which failed to take into account a possible restriction of potential competition.

[454] Ch 21, pp 826–827.   [455] See ch 6, pp 233–239.   [456] OJ [1985] L 85/1, [1985] 3 CMLR 474.

[457] OJ [1987] L 5/13, [1988] 4 CMLR 444, para 25.   [458] OJ [1985] L 92/1, [1987] 3 CMLR 813.

[459] OJ [1982] L 232/1, [1982] 3 CMLR 702.

of them. The Commission rejected this argument, holding that the Government had not compelled any particular form of behaviour or required them to enter into agreements prohibited by Article 81. The Commission's decision was upheld on appeal[460]. In *French-West African Shipowners' Committee*[461] the Commission rejected the Committee's argument that the cargo-sharing system they operated fell outside Article 81 as it was imposed upon them by public authorities in various African states. In *CNSD v Commission*[462] the CFI explained that if anti-competitive conduct is required of undertakings by national legislation, or if the latter creates a legal framework which itself eliminates any possibility of competitive activity on their part, Articles 81 and 82 do not apply; however, where the legislation does not preclude them from engaging in autonomous conduct, the competition rules can apply to their behaviour.

It is clear from the foregoing that the defence of state compulsion will succeed only rarely. For a successful defence it would seem that three requirements must be satisfied. First, the state must have made certain conduct *compulsory*: mere persuasion is insufficient; secondly, the defence is available only where there is a legal basis for this compulsion: this was considered by the Commission to be relevant in *Aluminium Producers*[463]; and thirdly, there must be no latitude for individual choice as to the implementation of the governmental policy.

(H) Highly regulated markets

In some cases undertakings accused of infringing Article 81 have argued that the market on which they were operating was so highly regulated by the state that there was no latitude left for competition; therefore they could not be found guilty of agreeing to restrict competition. In *Suiker Unie v Commission*[464] such a plea succeeded. In Italy the sugar industry was highly regulated in order that supply and demand be kept in balance; for example suppliers and customers were not allowed to negotiate with one another at all. The ECJ accepted that there was no competition capable of being distorted[465]. On subsequent occasions, however, this defence has failed. It was rejected by the ECJ in two judgments involving appeals against Commission decisions applying Article 81 to the Belgian[466] and Dutch[467] tobacco industries. In the latter decision, *Re Stichting Sigarettenindustrie Agreements*[468], the Commission refused to accept that the restriction of price competition in the Dutch cigarette market did not infringe Article 81(1) because Government regulations fixed the maximum price for retailing cigarettes: the regulations still left open the possibility of competing on price, albeit within a narrower band. Indeed if anything the Governmental restriction of competition meant

---

[460] Cases 240/82 etc *SSI v Commission* [1985] ECR 3831, [1987] 3 CMLR 661.

[461] OJ [1992] L 134/1, [1993] 5 CMLR 446, paras 32–38.

[462] Case T-513/93 [2000] ECR II-1807, [2000] 5 CMLR 614, paras 58–59; see also Cases C-359/95 and 379/95 P *Commission v Ladbroke Racing* [1997] ECR I-6265, [1998] 4 CMLR 27, para 33; Case T-228/97 *Irish Sugar v Commission* [1999] ECR II-2969, [1999] 5 CMLR 1300, para 130.

[463] OJ [1985] L 92/1, [1987] 3 CMLR 813.   [464] Cases 40/73 etc [1975] ECR 1663, [1976] 1 CMLR 295.

[465] In different proceedings the national regulations were themselves held to be unlawful under the Treaty provisions on the free movement of goods: Cases 65/75 and 88/75 *Tasca and SADAM v Comitato Interministeriale dei Prezzi* [1976] ECR 291 and 323, [1976] 2 CMLR 183.

[466] Cases 209/78 etc *Van Landewyck v Commission* [1980] ECR 3125, [1981] 3 CMLR 134.

[467] Cases 240/82 etc *SSI v Commission* [1985] ECR 3831, [1987] 3 CMLR 661 and Case 260/82 *NSO v Commission* [1985] ECR 3801, [1988] 4 CMLR 755.

[468] OJ [1982] L 232/1, [1982] 3 CMLR 702.

that it was all the more important to preserve what latitude for competition remained. The Commission also rejected similar arguments in *Greek Ferry Services Cartel*[469] and in *Raw Tobacco Italy*[470].

In *DaimlerChrysler AG v Commission*[471] the CFI annulled a decision of the Commission that DaimlerChrysler had infringed Article 81 by prohibiting its Spanish dealers from supplying cars to leasing companies in the absence of an identified customer for a leasing contract: since it was a requirement of Spanish law that there should be an identified customer, the DaimlerChrysler agreements were not themselves restrictive of competition[472].

(I) Commission Notices

There are a number of Commission Notices, some of which have been mentioned in the course of the preceding text, in which the Commission has provided guidance on the application of Article 81(1) to various types of agreement. It might be helpful to provide a checklist of these Notices, arranged chronologically, with some brief comments where appropriate.

(i) Notice on sub-contracting agreements[473]
Article 81(1) does not apply to some sub-contracting agreements.

(ii) Notice on the application of the competition rules to cross-border credit transfers[474]
This Notice has specific application in the banking sector.

(iii) Notice on the application of the competition rules to the postal sector[475]
This Notice has specific application in the postal sector.

(iv) Notice on the application of the competition rules to access agreements in the telecommunications sector[476]
This Notice has specific application in the telecommunications sector.

(v) *Guidelines* on vertical restraints[477]
These *Guidelines* deal, at length, with the application of Article 81(1) and Article 81(3) to vertical agreements. Paragraphs 12 to 20 of the *Guidelines* provide guidance on the application of Article 81(1) to agreements between principal and agent.

---

[469] OJ [1999] L 109/24, [1999] 5 CMLR 47, paras 98–108, upheld on appeal Cases T-56/99 etc *Marlines SA v Commission* [2003] ECR II-5225, [2005] 5 CMLR 1761; see also *French-West Africa Shipowners' Committees* OJ [1992] L 134/1, [1993] 5 CMLR 446; Cases C-359/95 P *Commission and France v Ladbroke Racing Ltd* [1997] ECR I-6265, [1998] 4 CMLR 27; Cases T-202/98 etc *Tate & Lyle plc v Commission* [2001] ECR II-2035, [2001] 5 CMLR 859, paras 44–45.

[470] Commission decision of 20 October 2005, paras 315–324.

[471] Case T-325/01 [2005] ECR II-3319, [2007] 4 CMLR 559.   [472] Ibid, para 156.

[473] OJ [1979] C1/2, [1979] 1 CMLR 264.   [474] OJ [1995] C 251/3.

[475] OJ [1998] C 39/2, [1998] 5 CMLR 108; see ch 23, pp 977–980.

[476] OJ [1998] C 265/2, [1998] 5 CMLR 821; see ch 23, pp 974–975.

[477] OJ [2000] C 291/1, [2000] 5 CMLR 1074; see ch 16, pp 612–618.

(vi) *Guidelines* on horizontal cooperation agreements[478]

These *Guidelines* deal, Notice deals, at length, with the application of Article 81(1) and Article 81(3) to horizontal cooperation agreements, that is to say agreements other than hard-core cartels.

(vii) Notice regarding restrictions directly related and necessary to the concentration[479]

Article 81(1) does not apply to ancillary restrictions; this Notice is specifically of relevance to the analysis of concentrations under the EC Merger Regulation, but it provides useful insights into the Commission's thinking more generally[480].

(viii) Notice on agreements of minor importance[481]

This Notice is concerned with the *de minimis* doctrine and is examined below.

(ix) *Guidelines* on the application of Article 81(3) of the Treaty[482]

Although these *Guidelines* are predominantly concerned with the application of Article 81(3), paragraphs 13 to 37 contain useful discussion of the principles behind Article 81(1).

(x) *Guidelines* on the application of Article 81 of the EC Treaty to technology transfer agreements[483]

These *Guidelines* deal at length with the application of Article 81(1) and Article 81(3) to technology transfer agreements. They also examine matters such as technology pools.

(xi) The Commission's Consolidated Jurisdictional Notice[483a]

Article 81 does not apply to full-function joint ventures. Paragraphs 91 to 109 examine the concept of full-functionality.

(xii) *Draft guidelines* on the application of Article 81 of the EC Treaty to maritime transport services[484]

These *Draft guidelines* set out the principles to be applied when assessing cooperation agreements in the maritime transport sector; in particular they consider the extent to which the exchange of information between competing undertakings may infringe Article 81.

5. THE *DE MINIMIS* DOCTRINE

(A) Introduction

Some agreements that affect competition within the terms of Article 81(1) may nevertheless not be caught because they do not have an appreciable impact either on

---

[478] OJ [2001] C 3/2, [2001] 4 CMLR 819; see ch 15, pp 575–581.   [479] OJ [2005] C 56/244.
[480] The Notice is discussed in ch 21, pp 870–871.   [481] OJ [2001] C 368/13, [2002] 4 CMLR 699.
[482] OJ [2004] C 101/97.   [483] OJ [2004] C 101/2: see ch 19, pp 771–786.   [483a] See ch 21, pp 826–827.
[484] OJ [2007] C 215/3.

competition or on inter-state trade. This *de minimis* doctrine was first formulated by the ECJ in *Völk v Vervaecke*[485]. There a German producer of washing-machines granted an exclusive distributorship to Vervaecke in Belgium and Luxembourg and guaranteed it absolute territorial protection against parallel imports. Volk's market share was negligible[486]. In an Article 234 reference the ECJ held that:

an agreement falls outside the prohibition in Article [81(1)] where it has only an insignificant effect on the market, taking into account the weak position which the persons concerned have on the market of the product in question.

The *de minimis* doctrine applies both to agreements whose object and whose effect is to prevent competition, which means that even horizontal restraints of a clearly anti-competitive nature or export bans in a vertical agreement could fall outside Article 81 because of their diminutive impact; having said this, it is to be expected that a stricter approach will be taken to agreements in the 'object' category within Article 81(1) than those that have as their effect the restriction of competition. Formal decisions applying the doctrine are rare: the Commission would normally not initiate proceedings in relation to a *de minimis* agreement, and if it were to do so it would be likely to settle the case informally.

The Commission has provided guidance on the *de minimis* doctrine in a series of Notices, the most recent of which appeared in 2001 and is discussed in the text below[487]. This Notice will in many cases give a reasonably clear idea of whether an agreement is *de minimis*. However in some circumstances an agreement might be held to fall within Article 81(1) even though it is below the quantitative criteria established by it; and an agreement may be found not to have an appreciable effect on competition even where the thresholds in the Notice are exceeded[488].

(B) The Commission's *Notice on Agreements of Minor Importance*

(i) Part I of the Notice: introductory paragraphs
Part I of the Notice contains important statements on the application of the *de minimis* doctrine. Paragraph 1 refers to the case law of the ECJ on appreciability. Paragraph 2 states that the Notice sets out the market share thresholds for determining when a restriction of competition is not appreciable. It points out that this 'negative' definition of appreciability (that is to say the explanation of what is *not* an appreciable restriction of competition) does not imply that agreements above the thresholds are caught by Article 81(1): agreements above the thresholds may have only a negligible effect on competition and so not be caught[489]; another way of putting this point is that the Notice

---

[485] Case 5/69 [1969] ECR 295, [1969] CMLR 273.
[486] 0.2 per cent and 0.5 per cent of production in Germany in 1963 and 1966 respectively.
[487] *Notice on Agreements of Minor Importance* OJ [2001] C 368/13, [2002] 4 CMLR 699, replacing the previous Notice OJ [1997] C 372/13, [1998] 4 CMLR 192; on the 2001 Notice see Peeperkorn 'Revision of the 1997 Notice on Agreements of Minor Importance' Commission's *Competition Policy Newsletter*, June 2001, p 4.
[488] See the text below.
[489] The Notice refers to Cases C-215/96 etc *Bagnasco* [1999] ECR I-135, [1999] 4 CMLR 624, paras 34–35 in support of this proposition; the same point will be found in two CFI judgments, Case T-7/93 *Langnese-Iglo*

establishes a 'safe harbour' for agreements below the thresholds, but does not establish a dangerous one for agreements above it. Paragraph 3 makes the important point that the *de minimis* Notice does *not* deal with the concept of an appreciable effect on trade between Member States: this is dealt with by the Commission's *Guidelines on the effect on trade concept contained in Articles 81 and 82 of the Treaty*[490]; paragraph 3 adds, however, that agreements between small- and medium-sized enterprises ('SMEs') are unlikely to affect trade between Member States: such undertakings are currently defined as those having fewer than 250 employees and with an annual turnover not exceeding €50 million or an annual balance-sheet total not exceeding €43 million[491].

Paragraph 4 of the Notice is important: it states that the Commission will not institute proceedings either upon application or upon its own initiative in respect of agreements covered by the Notice; and that, where undertakings assume in good faith that an agreement is covered by the Notice, the Commission will not impose fines. Paragraph 4 of the Notice adds that, although not binding on them, it is intended to provide guidance to national courts and NCAs. Paragraph 5 explains that the Notice also applies to decisions by associations of undertakings and to concerted practices. Paragraph 6 states that the Notice is without prejudice to any interpretation of Article 81 by the Community Courts.

(ii) Part II of the Notice: the threshold

The main provision in the Notice is contained in Part II, at paragraph 7. It provides as follows:

The Commission holds the view that agreements between undertakings which affect trade between Member States do not appreciably restrict competition within the meaning of Article 81(1):

  (a) if the aggregate market share held by the parties to the agreement does not exceed 10 per cent on any of the relevant markets affected by the agreement, where the agreement is made between undertakings[492] which are actual or potential competitors on any of these markets (agreements between competitors); or
  (b) if the market share held by each of the parties to the agreement does not exceed 15% on any of the relevant markets affected by the agreement, where the agreement is made between undertakings which are not actual or potential competitors on any of these markets (agreements between non-competitors).

In cases where it is difficult to classify the agreement as either an agreement between competitors or an agreement between non-competitors the 10% threshold is applicable.

As can be seen the Notice treats vertical agreements more generously than horizontal ones, by providing a higher threshold.

A particular problem arises in some sectors where the cumulative effect of many vertical agreements may lead to foreclosure of the market[493]. The Notice provides guidance on appreciability in this situation (a) by indicating when a cumulative foreclosure effect is likely and (b) by providing a market share threshold indicating whether particular agreements contribute to that foreclosure effect. Paragraph 8 provides that a

---

GmbH v Commission [1995] ECR II-1533, [1995] 5 CMLR 602, para 98; Case T-374/94 etc *European Night Services v Commission* [1998] ECR II-3141, [1998] 5 CMLR 718, paras 102–103.

[490] See pp 142–146 below.   [491] See Commission Recommendation 2003/361/EC OJ [2003] L 124/36.

[492] Throughout the Notice the expression 'undertakings' includes 'connected undertakings' such as parents and subsidiaries: see paragraph 12.

[493] See ch 16, p 628.

cumulative foreclosure effect is unlikely to exist if less than 30 per cent of the relevant market is covered by parallel agreements having similar effects; where there is a fore-closure effect, individual suppliers or distributors will not be considered to contribute to that effect where their market share does not exceed 5 per cent.

A problem that may arise in application of the Notice is that firms may outgrow the market share thresholds established by paragraphs 7 and 8; marginal relief is pro-vided by paragraph 9 where the thresholds (of 10 per cent, 15 per cent and 5 per cent respectively) are exceeded by no more than two percentage points during two succes-sive years.

It is not clear what happens to an agreement when it has outgrown the Notice, includ-ing the provisions for marginal relief: one possibility is that it becomes retrospectively void; a second is that it becomes unenforceable from the moment that the Notice ceases to apply. The second suggestion appears to be consistent with the scheme of Article 81 of the EC Treaty. In the UK the Court of Appeal held in *Passmore v Morland plc*[494] that an agreement can infringe Article 81(1) at some times and at other times not do so, depend-ing on the surrounding facts: in other words it can drift into and out of voidness.

Paragraph 10 of the Notice notes that guidance on market definition is provided by the Commission's *Notice on the Definition of Relevant Market for the Purpose of Community Competition Law*[495] and adds that market shares are to be calculated on the basis of sales value data or, where appropriate, purchase value data; where value data are not available, other criteria, including volume data, may be used.

(iii) Part II of the Notice: the treatment of 'hard-core' restrictions

The Notice does not provide a safe harbour for so-called 'hard-core restrictions' of the kind blacklisted in Regulation 2790/99 on vertical agreements and Regulation 2658/00 on specialisation agreements. The judgment of the ECJ in *Völk v Vervaecke*[496] did con-cern a hard-core restriction, in that the distributor was granted absolute territorial pro-tection; and ultimately it is for the Court to interpret and apply Article 81. However the Commission specifically says in paragraph 11 that the Notice does not apply to certain restrictions: horizontal agreements to fix prices, limit output or sales and to allocate markets or customers[497]; vertical agreements, for example to fix prices, impose export bans and to restrict sales within a selective distribution system[498]; and vertical agree-ments between competitors[499]. Thus there is no assurance that the Commission would not proceed against a hard-core cartel where the market share of the parties was less than 10 per cent; even SMEs might be investigated: in *Greek Ferries*[500] the Commission imposed fines on Marlines and Ventouris, which were SMEs as defined in an earlier Notice of 1997, since they were party to price-fixing agreements, a particularly serious

---

[494] [1999] 1 CMLR 1129, CA.   [495] OJ [1997] C 372/5, [1998] 4 CMLR 177; see ch 1, p 26ff.

[496] See n 485 above.

[497] *De minimis* Notice, para 11(1).

[498] *De minimis* Notice, para 11(2); the list is the same as in Article 4 of Regulation 2790/99, as to which see ch 16, p 652–657; on this point note *Volkswagen* OJ [2001] L 262/14, [2001] 5 CMLR 1309, para 79 (resale price maintenance could infringe Article 81(1) even where the parties' market share was below the *de minimis* threshold).

[499] *De minimis* Notice, para 11(3).

[500] *Greek Ferry Services Cartel* OJ [1999] L 109/24, [1999] 5 CMLR 47, upheld on appeal Cases T-56/99 etc *Marlines SA v Commission* [2003] ECR II-5225, [2005] 5 CMLR 1761.

infringement[501]. Of course the Commission might decide, as a matter of prosecutorial discretion, not to proceed against hard-core restrictions below the thresholds, but that is a different matter from providing such restrictions with a safe harbour.

(C) Limitations of the Notice

It is important to note some limitations of this Notice. The ECJ has indicated that it is wrong to adopt a purely quantitative approach to the issue of *de minimis* agreements; in *Distillers Co Ltd v Commission*[502] it concluded that an agreement affecting the distribution of Pimms was of importance, notwithstanding the minute proportion of the market held by that drink, because Distillers was a major producer occupying an important position on the market for drinks generally. In *Musique Diffusion Française v Commission*[503] the ECJ held that a concerted practice was not within the *de minimis* doctrine where the parties' market shares were small but the market was a fragmented one, their market shares exceeded those of most competitors and their turnover figures were high.

(D) Other examples of non-appreciability

The *de minimis* doctrine described in the preceding sections stems from the judgment in *Völk v Vervaecke*[504], which referred to the 'weak position' that the persons had on the market in question; this is why the Commission's Notice giving expression to the doctrine does so in terms of market share thresholds, which are used as a proxy for undertakings' market power, or rather lack of market power. It should be noted however that appreciability may be relevant to the application of Article 81(1) in a different way: judgments of the Community Courts and decisions of the Commission can be found in which it was concluded that a restriction of competition was not appreciable not because the parties to an agreement lacked market power, but because the restriction itself was insignificant. For example in *Pavel Pavlov v Stichting Pensioenfonds Medische Specialisten*[505] the ECJ concluded that a decision by medical specialists to set up a pension fund entrusted with the management of a supplementary pension scheme did not appreciably affect competition within the common market: the cost of the scheme had only a marginal and indirect influence on the final cost of the services that they offered. This finding was not linked in any way to the market power of the specialists. In *Irish Banks' Standing Committee*[506] the Commission decided that an agreement on the opening hours of Irish banks did not appreciably restrict competition. In *Visa International*[507] the Commission considered that one of the rules of the Visa card system, which required a bank to issue a certain number of Visa cards before contracting with retailers for processing credit card payments, did not appreciably restrict competition since it improved the utility of the card system for traders and did not create

[501] OJ [1999] L 109/24, [1999] 5 CMLR 121, para 151.
[502] Case 30/78 [1980] ECR 2229, [1980] 3 CMLR 121; see similarly Case 19/77 *Miller International v Commission* [1978] ECR 131, [1978] 2 CMLR 334; Case 107/82 *AEG-Telefunken v Commission* [1983] ECR 3151, [1984] 3 CMLR 325, para 58.
[503] Cases 100/80 etc [1983] ECR 1825, [1983] 3 CMLR 221; see also *Yves Saint Laurent Parfums* OJ [1992] L 12/24, [1993] 4 CMLR 120.
[504] See n 485 above. [505] Cases C-180/98 etc [2000] ECR I-6451, [2001] 4 CMLR 30, paras 90–97.
[506] OJ [1986] L 295/28, [1987] 2 CMLR 601, para 16. [507] OJ [2001] L 293/24, [2002] 4 CMLR 168.

significant barriers to entry[508]. In UEFA's *broadcasting regulations*[509] the Commission concluded that regulations preventing the live transmission of football matches at certain times on a Saturday or Sunday afternoon, in order to protect amateur participation in sport and to encourage live attendance at football matches, did not result in an appreciable restriction of competition[510]. In *Identrus*[511] the Commission decided that a prohibition on the members of Identrus selling their equity interest in it to third parties without first offering to sell the interest to Identrus itself or its other members did not amount to an appreciable restriction of competition[512].

6. THE EFFECT ON TRADE BETWEEN MEMBER STATES

The application of Article 81 is limited to agreements, decisions or concerted practices *which may affect trade between Member States*. The scope of Article 82 is similarly limited. The inter-Member State trade clause is very important in EC competition law, since it defines 'the boundary between the areas respectively covered by Community law and the law of the Member States'[513].

Historically both the Commission and the Community Courts have adopted a liberal interpretation of the inter-state trade clause, thereby enlarging the scope of Articles 81 and 82[514]. This was of particular significance at a time when many Member States had no competition laws of their own, or competition laws that were weak in terms of powers of investigation and sanctions. This point does not have the same significance today, since all the Member States have effective competition laws, and for the most part these are modelled upon Articles 81 and 82[515]. It follows that a hard-core cartel or abusive behaviour by a dominant firm will be illegal either under domestic or EC law, and to this extent it matters little whether the infringement occurs under one system or the other (or both). However the concept of inter-state trade is of central importance since the entry into force of the Modernisation Regulation, Regulation 1/2003[516], and the creation of the European Competition Network. Determining whether an agreement or practice has an effect on trade between Member States is important for a series of reasons[517]:

- Where there is an effect on trade between Member States, national courts and NCAs that apply national competition law to agreements or practices have an *obligation* to also apply Articles 81 and 82[518].

- Where there is an effect on trade between Member States, national courts and NCAs cannot apply stricter national competition law to agreements, although they can apply stricter national law to unilateral conduct[519].

---

[508] Ibid, para 65; the same conclusion was reached in relation to the 'no-discrimination' rule: ibid, paras 54–58 and the principle of territorial licensing: ibid, paras 63–64.

[509] OJ [2001] L 171/12, [2001] 5 CMLR 654.   [510] Ibid, paras 49–58.   [511] OJ [2001] L 249/12.

[512] Ibid, paras 54–55.

[513] Case 22/78 *Hugin Kassaregister AB v Commission* [1979] ECR 1869, p 1899, [1979] 3 CMLR 345, p 373.

[514] Cf the position in the US where the inter-state commerce clause has also been construed flexibly: see eg *Manderville Island Farms v American Crystal Sugar Co* 342 US 143 (1951).

[515] See ch 2, pp 58–59.   [516] OJ [2003] L 1/1.

[517] For discussion of the Modernisation Regulation see further ch 2, pp 52–53 and ch 7 generally.

[518] Regulation 1/2003, Article 3(1).   [519] Ibid, Article 3(2).

- NCAs that apply Articles 81 and 82 have an obligation to inform the Commission of the fact no later than 30 days before the adoption of the decision[520]. Clearly an NCA could avoid this obligation by reaching the conclusion that there is no effect on trade between Member States.

- When the Commission is informed that an NCA intends to adopt a decision on the basis of Community competition law, the Commission has the power to initiate its own proceedings and thereby to terminate the proceedings of the NCA[521].

- The Commission and the NCAs have the right to exchange information for the purpose of applying Articles 81 and 82[522].

- There are cooperation provisions in place that facilitate the enforcement of Articles 81 and 82 by national courts, as well as an obligation for Member States to inform the Commission of court cases deciding on the application of those provisions[523].

- NCAs and national courts that apply Articles 81 and 82 must not take decisions that conflict with decisions adopted by the Commission[524].

Clearly these rules mean that it remains important to know whether an agreement or practice has an effect on trade between Member States. This is why the Commission has published *Guidelines on the effect on trade concept contained in Articles 81 and 82 of the Treaty* ('the *Guidelines on inter-state trade*')[525]. They draw substantially on the case law of the Community Courts, going back to *Consten and Grundig v Commission* in 1966[526]. In the account of the *Guidelines on inter-state trade* that follows this case law will not be cited, but the reader should be aware that references to the relevant cases will be found in the footnotes of the *Guidelines*.

Part 1 of the *Guidelines on inter-state trade* contain a brief introduction explaining, in particular, that they deal with the issue of what is meant by an appreciable effect on inter-state trade, but not with the separate question of what is meant by an appreciable restriction of competition[527]. Part 2 of the *Guidelines* explains the effect on trade criterion, and is divided into four parts: general principles, the concept of 'trade between Member States', the notion 'may affect', and the concept of appreciability. Part 3 considers the application of the effect on trade criterion to particular examples of agreements and practices.

(A) The effect on trade criterion

(i) General principles

Articles 81 and 82 are applicable only where any effect on trade between Member States is appreciable[528]. In the case of Article 81 the question is whether the agreement affects trade: it is not necessary that each part of the agreement does so[529]; and if the agreement affects trade between Member States it is irrelevant that a particular undertaking that is party to the agreement does not itself produce such an effect[530]. In the case of Article 82 the abuse must have an affect on trade between Member States, but this does not mean that each element of the behaviour must be assessed in isolation to determine its effect: the conduct must be assessed in terms of its overall impact[531].

---

[520] Ibid, Article 11(4). [521] Ibid, Article 11(6). [522] Ibid, Article 12. [523] Ibid, Article 15.
[524] Ibid, Article 16. [525] OJ [2004] C 101/81. [526] Cases C 56/64 and C 58/64 [1966] ECR 429.
[527] *Guidelines on inter-state trade*, para 4. [528] Ibid, para 13. [529] Ibid, para 14. [530] Ibid, para 15.
[531] Ibid, para 17.

(ii) The concept of 'trade between Member States'

The concept of 'trade' is not limited to traditional exchanges of goods and services across borders: it is a wider concept and covers all cross-border activity, including the establishment by undertakings of agencies, branches or subsidiaries in other Member States[532]. The concept of trade also covers situations where the competitive structure of the market is affected by agreements and/or conduct[533]. There can be an effect on trade between Member States where parts only of those States are affected: the effect does not need to extend to their entire territories[534]. The question of whether trade between Member States is affected is separate from the issue of the relevant geographical market: trade could be affected even though the geographical market is national or even smaller than national[535].

(iii) The notion 'may affect'

The ECJ has often said that the notion that an agreement or practice 'may affect' trade between Member States means that it must be possible to foresee, with a sufficient degree of probability on the basis of a set of objective factors of law or fact, that the agreement or practice may have an influence, direct or indirect, actual or potential, on the pattern of trade between Member States[536]. Subjective intent to affect trade is not required[537]; and it is sufficient that the agreement or practice is capable of having an effect: it is not necessary to prove that it actually will do so[538]. In determining whether the pattern of trade is influenced it is not necessary to show that trade is or would be restricted or reduced: an increase in trade also means that it has been influenced[539]: the effect on trade criterion is simply jurisdictional, determining whether an examination of an agreement or conduct under the Community competition rules is warranted[540].

The fact that the influence on trade may be 'direct *or indirect*, actual *or potential*' clearly means that the jurisdictional reach of Articles 81 and 82 can be extensive[541]. However, in the case of indirect and potential influence the analysis must not be based on remote or hypothetical effects: a person claiming that trade is affected in this way must be able to explain how and why this is the case[542].

(iv) The concept of appreciability

Any effect on trade must be appreciable. The stronger the market position of the undertakings concerned, the likelier it is that any effect will be appreciable[543]. An undertaking's market share, and the value of its turnover in the products concerned, are relevant to the appreciability of any effect[544]. An assessment of appreciability must be considered in the legal and economic context of any agreement or practice including, in the case of vertical agreements, the cumulative effect of parallel networks[545].

The *Guidelines on inter-state trade* do not provide general quantitative rules on when trade is appreciably affected; however they do provide two examples of situations where trade is normally *not* capable of being appreciably affected.

---

[532] Ibid, paras 19 and 30.   [533] Ibid, para 20.   [534] Ibid, para 21.   [535] Ibid, para 22.
[536] Ibid, para 23.   [537] Ibid, para 25.   [538] Ibid, para 26.   [539] Ibid, para 34.
[540] Ibid, para 35.   [541] See paras 36–42 of the *Guidelines*.   [542] Ibid, para 43.
[543] Ibid, para 45.   [544] Ibid, paras 46–47.   [545] Ibid, para 49.

(A) Small and medium-sized businesses The *Guidelines* state that agreements between small and medium-sized businesses, as defined in Commission Recommendation 2003/361/EC[546], would not normally affect trade between Member States; however they might do so where they engage in cross-border activity[547].

(B) A negative rebuttable presumption of non-appreciability The *Guidelines* also set out a negative rebuttable presumption of non-appreciability. This arises where:

- The aggregate market share of the parties on any relevant market within the Community affected by the agreements does not exceed 5 per cent; and
- The parties' turnover is below €40 million: turnover is calculated differently according to whether the agreement is horizontal or vertical[548].

The presumption continues to apply where the turnover threshold is exceeded during two successive calendar years by no more than 10 per cent and the market share threshold by no more than 2 per cent.

(C) A positive rebuttable presumption of appreciability The *Guidelines* also set out a positive rebuttable presumption of appreciability in the case of agreements which 'by their very nature' are capable of affecting trade between Member States, such as agreements on imports and exports. This arises where:

- The turnover thresholds set out above are exceeded; and
- The parties' market shares exceed 5 per cent.

This positive presumption does not apply where the agreement covers part only of a Member State[549].

(B) The application of the effect on trade criterion to particular agreements and conduct

The *Guidelines on inter-state trade* proceed to examine how the effect on trade criterion applies in relation to particular types of agreement and conduct. They do so by reference to three categories: first, agreements and abuse covering or implemented in several Member States[550]; second, cases covering a single, or only part of a, Member State[551]; and third, cases involving undertakings located in third countries[552]. It is important to understand that Articles 81 and 82 are capable of application irrespective of where the undertakings concerned are located, provided that the agreement or practice is implemented or has effects within the Community[553]. It is also possible that an export ban imposed by a Community supplier on a distributor in a third country, which prevents the latter from re-importing into the Community, could have an effect on trade between Member States in certain circumstances, for example where there is a significant price differential between prices in the different territories, where that differential would not be eroded by customs duties and transport costs, and where significant volumes of a product could be exported from the third country to the Community[554].

---

[546] OJ [2003] L 124/36: see p 139 above for the definition of SMEs in the Recommendation.
[547] *Guidelines on inter-state trade*, para 50.   [548] Ibid, para 52.   [549] Ibid, para 53.
[550] Ibid, paras 61–76.   [551] Ibid, paras 77–99.   [552] Ibid, paras 100–109.
[553] See further ch 12, pp 478–482.   [554] *Guidelines on inter-state trade*, paras 108–109.

In an interesting case on the inter-state trade criterion decided since the *Guidelines* were published, the CFI held in *Raiffeisen Zentralbank Österreich AG v Commission*[555] that a banking cartel in Austria had an effect on trade between Member States. In that case there was a series of regional committees within Austria; the Court held that it was not necessary to consider whether each individual committee had an affect on trade: rather it was necessary to look at the cumulative effect of all the committees[556]. The overall cartel in Austria affected the entire country, and the Court said that this raised a strong presumption that trade between Member States was affected[557]. The Court noted that there had been cases in which this presumption had been rebutted[558], but held that it was not rebutted on the facts of this case[559].

7. CHECKLIST OF AGREEMENTS THAT FALL OUTSIDE ARTICLE 81(1)

At the end of this chapter it may be helpful to set out a checklist of the circumstances in which an agreement might be found not to infringe Article 81(1): the list follows the order of the text of this chapter:

- Article 81(1) applies only to an agreement between undertakings[560]
- Article 81(1) does not apply to collective agreements between employers and workers[561]
- Article 81(1) does not apply to an agreement between two or more persons that form a single economic entity[562]
- Article 81(1) normally does not apply to agreements between a principal and agent[563]
- Article 81(1) normally does not apply to an agreement between a contractor and a sub-contractor[564]
- Article 81(1) does not apply to unilateral conduct that is not attributable to a concurrence of wills between two or more undertakings[565]
- Article 81(1) does not apply to an agreement that has neither the object nor the effect of preventing, restricting or distorting competition[566]
- Article 81(1) does not apply to contractual restrictions that enable undertakings to achieve a legitimate purpose and which are not disproportionate[567]
- Article 81 does not apply to full-function joint ventures[568]
- A realistic view must be taken of potential competition[569]
- Article 81(1) does not apply to an agreement if this would obstruct an undertaking or undertakings in the performance of a task of general economic interest entrusted to them by a Member State[570]

[555] Cases T-259/02 [2006] ECR II-5169, [2007] 5 CMLR 1142.   [556] Ibid, para 177.   [557] Ibid, para 181.
[558] See eg Cases C-215/96 and C-216/96 *Bagnasco and others* [1999] ECR I-135; *Netherlands Bank II* OJ [1999] L 271/28.
[559] Cases T-259/02 [2006] ECR II-5169, [2007] 5 CMLR 1142, paras 182–186.
[560] See pp 82–91 above.   [561] See pp 90–91 above.   [562] See pp 91–95 above.
[563] See p 95 above and ch 16, pp 609–612.   [564] See p 95 above and ch 16, pp 666–667.
[565] See pp 107–113 above.   [566] See pp 113–126 above.   [567] See pp 126–130 above.
[568] See ch 21, pp 826–827.   [569] See pp 133–134 above.   [570] See p 134 above and ch 6, pp 233–239.

- Article 81(1) does not apply to an agreement which undertakings were compelled to enter into by law[571]
- Article 81(1) does not apply to an agreement in a market that is so highly regulated that there is no latitude left for competition[572]
- Article 81(1) does not apply to an agreement that has no appreciable effect on competition[573]
- Article 81(1) does not apply to an agreement that does not have an appreciable effect on trade between Member States[574].

---

[571] See pp 134–135 above.   [572] See pp 135–136 above.   [573] See pp 137–142 above.
[574] See pp 142–146 above.

4

Article 81(3)[1]

CHAPTER CONTENTS

1. INTRODUCTION

An agreement which falls within Article 81(1) of the Treaty is not necessarily unlawful. Article 81(3) provides a 'legal exception' to the prohibition in Article 81(1) by providing that it may be declared inapplicable in respect of agreements, decisions or concerted practices[2], or of categories[3] of agreements, decisions or concerted practices, which satisfy four conditions, the first two positive and the last two negative. To satisfy Article 81(3) an agreement:

- must contribute to improving the production or distribution of goods or to promoting technical or economic progress;
- while allowing consumers a fair share of the resulting benefit.

Furthermore the agreement[4]:

- must not impose on the undertakings concerned restrictions which are not indispensable to the attainment of these objectives; nor
- afford such undertakings the possibility of eliminating competition in a substantial part of the products in question[5].

---

[1] For further reading on Article 81(3) readers are referred to Faull and Nikpay *The EC Law of Competition* (2nd ed, 2007), ch 3, paras 3.395–3.460; Bellamy & Child *European Community Law of Competition* (eds Roth and Rose, Oxford University Press, 6th ed, 2008), ch 3.

[2] The reference to decisions is useful since it means eg that the rules of a trade association may satisfy Article 81(3); it will only be rarely that Article 81(3) is applied to a concerted practice, but this can happen: see eg *Re International Energy Agency* OJ [1983] L 376/30, [1984] 2 CMLR 186; renewed in 1994, OJ [1994] L 68/35.

[3] The inclusion of 'categories' of agreements is important since it paves the way for block exemptions: see further pp 164–169 below.

[4] This term should be taken to include decisions and concerted practices in the rest of this chapter.

[5] Note that the UK Competition Act 1998 contains a similar provision in s 9: see ch 9, pp 350–353.

Under Regulation 17 of 1962[6] the Commission had the exclusive right to grant so-called 'individual exemption' under Article 81(3) to agreements notified to it[7]. However the system of notification of agreements to the Commission and the grant of individual exemption was abolished with effect from 1 May 2004 by Council Regulation 1/2003[8] ('the Modernisation Regulation'); since then Article 81(3) has been directly applicable[9], and the Commission shares the competence to apply Article 81(3) with the national competition authorities ('the NCAs')[10] and national courts[11]. In order to provide guidance to national courts and NCAs, as well as to undertakings and their professional advisers, the Commission has published *Guidelines on the application of Article 81(3) of the Treaty* ('the *Article 81(3) Guidelines*')[12]. The *Guidelines* should be applied 'reasonably and flexibly' rather than in a mechanical manner[13]. Additional guidance on the application of Article 81(1) and (3) to agreements is provided by the Commission's guidelines on vertical agreements[14], on horizontal cooperation agreements[15] and on technology transfer agreements[16].

An alternative way of satisfying Article 81(3) is to draft an agreement to satisfy one of the so-called 'block exemptions' issued by the Council of the European Union (the Council') or by the Commission under powers conferred on it by the Council; the system of block exemptions is unaffected by the Modernisation Regulation.

After discussing the burden of proof under Article 81(3) and the implications of the CFI's judgment in *Matra Hachette v Commission*, section 2 of this chapter will discuss the criteria in Article 81(3). It will then consider the implications of the Modernisation Regulation for undertakings and their legal advisers. The final section in this chapter describes the system of block exemptions.

(A) The burden of proving that the conditions of Article 81(3) are satisfied

Article 2 of the Modernisation Regulation confirms well-settled case law that the burden of proof is on the Commission, the national competition authorities or the person opposing an agreement in a national court to show that it infringes Article 81(1), but that it is on the undertaking or undertakings seeking to defend an agreement to demonstrate that it satisfies the four conditions in Article 81(3). The Commission must examine the arguments and evidence put forward by the undertakings relying on Article 81(3); if it is unable to refute them it may be that the undertakings will be taken to have discharged the burden of proof upon them[17]. All four of the conditions must be satisfied if an agreement is to benefit from Article 81(3): the Community Courts have stressed this on a number of occasions[18], and the *Article 81(3) Guidelines* contain a statement to the same

---

[6] JO [1962] 204/62, OJ Sp Ed [1962] p 87.   [7] Ibid, Article 9(1).   [8] OJ [2003] L 1/1, [2003] 4 CMLR 551.
[9] Ibid, Article 1(1) and 1(2).
[10] Ibid, Article 5.   [11] Ibid, Article 6.   [12] OJ [2004] C 101/97.   [13] Ibid, para 6.
[14] *Guidelines on Vertical Restraints* OJ [2000] C 291/1.
[15] *Guidelines on the applicability of Article 81 to horizontal co-operation agreements* OJ [2001] C 3/2.
[16] *Guidelines on the application of Article 81 to technology transfer agreements* OJ [2004] C 101/2.
[17] Cases 56/64 and 58/64 *Consten and Grundig v Commission* [1966] ECR 299, p 347, [1966] CMLR 418, p 478; Cases C-204/00 P *Aalborg Portland and Others v Commission* [2004] ECR I-123, para 55; Case T-168/01 *GlaxoSmithKline Services Ltd v Commission* [2006] ECR II-2969, [2006] 5 CMLR 29, para 236.
[18] See eg Cases 43/82 and 63/82 *VBVB and VVVB v Commission* [1984] ECR 19, para 61; Case C-238/05 *Asnef-Equifax v Asociación de Usuarios de Servicios Bancarios (Ausbanc)* [2006] ECR I-11125, [2007] 4 CMLR 6, para 65.

effect[19]. For example the CFI annulled a Commission decision that an agreement satisfied Article 81(3) in *Métropole télévision SA v Commission*[20] because the Commission had failed to demonstrate that restrictions in the agreement were indispensable; the CFI did so again in *M6 v Commission*[21] where it considered that the Commission had incorrectly concluded that an agreement would not substantially eliminate competition. Paragraph 35 of the *Article 81(3) Guidelines* points out, however, that parties to an agreement covered by a block exemption do not have to show that each of the conditions of Article 81(3) is satisfied: there is a presumption that agreements falling within the scope of a block exemption satisfy all four conditions.

Paragraph 44 of the *Article 81(3) Guidelines* explains that Article 81(3) applies only for so long as the four conditions contained in it are satisfied; however when applying this rule due consideration must be given to the time that it will take, and the restrictions that may be needed, when firms make sunk investments to realise economic efficiencies.

(B) *Matra Hachette v Commission*

A very important point about Article 81(3) is that, as the CFI stated in *Matra Hachette v Commission*[22], there are no anti-competitive agreements which, *as a matter of law*, could never satisfy the four conditions set out in that provision: it is possible for the parties to any type of agreement to argue that the conditions of Article 81(3) are satisfied. Even an agreement that has as its *object* the restriction of competition in the sense of Article 81(1) is capable, in principle, of satisfying the conditions of Article 81(3): in this sense EC law differs from US law, since there are no agreements that are '*per se*' illegal in the EC system[23]. An example of an agreement restrictive of competition by object being granted individual exemption can be found in *Société Air France/Alitalia Linee Aeree Italiane SpA*[24] where the Commission authorised an extensive strategic alliance between those two airlines. Of course it would require extremely convincing evidence to satisfy the Commission, an NCA or a national court that hard-core restrictions such as horizontal price-fixing and market-sharing satisfy Article 81(3)[25], but in exceptional circumstances even this may be possible: indeed Articles 3 to 5 of Council Regulation 4056/86 on maritime transport[26] provide block exemption for horizontal price-fixing in the case of international liner conferences[27] due to the particular characteristics of that industry[28]. In *Reims II*[29] the Commission granted individual exemption to an agreement between the public postal operators in Europe as to the amount that one operator would pay to another for the onward delivery of letters in the latter's territory. The agreement did entail the 'fixing' of prices, in that participants in the scheme were committed to its principles; but this was price fixing of an 'unusual' nature[30], and the

[19] *Article 81(3) Guidelines*, para 42.
[20] Cases T-528/93 etc [1996] ECR II-649, [1996] 5 CMLR 386, para 93.
[21] Cases T-185/00 *Métropole télévision SA (M6) v Commission* [2002] ECR II-3805, [2003] 4 CMLR 707, para 86.
[22] Case T-17/93, [1994] ECR II-595, para 85; see also Case T-168/01 *GlaxoSmithKline Services Ltd v Commission* [2006] ECR II-2969, [2006] 5 CMLR 29, para 233, and para 46 of the *Article 81(3) Guidelines*.
[23] See further ch 3, pp 131–133.   [24] Commission decision of 7 April 2004.
[25] See the *Article 81(3) Guidelines*, para 46.   [26] OJ [1986] L 378/1.   [27] See ch 23, p 964.
[28] This block exemption will expire in 2008 as a result of Article 1 of Regulation 1419/2006, OJ [2006] L 269/1: see ch 23, pp 964–965.
[29] OJ [1999] L 275/17, [2000] 4 CMLR 704.   [30] Ibid, para 65.

Commission could identify a number of economic efficiencies that would follow from it[31]. The exemption was renewed in October 2003[32]. Similarly in *Visa International – Multilateral Interchange Fee*[33] the Commission stated that it is not the case that an agreement concerning prices is always to be classified as a cartel and therefore as inherently incapable of satisfying Article 81(3)[34]: in that decision the Commission granted individual exemption to a 'multilateral interchange fee' agreed upon between 'acquiring' and 'issuing' banks within the Visa system.

2. THE ARTICLE 81(3) CRITERIA

Each of the four requirements of Article 81(3) will now be examined. It is essential to consider them in conjunction with the *Article 81(3) Guidelines*. The text that follows will emulate the *Guidelines* by reversing the treatment of the second and third conditions set out in Article 81(3) (a fair share to consumers and indispensability): the Commission's view is that consideration of whether consumers would obtain a fair share of any resulting benefit does not arise in the event that an agreement fails the indispensability test, so that it is logical to consider the latter first[35].

(A) First condition of Article 81(3): an improvement in the production or distribution of goods or in technical or economic progress

The 'benefit' produced by an agreement must be something of objective value to the Community as a whole, not a private benefit to the parties themselves; cost savings that arise simply from the exercise of market power, for example by fixing prices or sharing markets, cannot be taken into account[36]. Any advantages claimed of the agreement must outweigh the detriments it might produce[37]; the Commission has declined to accept that an agreement produces an improvement if, in practice, its effect is a disproportionate distortion of competition in the market in question[38]. The benefits that may be claimed are specified in Article 81(3): the agreement must either contribute to an improvement in the production or distribution of goods[39] or promote technical or economic progress. These concepts overlap, and in many cases the Commission has considered that more

---

[31] Ibid, paras 69–76.   [32] OJ [2004] L 56/76, [2004] 5 CMLR 2.

[33] OJ [2002] L 318/17, [2003] 4 CMLR 283.

[34] Ibid, para 79; the Commission's suggestion in this paragraph that some agreements are inherently incapable of satisfying Article 81(3) is clearly wrong given the judgment of the CFI in the *Matra Hachette* case.

[35] *Article 81(3) Guidelines*, para 39.

[36] See Cases 56/64 and 58/64 *Consten and Grundig v Commission* [1966] ECR 299, p 348, [1966] CMLR 418, p 478; Case T-168/01 *GlaxoSmithKline Services Ltd v Commission* [2006] ECR II-2969, [2006] 5 CMLR 29, para 247 and para 49 of the *Article 81(3) Guidelines*.

[37] Cases 56/64 and 58/64 *Consten and Grundig v Commission* [1966] ECR 299, p 348, [1966] CMLR 418, p 478.

[38] *Screensport/EBU* OJ [1991] L 63/32, [1992] 5 CMLR 273, para 71.

[39] Note that services are not explicitly referred to here; however para 48 of the *Article 81(3) Guidelines* states that Article 81(3) applies, by analogy, to services; in the UK s 9 of the Competition Act 1998 specifically includes improvements in the production or distribution of goods *or services*.

than one – or even that all – the heads were satisfied[40]. In other cases a particular type of benefit may be obviously appropriate for the agreement in question. When permitting specialisation agreements, which can lead to economies of scale and other efficiencies, the Commission has considered that there would be an improvement in the production of goods[41], while it has often held that research and development projects would lead to technical and economic progress[42]. Vertical agreements between suppliers and distributors naturally come under the head of improvements in distribution[43]. The Commission has recognised network externalities as contributing to technical and economic progress from which consumers derive a benefit[44].

An important question is to determine how broad the criteria in the first condition of Article 81(3) are: to use an analogy from many card games, in what circumstances can a 'benefit' under Article 81(3) 'trump' a restriction of competition under Article 81(1), with the result that an agreement which would have been prohibited under Article 81(1) is in fact permitted as a result of the legal exception provided by Article 81(3)? The issue is of particular significance given that the Modernisation Regulation means that decisions under Article 81(3) are now made by NCAs and national courts as well as the Commission: concern was expressed when the Modernisation Regulation was in gestation that the criteria in Article 81(3) were so broad that they were not appropriate to be decided upon by NCAs and national courts; and that there was a risk that the criteria would be applied inconsistently from one Member State to another.

(i) A narrow view of Article 81(3)

A narrow view of Article 81(3) is that it permits only agreements that would bring about improvements in economic efficiency: the very wording of Article 81(3), which speaks of improvements to production and distribution and to technical and economic progress, is clearly suggestive of an efficiency standard. Article 81(3), therefore, simply allows a balancing of the restrictive effects of an agreement under Article 81(1) against the enhancement of efficiency under Article 81(3); in striving to achieve the right balance the other criteria of Article 81(3) – a fair share to consumers, no dispensable restrictions and no substantial elimination of competition – are there to ensure that a reasonable outcome in terms of consumer welfare is achieved. The Commission's *White Paper on Modernisation*[45], which began the process that culminated in the adoption of the Modernisation Regulation, explained Article 81(1) and 81(3) in precisely this way[46]; and the *Article 81(3) Guidelines* are drafted explicitly in terms of economic efficiency[47]. An attractive way of thinking of Article 81 as a whole is that Article 81(1) is concerned to establish whether an agreement could lead to allocative inefficiency, and that Article 81(3) permits such an agreement where there would be a compensating enhancement of productive efficiency[48].

---

[40] See eg *Re United Reprocessors GmbH* OJ [1976] L 51/7, [1976] 2 CMLR D1.

[41] On specialisation agreements see ch 15, pp 588–592.

[42] On research and developments agreements see ch 15, pp 581–588.

[43] On vertical agreements see ch 16 generally.

[44] *Visa International – Multilateral Interchange Fee* OJ [2002] L 318/17, [2003] 4 CMLR 283, para 83; on network effects see ch 1, pp 11–12; see similarly, under UK law, OFT Decision *LINK Interchange Network Ltd*, 16 October 2001, [2002] UKCLR 59, available at www.oft.gov.uk.

[45] OJ [2000] C 365 E/28, [2001] 5 CMLR 1148.   [46] Ibid, para 57.   [47] See pp 155–157 below.

[48] See Odudu *The Boundaries of EC Competition Law: The Scope of Article 81* (Oxford University Press, 2006), in particular ch 6.

(ii) A broader approach to Article 81(3)

However an alternative, and broader, view of Article 81(3) is possible: that it allows policies other than economic efficiency to be taken into account when deciding whether to allow agreements that are restrictive of competition. There are many important policies in the Community, for example on industry[49], the environment[50], employment[51], the regions[52] and culture[53], which go beyond the simple enhancement of economic efficiency. According to a broad view of Article 81(3) a benefit in terms of any of these policies may be able to 'trump' a restriction of competition under Article 81(1)[54].

Some of these broader considerations do seem to have had an influence on the application of Article 81(3) during the years when the Commission enjoyed a monopoly over decision-making under that provision[55]. For example industrial policy can be detected in some competition law developments[56]: Amato suggests that the block exemption for specialisation agreements, with its acceptance that rationalisation in production fulfils the Article 81(3) criteria, reflects industrial policy rather than competition thinking[57]. In *Metro v Commission*[58] the ECJ considered that employment was a relevant factor under the first condition in Article 81(3), saying that the agreement under consideration was 'a stabilising factor with regard to the provision of employment which, since it improves the general conditions of production, especially when market conditions are unfavourable, comes within the framework of the objectives to which reference may be had pursuant to Article [81(3)]'. When considering whether an exemption might be given to a joint venture to produce a 'multi-purpose vehicle' in Portugal in *Ford/Volkswagen*[59] the Commission 'took note' of 'exceptional circumstances' in that it would bring a large number of jobs and substantial foreign investment to one of the poorest regions of the Community, promoting harmonious development, reducing regional disparities and furthering European market integration[60]. The Commission emphasised, however, that this would not be enough in itself to make an exemption possible unless the other conditions of Article 81(3) were fulfilled[61]. In its submissions to the CFI when the decision

[49] On industry under the EC Treaty note Article 157 (ex Title XIII).

[50] On environmental protection under the EC Treaty note Article 6 (ex Article 3(c)) and Articles 174–176 (ex Title XVI).

[51] On employment under the EC Treaty note Articles 125–130 (ex Title VIa).

[52] On economic and social cohesion under the EC Treaty note Articles 158–162 (ex Title XIV).

[53] On culture under the EC Treaty note Article 151 (ex Article 128).

[54] For powerful argument as to why these broader issues should not be brought within the internal regime of competition law see Odudu *The Boundaries of EC Competition Law: The Scope of Article 81* (Oxford University Press, 2006), ch 7.

[55] For an interesting discussion of the policies under consideration in this section see Monti *EC Competition Law* (Cambridge University Press, 2007), ch 4; Jones and Sufrin *EC Competition Law: Text, Cases and Materials* (Oxford University Press, 3rd ed, 2007), pp 271–277.

[56] Note however that Article 157 EC provides that the Community's industrial policy is to be conducted 'in accordance with a system of open and competitive markets'.

[57] Amato *Antitrust and the Bounds of Power* (Hart Publishing, 1997), pp 63–64; the relevant block exemption is now Regulation 2658/2000, OJ [2000] L 304/3, [2001] 4 CMLR 800.

[58] Case 26/76 [1977] ECR 1875, [1978] 2 CMLR 1, para 43; see similarly Case 42/84 *Remia BV and Verenigde Bedrijven Nutricia NV v Commission* [1985] ECR 2545, [1987] 1 CMLR 1, para 42.

[59] OJ [1993] L 20/14, [1993] 5 CMLR 617.

[60] OJ [1993] L 20/14, [1993] 5 CMLR 617, paras 23, 28 and 36; see also the Commission Press Release IP/92/1083, 23 December 1992.

[61] OJ [1993] L 20/14, [1993] 5 CMLR 617, para 36.

was challenged the Commission argued that it was possible to take into account factors other than those expressly mentioned in Article 81(3) including, for example, the maintenance of employment[62]. The CFI concluded that, since the Commission would have granted an individual exemption anyway, its decision could not be impugned for having taken into account improper criteria[63].

In *UEFA*, when granting an individual exemption to the sale of the media rights to the UEFA Champions League, the Commission took note of the financial solidarity that supports the development of European football (citing the ECJ's judgments in *Metro* and *Remia*)[64]. In *Laurent Piau v Commission*[65] the CFI seems to have accepted that rules of FIFA, the body that controls football worldwide, that required football players' agents to comply with a mandatory licensing system, could contribute to economic progress by raising professional and ethical standards for players' agents in order to protect football players who have a short playing career[66]. In *Stichting Baksteen*[67] the Commission considered that the restructuring of the Dutch brick industry, involving coordinated closures 'carried out in acceptable social conditions, including the redeployment of employees', promoted technical and economic progress[68]. In *CECED*[69] the Commission granted an individual exemption to an agreement between manufacturers of domestic appliances (washing-machines etc) which would lead to energy efficiencies, and in doing so noted not only individual economic benefits to consumers from lower energy bills but also the 'collective environmental benefits' that would flow from the agreement[70], referring specifically to the Community's environmental policy in its decision. The Commission reached a similar conclusion when it informally settled cases relating to 'environmental' agreements for water heaters and dishwashers[71].

It is clear, therefore, that a number of factors appear to have been influential in decisions under Article 81(3), not all of which can be considered to be 'narrow' improvements in economic efficiency. There are significant proponents of the view that Article 81(3) does admit broad, non-competition considerations[72], and the CFI, in *Métropole télévision SA v Commission*[73], said that 'in the context of an overall assessment, the Commission is entitled to base itself on considerations *connected with the pursuit of the public interest in order to grant exemption under Article [81(3)]*' (emphasis added)[74]. It is also worth mentioning in passing that 'public interest' criteria may also be relevant when deciding

---

[62] Case T-17/93 *Matra Hachette v Commission* [1994] ECR II-595, para 96; on this case generally see Swaak (1995) 32 CML Rev 1271.

[63] [1994] ECR II-595, para 139.

[64] *Joint selling of the commercial rights of the UEFA Champions League* OJ [2003] L 291/25, [2004] 4 CMLR 9.

[65] Case T-193/02 [2005] ECR II-209, [2005] 5 CMLR 42, upheld on appeal Case C-171/05, *Piau v Commission* [2006] ECR I-37.

[66] Ibid, paras 100–106.   [67] OJ [1994] L 131/15, [1995] 4 CMLR 646.   [68] Ibid, paras 27–28.

[69] OJ [2000] L 187/47, [2000] 5 CMLR 635.   [70] Ibid, paras 55–57.

[71] Commission Press Release IP/01/1659, 26 November 2001; see also the Commission's *Competition Policy Newsletter* February 2002, p 50.

[72] See eg Siragusa in *European Competition Law Annual 1997: Objectives of Competition Policy* (eds Ehlermann and Laudati, Hart Publishing, 1998), p 39; Wesseling 'The Draft Regulation Modernising the Competition Rules: the Commission is Married to One Idea' (2001) 26 EL Rev 357; Monti 'Article 81 EC and Public Policy' (2002) 39 CML Rev 1057; Faull, giving the Burrell lecture in London, 21 February 2000, said that social policy can 'reasonably credibly' be brought within Article 81(3); for an interesting discussion of the issues see Sufrin 'The Evolution of Article 81(3) of the EC Treaty' (2006) 51 Antitrust Bulletin 915, pp 952–967.

[73] Cases T-528/93 etc [1996] ECR II-649, [1996] 5 CMLR 386.   [74] Ibid, para 118.

whether Article 81(1) is infringed in the first place, as the ECJ's judgment in *Wouters*[75] has demonstrated. Indeed the suppression of non-economic considerations under Article 81(3) might result in their re-emergence under the *Wouters* case law.

(iii) The Commission's approach in the *Article 81(3) Guidelines*

This discussion shows that, over a number of years, there has been uncertainty – even confusion – as to the proper application of Article 81(3). As long as the Commission enjoyed a monopoly over decision-making under Regulation 17 this may not have been too serious a problem: the Commission undoubtedly enjoyed a 'margin of appreciation' when applying Article 81(3)[76] under Regulation 17 and it would hardly be surprising if, when making decisions in individual cases over the period from 1962 to 2004, it was influenced, at least sometimes, by issues other than 'pure' economic efficiency. However the Modernisation Regulation makes it necessary to decide on the true content of Article 81(3) because decisions since 1 May 2004 can be made by NCAs and national courts as well as by the Commission itself. These institutions, and the undertakings that enter into agreements that might be challenged under Artcle 81, need to know the limits of what can be justified under Article 81(3); and the NCAs and national courts are not well-placed to balance a restriction of competition under Article 81(1) against a variety of Community policies ranging from industrial and environmental policy to social and cultural issues under Article 81(3). It seems reasonable to suppose that NCAs and national courts would have less difficulty in applying a 'narrow' interpretation of Article 81(3), limited to a consideration of economic efficiencies. These considerations suggest that, in the post-Modernisation Regulation world, Article 81(3) should be interpreted in a narrow rather than a broad manner, according to standards and by reference to principles that are justiciable in courts of law.

It is absolutely clear from the Commission's *Article 81(3) Guidelines* that it intends Article 81(3) to be applied according to the narrow approach based on economic efficiency[77]. Paragraph 11 of the *Guidelines* states that Article 81(3) allows 'pro-competitive benefits' to be taken into account under Article 81(3), and that these may outweigh any 'anti-competitive effects' under Article 81(1). Paragraph 32 of the *Guidelines* again speaks of the 'positive economic effects' of agreements that can be taken into consideration under Article 81(3). Paragraph 33 refers to the achievement of 'pro-competitive effects by way of efficiency gains', explaining that efficiencies may create additional value by lowering the cost of producing an output, improving the quality of the product, or creating a new product. Significantly paragraph 42 of the *Guidelines* explicitly states that '[g]oals pursued by other Treaty provisions can be taken into account only to the extent that they can be subsumed under the four conditions of Article 81(3)'. When the *Guidelines*, at paragraphs 48 to 72, reach the point of discussing the first condition of Article 81(3) – an improvement in production or distribution or in technical or economic progress – they do so specifically under the heading of 'efficiency gains', thereby

---

[75] Case C-309/99 [2002] ECR I-1577, [2002] 4 CMLR 27; see also Case C-519/04 P *Meca-Medina v Commission* [2006] ECR I-6991; this case law is discussed in ch 3, pp 126–131.

[76] See Cases 56/64 and 58/64 *Consten and Grundig v Commission* [1966] ECR 299, p 347, [1966] CMLR 418, p 477.

[77] It should be added that the Commission is in the process of harmonising its approach to efficiencies under Article 82 and under the ECMR with the *Article 81(3) Guidelines*: see ch 5, pp 207–208 and ch 21, pp 863–864.

removing any lingering doubt that might still remain that other, non-economic, considerations could be relevant to the assessment. It would not be unreasonable to expect that NCAs and national courts will take – and will be happy to take – a strong lead from the *Article 81(3) Guidelines*, although it is obviously open to undertakings to argue that they do not fully reflect the jurisprudence of the Community Courts. There may be litigation in the future in which the Community Courts will have to reconsider some of the statements in cases such as *Metro*[78] and *Remia and Nutricia*[79] and to decide whether to allow a broader approach to Article 81(3) than the *Guidelines* envisage; or whether to adopt the narrower, and more justiciable, approach suggested by the Commission. In *GlaxoSmithKline Services Ltd v Commission*[80] the CFI's analysis of whether GSK had satisfied the first condition of Article 81(3) was conducted under the heading 'Evidence of a gain in efficiency', suggesting that it was comfortable with a narrow approach to that provision[81].

Paragraph 51 of the *Article 81(3) Guidelines* stresses that all efficiency claims must be substantiated in order to verify:

- the *nature* of the claimed efficiencies, so that it is possible for the decision-maker to verify that they are objective in nature[82];
- the *link* between the agreement and the efficiencies which, as a general proposition, should be direct rather than indirect[83];
- the *likelihood* and *magnitude* of each claimed efficiency; and
- *how* and *when* each claimed efficiency would be achieved.

The decision-maker must be able to verify the value of the claimed efficiencies in order to be able to balance them against the anti-competitive effects of the agreement[84]. The Commission's requirement that undertakings must substantiate their claims is an important feature of the *Article 81(3) Guidelines*. Mere speculation or conjecture will be insufficient: there must be 'convincing arguments and evidence'[85] that the agreement will lead to the efficiencies claimed, the burden being on the parties seeking to defend it.

The Commission identifies two broad categories of efficiencies in the *Guidelines*, while acknowledging that it is not appropriate to draw clear and firm distinctions between the various categories[86].

(A) Cost efficiencies Paragraphs 64 to 68 consider cost efficiencies which may result, for example, from the development of new production technologies and methods[87], synergies arising from the integration of existing assets[88], from economies of scale[89], economies of scope[90] and from better planning of production[91].

(B) Qualitative efficiencies Paragraphs 69 to 72 consider qualitative efficiencies as opposed to cost reductions: research and development agreements are particularly cited in this

[78] Case 26/76 [1977] ECR 1875, [1978] 2 CMLR 1.   [79] Case 42/84 [1985] ECR 2545, [1987] 1 CMLR 1.
[80] Case T-168/01 *GlaxoSmithKline Services Ltd v Commission* [2006] ECR II-2969, [2006] 5 CMLR 29.
[81] Ibid, paras 247–308.   [82] *Article 81(3) Guidelines*, para 52.   [83] Ibid, paras 53 and 54.
[84] Ibid, paras 55–58.
[85] See Case T-168/01 *GlaxoSmithKline Services Ltd v Commission* [2006] ECR II-2969, [2006] 5 CMLR 29, para 235.
[86] *Article 81(3) Guidelines*, para 59.   [87] Ibid, para 64.   [88] Ibid, para 65.   [89] Ibid, para 66.
[90] Ibid, para 67.   [91] Ibid, para 68.

respect[92], as are licensing agreements and agreements for the joint production of new or improved goods or services[93]; there is also a reference to the possibility of distribution agreements delivering qualitative efficiencies[94].

(B) Third condition of Article 81(3): indispensability of the restrictions

The *Article 81(3) Guidelines* deal with the indispensability of restrictions before the question of a fair share for consumers, since the latter issue would not arise if the restrictions are not indispensable[95]. Paragraph 73 of the *Guidelines* states that the indispensability condition implies a two-fold test: first, whether the restrictive agreement itself is necessary in order to achieve the efficiencies; and secondly whether the individual restrictions of competition flowing from the agreement are reasonably necessary for the attainment of the efficiencies. Paragraph 30 of the *Guidelines* explains that the requirement of indispensability in Article 81(3) is conceptually distinct from the ancillary restraints doctrine: Article 81(3) involves a balancing of pro- and anti-competitive effects, which is not the case when determining whether a restraint is ancillary.

(A) The efficiencies must be specific to the agreement   Paragraphs 75 to 77 consider the first part of the two-fold test: the requirement that the efficiencies are specific to the agreement or, to put the point another way, that there are no other economically practicable and less restrictive means of achieving them[96]. The parties should explain, for example, why they could not have achieved the same efficiencies acting alone[97].

(B) The indispensability of individual restrictions   Paragraphs 78 to 82 consider whether any individual restrictions of competition flowing from the agreement are indispensable. The parties must demonstrate both that the nature of any restriction and that its 'intensity' are reasonably necessary to produce the claimed efficiencies[98]. A restriction is indispensable if its absence would eliminate or significantly reduce the efficiencies that follow from the agreement or make it significantly less likely that they will materialise; restrictions of the kind 'black-listed' in any of the block exemptions – for example horizontal price-fixing and market-sharing and the imposition of export bans in vertical agreements – would be unlikely to be considered indispensable[99]. A restriction may be indispensable only for a certain period of time; once that time has expired, it will cease to be so[100].

(C) Second condition of Article 81(3): fair share for consumers

The undertakings concerned must show that a fair share of the benefit that results from an agreement will accrue to consumers if Article 81(3) is to apply: it is helpful to think

---

[92] Ibid, para 70.   [93] Ibid, para 71.   [94] Ibid, para 72.   [95] Ibid, para 39.

[96] Ibid, para 75; note that under para 85 of the Commission's *Guidelines on the assessment of horizontal mergers* OJ [2004] C 31/5 efficiences are recognised in the assessment of mergers only where they can be shown to be merger-specific.

[97] *Article 81(3) Guidelines*, para 76.   [98] Ibid, para 78.

[99] Ibid, para 79; for 'black-listed' clauses in block exemptions see ch 15, p 592 (specialisation agreements) and p 587 (research and development agreements); ch 16, pp 652–657 (vertical agreements); and ch 19, pp 776–779 (technology transfer agreements).

[100] Ibid, para 81.

of this as the 'pass-on' requirement. Paragraph 84 of the *Article 81(3) Guidelines* states that the concept of consumers in Article 81(3) encompasses all direct or indirect users of the products covered by the agreement, including producers that use the products as an input, wholesalers, retailers, and final consumers; 'undertakings', in the competition law sense of the term[101], can be consumers for this purpose just as much as a natural person who purchases as a consumer in the lay sense. It is the beneficial nature of the effect on all consumers in the relevant markets that must be taken into consideration under this part of Article 81(3), not the effect on each member of that category of consumers[102]. Negative effects on consumers in one geographic or product market cannot normally be balanced against and compensated by positive effects for consumers in unrelated markets, although this may be possible where markets are related provided that the consumers affected by the restriction and benefiting from the efficiency gains are substantially the same[103].

If an agreement would leave consumers worse off than they would otherwise have been the pass-on condition of Article 81(3) will not have been satisfied[104]; however consumers do not have to gain from each and every efficiency achieved provided that they receive a fair share of the overall benefits[105]. It could be the case that an agreement, for example to produce a new product more quickly than if the parties had proceeded alone, might also lead to greater market power and therefore higher prices; the Commission does not rule out that early access to the new products might amount to a 'fair share' for consumers, notwithstanding the higher prices[106]. The greater the restriction of competition under Article 81(1), the greater must be the efficiency and the pass-on under Article 81(3)[107]; and where an agreement has substantial anti-competitive and substantial pro-competitive effects paragraph 92 of the *Guidelines* states that the decision-maker should take into account that competition is an important long-term driver of efficiency and innovation. The *Guidelines* proceed to discuss the pass-on requirement in relation to cost efficiencies and qualitative efficiencies respectively.

(A) Cost efficiencies Paragraphs 95 to 101 consider pass-on and the balancing of cost efficiencies. Paragraph 96 notes that cost efficiencies may lead to increased output and lower prices for consumers: in assessing whether this is likely the following factors should be taken into account:

- the characteristics and structure of the market;
- the nature and magnitude of the efficiency gains;
- the elasticity of demand; and
- the magnitude of the restriction of competition.

Paragraph 98 points out that consumers are more likely to benefit from a reduction in the parties' variable costs than in their fixed costs, since pricing and output decisions are determined predominantly by variable costs and demand conditions. Paragraph 99 explains that the actual rate of any pass-on to consumers will depend on the extent to which consumers will expand their demand in response to a lowering of price; this

---

[101] See ch 3, p 82–91.
[102] Case C-238/05 *Asnef-Equifax v Asociación de Usuarios de Servicios Bancarios (Ausbanc)* [2006] ECR I-11125, [2007] 4 CMLR 6, para 70.
[103] *Article 81(3) Guidelines*, para 43. [104] Ibid, para 85. [105] Ibid, para 86.
[106] Ibid, para 89. [107] Ibid, para 90.

will depend, among other things, on the extent to which sellers are able to discriminate in price between different categories of customers. Paragraph 101 cautions that any reduction in costs, and therefore any prospect of lower prices for consumers, must be balanced against the fact that an agreement being considered under Article 81(3) must necessarily involve a restriction of competition under Article 81(1), which in itself is likely to mean that the parties have the ability to raise their prices as a result of their increased market power: these 'opposing forces' must be balanced against one another.

(B) Qualitative efficiencies Paragraphs 102 to 104 consider pass-on and the balancing of other types of efficiencies: for example the emergence of a new and improved product might compensate for the fact that an agreement leads to higher prices. Paragraph 103 concedes that this involves a value judgment and that it is difficult to assign precise values to a balancing exercise of this nature. Paragraph 104 acknowledges that new and improved products are an important source of consumer welfare; it continues that, where prices will be higher as a result of the restrictive effect of the agreement on competition, it is necessary to consider whether the claimed efficiencies will create 'real value' for consumers that will compensate for this.

(D) Fourth condition of Article 81(3): no elimination of competition in a substantial part of the market

Paragraph 105 of the *Article 81(3) Guidelines* states that ultimately the protection of rivalry and the competitive process is given priority over pro-competitive efficiency gains that result from restrictive agreements.

(A) The relationship between Article 81(3) and Article 82 Paragraph 106 of the *Guidelines* explains that the concept of elimination of competition in a substantial part of the market is an autonomous Community concept specific to Article 81(3). Paragraph 106 then considers the relationship between Article 81(3) and Article 82. It refers to well-established case law that establishes that Article 81(3) cannot prevent the application of Article 82 EC[108] and that Article 81(3) cannot apply to agreements that constitute an abuse of a dominant position[109]. Paragraph 106 goes on to explain, however, that not all restrictive agreements concluded by a dominant undertaking necessarily constitute an abuse of a dominant position. The fact that most block exemptions contain market share caps means that dominant firms will rarely be in a position to rely on them[110].

(B) Determining whether competition will be substantially eliminated Paragraphs 107 to 116 explain how to assess whether an agreement will substantially eliminate competition. Paragraph 107 states that it is necessary to evaluate the extent to which competition will be reduced as a result of the agreement: the more that competition is already weakened

---

[108] See Cases C-395/96 P etc *Compagnie Maritime Belge Transports SA v Commission* [2000] ECR I-1365, [2000] 4 CMLR 1076, para 130.

[109] Case T-51/89 *Tetra Pak Rausing SA v Commission* [1990] ECR II-309, [1991] 4 CMLR 334 and Cases T-191/98 etc. *Atlantic Container Line v Commission* [2003] ECR II-3275, [2005] 4 CMLR 20, para 1456; in *Decca Navigator System* OJ [1989] L 43/27, [1990] 4 CMLR 627, para 122, the Commission refused individual exemption to an agreement that involved an abuse of a dominant position.

[110] See p 167 below.

in the market before the agreement, and the more that the agreement will reduce competition in the market, the more likely it is that the agreement will be considered to eliminate competition substantially. Both actual and potential competition should be taken into account when making the assessment[111]. The degree of actual competition in the market should not be assessed on the basis of market shares alone, but should be based on more extensive qualitative and quantitative analysis[112]. The *Article 81(3) Guidelines* set out a series of factors that should be taken into account when assessing entry barriers and the possibility of entry into the market on a significant scale, including, for example, the cost of entry including sunk costs, the minimum efficient scale within the industry and the competitive strengths of potential entrants[113].

(E) Review by the CFI[114]

The Commission's decisions on the application of Article 81(3) are subject to review by the CFI and (on a point of law) by the ECJ. In *Consten and Grundig v Commission*[115] the ECJ indicated that it would not adopt an interventionist stance on applications for review; Article 81(3) involves complex evaluations of economic issues, and the ECJ considered that this task is essentially one for the Commission: the Court would confine itself to examining the relevant facts and the legal consequences deduced therefrom; it would not substitute its decision for the Commission's. The Community Courts have maintained this approach, emphasising the extent of the margin of appreciation available to the Commission when dealing with notifications for exemption and (by implication) their unwillingness to interfere with the exercise of this appreciation[116]. However it is essential that the Commission's decision should be adequately reasoned, and where there is a defect in this respect the Courts will be prepared to annul the decision in question[117]. Similarly the CFI will annul a Commission decision where it has seriously misapprehended the facts of a particular case[118]. The CFI summed up the position in *GlaxoSmithKline Services Ltd v Commission*[119] as follows:

241 ...the Court dealing with an application for annulment of a decision applying Article 81(3) EC carries out, in so far as it is faced with complex economic assessments, a review confined, as regards the merits, to verifying whether the facts have been accurately stated, whether there has been any manifest error of appraisal and whether the legal consequences deduced from those facts were accurate (*Consten and Grundig* v *Commission*, paragraph 110 above, p. 347; *Metro I*, paragraph 109 above, paragraph 25; *Remia and Others* v *Commission*, paragraph 57 above, paragraph 34; and *Aalborg Portland and Others* v *Commission*, paragraph 55 above, paragraph 279).

242 It is for the Court to establish not only whether the evidence relied on is factually accurate, reliable and consistent, but also whether it contains all the information which must be taken into account for the purpose of assessing a complex situation and whether it is capable of substantiating the conclusions drawn from it (Case C-12/03 P *Commission* v *Tetra Laval* [2005] ECR I-987, paragraph 39, and Case T-210/01 *General Electric* v *Commission* [2005] ECR II-5575, paragraphs 62 and 63).

---

[111] *Article 81(3) Guidelines*, paras 108 and 114.   [112] Ibid, para 109.   [113] Ibid, para 115.
[114] See generally Bailey 'Scope of Judicial Review under Article 81 EC' (2004) 41 CMLR 1327.
[115] Cases 56/64 and 58/64 [1966] ECR 299, [1966] CMLR 418.
[116] See eg Case 26/76 *Metro SB-Grossmärkte v Commission* [1977] ECR 1875, [1978] 2 CMLR 1, paras 45 and 50; Case T-7/93 *Langnese-Iglo GmbH v Commission* [1995] ECR II-1533, [1995] 5 CMLR 602, para 178.
[117] See eg Case C-360/92 P *Publishers' Association v Commission* [1995] ECR I-23, [1995] 5 CMLR 33.
[118] Cases T-79/95 R etc *SNCF and BRB v Commission* [1996] ECR II-1491, [1997] 4 CMLR 334.
[119] Case T-168/01 [2006] ECR II-2969, [2006] 5 CMLR 29.

243 On the other hand, it is not for the Court to substitute its own economic assessment for that of the institution which adopted the decision the legality of which it is requested to review.

In the *Glaxo* case the CFI annulled the Commission's decision not to grant individual exemption to GSK's standard conditions of sale which were intended to prevent parallel trade from the low-priced Spanish pharmaceutical market to the higher-priced UK one: GSK argued that the restriction of trade was necessary to promote investment into research and development in the sector. The CFI held that the Commission had failed to carry out a proper examination of the factual arguments and evidence put forward by GSK or to refute its arguments[120]. Both the Commission[121] and GSK[122] have appealed to the ECJ against this judgment.

In *Métropole télévision SA v Commission*[123] a third party successfully persuaded the CFI that an individual exemption granted by the Commission should be annulled due to an error of law on the Commission's part. The Commission had granted individual exemption to the regulations of the European Broadcasting Union governing the joint negotiation, acquisition and sharing of television rights to sports events, subject to conditions designed to permit third parties to have access to the television rights in question and to ensure that the Commission would be kept informed of the practical application of the regulations[124]. A number of television companies, not members of the EBU, sought the annulment of the Commission's decision granting individual exemption. The CFI, having decided that the applications were admissible (in so far as the Commission had contested this in the first place), considered, first, whether the restrictions on competition arising from the rules on membership of the EBU were 'indispensable' in the sense of Article 81(3)(a); and, second, whether the 'particular public mission' of members of the EBU was relevant to an assessment of the EBU regulations under Article 81(3), and in particular paragraph (a) thereof, as opposed to Article 86(2).

As to the first issue the CFI considered, as in its view the Commission was obliged to do, whether the EBU membership rules were objective and sufficiently determinate so as to enable them to be applied uniformly and in a non-discriminatory manner vis-à-vis all potential active members: unless this precondition was satisfied it would be impossible to be sure that the restriction of competition inherent in the rules was indispensable. The CFI found that the Commission had not carried out such an investigation, and had consequently not considered whether the rules were indispensable: it had therefore committed an error of law warranting the annulment of the exemption. On the second point the CFI found that, in as much as the Commission had concluded in its decision that Article 86(2) was not applicable, it could not then take into account factors coming within its ambit in the context of Article 81(3). This also constituted an error of law.

This judgment demonstrates that a third party may be able successfully to challenge a finding that the terms of Article 81(3) are satisfied. In the *Métropole* case the Commission at a later stage adopted a further decision granting exemption to the rules in question; this decision was also successfully challenged on appeal by Métropole as the Commission had wrongly concluded that the agreement in question would not substantially eliminate competition[125].

---

[120]   Ibid, paras 247–308.   [121]   Case C-513/06 P, not yet decided.

[122]   Case C-501/06 P, not yet decided.   [123]   Cases T-528/93 etc [1996] ECR II-649, [1996] 5 CMLR 386.

[124]   OJ [1993] L 179/23, [1995] 4 CMLR 56.

[125]   Cases T-185/00 *Métropole télévision SA (M6) v Commission* [2002] ECR II-3805, [2003] 4 CMLR 707, paras 51–86.

3. THE MODERNISATION REGULATION

(A) The Commission's former monopoly over the grant of individual exemptions

Under Regulation 17 of 1962 the Commission had sole power (subject to review by the Community Courts) to grant individual exemptions to agreements on the basis of the criteria in Article 81(3)[126]. This monopoly over the grant of individual exemptions meant that the Commission had the opportunity to develop its policy towards various types of agreement over a period of time, and in some cases to give expression to this policy in its block exemption regulations. However the monopoly had many drawbacks: the Commission never had sufficient staff to deal with the enormous volume of agreements that were notified to it: the result was that severe delays were experienced; considerable business time was spent collecting the data and preparing the so-called 'Form A/B' on which notifications had to be submitted; substantial expense was incurred, not least on legal and other professional fees; and businesses faced a long period of uncertainty as to the lawfulness of their agreements. The Commission was overburdened with notifications, many of which concerned agreements that had no seriously anti-competitive effect, with the consequence that it was distracted from other tasks, such as the pursuit of cartels and abusive behaviour, which are of much greater significance for the public interest: as Recital 3 of the Modernisation Regulation says, 'the system of notification...prevents the Commission from concentrating its resources on curbing the most serious infringements. It also imposes considerable costs on undertakings.' The problems associated with the process of notification for individual exemption were ameliorated to some extent, for example by the adoption of block exemption regulations and by the informal settlement of some cases. However the 'problem' of the monopoly over the grant of individual exemptions was a real one, and this led the Commission, in the White Paper of 1999, to propose abolition of the process of notification altogether; this policy was carried into effect by the Modernisation Regulation.

(B) The end of the system of notification for individual exemption

The Modernisation Regulation ended the system of notification for individual exemption with effect from 1 May 2004. Previous editions of this book explained in detail how the system of individual exemptions operated[127]. There is little point devoting valuable space here to a system that is no longer in operation, except to point out that agreements that were formally granted individual exemption under the old regime continue to enjoy exemption even after the Modernisation Regulation takes effect. This is not stated explicitly in the Regulation but is undoubtedly the case; earlier drafts had said that existing exemptions would lapse, but this was thought to be unfair to undertakings that had notified and received an individual exemption and was therefore dropped. However

---

[126] Regulation 17, Article 9(1).

[127] See the fourth edition, ch 4, pp 136–141; see also Bellamy and Child *European Community Law of Competition* (Sweet & Maxwell, 6th ed, 2007, eds Roth and Rose), paras 13.004–13-016.

all individual exemptions were subject to a time limitation[128], and will therefore expire by effluxion of time in due course. In so far as individual exemptions were granted subject to conditions and obligations they are maintained in force by the Modernisation Regulation, which repeals the earlier legislation except for this purpose[129].

(C) Self-assessment

The fact that undertakings and their lawyers can no longer notify agreements to the Commission and await an administrative 'stamp of approval' certifying that the criteria of Article 81(3) are satisfied means that they must now be self-reliant and conduct their own 'self-assessment' of the application of that provision. This caused some consternation in the business and legal communities at the time that the Modernisation Regulation was being debated; some people expressed the fear that a lack of legal certainty might follow. However the old system was itself renowned for delay and uncertainty[130], and, given that lawyers have always had to provide advice to clients on the application of Article 81(1), Article 82 and Article 86(2), in relation to which the Commission has never enjoyed a 'monopoly' of the kind it did under Article 81(3), it is hard to see why they should not be able to provide similar advice under Article 81(3)[131]. The questions raised by Article 81(3) do not appear to be any more difficult than those that arise under those other provisions, if Article 81(3) is applied according to the narrow rather than the broad approach discussed above[132]. Since the Modernisation Regulation entered into effect there has been nothing to suggest that the direct applicability of Article 81(3) is causing difficulties in practice. A helpful Report, *Practical methods to assess efficiency gains in the context of Article 81(3) of the EC Treaty*[133], provides a structured framework on how to conduct a self-assessment of efficiency claims under Article 81(3). The mechanism in Article 10 of the Modernisation Regulation on findings of inapplicability, and the Commission's offer of 'informal guidance' in certain cases of uncertainty, have yet to be used[134].

(D) Notification and individual exemptions under domestic law

The Modernisation Regulation does not *require* Member States to abolish systems of notification for exemption under *domestic* law; however it would seem in principle to be undesirable to maintain a domestic system of notification following the reforms at Community level. The provisions in the UK Competition Act 1998 on notification and individual exemption were repealed by the *Competition Act 1998 and Other Enactments*

---

[128] This was required by Article 8(1) of Regulation 17.

[129] See Articles 36, 38, 39 and 43 of the Modernisation Regulation.

[130] See Commission's *Competition Policy Newsletter*, Spring 2003, p 4.

[131] See, to the same effect, Gyselen 'The Substantive Legality Test Under Article 81(3) EC Treaty – Revisited in Light of the Commission's Modernisation Initiative' in *Studies in Transnational Economc Law in Honour of Claus-Dieter Ehlermann* (Kluwer Law International, 2002, eds von Bogdandy, Mavroidis and Mény), 181.

[132] See pp 152–157 above.

[133] Available at www.ec.europa.eu/enterprise/library/lib-competition/doc/efficiency_guidance.pdf; note that this Report was commissioned by DG Enterprise and Industry rather than DG COMP.

[134] On findings of inapplicability and informal guidance see ch 7, pp 257–258; in the UK the OFT has issued a draft Opinion in relation to the distribution of newspapers and magazines: see ch 10, p 395.

(Amendment) Regulations 2004[135]. In May 2007 the Commission published on its website[136] the results of a questionnaire sent by the European Competition Network Working Group on Cooperation Issues that showed that most, though by no means all, Member States had achieved convergence with the position at EC level by abolishing domestic systems of notification and individual exemption.

4. BLOCK EXEMPTIONS[137]

(A) Role of block exemptions

Article 81(3) foreshadowed the advent of block exemptions by providing that the pro-hition in Article 81(1) could be declared inapplicable both in relation to agreements and to *categories* of agreements; in other words the Treaty itself envisaged the generic authorisation of agreements as well as pursuant to individual assessment. Most block exemptions are adopted by the Commission, acting under powers conferred upon it by regulations of the Council[138]. There are two exceptions to this, where the Council itself has granted the block exemption: the block exemption for certain agreements in the road and inland waterway sectors is provided by Article 4 of Council Regulation 1017/68[139] and block exemption for various agreements in the maritime transport sector is granted by Articles 3 to 6 of Council Regulation 4056/86[140].

Agreements within the terms of a block exemption have never been, and do not need to be, notified to the Commission: they are valid without specific authorisation. The block exemptions therefore provide desirable legal certainty for firms. In practice there is much to be said for drafting, for example, a vertical agreement or a transfer of tech-nology licence so that it satisfies the terms of the relevant block exemption as this pro-vides a 'safe haven' for it. Lawyers' reference works containing draft standard terms and conditions for distribution agreements and licences of intellectual property rights and know-how track closely the wording of block exemptions. In the days of notifi-cation for individual exemption the block exemptions were also important from the Commission's point of view, since they relieved it of the need for a substantial number of notifications for individual exemption. It is important to note that, since the block exemptions involve a derogation from the application of Article 81(1), their provisions must be interpreted strictly[141].

As paragraph 2 of the Commission's *Article 81(3) Guidelines* points out the system of block exemptions remains in effect, notwithstanding the abolition of individual exemp-tions as a result of the Modernisation Regulation. Paragraph 2 of the *Guidelines* also points out that a national court cannot declare an agreement invalid which is covered by a block exemption. Article 29 of that Regulation provides the Commission and, in

---

[135] SI 2004/1261; see ch 10, pp 394–395.   [136] www.ec.europa.eu.
[137] The terms 'bloc' and 'group' exemptions are also used: the expression 'block exemption' is used here as it is the most common one, and the one normally used by the Commission.
[138] See pp 165–166 below.   [139] OJ [1968] L 175/1.
[140] OJ [1986] L 378/1; this block exemption will expire in October 2008: see ch 23, pp 964–965.
[141] See Case T-395/94 *Atlantic Container Line and others v Commission* [2002] ECR II-1011, [2002] 4 CMLR 28, para 146; Case C-126/05 *Vulcan Silkeborg A/S v Skandinavisk Motor Co A/S* [2006] ECR I-7637, para 27.

certain circumstances, NCAs, with a power to withdraw the benefit of a block exemption. However paragraph 31 of the *Guidelines* explains that a national court cannot withdraw the benefit of a block exemption.

(B) *Vires* and block exemptions currently in force

The Commission requires authority from the Council to issue block exemptions[142]. The Council has published a number of Regulations; these are listed below, along with the Commission Regulations currently in force under each Council Regulation.

(i) Council Regulation 19/65

Regulation 19/65[143], as amended by Regulation 1215/99[144], authorises the Commission to grant block exemption to vertical agreements and to bilateral licences of intellectual property rights. The following Commission Regulations are in force under Council Regulation 19/65:

- Regulation 2790/99 on vertical agreements[145]; this Regulation replaced, and is wider in effect than, Regulation 1983/83 on exclusive distribution agreements[146], Regulation 1984/83 on exclusive purchasing agreements[147] and Regulation 4087/88 on franchising agreements[148].

- Regulation 1400/02 on distribution agreements for motor cars[149]; this Regulation replaced Regulation 1475/95[150].

- Regulation 772/2004 on technology transfer agreements[151]; this Regulation replaced, and is wider in scope than, Regulation 240/96[152].

(ii) Council Regulation 2821/71

Regulation 2821/71[153] authorises the Commission to grant block exemption in respect of standardisation agreements, research and development agreements and specialisation agreements. The following Commission Regulations are in force under Council Regulation 2821/71:

- Regulation 2658/2000[154] on specialisation agreements; this Regulation replaced Regulation 417/85[155], as amended by Regulation 151/93[156].

- Regulation 2659/2000[157] on research and development agreements; this Regulation replaced Regulation 418/85[158], as amended by Regulation 151/93[159].

(iii) Council Regulation 1017/68

Council Regulation 1017/68[160] itself provides block exemption for certain agreements between small- and medium-sized undertakings in the road and inland waterway

---

[142] The Council has power to confer such *vires* by virtue of Article 83(2)(b) EC.
[143] JO [1965] p 533, OJ [1965–66] p 35.   [144] OJ [1999] L 148/1.
[145] OJ [1999] L 336/21, [2000] 4 CMLR 398; see ch 16, pp 640–662.
[146] OJ [1983] L 173/1.   [147] OJ [1983] L 173/5.   [148] OJ [1988] L 359/46.
[149] OJ [2002] L 203/30, [2002] 5 CMLR 777; see ch 16, pp 663–666.
[150] OJ [1995] L 145/25, [1996] 4 CMLR 69.   [151] OJ [2004] L 123/11.
[152] OJ [1996] L 31/2, [1996] 4 CMLR 405.   [153] JO [1971] L 285/46, OJ [1971] p 1032.
[154] OJ [2000] L 304/3, [2001] 4 CMLR 800; see ch 15, pp 589–592.   [155] OJ [1985] L 53/1.
[156] OJ [1993] L 121/8.   [157] OJ [2000] L 304/7, [2001] 4 CMLR 808; see ch 15, pp 583–588.
[158] OJ [1985] L 53/5.   [159] See n 156 above.   [160] OJ [1968] L 175/1.

sectors[161]. There are no Commission Regulations granting block exemption under Regulation 1017/68.

(iv) Council Regulation 4056/86

Regulation 4056/86[162] itself provides block exemption for certain liner conferences[163] and for certain agreements between transport users and conferences concerning the use of scheduled maritime transport services[164]; however this block exemption will expire in October 2008 as a result of Article 1 of Council Regulation 1419/2006[165]. There are no Commission Regulations granting block exemption under Regulation 4056/86.

(v) Council Regulation 3976/87

Regulation 3976/87[166] authorises the Commission to grant block exemptions for certain agreements in the air transport sector. Regulation 411/2004[167] amends Regulation 3976/87 so that it now has application to agreements concerning air transport between the EU and third countries: formerly it applied only to air transport between Member States. There are no Commission Regulations currently in force under Regulation 3976/87[168].

(vi) Council Regulation 1534/91

Regulation 1534/91[169] authorised the Commission to grant block exemptions in the insurance sector. In February 2003 the Commission adopted Regulation 358/2003[170], which replaced Regulation 3932/92[171], under the powers conferred by this Council Regulation.

(vii) Council Regulation 479/92

Regulation 479/92[172] authorised the Commission to grant block exemptions to consortia between liner shipping companies. The Commission adopted Regulation 823/2000[173] under the *vires* of this Regulation; it has since been amended, to bring it into line with the principles of the Modernisation Regulation, and prolonged in effect until 25 April 2010[174].

(C) The format of block exemptions

The typical format of block exemptions is that they begin with a series of recitals which explain the policy of the Commission in adopting the regulation in question; these recitals may themselves be of legal significance, as they may be referred to for the purpose of construing the substantive provisions of the regulation itself where there are problems of interpretation. Each regulation will then confer block exemption upon a

---

[161] See Article 4.   [162] OJ [1986] L 378/1.   [163] See Articles 3–5.   [164] See Article 6.

[165] OJ [2006] L 269/1; see ch 23, pp 964–965.   [166] OJ [1987] L 374/9.   [167] OJ [2004] L 68/1.

[168] See ch 23, p 969.   [169] OJ [1991] L 143/1.

[170] OJ [2003] L 53/8, [2003] 4 CMLR 734; see Ryan 'The new insurance block exemption Regulation' *Competition Policy Newsletter* Summer 2003, p 51.

[171] OJ [1992] L 398/7.   [172] OJ [1992] L 55/3.

[173] OJ [2000] L 100/24, [2000] 5 CMLR 92; this block exemption replaced the earlier Regulation 870/95, OJ [1995] L 89/7.

[174] See ch 23, p 965.

particular category of agreements: for example Regulation 2790/99 block exempts vertical agreements, as defined in Article 2(1) thereof. The older block exemptions were very specific as to the clauses that could benefit from block exemption: only those set out in the so-called 'white list' would do so. This was considered by many critics to be too prescriptive and formalistic, and the four most recent block exemptions of the Commission are significantly different. Regulations 2790/99, 2658/2000, 2659/2000 and 772/2004, on vertical agreements, specialisation agreements, research and development agreements and technology transfer agreements, eschew white lists. They do, however, contain black lists (as did all earlier regulations), setting out provisions that must not be included if an agreement is to enjoy block exemption.

Most block exemptions have market share thresholds. For example each of the four Regulations just referred to has one: Article 3 of Regulation 2790/99 provides that undertakings with a market share of more than 30 per cent will not qualify for block exemption, although they may still be able to satisfy the conditions of Article 81(3) when assessed individually. Article 4 of the Regulation for specialisation agreements has a market share cap of 20 per cent. Article 4 of the Regulation for research and development agreements has one of 25 per cent. Article 3 of the Regulation for technology transfer agreements has a 20 per cent cap for horizontal agreements and a 30 per cent cap for vertical ones.

Article 29(1) of the Modernisation Regulation confers power on the Commission to withdraw the benefit of a block exemption where it finds, in a particular case, that an agreement covered by a block exemption regulation has certain effects that are incompatible with Article 81(3). Block exemption has been withdrawn from an agreement on only one occasion, in *Langnese-Iglo GmbH*[175]; the Commission's decision to do so was upheld on appeal by the CFI[176].

Article 7 of Regulation 2790/99 on vertical agreements gives a Member State the power to withdraw the benefit of the block exemption from vertical agreements which have effects incompatible with the conditions of Article 81(3) within its territory or a part thereof, where that territory has all the characteristics of a distinct geographic market. Article 29(2) of the Modernisation Regulation gives to each Member State a similar power of withdrawal in relation to the other block exemptions in respect of its territory if this territory has all the characteristics of a distinct geographical market. Paragraph 36 of the *Article 81(3) Guidelines* explains that in such a situation the Member State must demonstrate both that the agreement infringes Article 81(1) and that it does not fulfil the conditions of Article 81(3).

Article 8 of Regulation 2790/99 gives power to the Commission, by regulation, to withdraw the benefit of the block exemption from an entire sector, where parallel networks of similar vertical restraints cover more than 50 per cent of a relevant market.

(D) Characterisation of agreements to determine if block exemption is available

In order to benefit from a block exemption an agreement must be generically of the type envisaged by the Commission when producing the regulation in question. This means that there is a need to ensure that the agreement is within the spirit as well as

175 OJ [1993] L 183/19, [1994] 4 CMLR 51.
176 Case T-7/93 [1995] ECR II-1533, [1995] 5 CMLR 602.

the letter of any particular regulation. On several occasions an agreement has failed at the point of 'characterisation'. For example in *Italian Cast Glass*[177] the Commission rejected an argument that what it regarded as a horizontal market-sharing agreement was within the block exemption on specialisation agreements; in *Boussois/Interpane*[178] the parties failed to persuade the Commission that a licence of know-how with associated patents fell within the block exemption on patent licensing; in *Siemens/Fanuc*[179] the Commission rejected an argument that a horizontal market-sharing agreement was covered by the block exemption on exclusive distribution agreements. In *Moosehead/Whitbread*[180] the Commission concluded that a licence agreement between those two undertakings related primarily to the Moosehead trade mark, to which any know-how was ancillary; the consequence of this was that the now-repealed Regulation 556/89 on know-how licences was inapplicable and the parties had to notify the agreement in order to obtain an individual exemption[181]. In the case of Regulation 2790/99 the definition of a vertical agreement is a broad one, with the result that a much wider range of agreements will be block exempted than under the Regulations it replaced[182]. In the case of *Canal+/Telenor* the Commission found that agreements providing media content to a pay-TV channel were neither vertical, in the sense of Regulation 2790/99, nor technology transfer, in the sense of the predecessor to Regulation 772/2004, and so required individual exemption[183].

(E) *Delimitis v Henninger Bräu*

In order to benefit from a block exemption an agreement must satisfy all the requirements of the relevant regulation. The ECJ held in *Delimitis v Henninger Bräu*[184] that where an agreement failed to do so, albeit only in a marginal way, block exemption was unavailable and individual exemption was required; since the adoption of the Modernisation Regulation an individual assessment would have to be made. Provisions in a block exemption derogating from the prohibition in Article 81(1) cannot be interpreted widely, nor in such a way as to extend the effects of the regulation further than is necessary for the protection of the interests that it is intended to safeguard[185].

(F) Compliance with a block exemption is not mandatory

It is not mandatory to comply with a block exemption. This point may seem obvious, but this did not prevent a French court referring this very question to the ECJ in *VAG France SA v Etablissements Magne SA*[186]. The Court held that the block exemption on the distribution of motor vehicles presented undertakings with the possibility of invoking its terms, but that it was not obligatory for them to do so. They might instead have

---

[177] OJ [1980] L 383/19, [1982] 2 CMLR 61.   [178] OJ [1987] L 50/30, [1988] 4 CMLR 124.
[179] OJ [1985] L 376/29, [1988] 4 CMLR 945.   [180] OJ [1990] L 100/32, [1991] 4 CMLR 391.
[181] See also *Quantel International-Continuum/Quantel SA* OJ [1992] L 235/9, [1993] 5 CMLR 497, paras 45–49 (non-application of Regulation 418/85).
[182] See ch 16, pp 641–645.   [183] Commission decision of 29 December 2003.
[184] Case C-234/89 [1991] ECR I-935, [1992] 5 CMLR 210.
[185] Case T-9/92 *Automobiles Peugeot SA v Commission (No 2)* [1993] ECR II-493, [1995] 5 CMLR 696, para 37.
[186] Case 10/86 [1986] ECR 4071, [1988] 4 CMLR 98; see similarly Case C-41/96 *VAG-Händlerbeirat eV v SYD-Consult* [1997] ECR I-3123, [1997] 5 CMLR 537, para 16.

wished, for example, to apply for an individual exemption if they found it impossible to comply with the terms of a block exemption. Of course they would not now be able to notify for an individual exemption, but they might still be willing to take the risk of 'self-assessment' of their agreement on an individual basis rather than bringing it within the terms of a block exemption.

(G) Expiry of block exemptions

Each block exemption regulation contains an expiry date. For example, Regulation 2790/99 will expire on 31 May 2010. This means that a vertical agreement that will endure beyond that date cannot be said, with certainty, to be exempt from 1 June 2010 onwards. Clearly this may present the parties with difficulty. The Commission is of course well aware of the need for legal certainty and so, if it subsequently adopts a new regulation, it will normally include in it transitional provisions for agreements already in force. Obviously it is necessary to examine the provisions of each particular regulation to find out what the position is on transition. It is also possible that, even if an agreement does not satisfy the terms of a new block exemption that replaces an old one, the agreement may either fall outside Article 81(1) or satisfy Article 81(3) on an individual basis.

5

Article 82[1]

CHAPTER CONTENTS

1. INTRODUCTION

Article 82 is an important companion of Article 81. Whereas Article 81 is concerned with agreements, decisions and concerted practices which are harmful to competition, Article 82 is directed towards the unilateral conduct of dominant firms which act in an abusive manner. Article 82 of the EC Treaty provides as follows:

Any abuse by one or more undertakings of a dominant position within the common market or in a substantial part of it shall be prohibited as incompatible with the common market in so far as it may affect trade between Member States. Such abuse may, in particular, consist in:

(a) directly or indirectly imposing unfair purchase or selling prices or unfair trading conditions;

(b) limiting production, markets or technical development to the prejudice of consumers;

(c) applying dissimilar conditions to equivalent transactions with other trading parties, thereby placing them at a competitive disadvantage;

(d) making the conclusion of contracts subject to acceptance by the other parties of supplementary obligations which, by their nature or according to commercial usage, have no connection with the subject of such contracts.

---

[1] For further reading on Article 82 readers are referred to O'Donoghue and Padilla *The Law and Economics of Article 82* (Hart Publishing, 2006); *European Competition Law Annual: What is an Abuse of a Dominant Position?* (eds Ehlermann and Atanasiu, Hart Publishing, 2006); Faull and Nikpay *The EC Law of Competition* (Oxford University Press, 2nd ed, 2007), ch 4; Bellamy and Child *European Community Law of Competition* (eds Roth and Rose, Oxford University Press, 6th ed, 2008), ch 10; see also *Dominance: the regulation of dominant firm conduct in 38 jurisdictions worldwide* (eds Janssens and Wessely, Global Competition Review, 2008).

Many of the most controversial decisions of the Commission have been taken under Article 82, the most notable being the finding of two abuses on the part of Microsoft – a refusal to supply interoperability information to competitors and the tying of a media player with its operating software – of 24 March 2004: for these infringements Microsoft was fined € 497 million[2]. The *Microsoft* decision is discussed at various places in this book[3].

The purpose of this chapter is to describe the main features of Article 82; its application in practice is discussed at various points later in the book. Section 2 briefly discusses the meaning of undertaking and section 3 examines the requirement of an effect on trade between Member States. Section 4 considers what is meant by a dominant position under Article 82. Section 5 looks at the requirement that any dominant position should be held in a substantial part of the common market. Section 6 makes the point that quite small firms might find themselves the subject of an Article 82 investigation; not least because of the possibility that relevant markets might be narrowly defined. Section 7 looks at the central – and most complex – issue in this chapter, the meaning of abuse. More detailed analysis of individual abusive practices will be found in later chapters of this book, in particular chapters 17, 18 and 19, which examine, first, non-pricing abuses, then pricing abuses, and finally abuses that can arise in relation to the exercise, or sometimes the non-exercise, of intellectual property rights. Section 8 considers defences to allegations of abuse, and section 9 briefly considers the consequences of infringing Article 82.

The final section of this chapter discusses the Commission's review of Article 82, commenced in 2004, which led to publication of DG COMP's[4] *Discussion paper on the application of Article 82 of the Treaty to exclusionary abuses* in December 2005 ('the *Discussion paper*')[5]. Publication of the *Discussion paper* led to a prolonged debate on the law and practice of the Commission and the Community Courts under Article 82: widely divergent opinions were expressed as to whether Article 82 was in need of 'reform'. As at March 12 2008 the Commission had not made any public statement as to the likely outcome of the review commenced in 2004.

2. UNDERTAKINGS

The term 'undertaking' has the same meaning in Article 82 as in Article 81, and reference should be made to the relevant section of chapter 3[6]. It may be worth pointing out in passing that several of the cases on the meaning of an undertaking have arisen in

---

[2] *Microsoft* Commission decision of 24 March 2004, upheld on appeal Case T-201/04 *Microsoft Corpn v Commission* [2007] ECR II-000, [2007] 5 CMLR 846; quite apart from the payment of this fine, it has been reported in the media that out-of-court settlements have been reached between Microsoft and various of the complainants against it for the payment of damages: a report in the Financial Times of October 2005 suggested that Microsoft had paid a total of $3.73 bn.

[3] See in particular ch 17, pp 684–685 on the tying abuse and ch 19, pp 790–792 on the refusal to provide interoperability information.

[4] It is important to note that the *Discussion paper* is **not** a publication of the Commission itself, but a staff working paper; and that it does **not** contain draft guidelines: it is what it says it is – a discussion paper.

[5] Available at www.ec.europa.eu/comm/competition/antitrust/art82/index.html.

[6] See ch 3, pp 82–91.

the context of Article 82, for example where complaints were made to the Commission about the monopsonistic power of the Spanish Health Service[7] or the standard-setting power of Eurocontrol[8].

The issue of the application of the competition rules to public undertakings or to undertakings entrusted with exclusive or special rights will be discussed in chapter 6[9]; a few particular points about Article 82 and the public sector should, however, be noted here. First, the fact that an undertaking has a monopoly conferred upon it by statute does not remove it from the ambit of Article 82[10]. Secondly, Member States have a duty under Article 10 of the Treaty not to do anything 'which could jeopardise the attainment of the objectives of this Treaty', one of which is expressed in Article 3(1)(g) to be the institution of a system ensuring that competition is not distorted[11]. This means that a Member State cannot confer immunity on undertakings from Article 82, except to the limited extent provided for in Article 86(2)[12]. Thirdly, the provisions in Article 86(2) permitting derogation from the competition rules to the extent that their application would 'obstruct the performance, in law or in fact, of the particular tasks assigned to them' have consistently been interpreted narrowly by both the Commission and the Community Courts[13]. Lastly, it is important in this context to bear in mind Article 31 of the Treaty, the function of which is to prevent Member States from discriminating in favour of their own state monopolies of a commercial character. This provides the Commission with a useful alternative weapon for dealing with some monopolies in the public sector[14].

3. THE EFFECT ON INTER-STATE TRADE

The meaning of this phrase was analysed in chapter 3, to which reference should be made[15]. For the purpose of Article 82 particular attention should be paid to the ECJ's judgment in *Commercial Solvents v Commission*[16] in which it held that the requirement of an effect on trade between Member States would be satisfied where conduct brought

---

[7] Case T-319/99 *FENIN v Commission* [2003] ECR II-357, [2003] 5 CMLR 34, on appeal to the ECJ Case C-205/03 P *FENIN v Commission* [2006] ECR I-6295, [2006] 5 CMLR 559.

[8] Case T-155/04 *SELEX Sistemi Integrati v Commission* [2006] ECR II-4797, [2007] 4 CMLR 372, on appeal to the ECJ Case C-113/07 P *SELEX Sistemi Integrati v Commission*, not yet decided.

[9] See ch 6, pp 220–242.

[10] Case 311/84 *Centre Belge d'Etudes de Marché Télémarketing v CLT* [1985] ECR 3261, [1986] 2 CMLR 558, para 16; see also Case 26/75 *General Motors v Commission* [1975] ECR 1367, [1976] 1 CMLR 95; Case 41/83 *Italy v Commission* [1985] ECR 873, [1985] 2 CMLR 368; Case 226/84 *British Leyland v Commission* [1986] ECR 3263, [1987] 1 CMLR 185; Case C-41/90 *Höfner v Macrotron* [1991] ECR 1–1979, [1993] 4 CMLR 306, para 28; Case C-18/93 *Corsica Ferries* [1994] ECR 1–1783, para 43; Case C-242/95 *GT-Link v De Danske Statsbaner (DSB)* [1997] ECR I-4349, [1997] 5 CMLR 601, para 35; see also the Commission's decision in *French-West African Shipowners' Committees* OJ [1992] L 134/1, [1993] 5 CMLR 446, para 64.

[11] See eg Case C-260/89 *Elliniki Radiophonia Tiléorassi-Anonimi Etairia (ERT) v Dimotiki Etairia Pliroforissis (DEP)* [1991] ECR I-2925, [1994] 4 CMLR 540, para 27; see ch 2, p 50–51 on the deletion of Article 3(1)(g) from the Treaty as a result of the Lisbon Treaty of 2007 if and when it enters into force.

[12] Case 13/77 *INNO v ATAB* [1977] ECR 2115, [1978] 1 CMLR 283; see ch 6, pp 214–220.

[13] See ch 6, pp 233–239.   [14] See ch 6, pp 242–244.   [15] See ch 3, pp 142–146.

[16] Cases 6/73 and 7/73 [1974] ECR 223, [1974] 1 CMLR 309, para 33; see also Cases T-24/93 etc *Compagnie Maritime Belge v Commission* [1996] ECR II-1201, [1997] 4 CMLR 273, para 203.

about an alteration in the structure of competition in the common market[17]. This test, which has been applied by both the Community Courts and the Commission on subsequent occasions[18], is of particular importance in Article 82 cases: Article 82 can be applied only where there is already a dominant position – that is to say significant market power – and it is unsurprising that the Commission will be concerned with the structure of the market in such cases. In the *Soda-ash* decisions under Article 82[19] the Commission held that rebates offered by ICI and Solvay in their respective markets had the effect of reinforcing the structural rigidity of the EC market as a whole and its division along national lines. What is of interest about these decisions is that it was US exporters who were excluded from the EC market, but the Commission still held that there was an effect on inter-state trade: imports would have helped to undermine the dominant positions of ICI and Solvay in their respective markets.

The Commission's *Guidelines on the effect on trade concept contained in Articles 81 and 82 of the Treaty*[20] contain paragraphs that give specific consideration to the circumstances in which abusive behaviour – for example exploitative abuses that harm downstream trading partners and exclusionary abuses that harm competitors – might have an effect on trade between Member States[21].

Under Regulation 1/2003[22], the Modernisation Regulation[23], national courts and national competition authorities have an obligation to apply Article 82 where an abuse of a dominant position has an effect on trade between Member States[24]. This, however, does not preclude them from adopting or applying on their own territories stricter national laws which prohibit or sanction unilateral conduct engaged in by undertakings[25]; and the obligation is without prejudice to the application of provisions of national law that predominantly pursue an objective different from those pursued by Articles 81 and 82[26].

4. DOMINANT POSITION

Article 82 applies only where one undertaking has a 'dominant position' or where two or more undertakings are 'collectively dominant'[27]. A finding of dominance – whether

---

[17] The Commission refers to the 'competitive structure' test at para 20 of its *Guidelines on the effect on trade concept contained in Articles 81 and 82 of the Treaty*, OJ [2004] C 101/7.

[18] See eg Case 27/76 *United Brands v Commission* [1978] ECR 207, [1978] 1 CMLR 429; *Tetra Pak 1 (BTG Licence)* OJ [1988] L 272/27, [1988] 4 CMLR 881, para 48; *Napier Brown – British Sugar* OJ [1988] L 284/41, [1990] 4 CMLR 196, paras 77–80; *London European – Sabena* OJ [1988] L 317/47, [1989] 4 CMLR 662, para 33.

[19] *Soda-ash/Solvay* OJ [1991] L 152/21 and *Soda-ash/ICI* OJ [1991] L 152/1; these decisions were annulled on procedural grounds by the CFI: Cases T-30/91 etc *Solvay SA v Commission* [1995] ECR II-1775, [1996] 5 CMLR 57; the Commission's appeal to the ECJ failed, Cases C-286/95 P etc [2000] ECR I-2341, [2000] 5 CMLR 413 and 454; the Commission readopted the decisions in December 2000: OJ [2003] L 10/1.

[20] OJ [2004] C 101/7.   [23] See ch 2, pp 75–77.   [24] *Modernisation Regulation*, Article 3(1).

[21] Ibid, paras 73–76 (dealing with abuses covering several Member States); paras 93–96 (abuses covering a single Member State); paras 97–99 (abuses covering part only of a Member State); and paras 106–109 (abuses involving undertakings located in third countries).

[22] OJ [2003] L 1/1.

[25] Ibid, Article 3(2).   [26] Ibid, Article 3(3); see further ch 2, pp 77–78.

[27] The issue of whether any dominance is *collective* is discussed in ch 14 of this book, which considers in general terms the issues of oligopoly and tacit coordination between independent undertakings.

individual or collective – involves a two-stage procedure. The first is to determine the relevant market: market definition has been discussed in detail in chapter 1, in particular the 'hypothetical monopolist' or 'SSNIP' test; the problem of the 'Cellophane Fallacy' in Article 82 cases which might lead to the inclusion of false substitutes in the market definition; and the types of evidence that may be of assistance when defining relevant product, geographical and temporal markets[28].

Having defined the market, it is necessary in an Article 82 case to determine what is meant by a dominant position. Chapter 1 has already discussed the concept of market power, that is to say:

the power to influence market prices, output, innovation, the variety of goods and services, or other parameters of competition on the market for a significant period of time[29].

In particular that chapter looked at the relevance of market shares and market concentration when determining whether a firm or firms have market power; the significance of barriers to expansion and entry in the assessment; and the relevance of buyer power[30]. The text that follows will examine the approach that has been taken to determining dominance in the decisional practice of the Commission, in DG COMP's *Discussion paper*, and in the jurisprudence of the Community Courts under Article 82.

(A) The legal test

The ECJ in *United Brands v Commission*[31] laid down the following test of what is meant by a dominant position:

65 The dominant position thus referred to by Article [82] relates to a position of economic strength enjoyed by an undertaking which enables it to prevent effective competition being maintained on the relevant market by affording it the power to behave to an appreciable extent independently of its competitors, customers and ultimately of its consumers[32].

This definition contains two elements – the ability to prevent competition and the ability to behave independently – without explaining how these two ideas relate to each other. Does the ECJ mean that they are cumulative, that is to say that both elements must be proved? Or that one idea is parasitic upon the other, in which case which is the

---

[28] See ch 1, pp 26–40.

[29] See DG COMP's *Discussion Paper*, para 24; the expression 'other parameters of competition' presumably refers to other methods of, or manifestations of, competition.

[30] See ch 1, pp 40–43.

[31] Case 27/76 [1978] ECR 207, [1978] 1 CMLR 429; it has used the same formulation on several other occasions, eg in Case 85/76 *Hoffmann-La Roche v Commission* [1979] ECR 461, [1979] 3 CMLR 211, para 38.

[32] This definition does not adequately reflect (what is undoubtedly true) that Article 82 also applies to market power on the buying as well as the selling side of the market, since that was not in issue in *United Brands*; a powerful purchaser may be able to behave independently of its sellers who are not 'customers' in the normal sense of that word; for action taken against undertakings with buyer power see *Re Eurofima* [1973] CMLR D217; *Re GEMA* OJ [1971] L 134/15, [1971] CMLR D35; Case 298/83 *CICCE v Commission* [1985] ECR 1105, [1986] 1 CMLR 486; *UK Small Mines* Commission's XXIst *Report on Competition Policy* (1991), point 107; *Virgin/British Airways* OJ [2000] L 30/1, [2000] 4 CMLR 999, upheld on appeal to the CFI, Case T-219/99 *British Airways plc v Commission* [2003] ECR II-5917, [2004] 4 CMLR 1008: the CFI stated specifically at para 101 of its judgment that Article 82 can apply to undertakings with a dominant position on either side of the market; and on appeal to the ECJ, Case C-95/04 P *British Airways plc v Commission* [2007] ECR I-2331, [2007] 4 CMLR 982; see also ch 1, p 36 on procurement markets.

parasite? It is suggested that the essential issue is the ability to act independently on the market, that is to say with freedom from competitive constraint; in its *Discussion paper* DG COMP refers to independence as 'the special feature of dominance'[33]; it adds that for an undertaking (or undertakings) to be dominant they must not be subject to effective competitive constraints, and that this means that they must have substantial market power. The inclusion of the phrase about the power 'to prevent effective competition' in the *United Brands* judgment is therefore to be regarded as descriptive rather than prescriptive: it may have been inserted because of the application of Article 82 to exclusionary as well as exploitative behaviour.

(B) Measuring market power[34]

True monopoly is rare, except where conferred by the State. The majority of cases have therefore had to deal with the problem of deciding at what point an undertaking, though not a true monopolist, has sufficient power over the market to fall within the ambit of Article 82.

(i) Statutory monopolies

Various cases have concerned undertakings with a statutory monopoly in the provision of goods or services. The ECJ has rejected the argument that, because a monopoly is conferred by statute, this immunises the undertaking from Article 82[35]; where an undertaking has a statutory monopoly it must comply with Article 82, its only special privilege being that conferred by Article 86(2)[36]. A different point is that the fact that an undertaking has a dominant position as a result of rights derived from national legislation does not in itself mean that it has exclusive rights in the sense of Article 86[37].

(ii) The relevance of market shares

In cases where there is no statutory monopoly, market shares are an important issue in assessing market power, but not to the exclusion of other 'factors indicating dominance' which must also be taken into account, namely barriers to expansion and entry[38] and buyer power[39]. Market shares are not conclusive: mere numbers cannot in themselves determine whether an undertaking has power over the market. This point was stressed several times in chapter 1, and it should be borne firmly in mind in the discussion that follows[40]. Having said this, however, it is natural that market shares are looked at, and that they may be regarded as a proxy, albeit an imperfect one, for determining dominance: the range of situations in which market shares are used in competition law analysis was set out at the end of chapter 1[41].

---

[33] DG COMP cites paras 42–48 of the ECJ's judgment in Case 85/75 *Hoffmann-La Roche & Co AG v Commission* [1979] ECR 461, [1979] 3 CMLR 211, in support of this proposition.

[34] See *Bishop and Walker*, ch 3.   [35] See the cases cited at p 172, n 10 above.   [36] See ch 6, pp 233–239.

[37] See ch 6, pp 222–223.   [38] See pp 179–183 below.   [39] See p 183 below.

[40] See also Landes and Posner 'Market Power in Antitrust Cases' (1981) 94 Harvard Law Review 937; Vickers 'Market Power in Competition Cases' (2006) 2 (1) Supp (Special issue) European Law Journal 3; see also the speech of the Commissioner for Competition at the Fordham Corporate Law Institute on 23 September 2005, SPEECH/05/537, available at www.ec.europa.eu/comm/competition/speeches/index_2005. html: 'high market shares are not – on their own – sufficient to conclude that a dominant position exists'.

[41] See ch 1, pp 43–47.

As far as Article 82 is concerned, it is obvious that the larger the market share, the more likely the finding of dominance. A market share of 100 per cent is rare in the absence of statutory privileges, although not unheard of[42]. However some firms have been found to have very large market shares. For example in *Tetra Pak 1 (BTG Licence)*[43] Tetra Pak's market share in the market for machines capable of filling cartons by an aseptic process was 91.8 per cent; and in *BPB Industries plc*[44] BPB was found to have a market share in plasterboard of 96 per cent–98 per cent in Great Britain and of 92 per cent–100 per cent in Ireland, although the Commission had excluded wet plastering from the market definition. In the *Microsoft* decision[45] the Commission concluded that Microsoft had over 90 per cent of the market for personal computer operating software systems and at least 60 per cent of the market for work group server operating systems[46].

(A) The ECJ's Judgment in Hoffmann-La Roche v Commission In *Hoffmann-La Roche v Commission*[47] the ECJ said:

41 ...Furthermore although the importance of the market shares may vary from one market to another the view may legitimately be taken that very large shares are in themselves, and save in exceptional circumstances, evidence of the existence of a dominant position. An undertaking which has a very large market share and holds it for some time...is by virtue of that share in a position of strength....

The Court says here that large market shares may in themselves be evidence of a dominant position, but this assertion is qualified in two ways: first, by recognising that in 'exceptional circumstances' large market shares may not mean that a firm is dominant; and secondly, by referring to the notion that the market share must exist 'for some time'. In assessing market power, economists would argue that it is the exercise of market power *over time* which is of particular significance. A large market share held only briefly before the emergence of new competition would suggest that there was never any market power. This extract from *Hoffmann-La Roche* makes clear that a firm could argue, for example, that barriers to entry into a market are low so that new competition might soon emerge or that it was charging only at marginal cost so that its market share did not reflect true power over the market. In practice the Community Courts and the Commission habitually look to see what other factors indicate market power: they do not content themselves merely with quantifying market shares[48]. This is correct in

---

[42] In *GVL* OJ [1981] L 370/49, [1982] 1 CMLR 221 that body had a 100 per cent market share in the market in Germany for the management of performing artists' rights of secondary exploitation; see also *Amministratzione Autonoma del Monopoli di Stato ('AAMS')* OJ [1998] L 252/47, [1998] 5 CMLR 786, para 31, where the Commission found AAMS held a *de facto* monopoly of the Italian market for the wholesale distribution of cigarettes, upheld on appeal to the CFI, Case T-139/98 *AAMS v Commission* [2001] ECR II-3413, [2002] 4 CMLR 302, para 52.

[43] OJ [1988] L 272/27, [1988] 4 CMLR 881, para 44, upheld on appeal to the CFI Case T-51/89 *Tetra Pak Rausing SA v Commission* [1990] ECR II-539, [1991] 4 CMLR 334.

[44] OJ [1989] L 10/50, [1990] 4 CMLR 464, upheld on appeal to the CFI Case T-65/89 *BPB Industries Plc and British Gypsum Ltd v Commission* [1993] ECR II-389, [1993] 5 CMLR 33 and to the ECJ Case C-310/93 P *BPB Industries Plc and British Gypsum Ltd v Commission* [1995] ECR I-865, [1997] 4 CMLR 238.

[45] *Microsoft* Commission decision of 24 March 2004.   [46] Ibid, paras 430–435 and 473–499.

[47] Case 85/76 [1979] ECR 461, [1979] 3 CMLR 211; the Commission specifically referred to this paragraph in *Van den Bergh Foods Ltd* OJ [1998] L 246/1, [1998] 5 CMLR 530, para 258.

[48] In an interim case where it was necessary to act expeditiously the Commission considered that high market shares sufficed: see *ECS/AKZO* OJ [1983] L 252/13, [1983] 3 CMLR 694; see similarly *NDC Health/IMS Health: (Interim Measures)* OJ [2002] L 59/18, [2002] 4 CMLR 111, paras 57–62.

principle, in particular as market shares cannot say anything about *potential* entrants to the market, nor about buyer power.

(B) The AKZO *presumption of dominance where an undertaking has a market share of 50 per cent or more* In *AKZO v Commission*[49] the ECJ referred to the passage from *Hoffmann-La Roche* quoted above and continued that a market share of 50 per cent could be considered to be very large so that, in the absence of exceptional circumstances pointing the other way, an undertaking with such a market share will be presumed dominant; that undertaking will bear the burden of establishing that it is not dominant. The CFI applied this test in *Hilti AG v Commission*[50]. Clearly this is a very significant rule, which indicates that firms are at risk of being found to be dominant where they fall considerably short of being monopolists in the strict sense of that term. Some critics of Article 82, who believe that it is applied in too intrusive a manner, would like to see the 50 per cent threshold in *AKZO* raised: perhaps to 75 per cent. It remains to be seen whether, at some point in the future, the Community Courts might be prepared to do this; as far as the Commission itself is concerned it is, of course, bound by the case law of the Courts, although it could, as a matter of its own prosecutorial discretion, decide only to investigate cases where the dominant firm clearly has very substantial market power, perhaps where their market share was in excess of 75 per cent.

(C) Findings of dominance below the 50 per cent threshold It is necessary to consider at what point a firm's market share is so small that it could not be considered to have a dominant position. Both the ECJ and the Commission held in *United Brands* that a firm with a market share in the 40 per cent to 45 per cent range was dominant. In that case other factors were considered to be significant: the market share alone would not have been sufficient to sustain a finding of dominance. The case shows that a firm supplying less than 50 per cent of the relevant products may be held to have a dominant position. Even an undertaking subject to lively competition on the market, as UBC was at certain periods of the year, may be held to be dominant for the purposes of Article 82. In *United Brands* there was argument over the definition of the product, geographical and temporal markets: if they were drawn too narrowly or widely, United Brand's market share of between 40 per cent and 45 per cent may have considerably overstated its position, especially as it had faced fierce competition from other undertakings from time to time[51]. Given that it was subject to this competition, that its market share had been falling, and that it had not been in profit in its banana operations, one might say that UBC was as close to the threshold of dominance as one could get. Not everyone has been so charitable about the findings of the Commission and the ECJ in this case[52].

In *Hoffmann-La Roche v Commission*[53] the ECJ quashed the Commission's decision[54] that Roche was dominant in the vitamin B3 market where its market share was 43 per cent, as it was not satisfied that there were sufficient additional factors indicating

---

[49] Case C-62/86 [1991] ECR I-3359, [1993] 5 CMLR 215.

[50] Case T-30/89 [1991] ECR II-1439, [1992] 4 CMLR 16.

[51] The ECJ itself accepted that UBC had at times faced lively competition: Case 27/76 [1978] ECR 207, [1978] 1 CMLR 429, paras 113–117.

[52] See eg Valgiurata 'Price Discrimination under Article [82] of the [EC] Treaty: the *United Brands* case' (1982) 31 ICLQ 36.

[53] Case 85/76 [1979] ECR 461, [1979] 3 CMLR 211.

[54] *Hoffmann-La Roche AG* OJ [1976] L 223/27, [1976] 2 CMLR D25.

dominance for so deciding. The Commission has said that it takes the view that a dominant position can generally be taken to exist when a firm has a market share of 40 per cent–45 per cent and even that one cannot be ruled out in the region of 20 per cent to 40 per cent[55]. Its decision in *Virgin/British Airways*[56] marked the first occasion on which an undertaking with a market share of less than 40 per cent was found to be in a dominant position under Article 82. BA was held to be dominant in the UK market for the procurement of air travel agency services with a market share of 39.7 per cent. When the Commission's decision was challenged before the CFI the Court agreed that BA was dominant, noting that its market share was considerably larger than its rivals, and that this was reinforced by the world rank held by BA in terms of international scheduled passenger-kilometres flown, the extent of the range of its transport services and its hub network; the CFI also considered that BA was an obligatory business partner for travel agents[57]. The CFI stated specifically that the fact that BA's market share was in decline could not, in itself, constitute proof that it was not dominant[58].

Just as some commentators would prefer to see the presumption of dominance raised to a higher level than the 50 per cent in the *AKZO* judgment, so too there are those that would like to see a 'safe harbour' figure, below which the application of Article 82 would not be possible. In its *Discussion paper* DG COMP suggests that undertakings with less than 25 per cent of the market are 'unlikely' to be dominant[59]; however this offers more discomfort than comfort, since it suggests that it is at least possible that an undertaking could be found to be dominant below 25 per cent. It goes without saying that any harbour would be considerably safer if the figure was set at 40 per cent, or perhaps even 50 per cent. Ultimately it is for the Community Courts to decide whether such a safe harbour should be created.

(D) The relativity of market shares When looking at market shares it is relevant to look at the largest firm's share relative to its competitors': the smaller the shares of the competitors, the likelier the Commission will be to hold that the largest firm is dominant[60]. This was a significant point in the *Virgin/British Airways* case: in its judgment upholding the Commission's decision the CFI specifically noted that BA's market share constituted a multiple of the market shares of each of its five main competitors[61]. A different point is that where one firm has a market share of, say, 45 per cent, and its nearest rival has a similar market share of, say, 40 per cent, this would open up the possibility of the Commission reaching a finding that they are collectively dominant[62].

(E) How to calculate market shares In its *Notice on Market Definition*[63] the Commission deals with the method of calculating market shares at paragraphs 53 to 55. Data on

---

[55] See the Commission's Xth *Report on Competition Policy* (1980), point 50.

[56] OJ [2000] L 30/1, [2000] 4 CMLR 999.

[57] Case T-219/99 *British Airways v Commission* [2003] ECR II-5917, [2004] 4 CMLR 1008, paras 189–225, upheld on appeal to the ECJ , Case C-95/04 P *British Airways plc v Commission* [2007] ECR I-2331, [2007] 4 CMLR 982.

[58] Ibid, para 224.   [59] *Discussion paper*, para 31.

[60] See Case 322/81 *Nederlandsche Banden-Industrie Michelin v Commission* [1983] ECR 3461, [1985] 1 CMLR 282 where the nearest rivals of NBIM had shares between 4 per cent and 8 per cent; see also *Michelin* OJ [2002] L 143/1, [2002] 5 CMLR 388, para 178, upheld on appeal to the CFI Case T-203/01 *Michelin v Commission* [2003] ECR II-4071, [2004] 4 CMLR 923.

[61] Case T-219/99 *British Airways v Commission* [2003] ECR II-5917, [2004] 4 CMLR 1008, para 211.

[62] On collective dominance see ch 14 generally.   [63] OJ [1997] C 372/5, [1998] 4 CMLR 177.

these may be available from market sources, for example trade association statistics or from studies commissioned within the industry. However it will often be necessary to calculate market shares within the context of a particular investigation – whether under Article 81, Article 82 or the EC Merger Regulation – and the Commission will normally expect to do so by reference to the sales figures of the firms operating on the market. However sales figures are not the only data capable of revealing market shares. For example paragraph 54 of the Notice indicates that in the aviation sector it may be informative to look at the relative size of airlines' fleets, and in a sector such as mining the reserves held by different operators may be of importance. As for sales data themselves, the Commission states in paragraph 55 of the Notice that both sales by volume and sales by value are significant, and in the case of differentiated products it considers that sales by value and their associated market share are more revealing.

The Commission is primarily interested in a firm's current market share figures, although in some cases historic data may be important, for example in markets where there are large, 'lumpy' orders; this refers to a situation where large orders are placed – for example for the building of a power station or an airport – relatively infrequently: in such a case it may require a review of the market over many years to form a correct impression of competitors' market shares[64].

(F) Product differentiation and market share In some product markets it may be that some of the products are 'premium' brands and others are of a lower quality. In such cases firm A, that produces a premium brand and has 10 per cent of the market, may represent a greater competitive constraint on the leading undertaking than firm B, which produces lower quality products but has a higher market share. The Commission will take this possibility into account when assessing market shares[65].

(iii) Barriers to expansion and entry

Market shares are not the sole issue in determining whether a firm has market power. As was stressed in chapter 1, market shares cannot indicate the competitive pressure exerted by firms not yet operating on the market but with the capacity to enter it in a reasonably timely manner: what amounts to timely entry will depend on the dynamics and characteristics of the market; nor do market share figures provide any insight into the possibility that firms already in the market might be able to expand their production. It follows that an important part of the analysis of market power is a consideration of any barriers to expansion or entry faced by potential competitors. Where it can be demonstrated that there is a history of frequent and successful entry into a market, the Commission is unlikely to consider that there are high barriers to expansion or entry[66].

(A) DG COMP's Discussion paper Barriers to expansion and entry have already been discussed in chapter one. It was noted there that DG COMP's *Discussion paper* lists a number of such barriers. These are set out below with examples, taken in some cases from the decisional practice of the Commission and the jurisprudence of the Community Courts under Article 82, of particular types of barrier: to some extent they overlap one another.

---

[64] See further ch 1, p 40.   [65] See the DG COMP's *Discussion paper*, para 33.
[66] Ibid, para 36.

- **Legal barriers** The ownership of patents, trade marks and other intellectual property rights may constitute barriers to entry, depending on their strength and duration[67], although they do not, in themselves, confer dominance. In *Tetra Pak 1 (BTG Licence)*[68] the acquisition by Tetra Pak of a company that had the benefit of an exclusive patent and know-how licence was regarded as a factor indicating dominance, as it made entry to the market more difficult for other firms that would be unable to gain access to the licensed technology. In *Hugin v Commission*[69] the ECJ seems to have accepted that Hugin was dominant in the market for spare parts for its cash registers because other firms could not produce spares for fear of being sued by Hugin in the UK under the Design Copyright Act 1968. Other obvious legal barriers to entry are Government licensing requirements and planning regulations, Governmental control of frequencies for the transmission of radio signals[70], statutory monopoly power[71] and tariffs and non-tariff barriers.

- **Capacity constraints** Where competitors have to incur substantial sunk costs to enter a market, this may amount to a significant barrier to entry.

- **Economies of scale and scope**[72] The ECJ in *United Brands v Commission*[73] considered scale to be a factor indicating dominance, and the Commission in *BPB Industries plc* referred to this matter specifically[74].

- **Absolute cost advantages** Legal provisions of the kind discussed above give an incumbent firm an absolute advantage, since they mean either that a would-be entrant to the market cannot gain access to an asset or resource at all, or that it can do so only at considerable cost (for example by paying for a licence of an intellectual property right). The control of an essential facility, which may or may not be attributable to legal provisions, could confer the same absolute advantage on an incumbent undertaking[75], as could preferential access to natural resources, innovation or R&D. The ECJ has considered an undertaking's superior technology to be an indicator of dominance in several cases, including *United Brands v Commission*[76], *Hoffmann-La Roche v Commission*[77] and *Michelin v Commission*[78].

  Access to capital may sometimes give rise to cost advantages. In *Continental Can*[79] the Commission regarded that firm's access to the international capital market as significant, and this factor was stressed in *United Brands v Commission*[80].

---

[67] See eg *Eurofix-Bauco v Hilti* OJ [1988] L 65/19, [1989] 4 CMLR 677, para 66; *Magill TV Guide/ITP, BBC and RTE* OJ [1989] L 78/43, [1989] 4 CMLR 757, para 22 (copyright protection of TV listings relevant to finding of dominance), upheld on appeal to the CFI Cases T-69/89 etc *RTE v Commission* [1991] ECR II-485, [1991] 4 CMLR 586, and further on appeal to the ECJ Cases C-241 and C-242/91 P [1995] ECR I-743, [1995] 4 CMLR 718.

[68] OJ [1988] L 272/27, [1988] 4 CMLR 881, para 44, upheld on appeal Case T-51/89 *Tetra Pak Rausing SA v Commission* [1990] ECR II-309, [1991] 4 CMLR 334.

[69] Case 22/78 [1979] ECR 1869, [1979] 3 CMLR 345.

[70] *Decca Navigator System* OJ [1989] L 43/27, [1990] 4 CMLR 627.

[71] Case 311/84 *Centre Belge d'Etudes de Marché Télémarketing v CLT* [1985] ECR 3261, [1986] 2 CMLR 558; see Marenco 'Legal Monopolies in the case law of the Court of Justice of the European Communities' (1991) Fordham Corp L Inst (ed Hawk), pp 197–222.

[72] Economies of scale and scope are discussed in ch 1, pp 10–11.

[73] Case 27/76 [1978] ECR 207, [1978] 1 CMLR 429.

[74] See p 176, n 44 above, para 116.   [75] On essential facilities see ch 17, pp 690–699.

[76] Case 27/76 [1978] ECR 207, [1978] 1 CMLR 429, paras 82–84.

[77] Case 85/76 [1979] ECR 461, [1979] 3 CMLR 211, para 48.

[78] Case 322/81 [1983] ECR 3461, [1985] 1 CMLR 282; see also *Eurofix-Bauco v Hilti* (n 67 above), para 69 and *Tetra Pak 1 (BTG Licence)* (n 68 above), para 44; *Michelin* OJ [2002] L 143/1, [2002] 5 CMLR 388, paras 182–183.

[79] JO [1972] L 7/25, [1972] CMLR D11.   [80] Case 27/76 [1978] ECR 207, [1978] 1 CMLR 429, para 122.

- **Privileged access to supply** In *United Brands v Commission*[81] the ECJ described the extent to which UBC's activities were integrated – it owned banana plantations and transport boats and it marketed its bananas itself – and said that this provided that firm with commercial stability which was a significant advantage over its competitors.

- **A highly-developed distribution and sales network** In *Hoffmann-La Roche v Commission*[82] the ECJ pointed to Roche's highly developed sales network as a relevant factor conferring upon it commercial advantages over its rivals. The Commission has treated both vertical integration and the benefit of well-established distribution systems as a barrier to entry in several other decisions[83], since this could impede access for a would-be entrant to the market.

- **The established position of the incumbent firms on the market** In *United Brands v Commission*[84] the ECJ considered that United Brand's advertising campaigns and brand image were significant factors indicating dominance: it had spent considerable resources establishing the Chiquita brand name which was well-protected by trade marks. In its second *Michelin* decision the Commission relied upon the 'indisputable' quality and reputation of the Michelin tyre brand in its finding of dominance[85]. The Commission has often noted (in cases under the ECMR) that advertising expenditure could make entry difficult into the market for fast-moving consumer goods such as soft drinks[86], sanitary protection[87], and toilet tissue[88].

- **Other strategic barriers to expansion or entry** Network effects may be a barrier to expansion or entry[89]. This was a relevant consideration in *Microsoft*[90]. The Commission said that the ubiquity of Microsoft in the personal computer operating systems market meant that nearly all commercial applications software was written first and foremost to be compatible with the Microsoft platform. This gave rise to a self-reinforcing dynamic: the more users there were of the Microsoft platform, the more software was written for it, and *vice versa*[91].

(B) Obligatory trading partner A customer may be so dependent upon a firm for the supply of goods or services that the supplier can be regarded as an 'obligatory trading partner'[92]. In some cases under Article 82 the Commission and the Community Courts have been influenced by such a relationship in reaching a finding of dominance; for example in *Deutsche Bahn v Commission*[93] the CFI, in upholding the Commission's finding of dominance, noted the economic dependence of railway operators on the statutory monopolist in the provision of railway services within Germany. In *Virgin/British Airways*[94] the Commission noted that BA's position on the markets for air transport

---

[81]   Ibid, paras 69–81, 85–90.   [82]   Case 85/76 [1979] ECR 461, [1979] 3 CMLR 211, para 48.

[83]   See eg *Eurofix-Bauco v Hilti* OJ [1988] L 65/19, [1989] 4 CMLR 677, para 69; *Napier Brown – British Sugar* OJ [1988] L 284/41, [1990] 4 CMLR 196, para 56; *Michelin* OJ [2002] L 143/1, [2002] 5 CMLR 388, paras 191–195.

[84]   Case 27/76 [1978] ECR 207, [1978] 1 CMLR 429, paras 91–94.

[85]   *Michelin* OJ [2002] L 143/1, [2002] 5 CMLR 388, para 184.

[86]   See eg Case M.190 *Nestlé/Perrier* OJ [1992] L 356/1, [1993] 4 CMLR M17.

[87]   See eg Case M.430 *Procter & Gamble/VP Schickendanz* OJ [1994] L 352/32.

[88]   See eg Case M.623 *Kimberly-Clark/Scott Paper* OJ [1996] L 183/1.

[89]   On network effects see ch 1, pp 11–12.

[90]   Commission decision of 24 March 2004, on appeal Case T-201/04 *Microsoft Corp v Commission* [2007] ECR II-000, [2007] 5 CMLR 846.

[91]   Ibid, paras 448–459.

[92]   The concept of a 'partenaire obligatoire' was found originally in French law on pricing policy: see Ordonnance No 86-1243 on Freedom in Pricing and Competition.

[93]   Case T-229/94 [1997] ECR II-1689, [1998] 4 CMLR 220, para 57.

[94]   OJ [2000] L 30/1, [2000] 4 CMLR 999, para 92; see also *Michelin* OJ [2002] L 143/1, [2002] 5 CMLR 388, paras 200–207.

made it an obligatory business partner for travel agents, a point with which the CFI agreed on appeal[95].

(C) Conduct The ECJ in *United Brands v Commission*[96] agreed with the idea that the conduct of an alleged dominant firm could be taken into account in deciding whether it is dominant. This means, for example, that it might be legitimate to take into account the fact that a firm has offered discriminatory rebates to certain customers in deciding whether it is dominant: the rebates may themselves prevent competitors entering the market and so constitute a barrier to entry. In *Michelin v Commission*[97] the Commission had relied on Michelin's price discrimination as an indicator of dominance. Michelin argued before the ECJ that this approach was circular: the Commission was saying that because it had offered discriminatory prices, it was dominant, and because it was dominant its discriminatory prices were an abuse. The ECJ did not explicitly deal with this issue in its judgment, but in affirming the Commission's decision there is at least tacit approval of considering conduct as a factor indicating dominance.

Despite criticism of the circularity of this approach, the Commission has continued to regard conduct as a relevant factor indicating dominance: for example in *Eurofix-Bauco v Hilti*[98] it regarded that firm's behaviour as 'witness to its ability to act independently of, and without due regard to, either competitors or customers...'[99]; in *AKZO* it found that that undertaking's ability to weaken or eliminate troublesome competitors was an indicator of dominance[100]; and in *Michelin* it considered that that firm's conduct was strong evidence that a dominant position existed[101]. There is increasing recognition that there are types of behaviour that may deter entry[102], and it would be wrong to discount such conduct from the consideration of whether an undertaking is dominant.

(D) Performance The economic performance of an undertaking, as well as its conduct, may be a factor indicating dominance. The fact that a firm had idle capacity was regarded as significant in *Hoffmann-La Roche v Commission*[103], as was the ability of a firm unilaterally to increase its prices, which the market followed, in *Napier Brown – British Sugar*[104].

---

[95] OJ [2000] L 30/1, [2000] 4 CMLR 999, on appeal Case T-219/99 *British Airways v Commission* [2003] ECR II-5917, [2004] 4 CMLR 1008, paras 215–217.

[96] Case 27/76 [1978] ECR 207, [1978] 1 CMLR 429, paras 67–68.

[97] Case 322/81 [1983] ECR 3461, [1985] 1 CMLR 282.   [98] OJ [1988] L 65/19, [1989] 4 CMLR 677.

[99] Ibid, para 71; the objection to the 'circularity' argument may be met if the Commission uses conduct as an indicator only in clear cases, and provided that it is not relied on exclusively to support a finding of dominance.

[100] *ECS/AKZO* OJ [1985] L 374/1, [1986] 3 CMLR 273, para 56, upheld on appeal Case 62/86 *AKZO Chemie BV v Commission* [1991] ECR I-3359, [1993] 5 CMLR 215, para 61; see also *Soda-ash/ICI* OJ [1991] L 152/40, paras 6 and 48.

[101] *Michelin* OJ [2002] L 143/1, [2002] 5 CMLR 388, paras 197–199.

[102] See eg Ordovar and Salonen 'Predation, Monopolisation and Antitrust' in *The Handbook of Industrial Organisation* (Amsterdam, North-Holland, 1989, eds Schmalensee and Willig); OFT Research Paper 2 *Barriers to Entry and Exit in UK Competition Policy* (London Economics, 1994) and *Assessment of Market Power*, OFT Guideline 415, December 2004, paras 5.23–5.28.

[103] Case 85/76 [1979] ECR 461, [1979] 3 CMLR 211.

[104] OJ [1988] L 284/41, [1990] 4 CMLR 196, para 55; on the treatment of this issue in the UK, see *Assessment of Market Power*, OFT Guideline 415, December 2004, paras 6.5–6.6.

(E) Evidence of managers In *BBI/Boosey and Hawkes: Interim Measures*[105] the Commission regarded internal documents of Boosey and Hawkes, in which it had described its instruments as 'automatically first choice' of all the top brass bands, as significant in its finding that Boosey and Hawkes was dominant. In *Prokent-Tomra*[106] the Commission referred to several documents found during its inspection of Tomra's premises containing statements such as that Tomra's overall goal was to 'maintain market dominance and market share'[107]. Statements of this kind could not be probative of dominance in themselves. However it is clearly advisable for in-house lawyers to exercise restraint over hawkish commercial personnel, given to describing their position in the global widget market in memoranda and advertising copy as 'world-beating', 'the biggest' or 'clearly the dominant player'. Whilst shareholders might like to hear this, and whilst no doubt individuals' bonuses may be linked to their performance, it is not always easy to convince Commission officials that one's market power is insignificant in the face of such assertions.

(iv) Buyer power

As has been explained in chapter 1, a further issue of significance is whether a supplier or suppliers are confronted with buyer power; buyer power exists only where the buyer is well informed about and has a genuine choice between different suppliers, and is able to switch between them[108].

(C) Previous findings of dominance

In *Coca-Cola Co v Commission*[109] the CFI held that, whenever the Commission adopts a decision applying Article 82 (or the ECMR), it must define the relevant market and make a fresh analysis of the conditions of competition within it on the basis of the available evidence at the appropriate time; this may lead to a determination of the market which is different from a previous finding[110]. Furthermore a national court (or a national competition authority) would not be bound in a later case by a previous finding of dominance by the Commission in a different case[111]. However the actual decision in an Article 82 case may serve as a basis for an action for damages brought by a third party before a national court in relation to the same facts, even where the Commission's decision did not impose a fine[112].

(D) The 'special responsibility' of dominant firms

It is not an offence for a firm to have a dominant position; what is offensive is to abuse the position of dominance. However the ECJ in *Michelin v Commission*[113] stated that a firm

---

[105] OJ [1988] L 286/36, [1988] 4 CMLR 67, para 18.

[106] Commission decision of 29 March 2006; the case is on appeal to the CFI, Case T-155/06 *Tomra Systems and others v Commission*, not yet decided.

[107] Ibid, para 91.　　[108] See ch 1, p 43.

[109] Case T-125/97 etc [2000] ECR II-1733, [2000] 5 CMLR 467; the Commission defined the relevant product and geographic market afresh in its second *Michelin* decision: OJ [2002] L 143/1, [2002] 5 CMLR 388, paras 109–171.

[110] [2000] ECR II-1733, [2000] 5 CMLR 467, para 82.　　[111] Ibid, para 85.

[112] Ibid, para 86; see also Case C-344/98 *Masterfoods Ltd v HB Ice Cream Ltd* [2000] ECR I-11369, 130, [2001] 4 CMLR 449 and Article 16(1) of the *Modernisation Regulation*, discussed in ch 8, p 298.

[113] Case 322/81 *Michelin v Commission* [1983] ECR 3461, [1985] 1 CMLR 282.

in a dominant position 'has a special responsibility not to allow its conduct to impair undistorted competition on the common market'[114]. This statement is routinely repeated in the judgments of the Community Courts and the decisions of the Commission on Article 82. In a sense it is a statement of the obvious: it is clear that Article 82 imposes obligations on dominant firms that non-dominant firms do not bear. Unilateral behaviour is not controlled under Article 81, which applies only to conduct which is attributable to a concurrence of wills; unilateral acts can however amount to an infringement of Article 82[115]. An issue that will be explored later in this chapter, and in the discussion of abusive practices in chapters 17 to 19 of this book, is whether this special responsibility has led the Commission and the Community Courts to apply Article 82 too widely: do dominant firms labour under a handicap that prevents them from competing as fiercely as their non-dominant competitors[116]?

(E) The emergence of super-dominance

It would appear to be the case that the responsibility of a dominant firm becomes greater, so that a finding of abuse becomes more likely, where the firm under investigation is not merely dominant, but rather 'enjoys a position of dominance approaching a monopoly'[117]. The ECJ has said that the scope of the special responsibility of a dominant firm must be considered in the light of the special circumstances of each case[118]. It follows that behaviour may be considered not to be abusive when carried out by some dominant firms but to be abusive when carried out by others. An example of the distinction is afforded by the practice of a dominant firm which selectively cuts its prices to some customers, but not to below cost in the sense of the law on predatory pricing[119], whilst charging higher prices to others. There are strong arguments for not condemning this practice: if the dominant firm is not losing money, it would appear to be competing on the basis of efficiency, which competition law should encourage[120]. In *Compagnie Maritime Belge Transports SA v Commission*[121] the ECJ refrained from deciding generally on the practice of selective price cutting[122]; however, at paragraph 119 it said that:

It is sufficient to recall that the conduct at issue here is that of a conference having a share of over 90 per cent of the market in question and only one competitor. The appellants have, moreover, never seriously disputed, and indeed admitted at the hearing, that the purpose of the conduct complained of was to eliminate G&C from the market.

---

[114] Ibid, para 57.

[115] The respective roles of Articles 81 and 82 are spelt out particularly clearly in the judgment of the CFI in Case T-41/96 *Bayer v Commission* [2000] ECR II-3383, [2001] 4 CMLR 126, paras 175–176.

[116] See pp 188–206 below on the meaning of abuse, and pp 210–212 below on the Commission's review of Article 82.

[117] See para 136 of the Opinion of Advocate General Fennelly in Cases C-395/96 P etc *Compagnie Maritime Belge Transports SA v Commission* [2000] ECR I-1365, [2000] 4 CMLR 1076.

[118] Case C-334/94 P *Tetra Pak v Commission* [1996] ECR I-5951, [1997] 4 CMLR 662, para 24; Cases 395/96 P etc *Compagnie Maritime Belge Transports SA v Commission* [2000] ECR I-1365, [2000] 4 CMLR 1076, para 114.

[119] See ch 18, pp 738–741.

[120] It is possible that this pricing policy may amount to a different type of abuse, namely price discrimination (see ch 18, pp 748–753), but the issue here is whether the selective price cutting *in itself* amounts to an abuse.

[121] Cases C-395/96 P etc [2000] ECR I-1365, [2000] 4 CMLR 1076.

[122] [2000] ECR I-1365, [2000] 4 CMLR 1076, para 118.

On this basis the ECJ upheld the finding that there had been an abuse of a dominant position, whilst leaving open the possibility that the same conduct on the part of an undertaking with less than 90 per cent of the market and facing more competition would not have been found to be unlawful.

The idea that the obligations on dominant firms become more onerous depending on the special circumstances of the case (to use the language of the ECJ in *Tetra Pak*), finds expression in decisions and judgments that seem to have turned on the degree of market power that the dominant undertaking enjoys. For example Tetra Pak's market share in the market for aseptic cartons and carton-filling machines was in the region of 90 per cent to 95 per cent, and it was found to have abused a dominant position where its conduct did not take place in the market in which it was dominant, and was not intended to benefit its position in that market[123]. In *Compagnie Maritime Belge* the conference's market share was 90 per cent or more[124], and in the *IMS* case[125] the Commission, when ordering IMS to grant a licence of its copyright to third parties on the market on a non-discriminatory basis, noted that IMS was in a 'quasi-monopoly situation'[126].

In *Deutsche Post AG – Interception of cross-border mail*[127] the Commission noted that:

[t]he actual scope of the dominant firm's special responsibility must be considered in relation to the degree of dominance held by that firm and to the special characteristics of the market which may affect the competitive situation[128].

In *Microsoft*[129] the Commission said that Microsoft, with a market share above 90 per cent, had an 'overwhelmingly' dominant position'[130]. The Commissioner for Competition said after the CFI's judgment upholding the Commission's decision that the Court's judgment 'sends a clear signal that super-dominant companies cannot abuse their position to hurt consumers and dampen innovation by excluding competition in related markets'[131].

The idea that firms with a position of dominance approaching a monopoly may be subject to particularly onerous responsibilities would also help to explain why firms that control 'essential facilities' have an obligation in certain circumstances to provide access to them, since their market power is particularly strong[132]. It may be helpful, therefore, to identify a concept over and above dominance, that we might call 'super-dominance', where the risks of being found to be acting abusively are correspondingly higher: if a dominant undertaking has a 'special' responsibility, a super-dominant has one that is even greater. The expression 'super-dominance' has not been used by the Community Courts, nor by the Commission, and it remains to be seen whether it will be[133]. However a dominance/super-dominance calibration may be a helpful one

---

[123] See pp 203–205 below.

[124] See similarly, on the responsibility of a monopolist, Case 7/82 *GVL v Commission* [1983] ECR 483, [1983] 3 CMLR 645, para 56; this was cited by the Commission in *1998 Football World Cup* OJ [2000] L 5/55, [2000] 4 CMLR 963, para 85.

[125] *NDC Health/IMS Health: Interim Measures* OJ [2002] L 59/18, [2002] 4 CMLR 111; see also *Deutsche Post AG – Interception of cross-border mail* OJ [2001] L 331/40, [2002] 4 CMLR 598, paras 103 and 124.

[126] OJ [2002] L 59/18, [2002] 4 CMLR 111, para 58; this decision was subsequently withdrawn by the Commission: see Commission Press Release IP/03/1159, 13 August 2003.

[127] OJ [2001] L 331/40, [2002] 4 CMLR 598.   [128] Ibid, para 103, citing the *Tetra Pak* case.

[129] Commission decision of 24 March 2004.   [130] Ibid, para 435.

[131] See SPEECH/07/539, 17 September 2007.   [132] On essential facilities see ch 17, pp 690–699.

[133] See Case No 1001/1/1/01 *Napp Pharmaceutical Holdings Ltd v Director General of Fair Trading* [2002] CAT 1, [2002] CompAR 13, paras 219 and 337, in which the UK Competition Appeal Tribunal accepted that

in understanding why certain types of behaviour, such as selective price cutting and refusal to supply, are treated more seriously in some cases than in others.

5. A SUBSTANTIAL PART OF THE COMMON MARKET

Once it has been established that a firm has a dominant position on the market, one further jurisdictional question must be answered before going on to the issue of abuse. Is that dominant position held in the whole or a substantial part of the common market? If not Article 82, by its own terms, does not apply. This issue is not the same as the delimitation of the relevant geographical market: that concept is used as part of the investigation into a firm's market power. The requirement that market power should exist over a substantial part of the common market is in a sense the equivalent of the *de minimis* doctrine under Article 81, according to which agreements of minor importance are not caught[134].

Obviously there is no problem with the issue of substantiality where it is decided that an undertaking is dominant throughout the EC. The position may be more difficult where dominance is more localised than this. Suppose that a firm is dominant in just one Member State, or even in a part of one Member State: when will that area be considered to constitute a substantial part of the EC? Three points must be noted.

The first is that the issue is not solely a geographical one. In *Suiker Unie v Commission*[135] the ECJ said that for this purpose:

the pattern and volume of the production and consumption of the said product as well as the habits and economic opportunities of vendors and purchasers must be considered[136].

This indicates that substantiality is not simply a question of relating the *physical* size of the geographical market to the EC as a whole. In *Suiker Unie* the ECJ considered the ratio of the volume of Belgian and South German production of sugar to Community production overall and concluded on this basis that each of those markets could be considered to be substantial.

The second point is that it is likely that each Member State would be considered to be a substantial part of the common market, in particular where an undertaking enjoys a statutory monopoly[137], and *Suiker Unie* further established that parts of a Member State can be[138].

The third point is that neither the Community Courts nor the Commission have laid down that any particular percentage of the common market as a whole is critical in

---

the special responsibility of a dominant undertaking is particularly onerous in a case of a super-dominant undertaking under s 18 of the Competition Act 1998 (the domestic equivalent of Article 82); see further ch 9, p 360.

[134] See ch 3, pp 137–142.   [135] Cases 40/73 etc [1975] ECR 1663, [1976] 1 CMLR 295.

[136] [1975] ECR 1663, [1976] 1 CMLR 295, para 371.

[137] Case 127/73 *BRT v SABAM* [1974] ECR 313, [1974] 2 CMLR 238, para 5; Case T-229/94 *Deutsche Bahn AG v Commission* [1997] ECR II-1689, [1998] 4 CMLR 220; Case T-228/97 *Irish Sugar v Commission* [1999] ECR II-2969, [1999] 5 CMLR 1300, para 99.

[138] It is important to remember however that the abuse must also have an effect on inter-state trade to fall within Article 82: see pp 172–173 above.

determining what is substantial. In *BP v Commission*[139] Advocate General Warner took the view that sole reliance should not be placed on percentages in such cases and was of the opinion that the Dutch market for petrol, which represented only about 4.6 per cent of the Community market as a whole, could be considered substantial. The ECJ did not comment on this issue, as it quashed the Commission's finding of abuse on other grounds.

There are numerous examples of the test of substantiality having been satisfied in relation to a single facility: in each of *Merci Convenzionali Porto di Genova v Siderugica Gabriella*[140], *Sealink/B and I – Holyhead: Interim Measures*[141], *Sea Containers v Stena Sealink – Interim Measures*[142], *Flughaven Frankfurt/Main*[143], *Corsica Ferries*[144], *Portuguese Airports*[145], *Ilmailulaitos/Luftfartsverket*[146] and *Spanish Airports*[147] ports or airports have been found to be sufficiently substantial. Furthermore the ECJ has held that, where national law confers a contiguous series of monopolies within a Member State which, taken together, cover the entire territory of that State, that law creates a dominant position in a substantial part of the common market[148].

6. SMALL FIRMS AND NARROW MARKETS

(A) Small firms

It might be assumed that Article 82 is applicable only to large undertakings. It is certainly true that the Commission has used it to investigate some of the industrial giants of the world such as Roche, Commercial Solvents, United Brands, IBM and Microsoft. However it would be wrong to suppose that only firms such as this fall within the risk of Article 82. The significant issue under Article 82 is market power, not the size of an undertaking. Given that the relevant market may be drawn very narrowly, small firms may be found guilty of an abuse of Article 82. In *Hugin*[149] that firm was fined by the Commission for refusing to supply its spare parts to Liptons, the market for these purposes being spare parts for Hugin machines; Hugin's share of the cash register market was 12 per cent to 14 per cent, but its share of the spare parts market for its machines was 100 per cent. On appeal[150] the ECJ quashed the Commission's decision because it considered there to be no effect on inter-state trade, but it upheld the finding on dominance. A vivid illustration of the vulnerability of small firms under Article 82 is afforded by *BBI/Boosey and Hawkes: Interim Measures*[151]. Boosey and Hawkes was

---

[139] Case 77/77 [1978] ECR 1513, [1978] 3 CMLR 174.
[140] Case C-179/90 [1991] ECR I-5889, [1994] 4 CMLR 422, para 15.
[141] [1992] 5 CMLR 255, para 40.   [142] OJ [1994] L 15/8, [1995] 4 CMLR 84.
[143] OJ [1998] L 72/30, [1998] 4 CMLR 779.   [144] Case C-18/93 [1994] ECR I-1783.
[145] OJ [1999] L 69/31, [1999] 5 CMLR 103, upheld on appeal Case C-163/99 *Portugal v Commission* [2001] ECR I-2613, [2002] 2 CMLR 1319.
[146] OJ [1999] L 69/24, [1999] 5 CMLR 90.   [147] OJ [2000] L 208/36, [2000] 5 CMLR 967.
[148] Case C-323/93 *La Crespelle* [1994] ECR I-5077, para 17; this reasoning was applied by the Commission in, for example, *Portuguese Airports* OJ [1999] L 69/31, [1999] 5 CMLR 103, paras 21–22.
[149] OJ [1978] L 22/23, [1978] 1 CMLR D19.
[150] Case 22/78 *Hugin v Commission* [1979] ECR 1869, [1979] 3 CMLR 345.
[151] OJ [1987] L 286/36, [1988] 4 CMLR 67.

found by the Commission, in an interim decision, to have abused its dominant position when it refused to supply musical instruments to customers who were threatening to enter into competition with it. Boosey and Hawkes' world-wide sales in all products were worth £38 million in 1985, and the market it was accused of dominating was defined as instruments for British-style brass bands, in which its market share was 80 per cent to 90 per cent.

(B) Narrow markets

In the *Hugin* case a small part of Hugin's activities, the supply of spare parts, constituted the relevant market within which it was dominant. Similarly in *General Motors v Commission*[152], where the Belgian Government had given General Motors the exclusive power to grant test certificates to second-hand imports of Opel cars, this function was held to constitute a separate market, and General Motors' exclusive right meant that it was in a dominant position. The decision in *British Leyland v Commission*[153] was similar, that firm being held to have a dominant position in the provision of national type-approval certificates for its vehicles. Two further cases illustrate how narrowly a market can be defined. In *Porto di Genova v Siderurgica Gabrielli*[154] the ECJ held that the organisation of port activities at a single port could constitute a relevant market; and in *Corsica Ferries*[155] it reached the same conclusion in relation to the provision of piloting services at the same port. Similarly narrow markets have been found by the Commission in a series of decisions on services linked to access to airports[156].

The *Football World Cup 1998*[157] decision epitomises the possibility of narrow market definitions. The Commission proceeded on the basis of abuse in the market for 574,300 'blind pass' tickets to matches at the 1998 World Cup, a blind pass consisting of a ticket where the consumer does not know, at the time of purchase, what game he or she will be seeing[158]. The CFO, responsible for the ticketing arrangements, was found to have abused its dominant position by selling tickets only to customers having a postal address in France: this had caused complaints, not surprisingly, that it was guilty of discrimination in favour of French nationals. A token fine of €1,000 was imposed.

7. ABUSE

Once it has been decided that a firm has a dominant position in a substantial part of the common market it is necessary to consider what constitutes an abuse of that position. Article 82 gives examples – charging unfair prices, limiting production and discrimination – but this list is not exhaustive[159], and the Commission's decisions and

---

[152] OJ [1975] L 29/14, [1975] 1 CMLR D20; the decision was quashed by the ECJ on the issue of whether General Motors was guilty of excessive pricing issue: Case 26/75 *General Motors Continental NV v Commission* [1975] ECR 1367, [1976] 1 CMLR 95: see ch 18, p 712.

[153] Case 226/84 [1986] ECR 3263, [1987] 1 CMLR 185.

[154] Case C-179/90 [1991] ECR I-5889, [1994] 4 CMLR 422.   [155] Case C-18/93 [1994] ECR I-1783.

[156] See p 187 above.   [157] OJ [2000] L 5/55, [2000] 4 CMLR 963.

[158] For example, the third place play-off between, as yet, unidentified teams.

[159] Case 6/72 *Continental Can v Commission* [1973] ECR 215, [1973] CMLR 199, para 26; Cases C-395/96 P etc *Compagnie Maritime Belge Transports SA v Commission* [2000] ECR I-1365, [2000] 4 CMLR 1076, para 112; Case T-201/04 *Microsoft Corpn v Commission* [2007] ECR II-000, [2007] 5 CMLR 846, para 860.

the case law of the Community Courts have applied Article 82 to practices not specifically mentioned in it. Of particular importance is the ECJ's teleological interpretation of the Treaty whereby it applies the competition rules against the backdrop of the overall objectives expressed in Articles 2 and 3(1)(g); this has been highly significant in the case of so-called exclusionary abuses[160].

The law of abuse is complex and controversial, and a great deal of intellectual effort has been expended, particularly since the initiation of the Commission's review of Article 82 in 2004, in trying to clarify the underlying purpose of and the guiding principles behind this provision. This section of the chapter discusses in general terms what is meant by abuse, and notes the controversy that surrounds it.

(A) The Article 82 controversy

It is not controversial to say that Article 82 is controversial. In the case of Article 81 undertakings are liable only where they enter into agreements that restrict competition; the main focus of the Commission's (and of national competition authorities') attention is the deliberate and secret cartelisation of markets, and there are few apologists today for this kind of behaviour[161]. Article 82, on the other hand, bears upon the individual behaviour of a dominant firm[162]; by its nature the application of Article 82 involves a competition authority or a court having to decide whether that behaviour deviates from 'normal' or 'fair' or 'undistorted' competition, or from 'competition on the merits', none of which expressions is free from difficulty[163].

Transgression of Article 82 has serious consequences: fines, damages claims, the imposition of remedies such as a duty to deal or to raise or lower prices, and even the possibility of a structural change in the dominant undertaking[164]. It follows that there must be rules that are reasonably certain in scope and that are administrable in practice that enable undertakings and their professional advisers to know on which side of legality they stand; competition authorities and courts also need to know what is lawful and what is unlawful. An obvious danger is that the rules on what amounts to an abuse might be too broad – that is to say they might apply to some practices that are not anti-competitive at all. It is a truism that competition policy is in favour of firms competing, on price, quality and innovation; and that dominant firms should compete – and be able to compete – as well as non-dominant ones. However it is also the case that competition law prohibits various practices, including some price cuts by dominant firms: the most obvious example is predatory pricing which means, in essence, selling at a loss[165]. If the rule on predatory pricing is broader than is appropriate there is an obvious possibility that dominant firms – as well as non-dominant ones that fear that they might (wrongly) be found to be dominant – will refrain from reducing their prices because of the risk of being accused of abusive behaviour. The paradox of this situation is obvious: that competition law may act as a deterrent to competition.

---

[160] See pp 200–201 below.   [161] See ch 13 generally on cartels.

[162] Article 82 can also apply to the abuse of collective dominance, although this is not a concept that has been explored in much detail in the case law: see ch 14, pp 565–567.

[163] See *Competition on the Merits* OECD DAF/COMP(2005) 27 for a general discussion of this topic, available at www.oecd.org.

[164] See generally chs 7 and 8 on the public and private enforcement of the competition rules, including Article 82.

[165] Predatory pricing, and the complexities associated with it, is discussed in ch 18, pp 729–743.

(B) Type I errors (false negatives) and Type II errors (false positives)

A more stylised way of presenting this problem is to consider the difference between what are sometimes referred to as 'Type I errors' and 'Type II errors'.

A **Type I error** – sometimes referred to as a **false negative** or under-inclusiveness – occurs where a competition authority incorrectly concludes that anti-competitive behaviour is not illegal and therefore permits it: a harm to consumers. A **Type II error** – also known as a **false positive** or over-inclusiveness – occurs where a competition authority incorrectly concludes that pro-competitive behavior is illegal: a harm to the firm(s) found guilty, and also to consumers, since the pro-competitive behavior will be prohibited. Given the inherent difficulty of determining which unilateral acts are anti-competitive and which are pro-competitive, it is inevitable that competition authorities will sometimes make errors. An important policy question when framing the rules on unilateral behaviour is to decide which of the two errors is preferable. There is an undoubted perception that the enforcement authorities and the courts in the US today are more concerned about Type II errors than Type I: that is to say that they err on the side of non-intervention under section 2 of the Sherman Act 1890, which forbids the monopolisation of markets[166], whereas the Commission and the Community Courts tend the other way[167]. In *Verizon Communications Inc v Law Offices of Curtis Trinko*[168] the Supreme Court, in a refusal to supply case, was explicit about its fear of Type II errors:

Against the slight benefits of antitrust intervention here, we must weigh a realistic assessment of its costs...Mistaken inferences and the resulting false condemnations are "especially costly, because they chill the very conduct the antitrust laws are designed to protect"...The cost of false positives counsels against an undue expansion of s. 2 liability[169].

In contrast one might note that on many occasions when the Community Courts have been invited to expand Article 82 liability they have done so: for example when apparently adopting *per se* rules[170]; when establishing that Article 82 could apply to mergers[171]; when deciding that there did not need to be any causation between the market power held by a dominant firm and its abusive behaviour[172]; when accepting that the dominance, abuse and effects of the abuse can be in different markets[173]; when extending the application of Article 82 to collective, as well as to individual,

---

[166] For discussion of section 2 of the Sherman Act see Sullivan and Harrison *Understanding Antitrust and Its Economic Implications* (LexisNexis, 4th ed, 2003), ch 6; Sullivan and Hovenkamp *Antitrust Law, Policy and Procedure: Cases, Materials, Problems* (LexisNexis, 5th ed, 2004), ch 6; Fox, Sullivan and Peritz *Cases and Materials on U.S. Antitrust in Global Context* (Thomson/West, 2nd ed, 2004), ch 3; Hovenkamp *Federal Antitrust Policy: The Law of Competition and Its Practice* (Thomson/West, 3rd ed, 2005), chs 6–10; Kovacic 'The Intellectual DNA of Modern US Competition Law for Dominant Firm Conduct: The Chicago/Harvard Double Helix' (2007) Columbia Business Law Review 1; for a critique of the 'vacuous standards and conclusory labels that provide no meaningful guidance about which conduct will be condemned as exclusionary' under section 2 of the Sherman Act see Elhauge 'Defining Better Monopolization Standards' (2003) 56 Stanford Law Review 253.

[167] For an interesting discussion of the differences in approach in the US and the EU, suggesting that the position in the US can lead to anti-competitive behaviour escaping sanction, see Fox 'A Tale of Two Jurisdictions and an Orphan Case: Antitrust, Intellectual Property, and Refusals to Deal' (2005) 28 Fordham International Law Journal 952

[168] 540 US 398 (2004).   [169] Ibid, p 414.   [170] See pp 195–197 below.   [171] See pp 200–201 below.

[172] See pp 201–202 below.   [173] See pp 203–205 below.

dominance[174]; and when acknowledging the possibility of an individual abuse of a collective dominant position[175]. This record does not suggest the same reticence as that of the Supreme Court in *Verizon*.

(C) What is the purpose of Article 82?

In determining what behaviour is capable of infringing Article 82, it is necessary to begin with a consideration of what the underlying purpose of this provision is[176]. Article 3(1)(g) tells us that one of the activities of the Community is the institution of a system ensuring that competition in the internal market is not distorted, but this does not explain the purpose of undistorted competition. Nor does Article 82 provide us with a definition of abuse: as with many expressions in Community competition law – what is an undertaking? what is a restriction of competition? – the Treaty is drafted in broad and non-specific language, leaving it to the Community institutions, and in particular the Courts, to put flesh on the bare bones.

Critics of the way that Article 82 is applied in practice often argue that it has been, and is, used to protect competitors, including inefficient competitors, rather than to protect competition. The Commission, in particular in recent years, protests that it does not act to protect competitors, but to promote consumer welfare through the process of competition. These two competing claims will be examined in the text that follows, and an attempt to resolve the debate as to the underlying purpose of Article 82 will then be made.

(i) Is the purpose of Article 82 to protect competitors rather than competition?

Proponents of the view that Article 82 is used to protect competitors rather than competition protest that this means that efficient dominant firms are, in effect, subjected to a handicap; competitive acts, such as price reductions or the bundling of different products, that are perfectly legal for non-dominant firms, become illegal when a firm is dominant. The complaint is that this means that firms that possess superior efficiency are restrained in order to provide a place in the competitive arena for less efficient ones. This criticism brings to mind Robert Bork's attack on the antitrust rules as they were applied in the US in the 1960s and 1970s, and in particular the 'uncritical sentimentality in favour of the small guy' of the enforcement authorities and the courts there at that time[177]. The most high-level accusation of the EU's predilection for protecting competitors rather than competition came from the Assistant Attorney General for Antitrust at the US Department of Justice in response to the judgment of the CFI in September 2007 upholding the Commission's decision that Microsoft had abused its dominant position[178]. After expressing 'concern' about the standard applied to unilateral conduct in Europe, Mr Barnett said that:

In the United States, the antitrust laws are enforced to protect consumers by protecting competition, not competitors[179].

---

[174] See ch 14, pp 556–564.   [175] Ibid, pp 565–567.

[176] For a discussion of the purpose of unilateral conduct laws generally see the *Report on the Objectives of Unilateral Conduct Laws* prepared by the Unilateral Conduct Working Group of the ICN, May 2007, available at www.internationalcompetitionnetwork.org.

[177] Bork *The Antitrust Paradox* (The Free Press, 1993).

[178] Case T-201/04 *Microsoft Corpn v Commission* [2007] ECR II-000, [2007] 5 CMLR 846.

[179] See the Press Release of 17 September 2007, available at www.usdoj.atr/public/press_releases.

Without saying more, his meaning could hardly have been clearer: that in the EU the prime concern is not with the protection of consumers through competition, but with the protection of competitors.

Some commentators lay the blame for what they see as an unduly interventionist application of Article 82 at the door of the school of ordoliberalism which, through its concern to protect economic freedom, including the right of access to markets unconstrained by barriers such as exclusive agreements or rebating and discounting practices having analogous effects, led to the adoption of formalistic rules capable of having perverse consequences[180]. We will return to this criticism, and consider whether it is valid, below[181].

(ii) Is the purpose of Article 82 to promote consumer welfare through the process of competition?

A quite different view is that Article 82 is not a provision designed for the protection of competitors as such; rather that it is predominantly concerned with economic efficiency. In recent years the Commission has stated on numerous occasions, and in relation to various aspects of Community competition law, that the underlying purpose of the law is to maximise consumer welfare[182]. A clear statement to this effect can be found in paragraph 54 of DG COMP's *Discussion paper on exclusionary abuses*:

The essential objective of Article 82 when analysing exclusionary conduct is the protection of competition on the market as a means of enhancing consumer welfare and of ensuring an efficient allocation of resources.

Perhaps as important is a later sentence in the same paragraph:

This means that it is competition, and not competitors as such, that is to be protected.

The Commissioner for Competition said the same thing in a speech at Fordham in September 2005[183]:

My own philosophy on this is fairly simple. First, it is competition, and not competitors, that is to be protected. Second, ultimately the aim is to avoid consumers harm.
   I like aggressive competition – including by dominant companies – and I don't care if it may hurt competitors – as long as it ultimately benefits consumers. That is because the main and ultimate objective of Article 82 is to protect consumers, and this does, of course, require the protection of an undistorted competitive process on the market.

(iii) Resolution of the debate

Clearly there is a considerable difference between the two positions just outlined, and there is a need to resolve the debate as to the underlying purpose of Article 82. As noted in chapter 1, different policy objectives have been pursued in the name of competition law over the years. Neither time nor competition policy stand still, and it would be naive to suppose that all competition law decisions in the European Union, over a period

---

[180] For a discussion of ordoliberalism see ch 1, pp 21–22; for an example of criticism of the impact of ordoliberalism see eg Kallaugher and Sher 'Rebates Revisited: Anti-Competition Effects and Exclusionary Abuse Under Article 82' (2004) 25 ECLR 263; Venit 'Article 82: The Last Frontier – Fighting Fire with Fire' (2005) 28 Fordham International Law Journal 1157.
[181] See p 193 below.   [182] See ch 1, p 19.   [183] SPEECH/05/537, 23 September 2005.

of 50 years, have been adopted by reference to a single principle or policy. Without naming any particular cases, it is possible to imagine that in some the Commission or the Community Courts had greater or lesser concerns, for example, about small or medium-sized firms that appeared to be the 'victim' of aggressive behaviour by a dominant firm; about apparent violations of the 'single market imperative'; or about the exploitation of a 'locked-in' customer. However competition policy evolves, and the experience acquired over time leads (one would hope) to a better understanding of economic principles, a more refined set of rules and a more focused selection of cases for investigation. In this author's view a search for the underlying purpose of Article 82 through a microscopic analysis of all the decisions and judgments in Article 82 cases of the last 50 years – many of which were highly fact-specific, and some of which were not well reasoned – is not a particularly rewarding exercise. However the assertion that the fingerprints of the ordoliberal school are to be found on the case law of Article 82, and that this has led to a systematic bias in favour of competitors and against efficient dominant firms, is at best a misdescription of the true position and at worst little more than a slogan by protagonists of minimalist intervention. A recent research paper, published in 2007, examines the travaux préparatoires of Article 82 and concludes that its drafters were mainly concerned with increasing efficiency; their intention was not to protect competitors, but their customers[184]. This explains why the language of Article 82 is predominantly focused on exploitative behaviour, such as the imposition of unfair selling prices, terms and conditions and the limitation of markets to the prejudice of consumers, rather than exclusionary abuses[185]. The research paper seeks to defy the widely-held belief in the English-language literature that Article 82 is based on ordoliberal foundations.

What matters today is that Article 82 should be applied in a manner that is appropriate in current economic conditions, based on sound economic principles derived from experience gained from the past. The suggestion that efficiency has always been an underlying objective of Article 82 provides a solid foundation for contemporary policy; and the consistent approach of the Commission in recent years that the purpose of the competition rules is to promote consumer welfare through the process of competition can be seen as a natural development of that policy.

(D) Is there a single definition of what amounts to an abuse?

If the debate as to the purpose of Article 82 can be resolved in favour of the proposition that it is to increase efficiency which, in the parlance of today has come to mean the promotion of consumer welfare, there remains the question of whether there exists a definition of what is meant by an abuse of a dominant position. No such definition has been provided by the Community Courts. In a discussion of exclusionary conduct under Article 82 the ECJ in *Hoffmann-la Roche v Commission*[186] gave a definition of abuse as:

An objective concept relating to the behaviour of an undertaking in a dominant position which is such as to influence the structure of a market where, as a result of the very presence of the undertaking in question the degree of competition is weakened and which, through recourse to

---

[184] See Akman 'Searching for the Long-Lost Soul of Article 82 EC' (CCP Working Paper 07–5, available at http://www.ccp.uea.ac.uk).

[185] See p 199 below on the distinction between exploitative and exclusionary abuses.

[186] Case 85/76 [1979] ECR 461, [1979] 3 CMLR 211.

methods different from those which condition normal competition in products or services on the basis of the transaction of commercial operators, has the effect of hindering the maintenance of the degree of competition still existing in the market or the growth of that competition.

This paragraph has been regularly cited in judgments and decisions on the meaning of abuse and in the literature on the subject, but it does not provide an overarching definition of the term; quite apart from the fact that it does not capture the exploitative practices of a dominant firm, for example to charge customers excessively high prices, which cannot be said to *hinder* competition, reference to the idea of 'methods different from those which condition normal competition' is too indeterminate to provide a coherent definition.

A quite different approach to defining abuse would be to suggest that it consists of all those practices that the Community Courts have found to be abusive in the cases that have come before them: not a very satisfying intellectual resolution to a complex problem, particular to commentators, of which there are many, who criticise many of those judgments. A particular problem with such an approach is that it is formalistic and devoid of economic content; as such it tends to encourage a *per se* approach to the definition of abuse; furthermore it provides little insight into types of conduct that may be abusive, but which have not yet been found to be so.

The truth of the matter is that no overarching definition of abuse has yet been found. As the Director General of DG COMP said in his remarks on unilateral conduct in Washington in September 2006:

[J]ust as physicists strive to find the theory that unifies Newtonian physics and quantum mechanics, so economists strive to find the theory that unifies the various aspects of anti-competitive unilateral conduct. And the economists, just as the physicists, have not yet found it.[187]

(E) Some guiding principles

In the absence of a definition that successfully embraces all abusive behaviour, it is desirable to identify some guiding principles that should inform the content of specific rules[188].

The first guiding principle could be that behaviour is only abusive where it causes or is likely to cause clear and demonstrable harm to consumers. The attraction of such a test is that it is linked to the underlying purpose identified above – the promotion of consumer welfare through protecting the process of competition – and that it requires the rejection of *per se* rules under Article 82, an issue that is discussed in the next section. A requirement to demonstrate harm to consumers responds to the criticism that some cases in the past have proceeded on too formalistic a basis, and that a 'more economic approach' is required. The important issue to focus on when considering harm to consumers is the standard of proof required: how far must a competition authority go to prove its case? Should it actually have to prove that the behaviour under investigation will lead to higher prices? This would be a very high standard, and could lead

---

[187] See speech of 11 September 2006, available at www.ec.europa.eu/comm/competition/speeches/index_2006.html.

[188] Two particular articles are recommended reading: Vickers 'Abuse of Market Power' (2005) 115 Economic Journal 244, based on a speech given in Berlin in September 2004, available at www.oft.gov.uk; and Werden 'Competition Policy on Exclusionary Conduct: Towards an Effects-based Analysis' (2006) 2 European Competition Journal, Supp (Special issue) 53.

to a large number of Type I errors. Would it be sufficient to show that the behaviour will eliminate competitors from the market, and should this mean all competitors or just some? Should the case be proved on the basis of a balance of probabilities, or a possibility?

A second guiding principle, which follows from the first, would be that Article 82 should not be applied simply to protect competitors: its purpose is to promote consumer welfare, and consumers do not normally benefit from the protection of inefficient firms. Of course a rule, for example, that forbids long-term exclusive dealing agreements between a dominant firm and its customers might, incidentally, benefit competitors, since they can therefore have access to those customers that they would not otherwise have; but this does not mean that the *purpose* of the rule is to protect competitors. It is because of the principle that Article 82 should not be applied to protect inefficient competitors that individual rules on abuse increasingly address the question of whether a dominant firm's unilateral behaviour could harm 'as efficient' competitors[189].

A further principle might be that the law of abuse should not focus purely on the short term. Where a dominant firm offers predatorily low prices for a period of time in order to prevent a competitor from entering the market or expanding within it, customers during the period of predation obviously benefit: they pay lower fares. However this cannot be sufficient in itself to justify the low fares: a longer-term consideration is whether these lower fares will lead to less competition – and therefore higher prices – in the longer term.

(F) Are there or should there be any *per se* rules under Article 82?

One of the most common complaints about Article 82 is that the Commission and the Community Courts apply it in too formalistic a manner. This criticism can be articulated in various ways. One is the argument that some practices appear to be unlawful *per se*, but that this is inappropriate for behaviour such as price cutting and refusals to deal which may, depending on the facts of a particular case, be pro-competitive, anticompetitive, or neutral. Another way of voicing the same criticism is to argue that the Commission and the Courts often fail to demonstrate how a particular practice could have significant effects on the market: too often they fail to articulate a convincing theory of economic harm and/or to produce evidence that adverse effects would follow from the practice under investigation. A further variant of the basic criticism is that the way the law is applied in practice is too distanced from sound economic principles and that this leads, for example, to pro-competitive rebating practices sometimes being condemned as abusive.

(i) What is meant by a *per se* rule?

It is necessary to begin a discussion of this criticism by considering what is meant by a *per se* rule in the context of Article 82. Article 81(1) distinguishes between agreements that have as their object the restriction of competition and those that restrict competition by effect; where an agreement restricts by object, there is no need for the

---

[189] This idea will recur throughout chs 17 to 19 on individual abuses, particularly when considering pricing abuses such as predatory pricing and margin squeezing.

Commission to prove anti-competitive effects[190]. Only a limited class of agreements fall into the 'object' box: horizontal price fixing and market sharing are obvious examples. These agreements are so obviously likely to harm consumer welfare that there is no point in asking the Commission to demonstrate adverse effects. A *per se* approach to Article 82 would mean that some practices would be regarded as so obviously harmful that proof of adverse effects could similarly be dispensed with. Illegality would be established simply by a particular practice's inclusion in the *per se* list.

Before considering whether any practices are regarded as unlawful under Article 82 it is important to recall that any agreement – including an agreement that restricts by object – can be defended under Article 81(3): it is highly unlikely that a horizontal price-fixing agreement would be found to satisfy that provision, but this is different from saying that it cannot, as a matter of law, do so[191]. In this sense there is no *per se* illegality under Article 81 as a whole, only presumptive illegality under Article 81(1).

(ii) Are there any *per se* rules?

Language can be found in judgments of the Community courts that suggests that some unilateral practices are *per se* illegal. A few extracts from the CFI's judgment in *Michelin v Commission*, summarising earlier case law, illustrate this[192]:

[I]t is apparent from a consistent line of decisions that a loyalty rebate, which is granted in return for an undertaking by the customer to obtain his stock exclusively or almost exclusively from an undertaking in a dominant position, is contrary to Article 82 EC[193].

Later the CFI says that:

[I]t may be inferred generally from the case law that any loyalty-inducing rebate system applied by an undertaking in a dominant position has foreclosure effects prohibited by Article 82 EC[194].

Later again the CFI says that:

[D]iscounts granted by an undertaking in a dominant position must be based on a countervailing advantage which may be economically justified[195].

If these statements are correct, then it would seem that there are, indeed, *per se* rules under Article 82; in particular it is noticeable that the CFI says here that foreclosure effects can be inferred: that is to say that they do not need to be proved; in the language of Article 81(1), a loyalty-inducing rebate system abuses *by object*, so that there is no need to prove effects.

(iii) Should there be any *per se* rules?

In the opinion of this author there should be no *per se* rules under Article 82; to put the point another way, behaviour should be held to be abusive only where the Commission can demonstrate, to the required degree[196], that it has or would lead to harm to consumers. There are various reasons for rejecting *per se* rules[197].

---

[190] See ch 3, pp 116–117.   [191] See ch 4, pp 150–151.

[192] Case T-203/01 [2003] ECR II-4071, [2004] 4 CMLR 923; for comment see Waelbroeck 'Michelin II: A *per-se* rule against rebates by dominant companies?' (2005) 1 Journal of Competition Law and Economics 149.

[193] Ibid, para 56.   [194] Ibid, para 65.   [195] Ibid, para 100.

[196] See p 198 below on the standard of proof in abuse cases.

[197] Note that, just as US courts have tended to reduce the range of agreements that are *per se* illegal under section 1 of the Sherman Act, so too *per se* analysis of practices such as tying has been rejected under section 2: see eg *US v Microsoft* 253 F 3d (D.C. Circuit 2001).

The first point is that the economics of unilateral behaviour are complex and con-troversial, considerably more so, for example, than those of horizontal price fixing. There is sufficient consensus that price fixing harms consumer welfare to place it in the 'object box' of Article 81(1); and even then it can be defended, at least in theory, under Article 81(3). The same consensus does not exist in relation to unilateral behaviour. Price cuts may be pro-competitive, anti-competitive or neutral: empirical analysis is needed to reach a conclusion on the facts of any particular case.

A second point is that *per se* analysis greatly increases the chances of Type II errors. Without deciding whether Type II errors are better than Type I errors, one can suggest that a method of analysis that systemically leads to Type II errors is best avoided. This point can be demonstrated by the fact that, if a particular practice is *per se* abusive, it will be *per se* illegal when practised by a dominant firm and *per se* legal if practised by a non-dominant one. Given the inherent difficulty of determining whether a firm is dom-inant, it is highly questionable that this is sound policy.

A third reason for rejecting *per se* analysis is that it is inconsistent with the general direction of competition policy in the last decade, which has seen a systematic change towards a 'more economic approach'. Article 81 and the ECMR are applied with much greater sensitivity to economic principles today than was formerly the case, and it would be perverse if Article 82 were to be isolated from this trend. The Commission's Economic Advisory Group for Competition Policy called for an economics-based approach to Article 82 to match the reforms of Article 81 and the ECMR[198], and Section 5 of DG COMP's *Discussion paper on exclusionary abuses* is consistent with the move towards a more economic approach to the application of Article 82. It is ultimately for the Community Courts to determine whether *per se* rules are appropriate under Article 82. In a case currently before the CFI, *Tomra Systems v Commission*, one of Tomra's specific grounds of appeal against the Commission's decision is that the Commission commit-ted a manifest error in holding that exclusivity arrangements, individualised quan-tity commitments, and individualised retroactive rebates were unlawful *per se* under Article 82[199].

A fourth point is that it is always possible for a dominant firm accused of abusive behaviour to argue that it had an objective justification for that behaviour[200]; in a sense, therefore, there is something like an Article 82(3) that allows a firm under investigation to mount a defence to an allegation of abuse. In this sense, the most that can be said is that there is a *presumptive* illegality under Article 82, in the same way that agreements that restrict competition by object are presumptively illegal under Article 81(1); but this is a presumption that can, in the case of Article 82, be rebutted by a defence of objective justification.

(G) Effects analysis

If *per se* analysis is inappropriate for Article 82 cases, it follows that a more searching enquiry should be conducted before concluding that unilateral behaviour amounts to

[198] 'An economic approach to Article 82', July 2005, available at www.ec.europa.eu/comm/competition/antitrust/art82/index.html.

[199] Commission decision of 29 March 2006; the case is on appeal to the CFI, Case T-155/06 *Tomra Systems and others v Commission*, not yet decided.

[200] See pp 206–209 below on defences under Article 82.

an abuse[201]. In particular the Commission should have to propose a theory of harm and demonstrate actual or potential adverse effects. This is sometimes referred to as 'rule of reason' analysis, to distinguish it from the formalistic nature of *per se* rules.

The complexity of rule of reason analysis is to determine how far the Commission should have to go in demonstrating effects: whatever rule is adopted must be 'operational', that is to say it must be capable of being applied by the Commission and Courts with reasonable ease and understood by undertakings and their professional advisers.

It is obvious that the Commission should not have to show that actual adverse effects *have already occurred*: that would mean that Article 82 can be applied only after the damage is done. The next question is to decide what effects the Commission is required to show. A very high standard would be to require it to demonstrate that the behaviour under scrutiny has led or will lead to the dominant firm raising its prices to the detriment of consumers. In this author's opinion this would be to raise the bar too high, since this would be a very difficult matter to prove: to put the point another way, this could lead to a number of Type I errors. Rather, the effects that have to be proved will vary from one kind of abuse to another: for example, as we shall see in chapter 17 and 19, what amounts to an unlawful refusal to supply varies according to whether the dominant firm is refusing to deal with an existing customer or a new one; and a particularly high standard must be satisfied before a refusal to licence intellectual property can be condemned: in the latter situation it is necessary to show that the refusal will have as its consequence the prevention of a new product being introduced to the market or the limitation of technical development to the prejudice of consumers[202].

A separate, though related, issue is the *standard* of proof that the Commission should satisfy. It is a statement of the obvious that if the standard is too low Type II errors may follow; and if it is too high there will be Type I errors. In some cases the Courts have required the Commission merely to show that a practice would 'tend' to foreclose the market: a very low standard[203]. It would be too strict to require proof beyond reasonable doubt, a standard used in criminal law. An intermediate position would be to require proof of harmful effects on the balance of probabilities, the standard required by the CFI in merger cases[204].

(H) Dominance is not an offence in itself

The discussion above has been somewhat abstract and theoretical. The text that follows contains a more prosaic examination of the actual legal rules on the abuse of dominance.

The first point that needs to be stressed is that it is not an offence for a firm to have a dominant position; it is only the abuse of dominance that can be challenged. However, as has already been noted, a firm in a dominant position has a special responsibility not to allow its conduct to impair undistorted competition on the common market[205]; and it would appear that this responsibility becomes greater, so that a finding of abuse

---

[201] For a thoughtful discussion of this problem see Eilmansberger 'How to Distinguish Good from Bad Competition under Article 82 EC: In Search of Clearer and More Coherent Standards for Anti-competitive Abuses' (2005) 42 CML Rev 129.

[202] See ch 19, pp 786–792.

[203] See eg Case T-219/99 *British Airways plc v Commission* [2003] ECR II-5917, [2004] 4 CMLR 1008, where the CFI said, at para 293, that 'it is sufficient in that respect to demonstrate that the abusive conduct is a dominant position *tends to restrict competiton*' (emphasis added).

[204] See ch 21, p 881.　　[205] See pp 183–184 above.

becomes more likely, where the firm under investigation is not merely dominant, but super-dominant[206].

(I) Exploitative, exclusionary and single market abuses

When reviewing the decisional practice of the Commission and the jurisprudence of the Community Courts, it is possible to identify at least two, and perhaps three, types of abuse. The first consists of **exploitative abuses**. The most obvious objection to a monopolist is that it is in a position to reduce output and increase the price of its products above the competitive level, thereby exploiting customers[207]. However in the absence of barriers to entry a monopolist earning monopoly profits would be expected to attract new entrants to the market: in other words exploitation of a monopoly position may in itself increase competition.

Of greater long-term significance is behaviour by a dominant firm designed to, or which might have the effect of, preventing the development of competition, and much of the case law of the Community Courts and the decisional practice of the Commission has been concerned with **exclusionary abuses** of this kind: Neelie Kroes, the Commissioner for Competition, said in September 2005 that:

We think that it is sound for our enforcement policy to give priority to so-called exclusionary abuses[208].

In order to illustrate the kind of behaviour which falls within the mischief of Article 82 it is therefore helpful to consider exploitative and exclusionary abuses separately[209], although this is not to suggest that there is a rigid demarcation between these two categories: the same behaviour may exhibit both characteristics. For example a dominant firm which charges discriminatory prices may be both exploiting its position by earning the maximum profit it can at the expense of customers and harming competition by making it harder for other firms to enter the market. In the same way a refusal to supply may have an exploitative purpose (for example where it is threatened or effected in order to make a customer pay a higher price) and an exclusionary one (where it is intended to remove a competitor from the market).

A possible third category of cases under Article 82 is concerned with **single market abuses**. For example excessive pricing, as well as being exploitative, may be a ploy to impede parallel imports and to limit intra-brand competition, as in the case of *British Leyland v Commission*[210].

(J) Exploitative abuses

It is clear from its very wording that Article 82 is capable of application to exploitative behaviour: Article 82(2)(a) gives as an example of an abuse the imposition of unfair purchase or selling prices or other unfair trading conditions. Exploitative pricing practices

---

[206] See pp 184–186 above   [207] See the analysis of price theory in ch 1, pp 3–7.

[208] SPEECH/05/537, 23 September 2005, available at www.ec.europa.eu/comm/competition/speeches/index_2005.html.

[209] The distinction between exploitative and exclusionary abuses is recognised in para 3 of DG COMP's *Discussion paper*, which is specifically limited to the latter type of abuse.

[210] Case 226/84 [1986] ECR 3263, [1987] 1 CMLR 185; see pp 205–206 below and ch 18, pp 753–755.

are considered further in chapter 18[211]. There have also been cases on the activities of collecting societies in which their rules have been scrutinised in order to ensure that they do not act in a way that unfairly exploits the owner of the copyright or the would-be licensee of it; collecting societies are considered in chapter 19[212]. Unfair trading conditions were condemned by the Commission in *AAMS*[213] and in *1998 Football World Cup*[214], where it considered that the arrangements for the sale of tickets were unfair to consumers resident outside France.

In its colloquial sense, exploitation suggests the earning of monopoly profits at the expense of the customer. One of the other 'benefits' of the monopolist is the 'quiet life' and the freedom from the need to innovate and improve efficiency in order to keep up with or ahead of competitors[215]. This raises the question whether inefficiency or inertia could be considered to be an abuse under Article 82. Article 82(2)(b) gives as an example of abuse the limitation of production, markets or technical development to the prejudice of the consumer, and in *British Telecommunications*[216] the Commission objected to behaviour on BT's part which, inter alia, meant that the possible use of new technology was impeded. This is dealt with in chapter 6[217].

(K) Exclusionary abuses

Article 82 has most frequently been applied to behaviour which the Commission and Community Courts consider to be exclusionary.

(i) *Continental Can v Commission*[218]

The ECJ established in *Continental Can v Commission* that Article 82 was capable of application to exclusionary abuses as well as exploitative ones. The specific question before the Court was whether mergers could be prohibited under Article 82. One argument against this was that Article 82 was concerned only with the direct exploitation of consumers and not with the more indirect adverse effects that might be produced by harming the competitive process[219]; according to this argument structural changes in the market could not be caught. The ECJ rejected this. It was not possible to draw a distinction between direct and indirect effects on the market; instead it was necessary to interpret Article 82 in the light of the spirit of the Treaty generally. Article 3(1)(g)

---

[211] See ch 18, pp 709–718.   [212] See ch 19, pp 792–793.

[213] OJ [1998] L 252/47, [1998] 5 CMLR 786, paras 33–46, upheld on appeal to the CFI Case T-139/98 *Amministratzione Autonoma dei Monopoli di Stato v Commission* [2001] ECR II-3413, [2002] 4 CMLR 302, paras 73–80.

[214] OJ [2000] L 5/55, [2000] 4 CMLR 963, para 91; see also paras 99–100.

[215] See ch 1, pp 6–7.

[216] OJ [1982] L 360/36, [1983] 1 CMLR 457, upheld on appeal Case 41/83 *Italy v Commission* [1985] ECR 873, [1985] 2 CMLR 368.

[217] Ch 6, p 229.

[218] Case 6/72 *Europemballage Corpn and Continental Can Co Inc Commission* [1973] ECR 215, [1973] CMLR 199; the impact of the judgment is discussed in Vogelenzang 'Abuse of a Dominant Position in Article [82]: the Problem of Causality and Some Applications' (1976) 13 CML Rev 61.

[219] See eg Joliet *Monopolisation and Abuse of Dominance* (Martinus Nijhoff, 1970); it was also argued in *Continental Can* that mergers were not caught by Article 82 as the former ECSC Treaty dealt with them explicitly so that, by inference, the EC Treaty, which was silent on the issue, could not apply to them; and that anyway behaviour could not be abusive unless it was attributable to and caused by the use of the position of dominance (see below).

required the institution of a system ensuring that competition in the common market is not distorted and Article 2 called for the promotion of a continuous and balanced expansion in economic activities. Articles 81 and 82 had to be interpreted with these aims in mind: it would be futile to prevent agreements which distort competition under Article 81 but then to allow mergers which resulted in the elimination of competition. The adoption in 1989 of the EC Merger Regulation means that Article 82 is now largely redundant in respect of mergers[220]; however *Continental Can* remains immensely important to the law on Article 82, since it confirmed that it could be applied to exclusionary abuses as well as to exploitative ones.

(ii) Causation

One of the arguments raised by Continental Can was that, even if mergers were caught by Article 82, it had not *used* its market power to effect the merger in question; thus there was a break in the chain of causation between its position on the market and the behaviour alleged to amount to an abuse. It had not, for example, threatened to drive the target firm out of the market by predatory price cutting if it refused to merge. The ECJ rejected this argument as well. It was possible to abuse a dominant position without actually exercising or relying on market power. It was an abuse simply for a dominant firm to strengthen its position and substantially to eliminate competition by taking over a rival. Abuse is an objective concept, and the conduct of an undertaking may be regarded as abusive in the absence of any fault and irrespective of the intention of the dominant undertaking. The scope of Article 82 would obviously be reduced if the Commission could apply it only to practices which were attributable to the exercise of market power that a dominant undertaking enjoys[221]. In *Hoffmann-La Roche* the ECJ said that:

The interpretation suggested by the applicant that an abuse implies that the use of the economic power bestowed by a dominant position is the means whereby the abuse has been brought about cannot be accepted[222].

In *Tetra Pak II*[223] the ECJ stated at paragraph 27 of its judgment that 'application of Article [82] presupposes a link between the dominant position and the alleged abusive conduct'. This may appear to contradict the causation point in *Continental Can*. However, the issue in *Tetra Pak* was whether it is possible for the abuse to take place in a market different from the one in which an undertaking is dominant[224]; the Court was not concerned with the issue of whether the market power had to have been used in order to bring about the abuse.

It is interesting to note in passing that some systems of law – for example Australia and New Zealand – do require a causal connection between the position of dominance and the abusive behaviour: the majority judgment of the UK Privy Council in *Carter Holt Harvey Building Products Group Ltd v The Commerce Commission*[225] contains an

---

[220] See ch 21, p 832, n 117.

[221] See Vogelenzang 'Abuse of a Dominant Position in Article [82]: the Problem of Causality and Some Applications' (1976) 13 CML Rev 61; the Commission relied specifically on this aspect of the *Continental Can* judgment in para 46 of its decision in *Tetra Pak 1 (BTG Licence)* OJ [1988] L 272/27, [1988] 4 CMLR 881.

[222] At para 91; note the suggestion by Advocate General Reischl at para 7c of his Opinion in *Hoffmann-La Roche* that causation might be treated differently according to the nature of the abuse in question.

[223] Case C-333/94 P *Tetra Pak International v Commission* [1996] ECR I-5951, [1997] 4 CMLR 662.

[224] See pp 202–204 below.   [225] Privy Council Appeal No 6 of 2004, 14 July 2004 [2004] UKPC 37.

interesting discussion of the case law in those two countries. Clearly such an approach will result in fewer findings of abuse; however the *Continental Can* judgment is clear that causation is not required under Article 82.

(iii) Horizontal and vertical foreclosure[226]

The concern about exclusionary abuses is that a dominant firm is able to behave in a way that forecloses competitors in an anti-competitive way[227] from entering the market, or prevents existing competitors from growing within it. The foreclosure might occur 'upstream' or 'downstream' in the market. Suppose that a firm is vertically integrated: it extracts a raw material, widgets, from its widget mines, and processes widgets into widget dioxide: the upstream market is raw widgets, the downstream one is widget dioxide. Harm to competition could occur at either level of the market:

- **Horizontal foreclosure** arises where the dominant firm takes action to exclude a competitor that supplies widgets

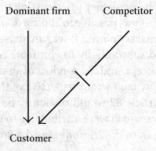

Fig. 5.1 Horizontal foreclosure

- **Vertical foreclosure** arises where the dominant firm takes action to exclude a competitor in the downstream market for widget dioxide

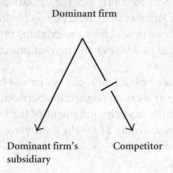

Fig. 5.2 Vertical foreclosure

---

[226] The distinction between horizontal and vertical foreclosure is helpfully discussed in DG COMP's *Discussion paper* at paras 69–73; alternative expressions found in the literature are 'primary-line injury' (horizontal foreclosure) and secondary-line injury (vertical foreclosure).

[227] If a competitor is foreclosed by the superior efficiency of the dominant firm, the foreclosure would not be abusive.

Many exclusionary abuses are concerned with horizontal foreclosure: for example single branding agreements, rebates and predatory pricing. Others however, for example refusal to supply and margin squeezing, are predominantly[228] concerned about harm to competition in the downstream market.

(iv) The dominant position, the abuse and the effects of the abuse may be in different markets

It is not necessary for the dominance, the abuse and the effects of the abuse all to be in the same market. In a simple case, X may be dominant in the market for widgets and charge high prices to exploit its customers or drop its prices in order to eliminate competitors from the widget market: clearly Article 82 can apply to this behaviour. However more complex situations may occur. X might be present on both the widget market and the downstream widget dioxide market, and may act on one of those markets in order to derive a benefit in the other: as we have just seen, there may be a horizontal or a vertical foreclosure of the market.

Some examples will illustrate the range of possibilities.

(A) Michelin v Commission[229] Michelin was dominant in the market for replacement tyres and committed various abuses in order to protect its position in that market.

(B) Commercial Solvents[230] Commercial Solvents supplied a raw material in which it was dominant to a customer which used it to make an anti-tuberculosis drug. The raw material was the upstream product; the drug was the downstream product. Commercial Solvents decided to produce the drug itself and ceased to supply the customer. Commercial Solvents was found to have abused its dominant position: it refused to supply the raw material in relation to which it was dominant, but this was done to benefit its position in the drug market, where it was not yet present at all.

(C) De Poste-La Poste[231] The Belgian Post Office, dominant in the market for the delivery of 'normal' letters, abused its dominant position in that market in order to eliminate a competitor in the neighbouring market for business-to-business mail services.

(D) Télémarketing[232] The dominant undertaking, a broadcasting authority with a statutory monopoly, decided to enter the downstream telemarketing sector. It ceased to supply broadcasting services to the only other telemarketer, thereby eliminating it from the market and effectively reserving the telemarketing business to itself.

(E) Sealink/B&I – Holyhead: Interim Measures[233] Sealink, which owned and operated the port at Holyhead, was considered to have committed an abuse on the market for the provision of port facilities for passenger and ferry services, in which it was dominant, by structuring the sailing schedules there to the advantage of its own downstream ferry

---

[228] A refusal to supply may sometimes have a horizontal effect: see ch 17, pp 699–700.
[229] Case 322/81 [1983] ECR 3461, [1985] 1 CMLR 282.
[230] Case 6/73 etc [1974] ECR 223, [1974] 1 CMLR 309.
[231] OJ [2002] L 61/32, [2002] 4 CMLR 1426, paras 36–51.
[232] Case 311/84 *Centre Belge d'Etudes de Marché Télémarketing v CTL* [1985] ECR 3261, [1986] 2 CMLR 558.
[233] [1992] 5 CMLR 255.

operations and to the disadvantage of its competitor at that level of the market, B&I. The same point can be noted in *Sea Containers v Stena Sealink – Interim Measures*[234].

(F) British Gypsum v Commission[235] British Gypsum was dominant in the plasterboard market, but not dominant in the neighbouring plaster market (these markets were horizontally, rather than vertically, related). Among its abuses, British Gypsum gave priority treatment to customers for plaster who remained loyal to it in relation to plasterboard. This differs from the above examples, since in *British Gypsum* the abuse was committed in the non-dominated market in order to protect British Gypsum's position in its dominated market.

(G) Tetra Pak II[236] The ECJ concluded that Tetra Pak had infringed Article 82 by tying practices and predatory pricing in the market for non-aseptic liquid repackaging machinery and non-aseptic cartons. It was not dominant in this market, but the abusive conduct was intended to benefit its position in that market. Tetra Pak was dominant in the (horizontally) associated market for aseptic machinery and cartons. The ECJ, after citing *Commercial Solvents*, *Télémarketing* and *British Gypsum*, held that 'in special circumstances'[237], there could be an abuse of a dominant position 'where conduct on a market distinct from the dominated market produces effects on that distinct market'[238]. The ECJ then went on to describe the 'close associative links' between the aseptic and non-aseptic markets which amounted to sufficiently special circumstances to engage Article 82: for example Tetra Pak had or could have customers in both markets, it could rely on having a favoured status in the non-dominated market because of its position in the dominated one, and it could concentrate its efforts on the non-aseptic market independently of other economic operators because of its position in relation to the aseptic market. This case extends the scope of application of Article 82 beyond, even, *British Gypsum*.

A table may help to explain the propositions set out in this paragraph.

5.3 Dominance, abuse and neighbouring markets

Case	Market A	Market B
Michelin v Commission	Dominance Abuse Benefit	
Commercial Solvents; *Télémarketing*; *De Poste-La Poste*; *Sealink decisions*	Dominance Abuse	Benefit
British Gypsum	Dominance Benefit	Abuse
Tetra Pak v Commission	Dominance	Abuse Benefit

---

[234] OJ [1994] L 15/8, [1995] 4 CMLR 84.   [235] Case C-310/93 P [1995] ECR I-865, [1997] 4 CMLR 238.
[236] Case C-333/94 P [1996] ECR I-5951, [1997] 4 CMLR 662; the ECJ's approach to the issue of abuse was different from that of the Commission's in its decision.
[237] Case 333/94 P [1996] ECR I-5951, [1997] 4 CMLR 662, paras 25–31.
[238] [1996] ECR I-5951, [1997] 4 CMLR 662.

Many of the Commission's decisions under Article 82 in recent years have involved two rather than one markets. A good example is *Virgin/British Airways*[239]: BA's dominant position was in the market for the procurement of travel agents' services; its abuse in that market was found by the Commission to have effects on the neighbouring market for air transport[240]. The CFI specifically upheld this point in the appeal against the Commission's decision[241].

The Commission could presumably apply the reasoning just described in the context of neighbouring product markets to dominance, abuse and benefits in neighbouring geographical markets[242].

(v) Examples of exclusionary abuses

The Commission and the Community Courts have condemned many practices which could have anti-competitive effects. These will be examined in detail in chapters 17 to 19, which will consider in turn the following abuses:

- Exclusive dealing agreements[243]
- Tying[244]
- Refusals to supply[245]
- Miscellaneous other non-pricing abuses[246]
- Rebates and other practices having effects similar to single branding agreements[247]
- Bundling[248]
- Predatory pricing[249]
- Margin squeezing[250]
- Price discrimination[251]
- Refusals to licence intellectual property rights or to provide proprietary information[252].

(L) Abuses that are harmful to the single market

As one would expect, abuses that are harmful to the single market are condemned[253]. The pressure not to export sugar to other Member States applied to Belgian customers by Raffinerie Tirlemontoise was held to be an abuse within Article 82 in *Suiker Unie v Commission*[254] and, had the evidence supported the allegation, the Court would have condemned import bans in that case too[255]. In *British Leyland v Commission*[256]

---

[239] OJ [2000] L 30/1, [2000] 4 CMLR 999. [240] Ibid, paras 96–111.

[241] Case T-219/99 *British Airways plc v Commission* [2003] ECR II-5917, [2004] 4 CMLR 1008, paras 127–135.

[242] See eg *Interbrew* in the Commission's XXVIth *Report on Competition Policy* (1996), point 53, where Interbrew was considered to have acted in non-dominated geographical markets to protect its dominant position in Belgium.

[243] Ch 17, pp 673–679. [244] Ibid, pp 679–687. [245] Ibid, pp 687–702.

[246] Ibid, pp 703–705. [247] Ch 18, pp 719–727. [248] Ibid, pp 727–729.

[249] Ibid, pp 729–743. [250] Ibid, pp 744–748. [251] Ibid, pp 748–753.

[252] Ch 19, pp 786–792. [253] See ch 1, pp 22–23 and ch 2, pp 51–52 on the single market imperative.

[254] Cases 40/73 etc [1975] ECR 1663, [1976] 1 CMLR 295.

[255] See also the fate of the 'green banana' clause in Case 27/76 *United Brands v Commission* [1978] ECR 207, [1978] 1 CMLR 429.

[256] Case 226/84 [1986] ECR 3263, [1987] 1 CMLR 185.

BL's pricing policy in respect of type approval certificates had the effect of reducing imports of BL cars from the continent into the UK, and the Commission's condemnation of this conduct was upheld on appeal by the ECJ. In *Eurofix-Bauco v Hilti*[257] one of Hilti's abuses was to have imposed pressure on its distributors in the Netherlands not to supply Hilti compatible cartridge strips to the UK. In *AAMS*[258] the Commission concluded that both contractual and unilateral practices on the part of an Italian cigarette producer and distributor intended to limit access for foreign cigarettes to the Italian market amounted to an abuse of a dominant position; a fine of €6 million was imposed. The Commission took action in *Deutsche Post AG – Interception of cross-border mail*[259] to prevent the German Post Office from delaying incoming mailings from the UK. Rebates and discounts intended to keep imports out of a dominant firm's territory will be condemned[260].

8. DEFENCES

There is no Article 82(3), in the way that Article 81(3) provides an efficiency defence for agreements that infringe Article 81(1). However it is clear that a dominant undertaking can raise a defence to an accusation of abuse where it can show that it had an 'objective justification' for its behaviour. Advocate General Jacobs pointed out in his Opinion in the *Syfait* case[261] that, given the absence of an Article 82(3), there is a certain artificiality about claiming a defence to an allegation of abuse: rather, the objective justification means that there is no abuse in the first place[262]. Article 81 operates differently, in that a successful defence under Article 81(3) does not mean that the agreement did not restrict competition in the first place: it is rather that the economic efficiency identified under Article 81(3) outweighs the restriction of competition. The logic of the Advocate General's Opinion is undeniable; nevertheless there is a convenience in analysing objective justification as a separate matter, as indeed he did in *Syfait*[263]. DG COMP's *Discussion paper* also contains a separate section on defences[264].

This section will examine what is meant by objective justification; it will briefly consider the question of whether a defence can be based on the principle of non-interference with property rights; and will conclude with a discussion of the burden of proving a defence.

[257] OJ [1988] L 65/19, [1989] 4 CMLR 677.

[258] OJ [1998] L 252/47, [1998] 5 CMLR 786, upheld on appeal Case T-139/98 *Amministratzione Autonoma dei Monopoli di Stato v Commission* [2001] ECR II-3413, [2002] 4 CMLR 302.

[259] OJ [2001] L 331/40, [2002] 4 CMLR 598.

[260] *BPB Industries* OJ [1989] L 10/50, [1990] 4 CMLR 464, upheld on appeal to the CFI Case T-65/89 *BPB Industries plc and British Gypsum v Commission* [1993] ECR II-389, [1993] 5 CMLR 32 and further on appeal to the ECJ Case 310/93P *BPB Industries plc and British Gypsum v Commission* [1995] ECR I-865, [1995] 4 CMLR 238; *Michelin* OJ [2002] L 143/1, [2002] 5 CMLR 388, paras 312–314.

[261] Case C-53/03 [2005] ECR I-4609, [2005] 5 CMLR 7.   [262] Ibid, para 72.

[263] Ibid, paras 73–104.   [264] *Discussion paper*, paras 77–92.

(A) Objective justification[265]

The language of objective justification can be found in many judgments and decisions, coupled with the proposition that, to be objectively justified, the conduct in question must be proportionate. For example in *Centre Belge d'Etudes de Marché Télémarketing v CLT*[266] the ECJ held that an undertaking in a dominant position in television broadcasting which entrusted 'telemarketing' to its own subsidiary, thereby excluding other firms from entering this market, would be guilty of an abuse where there was no objective necessity for such behaviour[267]. The Commission in *Eurofix-Bauco v Hilti*[268] considered whether there was any objective justification, such as safety considerations and the prevention of false and misleading advertising, for Hilti's practice of requiring purchasers of Hilti nail cartridges to also purchase Hilti nails, but concluded that there was no such justification. When dismissing Hilti's appeal, the CFI concluded that there are laws in the UK attaching penalties to the sale of dangerous products and to the use of misleading claims as to the characteristics of products, as well as authorities vested with powers to enforce those laws; it was not for Hilti to take steps on its own initiative to eliminate products which, rightly or wrongly, it regarded as dangerous or inferior to its own[269]. The Commission rejected claims in *Tetra Pak II* that the tie-in provisions were necessary to protect health and to avoid product liability[270]. In *Portuguese Airports*[271] the Commission rejected as an objective justification for the discount system operated for the use of airports in Portugal that Barcelona and Madrid operated a similar system; the Commission was proceeding against them anyway, and a Member State cannot justify an infringement of the Treaty by arguing that another Member State was guilty of the same infringement. In *Prokent-Tomra*[272] the Commission rejected arguments by Tomra that its exclusive agreements, quantity commitment and rebate schemes had an objective justification[273]. The principles of objective justification and proportionality have been invoked on other occasions[274] and are firmly part of Article 82 analysis.

DG COMP's *Discussion paper* is particularly interesting on the issue of defences under Article 82. It acknowledges the idea of an objective justification defence, which

[265] For discussion see Loewenthal 'The Defence of "Objective Justification" in the Application of Article 82 EC' (2005) 28(4) World Competition 455; Albors-Llorens 'The role of objective justification and efficiencies in the application of Article 82 EC' (2007) 44 Common Market Law Review 1727.

[266] Case 311/84 [1985] ECR 3261, [1986] 2 CMLR 558.

[267] [1985] ECR 3261, [1986] 2 CMLR 558, para 26. [268] OJ [1988] L 65/19, [1989] 4 CMLR 677.

[269] Case T-30/89 *Hilti AG v Commission* [1991] ECR II-1439, [1992] 14 CMLR 16, paras 102–119.

[270] OJ [1992] L 72/1, [1992] 4 CMLR 551, paras 118–120, upheld on appeal to the CFI Case T-83/91 *Tetra Pak International SA v Commission* [1994] ECR II-755, [1997] 4 CMLR 726, paras 136–140, and on appeal to the ECJ Case 333/94 *Tetra Pak International SA v Commission* [1996] ECR I-5951, [1997] 4 CMLR 662, para 37.

[271] OJ [1999] L 69/31, [1999] 5 CMLR 103, para 29.

[272] Commission decision of 29 March 2006; the case is on appeal to the CFI, Case T-155/06 *Tomra Systems and others v Commission*, not yet decided.

[273] Ibid, paras 347–390.

[274] See eg *BBI/Boosey and Hawkes* OJ [1987] L 286/36, [1988] 4 CMLR 67; *BPB Industries plc* OJ [1989] L 10/50, [1990] 4 CMLR 464, para 132, upheld on appeal Case T-65/89 *BPB Industries plc and British Gypsum v Commission* [1993] ECR II-389, [1993] 5 CMLR 32 and further on appeal to the ECJ Case C-310/93 P *BPB Industries plc and British Gypsum v Commission* [1995] ECR I-865, [1997] 4 CMLR 238; *Napier Brown – British Sugar* OJ [1988] L 284/41, [1990] 4 CMLR 196, paras 64 and 70; *NDC Health/IMS Health: Interim Measures* OJ [2002] L 59/18, [2002] 4 CMLR 111, paras 167–174.

it says should be applied strictly, as in the *Hilti* case[275]. It also notes that case law provides a 'meeting competition' defence, which again is limited in scope[276]. The *Discussion paper* also suggests that a dominant firm could plead an efficiency defence: in other words, DG COMP suggests, in effect, that there is an Article 82(3)[277]. In considering whether such a defence might be available, the *Discussion paper* applies the criteria found in Article 81(3). In its decision in *Wanadoo de España v Telefónica*[278] the Commission included a lengthy discussion of possible defences including, from paragraphs 641 to 663, efficiencies, which it rejected on the facts of the case. In the opinion of this author it is very much to be welcomed that efficiencies should be taken into consideration in cases of abuse, and, notwithstanding the lack of an explicit legal basis for this, the creation of an imaginary Article 82(3) creates a useful template within which to do so.

(B) Abuse of dominance and property rights

In a number of cases under Article 82 a particular issue has been the extent to which a dominant undertaking could be held to have acted abusively in relation to the way in which it chose to use, or not to use, its own property. Article 295 EC provides that:

This Treaty shall in no way prejudice the rules in Member States governing the system of property ownership.

If it is possible for the Commission, under Article 82, to order the owner, for example, of an essential facility to provide access to it to a third party[279], this clearly affects that undertaking's property rights; but has it affected them to the point where the rules on property ownership in Member States have been prejudiced? The issue arose in relation to *Frankfurt Airport*[280] where the Commission required FAG, the owner and operator of that airport, to allow competition in the market for ground-handling services there. The Commission rejected the argument that this would interfere with the property rights of FAG. The Commission noted that the ECJ in *Hauer v Land Rheinland Pfalz*[281] had acknowledged the existence of a fundamental right to property in the Community legal order; however it had also noted that the constitutions of the Member States recognised that the exercise of property rights may be restricted in the public interest. In the *Frankfurt Airport* decision the Commission said that it followed from the *Hauer* judgment that the competition rules in the Treaty may be considered to constitute restrictions on the right of property which correspond to objectives of general interest pursued by the Community[282]. In the Commission's view, allowing the provision of ground-handling services within the airport would not constitute an excessive or intolerable interference with FAG's rights as owner of the airport; it would not interfere with FAG's own ability to provide these services, and FAG could charge a reasonable fee to third parties for their right to do so.

---

[275] *Discussion paper*, para 80.   [276] Ibid, paras 81–83.   [277] Ibid, paras 84–92.
[278] Commission decision of 4 July 2007; on appeal Case T-336/07 *Telefónica de España v Commission*, not yet decided.
[279] See ch 17, pp 690–699.   [280] *Flughafen Frankfurt* OJ [1998] L 72/30, [1998] 4 CMLR 779.
[281] Case 44/79 [1979] ECR 3727, [1980] 3 CMLR 42, para 17.
[282] *Flughafen Frankfurt* OJ [1998] L 72/30, [1998] 4 CMLR 779, para 90.

In his Opinion in *Masterfoods Ltd v HB Ice Cream Ltd*[283] Advocate General Cosmas had no doubt that:

> it is perfectly comprehensible for restrictions to be placed on the right to property ownership pursuant to Articles [81] and [82] of the EC Treaty, to the degree to which they might be necessary to protect competition[284].

In *Van den Bergh Foods Ltd v Commission*[285] the CFI rejected an argument that the Commission's decision in *Van den Bergh Foods Ltd*[286], requiring that space be made available in Van den Bergh's freezer cabinets for the ice-cream of competitors, amounted to a disproportionate interference with its property rights[287]. In *Microsoft v Commission* the CFI rejected the argument that Microsoft was entitled to refuse to supply interoperability information to competitors because it was protected by intellectual property rights: this would be inconsistent with the rule, derived from the *Magill* and *IMS Health* cases, that, in exceptional circumstances, there can be an obligation to grant licences to third parties[288].

(C) Burden of proof

In *Microsoft v Commission*[289] the CFI stated that:

> it is for the dominant undertaking concerned, and not for the Commission, before the end of the administrative procedure, to raise any plea of objective justification and to support it with arguments and evidence. It then falls to the Commission, where it proposes to make a finding of an abuse of a dominant position, to show that the arguments and evidence relied on by the undertaking cannot prevail and, accordingly, that the justification cannot be accepted[290].

The CFI went on to state that it was not sufficient for the dominant undertaking to put forward 'vague, general and theoretical arguments' in support of its objective justification[291].

9. THE CONSEQUENCES OF INFRINGING ARTICLE 82

(A) Public enforcement[292]

Where the Commission finds an abuse of a dominant position it has power, pursuant to Article 23 of the Modernisation Regulation, to impose a fine[293], and to order the

---

[283] [2000] ECR I-11369, [2001] 4 CMLR 449; see also Case C-163/99 *Portugal v Commission* [2001] ECR I-2613, [2002] 2 CMLR 1319, paras 58–59.

[284] [2001] ECR I-2613, [2002] 2 CMLR 1319, para 105.

[285] Case T-65/98 [2003] ECR II-4653, [2004] 4 CMLR 14.   [286] OJ [1998] L 246/1, [1998] 5 CMLR 530.

[287] Ibid, paras 170–171.   [288] Ibid, paras 690–691; see ch 19, pp 790–792.

[289] Case T-201/04 *Microsoft Corpn v Commission* [2007] ECR II-000, [2007] 5 CMLR 846.

[290] Ibid, para 688.

[291] Ibid, para 698; for discussion of proof generally in Article 82 cases see Paulis 'The burden of proof in Article 82 cases' [2006] Fordham Corporate Law Institute (ed Hawl), ch 20; Nazzini 'The wood began to move: an essay on consumer welfare, evidence and burden of proof in Article 82 EC cases' (2006) 31 ELR 518.

[292] See *Remedies and Sanctions in Abuse of Dominance Cases* OECD DAF/COMP(2006)19 for a general discussion of this topic, available at www.oecd.org.

[293] See ch 7, pp 272–278.

dominant undertaking to cease and desist from the conduct in question[294]; where necessary, it may also order a dominant undertaking to adopt positive measures in order to bring an infringement to an end[295]. It is even possible for the Commission to order the divestiture of an undertaking's assets, or to break an undertaking up, under the powers conferred by Article 7 of the Modernisation Regulation[296], provided it is proportionate and necessary to bring the infringement to an end and provided that there is no equally effective behavioural remedy or that such a remedy would be more burdensome[297].

In a number of cases the Commission has negotiated a settlement with the undertaking under investigation, without reaching a formal decision and imposing a fine, in return for an agreed remedy. Through the use of informal settlements of this kind the Commission can sometimes achieve as much if not more than it would have done if it had gone through the formal procedure and reached a final decision: an undertaking may agree to change its conduct in the future, and perhaps agree even to a structural remedy, that might not have been forced upon it by formal decision. It is noticeable that a number of important cases have been settled in this way. An important example in the early 1980s was the settlement in the *IBM* case[298]. Subsequent examples include *IRI/Nielsen*[299], *SWIFT*[300], *Belgacom*[301], *Digital*[302], *Athens Airport*[303] and *IRE/Nordion*[304]. Until 2004 there was no legal basis for the settlement of cases in this way. However Article 9 of the Modernisation Regulation now provides a legal basis for the acceptance by the Commission of legally binding commitments from undertakings[305]. A significant case settled in this way was the *Coca-Cola* case, where The Coca-Cola Company offered a series of commitments in relation to the sale of carbonated soft drinks[306].

(B) Private enforcement

The civil law consequences of infringing Article 82 are discussed in chapter 8[307].

10. THE COMMISSION'S REVIEW OF ARTICLE 82

In December 2005 Dg comp published its *Discussion paper on the application of Article 82 EC to exclusionary abuses*: it did not discuss exploitative or discriminatory

---

[294] See ch 7, pp 250–252.   [295] See ch 7, p 251.   [296] OJ [2003] LI/1.

[297] See ch 7, p 252.   [298] See the Commission's XIVth *Report on Competition Policy*, pp 77–79.

[299] See the Commission's XXVIth *Report on Competition Policy* (1996), pp 144–148 (termination of exclusivity contracts, unbundling of products).

[300] XXVIIth *Report on Competition Policy* (1997), pp 143–145 (non-discriminatory access to cross-border payment services).

[301] XXVIIth *Report on Competition Policy* (1997), pp 152–153 (access to date regarding subscribers to Belgacom's voice telephony services).

[302] XXVIIth *Report on Competition Policy* (1997), pp 153–154 (unbundling of products and amendment to pricing policies); see Dolmans and Pickering 'The 1997 Digital Undertaking' (1998) 19 ECLR 108; Andrews 'Aftermarket Power in the Computer Services Market: The Digital Undertaking' (1998) 19 ECLR 176.

[303] Commission's XXVIIth *Report on Competition Policy* (1997), points 131–134 (improvements to airport terminal, abolition of monopoly over ground-handling services).

[304] Commission's XXVIIIth *Report on Competition Policy* (1998), point 74 and pp 169–170 (renunciation of exclusivity clauses in sales contracts).

[305] See ch 7, pp 253–257.   [306] Commission decision of 22 June 2005.   [307] See pp 315–316.

abuses[308]. This followed a review of Article 82 launched by the Commission in 2004: by then most other aspects of competition law had been the subject of extensive reform – for example the adoption of new block exemptions for vertical agreements and technology transfer agreements, the recast Merger Regulation, the Modernisation Regulation and the publication of extensive guidelines on a variety of different matters. A review of Article 82 was therefore due. The *Discussion paper* stated clearly that the objective of Article 82 is to protect competition on the market as a means of enhancing consumer welfare and of ensuring an efficient allocation of resources; it stressed that the purpose of Article 82 is to protect competition and not competitors; and said that conduct should be prohibited only where it produces actual or likely anti-competitive effects on the market[309]. It then proceeded to discuss specific practices – predation, exclusive dealing and rebates, tying, and refusals to supply. Publication of the *Discussion paper* was followed by a period of intense debate: conferences, seminars and 'webinars', lectures, lunches, and dinners dominated the early months of 2006, and DG COMP received a huge number of responses, which can be found on its website[310]. There was a widely-held assumption that the process would culminate in the Commission publishing draft Guidelines on Article 82; no such Guidelines had emerged by 12 March 2008, the date of the submission of the manuscript of this book. A number of points should be made.

First, the *Discussion paper* is a staff working paper of DG COMP. It is not, and should not be treated as, draft Guidelines, still less as actual Guidelines. Much of the discussion is extremely interesting and insightful, but it would be quite wrong for professional advisers and businesses to rely on it as a statement of the law: the *Discussion paper* states this explicitly at paragraph 7.

A second point is that it is well-known that there are a number of views as to what is wrong – and what is right – with Article 82. As we have seen earlier in this chapter, some commentators are highly critical of Article 82 case law, in particular because of what is seen as its formalism and lack of economic analysis. Others, however, are much less critical: indeed the judgments of the Community Courts in recent years, in cases such as *Michelin II*, *British Airways*, and *Microsoft*, do not seem to suggest that they have any fundamental anxiety about the existing case law. It is known to be the case that there are different views within the Commission, and between the Member States, as to the need for and nature of any reform of the law.

A third point is that, ultimately, any reform of the law, short of a change in the Treaty itself, is for the Community Courts: Article 82 is not like Article 81 where the Commission makes significant changes on its own initiative by introducing new or amending existing block exemptions. There are no block exemptions under Article 82. The law is what the Community Courts say it is.

It is not surprising, therefore, that the Commission has not produced draft Guidelines. In particular, *if* the Commission were to decide that it disapproves of the existing law – and there is no reason to believe that the Commission itself, as opposed to individuals within it, does disapprove of the law – it would be very difficult for it to write Guidelines that directly contradict the case law of the Community Courts; and if it were to do so, this could cause considerable confusion, in particular in national courts, where a judge

---

[308] Available at www.ec.europa.eu/comm/competition/antitrust/art82/index.html.
[309] Ibid, paras 54–55.
[310] See www.ec.europa.eu/comm/competition/antitrust/art82/contributions.html.

might find him- or herself confronted with judgments of the Courts and Guidelines of the Commission that pull in opposite direction.

In the opinion of this author, the best solution to this problem would be for the Commission to publish a statement of its own enforcement prioritisation criteria. It could state which types of abuse, or which economic sectors, it intends to investigate with the resources at its disposal. Cases that the Commission does not investigate would then be dealt with, if at all, by national competition authorities, which would have their own prioritisation criteria; or would be litigated in a national court, where judges would proceed on the basis of the existing jurisprudence.

6

The obligations of Member States under the EC competition rules

CHAPTER CONTENTS

1. INTRODUCTION

This chapter will examine the obligations of Member States in relation to the competition rules in the EC Treaty. Specifically it will consider the obligations that Articles 10, 31 and 86 place upon Member States; Articles 87 to 89 on state aid will be briefly mentioned at the end of the chapter. Article 10 imposes a general duty of 'sincere cooperation' or 'loyalty' on Member States; Article 31 deals specifically with state monopolies of a commercial character; and Article 86 is concerned with measures that are contrary to the Treaty. In *France v Commission*[1] Advocate General Tesauro spoke of the 'obscure clarity' of Article 31 as opposed to the 'clear obscurity' of Article 86. These provisions are complex and the law has taken a long time to develop: the encroachment of the Treaty on national monopolies and state activity is inevitably political and contentious.

The Treaty itself provides, in Article 3(1)(g), that one of the activities of the Community shall be to institute 'a system ensuring that competition in the internal market is not distorted'[2]. Article 4 provides that the activities of the Member States and the Community shall be conducted in accordance with the principle of an open market economy with free competition[3]. State involvement in economic activities may work against this goal; however Member States may take offence at too much interference at an EC level in domestic economic and social policy. Articles 81 and 82 are essentially private law provisions, conferring rights and imposing obligations on undertakings;

---

[1] Case C-202/88 [1991] ECR I-1223, [1992] 5 CMLR 552, at para 11 of his Opinion.
[2] Note that Article 3(1)(g) will be dropped from the Treaty if and when the Lisbon Treaty is ratified: see ch 2, pp 50–51.
[3] Note that the ECJ stressed the importance of Article 4 EC in its judgment in Case C-198/01 *Consorzio Industrie Fiammiferi (CIF)* [2003] ECR I-8055, [2003] 5 CMLR 829, para 47.

many other Articles in the Treaty are primarily of a public law nature, imposing obligations on Member States. The extent to which Member States and undertakings which enjoy special or exclusive rights are subject to Articles 81 and 82 is an issue that is still being explored by the Commission and the Community Courts.

The Treaty is neutral on the issue of public ownership of industry in itself. Article 295 provides that the Treaty 'shall in no way prejudice the rules in Member States governing the system of property ownership'. This means that Member States may confer legal monopolies on organs of the State or on undertakings that are not publicly owned, and in cases under Article 86(1) such as *Sacchi*[4], *ERT v Dimotiki*[5] and *Höfner & Elser v Macrotron GmbH*[6] the ECJ has held that the conferment of special or exclusive rights on an undertaking is not, in itself, an infringement of the Treaty. However there is a tension between this principle and the obligation imposed on Member States by Article 86(1) not to enact nor to maintain in force measures contrary to the competition rules in the Treaty, with the result that property rights are not as inviolable as the wording of Article 295 suggests[7].

2. ARTICLE 10

Article 10(1) requires Member States to take all appropriate measures to ensure fulfilment of the obligations arising out of the Treaty; Article 10(2) imposes an obligation on Member States to abstain from any measure which could jeopardise the attainment of the objectives of the Treaty. There have been many cases in which individuals and undertakings have invoked Article 10(2) in proceedings in the criminal and civil courts of Member States, both as plaintiff and defendant, to claim that a particular law of a Member State is unenforceable because of its incompatibility with the competition rules in the Treaty; many of these cases have led to references to the ECJ under Article 234, and will be discussed in this section of the chapter. The ECJ has established that the obligation of Member States to disapply national legislation that contravenes Community law attaches not only to national courts but also to administrative bodies, including national competition authorities[8]. Where a Member State is in breach of its Treaty obligations under Article 10 it would also be possible for the Commission to take action against it, either under Article 226, as in the case of *Commission v Italy*[9], or, where there is an infringement of Article 86(1), under Article 86(3)[10].

(A) The relationship between Article 10 and Articles 81 and 82

The case law on Article 10 is complex, for reasons that are not difficult to understand[11]. It is obvious that measures adopted by Member States may distort competition: they might

---

[4] Case 155/73 [1974] ECR 409, [1974] 2 CMLR 177, para 14.

[5] Case C-260/89 [1991] ECR I-2925, [1994] 4 CMLR 540, para 16.

[6] Case C-41/90 [1991] ECR I-1979, [1993] 4 CMLR 306, para 29.   [7] See further pp 227–232.

[8] See Case C-198/01 *Consorzio Industrie Fiammiferi (CIF)* [2003] ECR I-8055, [2003] 5 CMLR 829, paras 49–50.

[9] Case C-35/96 [1998] ECR I-3851, [1998] 5 CMLR 889; see pp 239–242 below.

[10] See further pp 239–242.

[11] For interesting discussions of the issues involved see Bacon 'State Regulation of the Market and EC Competition Rules: Articles [81] and [82] Compared' (1997) 18 ECLR 283; Ehle 'State Regulation under the US Antitrust State Action Doctrine and under EC Competition Law: a Comparative Analysis' (1998)

do so for example by imposing minimum or maximum prices for goods or services; by adopting discriminatory measures of taxation; by imposing regulatory rules that make it difficult for undertakings to enter markets; or by operating restrictive licensing regimes for particular economic activities. Each of these measures might have serious implications for the competitiveness of markets. However the issue that arises in relation to Article 10, when read in conjunction with Articles 81 and 82, is the extent to which those measures can be challenged, and be found to be unlawful, under EC law.

Article 10 is addressed to Member States; Articles 81 and 82 are directed to undertakings. The conundrum is to decide when a Member State can be held liable for behaviour of undertakings that infringes the competition rules. On the one hand Member States are naturally jealous of their sovereignty, and do not welcome the use of Article 10 to undermine national laws, delegated legislation, regulatory regimes and other measures because they happen to have an effect on the competitiveness of markets; a broad use of Article 10 would be particularly objectionable given that there are clear legal bases for proceeding against Member States under other parts of the Treaty dealing, for example, with the free movement of goods and services. On the other hand the full effectiveness of Articles 81 and 82 could be seriously undermined if Member States could act as the agent of cartels and dominant undertakings that act abusively by adopting measures that have the same effect on the market as the undertakings would have achieved themselves. The case law of the ECJ has sought to achieve a balance and to identify those infringements of Articles 81 and 82 for which Member States must bear responsibility.

(B) The case law predominantly concerns Article 10 in conjunction with Article 81

It is noticeable that state measures that raise issues in relation to abusive behaviour under Article 82 usually arise in the context of Article 86(1), which imposes a specific duty on Member States not to enact nor to maintain in force measures in the case of 'public undertakings and undertakings to which Member States grant special or exclusive rights' which infringe the Treaty and, specifically, the competition rules[12]. The case law on Article 10 therefore has been predominantly concerned with the liability of Member States for infringements of Article 81. Before considering the cases themselves it may be helpful to illustrate the type of problem that arises. Suppose the following:

- In Member State A all lawyers belong to a privately-established bar association and agree to comply with the fees that it recommends for legal services
- In Member State B the State itself fixes legal fees
- In Member State C the bar association is established by law but the association is free to decide whether to recommend fees and, if so, to determine the level of those fees

---

19 ECLR 380; Neergaard *Competition Competences: The Tensions between European Competition Law and Anti-competitive Measures by the Member States* (DJØF Publishing, 1998); Gagliardi 'United States and European Union Antitrust Versus State Regulation of the Economy: Is There a Better Test?' (2000) 25 EL Rev 353; Schepel 'Delegation of Regulatory Powers to Private Powers under EC Competition Law: Towards a Procedural Public Interest' (2002) 39 CML Rev 31; on the position in the US in relation to state regulatory measures see *Parker v Brown* 317 US 341 (1943) and the *Schepel* article cited above.

[12] See pp 220–232 below.

- In Member State D the State requires the bar association to fix fees but leaves it to determine what they should be

- In Member State E a Government Minister has the power, by order, to decree that all lawyers will comply with a draft tariff of fees prepared by the bar association.

In each of these cases the likely outcome will be that there is little competition in relation to legal fees: the effect is that of a horizontal cartel. However in EC competition law the important question is which, if any, of these situations is unlawful; and, specifically in the case of Article 10, whether there is a state measure that violates the Treaty with the consequence that it is void and unenforceable. These questions will be considered after the case law has been analysed.

(C) The case law of the ECJ on Article 10 and the competition rules

(i) The *INNO* doctrine

In *INNO v ATAB*[13] the ECJ, dealing in that case with the taxation of tobacco in the Netherlands, held that the combined effect of Articles 3(1)(g), 10, 81 and 82 meant that a Member State could infringe the Treaty by maintaining in force legislation which could deprive the competition rules of their effectiveness. Subsequent cases have had to search out the implications of this judgment. A challenge to French legislation requiring retailers of books to comply with minimum resale prices imposed by publishers failed since the ECJ was not certain that this practice was unlawful under Article 81 anyway[14]; a challenge to fixed minimum prices for petrol also failed, since this was a pure state measure unrelated to any agreement between undertakings[15]. Opposition to a French law forbidding the undercutting of tariffs for air fares approved by the Minister for Civil Aviation and made binding upon all traders also failed since, at the time, there was no implementing regulation for the application of the competition rules to the air transport sector; this meant that there was no mechanism in place for determining whether any agreements satisfied the terms of Article 81(3)[16]. In *BNIC v Clair*[17] a French trade association, BNIC, sued Clair for undercutting minimum prices established by it, but then extended by Ministerial decree to the entire industry. Under French law these 'extension orders' became binding on everyone in the industry, and BNIC was given the right to bring an action against anyone selling at less than the fixed price. The ECJ, in an Article 234 reference from a French court, held that the involvement of the Minister did not deprive the activities of BNIC of illegality under Article 81(1). This confirmed

---

[13] Case 13/77 [1977] ECR 2115, [1978] 1 CMLR 283.

[14] See Case 229/83 *Association des Centres Distributeurs Edouard Leclerc v Au Ble Vert* [1985] ECR 1, [1985] 2 CMLR 286; Case 254/87 *Syndicat des Libraires de Normandie v L'Aigle Distribution SA* [1988] ECR 4457, [1990] 4 CMLR 37.

[15] Case 231/83 *Cullet v Centre Leclerc, Toulouse* [1985] ECR 305, [1985] 2 CMLR 524.

[16] Cases 209/84 etc *Ministère Public v Asjes* [1986] ECR 1425, [1986] 3 CMLR 173, paras 46–69; however the ECJ continued that, if an adverse finding had been made under Articles 84 or 85(2), it would have been contrary to Article 10 for France to have reinforced the effects of an unlawful agreement: ibid, paras 70–77; Council Regulation 3975/87 OJ [1987] L 374/1 was subsequently adopted in relation to air transport: see ch 23, pp 968–969.

[17] Case 123/83 [1985] ECR 391, [1985] 2 CMLR 430.

the Commission's decisions in *BNIA*[18] and *BNIC*[19]; however the ECJ was not asked in this reference to consider the legality of the French legislation or of the Ministerial order themselves, so that Article 10 was not discussed.

(ii) Successful application of the *INNO* doctrine

(A) BNIC v Yves Aubert The *INNO* doctrine was successfully applied in a similar case, *BNIC v Yves Aubert*[20]. There the ECJ held that the Minister's extension order, which in this case fixed quotas for wine-growers and permitted fines to be imposed on anyone who exceeded them, was itself unlawful. The order had the effect of strengthening the impact of the prior agreement made within the membership of BNIC and was a breach of France's obligations under the Treaty; it followed that an action brought against Yves Aubert by BNIC for infringement of the extension order failed.

(B) Vlaamse Reisbureaus v Sociale Dienst In *Vlaamse Reisbureaus v Sociale Dienst*[21] a tour operator in Belgium brought an action against an association of travel agents which was passing on to its customers the commission it received from tour operators. By Belgian law the tour operator was permitted in these circumstances to bring an action for unfair competition against the price-cutter. The defendant raised the incompatibility of this law with Article 81(1). The ECJ held that there was a constellation of agreements in the industry between tour operators and agents intended to dampen price competition and which infringed Article 81(1); the Belgian legislation buttressed this anti-competitive system by giving it permanent effect, extending it to non-participating undertakings, and by providing penalties for firms which passed on their commission. Therefore the legislation violated the Treaty and the plaintiff's action for unfair competition should fail.

(C) Ahmed Saeed In *Ahmed Saeed Flugreisen v Zentrale zur Bekämpfung Unlauteren Wettbewerbs eV*[22] the ECJ held that the approval by aeronautical authorities of air tariffs fixed by agreement by airlines involved a breach by Member States of their obligations under Articles 3(1)(g), 10, 81 and 82 of the Treaty. The material distinction between this case and *Ministère Public v Asjes*[23] was that by the time of the litigation in *Ahmed Saeed* the implementing regulation in the air transport sector had come into effect[24], so that there was no longer the problem that existed at the time of the earlier case[25].

(D) Consorzio Industrie Fiammiferi In *Consorzio Industrie Fiammiferi*[26] the ECJ held that the Italian competition authority was required by Article 10 of the Treaty to

[18] OJ [1976] L 231/24, [1976] 2 CMLR D63.   [19] OJ [1982] L 379/1, [1983] 2 CMLR 240.
[20] Case 136/86 [1987] ECR 4789, [1988] 4 CMLR 331.
[21] Case 311/85 [1987] ECR 3801, [1989] 4 CMLR 213.
[22] Case 66/86 [1989] ECR 803, [1990] 4 CMLR 102.
[23] Cases 229/84 etc [1986] ECR 1425, [1986] 3 CMLR 173.
[24] See n 16 above.   [25] See p 216 above.
[26] Case C-198/01 [2003] ECR I-8055, [2003] 5 CMLR 829; for comment see Nebbia (2004) 41 Common Market Law Review 839; Kaczorowska 'The Power of a National Competition Authority to Disapply National Law Incompatible with EC Law – and its Practical Consequences' (2004) 25 ECLR 591; for discussion of the *CIF* judgment in the UK Competition Appeal Tribunal see Case 1024/2/3/04 *Floe Telecom Ltd (in administration) v OFCOM* [2006] CAT 17, paras 317–348.

disapply an Italian law of 1923 which regulated the manufacture and sale of matches in Italy in so far as that law required or facilitated price fixing and market sharing contrary to Article 81; it added that penalties could be imposed on the undertakings involved in the unlawful period, except to the extent that the behaviour in question was required as opposed to merely being permitted by the legislation.

In each of these cases an infringement of Article 10 was found where the legislation of a Member State strengthened or encouraged anti-competitive agreements that were already in existence; in *Yves Aubert* and *Ahmed Saeed* the Member States had delegated the power to fix prices to private operators, subsequently reinforcing the effect of their decisions. In *P Van Eycke v ASPA* a plaintiff, disappointed at the interest rate payable on a deposit of his savings, claimed that the rate had been reduced below his expectations because of tax legislation which contravened Article 81. The ECJ held that the *INNO* doctrine was inapplicable as there was no suggestion that the legislation in question encouraged or extended a prior anti-competitive private agreement. In its judgment the ECJ said that the case law showed that a Member State would be in breach of Article 10 in conjunction with Article 81 if it were:

to require or favour the adoption of agreements, decisions or concerted practices contrary to Article [81] or to reinforce their effects, or to deprive its own legislation of its official character by delegating to private traders responsibility for taking decisions affecting the economic sphere[27].

This is a formulation that the ECJ has repeated on subsequent occasions[28]. A particularly clear application of the doctrine is to be found in *Commission v Italy*[29], an action brought by the Commission under Article 226, challenging – successfully – Italian legislation which required the National Council of Customs Agents to set compulsory tariffs for customs agents. The ECJ concluded that the National Council had itself infringed Article 81(1) by adopting the tariff[30]. However it held further that Italy had also infringed the Treaty by requiring the Council to compile a compulsory, uniform tariff[31]: by wholly relinquishing to private economic operators the powers of the public authorities to set tariffs[32]; by prohibiting, in the primary legislation, any derogation from the tariff[33]; and by adopting a Decree having the appearance of approving the tariff by public regulation[34].

(iii) No liability where there is no agreement between undertakings

Several challenges to national legislation have failed where the final determination of prices remained with a Member State: Article 10 in conjunction with Article 81 is infringed only where a Member State requires, favours or reinforces an anti-competitive agreement or abandons its own price-setting powers and delegates them to private operators. Thus in *Meng*[35] the ECJ declined to strike down a German regulation which

---

[27] Ibid, para 16.
[28] See eg Case C-185/91 *Reiff* [1993] ECR I-5801, [1995] 5 CMLR 145, para 14; Case C-153/93 *Delta Schiffahrts- und Speditionsegesellschaft* [1994] ECR I-2517, [1996] 4 CMLR 21, para 14; Case C-38/97 *Autotrasporti Librandi v Cuttica Spedizioni e Servizi Internazionali* [1998] ECR I-5955, [1998] 5 CMLR 966, para 26.
[29] Case C-35/96 [1998] ECR I-3851, [1998] 5 CMLR 889; the Commission's decision finding that the National Council itself had infringed Article 81(1), OJ [1993] L 203/27, [1995] 5 CMLR 495, was upheld on appeal by the CFI in Case T-513/93 *CNSD v Commission* [2000] ECR II-1807, [2000] 5 CMLR 614.
[30] [1998] ECR I-3851, [1998] 5 CMLR 889, para 51.   [31] Ibid, para 56.
[32] Ibid, para 57.   [33] Ibid, para 58.   [34] Ibid, para 59.
[35] Case C-2/91 [1993] ECR I-5751; note that *Meng* was decided at about the same time as *Keck and Mithouard*, Case C-267/91 [1993] ECR I-6097, [1995] 1 CMLR 101, in which the ECJ declined to apply

prohibited insurance companies from passing on commissions to their customers: unlike the position in *Vlaamse*, where Belgium had acted to reinforce prior agreements between travel agents, there was no agreement in *Meng*[36]; similar conclusions were reached in *Ohra*[37], *Reiff*[38] and in a number of later judgments[39]. In *Arduino*[40] the ECJ held that the involvement of the Italian National Bar Council in the production of a draft tariff for legal fees did not divest the tariff adopted by the Minister of the character of legislation[41]. The insistence that there must be an agreement contrary to Article 81 before a Member State can be found to have infringed Article 10 places an obvious limit on the extent to which it is possible to use the *INNO* doctrine to challenge state measures; in particular it is clear that Article 10 cannot be used simply because a state measure produces effects similar to those of a cartel.

(D) Application of the case law to lawyers' fees

Having analysed the case law under the *INNO* doctrine we should return briefly to the alternative situations set out above in relation to legal fees[42].

- In the case of Member State A lawyers agreed to comply with the recommendations of a private-ly-established bar association: this could clearly amount to an infringement of Article 81(1), assuming an appreciable effect on competition and inter-state trade; however there is no involvement on the part of the State, so the application of Article 10 does not arise[43].

- In the second situation Member State B itself fixed the fees: however in this case there is no suggestion of an agreement, and so there can be no infringement of Article 10.

- In the third case Member State C established a regulatory mechanism, but left it to the bar association to decide whether to recommend fees and, if so, to determine what their level should be: the association in doing so would be infringing Article 81, but it is not clear whether the Member State has acted unlawfully; it has given freedom to the bar association to decide how to act, rather than requiring it to act.

- In the case of Member State D, however, it has delegated its regulatory role to the bar association and required it to fix fees, so that it would be held responsible for the price fixing that ensues.

Article 28 to national marketing rules forbidding the use of loss-leaders (selling below cost) in retail outlets: see Reich 'The "November Revolution" of the European Court of Justice: *Keck, Meng* and *Audi* Revisited' (1994) 31 CML Rev 459.

[36] [1993] ECR I-5751, para 14.   [37] Case C-245/91 [1993] ECR I-5851.

[38] Case C-185/91 [1993] ECR 5801, [1995] 5 CMLR 145.

[39] See eg Case C-153/93 *Delta Schiffahrts- und Speditionsgesellschaft* [1994] ECR I-2517, [1996] 4 CMLR 21; Case C-412/93 *Société d'Importaton Edouard Leclerc-Siplec v TF1 and M6* [1995] ECR I-179, [1995] 3 CMLR 422; Case C-96/94 *Centro Servizi Spediporto v Spedizioni Marittima del Golfo* [1995] ECR I-2883, [1996] 4 CMLR 613; Cases C-140/94 etc *DIP SpA v Commune di Bassano del Grappa* [1995] ECR I-3257, [1996] 4 CMLR 157; Case C-38/97 *Autotrasporti Librandi v Cuttica Spedizioni e Servizi Internazionali* [1998] ECR I-5955, [1998] 5 CMLR 966; Case C-266/96 *Corsica Ferries* [1998] ECR I-3949, [1998] 5 CMLR 402.

[40] Case C-35/99 [2002] ECR I-1529, [2002] 4 CMLR 866; for discussion of this case see Thunstrom, Carle and Lindeborg 'State Liability Under the EC Treaty Arising from Anti-competitive State Measures' (2002) 25 World Competition 515.

[41] [2002] ECR I-1529, [2002] 4 CMLR 866, paras 40–44; see to similar effect Case C-250/03 *Mauri*, order of 17 February 2005, [2005] ECR I-1267, [2005] 4 CMLR 723, paras 31–38; Cases C-94/04 etc. *Cipolla* [2006] ECR I-11421, [2007] 4 CMLR 286, paras 48–54.

[42] See pp 215–216 above.

[43] On the application of the competition rules to the professions see ch 3, pp 89–90.

- Member State E could be considered to be strengthening the effect of an agreement contrary to Article 81 by issuing a decree compelling compliance with the bar association's recommendations. However the ECJ has held that if the Minister is free to vary the tariff, acting on the advice of other public bodies, there would be no infringement; the decree retains the character of legislation rather than amounting to the encouragement or reinforcement of an agreement[44].

3. ARTICLE 86[45]

Article 86 provides that:

1. In the case of public undertakings and undertakings to which Member States grant special or exclusive rights, Member States shall neither enact nor maintain in force any measure contrary to the rules contained in this Treaty, in particular to those rules provided for in Article 12 and Articles 81 to 89.

2. Undertakings entrusted with the operation of services of general economic interest or having the character of a revenue-producing monopoly shall be subject to the rules contained in this Treaty, in particular to the rules on competition, in so far as the application of such rules does not obstruct the performance, in law or in fact, of the particular tasks assigned to them. The development of trade must not be affected to such an extent as would be contrary to the interests of the Community.

3. The Commission shall ensure the application of the provisions of this Article and shall, where necessary, address appropriate directives or decisions to Member States.

Article 86(1) is a prohibition addressed to Member States themselves; Article 86(2) provides a limited exception for certain undertakings from the application of the competition rules; Article 86(3) provides the Commission with important powers to ensure compliance with the provisions of Article 86. The law of Article 86 is complex and still developing. After a long period when it was little used it has proved to be a formidable provision in the process of liberalising numerous markets in Europe, in particular in 'utility' sectors such as telecommunications, energy and post and related services. The ECJ has said in *Spain v Commission* that:

[P]aragraph 2 of Article 86 EC, read with paragraph (1) thereof, seeks to reconcile the Member States' interest in using certain undertakings, in particular in the public sector, as an instrument of economic or social policy with the Community's interest in ensuring compliance with the rules on competition and the preservation of the unity of the common market.[46]

(A) Article 86(1)

Article 86(1) is closely related to Article 10: each seeks to ensure effective adherence to the Treaty on the part of Member States. However Article 86 goes beyond Article 10

---

[44] Case C-35/99 *Arduino* [2002] ECR I-1529, [2002] 4 CMLR 866; Cases C-94/04 etc *Cipolla* [2006] ECR I-11421, [2007] 4 CMLR 286.

[45] For further reading on Article 86 see Buendia Sierra *Exclusive Rights and State Monopolies under EC Law* (Oxford University Press, 1999): this book contains an extensive bibliography of literature on Article 86 at pp 431–451; Faull and Nikpay *The EC Law of Competition* (2nd ed, 2007), ch 6; Bellamy and Child *European Community Law of Competition* (eds Roth and Rose, Oxford University Press, 6th ed, 2008), paras 11.009–11.028; see also Blum and Logue *State Monopolies under EC Law* (Wiley, 1998); Edwards and Hoskins 'Article [86]: Deregulation and EC Law: Reflections Arising from the XVI FIDE Conference' (1995) 32 CML Rev 157; Holmes 'Fixing the Limits of EC Competition Law: State Action and the Accommodation of the Public Services' (2004) 57 Current Legal Problems 149.

[46] Case C-463/00 [2003] ECR I-4581, [2003] 2 CMLR 557, para 82.

in that it has its own sphere of application and is not limited to compliance with general principles of law. Article 86(1) imposes an obligation on Member States not to enact nor to maintain in force measures 'contrary to those rules contained in this Treaty, in particular to those rules provided for in Article 12 and Articles 81 to 89'. Two important features of Article 86(1) should be noted at the outset. The first is that Article 86(1) is a 'renvoi' provision or a 'reference rule', that is to say it does not have an independent application but applies only in conjunction with another Article or other Articles of the Treaty. The second point is that Article 86(1) is not limited in its scope only to infringements of the competition rules; although the competition rules (and the rule of non-discrimination in Article 12) are specifically mentioned, measures that infringe, for example, Article 28 on the free movement of goods[47], Article 39 on the free movement of workers[48], Article 43 on the freedom of establishment[49] and Article 49 on the free movement of services[50], could all result in an infringement of Article 86(1). It follows that Article 86(1) did not need to have been placed in the chapter of the Treaty on competition law; however the fact that it is there indicates that the Treaty's authors were aware of the potential for Member States to distort competition through the legislative and other measures that they adopt. The importance of Article 86(1) in relation to the competition rules is that, in certain circumstances, a Member State can be liable for the abuses that have been, or would be, carried out by undertakings.

(i) Undertakings

Article 86(1) applies to measures concerning 'public undertakings and undertakings to which Member States grant special or exclusive rights'. The term 'undertaking' has been considered in the context of Articles 81 and 82 in earlier chapters[51]. In particular it should be noted that state-owned bodies can be undertakings, but that organs of the state that are not involved in any economic activity fall outside the definition[52].

(ii) Public undertakings[53]

The term 'public undertaking' appears only in Article 86(1) of the Treaty, and is not defined. There is no uniform notion of this expression among the Member States, and state intervention in and control of economic behaviour takes many different forms. For this reason Advocate General Reischl has stated that the term must be a concept of Community law which should be given a uniform interpretation for all Member States[54]. In Article 2(1)(b) of the Transparency Directive[55] the Commission said that a public undertaking means:

any undertaking over which the public authorities may exercise, directly or indirectly, a dominant influence by virtue of their ownership of it, their financial participation therein, or the rules which govern it.

---

[47] See eg Case C-18/88 *RTT* [1991] ECR I-5941.

[48] See eg Case C-179/90 *Merci* [1991] ECR I-5889, [1994] 4 CMLR 422.

[49] See eg *Greek Insurance* OJ [1985] L 152/25.

[50] See eg Case C-260/89 *ERT v Dimotiki* [1991] ECR I-2925, [1994] 4 CMLR 540.

[51] See ch 3, pp 82–91 and ch 5, pp 171–172   [52] See in particular ch 3, pp 85–88.

[53] For detailed discussion of this concept see *Buendia Sierra*, paras 1.113–1.139.

[54] Cases 188/80 etc *France v Commission* [1982] ECR 2545, p 2596.

[55] OJ [1980] L 195/35, as amended most recently by Directive 2006/111/EC OJ [2006] L 318/17.

On appeal the ECJ approved this, without providing a more exhaustive definition[56]. The crucial question in each case should be whether the State does have such influence, not the legal form of the undertaking in question.

(iii) Undertakings with 'special or exclusive rights'

Article 86(1) applies to measures in the case both of public undertakings and of undertakings having 'special or exclusive rights': sometimes the latter are referred to as 'privileged undertakings' to distinguish them from public undertakings. It is important to understand what each of the expressions 'special' and 'exclusive' means. The Treaty does not define them, but definitions can be found in Article 2(1)(f) and (g) of the Transparency Directive[57]. Often special or exclusive rights will have been given to a public undertaking, in which case it is unnecessary to give separate consideration to this head of Article 86(1). However many undertakings may have exclusive or special rights without being 'public'.

(A) Exclusive rights[58]   A company established by insurance undertakings to perform a specific statutory task[59], an agricultural marketing board[60], an entity granted a monopoly over the provision of recruitment services[61], a dock-work undertaking entrusted with the exclusive right to organise dock work for third parties[62] and a limited partnership between a Member State, a district authority and eight industrial undertakings responsible for waste management[63] are examples of bodies that were considered to have been granted exclusive rights. It would appear that an 'exclusive' right can be granted to more than one undertaking: in *Entreprenørforeningens Affalds v Københavns Kommune*[64] the ECJ held that three undertakings authorised to receive building waste in Copenhagen had been granted an exclusive right, but it did not explain why these rights were exclusive rather than special, which would have been a more natural finding.

In principle it seems appropriate that a functional rather than a formalistic approach should be taken to the meaning of 'exclusive rights'. Rights may be exclusive in substance, even though they are not described as such (or as monopolies) in the measure in question. For example in *La Crespelle*[65] the ECJ concluded that a scheme for the artificial insemination of cattle in France involved exclusive rights because of the way the national legislation was operated in practice[66]. Furthermore the exclusive rights may derive from a series of different legislative and administrative measures rather than just one[67]. On the other hand the ECJ has held that the mere fact that a body exercises powers conferred upon it by the state and that it has a dominant position in the market

---

[56]   Cases 188/80 etc *France v Commission* [1982] ECR 2545, [1982] 3 CMLR 144.
[57]   See p 210, n 55 above.   [58]   On the concept of exclusive rights see *Buendia Sierra*, paras 1.01–1.214.
[59]   Case 90/76 *Van Ameyde v UCI* [1977] ECR 1091.
[60]   Case 83/78 *Pigs Marketing Board v Redmond* [1978] ECR 2347, [1979] 1 CMLR 177.
[61]   Case C-41/90 *Höfner & Elser v Macrotron* [1991] ECR I-1979, [1993] 4 CMLR 306, para 34.
[62]   Case C-179/90 *Merci* [1991] ECR I-5889, [1994] 4 CMLR 422.
[63]   Case C-203/96 *Dusseldorp* [1998] ECR I-4075, [1998] 3 CMLR 873, para 58.
[64]   Case C-209/98 [2000] ECR I-3743, [2001] 2 CMLR 936.   [65]   Case C-323/93 [1994] ECR I-5077.
[66]   Although the ECJ did not address the point directly, the Opinion of Advocate General Gulmann indicates that it was common ground between the parties that exclusive rights existed.
[67]   See *Exclusive Rights to Broadcast Television Advertising in Flanders* OJ [1997] L 244/18, [1997] 5 CMLR 718, paras 1 and 2, upheld on appeal Case T-266/97 *Vlaamse Televisie Maatschappij NV v Commission* [1999] ECR II-2329, [2000] 4 CMLR 1171.

is not sufficient in itself to establish that it has exclusive rights[68]. This is consistent with an early Commission decision that a copyright collecting society that could derive benefits from national copyright legislation did not have exclusive rights where there was no impediment to other such societies claiming the same benefit[69]; nevertheless the Commission did conclude that the society in question had a dominant position for the purpose of Article 82. The concepts of 'exclusive rights' and 'dominant position' are independent of one another.

Intellectual property rights are not exclusive rights in the sense of Article 86(1). Although it is true to say, for example, that a patent gives an exclusive right (to exclude others from the patented product or process), the patent itself was available to anyone who applied for it and who satisfied the relevant legal requirements. For a measure to fall within Article 86(1) it must entail some element of discretion on the part of the State: where an intellectual property right is given pursuant to the terms of a given Act there is no *discretion* on the part of the State. The same is true in the case of public procurement when practised in accordance with the law[70]; the fact that an undertaking is awarded a contract does not give it an exclusive right in the sense of Article 86(1), since the award is not discretionary. This is a helpful, and perhaps overlooked, way of explaining why some state-conferred exclusivities are not covered by Article 86(1).

(B) Special rights[71]   The ECJ's judgment in *France v Commission*[72] indicates that there is a distinction between exclusive and special rights. The Court held that the provisions in the Commission's Directive on *Telecommunications Equipment*[73] were void in so far as they required Member States to remove special rights from national telecommunications services providers, since it had failed to specify which rights were special or why they were incompatible with the Treaty. In the subsequent amended Directive on *Telecommunications Liberalisation*[74] the Commission stated at recital 11 that, in the telecommunications sector, special rights are:

rights that are granted by a Member State to a limited number of undertakings, through any legislative, regulatory or administrative instrument which, within a given geographical area, limits to two or more, otherwise than according to objective, proportional and non-discriminatory criteria, the number of undertakings which are authorised to provide any such service[75].

This definition can presumably be carried over to other sectors of the economy. In *Second Operator of GSM Radiotelephony Services in Italy*[76] the Commission decided that the grant to Telecom Italia of the right to operate a GSM radiotelephony network qualified as a special right, since the operator had been designated otherwise than according to objective and non-discriminatory criteria.

---

[68] Case C-387/93 *Banchero* [1995] ECR I-4663.   [69] *GEMA* OJ [1971] L 134/15, [1971] CMLR D35.

[70] See ch 2, p 49, n 7 for relevant literature on public procurement law.

[71] On the concept of special rights see *Buendia Sierra* (p 220, n 45), paras 2.01–2.22.

[72] Case C-202/88 [1991] ECR I-1223, [1992] 5 CMLR 552, paras 31–47; see similarly Cases C-271/90 etc *Spain v Commission* [1992] ECR I-5833, paras 32 and 34.

[73] Commission Directive (EEC) 88/301 on competition in the markets for telecommunications terminal equipment OJ [1988] L 131/73, [1991] 4 CMLR 922.

[74] Commission Directive (EC) 94/46 amending Directive (EEC) 88/301 and Directive (EEC) 90/388 in particular with regard to satellite communications OJ [1994] L 268/15.

[75] See similarly Article 2(1)(g) of the Commission's Transparency Directive, p 210, n 55 below.

[76] OJ [1995] L 280/49, para 6; see similarly *Second Operator of GSM Radio Telephony Services in Spain* OJ [1997] L 76/19, para 10.

(iv) 'Measures'

For a Member State to be in breach of Article 86(1) it must have adopted a 'measure'. This expression has been given a wide meaning by the Commission, and its approach has been endorsed by the ECJ. In an early Directive under Article 28[77] the Commission said that measures in that Article included 'laws, regulations, administrative provisions, administrative practices, and all instruments issued from a public authority, including recommendations'; there is no reason to suppose that the expression should have a different meaning under Article 86(1). In another case under Article 28, *Commission v Ireland*[78], the ECJ said that a measure did not have to be legally binding, provided that it might be capable of exerting an influence and of frustrating the aims of the Community as set out in Articles 2 and 3 of the Treaty[79]. The measure does not have to have been adopted by central Government or by a national Parliament: a measure of any body that is a manifestation of the state could fall within Article 86(1), such as the local communes in *Corinne Bodson v Pompes Funèbres*[80].

Numerous examples can be given to support the view that the expression 'measures' has a wide meaning under Article 86(1): for example in *Second Operator of GSM Radio Telephony in Italy*[81] and *Second Operator of GSM Radio Telephony in Spain*[82] the grant of a second mobile licence subject to a substantial licence fee which had not been levied on the incumbent operator amounted to a measure; in *Port of Rødby*[83] the refusal to grant a ferry company access to a state-run Danish port was a measure; and in *Brussels National Airport (Zaventem)*[84], *Portuguese Airports*[85] and *Spanish Airports*[86] systems of stepped landing fee discounts at various national airports were measures.

In each of the above cases the Member State had adopted specific measures which affected the conduct of the public undertaking or the undertaking given special or exclusive rights. In some cases a public authority enters into an agreement with an undertaking granting the latter an exclusive right to perform a particular task: for example to provide funeral services[87]. The question here is whether this amounts to a measure granting exclusive rights, in which case Article 86(1) may apply, or an agreement between undertakings that restricts competition, in which case Article 81(1) may apply. In *Bodson* the ECJ considered that Article 81(1) would not be applicable where a local authority was acting pursuant to its public law powers, since it would not be acting as an undertaking[88]. In *British Telecommunications*[89], however, BT was acting as an undertaking, and so subject to Article 82 when, notwithstanding that it had a regulatory function, it was carrying on a business activity in retransmitting messages.

---

[77] Commission Directive (EEC) 70/50 based on the provisions of Article 33(7) on the abolition of measures which have an effect equivalent to quantitative restrictions on imports and are not covered by other provisions adopted in pursuance of the EEC Treaty JO [1970] L 13/29.

[78] Case 249/81 [1982] ECR 4005 (the '*Buy Irish*' case).   [79] [1982] ECR 4005, para 28.

[80] Case 30/87 [1988] ECR 2479, [1989] 4 CMLR 984.   [81] OJ [1995] L 280/49.

[82] OJ [1997] L 76/19.   [83] OJ [1994] L 55/52.   [84] OJ [1995] L 216/8, [1996] 4 CMLR 232.

[85] OJ [1999] L 69/31, [1999] 5 CMLR 103, upheld on appeal Case C-163/99 *Portugal v Commission* [2001] ECR I-2613, [2002] 2 CMLR 1319.

[86] OJ [2000] L 208/36, [2000] 5 CMLR 967.

[87] Case 30/87 *Corinne Bodson v Pompes Funèbres* [1988] ECR 2479, [1989] 4 CMLR 984.

[88] See ch 3, pp 87–88.

[89] *British Telecommunications* [1982] OJ L 360/36, upheld on appeal Case 41/83 *Italy v Commission (British Telecommunications)* [1985] ECR 873, [1985] 2 CMLR 368.

(v) The obligations on Member States under Article 86(1)

Article 86(1) requires Member States to refrain from enacting or maintaining in force any measure contrary to the Treaty, and in particular one which would contravene Article 12, Article 81 or Article 82. The relationship of Article 86(1) with Articles 81 and 82 is one of the most difficult areas of competition law. Articles 81 and 82 are addressed to undertakings, but Article 86 to Member States: as in the case of Article 10[90] the conceptual issue is to determine how, and in what circumstances, these provisions can operate in such a way as to lead to an infringement of the Treaty by a Member State. As has been seen, under Article 10 the liability of Member States in relation to Article 81 is quite limited; however the jurisprudence of the ECJ has been more dramatic in cases dealing with Article 86(1) in conjunction with Article 82. For many years this issue was barely addressed at all; however the position began to change as a result of a remarkable series of cases in 1991 in which the ECJ delivered four judgments on the relationship between Article 86(1) and other Treaty Articles, including in particular Article 82. A further landmark judgment, in the *Corbeau* case, followed in 1993[91].

(vi) The judgments of 1991

(A) Höfner & Elser v Macrotron   In April 1991 the ECJ held in *Höfner & Elser v Macrotron GmbH*[92] that a Member State which had conferred exclusive rights on a public employment agency could be in breach of Article 86(1) where the exercise by that agency of its rights would inevitably involve an infringement of Article 82. In Germany the Federal Employment Office ('the FEO') had a legal monopoly as an intermediary in the employment market, though in practice it was unable to satisfy demand and tolerated 'headhunting' agencies which, strictly, were acting illegally. An agency seeking payment of its fee for having successfully recruited on behalf of a client was met with the defence that, as the agency was acting unlawfully, it could not enforce the contract; thus the alleged infringement by Germany of the Treaty was raised as a defence to a contract action between two private undertakings. The matter was referred to the ECJ pursuant to Article 234. The conclusion of the ECJ was that the fact that Germany had granted a legal monopoly to the FEO did not in itself entail a breach of Articles 82 and 86(1)[93]; however there would be a breach if the mere exercise of its right would inevitably lead to an abuse under Article 82. This could be the case if the undertaking was manifestly unable to satisfy demand, as was the case here by the admission of the FEO, and if the legal monopoly prevented a competitor from trying to satisfy that demand[94].

(B) ERT v Dimotiki   In June 1991 the ECJ considered in *ERT v Dimotiki*[95] the compatibility with the Treaty of the Greek television and radio station's monopoly over broadcasting. The Court held that the existence of the monopoly in itself was not contrary to the Treaty, but that the manner in which it was exercised could be so[96]. Specifically on Article 82 the ECJ held that, if a Member State which had granted the exclusive right to transmit television broadcasts then granted the same undertaking the right to

---

[90] See pp 214–220 above.   [91] Case C-320/91 [1993] ECR I-2533, [1995] 4 CMLR 621.
[92] Case C-41/90 [1991] ECR I-1979, [1993] 4 CMLR 306.   [93] Ibid, para 29.
[94] Ibid, paras 30–31.   [95] Case C-260/89 [1991] ECR I-2925, [1994] 4 CMLR 540.
[96] [1991] ECR I-2925, [1994] 4 CMLR 540, paras 12 and 32.

retransmit broadcasts, it would infringe Article 86(1) if this created a situation in which the broadcaster would be led to infringe Article 82 by virtue of a discriminatory policy which favours its own broadcasts.

(C) Merci Convenzionale Porto di Genova v Siderurgica Gabrielli In December 1991 the ECJ gave its judgment in *Merci Convenzionale Porto di Genova v Siderurgica Gabrielli*[97]. Merci was a private undertaking given an exclusive concession for the handling of loading operations in the harbour of Genoa. As a result of a strike at Merci, Siderurgica was unable to unload goods imported in a ship from Germany. Siderurgica sued for damages. The ECJ stated that the simple fact of creating a dominant position by granting exclusive rights is not as such incompatible with Article 86(1)[98]; however the Court repeated the ideas in *Höfner* and *ERT* that there could be an infringement by a Member State if the undertaking in question, merely by exercising the exclusive rights granted to it, cannot avoid abusing its dominant position (*Höfner*), or when such rights are liable to create a situation in which that undertaking is induced to commit such abuses (*ERT*)[99]. In this case the Court observed that Merci appeared to have been induced to demand payment for services which had not been requested, to charge disproportionate prices, to refuse to have recourse to modern technology and to treat customers in a discriminatory manner: matters which are specifically mentioned as possible abuses in Article 82(2)(a), (b) and (c) of the Treaty[100].

(D) RTT v GB-Inno-BM The ECJ delivered a further judgment in December 1991, three days after the judgment in *Merci*, in *RTT v GB-Inno-BM*[101]. RTT had exclusive rights in Belgium for the operation of telephone services and for the approval of telecommunications terminal equipment such as telephones; it was also a supplier of telephones itself. GB-Inno sold telephones in Belgium which had been imported from the Far East. RTT asked for an injunction to prevent such sales, since this encouraged people to connect equipment which had not been approved according to Belgian law. The ECJ referred to earlier case law, that an abuse is committed where an undertaking holding a dominant position on a particular market reserves to itself an ancillary activity which might be carried out by another undertaking as part of its activities on a neighbouring but separate market, with the possibility of eliminating all competition from such an undertaking[102]. The ECJ went on to say that, where a state measure brings about such a reservation of an ancillary activity, the measure in question infringes Article 86(1)[103]. RTT argued that there would be an infringement of Article 86(1) only where the Member State favoured an abuse, for example by acting in a discriminatory manner[104], but the ECJ rejected this, stating that the extension of RTT's monopoly was itself a state measure contrary to Article 86(1)[105]. The establishment of a regulatory system which gave RTT the power to determine at will which telephone equipment could be connected to the public telephone network, thereby placing itself at an obvious advantage over its competitors, was unlawful[106].

---

[97] Case C-179/90 [1991] ECR I-5889, [1994] 4 CMLR 422; see Gyselen (1992) 29 CML Rev 1229.
[98] [1991] ECR I-5889, [1994] 4 CMLR 422, para 16.   [99] Ibid, para 17.
[100] Ibid, paras 18 and 19.   [101] Case C-18/88 [1991] ECR I-5941; see *Gyselen*, n 97 above.
[102] [1991] ECR I-5941, para 18, referring to Case 311/84 *CBEM* (the *Télémarketing* judgment) [1985] ECR 3261, [1986] 2 CMLR 558.
[103] [1991] ECR I-5941, para 21.   [104] Ibid, para 22.   [105] Ibid, para 23.
[106] In reaching this finding the ECJ relied on another of its judgments in 1991, the *Telecommunications Directive* case, p 223, n 72 above, at para 51.

(vii) The *Corbeau* judgment

A further judgment of great significance was *Corbeau* in 1993[107]. Criminal proceedings had been brought against Corbeau, a businessman from Liège, for infringing the Belgian legal monopoly for postal services. Corbeau was operating a door-to-door express delivery service in the Liège area: he was not conducting the service of delivering letters on a daily-delivery basis. The ECJ, after referring to the requirement in Article 86(1) not to enact nor to maintain in force measures contrary to the competition rules[108], spent the rest of its judgment considering, under Article 86(2), whether the breadth of the monopoly given to the Belgian Post Office was greater than was necessary to enable it to carry out the task of general economic interest entrusted to it[109]. The significance of the judgment for Article 86(1) was that the ECJ, in effect, was ruling that the breadth of the monopoly granted to the Belgian Post Office was, to the extent that it could not be justified under Article 86(2), unlawful under the Treaty. In other words the Court was challenging the exclusive rights themselves, despite its numerous statements that the creation of dominance is not in itself incompatible with the Treaty.

(viii) Making sense of the case law on Article 82 in conjunction with Article 86(1)

The difficulty with these cases, and with the ECJ's subsequent judgments[110], is to determine the circumstances in which a Member State can be liable under Article 86(1) for an infringement of Article 82. Two points can be made at the outset. First, as Advocate General Jacobs explained at paragraph 388 of his Opinion in *Albany*[111], a Member State cannot be held responsible for independent anti-competitive behaviour on the part of an undertaking simply because it takes place within its jurisdiction. Article 86(1) can be infringed 'only where there is a causal link between a Member State's legislative or administrative intervention on the one hand and anti-competitive behaviour of undertakings on the other hand'. Secondly, the mere creation of a dominant position by the grant of exclusive rights does not infringe Article 86(1); this has been said by the ECJ on

---

[107] Case C-320/91 [1993] ECR I-2533, [1995] 4 CMLR 621; see Hancher (1994) 31 CML Rev 105.

[108] [1993] ECR I-2533, [1995] 4 CMLR 621, para 12.

[109] For discussion of Article 86(2), and of the *Corbeau* judgment on this issue, see pp 233–239 below.

[110] There have been several subsequent judgments on the relationship between Article 82 and Article 86(1): see in particular Case C-393/92 *Almelo* [1994] ECR I-1477; Case C-18/93 *Corsica Ferries Italia srl v Corpo del Piloti del Porto de Genoa* [1994] ECR I-1783; Case C-323/93 *Centre d'Insémination de la Crespelle v Coopérative de la Mayenne* [1994] ECR I-5077; Case C-111/94 *Job Centre (I)* [1995] ECR I-3361; Case C-242/95 *GT-Link A/S v De Danske Statsbaner* [1997] ECR I-4349, [1997] 5 CMLR 601; Case C-387/93 *Banchero* [1995] ECR I-4663; Case C-55/96 *Job Centre (II)* [1997] ECR I-7119, [1998] 4 CMLR 708; Case C-70/95 *Sodemare v Regione Lombardia* [1997] ECR I-3395, [1998] 4 CMLR 667; Case C-163/96 *Silvano Raso* [1998] ECR I-533, [1998] 4 CMLR 737; Case C-266/96 *Corsica Ferries France SA v Gruppo Antichi Ormeggiatori del Porto di Genova* [1998] ECR I-3949, [1998] 5 CMLR 402; Case C-203/96 *Dusseldorp* [1998] ECR I-4075, [1998] 3 CMLR 873; Cases C-67/96 etc *Albany International BV v SBT* [1999] ECR I-5751, [2000] 4 CMLR 446; Cases C-147/97 and C-148/97 *Deutsche Post Ag v GZS* [2000] ECR I-825, [2000] 4 CMLR 838; Case C-258/98 *Giovanni Carra* [2000] ECR I-4217, [2002] 4 CMLR 285; Case C-209/98 *Entreprenørforeningens Affalds/ Miljøsektion v Københavns Kommune* [2000] ECR I-3743, [2001] 2 CMLR 936, on which see van Calster 'Exclusive Rights Ruling No Safe Harbour for Export Restrictions' (2001) 26 CML Rev 502; Case C-340/99 *TNT Traco SpA v Poste Italiane SpA* [2001] ECR I-4109, [2003] 4 CMLR 663; Case C-475/99 *Ambulanz Glöckner v Landkreis Südwestpfalz* [2001] ECR I-8089, [2002] 4 CMLR 726.

[111] Cases C-67/96 etc *Albany International BV v SBT* [1999] ECR I-5751, [2000] 4 CMLR 446.

many occasions[112]: the point is exemplified by the judgment in *Crespelle*[113], where the Court concluded that French legislation conferring legal monopolies on insemination centres for the provision of certain services to cattle breeders did not lead to an abuse for which France was responsible.

Helpful though these two points are, they do not shed any light on the circumstances in which a Member State will be found to have infringed Article 86(1) as a result of an abuse that infringes Article 82. Furthermore, the frequently-repeated statement that the mere creation of dominance does not in itself infringe Article 86(1) does not sit easily with judgments such as *ERT, RTT* and *Corbeau* which do seem, in effect, to have concluded that the monopoly rights in question were incompatible with the Treaty. The judgments of the ECJ on the necessary causal link between the measure under Article 86(1) and the abuse under Article 82 are neither clear nor consistent: in *Höfner* the Court considered that a measure would be unlawful where it led to an 'inevitable' abuse; in *ERT* if it would induce an infringement; in *Banchero*[114] the ECJ considered that there would be an infringement only if the Member State created a situation in which the undertaking in question 'cannot avoid abusing its dominant position'[115]. In *Dusseldorp*[116] the Court was much less guarded: a Member State infringes Article 86(1) in conjunction with Article 82 'if it adopts any law, regulation or administrative provision which enables an undertaking on which it has conferred rights to abuse its dominant position'[117]. Some formulations of the necessary causal link impose quite a high threshold before a Member State will be found liable; others, such as the one in *Dusseldorp*, suggest a lower threshold. What seems clear is that the causal link must be stronger in some kinds of cases than others, depending on how likely it is that abusive behaviour will follow from the measure in question.

Many attempts have been made to make sense of the cases, in particular by identifying specific categories[118]; this is a natural response to the case law, but it is noticeable that different commentators have devised different categories, or have assigned the cases differently. This is not surprising: the cases can be explained in different, and sometimes in overlapping, ways, and the jurisprudence is still evolving. As Advocate General Fennelly stated in his Opinion in *Silvano Raso*[119]:

I do not think that any general test can be enunciated for determining in advance the existence of such a [causal] link. Instead, in each individual case, it will be necessary to assess the impact of impugned national rules in the economic and factual circumstances in which they operate[120].

---

[112] Specific paras in which the ECJ has said this were cited above in relation to the 1991 judgments in *Höfner, ERT* and *Merci*: see pp 225–226 above.

[113] Case C-323/93 *Centre d'Insémination de la Crespelle v Coopérative de la Mayenne* [1994] ECR I-5077; see also Cases C-180/98 etc *Pavel Pavlov v Stichting Pensioenfonds Medische Specialisten* [2000] ECR I-6451, [2001] 4 CMLR 30, para 127.

[114] Case C-387/93 [1995] ECR I-4663.   [115] [1995] ECR I-4663, para 51.

[116] Case C-203/96 [1998] ECR I-4075, [1998] 3 CMLR 873.

[117] Ibid, para 61, citing the *RTT* judgment (see p 226, n 101 above).

[118] See eg *Buendia Sierra* (p 220, n 45 above), paras 5.68–5–109; see also Buendia Sierra in Faull and Nikpay *The EC Law of Competition* (Oxford University Press, 2nd ed, 2007), paras 5.52–5.79; Edward and Hoskins 'Article [86]: Deregulation and EC Law: Reflections arising from the XVI FIDE Conference' (1995) 32 CML Rev 157; Advocate General Jacobs in his Opinion in *Albany* (n 111 above), paras 396–440; Ritter, Braun and Rawlinson *European Competition Law: a Practitioner's Guide* (Kluwer Law International, 3rd ed, 2005), pp 764–767; see also, on the issue of causation, the Opinion of Advocate General Fennelly in Case C-163/96 *Silvano Raso* [1998] ECR I-533, [1998] 4 CMLR 737, paras 57–66.

[119] [1998] ECR I-533, [1998] 4 CMLR 737.   [120] Ibid, para 65.

The text that follows attempts a categorisation, but must be read subject to the caveat that it is simply one way, among several others, of trying to make sense of the jurisprudence of the ECJ and the decisional practice of the Commission.

(A) Manifest inability to meet demand In *Höfner & Elser v Macrotron GmbH*[121] the ECJ held that there would be an infringement of Article 86(1) where Germany had created a situation in which the FEO was 'manifestly not in a position to satisfy demand' for recruitment services, and its legal monopoly prevented a competitor from satisfying that demand. The idea that inability to meet demand can be abusive can be traced back to Article 82(2)(b), which gives as an example of abuse 'limiting production, markets or technical development to the prejudice of consumers'. On similar facts to *Höfner*, in *Job Centre (II)*[122] the ECJ concluded that the enforcement of an employment procurement monopoly enforced in Italy through criminal proceedings was a measure contrary to Article 86(1). In the *Albany* judgment[123] the ECJ seems to have considered that the exclusive right given to the operator of a sectoral pension fund amounted to a limitation of demand[124], although it went on to decide that this could be justified under Article 86(2)[125]. The judgment in *Merci*[126] can be explained, in part, on the basis that the entrusted undertaking had refused to have recourse to modern technology, which resulted in a failure to satisfy the demand of customers. In *Dusseldorp*[127] a requirement that waste for recovery could be supplied only to the entrusted undertaking, and could not be exported to a third undertaking, was held to restrict outlets and to contravene Article 86(1) in conjunction with Article 82[128]. However in *Ambulanz Glöckner v Landkreis Südwestpfalz*[129] Advocate General Jacobs suggested that a Member State would be liable under Article 86(1) only where there is a systemic failure to meet demand and not where there is a failure merely due to inefficient management[130]. The Commission's decisions on courier services, *Dutch Express Delivery Services*[131] and *Spanish International Courier Services*[132], and on licences for mobile telephony operators, *Second Operator of GSM Telephony Services in Italy*[133] and *Second Operator of GSM Telephony Services in Spain*[134], can be included, in part, in this category of cases[135].

---

[121] Case C-41/90 [1991] ECR I-1979, [1993] 4 CMLR 306.

[122] Case C-55/96 [1997] ECR I-7119, [1998] 4 CMLR 708; see also Case C-258/98 *Giovanni Carra* [2000] ECR I-4217, [2002] 4 CMLR 285.

[123] Cases C-67/96 etc [1999] ECR I-5751, [2000] 4 CMLR 446.

[124] [1999] ECR I-5751, [2000] 4 CMLR 446, para 97.   [125] On Article 86(2) see pp 233–239 below.

[126] Case C-179/90 [1991] ECR I-5889, [1994] 4 CMLR 422.

[127] Case C-203/96 [1998] ECR I-4075, [1998] 3 CMLR 873.

[128] [1998] ECR I-4075, [1998] 3 CMLR 873, para 63.

[129] Case C-475/99 [2001] ECR I-8089, [2002] 4 CMLR 726.

[130] [2001] ECR I-8089, [2002] 4 CMLR 726, para 148 of his Opinion; the ECJ did not deal with this point explicitly, though the tone of its comments at paras 62–65 appear to be consistent with the views of the Advocate General.

[131] OJ [1990] L 10/47, [1990] 4 CMLR 947 quashed on appeal Cases C-48/90 and C-66/90 *Netherlands and Koninklijke PTT Nederland v Commission* [1992] ECR I-565, [1993] 5 CMLR 316.

[132] OJ [1990] L 233/19, [1991] 4 CMLR 560, para 11.

[133] OJ [1995] L 280/49, [1996] 4 CMLR 700, para 17(ii).   [134] OJ [1997] L 76/19, para 21(ii).

[135] The same decisions can also be included in the 'reservation of an ancillary activity' category: see below.

(B) Conflict of interest In *ERT v Dimotiki*[136] the ECJ held that there would be an infringement of Article 86(1) where Greece had created a situation in which the broadcaster ERT would be led to infringe Article 82 by virtue of a discriminatory policy in favour of its own broadcasts. A notable feature of this case was that it was not necessary for ERT to have actually abused its dominant position in the manner suggested: the granting of the exclusive right made this sufficiently likely that the measure in question infringed Article 86(1). The ECJ seems to have considered it to be inevitable that an undertaking in the position of ERT, because of its conflict of interest, would act abusively. The same idea was presumably present in *RTT v GB-Inno-BM*[137], since the regulatory function of RTT inevitably gave rise to a conflict of interest, although the ECJ specifically relied there on the extension of monopoly rights to neighbouring markets[138]. A further example of a conflict of interest case is *Silvano Raso*[139], where a dock-work scheme granted an undertaking the exclusive right to supply temporary labour to terminal concessionaires, but also enabled it to compete with them on the market for the provision of dock services: merely by exercising its monopoly rights the entrusted undertaking would be able to distort competition in its favour, for example by imposing on its competitors unduly high costs or by supplying them with labour less suited to the work to be done[140]; the ECJ specifically mentioned the conflict of interest of the entrusted undertaking in this judgment[141]. The ECJ would be less likely to find an infringement of Article 86(1) where provision exists for judicial review of the decisions made by an apparently conflicted undertaking[142].

(C) Reservation of an ancillary activity In *RTT v GB-Inno-BM*[143] the ECJ held that a measure that resulted in the extension of RTT's monopoly to an ancillary activity on a neighbouring but separate market infringed Article 86(1). As noted in the preceding paragraph, the ECJ could have reached the same conclusion on the basis of a conflict of interest, but it decided the case specifically on the basis of its earlier judgment in the *Télémarketing* case[144]. In *Ambulanz Glöckner v Landkreis Südwestpfalz*[145] the ECJ held that a law adopted by Länder in Germany concerning the provision of ambulance services infringed Article 86(1) because medical aid organisations that had an exclusive right to provide emergency ambulance services were enabled to also offer non-emergency patient transport services, which could have been carried out by independent operators[146]. The Commission considered that there were abuses under this head in *Dutch Express Delivery Services*[147] and *Spanish International Courier Services*[148]. In

---

[136] Case C-260/89 [1991] ECR I-2925, [1994] 4 CMLR 540.
[137] Case C-18/88 [1991] ECR I-5941.   [138] See below.
[139] Case C-163/96 [1998] ECR I-533, [1998] 4 CMLR 737; the Commission condemned various aspects of the same dock-work legislation in *Provisions of Italian Ports Legislation Relating to Employment* OJ [1997] L 301/17; it noted the conflict of interest created by the legislation at paras 30(b) and (c) of its decision, referring to this as 'inherently an abuse'.
[140] Case C-163/96 [1998] ECR I-533, [1998] 4 CMLR 737, paras 28–31.
[141] [1998] ECR I-533, [1998] 4 CMLR 737, para 28.
[142] Case C-67/96 *Albany International BV v SBT* [1999] ECR I-5751, [2000] 4 CMLR 446, paras 116–121.
[143] Case C-18/88 [1991] ECR I-5941.
[144] Case 311/84 [1985] ECR 3261, [1986] 2 CMLR 558; see also Cases C-271/90 etc *Spain v Commission* [1992] ECR I-5833, para 36.
[145] Case C-475/99 [2001] ECR I-8089, [2002] 4 CMLR 726.
[146] [2001] ECR I-8089, [2002] 4 CMLR 726, para 43.
[147] OJ [1990] L 10/47, annulled on appeal Cases C-48/90 and C-66/90 *Netherlands and Koninklijke PTT Nederland v Commission* [1992] ECR I-565, [1993] 5 CMLR 316.
[148] OJ [1990] L 233/19, [1991] 4 CMLR 560, para 10.

each of *Second Operator of GSM Telephony Services in Italy*[149] and *Second Operator of GSM Telephony Services in Spain*[150] the Commission decided that, in requiring a second mobile operator to make a substantial payment for a mobile telephony licence that had not been paid by the incumbent telecommunications companies, there had been state measures capable of extending the monopoly rights of the latter. The judgment of the ECJ in *Connect Austria Gesellschaft für Telekommunications GmbH v Telekom-Control-Kommission*[151], an Article 234 reference from a court in Austria, points to the same conclusion. The Commission also considered that there was an abuse under this head in *Port of Rødby*[152] where the refusal by a port operator, DSD, to allow Euro-Port A/S access to the port of Rødby eliminated competition in the downstream market for ferry services from Rødby to Puttgarden, in which it was collectively dominant with Deutsche Bahn. A further decision under this head is *New Postal Services in Italy*[153].

(D) Corbeau In *Corbeau*[154] the ECJ did not discuss Article 86(1) in any detail, but instead considered the extent to which the postal monopoly of the Belgian Post Office could be justified under Article 86(2)[155]. However the interest of the case under Article 86(1) is that, to the extent that the monopoly was not justifiable under Article 86(2), the ECJ seems to have considered that it would amount to a measure contrary to Article 86(1). This could be seen as an example of the unlawful extension of a monopoly right to an ancillary activity, as in the cases just discussed. More radically, however, the case seems to suggest that it is possible to strike down monopolies that are too broad: in *RTT*, for example, that company would be able to use its monopoly right to extend its activities into the neighbouring market; in *Corbeau* the Court seems simply to have regarded the monopoly of the Belgian Post Office as too broad in itself. To the extent that this is a correct interpretation of *Corbeau* the judgment is very radical, and seems to go beyond the often-repeated assertion that the grant of an exclusive right is not, in itself, unlawful. Since *Corbeau* a specific Directive has been adopted in the postal sector determining the permitted extent of the 'reserved area' (that is to say the monopoly) in the postal sector[156]. As for the judgment itself, it is possible that this was the 'high-tide' of intervention under Article 86(1), and that the ECJ has since taken a more cautious approach, as the judgments in *Crespelle*[157] and *Banchero*[158] seem to suggest[159].

(E) Discrimination In *Merci*[160] the ECJ referred to the discriminatory treatment of customers as an abuse for which a Member State could be responsible under Article 86(1). In *GT-Link A/S v De Danske Statsbaner*[161] the Court stated that, where a public undertaking which owns and operates a commercial port waives the port duties on its own ferry services and some of its trading partners whilst charging the full duties to other customers, there could be an infringement of Article 82(2)(c), which refers to the application of dissimilar conditions to equivalent transactions placing other trading parties at

---

[149] OJ [1995] L 280/49, [1996] 4 CMLR 700, para 17(i).   [150] OJ [1997] L 76/19, para 21(i).
[151] Case C-462/99 [2003] ECR I-5147, [2005] 5 CMLR 302.   [152] OJ [1994] L 55/52.
[153] OJ [2001] L 63/59.   [154] Case C-320/91 [1993] ECR 1–2533, [1995] 4 CMLR 621.
[155] See p 237 below.   [156] See ch 23, pp 977–978.
[157] Case C-323/93 *Centre d'Insémination de la Crespelle v Coopérative de la Mayenne* [1994] ECR I-5077.
[158] Case C-387/93 [1995] ECR I-4663.
[159] On these two judgments see Buendia Sierra *Exclusive Rights and State Monopolies under EC Law*, paras 5.110–5.128.
[160] Case C-179/90 [1991] ECR I-5889, [1994] 4 CMLR 422.
[161] Case C-242/95 [1997] ECR I-4349, [1997] 5 CMLR 601.

a competitive disadvantage[162]. Appropriately transparent accounting would be needed to show that this was not the case[163]. In a series of decisions in relation to charges levied for the use both of airports[164] and ports[165] the Commission has expressly condemned price discrimination contrary to Article 82(2)(c), and found the Member State in question to have adopted a measure contrary to Article 86(1). In these cases the airport or port was a natural monopoly, which would result in a particularly strict responsibility not to act in an abusive manner[166]; and it may be necessary, under the essential facilities doctrine[167], for the owner of such infrastructure to grant access to third parties on non-discriminatory terms[168].

(F) The categories are not closed The caveat has already been entered that this categorisation of the cases is simply an attempt to make sense of the judgments and decisions on Article 86(1) in conjunction with Article 82. It should be added that there is no reason why there should not be further cases in the future that do not fall into any of these categories at all. In each case the question is whether a Member State has adopted a measure that infringes or might infringe Article 82 for which it bears responsibility under Article 86(1): the categories set out above do not include all the examples of abusive behaviour found to have infringed Article 82[169].

(ix) Remedies and direct effect

Article 86(1) has direct effect when applied in conjunction with another directly applicable provision of Community law, with the consequence that individuals can bring an action in a national court against a Member State which has infringed it[170]. Furthermore, the direct effect of Article 86(1) means that, as in the case of *Höfner & Elser v Macrotron GmbH*[171], one undertaking may be able to invoke it against another in domestic litigation.

An interesting question is whether an individual or a third party is able to bring an action for damages against a Member State which has acted in breach of Article 86(1). After the *Factortame* litigation on 1996[172], in which the ECJ held that in certain circumstances a Member State may have to compensate individuals who suffer as a result of infringing EU law, this must at least be arguable.

---

[162] [1997] ECR I-4349, [1997] 5 CMLR 601, para 41; on Article 82(2)(c) generally, see ch 18, pp 748–753.

[163] [1997] ECR I-4349, [1997] 5 CMLR 601, para 42.

[164] See *Brussels National Airport (Zaventem)* OJ [1995] L 216/8, [1996] 4 CMLR 232, paras 12–18; *Portuguese Airports* OJ [1999] L 69/31, [1999] 5 CMLR 103, paras 24–40; *Spanish Airports* OJ [2000] L 208/36, [2000] 5 CMLR 967, paras 45–56.

[165] See *Tariffs for Piloting in the Port of Genoa* OJ [1997] L 301/27, paras 11–21.

[166] See ch 5, pp 183–186 on the responsibilities of dominant, and 'super-dominant', undertakings.

[167] See ch 18, pp 690–699.

[168] See eg *Port of Rødby* OJ [1994] L 55/52, where the Commission decided that a refusal to allow access to the port was an unlawful extension of the monopoly right enjoyed by the port operator: see p 231 above.

[169] On abusive behaviour under Article 82 see further ch 5, pp 188–206 and chs 18 and 19 generally.

[170] See for example Case 155/73 *Sacchi* [1974] ECR 409, [1974] 2 CMLR 177, para 18; Case C-179/90 *Merci Convenzionale Porto di Genova SpA v Sidururgica Gabrielli SpA* [1991] ECR I-5889, [1994] 4 CMLR 422, para 23; for a more recent statement to the same effect, and citing other judgments of the ECJ on the point see Case C-258/98 *Giovanni Carra* [2000] ECR I-4217, [2002] 4 CMLR 285, para 11.

[171] See n 92 above.

[172] Cases C-46/93 and C-48/93 *Brasserie du Pêcheur SA v Bundesrepublik Deutschland* [1996] ECR I-6297, [1996] 1 CMLR 889.

(B) Article 86(2)

Article 86(2) is a somewhat awkwardly drafted provision[173]. It is in three parts. To begin with, it states that undertakings entrusted with the operation of services of general economic interest or having the character of a revenue-producing monopoly shall be subject to the rules in the Treaty, and in particular to the competition rules. It then states, however, that this subjection to the rules applies only 'in so far as the application of such rules does not obstruct the performance, in law or in fact, of the particular tasks assigned to them'. Perhaps an easier way to think of Article 86(2) is to ask whether it provides a way of justifying what would otherwise amount to an infringement of the competition rules[174]. Since Article 86(2) results in the non-application of Articles 81 and 82, it must be interpreted strictly[175]. Article 86(2) requires that any restriction of competition should satisfy the principle of proportionality[176]. The burden of proof is on the undertaking seeking to rely on this provision[177]; however to succeed under Article 86(2) it is not necessary to show that an undertaking's survival would be threatened if it were to be subjected to the competition rules[178]; nor to prove that there is no other conceivable measure that could secure that the task in question could be performed[179]. A third limb to Article 86(2) adds that the development of trade must not be affected to such an extent as would be contrary to the interests of the Community. The burden is on the Commission or third party complainants to prove this[180].

The effect of Article 86(2) is that some undertakings can successfully claim that Articles 81 and 82 do not apply where their application would prevent them from carrying on the tasks assigned to them by a Member State; however a Member State's interest in doing this must be balanced against the Community's interest in ensuring free competition and a single market. A good example of circumstances in which Article 86(2) may be applicable is afforded by postal services: all Member States require their national postal operator to observe a 'minimum service obligation': this is defined in Article 1 of the Postal Services Directive[181] as 'a universal service involving the permanent provision of a postal service of specified quality at all points in their territory at affordable prices for all users'. The postal operator will charge the same price for the delivery of letters to all parts of the country. In effect, this means that the inhabitants of urban areas subsidise the postal services of those living in rural ones: delivering a letter from one part of London to another is cheaper than from the south-west of England to the

---

[173] Its counterpart in UK law will be found in the Competition Act 1998, Sch 3, para 4, although that provision is drafted rather more elegantly; for detailed discussion of Article 86(2) see *Buendia Sierra* (p 220, n 45 above) paras 8.01–8.324; see also Buendia Sierra in *Faull and Nikpay* (p 220, n 45 above) paras 6.131–6.216; Auricchio 'Services of General Economic Interest and the Application of EC Competition Law' (2001) 24 World Competition 65.

[174] See Case C-475/99 *Ambulanz Glöckner v Landkreis Südwestpfalz* [2001] ECR I-8089, [2002] 4 CMLR 726.

[175] See Cases C-157/94 etc *Commission v Netherlands* [1997] ECR I-5699, [1998] 2 CMLR 373, para 37; see also *Reims II* OJ [1999] L 275/17, [2000] 4 CMLR 704, para 92.

[176] See *Buendia Sierra* (p 220, n 45 above) paras 8.115–8.261; also Buendia Sierra in *Faull and Nikpay* (p 220, n 45 above) paras 6.162–6.204.

[177] See Cases 157/94 etc *Commission v Netherlands* [1997] ECR I-5699, [1998] 2 CMLR 373, para 51.

[178] Ibid, para 43.   [179] Ibid, para 58.   [180] See pp 238–239 below.

[181] Directive 97/67/EC of the European Parliament and of the Council on *Common Rules for the Development of the Internal Market of Community Postal Services and the Improvement of Quality of Service* OJ [1998] L 15/14.

north-east of Scotland. In a sense, therefore, the uniform tariff is discriminatory and could be attacked as such under Article 82. However, in so far as the uniform tariff provides an income to the postal operator that enables it to maintain the universal service, Article 86(2) is applicable and the undertaking is not subject to the competition rules.

A number of points require consideration.

(i) Services of general economic interest

An undertaking can claim to be excluded from the rules in the Treaty only if it has been entrusted with services of general economic interest or if it has the character of a revenue producing monopoly. It is not enough in itself that the undertaking performs that service; it must have been entrusted with that performance, which will mean that it is under certain obligations[182]. It is not necessary that the undertaking has been entrusted with the performance of the service by a legislative measure; this could have come about, for example, as a result of the terms and conditions of a concession agreement[183]. The fact that an undertaking is entrusted at its own request does not mean that Article 86(2) is inapplicable as long as its position derives from an act of public authority[184].

The expression 'services of general economic interest' is not defined in the Treaty. Obvious examples of such services are the operation of the basic postal service[185] and the provision of services, for example in the transport sector, which are not economically viable in their own right[186]. However it is noticeable that, in recent judgments, the ECJ has recognised that the 'protection' of Article 86(2) can extend beyond the conventional utilities: for example it has been found to be capable of application to pension schemes[187], ambulance services[188], and the treatment of waste material[189]. The CFI has held that Member States enjoy a wide discretion to define what they regard as services of general economic interest[190]

The protection afforded to services of general economic interest is a sensitive political issue and was addressed at the 1997 Inter-Governmental Conference. Proposals to amend Article 86(2) itself were rejected in favour of the insertion of Article 16 EC by the Treaty of Amsterdam. This expressly preserves the application of Article 86 because of:

the place occupied by services of general economic interest in the shared values of the Union as well as their role in promoting social and territorial cohesion[191].

---

[182] See the Opinion of Advocate General Jacobs in Case 203/96 *Dussesldorp* [1998] ECR I-4075, [1998] 3 CMLR 873, para 103.

[183] Case 30/87 *Corinne Bodson v Pompes Funèbres* [1988] ECR 2479, [1989] 4 CMLR 984.

[184] Case T-17/02 *Fred Olsen SA v Commission* [2005] ECR II-2031, paras 187–190.

[185] Case 320/91 *Corbeau* [1993] ECR I-2533, [1995] 4 CMLR 621, para 15: 'it cannot be disputed that Régie des Postes is entrusted with a service of general economic interest consisting in its obligation to collect, carry and distribute mail on behalf of all users throughout the territory of the Member State concerned, at uniform tariffs…'.

[186] See eg Case 66/88 *Ahmed Saeed* [1989] ECR 803, [1990] 4 CMLR 102, para 55.

[187] Cases C-67/96 etc *Albany International BV v Stichting Bedrijfspensioenfonds Textielindustrie* [1999] ECR I-5751, [2000] 4 CMLR 446.

[188] Case C-475/99 *Ambulanz Glöckner v Landkreis Südwestpfalz* [2001] ECR I-8089, [2002] 4 CMLR 726.

[189] Case C-203/96 *Dusseldorp* [1998] ECR I-4075, [1998] 3 CMLR 873; Case C-209/98 *Entreprenørforeningens Affalds/Miljøsektion v Københavns Kommune* [2000] ECR I-3743, para 75.

[190] See Case T-106/95 *FFSA v Commission* [1997] ECR II-229, para 99 and Case T-17/02 *Fred Olsen SA v Commission* [2005] ECR II-2031, paras 215–228.

[191] Article 16 EC; see further the Commission's XXVIIth *Report on Competition Policy* (1997), points 96–98; Ross 'Article 16 EC and Services of General Economic Interest: from Derogation to Obligation'

Article 16 reinforces the commitment of the Community and Member States to support undertakings required to provide services of general economic interest[192]. In 1996 the Commission adopted a communication on services of general interest in Europe[193] in which it confirmed that both public and private undertakings can be entrusted with the operation of services of general economic interest;[194] a further communication (replacing the 1996 one) was adopted in September 2000[195]. In November 2002 the Commission published a 'non-paper' on *Services of general economic interest and state aid*[196] setting out further thoughts on the matter for the purpose of encouraging further discussion with the Member States. A *Green Paper on services of general interest* was published in May 2003[197]. This was followed in 2004 by the publication of a *White Paper on services of general interest*[198] which recognised the importance of well-functioning, accessible, affordable, and high-quality services of general interest for the quality of life of European citizens, the environment, and the competitiveness of European enterprises. The White Paper explained the further action that the Commission intended to take in relation to services of general interest, including a reexamination of the need for a framework law on them, a review of the procurement aspects of public–private partnerships and the submission of a communication on social and health services. In 2006 the Commission published a Communication on *Social services of general interest in the EU*[199]; and in 2007 it published a further Communication on *Services of general interest, including social services of general interest: a new European commitment*[200].

(ii) Undertakings having the character of a revenue-producing monopoly

This expression is not defined in the Treaty. It would apply to a monopoly created in order to raise revenue for the State; usually this monopoly would be conferred upon a public undertaking which would contribute its profits to the State, but it could also be conferred upon a private undertaking in exchange for revenue. Undertakings that have the character of a revenue-earning monopoly may also be subject to Article 31, and the ECJ has established that Article 86(2) may be invoked as a defence in an action under that provision[201].

(2000) 25 EL Rev 22; Szyszczak 'Public Services in Competition Markets' [2001] Yearbook of European Law (Oxford University Press, eds Eeckhout and Tridimas), ch 2; Ross 'Promoting solidarity: From public services to a European model of competition?' (2007) 44 Common Market Law Review 1057; Boeger 'Solidarity and EC competition law' (2007) ELR 319.

[192] Note that Article 16 will be reformulated, and renumbered as Article 14, if and when the Lisbon Treaty is ratified and enters into force.
[193] Commission Communication OJ [1996] C 281/3; see further the Commission's XXVIIth *Report on Competition Policy* (1997), point 99.
[194] Ibid, para 10.   [195] OJ [2001] C 17/4, [2001] 4 CMLR 882.
[196] Available at www.europa.eu.int/comm/competition/state_aid/others.
[197] COM(2003)270 final, available at www.ec.europa.eu/services_general_interest/index_en.htm.
[198] COM(2004)374, available at www.ec.europa.eu/services_general_interest/index_en.htm.
[199] COM(2006)177 final, available at www.ec.europa.eu/employment_social/social_protection/docs.
[200] COM(2007)725 final, available at www.ec.europa.eu/services_general_interest.
[201] See p 242–244 below.

(iii) Scope of the exception: obstruction of the performance of the tasks assigned

In a number of cases undertakings have argued that they were shielded from the competition rules by virtue of Article 86(2); in *BRT v SABAM*[202] the ECJ ruled that, as Article 86(2) involves a derogation from the application of the competition rules, it should be construed narrowly, and the Commission and the Community courts have consistently done so, thereby maximising the application of Articles 81 and 82. In particular they have been sceptical of the assertion that anti-competitive behaviour is *necessary* to enable undertakings to carry out the tasks assigned to them.

(A) Unsuccessful claims based on Article 86(2) Claims based on Article 86(2) have often been rejected[203]. For example, in *EEC v ANSEAU-NAVEWA*[204] the Commission held that an agreement requiring purchasers in Belgium to acquire 'conformity labels' before washing-machines and dishwashers could be plumbed in infringed Article 81(1) because it had the effect of discriminating against imports from other Member States. The association of Belgian water authorities involved in running the scheme claimed the benefit of Article 86(2). The Commission accepted that they qualified as a body to whom services of a general economic interest had been entrusted, but went on to hold that the scheme in question was much more restrictive than necessary, saying that:

a possible limitation of the application of the rules on competition can only be envisaged in the event that the undertaking concerned has no other technically and economically feasible means of performing its particular task[205].

Similarly in *British Telecommunications*[206] the Commission rejected British Telecommunications's defence based on Article 86(2); when the Italian Government challenged this decision before the ECJ the Commission's decision was upheld[207]. The ECJ held that Italy had failed to show that the Commission's censure of BT, for prohibiting private message-forwarding agencies from using its network to forward messages from other EC Member States, put the performance of its tasks in jeopardy. Article 86(2) also failed in *Air Inter v Commission*[208], where the CFI rejected TAT's appeal against a Commission decision requiring the termination of exclusive rights on French air routes. The CFI accepted that the airline was entrusted with a public task of maintaining

---

[202] Case 127/73 [1974] ECR 313, [1974] 2 CMLR 238.

[203] As well as the cases mentioned in the text see Case 172/80 *Züchner v Bayerische Vereinsbank* [1981] ECR 2021, [1982] 1 CMLR 313 and *Uniform Eurocheques* OJ [1985] L 35/43, [1985] 3 CMLR 434, paras 29 and 30 (both cases on banking); *Decca Navigator System* OJ [1989] L 43/27, [1990] 4 CMLR 627, para 128; *Magill TV Guide/ITP, BBC and RTE* OJ [1989] L 78/43, [1989] 4 CMLR 757, para 25; *Dutch Express Delivery Services* OJ [1990] L 10/47, paras 16–18; *Spanish International Courier Services* OJ [1990] L 233/19, [1991] 4 CMLR 560, paras 13–14; Case C-179/90 *Merci Convenzionale Porto di Genova v Siderurgica Gabrielli* [1991] ECR I-5889, [1994] 4 CMLR 540, paras 25–28; Case C-18/88 *RTT v GB-Inno-BM* [1991] ECR I-5941, paras 14–28; *IJsselcentrale* OJ [1991] L 28/32, [1992] 5 CMLR 154, paras 39–42; Case C-242/95 *GT-Link A/S v De Danske Statsbaner* [1997] ECR I-4349, [1997] 5 CMLR 601, paras 47–55; Case C-393/92 *Almelo* [1994] ECR I-1477, paras 46–51; when this case returned to the Dutch court the claim based on Article 86(2) was unsuccessful: see Hancher (1997) 34 CML Rev 1509.

[204] OJ [1982] L 167/39 as amended at L 325/20, [1982] 2 CMLR 193; upheld on appeal, Cases 96/82 etc *IAZ International Belgium SA v Commission* [1983] ECR 3369, [1984] 3 CMLR 276.

[205] OJ [1982] L 167/39, [1982] 2 CMLR 193, para 66.   [206] OJ [1982] L 360/36, [1983] 1 CMLR 457.

[207] Case 41/83 *Italy v Commission* [1985] ECR 873, [1985] 2 CMLR 368.

[208] Case T-260/94 [1997] ECR II-997, [1997] 5 CMLR 851.

unprofitable domestic air routes. However it held that subjection to the competition rules would merely hinder or make more difficult the performance of this task; for Article 86(2) to apply it was necessary to show that this would obstruct it, in fact or in law[209].

A particularly important judgment on Article 86(2) is *Corbeau*[210]. As we have seen, the case concerned the operation of an express delivery service, in contravention of the Belgian Post Office's postal monopoly[211]. The core of the ECJ's judgment dealt with the extent to which the postal monopoly could be justified under Article 86(2)[212]. The Court acknowledged that the Post Office was entrusted with a service of general economic interest[213], and that it might be necessary for it to benefit from a restriction of competition in order to be able to offset less profitable activities against profitable ones[214]: put more colloquially, it may be legitimate to prevent an entrant into the market from 'cream-skimming' or 'cherry-picking', leaving the incumbent postal operator to carry out unprofitable services pursuant to its universal service obligation. However the Court continued that:

the exclusion of competition is not justified as regards specific services dissociable from the service of general interest which meet special needs of economic operators and which call for certain additional services not offered by the traditional postal service, such as collection from the senders' address, greater speed or reliability of distribution or the possibility of changing the destination in the course of transit, in so far as such services, by their nature and the conditions in which they are offered, such as the geographical area in which they are provided, do not compromise the economic equilibrium of the service of general economic interest performed by the holder of the exclusive right[215].

Since this was a reference under Article 234, the ECJ then stated that it would be for the national court to make a decision under Article 86(2) on the particular facts of the case[216], but it is clear that it was giving a strong indication that it should not be possible to maintain a monopoly over express courier services in order to sustain the basic service of the daily delivery of letters.

(B) Successful claims based on Article 86(2) It would be wrong to suppose from the foregoing that claims based on Article 86(2) are always unsuccessful. In particular, as the competition rules have come to be applied with greater regularity to the utilities (gas, electricity, water and similar sectors) and to areas of activity for which the state has historically taken responsibility, so too Article 86(2) has been invoked more often with successful effect. This point can be demonstrated by reference to five judgments of the ECJ from 1998 to 2001. In *Corsica Ferries France SA v Gruppo Antichi Ormeggiatori del Porto di Genova*[217] the Court was concerned with Italian legislation requiring ships from other Member States using the ports of Genoa and La Spezia in Italy to use the services of local mooring companies. It considered that mooring operations were of general economic interest: mooring groups are obliged to provide at any time and to any user a universal mooring service, for reasons of safety in port waters[218]. As a result it was not incompatible with Article 86(1) in conjunction with Article 82 to include in the

[209] [1997] ECR II-997, [1997] 5 CMLR 851, paras 134–141.
[210] Case C-320/91 [1993] ECR I-2533, [1995] 4 CMLR 621.   [211] See p 227 above.
[212] Case C-320/91 [1993] ECR I-2533, [1995] 4 CMLR 621, paras 13–21.   [213] Ibid, para 15.
[214] Ibid, paras 17–18.   [215] Ibid, para 19.   [216] Ibid, para 20.
[217] Case C-266/96 [1998] ECR I-3949, [1998] 5 CMLR 402.   [218] Ibid, para 45.

price of the service a component designed to cover the cost of maintaining the universal mooring service, and Article 86(2) was applicable[219].

In the *Albany* judgment[220] the ECJ held that the exclusive right of a pension fund to manage supplementary pensions in a particular sector could be justified under Article 86(2), since otherwise 'young employees in good health engaged in non-dangerous activities' would leave the scheme, leaving behind members who would be bad insurance risks, thereby undermining the success of the system[221]. In *Deutsche Post AG v Gesellschaft für Zahlungssysteme mbH and Citicorp Kartenservice GmbH*[222] the ECJ considered that Article 86(2) justified the grant by a Member State to its postal operators of a statutory right to charge internal postage on items of so-called 'remail'[223]. Environmental considerations led to the successful application of Article 86(2) in *Entreprenørforeningens Affalds/Miljøsektion v Københavns Kommune*[224]. In *Ambulanz Glöckner v Landkreis Südwestpfalz*[225] the ECJ considered that a national law which protected the providers of emergency ambulance services against competition from independent operators, even on a related non-emergency transport market, could be justified under Article 86(2) if this was necessary for them to perform their tasks in economically acceptable conditions[226].

Although Article 86(2) is drafted in terms of the position of undertakings, it has become clear that Member States themselves can rely on it. For example in *Dusseldorp*[227] the ECJ, following the Opinion of Advocate General Jacobs, confirmed that the Netherlands could rely on Article 86(2) in relation to its 'Long Term Plan' relating to waste disposal. The same point arose in *Commission v Netherlands*[228]. The ECJ has also held that Article 86(2) may be invoked by a Member State in defence of state aid that might otherwise contravene Article 87[229]. The implications of this judgment are considered in a Commission decision[230].

(iv) Adverse development of trade

It is not possible to rely on Article 86(2) if the development of trade would be affected to such an extent as would be contrary to the interest of the Community. This must mean something more than an effect on trade in the sense of Articles 81 and 82, since without such an effect the EC competition rules would not be applicable anyway. The ECJ has held in *Commission v Netherlands* that the Commission must prove whether the exclusive right has affected and continued to affect the development of intra-Community trade 'to an extent which is contrary to the interests of the Community'[231]. An application will be dismissed where it fails to do so[232]. If the matter were to arise

---

[219] Ibid, paras 46–47.
[220] Cases C-67/96 etc *Albany International BV v SBT* [1999] ECR I-5751, [2000] 4 CMLR 446.
[221] Ibid, paras 98–111.   [222] Cases C-147/97 etc [2000] ECR I-825, [2000] 4 CMLR 838.
[223] Ibid, paras 41–54.   [224] Case C-209/98 [2000] ECR I-3743, [2001] 2 CMLR 936, paras 74–83.
[225] Case C-475/99 [2001] ECR I-8089, [2002] 4 CMLR 726.   [226] Ibid, paras 51–65.
[227] Case C-203/96 [1998] ECR I-4075, [1998] 3 CMLR 873, para 67.
[228] Cases C-157/94 etc [1997] ECR I-5699, [1998] 2 CMLR 373, paras 51–64.
[229] See Case C-280/00 *Altmark Trans GmbH* [2003] ECR I-7747, [2003] 3 CMLR 339.
[230] Commission Decision of 28 November 2005 on the application of Article 86(2) of the EC Treaty to State aid OJ [2005] L 312/67; see also the Commission Staff Working Document *Frequently asked questions on the application of Article 86(2) of the EC Treaty to state aid*, available at www.ec.europa.eu/services_general_interest.
[231] [1997] ECR I-5699, [1998] 2 CMLR 373, paras 65–68.
[232] See Case C-159/94 *Commission v France* [1997] ECR I-5815, [1998] 2 CMLR 373, paras 109–116.

in domestic litigation, not involving the Commission, it would presumably fall upon the complainant, as opposed to the dominant undertaking, to demonstrate an adverse effect on the development of trade.

(v) Direct effect

In *Belgische Radio en Televisie (BRT) v SABAM*[233] the ECJ established that Articles 81 and 82 are directly applicable to the undertakings described in Article 86(2) so that an action may be brought against them in domestic proceedings, whether the Commission has acted under Article 86(3) or not. A national court should investigate whether the undertaking falls within Article 86(2); if it does not, the court may go ahead and apply the competition rules[234]. In this sense, Article 86(2) could be said to be 'negatively' directly effective. What was not clear was whether a national court should proceed if satisfied that an undertaking is within Article 86(2): could the court in those circumstances ask whether application of the competition rules would obstruct the undertaking in the performance of the tasks assigned to it? It was arguable that this matter was exclusively within the competence of the Commission, so that the court could not deal with it[235]; a preferable solution was that the national court could address this issue and, in clear cases, reach a conclusion on it: in other words, that Article 86(2) should be 'positively' as well as 'negatively' directly effective. In cases of doubt the national court could stay the action whilst the opinion of the Commission is sought. The latter view was apparently favoured by the ECJ in *Ahmed Saeed*[236] and was actually decided in *ERT v Dimotiki*[237]; it was affirmed by the Court in *Almelo*[238].

It remains uncertain whether the final sentence of Article 86(2), which requires that trade must not be affected contrary to the interests of the Community, has direct effect. It is arguable that only the Commission should be entitled to carry out the task of assessing the interests of the Community.

(C) Article 86(3)[239]

Article 86(3) provides that the Commission shall ensure the application of Articles 86(1) and (2) and that, where necessary, it shall address appropriate decisions or directives to Member States. This is a power which for many years lay dormant; however the Commission began to employ it in the 1980s, most notably in the context of the telecommunications sector[240], and it is now an important part of its armoury. The advantage of Article 86(3) from the Commission's perspective is that it can adopt a decision or directive itself; in doing so, it is not subject to any particular procedural framework, although it must of course comply with the general principles of EC law, and must provide adequate reasons for its action, in accordance with Article 253 EC[241].

---

[233] Case 127/73 [1974] ECR 313, [1974] 2 CMLR 238.

[234] Case 155/73 *Italy v Sacchi* [1974] ECR 409, [1974] 2 CMLR 177.

[235] See Case 10/71 *Public Prosecutor v Müller* [1971] ECR 723.   [236] Case 66/86 [1989] ECR 803.

[237] Case C-260/89 [1991] ECR I-2925, [1994] 4 CMLR 540, para 34.

[238] Case C-393/92 [1994] ECR I-1477, para 50.

[239] On Article 86(3) generally, see Buendia Sierra *Exclusive Rights and State Monopolies under EC Law*, paras 10.01–10.184 and Buendia Sierra in *Faull and Nikpay* (p 220, n 45 above) paras 6.217–6.257.

[240] See pp 241–242 below.

[241] The Commission's decision in *Dutch Express Delivery Services* was quashed for various procedural improprieties: see n 246 below.

The Commission liaises with other interested parties, including the Parliament, when exercising its powers under Article 86(3), and particularly when adopting a Directive[242]. If the Commission did not have its Article 86(3) powers, it would be able to proceed against measures that offend Article 86(1) only by taking proceedings before the ECJ under Article 226 or by persuading the Council of Ministers to adopt the measures it favours.

Article 86(3) enables the Commission to adopt both decisions and directives: a decision can be adopted, establishing that a Member State is in breach of a Community obligation; but a directive can go further and legislate for the elimination of existing violations of the Treaty and the prevention of future ones.

(i) Decisions

In *Greek Public Property Insurance*[243] the Commission required Greece, by decision under Article 86(3), to alter its domestic legislation requiring that all public property in Greece be insured by Greek public sector insurance companies and that staff of Greek state-owned banks recommend to their customers insurance with companies affiliated to the public banking sector and controlled by it. When Greece failed to take the necessary measures to do this within the prescribed period the Commission brought an action under Article 226 for failure to fulfil its Treaty obligations. The ECJ made the declaration[244], holding in the course of its judgment that a decision by the Commission under Article 86(3) is 'binding in its entirety' on the person to whom it is addressed so that the addressee must comply with it until it obtains from the ECJ a suspension of its operation or a declaration that it is void. In *Spanish Transport Fares*[245] the Commission addressed a decision to Spain condemning its discriminatory fares for passengers from mainland Spain to the Balearic and Canary Islands. The Commission also adopted decisions under Article 86(3) in:

- *Dutch Express Delivery Services*[246]
- *Spanish International Courier Services*[247]
- *Port of Rødby*[248]
- *Second Operator of GSM Radiotelephony Services in Italy*[249]
- *Second Operator of GSM Radiotelephony Services in Spain*[250]
- *Brussels National Airport (Zaventem)*[251]
- *Exclusive Right to Broadcast Television Advertising in Flanders*[252]
- *Italian Ports Legislation Relating to Employment*[253]
- *Tariffs for Piloting in the Port of Genoa*[254]

---

[242] See XXVth *Report on Competition Policy* (1995), point 100.   [243] OJ [1985] L 152/25.
[244] Case 226/87 *Commission v Greece* [1988] ECR 3611, [1989] 3 CMLR 569.   [245] OJ [1987] L 194/28.
[246] OJ [1990] L 10/47, quashed on appeal Cases C-48/90 and C-66/90 *Netherlands and Koninklijke PTT Nederland v Commission* [1992] ECR I-565, [1993] 5 CMLR 316 as the Commission had failed to give the Dutch Government a fair hearing.
[247] OJ [1990] L 233/19, [1991] 4 CMLR 560.   [248] OJ [1994] L 55/52.
[249] OJ [1995] L 280/49, [1996] 4 CMLR 700.   [250] OJ [1997] L 76/19.
[251] OJ [1995] L 216/8, [1996] 4 CMLR 232.
[252] OJ [1997] L 244/18, [1997] 5 CMLR 718, upheld on appeal Case T-266/97 *Vlaamse Televisie Maatschappij NV v Commission* [1999] ECR II-2329, [2000] 4 CMLR 1171.
[253] OJ [1997] L 301/17.   [254] OJ [1997] L 301/27.

- *Portuguese Airports*[255]
- *Spanish Airports*[256]
- *New Postal Services in Italy*[257]
- *La Poste*[258]
- *German postal legislation*[259]
- *French savings accounts*[260]
- *Greek lignite*[261]

(ii) Directives

The competence of the Commission to adopt directives under Article 86(3) has been considered by the ECJ on three occasions. The Transparency Directive[262] was challenged in *France v Commission*[263] on the basis that, since it concerned the surveillance of state aids, it should have been adopted under Article 89 rather than Article 86(3). The ECJ ruled that the fact that the Commission could have proceeded under Article 89 did not mean that it could not also do so under Article 86(3). Towards the end of the 1980s, the Commission's concern about the fragmented nature of the telecommunications market in the EC and the consequent lack of competition led to the adoption of two directives, the first on the telecommunications terminal equipment market[264] and the second on telecommunications themselves[265]. Opposition from Member States to these Directives was considerable and both were challenged before the ECJ. In each case the ECJ upheld the competence of the Commission to have proceeded under Article 86(3)[266]. In *France v Commission*[267] three Member States complained that the Commission should have proceeded under Article 226 rather than Article 86(3). The ECJ held that there had been no misuse of powers: the Commission may use the powers conferred upon it by Article 86(3) to specify in general terms the obligations that arise under Article 86(1); however the Commission may not use a directive under Article 86(3) to rule upon specific infringements of the Treaty, for which the Article 226 procedure must be used[268]. The ECJ also held that the fact that the Council had competence to adopt legislation relating to telecommunications did not mean that the Commission

---

[255] OJ [1999] L 69/31, [1999] 5 CMLR 103, upheld on appeal Case C-163/99 *Portugal v Commission* [2001] ECR I-2613, [2002] 4 CMLR 1319.

[256] OJ [2000] L 208/36, [2000] 5 CMLR 967.   [257] OJ [2001] L 63/59.   [258] OJ [2002] L 120/19.

[259] Commission decision of 20 October 2004, available at www.ec.europa.eu/comm/competition/liberalisation/cases.html, on appeal Cases T-490/04 etc *Germany v Commission*, not yet decided.

[260] Commission decision of 10May 2007, on appeal Case T-289/07 *Caisse Nationale des Caisses d'Épargne et de Prévoyance*, not yet decided.

[261] Commission Press release IP/08/386, 5 March 2008; Summary of decision OJ [2008] C 93/3.

[262] Commission Directive (EEC) 80/723 OJ [1980] L 195/35, amended most recently by OJ [2000] L 193/75.

[263] Cases 188/80 etc [1982] ECR 2545, [1982] 3 CMLR 144; for a later challenge related to this Directive, see Case C-325/91 *France v Commission* [1993] ECR I-3283.

[264] Commission Directive (EEC) 88/301 OJ [1988] L 131/73, [1991] 4 CMLR 922.

[265] Commission Directive (EEC) 90/388 OJ [1990] L 192/10, [1991] 4 CMLR 932.

[266] See Case C-202/88 *France v Commission* [1991] ECR I-1223, [1992] 5 CMLR 552 (terminal equipment); Cases C-271/90 etc *Spain, Belgium and Italy v Commission* (telecommunications) [1992] ECR I-5833, [1993] 4 CMLR 100.

[267] See n 263 above.   [268] [1991] ECR I-1223, [1992] 5 CMLR 552, paras 16–18.

had no competence[269]. The ECJ annulled Articles 2, 7 and 9 of the Directive on terminal equipment since the Commission had failed to explain which rights were 'special' and why they were contrary to Community law[270]. It is not possible to use Article 86(3) for the purpose of achieving harmonisation, the legislative base for which is provided by Articles 94 and 95 EC: this explains why in the telecommunications sector there are Article 86(3) Directives, dealing with the conditions of competition, and a raft of separate measures under Article 94 and 95 on harmonisation[271].

(iii) Judicial review of the Commission's powers under Article 86(3)

The Commission enjoys a wide discretion in the field covered by Article 86(1) and (3)[272]. Third parties cannot, except in an exceptional situation, bring an action against a Commission decision not to use its powers under Article 86(3)[273].

4. ARTICLE 31 – STATE MONOPOLIES OF A COMMERCIAL CHARACTER[274]

Article 31(1) of the Treaty provides that:

Member States shall adjust any State monopolies of a commercial character so as to ensure that no discrimination regarding the conditions under which goods are procured and marketed exists between nationals of Member States[275].

Article 31(1) goes on to state that it applies to any body through which a Member State supervises, determines or appreciably influences imports or exports between Member States, and also that it applies to monopolies delegated by the State to others. Article 31(2) obliges Member States not to introduce any new measure contrary to the principles in Article 31(1) or which restricts the scope of the Treaty Articles dealing with the prohibition of customs duties and quantitative restrictions between Member States. However Article 31 does not require the abolition of existing monopolies; only that they should be adjusted to prevent discrimination.

---

[269] Ibid, paras 19–27; see similarly Cases 188/80 etc *France v Commission* [1982] ECR 2545, [1982] 3 CMLR 144, para 14.

[270] Case C-202/88 (n 266 above), paras 45–47 and 53–58. [271] See ch 23, pp 973–974.

[272] Case C-107/95 P *Bundesverband der Bilanzbuchhalter v Commission* [1997] ECR I-947, [1997] 5 CMLR 432 , para 27; see also Case T-266/97 *Vlaamse Televisie Maatschappij NV v Commission* [1999] ECR II-2329, [2000] 4 CMLR 1171, para 75 and Case T-52/00 *Coe Clerici Logistics SpA v Commission* [2003] ECR II-2123, [2003] 5 CMLR 539, paras 86–89.

[273] Case C-107/95 P *Bundesverband der Bilanzbuchhalter v Commission* [1997] ECR I-947, [1997] 5 CMLR 432, para 28; see also Case C-141/02 P *Commission v T-Mobile Austria GmbH, formerly max. mobil Telecommunications service GmbH* [2005] ECR I-1283, [2005] 4 CMLR 735, paras 69–73 where the ECJ annulled a judgment of the CFI which had suggested greater rights for third parties to challenge the Commission's decision not to act; for comment see Hocepied 'The *Max.mobil* Judgment: the Court of Justice clarifies the role of complainants in Article 86 procedures' *Competition Policy Newsletter*, Summer 2005, 53: 'the judgment...clarifies a question which had been debated nearly 15 years'.

[274] See generally Buendia Sierra *Exclusive Rights and State Monopolies under EC Law* (OUP, 1999) paras 3.01–3.201; also Buendia Sierra in *Faull and Nikpay*, paras 6.106–6.121.

[275] Note that Article 31 of the Treaty is not identical to the original Article 37, which contained transitional rules that had become redundant.

Article 31 is designed to prevent state monopolies of a commercial character discriminating against nationals of other Member States. This provision appears in the chapter of the Treaty on the free movement of goods rather than on the competition rules: it might have been more natural for it to appear alongside Article 86, which was contemplated at one stage during the writing of the Treaty. At some stage, however, these siblings became separated, and subsequent amendments to the Treaty have not reunited them. One way of ensuring that Member States do not discriminate in this way is to alter their public procurement policies, in which area the Council has been active[276]. The Commission continues to monitor the conduct of Member States under Article 31; details of its application of Article 31 will be found in its annual reports on competition policy[277]. In *Commission v Greece*[278] the ECJ held that Greece was obliged to terminate exclusive rights to import and sell petroleum derivatives since those rights discriminated against exporters of such products in other Member States and since they upset the normal conditions of competition between Member States. Where the Commission suspects infringement of Article 31 it may take proceedings against the Member State under Article 226 of the Treaty or it could make use of the powers available to it under Article 86(3)[279]. Where the Commission brings Article 226 proceedings it must prove that a Member State has failed to fulfil its obligations and it must place before the ECJ the information needed to enable it to decide whether this is the case[280]. An injured undertaking could bring an action in a national court, as Article 31 is directly effective[281].

In *Commission v Netherlands* the ECJ found that import and export monopolies for gas and electricity in the Netherlands, Italy, and France amounted to an infringement of Article 31(1)[282]. However the Court considered that Article 86(2) could be invoked by Member States in proceedings brought under Article 31 to justify such monopolies. Justification was possible, provided that the maintenance of monopoly rights was necessary to enable the undertaking in question to perform the tasks of general economic interest entrusted to it under economically acceptable conditions; it was not necessary to demonstrate that the survival of the undertaking itself would be threatened in the absence of such a monopoly. On the facts the Commission failed to satisfy the ECJ that the monopolies could not be justified under Article 86(2). In *Krister Hanner*[283] the ECJ considered, in an Article 234 reference from a Swedish court, that Article 31(1) precluded a sales regime that conferred a legal monopoly at the retail level of trade in medicinal preparations on Apoteket, an entity in which the Swedish state had a majority shareholding and the management of which was predominantly in the hands of politicians and civil servants. The Court's concern was that Apoteket's procurement arrangements were liable to discriminate against medicinal preparations from outside Sweden[284]. In October 2007 the Commission announced that it would bring proceedings under Article 31 against Malta unless it adjusted a monopoly for the importation,

---

[276] See ch 2, p 49, n 7.

[277] See eg the Commission's XXVIth *Report on Competition Policy* (1996), points 132–135; XXVIIth *Report on Competition Policy* (1997), points 137–144; XXXIInd *Report on Competition Policy* (2002), point 636.

[278] Case C-347/88 [1990] ECR I-4747.   [279] See pp 239–242 above.

[280] See eg Cases C-157/94 etc *Commission v Netherlands* [1997] ECR I-5699, [1998] 2 CMLR 373, para 59.

[281] Case 91/78 *Hansen v Hauptzollamt Flensberg* [1979] ECR 935.

[282] See Cases C-157/94 etc *Commission v Netherlands* [1997] ECR I-5699, [1998] 2 CMLR 373: the nature of the monopolies varied from state to state.

[283] Case C-438/02 [2005] ECR I-4551, [2005] 2 CMLR 1010.   [284] Ibid, paras 32–49.

storage and wholesale of petroleum products[285]; the case was closed after Malta took steps to open the market to third parties[286].

5. ARTICLES 87 TO 89 – STATE AIDS[287]

The Treaty provides the Commission with power under Articles 87 to 89 of the Treaty to deal with state aids that could distort competition in the common market. A considerable amount of DG COMP's energies go into this issue, but lack of space prevents a detailed discussion of the topic here.

Article 87(1) provides that:

Save as otherwise provided in this Treaty, any aid granted by a Member State or through State resources in any form whatsoever which distorts or threatens to distort competition by favouring certain undertakings or the production of certain goods shall, in so far as it affects trade between Member States, be incompatible with the common market.

Article 87(2) provides that aids having a social character granted to individual consumers, aids to make good the damage caused by national disasters or exceptional occurrences and aids granted to the economy of certain areas of Germany affected by the division of that country after the Second World War shall be compatible with the common market. Article 87(3) gives the Commission discretion to permit other aids, for example to promote the economic development of areas where the standard of living is abnormally low or where there is serious unemployment, or to promote the execution of an important project of common European interest or to remedy a serious disturbance in the economy of a Member State.

Article 88 deals with procedure. The Commission may, by Article 88(2)(i), adopt a decision that a state aid which is incompatible with the common market shall be abolished or altered. If the Member State does not comply with this decision within the stated time, the Commission or another Member State may take the matter to the ECJ under Article 87(3)(ii) without having to resort to the procedure under Articles 226 and 227 of the Treaty[288]. Repayment of state aids will usually be demanded. Article 88(3) requires plans to grant or alter aids to be notified to the Commission in sufficient time to enable it to submit its comments. The aid may not be implemented until the Commission has reached a decision. Article 88(3) is directly effective[289] and an individual may seek relief

---

[285] Commission Press Release IP/07/1544, 18 October 2007.

[286] Commission Press release IP/07/1952, 18 December 2007.

[287] For further reading on state aids see Quigley and Collins *EC State Aid Law and Policy* (Hart Publishing, 2003); Hancher, Ottervanger and Slot *EC State Aids* (Sweet & Maxwell, 3rd ed, 2006); Wyatt and Dashwood *European Union Law* (Sweet & Maxwell, 5th ed, 2006), ch 24; Faull and Nikpay *The EC Law of Competition* (Oxford University Press, 2nd ed, 2007), ch 16; Bellamy and Child *European Community Law of Competition* (Sweet & Maxwell, 6th ed, 2008, ed Roth), ch 15; the Commission's *Annual Report on Competition Policy* contains a detailed account of its activities under the state aids provisions; see eg the XXXVth *Report on Competition Policy* (2005), pp 119–186 and XXXVIth *Report on Competition Policy* (2006), pp 30–43.

[288] It cannot proceed under Article 88(2)(ii) in respect of a later state aid which was not within the scope of an earlier decision: Case C-294/90 *British Aerospace plc v Commission* [1992] ECR I-493, [1992] 1 CMLR 853.

[289] Case 120/73 *Lorenz v Germany* [1973] ECR 1471.

in a domestic court where aid is granted without notification under Article 88(3) or put into effect before the Commission's decision[290].

It can be difficult to tell, in the absence of relevant information, whether competition is being distorted where a Member State controls part of the economy directly or grants financial aids to certain firms. To overcome this problem the Commission issued a Directive in 1980 to increase the transparency of the relationship between Member States and public undertakings[291], which was unsuccessfully challenged in *France v Commission*[292]; the Directive has been amended a number of times, most recently in November 2006[293]. The Commission uses the data that it receives through this Directive to monitor the compatibility of state aids with Article 87.

Council Regulation 994/98[294] confers powers on the Commission to adopt 'group exemptions' for certain categories of state aid, and to adopt a regulation on *de minimis* aids. Several regulations have been adopted under Regulation 994/98: they can be accessed on the website of DG COMP[295]. That website provides a considerable amount of other information about state aid policy, including details of current developments, a register of cases, reports on state aid matters and discussion of possible reforms.

The procedural powers of the Commission in relation to state aids are set out in Regulation 659/1999[296].

[290] See eg *R v A-G, ex p ICI* [1987] 1 CMLR 72, CA.   [291] OJ [1980] L 195/35.
[292] See p 222, n 56 above.   [293] Commission Directive 2006/111/EC OJ [2006] L 318/17.
[294] OJ [1998] L 142/1.   [295] www.ec.europa.eu/comm/competition/index_en.html.
[296] OJ [1999] L 83/1, as amended by Regulation 794/2004, OJ [2004] L 140/1.

7

Articles 81 and 82: public enforcement by the European Commission and national competition authorities under the Modernisation Regulation

CHAPTER CONTENTS

Infringement of Articles 81 and 82 has serious consequences for guilty undertakings. Such is the importance of competition law that undertakings are well-advised to put in place effective compliance programmes to ensure that the competition rules are not infringed and that employees understand what types of behaviour must be avoided. The powers of the Commission to enforce Articles 81 and 82 were originally contained in Regulation 17[1]. Major changes in the enforcement of Articles 81 and 82 were effected by Regulation 1/2003[2] ('the Modernisation Regulation'), which entered into force on 1 May 2004. This chapter will explain the main features of the public enforcement system: there are several practitioners' books that provide a more detailed analysis of the position[3]. The chapter will begin with a brief overview of the Modernisation Regulation. Section 2 provides a detailed examination of the Commission's enforcement powers; it also notes the possibility that the Commission might, in the fairly near future, introduce a system of settling some cartel cases whereby, in return for a reduced penalty, undertakings would admit to their unlawful behaviour and agree to cooperate with the Commission in bringing a case to a speedy conclusion. Section 3 discusses the operation of the European Competition Network ('the ECN') that brings together the Commission

---

[1] JO 204/62, OJ (Special Edition 1959–62), p 57. [2] OJ [2003] L 1/1, [2003] 4 CMLR 551.

[3] See in particular Kerse and Khan *EC Antitrust Procedure* (Sweet & Maxwell, 5th ed, 2005); Ortiz Blanco *European Community Competition Procedure* (Oxford University Press, 2nd ed, 2006); Faull and Nikpay *The EC Law of Competition* (Oxford University Press, 2nd ed, 2007), ch 2; Bellamy and Child *European Community Law of Competition* (eds Roth and Rose, Oxford University Press, 6th ed, 2008), ch 13; for a series of seminal essays on all aspects of public enforcement see Wils *The Optimal Enforcement of EC Antitrust Law* (Kluwer Law International, 2002), Wils 'Principles of European Antitrust Enforcement' (2005, Hart Publishing); Wils *Efficiency and Justice in European Antitrust Enforcement* (Hart Publishing, 2008).

and the national competition authorities of the Member States ('the NCAs'). The final section of the chapter will provide a brief account of judicial review of the Commission's decisions. Articles 81 and 82 are directly applicable and may be invoked in proceedings in the domestic courts of the Member States: the private enforcement of the competition rules will be considered in chapter 8.

In understanding the extent of – or rather the limits to – the Commission's powers, it is important to have reference to the general principles of Community law some of which, such as respect for the rights of the defence and the principles of proportionality, equal treatment, the protection of legitimate interests, legal certainty and non-retro-activity, have obvious significance for the enforcement of the competition rules[4]. Two further important issues are the relationship between the Commission's procedures and the standards required by the European Convention on Human Rights[5] and by the Charter of Fundamental Rights of the European Union[6]; recital 37 of the Modernisation Regulation states that it should be interpreted in accordance with the rights and principles recognised in the Charter. However whilst it is important to ensure that the rights of the defence are properly respected, it is also important to avoid them being so elevated that it becomes disproportionately difficult for the Commission to enforce the law: a balance has to be struck between the private interest of undertakings not to be found guilty of behaviour of which they are innocent and the public interest of punishing serious infringements of the law. A related point is that the law of 'human' rights was developed with the laudable goal of protecting natural persons from arbitrary and oppressive behaviour, including physical maltreatment. It would not be surprising if the Community Courts were to develop different standards of human rights for natural persons on the one hand and for well-resourced multinational corporations on the other with access to sophisticated legal advice in the context of administrative proceedings based on Articles 81 and 82 EC[7].

1. OVERVIEW OF THE MODERNISATION REGULATION

The Modernisation Regulation abolished the notification of agreements to the Commission for individual exemption and the Commission's exclusive power to make decisions on the application of Article 81(3) in individual cases: that provision is now directly applicable in the same way that Articles 81(1), 81(2) and 82 have always been[8]. One

---

[4] On general principles of EC law see the books cited in n 3 above and Usher *General Principles of EC Law* (Addison Wesley Longman, 1998); Tridimas *The General Principles of EU Law* (Oxford University Press, 2006); Wyatt and Dashwood's *European Union Law* (Sweet & Maxwell, 5th ed, 2006), ch 6; Hartley *The Foundations of European Community Law* (Oxford University Press, 6th ed, 2007), ch 5.

[5] Available at www.echr.coe/Eng/BasicTexts.htm.

[6] OJ [2000] C 364/1, available at www.ue.eu.int/df/default.asp?lang=en.

[7] See eg the Opinion of Advocate General Geelhoed in Case C-301/04 P *Commission v SGL* [2006] ECR I-5915, [2006] 5 CMLR 877, paras 62–69 and the judgment of the ECJ in Case C-411/04 P *Salzgitter v Commission* [2007] ECR I-965, [2007] 4 CMLR 682, paras 40–50; note also the judgment of the European Court of Human Rights in *Neste St Petersburg v Russia*, 3 June 2004, concluding that proceedings under Russian competition law were not criminal proceedings for the purpose of Article 6 of the European Convention on Human Rights.

[8] See ch 4, pp 162–164.

of the reasons for this fundamental change in the procedural regime was to enable the Commission to use its resources for investigating serious infringements of the competition rules, such as price-fixing and market-sharing cartels, rather than having to devote a large amount of time to examining agreements and practices notified to it which, for the most part, did not raise serious competition problems[9]. However the Modernisation Regulation did not deal only with these matters: the opportunity was taken to refresh the enforcement powers of the Commission generally, and the Regulation adopted a number of new provisions including, for example, the possibility of the Commission adopting decisions on the basis of legally-binding commitments as to undertakings' future behaviour (Article 9) and the power to conduct inspections at people's homes (Article 21).

(A) The content of the Modernisation Regulation

The Modernisation Regulation consists of 11 chapters:

- Chapter I is entitled 'Principles': Article 1 provides for the direct applicability of Articles 81 and 82, Article 2 explains who bears the burden of proof in cases under Articles 81 and 82 and Article 3 deals with the relationship between those provisions and national competition law[10]
- Chapter II of the Regulation sets out the powers of the Commission, the NCAs and national courts
- Chapter III provides for various types of Commission decision: findings of infringement, interim measures, the acceptance of commitments and declarations of inapplicability
- Chapter IV is concerned with cooperation between the Commission, NCAs and national courts
- Chapter V deals with the Commission's powers of investigation
- Chapter VI deals with penalties
- Chapter VII is concerned with limitation periods for the imposition and enforcement of penalties
- Chapter VIII deals with hearings and professional secrecy
- Chapter IX provides for the withdrawal of the benefit of block exemption regulations in certain circumstances
- Chapter X contains general provisions
- Chapter XI contains transitional, amending and final provisions.

(B) Supporting measures

The Commission has adopted a number of supporting measures necessary for the successful application of the Modernisation Regulation. These measures consist of one Commission Regulation and a number of Notices, as follows:

- Commission Regulation 773/2004 relating to the conduct of proceedings under Articles 81 and 82[11]

---

[9] For a discussion of the background to the adoption of the Modernisation Regulation, including the Commission's *White Paper on Modernisation*, see the fifth edition of this book, ch 7, pp 245–251 and the extensive list of literature cited there.

[10] The relationship between EC and domestic competition law is discussed in ch 2, pp 74–77.

[11] OJ [2004] L 123/18.

- *Notice on cooperation within the network of competition authorities[12]*
- *Notice on the cooperation between the Commission and courts of the EU Member States in the application of Articles 81 and 82 EC[13]*
- *Notice on the handling of complaints by the Commission under Articles 81 and 82 of the EC Treaty[14]*
- *Notice on informal guidance relating to novel questions concerning Articles 81 and 82 of the EC Treaty that arise in individual cases (Guidance letters)[15]*
- *Notice on the effect on trade concept contained in Articles 81 and 82 of the Treaty[16]*
- *Guidelines on the application of Article 81(3) of the Treaty[17]*
- *Settlements Notice (it is anticipated that this will be adopted by the end of 2008)[17a]*

2. THE COMMISSION'S ENFORCEMENT POWERS UNDER THE MODERNISATION REGULATION

(A) Burden of proof

Article 2 of the Regulation provides that the burden of proving an infringement of Article 81(1) or Article 82 is on the person or competition authority alleging the infringement and that the burden of showing that Article 81(3) is satisfied is on the person making that claim. There may be circumstances where the party bearing the burden of proof produces evidence that requires the other party to provide an explanation or justification, failing which it is permissible to conclude that the burden of proof has been satisfied[18]. The *Guidelines on the application of Article 81(3) of the Treaty[19]* explain the kind of evidence that undertakings should provide when defending an agreement under Article 81(3).

The Regulation does not discuss the burden of proof where an undertaking raises objective justification as a defence under Article 82. The position is that the evidential burden in such a situation rests with the undertaking asserting the justification, and that it is then incumbent on the Commission to show why that justification is inapplicable[20]. Similarly it would seem that an undertaking that asserts that a contractual restriction is ancillary bears the evidential burden of showing that this is so, and that the Commission should then have to show why this is not so[21].

(B) Chapter II: powers

Articles 4 to 6 deal with the powers of the Commission, the NCAs and national courts respectively.

---

[12] OJ [2004] C 101/43. [13] OJ [2004] C 101/54. [14] OJ [2004] C 101/65.
[15] OJ [2004] C 101/78. [16] OJ [2004] C 101/81. [17] OJ [2004] C 101/97. [17a] See pp 258–261 below.
[18] Case C-204/00 P *Aalborg Portland A/S* [2004] ECR I-123, para 79. [19] OJ [2004] C 101/97.
[20] See eg Case T-201/04 *Microsoft Corpn v Commission* [2007] ECR II-000, para 688.
[21] On this point see a case under the UK Competition Act 1998, Case Nos 1035/1/1/04 and 1041/2/1/04 *The Racecourse Association and Others v OFT* [2005] CAT 29, [2006] CompAR 99, paras 130–134.

(i) Article 4: powers of the Commission

Article 4 states that the Commission shall have the powers provided for by the Modernisation Regulation: of particular importance are the decision-making powers in Chapter III; the powers of investigation contained in Chapter V; and the powers to impose penalties provided by Chapter VI; these are described below.

(ii) Article 5: powers of the NCAs

Recital 6 of the Regulation states that, to ensure the effective application of the competition rules, NCAs should be associated more closely with their application. Article 5 therefore provides that NCAs shall have the power to apply Articles 81 and 82 in individual cases. For this purpose the NCAs may make decisions requiring the termination of an infringement, ordering interim measures, accepting commitments and imposing fines and periodic penalty payments; they may also decide that there are no grounds for action on their part. Article 35 of the Regulation requires Member States to designate the competition authority or authorities responsible for the application of Articles 81 and 82 in such a way that its provisions are effectively complied with; the designated authorities can include courts. The Commission works with the NCAs through the medium of the ECN, the work of which is discussed in section 3 below.

(iii) Article 6: powers of the national courts

Article 6 provides specifically that national courts shall have the power to apply Article 81, in its entirety, and Article 82: the role of national courts is discussed in chapter 8.

(C) Chapter III: Commission decisions

Articles 7 to 10 deal with Commission decisions. The Commission has also issued a *Notice on informal guidance relating to novel questions concerning Articles 81 and 82 of the EC Treaty that arise in individual cases (Guidance letters)*[22] explaining the (rare) circumstances in which it might be prepared to give undertakings informal guidance on the application of the competition rules. It is possible that the Commission will introduce a system of settlements for cartel cases. Informal guidance and settlements will be discussed after the powers conferred by Articles 7 to 10 have been described.

(i) Article 7: finding and termination of an infringement

Article 7(1) provides that where the Commission, acting on a complaint or on its own initiative, finds an infringement of Article 81 or 82, it may by decision require an end to it. Article 7(1) continues by stating that the Commission may impose on undertakings behavioural or structural remedies which are proportionate to the infringement and necessary to bring the infringement effectively to an end.

(A) Behavioural remedies A behavioural remedy may be negative, for example to stop a certain kind of conduct, or positive, to order an undertaking to do something. In a typical cartel case the Commission will require the participants in the cartel to stop the

---

[22] OJ [2004] C 101/78.

illegal behaviour, insofar as they have not already done so, and to refrain from any act or conduct having the same or a similar object or effect in the future[23].

The ability of the Commission to make a positive order under Regulation 17 was confirmed by the ECJ in *Commercial Solvents Co v Commission*[24]; there is no reason to suppose that its powers would be any different under the Modernisation Regulation. In *Commercial Solvents* that firm was found guilty of an unlawful refusal to supply contrary to Article 82 and was ordered to resume supplies to a former customer. In *Microsoft*[25] the Commission ordered Microsoft to disclose to competitors the interfaces required for their products to be able to interoperate with Microsoft's Windows operating software, and to offer a version of its operating software without a Windows media player to PC manufacturers or when selling directly to end users. The Commission appointed a monitoring trustee to oversee Microsoft's compliance with these requirements. On appeal the CFI upheld the Commission's decision as to substance, but held that the Commission did not have the right to appoint an independent monitoring trustee to enforce the remedy: this went 'far beyond' retaining an expert to advise it on implementation of the remedies[26]. However the Commission was entitled to monitor Microsoft's compliance with the remedies required and to use an external expert in order to resolve technical issues[27].

Whereas an undertaking can be ordered to supply a distributor or customer where it has infringed Article 82, this cannot be done following an infringement of Article 81. In *Automec v Commission (No 2)*[28] Automec complained to the Commission that it had been wrongly excluded from BMW's distribution system and asked it to order BMW to make supplies of BMW cars available. The Commission told Automec that it had no power to make such an order, and this was upheld on appeal by the CFI. Articles 81 and 82 have a different logic: Article 81 prohibits agreements, and the Commission may make an order to terminate them; Article 82 prohibits abuse, and again the Commission can make an order to terminate an abuse. However a refusal to supply under Article 81 cannot in itself be unlawful. The Commission could order an undertaking to terminate an agreement not to supply, but it does not follow that it can also make an order to supply. Any further civil law consequences of an infringement of Article 81 should be determined in the domestic courts of Member States[29].

In *Atlantic Container Line AB v Commission*[30] the CFI upheld the Commission's decision prohibiting a horizontal agreement to fix prices in the maritime transport sector[31]; however it annulled Article 5 of the decision, which had required the parties to the agreement to inform their customers that they were now able to renegotiate their service agreements with the members of the cartel, since this went beyond what was necessary to bring the infringement in question to an end[32].

---

[23] See eg Article 3 of the Commission's decision in *Gas Insulated Switchgear* of 24 January 2007, available at www.ec.europa.eu/comm/competition/antitrust/cases.

[24] Cases 6/73 and 7/73 [1974] ECR 223, [1974] 1 CMLR 309.

[25] Commission decision of 24 March 2004 available at www.ec.europa.eu/comm/competition/antitrust/cases, upheld on appeal Case T-201/04 *Microsoft Corpn v Commission* [2007] ECR II-000, judgment of 17 September 2007.

[26] Ibid, paras 1251–1279.   [27] Ibid, para 1265.   [28] Case T-24/90 [1992] ECR II-2223, [1992] 5 CMLR 431.

[29] Ibid, para 50; see also Cases C-377/05 and C-376/05 *A. Brunsteiner Gmbh v Bayerische Motorenwerke AG* [2006] ECR I-11383, [2007] 4 CMLR 259, paras 48–51.

[30] Case T-395/94 [2002] ECR II-875, [2002] 4 CMLR 1008.   [31] *TAA* OJ [1994] L 376/1.

[32] [2002] ECR II-875, [2002] 4 CMLR 1008, paras 410–420.

(B) Structural remedies Regulation 17 did not specifically provide for a structural remedy, and the explicit inclusion of this possibility in the Modernisation Regulation was controversial. Article 7(1) states that structural remedies can be imposed only where there is no equally effective behavioural remedy or where a behavioural remedy would be more burdensome for the undertaking concerned than the structural remedy. Recital 12 adds that changes to the structure of an undertaking as it existed before the infringement was committed would be proportionate only where there is a substantial risk of a lasting or repeated infringement that derives from the very structure of the undertaking. A possible example of this could arise where a vertically-integrated undertaking consistently denies access to an essential facility or discriminates against downstream competitors in relation to a vital input; another example could be where an undertaking repeatedly indulges in margin-squeezing[33]. The Commission might be tempted to adopt a structural remedy if it were to find that undertakings in the energy sector, as to which it has significant concerns about anti-competitive behaviour, repeatedly refuse access on reasonable and non-discriminatory terms to vital infrastructure such as a gas transmission network[34].

(C) Past infringements Article 7(1) of the Regulation ends by providing that the Commission, where it has a legitimate interest in doing so, may adopt a decision that an infringement has been committed in the past[35]. There might be an interest in doing so, for example, in order to clarify an important point of principle or as a way of facilitating a follow-on action for damages[36]. However the Commission must explain why there is a Community interest in the adoption of a decision relating to past behaviour, and a failure to do so could lead to the decision being annulled on appeal[37]. The Commission cannot state in the narrative of its decision that an undertaking has committed an infringement of the competition rules unless it also reaches a conclusion to that effect in the operative part of its decision: the undertaking has a right to appeal only in relation to the operative part of the decision and should not be exposed to the risk, for example, of a damages claim in relation to assertions of fact which it has no ability to challenge[38].

(D) Complainants Article 7(2) of the Regulation provides that those entitled to lodge a complaint for the purpose of Article 7(1) are natural or legal persons who can show a legitimate interest and Member States. The position of complainants is considered below[39].

---

[33] See ch 17 pp 690–699 and ch 18, pp 744–748 on these practices.

[34] See p 265 on the Commission's sectoral review of the energy sector and ch 23, pp 981–984.

[35] This was possible under Regulation 17 see Case 7/82 *GVL v Commission* [1983] ECR 483, [1983] 3 CMLR 645; *Bloemenveilingen Aalsmeer* OJ [1988] L 262/27, [1989] 4 CMLR 500, paras 164–168; *Distribution of Package Tours During the 1990 World Cup* OJ [1992] L 326/31; *Zera/Montedison* OJ [1993] L 272/28, [1995] 5 CMLR 320, para 132; *Europe Asia Trades Agreement* OJ [1999] L 193/23, [1999] 5 CMLR 1380, paras 182–185.

[36] See ch 8, pp 298–299.

[37] See Joined Cases T-22/02 and 23/02 *Sumitomo Chemical Co Ltd v Commission* [2005] ECR II-4065, [2006] 4 CMLR 42, paras 129–140.

[38] Case T-474/04 *Pergan Hilfsstoffe für Industrielle Prozesse GmbH v Commission*, judgment of 12 October 2007, [2007] ECR II-000.

[39] See pp 280–281 below.

(ii) Article 8: interim measures

Article 8(1) of the Regulation provides that, in cases of urgency due to the risk of serious and irreparable damage to competition, the Commission, acting on its own initiative[40], may, on the basis of a *prima facie* finding of infringement, order interim measures. Article 8(2) states that an order shall be for a specified period of time, and may be renewed in so far as this is necessary and appropriate. Regulation 17 was silent on the issue of interim measures, but the ECJ established in *Camera Care v Commission*[41] that the Commission did have power under Article 3 of that Regulation to grant interim relief. Recital 11 of the Modernisation Regulation says that explicit provision should now be made for interim measures. In practice the Commission did not often adopt interim measures under the *Camera Care* judgment: it preferred third parties to seek interim relief in their domestic courts[42] or from NCAs[43]. The decisions that the Commission did adopt – for example *Ford Werke AG-Interim Measure*[44], *ECS/AKZO*[45], *BBI/Boosey and Hawkes: Interim Measures*[46], *Ecosystem SA v Peugeot SA*[47], *Langnese-Iglo/Mars*[48], *Sealink/B & I – Holyhead: Interim Measures*[49], *Sea Containers v Stena Sealink – Interim Measures*[50], *Irish Continental Group v CCI Morlaix*[51], *NDC Health/ IMS Health: Interim Measures*[52] – will be of relevance to the way in which it exercises its powers under Article 8 of the Modernisation Regulation. On a few occasions the Commission has negotiated an interim settlement with undertakings without formally adopting an interim decision. This happened for example in *Hilti*[53]; the terms of the undertaking were subsequently broken and the Commission took this into account in its final decision.

(iii) Article 9: commitments

Article 9 provides for the adoption of decisions by the Commission whereby undertakings under investigation make legally-binding commitments as to their future behaviour; the Commission then closes its file without making a finding as to whether there has been or continues to be an infringement of Article 81 and/or 82. The Article 9

---

[40] Note that interim measures are adopted, if at all, at the initiative of the Commission and not pursuant to any 'right' of complainants to ask the Commission to act: see Nordsjo 'Regulation 1/2003: Power of the Commission to Adopt Interim Measures' (2006) 27 ECLR 299.

[41] Case 792/79 R [1980] ECR 119, [1980] 1 CMLR 334.

[42] On applications for interim measures in the UK courts see ch 8, pp 305–306.

[43] On the powers of the OFT in the UK to adopt interim measures see ch 10, p 398.

[44] OJ [1982] L 256/20, [1982] 3 CMLR 263; this decision was annulled on appeal to the ECJ Cases 228/82 and 229/82 *Ford Werke AG v Commission* [1984] ECR 1129, [1984] 1 CMLR 649.

[45] OJ [1983] L 252/13, [1983] 3 CMLR 694.   [46] OJ [1987] L 286/36, [1988] 4 CMLR 67.

[47] [1990] 4 CMLR 449, upheld on appeal Case T-23/90 *Peugeot v EC Commission* [1991] ECR II-653, [1993] 5 CMLR 540.

[48] Unreported decision of 25 March 1992; see XXIInd *Report on Competition Policy* (1992), point 195; this decision was suspended in part in Cases T-24/92 and 28/92 R *Langnese-Iglo GmbH v Commission* [1992] ECR II-1839.

[49] [1992] 5 CMLR 255.   [50] OJ [1994] L 15/8, [1995] 4 CMLR 84.   [51] [1995] 5 CMLR 177.

[52] OJ [2002] L 59/18: for discussion of this case, including the suspension of the Commission's interim measures decision, see ch 19, p 789.

[53] The undertakings given by Hilti were attached as an Annex to the Commission's final decision: *Eurofix-Bauco v Hilti* OJ [1988] L 65/19, [1989] 4 CMLR 677; other examples of interim undertakings include *Ford Motor Co* XVth *Report on Competition Policy* (1985), point 49; *British Sugar/Napier Brown* XVIth *Report on Competition Policy* (1986), point 74; *Irish Distillers Group v G C & C Brands Ltd* [1988] 4 CMLR 840.

procedure is influenced by the practice in the US of settling cases on the basis of 'consent decrees'[54]. Article 9 was an innovatory provision in the Modernisation Regulation: there were no provisions in Regulation 17 whereby a case could be settled on the basis of legally-binding commitments. Despite this there were several cases in which the Commission did close its file on the basis of commitments, some of which were clearly of great significance: among the best known were *IBM*[55], *Microsoft (licensing agreements)*[56], *Interbrew*[57], *IRI/Nielsen*[58], and *Digital*[59]. Article 9 of the Regulation for the first time provides a legal basis for commitments; it has generated quite a lot of literature in a short period of time[60]. By the 12 March 2008 commitments have been accepted in eight cases, as shown in the *Table of Commitment Decisions* below (p 266).

(A) Article 9: substantive rules Article 9(1) of the Regulation provides that, where the Commission intends to adopt a decision requiring that an infringement of Article 81 and/or 82 be brought to an end and the undertakings concerned offer commitments to meet the concerns expressed by the Commission in its preliminary assessment, the Commission may adopt a decision that makes those commitments binding on the undertakings. The final sentence of Article 9(1) provides that the decision may be for a specified period (though this is not a requirement[61]) and shall conclude that there are no longer grounds for action by the Commission. Article 9(2) provides that the Commission may reopen the proceedings in certain specified circumstances, for example where the undertakings concerned act contrary to their commitments. Recital 13 of the Regulation states that the Article 9 procedure is not appropriate in cases where the Commission intends to impose a fine: commitment decisions are therefore excluded in the case of hard-core cartels. In a memorandum of 17 September 2004 the Commission said that commitments may be behavioural or structural and may be limited in time[62]. The CFI has held that the Commission is bound by the principle of proportionality when determining whether a commitment is appropriate for the purpose of Article 9[63].

---

[54] See Sullivan and Hovenkamp *Antitrust Law, Policy and Procedure: Cases, Materials, Problems* (Lexis Nexis, 5th ed, 2003), pp 147–152.

[55] See the Commission's XIVth *Report on Competition Policy* (1984), pp 77–79.

[56] See the Commission's XXIVth *Report on Competition Policy* (1994), pp 364–365.

[57] See the Commission's XXVIth *Report on Competition Policy* (1996), pp 139–140.

[58] See the Commission's XXVIth *Report on Competition Policy* (1996), pp 144–148.

[59] See the Commission's XXVIIth *Report on Competition Policy* (1997), pp 153–154.

[60] See eg Temple Lang 'Commitment Decisions under Regulation 1/2003: Legal Aspects of a New Kind of Competition Decision' (2003) 24 ECLR 347; Furse 'The Decision to Commit: Some pointers from the US' (2004) 25 ECLR 5; Temple Lang 'Commitment Decisions and Settlements with Antitrust Authorities and Private Parties under European Antitrust Law' [2005] Fordham Corporate Law Institute (ed Hawk, 2006), 265; Kerse and Khan *EC Antitrust Procedure* (Sweet & Maxwell, 5th ed, 2005), pp 357–360; Davies and Das 'Private Enforcement of Commission Commitment Decisions: a Steep Climb not a Gentle Stroll' [2005] Fordham Corp L Inst (ed Hawk, 2006), 199, also published in (2006) 29 Fordham International Law Journal 917; Wils 'Settlements of EU Antitrust Investigations: Commitment Decisions under Article 9 of Regulation 1/2003' (2006) 29(3) World Competition, 345; Whish 'Commitment Decisions under Article 9 of the EC Modernisation Regulation: Some Unanswered Questions', in *Liber Amicorum in Honour of Sven Norberg* (2006, Bruylant, Brussels), pp 555–572.

[61] See Case T-170/06 *Alrosa Company Ltd v Commission* [2007] ECR II-000, para 91; this case is on appeal to the ECJ, Case C-441/07 P *Commission v Alrosa*, not yet decided.

[62] Commission MEMO/04/217, available at www.europa.eu/rapid.

[63] Case T-170/06 *Alrosa Company Ltd v Commission* [2007] ECR II-000, paras 92–158.

Article 23(2)(c) of the Regulation provides that fines can be imposed on an undertaking that fails to comply with a commitment of as much as 10 per cent of its total turnover in the preceding business year. Article 24(1)(c) provides for the imposition of periodic penalty payments of up to 5 per cent of average daily turnover in the previous business year for a continuing infringement of a commitment decision.

(B) Article 9: procedure The Article 9 procedure is a formal one and entails the initiation of proceedings by the Commission. However the Commission does not necessarily have to issue a statement of objections: it would suffice that it sends the undertakings concerned a 'preliminary assessment' of its case which may be shorter and less formal than a statement of objections. The preliminary assessment may be contained in a letter or may be sent as an independent document, more like a statement of objections. The preliminary assessment or statement of objections will give the undertakings concerned a period of time within which to respond to the Commission's concerns and to offer draft commitments. The CFI has held that there is a right of access to the file in a case being conducted under the commitments procedure[64].

Article 27(4) of the Implementing Regulation provides that where the Commission intends to adopt an Article 9 decision it must publish a concise summary of the case and the main content of the commitments; third parties are then given an opportunity to comment within a fixed time limit of not less than one month. In its memorandum of 17 September 2004 the Commission says that it will publish the full text of the draft commitments in their original language on the Internet. It adds that the process of 'market testing' the draft commitments may reveal weaknesses in them that could lead the Commission to renegotiate or abandon the settlement option and revert to the possibility of proceeding to a prohibition decision. Article 30 of the Modernisation Regulation provides that the Commission must publish its Article 9 decisions.

(C) Article 9: practical considerations Various practical points should be noted about Article 9 commitments. First, Recital 13 of the Modernisation Regulation says that commitment decisions will not conclude whether or not there has been or still is an infringement of the competition rules, and adds that commitment decisions are without prejudice to the powers of NCAs and national courts to decide upon the case, a point repeated in the final sentence of recital 22. It follows that the fact that the Commission accepts commitments from undertakings as to their future behaviour in no way immunises them from the possibility of a challenge as to their past behaviour; in particular they remain vulnerable to an action for damages in a national court.

Where undertakings give commitments to the Commission as to their future behaviour the question arises of whether third parties could challenge conduct that is consistent with the commitments as being unlawful under Articles 81 and/or 82. Article 9 of the Regulation simply states that the Commission's decision 'shall conclude that there are no longer grounds for action by the Commission'. However this does not in itself mean that the Commission has concluded that there is no longer an infringement: it could mean that it has decided, having been offered suitable commitments, that the case is no longer one that, as a matter of administrative priority, it wishes to pursue. It would

---

[64] Ibid, paras 197–204.

seem to follow therefore that a commitment decision does not provide immunity as to future behaviour either.

Given that the Article 9 procedure is voluntary on the part of the parties that offer commitments it is unlikely that they would appeal against an Article 9 decision, although they may wish to challenge aspects of the Commission's procedure, such as their right of access to the file. Third parties may wish to bring Article 9 cases to the CFI. This might happen where they have complained to the Commission of anti-competitive behaviour, but where they believe that a commitment has been accepted which is inadequate to bring an end to the infringement. Third party appeals against commitment decisions under the EC Merger Regulation occur quite frequently[65]; however there is a material distinction between the ECMR and Article 9 of the Modernisation Regulation in that decisions in merger cases are final and binding, whereas an Article 9 decision does not contain a finding of an infringement and is not binding on NCAs or national courts. A different issue arose in *Alrosa v Commission*[66] where a third party considered that the Commission's Article 9 commitments decision was too strict and disproportionately harmed its interest. Alrosa was a supplier of rough diamonds to De Beers, a firm with which it competed. The Commission objected to there being a long-term supply agreement between competitors and commenced proceedings on the basis of both Article 81 and 82. In the end it accepted commitments from De Beers to bring an end to the Article 82 proceedings against it: De Beers would cease to purchase rough diamonds at all from Alrosa with effect from 2009. Alrosa considered that this was a disproportionate remedy as it meant that it could not supply De Beers in any circumstances. The CFI agreed that the Commission should have looked for a less Draconian remedy[67]. The CFI also upheld Alrosa's argument that it had been improperly denied the right to be heard[68]. The Commission has appealed against the CFI's judgment to the ECJ[69].

The following table provides details of cases in which the Commission had accepted commitments by 12 March 2008.

7.1 Table of Article 9 Commitment Decisions

Case name	Date of publication of proposed commitments	Date upon which commitments were made legally binding	Date until which commitments will remain in force
Joint selling of the media rights to the German Bundesliga	14.9.2004	19.1.2005	30.6.2009
Coca-Cola	19.10.2004	22.6.2005	31.12.2010
Repsol C.P.P.	20.10.2004	12.4.2006	31.12.2011

---

[65] See ch 21, p 884.   [66] Case T-170/06, [2007] ECR II-000, judgment of 11 July 2007.
[67] Ibid, paras 112–157.   [68] Ibid, paras 175–205.
[69] Case C-441/07 P *Commission v Alrosa Company Ltd*, not yet decided.

Case name	Date of publication of proposed commitments	Date upon which commitments were made legally binding	Date until which commitments will remain in force
De Beers	3.6.2005	22.2.2006	Infinite duration
Decision annulled on appeal, Case T-170/06 *Alrosa Co Ltd v Commission*, judgment of 11 July 2007			
On appeal to the ECJ, Case C-441/07 P *Commission v Alrosa Co* (judgment pending)			
BUMA/SABAM (Santiago Agreement)	17.8.2005	No decision taken	
Austrian Airlines/SAS cooperation agreement	22.9.2005	No decision taken	
Joint selling of the media rights to the FA Premier League	30.4.2004	22.3.2006	30.6.2013
The Cannes Extension Agreement	23.5.2006	4.10.2006	Infinite duration
Carmakers (DaimlerChrysler, Opel, Toyota and Fiat)	22.3.2007	14.9.2007	May 2010
Distrigaz	5.4.2007	11.10.2007	31.12.2010
CISAC	9.6.2007	No decision taken	
SkyTeam	19.10.2007	No decision taken	

(iv) Article 10: finding of inapplicability

Article 10 provides that, where the Community public interest requires, the Commission may adopt a 'finding of inapplicability' that Article 81 and/or Article 82 do not apply to an agreement or practice. Firms do not have a right to ask for such a decision, but the Commission might decide to adopt one (in 'exceptional cases', as recital 14 says) where this would clarify the law and ensure its consistent application throughout the Community; the same recital adds that this might be particularly useful where new types of agreements or practices occur in relation to which there is no case law or administrative practice. The Commission had not adopted any Article 10 decisions by 12 March 2008.

(v) Informal guidance

The need for undertakings to have legal certainty in order to promote innovation and investment is acknowledged in recital 38 of the Modernisation Regulation: it says that where there is genuine uncertainty because of novel or unresolved questions of competition law undertakings may seek informal guidance from the Commission. Both Article 10 and recital 38 address the anxieties of those that were concerned that the procedure of notifying agreements for individual exemptions under Article 81(3) was to be abolished. The Commission has issued a *Notice on informal guidance relating to novel questions arising under Articles 81 and 82 (Guidance letters)*[70]. The Notice points out that undertakings have access to a substantial body of case law, decisional practice, block exemptions, guidelines, and notices enabling them to undertake a self-assessment of the legality of their commercial plans[71]; however it also notes that there might be cases in which a guidance letter would be appropriate[72]. The Commission says that issuing a guidance letter would be considered only where the following cumulative criteria are satisfied:

- there is no current case law, guidance or precedent in relation to a particular type of agreement or practice
- guidance would be useful taking into account
  - the economic importance from the point of view of the consumer of the goods or services to which the agreement or practice relates; and/or
  - the extent to which the agreement or practice corresponds to more widely spread economic usage in the marketplace; and/or
  - the scope of the investments linked to the transaction in relation to the size of the undertakings concerned and the extent to which the transaction relates to a structural operation such as the creation of a non-full-function joint venture
- guidance can be given on the basis of information already provided to the Commission and no further fact-finding is required[73].

The Commission will not issue guidance letters in relation to purely hypothetical questions[74]. A memorandum should be submitted with a request for a guidance letter containing information specified by the Commission[75]. A guidance letter will set out a summary of the facts on which it is based and the principle legal reasoning underlying the Commission's understanding of the novel questions raised by the request[76]. Guidance letters will be published on the Commission's website, subject to the deletion of business secrets[77]. Guidance letters are not Commission decisions and do not bind NCAs or national courts[78]. No such letters had been issued by 12 March 2008.

(vi) A system of settlements for cartel cases?[79]

In October 2007 the Commission launched a public consultation, which ended on 21 December of that year, on the possibility of introducing a system for settling cartel

[70] OJ [2004] C 101/78. [71] Ibid, para 3. [72] Ibid, para 5. [73] Ibid, para 8.
[74] Ibid, para 10. [75] Ibid, para 14. [76] Ibid, para 19. [77] Ibid, para 21. [78] Ibid, para 25.
[79] See Whish 'Settlements – the Future of Competition Litigation?' *Current Developments in European and International Competition Law* (14th St. Gallen International Competition Law Forum, ed Baudenbacher, Helbing Lichtenhahn, 2008); Lawrence and Sansom 'The Increasing Use of Administrative Settlement Procedures in UK and EC Competition Investigations' (2007) 3 Competition Law Journal 163; some papers on settlements will be found in *European Competition Law Annual 2006: Enforcement*

cases: the package consisted of a press release and a memorandum of 'frequently asked questions', a draft *Settlements Notice* and a draft regulation amending Regulation 773/2004[80]. The essence of such a system would be that undertakings involved in a cartel would acknowledge their participation and liability and would agree to a faster and simplified procedure; in return for this cooperation the Commission would impose lower penalties than would otherwise have been the case. This would mean that the Commission would be able to handle more cases than it does at the moment, but with the same resources. The intention is that the settlements package will be adopted in the course of 2008.

It is important that any settlements procedure does not undermine the central importance of deterrence, which is necessary to make undertakings comply with the law; nor must it reduce the incentive for members of cartels to 'blow the whistle' in return for immunity from penalties or a significantly reduced penalty[81]: this incentive is itself linked to the issue of deterrence. If the settlement of cases were to lead to much lower penalties there is a danger that these two important features of the current system could be harmed. From the Commission's point of view it is possible to describe a virtuous circle:

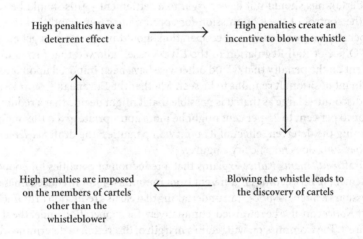

However this circle would be severely damaged if the effect of a settlement policy were to lead to the imposition of inappropriately low penalties thereby undermining the incentive for undertakings to blow the whistle. For the Commission the following would be a

of Prohibition of Cartels (eds Ehlermann and Atansiu, Hart Publishing, 2007), 597ff; Wils 'The Use of Settlements in Public Antitrust Enforcement: Objectives and Principles' (2008) 31(3) World Competition. The OECD held a roundtable discussion on 'Plea Bargaining/Settlement of Cases' in 2006: the papers are available at www.oecd.org.

[80] See Commission Press Release IP/07/1608; MEMO/07/433; the draft *Notice on the conduct of settlement proceedings in view of the adoption of Decisions pursuant to Article 7 and Article 23 of Council Regulation (EC) No 1/2003 in cartel cases*; and the *Proposal for a Commission Regulation amending Regulation (EC) No 773/2994, as regards the conduct of settlement procedures in cartel cases.*

[81] See pp 275–278 below on leniency applications to the Commission.

vicious rather than a virtuous circle:

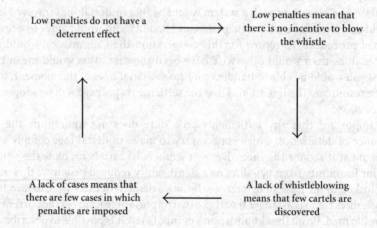

The need to maintain adequate deterrence and the incentive to blow the whistle implies that undertakings should not have a *right* to a settlement – this should be something within the control of the Commission for appropriate cases – and that the reduction in the penalty for confession and cooperation should not be unduly generous. In the UK the Office of Rail Regulation in the *EW&S* case[82] allowed that firm a discount of 35 per cent on the penalty that would otherwise have been imposed upon it for abusing its dominant position. It remains to be seen whether the European Commission would allow a discount as large as that; it is possible that it might decide that a reduction in the region of 10 per cent to 25 per cent might be more appropriate given the importance of maintaining the deterrent effect of its policy on penalties: the draft *Settlements Notice* of October 2007 does not specify a figure.

The draft *Settlements Notice* explains that a reduction of penalties for cooperation in the settlement of proceedings is different from immunity and/or reduced fines under the Commission's *Leniency Notice*[83]; an undertaking that earns a reduction in its fine under the *Leniency Notice* can also be rewarded, cumulatively, for cooperation under the settlements procedure[84]. The Commission will retain a margin of discretion to determine which cases are suitable for settlement[85]; undertakings will not have a *right* to settle[86]. Undertakings involved in settlement discussions with the Commission will be required not to disclose this fact to anyone else except with the express authorisation of the Commission[87].

The draft Notice makes provision for the Commission to initiate proceedings and for it to take exploratory steps towards the possibility of a settlement[88]. Where an undertaking requests settlement discussions, these would be handled by DG COMP[89]. DG COMP would disclose to the undertaking the essential elements of the case against it, including the facts alleged, the gravity and duration of the alleged cartel and an estimation of the range of likely fines[90]; the undertaking would then make a written settlement submission within a time-limit fixed by the Commission and would be given limited

---

[82] Available at www.oft.gov.uk/advice_and_resources/resource_base/ca98/decisions.
[83] See pp 275–278 below on the *Leniency Notice*.   [84] Draft *Settlements Notice*, para 1.
[85] Ibid, para 5.   [86] Ibid, para 6.   [87] Ibid, para 7.   [88] Ibid, paras 8–13.
[89] Ibid, para 14.   [90] Ibid, para 16.

access to key documents in the Commission's possession[91]. The written settlement submission would contain:

- An unequivocal acknowledgement of the undertaking's liability for the infringement
- An indication of the maximum amount of the fine that the undertaking foresees that the Commission could impose and which it accepts in the framework of the settlement procedure
- Confirmation that the undertaking has been sufficiently informed of the Commission's objections and has been given sufficient opportunity to make its views known to the Commission
- Confirmation that the undertaking does not envisage seeking access to the file or requesting an oral hearing
- Agreement to receive a statement of objections and a final decision in an official language of the European Community[92].

The Commission would issue a statement of objections in a settlement case, although this would be a shorter document than in the case of adversarial proceedings, and there would be a right to reply[93]. The Commission would then proceed to a final decision[94]. The possibility would exist that the Commission would decide not to determine a case on the basis of the settlement discussions; in this situation the undertaking(s) would be informed and the matter would proceed under the general rules of procedure[95]. The settlement procedure would be available for any case pending at the time that the *Settlements Notice* is published in the Official Journal[96].

It would be possible to appeal to the CFI against a decision of the Commission adopted pursuant to the settlement procedure[97]. However this would presumably be unlikely to happen often, if at all, given that undertakings will have conceded liability and acknowledged the key facts in their written settlement submission. Under current practice almost every cartel decision is appealed to the CFI, and numerous points are argued on law, fact and procedure. Such appeals are beneficial to lawyers' welfare, though not necessarily to consumer welfare, and their eradication as a result of a settlements procedure is one of the attractions of such a system.

(D) Chapter IV: cooperation

Recital 15 of the Modernisation Regulation states that the Commission and the NCAs should form a 'network of public authorities'. The network is known as the European Competition Network; its composition and operation in practice are described in section 3 below[98]. The members of the ECN are linked by a secure Intranet. Recital 21 of the Regulation adds that cooperation between the Commission and the national courts is also necessary, and recital 22 stresses the need for uniform application of the competition rules on the part of the Commission, NCAs and national courts. Articles 11 to 16 of the Regulation contain provisions to promote cooperation between the Commission, NCAs and national courts. The Commission has issued two important notices on cooperation, the *Notice on cooperation within the network of competition authorities* ('the *Notice on NCA cooperation*')[99] and the *Notice on the cooperation between the Commission and*

---

[91] Ibid, para 17. [92] Ibid, para 20. [93] Ibid, paras 23–27. [94] Ibid, para 28.
[95] Ibid, para 29. [96] Ibid, para 34. [97] Ibid, para 36. [98] See pp 283–284.
[99] OJ [2004] C 101/43; note that this Notice is subject to periodic review by the Commission and the NCAs: ibid, para 70.

courts of the EU Member States in the application of Articles 81 and 82 EC[100]. The latter of these two Notices is discussed in chapter 8 on the private enforcement of the competition rules.

(i) Article 11: cooperation between the Commission and the NCAs[101]

Article 11(1) of the Regulation provides that the Commission and the NCAs are to apply the competition rules in close cooperation. Article 11(2) requires the Commission to transmit to NCAs the most important documents it has collected with a view to the adoption of decisions under Articles 7 to 10 (above) or Article 29(1) (below). Article 11(3) requires NCAs to inform the Commission in writing before or without delay after commencing proceedings under Article 81 or Article 82; this information may also be made available to the NCAs via the Intranet. The *Notice on NCA cooperation* explains that the purpose of Article 11(2) and 11(3) is to ensure that cases can be allocated to a 'well placed' authority[102]. The Notice sets out the principles by reference to which a well-placed authority is to be identified[103]. The Commission is particularly well placed where an agreement or practice has effects in more than three Member States[104].

Article 11(4) and Article 11(6) are of particular importance. Article 11(4) provides that, not later than 30 days before adopting an infringement decision, accepting commitments or withdrawing the benefit of a block exemption, NCAs must inform the Commission: guidance on the application of Article 11(4) will be found in the *Notice on NCA cooperation*[105]. Article 11(6) provides that the initiation by the Commission of proceedings shall relieve NCAs of their competence to apply Articles 81 and 82[106]; the Notice provides guidance on how this provision is to be applied in practice[107]. Articles 11(4) and (6) are central to the functioning of the Modernisation Regulation system and mean that the Commission can halt the proceedings of an NCA and take a case over itself. This power of the Commission is sometimes referred to as 'the nuclear option' since it is so profound in its effect: the *Notice on NCA cooperation* explains the limited range of circumstances in which the Commission is likely to make use of Article 11(6)[108]. The power had not been exercised in any case as at 12 March 2008.

Article 11(5) provides that NCAs may consult with the Commission on any case involving the application of Community competition law.

(ii) Article 12: exchange of information

(A) Free movement of information Article 12 of the Regulation is a sensitive provision for undertakings since it provides for the exchange of information between the

---

[100] OJ [2004] C 101/54.
[101] See Wils 'The EU Network of Competition Authorities, the European Convention on Human Rights and the Charter of Fundamental Rights of the EU' *European Competition Law Annual 2002: Constructing the EU Network of Competition Authorities* (eds Ehlermann and Atanasiu, Hart Publishing, 2003), pp 433–464; Brammer 'Concurrent jurisdiction under Regulation 1/2003 and the issue of case allocation' (2005) 42 Common Market Law Review 1383; Andreangeli 'The impact of the Modernisation Regulation on the guarantees of due process in competition proceedings' (2006) 331 ELR 342.
[102] OJ [2004] C 101/43, paras 16 and 17.   [103] Ibid, paras 5–15.
[104] Ibid, para 14.   [105] Ibid, paras 43–49.
[106] Article 11(6) of the Regulation requires that, if an NCA is already acting on a case, the Commission shall initiate proceedings only following consultation.
[107] OJ [2004] C 101/43, paras 50–57.   [108] Ibid, para 54.

Commission and NCAs. It must be read in conjunction with Article 28 which contains provisions restricting the use or disclosure of information covered by an obligation of professional secrecy[109]. The Commission's view is that Article 12 is a key element in the proper functioning of the ECN and a precondition to the efficient and effective allocation of cases[110]. Article 12(1) provides that the Commission and NCAs have the power to provide one another with and use in evidence any matter of fact or law, including confidential information: the exchange of information can take place both between the Commission and the NCAs and also between NCAs[111]. Article 12(2), however, states that information exchanged can be used only for the purpose of applying Articles 81 and 82 and in respect of the subject-matter for which it was collected; an exception to this is that an NCA can use information received in order to apply its domestic law, where the same case involves the parallel application of Article 81 or Article 82 and the outcome would be the same under both systems of law.

(B) Restrictions on the use of information In some Member States natural persons can be the subject of fines, or even terms of imprisonment: this is true, for example, where the 'cartel offence' is committed under the Enterprise Act 2002 in the UK[112]. There are restrictions on the use of information exchanged between competition authorities in these circumstances[113]. The first indent of Article 12(3) provides that information exchanged pursuant to Article 12(1) can be used in evidence to impose sanctions on natural persons only where the law of the transmitting authority foresees sanctions of a similar kind in relation to an infringement of Article 81 or Article 82; this means, for example, that if the law of both the transmitting and the receiving authority were to provide for terms of imprisonment to be imposed, the information exchanged could be used as evidence in a criminal case leading to imprisonment. The second indent of Article 12(3) provides that, where it is not the case that the law of the transmitting authority foresees sanctions of the same kind as the law of the receiving authority, the information can be used by the latter only where it has been collected by the former in a way which respects the same level of protection of the rights of defence of natural persons as provided for under the national rules of the receiving authority; however in this case the information cannot be used to impose custodial sentences at all, but only for other sanctions such as fines.

(C) The exchange of information with third countries Article 12 does not discuss the issue of information exchange between the European Commission and institutions outside the EU. To some extent this is dealt with in cooperation agreements entered into, for example, with the US, Canada and Japan[114]. An attempt by AMD, a plaintiff in proceedings brought in the US, to obtain an order from a court there against Intel requiring it to produce information about alleged violations of EC competition law being investigated by the European Commission failed in *AMD Inc v Intel Corporation*[115]; the Commission indicated in an *amicus curiae* brief to the US court that it did not want it to make such an order.

---

[109] See p 281 below.   [110] *Notice on NCA cooperation*, para 26.   [111] Ibid, para 27.
[112] See ch 10, pp 415–422.   [113] See the *Notice on NCA cooperation*, para 28(c).
[114] See ch 12, pp 493–495.
[115] Order of 4 October 2004, Case No C 01–7033 MISC JW; see the earlier judgment of the Supreme Court in *Intel Corporation v Advanced Micro Devices* 124 S Ct 2466 (2004).

(iii) Article 13: suspension or termination of proceedings

Article 13 contains provisions to avoid the duplication of investigations; the *Notice on NCA cooperation* provides additional guidance[116]. Article 13(1) provides that, where an NCA is dealing with a case, this is a sufficient ground for another NCA or the Commission to suspend proceedings or to reject a complaint; however there is no obligation to do so, thereby leaving the NCAs with some discretion as to whether to proceed or not[117]. Article 13(2) states that an NCA or the Commission may reject a complaint which has already been dealt with by another competition authority. Recital 18 of the Regulation adds that the provisions of Article 13 are without prejudice to the right of the Commission to reject a complaint due to lack of Community interest[118].

(iv) Article 14: Advisory Committee

Regulation 17 established the Advisory Committee on Restrictive Practices and Dominant Positions[119] which, according to recital 19 of the Modernisation Regulation, 'has functioned in a very satisfactory manner': this recital adds that the Advisory Committee will fit well into the new enforcement system, and that certain aspects of its procedure should be developed further. Article 14(1) of the Regulation requires the Commission to consult with the Advisory Committee when taking key decisions, such as findings of an infringement or the imposition of a fine. Article 14(2) deals with the constitution of the Advisory Committee. Article 14(3) and (4) explain the consultation procedure, which may take place at a meeting or (an innovation introduced by the Regulation) in writing. Article 14(5) requires the Commission to take the 'utmost account' of the Advisory Committee's opinion. Article 14(7) provides that cases being decided by an NCA may be discussed at the Advisory Committee, and that an NCA may request that the Advisory Committee should be consulted when the Commission is contemplating the initiation of proceedings under Article 11(6). Part 4 of the Commission's *Notice on NCA cooperation* explains further the role of the Advisory Committee[120].

(v) Article 15: cooperation with national courts

Article 15 deals with cooperation with national courts: this is discussed in chapter 8[121].

(vi) Article 16: uniform application of Community competition law

Article 16 of the Regulation deals with the effect of Commission decisions on national courts (Article 16(1)) and NCAs (Article 16(2)). The position of national courts is discussed in chapter 8[122]. Article 16(2) provides that NCAs cannot take decisions which would run counter to a decision adopted by the Commission.

(E) Chapter V: powers of investigation

Chapter V of the Regulation gives the Commission various powers of investigation: of particular importance are Article 18, which enables it to request information, and Articles 20 and 21, which enable it to conduct inspections, even of an individual's home.

---

[116] OJ [2004] C 101/43, paras 20–25. [117] Ibid, para 22. [118] See p 281 below.
[119] See ch 2, pp 56–57. [120] *Notice on NCA cooperation*, paras 58–68.
[121] See ch 8, pp 296–298. [122] Ibid.

(i) Article 17: investigations into sectors of the economy and into types of agreements

Article 17(1) enables the Commission to conduct an investigation into a sector of the economy or a type of agreement where it appears that there may be a restriction or distortion of competition, for example because of the lack of new entrants into a market or the rigidity of prices[123]. Article 17(2) gives the Commission the power to request information and to conduct inspections of business (not residential) premises for the purpose of conducting a sectoral investigation. The third indent of Article 17(1) states that the Commission may publish a report on the results of its inquiry and invite comments from interested parties. It is important to understand that the Commission does not have any remedial powers following such a sectoral investigation. An Article 17 investigation is not like a market investigation by the Competition Commission under the Enterprise Act in the UK, where that Commission has the power to impose behavioural and structural remedies on undertakings to deal with any adverse effect on competition that it identifies[124]. An Article 17 investigation is more like an OFT market study, whereby the OFT conducts a study to inform itself about how well a market is operating; at the end of the study the OFT decides on what further action, if any, needs to be taken[125]. In the same way the European Commission conducts a sectoral investigation under Article 17 in order to obtain a better understanding of the competition conditions within a sector, and decides at the end of the process what should happen next.

In recent years the Commission has conducted two particularly significant sectoral investigations, one into financial services and one into energy markets. The investigation of financial services focused on payment cards, core retail banking and business insurance. The final report on retail banking was published on 31 January 2007 and on business insurance on 25 September 2007. The final report on energy was adopted on 10 January 2007. Full information about these two investigations, including the reports themselves, can be obtained from DG COMP's website[126]; useful discussion of the energy and retail banking reports will also be found in the Commission's *Competition Policy Newsletter* of Spring 2007[127]. Further action, including enforcement action under Articles 81 and 82, can be anticipated in the wake of these reports[128].

The Commission initiated a new sectoral inquiry, into the practices, such as vexatious litigation and misuse of the patent system, on the part of pharmaceutical companies that might have the effect of hindering producers of 'generic' products from entering the market[129].

(ii) Article 18: requests for information

(A) The Commission's powers Article 18 of the Regulation enables the Commission, in order to carry out its duties under the Regulation, to require 'all necessary

---

[123] A similar power had existed in Article 12 of Regulation 17, although it was not used on many occasions; the last investigation under Article 12 was of *Sports content over third generation mobile networks*, Commission Report of 21 September 2005, available at www.ec.europa.eu/comm/competition/antitrust/others/sector_inquiries/new_media/3g/index.html.

[124] See ch 11, pp 452–459 and Enterprise Act 2002, Sch 8.   [125] See ch 11, pp 445–452.

[126] See www.ec.europa.eu/comm/competition/antitrust/sector_inquiries.html.

[127] See p 55 (energy) and p 60 (retail banking).

[128] See in particular ch 23, pp 981–984 on issues in the energy sector.

[129] Commission Press Release IP/08/49, 16 January 2008.

information"[130]; Article 18 is similar to, though not identical to, Article 11 of Regulation 17/62. Article 18(1) of the Modernisation Regulation provides that the Commission may simply request information, or may require it by decision.

Article 18(2) deals with simple requests: the Commission must state the legal basis and the purpose of the request, specify what information is required and fix the time-limit within which it is to be provided; it must also explain the penalties in Article 23 of the Regulation for supplying incorrect or misleading information[131]. There is no obligation to comply with a simple request. However, undertakings must respond to a Commission decision requiring information: Article 18(3) says that, where the Commission requires information by decision, it must also explain that a penalty can be imposed under Article 23 for not supplying the information at all, and that the undertaking required to provide the information may seek a judicial review of the decision by the CFI. The fact that an undertaking considers that the Commission has no grounds for action under Article 81 does not entitle it to resist a request for information[132]. However the Commission would not be entitled to request information for a purpose other than the enforcement of the competition rules, and in exercising its discretion under Article 18 it must have regard to the principle of proportionality[133].

Article 18(4) explains who should provide the information: an innovation in Article 18 is that authorised lawyers can supply information on behalf of a client, although the client remains responsible for incomplete, incorrect or misleading information. Article 18(5) requires the Commission to inform NCAs in the relevant Member State of information required of undertakings by decision, and Article 18(6) provides that the Commission can request information from governments and NCAs.

Quite often the Commission will request information under Article 18 *after* it has carried out an on-the-spot investigation under Article 20 or 21[134], for example because it needs to check particular points that have arisen out of the inspection or to pursue certain matters further.

The issue arises under Article 18 (and also where the Commission conducts an inspection under Article 20 or Article 21) of whether it is possible to resist answering questions or providing information on the basis that this would be self-incriminating, or that the information sought is protected by legal professional privilege. Recital 23 of the Modernisation Regulation (in acknowledgement of the case law discussed below) states that undertakings, when complying with a decision requesting information, cannot be forced to admit that they have committed an infringement; however it adds that they are obliged to answer factual questions and to provide documents, even if this information may be used to establish an infringement against them or another undertaking.

---

[130] Information for this purpose includes documents: Case 374/87 *Orkem v Commission* [1989] ECR 3283, [1991] 4 CMLR 502, paras 13–14; Case 27/88 *Solvay & Cie v Commission* [1989] ECR 3355, [1991] 4 CMLR 502, paras 13–14; on the meaning of 'necessary information' see Case C-36/92 P *SEP v Commission* [1994] ECR I-1911; see also Case T-46/92 *Scottish Football Association v Commission* [1994] ECR II-1039.

[131] Penalties were imposed on a number of occasions for the provision of misleading information under Article 11 of Regulation 17: see eg *Telos* OJ [1982] L 58/19, [1982] 1 CMLR 267; *National Panasonic (Belgium) NV* OJ [1982] L 113/18, [1982] 2 CMLR 410; *National Panasonic (France) SA* OJ [1982] L 211/32, [1982] 3 CMLR 623; *Comptoir Commercial d'Importation* OJ [1982] L 27/31, [1982] 1 CMLR 440; *Peugeot* OJ [1986] L 295/19, [1989] 4 CMLR 371; *Anheuser-Busch Incorporated/Scottish & Newcastle* OJ [2000] L 49/37, [2000] 5 CMLR 75.

[132] See eg *Fire Insurance* OJ [1982] L 80/36, [1982] 2 CMLR 159 and *Deutsche Castrol* OJ [1983] L 114/26, [1983] 3 CMLR 165.

[133] Case C-36/92 P *SEP v Commission* [1994] ECR I-1911.   [134] See pp 269–271 below.

The Regulation is silent on the issue of legal professional privilege. There was case law of the Community Courts on both types of privilege under Regulation 17, and it will continue to apply under the Modernisation Regulation.

(B) Privilege against self-incrimination In the *Orkem* and *Solvay* cases[135] the ECJ considered whether undertakings could refuse to answer certain questions in a Commission request for information on the basis that to do so would be self-incriminating. The ECJ's conclusion was that there is a limited privilege against self-incrimination in Community law, which entitles undertakings to refuse to answer questions that would require them to admit to the very infringement the Commission is seeking to establish; however this privilege does not entitle them to refuse to hand over documents to the Commission which might serve to establish an infringement by the undertaking concerned or by another one. It is presumably the case that the same doctrine applies in the case of inspections under Articles 20 and 21. The ECJ has held that privilege against self-incrimination can be claimed only where the Commission requires information under compulsion, that is to say in an Article 18(3) case; privilege does not attach to information provided in response to a mere request under Article 18(2)[136].

In *Mannesmann-Röhrenwerke AG v Commission*[137] the CFI held that there is no absolute right to silence in competition proceedings[138], except in so far as a compulsion to provide answers would involve an admission of the existence of an infringement[139]; in the Court's view certain questions asked by the Commission did go beyond what it was entitled to ask[140]. Judgments of the European Court of Human Rights in *Funke v France*[141] and *Saunders v United Kingdom*[142] have recognised a right to remain silent in criminal cases, but it seems after the *Mannesmann* judgment that Community law will not extend privilege this far in relation to cases under Articles 81 and 82, unless at some point in the future the ECJ overrules the judgment of the CFI.

In *Commission v SGL Carbon AG*[143] the ECJ held that undertakings are required to produce documents in their possession, even if those documents can be used to establish the existence of an infringement: privilege against self-incrimination applies only

---

[135] Case 374/87 *Orkem v Commission* [1989] ECR 3283, [1991] 4 CMLR 502: see Lasok 'The Privilege against Self-incrimination in Competition Cases' (1990) 11 ECLR 90; Case 27/88 *Solvay & Cie v Commission* [1989] ECR 3355, [1991] 4 CMLR 502; see also Case T-34/93 *Société Générale v Commission* [1995] ECR II-545, [1996] 4 CMLR 665, paras 72–74; as to privilege against self-incrimination in domestic courts see Case C-60/92 *Otto v Postbank* [1993] ECR I-5683: for comment on this case see Kerse (1994) 31 CML Rev 1375; Cumming '*Otto v Postbank* and the Privilege Against Self-Incrimination in Enforcement Proceedings of Articles [81] and [82] before the English Courts' (1995) 16 ECLR 401; on self-incrimination generally see Wils 'Self-incrimination in EC antitrust enforcement: A legal and economic analysis' (2003) 26 World Competition, pp 566–588; Gippini-Fournier 'Legal Professional Privilege in Competiton Proceedings before the European Commission: Beyond the Cursory glance' [2004] Fordham Corporate Law Institute (ed Hawk) 587; Vesterdorf 'Legal Professional Privilege and the Privelege against Self-incrimination in EC Law: Recent Developments and Current Issues' [2004] Fordham Corporate Law Institute (ed Hawk), 701; MacCulloch 'The privilege against self-incrimination in competition investigations: theoretical foundations and practical implications' (2006) 26(2) Legal Studies 211.

[136] Case C-407/04 P *Dalmine v Commission* [2007] ECR I-835, paras 33–36.

[137] Case T-112/98 [2001] ECR II-729, [2001] 5 CMLR 54.   [138] Ibid, para 66.

[139] Ibid, para 67.   [140] Ibid, paras 69–74.

[141] [1993] 1 CMLR 897; for comment on *Funke* see van Overbeek 'The Right to Remain Silent in Competition Investigations' (1994) 15 ECLR 127.

[142] (1996) 23 EHRR 313.   [143] Case C-301/04 P [2006] ECR I-5915, [2006] 5 CMLR 877.

where the Commission requires answers to questions addressed to undertakings under investigation[144].

(C) Legal professional privilege That some documents are covered by legal professional privilege under Community law was established by the ECJ in *AM and S Europe Ltd v Commission*[145], where certain papers had been withheld from Commission officials during an inspection; the same principle must surely apply to a request for information under Article 18. The *AM & S* case dealt with two issues: first, whether there is a doctrine of privilege in Community law; secondly, if there is one, what mechanism should be adopted to ascertain whether any particular document is privileged. On the first question the ECJ held that some, but not all, correspondence between a client and an independent lawyer based in the EC was privileged, but that dealings with an in-house lawyer or with a lawyer in a third country were not. Privilege mainly extends to correspondence relating to the defence of a client after the initiation of proceedings by the Commission, although it also applies to correspondence before the initiation of proceedings though intimately linked with their subject-matter. The privilege belongs to the client, not the lawyer.

The ECJ limited privilege to dealings with independent lawyers because in many Member States employed lawyers are not subject to professional codes of discipline. In some Member States, for example the UK, in-house counsel may remain subject to the rules of the Bar Council or the Law Society, so that this reason for excluding privilege ought not to apply; however the ECJ's judgment is quite clear that there is no privilege in these circumstances[146]. The position was slightly relaxed in *Hilti v Commission*[147] where the CFI held that privilege does extend to an internal memorandum prepared by an in-house lawyer which simply reports what an independent lawyer has said. In *John Deere*[148] the Commission relied on written advice by an in-house lawyer to show that an undertaking knew that it was infringing Article 81.

The limitation of privilege to correspondence with EC lawyers is overtly discriminatory, and the Commission at one point intended to try to persuade the Council to rectify this[149]; it is understood that this has since been dropped.

In *Akzo Nobel Chemicals Ltd v Commission*[150] the CFI was invited to reconsider the ECJ's ruling in *AM & S* but it very clearly declined to do so[151]. Akzo has appealed against the CFI's judgment to the ECJ[152].

On the question of how claims to privilege should be adjudicated the ECJ, in effect, held that it (or, now, the CFI) should fulfil this task. This seems cumbersome, but is better than allowing the Commission itself to see the documents: even if a Commission official were to accept that they were privileged, a firm would be bound to suspect that

---

[144] Ibid, paras 33–51.   [145] Case 155/79 [1982] ECR 1575, [1982] 2 CMLR 264.

[146] See however the cogent argument of Advocate General Slynn to the contrary in the *AM & S* case; note that under s 30 UK Competition Act 1998 communications with in-house lawyers do enjoy privilege: see ch 10, pp 389–390.

[147] Case T-30/89 [1990] ECR II-163, [1990] 4 CMLR 16.

[148] OJ [1985] L 35/58, [1985] 2 CMLR 554; see similarly *London European-Sabena* OJ [1988] L 317/47, [1989] 4 CMLR 662; privilege was unsuccessfully claimed in *VW* OJ [1998] L 124/60, [1998] 5 CMLR 55, para 199.

[149] See the XIIIth *Report on Competition Policy* (1983), point 78 and Faull 'Legal Professional Privilege *(AM and S)*: the Commission Proposes International Negotiations' (1985) 10 EL Rev 119.

[150] Cases T-125/03 etc [2007] ECR II-000, judgment of 17 September 2007.

[151] Ibid, paras 165–179.   [152] Case C-550/07 P *Akzo Nobel Chemicals Ltd v Commission*, not yet decided.

he or she had been influenced by what had been seen. It follows that, as a matter of law, what has to happen in the case of a dispute as to privilege is that the Commission must make a formal decision, requiring the documents in question; this decision may then be appealed to the CFI, which will resolve the issue. It is understood that, in practice, a more pragmatic line is sometimes taken: for example, one solution is for the document(s) in question to be sealed in an envelope and handed over to the Hearing Officer for him or her to determine whether the claim of privilege is a sound one[153].

(iii) Article 19: power to take statements

A novel provision in the Modernisation Regulation is the power conferred on the Commission by Article 19 to interview natural or legal persons, with their consent, for the purpose of collecting information relating to the subject-matter of an investigation. NCAs must be informed of interviews within their territory, and they have a right to be present. An important point is that there are no penalties for providing incorrect or misleading information at an interview.

(iv) Article 20: the Commission's powers of inspection[154]

An important part of a competition authority's armoury is the ability to conduct a 'dawn raid' – better described as a 'surprise inspection' – on undertakings: those responsible for hard-core cartels, for example, are perfectly aware that what they are doing is illegal, and they may go to great lengths to suppress evidence of their activities. Article 20 of the Modernisation Regulation, similar to Article 14 of Regulation 17, enables the Commission to conduct inspections of business premises, either by agreement or by surprise; Article 21 allows an inspection of 'other premises', including an individual's home: this had no counterpart in Regulation 17.

Article 20(1) enables the Commission, in order to be able to carry out its duties under the Regulation, to conduct 'all necessary inspections'. Article 20(2) empowers those conducting the inspection:

- To enter premises
- To examine books and other records, including data stored in electronic form, for example on a hard disk, a CD-ROM or a memory stick
- To take or obtain copies or extracts from them: it is sensible to make photocopying facilities available to the inspectors and to make a duplicate set of all items copied for retention by the undertaking that is being investigated
- To seal premises, books or records to the extent necessary for the inspection: this can be important, for example, where an inspection will go into a second day and the inspectors wish to ensure that evidence will not be interfered with overnight[155]
- To ask for explanations of facts or documents and to record the answers.

---

[153] On the position of the Hearing Officer see p 279 below.

[154] On the position of dawn raids under the Convention for the Protection of Human Rights and Fundamental Freedoms see Case 37971/97 *Société Colas Est v France* judgment of 16 April 2002, European Court of Human Rights, finding France to have infringed the applicants' fundamental rights and awarding damages as the inspectors' had entered without prior judicial warrant.

[155] Recital 25 of the Regulation states that seals should not normally be affixed for more than 72 hours; in January 2008 the Commission imposed a fine of €38 million on E.ON Energie AG for breaching a seal that had been affixed to documents during an inspection in May 2006: see Commission Press Release IP/08/108 of 30 January 2008.

The rules on self-incrimination and legal professional privilege, discussed above, would apply to inspections. Undertakings may submit to an inspection voluntarily; however they must submit to an inspection ordered by decision under Article 20(4), which may be conducted without prior announcement: the so-called 'dawn raid'. The Commission does not have an obligation to attempt a voluntary inspection prior to a dawn raid[156].

(A) Voluntary investigations In the case of a voluntary investigation Article 20(3) requires the Commission's officials and other accompanying persons authorised by the Commission (for example a forensic IT specialist, whose function is to search computer records, e-mails and other electronic media) to produce an authorisation in writing; it must specify the subject-matter and purpose of the investigation and the penalties which may be imposed for incomplete production of the required books and business records or the provision of incorrect or misleading information. NCAs must be informed of inspections in their territory. The Commission held (in decisions under Regulation 17) that a firm being investigated is under a positive duty to assist the Commission's officials in finding the information they want: it is not sufficient simply to grant them unlimited access to all the filing cabinets or the IT system[157]; this has been confirmed in the case law of the Community Courts[158].

(B) Mandatory investigations The Commission may adopt a decision under Article 20(4) requiring an undertaking to submit to an inspection. The Commission must consult with the local NCA before carrying out such an inspection in its territory, but this can be done in an informal manner, by telephone if necessary[159]. There is no entitlement to the presence of a lawyer, although the Commission may be prepared to wait for a reasonable period for one to arrive if there are no in-house lawyers[160]. The Commission's decision must explain the penalties for non-compliance with the decision ordering the inspection, and that the decision can be reviewed by the CFI. Under Regulation 17 the Commission imposed a fine of €3,000 on CSM NV for preventing Commission officials from taking copies of particular documents during the course of an investigation. The Commission stressed in its decision that, if the undertaking concerned considered that the Commission was not entitled to certain documents, the matter should be determined by the CFI: the undertaking cannot decide this itself. In the maritime transport sector a fine of €5,000 was imposed on *Ukwal*[161] for refusing to submit to an investigation. In *AKZO*[162] the Commission imposed a fine of €5,000 for failing to submit fully to an investigation and rejected arguments that it could investigate the offices of AKZO Chemicals only at two named sites, and not at premises that belonged to AKZO NV, a different undertaking.

Quite apart from these penalties the Commission's recent practice has been to regard a lack of cooperation during an inspection as an aggravating factor when it comes to

---

[156] Case 136/79 *National Panasonic (UK) Ltd v Commission* [1980] ECR 2033, [1980] 3 CMLR 169, paras 8–16.

[157] See *Fabbrica Pisana* OJ [1980] L 75/30, [1980] 2 CMLR 354 and *Pietro Sciarra* OJ [1980] L 75/35, [1980] 2 CMLR 362; the same would be true of an investigation under Article 20(4).

[158] See eg Case C-301/04 P *Commission v SGL Carbon* [2006] ECR I-5915, [2006] 5 CMLR 877, para 40.

[159] Case 5/85 *AKZO Chemie BV v Commission* [1986] ECR 2585, [1987] 3 CMLR 716, para 24.

[160] See the Commission's XIIth *Report on Competition Policy* (1982), point 32.

[161] OJ [1992] L 121/45, [1993] 5 CMLR 632; see also *Mewac* OJ [1993] L 20/6, [1994] 5 CMLR 275.

[162] OJ [1994] L 294/31.

determining the level of the fine for the substantive infringement of Article 81 or 82. For example in *Bitumen*[163] the fine on KWS was increased by 10 per cent because it refused to allow the Commission officials access to the premises and in *Professional videotapes* the fine on Sony was increased by 30 per cent because one of its employees refused to answer questions during an inspection and another shredded documents during it[164].

(C) The involvement of Member States Article 20(5) of the Regulation provides that officials of NCAs shall, at the request of the Commission, actively assist its officials with their inspections. Where an undertaking refuses to submit to an inspection, Article 20(6) requires the Member State concerned to afford the Commission the necessary assistance to enable the inspection to take place: this may require the involvement of the police or an equivalent enforcement authority. Article 20(7) states that, if judicial authorisation is required, for example to obtain entry to premises, this must be applied for. Article 20(8), which gives expression to the judgment of the ECJ in *Roquette Frères SA v Commission*[165], sets out the role of the judicial authority in circumstances where it is asked, for example, to issue a warrant ordering entry into premises. The court should ensure that the Commission's decision is authentic and that the coercive measures sought are neither arbitrary nor excessive; for this purpose the court may address questions to the Commission. However the court may not call into question the necessity for the inspection, nor demand that it be provided with all the information in the Commission's file.

The OFT has power under Part II of the Competition Act 1998 to conduct inspections in relation to possible infringements of Articles 81 and 82[166].

(v) Article 21: inspection of other premises

Recital 26 of the Modernisation Regulation states that experience has shown that there are cases where business records are kept in people's homes, and that therefore it should be possible, subject to judicial authorisation, to conduct inspections there. The *SAS/Maersk Air*[167] decision provides an example of this, where important documents relating to a market-sharing agreement were kept in individuals' homes. Article 21 therefore confers a power on the Commission to inspect 'other premises', which can include homes; Article 21(3) requires prior authorisation by a court. It is reasonable to predict that this power will be exercised rarely, but in principle it seems correct that the Commission should be able to conduct such inspections where it has reason to believe that the individuals responsible for cartels (or, less likely, abusive practices) are keeping relevant information at home.

(vi) Article 22: investigations by competition authorities of Member States

Article 22(1) of the Regulation enables an NCA to conduct an inspection in its territory on behalf of an NCA in another Member State. Article 22(2) provides that NCAs

---

[163] See paras 340–341 of the decision in this case, Commission decision of 13 September 2006.
[164] Commission Press Release IP/07/1724, 20 November 2007.
[165] Case C-94/00 [2002] ECR I-9011, [2003] 4 CMLR 46.   [166] See ch 10, p 393.
[167] OJ [2001] L 265/15, [2001] 5 CMLR 1119, paras 7, 89 and 123.

shall carry out inspections which the Commission considers to be necessary under Article 20(1) or Article 20(4)[168].

(F) Chapter VI: penalties

Articles 23 and 24 provide for fines and periodic penalty payments. The Commission cannot impose fines on individuals, except in so far as an individual acts as an undertaking[169], nor can it sentence them to terms of imprisonment. Some Member States, including the UK, do have powers to impose sanctions on individuals[170].

(i) Article 23: fines[171]

Article 23 enables fines to be imposed on undertakings both for procedural and for substantive infringements. Procedural fines can be imposed under Article 23(1) on undertakings that commit offences in relation to requests for information or inspections under Articles 17, 18 or 20 of the Regulation (fines cannot be imposed on individuals whose homes are inspected under Article 21). A typical infringement would be the supply of incorrect or misleading information, or the refusal by an undertaking to submit to an inspection. The fines under Regulation 17 for these infringements were very low; under the Modernisation Regulation they can be substantially higher: up to 1 per cent of an undertaking's total turnover in the preceding business year.

Article 23(2) provides for very substantial fines to be imposed where undertakings infringe Articles 81 and 82 EC, where they contravene an interim measures decision made under Article 8 of the Regulation, or where they fail to comply with a commitment made binding by a decision under Article 9. In these cases the maximum fine that can be imposed is €1 million or 10 per cent of an undertaking's worldwide turnover in the preceding business year[172]: clearly this can be an enormous amount, in particular since it is not limited to turnover in the market affected by the infringement, nor to turnover in the EU.

In fixing the level of a fine, the Commission is required by Article 23(3) to have regard to the gravity and to the duration of the infringement. Where a fine is imposed on a trade association Article 23(4) provides that, if the association is insolvent, the association must call for contributions from its members to cover the fine; in case of default the Commission can impose the fine on the members themselves.

Reference has been made elsewhere in this book to the fact that very large fines have been imposed by the Commission, particularly in recent years, for participation in hard-core cartels[173], for the imposition of resale price maintenance and export bans in vertical agreements[174], and for the abuse of a dominant position[175]. It is noticeable

---

[168] On the position in the UK see ch 10, p 393.

[169] See ch 3, p 85; the Commission has never imposed a fine on an individual, although in *French beef* it imposed fines on trade unions representing individual farmers: OJ [2003] L 209/12, upheld on appeal Cases T-217/03 and T-245/03 *FNCBV v Commission*, judgment of 13 December 2006, [2006] ECR II-4987, on appeal Case C-110/07, not yet decided.

[170] See ch 10, pp 415–423.

[171] See Wils *The Optimal Enforcement of EC Antitrust Law* (Kluwer Law International, 2002); Wils *Efficiency and Justice in European Antitrust Enforcement* (Hart Publishing, 2008).

[172] Where an undertaking had no turnover in the preceding years an earlier year can be used: Case C-76/06 *Britannia Alloys v Commission* [2007] ECR I-000, [2007] 5 CMLR 251, paras 10–33.

[173] See ch 13, pp 502–504.

[174] See ch 16, pp 622–624.   [175] See ch 5, p 171.

that the cartel cases in recent years that have been taken on appeal to the CFI contain at least as much, if not more, analysis of the level of fines than on the finding of the substantive infringement. A detailed study of the 'science' of setting the right level of a fine is beyond the scope of this book: the practitioners' works cited earlier contain extensive commentary on the subject[176].

The CFI has an unlimited jurisdiction on appeal to determine the level of fines; this includes the power to increase as well as to decrease the fines imposed by the Commission[177].

In 2006 the Commission adopted two important Notices (replacing earlier ones) on its fining policy. The first concerned its method of calculating the level of a fine and the second its policy of allowing leniency towards whistleblowers.

(ii) The Commission's guidelines on the method of setting fines[178]

The Commission enjoys a wide margin of appreciation when determining the level of fines[179]. However, in the interests of transparency and impartiality, it decided in 1998 to publish guidelines on its methodology when setting fines[180]; they were replaced in 2006 by new guidelines building on the Commission's subsequent experience[181]. The new *Fining Guidelines* apply in relation to cases in which the Commission issues a statement of objections after 1 September 2006, the date on which they were published in the Official Journal[182]. The *Fining Guidelines* respond to the criticism that, even if the Commission has a wide margin of appreciation, it is not an unfettered one; in the US, for example, there are sentencing guidelines that enable the level of a fine (and the duration of a prison sentence) to be predicted with a fairly high degree of accuracy[183]. Guidance on the amount of a penalty is also available in various Member States, including the UK[184]. The Commission points out in the *Guidelines* of 2006 that fines should have a sufficiently deterrent effect both on the undertakings involved in a particular infringement of the competition rules ('specific deterrence') and also on other undertakings that might be inclined to act unlawfully ('general deterrence')[185]. The ECJ has repeatedly held that the need to deter infringements of the competition rules is one of the factors to be taken into account when determining the level of fines[186] and has established that the Commission is entitled to change its methodology for the setting of fines, including

---

[176] See p 246, n 3 above.   [177] See pp 288–289 below.

[178] See Wils 'The European Commission's 2006 Guidelines on Antitrust Fines: A Legal and Economic Analysis' (2007) 30(2) World Competition 197; Motta 'On Cartel Deterrence and Fines in the European Union' (2008) 29 ECLR 209; Manzini 'European Antitrust in Search of the Perfect Fine' (2008) 31(1) World Competition 3.

[179] See eg Cases C-189/02 P etc. *Dansk Rørindustri A/S and others v Commission* [2005] ECR I-5425, [2005] 5 CMLR 796, para 172.

[180] *Guidelines on the method of setting fines imposed pursuant to Article 15(2) of Regulation No 17 and Article 65(3) of the ECSC Treaty* OJ [1998] C 9/3.

[181] *Guidelines on the method of setting fines imposed pursuant to Article 23(2)(1) of Regulation 1/2003* OJ [2006] C 210/2, available at ec.europa.eu/comm/competition/antitrust/legislation/fines.html.

[182] Ibid, para 38.

[183] See the Sentencing Reform Act 1984 and the US Sentencing Commission *Guidelines Manual*, available at www.ussc.gov/2006guid/TABCON06.htm.

[184] See ch 10, pp 400–404.   [185] *Fining Guidelines* OJ [2006] C 210/2, para 4.

[186] See eg Case s 100/80 *Musique Diffusion Française v Commission* [1983] ECR 1825, paras 105–106; Case C-289/04 P *Showa Denko KK v Commission* [2006] ECR I-5859, [2006] 5 CMLR 840, para 16.

introducing higher fines, where this is necessary for the effective enforcement of the competition rules[187].

The *Guidelines* of 2006 propose a two-step methodology when setting fines.

(A) Basic amount of the fine The Commission begins by setting a 'basic amount' for the fine, which is determined by reference to the value of the sales of the goods or services to which the infringement relates[188]. It is not necessary for the Commission to conduct a full definition of the relevant market for these purposes[189]. The basic amount will be related to a proportion of the value of such sales, depending on the degree of gravity of the infringement, multiplied by the number of years of infringement[190]. The gravity of the infringement is determined on a case-by-case basis[191]; as a general rule it will be set at a level of up to 30 per cent of the value of sales[192]. Hard-core cartel infringements are likely to be at the top end of the scale[193]. The amount determined as a result of the rules just mentioned will then be multiplied by the number of years of participation in the cartel[194]. Furthermore an amount of between 15 per cent and 25 per cent of the basic amount will be imposed as a sanction for participating in the infringement in the first place, a so-called 'entry fee' intended to act as an additional deterrent[195]. Clearly these rules can lead to enormous fines, in particular where a cartel has lasted for a long time: the Commission's Press Release in relation to the *Organic Peroxides* cartel suggested that it had lasted for 29 years, a very significant 'multiplier'[196]. However it should be recalled that Article 23(2) of the Regulation provides that a fine cannot exceed 10 per cent of an undertaking's worldwide turnover.

(B) Adjustments to the basic amount Having determined the basic amount of the fine, the Commission then takes into account various aggravating and mitigating circumstances[197]. Aggravating circumstances are set out in paragraph 28 of the *Guidelines* and include:

- The fact that an undertaking is a recidivist: the basic amount will be increased by up to 100 per cent for each past finding of an infringement of Article 81 or 82, whether by the Commission or an NCA[198]. The previous infringements do not have to have been in the same product market[199], and there is no limitation period for taking them into account[200]

---

[187] See eg Case C-213/02 *Dansk Rørindustri v Commission* [2005] ECR I-5425, [2005] 5 CMLR 796, paras 227–228; Case C-397/03 P *Archer Daniels Midland Co v Commission* [2006] ECR I-4429, [2006] 5 CMLR 230, paras 21–22.

[188] *Fining Guidelines* OJ [2006] C 210/2, paras 12–26.

[189] Case T-48/02 *Brouwerij Haacht NV v Commission* [2005] ECR II-5259, [2006] 4 CMLR 621, para 59.

[190] Ibid, para 19.   [191] Ibid, para 20.

[192] Ibid, para 21; the Commission adds that the particularities of a given case might mean that it would depart from the methodology in the *Guidelines*, including the 30 per cent figure: ibid, para 37.

[193] Ibid, para 23.   [194] Ibid, para 24.   [195] Ibid, para 25; see also para 7.

[196] Commission Press Release IP/03/1700, 10 December 2003.

[197] *Fining Guidelines* OJ [2006] C 210/2, paras 27–29.

[198] The ECJ has confirmed in Case C-3/06 P *Groupe Danone v Commission* [2007] ECR I-0000, [2007] 4 CMLR 701, that the Commission is entitled to treat recidivism as an aggravating circumstance where past infringers need to be induced to change their behaviour: see paras 26–29 of the judgment; there is no limitation period to considering past infringements (ibid, para 38), and an uplift can be applied for recidivism even if no fine was imposed on a previous occasion (ibid, para 41). It would appear to be the case that the fine could be increased for a past infringement even where a firm had blown the whistle on that occasion.

[199] Cases T-101/05 and T-111/05 *BASF AG v Commission* [2007] ECR II-000, para 64.   [200] Ibid, para 67.

- Refusal to cooperate with or obstruction of the Commission in its investigation[201]
- Acting as leader or instigator of the infringement.

Mitigating circumstances are set out in paragraph 29 and include:

- Early termination of infringing behaviour as soon as the Commission began its investigation (this does not apply to secret agreements or concerted practices, in particular cartels[202])
- Negligent, as opposed to intentional, infringements
- Having a limited role in the infringement
- Cooperating with the Commission outside the scope of the *Leniency Notice*
- Authorisation or encouragement of the infringement by public authorities or by legislation.

In exceptional cases the inability of an undertaking to pay a fine, to the point that its economic viability would be jeopardised, might be taken into account by the Commission[203]. The fact that an undertaking adopts a competition law compliance programme is not a factor that the Commission is obliged to take into account as an attenuating factor[204]. Nor is the Commission required to reduce a fine on the basis that a defendant has paid damages to the victims of its anti-competitive behaviour[205].

The principle of *ne bis in idem* prevents the same person from being fined more than once for the same unlawful conduct. The principle is subject to three cumulative conditions: the facts must be identical, the offender must be the same undertaking, and the legal interest protected must be the same[206]. It follows that the principle does not apply where a fine has been imposed, for example, in the US, since it does not relate to the same interest as that protected by EC law[207].

(iii) The Commission's *Leniency Notice*[208]

The detection and punishment of cartels is a major priority of competition authorities throughout the world[209]. Undertakings that participate in cartels are usually fully aware that their behaviour is unlawful and go to great lengths to maintain secrecy and to avoid

---

[201] See the *Bitumen* and *Professional Videotapes* decisions discussed at p 271 above.

[202] See eg Case T-329/01 *Archer Daniels Martin Co. v Commission* [2006] ECR II-3255, [2006] 5 CMLR 230, paras 272–287 in which the CFI upheld the Commission's refusal to recognise termination of participation in a secret cartel as an attenuating circumstance.

[203] *Fining Guidelines* OJ [2006] C 210/2, para 35.

[204] Case T-329/01 *Archer Daniels Midland Co v Commission* [2006] ECR II-3255, [2007] 4 CMLR 43, paras 299–302; Case T-59/02 *Archer Daniels Midland Co v Commission* [2006] ECR II-3627, para 359.

[205] Case T-59/02 *Archer Daniels Midland Co v Commission* [2006] ECR II-3627, para 354.

[206] Cases C-204/00 etc *Aalborg Portland and others v Commission* [2004] ECR I-123, [2005] 4 CMLR 251, para 338; see generally Wils 'The Principle of "Ne Bis in Idem" in EC Antitrust Enforcement: A Legal and Economic Analysis' (2003) 26(2) World Competition 131.

[207] See eg Case C-308/04 P *SGL Carbon AG v Commission* [2006] ECR I-5977, [2006] 5 CMLR 922, paras 26–39; Case C-289/04 P *Showa Denko KK v Commission* [2006] ECR I-5858, [2006] 5 CMLR 840, paras 50–63; Case T-329/01 *Archer Daniels Midland Co v Commission* [2006] ECR II-3255, [2007] 4 CMLR 43, (the *Sodium Gluconate* case), paras 290–295; Case T-59/02 *Archer Daniels Midland Co v Commission* [2006] ECR II-3627, [2006] 5 CMLR 1528 (the *Citric Acid* case), paras 61–73.

[208] See Wils 'Leniency in Antitrust Enforcement: Theory and Practice' (2007) 30(1) World Competition 25; for a global review see *Leniency Regimes: Jurisdictional comparisons* (eds Arquit, Buhart and Antoine) European Lawyer Reference 2007; Global Antitrust Leniency Manual (ed Mobley) Baker & McKenzie 2008; see also Botana 'Antitrust Enforcement and Deterrence of Collusive Behaviour: The Role of Leniency Programs' (2006/2007) 13(1) Columbia Journal of Law 47.

[209] See ch 13, pp 497–501.

detection. Competition authorities therefore face considerable difficulties in detecting cartels. A crucial tool in practice is to incentivise participants in cartels to 'blow the whistle' to the relevant competition authority or authorities. The Commission's policy is to allow total immunity – a fine of zero – to the first undertaking in a cartel to blow the whistle, and to impose lower fines than would otherwise be the case on undertakings that provide it with further evidence that enables it to proceed more effectively with the investigation of a case. The encouragement of whistleblowing has proved to be immensely successful in the US in prosecuting cartels[210]; the US policy can be accessed on the home page of the Department of Justice[211]. Nearly all of the cartel cases brought by the Commission in recent years began with a whistleblower[212]. However it should be noted that some major cases are brought on the Commission's own initiative: it is not dependent on whistleblowers[213]. The relationship between the level of penalties and the incidence of whistleblowing has been referred to earlier in this chapter in the discussion of settlements, where both 'virtuous' and 'vicious' circles were identified. It is important to point out that whistleblowing does not affect the liability of a whistleblower to pay damages to victims of a cartel as a matter of civil law[214].

The Commission first adopted a Notice on leniency in 1996[215] which was replaced in 2002[216]. A new Notice was published in the Official Journal in December 2006 setting out the Commission's current policy on this important topic; the new Notice is intended to provide greater transparency as to what is expected of undertakings when they apply for leniency; it also introduced some procedural innovations[217]. The Notice is in line with the principles of the European Competition Network's *Model Leniency Programme* which was adopted by the heads of the NCAs in September 2006[218]. After some introductory comments, Section II of the *Leniency Notice* explains the circumstances in which an undertaking may qualify for immunity from fines; Section III deals with the possibility of reduced fines; Section IV discusses ways of making 'corporate statements', including the possibility of doing so orally in order to avoid problems that might arise in civil litigation.

(A) Section I: introduction The Notice sets out the framework for the Commission to reward undertakings that are or have been members of secret cartels that cooperate with it in its investigation[219]. The Notice recognises two types of leniency: immunity

---

[210] Major cases in the US such as *Vitamins*, *Citric Acid* and *Sotheby's/Christies* all came to light as a result of whistleblowing.

[211] See www.usdoj.gov/atr/public/guidelines.

[212] In 2005 out of 5 decisions adopted by the Commission 3 started with a whistleblower, see the Commission's XXXVth *Report on Competition Policy* (2005), paras 174; in 2006 out of 7 decisions adopted by the Commission 5 started with a whistleblower, see the Commission's XXXVIth *Report on Competition Policy* (2006), para 8; in 2007 out of 8 decisions adopted by the Commission 6 started with a whistleblower.

[213] See eg *Flat Glass*, Commission decision of 28 November 2007, discussed at p 284 below.

[214] See Commission's *Leniency Notice* OJ [2002] C 45/3, [2002] 4 CMLR 906, para 31.

[215] OJ [1996] C 207/4, [1996] 5 CMLR 362.   [216] OJ [2002] C 45/3.

[217] *Notice on Immunity from fines and reduction of fines in cartel cases* OJ [2006] C 298/17, available at www.ec.europa.eu/comm/competition/cartels/legislation/leniency_legislation.html; for discussion of the 2006 Notice see Suurnäkki and Tierno Centella 'Commission adopts revised Leniency Notice to reward companies that report hard-core cartels' Commission *Competition Policy Newsletter*, Spring 2007, p 7.

[218] See p 284 below.

[219] Note that the Notice does not apply to cooperation in relation to vertical agreements, for example involving resale price maintenance; however para 29 of the *Fining Guidelines* (n 180 above) provide for reductions in fines for cooperation with the Commission 'outside the scope of the Leniency Notice'.

from fines and a reduction of fines. It states that immunity from fines may be justified where an undertaking makes a decisive contribution to the opening of an investigation or to the finding of an infringement[220]; a reduction of a fine may be justified where an undertaking provides the Commission with evidence that adds 'significant value' to that already in its possession[221]. The ECJ has held that a reduction under the leniency programme can be justified only where the conduct of the undertaking concerned demonstrates a genuine spirit of cooperation on its part[222]. The Commission acknowledges in the introduction to the *Leniency Notice* that the making of corporate statements ought not to expose undertakings to risks in civil litigation not experienced by undertakings that do not cooperate with it[223].

(B) Section II: immunity from fines Immunity from a fine will be granted to the first undertaking in a cartel to submit information to the Commission that will enable it to carry out an inspection or to find an infringement of Article 81 in connection with the cartel[224]; immunity will not be granted if the Commission already had sufficient evidence to proceed to an inspection or to a final decision[225]. The whistleblower must make a corporate statement to the Commission containing specified information such as a description of the cartel, the names, positions, office locations and, where necessary, home addresses of the individuals involved in the cartel and details of any other competition authorities that have been contacted as well as any other relevant evidence in the whistleblower's possession[226]. The whistleblower must comply with a series of conditions in order to qualify for immunity:

- Genuine, continuous and expeditious cooperation
- Termination of any involvement in the cartel, unless the Commission considers that continuing involvement might be useful for the preparation of inspections: if the whistleblower were to be absent from cartel meetings, for example, the other participants might guess what has happened and realise that inspections are imminent
- It must not have destroyed, falsified or concealed any relevant evidence when contemplating its application for immunity[227].

The *Leniency Notice* explains the procedure for making an application for immunity[228], including the so-called 'marker system' whereby an undertaking can contact the Commission and agree with it a date by when it will provide the evidence needed to pass the threshold for leniency. If the undertaking 'perfects' the marker by the agreed date its application will be deemed to have been made at the time of the original approach to the Commission, and will therefore rank higher in the queue of leniency applicants than an undertaking that made an application before the marker was perfected[229].

(C) Section III: reduction of fines An undertaking that does not qualify for immunity, for example because it was not the first to blow the whistle, may nevertheless qualify for a reduced fine where it provides evidence to the Commission 'which represents significant added value'[230]. Reductions in the range of 20 per cent to 50 per cent are available for such an undertaking[231]. The *Leniency Notice* explains the procedure for such cases[232].

[220] *Leniency Notice* OJ [2006] C 298/17, para 4.   [221] Ibid, para 5.
[222] Case C-301/04 P *Commission v SGL Carbon AG* [2006] ECR I-5915, [2006] 5 CMLR 877, paras 66–70.
[223] *Leniency Notice*, para 6.   [224] Ibid, para 8.   [225] Ibid, paras 10 and 11.   [226] Ibid, para 9.
[227] Ibid, para 12.   [228] Ibid, paras 14–22.   [229] Ibid, para 15.   [230] Ibid, paras 24 and 25.
[231] Ibid, para 26.   [232] Ibid, paras 27–30.

(D) Section IV: corporate statements The *Leniency Notice* discussed how corporate state-ments may be made[233], and makes specific provision for such statements to be oral rather than written[234]. The reason for this is the fear that, if an undertaking were to prepare a written corporate statement, this might be discoverable in the event of a treble damages action in the US: this might deter the undertaking from blowing the whistle at all, in which case the cartel might go undetected. An oral statement is rendered into writing by the Commission. As it is not a document of the whistleblower it cannot be discovered from it; and any attempt by a US court to demand that the Commission should hand its own document over would probably fail on public interest grounds.

(iv) Article 24: periodic penalty payments

Article 24 provides for the imposition of periodic penalty payments on undertakings, for example where they persist in an infringement of Article 81 or Article 82 even after a decision requiring it to end, or where they continue to fail to supply complete and accur-ate information in response to a Commission request. The fines are much higher than under Regulation 17: up to 5 per cent of an undertaking's daily turnover. In July of 2006 the Commission adopted a decision that Microsoft had failed to comply with its obliga-tion to supply full interoperability information in accordance with its decision of March 2004 and imposed a fine of €280.5 million, €1.5 million per day from 16 December 2005 to 20 June 2006[235]. This was followed by a second fine, of €899 million, in February 2008 for charging unreasonable prices for access to interface documentation[236].

(G) Chapter VII: limitation periods

(i) Article 25: limitation periods for the imposition of penalties

Article 25, which replaces the rules formerly contained in Regulation 2988/74[237], estab-lishes limitation periods for action on the part of the Commission against competition law infringements: the period is three years in the case of provisions concerning requests for information or the conduct of inspections, and five years in the case of all other infringements. The burden of proving the duration of an infringement of the competition rules – and therefore of demonstrating that the limitation period has not expired – rests with the Commission[238]. The Commission sometimes addresses a decision to an under-taking, stating that it has been in a cartel, but does not impose a fine because of the limita-tion rule. The Commission's interest in doing so includes that the undertaking might be sued for damages on a follow-on basis in the courts of a Member State: the fact that the Commission no longer has the ability to impose a fine does not preclude the possibility that, under the relevant civil law, a damages claim might still be possible. However the Commission must explain its reason for addressing the decision to the undertaking[239].

(ii) Article 26: limitation period for the enforcement of penalties

Article 26 provides that the limitation period for enforcing fines and periodic pen-alty payments is five years. In *Ferrière Nord SpA v Commission*[240] the CFI held that the

---

[233] Ibid, paras 31–35.   [234] Ibid, para 32.   [235] Commission Decision of 12 July 2006.
[236] Commission Decision of 27 February 2008.   [237] OJ [1974] L 319/1.
[238] Case T-120/04 *Peróxidos Orgánicos SA v Commission* [2006] ECR II-4441, [2007] 4 CMLR 153, para 52.
[239] See p 252 above.   [240] Case T-153/04 [2006] ECR II-3889, [2006] 5 CMLR 1416.

Commission was unable to enforce a fining decision against Ferrière Nord as it had become time-barred under Regulation 2988/74, the predecessor of Article 26; the ECJ set this judgment aside on the ground that the Commission had not committed an 'act' capable of judicial review[241].

(H) Chapter VIII: hearings and professional secrecy

Articles 26 and 27 deal respectively with hearings and with professional secrecy.

(i) Article 27: hearing of the parties, complainants and others

(A) The provisions of Article 27 Article 27(1) provides that, before decisions are taken under Articles 7 and 8 (infringement and interim measures decisions) or under Articles 23 and 24 (fines and periodic penalty payments), the undertakings which are the subject of the proceedings have a right to be heard. The Commission may base its decisions only on objections on which the parties have had an opportunity to comment. Complainants 'shall be closely associated with the proceedings'.

Article 27(2) provides that the rights of the defence shall be fully respected during the Commission's proceedings, including the right to have access to the Commission's file. Article 27(2) of the Regulation makes clear that there is no right of access to confidential information, nor to internal documents of the Commission and the NCAs and correspondence within the ECN. Article 27(3) provides that the Commission may hear third parties with a sufficient interest, and Article 27(4) provides that, where the Commission intends to close a case subject to binding commitments, pursuant to Article 9, or to make a finding of inapplicability, under Article 10, it must publish the fact of its intention and allow third parties an opportunity to be heard.

(B) The conduct of proceedings Commission Regulation 773/2004[242] ('the Implementing Regulation') explains how and when the Commission may initiate proceedings, and how the right to be heard is exercised, in competition cases. Specifically it sets out the rules in relation to the statement of objections that must be sent to the parties and the right to be heard, and confers upon the parties a right to an oral hearing; third parties with a sufficient interest may also be heard[243]. The Regulation sets out the rules for the oral hearing, which is conducted by a Hearing Officer: a Commission decision of May 2001 sets out the terms of reference of the Hearing Officers in competition cases[244]. The Regulation also explains how confidential information is to be dealt with during proceedings, and how disputes should be resolved.

The Commission's *Notice on the rules for access to the Commission's file*[245] explains its current policy on access to the file in the context of the relevant Community legislation,

[241] Case C-516/06 P *Commission v Ferriere Nord SpA* [2007] ECR II-000, paras 27–34.
[242] OJ [2004] L 123/18.
[243] They are also entitled to receive a non-confidential version of the statement of objections: Cases T-213/01 and T214/01 *Österreichische Postsparkasse AG v Commission* [2006] ECR II-1601, [2007] 4 CMLR 506.
[244] OJ [2001] L 162/21, available at www.europa.eu.intcomm/competition/antitrust/others; on the role of the Hearing Officer see Durande and Williams 'The practical impact of the exercise of the right to be heard: A special focus on the effect of Oral Hearings and the role of the Hearing Officers' Commission *Competition Policy Newsletter*, Summer 2005, 22.
[245] OJ [2005] C 325/7; this Notice replaces an earlier one, OJ [1997] C 27/3.

including the Modernisation Regulation and the Implementing Regulation and the jurisprudence of the Community courts. Access to the file for competition law purposes is subject to different criteria and exceptions from the right of access to Community documents under Regulation 1049/2001[246]. The *Notice on access to the file* explains who is entitled to access to the file; which documents can be accessed; and when access may be granted. The provision of documents to complainants and other third parties is also discussed, as is the procedure for implementing access to the file. Access may be given to the paper file, but this may also be effected by DVD or by CD-ROM.

Where the Commission is in possession of documents that might provide exculpatory evidence for a defendant undertaking, it must make them available, although a failure to do so would only lead to the annulment of the Commission's decision if their availability would have led to a different outcome[247]. In *Salzgitter v Commission*[248] the ECJ confirmed that the Commission may attach probative value to evidence provided by a source that insists on anonymity.

The ECJ has established that undertakings are entitled to expect that competition law proceedings will be concluded within a reasonable period[249].

(C) A typical case In a typical cartel case[250] the Commission's procedure would be as follows:

- A whistleblower applies to the Commission for immunity from fines, or the Commission decides to start an investigation on its own initiative
- The Commission conducts surprise inspections
- The Commission considers the evidence it has obtained and sends requests for or requires further information
- The Commission issues statements of objections to the undertakings it considers to be in the cartel
- The undertakings submit written replies to the statements of objections
- An oral hearing is held[251]
- DG COMP prepares a draft decision
- The draft decision goes to the Commissioner for Competition
- The Advisory Committee is consulted on the draft decision
- The draft decision is seen by the College of Commissioners
- The College adopts the final decision.

(D) The position of complainants Various provisions in the Modernisation Regulation, including Article 27(3), acknowledge that third parties with a sufficient interest have

---

[246] OJ [2001] L 145/43; see the *Notice on access to the file*, para 2.

[247] See eg Case T-314/01 *Coöperatieve Verkoop- en Productievereniging van Aardappelmeel en Derivaten Avebe BA v Commission* [2006] ECR II-3085, [2007] 4 CMLR 9, paras 66–67 and the case-law cited therein.

[248] Case C-411/04 P, [2007] ECR I-965, [2007] 4 CMLR 682, paras 40–50.

[249] Case C-185/95 P *Baustahlgewebe v Commission* [1998] ECR I-8417; [1999] 4 CMLR 1203, paras 28–49; see similarly Cases C-105/04 and C-113/04 P *Nederlandse Federatieve Vereniging voor de Groothandel op Elektrontechnisch Gebied v Technische Unie BV v Commission* [2006] ECR I-8725, [2006] 5 CMLR 1257, paras 35–52.

[250] An Article 82 case would be very similar but, for obvious reasons, would not involve a whistleblower.

[251] In some cases undertakings waive their right to an oral hearing.

a right to participate in proceedings, although these rights are, of course, less than those of the undertakings accused of an infringement. Chapter IV of the Implementing Regulation[252] also deals with the handling of complaints, including the admissibility of complaints, the participation of complainants in proceedings, the rejection of complaints, and complainants' access to information. The Commission has also published a *Notice on the handling of complaints by the Commission under Articles 81 and 82 of the EC Treaty*[253]. Part II of the *Notice on Complaints* discusses the complimentary roles of public and private enforcement of the competition rules, pointing out the benefits for complainants, in some circumstances, to go to a court rather than a competition authority: for example only a court can award damages or determine the effect on a contract of the voidness provided for by Article 81(2)[254]. It also explains the provisions on case-allocation within the ECN, which should assist a complainant in deciding which public authority it would be sensible to approach if that is preferred to private litigation[255]. Part III of the *Notice on Complaints* explains in considerable detail how the Commission goes about handling complaints, and specifies the information that must be supplied on Form C, the form that must be used when making a complaint[256]. The Notice discusses the Commission's right to prioritise its enforcement efforts and to concentrate on cases that have a 'Community interest'[257]; the right of the Commission to do so has been clearly restated in a judgment early in 2008, *Scippecercola v Commission*[258]. The final part of the Notice explains the Commission's procedure when dealing with complaints, including the procedural rights of complainants and Commission decisions to reject complaints[259].

The Commission is entitled to make use of evidence provided by third parties on condition of their anonymity being maintained, although such evidence would not be sufficient in itself to sustain a finding of infringement but would have to be part of a body of evidence[260].

(ii) Article 28: professional secrecy

Article 28 contains two provisions: first, information collected under the Regulation may be used only for the purpose for which it was acquired; second, the Commission and the NCAs must not disclose information acquired or exchanged by them under the Regulation if that information is covered by an obligation of professional secrecy. Quite apart from the provisions of Article 28 of the Regulation, Article 287 of the Treaty itself imposes restrictions on the transmission of such information: Paragraph 28(a) of the Commission's *Notice on NCA cooperation* provides guidance on the practical application of Article 28.

(l) Chapter IX: exemption regulations

Article 29 of the Regulation provides power for the Commission and the NCAs to withdraw the benefit of block exemptions in individual cases: there were provisions to

---

[252] OJ [2004] L 123/18. [253] OJ [2004] C 101/65 [254] Ibid, para 16. [255] Ibid, paras 19–25.
[256] Ibid, paras 29–32. [257] Ibid, paras 41–45. [258] Case T-306/05 [2008] ECR II-000, paras 91–93.
[259] Ibid, paras 53–81.
[260] Case C-411/04 P *Salzgitter Mannesmann GmbH v Commission* [2007] ECR I-965, [2007] 4 CMLR 682, paras 47 and 50.

this effect in earlier Regulations, but these are repealed by Article 40 of the Modernisation Regulation in the light of the 'overarching' power conferred by Article 29.

(J) Chapter X: general provisions

(i) Article 30: publication of decisions

Article 30(1) requires the Commission to publish its decisions under Articles 7 to 10, 23 and 24, having regard to the legitimate interests of the parties in the protection of their business secrets.

(ii) Article 31: review by the Court of Justice

Article 31 provides that the Community Courts have unlimited jurisdiction to review decisions in which the Commission has imposed a fine or a periodic penalty payment.

(K) Chapter XI: transitional, amending and final provisions

Articles 35 to 42 contain transitional and final provisions.

(i) Article 34: transitional provisions

Article 34(1) provides that all existing notifications for an individual exemption to the Commission lapsed on 1 May 2004. Individual exemptions granted under Regulation 17 continue in force[261].

(ii) Article 35: designation of competition authorities of Member States

Article 35 requires Member States to designate the competition authority or authorities responsible for the application of Articles 81 and 82[262].

(iii) Articles 36–42: miscellaneous amendments

The provisions on the transport Regulations in Articles 36, 38, 39 and 41 have been overtaken by subsequent events[263]. Article 37 repeals the provisions of Regulation 2988/74 on limitation periods, since they are now dealt with by Articles 25 and 26. Article 40 of the Modernisation Regulation repeals the powers in earlier Regulations to enable the withdrawal of the benefit of block exemptions, since the power to do this is now conferred by Article 29[264], Article 42 is no longer significant.

(iv) Article 43: repeal of Regulations 17 and 141

Article 43(1) repeals Regulation 17, except in relation to conditions and obligations attached to individual exemptions already granted by the Commission[265]. Article 43(2) repeals Regulation 141, which had exempted the transport sector from Regulation 17[266].

(v) Article 44: Report on the application of the Modernisation Regulation

The Commission is required to report to the Parliament and the Council in 2009 on the functioning of the Regulation, in particular on Article 11(6) and Article 17, and assess whether it is appropriate to propose any revisions.

---

[261] See ch 4, pp 162–163. [262] See p 250 above. [263] See ch 23, pp 961–970.
[264] See p 281 above. [265] See ch 4, pp 162–163. [266] See ch 23, pp 961–970.

3. THE MODERNISATION REGULATION IN PRACTICE[267]

The adoption of the Modernisation Regulation was an extremely bold and imaginative moment in the evolution of competition policy in the EU. The European Commission now shares the task of enforcing the competition rules in the EC Treaty with the NCAs of the 27 Member States and with the national courts. The Commission and the NCAs together operate within the framework of the European Competition Network ('the ECN'). In the future Articles 81 and 82 will be applied with far greater frequency by the NCAs than by the Commission.

(A) The European Competition Network

The ECN does not have legal identity nor is it an international organisation as such. Rather it provides a framework within which the Commission and the NCAs discuss the sharing of work: for example which authority is best placed to handle a particular investigation. Information is exchanged between competition authorities within the framework of the ECN, as is experience gathered both in relation to actual cases and the development of policy. Members of the ECN are linked by a secure Intranet. The Commission takes the lead role in ensuring coherence in the application of the competition rules, in particular as a result of its examination of draft decisions of the NCAs in conjunction with its power to initiate its own proceedings, and thereby to suspend those of an NCA, under Article 11(6) of the Regulation. Information about the work of the ECN is obtainable from the website of DG COMP including, for example, the number of investigations under Articles 81 and 82 reported to the ECN and the proportion of them that had been started by an NCA on the one hand or the Commission on the other[268]. The Directors General of the NCAs meet once a year to discuss major policy issues within the ECN: this is the top level of the ECN framework. The so-called 'ECN Plenary' consisting of officials in the NCAs and the Commission meets four times a year. It has a number of working groups, for example on issues of cooperation, leniency, and sanctions, and it also has a number of sectoral sub-groups, for example on the liberal professions, energy, and financial services.

(B) Case-allocation under the Modernisation Regulation

The *Notice on NCA cooperation*[269] sets out the jurisdictional principles according to which cases should be allocated within the ECN[270]. An example of a case being reallocated from an NCA to the Commission is *iTunes*, where the OFT in the UK considered

---

[267] See DeKeyser and Gauer 'The new enforcement system for Articles 81 and 82 EC and the rights of defence' in *2004 Annual Proceedings of the Fordham Corporate Law Institute* (ed Hawk, Juris Publishing 2005), 549; DeKeyser and Jaspers 'A New Era of ECN Cooperation' (2007) 30(1) World Competition 3; Commission's *Report on Competition Policy 2006*, COM(2007)358 final, pp 86–89; Reichelt 'To what extent does the cooperation within the European Competition Network protect the rights of undertakings?'(2005) 42 Common Market Law Review 745; the Commission's *Annual Report on Competition Policy* also provides helpful detail on the operation of the ECN.

[268] See www.ec.europa.eu/comm/competition/ecn/index_en.html.

[269] OJ [2004] C 101/43. [270] Ibid, paras 5–15.

that the Commission was in a better position to consider a complaint by Which? (formerly the Consumers' Association) that Apple's iTunes service discriminated on price according to the user's country of residence, in particular since this gave rise to issues concerning the wider single market in Europe[271]. The Commission announced that Apple had agreed to equalise the prices of its downloads across Europe in January 2008[272]. Another interesting case is *Flat Glass*, where several NCAs cooperated with the Commission within the ECN, leading to the imposition by the Commission of fines totaling €488 million[273].

(C) 'Soft' convergence

An interesting by-product of the Modernisation Regulation and the establishment of the ECN has been the considerable amount of soft convergence that has taken place in relation to national competition laws and procedures. Although the Regulation did not explicitly require there to be convergence, the reality is that in many respects – for example the abolition of national systems of notification and individual exemption, the alignment of investigative procedures, the introduction of leniency programmes and of commitments procedures similar to those in Article 9 – national laws have been brought into alignment with those of the EC. Information about the reform of the competition laws of the Member States since the Modernisation Regulation came into force is available on the website of the ECN[274].

(D) Leniency

The work of the ECN in the area of leniency has been of particular importance. Its central role in the Commission's policy of detecting and penalising cartels has already been noted. It was recognised from the outset of the modernisation project that the existence of different leniency policies in different Member States, and the non-existence of such policies in some, presented real difficulties. Given that the success of a leniency policy depends on maximisation of the incentive of firms to come forward on a voluntary basis with information about a cartel, it is obvious that the more complex the rules are the less likely it is that a firm will blow the whistle. The Commission does not have the legal power to require Member States to adopt a leniency programme; nor can it dictate the content of any such programme. However, under the aegis of the ECN, 25 of the 27 NCAs now have a leniency programme[275], and the ECN has produced a *Model Leniency Programme* aimed at achieving soft harmonisation through convergence. The *Model Leniency Programme* has been endorsed by the heads of all the NCAs and is available on the ECN's website[276]. The ECN will conduct a review in 2008 to find out the extent to which convergence has in fact been achieved.

---

[271] OFT Press Release, 3 December 2004, available at www.oft.gov.uk/news/press/2004/itunes.

[272] Commission Press Release IP/08/22, 9 January 2008.

[273] Commission decision of 28 November 2007; see Commission Press Release IP/07/1781.

[274] See www.ec.europa.eu/comm/competition/ecn/index_en.html.

[275] The only two not to do so are Malta and Slovenia.

[276] See www.ec.europa.eu/comm/competition/ecn/index_en.html; for discussion see Gauer and Jaspers 'ECN Model Leniency Programme – a first step towards a harmonised leniency policy in the EU' Commission *Competition Policy Newsletter*, Spring 2007, p 35.

4. JUDICIAL REVIEW[277]

It is possible to bring an action before the CFI (and ultimately the ECJ on points of law) in respect of Commission decisions on competition matters; Article 232 of the Treaty deals with failures to act, Article 230 with actions for annulment and Article 229 with penalties. The Community Courts have exclusive competence to consider whether acts of the Commission are lawful or not[278]. Proceedings before the CFI must be completed within a reasonable time; reasonableness is tested by reference to the importance of the case for the person concerned, its complexity and the conduct of the applicant and the competent authorities[279].

(A) Article 232: failure to act

Under Article 232 it is possible to bring an action against the Commission where, in infringement of the Treaty, it has failed to act. The Commission must have been under a specific duty to carry out the act in question. An action may be brought only where the Commission has been required to act and has failed to do so within two months; the action itself must be brought within the following two months[280]. If an action for failure to act is commenced under Article 232 and the Commission subsequently performs the act required of it, the action becomes devoid of purpose and the CFI will not give a ruling on it[281]. Article 232 is sometimes invoked by complainants wishing to force the Commission to investigate complaints against undertakings suspected of infringing the competition rules[282].

Where the Commission is guilty of a failure to act, an undertaking that suffers damage in consequence may bring an action against the Commission for compensation under Article 288 EC; to date such actions in the context of the competition rules have failed, for example because the undertaking omitted to specify the damage it had suffered[283] or because it calculated damage in respect of an incorrect period[284].

(B) Article 230: action for annulment

Under Article 230 it is possible to bring an action to have various 'acts' of the Commission annulled. Proceedings must be commenced within two months of the applicant hearing

---

[277] See Kerse and Khan *EC Antitrust Procedure* (Sweet & Maxwell, 5th ed, 2005), ch 8; Bailey 'Scope of Judicial Review Under Article 81 EC' (2004) 41 Common Market Law Review 1328; Vesterdorf 'Judicial Review in EC Competition Law: Reflections on the Role of the Community Courts in the EC System of Competition Law Enforcement' (2005) 1(2) Competition Policy International 3.

[278] See Case C-344/98 *Masterfoods* [2000] ECR I-11369, [2001] 4 CMLR 449.

[279] Case C-185/95 P *Baustahlgewebe GmbH v Commission* [1998] ECR I-8417, [1999] 4 CMLR 1203; the fine was reduced by €50,000 in this case because of the delay in the proceedings.

[280] Article 232(2); time-limits are applied strictly by the CFI: see Case T-12/90 *Bayer v Commission* [1991] ECR II-219, [1993] 4 CMLR 30, paras 14, 16 and 46.

[281] Case T-28/90 *Asia Motor France v Commission* [1992] ECR II-2285, [1992] 5 CMLR 431, paras 34–38.

[282] On the position of complainants see pp 280–281 above.

[283] Case T-64/89 *Automec Srl v Commission* [1990] ECR II-367, [1991] 4 CMLR 177.

[284] Case T-28/90 *Asia Motor France v Commission* [1992] ECR I-2285, [1992] 5 CMLR 431, paras 48–51.

of the act in question[285]. Where an action succeeds in part only, Article 231 enables the unlawful parts of a decision to be severed and annulled, leaving the remainder intact. Four issues in particular need consideration: who may sue; what 'acts' may be challenged; on what grounds an action may be brought; and whether damages are available once a decision has been annulled.

(i) Standing

Apart from Member States and the Council, Article 230(4) provides that any undertaking may challenge a decision addressed to it or to another person if it is of 'direct and individual concern' to it. This clearly entitles third parties in some situations to sue. In *Metro v Commission*[286] the ECJ confirmed that a complainant under Article 3(2) of Regulation 17 (Article 7(2) of the Modernisation Regulation) could proceed under Article 230[287]; if one applicant has standing, it is not necessary for other applicants concerned in the same application do so[288]. It is presumably the case that in appropriate circumstances a third party who has not actually complained under the relevant Regulation could do so. In some cases however the applicant's interest may be altogether too vague to give standing[289]. The recipients of adverse decisions may themselves bring an action under Article 230, and their right to do so is not limited to cases in which fines have been imposed.

(ii) Acts

It is not only decisions, but other 'acts' which may be challenged under Article 230. Formal decisions of the Commission applying Articles 81 and 82 of course can be challenged. In *Coca-Cola Co v Commission*[290] the CFI held that it is settled law that any measure which produces binding legal effects such as to affect the interest of an applicant by bringing about a distinct change in its legal position is an act or decision which may be the subject of an action under Article 230[291]. In *IBM v Commission*[292] the ECJ held that a statement of objections could not normally be challenged, because it was simply a preliminary step in the formal procedure[293]. In *BAT v Commission*[294]

---

[285] Article 230(5); see n 280 above on the CFI's approach to time-limits.

[286] Case 26/76 [1977] ECR 1875, [1978] 2 CMLR 1.

[287] See also Case 43/85 *ANCIDES v Commission* [1987] ECR 3131, [1988] 4 CMLR 821; a third party successfully challenged the grant of an individual exemption in Cases T-528/93 etc *Métropole v Commission* [1996] ECR II-649, [1996] 5 CMLR 386.

[288] Case T-306/05 *Scippacercola v Commission* [2008] ECR II-000, para 71.

[289] See eg Case 246/81 *Bethell v Commission* [1982] ECR 2277, [1982] 3 CMLR 300; Case C-70/97 P *Kruidvat BVBA v Commission* [1998] ECR I-7183, [1999] 4 CMLR 68.

[290] Joined Cases T-125/97 and T-127/97 [2000] ECR II-1733, [2000] 5 CMLR 467.

[291] The CFI cited for this proposition the judgments in Case 60/81 *IBM v Commission* [1981] ECR 2639, [1981] 3 CMLR 635, para 9; Joined Cases C-68/94 and C-30/95 *France v Commission* [1998] ECR I-1375, [1998] 4 CMLR 829, para 62; and Case T-87/95 *Assuriazioni Generali v Commission* [1999] ECR II-203, [2000] 4 CMLR 312, para 37.

[292] Case 60/81 [1981] ECR 2639, [1981] 3 CMLR 635.

[293] See similarly Cases T-10/92 etc *SA Cimenteries CBR v Commission* [1992] ECR II-2667, [1993] 4 CMLR 259; Cases T-377/00 etc *Philip Morris International Inc v Commission* [2003] 1 CMLR 676; Case T-48/03 *Schneider Electric v Commission*, order of 31 January 2006 [2006] ECR II-111, which held that a Commission decision under the ECMR to take a case into Phase II is not susceptible to judicial review: an appeal to the ECJ was dismissed in Case C-188/06 P, 9 March 2007; see also Case C-516/06 P *Commission v Ferriere Nord SpA* [2007] ECR II-000: no Commission act capable of judicial review.

[294] Cases 142, 156/84 [1987] ECR 4487, [1988] 4 CMLR 24; see also Case 210/81 *Demo-Studio Schmidt v Commission* [1983] ECR 3045, [1984] 1 CMLR 63.

the ECJ held that letters from the Commission to two complainants, finally rejecting their complaints, were acts capable of challenge under Article 230. The CFI held in the *Omni-Partijen Akkoord* judgments[295] that a letter from the Commissioner responsible for competition policy to a Member State that was purely factual in nature produced no legal effects and could not be challenged under Article 230. Mere silence on the part of a Community institution cannot produce binding legal effects unless express provision to this effect is made for it in Community law[296].

(iii) Grounds of review

The Community Courts must assess the legality of the Commission's decision according to the grounds of review specified in Article 230(1). The Commission may be challenged on grounds of:

lack of competence, infringement of an essential procedural requirement, infringement of this Treaty or of any rule of law relating to its application, or misuse of powers.

To some extent these grounds overlap with one another, and their cumulative effect is to provide a basis of review which is not dissimilar to the position in the administrative law of the UK. Of particular significance will be a failure by the Commission to give a fair hearing[297]; a failure to articulate properly the reasoning behind its decision[298]; and a failure to base a decision on adequate evidence[299]. The Commission is not required to set out in its decision exhaustively all the evidence available; it is sufficient if it refers to the conclusive evidence[300].

The Community Courts have tended to review the decisions of the Commission with a degree of self-restraint, having due regard to the margin of appreciation enjoyed by the Commission when making complex technical and economic assessments[301]. The position is succinctly summed up in the judgment of the CFI in *Microsoft Corpn v Commission*[302] where it said that the review carried out by the Community Courts:

is necessarily limited to checking whether the relevant rules on procedure and on stating reasons have been complied with, whether the facts have been adequately stated and whether there has been any manifest error of assessment or a misuse of powers...

[I]n so far as the Commission's decision is the result of complex technical appraisals, those appraisals are in principle subject to only limited review by the Court, which means that the Community Courts cannot substitute their own assessment of matters of fact for the Commission's.

---

[295] Cases T-113/89 etc *Nefarma v Commission* [1990] ECR II-797.

[296] Cases T-189/95 etc *Service pour le Groupement d'Acquisitions v Commission* [1999] ECR II-3587, [2001] 4 CMLR 215, paras 26–29.

[297] See eg Case 17/74 *Transocean Marine Paint Association v Commission* [1974] ECR 1063, [1974] 2 CMLR 459 where the members of the association were not given an opportunity to be heard on the conditions which the Commission intended to attach to an individual exemption.

[298] See eg Case 73/74 *Groupement des Fabricants des Papiers Peints de Belgique v Commission* [1975] ECR 1491, [1976] 1 CMLR 589 where the Commission failed to explain the mechanism whereby the agreement in question could affect inter-state trade.

[299] See eg Case 41/69 *ACF Chemiefarma v Commission* [1970] ECR 661, [1970] CMLR 43 where the Commission's decision was partially annulled for lack of evidence.

[300] Case T-2/89 *Petrofina SA v Commission* [1991] ECR II-1087.

[301] See eg Case 42/84 *Remia BV and Verenigde Bedrijven and Nutricia v Commission* [1985] ECR 2545, [1987] 1 CMLR 1, para 34; Cases 142/84 and 156/84 *BAT and Reynolds v Commission* [1987] ECR 4487, [1988] 4 CMLR 24, para 62.

[302] Case T-201/04 [2007] ECR II-000.

The Community courts must not only establish whether the evidence put forward is factually accurate, reliable and consistent but must also determine whether that evidence contains all the relevant data that must be taken into consideration in appraising a complex situation and whether it is capable of substantiating the conclusions drawn from it[303].

However, within the limits of the review that it may carry out under Article 230, the CFI has been prepared to exercise its power of review of the substance of Commission decisions in a comprehensive and exacting manner. This is exemplified by a series of judgments rendered by the CFI on the application of the EC Merger Regulation: *Airtours v Commission*[304], *Schneider Electric v Commission*[305] and *Tetra Laval v Commission*[306] at a time when considerable disquiet was being expressed about the fact that the Commission had the combined powers to investigate and prohibit mergers. In each case the CFI engaged in an exhaustive review of the substantive as well as the procedural propriety of the Commission's decision and, again in each case, annulled the decision. These cases, as well as the later judgment in *General Electric v Commission*[307], demonstrate that the Commission must provide adequate reasoning in its decisions, based on accurate and persuasive evidence; the margin of appreciation accorded to the Commission in competition cases will not prevent effective judicial review by the CFI.

(iv) Actions for damages

In the event that the CFI annuls a decision of the Commission under Article 288 EC it may be possible for the successful applicants to bring an action for damages for any losses they have suffered as a result of the unlawful decision. This has occurred in a case under the EC Merger Regulation[308]; the case is on appeal to the ECJ[309]. A claim for damages was rejected in *SELEX v Commission*[310].

(C) Article 229: penalties

Under Article 229 the CFI has unlimited jurisdiction in respect of penalties imposed by the Commission. Article 31 of the Modernisation Regulation provides that the Community Courts may cancel, reduce or increase fines or periodic penalties imposed. In the exercise of its unlimited jurisdiction the Courts may review a decision in its entirety – on factual as well as legal grounds – and many of its judgments have dealt exhaustively with the facts of the case. When the CFI finds that there is a factual error in the Commission's assessment it will not hesitate to adjust the fine. This can occur, for example, where the CFI considers that the Commission has exaggerated the duration of an undertaking's participation in a cartel[311] or has wrongly attributed to an undertaking the role of instigator or ringleader of a cartel[312]. The CFI will also make adjustments to fines where it feels that an undertaking has been the victim of unequal treatment

[303] Ibid, paras 87–88.   [304] Case T-342/99 [2002] ECR II-2585, [2002] 5 CMLR 317.
[305] Case T-310/01 [2002] ECR II-4071, [2003] 4 CMLR 768.
[306] Case T-5/02 [2002] ECR II-4381, [2002] 5 CMLR 1182.
[307] Case T-210/01 [2005] ECR II-5575, [2006] 4 CMLR 686.
[308] Case T-351/03 *Schneider Electric SA v Commission*, judgment of 11 July 2007.
[309] Case C-440/07 *Commission v Schneider Electric SA*, not yet decided.
[310] Case T 186/05, Order of 29 August 2007.
[311] See eg Case T-44/00 etc. *Mannesmannröhren-Werke AG v Commission* [2004] ECR II-2223.
[312] Case T-15/02 *BASF v Commission* [2006] ECR II-497, [2006] 5 CMLR 27, paras 280–464.

compared with other members of the same cartel[313]. The CFI has not actively sought to substitute its own opinion on the level of the fine for that of the Commission, where the Commission has a margin of appreciation[314]. However it is important to understand that the CFI has the power to increase, as well as to decrease the level of a fine, and that it has on a few occasions done so[315].

(D) Accelerated procedure

An important development for the way in which cases are handled by the CFI is the introduction of the so-called 'accelerated procedure' which entered into force on 1 February 2001[316]. This procedure enables the CFI to expedite the hearing and determination of appeals and was used to dramatic effect in *Schneider Electric v Commission*[317] and *Tetra Laval v Commission*[318].

(E) Interim measures

It is possible to apply to the CFI for interim measures suspending the operation of a Commission decision pending an appeal. Three conditions must be fulfilled in order for interim relief to be granted: first, the applicant must establish a *prima facie* case that the Commission's assessment is unlawful; secondly, it must demonstrate the urgency of interim measures to prevent it from suffering serious and irreparable damage; and thirdly it must explain why the balance of interests favours the adoption of such measures. Examples of cases in which interim measures have been granted are *Magill*[319]; *Atlantic Container Line AB v Commission*[320]; *Bayer v Commission*[321]; and *Van den Bergh Foods Ltd v Commission*[322]. In cases where there is an imminent risk of severe and lasting harm to one or more of the parties, the CFI may suspend the operation of a Commission decision *ex parte*, pending the outcome of the proceedings for interim relief; this happened, for example, in *NDC Health/IMS Health: Interim Measures*[323].

---

[313] See eg Cases T-109/02 etc *Bolloré SA v Commission* [2007] ECR II-000 where the fine on Arjo Wiggins Appleton was reduced by €33 million as a result of unequal treatment.

[314] See ch 13, pp 504–505.

[315] See eg Cases T-101/05 and T-111/05 *BASF AG v Commission* [2007] ECR II-000, paras 212–223 where the fine on BASF was marginally increased.

[316] OJ [2000] L 322/4; see further ch 21, pp 882–883.

[317] Case T-310/01 [2002] ECR II-4071, [2003] 4 CMLR 768.

[318] Case T-5/02 [2002] ECR II-4381, [2002] 5 CMLR 1182.

[319] Cases 76/89 R etc *Radio Telefis Eireann v Commission* [1989] ECR 1141, [1989] 4 CMLR 749; the appeal was unsuccessful in this case: see Cases T-69/89 etc *RTE v Commission* [1991] ECR II-485, [1991] 4 CMLR 586, upheld by the ECJ Cases 241/91 P etc *RTE and ITP v Commission* [1995] ECR I-743, [1995] 4 CMLR 718; see further ch 19, pp 787–788.

[320] Case T-395/94 R [1995] ECR II-595, upheld on Case C-149/95 P R [1995] ECR I-2165, [1997] 5 CMLR 167; the appeal in this case was mostly unsuccessful: Case T-395/94 *Atlantic Container Line AB v Commission* [2002] ECR II-875, [2002] 4 CMLR 1008.

[321] Case T-41/98 R [1997] ECR II-381; Bayer's appeal in this case was successful: see Case T-41/96, [2001] 4 CMLR 126; the CFI's judgment was upheld on appeal to the ECJ, Cases C-2/01 P and C-3/01 P *Commission v Bayer* [2004] ECR I-23, [2004] 4 CMLR 653.

[322] Case T-65/98 R [1998] ECR II-2641, [1998] 5 CMLR 475.

[323] Case T-184/01 R *IMS Health v Commission* [2001] ECR II-3193, [2002] 4 CMLR 58, upheld on appeal Case C-481/01 P R [2002] ECR I-3401, [2002] 5 CMLR 44.

8

Articles 81 and 82: private enforcement in the courts of Member States

CHAPTER CONTENTS

1. INTRODUCTION[1]

Chapter 7 was concerned with the public enforcement of Articles 81 and 82 by the European Commission and the national competition authorities ('the NCAs'). This chapter discusses the private enforcement of the competition rules, that is to say the situation where litigants take their disputes to a domestic court or, quite often, to arbitration.

Historically within the EU public enforcement of competition law has been infinitely more important than private enforcement[2]. However the competition authorities in the EU have limited resources and they are unable to investigate every alleged infringement of the competition rules. Private enforcement can therefore be an important complement to their activities[3]. The Commission has for a long time been eager that Articles 81

---

[1] See generally Jones *Private Enforcement of Antitrust Law in the EU, UK and USA* (Oxford University Press, 1999); *European Competition Law Annual 2001: Effective Private Enforcement of EC Antitrust Law* (eds Ehlermann and Atanasiu, 2003); Kerse and Khan *EC Antitrust Procedure* (Sweet & Maxwell, 5th ed, 2005), ch 5, paras 5-054–5-068; Komninos *EC Private Antitrust Enforcement: Decentralised Application of EC Competition Law by National Courts* (Hart Publishing, 2007); Bellamy and Child *European Community Law of Competition* (Oxford University Press, 6th ed, 2008, eds Roth and Rose), paras 14.042–14.142; *Private Antitrust Litigation* (Global Competition Review, 2008, ed Mobley).

[2] See Jones *Private Enforcement of Antitrust Law in the EU, UK and USA* (Oxford University Press, 1999) who estimates that approximately 90 per cent of all antitrust cases in the US involve private rather than public action, and that as many as 2,000 cases have been brought in a single year (ibid, p 79); however this figure includes a large number of follow-on actions pursuant to earlier public enforcement, so that the contrast is not as great as these figures may suggest.

[3] For a study of the complementary role of damages actions in the US see Lande and Davis *Report of the American Institute's Private Enforcement Project: Benefits From Private Antitrust Enforcement: An Analysis of Forty Cases* (American Antitrust Institute, 2007).

and 82 should be applied more frequently in national courts, thereby relieving it of some of the burden of enforcement. Statements to this effect can be found more than twenty years ago[4]. Commissioner Monti reaffirmed the Commission's desire for more private enforcement in a speech to the Sixth EU Competition Law and Policy Workshop in Florence in June 2001[5]. One of the driving forces behind Regulation 1/2003 ('the Modernisation Regulation') was the Commission's desire that national courts and NCAs should share with it the task of enforcing the competition rules, thereby enabling the Commission to concentrate its resources on pursuing the most serious infringements of the law[6]. Articles 6, 15, and 16 of the Modernisation Regulation contain important provisions dealing respectively with the powers of national courts, cooperation between national courts and the Commission and the uniform application of Community competition law. These provisions, and the accompanying Commission *Notice on the co-operation between the Commission and the courts of the EU Member States in the application of Articles 81 and 82 EC*[7] ('the *Co-operation Notice*'), are incorporated into the text that follows. The Modernisation Regulation and the *Co-operation Notice* are silent on the subject of arbitration[8].

A study published in August 2004, usually referred to as the *Ashurst report*[9], was carried out for the Commission to identify and analyse the obstacles to successful damages actions in the Member States based on infringements of competition law. The Report concluded that the picture was one of 'astonishing diversity and total underdevelopment'; on the latter point the Report found only 60 or so cases leading to a judgment on damages, 28 of which had actually led to an award of damages[10]. These figures to some extent misrepresent the number of damages actions that have been brought, since it is well known that many cases are settled out-of-court on the basis of confidentiality[11]; nevertheless the *Ashurst Report* did highlight numerous obstacles to private enforcement of the competition rules. This led the Commission to publish a Green Paper in December 2005, *Damages actions for breach of the EC antitrust rules*[12], the purpose of which was to identify the main obstacles to a more efficient system of damages claims and to set out different options to promote more such claims; this was followed in

---

[4] See eg the Commission's XIIIth *Report on Competition Policy* (1983), point 217.

[5] The speech is available at www.europa.eu.int/comm/competition/speeches; see further *European Competition Law Annual 2001: Effective Private Enforcement of EC Antitrust Law* (Hart Publishing, 2003, eds Ehlermann and Atanasiu); for a contrary view, arguing that 'public antitrust enforcement is inherently superior to private enforcement', see Wils 'Should Private Antitrust Enforcement Be Encouraged in Europe?' (2003) 26(3) World Competition 473–488 and Wils 'Should Private Antitrust Enforcement be Encouraged', in ch 4 of his book *Principles of European Antitrust Enforcement* (Hart Publishing, 2005).

[6] See Recitals 3 and 7 of the Modernisation Regulation.   [7] OJ [2004] C 101/4.

[8] On arbitration see pp 317–318 below.

[9] Study on the conditions of claims for damages in case of infringement of EC competition rules, August 2004, available at www.ec.europa.eu/comm/competition/antitrust/others/actions_for_damages/study.html.

[10] Ibid, p 1; there have been a few examples of awards of damages in competition law cases since the Ashurst Report: see eg judgment of the District Court of Dortmund of April 2004 (13 O 55/02) awarding damages of €1.6 million to August Storck KG against Hoffmann-La Roche following the Commission's decision in the *Vitamins* case; Case 85/2005 *Conduit Europe v Telefónica*, judgment of the Commercial Court of Madrid of 11 November 2005, awarding damages of €639,000 for refusal to supply contrary to Article 82.

[11] See eg Rodger 'Private Enforcement of Competition Law, the Hidden Story: Competition Law Litigation Settlements 2000–2005' (2008) 29 ECLR 96.

[12] COM(2005) 672 final, 19.12.2005, available at www.ec.europa.eu/comm/competition/antitrust/actionsdamages; see also the accompanying Staff Working Paper which contains a rich source of research material.

April 2008 by a White Paper bearing the same title.[12a] The Green and White Papers are discussed in the final section of this chapter; so too is a Discussion Paper produced by the Office of Fair Trading in the UK in April 2007, *Private actions in competition law: effective redress for consumers and business* and the OFT's subsequent recommendations to the Government in November 2007[13].

Section 2 of this chapter will deal with actions for an injunction and/or damages based on infringements of Article 81 and/or 82 EC. Section 3 deals with damages actions in the UK courts including, specifically, so-called 'follow-on' actions for damages in the UK Competition Appeal Tribunal under section 47A of the Competition Act 1998. Section 4 deals with the use of competition law not as a 'sword', where the claimant's cause of action is based on an infringement of competition law, but rather as a 'shield', that is to say as a defence, for example to an action for breach of contract or infringement of an intellectual property right. Section 5 contains a brief discussion of issues that can arise where competition law disputes are referred to arbitration rather than to a court for resolution. Section 6 discusses the options for reform that are currently under consideration in the EU and the UK.

2. ACTIONS FOR AN INJUNCTION AND/OR DAMAGES

(A) Is there a right to damages under Articles 81 and 82?

Articles 81 and 82 are directly applicable and produce direct effects: they give rise to rights and obligations which national courts have a duty to safeguard and enforce[14]. However until 2001 there had not been a judgment of the ECJ dealing specifically with the question of whether Member States have an obligation, as a matter of Community law, to provide a remedy in damages where harm has been inflicted as a result of an infringement of the competition rules. The issue is particularly important given that the Commission has no power to award damages, although it may be able to encourage a defendant to compensate its victims in return for a reduction in its fine[15]. The principles of non-discrimination and full effectiveness ('*effet utile*')[16], the judgment of the ECJ in *Francovich v Italy*[17] and the opinion of Advocate General van Gerven in *HJ Banks v British Coal Corpn*[18] all pointed towards the possibility of an action for damages; and the courts in the UK had assumed, in several cases, that such an action was

---

[12a] COM(2008) 154 final, 2.4.2008.

[13] OFT 916, available at www.oft.gov.uk/shared_oft/reports/comp_policy/oft916.pdf.

[14] Case 127/73 *BRT v SABAM* [1974] ECR 51, [1974] 2 CMLR 238, para 16; Case C-453/99 *Courage Ltd v Crehan* [2001] ECR I-6297, [2001] 5 CMLR 1058, para 23.

[15] See eg Nintendo Commission Decision of 30 October 2002, OJ [2003] L 255/33, paras 440–441.

[16] See Case 106/77 *Simmenthal* [1978] ECR 629, [1978] 3 CMLR 263, para 16; Case 158/80 *REWE v Hauptzollamt Kiel* [1981] ECR 1805, [1982] 1 CMLR 449, para 44; Case 199/82 *Amministrazione delle Finanze dello Stato v San Giorgio* [1983] ECR 3595, [1985] 2 CMLR 658; Case C-213/89 *Factortame* [1990] ECR I-2433, [1990] 3 CMLR 1, para 19.

[17] Cases C-6/90 and 9/90 [1991] ECR I-5357, [1993] 2 CMLR 66; see also Case C-5/94 *R v Ministry of Agriculture, Fisheries and Food, ex p Hedley Lomas* [1996] ECR I-2553, [1992] 2 CMLR 391; Cases C-178/94 etc, *Dillenkofer v Germany* [1996] ECR I-4845, [1996] 3 CMLR 469.

[18] Case C-128/92 [1994] ECR I-1209, [1994] 5 CMLR 30; for comment on this case see Friend 'Enforcing the ECSC Treaty in National Courts' (1995) 20 EL Rev 59.

available[19]. In 2001 the ECJ's judgment in *Courage Ltd v Crehan*[20] clarified the position, emphatically establishing a right to damages. A subsequent judgment of the ECJ in 2006, *Manfredi*[21], was equally emphatic.

(B) *Courage Ltd v Crehan*

In *Courage Ltd v Crehan* the ECJ held that:

The full effectiveness of Article 81 of the Treaty and, in particular, the practical effect of the prohibition laid down in Article 81(1) would be put at risk if it were not open to any individual to claim damages for loss caused to him by a contract or by conduct liable to restrict or distort competition.

Indeed the existence of such a right strengthens the working of the Community competition rules and discourages agreements or practices, which are frequently covert, which are liable to restrict or distort competition. From that point of view, actions for damages before the national courts can make a significant contribution to the maintenance of effective competition in the Community[22].

The judgment in *Courage Ltd v Crehan* was a landmark in the private enforcement of Articles 81 and 82. It was a particularly striking case in that the claimant, Crehan, was not, for example, a customer of a cartel seeking damages for harm inflicted by a horizontal agreement the object of which was to restrict competition. Rather Crehan was himself party to a vertical agreement for the supply of beer by a brewer to him. At most the agreement was one that restricted competition by effect rather than by object, and, as a co-contractor, it was arguable that Crehan should not be able to recover damages as a result of losses caused by an unlawful agreement for which he was himself partly responsible. In English law there is a rule that one party to an agreement cannot recover damages from another party if they are both equally responsible for it ('*in pari delicto*')[23]. The ECJ's view was that there should not be an absolute bar to a person in the position of Crehan bringing an action[24]: the national court should take into account matters such as the economic and legal context in which the parties find themselves and the respective bargaining power and conduct of the two parties to the contract[25]. Of particular importance would be whether a person in the position of Crehan found himself in a markedly weaker position than a brewer such as Courage, so as seriously to compromise or even eliminate his freedom to negotiate the terms of the contract and his capacity to avoid the loss or reduce its extent[26]. A further point was that, in a situation

---

[19] See p 299 below.

[20] Case C-453/99 [2001] ECR I-6297, [2001] 5 CMLR 1058; see Komninos 'New prospects for private enforcement of EC competition law: Courage v Crehan and the Community right to damages' (2002) 39 CML Rev 447; Reich 'The "Courage" doctrine encouraging or discouraging compensation for antitrust injuries' (2005) 42 CML Rev 35; Drake 'Scope of Courage and the principle of "individual liability" for damages: further development of the principle of effective judicial protection by the Court of Justice' (2006) 31 ELR 841.

[21] Cases C-295/04 etc *Vincenzo Manfredi v Lloyd Adriatico Assicurazioni SpA* [2006] ECR I-6619, [2006] 5 CMLR 17.

[22] Case C-453/99 [2001] ECR I-6297, [2001] 5 CMLR 1058, paras 26–27.

[23] See Monti 'Anticompetitive Agreements: the Innocent Party's Right to Damages' (2002) 27 EL Rev 282 (critical of the judgment); Odudu and Edelman, ibid, 327; Cumming 'Courage Ltd v Crehan' (2002) 27 ECLR 199; Jones and Beard 'Co-contractors, Damages and Article 81: The ECJ Finally Speaks' (2002) 23 ECLR 246; on the position in the US, see *Perma Life Mufflers Inc v International Parts Corpn* 392 US 134 (1968).

[24] Case C-453/99 [2001] ECR I-6297, [2001] 5 CMLR 1058, para 28.   [25] Ibid, para 32.

[26] Ibid, para 33.

such as that in *Courage*, the restrictive effect of Courage's agreement with Crehan arose from the fact that it was one of many similar agreements having a cumulative effect on competition[27]: in those circumstances Crehan could not be considered to bear significant responsibility for the infringement of the competition rules[28].

Unfortunately for Crehan when the case reverted to the Chancery Division in the UK Park J held that the agreement did not infringe Article 81 anyway and dismissed his claim[29]; this finding was ultimately upheld on appeal to the House of Lords[30]. After 13 years of litigation Crehan recovered no damages whatsoever; however he made a crucial contribution to the important issue of the private enforcement of competition law.

(C) *Manfredi*

In *Manfredi* the Italian Competition Authority had held that various insurance companies had violated Italian competition law through the unlawful exchange of information; the decision was upheld on appeal to the Council of State. Customers of the insurance companies sued for damages for breaches of both Italian and EC competition law. Various questions were submitted to the ECJ under Article 234, partly as to the right to damages under Article 81 and partly as to specific Italian provisions concerning damages claims under internal Italian law. On the right to damages the ECJ repeated what it had said in *Courage*. The full effectiveness of Article 81(1) required that:

any individual can claim compensation for the harm suffered where there is a causal relationship between that harm and an agreement or practice prohibited under Article 81 EC[31].

In *Manfredi* there were some specific points about Italian procedural law that seemed to complicate the claimants' actions: for example there were rules that allocated jurisdiction in actions for damages based on competition law to a different court from the one that would deal with 'normal' damages claims, thereby increasing the cost and length of the litigation; there were limitation periods that could be harmful to their cause; and there were rules that might prevent them from recovering the full amount of their losses. The Article 234 reference asked the ECJ whether these domestic rules were compatible with Community law. The ECJ's answer, in essence, was that these were matters of internal Italian law, provided that they did not offend the Community principles of non-discrimination and *effet utile*. What the *Manfredi* judgment did was to reveal that, despite the ECJ's enthusiasm for damages actions, there remains the 'problem' that Member States retain autonomy in relation to the procedural rules of their domestic judicial systems, as well as the substantive rules of recovery in tort, delict, restitutionary and other actions, and that these rules might inhibit successful damages claims[32]. This is precisely why the Commission's Green Paper set out to identify the 'obstacles' that lie

---

[27] On this point see ch 16, p 628.

[28] [2001] ECR I-6297, [2001] 5 CMLR 1058, para 34; it is interesting to speculate as to what would have happened if a third party had sued Courage and Crehan for harm suffered as a result of the agreement: the ECJ's reasoning would suggest that Courage, but not Crehan, should be liable.

[29] *Crehan v Inntrepreneur Pub Co* [2003] EWHC 1510 (Ch), [2003] 27 EG 138 (CS), ChD.

[30] [2006] UKHL 38, [2006] UKCLR 1232

[31] Cases C-295/04 etc *Vincenzo Manfredi v Lloyd Adriatico Assicurazioni SpA* [2006] ECR I-6619, [2006] 5 CMLR 17, para 61.

[32] When the case returned to Italy Mr Manfredi was awarded €889.10 and €500 for legal costs by the small claims court: see Nebbia 'So What Happened to Mr Manfredi? The Italian Decision Following the Ruling of the European Court of Justice' (2007) 28 ECLR 591.

in the way of damages actions and to consider ways of reducing or eliminating them. This issue will be returned to in the final section of this chapter.

(D) Interim relief

Crehan and *Manfredi* establish that there is a right to damages for harm caused by an infringement of the competition rules. Quite often a claimant is as interested in obtaining an injunction to bring anti-competitive behaviour to an end as in receiving damages; more specifically the claimant may seek interim relief pending the outcome of a competition investigation by a competition authority.

The Commission has power under Article 8 of the Modernisation Regulation to adopt interim measures[33]; NCAs have similar powers[34]. However the public authorities, acting in the public interest, are sparing in their adoption of interim measures; a claimant in need of interim relief may find that an application to a national court is a more effective way to proceed, the function of the court being to achieve justice between the parties. In his Opinion in *AOK Bundersverbund*[35] Advocate General Jacobs considered that the *Crehan* principles that damages should be available to protect the *effet utile* of Article 81 applied equally to applications for interim relief[36]. In the UK, courts have sometimes rejected applications for interim relief on the ground that an award of damages at the trial of the action would be an adequate remedy[37]. However some applications have been successful, particularly where individuals' livelihoods were at stake[38], but also sometimes between more substantial litigants[39]. A particularly striking example of a successful application for interim relief is the case of *Adidas-Salomon AG v Roger Draper and Paul Howorth*[40] in which Adidas was granted an interim injunction against the International Tennis Federation and the 'Grand Slam' tennis tournaments in relation to the dress rules for tennis players; a settlement was subsequently reached so that the case did not go to trial[41]. Interim orders were also successfully obtained in relation to a dispute in the mobile telephony sector in *Software Cellular Network Ltd v T-Mobile (UK) Ltd*[42].

An application for an interim injunction was unsuccessful in *AAH Pharmaceuticals Ltd v Pfizer Ltd*[43] where the claimants were considered to have unduly delayed their application to the court, having earlier sought (and failed to obtain) interim measures from the OFT. The court held in this case that the correct test for the grant of an interim injunction in competition cases was to decide which course (that is to say the grant

---

[33] See ch 7, p 253.
[34] On the OFT's powers under UK law to adopt interim measures see ch 10, p 398.
[35] Case C-264/01 [2004] ECR I-2493.   [36] See para 104 of the Opinion.
[37] See eg *Garden Cottage Foods v Milk Marketing Board* [1984] AC 130, [1983] 3 CMLR 43; *Argyll Group plc v Distillers Co plc* [1986] 1 CMLR 764; *Plessey Co plc v General Electric Co* [1990] ECC 384; *Megaphone v British Telecom* 28 February 1989, unreported, QBD; *Macarthy v UniChem* [1991] ECC 41, ChD.
[38] *Cutsforth v Mansfield Inns* [1986] 1 CMLR 1; *Holleran and Evans v Thwaites plc* [1989] 2 CMLR 917.
[39] For example ECS succeeded in obtaining an interim injunction against AKZO in the High Court as well as persuading the Commission to proceed under Article 82 in *ECS/AKZO* OJ [1983] L 252/13, [1983] 3 CMLR 694; see also *Sockel GmbH v Body Shop International plc* [1999] Eu LR 276, ChD.
[40] [2006] EWHC 1318 (Ch), [2006] UKCLR 823, [2006] ECR 411.
[41] See press release by International Tennis Federation of 4 October 2006, available at www.itftennis. com/abouttheitf/news/newsarticle.asp?articleid=17019.
[42] Claim No HC07C, judgment of 17 July 2007.
[43] [2007] EWHC 565 (Ch D), judgment of 5 March 2007.

or the refusal of the injunction) would involve less risk of injustice if it turns out to be wrong[44].

(E) Private enforcement and the Modernisation Regulation

Recital 7 of the Modernisation Regulation states that national courts have an 'essential part' to play in applying the competition rules. Article 6 of the Regulation states simply that:

National courts shall have the power to apply Articles 81 and 82 of the Treaty.

There are two further provisions in the Modernisation Regulation of considerable importance to private enforcement: Article 15 on cooperation with national courts and Article 16 on the uniform application of Community competition law. They should be read in conjunction with the Commission's *Co-operation Notice*.

(i) Article 15: cooperation with national courts

Recital 21 of the Modernisation Regulation refers to the importance of consistency in the application of the competition rules across the Community, and to the consequent need to establish arrangements for cooperation between the Commission and national courts, whether those courts are dealing with litigation between private parties, are acting as enforcers of the law or are sitting as courts of appeal or judicial review. Article 15 of the Regulation provides for various types of cooperation with national courts, as set out below. The cooperation envisaged under Article 15 is between the Commission and the national courts, not between the Commission and the litigants themselves: when asked to assist a national court the Commission will not have any direct dealings with the parties to the litigation and, if approached by them, it will inform the national court of the fact[45]. The Commission publishes a summary of its cooperation with national courts in its annual Report on Competition Policy[46]; two opinions were provided, to a Dutch and Belgian court respectively, in the course of 2006[47].

The Modernisation Regulation does not provide for a 'network of national courts' in the way that it establishes a 'network of national competition authorities'[48]; however, an 'Association of European Competition Law Judges' has been established which brings together judges of the Community and national courts to discuss and debate points of common interest. It is understood that a website is in the course of development to which the judges will have access.

(A) Requests by national courts for information or an opinion Article 15(1) of the Modernisation Regulation provides that a national court may request the Commission to transmit to it information in the Commission's possession or to provide it with an opinion concerning the procedural or substantive application of the Community competition rules. The Commission will endeavour to reply to a request for information

---

[44] See to similar effect an earlier judgment of the Court of Appeal in *Zockoll Group Ltd v Mercury Communications Ltd* [1998] FSR 254.

[45] *Co-operation Notice*, para 19.

[46] See eg Commission's XXXVIth *Report on Competition Policy* (2006), paras 70–73.

[47] Ibid, paras 327–330.   [48] See ch 7, pp 283–284.

within one month[49]. An important point is that Article 287 EC provides that the Commission is not allowed to transmit information covered by the obligation of professional secrecy, which may be both confidential information and business secrets: the Commission will not provide such information to a national court unless the latter can guarantee that it will protect it[50]. The Commission will not transmit to a national court information voluntarily submitted to it by a leniency applicant without its consent[51]. The Commission will endeavour to reply to a request for an opinion within four months[52]. When giving its opinion the Commission will limit itself to providing the national court with the factual information or the economic or legal clarification asked for without considering the merits of the case[53]. Of course a national court requiring advice on a point of law could also, should it prefer to do so, make a preliminary reference under Article 234 EC to the ECJ[54].

A national court wishing to approach the Commission for assistance may do so by post, but may also do so by sending an e-mail to a bespoke address, comp-amicus@cec.eu.int.

(B) Submission of judgments to the Commission Article 15(2) of the Modernisation Regulation requires Member States to submit any written judgment deciding on the application of Articles 81 and 82 to the Commission, without delay after the full written judgment is notified to the parties. The Commission has created a database of all such judgments which is accessible on its website; it contains non-confidential versions of judgments in their original language, classified according to the Member State of origin[55]. Unfortunately little attempt seems to be made to keep it up to date.

(C) Observations by national competition authorities and the Commission Article 15(3) of the Modernisation Regulation makes provision for NCAs and the Commission to make observations to national courts. Each may make written observations acting on their own initiative; oral observations may be made with the permission of the court. In order to enable them to make such observations NCAs and the Commission may request the relevant court to transmit or ensure the transmission to them of documents necessary for an assessment of the case. This provision is similar to the practice in some Member States that enables an NCA to intervene in cases before the national courts; in France for example the Conseil de la Concurrence may give expert testimony in civil proceedings[56]. The Modernisation Regulation does not provide a procedural framework for the submission of observations; this is therefore a matter for the rules and practices of the court of the Member State to which they are made[57]. The ORR, relying on Article 15 of the Modernisation Regulation, made observations to the court in the case of *EW&S v E.ON*[58].

(D) Wider national powers Article 15(1) to (3) of the Modernisation Regulation establishes Community rules on cooperation; Article 15(4) states that the rules therein are

[49] *Co-operation Notice*, para 22.   [50] Ibid, paras 23–25.   [51] Ibid, para 26.   [52] Ibid, para 28.
[53] Ibid, para 29.   [54] On Article 234 references see ch 2, p 72 and ch 10, p 437.
[55] www.ec.europa.eu/comm/competition/antitrust/national_courts/index_en.html.
[56] Commission's White Paper on modernisation of the rules implementing [Articles 81 and 82] of the EC OJ [1999] C 132/1, [1999] 5 CMLR 208, para 107.
[57] *Co-operation Notice*, paras 34–35.
[58] Judgment of 23 March 2007, [2007] EWHC 599 (Comm), [2007] UKCLR 1653.

without prejudice to any wider powers that might exist under national law in a particular Member State allowing competition authorities to make observations.

(ii) Article 16: uniform application of Community competition law

Article 16(1) of the Modernisation Regulation, which is concerned with the uniform
application of the Community competition rules, explains the effect of Commission
decisions on national courts. As Recital 22 of the Regulation points out it is important
that the competition rules should be applied uniformly throughout the Community
and that conflicting decisions should be avoided. The Regulation therefore clarifies,
in accordance with the case law of the ECJ[59], the effect of Commission decisions on
national courts (and NCAs). The Regulation also addresses the position of a national
court dealing with a case which the Commission is investigating at the same time, without having yet reached a decision.

(A) The effect of Commission decisions The first sentence of Article 16(1) gives expression
to Article 249 EC and the ECJ's judgment in *Masterfoods*[60]. It states that, where national
courts rule on a matter which has already been the subject of a Commission decision
under Article 81 or Article 82, they cannot reach conclusions running counter to that of
the Commission. The Regulation does not state specifically that an appellate court in a
Member State would be bound by a Commission decision even where a lower court had
reached a contrary conclusion prior to the Commission's decision; however this point
was established by the ECJ in *Masterfoods*[61]. If the Commission's decision is on appeal
to the CFI or the ECJ the national court should stay its proceedings pending a definitive
decision on the matter by the Community Courts[62]. If a national court considers that
a Commission decision is wrong, and if it has not been the subject of an appeal to the
Community Courts, the only option available to the national court would be to make
an Article 234 reference to the ECJ[63].

Sometimes the Commission states that an undertaking has participated in a cartel,
but does not impose a fine because this has become time-barred: the undertaking may
challenge the reference to it in the decision because the fact renders it vulnerable to a
damages claim[64].

(B) Parallel proceedings The second sentence of Article 16(1) states that, where a national
court is hearing an action, it must avoid giving a decision which would conflict with
a decision contemplated by the Commission in proceedings that it has initiated.
Article 16(1) adds that the national court in this situation should consider whether to
stay its proceedings; if it were to do so, it is likely that the Commission would expedite
its own proceedings in order to enable the outcome of the civil dispute to be decided.
The national court could order interim measures to protect the interests of the parties
while awaiting the Commission's decision[65].

---

[59] Of particular importance is the judgment of the ECJ in Case C-344/98 *Masterfoods Ltd v HB Ice Cream
Ltd* [2000] ECR I-11369, [2001] 4 CMLR 449; see generally Nazzini *Concurrent Proceedings in Competition
Law* (OUP, 2004), esp ch 7.

[60] See n 59 above.   [61] *Masterfoods*, para 60.

[62] *Masterfoods*, paras 52 and 57; *Co-operation Notice*, para 13.   [63] *Co-operation Notice*, para 13.

[64] See ch 7, p 252.   [65] *Masterfoods*, para 58; *Co-operation Notice*, para 14.

Where a national court has reason to believe that the Commission is conducting a parallel investigation of a possible infringement of Article 81 or 82 it could seek information from the Commission about any proceedings it may have in motion, what it is likely to decide in that case and when, under the provisions of Article 15 of the Modernisation Regulation discussed above. The Commission has a duty under Article 10 EC to cooperate with the judicial authorities in Member States in matters of this kind[66].

(F) The duty of national courts

An important issue is whether a national court has a duty, of its own motion, to raise issues of competition law irrespective of whether one or more of the litigants do so. This matter was considered by the ECJ in *van Schijndel*[67] and is summarised in paragraph 3 of the Commission's *Co-operation Notice*. Where domestic law requires a national court to raise points of law based on binding domestic rules which have not been raised by the parties the same obligation also exists where binding EC rules, such as those on competition, exist; the same is the case where the national court has a discretion to raise such points of law. However Community law does not require national courts to raise a point of Community law where this would require them to abandon the passive role assigned to them by going beyond the ambit of the dispute defined by the parties.

3. DAMAGES ACTIONS IN THE UK COURTS[68]

The UK courts accepted more than 20 years ago (long before the *Crehan* judgment) that damages could be available for harm caused by infringements of Articles 81 and 82[69]. The Competition Act 1998 does not explicitly confer a right to damages where the Chapter I and II prohibitions are infringed. However the *Crehan* and *Manfredi* judgments, read in conjunction with section 60 of the Act, requiring consistency with the jurisprudence of the Community Courts[70], section 47A, which provides for follow-on

[66] See Case C-234/89 *Delimitis v Henninger Bräu* [1991] ECR I-935, [1992] 5 CMLR 210, para 53; see also Cases C-319/93 etc *Hendrik Evert Dijkstra v Friesland (FRICO Domo) Coöperatie BA* [1995] ECR I-4471, [1996] 5 CMLR 178, para 34; on the Commission's duty of sincere cooperation under Article 10 EC see Case C-2/88 R *Zwartveld* [1990] ECR I-3365, [1990] 3 CMLR 457.

[67] Cases C-430/93 etc. [1995] ECR-4705; on this case see Prechal 'Community Law in National Courts: The Lessons from Van Schijndel' (1998) 35 CML Rev 681.

[68] See Rodger 'Competition Law Litigation in the UK Courts: A Study of All Cases to 2004' [2006] 27 ECLR 241, 279 and 341.

[69] See eg *Garden Cottage Foods v Milk Marketing Board* [1984] AC 130, [1983] 3 CMLR 43; *An Bord Bainne Co-operative Ltd v Milk Marketing Board* [1984] 1 CMLR 519, affd [1984] 2 CMLR 584, CA; *Bourgoin S A v Minister of Agriculture Fisheries and Food* [1985] 1 CMLR 528, on appeal [1986] 1 CMLR 267, CA (this case was concerned with whether damages could be recovered from a Member State that had acted in breach of Article 28 of the Treaty, but the judgments in the Court of Appeal deal also with actions under the competition rules: the case was settled after the Court of Appeal's judgment, the claimant recovering substantial damages, and before an appeal to the House of Lords had been heard: see [1987] 1 CMLR 169); *Plessey v GEC* [1990] ECC 384, para 37 (injunction refused *inter alia* on grounds that damages at the trial would be an adequate remedy); *Norbain SD Ltd v Dedicated Micros Ltd* [1998] Eu LR 266 (QBD: interlocutory injunction refused partly because this would complicate rather than simplify the calculation of damages) *Arkin v Borchard Lines Ltd* [2001] Eu LR 232, QBD (preliminary issues); final judgment was given in *Arkin v Borchard Lines Ltd* [2003] EWHC 687 (Comm Ct).

[70] See ch 9, pp 362–367.

actions pursuant to findings of an infringement of EC or UK competition law by the competition authorities, and the debate in Parliament on the Bill[71], leave no room for doubt that damages are available[72].

Public policy in the UK has moved in favour of more private enforcement of the competition rules: in particular various provisions in the Enterprise Act 2002 were designed to facilitate damages claims, as will be seen in the text that follows. In April 2007 the OFT published a Discussion Paper, *Private actions in competition law: effective redress for consumers and business*[73]; this was followed in November of the same year by *Private actions in competition law: effective redress for consumers and business: Recommendations from the Office of Fair Trading*: the Discussion Paper and the OFT's recommendations will be briefly considered at the end of this chapter[74]. It is possible that the UK Government will introduce legislative changes to facilitate more private actions in the fairly near future.

A claimant seeking damages in the UK has two options: to bring a 'standalone' action in the High Court, or, where the OFT, a sectoral regulator or the European Commission has adopted a decision finding an infringement of EC or UK competition law, to bring a 'follow-on' action in the High Court or the Competition Appeal Tribunal ('the CAT'). Each of these possibilities will now be considered.

(A) Standalone actions in the High Court

(i) Actions must be brought in the Chancery Division

A standalone action is one where the claimant must prove an infringement of the competition rules without the benefit of a prior decision to that effect by a public authority. Standalone actions that involve issues of competition law must usually be brought in the Chancery Division of the High Court[75]. Section 16 of the Enterprise Act 2002 makes provision for the Lord Chancellor to make regulations for the transfer of standalone cases to the CAT[76]; to date no such regulations have been made[77].

[71] See eg Lord Simon, HL 2R, 30 October 1997, col 1148; Margaret Beckett, HC 2R, 11 May 1998, col 35; see also DTI Press Release P/98/552, 9 July 1998.

[72] See generally Yeung 'Privatizing Competition Regulation' (1998) 18 Oxford Journal of Legal Studies 581; Kon and Maxwell 'Enforcement in National Courts of the EC and New UK Competition Rules: Obstacles to Effective Enforcement' (1998) 19 ECLR 443; Turner 'The UK Competition Act 1998 and Private Rights' (1999) 20 ECLR 62; MacCulloch 'Private Enforcement of the Competition Act Prohibitions' in *The Competition Act: A New Era for UK Competition Law* (Hart Publishing, 2000, eds Rodger and MacCulloch); Roth 'The New UK Competition Act – The Private Perspective' in [2000] Fordham Corporate Law Institute (ed Hawk), ch 7; Rodger 'Private Enforcement and the Enterprise Act: An Exemplary System of Awarding Damages?' (2003) 24 ECLR 103; see also the Government's White Paper *Productivity and Enterprise – A World Class Competition Régime* Cm 5233 (2001), ch 8.

[73] OFT 916, available at www.oft.gov.uk/shared_oft/reports/comp_policy/oft916.pdf.

[74] See pp 320–322 below.

[75] Civil Procedure Rules, Rule 30.8; see also the CPR Practice Direction – Competition Law – Claims relating to the application of Articles 81 and 82 of the EC Treaty and Chapters I and II or Part I of the Competition Act 1998, January 2007, which deals, among other matters, with Articles 15 and 16 of the Modernisation Regulation; it is available at www.justice.gov.uk/civil/procrules_fin/contents/practice_directions/competitionlaw_pd.htm.

[76] See Lever 'Restructuring Courts and Tribunals Hearing UK and EC Competition Law Cases' (2002) 1 Competition Law Journal 47; Brown 'Section 16 Enterprise Act 2002 – Time for Activation?' (2007) 28 ECLR 488.

[77] Note however that there is provision for the transfer between the High Court and the CAT of follow-on actions under section of the 47A Competition Act: see pp 307–308 below.

(ii) Private international law

The jurisdictional issue of which Member State's courts have jurisdiction in relation to a competition law case are determined by reference to the *Brussels Regulation on Jurisdiction and the Recognition and Enforcement of Judgments in Civil and Commercial Matters*[78]: the basic rule is that the defendant should be sued where it is domiciled, but there are a number of exceptions to this. The substantive issue of which law should actually be applied in a case of non-contractual obligations arising out of a restriction of competition will, with effect from 11 January 2009, be determined by reference to the *Regulation on the Law Applicable to Non-contractual Obligations ('Rome II')*[79]: the basic rule is that the law of the place where the market is affected or likely to be affected should be applied.

It is possible under the Brussels Regulation that the courts of England and Wales may be able to assume jurisdiction over non-UK undertakings that were involved in an international cartel where it is appropriate to join them in an action against UK undertakings, as is demonstrated by the judgment of the High Court in *Roche Products Ltd & Others v Provimi Ltd*[80]. This case, and two of the follow-on cases brought under section 47A of the Competition Act 1998[81], suggest that litigants see certain advantages to litigating in England and Wales (for example because of the rules for discovery of evidence, effective case management procedures and considerable experience of handling complex international litigation), and the *Provimi* judgment shows that creative application of the Brussels Regulation may make jurisdiction there possible. However an attempt to claim jurisdiction on the basis of Article 5(3) of the Regulation, which allows a claimant to sue in the courts of the country in which it suffered harm, failed in *Sandisk Corporation v Koninklijke Philip Electronics NV*[82] where the claimant failed to demonstrate a 'good arguable case' and where other Member States indisputably had jurisdiction[83].

In some circumstances a claimant may be able to sue in the US, where it may obtain the benefit of treble damages[84]; however this may not be possible if no antitrust harm has been suffered within the US[85].

(iii) The cause of action

The claimant's cause of action is generally considered to be for breach of statutory duty, the statute in question being the European Communities Act 1972 or the Competition Act 1998[86]. The point is not free from doubt. In *Courage Ltd v Crehan*[87] the Court of

---

[78] Council Regulation 44/2001, OJ [2001] L 12/1; for commentary on the Brussels Regulation see Dicey, Morris and Collins *The Conflict of Laws* (Sweet & Maxwell, 15th ed, 2006), ch 11.

[79] Regulation 864/2007, OJ [2007] L 199/40.

[80] [2003] EWHC 961 (Comm), [2003] All ER (D) 59 (May); for comment on this case see Bulst 'The Provimi Decision of the High Court: Beginnings of Private Antitrust Litigation in Europe' (2003) European Business Organisation Law Review 623.

[81] See pp 307–308 below. [82] [2007] EWHC 332, Ch D. [83] Ibid, para 41.

[84] On the treble damages action in US law see Jones *Private Enforcement of Antitrust Law in the EU, UK and USA* (Oxford University Press, 1999), pp 79–84.

[85] See *Hoffmann-La Roche v Empagran* 542 US 155 (2004).

[86] This was the approach taken by the House of Lords in *Garden Cottage Foods v Milk Marketing Board* [1984] AC 130, [1983] 3 CMLR 43 and in most cases since.

[87] [2004] EWCA 637, judgment of 21 May 2004, [2004] UKCLR 1500.

Appeal noted that Crehan would not have been able to recover damages according to the rules of that tort, since the harm he had suffered was not of the kind that Article 81 intended to prevent. However the Court of Appeal recognised that Crehan should be able to recover damages because of the direction to that effect from the ECJ: the Community principle of *effet utile* overrode the position at common law[88]. In *Devenish Nutrition Ltd v Sanofi-Aventis SA*[89] the High Court held that, unless and until a higher court decides to the contrary, it is not possible to bring a restitutionary claim in a competition law case[90]; permission has been given to appeal to the Court of Appeal on this point.

There are numerous questions that remain to be answered about damages actions in competition law cases under English law. The first is whether English law allows a 'passing on' defence. For example it is undecided whether a purchaser that purchases goods or services from a cartel at an inflated price, but which then passes that price on to its own customers, has a right to damages: arguably, since it has suffered no harm, the defendants should be able to rely on a passing on defence. On the other hand it can be argued that the members of the cartel have been unjustly enriched as a result of their unlawful behaviour, so that the purchaser should have the right to bring an action to force them to disgorge their undeserved profits[91]. A related issue is whether an 'indirect purchaser' – for example the customer that purchased from the immediate victim of the cartel and to whom the higher price was passed – should be able to sue for damages[92]. The policy issues around these inter-related issues are complex, and a ruling on them is eagerly awaited[93].

Another issue is the question of causation and the quantification of damages. A claimant must be able to demonstrate that the anti-competitive behaviour of which it complains caused the loss it suffered[94]. As to quantum the claimant should be able to recover the difference between the price it actually paid and the price that would have prevailed in competitive market conditions: a simple principle to state, but something that can be very hard to establish in practice. A helpful guide to the methodology to be applied will be found in paragraph 19 of the judgment of the High Court in *Devenish Nutrition Ltd v Sanofi-Aventis SA*[95].

---

[88] Ibid, paras 154–168.   [89] [2007] EWHC 2394, Ch D, [2008] ECC 28.   [90] Ibid, para 108.

[91] See Kennelly 'Damages Actions before the CAT and the Passing On Defence' (2004) 3 Competition Law Journal 238; Petrucci 'The Issues of the Passing-on Defence and Indirect Purchasers' Standing in European Competition Law' (2008) 29 ECLR 33; on the position in the US see *Hanover Shoe Inc v United Shoe Machinery Corp* 392 US 481 (1968) in which the Supreme Court rejected the passing on defence.

[92] On the position in the US see *Illinois Brick Co v Illinois* 431 US 720 (1977) in which the Supreme Court held that in general claims by indirect purchasers should not be allowed; see Brealey 'Adopt Perma Life, but Follow Hanover Shoe to Illinois? – Who Can Sue for Damages for Breach of EC Competition Law?' (2002) 1 Competition Law Journal 127. The US Antitrust Modernisation Commission recommended legislative action to improve the law on indirect purchasers: see Chapter IIIB of the Report, available at www.amc.gov/report_recommendation/toc.htm.

[93] For a helpful discussion of the issues see Beard 'Damages in Competition Law Litigation' in *Competition Litigation in the UK* (eds Ward and Smith, Sweet & Maxwell, 2005), paras 7-049–7-061; see also Hoseinian 'Passing-on Damages and Community Antitrust Policy – An Economic Background' (2005) 28(1) World Competition 3–23; Petrucci 'The Issues of the Passing-on Defence and Indirect Purchasers' Standing in European Competition Law' (2008) 29 ECLR 33.

[94] See eg the judgment of the Queen's Bench Division in *Arkin v Bochard Lines Ltd* [2003] EWHC 687 (Comm Ct), paras 489–570, where the court found that there was no causation between the conduct complained of and the harm suffered by the claimant.

[95] [2007] EWHC 2394, Ch D, [2008] ECC 28.

The date at which damages are to be calculated can have an important effect on the outcome of a case. In *Courage Ltd v Crehan*[96] the High Court held that, if Crehan was entitled to damages, these should be assessed at the time of the trial of the action, which took place 10 years after the action was commenced: on that basis the Court would have awarded Crehan £1,311,500. However on appeal the Court of Appeal held that the correct time for determining damages was the (much earlier) time of the loss, and on that basis would have awarded the claimant only £131,336[97]. This specific issue was not dealt with in the opinions of the Law Lords in the House of Lords; their Lordships upheld the finding of the High Court that there had been no infringement of competition law, so that Crehan did not even recover the much lower amount suggested by the Court of Appeal[98].

A further issue in relation to damages actions is whether a claimant is able to recover 'punitive' or 'exemplary', as well as compensatory, damages. English law does provide for exemplary damages[99]. Where a defendant has already been ordered to pay a substantial penalty, for example by the OFT or the European Commission, for infringing competition law the High Court has held that exemplary damages are not available as this would violate the principle of *ne bis in idem*[100]; the Court was of the view that Article 16 of the Modernisation Regulation also precludes an award of exemplary damages[101]. On the other hand where a claimant is harmed by particularly serious anti-competitive behaviour, such as targeted and sustained predatory pricing, and there have been no administrative proceedings, a court might be inclined to include such an award. It is worth pointing out that the courts in England and Wales can award pre-judgment interest to be added to any damages payable, and that this can lead to a substantial increase in the amount that a claimant can recover.

(iv) Sections 58 and 58A of the Competition Act 1998: findings of fact and findings of infringements

(A) Section 58: findings of fact Section 58(1) of the Competition Act provides that, unless the court directs otherwise, findings of fact by the OFT[102] in proceedings based on UK or EC competition law are binding on the parties in court proceedings brought by the infringing parties or third parties, provided that the time for appeal against the finding has expired, or that the OFT's findings are confirmed on appeal. This means that parties that initiate such proceedings will not have to go through the process of producing all the evidence once again, but can proceed on the 'coat-tail' of the OFT's findings. The wording of the OFT's decision is obviously very important for the purposes of section 58. There is a significant distinction between a statement that 'A and B agreed to

---

[96] [2003] EWHC 1510 Ch D, [2003] UKCLR 834, [2004] ECC 78.

[97] [2004] EWCA 637, [2004] UKCLR 1500, [2004] ECC 407.

[98] [2007] 1 AC 333, [2006] UKHL 38, [2006] UKCLR 1232, [2008] ECC 45; see Beal 'Crehan and Postmodern Malaise' [2007] Competition Law 17; Hanley (2007) 44 CMLRev 817.

[99] *Rookes v Barnard* [1964] AC 1129; *Kuddas v Chief Constable of Leicestershire* [2002] 2 AC 122; see also Clerk & Lindsell *Torts* (Sweet & Maxwell, 19th ed, 2006), paras 29.137–29.150.

[100] *Devenish Nutrition Ltd v Sanofi-Aventis SA* [2007] EWHC 2394, [2008] ECC 28, para 52, Ch D.

[101] Ibid, para 55.

[102] Or a sectoral regulator: see section 371 of the Communications Act 2003 in relation to OFCOM and section 54 and Schedule 10 of the Competition Act 1998 in relation to the other regulators.

fix prices' and one that says 'it appears to the OFT that A and B may have fixed prices': only the former involves a finding of fact. Section 58(3) of the Act enables rules of court to be made for the OFT to provide assistance to the court in private actions; no such rules have been made. When the OFT reached a settlement with a number of independent schools accused of price fixing it adopted a decision saying that the agreement in question had the object of restricting competition; however the OFT made no finding of effect. From the perspective of the schools it was preferable that the agreement was found to restrict by object rather than effect since an explicit finding that the agreement had led to higher school fees might have encouraged damages actions[103].

(B) Section 58A: findings of infringement Section 58A of the Competition Act 1998, added by the Enterprise Act 2002, provides that findings by the OFT[104] or the CAT of infringements of UK or EC competition law are binding on courts in which damages or other sums of money are claimed once any appeal periods have elapsed. Section 58A goes beyond section 58 of the Act, which simply relates to findings of fact; section 58A means that the substantive assessment of the OFT and the CAT binds the court hearing the claim.

(C) Article 16(1) of the modernisation regulation Section 58A of the Competition Act does not say anything about the effect of findings of infringement by the European Commission. However this matter is dealt with by Article 16(1) of the Modernisation Regulation: it gives effect to the judgment of the ECJ in the *Masterfoods* case to the effect that a national court cannot reach a conclusion different from that of the Commission[105]. The *Crehan* litigation shed interesting light on the operation of this provision. In that case the Commission had reached the conclusion, in relation to beer supply agreements entered into by, for example, Whitbread[106], Bass[107] and Scottish and Newcastle[108], that access to the retail level of the beer market in the UK market was foreclosed. However Crehan's agreement was not with any of those brewers, but with Courage, and the Commission had not reached a finding of foreclosure in relation to Courage's agreements. An issue in the litigation, therefore, was whether the court was 'bound' by the Commission's findings in the *Whitbread* case. The answer given by Park J[109] and the House of Lords on appeal[110] (disagreeing with the Court of Appeal[111]) was that, since those decisions did not deal with the same facts and the same parties, they were not binding on the court, although they were admissible as evidence[112]. Park J conducted his own assessment of the market and reached the conclusion that there was no foreclosure of the UK beer market, and that therefore the agreements in question did not infringe Article 81; the House of Lords upheld this finding.

---

[103] Exchange of information on future fees by certain independent fee-paying schools, OFT decision of 20 November 2006, [2007] UKCLR 361.

[104] Or a sectoral regulator: see n 102 above.   [105] See pp 298–299 above.

[106] OJ [1999] L 88/26, [1999] CMLR 118, upheld on appeal in Case T-131/99 *Shaw and others v Commission* [2002] ECR II-2023, [2002] 5 CMLR 81.

[107] OJ [1999] L 186/1, [1999] 5 CMLR 782, upheld on appeal in Case T-231/99 *Joynson v Commission* [2002] ECR II-2085, [2002] 5 CMLR 123.

[108] OJ [1999] L 186/28, [1999] 5 CMLR 831.   [109] [2003] EWHC 1510, [2003] EuLR 663, [2004] ECC 78.

[110] [2006] UKHL 38, UKCLR 1232, [2007] ECC 45.   [111] [2004] EWCA 637, [2004] ECC 407.

[112] On this point see *Iberian UK Ltd v BPB Industries and British Gypsum* [1996] 2 CMLR 601, [1997] Eu LR 1 (per Laddie J).

(v) Group litigation orders and conditional fees

Actions for damages may be facilitated by resort to the concept of a 'group litigation order', a procedure available in England and Wales since 2 May 2000[113] which provides for the case management of claims that give rise to common or related issues of fact or law; the fact that lawyers are entitled to work on a conditional fee basis may also be of assistance to would-be claimants[114].

(vi) High Court litigation in practice

(A) The standard of proof required As a preliminary matter the question arises of the standard of proof to be satisfied by the claimant. As long ago as 1989 in *Shearson Lehman Hutton Inc v Watson Co Ltd*[115] Webster J was of the view that, as an infringement of Article 81 carries with it a liability to penalties, he should apply the standard of 'a high degree of probability': this is a higher standard than in civil proceedings generally but lower than the requirement in a criminal case. In *Masterfoods Ltd v HB Ice Cream Ltd*[116], however, Kean J in the Irish High Court decided to apply the standard of proof normally applicable in civil proceedings, namely proof on the balance of probabilities; the same standard was applied by the Queen's Bench Division in *Arkin v Borchard Lines Ltd*[117]. In *Chester City Council v Arriva plc*[118] the High Court held that 'strong and compelling evidence'[119] was needed before Arriva could be found to have abused its dominant position, bearing in mind that, quite apart from the damages claim against it, a finding of abusive predatory pricing could lead to the imposition of severe financial penalties[120]. The *Chester City* approach would seem to be consistent with that taken in *Shearson* and is likely to be followed.

(B) Duty of disclosure The High Court suggested in *Ineos Vinyls Ltd v Hunstman Petrochemicals (UK) Ltd*[121] that a claimant before the court has a duty to inform it of any contact that it may have had with the OFT (or presumably the European Commission)[122].

(C) Successful claims Successful claims under UK and EC competition law have been fairly rare in the UK, although it is well known that many cases have been settled out of court in which the claimant has received substantial damages[123]. There are no final

---

[113] Civil Procedure Rules, Rule 19.10–19.15; for cases brought under the group litigation order procedure see www.hmcourts-service.gov.uk/cms/150.htm.

[114] Courts and Legal Services Act 1990, s 58; Conditional Fee Agreements Regulations 2000, SI 2000/692; Conditional Fee Agreements Order 2000, SI 2000/823.

[115] [1989] 3 CMLR 429 at 570; see also Application by Anley Maritime Agencies Ltd for Judicial Review [1999] EuLR 97.

[116] [1992] 3 CMLR 830 at 873.

[117] [2001] Eu LR 232, QBD (preliminary issues); final judgment was given in *Arkin v Borchard Lines Ltd* [2003] EWHC 687 (Comm Ct).

[118] [2007] EWHC 1373 (Ch), judgment of 15 June 2007.

[119] The expression is taken from the CAT judgment in Case No 1000/1/1/01 *Napp Pharmaceutical Holdings Ltd v Director General of Fair Trading* [2002] CAT 1, [2002] CompAR 13.

[120] Ibid, para 10.   [121] [2006] EWHC 1241 (Ch), judgment of 26 May 2006.   [122] Ibid, paras 210–211.

[123] For example some damages claims have been settled between pharmaceutical producers and the Department of Health: see eg Department of Health Press Notice of 1 April 2005, announcing the payment

judgments in which damages have been awarded. A partially successful action was *Hendry v World Professional Billiards and Snooker Association*[124] in which Lloyd J held that, for the most part, the rules of the association did not infringe competition law; however one rule, which restricted the tournaments in which players could participate in certain circumstances, was found to infringe both the Chapter I and II prohibitions[125], as well, probably, as Articles 81 and 82 EC[126]. An interim injunction was granted to the claimant in *Jobserve Ltd v Network Multimedia Television*[127], where the judge was of the view that there was an arguable case that it was an abuse of a dominant position for Jobserve to refuse to accept job vacancy advertisements on its website: pending trial the balance of justice lay in the claimant's favour. An important case was *Attheraces v British Horse Racing Board*[128] in which the High Court concluded that the British Horseracing Board had abused its dominant position under Article 82 by charging excessive and/or discriminatory prices for the supply of information to Attheraces about horse-racing events conducted under its auspices; however this judgment was reversed on appeal[129]. A successful application for an interim injunction was made in *Adidas-Salomon AG v Roger Draper and Paul Howorth*[130]; the same was the case in *Soft Cellular Network Ltd v T-Mobile (UK) Ltd*[131].

(D) Unsuccessful claims In *Claritas (UK) Ltd v Post Office* an application by Claritas Ltd for an interim injunction against the Post Office under the Chapter II prohibition was rejected[132]; subsequently the OFT also rejected the Claritas complaint, albeit on different grounds from those of the High Court[133]. An action for a declaration, injunction and damages under the Chapter II prohibition failed in *Chester City Council v Arriva plc*[134] where the Court held that the claimant had failed to adduce any evidence demonstrating that Arriva plc enjoyed a dominant position in the market for local bus services in the area of Chester. Several other attempts to invoke the Competition Act in litigation have failed[135].

by Ranbaxy (UK) Ltd of £4.5 million, and the Press Releases of 4 April 2006 and 22 June 2007; see similarly Scottish Government Press Release of 4 March 2008, announcing that the Goldshield Group had agreed to pay damages of £750,000. In a different case it was announced in February 2008 that British Airways and Virgin Atlantic had made £73.5 million available to settle cases in the UK arising out of the air fuel surcharge cartel: see www.airpassengerrefund.co.uk. See further Rodger 'Private Enforcement of Competition Law, the Hidden Story: Competition Litigation Settlements in the United Kingdom, 2000–2005' (2008) 29 ECLR 96.

[124] [2002] UKCLR 5, [2002] EuLR 770, [2002] ECC 96; for (critical) comment see Harris 'Abusive Sports Governing Bodies: Hendry v WPBSA' (2002) 1 Competition Law Journal 101; on the market definition in this case see Veljanovski 'Markets in Professional Sports: Hendry v WPSBA and the Importance of Functional Markets' (2002) 23 ECLR 273.

[125] Ibid, para 112.   [126] Ibid, para 113.

[127] [2001] UKCLR 814, upheld on appeal [2002] UKCLR 184, CA.

[128] [2005] EWHC 3015, [2006] UKCLR 167.

[129] [2007] EWCA Civ 38, [2007] UKCLR 309, [2007] ECC 98; for further discussion of this case see ch 18, p 718.

[130] [2006] EWHC 1318 (Ch), [2006] UKCLR 823, [2006] ECR 411.

[131] Judgment of 17 July 2007, Claim No HC07C.   [132] [2001] UKCLR 2, [2001] ECC 117.

[133] OFT Decision Consignia plc/Postal Preference Service Ltd 15 June 2001, available at www.oft.gov.uk.

[134] [2007] EWHC (Ch), [2007] UKCLR 1582.

[135] *Synstar Computer Services (UK) Ltd v ICL (Sorbus) Ltd* [2001] UKCLR 585; *Land Rover Group Ltd v UPF (UK) Ltd (in receivership)* [2002] All ER (D) 323; *Getmapping plc v Ordnance Survey* [2002] EWHC 1089 (Ch), [2002] UKCLR 410; *Intel Corpn v VIA Technologies* [2002] EWHC 1159, Ch D, reversed on appeal by the Court of Appeal [2002] EWCA Civ 1905; *Suretrack Rail Services Ltd v Infraco JNP Ltd* [2002] EWHC 1316, [2002] All ER (D) 261 (Jun).

(vii) Mediation

It is understood that in some cases the High Court encourages the parties to consider the possibility of mediation of their dispute, and that this process has led to several settlements out of court.

(viii) OFT competition law cases database

It is important that information about the enforcement of the Competition Act and Articles 81 and 82 in civil proceedings should be readily available. The OFT has established a page on its website which is intended to provide brief outlines of the competition law judgments handed down under the 1998 Act[136]. Lawyers who are involved in such cases may submit details of them to the OFT in a pro-forma notification form. Unfortunately no cases have been added to this database since 2003.

(B) Follow-on actions in the Competition Appeal Tribunal

The Enterprise Act 2002 amended the Competition Act 1998 in order to facilitate 'follow-on' damages actions that can be brought in the CAT. Several actions have been initiated under these provisions (see below).

(i) Monetary claims before the CAT

Section 47A of the Competition Act, added by the Enterprise Act, provides for follow-on actions for damages or any other sum of money to be brought before the CAT where there has been a finding of an infringement of UK or EC competition law by the OFT[137], the CAT, or the European Commission; proceedings can be brought only after any appeal periods have elapsed[138]. The Act does not provide for a follow-on action where an NCA of another Member State has found an infringement of Articles 81 and/ or 82 EC. The right to bring a follow-on action before the CAT is without prejudice to the right to bring proceedings before the 'normal' courts[139]. Part IV of the *Competition Appeal Tribunal Rules 2003*[140] contains provisions on claims for damages under section 47A; in the CAT's view these rules are a coherent and self-standing set of procedural rules and are more general and flexible than the Civil Procedure Rules[141]. The usual limitation period for civil proceedings in the Limitation Act 1980 does not apply to section 47A proceedings; rather proceedings must be commenced within two years of the 'relevant date'[142], which will usually be the date of the decision plus any appeal period[143]. Provision is made for the transfer of follow-on actions from the CAT to the High Court[144] and from the High Court to the CAT[145]. Section 49 of the Act provides

---

[136] Available at www.oft.gov.uk/advice_and_resources/resource_base/competition-courts.
[137] Or a sectoral regulator: see n 102 above. [138] Competition Act 1998, s 47A(7) and (8).
[139] Ibid, s 47A(10). [140] SI 2003/1372.
[141] Case 1028/5/7/04 *BCL Old Co Ltd v Aventis SA* [2005] CAT 1, [2005] CompAR 470, para 41.
[142] Competition Appeal Tribunal Rules 2003, Rule 31.
[143] For an interpretation of rule 31 of the CAT's rules see *Emerson Electric Co v Morgan Crucible Company plc* Case 1077/4/7/07 [2007] CAT 28; the CAT gave Emerson permission to make a claim for damages on 16 November 2007: [2007] CAT 30.
[144] Ibid, Rule 48. [145] Ibid, Rule 49.

for an appeal on a point of law, with permission, to the Court of Appeal from a decision of the CAT on damages.

(ii) Claims brought on behalf of consumers

Section 47B of the Competition Act 1998, added by the Enterprise Act 2002, provides for a specified consumer body to bring a 'representative' or 'collective' follow-on action before the CAT on behalf of two or more consumers[146]; it is for the Secretary of State to specify consumer bodies for this purpose[147]. The Rules of the CAT contain provisions on claims under this section[148]. The *Specified Body (Consumer Claims) Order 2005*[149] names The Consumers' Association (now known as Which?) for the purpose of section 47B. The advantage of representative claims is that, in some cases, the economic loss suffered by individual consumers may be so small as to make litigation uneconomic. However if enough individual claims can be aggregated litigation may become realistic. The representative claimant then apportions any damages recovered between the consumers that consented to the action[150]. It is important to note that section 47B provides for the recovery of damages only on behalf of consumers that give their consent: this is often referred to as the 'opt-in' model. This differs from a possible alternative, the so-called 'opt-out' model, where the action is brought on behalf of a defined category of consumers; in this system consumers can opt out of the litigation and, should they so wish, bring their own claims.

One representative action has been brought under section 47B, *The Consumers' Association v JJB Sports*[151]; this case arose out of the *Football Replica Kit* decision of the OFT[152]. It was settled by agreement early in 2008 and the action was withdrawn[153].

(iii) Examples of follow-on actions in the CAT

The first follow-on action to be brought to the CAT arose from the European Commission's decision in the *Vitamins* case[154]. In *BCL Old Co Ltd v Aventis SA: security for costs*[155] the CAT declined the defendants' request that the claimants should be required to give security for costs; the CAT was obviously concerned not to place undue obstacles in the way of the claimants, in particular in circumstances where the defendants had undoubtedly infringed Article 81 and were therefore almost inevitably going to have to pay damages, albeit that quantum was a matter of dispute. The case was settled before the CAT had given a final judgment.

In *Healthcare at Home v Genzyme* a follow-on action was brought before the CAT by a firm that had been the victim of a margin squeeze by Genzyme Ltd[156]. Interestingly in this case an award of interim damages was made, the first time that this has happened in a competition law case in the UK[157]. The CAT held in its judgment that the claimant could claim damages not only for the period that the OFT and the CAT itself had held

---

[146] There are no provisions for representative actions to be brought on behalf of businesses as opposed to consumers.

[147] Competition Act 1998, s 47B(9).   [148] SI 2003/1372, Rule 33.   [149] SI 2005/2365.

[150] See s 47B(3) of the Competition Act 1998.   [151] Case 1078/7/9/07.

[152] Football kit price-fixing, OFT decision of 1 August 2003, [2004] UKCLR 6.

[153] See the Order of the CAT of 14 January 2008.   [154] OJ [2003] L 6/1, [2003] CMLR 1030.

[155] Case No 1028/5/7/04 [2005] CAT 2, [2005] CompAR 485.

[156] *Genzyme Ltd*, OFT decision of 27 March 2003, upheld on appeal to the CAT, Case No 1016/1/1/03 *Genzyme Ltd v OFT* [2004] CAT 4, [2004] CompAR 358.

[157] Case No 1060/5/7/06 [2006] CAT 29, [2007] CompAR 474.

that the Chapter II prohibition had been infringed, but also for the subsequent period in which the infringement continued, a very sensible interpretation of the Act[158].

In *Emerson Electric Co and others v Morgan Crucible Company plc and others*[159] Emerson brought an action for damages arising from the European Commission's decision in the *Electrical and Mechanical Carbon and Graphite Products* cartel[160]. In *ME Burgess v W Austin & Sons Ltd*[161] Burgess brought an action for damages arising from the CAT's own judgment in *JJ Burgess & Sons v OFT*[162]. The case brought by the Consumers' Association following the *Football Replica Kit* case was referred to above.

4. COMPETITION LAW AS A DEFENCE

(A) Article 81(2)

(i) The sanction of voidness

Many systems of competition law deploy an important sanction, in addition to the imposition of fines and damages actions, in order to persuade undertakings to obey the law: the sanction of voidness. Article 81(2) of the EC Treaty and section 2(4) of the Competition Act 1998 provide that an agreement that restricts competition in the sense of Article 81(1) and that does not satisfy the terms of Article 81(3) is void. In some cases the sanction of voidness may not be a very real one: the members of a price-fixing or a market-sharing cartel would not normally think of trying to enforce their agreement in a court. Their main concern will be to conceal the cartel from the competition authorities, although the latter have considerable powers to unearth this type of practice[163] and to penalise the recalcitrant firms[164]. In other cases, however, the sanction of voidness may be much more significant. If a patentee grants a licence of a patent it will calculate carefully what rate of royalties the licensee should pay and protracted negotiations may take place to settle the other terms of the bargain, for example on the quantities to be produced, the areas in which the products are to be sold and the treatment and ownership of any improvements made by the licensee. For its part the licensee will often have been granted an exclusive territory in which to manufacture and sell. If it transpires that certain aspects of the licence are void and unenforceable this will undermine the deal struck between the parties. The same would be true of an exclusive purchasing term imposed by a supplier on a distributor, as typically occurs in agreements for the sale and purchase of beer and petrol; and of non-competition covenants imposed, for example, when a vendor sells a business as a going concern to a purchaser. In these cases the threat that competition law poses is not that the Commission or some other competition authority will impose a fine, but that a key term of a contract will be unenforceable in commercial litigation. It will be noted from this that the sanction of voidness, as a general proposition, impacts not on serious infringements of the competition rules, such as the operation of cartels, but on more innocuous agreements where the harm

[158] Ibid, para 59.   [159] Case 1077/5/7/07, not yet decided,
[160] Commission Decision of 3 December 2003, OJ [2004] L 125/45, [2005] 5 CMLR 20.
[161] Case 1087/2/3/07, not yet decided.   [162] Case 1044/2/1/04 [2005] CAT 25, [2005] CompAR 1151.
[163] For the Commission's powers of investigation see ch 7, pp 264–272.   [164] See ch 7, pp 272–278.

to competition is much less obvious; this is a powerful reason for urging competition authorities to adopt a 'realistic' approach to the application of Article 81(1) and its progeny in the Member States to agreements[165].

(ii) *Eco Swiss China Time Ltd v Benetton*

Judges tend to be hostile by instinct to what may be seen as technical – even scurrilous – attempts to avoid contractual obligations by invoking points of competition law. However the ECJ's judgment in *Eco Swiss China Time Ltd v Benetton*[166] has confirmed how significant the sanction of voidness is in the legal system of the Community: where an agreement infringes Article 81(1), voidness is an important consequence. At the risk of over-simplification, the ECJ was asked by the Dutch Supreme Court to determine whether the competition rules in the Treaty could be considered to be rules of public policy: on this question turned the possibility of an appeal being brought against an arbitral award[167]. The ECJ was quite clear:

36. However, according to Article 3(g) of the EC Treaty (now, after amendment, Article 3(1)(g) EC), Article 81 EC (ex Article 85) constitutes a fundamental provision which is essential for the accomplishment of the tasks entrusted to the Community and, in particular, for the functioning of the internal market. The importance of such a provision led the framers of the Treaty to provide expressly, in Article 81(2) EC (ex Article 85(2)), that any agreements or decisions prohibited pursuant to that Article are to be automatically void.

37. It follows that where its domestic rules of procedure require a national court to grant an application for annulment of an arbitration award where such an application is founded on failure to observe national rules of public policy, it must also grant such an application where it is founded on failure to comply with the prohibition laid down in Article 81(1) EC (ex Article 85(1)).

(B) The 'problem' of Article 81(3) and the Commission's role in relation to individual exemptions

Previous editions of this book, at this point, dealt at length with the fact that only the Commission could apply Article 81(3) to individual agreements, and that this threw up numerous problems as to the enforceability of agreements between the parties; these problems concerned the rules on notification, the retrospectivity of individual exemptions, the concept of provisional validity and parallel Commission and national court proceedings. However the entry into force of the Modernisation Regulation on 1 May 2004 abolished the process of notifying agreements to the Commission for an individual exemption[168], and the Regulation itself contains several provisions on the role of national courts in the new regime[169]. For this reason the text on the 'problem' of applying Article 81(3) has been dropped from this edition of the book. Of course, the enforceability of an unnotified restrictive agreement prior to 1 May 2004 could still arise in domestic litigation, and readers are referred to a number of practitioners' textbooks should this problem arise in practice[170].

---

[165] See ch 3, pp 116–134, in particular on what is meant by an agreement having as its 'effect' the restriction of competition.

[166] Case C-126/97 [1999] ECR I-3055, [2000] 5 CMLR 816; see also Case C-453/99 *Courage Ltd v Crehan* [2001] ECR I-6297, [2001] 5 CMLR 1058, paras 20–22.

[167] The case is discussed further at pp 317–318 below.   [168] See in particular ch 4, pp 162–164.

[169] See pp 296–299 above.

[170] See eg Bellamy and Child *European Community Law of Competition* (Oxford University Press, 6th ed, 2008, eds Roth and Rose), paras 13-004–13-007.

(C) The classic 'Euro-defence'

As suggested above there seems little doubt that the judicial mind is unsympathetic to an Article 81(2) defence where one party to an agreement freely entered into, attempts to walk away from it on the ground that it is void under competition law. The maxim 'pacta sunt servanda' – contracts should be honoured – has a powerful influence where an undertaking purports, on the basis of a 'technicality' of competition law, to avoid a contractual obligation. The remainder of this section will look at cases in which Euro-defences failed under Article 81. However a recent case reveals that the Euro-defence can succeed: in *Calor Gas Ltd v Express Fuels (Scotland) Ltd*[171] the Outer House of the Scottish Court of Session held that an exclusive dealing agreement was unenforceable by the supplier, Calor Gas, as it infringed Article 81.

In the *George Michael* case[172] the singer argued that his recording contract with Sony was in restraint of trade at common law and amounted to an infringement of Article 81(1), and that it was therefore void and unenforceable: on this occasion the matter came before the court not as a Euro-defence, but in an action by George Michael for a declaration. The court rejected both claims; as to Article 81(1) Parker J was not satisfied that the recording contract was capable of producing an appreciable effect on trade between Member States. More generally the judge was clearly unimpressed at an attempt to avoid an agreement which had been entered into as a settlement of earlier litigation between the parties, the singer at the time of such settlement having received legal advice from leading lawyers in the UK and US with specialisation in the law of publishing agreements. The maxim *interest rei publicae ut finis litium sit* – it is in the public interest that litigation should be settled – in conjunction with *pacta sunt servanda* formed a powerful combination on this occasion.

Euro-defences were invoked in two cases arising from the plight of individuals – known as 'names' – called upon by Lloyd's of London to contribute substantial sums of money as a result of insurance losses, *Society of Lloyd's v Clementson*[173] and *Higgins v Marchant & Eliot Underwriting Ltd*[174]. In *Clementson* Lloyds itself was suing Clementson; his defence was that the Central Fund Byelaw of the Society of Lloyds infringed Article 81(1). The Court of Appeal had concluded that it was at least arguable that Clementson would be able to run such a Euro-defence, and therefore allowed an appeal against its having been struck out. Subsequently, however, the defence did indeed fail. In the *Marchant* case two cash calls had been made on a Lloyds name, Higgins, by Marchant & Elliott Underwriting Ltd. Higgins' case was that the agreement between him and Marchant & Elliott infringed Article 81(1) and was therefore unenforceable. Rix J considered that *Clementson* was distinguishable, as what was in issue in that case was whether the Central Fund Byelaw of Lloyds itself infringed Article 81(1). In the *Higgins* case the agreement that Marchant & Elliott sought to enforce was a separate agreement between it and Higgins. For Higgins it was argued that this agreement was entered into pursuant to the Lloyds regime, and that it amounted, effectively, to an

[171] [2007] CSOH 170.
[172] *Panayiotou v Sony Music Entertainment (UK) Ltd* [1994] ECC 395, [1994] EMLR 229, ChD.
[173] [1995] 1 CMLR 693, [1995] ECC 390, CA.
[174] [1996] 1 Lloyd's Rep 313, [1996] 3 CMLR 314, QBD.

attempt to enforce the rules of the overall system; as a result it was also tainted and unenforceable. This was rejected by Rix J[175]:

No case has been cited to me in which A has been unable to enforce his lawful rights under contract with B because A has been instigated to litigate against B by C in furtherance of C's unlawful agreement or decision. Such a doctrine would be immensely far-reaching and damaging to lawful rights.

In the Court of Appeal the judgment of Rix J was upheld[176]. Judicial disfavour of Euro-defences shone through: 'through the ingenuity of his lawyers [Higgins] relies upon the Article to evade payment of his debts. It is our task to see whether that ingenuity has been well directed and will avail him' (per Leggatt LJ).

Another failed Euro-defence can be seen in *Oakdale (Richmond) Ltd v National Westminster Bank plc*[177]. Chadwick J dismissed an argument that the restrictive terms of an all-moneys debenture arrangement, which provided for a lender to have control over the borrower company's book debts and which was necessary to protect the bank against the risks it had assumed, were anti-competitive. On the contrary the judge was satisfied that these terms were necessary to such agreements and, as such, promoted competition. This judgment is of interest in that the judge did not 'merely' reject the defence, but positively recognised that contractual restrictions can be pro-competitive: as such it sits happily with judgments of the ECJ such as *Delimitis v Henninger Bräu*[178] and *Gøttrup Klim v DLG*[179] in which that court has provided an important lead in showing that contractual restrictions are not necessarily restrictions of competition; indeed contractual restrictions often provide a positive contribution to the competitive process[180]. A Euro-defence also failed in *Leeds City Council v Watkins*[181] where the judge concluded that the defendants had failed to produce any evidence that the claimants had infringed UK or EC competition law. The judge in this case was highly critical of both parties' economics experts[182].

(D) Severance

The preceding section reveals that judges may view with distaste technical invocations of the competition rules in order to avoid contractual obligations. However there will be occasions when voidness does follow from an infringement of Article 81(1); the facts of *Eco Swiss China Time v Benetton*[183] reveal how this might happen. Where Article 81(1) is successfully invoked in litigation a problem can arise over the effect of the voidness upon the remainder of the agreement. The ECJ has held that, provided that it is possible to sever the offending provisions of the contract from the rest of its terms, the latter

---

[175] [1996] 1 Lloyd's Rep 313, 324, [1996] 3 CMLR 313, p 331.
[176] [1996] 2 Lloyd's Rep 31, [1996] 3 CMLR 349, CA.
[177] [1997] ECC 130, [1997] Eu LR 27, ChD, affd on appeal [1997] 3 CMLR 815, CA.
[178] Case C-234/89 [1991] ECR I-935, [1992] 5 CMLR 210.
[179] Case C-250/92 [1994] ECR I-5641, [1996] 4 CMLR 191.   [180] See ch 3, pp 124–126.
[181] [2003] EWHC 598 (Ch), [2003] UKCLR 467.
[182] Ibid, paras 88–117; Euro-defences also failed in *LauritzenCool AB v Lady Navigation Inc* [2004] EWHC 2607, (Comm); in *Days Medical Aids v Pihsiang* [2004] EuLR 477, [2004] ECC 297 (QBD); and in *The Qualifying Insurers Subscribing to the ARP v Ross* [2006] ECC 33.
[183] See Case C-126/97 [1999] ECR I-3055, [2000] 5 CMLR 816; the facts of the case are discussed at pp 317–318 below.

remain valid and enforceable[184]. However the Court did not lay down a Community-wide principle of severance, so that the mechanism whereby this is to be effected is a matter to be decided according to the domestic law of each Member State[185]. This in turn gives rise to issues under the Brussels Regulation[186] and the Rome Convention[187]; the former determines where litigation may take place in civil and commercial cases, while the latter determines the law that should be applied in contractual disputes. Assuming that severability is regarded as a matter of substance rather than procedure the Brussels Regulation ought not to affect the outcome of litigation, since in principle the Rome Convention should lead to the same finding of the applicable law, wherever the litigation takes place; however the determination of the applicable law may be crucial to the outcome of the litigation, since different Member States have different methods of severing unlawful restrictions from contracts.

As a matter of English contract law severance is possible in certain circumstances, although the rules on this subject are complex[188]. The Court of Appeal was called upon to examine severability in a competition law context in *Chemidus Wavin Ltd v Société pour la Transformation*[189]. A patentee was suing for royalties payable under an agreement that arguably infringed Article 81(1). The Court held that the minimum royalties provision was enforceable, irrespective of whether other parts of the agreement might infringe Article 81(1). Buckley LJ said:

It seems to me that, in applying Article [81] to an English contract, one may well have to consider whether, after the excisions required by the Article of the Treaty have been made from the contract, the contract could be said to fail for lack of consideration or on any other ground, or whether the contract would be so changed in its character as not to be the sort of contract that the parties intended to enter into at all.

In *Inntrepreneur Estates Ltd v Mason*[190] M Barnes QC, sitting as a Deputy Judge of the High Court, held that, where a beer tie infringed the competition rules, it did not follow that a covenant to pay rent would also be unenforceable. Applying the test in *Chemidus Wavin* the judge had no difficulty in severing the tie, leaving the rest of the agreement intact. A similar result was reached by the Court of Appeal in *Inntrepeneur Estates (GL) Ltd v Boyes*[191]. It is unsurprising that the judges in these cases found the argument unappealing that the tenant of a public house could be relieved of the obligation to pay rent to the landlord as a collateral consequence of an (arguably) unlawful beer tie.

[184] Case 56/65 *Société Technique Minière v Maschinenbau Ulm* [1966] ECR 235, [1966] CMLR 357; Case 319/82 *Société de Vente de Ciments et Bétons de l'Est v Kerpen and Kerpen GmbH* [1983] ECR 4173, [1983] ECR 4173, [1985] 1 CMLR 511.

[185] Case 319/82 *Ciments et Bétons* (n 184 above); Case 10/86 *VAG France SA v Etablissements Magne SA* [1986] ECR 4071, [1988] 4 CMLR 98.

[186] Council Regulation 44/2001 on Jurisdiction and the recognition and enforcement of judgments in civil and commercial matters OJ [2001] L 12/1.

[187] Rome Convention on the Law Applicable to Contractual Obligations 1980; note also the Regulation on the Law Applicable to Non-contractual Obligations, Regulation 864/2007, OJ [2007] L 199/40.

[188] See *Chitty on Contracts* (Sweet & Maxwell, 29th ed, 2004), chapter 16, paras 16.188–16.197; for discussion of the obligations of a national court to comply with EC law when determining whether to sever clauses in an agreement that infringes Article 81(1) see also *Re The Nullity of a Beer Agreement* [2002] ECC 26 (Austrian Supreme Court).

[189] [1977] FSR 181, [1978] 3 CMLR 514, CA.   [190] [1994] 68 P & CR 53, [1993] 2 CMLR 293, QBD.

[191] [1995] ECC 16, [1993] 2 EGLR 112, CA; see similarly *Trent Taverns Ltd v Sykes* [1998] Eu LR 571, QBD, upheld on appeal [1999] Eu LR 492, CA.

A contrary finding would have devastating consequences for landlords holding large portfolios of public houses.

If the effect of severing certain clauses from an agreement would be that its scope and intention would be entirely altered, bringing about a fundamental change in the bargain between the parties, the entire agreement would become unenforceable[192]. This was the conclusion in *English Welsh & Scottish Railway Ltd v E.ON UK plc*[193] where Field J held that the directions of the Office of Rail Regulation, that various terms of a coal carriage agreement between the parties were unlawful under the Chapter II prohibition and Article 82 and should be removed or modified, altered the contract so fundamentally that it became void and unenforceable in its entirety.

(E) Void or illegal?

Agreements which infringe Article 81(1) are stated by Article 81(2) to be void; however an important question is whether they are 'merely' void or whether they are also illegal. On this classification turn the important issues of whether any money paid under the contract by one party to the other would be irrecoverable, applying the principle *in pari delicto potior est conditio defendentis* (which roughly translates as 'where both parties are to blame the defendant's position is more powerful')[194], and whether one party to the agreement could bring an action against the other for damages for harm suffered as a result of the operation of the agreement. This issue was discussed above in relation to the judgment in *Courage Ltd v Crehan*[195].

(F) Transient voidness

One issue to have come before the Court of Appeal is whether the statutory prohibition in Article 81(2) may be 'turned on and off' depending on the surrounding facts[196]. In *Passmore v Morland plc*[197] the Court of Appeal upheld the Chancery Division's judgment that an agreement could move from voidness to validity (and back again) according to the effect that it might be having on the market. Passmore was the publican of a pub in Aldershot, under a tenancy granted by the Inntrepreneur Pub Co ('IPC'). The tenancy contained an exclusive purchasing term that Passmore should purchase beer exclusively from IPC. Subsequently the reversion of the lease was acquired by Morland plc, a relatively small brewer. In a dispute between Morland and Passmore the latter claimed that the beer tie was unenforceable as a result of the application of Article 81. Essentially the question for the Court of Appeal was as follows: Suppose that the exclusive purchasing term was unenforceable when entered into, since IPC owned 4,500 pubs containing similar ties which, cumulatively, could foreclose access to the market by

---

[192] See *Richard Cound Ltd v BMW (GB) Ltd* [1997] Eu LR 277, QBD and CA; *Benford Ltd v Cameron Equipment Ltd* [1997] Eu LR 334 (Mercantile Court); *Clover Leaf Cars Ltd v BMW (GB) Ltd* [1997] Eu LR 535, CA; *First County Garages Ltd v Fiat Auto (UK) Ltd* [1997] Eu LR 712, ChD; *Fulton Motors Ltd v Toyota (GB) Ltd* [1998] Eu LR 327, ChD.

[193] [2007] EWHC 599 (Comm), [2007] UKCLR 1653.

[194] See Goff and Jones *The Law of Restitution* (Sweet & Maxwell, 7th ed, 2006), ch 24.

[195] See pp 293–294 above.

[196] See the Commission's Guidelines on the application of Article 81(3) of the Treaty, OJ [2004] C 101/8, para 44.

[197] [1998] 4 All ER 468, [1998] Eu LR 580, ChD; affd [1999] Eu LR 501, [1999] 1 CMLR 1129, CA.

other brewers (this being the essential issue according to the judgment of the ECJ in *Delimitis*[198]). If some of those pubs were subsequently to come into the hands of a small brewer such as Morland might it follow that, because those agreements did not contribute to any foreclosure because of its much weaker position in the market, they would cease to be unenforceable? In other words is the logic of the prohibition in Article 81(1), in conjunction with the declaration of voidness in Article 81(2), that agreements can, over a period of time, float into and out of voidness, depending on market conditions? The Court of Appeal, upholding the order of Laddie J below[199], was clear that this was indeed the position. Three passages of the judgment of Chadwick LJ state the position clearly:

[A]n agreement which is not within Article [81(1)] at the time when it is entered into – because, in the circumstances prevailing in the relevant market at that time, it does not have the effect of preventing, restricting or distorting competition – may, subsequently and as the result of change in those circumstances, come within Article [81(1)], because, in the changed circumstances, it does have that effect[200].

Later:

It must follow, also, by a parity of reasoning, that an agreement which is within the prohibition of Article [81(1)] at the time when it is entered into – because, in the circumstances prevailing in the relevant market at that time, it does have the effect of preventing, restricting or distorting competition – may, subsequently and as a result of a change in those circumstances, fall outside the prohibition contained in that Article, because, in the changed circumstances, it no longer has that effect[201].

Later again:

The prohibition is temporaneous (or transient) rather than absolute, in the sense that it endures for a finite period of time – the period of time for which it is needed – rather than for all time[202].

Towards the end of his judgment Chadwick LJ dealt with an argument on behalf of Passmore that the principle of legal certainty should have as its consequence that the tie was and remained unenforceable, consistently with the Court of Appeal's judgment in *Shell UK Ltd v Lostock Garage*[203]: the Court of Appeal (Lord Denning MR dissenting) held there that a restrictive covenant that was valid when entered into should remain valid, even if subsequent circumstances made it unreasonable or unfair to enforce it. Ormrod LJ felt that the opposite conclusion 'would introduce into the law an unprecedented discretion in the court to suspend for a time a term in a contract; the repercussions of this are quite unforeseeable and unmanageable'[204]. On this point Chadwick LJ concluded in *Passmore* that 'it has to be recognised that what was seen, in *Shell UK Ltd v Lostock Garage Ltd*, as a wholly novel doctrine is now enshrined in Community competition law'[205].

(G) Article 82

It may be that a contractual term infringes Article 82, because it amounts to an abuse of a dominant position, as well as infringing Article 81. For example an agreement to

---

[198] See ch 3, p 123.   [199] [1998] 4 All ER 468.
[200] [1999] Eu LR 501, p 511, [1999] 1 CMLR 1129, para 26.   [201] Ibid, para 26.   [202] Ibid, para 28.
[203] [1977] 1 All ER 481, [1976] 1 WLR 1187, CA.   [204] Ibid, pp 492, 1202 respectively.
[205] [1999] Eu LR 501, [1999] 1 CMLR 1129, para 54.

purchase one's entire requirements of a particular product from a dominant firm is quite likely to infringe both Article 81 and Article 82[206], because it might foreclose access to the market on the part of competitors; it is irrelevant for this purpose whether the undertaking that accepts the obligation is willing or unwilling to accept it[207]. Similarly a system of loyalty rebates, which falls short of a contractual requirement not to buy from competitors but which may have the same effect, may amount to an abuse[208]. In this situation it has been assumed that the prohibition of Article 82 means that the offending provisions are void, although there is nothing on the face of Article 82, as there is in the case of Article 81(2), to say so. It would follow that a customer tied by an exclusive purchasing commitment which infringes Article 82 could safely ignore it and purchase supplies elsewhere. The impact of any such invalidity on the remainder of the agreement would raise the same question of severability discussed above[209]. In *English Welsh & Scottish Railway Ltd v E.ON UK plc*[210] the High Court concluded that abusive terms in coal carriage agreements rendered them void and unenforceable[211].

(H) Third party as defendant

The discussion so far has concerned contractual actions where a defendant raises UK or EC competition law as a defence. However on some occasions the competition rules (usually Article 82) are raised as a defence by a third party. In several cases the owner of an intellectual property right such as a patent, registered design or copyright has brought an action against a defendant for infringement; the defendant has then claimed that it has a defence under Article 82 on the basis that the claimant is guilty of abusing its dominant position. In particular, the defendant may claim that, by refusing to grant a licence of the intellectual property right in question, it (the claimant) is guilty of an abuse under Article 82. Whether or not a refusal to license can be abusive is itself a vexed question; it is considered in chapter 19[212]. However even if the claimant is abusing its dominant position, this will not in itself confer on the defendant a valid defence. The courts have established that there must be a sufficient nexus between the claimant's abusive behaviour and the defendant to entitle it to rely on Article 82. In *Chiron Corpn v Organon Teknika Ltd*[213] Aldous J said (at paragraph 44) that:

The fact that a person is abusing a dominant position does not mean that all wrongdoers have a defence in respect of all actions brought by that person. It is only in those cases where the exercise or existence of that right creates or buttresses the abuse will the court refuse to give effect to the exercise of the right.

In several cases the necessary nexus has been lacking[214] and the defence therefore struck out. Where there is a sufficient nexus between the parties, for example where

---

[206] See eg Case 85/76 *Hoffmann-La Roche v Commission* [1979] ECR 461, [1979] 3 CMLR 211.
[207] On agreements of this kind see ch 17, pp 679–687.
[208] On practices of this kind see ch 18, pp 719–727.   [209] See pp 312–314 above.
[210] [2007] EWHC 599 (Comm), [2007] UKCLR 1653.   [211] See p 314 above.
[212] See ch 19, pp 786–792.
[213] [1993] FSR 324, [1992] 3 CMLR 813, upheld on appeal [1993] FSR 567, CA.
[214] See eg *ICI v Berk Pharmaceuticals* [1981] 2 CMLR 91, [1981] FSR 1; *British Leyland Motor Corpn v Armstrong Patents Co Ltd* [1984] 3 CMLR 102 (this decision was overturned in the House of Lords on the issue of copyright protection for functional objects: [1986] AC 577); *Ransburg-GEMA AG v Electrostatic Plant Systems* [1989] 2 CMLR 712, QBD; *Philips Electronics v Ingman Ltd* [1998] Eu LR 666, ChD; *Sandvik Aktiebolag v KR Pfiffner (UK) Ltd* [1999] Eu LR 755, ChD; *HMSO v Automobile Association Ltd* [2001] Eu LR

the dominant undertaking is abusing its market power specifically in order to harm the defendant, a defence based on Articles 81 and/or 82 may be pleaded[215].

5. ARBITRATION

Commercial agreements very often provide for the arbitration of disputes, and it is not uncommon for competition law issues – for example the enforceability of a non-compete clause or of an exclusive purchasing obligation – to be referred to arbitration. The subject is complex; there is a growing body of literature on it[216]. The European Commission is conscious of the amount of arbitration (and of other forms of alternative dispute resolution) that takes place; indeed in its own remedies it quite often provides mechanisms for the settlement of disputes[217]. The Commission has been known to investigate cases *after* parties have settled a dispute in arbitration proceedings[218].

In *Eco Swiss China Time Ltd v Benetton International NV*[219] the ECJ was asked to consider the impact of the competition rules on arbitration proceedings. Benetton had granted a trade mark licence to Eco Swiss to market watches under the Benetton name. Benetton subsequently terminated the licence and Eco Swiss referred the matter to an

---

80, [2001] ECC 273, ChD; *P&S Amusements Ltd v Valley House Leisure Ltd* [2006] EWHC 99 (Ch), [2006] UKCLR 855.

[215] See eg *British Leyland v TI Silencers* [1981] 2 CMLR 75, CA; *Lansing Bagnall v Buccaneer Lift Parts* [1984] 1 CMLR 224, [1984] FSR 241, CA; *Pitney Bowes Inc v Francoyp-Postalia GmbH* [1990] 3 CMLR 466, [1991] FSR 72; *Intel Corpn v Via Technologies* [2002] EWCA Civ 1905, [2002] All ER (D) 346 (Dec): see Curley 'Eurodefences and Chips: "A Somewhat Indigestible Dish"' (2003) 25 EIPR 282; see also *Intergraph Corpn v Solid Systems* [1998] Eu LR 221, ChD; *Sportswear SpA v Stonestyle Ltd* [2006] EWCA 380, [2006] UKCLR 893, [2006] ECC 373 (a case under Article 81 rather than Article 82).

[216] See *Competition and Arbitration Law* (International Chamber of Commerce, 1993); Atwood 'The Arbitration of International Antitrust Disputes: A Status Report and Suggestions' [1994] Fordham Corporate Law Institute (ed Hawk), ch 15; von Mehren 'Some Reflections on the International Arbitration of Antitrust Issues' ibid, ch 16; Atwood, von Mehren and Temple Lang 'International Arbitration' ibid, ch 17; Schmitthoff 'The Enforcement of EC Competition Law in Arbitral Proceedings' [1996] Legal Issues in European Integration 101; Lugard 'EC Competition Law and Arbitration: Opposing Principles?' (1998) 19 ECLR 295 (written prior to the judgment in *Eco Swiss*); Komninos 'Arbitration and the Modernisation of European Competition Law Enforcement' (2001) 24 World Competition 211; Baudenbacher and Higgins 'Decentralization of EC Competition Law Enforcement and Arbitration' [2002] Columbia Journal of Community Law 1; Baudenbacher 'Enforcement of EC and EEA Competition Rules by Arbitration Tribunals Inside and Outside the EU' in *European Competition Law Annual 2001: Effective Enforcement of EC Antitrust Law* (eds Ehlermann and Atansiu, Hart Publishing, 2003); Dolmans and Grierson 'Arbitration and the Modernisation of EC Antitrust Law: New Opportunities and New Responsibilities' (2003) 14 ICC International Court of Arbitration Bulletin, p 37; Blessing Arbitrating Antitrust and Merger Control Issues (Helbing & Lichtenhahn, 2003); Nazzini 'International Arbitration and Public Enforcement of Competition Law' (2004) 25 ECLR 153; Nazzini *Concurrent Proceedings in Competition Law: Procedure, Evidence and Remedies* (Oxford University Press, 2004), chs 10 and 11; Bowsher 'Arbitration and Competition' in *Competition Litigation in the UK* (eds Ward and Smith, Sweet & Maxwell, 2005), ch 11; Landolt *Modernised EC Competition Law in International Arbitration* (Kluwer Law International, 2006); on arbitration and the antitrust rules in the US see *Mitsubishi Motors v Soler Chrysler-Plymouth Inc* 473 US 614 (1985) and *JLM Industries Inc v Stolt-Nielsen SA* 387 F.3d 163 (2004).

[217] See Bowsher, n 216 above, paras 11-036–11-042.

[218] See eg the discussion of the *Marathon* case in Competition Policy Newsletter (Summer 2004) pp 41–43.

[219] Case C-126/87 [1999] ECR I-3055, [2000] 5 CMLR 816; see Komninos (2000) 37 CML Rev 459.

arbitrator, under Dutch law, in accordance with the agreement. The arbitrator awarded
Eco Swiss substantial damages. No competition law point was taken by the parties, and
the arbitrator did not raise one. In fact the trade mark licence infringed Article 81(1)
and was ineligible for block exemption under Regulation 240/96 on technology transfer
agreements[220]. Benetton subsequently decided to argue that the award of damages to
Eco Swiss amounted to enforcing an agreement that was contrary to EC competition
law. Under Dutch law an arbitration award can be challenged before the courts, in the
absence of agreement between the parties, only on grounds of public policy. The Dutch
Supreme Court held that the enforcement of competition rules did not amount to public policy in Dutch law, so that if the matter were purely domestic Benetton would be
unsuccessful. However, since Benetton's case rested on the Community competition
rules, the matter was referred to the ECJ under Article 234.

As noted above the ECJ stressed the fundamental importance of the competition
rules in the Treaty, and the importance of the sanction of voidness in ensuring compliance with them[221]. A consequence of this was that, if domestic law allowed an appeal
against an arbitration award on grounds of public policy, the possibility that there might
be a breach of the Community competition rules should be investigated. On a separate
point the ECJ recognised that domestic procedural rules which prescribe time limits for
the challenging of arbitral awards could have the effect of preventing an appeal based
on the competition rules; provided that the time limits were not so fierce as to infringe
the requirement of effective application of the competition rules they would themselves
be valid.

The ECJ did not say anything specifically about the obligations of arbitrators
themselves, but the case is of obvious importance to their role. Arbitration is intended
to enable parties to disputes to reach a reasonably rapid and cheap settlement of disputes. If an arbitrator ignores points of competition law, but these can subsequently be
raised on appeal as, subject to the time limit point, in *Eco Swiss*, the speedy and cheap
conclusion of cases would be undermined. It seems sensible therefore that the arbitrator should apply his or her mind to the issue; however the ECJ's judgment in *Van
Schijndel*[222] established that there is no obligation upon a national court (nor therefore upon an arbitral panel) pro-actively to root out infringements of the competition
rules[223].

It would appear to be the case that an arbitrator could not refer an issue of competition law to the ECJ under Article 234; the establishment of an arbitration panel
is a consensual process, with the result that it is not a 'court or tribunal of a Member
State'[224].

[220] This Regulation has since been replaced by Regulation 772/2004, OJ [2004] L 123/11; it is discussed in
ch 19, pp 771–781.
[221] See pp 309–310 above.
[222] Cases C-430/93 etc. [1995] ECR I-4705, [1996] 1 CMLR 801: see p 299 above; on the point in the text see
Thalès Air Defense v Euromissile, judgment of the Paris Court of Appeal of 18 November 2004, [2006] ECC
6, where an appeal against an award of damages by an arbitral panel was dismissed since the Article 81 point
had not been raised during the course of the arbitration but was only raised after the event.
[223] An interesting question is whether an arbitrator in a non-EU country would apply the competition
rules, as a matter of public policy, where an agreement infringes Article 81 (or Article 82); on this point see
Bowsher, n 216 above, paras 11-063–11-069.
[224] Case 102/81 *Nordsee Deutsche Hochseefischerei GmbH v Reederei Mond* [1982] ECR 1095; see further
the Opinion of Advocate General Colomer in Case C-17/00 *de Coster v Collège des Bourgmestres* [2001] ECR
I-9445, [2002] 1 CMLR 285.

6. PROPOSALS FOR REFORM

(A) The European Commission's Green and White Papers

In December 2005 the European Commission published a Green Paper, *Damages actions for breach of the EC antitrust rules*[225], the purpose of which was to identify the main obstacles to a more efficient system of damages claims and to set out different options to promote more damages claims. Commissioner Kroes has spoken on numerous occasions of the need to ensure that consumers should be able to seek damages for the harm that they suffer as a result of anti-competitive behaviour[226]. Prior to the adoption of the Green Paper three Commission officials set out a number of reasons why the greater use of private enforcement might be beneficial[227]:

- It would increase deterrence against infringements and increase compliance with the law
- The victims of illegal anti-competitive behaviour would be compensated for loss suffered
- Some cases – for example between just two parties – are more appropriate for determination by private than public enforcement
- Public authorities do not have the resources to investigate every complaint of anti-competitive behaviour
- Interim relief may be obtained more quickly from courts than from public authorities
- Courts can order unsuccessful parties to pay the successful party's costs, something which public authorities cannot do
- Private actions assist the development of a 'competition culture'.

The Green Paper identified a number of possible obstacles to private enforcement and considered various options as to how they might be addressed; the staff working paper that accompanied the Green Paper provides very useful additional information about the matters raised. These included the issue of access to evidence; the question of whether liability to damages should depend on a finding of fault; the nature and level of damages; the position of indirect purchasers and the 'passing-on' defence; representative actions on behalf of consumers; costs; the relationship between public and private enforcement; and jurisdiction and the applicable law. The Commission received

---

[225] COM(2005) 672 final, 19.12.2005, available at www.ec.europa.eu/comm/competition/antitrust/actionsdamages/documents.html#greenpaper; see also the accompanying Staff Working Paper which contains a rich source of research material; see Diemer 'The Green Paper on Damages Actions for Breach of the EC Antitrust Rules' (2006) 27 ECLR 309; Pheasant 'Damages Actions for Breach of the EC Antitrust Rules: The European Commission's Green Paper' (2006) 27 ECLR 365; Homes and Doig 'Views on the Commission's Green Paper on Damages Actions for Breach of EC Antitrust Rules: Causation and Passing-on Defence' (2006) 5 Competition Law Journal 123; Eilmansberger 'The Green Paper on damages actions for breach of the EC antitrust rules and beyond: Reflections on the utility and feasibility of stimulating private enforcement through legislative action' (2007) 44 Common Market Law Review 431; Nebbia 'Damages actions for the infringement of EC competition law: compensation or deterrence?' (2007) 33 ELR 23.

[226] See eg 'Reinforcing the fight against cartels and developing antitrust damage actions: two tools for a more competitive Europe', speech of 8 March 2007, available at www.ec.europa.eu/comm/competition/speeches/index_2007.html.

[227] Woods, Sinclair and Ashton 'Private enforcement of Community competition law: modernisation and the road ahead' Competition Policy Newsletter, Summer 2004, p 31; see also Baker 'Revisiting History – What have we Learned about Private Antitrust Enforcement that we would Recommend to Others' (2004) 16 Loyola Consumer Law Review.

a large number of responses to the Green Paper[228]. The UK Government gave a warm welcome to it[229].

In April 2008 the Commission published a White Paper, *Damages actions for breach of the EC Antitrust Rules*[230]. At the same time it also published a Staff Working Paper[231] and an *Impact Assessment*[232]. The key recommendations of the White Paper are that:

- victims of anti-competitive behaviour should be able to claim **single damages** for their harm, but not multiple damages; indirect purchasers should be able to claim as well as purchasers that have direct dealings with those responsible for the infringement

- **collective redress** should be available to consumers and small and medium-sized businesses through representative actions by qualified bodies such as consumer associations, state bodies and trade associations and opt-in collective actions in which victims expressly decide to combine their individual claims into a single action

- there should be a **minimum level of disclosure of evidence** across the EU between parties involved in litigation, subject to strict judicial control; adequate protection should be given to corporate statements by leniency applicants and to the investigations of competition authorities

- decisions of NCAs should have a **binding effect** on courts in the same way that Commission decisions are binding by virtue of Article 16(1) of the Modernisation Regulation

- where a Member State's national law requires a finding of fault before damages can be awarded, there should be a rule that, once the victim has shown a breach of Article 81 or 82, the infringer should be liable in damages unless it can show that the infringement was the result of **excusable error.**

The Commission invited comments on these (and other) recommendations by 15 July 2008. It does not say in the White Paper how its recommendations would be effected: it may be that a degree of convergence will come about as a result of voluntary action on the part of Member States to amend their own laws. 'Soft convergence' of this kind has been pronounced in the case of the public enforcement of the competition rules in the EU. It may be that the Commission will propose a directive in relation to some of its recommendations: for example there is a relevant precedent on access to evidence in civil litigation in the form of the *Directive on the enforcement of intellectual property rights*[233].

(B) The Office of Fair Trading's Discussion Paper

In April 2007 the OFT published a Discussion Paper, *Private actions in competition law: effective redress for consumers and business*[234]. The Discussion Paper discussed the principles that should inform any proposals designed to make private competition law actions more effective. These principles are that:

- Consumers and businesses suffering losses as a result of breaches of competition law should be able to recover compensation, both on a standalone basis as well as in follow-on actions following public enforcement action.

---

[228] Available at www.ec.europa.eu/comm/competition/antitrust/actionsdamages/green_paper_comments.html.
[229] See www.berr.gov.uk/files/file28534.pdf.   [230] COM(2008) 154 final, 2.4.2008.
[231] SEC (2008) 404.   [232] SEC (2008) 405.   [233] Directive 2004/48/EC OJ [2004] L 195/16.
[234] OFT 916, available at .oft.gov.uk/shared_oft/reports/comp_policy/oft916.pdf.

- Representative bodies should be allowed to bring actions on behalf of those persons.
- Private competition law actions should exist alongside, and in harmony with, public enforcement.
- Any changes in the law to facilitate private actions must guard against the risk of creating a 'litigation culture' which is costly and unduly diverts management time.
- Processes and systems should be devised to encourage the settlement of cases without going to court or trial wherever possible.
- The right balance should be struck between requiring defendants and others to disclose relevant materials to claimants and ensuring that the process is not abused.

The Discussion Paper proceeded to discuss representative actions, including the possibility that representative bodies should be allowed to bring standalone actions on behalf of consumers as well as follow-on ones, and that they should be able to bring both standalone and follow-on actions on behalf of businesses. It also discussed costs and funding arrangements, including the introduction of conditional fee arrangements under which it may be possible to allow a percentage increase on fees of greater than 100 per cent if a case is won; a further idea was to make provision for clearer guidance on costs-capping orders, allowing the court to cap the parties' liability for each other's costs. The Discussion Paper then addressed evidential issues, including the suggestion that the burden of proving that a claimant has 'passed on' any higher prices to its customers should lie with the defendant. Other matters covered included the applicable law, effective claims resolution, and the interface with public enforcement and consistency of policy.

The OFT received a large number of responses to its Discussion Paper: these can be accessed on its website[235]. Most of the responses were favourable to steps being taken to facilitate more private actions, although there was a general recognition that care should be taken to ensure that vexatious and frivolous cases should be avoided: establishing a 'competition culture' in which victims of anti-competitive behaviour can sue for compensation should not lead to a 'litigation culture' in which unmeritorious claims are made. The responses were also clear that private actions should be a complement to, but not a replacement for, effective public enforcement by the OFT and sectoral regulators.

In November 2007 the OFT published its recommendations to the Government[236]. These were that the Government should consult on the following measures, to be designed and implemented is such a way as to comply with the principles outlined above:

- Modify existing or introduce new procedures to allow representative bodies to bring standalone and follow-on actions for damages and injunctions on behalf of consumers
- Modify existing or introduce new procedures to allow representative bodies to bring standalone and follow-on actions for damages and injunctions on behalf of businesses
- Introduce conditional fee arrangements in representative actions which allow for an increase of greater than 100 per cent on lawyers' fees
- Codify courts' discretion to cap parties' costs liabilities and to provide for the courts' discretion to give the claimant cost-protection in appropriate cases

[235] Available at www.oft.gov.uk/advice_and_resources/resource_base/consultations/private.
[236] Private actions in competition law: effective redress for consumers and business.

- Establish a merits-based litigation fund
- Require UK courts and tribunals to 'have regard' to decisions and guidance of the OFT and the sectoral regulators
- Confer power on the Secretary of State to exclude leniency documents from use in litigation without the consent of the leniency applicant
- Confer power on the Secretary of State to remove joint and several liability for immunity recipients in private actions for damages in competition law cases.

9

Competition Act 1998 – substantive provisions

CHAPTER CONTENTS

1. INTRODUCTION

The Competition Act 1998, the main provisions of which entered into force on 1 March 2000, radically reformed the domestic law of the UK on restrictive agreements and anti-competitive practices. The Competition Act swept away much of the system that had been established over the preceding 50 years: the Restrictive Trade Practices Acts 1976 and 1977, the Resale Prices Act 1976 and the provisions on anti-competitive practices in the Competition Act 1980 were all repealed. The Enterprise Act 2002 implemented further changes to UK competition law including the creation of a new system of market investigations[1] and merger control[2], the introduction of criminal sanctions for individuals involved in cartel cases[3] and the disqualification of directors of companies that infringe competition law[4]. Further changes, in particular to the Competition Act 1998, were effected by the *Competition Act 1998 and Other Enactments (Amendment) Regulations 2004*[5] ('the *Amendment Regulations*') in order to bring domestic law into alignment with the principles of the EC Modernisation Regulation[6]; these changes are incorporated in the text that follows.

Section 2 of this chapter will provide an overview of the Competition Act. Sections 3 and 4 will consider in turn the so-called Chapter I and Chapter II prohibitions in the Competition Act which are modelled upon Articles 81 and 82 EC respectively. Section 5 discusses the relationship between EC and domestic competition law, including the important 'governing principles' clause in section 60 of the Competition Act, which is intended to achieve consistency with EC law. Section 6 contains a table of all the

---

[1] See ch 11. [2] See ch 22. [3] See ch 10, pp 415–422. [4] See ch 10, pp 422–423.
[5] SI 2004/1261. [6] OJ [2003] L 1/1.

decisions under the Competition Act to have been published on the website of the Office of Fair Trading ('the OFT') by the end of January 2008 and discussion of the application of the Competition Act in practice. Many of the decisions of the OFT and the sectoral regulators under the Competition Act will be discussed further in the contextual chapters in the second half of this book[7]. Private enforcement of the Act is discussed in chapter 8; public enforcement by the OFT and the sectoral regulators is considered in chapter 10.

2. THE COMPETITION ACT 1998 – OVERVIEW

(A) Outline of the Act

The Competition Act 1998 is a complex piece of legislation; a number of amendments to it were made by the Enterprise Act 2002, and more by the *Amendment Regulations* of 2004. The Competition Act is divided into four parts, consisting of 76 sections. It contains numerous schedules which contain important detail, for example on exclusions, commitments and the role of the sectoral regulators.

(i) Part 1: the Chapter I and Chapter II prohibitions

The most important provisions are found in Part 1 of the Act, which is divided into five chapters. In particular it introduces prohibitions that are modelled upon Article 81 EC ('the Chapter I prohibition') and Article 82 EC ('the Chapter II prohibition'). The Act confers substantial powers of investigation and enforcement on the OFT and the sectoral regulators such as the OFCOM[8]. The Act established the Competition Commission as a successor to the former Monopolies and Mergers Commission[9]; the Competition Commission is responsible for carrying out merger inquiries and market investigations. The Competition Appeal Tribunal ('the CAT'), a successor to the former Competition Commission Appeal Tribunal, hears appeals against decisions of the OFT and the regulators under the Competition Act; it also has various other functions under the Enterprise Act[10].

(ii) Part 2: European investigations

Part 2 of the Competition Act is concerned with investigations in relation to Articles 81 and 82 EC, giving specific powers to a High Court judge to issue a warrant authorising the OFT to enter premises in connection with an investigation ordered or requested by the European Commission[11]. Part 2A of the Act is concerned with investigations conducted by the OFT on behalf of a competition authority of another Member State of the EU pursuant to Article 22 of the EC Modernisation Regulation[12].

---

[7] See eg ch 13, pp 538–543 on cartels cases and ch 18 generally on pricing abuses.
[8] See ch 10, pp 424–426 on the concurrent powers of the OFT and the sectoral regulators.
[9] Competition Act 1998, s 45.
[10] On the OFT, the Competition Commission and the CAT see ch 2, pp 64–73.
[11] See ch 10, p 393. [12] Ibid.

(iii) Part 3: amendments to the FTA

Part III of the Act made some amendments to the monopoly provisions of the Fair Trading Act 1973; these, however, have been repealed and replaced by the market investigation provisions in the Enterprise Act 2002: they are described in chapter 11.

(iv) Part IV: miscellaneous amendments

Part IV of the Competition Act 1998 contains supplemental and transitional provisions, including the repeal of sections 44 and 45 of the Patents Act 1977[13], and provisions on Crown application.

(B) OFT guidance

The Competition Act 1998 requires the OFT to publish general advice and information as to how it will apply the law in practice[14]. The sectoral regulators may issue similar advice and information in relation to their respective sectors and have done so in conjunction with the OFT. A number of guidelines were published in 2000, when the Act first entered into force; most of these have been revised to take into account changes introduced as a result of the adoption of the EC Modernisation Regulation. On 12 March 2008 the following guidelines had been published under the Competition Act[15]:

- *Agreements and concerted practices*[16]
- *Abuse of a dominant position*[17]
- *Market definition*[18]
- *Powers of investigation*[19]
- *Concurrent application to regulated industries*[20]
- *Enforcement*[21]
- *Trade associations, professional bodies and self-regulatory organisations*[22]
- *Assessment of market power*[23]
- *The application of the Competition Act in the telecommunications sector*[24]
- *Vertical agreements and restraints*[25]
- *Land agreements*[26]
- *Services of general economic interest*[27]
- *The application of the Competition Act in the water and sewerage sectors*[28]
- *OFT's Guidance as to the appropriate amount of a penalty*[29]
- *Application in the energy sector*[30]

---

[13] See ch 19, p 796. [14] Competition Act, s 52.
[15] The guidelines are available at www.oft.gov.uk/advice_and_resources/resource_base/legal/competition-act-1998/publications#named1.
[16] OFT 401, December 2004. [17] OFT 402, December 2004. [18] OFT 403, December 2004.
[19] OFT 404, December 2004. [20] OFT 405, December 2004. [21] OFT 407, December 2004.
[22] OFT 408, December 2004. [23] OFT 415, December 2004. [24] OFT 417, February 2000.
[25] OFT 419, December 2004. [26] OFT 420, December 2004. [27] OFT 421, December 2004.
[28] OFT 422, February 2000. [29] OFT 423, December 2004. [30] OFT 428, January 2005.

- *Application to services relating to railways*[31]
- *Application to the Northern Ireland energy sectors*[32]
- *Public transport ticketing schemes block exemption*[33]
- *Modernisation*[34]
- *The Competition Act 1998 and public bodies*[35]
- *Involving third parties in Competition Act investigations*[36]
- *Leniency and no-action*[37], which deals with leniency applications under both the Competition Act 1998 and the Enterprise Act 2002.

The OFT also published a draft guideline on *Assessment of conduct*[38] which is still available on its website, although it has not been adopted pending the outcome of the European Commission's review of Article 82 EC[39].

The following guidelines explain the application of the cartel offence and company director disqualification under the Enterprise Act 2002:

- *Competition disqualification orders*[40]
- *The cartel offence*[41]
- *Powers for investigating criminal cartels*[42]

(C) Other information about the Competition Act

The OFT's website[43] contains a large amount of information about the Competition Act 1998. The guidelines listed above will be found there, as will a register of decisions adopted by the OFT and the sectoral regulators. It is also possible to follow OFT consultations on the website.

(D) Delegated legislation under the Act

The Secretary of State has made a number of Orders, Rules and Regulations pursuant to his powers under the Competition Act 1998, including in particular:

- *The Competition Act 1998 (Small Agreements and Conduct of Minor Significance) Regulations*[44]
- *The Competition Act 1998 (Determination of Turnover for Penalties) Order*[45]
- *The Competition Act 1998 (Concurrency) Regulations 2004*[46]
- *The Competition Act 1998 (Appealable Decisions and Revocation of Notification of Excluded Agreements) Regulations 2004*[47]
- *The Competition Act 1998 (Land Agreements Exclusion and Revocation) Order 2004*[48]
- *The Competition Act 1998 and Other Enactments (Amendment) Regulations 2004*[49]
- *The Competition Act 1998 (Office of Fair Trading's Rules) Order 2004*[50]

---

[31] OFT 430, October 2005. [32] OFT 437, July 2001. [33] OFT 439, November 2006.
[34] OFT 442, December 2004. [35] OFT 443, August 2004. [36] OFT 451, April 2006.
[37] OFT 803, January 2008. [38] OFT 414a, April 2004. [39] See ch 5, pp 210–212.
[40] OFT 510, May 2003. [41] OFT 513, April 2003. [42] OFT 515, January 2004.
[43] www.oft.gov.uk. [44] SI 2000/262. [45] SI 2000/309, as amended by SI 2004/1259.
[46] SI 2004/1077. [47] SI 2004/1078. [48] SI 2004/1260. [49] SI 2004/1261. [50] SI 2004/2751.

(E) Literature

A large number of books and articles have been written on the Competition Act[51].

3. THE CHAPTER I PROHIBITION

The provisions on the Chapter I prohibition are contained in sections 1 to 11 of the Act. Section 50 provides for the exclusion, by order, of agreements relating to land: this was effected originally by SI 2000/310 and subsequently by SI 2004/1260[52]. Section 1 repealed the Acts referred to at the start of this chapter with effect from 1 March 2000. The OFT's Guidelines *Agreements and concerted practices*[53] and *Modernisation*[54] provide a useful overview of the Chapter I prohibition.

Section 2 contains the actual Chapter I prohibition[55]. Section 3 provides for excluded agreements. Sections 4 and 6 provide for the making of block exemptions. Section 9 reflects Article 81(3) EC, setting out the criteria that an agreement must satisfy to be exempt from the Chapter I prohibition. Section 10 provides for so-called 'parallel exemption' and section 11 provided exemption for certain other agreements, but this provision is now otiose[56]. Sections 4, 5 and 12 to 16, which dealt with the notification of agreements to the OFT for individual exemption, have been repealed by the *Amendment Regulations*: given that the Modernisation Regulation abolished the notification of agreements to the European Commission as a matter of EC law, it was thought appropriate to do the same as a matter of domestic law. The Chapter I prohibition is

---

[51] On the background to the reform of domestic competition law see the fifth edition of this book, pp 306–308; Wilks 'The Prolonged Reform of UK Competition Policy' in *Comparative Competition Policy* (Clarendon Press, 1996, eds Doern and Wilks); Wilks *In the Public Interest* (Manchester University Press, 1999), pp 296–305; Whish 'The Competition Act 1998 and the Prior Debate on Reform' in *The Competition Act: A New Era for UK Competition Law* (Hart Publishing, 2000, eds Rodger and MacCulloch); on the Act itself see Coleman and Grenfell *The Competition Act 1998* (Oxford University Press, 1999); Flynn and Stratford *Competition: Understanding the 1998 Act* (Palladian Law Publishing, 1999); Frazer and Hornsby *The Competition Act 1998: A Practical Guide* (Jordans, 1999); Freeman and Whish *A Guide to the Competition Act 1998* (Butterworths, 1999); Latham *A Practitioner's Guide to the Competition Act 1998* (Sweet & Maxwell, 2000); Livingstone *The Competition Act 1998: A Practical Guide* (Sweet & Maxwell, 2001); Singleton *Blackstone's Guide to the Competition Act 1998* (Blackstone Press, 1999); SJ Berwin and Co *Competition Law of the UK* (Juris Publishing, Inc, 2000); Kellaway and Rose *Tolley's Competition Act 1998: A Practical Guide* (Tolley's, 1999); Roger & MacCulloch *The UK Competition Act 1998: A New Era for UK Competition Law* (Hart, 2000); Willis *The Competition Act 1998: A Guide for Businesses* (Monitor Press Ltd, 2nd ed, 2000); Ward and Smith *Competition Litigation in the UK* (Sweet & Maxwell, 2003); O'Neill and Sanders *UK Competition Procedure* (OUP, 2007); Maher 'Juridification, Codification and Sanction in UK Competition Law' (2000) 63 MLR 544; Parker 'The Competition Act 1998: Change and Continuity in UK Competition Policy' [2000] JBL 283; Gordon *A Practical Guide to the United Kingdom Competition Act 1998* (European Legal Publishing, 2001).

[52] See pp 348–350 below; vertical agreements were also excluded from the Chapter 1 prohibition between 2000 and May 2005, but this is no longer the case: see ch 16, pp 668–669.

[53] OFT Guideline 401, December 2004. [54] OFT Guideline 442, December 2004.

[55] See also *Agreements and concerted practices*, OFT Guideline 401; *Trade associations, professional bodies and self-regulatory organisations*, OFT Guideline 408; *Vertical agreements and restraints*, OFT 419; *Land agreements*, OFT Guideline 420; and *Modernisation*, OFT Guideline 442.

[56] See ch 23, pp 968–969.

closely modelled upon Article 81 EC, although it is not identical in every respect[57]. Where an agreement has an effect on trade between Member States the OFT is obliged, if it decides to proceed under UK law, also to apply EC law as a result of Article 3(1) of the Modernisation Regulation, and Article 3(2) prevents it from reaching a stricter conclusion under domestic than under EC law[58].

The OFT has imposed penalties in several Chapter I prohibition decisions, including some in which it also found an infringement of Article 81 EC[59].

(A) Section 2(1): the prohibition

Section 2(1) provides that:

Subject to section 3, agreements between undertakings, decisions by associations of undertakings or concerted practices which–

  (a) may affect trade within the UK, and
  (b) have as their object or effect the prevention, restriction or distortion of competition within the UK,

 are prohibited unless they are exempt in accordance with the provisions of this Part.

Section 2(2) provides an illustrative list of the kinds of agreements that might be caught by section 2(1)[60].

(i) 'Subject to section 3'

Section 3 provides for various agreements to be excluded from the Chapter I prohibition. These exclusions are considered below[61]. It is also necessary to bear in mind the exclusion for land agreements under section 50[62].

(ii) Agreements between undertakings, decisions by associations of undertakings or concerted practices

These words are identical to those in Article 81(1). These expressions are ones that have been considered in numerous judgments of the Community Courts which, as a general proposition, the OFT and sectoral regulators, the CAT and the domestic courts in the UK are obliged to follow as a result of section 60 of the Act[63].

(iii) 'Undertakings'

(A) *General comments* As in the case of Community law[64], the term 'undertaking' is interpreted by the OFT to include any natural or legal person capable of carrying on commercial or economic activities relating to goods or services; an entity may engage in economic activity in relation to some of its functions but not others[65]. It is possible that the OFT will publish a guideline on the meaning of undertakings in due course; in the meantime it has issued a policy note on *The Competition Act 1998 and public bodies*[66]. In

---

[57] For a detailed discussion of Article 81 EC see chs 3 and 4.   [58] See ch 2, pp 74–78.
[59] See the Table of Competition Act decisions, pp 367–381 below.   [60] See p 338 below.
[61] See pp 341–347 below.   [62] See pp 348–350 below.   [63] For discussion of s 60 see pp 362–367 below.
[64] On the meaning of undertakings in Community law see ch 3, pp 82–91 and ch 5, pp 171–172.
[65] *Agreements and concerte*d practices, OFT Guideline 401, para 2.5.   [66] OFT 443, August 2004.

Institute of Independent Insurance Brokers v Director General of Fair Trading[67] the CAT considered that the General Insurance Standards Council, GISC, established upon the private initiative of its members rather than pursuant to a statutory requirement, was probably an undertaking for the purposes of the Chapter I prohibition, although this was not a necessary finding for the judgment[68].

A parent company and its subsidiaries will be treated as one undertaking where the subsidiaries lack economic independence with the result that agreements between them would not be subject to the Chapter I prohibition; the same would be true of agreements between two companies under the control of a third[69]. Similarly an agreement between entities which form a single economic unit are not subject to the Chapter I prohibition; this was one of the OFT's conclusions in *Anaesthetists' groups*[70], where the OFT said that a group of individuals would be treated as a single entity only if they operate and present themselves as a single entity on the market. Individuals acting under a contract of employment do not do so as undertakings[71]. Where entities form a single undertaking, companies within the group may be jointly and severally liable for an infringement of the competition rules[72].

The Chapter I prohibition applies to agreements 'between undertakings', but certain provisions of the Act refer to 'persons' rather than undertakings. The reason for this is that in some contexts the word 'person' is a more appropriate expression; however, in order to prevent undertakings arguing to the contrary, section 59 provides that the expression 'persons' includes 'undertakings'[73].

An unusual finding in *Exchange of information on future fees by certain independent fee-paying schools*[74] was that the Secretary of State for Defence, in his capacity as the person responsible for the governance of the Royal Hospital School, was acting as an undertaking but that, as he constituted the Crown for this purpose, no penalty could be imposed as a result of section 73(1)(b) of the Competition Act[75]. The OFT held that the other schools involved in this case were undertakings, their charitable status notwithstanding[76].

(B) The BetterCare *case* The scope of application of the competition rules to public-sector organisations, both as purchasers and as providers of goods and services, is clearly a matter of major significance. The issue arose in *BetterCare Group v Director General of Fair Trading*[77]. The OFT had received a complaint from BetterCare that the North & West Belfast Health and Social Services Trust had abused a dominant position by offering unfairly low prices and unfair terms in its purchases of social care from BetterCare. The Trust had a statutory duty to provide nursing and residential care to elderly people: it had nursing homes of its own, but also 'contracted out' to the private sector. The Trust charged for the provision of care, although it did not recover from patients the full cost.

---

[67] Case No 1002/2/1/01 [2001] CAT 4, [2001] CompAR 62.   [68] Ibid, paras 252–258.

[69] *Agreements and concerted practices*, OFT Guideline 401, para 2.6.

[70] OFT decision of 15 April 2003, [2003] UKCLR 695.

[71] See *ET Plus SA v Welter* [2005] EWHC 2115, [2006] 1 Lloyd's Rep 251, para 84.

[72] See Case 1072/1/1/06 *Sepia Logistics Ltd v OFT* [2007] CAT 13, [2007] CompAR 747, paras 70–80.

[73] See HL Report Stage, 23 February 1998, cols 511–512.

[74] OFT decision of 20 November 2006, [2007] UKCLR 361.

[75] Ibid, para 174.   [76] Ibid, paras 1311–1320.

[77] Case No 1006/2/1/01 [2002] CAT 7, [2002] CompAR 299; for comment see Skilbeck '*BetterCare*; The Conflict Between Social Policy and Economic Efficiency' (2002) 1 Competition Law Journal 260.

The OFT considered, for a variety of reasons[78], that the Trust was not an undertaking for the purpose of the Competition Act when it purchased residential and nursing care, and therefore closed its file[79]. BetterCare appealed to the CAT which, in its first judgment in the case, held that the OFT had made an 'appealable decision' which it had jurisdiction to review[80]. In its second judgment[81], dealing with the substantive matter, the CAT concluded that the Trust was, indeed, an undertaking when purchasing care, and remitted the matter to the OFT to address the question of whether it had acted in an abusive manner. In reaching its decision the CAT, after a thorough review of the case law of the Community Courts, concluded that no precedent addressed the factual circumstances of the case in hand[82]. In the CAT's view the contracting-out activities of the Trust amounted to an economic activity[83]: the fact that it was a purchaser rather than a provider did not affect the analysis[84]; and the Trust was active on 'a market', namely for the supply of residential and nursing care services in Northern Ireland[85]. Furthermore the Trust did not provide its services gratuitously, but sought to recover as much as possible as it could of the cost of providing care[86]. The CAT stressed that its finding that the Trust was an undertaking was quite separate from the question of whether it was guilty of abusive behaviour[87].

The subsequent judgments of the CFI and the ECJ in *FENIN v Commission*[88] cast doubt on the correctness of *BetterCare*, in that both Community Courts took a rather robust view that, where a public-sector body purchases goods or services in order to provide a social service, it does not do so as an undertaking. There are factual differences between the two cases, in particular given that the Trust in *BetterCare* did charge for its services, albeit not at a full market rate; this was not the case in *FENIN*. However, at a policy level, there seems to be an unwillingness in the *FENIN* judgments to extend the application of the competition rules to the procurement activities of the Spanish Health Service, but less of an unwillingness on the CAT's part in *BetterCare* in relation to the Health Trust. When the matter in *BetterCare* was remitted to the OFT for further consideration it reached the conclusion that the Health Trust was not abusing a dominant position anyway; it therefore did not need to decide whether the Trust was acting as an undertaking[89]. This meant that the OFT avoided the conundrum of deciding whether it should apply the CAT's judgment in *BetterCare* or, as a result of the governing principles clause in section 60 of the Competition Act, maintain consistency with the CFI's judgment in *FENIN* which by then had been decided[90].

---

[78] The OFT's arguments as to why the Trust was not an undertaking are set out at paras 221–276 of the CAT's judgment.

[79] *North & West Belfast Health and Social Services Trust*, 30 April 2002, [2002] UKCLR 428.

[80] Case No 1006/2/1/01 *BetterCare Group v Director General of Fair Trading* [2002] CAT 6, [2002] CompAR 226; on appealable decisions under the Competition Act see ch 10, pp 426–436.

[81] See n 77 above.

[82] Case No 1006/2/1/01 *BetterCare Group Ltd v Director General of Fair Trading* [2002] CAT 7, [2002] CompAR 299, para 176.

[83] Ibid, paras 191–192.   [84] Ibid, paras 193–194.   [85] Ibid, paras 195–200.

[86] Ibid, para 201.   [87] Ibid, paras 210–217.

[88] Case T-319/99 *FENIN v Commission* [2003] ECR II-357, [2003] 5 CMLR 34, upheld on appeal Case C-205/03 P *FENIN v Commission* [2006] ECR I-6295, [2006] 5 CMLR 559: see ch 3, p 88 for discussion of this case, and the comments on it in relation to the *BetterCare* judgment.

[89] *BetterCare Group Ltd/North & West Belfast Health & Social Services Trust*, OFT decision of 18 December 2003, [2004] UKCLR 455.

[90] On s 60 of the Act see pp 362–367 below.

(C) The OFT's subsequent decisional practice The OFT has not refrained from considering the application of the competition rules to other public-sector entities. For example it investigated Companies House, an executive agency of the former Department of Trade and Industry, which is required by statute to maintain a register of information about companies; it also acts commercially in markets for the provision of information[91]. In the OFT's view Companies House was acting as an undertaking when operating on these commercial markets[92]; however it found no evidence that it was cross-subsidising from its statutory operations in order to predate or to impose a margin squeeze in the commercial markets[93].

(iv) 'Agreements'

This term is construed widely in Community law[94]. Agreements may be spoken or written and need not be legally binding[95]; a reluctant participant in an agreement can still be liable, although such reluctance may be relevant to the level of any penalty[96]. In Community law there is no need for the European Commission to make a formal distinction between an agreement on the one hand and a concerted practice on the other; and in some cases it has been able to find a 'single overall agreement' to which a number of undertakings are party[97]. The OFT has taken the same approach in some of its cartel decisions[98]; however the 'single overall agreement' analysis does not always apply in the case of bid-rigging, where there may be a series of discrete agreements in relation to particular contracts, each one requiring individual analysis, rather than an overall plan[99].

Two cases, best referred to as *Football Shirts* and *Toys and Games*, are of considerable interest to the meaning of agreement (and concerted practice) under the Act. In each case the OFT had found there to be agreements and/or concerted practices as to the retail prices at which these consumer goods were sold to the public[100]. The interesting feature of the cases is that the OFT claimed not only that there were bilateral vertical agreements between the suppliers and their dealers, but also that there were horizontal agreements between the dealers themselves, and that these agreements had come about not, or not only, from direct contact between the dealers but also through the role played by the supplier in each case.

[91] OFT decision of 25 October 2002, [2003] UKCLR 24.   [92] Ibid, para 12.
[93] On predatory pricing see ch 18, pp 729–743 and on vertical margin squeezes see ch 18, pp 744–748.
[94] See ch 3, pp 97–102.
[95] *Agreements and concerted practices*, OFT Guideline 401, para 2.7, and see *Arriva/First Group*, [2002] UKCLR 322, 5 February 2002, paras 29–33.
[96] *Agreements and concerted practices*, OFT Guideline 401, para 2.8.   [97] See ch 3, pp 99–102.
[98] See eg *UOP Limited/UKae Limited/Thermoseal Supplies Ltd/Double Quick Supplyline Ltd/Double Glazing Supplies Ltd*, OFT decision of 8 November 2004, [2005] UKCLR 227, paras 50–55.
[99] See eg *West Midland Roofing Contractors*, OFT decision of 17 March 2004, [2004] UKCLR 1119, upheld on appeal in Case Nos 1032/1/1/04 etc *Apex Asphalt & Paving Co Ltd v OFT* [2005] CAT 4, [2005] CompAR 507; see ch 13, pp 541–542 for discussion of the OFT's decisions on bid-rigging.
[100] *Football Kit price-fixing*, OFT decision of 1 August 2003, [2004] UKCLR 6 and *Hasbro UK Ltd/Argos Ltd/Littlewoods Ltd*, OFT decision of 2 December 2003, [2004] UKCLR 717; note that, in the case of *Football Shirts*, Which? (formerly the Consumers' Association) brought a follow-on action for damages in the CAT on behalf of consumers that were overcharged: see ch 8, p 308.

This can be presented in diagrammatic form:

The OFT's case was that not only were there bilateral agreements between B and A and between B and C. It also found that there were trilateral agreements in each case between A, B and C which, as between A and C, were horizontal rather than vertical. These horizontal agreements had come about as a result of indirect contact between A and C through the medium of B. This phenomenon is sometimes referred to as one of 'hub and spokes', where B represents the 'hub' and each of A and C is on the end of a 'spoke'.

The CAT agreed with the OFT's findings of a trilateral agreement in each of the cases[101]. Further appeals were taken to the Court of Appeal; the two cases were heard together and a single judgment was given[102]. The Court of Appeal agreed that there had been trilateral agreements[103]. However it suggested that the CAT's formulation of how a trilateral agreement could come about in these circumstances 'may have gone too far'[104]. The CAT had suggested that, if A were to disclose its future pricing intentions to B in circumstances in which it was 'reasonably foreseeable' that B might make use of that information and pass it on to C, there would be a concerted practice between A, B and C[105]. The Court of Appeal preferred a slightly narrower formulation, omitting the reference to reasonable foreseeability:

If (i) retailer A discloses to supplier B its future pricing intentions in circumstances where A may be taken to intend that B will make use of that information to influence market conditions by passing that information to other retailers (of whom C is one or may be one), (ii) B does, in fact, pass that information to C in circumstances where C may be taken to know the circumstances in which the information was disclosed by A to B and (iii) C does, in fact, use the information in determining its own future pricing intentions, then A, B and C are all to be regarded as parties to a concerted practice having as its object the restriction or distortion of competition. The case is all the stronger

---

[101] Some of the OFT's findings of fact were annulled in *Football Shirts*, Case Nos 1021/1/1/03 and 1022/1/1/03 *JJB Sports PLC v OFT* [2004] CAT 17, [2005] CompAR 29; the decision in *Toys and Games* was upheld in its entirety on substance, although the CAT adjusted the level of the penalties, Case Nos 1014 and 1015/1/1/03 *Argos Ltd v OFT* [2004] CAT 24, [2005] CompAR 588 (judgment on liability) and Case Nos 1014 and 1015/1/1/03 *Argos Ltd v OFT* [2005] CAT 13, [2005] CompAR 834 (judgment on penalty).

[102] *Argos Ltd v OFT* (the *Toys and Games* appeal) and *JJB Sports plc v OFT* (the *Football Shirts* appeal), [2006] EWCA Civ 1318, [2006] UKCLR 1135; see Bailey 'Contours of Collusion: Football Shirts and Toys and Games' (2006) 4 Competition Law Journal 236.

[103] See paras 92–106 of the judgment in the case of *JJB Sports* and paras 138–145 in the case of *Argos Ltd*.

[104] Ibid, paras 91 and 140.

[105] See para 659 of the CAT's judgment in the *Football Shirts* appeal.

where there is reciprocity: in the sense that C discloses to supplier B its future pricing intentions in circumstances where C may be taken to intend that B will make use of that information to influence market conditions by passing that information to (amongst others) A, and B does so.

Clearly these cases mean that an undertaking in the position of B must take care to ensure that it does not, consciously or unconsciously, act as the agent of a horizontal agreement between A and C. The point was put to the Court of Appeal that the formulation of an agreement and/or concerted practice in these cases could jeopardise normal commercial dealings between suppliers and dealers. The Court of Appeal rejected this: bilateral discussions between a supplier and a dealer of a purely vertical nature about matters such as likely retail prices, profit margins and wholesale prices and terms of sale would not give rise to problems of unlawfulness: what would be problematic would be discussions which clearly have 'a horizontal element'[106]. Permission to appeal to the House of Lords was rejected[107].

Where there is direct contact between two undertakings – between A and C in the example above – involving the disclosure of pricing information it is much easier to establish an agreement and/or concerted practice[108].

(v) 'Decisions by associations of undertakings'

This expression has been broadly interpreted in Community law[109]. A body can be classified as an association of undertakings irrespective of whether it carries on any commercial or economic activity of its own[110], and the fact that it is a 'loose knit association' does not prevent it from being an association of undertakings[111]. The term 'decision' has a broad meaning, including the rules of trade associations, recommendations, resolutions of the management committee and rulings of the chief executive; the crucial issue is whether the object or effect of the decision is to influence the conduct or coordinate the activity of the members[112]. The Guideline on *Trade associations, professions and self-regulating bodies*[113] provides additional guidance on the meaning of decisions[114]; it also discusses the extent to which activities such as information sharing, advertising, the promulgation of codes of conduct, the formulation of standard terms and conditions and certification activities, each of which trade associations typically become involved in, can infringe Article 81 EC and the Chapter I prohibition[115]. This Guideline also has a specific section on the position of the professions[116] and of self-regulating bodies[117].

In *Northern Ireland Livestock and Auctioneers' Association*[118] the OFT concluded that a non-binding recommendation by the Association as to the commission that its members should charge for the purchase of livestock in Northern Ireland cattle marts amounted to a decision within the Chapter I prohibition[119]. The Standard Conditions

---

[106] See para 106 of the Court of Appeal judgment.
[107] See OFT Press Release 17/07 of 7 February 2007.
[108] Case 1061/1/1/06 *Makers UK Ltd v OFT* [2007] CAT 11, [2007] CompAR 699, paras 99–100, distinguishing such a situation from the ones in *Football Shirts* and *Toys and Games*.
[109] See ch 3, pp 102–104.   [110] See *GISC*, n 67 above, paras 248–250.
[111] *Northern Ireland Livestock and Auctioneer's Association* OFT decision of 3 February 2003, [2003] UKCLR 433, para 35.
[112] *Agreements and concerted practices*, OFT Guideline 401, para 2.9.
[113] OFT Guideline 408.   [114] Ibid, paras 2.1–2.5.   [115] Ibid, paras 3.1–3.20.   [116] Ibid, paras 6.1–6.7.
[117] Ibid, paras 7.1–7.3.   [118] OFT decision of 3 February 2003, [2003] UKCLR 433.
[119] Ibid, paras 37–49.

of the Film Distributors' Association were found to be a decision of an association of undertakings; certain clauses to which the OFT objected, including those that limited the ability of cinemas to determine their own prices and promotional activities, were dropped[120].

Standard conditions drawn up by a trade association will be less likely to have an appreciable effect on competition where its members have the freedom to adopt different conditions if they so wish[121].

The effect that a decision of an association might have on the UK market will depend to a certain extent on the size of the membership of the association concerned: the broader the membership of an association, the greater the influence of the association is likely to be[122].

(vi) 'Concerted practices'

This expression will be interpreted in line with the jurisprudence of the Community Courts[123] which identifies the main elements of a concerted practice as a form of practical cooperation, knowingly entered into by the parties, which is intended to amount to a substitution for competition in the market[124]. Contacts or communications which influence market behaviour, depending on the nature of the contact or the effect, or even potential effect, on competition, may be caught if the conduct leads to, or would have led to, a different result had the undertakings not embarked on this conduct[125].

The OFT will take into account the following factors in establishing whether a concerted practice exists:

- Whether the parties knowingly entered into practical cooperation
- Whether behaviour in the market is influenced as a result of direct or indirect contact between undertakings
- Whether parallel behaviour is a result of contact between undertakings leading to conditions of competition which do not correspond to normal conditions of the market
- The structure of the relevant market and the nature of the product involved
- The number of undertakings in the market and, where there are only a few undertakings, whether they have similar cost structures and outputs[126].

In *Apex Asphalt and Paving Co Ltd v OFT*[127] the CAT considered the meaning of a concerted practice in a case where the OFT had imposed fines on undertakings for participating in collusive tendering in relation to roofing contracts in the west

---

[120] *Notification by the Film Distributors' Association of its Standard Conditions for Licensing the Commercial Exhibition of Films*, OFT decision of 1 February 2002, [2002] UKCLR 343, paras 43–45.

[121] *Trade associations, professionals and self-regulating bodies*, OFT Guideline 408, para 3.18: see OFT Press Release PN 02/03, 9 January 2003, for details of amendment to three trade associations' rules to provide such freedom; see also *Royal Institute of British Architects* 17–23, Weekly Gazette of the OFT, Competition case closure summaries, available at www.oft.gov.uk.

[122] *Trade associations, professions and self-regulating bodies*, OFT Guideline 408, para 5.3.

[123] See ch 3, pp 104–107.

[124] Case 48/69 *ICI v Commission ('Dyestuffs')* [1972] ECR 619, [1972] CMLR 557.

[125] Cases 40/73 etc *Suiker Unie v Commission* [1975] ECR 1663, [1976] 1 CMLR 295.

[126] *Agreements and concerted practices*, OFT Guideline 401, para 2.13.

[127] Case No 1032/1/1/04 [2005] CAT 4, [2005] CompAR 507.

Midlands[128]. Having analysed the case law of the Community Courts[129] the CAT distilled a number of principles, including that a concerted practice can arise where there are reciprocal contacts between undertakings which remove or reduce uncertainty as to their future conduct. The CAT continued that:

reciprocal contacts are established where one competitor discloses its future intentions or conduct on the market to another when the latter requests it or, at the very least, accepts it.

After noting that these principles had never, in the case law of the Community Courts or the Commission, been applied to collusive tendering, the CAT proceeded to uphold the finding of the OFT that there had been an infringement in this case[130]. The OFT has adopted a number of subsequent decisions on collusive tendering[131].

(vii) 'Object or effect the prevention, restriction or distortion of competition within the UK'

This concept is understood and applied in the same way as Article 81(1)[132]. In the *GISC* case[133] the CAT said that the first step is normally to determine the object of an agreement; if it is not plain that the object is to restrict competition one should then move on to consider the effects[134]. In several decisions the OFT has found that an agreement had the object of restricting competition and that therefore it did not need to demonstrate that it had the effect of doing so; the first OFT decision on a 'hard-core' cartel stated that an agreement sharing bus routes in Leeds had as its object the restriction of competition[135]. The OFT has also stated that it does not consider that the subjective intentions of the parties to an agreement are relevant to determining whether an agreement has as its object the restriction of competition[136]. In *Exchange of information on future fees by certain independent fee-paying schools*[137] the OFT found that the exchange of future price information between 50 independent schools about the level of their intended fees had as its object the restriction of competition and made no finding on effects[138]; this case was settled by agreement between the OFT and the schools, and it actually benefited the schools that the OFT did not find anti-competitive effects – that is to say higher school fees – since that might have encouraged follow-on damages actions against them.

In the *GISC* case[139] the CAT's view was that the rules of GISC, which prevented its insurer members from dealing with insurance intermediaries unless they were themselves members of GISC, 'clearly' fell within section 2(1)(b) of the Competition Act[140]. The Tribunal did not say specifically that the rules had the object of restricting competition, but the tenor of its comments from paragraphs 179 to 192 suggests that this

---

[128] OFT decision of 17 March 2004, [2004] UKCLR 1119

[129] Case No 1032/1/1/04 [2005] CAT 4, [2005] CompAR 507, paras 195–205.

[130] For further discussion of this case see ch 13, p 542 and Kar and Bailey 'The Apex Judgment: When does a Practice become Concerted?' (2005) 4 Competition Law Journal 17; on concerted practices see also Case 1061/1/1/06 *Makers UK Ltd v OFT* [2007] CAT 11, [2007] CompAR 699, paras 99–110.

[131] See ch 13, pp 541–542.   [132] See ch 3, pp 116ff.

[133] Case No 1003/2/1/01 [2001] CAT 4, [2001] CompAR 62.

[134] [2001] CAT 4, [2001] CompAR 62, paras 169–170.

[135] See *Market Sharing by Arriva plc and FirstGroup plc*, 20 January 2002, [2002] UKCLR 322, para 42; the same approach will be seen in all the cartel decisions of the OFT: these are discussed in ch 13, pp 538–543.

[136] *Memorandum of Understanding on the Supply of Oil Fuels in an Emergency*, 25 October 2001, paras 39–40.

[137] OFT decision of 20 November 2006, [2007] UKCLR 361.   [138] Ibid, paras 1348–1358.

[139] Case No 1003/2/1/01 [2001] CAT 4, [2001] CompAR 62.   [140] Ibid, para 192.

was its view, and paragraphs 214 and 215 very nearly say so in those terms. The CAT annulled the OFT's decision that there was no infringement, and the matter was remitted to it for a consideration of whether the rules satisfied the terms of section 9 of the Competition Act, the equivalent of Article 81(3) EC[141]. Subsequently the offending rule was dropped, and the OFT adopted a second decision finding no infringement of the Chapter I prohibition[142].

Where an agreement does not have the object of restricting competition there remains the possibility that its effect, considered within its market and economic context, might be to do so[143]. An interesting judgment on this is *The Racecourse Association v OFT*[144], where the CAT reached the conclusion that the OFT had failed to demonstrate that the collective selling of broadcasting rights to horse-racing events had an anti-competitive effect: in particular the Tribunal considered that the OFT had proceeded on the basis of a 'somewhat shifting, hypothetical counterfactual situation'[145].

In *P&S Amusements Ltd v Valley House Leisure Ltd*[146] the Chancery Division of the High Court concluded that there was no prospect of it being found that a beer tie in a lease of a public house in Blackpool would be found to have as its effect an appreciable restriction of competition[147]. In *Mastercard UK Members Forum Ltd*[148] the OFT investigated two restrictions, one into the collective setting of the multilateral interchange fee within the Mastercard system and the other into the unjustified inclusion of extraneous costs as a result of the fee. In each case the OFT explicitly stated that it had *not* reached a finding that the agreement had an anti-competitive object; instead it concluded that there were restrictions by effect[149]. In *Independent Media Support*[150] OFCOM reached the conclusion that an exclusive agreement between BBC and Channel 4 to provide television access services did not have an anti-competitive effect[151].

The OFT's Guideline on *Agreements and concerted practices*[152] provides examples of types of agreements that could have as their object or effect the restriction of competition, including agreements of the kind set out in the illustrative list in section 2(2) of the Competition Act[153].

(viii) Appreciability

The Chapter I prohibition (and Article 81 EC) applies only where an agreement brings about an *appreciable* restriction of competition. In determining whether an agreement

---

[141] It is interesting to speculate whether, if the *GISC* case had been heard after the ECJ's judgment in Case C-309/99 *Wouters v Algemene Raad van de Nederlandse Orde van Advocaten* [2002] ECR I-1577, [2002] 4 CMLR 913, the CAT might have asked whether GISC's rules fell outside the Chapter I prohibition, subject to their satisfying a test of proportionality; on the *Wouters* judgment see ch 3, pp 126–130.

[142] *General Insurance Standards Council*, 22 November 2002, [2003] UKCLR 39.

[143] OFT Guideline 401, para 7.2; see also Case No 1003/2/1/01 *Institute of Independent Insurance Brokers v Director General of Fair Trading* [2001] CAT 4, [2001] CompAR 62, para 170.

[144] Case Nos 1035/1/1/04 and 1041/2/1/04 [2005] CAT 29, [2005] CompAR 99.

[145] Ibid, paras 177–202. [146] [2006] EWHC 1510 (Ch), [2006] UKCLR 867.

[147] Ibid, paras 23–26. [148] OFT decision of 6 September 2005, [2006] UKCLR 236.

[149] Ibid, paras 389–393 and 677–680; note that the OFT's decision was appealed to the CAT and subsequently withdrawn: Case Nos 1054/1/1/05–1056/1/1/05 *Mastercard UK Members Forum Ltd v OFT* [2006] CAT 14, [2006] CompAR 595.

[150] OFCOM decision of 30 May 2007, [2007] UKCLR 1357, upheld on appeal *Independent Media Support Ltd v OFCOM* [2008] CAT 13.

[151] Ibid, paras 8.1–8.25.

[152] OFT Guideline 401. [153] Ibid, paras 3.3–3.27; the illustrative list is set out at p 338 below.

has an appreciable effect the OFT has said[154] that it will have regard to the European Commission's approach as set out in the *Notice on Agreements of Minor Importance*[155]. Essentially that Notice states that agreements between actual or potential competitors do not appreciably restrict competition where the parties' market shares are below 10 per cent and that agreements between undertakings that are not actual or potential competitors do not do so where both parties' market share is below 15 per cent: however the Notice does not apply in the case of serious restrictions of competition such as horizontal price fixing, market sharing and output restriction, nor to vertical agreements for example to fix minimum prices or to restrict passive sales[156]. The OFT would not impose financial penalties on undertakings that have relied in good faith on the Commission's *Notice on Agreements of Minor Importance*[157]. The fact that an agreement exceeds the thresholds of the Commission's Notice does not mean, in itself, that any restriction of competition is appreciable: such a finding would require further analysis, in particular to determine how much market power the parties to the agreement possess[158]. In determining undertakings' turnover the OFT will take into account the turnover of connected undertakings[159].

In the *GISC* case[160] the CAT held that the rule of GISC prohibiting insurer members from dealing with intermediaries who were not themselves members of GISC resulted in an appreciable restriction of competition; in doing so it did not proceed solely on the basis of the market share of GISC's members, but also by reference to the number of insurers subject to the rule in question, the size of the general insurance market and the number of intermediaries affected[161].

(ix) Applicable law and territorial scope

Where the OFT intends to take action in relation to an agreement that it considers may be anti-competitive it must decide whether to do so on the basis of the Chapter I prohibition alone or whether it should also proceed under Article 81 EC. Where an agreement may affect trade between Member States Article 3(1) of the Modernisation Regulation requires it to apply Article 81[162]. As the OFT notes in *Agreements and concerted practices*[163] the case law of the Community Courts interprets the meaning of effect on trade between Member States broadly; it adds that it will have regard to the European Commission's *Guidelines on the Effect on Trade Concept contained in Articles 81 and 82 of the Treaty*[164] when considering whether an agreement might infringe Article 81 EC.

As far as the Chapter I prohibition is concerned, this applies only where trade *within the UK* is affected. The OFT has said that its focus will be on whether an agreement appreciably restricts competition within the UK since, if it does so, it will also affect trade there[165]. The CAT has held that the requirement that there should be an effect on trade within the UK does not require that that effect should be appreciable[166]. Its reasoning was that in Community law the requirement of an appreciable effect on trade was

[154] *Agreements and concerted practices*, OFT Guideline 401, para 2.18.
[155] OJ [2001] C 368/13; see ch 3, pp 137–142.   [156] See para 11 of the Notice.
[157] *Agreements and concerted practices*, OFT Guideline 401, para 2.19.   [158] Ibid, para 2.20.
[159] Ibid, para 2.21.   [160] Case No 1003/2/1/01 [2001] CAT 4, [2001] CompAR 62.
[161] Ibid, paras 185–189.   [162] See ch 2, pp 74–78.   [163] OFT Guideline 401, para 2.23.
[164] Ibid.   [165] Ibid, para 2.25.
[166] Case No 1009/1/1/02 *Aberdeen Journals Ltd v Office of Fair Trading* [2003] CAT 11, [2003] CompAR 67, paras 459–462; this was a case on the Chapter II prohibition, but there is no reason in principle to suppose that it would have reached a different conclusion in the case of the Chapter I prohibition.

a jurisdictional rule to demarcate the respective spheres of application of Community and domestic competition law, and that there was no need to transcribe that reasoning to a purely domestic context. However it is of interest to note that the Chancellor of the High Court felt 'considerable misgivings' as to whether the CAT was correct on this point in *P&S Amusements Ltd v Valley House Leisure Ltd*[167]. This is a matter on which a ruling of the Court of Appeal is required.

(B) Section 2(2): illustrative list

Section 2(2) provides that:

Subsection (1) applies, in particular, to agreements, decisions or practices which—

  (a) directly or indirectly fix purchase or selling prices or any other trading conditions;
  (b) limit or control production, markets, technical development or investment;
  (c) share markets or sources of supply;
  (d) apply dissimilar conditions to equivalent transactions with other trading parties, thereby placing them at a competitive disadvantage;
  (e) make the conclusion of contracts subject to acceptance by the other parties of supplementary obligations which, by their nature or according to commercial usage, have no connection with the subject of such contracts.

This list, which exemplifies the sorts of agreement which would infringe section 2(1), is identical to the list in Article 81(1) EC. However it is important to stress that Article 81(1) has been applied to many other agreements that are *not* explicitly mentioned in the list, and that the same will be true in the case of the Chapter I prohibition. For example an agreement to exchange information about sales, which enables manufacturers to know the market position and strategy of their competitors in an oligopolistic market, has been found by the ECJ to be caught by Article 81(1)[168], although there is no specific reference to information exchanges in the Article itself[169]. This is because the list is merely illustrative and in each case the critical issue is whether the agreement has as its object or effect the prevention, restriction or distortion of competition. The OFT's Guideline *Agreements and concerted practices* sets out numerous examples of agreements that could infringe the Chapter I prohibition at paragraphs 3.3 to 3.27; these will be examined further in chapter 13 on cartels and hard-core restrictions of competition[170].

Section 2(2)(d) and (e) suggest that agreements to discriminate and tie-ins may amount to infringements of Article 81 or the Chapter I prohibition. It is fair to point out, however, that in the history of the application of Article 81 by the Commission there have been few cases under Article 81(1)(d) and (e). Discrimination and tie-ins are matters which usually give rise to concern in competition policy only where there is significant market power on the part of the party which is practising discrimination or which is imposing the tie. For this reason these phenomena are usually investigated, if at all, under Article 82 rather than under Article 81[171].

---

[167] [2006] EWHC 1510 (Ch), [2006] UKCLR 867, paras 21–22 and 34.
[168] Case C-7/95 P *John Deere Ltd v Commission* [1998] ECR I-3111, [1998] 5 CMLR 311.
[169] Another example would be restrictions imposed on advertising: see *Lladró Comercial*, OFT decision of 31 March 2003, [2003] UKCLR 652, paras 68–71.
[170] See ch 13, pp 538–543.
[171] On price discrimination see ch 18, pp 748–753 and on tie-ins see ch 17, pp 679–687.

(C) Section 2(3): extra-territorial application

The extra-territorial scope of the Act is considered in chapter 12[172].

(D) Section 2(4): voidness

Section 2(4) provides that:

Any agreement or decision which is prohibited by subsection (1) is void.

This mirrors Article 81(2) EC. The possibility that agreements may be void is of considerable significance: for many firms it is the possibility that their agreements may turn out to be unenforceable that has as much, and in many cases more, significance than the possibility of being fined. A considerable compliance effort has to be maintained in order to ensure that important commercial transactions will not be undermined by one or more parties to an agreement subsequently reneging on it and claiming it to be unenforceable. These issues are considered in chapter 8[173]. A couple of points are worthy of mention here.

(i) Severance[174]

Section 2(4) provides that 'any agreement' which violates section 2(1) is void. It does not say that the voidness might relate only to the provisions in the agreement that violate the Chapter I prohibition, nor does it say anything about the consequence of such voidness on the remaining provisions of the agreement. However, despite the clear wording of both section 2(4) and Article 81(2) EC that the agreement is void, it has been established by the ECJ that it may be possible to sever the offending clauses, leaving the remainder of the agreement enforceable[175]. The intention is that the courts in the UK should interpret section 2(4) in the same way as the ECJ has interpreted Article 81(2)[176], and this will be possible by virtue of section 60 of the Act.

English contract law provides that severance is possible in certain circumstances, although the rules on this subject are complex[177]. It is a matter for the applicable law of the contract, rather than the *lex fori* of the court in which the action is brought, to determine whether, and, if so, by what criteria, severance is to be effected[178].

(ii) Void or illegal?

In *Gibbs Mew plc v Gemmell*[179] the Court of Appeal concluded that an agreement that infringes Article 81(1) is not only void and unenforceable, but is also illegal. This has serious consequences: for example a party who has paid money to another under an illegal agreement cannot recover that money unless it can be shown that the parties

---

[172] See ch 12, pp 484–486.
[173] See also Whish 'The Enforceability of Agreements under EC and UK Competition Law' in *Lex Mercatoria: Essays on International Commercial Law in Honour of Francis Reynolds* (LLP, ed Rose, 2000).
[174] See generally ch 8, pp 312–314.   [175] See ch 8, pp 312–313.
[176] HL Report Stage, 9 February 1998, col 890.
[177] See *Chitty on Contracts* (Sweet & Maxwell, 29th ed, 2004, ed Beale), paras 16.188–16.197.
[178] See Rome Convention on the law applicable to contractual obligations 1980 (consolidated version OJ [1998] C 27/34, p 34); *Dicey and Morris on the Conflict of Laws* (Sweet & Maxwell, 14th ed, 2006, ed Collins), chs 32 and 33.
[179] [1998] Eu LR 588; see also *Trent Taverns Ltd v Sykes* [1999] Eu LR 492, CA.

were not *in pari delicto*[180]. In *Crehan v Courage Ltd*[181], a case concerning Article 81 EC referred to the ECJ by the Court of Appeal under Article 234 EC, the ECJ held that it would be contrary to the effective application of Article 81 for national law to impose an absolute bar on an action by one party to an agreement that restricts competition against another party to it[182]; however, Community law does not prevent national law from denying a party who has significant responsibility for the restriction of competition the right to obtain damages from the other contracting party[183]. The principles in *Courage Ltd v Crehan* would presumably be applied in a case concerning section 2(4) of the Competition Act, pursuant to the governing principles clause in section 60 of the Competition Act[184].

(iii) Transient voidness

In *Passmore v Morland plc*[185] the Court of Appeal held that an agreement may, in its lifetime, drift into and out of unlawfulness under Article 81(1), and therefore be void and unenforceable at some times but not at others. The same presumably will be true of section 2(4) of the Competition Act.

(E) Sections 2(5) and 2(6): interpretation

These provisions explain that, except where the context otherwise requires, any reference in the Act to an agreement includes a reference to a concerted practice and a decision by an association of undertakings. This overcomes the clumsiness of having to use all three expressions throughout the text of the Act.

(F) Section 2(7): the UK

Section 2(7) provides that ' "the UK" means, in relation to an agreement which operates or is intended to operate only in a part of the UK, that part'[186]. The UK for this purpose includes England, Wales, Scotland plus the subsidiary islands (excluding the Isle of Man and the Channel Islands) and Northern Ireland.

(G) Section 2(8): the 'Chapter I prohibition'

Section 2(8) provides that:

The prohibition imposed by subsection (1) is referred to in this Act as 'the Chapter I prohibition'.

The expression 'the Chapter I prohibition' is therefore a legislative one, and is mirrored by section 18(4) which recognises the companion 'Chapter II prohibition'.

---

[180] See Goff and Jones *Law of Restitution* (Sweet & Maxwell, 7th ed, 2006), ch 24.
[181] Case C-453/99 [2001] ECR I-6297, [2001] 5 CMLR 1058; for discussion of *Crehan* see ch 8, pp 293–294.
[182] [2001] ECR I-6297, [2001] 5 CMLR 1058, para 28.   [183] Ibid, paras 31–33.
[184] On s 60 of the Act see pp 362–367 below.
[185] [1999] 3 All ER 1005, [1999] 1 CMLR 1129, CA; see ch 8, pp 314–315.
[186] See eg *Arrival/First Group*, decision of 5 February 2002, [2002] UKCLR 322, paras 44–45.

(H) The Chapter I prohibition: excluded agreements

Section 3 provides for a number of exclusions from the Chapter I prohibition. Some, but not all, of these exclusions apply also in the case of the Chapter II prohibition[187]. Section 50 provides for the possibility of vertical and land agreements to be excluded, and this power has been exercised in relation to some land agreements[188]. Section 59(2) provides that if the effect of one or more exclusions is that the Chapter I prohibition is inapplicable to one or more provisions of an agreement, those provisions do not have to be disregarded when considering whether the agreement itself infringes the prohibition for other reasons. In other words, the effect of the agreement as a whole can be considered.

Section 3(1) provides that the Chapter I prohibition does not apply in any of the cases in which it is excluded by or as a result of Schedule 1 on mergers and concentrations; Schedule 2 on competition scrutiny under other enactments; and Schedule 3 on planning obligations and other general exclusions. Schedule 4, which excluded from the Competition Act 1998 the regulatory rules of various professions, such as lawyers and accountants, was repealed by section 207 of the Enterprise Act 2002: such rules may now infringe the Chapter I prohibition, though they must be tested not only by reference to the general principles of Articles 81(1) and (3) but also according to the judgment of the ECJ in *Wouters*[189]. The regulatory rules of the legal profession will be subject to competition scrutiny under sections 57 to 61 of the Legal Services Act 2007. Sections 3(2) to (5) of the Competition Act make provision for the Secretary of State to amend Schedules 1 and 3 in certain circumstances, whether by adding additional exclusions or by amending or removing existing ones[190]. Section 3(6) notes that Schedule 3 itself enables the Secretary of State in certain circumstances to exclude agreements from the Chapter I prohibition[191].

(i) Schedule 1: mergers and concentrations

Schedule 1 of the Competition Act deals with the application of the Chapter I and II prohibitions to mergers and concentrations. The basic policy of the Schedule is that the prohibitions do not apply to mergers under the Enterprise Act nor to concentrations in respect of which the European Commission has exclusive jurisdiction under the EC Merger Regulation ('the ECMR')[192]. The exclusion in Schedule 1 is automatic and does not require an application to the OFT.

(A) Relationship of the Chapter I and II prohibitions with UK merger control[193] Schedule 1, paragraph 1(1) provides that the Chapter I prohibition does not apply to an agreement or combination of agreements which results or would result in any two enterprises 'ceasing to be distinct enterprises' for the purposes of Part 3 of the Enterprise Act[194]. The exclusion applies to any transaction whereby enterprises cease to be distinct,

---

[187] See p 362 below. [188] See pp 348–350 below and ch 16, pp 668–669.

[189] Case C-309/99 [2002] ECR I-1577, [2002] 4 CMLR 913; see further pp 347–348 below and ch 3, pp 126–130.

[190] This order-making power is subject to s 71 of the Act, which requires an affirmative resolution of each House of Parliament.

[191] See pp 346–347 below on Sch 3, para 7. [192] Council Regulation 139/2004 EC, OJ [2004] L 24/1.

[193] See the OFT's *Mergers – Substantive assessment guidance*, OFT Guideline 516, paras 11.1–11.24.

[194] For the meaning of 'ceasing to be distinct' see s 26 Enterprise Act 2002 and ch 22, pp 908–910; the UK exclusion is wider than the disapplication of Article 81 to concentrations in the EC, effected by

irrespective of whether there is a 'relevant merger situation' capable of being investigated under the Enterprise Act[195]. If this were otherwise the Competition Act would have revolutionised the control of mergers in the UK by bringing all those transactions that are not subject to the Enterprise Act, because they fall below the relevant thresholds, within the scope of the 1998 Act, which would be an absurdity.

Schedule 1, paragraph 1(2) provides in addition that the exclusion of the Chapter I prohibition extends to 'any provision directly related and necessary to the implementation of the merger provisions': this means that 'ancillary restraints' also fall outside the Chapter I prohibition. To be ancillary the restraint must be both 'directly related [to]' and 'necessary to the implementation of' the merger provisions. Examples of ancillary restraints are given in the OFT's guideline[196] which generally follows the position of the European Commission under the ECMR[197]; ancillary restraints include, for example, appropriately limited non-compete clauses, licences of intellectual property rights and know-how and purchase and supply agreements. Procedural issues in relation to ancillary restraints are discussed in Annexe B of the OFT's guidance on the procedural aspects of mergers[198].

(B) Newspaper mergers Schedule 1, paragraph 3 of the Competition Act as originally drafted provided the same exclusion from the Chapter I prohibition for newspaper mergers as defined in section 57 of the Fair Trading Act 1973, and any ancillary restraints; however section 57 was repealed by the Communications Act 2003[199].

(C) Clawback Schedule 1, paragraph 4 provides for the possibility of 'withdrawal of the paragraph 1 exclusion' by the OFT. The 'clawback' provision applies only to the Chapter I prohibition; it does not apply to the Chapter II prohibition. In the House of Lords Lord Simon explained the reason for the inclusion of the clawback provision: that the breadth of the exclusion – even to include the acquisition of control or material influence by one business over another – 'creates some risk of providing a loophole for anti-competitive agreements'[200]. Paragraph 4(5) therefore provides that the OFT may, by a direction in writing[201], remove the benefit of the exclusion where it considers that (a) an agreement would, if not excluded, infringe the Chapter I prohibition; and (b) the agreement is not a protected agreement[202].

These provisions will be exercised only rarely, which is acknowledged in the OFT Guideline[203]. The procedure for withdrawing the benefit of this exclusion is set out in Annexe B of the OFT's guidance on the procedural aspects of mergers[204].

(D) Protected agreements The OFT cannot exercise the right of clawback in relation to a 'protected agreement'. The Act defines four categories of protected agreement. First,

---

Article 21(1) of the ECMR, since 'ceasing to be distinct' is a broader concept than that of a concentration under Article 3(2) of the ECMR: see ch 22, p 909; see also HL Third Reading, 5 March 1998, col 1365 (Lord Simon of Highbury).

[195] See ch 22, pp 908–912 on the meaning of a relevant merger situation.
[196] See *Mergers – Substantive assessment guidance*, OFT Guideline 516, paras 11.1–11.24.
[197] On ancillary restraints under the ECMR see ch 21, pp 870–871.
[198] *Mergers – procedural guidance*, OFT 526, May 2003.   [199] See ch 22, pp 951–953.
[200] HL Committee, 13 November 1997, col 328.
[201] Competition Act 1998, Sch 3, para 4(7)(a); the direction cannot be retrospective: see para 4(7)(b).
[202] Ibid, Sch 3, para 5; on protected agreements, see below.
[203] See *Mergers – Substantive assessment guidance*, OFT Guideline 516, para 11.9.
[204] *Mergers – procedural guidance*, OFT 526, May 2003.

an agreement in relation to which the OFT or Secretary of State, as the case may be, has published its or his decision not to make a reference to the Competition Commission; the OFT cannot override the decision not to refer a merger under the Enterprise Act by instituting its own investigation under the Competition Act 1998. Second, an agreement in relation to which the Competition Commission has found there to be a relevant merger situation. Third, an agreement that would result in enterprises ceasing to be distinct in the sense of section 26 of the Enterprise Act, other than as a result of subsection (3) and (4)(b) of that section[205]. Fourth, an agreement which the Competition Commission has found gives rise to a merger in the sense of section 32 of the Water Industry Act 1991.

(E) Relationship of the Chapter I and II prohibitions with EC merger control[206] Paragraph 6 of Schedule 1 provides that the Chapter I prohibition does not apply to concentrations which have a Community dimension. This provision is necessary in order to comply with Article 21(3) of the ECMR[207]; it provides that no Member State may apply its national legislation on competition to any concentration that has a Community dimension, since the European Commission has exclusive jurisdiction in such cases. Paragraph 6 does not mention ancillary restraints specifically, but since they are deemed to be cleared by a Commission decision permitting a concentration it presumably follows that Member States cannot take action in relation to them[208].

(F) No clawback Since Schedule 1, paragraph 6 deals with matters that are within the exclusive jurisdiction of the European Commission, it follows that the OFT does not in this situation enjoy a right of clawback as it does under paragraph 4 in relation to mergers that are subject to the Enterprise Act 2002.

(ii) Schedule 2: competition scrutiny under other enactments[209]

Schedule 2 excludes agreements which are subject to 'competition scrutiny' under some other piece of legislation: the Government explained during the passage of the Competition Bill that, in so far as particular agreements are subject to competition scrutiny under regimes constructed to deal with the circumstances of specific sectors, it is inappropriate to subject them to the Chapter I prohibition as well, as 'that would just create an unwelcome and unjustified double jeopardy'[210].

(A) Communications Act 2003 Section 293 of the Communications Act 2003 requires that the Office of Communications ('OFCOM') periodically should review the 'networking arrangements' between Independent Television Ltd and the 13 regional Channel 3 licensees, including an assessment of their effect on competition. OFCOM published its most recent review of these arrangements in March 2007[211].

---

[205] See above.

[206] See the OFT's *Mergers – Substantive assessment guidance*, OFT 516, paras 12.1–12.10; on the ECMR generally see ch 21.

[207] See ch 21, pp 832–834.   [208] On ancillary restraints see ch 21, pp 870–871.

[209] Note that the provisions in the Competition Act, as originally enacted, excluding the supervision and qualification of auditors (Sch 2, paras 2 and 3) and of certain environmental matters (Sch 2, para 6) from the Chapter I prohibition, were repealed by the *Competition Act 1998 and Other Enactments (Amendment) Regulations 2004*, SI 2004/1261.

[210] HL Committee, 13 November 1997, col 342.

[211] *Review of ITV Networking Arrangements 2006*, available at www.ofcom.org.uk/consult/condocs/itv_network/statement/statement.pdf.

(B) Financial Services and Markets Act 2000 This Act established the Financial Services Authority ('the FSA') with the regulatory objectives of achieving market confidence, public awareness, the protection of consumers and the reduction of financial crime[212]. Section 95 makes provision for the Treasury, by order, to establish competition scrutiny of the FSA in relation to the official listing of securities. Sections 159 to 163 provide for competition scrutiny in relation to regulating provisions and practices adopted by the FSA. The OFT must keep them under review and may report on provisions and practices having a significant adverse effect on competition[213]. Where the OFT makes a report to this effect, the Competition Commission will investigate the matter further[214]. Where the Commission's report is adverse, the Treasury is given power to give directions, although it is not always bound to do so[215]. Section 164 provides for exclusion from both the Chapter I and Chapter II prohibitions for agreements, practices or conduct that are encouraged by any of the FSA's regulating provisions. Similar provisions are to be found in sections 302 to 312 in relation to recognised investment exchanges and clearing houses. The OFT published a report under section 304(3) of the FSMA 2000 in July 2004 into the issuer fees of the London Stock Exchange; this investigation led to a significant reduction of earlier fee increases[216].

The OFT, acting under its general function of keeping markets under review, conducted a market study into the effects of the FSMA in March 2004 in which it concluded that there were no indications that the FSMA had had a significant negative impact on competition[217].

(C) Legal Services Act 2007 Sections 57 to 61 of this legislation make provision for competition scrutiny of the regulatory rules of the legal profession by the OFT and the CC.

(D) No power to amend Schedule 2 There is no power to amend Schedule 2. Section 3 of the Competition Act provides the power to amend only in relation to Schedule 1 and Schedule 3.

(iii) Schedule 3: planning obligations and other general exclusions

Schedule 3 is entitled 'General Exclusions' and sets out various matters that are excluded, some of which are of considerable importance.

(A) Planning obligations Paragraph 1 of Schedule 3 provides that the Chapter I prohibition does not apply to agreements involving planning obligations, for example where planning permission is given subject to the developer agreeing to provide certain services or access to facilities[218].

(B) Section 21(2) Restrictive Trade Practices Act 1976 Paragraph 2 of Schedule 3 provided that agreements that were the subject of directions under section 21(2) of the Restrictive Trade Practices Act 1976 were excluded from the Chapter I prohibition; however this provision was repealed with effect from 1 May 2007[219].

---

[212] Financial Services and Markets Act 2000, ss 1 and 2.   [213] Ibid, ss 159 and 160.
[214] Ibid, s 162 and Sch 14.   [215] Ibid, s 163.
[216] Available at www.oft.gov.uk/advice_and_resources/publications/reports/financial/oft713.
[217] Available at www.oft.gov.uk/advice_and_resources/resource_base/market-studies/fsma.
[218] See Town and Country Planning Act 1990, s 106.
[219] *Competition Act 1998 and Other Enactments (Amendment) Regulations 2004*, SI 2004/1261, reg 4, Sch 1, para 50a; for a discussion of s 21(2) of the RTPA see Volume 47 of *Halsbury's Laws of England*, para 269.

(C) EEA regulated markets Paragraph 3 of Schedule 3 provides that the Chapter I prohibition does not apply to various matters concerning 'EEA regulated [financial services] markets'. This expression is defined in paragraph 3(5) as meaning a market which is listed by another EEA state[220] and which does not require a dealer on the market to have a presence where trading facilities are provided or on any other trading floor of that market.

(D) Services of general economic interest Paragraph 4 of Schedule 3 provides that neither the Chapter I nor the Chapter II prohibition shall apply to an undertaking:

entrusted with the operation of services of general economic interest or having the character of a revenue-earning monopoly in so far as the prohibition would obstruct the performance, in law or in fact, of the particular tasks assigned to it.

This important provision is modelled upon Article 86(2) EC[221], although the language of the Schedule is somewhat less tortuous than that to be found in the Treaty.

The OFT has published *Services of general economic interest exclusion*[222] containing important guidance on this provision. The OFT will interpret the exclusion strictly[223]. The guidance notes that, as various public-sector activities become exposed to competition or economic regulation, it is possible that certain functions that once might have been considered to be administrative or social become regarded as economic; this can have the result that an entity engaged in those activities might come to be regarded as an undertaking, and therefore fall within the purview of competition law[224]. The guidance discusses what is meant by the notion of 'entrusting' an undertaking with performance of services[225]; it also considers the meaning both of 'services'[226] and of 'general economic interest'[227]. The OFT notes that in a number of EC cases Article 86(2) has been held to be applicable where an undertaking was subject to a universal service obligation and needed to be protected from 'cream-skimming' or 'cherry-picking'[228]. However it also notes that in the UK the combined effect of privatisation, liberalisation and EC initiatives has been that the number of exclusive rights held by undertakings has been significantly reduced[229]. The OFT's view is that, in general, effective competition will best serve the interests of consumers over time, which is why it will interpret the exclusion narrowly. The OFT's guidance concludes by saying that it is unlikely that there are any 'revenue-earning monopolies' of the kind referred to in Schedule 3, paragraph 4 in the UK[230].

(E) Compliance with legal requirements Paragraph 5 of Schedule 3 provides that neither the Chapter I nor the Chapter II prohibition applies to an agreement or to conduct that is required to comply with a legal requirement. For this purpose a legal requirement is one imposed by or under any enactment in force in the UK, by or under the EC Treaty or the EEA Agreement and having legal effect in the UK without further enactment, or under the law in force in another Member State having legal effect in the UK. An example of the operation of this exclusion occurred in *Vodafone*[231]. In that case the mobile phone operator sold 'pre-pay mobile phone vouchers' to wholesalers, who resold

---

[220] Pursuant to Article 16 of Council Directive 93/22/EEC, OJ [1993] L 141/27.
[221] See ch 6, pp 233–239.   [222] OFT Guideline 421, December 2004.   [223] Ibid, para 1.9.
[224] Ibid, para 2.7.   [225] Ibid, paras 2.9–2.15.   [226] Ibid, paras 2.16–2.18.
[227] Ibid, paras 2.19–2.22.   [228] Ibid, para 3.4.   [229] Ibid, para 3.5.   [230] Ibid, paras 4.1–4.4.
[231] OFTEL decision of 5 April 2002.

them to retailers. The vouchers had a 'face value', for example of £5 or £10. The whole-salers complained that this amounted to resale price maintenance, and OFTEL (now OFCOM) investigated whether Vodafone was guilty of infringing the Chapter I prohibition. However it transpired that Vodafone had printed the prices in order to comply with a licence condition imposed upon it by OFTEL: it followed that Vodafone could not be guilty of infringing the Competition Act by virtue of the operation of Schedule 3, paragraph 5(1)[232]. OFTEL therefore removed the price publication requirement from Vodafone's licence, so that the exclusion no longer applied. Similarly an undertaking could not be found liable under the Act where it had done something required, for example, by a Commission Directive adopted under Article 86(3) of the Treaty[233].

The exclusion in paragraph 5 of Schedule 3 applies only where the regulated undertaking is required to act in a certain way; it does not apply to the discretionary behaviour of that undertaking. In *Re-investigation of a complaint from VIP Communications Ltd*[234] OFCOM considered that T-Mobile was able to rely on Schedule 3(5) in refusing to supply certain services to VIP Communications in circumstances where it knew that VIP would use those services in order to act unlawfully in violation of the Wireless Telegraphy Act 1949: OFCOM considered that T-Mobile was required by law to desist from conduct that would result in illegal behaviour[235].

(F) Avoidance of conflict with international obligations   Paragraph 6(1) of Schedule 3 gives to the Secretary of State the power to make an order to exclude the application of the Chapter I prohibition from an agreement or a category of agreements where this would be appropriate in order to avoid a conflict between the provisions of the Competition Act and an international obligation of the UK. The order can provide that the exclusion shall apply only in specified circumstances[236] and may be retrospective[237]. Similar provisions are contained in Schedule 3 paragraphs 6(4) and (5) for exclusion from the Chapter II prohibition. Schedule 3 paragraph 6(6) was introduced in the House of Lords as a Government amendment to extend the meaning of the term 'international obligation' to include inter-Governmental arrangements relating to civil aviation: the reason for this is that such arrangements, permitting flights between the UK and other countries, are often not made as treaties[238] and so do not give rise to international 'obligations' as such.

(G) Public policy   Paragraph 7 of Schedule 3 gives power to the Secretary of State to make an order to exclude the application of the Chapter I prohibition from an agreement or a category of agreements where there are 'exceptional and compelling reasons of public policy' for doing so. The order can provide that the exclusion shall apply only in specified circumstances[239], and may be retrospective[240]. Similar provisions are contained in paragraph 7(4) and (5) of Schedule 3 for exclusion from the Chapter II prohibition. Two orders have been made under paragraph 7 in relation to the defence industry: the first excludes agreements relating to the maintenance and repair of warships from

---

[232]   Ibid, para 47.   [233]   On Article 86(3) see ch 6, pp 239–242.
[234]   OFCOM decision of 28 June 2005, [2005] UKCLR 914; OFCOM's decision is on appeal to the CAT in Case 1027/2/3/04 *VIP Communications Ltd (in administration) v OFCOM*, not yet decided.
[235]   Ibid, para 205.   [236]   Competition Act, Sch 3, para 6(2).   [237]   Ibid, Sch 3, para 6(3).
[238]   HL Deb 9 February 1998, cols 972–3.   [239]   Competition Act, Sch 3(7)(2).   [240]   Ibid, Sch 3(7)(3).

THE CHAPTER I PROHIBITION 347

the Chapter I prohibition[241]; the second excludes the application of the Chapter I and Chapter II prohibitions to agreements and conduct affecting strategic and tactical weapons and their supporting technology[242]. The EC Treaty provides a specific exclusion from the competition rules for certain matters related to defence in Article 296, but there are no specific exclusions for this area from the Competition Act.

(H) Coal and steel Paragraph 8 of Schedule 3 provides that the Chapter I and Chapter II prohibitions do not apply to agreements and conduct within the exclusive jurisdiction of the European Commission under the ECSC Treaty. These exclusions ceased to have effect when the ECSC Treaty expired on 23 July 2002[243].

(I) Agricultural products Paragraph 9 of Schedule 3 provides exclusion from the Chapter I prohibition for agreements that fall outside Article 81 EC by virtue of Regulation 1184/2006[244]. If the European Commission decides that an agreement is not excluded from Article 81 by Regulation 1184/2006, the exclusion from paragraph 9 of Schedule 3 ceases on the same date[245]. Provision is made for clawback[246].

(iv) Professional rules

When the Competition Act 1998 was passed, paragraph 1(1) of Schedule 4 provided that the Chapter I prohibition did not apply to designated professional rules. The Government felt that professional rules which served to protect the public, which contained disciplinary arrangements and which were liable to judicial review should be excluded[247]. The level of competition in the professions was kept under review, and in the spring of 2000 the OFT published a consultation document, *A review of competition restrictions in the professions*[248]. This was followed by an OFT report in March 2001, *Competition in professions*, in which it recommended that a number of restrictions on competition in three professions – lawyers (in particular barristers), accountants and architects – should be removed[249]; the OFT considered that there was a strong case for repealing Schedule 4 of the Competition Act 1998, a view with which the Secretary of State agreed[250]. Section 207 of the Enterprise Act 2002 therefore repealed Schedule 4 with effect from 1 April 2003. The application of the Chapter I prohibition to professional rules must now be considered in the light of the judgment of the ECJ in *Wouters*[251], where it held that certain restrictions of competition might fall outside Article 81 EC in so far as they are necessary for the proper practice of a profession.

The OFT remains active in reviewing the conditions of competition in the professional services sector. The OFT's work in this area was usefully reviewed in a speech

---

[241] Competition Act 1998 (Public Policy Exclusion) Order 2006, SI 2006/605.

[242] Competition Act 1998 (Public Policy Exclusion) Order 2007, SI 2007/1896.

[243] Competition Act, Sch 3(8)(2) and (4); see ch 23, p 961.

[244] See ch 23, pp 957–961.   [245] Competition Act, Sch 3, para 9(2).   [246] Ibid, para 9(6) and (7).

[247] HL Committee, 13 November 1997, col 292; see also HL Deb 9 February 1998, cols 896–898.

[248] www.oft.gov.uk/html/new/professions5–00.htm.

[249] The report is available at www.oft.gov.uk/html/rsearch/reports/oft328.htm and was concluded under s 2 of the Fair Trading Act 1973.

[250] DTI Press Release P/2001/141, 9 March 2001; see also White Paper *Productivity and Enterprise: A World Class Competition Regime* Cm 5233, (DTI, 31 July 2001), para 9.4.

[251] Case C-309/99 *Wouters v Algemene Raad van de Nederlandsche Orde van Advocaten* [2002] ECR I-1577, [2002] 4 CMLR 913; on this judgment see further ch 3, pp 126–130.

by its chairman in September 2006[252]. The OFT received a super-complaint from the consumer organisation *Which?* in May 2007 concerning restrictions imposed on the providers of legal services in Scotland; the OFT made recommendations to the Scottish Government in July 2007 that various restrictions which could be harming consumers – for example on solicitors and advocates providing services jointly, third party entry into the market and direct consumer access to advocates – should be lifted[253]. In December 2004 the 'Clementi Review' was published recommending the establishment of a Legal Services Board to act as the single external regulator of legal services in England and Wales[254]. The OFT welcomed these proposals[255] which have been passed into law by the Legal Services Act 2007. It provides for competition scrutiny of the regulatory rules of the legal profession.

(v) Section 50: vertical agreements[256]

Section 50 of the Act makes provision for the exclusion or exemption of vertical agreements from the Chapter I, but not the Chapter II, prohibition. This was effected, except in relation to vertical price fixing, by the Competition Act 1998 (Land and Vertical Agreements Exclusion) Order 2000[257]. However the adoption of the EC Modernisation Regulation meant that it was desirable that the treatment of vertical agreements in domestic and EC law should be brought into alignment with one another. As a result of this the exclusion of vertical agreements from the Chapter I prohibition was repealed[258]; however they may enjoy the benefit of the EC block exemption for vertical agreements[259].

(vi) Section 50: land agreements

As the Competition Bill passed through Parliament the Government recognised that there was a compelling case for excluding certain agreements relating to land from the Chapter I, though not the Chapter II[260], prohibition: an obvious case would be commercial leases containing covenants and conditions imposed for the sake of good estate management[261]. In particular it would be undesirable if there was widespread uncertainty as to whether such covenants and conditions might be rendered void and unenforceable as a result of section 2(4) of the Act. However the difficulties of framing a

---

[252] See Collins 'Promoting competition in professions: Development in the UK', available at www.oft. gov.uk/shared_oft/speeches/sp0906.pdf; see also the OFT's *Annual Report 2005–06*, p 48 for discussion of action taken in relation to legal services in parts of the UK.

[253] www.oft.gov.uk/news/press/2007/110-07.

[254] *Report of the Review of the Regulatory Framework for Legal Services in England and Wales*, available at www.legal-services-review.org.uk.

[255] www.oft.gov.uk/news/press/2004/91-04.

[256] On vertical agreements generally see ch 16.   [257] SI 2000/310.

[258] This was effected by the Competition Act 1998 (Land Agreements Exclusion and Revocation) Order 2004, SI 2004/1260, which repealed SI 2000/310 that had created the exclusion for vertical agreements in the first place.

[259] See ch 16, pp 640–662.

[260] On the application of the Chapter II prohibition and Article 82 EC to land agreements see *Land agreements*, OFT Guideline 420, December 2004, paras 5.1–5.9.

[261] The registrability of restrictive covenants in commercial leases under the Restrictive Trade Practices Act 1976 was the subject of a test case in *Re Ravenseft Property Ltd's Application* [1978] QB 52, [1977] 1 All ER 47, RPC; on the position of shopping centre leases in Ireland see Maher *Competition Law: Alignment and Reform* (Round Hall Sweet & Maxwell, 1999), pp 430–431.

specific exclusion were noted by Lord Simon in the House of Lords[262]; rather than defining land agreements in the Act itself, power was given to exclude or exempt them in section 50. The Competition Act 1998 (Land and Vertical Agreements Exclusion) Order 2000 excluded land agreements from the Chapter I prohibition from 1 March 2000 until 30 April 2005[263]. Since 1 May 2005 the Competition Act 1998 (Land Agreements Exclusion and Revocation) Order 2004 has been in effect[264]. It should be read in conjunction with the OFT's Guideline *Land agreements*[265].

(A) The exclusion Article 4 of the Order provides that the Chapter I prohibition shall not apply to an agreement to the extent to which it is a land agreement. To the extent that an agreement is not a land agreement it could be subject to the Chapter I prohibition[266]; this would require an analysis of the various criteria for application of that provision[267]. It will be recalled that there is a specific exclusion in paragraph 1 of Schedule 3 for planning obligations[268].

Article 3 of the Order provides that a land agreement means:

an agreement between undertakings which creates, alters, transfers or terminates an interest in land, or an agreement to enter into such an agreement, together with any obligation and restriction to which Article 5 applies.

The same Article defines further what is meant by an 'interest in land', which includes licences and references to Scottish property concepts; and 'land', which includes buildings and other structures and land covered with water. Examples of land agreements include transfers of freeholds, leases or assignments of leasehold interests and easements[269]. The exclusion applies only to an agreement as defined in Article 2; an agreement between landlords to fix rents, or between tenants as to the goods they will sell from their properties, would not be land agreements since they do not *create, alter, transfer or terminate* an interest in land[270].

(B) Article 5 obligations and restrictions The exclusion of land agreements extends, by virtue of Article 5, to obligations[271] and restrictions[272] which relate to 'relevant land'[273]. Examples of such obligations and restrictions are covenants in commercial property agreements relating to payment of rent, service charges, user clauses and alienation. Restrictions on a tenant relating to alterations, repairs, applications for planning permission, the presence of shop signs, advertisements or the hours of use of the premises may also benefit from the exclusion[274].

For obligations to be excluded they must be accepted by a party to a land agreement 'in its capacity as holder of an interest' in relevant land: if the obligation is not accepted in this capacity it may amount to a restriction of competition and must be tested according to the criteria of the Chapter I prohibition[275]. The critical term here is 'capacity', which is considered in paragraphs 2.6 to 2.9 of the Guideline. For restrictions to be excluded they must restrict the activity that may be carried out on or in connec-

[262] HL Committee, 13 November 1997, col 340.   [263] SI 2000/310.   [264] SI 2004/1260.
[265] OFT Guideline 420, December 2004.
[266] On the expression 'to the extent that' see paras 3.3 and 3.4 of the Guideline.
[267] OFT Guideline 420, paras 1.9–1.14.   [268] See p 344 above.   [269] OFT Guideline 420, para 2.3.
[270] Ibid, para 2.4.   [271] SI 2004/126, Article 5(1).   [272] Ibid, Article 5(2).
[273] Relevant land is defined in Article 3 of the Order.   [274] OFT Guideline 420, para 2.5.
[275] *Land Agreements*, OFT Guideline 420, paras 1.9–1.14.

tion with the relevant land, and again must be accepted by a party to the agreement in its capacity as holder of an interest in that land; here again the term 'capacity' is critical, as is the expression 'activity': the latter term is considered in paragraphs 2.10 and 2.11 of the Guideline. Paragraph 2.12 states that reciprocal restrictions may benefit from the exclusion: for example a restriction imposed on one tenant of premises in a shopping centre only to sell widgets on condition that other tenants in the same centre will not sell widgets[276].

(C) The application of Article 81 EC Insofar as an agreement is subject to Article 81 EC it would not benefit from the exclusion for land agreements; however since land agreements are localised in effect it is unlikely that they would have an appreciable effect on trade between Member States, with the result that Article 81 would be unlikely to be applicable anyway[277].

(D) Clawback Provision is made for clawback of the exclusion for land agreements by Article 6 of the Order. Where a direction for clawback is made Article 7 provides that the exclusion for land agreements will not apply to any agreement that is made 'to the like object or effect' as the one that was the subject of the direction. The OFT has indicated that this power will rarely be used[278]. Where it is used, it does not follow that the agreement automatically will infringe the Chapter I prohibition: it simply enables the OFT to consider whether there is an infringement[279]. Any infringement would be found only from the date of withdrawal; any voidness of the agreement would start from that date, and penalties could be imposed only from then[280].

(I) The Chapter I prohibition: exemptions

(i) Introduction

As in the case of Article 81(3) EC the Competition Act makes provision for exemption from the Chapter I prohibition. The provisions in sections 4 and 5 of the Act whereby the OFT could grant an individual exemption to an agreement notified to it were repealed by the *Amendment Regulations*: as in the case of EC law undertakings must conduct a self-assessment of whether an agreement that infringes the Chapter I prohibition satisfies the criteria of section 9 of the Act, which mirrors Article 81(3)[281]. Sections 6 and 8 of the Competition Act make provision for the adoption of block exemptions, while section 10 provides for so-called 'parallel exemption' where an agreement satisfies one of the EC block exemptions, or would do if it were to affect trade between Member States[282]. Section 11 of the Act, which provided 'exemptions for other agreements', and which was primarily concerned with certain agreements in the air transport sector, is now obsolete[283].

The operation of these provisions will be explained below, after a consideration of the criteria according to which exemption may be available.

---

[276] If the tenants were to agree this between themselves the exclusion would not apply (see n 275 above); however it seems that the same effect can be achieved where the restrictions are agreed with the landlord.
[277] OFT Guideline 420, paras 3.1–3.2.   [278] Ibid, para 4.2.   [279] Ibid, para 4.4.
[280] Ibid, para 4.5.   [281] On self-assessment under Article 81(3) EC see ch 4, p 163.
[282] On the EC block exemptions see ch 4 pp 164–169.   [283] See ch 23, pp 967–969.

(ii) Exemption criteria

The exemption criteria are set out in section 9(1) of the Competition Act. Exemption is available for any agreement which:

(a) contributes to –
   (i) improving production or distribution, or
   (ii) promoting technical or economic progress, while allowing consumers a fair share of the resulting benefit; but

(b) does not –
   (i) impose on the undertakings concerned restrictions which are not indispensable to the attainment of those objectives; or
   (ii) afford the undertakings concerned the possibility of eliminating competition in respect of a substantial part of the products in question.

The wording of section 9 is very similar to, but not quite identical with, Article 81(3) EC. The latter refers to 'improving the production or distribution *of goods*' (emphasis added), but the domestic provision is not so limited, and can therefore be applied to services as well. Section 9(2) of the Act provides that undertakings claiming the benefit of section 9(1) bear the burden of proving that the conditions it contains are satisfied[284]. In applying section 9(1) the OFT has said[285] that it will have regard to the European Commission's *Guidelines on the Application of Article 81(3) of the Treaty*[286]. The OFT's own guidance on *Agreements and concerted practices* does not provide a commentary on the constituent parts of section 9(1), presumably since this would be likely simply to duplicate what is in the Commission's *Guidelines*.

There have been only a few applications of section 9(1) by the OFT in the years since it has been in force. In *LINK Interchange Network Ltd*[287] the OFT granted individual exemption to arrangements that provided for a centrally-set multilateral interchange fee for the operation of the LINK network of automated teller machines, in which the major banks and building societies in the UK participate. The OFT recognised that charging such a fee could lead to an improvement in distribution by preventing one bank from taking a free ride on the investment of others[288]. The OFT considered whether the level of the multilateral interchange fee exceeded the cost of operating the network of cash machines but found that it did not[289]. However in *Mastercard UK Members Forum Ltd*[290] the OFT concluded that the collective fixing of the interchange fee did not satisfy the requirement in section 9 (and Article 81(3)) of indispensability since it extended to services that were not within the scope of the payment system[291]. It followed that there was no need for the OFT to consider whether consumers would get a fair share of any benefit, since the restriction was too wide anyway[292].

[284] This mirrors Article 2 of the EC Modernisation Regulation OJ [2003] L 1/1, [2003] 4 CMLR 551: see ch 4, pp 149–150.

[285] *Agreements and concerted practices*, OFT Guideline 401, December 2004, para 5.5.

[286] OJ [2004] C 101/97; these *Guidelines* are discussed in ch 4, pp 151–160.

[287] OFT decision of 16 October 2001, [2002] UKCLR 59. [288] Ibid, paras 42–45.

[289] OFT decision of 16 October 2001, [2002] UKCLR 59, paras 47–49.

[290] OFT decision of 6 September 2005, [2006] UKCLR 236; for discussion see Vickers 'Public Policy and the Invisible Price: Competition Law, Regulation and the Interchange Fee' (2005) 4 Competition Law Journal 5.

[291] OFT decision of 6 September 2005, [2006] UKCLR 236, para 519 and paras 533–649.

[292] Ibid, paras 650–651.

In *Memorandum of Understanding on the supply of oil fuels in an emergency*[293] the OFT granted an individual exemption to an agreement which would improve distribution by enabling the Government to direct supplies of fuel to 'essential users' such as providers of emergency services in the event of a fuel shortage[294]. In *Lucite International UK Ltd and BASF plc*[295] the OFT concluded that the restrictions inherent in a long-term agreement for the supply of hydrogen cyanide were indispensable because they helped solve the 'hold-up problem' that may occur when one party is required to invest in client-specific investment[296]. In *Pool Reinsurance Company Ltd*[297] the OFT concluded that rules designed to provide reinsurance against acts of terrorism in the UK restricted competition but satisfied the conditions of section 9. In *Association of British Insurers' General Terms of Agreement*[298] the OFT considered that, if certain provisions of the General Terms of Agreement were amended, it might be eligible for exemption under section 9. The decision was set aside on appeal to the CAT[299]. The OFT subsequently decided to close the file since the case did not constitute an administrative priority[300].

During the Parliamentary debates on section 9 Lord Simon stated twice in the House of Lords that he expected the criteria in section 9 to be interpreted in the same broad way as Article 81(3) EC[301]. The OFT gave an indication of the breadth of the exemption criteria in *Lucite International UK Ltd and BASF plc*[302], where it considered that the agreement under consideration would have beneficial environmental effects. However it is interesting to contemplate whether the OFT would, since the Modernisation Regulation, interpret section 9(1) in such a broad manner: it seems clear that the European Commission's intention is that, since Article 81(3) has become directly applicable, it should be interpreted according to an economic efficiency standard, and, as already noted, the OFT's intention (and legal duty) is to have regard to the Commission's position.

(iii) Block exemptions

Section 6 of the Competition Act allows the Secretary of State, acting upon a recommendation from the OFT, to adopt block exemptions. A block exemption may contain conditions and obligations and may be of limited duration, by virtue of sections 6(5) and 6(7) respectively. The procedure for adopting block exemptions is set out in section 8. There are a number of EC block exemptions, and these will be applicable to agreements caught by the Chapter I prohibition by virtue of the parallel exemption provisions in section 10[303]. One block exemption has been adopted under the Competition Act, for public transport ticketing schemes that allow passengers to purchase tickets that can be used on the services of the participating travel operators. The block exemption entered

---

[293] OFT decision of 25 October 2001, [2002] UKCLR 74.   [294] Ibid, paras 62–63.
[295] OFT decision of 29 November 2002, [2003] UKCLR 176, paras 45–46; on the hold-up problem see ch 16, p 617.
[296] See ch 16, p 669.   [297] OFT decision of 15 April 2004, [2004] UKCLR 893.
[298] OFT decision of 22 April 2004, [2004] 917.
[299] Case No 1036/1/1/04 *Association of British Insurers v OFT*, Order of 30 July 2004.
[300] Case closure notice of 29 January 2007, available at www.oft.gov.uk/advice_and_resources/resource_base/ca98/closure.
[301] On the exemption criteria under Article 81(3) see ch 4, pp 151–160.
[302] OFT Decision, 29 November 2002, [2003] UKCLR 176, paras 39–41, referring to the Commission decision in *CECED* on environmental agreements; see ch 15, pp 598–599.
[303] See below.

THE CHAPTER II PROHIBITION

into force on 1 March 2001[304] and was amended with effect from 23 January 2006[305]; the OFT produced an updated guideline on 30 November 2006[306]. Annex A of the guideline contains a consolidated text of the block exemption as amended.

(iv) Parallel exemptions

Section 10 of the Competition Act 1998 makes provision for 'parallel exemptions'. Many agreements are block exempted by a Community block exemption[307]; there are others that would be exempt but for the fact that they do not produce an effect on trade between Member States: since such agreements would not infringe Article 81(1) they would not require or benefit from block exemption under Article 81(3). Sections 10(1) and (2) of the Act provide that any agreement that benefits from a block exemption under Community law, or that would do if it were to affect trade between Member States, will also be exempted from the Chapter I prohibition under domestic law.

A consequence of the availability of parallel exemption is that the parties to such agreements do not need a block exemption under domestic law. Section 10(4) ensures that the duration of any parallel exemption is in line with the position in EC law. The most important effect of section 10 is that vertical agreements may benefit from Regulation 2790/99[308] and that licences of intellectual property rights may benefit from Regulation 772/2004[309]. Specialisation agreements or research and development agreements could benefit from Regulations 2658/2000[310] and Regulation 2659/2000[311] respectively.

Section 10(5) makes provision for the OFT, in accordance with rules made under section 51 of the Act, to impose, vary or remove conditions and obligations subject to which a parallel exemption is to have effect, or even to cancel a parallel exemption. Section 10(6) enables this cancellation to be retrospective from before the date of the OFT's notice. However Article 3(2) of the EC Modernisation Regulation makes clear that, as a matter of Community law, it is not open to the OFT to impose stricter standards to an agreement that fulfils the conditions under Article 81(3) of the Treaty[312]. A different point is that Article 29(2) of the Modernisation Regulation[313] specifically authorises a Member State to withdraw the benefit of an EC block exemption in certain, specified, circumstances.

4. THE CHAPTER II PROHIBITION

The Chapter II prohibition is contained in section 18 of the Competition Act 1998. The OFT's Guidelines *Abuse of a dominant position*[314], *Assessment of market power*[315] and

---

[304] Competition Act 1998 (Public Transport Ticketing Schemes Block Exemption) Order 2001, SI 2001/319.
[305] Competition Act 1998 (Public Transport Ticketing Schemes Block Exemption)(Amendment) Order 2005, SI 2005/3347.
[306] *Public transport ticketing schemes block exemption*, OFT Guideline 439.
[307] For discussion of the EC block exemptions see ch 4, pp 164–169.   [308] See ch 16, pp 640–662.
[309] See ch 19, pp 771–781.   [310] See ch 15, pp 589–592.   [311] Ibid, pp 583–588.
[312] See ch 2, pp 74–78; the OFT would presumably be under no constraint in a s 10(2) case, where there is, *ex hypothesi*, no Community jurisdiction.
[313] Council Regulation 1/2003 OJ [2003] L 1/1, [2003] 4 CMLR 551; see also Article 7 of Commission Regulation 2790/99 OJ [1999] L 336/21, [2000] 4 CMLR 398; for a detailed account of this Regulation, see ch 16, pp 640–662.
[314] OFT Guideline 402, December 2004.   [315] OFT Guideline 415, December 2004.

Modernisation[316] provide a useful overview of the Chapter II prohibition. The OFT has imposed fines for infringements of the Chapter II prohibition in three cases: it imposed a penalty of £3.21 million for abusive pricing in *Napp*[317], reduced to £2.2 million on appeal[318]; in *Aberdeen Journals*[319] it imposed a fine of £1.32 million for predatory pricing, reduced to £1 million on appeal[320]; and in *Genzyme*[321] it fined Genzyme £6.8 million for engaging in various exclusionary practices. The Office of Rail Regulation imposed a fine of £4.1 million in the case of *English Welsh and Scottish Railway Ltd*[322], and the Gas and Electricity Markets Authority imposed a fine of £41.6 million in *National Grid*[323]. On two occasions the CAT has found an abuse of a dominant position in circumstances where the OFT and/or OFWAT had decided that there was not one[324]. The OFT has published research into the costs of inappropriate intervention and non-intervention under the law of abuse of dominance[325].

(A) The prohibition

(i) Section 18

The prohibition of the abuse of a dominant position is contained in section 18 of the Competition Act. Section 18 draws heavily on the text of Article 82[326]:

(1) Subject to section 19, any conduct on the part of one or more undertakings which amounts to the abuse of a dominant position in a market is prohibited if it may affect trade within the UK.
(2) Conduct may, in particular, constitute such an abuse if it consists in-
   (a) directly or indirectly imposing unfair purchase or selling prices or other unfair trading conditions;
   (b) limiting production, markets or technical development to the prejudice of consumers;
   (c) applying dissimilar conditions to equivalent transactions with other trading parties, thereby placing them at a competitive disadvantage;
   (d) making the conclusion of contracts subject to acceptance by the other parties of supplementary obligations which, by their nature or according to commercial usage, have no connection with the subject of the contracts.
(3) In this section-
   'dominant position' means a dominant position within the UK; and 'the UK' means the UK or any part of it.
(4) The prohibition imposed by subsection (1) is referred to in this Act as 'the Chapter II prohibition'.

---

[316] OFT Guideline 442, December 2004. [317] OFT Decision, 30 March 2001, [2001] UKCLR 597.
[318] Case No 1000/1/1/01 *Napp Pharmaceutical Holdings Ltd v Director General of Fair Trading* [2002] CAT 1, [2002] CompAR 13.
[319] *Aberdeen Journals Ltd – remitted case*, OFT decision of 16 September 2002, [2002] UKCLR 740.
[320] Case No 1009/1/1/02 *Aberdeen Journals Ltd v Office of Fair Trading* [2003] CAT 11.
[321] OFT Decision of 27 March 2003, [2003] UKCLR 950, on appeal Case No 1016/1/1/03 *Genzyme Ltd v Office of Fair Trading* [2004] CAT 4, [2004] CompAR 358; interim relief was granted against the directions imposed by the OFT: Case No 1013/1/03 (IR) *Genzyme Ltd v Office of Fair Trading* [2003] CAT 8, [2003] CompAR 290.
[322] ORR decision of 17 November 2006, [2007] UKCLR 937.
[323] OFGEM press release of 25 February 2008.
[324] Case No 1044/2/1/04 *M.E. Burgess, J.J. Burgess and S.J. Burgess v OFT* [2005] CAT 25, [2005] CompAR 1151 and Case No 1046/2/4/04 *Albion Water Ltd v Director General of Water Services* [2006] CAT 36, [2007] CompAR 328, upheld on appeal *Dwr Cymru Cyfyngedig v Water Services Regulation Authority* [2008] EWCA Cia 536.
[325] OFT 864, September 2006, available at www.oft.gov.uk/shared_oft/economic_research/oft864.pdf.
[326] For detailed discussion of EC law on the abuse of a dominant position see chs 5, 17, and 18.

(ii) 'The Chapter II prohibition'

Section 18(4) of the Act establishes the term 'the Chapter II prohibition' to refer to the prohibition set out in section 18.

(iii) 'Undertakings'

This term has the same meaning as in the Chapter I prohibition and in Articles 81 and 82 EC[327]. The *BetterCare*[328] case, in which the CAT ruled that the North & West Belfast Health and Social Services Trust was an undertaking for the purpose of the Competition Act, was a case on the Chapter II prohibition[329].

(iv) Affecting trade within the UK

As with the Chapter I prohibition there is a requirement that trade within the UK be affected; most conduct that is an abuse of a dominant position within the UK will also affect trade there. The CAT has held that there is no need to show an *appreciable* effect on trade within the UK[330], although the Chancery Division of the High Court has questioned the correctness of this[331]. The requirement of an effect on trade within the UK could exclude from the scope of the prohibition an abuse of a dominant position within the UK that has its effects entirely outside the UK[332].

(v) Voidness

The Competition Act does not refer explicitly to voidness in the case of the Chapter II prohibition. Prohibited conduct can nevertheless include agreements. In *English Welsh & Scottish Railway Ltd v E.ON UK plc*[333] the High Court held that coal carriage agreements that infringed Chapter II (and Article 82 EC) were void and unenforceable.

(vi) Market size

Section 18(3) provides that a dominant position means a dominant position in the UK, and that the UK means the UK 'or any part of it'. Unlike Article 82, which refers to a dominant position '...within the common market *or in a substantial part of it*'[334], there is no need for the dominant position to be in the whole or a 'substantial' part of the UK, and a relatively small part of the UK could constitute a 'market' within the meaning of section 18. The Chapter II prohibition is therefore a potentially far-reaching instrument for competition authorities and litigants alike. Firms that have market power which is on only a local scale and which therefore run little risk of infringing Article 82 for lack of any effect on inter-state trade, or are dominant only in an insubstantial part of the common market, might find that they are infringing the Chapter II prohibition. Local dominance can be expected to be found in some sectors, such as the operation of bus services: there were numerous investigations of bus services under

[327] See pp 328–331 above.
[328] Case No 1006/2/1/01 *BetterCare Group Ltd v Director General of Fair Trading* [2002] CAT 7, [2002] CompAR 299.
[329] The case is discussed at pp 329–330 above.
[330] Case No 1009/1/1/02 *Aberdeen Journals Ltd v Office of Fair Trading* [2003] CAT 11, [2003] CompAR 67, paras 459–462.
[331] See p 338 above.   [332] See ch 12, pp 485–486.
[333] [2007] EWHC 599 (Comm), [2007] UKCLR 1653.   [334] See ch 5, pp 186–187.

the old Competition Act 1980[335] and the now-repealed monopoly provisions of the Fair Trading Act 1973[336]. In *First Edinburgh*[337] the OFT concluded that that company had not infringed the Chapter II prohibition by charging predatory prices or by increasing the frequency of bus services in order to foreclose access to the market to a rival bus operator, Lothian Buses plc. In May 2007 the OFT announced that it had sent a statement of objections to Cardiff Bus Company for engaging in predatory pricing[338]. In the case of *JJ Burgess & Sons v OFT*[339] the CAT concluded that W. Austin & Sons had abused a dominant position by refusing access to a crematorium in the Stevenage/Knebworth area of Hertfordshire.

(vii) The relevant market

As in the case of Community law, a finding of dominance requires an assessment of the relevant market. Market definition has been discussed in chapter 1[340]. In the UK guidance on market definition can be found in the first judgment of the CAT in the *Aberdeen Journals* case[341] and in its judgment of December 2006 in *Albion Water v Water Services Regulation Authority*[342]; the OFT has also issued a Guideline on *Market definition*[343]. In general the OFT's Guideline on *Market definition* follows the approach of the European Commission's *Notice on the definition of the relevant market for the purposes of Community competition law*[344].

The OFT's Guideline explains that market definition is not an end in itself but a key step in identifying the competition constraints acting on a supplier of a given product or service[345]. As the CAT said in *Aberdeen Journals*:

the key idea is that of competitive constraint: do the other products alleged to form part of the same market act as a competitive constraint on the conduct of the allegedly dominant firm?[346]

In that case the CAT set aside the OFT's decision that Aberdeen Journals had abused its dominant position in the market for the supply of advertising space for paid-for and free local newspapers in the Aberdeen area since it considered that the analysis of the relevant product market was inadequate. The CAT noted in particular that it had been placed in an unsatisfactory position since the OFT's decision had not contained a description of the newspapers in question or the advertising that they carried[347]. The CAT remitted the case to the OFT for further consideration; the OFT adopted a second

---

[335] See eg *Thamesway Ltd*, OFT, August 1993; *Fife Scottish Omnibuses Ltd*, OFT, March 1994; *United Automobile Services Ltd*, OFT, March 1995.

[336] See eg *The supply of bus services in the north-east of England* Cm 2933 (1995); on the application of the competition rules to the bus industry, see OFT information leaflets: *Frequently asked questions on competition law and the bus industry*, OFT 448, updated July 2006, and *A brief guide to the role of the OFT in the bus industry* and *The OFT and the bus industry*, OFT 397, February 2003.

[337] OFT decision of 29 April 2004, [2004] UKCLR 1554.

[338] OFT press release 74/07 of 15 May 2007.

[339] Case No 1044/2/1/04, [2005] CAT 25, [2005] CompAR 1151. [340] See ch 1, pp 26–40.

[341] Case No 1005/1/1/01 *Aberdeen Journals Ltd v Director General of Fair Trading* [2002] CAT 4, [2002] CompAR 167.

[342] Cases No 1046/2/4/04 and 1032/2/4/04 (IR) [2006] CAT 36, [2007] CompAR 328, paras 90–117.

[343] OFT Guideline 403, December 2004; the OFT's Guideline *Abuse of a dominant position*, OFT 402, December 2004, contains a brief discussion of market definition at paras. 4.4–4.9.

[344] OJ [1997] C 372/5, [1998] 4 CMLR 177. [345] *Market definition*, OFT Guideline 403, para 2.1.

[346] Case No 1005/1/1/01 *Aberdeen Journals Ltd v Director General of Fair Trading* [2002] CAT 4, [2002] CompAR 167, para 97.

[347] Ibid, para 184.

decision in September 2002, in which it again found that Aberdeen Journals had been guilty of abusive behaviour[348]. As would be expected the second decision contained a much longer discussion of the relevant product market; however it reached the same conclusion as in the first decision[349]. On appeal the CAT upheld the second decision of the OFT, on market definition, dominance and abuse, although it reduced the level of the penalty from £1.3 million to £1 million[350].

Market definition is important in assessing whether an agreement has an appreciable effect on competition for the purpose of Article 81 EC or the Chapter I prohibition and in determining whether a firm is dominant for the purpose of Article 82 EC or the Chapter II prohibition[351]. The OFT applies the 'hypothetical monopolist' or 'SSNIP' test to ascertain which group of products could be supplied at prices maintained above competitive levels, and it will usually apply the narrowest potential definition[352]. Part 3 of the Guideline on *Market definition* deals specifically with the product market. It begins with a discussion of demand substitution[353], including the types of evidence on substitution that might be of assistance[354]. The Guideline then discusses the relevance of price discrimination: if a firm can prevent arbitrage between different groups of customers it may be that there are two different product markets[355]. The Guideline also considers the extent to which supply-side substitution may be relevant to product market definition and evidence that may be of value[356]. Part 4 of the Guideline deals with geographic market definition. Part 5 of the Guideline discusses various other issues. After explaining what is meant by a temporal market[357], it addresses the problem of the 'Cellophane fallacy': the hypothetical monopolist test should consider the effect of an increase in price from the competitive level, not a price that is already distorted because of market power[358]. The OFT says that the *Cellophane fallacy* will be accounted for 'when all the evidence on market definition is weighed in the round'. In its second *Aberdeen Journals* judgment[359] the CAT noted the problem of the *Cellophane fallacy* in abuse cases and said that the relevant market to be defined is the market that would exist where prices are competitive[360]. Part 5 of the Guideline also discusses the relevance of market definitions in previous cases[361]. While they may be informative, undue reliance should not be placed on previous decisions, not least since competitive conditions may change over time so that an earlier market definition may no longer be appropriate[362]. Part 6 of the Guideline deals with market definition in 'after markets'[363].

Where the OFT concludes that an allegation of abusive behaviour cannot be substantiated, it may refrain from reaching a conclusion as to the relevant product and geographic

---

[348] *Predation by Aberdeen Journals Ltd (Remitted Case)*, 16 September 2002, [2002] UKCLR 740.

[349] Ibid, paras 19–143; note that the OFT discussed the possibility of the abuse of dominance being in a different market from the dominance itself: see paras 133–139; this aspect of the decision was upheld on appeal by the CAT in Case No 1009/1/1/02 *Aberdeen Journals Ltd v Office of Fair Trading* [2003] CAT 11, [2003] CompAR 67, paras 314–326.

[350] Case No 1009/1/1/02 *Aberdeen Journals Ltd v Office of Fair Trading* [2003] CAT 11, [2003] CompAR 67.

[351] *Market definition*, OFT Guideline 403, para 2.2. [352] Ibid, para 2.7.

[353] Ibid, paras 3.1–3.6. [354] Ibid, para 3.7. [355] Ibid, paras 3.8–3.10.

[356] Ibid, paras 3.12–3.18. [357] Ibid, paras 5.1–5.3.

[358] Ibid, paras 5.4–5.6; see further ch 1, pp 30–31 above.

[359] Case No 1009/1/1/02 *Aberdeen Journals Ltd v Office of Fair Trading* [2003] CAT 11, [2003] CompAR 67.

[360] Ibid, para 276. [361] Ibid, paras 5.7–5.9.

[362] Ibid, para 5.7; this accords with the judgment of the CFI in Case T-125/97 *Coca-Cola Co v Commission* [2000] ECR II-1733, [2000] 5 CMLR 467.

[363] See ch 1, pp 35–36.

markets[364]. However in *Freeserve.com plc v Director General of Telecommunications* the CAT emphasised that it will often be appropriate, for clarity of analysis, for the OFT or sectoral regulator to indicate which markets seem to be potentially relevant in a particular case[365].

(viii) Assessing dominance

The OFT has issued a Guideline *Assessment of market power*[366]. As paragraph 1.2 of the Guideline points out the concept of market power is not part of the statutory framework of the Competition Act, which forbids restrictive agreements and the abuse of dominance; however market power is a useful tool in assessing potentially anti-competitive behaviour. The Guideline states that market power arises where an undertaking does not face effective competitive pressure[367] and can be thought of as the ability profitably to sustain prices above competitive levels or to restrict output or quality below competitive levels[368]. The Guideline quotes the well-known definition of a dominant position from *United Brands v Commission*[369], the ability to 'prevent effective competition being maintained on the relevant market'[370]. In *Napp Pharmaceutical Holdings Ltd v Director General of Fair Trading* (and in subsequent cases) the CAT has adopted the same definition[371]. In *Albion Water v Water Services Regulation Authority*[372] the CAT, perhaps concerned at the lack of findings of infringement of the Chapter II prohibition by the OFT and the sectoral regulators, said that:

when assessing dominance under the Competition Act, it is unnecessary for the competition authority to investigate distant or theoretical possibilities with a view to dotting every 'i' or crossing every 't' that could conceivably be imagined. While a sensible analysis is required, there is no need to make the issue of dominance more complicated than it really is[373].

The OFT's Guideline on the *Assessment of market power* says that an undertaking will not be dominant unless it enjoys 'substantial market power'[374]: it will be recalled that DG COMP's *Discussion Paper on exclusionary abuses* of December 2005[375] made the same equation[376]. The Guideline adds that assessing market power requires an examination of the competitive constraints that an undertaking faces, and it proceeds to discuss market shares (Part 4), entry barriers (Part 5) and other factors relevant to an assessment of market power (Part 6).

(A) Market shares Paragraph 2.11 of the Commission's Guideline makes the point that there is no fixed market share threshold for the determination of market power: market power depends on a variety of factors of which market share is one; paragraph 2.12 notes that there is a presumption in Community law of dominance at 50 per cent or above[377], and adds that the OFT considers it unlikely that an undertaking would be dominant

[364] See eg *Association of British Travel Agents and British Airways plc*, 11 December 2002, [2003] UKCLR 136, paras 10–19.
[365] Case No 1007/2/3/02 [2003] CAT 5, [2003] CompAR 202, para 131.
[366] OFT Guideline 415 the OFT's Guideline *Abuse of a dominant position*, OFT 402, December 2004, contains a briefer discussion of market definition at paras 4.10–4.22.
[367] *Assessment of market power*, para 1.3.   [368] Ibid, para 1.4.
[369] Case 27/76 [1978] ECR 207, [1978] 1 CMLR 429.   [370] See ch 5, p 174.
[371] Case No 1000/1/1/01 [2002] CAT 1, [2002] CompAR 13, para 164.
[372] Cases No 1046/2/4/04 and 1032/2/4/04 (IR) [2006] CAT 36, CompAR 328.
[373] Ibid, para 185.   [374] *Assessment of market power*, para 2.9.
[375] See ch 5, pp 210–212.   [376] *Discussion Paper*, para 23.   [377] See ch 5, p 177.

with a market share below 40 per cent. Paragraph 3.3 points out that one of the competitive constraints upon an undertaking comes from existing competitors within the relevant market, and market shares help[378] to assess the extent of this constraint. Part 4 of the Guideline discusses market shares in more detail. Market power is more likely to exist where an undertaking has a persistently high market share[379]. It is the development of market shares over a period of time that is important, not their calculation at a single point in time[380]. The Guideline explains various reasons why market shares might not be a reliable guide to market power, for example because barriers to entry are low or because the market is a 'bidding market'[381]. Paragraphs 4.6 to 4.8 provide insights into methods of calculating market shares.

(B) Entry barriers Paragraph 3.3 of the Guideline points out that one of the competitive constraints upon an undertaking comes from potential competition, and entry barriers are relevant to an examination of this issue. Part 5 of the Guideline discusses barriers to entry; paragraph 5.1 explains that firms already in the market may experience barriers to expansion, and that such barriers can be analysed in the same way as barriers to entry. Entry barriers are important to the assessment of potential competition: the lower they are, the more likely it is that potential competition will prevent undertakings already in the market from profitably sustaining prices above competitive levels[382].

The Guideline acknowledges that there are various ways of classifying barriers to entry; it examines the issue under six heads[383]:

- **Sunk costs**: sunk costs – that is to say costs that must be incurred to enter a market but which are not recoverable on exiting the market – may give incumbent firms an advantage over potential entrants[384]

- **Poor access to key inputs and distribution outlets**: there can be a barrier to entry where an incumbent has privileged access to a scarce input or distribution outlet, for example to essential facilities or intellectual property rights[385]

- **Regulation**: regulation – for example a limitation of the numbers of undertakings licensed to operate in a market or standards that an incumbent can satisfy but that new entrants find it difficult to – can amount to a barrier to entry[386]

- **Economies of scale**: the fact that an undertaking may need to enter the market on a large scale can constitute a barrier to entry[387]

- **Network effects**: as in the case of economies of scale, network effects can make it hard for a new firm to enter the market where the minimum viable scale of the network is large in relation to the size of the market[388]

- **Exclusionary behaviour**: behaviour such as predation, margin squeezes and refusals to supply may act as barriers to entry[389]

The Guideline discusses ways of assessing the effects of barriers to entry and the type of evidence that a firm should adduce where it wishes to argue that potential competition (that is to say an absence of barriers to entry) amounts to an effective competitive constraint upon its behaviour[390].

---

[378] Market share figures do not yield any information about the competitive constraint that arises from the ability of existing firms within the market to expand.

[379] *Assessment of market power*, para 4.2.   [380] Ibid, para 4.2.   [381] See ch 1, p 40.

[382] *Assessment of market power*, para 5.2.   [383] Ibid, para 5.6.   [384] Ibid, paras 5.8–5.11.

[385] Ibid, paras 5.12–5.15.   [386] Ibid, paras 5.16–5.17.   [387] Ibid, paras 5.18–5.20.

[388] Ibid, paras 5.21–5.22.   [389] Ibid, paras 5.23–5.28.   [390] Ibid, paras 5.29–5.36.

(C) Other factors in the assessment of market power Part 6 of the Guideline considers other matters that are relevant to an assessment of market power. These include:

- **buyer power**: buyer power may act as a constraint on an undertaking's market power; however buyer power does not come from size alone: the buyer must have a choice of supplier[391];

- **behaviour and performance**: the behaviour and performance of the undertaking under investigation may provide evidence of market power, for example where it can set prices consistently above an appropriate measure of cost or where it can persistently earn excessive profits[392]; and

- **economic regulation**: economic regulation may prevent an undertaking from raising prices above a competitive level, although this does not in itself mean that that undertaking does not have market power[393]. In the *Napp* case[394] the CAT rejected the argument that the Pharmaceutical Price Regulation Scheme, which limits the rate of return on a company's total sales of all its branded prescription medicines to the National Health Service, meant that Napp did not enjoy a dominant position[395].

(D) Super-dominance In the *Napp* case[396] the CAT recognised that certain firms may be 'super-dominant', with the result that the 'special responsibility' that they bear may be particularly onerous[397]. This means that the application of Article 82 may be stricter for super-dominant undertakings or undertakings which hold a position of dominance approaching monopoly. In *BT Broadband*[398] OFTEL (the predecessor of OFCOM) concluded that BT, with a market share in the relevant market of 65 per cent to 70 per cent, was not in a super-dominant position[399].

(ix) Abuse

(A) Examples of abuse Section 18(2) sets out a non-exhaustive list of abuses, in identical terms to those in Article 82 EC. Unlike Article 82, sections 18(1) and 18(2) refer to 'conduct' which amounts to an abuse, rather than merely an abuse. It is hard to see how the use of the term 'conduct' improves on the EC version, and indeed it is not entirely apt: there is no doubt, for example, that a refusal to supply could, in certain circumstances, amount to an abuse of a dominant position; semantically it is somewhat strange to characterise inaction as conduct.

The CAT has pointed out that the primary interest to be protected under the Chapter II prohibition is the process of competition, and ultimately the interest of the consumer, rather than the private interest of a particular competitor; but that in some cases protecting the competitive process necessarily involves having regard to the situation of competitors[400].

---

[391] Ibid, paras 6.1–6.4.   [392] Ibid, paras 6.5–6.6.   [393] Ibid, para 6.7.
[394] Case No 1000/1/1/01 *Napp Pharmceutical Holdings Ltd v Director General of Fair Trading* [2002] CAT 1, [2002] CompAR 13.
[395] Ibid, paras 161–168.
[396] Case No 1000/1/1/01 *Napp Pharmaceutical Holdings Ltd v Director General of Fair Trading* [2002] CAT 1, [2002] CompAR 13, para 219.
[397] [2002] CAT 1, [2002] CompAR 13, para 219; on 'super-dominance' see further ch 5, pp 184–186.
[398] Decision of 11 July 2003, [2003] UKCLR 1141.   [399] Ibid, para 2.23.
[400] Case 1046/2/4/04 *Albion Water Ltd v Director General of Water Services* [2005] CAT 40, [2006] CompAR 269, para 262.

The OFT's Guideline *Abuse of a dominant position*[401] contains a brief discussion of the meaning of abuse, but does little more than to repeat what is contained in Article 82 EC and section 18. The OFT published a draft Guideline *Assessment of conduct* in April 2004 which, if adopted, would have provided much more detailed discussion of the concept of abuse. However the OFT decided not to proceed to the adoption of a final Guideline given that the European Commission was conducting its own review of Article 82[402]. The OFT's draft Guideline is still available on its website[403]. It is possible that, following a further period of consultation, the OFT will adopt a guideline on this subject at some point in the future. In the meantime the guidelines for particular sectors such as the energy sector and railways contain discussion of the concept of abuse in the circumstances of those markets[404].

Community jurisprudence on the meaning of abuse is highly influential in the application of the Chapter II prohibition, not least because of the 'governing principles' clause in section 60 of the Act[405]: as a result the reader is referred to chapter 5 for a general discussion of the meaning of abuse under Article 82[406]. Abusive practices themselves are considered in detail in chapter 17, which deals with non-pricing abuses, and chapter 18, which deals with pricing abuses. In each chapter specific attention is given to the application of the Chapter II prohibition[407].

(B) Objective justification Behaviour that appears to be abusive may be held to be lawful where it has an objective justification[408]. In *Floe Telecom Ltd (in administration) v OFCOM*[409] the CAT disagreed with OFCOM's view[410] that Vodafone's refusal to supply certain services in the mobile telephony sector to Floe was objectively justified since Floe required them in order to act illegally, in violation of the Wireless Telegraphy Act 1949. In the CAT's view if Floe's behaviour was clearly illegal, Vodafone would have been justified in refusing to deal with it[411]. However the CAT considered that the illegality of Floe's behaviour was far from clear, and that OFCOM should have conducted a much more extensive enquiry before concluding that Vodafone's refusal to supply was objectively justified[412]. OFCOM's decision was therefore set aside. When OFCOM reexamined the matter, in the light of the CAT's comments, it continued to believe that Vodafone's behaviour was objectively justified[413]. OFCOM's second decision in this case was also appealed to the CAT, but it did not reach a conclusion on this issue since it decided the case on different grounds from those of OFCOM[414]. In *Re-investigation of a complaint from VIP Communications Ltd*[415] OFCOM considered that T-Mobile's refusal to supply VIP was objectively justified for the same reason that applied in *Floe*[416]. The

---

[401] OFT Guideline 402, December 2004.   [402] See ch 5, pp 210–212.

[403] www.oft.gov.uk/shared_oft/business_leaflets/competition_law/oft414a.pdf.

[404] These guidelines are listed at pp 325–326 above.   [405] See pp 362–367 below.

[406] See ch 5, pp 188–206.   [407] See chs 17 and 18 generally.

[408] See ch 5, pp 207–208.   [409] Case No 1024/2/3/04 [2004] CAT 18, [2005] CompAR 290.

[410] Decision of 3 November 2003, [2004] CompAR 313; at that time OFCOM was known as OFTEL.

[411] Case No 1024/2/3/04 [2004] CAT 18, [2005] CompAR 290, para 333.

[412] Ibid, paras 334–339.   [413] Decision of 28 June 2005, [2005] UKCLR 1112, paras 246–312.

[414] Case 1024/2/3/04 [2006] CAT 17, [2006] CompAR 637; see in particular paras 349–372.

[415] OFCOM decision of 28 June 2005, [2005] UKCLR 1112; OFCOM's decision is on appeal to the CAT in Case 1027/2/3/04 *VIP Communications Ltd (in administration) v OFCOM*, not yet decided.

[416] Ibid, paras 239–254.

Office of Rail Regulation accepted a defence of objective justification in *Complaint from NTM Sales and Marketing Ltd against Portec Rail Products (UK) Ltd*[417].

(C) Conduct of minor significance Conduct of minor significance cannot be the subject of a financial penalty[418].

(D) Article 3(2) EC modernisation regulation Unilateral conduct that is not abusive may, nevertheless, be subject to a stricter rule of national law[419].

(B) Exclusions[420]

(i) Exclusions for mergers subject to UK or EC merger control

The Chapter II prohibition does not apply to conduct resulting in a relevant merger situation[421] or in a concentration having a Community dimension[422]. This exclusion is closely related to the exclusion of mergers from the Chapter I prohibition, which was described above[423].

(ii) Financial Services and Markets Act 2000

The Chapter II prohibition will not apply to certain conduct pursuant to the regulatory provisions of the FSMA[424].

(iii) Other exclusions

Section 19(1) provides that the Chapter II prohibition does not apply to cases excluded by Schedule 3[425]. Some of the exclusions in Schedule 3 apply only to the Chapter I prohibition; however paragraph 4 of Schedule 3 (services of general economic interest), paragraph 5 (compliance with legal requirements), paragraph 6 (avoidance of conflict with international obligations), and paragraph 7 (exceptional and compelling reasons of public policy) also exclude the application of the Chapter II prohibition.

5. 'GOVERNING PRINCIPLES CLAUSE': SECTION 60 OF THE COMPETITION ACT 1998

The EC Modernisation Regulation requires that, where the OFT, a sectoral regulator or a court apply domestic competition law they must, in so far as an agreement or conduct has an effect on trade between Member States, also apply Article 81 and/or 82 EC. The relationship between EC national competition law, and in particular the scope for applying stricter rules than those of the EC, has already been considered in the final

---

[417] ORR decision of 19 August 2005, [2006] UKCLR 12, paras 168–185.
[418] See ch 10, p 404.   [419] See ch 2, p 77.
[420] See the detailed discussion of exclusions in the context of the Chapter I prohibition at pp 341–347 above.
[421] Competition Act 1998, s 19 and Sch 1, para 2 ('normal' mergers).
[422] Ibid, s 19 and Sch 1, para 6.   [423] See pp 341–343 above.
[424] See p 344 above.   [425] For a discussion of Schedule 3 see pp 344–347 above.

section of chapter 2[426]. In the years since the Modernisation Regulation entered into force there has been no difficulty in applying the EC and domestic rules in a harmonious fashion.

This section of this chapter deals with a different point which is that UK law itself, as a result of the 'governing principles clause' found in section 60 of the Competition Act, requires that there should be consistency, where possible, in the application of domestic and Community competition law. Section 60 has been extremely important in practice and will continue to be so in cases where there is no effect on trade between Member States with the result that domestic law alone is applicable.

Section 60 of the Competition Act sets out the governing principles to be applied in determining questions which arise in relation to competition within the UK; essentially, the principle is that there should be close conformity between the Act and the EC regime; section 60 is also applicable in relation to questions arising under the provisions for the disqualification of company directors[427]. Section 60 enables the UK competition authorities and courts to apply Community competition law when making decisions under the Act.

(i) Section 60(1)

Section 60(1) sets out the purpose of the governing principles clause: the duties to which it gives rise are imposed by section 60(2) and (3). Section 60(1) provides that:

The purpose of this section is to ensure that so far as is possible (having regard to any relevant differences between the provisions concerned), questions arising under this Part in relation to competition within the UK are dealt with in a manner which is consistent with the treatment of corresponding questions arising in Community law in relation to competition within the Community[428].

The objective of consistency is not absolute: consistency is envisaged only 'so far as is possible', having regard to 'relevant differences' and is required as to 'corresponding questions' that arise 'in relation to competition'. The Government stated that 'we are satisfied that the drafting of [section] 60 accurately expresses the concept that Community jurisprudence is to be followed unless the court is driven to some different interpretation by some provision in that part of the [Act]'[429]. Where the factual circumstances of the case-law of the Community Courts differ from those in a UK case, the CAT in *BetterCare* nevertheless observed that its duty under section 60(1) was to approach an issue of competition law 'in the manner in which we think the European Court would approach it, as regards the principles and reasoning likely to be followed by that Court'[430].

(A) 'So far as is possible' The purpose of the Act is to achieve consistency 'so far as is possible'. Clearly this is not possible where the Act explicitly differs from EC law: examples of this are given in the next section. Where there is some doubt in a particular case, these words indicate that there is a policy preference towards maintaining consistency with EC law.

[426] See ch 2, pp 74–78.

[427] See s 9A(11) of the Company Directors Disqualification Act 1986, inserted by s 204 Enterprise Act 2002.

[428] For the meaning of 'the Community' see the Interpretation Act 1978 and European Communities Act 1972.

[429] HL Consideration of Commons' Amendments, 20 October 1998, col 1383 (Lord Simon of Highbury).

[430] Case No 1006/2/1/01 *BetterCare Group v Director General of Fair Trading* [2002] CAT 7, [2002] CompAR 299, para 32.

(B) 'Having regard to any relevant differences' A critical issue is the identification of any 'relevant differences' between Community law and the Act. Some examples appear on the face of the Act itself: for example it contains a few exclusions which are not available under EC law[431]; the Act provides a wider privilege for correspondence with lawyers than in the Community[432]; the exclusion under the Competition Act for mergers is wider than that provided for under EC law; and the Act makes specific provision for land agreements to be excluded, which has been done by statutory instrument[433]. Secondly, the procedural and enforcement rules under the Act are not identical to those in EC law. For example there is a full appeal to the CAT against decisions of the OFT and the CAT has a power to remit a case to the OFT[434] and the sectoral regulators; in the Community, judicial review may provide a less effective remedy to an applicant. Another procedural difference is that the provisions on leniency in the UK are different from those in the EC[435], as is the method of calculating the level of a fine[436].

A further example of a relevant difference, but one that is not apparent on the face of the Act, is that the EC competition rules are applied, in part, with the objective of single market integration in mind. The Competition Act, presumably, does not have to be applied for this purpose, since the goal of market integration is 'relevantly different' from one arising in relation to competition within the UK: this could lead to some divergence in the way in which the Chapter I and II prohibitions and Articles 81 and 82 are applied.

A further area in which relevant differences might exist will arise in the substantive analysis of particular cases; for example it is provided by the OFWAT Guidelines that a different measure of costs will be used to assess alleged predatory pricing[437] due to the 'specific nature of the water industry as a network industry' from the one suggested by the ECJ in the *AKZO* judgment[438].

In *Aberdeen Journals Ltd v Office of Fair Trading*[439] the CAT concluded that there was no need to import a rule of 'appreciability' into the expression 'affect trade' in section 18(1) of the Competition Act, and that this was a 'relevant difference' from the test of 'effect on trade' in Article 82 of the EC Treaty[440].

(C) 'Corresponding questions' In *Mastercard UK Members Forum Ltd*[441] the OFT considered that the questions under consideration in that case did not 'correspond with' those

---

[431] On the exclusions from the Chapter I and Chapter II prohibitions see pp 341–347 and p 362 above.

[432] See ch 10, pp 389–390.

[433] See pp 348–350 above on land agreements; in Case No 1006/2/1/01 *BetterCare Group v Director General of Fair Trading* [2002] CAT 7, [2002] CompAR 299, para 288, the CAT left open the question of whether paragraph 5 of Schedule 3 was relevantly different from EC law.

[434] See eg Case No 1005/1/1/01 *Aberdeen Journals v Director General of Fair Trading* [2002] CAT 4, [2002] CompAR 167, para 190.

[435] See ch 10, pp 404–407.

[436] Case No 1000/1/1/01 *Napp Pharmaceutical Holdings Ltd v Director General of Fair Trading* [2002] CAT 1, [2002] CompAR 13, para 503; note that the CAT did not consider that the slight differences between Article 15(2) of Regulation 17 and ss 36 and 38 of the Competition Act in relation to fines and penalties was sufficient to amount to a 'relevant difference' for the purposes of section 60: ibid, para 455.

[437] *Application in the water and sewerage sector* (OFT Guideline 422), paras 4.11–4.13, where instead of the Community assessment of predation using average variable costs and average total costs, the OFT and the sectoral regulator will consider long run marginal costs; see similarly *The application of the Competition Act 1998 in the telecommunications sector* (OFT Guideline 417), paras 7.6–7.19 and Case No 1007/2/3/02 *Freeserve.com plc v Director General of Telecommunications* [2003] CAT 5, [2003] CompAR 202, paras 212–225.

[438] OFT Guideline 417, para 4.12; on *AKZO* see ch 18, pp 732–733.

[439] Case No 1009/1/1/02 [2003] CAT 11, [2003] CompAR 67.

[440] Ibid, paras 459–460.   [441] OFT decision of 6 September 2005, [2006] UKCLR 236.

in the European Commission's decision in *Visa International – Multilateral Interchange Fee*[442] since the latter was explicitly concerned with a cross-border payment system whereas the OFT's decision was dealing with a payment system within the UK[443].

(D) 'Questions arising ... in relation to competition' The policy of maintaining consistency arises only where there are 'questions arising in relation to competition'. The view of the UK Government when the Bill was proceeding through Parliament was that it was not necessary for the OFT (or sectoral regulators) to follow the same detailed procedures as the European Commission: indeed that might be undesirable, given that it is a very different institution from the OFT; it can reasonably be argued that the procedural rules do not themselves raise questions 'in relation to competition'. However it was accepted in the House of Lords by Lord Simon of Highbury that section 60 does import the general principles of Community law as well as the specific jurisprudence on Articles 81 and 82 themselves, save where there is a relevant difference[444]. Examples of what have come to be termed in discussion of the Act as 'high level principles' are equality, legal certainty, legitimate expectation, proportionality and privilege against self-incrimination: each of these is well-established in Community law[445]. Other general principles noted by the Community Courts include the duty to state reasons for a decision with sufficient precision[446], the principle of good administration[447], the right of access to the file[448] and equality of arms[449]. In *Pernod-Ricard v OFT*[450] the CAT considered that the rights of a third party complainant in competition proceedings raised a question which arose 'in relation to competition' for the purposes of section 60 of the Act[451]. The Tribunal also referred extensively to the jurisprudence of the Community courts in *Apex Asphalt and Paving Co Ltd v OFT*[452] when considering whether there were procedural defects in a statement of objections issued by the OFT[453].

(ii) Section 60(2) and (3)

Section 60(2) and (3) provides that:

(2) At any time when the court[454] determines a question arising under this Part, it must act (so far as is compatible with the provisions of this Part[455] and whether or not it would otherwise be required to do so) with a view to securing that there is no inconsistency[456] between-
(a) the principles applied, and decision reached, by the court in determining that question; and

---

[442] OJ [2002] L 318/17, CMLR.   [443] Ibid, paras 97–106.

[444] HL Committee, 25 November 1997, cols 960–963.

[445] See *Wyatt and Dashwood's European Union Law* (Sweet & Maxwell, 5th ed, 2006, eds Arnull, Dashwood, Dougan, Ross, Spaventa and Wyatt), ch 7.

[446] Case T-241/97 *Stork Amsterdam BV v EC Commission* [2000] ECR II-309, [2000] 5 CMLR 31, para 74.

[447] Case T-127/98 *UPS Europe SA v EC Commission* [1999] ECR II-2633, [2000] 4 CMLR 94, para 37.

[448] Cases T-25/95 etc *Cimenteries CBR SA v Commission* [2000] ECR II-491, [2000] 5 CMLR 204, para 142.

[449] Ibid, para 143.   [450] Case No 1017/2/1/03 [2004] CAT 10, [2004] CompAR 707.

[451] Ibid, paras 228–234.   [452] Case No 1032/1/1/04 [2005] CAT 4, [2005] CompAR 507.

[453] Ibid, paras 92–100.

[454] 'Court' in this context includes the Competition Commission, the OFT and the sectoral regulators: Competition Act 1998, s 60(5).

[455] 'This Part' of the Act deals with all matters to do with the prohibitions and their enforcement of them, but not investigations under the Enterprise Act 2002.

[456] Section 60(1) puts the objective positively and is preferable to this double negative.

    (b) the principles laid down by the Treaty[457] and the European Court[458], and any relevant decision of that Court, as applicable at that time in determining any corresponding question arising in Community law.

  (3) The court must, in addition, have regard to any relevant decision or statement of the Commission.

(A) The duty of consistency Consistency must be maintained between the principles applied and the decision reached by the domestic authority and the principles laid down by the Treaty and the Community Courts and any decisions of those Courts in determining corresponding questions that may be applicable at that time. As already noted, 'high level' principles such as equality and proportionality will be imported by virtue of section 60(2).

(B) Having regard to decisions or statements of the Commission The competition authorities and courts under section 60(3) must 'have regard to' any relevant decision[459] or statement of the Commission; this is a lesser obligation than the obligation to ensure that there is no inconsistency under section 60(2). Decisions and statements of other bodies such as the Council of Ministers[460] or the European Parliament are not included. The Act itself does not explain what is meant by Commission statements. However the OFT's view is that the statements must carry the authority of the Commission as a whole such as, for example, decisions in individual cases under Articles 81 and/or 82, Commission Notices and clear statements about its policy approach as published in its Annual Report on Competition Policy[461]. In *Albion Water Ltd v Director General of Water Services*[462] the CAT was of the view that the Director General of Water Services seemed to have adopted an approach to the margin squeeze alleged in that case that was at variance with the methodology adopted by the European Commission in its *Telecommunications Notice*[463] and in its decision in *Deutsche Telekom*[464]; the CAT therefore needed to hear further argument on the point[465].

In *Mastercard UK Members Forum Ltd*[466] the OFT said that the duty to 'have regard' to Commission decisions and statements did not mean that it was bound to comply with them, but only to give serious consideration to them[467].

---

[457] 'Treaty' in this context refers to the EC Treaty: Competition Act 1998, s 59(1); it would not apply to jurisprudence or decisions under the ECSC Treaty, nor under the EEA Agreement.

[458] 'European Court' refers to both the ECJ and the CFI: ibid; it does not refer to the opinions of the Advocates General, as to which see Buxton LJ in *Napp Pharmaceutical Holdings Ltd v Director General of Fair Trading* [2002] EWCA Civ 796, [2002] 4 All ER 376, who nevertheless characterised such opinions as 'important and authoritative'; nor to the EFTA Court.

[459] On the meaning of decision see Competition Act 1998, s 60(6).

[460] Documents such as the Minutes of the Council's deliberations about the ECMR would therefore not need to be considered, although they could be relevant in a particular case.

[461] *Modernisation*, OFT Guideline 442, para 4.11.

[462] Case No 1046/2/4/04 [2005] CAT 40, [2006] CompAR 269.

[463] *Notice on the application of the competition rules to access agreements in the telecommunications sector* OJ [1988] C 265/2.

[464] Commission decision of 21 May 2003, OJ [2003] L 263/9.

[465] Case No 1046/2/4/04 [2005] CAT 40, [2006] CompAR 269, paras 394–419.

[466] OFT decision of 6 September 2005, [2006] UKCLR 236.   [467] Ibid, paras 107–116.

(C) References to the ECJ The CAT, the Court of Appeal and the House of Lords will be able to make references to the ECJ for a preliminary ruling under Article 234 of the EC Treaty. This is considered further in chapter 10[468].

6. THE COMPETITION ACT 1998 IN PRACTICE

The OFT maintains a register of decisions adopted by itself and by the sectoral regulators under the Competition Act. The following table sets out the decisions that had been published by 12 March 2008.

9.1 Table of published decisions of the OFT and sectoral regulators[1] and appeals to the CAT[2] under the Competition Act 1998 and/or Articles 81 and 82 EC

Case name	Date of decision	Outcome	On appeal to the CAT
General Insurance Standards Council NB: second decision adopted 13.11.2002 – see below	26.1.2001 and 11.5.2001	No infringement of Chapter I prohibition	Decision annulled[3]
Napp Pharmaceutical Holdings Ltd	5.4.2001	Infringement of Chapter II prohibition **Fine of £3.21m**	Finding of infringement upheld **Fine reduced to £2.2 million[4]**
Swan Solutions Ltd/ Avaya ECS Ltd **(OFCOM)**	6.4.2001	No infringement of Chapter I and II prohibitions	
DSG Retail Ltd ('Dixons')/Compaq Computer Ltd/ Packard Bell NEC Ltd	18.4.2001	No infringement of Chapter I and II prohibitions	
BT Surf Together and BT Talk & Surf Together pricing packages **(OFCOM)**	4.5.2001	No infringement of Chapter II prohibition	

---

[468] See ch 10, pp 436–438.

Case name	Date of decision	Outcome	On appeal to the CAT
Consignia and Postal Preference Service Limited	15.6.2001[5]	No infringement of Chapter II prohibition	
Aberdeen Journals Ltd **NB: second decision adopted 16.09.2002 – see below**	16.7.2001	Infringement of Chapter II prohibition **Fine of £1.3 million**	Decision annulled and remitted to the OFT for re-definition of relevant product market[6]
ICL/Synstar	24.7.2001	No infringement of Chapter II prohibition	
LINK Interchange Network Ltd	16.10.2001	Infringement of Chapter I prohibition Granted an individual exemption	
Memorandum of Understanding on the Supply of Oil Fuels	25.10.2001	Infringement of Chapter I prohibition Granted an individual exemption No infringement of Chapter II prohibition	
XDSL Wholesale Products of BT **(OFCOM)**	24.1.2002	No infringement of Chapter II prohibition	
Market sharing by Arriva plc and FirstGroup plc	30.1.2002	Infringement of Chapter I prohibition **Fines of £848,027** (before leniency) **Fines of £203,632** (after leniency)	
Notification by the Film Distributors' Association	1.2.2002	No infringement of Chapter I prohibition	
BT's Wholesale DSL Products: alleged anti-competitive pricing **(OFCOM)**	28.3.2002	No infringement of Chapter II prohibition	

Case name	Date of decision	Outcome	On appeal to the CAT
Vodafone's distribution agreements for pre-pay mobile phone vouchers **(OFCOM)**	05.4.2002	No infringement of the Chapter I prohibition	
The North & West Belfast Health and Social Services Trust **NB: second decision adopted 23.12.03 – see below**	30.4.2002	No infringement of Chapter II prohibition	(i) Judgment holding that the OFT had made an appealable decision when rejecting BetterCare's complaint[7] (ii) Judgment holding that the Health Trust was an undertaking and remitting the matter to the OFT[8]
John Bruce (UK) Ltd, Fleet Parts Ltd and Truck and Trailer Components	17.5.2002	Infringement of Chapter I prohibition **Fines of £33,737**	
Agreement refusing to supply interconnection services for BT Ignite's Multimedia Voice over Internet Protocol service **(OFCOM)**	12.7.2002	Parties renounced agreement so case was closed	
Harwood Park Crematorium Ltd **NB: decision withdrawn, 9.4.2003; second decision adopted 12.8.2004 – see below**	6.8.2002	No infringement of Chapter II prohibition	
Aberdeen Journals Ltd II **NB: second decision**	16.9.2002	Infringement of Chapter II prohibition Fine of £1.3 million	Finding of infringement upheld on appeal **Fine reduced to £1 million**[9]

Case name	Date of decision	Outcome	On appeal to the CAT
Companies House	25.10.2002	No infringement of Chapter II prohibition	
General Insurance Standards Council **NB: second decision**	13.11.2002	No infringement of Chapter I prohibition following amendment of the GISC rules	
Lucite International UK Ltd	29.11.2002	No infringement of Chapter I prohibition as the agreement was vertical and therefore covered by the Exclusion Order for vertical agreements; no reason to 'clawback' exclusion	
Hasbro I	6.12.2002	Infringement of Chapter I prohibition Fine of £4.95 million	Appeal withdrawn following grant of 100% leniency to Hasbro in *Hasbro II* – see below[10]
ABTA and British Airways plc	11.12.2002	No infringement of the Chapter II prohibition	
BSkyB investigation **NB: refusal to vary or withdraw decision 12.8.2003 – see below**	17.12.2002	No infringement of the Chapter II prohibition	
BT Group plc **NB: second decision adopted 19.12.2003 – see below** **(OFCOM)**	9.1.2003	No infringement of the Chapter II prohibition	(i) Judgment holding that OFTEL had made an appealable decision[11] (ii) Judgment partially annulling OFTEL's decision but otherwise dismissing the appeal[12]
Northern Ireland Livestock and Auctioneers's Association	4.2.2003	Infringement of the Chapter I prohibition **No fine**	

Case name	Date of decision	Outcome	On appeal to the CAT
Elite Greenhouses Ltd	14.2.2003	No infringement of the Chapter I prohibition	
Hasbro II **NB: fresh decision adopted 2.12.2003 – see below**	19.2.2003	Infringement of the Chapter I prohibition	Remitted to the OFT so that key witness statements may be put to the parties[13]
Lladró Comercial SA	31.3.2003	Infringement of the Chapter I prohibition **No fine**	
Thames Water Utilities Ltd/Bath House Albion Yard **(OFWAT)**	31.3.2003	No infringement of the Chapter II prohibition	
Anaesthetists Group	15.4.2003	No infringement of the Chapter I prohibition	
Genzyme Ltd	27.4.2003	Infringement of the Chapter II prohibition **Fine of £6.8 million**	(i) One finding of infringement annulled on appeal; second finding upheld **Fine reduced to £3 million**[14] (ii) Judgment on remedy given on 29 September 2005[15]
BT/BSkyB broadband promotion **(OFCOM)**	19.5.2003	No infringement of Chapter I and II prohibitions	
BT UK-SPN calls service alleged anticompetitive pricing **(OFCOM)**	23.5.2003	No infringement of the Chapter II prohibition	
Alleged cross-subsidy of BT's discounts **(OFCOM)**	28.5.2003	No infringement of the Chapter II prohibition	

Case name	Date of decision	Outcome	On appeal to the CAT
BT TotalCare **(OFCOM)**	10.6.2003	No infringement of the Chapter II prohibition	
BT Broadband **(OFCOM)**	11.7.2003	No infringement of the Chapter II prohibition	
Replica football kits	01.8.2003	Infringement of the Chapter I prohibition **Fines of £18.668 million** (before leniency) **Fines of £18.627 million** (after leniency)	(i) Finding of infringement substantially upheld[16] (ii) **Fine reduced to £14.92 million**[17] (iii) Judgment of Court of Appeal of 19 October 2006 upholding the CAT[18] (iv) House of Lords refused permission to appeal on 7 February 2007
BSkyB decision dated 17 December 2002: rejection of applications under section 47 Competition Act **NB: second decision**	12.8.2003	No infringement of the Chapter II prohibition	
London Electricity plc **(OFGEM)**	17.9.2003	No infringement of the Chapter II prohibition	
E.I. du Pont de Nemours & Co	22.9.2003	No infringement of the Chapter II prohibition	
Disconnection of Floe Telecom Ltd's Services by Vodafone Limited **NB: fresh decision adopted 30.6.2005 – see below (OFCOM)**	3.11.2003	No infringement of the Chapter II prohibition	(i) Judgment of 19 November 2004 requiring OFCOM to reconsider the matter[19]

Case name	Date of decision	Outcome	On appeal to the CAT
			(ii) Ruling of 20 July 2005 refusing permission to appeal to the CAP[20]
			(iii) The CAP gave permission to appeal, including intervener status to the OFT, leading to a judgment providing guidance on the CAT's jurisdiction on 15 June 2006[21]
Hasbro II **NB: second decision**	2.12.2003	Infringement of Chapter I prohibition **Fines of £38.25 million** (before leniency) **Fines of £22.66 million** (after leniency)	(i) Finding of infringement upheld[22] **(ii) Fine reduced to £19.50 million**[23] (iii) Ruling of 29 April 2005 refusing permission to appeal to the CAP[24] (iv) Judgment of Court of Appeal of 19 October upholding the CAT[25] (v) House of Lords refused permission to appeal on 7 February 2007
Alleged predatory pricing by English Welsh and Scottish Railway **(ORR)**	3.12.2003	No infringement of Chapter II prohibition	
BT/Openworld **NB: second decision (OFCOM)**	19.12.2003	No infringement of Chapter II prohibition	Appeal pending[26]
BetterCare Group Ltd/North & West Belfast Health & Social Services Trust **NB: second decision**	23.12.2003	No infringement of Chapter II prohibition	

Case name	Date of decision	Outcome	On appeal to the CAT
Disconnection of VIP Communications Limited's services by T-Mobile Limited **NB: fresh decision adopted 30.6.2005 – see below (OFCOM)**	31.12.2003	No infringement of Chapter II prohibition	Decision set aside by Order of the CAT[27]; OFCOM to re-consider the matter
BT publishing its 118500 directory enquiries number on the front of the BT phonebook **(OFCOM)**	31.12.2003	No infringement of Chapter II prohibition	
United Utilities Electricity plc **(OFGEM)**	10.2.2004	No infringement of Chapter II prohibition	
West Midlands roofing contractors	17.3.2004	Infringement of Chapter I prohibition **Fines of £971,186** (before leniency) **Fines of £297,625** (after leniency)	Finding of infringement upheld on appeal[28] **Fines reduced to £288,625**[29]
Pool Reinsurance Company Limited	15.4.2004	Infringement of Chapter I prohibition Granted an individual exemption	
Association of British Insurers	22.4.2004	Infringement of Chapter I prohibition Conditionally granted an individual exemption	Decision on exemption suspended; the OFT subsequently closed the case[30]
Attheraces	10.5.2004	Infringement of Chapter I prohibition	Judgment of 2 August 2005 annulling the OFT's decision[31]
Albion Water/Dŵr Cymru **(OFWAT)**	27.5.2004	No infringement of Chapter II prohibition	(i) Judgment finding infringement of the Chapter II prohibition on 18 December 2006[32]

Case name	Date of decision	Outcome	On appeal to the CAT
			(ii) Order of the Court of Appeal on 26 July 2007 granting permission to appeal[33] (iii) Judgment of the Court of Appeal upholding the CAT[34]
Suspected margin squeeze by Vodafone, O2, Orange and T-Mobile (OFCOM)	27.5.2004	No infringement of Chapter II prohibition	
Complaint against Network Rail by the Sub Contractors Welding Federation (ORR)	4.6.2004	No infringement of Chapter II prohibition	
First Edinburgh/ Lothian	9.6.2004	No infringement of Chapter II prohibition	
NPower (OFGEM)	9.6.2004	No infringement of Chapter II prohibition	
Suretrack Rail Services Ltd and P Way Services Ltd/London Underground Group (ORR)	5.7.2004	No infringement of Chapter II prohibition	
Investigation against BT about potential anti-competitive exclusionary behaviour (OFCOM)	12.7.2004	No infringement of Chapter II prohibition	
Southern Water Services Ltd/ Provision of new infrastructure in East Kent (OFWAT)	3.8.2004	No infringement of Chapter II prohibition	

Case name	Date of decision	Outcome	On appeal to the CAT
Refusal to supply JJ Burgess Ltd with access to Harwood Park Crematorium **NB: second decision**	12.8.2004	No infringement of Chapter II prohibition	Judgment of 6 July 2005 setting aside the OFT's decision and concluding that W. Austin and Sons had abused a dominant position in relation to access to Harwood Park[35]
BT 0845 and 0870 retail price change **(OFCOM)**	12.8.2004	No infringement of Chapter II prohibition	
TM Property Services Ltd/MacDonald Ltd	29.9.2004	No infringement of Chapter II prohibition **(NB: OFT market study launched, December 2004)**	
Pricing of BT Analyst **(OFCOM)**	28.10.2004	No infringement of Chapter II prohibition	
UOP Ltd/Ukae Ltd Etc (Desiccants)	9.11.2004	Infringement of Chapter I Prohibition **Fines of £2.433 million** (before leniency) **Fines of £1.707 million** (after leniency)	**Fines reduced to £1.635 million by Consent Order of 19 May 2005**[36]
United Utitilies Electricity plc **(OFGEM)**	21.12.2004	No infringement of Chapter II prohibition	
Collusive tendering for mastic asphalt flat-roofing contracts in Scotland	8.4.2005	Infringement of Chapter I Prohibition **Fines of £231,445** (before leniency) **Fines of £87,353** (after leniency)	

Case name	Date of decision	Outcome	On appeal to the CAT
Collusive tendering for felt and single ply flat-roofing contracts in the North East of England	8.4.2005	Infringement of Chapter I Prohibition **Fines of £598,223** (before leniency) **Fines of £471,029** (after leniency)	
Treatment of tankered landfill leachate **(OFWAT)**	20.5.2005	No infringement of Chapter II prohibition	
Complaint from Gamma Telecom Ltd against BT Wholesale **(OFCOM)**	16.6.2005	No infringement of Chapter II prohibition	
Re-investigation of Floe Telecom **NB: second decision (OFCOM)**	30.6.2005	No infringement of Chapter II prohibition	(i) Judgment of 31 August 2006 rejecting Floe's appeal[37] (ii) Judgment of 15 March 2007 refusing application by T-Mobile for permission to appeal[38] (iii) Judgment of 15 March 2007 refusing application by OFCOM for permission to appeal[39] (iv) Order of the Court of Appeal on 19 June 2007 granting OFCOM and T-Mobile permission to appeal[40]
Re-investigation of VIP Communications **NB: second decision (OFCOM)**	30.6.2005	No infringement of Chapter II prohibition	Appeal stayed pending the outcome of the judgment of the Court of Appeal in the *Floe Telecoms* case[41]

378 9 COMPETITION ACT 1998 – SUBSTANTIVE PROVISIONS

Case name	Date of decision	Outcome	On appeal to the CAT
Collusive tendering for felt and single ply roofing contracts in Western Central Scotland	12.7.2005	Infringement of Chapter I prohibition **Fines of £258,576** (before leniency) **Fines of £138,515** (after leniency)	
Complaint from NTM Sales and Marketing Against Portec Rail Products (UK) Ltd **(ORR)**	19.8.2005	No infringement of Chapter I or Chapter II prohibitions	
Investigation of the multilateral interchange fees – Mastercard	6.9.2005	Infringement of the Chapter I prohibition	Judgment of 10 July 2006 setting aside OFT's decision[42]
Collusive tendering for flat roof and car park surfacing contracts in England and Scotland	23.2.2006	Infringement of the Chapter I prohibition **Fines of £1.852 million** (before leniency) **Fines of £1,557 million** (after leniency)	Decision upheld on appeal[43]
London Metal Exchange – interim measures direction	27.2.2006	Interim measures direction issued to the London Metal Exchange: suspected infringement of Chapter II prohibition; decision subsequently withdrawn by OFT	Judgment of 8 September 2006 on costs[44]
Stock check pads	4.4.2006	Infringement of the Chapter I prohibition **Fines of £2,184,767** (before leniency) **Fines of £168,318** (after leniency)	Decision upheld on appeal[45]

Case name	Date of decision	Outcome	On appeal to the CAT
Aluminium spacer bars	29.6.2006	Infringement of the Chapter I prohibition **Fines of £1,384,050** (before leniency) **Fines of £898,470** (after leniency)	Judgment of 9 March 2006 rejecting DQS's appeal[46]
BT's pricing of digital and cordless phones **(OFCOM)**	7.8.2006	No infringement of Chapter II prohibition	
English Welsh and Scottish Railway Ltd **(ORR)**	17.11.2006	Infringement of the Chapter II prohibition **Fine of £4.1 million**	
Schools: exchange of information on future fees	20.11.2006	Infringement of the Chapter I prohibition **Fines of £10,000 for each school that participated in the infringement**	
EDF's electricity metering and related services **(OFGEM)**	24.1.2007	No infringement of the Chapter II prohibition	
BBC Broadcast access services **(OFCOM)**	5.6.2007	No infringement of the Chapter II prohibition	Judgment of 20 May 2008 rejecting Independent Media Support's appeal[47]
British Airways[48]	1.8.2007	Infringement of the Chapter I prohibition **Fine of £121.5 million**	
Dairy products	7.12.2007 15.2.2008	Early resolution of collusion case: seven undertakings agreed to pay fines of £120 million	

Case name	Date of decision	Outcome	On appeal to the CAT
National Grid (OFGEM)	25.2.2008	Infringement of Chapter II prohibition and Article 82 **Fine of £41.6 million**	Application for interim relief pending[49] Appeal pending[50]

[1] To avoid confusion the names 'OFCOM', 'ORR', 'OFGEM' and 'OFWAT' will be used throughout, although, at the relevant time, a decision may have been adopted by a different institution (for example OFTEL, which enforced competition law in the telecommunications sector prior to the creation of OFCOM).

[2] Note: in the course of an appeal the CAT may hand down a number of rulings and judgments on various matters: these will all be found on its website, www.catribunal.org.uk; this Table refers only to the key phases in any particular case.

[3] Cases 1002–1004/2/1/01 *Institute of Independent Insurance Brokers v Director General of Fair Trading* [2001] Comp AR 62.

[4] Cases 1000–1/1/1/01 *Napp Pharmaceutical Holdings Ltd v Director General of Fair Trading* [2002] Comp AR 13.

[5] Cf also the judgment of the Chancery Division of 2 November 2000, rejecting Claritas's application for interim measures.

[6] Case 1005/1/1/01 *Aberdeen Journals Ltd v Director General of Fair Trading* [2002] Comp AR 167.

[7] Case 1006/2/1/01 *BetterCare Group v Director General of Fair Trading* [2002] Comp AR 226.

[8] Case 1006/2/1/01 *BetterCare Group Ltd v Director General of Fair Trading* [2002] CAT 7.

[9] Case 1009/1/1/02 *Aberdeen Journals v Director General of Fair Trading* [2003] CAT 11.

[10] Case 1010/1/1/03 *Hasbro UK Limited v The Director General of Fair Trading.*

[11] Case 1007/2/3/02 *Freeserve v Director General of Telecommunications* [2002] CAT 8.

[12] Case 1007/2/3/02 *Freeserve v Director General of Telecommunications* [2003] CAT 5.

[13] Case 1014 and 1015/1/1/03 *Argos Ltd and Littlewoods Ltd v Office of Fair Trading* [2003] CAT 16.

[14] Case 1016/1/1/03 *Genzyme v Office of Fair Trading* [2004] CAT 4.

[15] Case 1016/1/1/03 *Genzyme v Office of Fair Trading* [2005] CAT 32.

[16] Cases 1021/1/1/03 etc *JJB v OFT* [2004] CAT 17.

[17] Case 1019/1/1/03 etc *Umbro Holdings Ltd* [2005] CAT 22.

[18] [2006] EWCA 1318.

[19] Case 1024/2/3/04 *Floe Telecom Ltd (in administration) v OFCOM* [2004] CAT 18.

[20] Case 1024/2/3/04 *Floe Telecom Ltd (in administration) v OFCOM* [2005] CAT 28.

[21] [2006] EWCA Civ 768.

[22] Cases 1014/1/1/03 and 1015/1/1/03 *Argos Ltd and Littlewoods Ltd v OFT* [2004] CAT 24.

[23] Cases 1014/1/1/03 and 1015/1/1/03 *Argos Ltd and Littlewoods Ltd v OFT* [2005] CAT 13.

[24] Cases 1014/1/1/03 and 1015/1/1/03 *Argos Ltd and Littlewoods Ltd v OFT* [2005] CAT 16.

[25] [2006] EWCA 768.

[26] Case 1026/2/3/04 *Wanadoo (UK) plc (formerly Freeserve.com plc) v OFCOM.*

[27] Case 1027/2/3/04 *VIP Communications Ltd v OFCOM*, Order of 1 December 2004.

[28] Cases 1032/1/1/04 etc *Apex Asphalt v OFT* [2005] CAT 4 and CAT [2005] 5.

[29] Cases 1032/1/1/04 etc *Apex Asphalt v OFT* [2005] CAT 11 and CAT [2005] 12.

[30] Case 1036/1/1/04 *Association of British Insurers v OFT.*

[31] Case 1035/1/1/04 *The Racecourse Association v OFT* and Case No. 1041/2/1/04 *British Horseracing Board v OFT* [2005] CAT 29.

[32] Case 1046/2/4/04 *Albion Water Limited v Director General of Water Services (Dŵr/Shotton Paper)* [2006] CAT 36.

[33] Cases C1/2007/0373 and C1/2007/0374.

[34] Judgment of 22 May 2008, [2008] EWCA Civ 536.

[35] Case 1044/2/1/04 *Burgess v OFT* [2005] CAT 25.

[36] Case 1048/1/1/05 *Double Quick Supplyline Ltd v OFT.*

[37] [2006] CAT 17.

[38] Case 1024/2/3/04 *Floe Telecom Ltd (in administration) v OFCOM* [2007] CAT 16.

[39] Case 1024/2/3/04 *Floe Telecom Ltd (in administration) v OFCOM* [2007] CAT 15.

[40] Cases C3/2007/0658 *OFCOM v Floe Telecom Ltd* and C3/2007/0665 *T-Mobile Ltd v Floe Telecom Ltd*

[41] Case 1027/2/3/04 *VIP Communications Ltd (in administration) v OFCOM*.

[42] Cases 1054–1056/1/1/05 *MasterCard UK Members Forum Limited v OFT* [2006] CAT 14.

[43] Case 1061/1/1/06 *Makers UK Ltd v OFT* and Case No. 1065/1/1/06 *Prater Ltd v OFT* [2007] CAT 11.

[44] Case 1062/1/1/06 *London Metal Exchange v OFT* [2006] CAT 19.

[45] Case 1067/1/1/06 *Achilles Group Ltd v OFT* [2006] CAT 24.

[46] Case 1072/1/1/06 *Double Quick Supplyline Ltd and Plastic Building Materials Ltd v OFT* [2007] CAT 13.

[47] Case 1087/2/3/07 *Independent Media Support Ltd v OFCOM* [2008] CAT 13.

[48] Note: formal decision to be adopted and published in due course.

[49] Case 1097/1/2/08 (IR) *National Grid plc v The Gas and Electricity Markets Authority (Interim Relief)*.

[50] Case 1099/1/2/08 *National Grid plc v The Gas and Electricity Markets Authority*.

A number of points can be made about the application of the Competition Act since 2000.

(A) Total number of infringements

The OFT has found infringements of the Chapter I prohibition and Article 81 on 18 occasions; two of these decisions were set aside on appeal to the CAT, *Attheraces* and *Mastercard*. The OFT will adopt formal decisions in the cases of *British Airways* and *Dairy products* in due course. Four individual exemptions were granted before the abolition of notification and exemption, one of which was suspended on appeal. The OFT has found infringements of the Chapter II prohibition on 3 occasions. The ORR has found an infringement of Chapter II and Article 82 EC on one occasion as has OFGEM[469].

(B) Findings of infringement by the CAT

In addition to the findings of infringement by the OFT and the ORR, on two occasions the CAT has made its own finding of an infringement of Chapter II; this happened in appeals from non-infringement decisions of the OFT and OFWAT respectively. In *JJ Burgess & Sons v OFT*[470] the CAT concluded that W Austin and Sons had abused a dominant position by refusing to grant access to a competing firm of funeral directors to its crematorium facilities at Harwood Park in Hertfordshire. In *Albion Water Ltd v Water Services Regulation Authority*[471] the CAT concluded that Dŵr Cymru had abused its dominant position in the market for the supply of water by applying a margin squeeze to Albion Water.

(C) Appeals against infringement decisions

Several of the OFT's infringement decisions have been appealed to the CAT. Most of them were upheld on substance. Some of the findings of infringements were set aside in the *Football Shirts* case[472]. The only infringement decision to have been overturned in its entirety was *Attheraces*[473]. The OFT had concluded that the collective selling by the

[469] For more detailed discussion of the penalties imposed to date see ch 10, pp 408–412.

[470] Case No 1044/2/1/04 [2005] CAT 25, [2005] CompAR 1151.

[471] Case No 1046/2/4/04 [2006] CAT 36, [2007] CompAR 328, upheld on appeal to the Court of Appeal *Dŵr Cymru Cyfyngedig v Water Services Regulation Authority* [2008] EWCA Civ 536.

[472] Case Nos 1021/1/1/03 etc *JJB v OFT* [2004] CAT 17, [2005] CompAR 29.

[473] OFT decision of 10 May 2004, [2004] UKCLR 995.

Racecourse Association of the non-licensed betting office ('non-LBO') media rights to horseracing at 59 racecourses in Great Britain infringed the Chapter I prohibition; and that it did not satisfy the criteria of section 9 of the Competition Act, which provides a defence for restrictive agreements that produce economic efficiencies. The Racecourse Association (and the British Horseracing Board) appealed to the CAT, which disagreed with the OFT's analysis[474]. In the CAT's view the OFT had failed to define the relevant market correctly. The OFT had defined a market for non-LBO media rights, but the CAT considered that this was too narrow: the CAT concluded that this was a sufficient reason in itself to set the decision aside[475]. However the CAT also went on to consider whether, assuming the OFT had correctly defined the relevant market, the collective selling amounted to an infringement of the Chapter I prohibition[476]. In the CAT's opinion, the collective selling of the media rights in question was objectively necessary:

an acquisition via a central negotiation was the only realistic way forward both from the viewpoint of both bidder and sellers (sic) and we regard it as probable that any initial attempt at a self-assembly exercise via individual negotiations would have led quickly to a centrally negotiated one[477].

The CAT also concluded that the OFT had failed to demonstrate that collective selling led to an appreciable increase in price[478]; nor that it resulted in a loss of non-price competition[479]. The CAT's judgment in this case is a most interesting one, in which it takes a robust, 'common-sense' approach to the question of whether competition was restricted on the facts of the case. The discussion of the necessity of collective selling acknowledges that the *evidential* burden of proving such necessity lay with the parties to the agreement rather than with the OFT, even though the overall burden of showing an infringement of Chapter I was on the OFT[480]. The CAT noted the difficulty of reconciling the judgments of the ECJ in *Wouters*[481] and *Gøttrup-Klim*[482] with the CFI's judgment in *Métropole v Commission*[483], concluding, in relation to the ECJ's judgments, that:

What these cases show is that ostensibly restrictive arrangements which are *necessary* to achieve a proper commercial objective will not, or may not, constitute an anti-competitive infringement at all. Whether or not they will do so requires an objective analysis of the particular arrangement entered into by the parties, assessed by reference to their subjective 'wants' and against the evidence of the particular market in which they made their arrangement. The task then is to consider whether the restrictive arrangement of which complaint is made is 'necessary' to achieve the objective[484].

(D) Appeals against non-infringement and case-closure decisions

On several occasions complaints have been made to the OFT or to one of the sectoral regulators of abusive behaviour contrary to the Chapter II prohibition and Article 82 EC. After a period of investigation a decision has then been taken either to close the file

---

[474] Case Nos 1035/1/1/04–1041/2/1/04 *The Racecource Association v Office of Fair Trading* [2005] CAT 29, [2006] CompAR 99.
[475] Ibid, paras 135–150.   [476] Ibid, paras 160–176.   [477] Ibid, para 171.
[478] Ibid, paras 177–202.   [479] Ibid, paras 207–211.   [480] Ibid, paras 130–134.
[481] Case C-309/99 *Wouters v Algemene Raad van de Nederlandse Orde van Advocaten* [2002] ECR I-5777, [2002] 4 CMLR 913.
[482] Case C-250/92 *Gøttrup-Klim Grovvareforreininger v DanskLandburgs Grovvareselskab AmbA* [1994] ECR-5641, [1996] CMLR 191.
[483] Case T-112/99 [2001] ECR II-2459, [2001] 5 CMLR 1236.   [484] See para 167 of the judgment.

and to proceed no further or that there was no infringement; the complainants have then appealed to the CAT in the hope of getting the decision overturned. These cases are discussed in chapter 10[485].

(E) Sectoral regulators

There have been only two findings of an infringement by a sectoral regulator. The first was the case of *English Welsh and Scottish Railway Ltd* and the second was the fine imposed on National Grid Co by the Gas and Electricity Markets Authority. In another case GEMA accepted commitments from SP Manweb, which had been accused by independent connection providers in the electricity sector of discriminatory behaviour in favour of its own affiliated connections business, that it would provide connection services in a non-discriminatory manner within recommended timescales[486]. As can be seen from the Table of Competition Act Decisions there have been a large number of non-infringement decisions by the sectoral regulators.

[485] See ch 10, pp 427–431.
[486] See OFGEM press release R/42 of 27 October 2005, available at www.ofgem.gov.uk.

10

Competition Act 1998 and the cartel offence: public enforcement and procedure

CHAPTER CONTENTS

1. INTRODUCTION

The Competition Act 1998 gives wide powers of enforcement to the Office of Fair Trading ('the OFT') and to the sectoral regulators. The exercise of these powers must satisfy the Human Rights Act 1998, which received the Royal Assent on the same day as the Competition Act 1998 (9 November 1998) and which entered into force on 2 October 2000[1]. The Enterprise Act 2002 amended and reinforced the Competition Act 1998 in significant ways: for example it simplified third party appeals[2] and made provision for monetary claims where an infringement of the Competition Act causes economic harm[3]; it provided for so-called 'super-complaints'[4]; it introduced a criminal 'cartel offence' which can result in the imprisonment of individuals for up to five years[5]; and it provided for company director disqualification where a director knew, or ought to have known, of a corporate infringement of EC or UK competition law[6]. Significant changes were made to the Competition Act by the Competition Act 1998 and Other Enactments (Amendment) Regulations 2004[7] (the 'Amendment Regulations') in order to bring domestic law into alignment with the principles of the EC Modernisation Regulation[8]; these changes are incorporated into the text that follows.

---

[1] On the Human Rights Act 1998 see pp 391–392 below and, more generally, Gordon and Ward *Judicial Review and the Human Rights Act* (Cavendish Publishing, 2000); for further discussion of procedural issues in the UK see Ward and Smith *Competition Litigation in the UK* (Sweet & Maxwell, 2003); O'Neill and Sanders *UK Competition Procedure* (Oxford University Press, 2007).

[2] See p 427 below. [3] See ch 8, pp 307–309. [4] See ch 11, pp 442–445.

[5] See pp 415–422 below. [6] See pp 422–423 below. [7] SI 2004/1261.

[8] Council Regulation 1/2003 OJ [2003] L 1/1, [2003] 4 CMLR 551.

This chapter will begin with a consideration of the way in which inquiries and investigations are carried out under the Competition Act. After a section on complaints and super-complaints it will consider the extent to which it may be possible to receive guidance from the OFT on the application of the Act. Section 4 deals with enforcement and section 5 with the cartel offence and company director disqualification. Section 6 considers the issue of concurrency. Section 7 contains a discussion of the appeal mechanism under the Competition Act and section 8 examines the possibility of Article 234 references to the European Court of Justice ('the ECJ'). The private enforcement of the Competition Act (and of Articles 81 and 82 EC) in the civil courts in the UK was discussed in chapter 8 of this book[9].

2. INQUIRIES AND INVESTIGATIONS

The purpose of the 1998 Act is to eradicate cartels and abusive behaviour and it provides the OFT and the sectoral regulators with wide powers to conduct inquiries and investigations on their own behalf. These powers are set out in sections 25 to 29 of the Act as modified by the Amendment Regulations. Pursuant to Articles 20 to 22 of the EC Modernisation Regulation the OFT also has powers to conduct investigations on behalf of the European Commission or at the request of a competition authority of a Member State of the EU: these powers are set out in sections 61 to 65 of the Competition Act, again as modified by the Amendment Regulations[10]. The OFT's powers to conduct inquiries and investigations are explained in some detail in the OFT's Guideline *Powers of investigation*[11]. The OFT has also published a 'Quick guide' *Under investigation?*[12]. The OFT has introduced a pilot project whereby rewards may be given to informants that provide it with intelligence about cartel behaviour[13]. These, and all the other guidance documents referred to in this chapter, are available on the OFT's website[14].

Section 25 of the Competition Act provides that the OFT may conduct an investigation if there are 'reasonable grounds for suspecting' that either of the prohibitions in the Competition Act or that Articles 81 or 82 EC have been infringed; this is often referred to as the 'section 25 threshold'[15], and is much more easily satisfied than the requirement that there should be 'strong and compelling evidence' to support an infringement decision imposing a fine where the Chapter I and/or II prohibition or Articles 81 and/or 82 EC have been infringed[16]. It is important to note that section 25 gives the OFT a discretion whether or not to conduct an investigation: it is not under a duty to conduct one. A report by the National Audit Office, *The Office of Fair Trading: Enforcing*

---

[9] See ch 8, pp 299–309.

[10] See p 393 below for a brief discussion of investigations under these provisions.

[11] OFT 404, December 2004. [12] OFT 426, March 2005.

[13] See OFT press release of 29 February 2008; more information is available at www.oft.gov.uk/advice_and_resources/resource_base/cartels/rewards.

[14] www.oft.gov.uk.

[15] On the circumstances in which the OFT's powers can be used see *Powers of investigation*, para 2; the OFT's powers are equally available to the sectoral regulators listed in s 54 of the Competition Act and it should be assumed throughout this chapter that anything which applies to the OFT applies equally to them unless otherwise stated.

[16] See further p 391 below.

competition in markets[17], published in November 2005, suggested that the OFT should do more to improve the resourcing and prioritisation of its casework and the transparency and speed of its case management. The OFT accepted the NAO's conclusions[18], and in October 2006 it published a *Competition prioritisation framework* which sets out the criteria that the OFT takes into account when selecting cases for investigation[19].

As in the case of the Modernisation Regulation, which gives the European Commission power to obtain information (Article 18) and to conduct on-the-spot investigations (Articles 20 and 21), the Act gives the OFT the power to make written inquiries (section 26) and to enter business and domestic premises (sections 27 to 29)[20]. These powers are also available to enable the OFT to decide whether to apply for a company director disqualification order[21].

(A) Written inquiries[22]

Where the section 25 threshold has been reached, a written request for information may be made by a notice under section 26 requiring a person to produce to the OFT a specified document or specified information which the OFT considers relevant to the investigation[23]. The notice must indicate the subject-matter and purpose of the investigation[24] and the offences involved in non-compliance[25]. Specification can be by reference to a particular item or by category and the notice may state when and where the document or information is to be provided as well as how and in what form[26]. The OFT has the further power to take copies or extracts from a document produced in response to the notice and to ask for an explanation of it, or, if the document is not produced, to ask where it is believed to be[27]. Notices can be addressed to any person, which is defined to include an undertaking[28]; they may be sent not only to the undertakings suspected of infringement, but also to third parties such as complainants, suppliers, customers, or competitors[29]. It should be noted that while section 26 applies equally to documents and to information, the Guideline on *Powers of investigation* makes clear that the power to obtain information means that the OFT can require a person to create a document incorporating that information: for example a person may be asked to provide market share information or to describe a particular market on the basis of their knowledge or experience or that of their staff[30]. Some section 26 notices are sent after on-site investigations in order to seek clarification of documents obtained[31].

---

[17] Available at www.nao.org.uk.

[18] See the OFT's evidence before the Public Accounts Committee, available at www.publications. parliament.uk/pa/cm200506/cmselect/cmpubacc/841/841.pdf.

[19] Available at www.oft.gov.uk/news/press/2006/146-06.

[20] Note that ss 61–64 deal with investigations under Articles 81 and 82 EC.

[21] Company Directors Disqualification Act 1986, s 9C, inserted by Enterprise Act 2002, s 204.

[22] See Powers of Investigation, para 3.   [23] Competition Act 1998, s 26(1), (2).

[24] Ibid, s 26(3)(a).   [25] Ibid, s 26(3)(b).

[26] Ibid, s 26(4) and (5); s 59(3) provides that, if information is not in legible form, the OFT may require a copy in legible form.

[27] Ibid, s 26(6); see p 390 below for discussion of the scope of the power to request explanations and the law on self-incrimination.

[28] Ibid, s 59(1), which refers to the Interpretation Act 1978 ('person' includes a body of persons corporate or unincorporate).

[29] Powers of investigation, para 3.4.   [30] Ibid, para 3.7.   [31] Ibid, para 3.2.

(B) Power to enter premises without a warrant[32]

Section 27(1) of the Act provides that any officer of the OFT who is authorised in writing by the OFT to do so ('an investigating officer') may enter any business premises[33] in connection with an investigation under section 25[34].

The operation of the power of entry varies depending on whether the premises are occupied by a 'third party', that is to say someone who is not suspected of an offence, or by a party under investigation for a possible infringement. In the case of a third party at least two working days' notice of the inspection must be given, together with a document explaining the subject-matter and the purpose of the investigation[35]. If, however, the officer has taken all reasonable steps to give notice but has been unable to do so he may dispense with the notice requirement[36]. In the case of a party under investigation there is no requirement to give prior warning or notice[37], but the subject-matter and purpose of the investigation must be explained. It is not necessary for the OFT first to have attempted to obtain information under the powers in section 26[38].

When entering the premises the officer may take with him any necessary equipment: this could be a laptop computer or tape-recording equipment[39]; may require 'any person'[40] to produce any documents which the officer considers relevant, to say where a document may be found, and, in relation to any document produced, may require an explanation of it; may take copies of or extracts from any document produced (but not the originals); may require the production in visible, legible and portable form of any relevant information that is held on computer; and may take any steps necessary to preserve or prevent interference with any document relevant to the investigation[41]. The procedure when conducting an inspection without a warrant is explained in the OFT's Guideline[42].

It is not permissible under section 27 to use force to enter or once on the premises; it follows that permitted equipment would not include crowbars or other tools. Section 27 entry may therefore be described as a 'right of peaceful entry'. Where force might be required to gain entry the powers in section 28 must be used. Section 27 does not give a power of search: again this is available only under section 28.

(C) Power to enter premises with a warrant[43]

The OFT may apply for a warrant giving a power of entry to business[44] or domestic premises[45] to named officers of the OFT[46] and to non-employees, such as IT experts, who

---

[32] Ibid, para 4.

[33] Competition Act 1998, s 27(6); premises includes any land or means of transport: ibid, s 59(1).

[34] As to investigations under s 27 on Crown land see the Competition Act 1998, s 73(4)(a) and the Competition Act 1998 (Definition of Appropriate Person) Regulations 1999, SI 1999/2282; the Secretary of State may certify in the interests of national security that specified Crown premises may not be entered under this section (see s 73(8)).

[35] Competition Act 1998, s 27(2).   [36] Ibid, s 27(3)(b).   [37] Ibid, s 27(3)(a).

[38] Powers of investigation, para 3.2.   [39] Ibid, para 4.6.

[40] In this instance this term presumably (although not necessarily) refers to an individual rather than to an undertaking, but there is no restriction as to who the person needs to be; it could include secretaries, IT personnel and messengers as well as directors; see HL Committee, 17 November 1997, col 391 (Lord Simon of Highbury).

[41] Competition Act 1998, s 27(5); see also s 59(3).   [42] Powers of investigation, paras 4.7–4.11.

[43] Ibid, para 5; see also Peretz 'Warrants under Section 28 of the CA 1998: *OFT v D*' (2003) 2 Competition Law Journal 129.

[44] Competition Act 1998, s 28.   [45] Ibid, s 28A.

[46] Ibid, s 28(2) (business premises) and s 28A(2) (domestic premises).

may be able to assist with the investigation[47]. Where the OFT wishes to enter domestic premises it can be anticipated that the Human Rights Act 1998 might be invoked, since one of the 'Convention Rights' protected by that Act is the right to respect for private and family life, the home, and correspondence[48]. A section 28 investigation cannot be conducted on Crown land[49]. The OFT also has powers to conduct inspections under the Enterprise Act 2002 where it has reasonable grounds for suspecting that the criminal cartel offence established by section 188 of that Act has been committed[50].

A warrant may be issued in specified circumstances by a judge of the High Court (Court of Session in Scotland) and in this case reasonable force may be used to obtain entry[51]. The circumstances are[52]: that there are reasonable grounds for suspecting that a document sought by written notice, or by an investigation without a warrant, but not produced, is on the premises; that there are reasonable grounds for suspecting that a document that the OFT could obtain by written notice or by peaceful entry is on the premises but would be interfered with if it were required to be produced; or (in the case of business premises) that entry without a warrant for the purpose of investigation has been impossible and there are reasonable grounds for suspecting that documents are on the premises that could have been required if entry had been obtained. The section 28 powers therefore confer a 'right of forcible entry'.

Investigation by warrant is a serious matter and the investigator's powers are more extensive than under sections 26 or 27. The subject-matter and purpose of the investigation, and the offences for non-compliance, must be indicated in the warrant itself[53]. It follows that the party being investigated should inspect this document carefully.

The investigators may use reasonable force to gain entry, but must lock the premises up in as secure a manner as they found them before leaving[54]. They may take 'equipment' to exercise such force but may not use force against any person[55]. As with investigations without a warrant the authorised officer may require documents to be produced, but the scope of this power depends on the situation in which the warrant was issued. The warrant will accordingly specify documents of 'the relevant kind'[56], that is to say those subject to a specific request under sections 26 or 27, or those of the kind that could have been required on investigation under section 27 but were not provided. In addition to all the powers investigators would have on entry without a warrant, including the power to require information to be accessed from computers[57], they can also take away *originals* of documents and retain them for three months if copying them on the premises is

[47] Ibid, s 28(3A) (business premises) and s 28A(4) (domestic premises).
[48] Human Rights Act, Sch 1, Article 8: on the interpretation of Article 8 of the European Convention for the Protection of Human Rights and Fundamental Freedoms 1950 see in particular *Niemietz v Germany* (1992) 16 EHRR 97, which suggested that it may apply in the case of business as well as domestic premises: ibid, paras 29–33, and, more significantly, Case 37971/97 *Société Colas Est v France and others* judgment of 16 April 2002, [2002] ECHR III-135, finding France to have infringed the applicants' fundamental rights and awarding damages as the inspectors had entered without prior judicial warrant; under EC law see Cases 46/87 and 227/88 *Hoechst AG v Commission* [1989] ECR 2859, [1991] 4 CMLR 410 and Case C-94/00 *Roquette Frères v Directeur Général de la Concurrence* [2002] ECR I-9011, [2003] 4 CMLR 46; see also Article 20(8) of the EC Modernisation Regulation.
[49] Competition Act 1998, s 73(4)(b). [50] See p 416 below.
[51] Competition Act 1998, s 28(2)(a) (business premises) and s 28A(2)(a) (domestic premises).
[52] Ibid, s 28(1) (business premises) and s 28A(1) (domestic premises). [53] Ibid, s 29(1).
[54] Ibid, s 28(5) (business premises), s 28A(6) (domestic premises). [55] Powers of investigation, para 5.5.
[56] Competition Act 1998, s 28(2)(b) (business premises) and s 28A(2)(b) (domestic premises).
[57] Ibid, s 28(3).

not practicable or if taking them away appears necessary to prevent their disappearance[58]. The investigators can also take any other necessary steps to preserve the existence of documents[59]. The procedure when conducting an inspection with a warrant is explained in the OFT's Guideline[60].

Of the 92 inspections conducted by the OFT in relation to seven cases in the period to which the Annual Report for 2005–2006 relates 34 were conducted under section 27 without a warrant and 58 under section 28 with a warrant[61]. During 2006–2007 the OFT visited 14 business premises, 11 without a warrant and three with a warrant[62].

(D) Powers of surveillance

The OFT also has powers of directed surveillance and to make use of covert human intelligence sources in order to investigate infringements of the Competition Act[63].

(E) Access to lawyers

There is no statutory right to obtain outside legal help in the case of an investigation with or without a warrant, and certainly none to delay the start of an investigation until an undertaking's external lawyer arrives on the scene. During the passage of the Competition Bill through Parliament the Government stated that, even though there was nothing in the statute itself, the OFT would follow European Commission practice in this regard by giving a firm without internal legal assistance a reasonable period (in practice usually an hour or so) to obtain external help[64]. The OFT's Rules provide expressly for this right 'if the officer considers it reasonable in the circumstances to do so and if he is satisfied that such conditions as he considers…appropriate…will be complied with'[65]. The Guideline *Powers of investigation* provides further guidance on this issue[66]. The investigating officer will not wait for an external lawyer to arrive if the firm being investigated has an internal legal adviser[67], apparently irrespective of whether he or she is specialised in competition law.

(F) Limitation on the use of the powers of investigation[68]

(i) Legal professional privilege

The requirement to produce documents, whether by written notice or during an inspection, does not extend to privileged communications[69]. These are defined as communications either between a professional legal adviser and his client or those made in connection with, or in contemplation of, legal proceedings and which, for the purposes of those proceedings, would be protected from disclosure in High Court proceedings (Court of Session in Scotland) on grounds of legal professional privilege (confidentiality

---

[58] Ibid, s 28(2)(c), (7) (business premises) and s 28A(2)(c), (8) (domestic premises).
[59] Ibid, s 28(2)(d) (business premises) and s 28A(2)(d) (domestic premises).
[60] Powers of investigation, paras 5.10–5.14.
[61] 2005–2006 Annual Report and Resource Accounts of the Office of Fair Trading p 41.
[62] 2006–2007 Annual Report and Resource Accounts of the Office of Fair Trading Annex C, p 1.
[63] See pp 417–418 below.   [64] HL Committee, 17 November 1997, col 404 (Lord Simon of Highbury).
[65] SI 2004/2751, r 3(1).   [66] Powers of investigation, paras 4.10–4.11.   [67] Ibid, para 4.11.
[68] Ibid, para 6.1.   [69] Competition Act 1998, s 30.

of communications in Scotland)[70]. 'Professional legal adviser' includes professionally qualified lawyers employed by firms (in-house counsel) as well as those practising in their own right, and in this respect privilege under the 1998 Act is more extensive than under EC competition law[71]. Not only does EC law not extend to correspondence with 'in-house' (that is to say employed) lawyers; nor does it apply to dealings with independent professional lawyers not qualified in a Member State[72]. It follows that some documents can legitimately be withheld where the inspection is one that the OFT conducts on its own behalf but not where it is assisting the European Commission's own inspections under Articles 20 and 21 of the Modernisation Regulation. The more generous UK rules on privilege do apply where the OFT conducts an inspection on behalf of the European Commission[73] or on behalf of a competition authority of a Member State[74].

(ii) Self-incrimination

The OFT acknowledges the EC jurisprudence on the subject of self-incrimination[75] and accepts that this is one of those 'high level' principles which will apply to its actions by virtue of section 60[76]. The OFT accepts that it may not ask for explanations that might involve admissions of an infringement and will instead seek explanations of matters of fact, such as whether a particular employee was at a particular meeting[77]; however the distinction between these two will not always be clear-cut. It may be, however, that an applicant for leniency will be prepared to waive privilege against self-incrimination in order to qualify for leniency which, for the first such applicant, may amount to 100 per cent[78]. A statement made by a person in response to a requirement arising from sections 26 to 28A of the Act cannot be used against him for the purposes of a prosecution under the criminal cartel offence unless he makes statements inconsistent with it or adduces evidence in relation to it[79].

The power to demand an 'explanation' of a document is expressly linked to and limited to documents that are produced[80]. However, in the case of an investigation, an explanation can be sought in relation to 'any document appearing to be of the relevant kind'[81] without any specific reference to the document having been produced: this is because, in the case of a search, documents may be found as well as produced. The investigator could in theory require explanation of a document that appears to exist but which he has been unable to find, but the OFT's guidelines do not indicate any intention to act in this way.

(iii) Confidentiality

There are detailed provisions in Part 9 of the Enterprise Act 2002 (replacing sections 55 and 56 and Schedule 11 of the Competition Act 1998) about restrictions on the disclosure of information obtained during the course of an investigation (and as a result of

---

[70] For the law of privilege in court proceedings see 13 *Halsbury's Laws* (4th edn), paras 71–85.

[71] See *Powers of investigation*, paras 6.1–6.2, 9.7–9.9 and 10.5.

[72] For a discussion of privilege in EC competition law see ch 7 pp 268–269.

[73] Competition Act 1998, s 65A.   [74] Ibid, s 65J.   [75] See ch 7, pp 227–268.

[76] *Powers of investigation*, para 6.5; note that in *OFT v X* [2003] EWHC 1042 (Comm), [2003] 2 All ER (Comm) 183 it was held that the jurisprudence of the EC on self-incrimination was consistent with the European Convention on Human Rights.

[77] Ibid, para 6.6.   [78] On leniency see pp 404–407 below.   [79] Competition Act 1998, s 30A.

[80] Ibid, ss 26(6)(a)(ii), 27(5)(b)(ii).

[81] Ibid, s 28(2)(e) (business premises) and s 28A(2)(b) (domestic premises).

the operation of Part I of the Act generally) and these provide a degree of reassurance to disclosing parties. However parties subject to an investigation or to a request for information should identify any confidential information that is supplied to the OFT or to its investigators in order to support any subsequent claim that it should not be published or disclosed to anyone else; indeed the OFT will usually ask them to do this, particularly where significant amounts of information or numbers of documents are sought. There is no right to withhold information from the investigators on grounds of confidentiality[82]. The OFT's Guideline explains the OFT's rights and obligations as regards publication[83].

(iv) Human Rights Act 1998 and Police and Criminal Evidence Act 1984 ('PACE')

In *Napp Pharmaceutical Holdings Ltd v Director General of Fair Trading*[84] the question arose whether proceedings under the Chapter I and Chapter II prohibitions were criminal proceedings for the purpose of the Human Rights Act 1998 ('the HRA 1998'). The Competition Appeal Tribunal ('the CAT') held that proceedings under the Competition Act 1998 are 'criminal' and that it followed from this that the undertaking concerned is entitled, amongst other things, to a fair and public hearing by an independent and impartial tribunal and to be presumed innocent: it is for the OFT to prove the infringements alleged. However the CAT also concluded that the fact that penalty proceedings under the Competition Act 1998 are criminal for the purpose of the HRA 1998 does not mean that they should be subject to the same rules of evidence or procedures as ordinary criminal proceedings[85]. In particular the CAT held that the HRA 1998 does not require that the criminal standard of proof 'beyond all reasonable doubt' should be applied; instead it concluded that the civil standard 'balance of probabilities' was the appropriate standard although, where a fine is imposed, this would require the OFT to provide 'strong and compelling evidence, ... the undertaking being entitled to the presumption of innocence, and to any reasonable doubt there may be'[86]. The CAT added that the fact that competition law has established certain presumptions, for example that a firm with a very high market share is dominant or that sales by a dominant firm at less than average variable cost are predatory, does not reverse the burden of proof or set aside the presumption of innocence. In subsequent judgments the CAT has stressed that the standard of proof is the balance of probabilities, laying less stress on the requirement that evidence should be 'strong and compelling'[87]. The CAT may have felt that the latter standard was having a chilling effect on findings of infringements by the OFT and the sectoral regulators.

On a separate point, in *Hasbro UK Ltd, Argos Ltd and Littlewoods Ltd*[88] the OFT rejected an argument that it should, when conducting interviews with employees of

---

[82] See r 6 of the OFT's Rules in relation to information provided by third parties.

[83] Powers of Investigation, paras 6.8–6.13.

[84] Case No 1000/1/1/01 [2002] CAT 1, [2002] CompAR 13; [2002] ECC 177, see also the interim judgment of the CAT in this appeal: Case No 1001/1/1/01, [2001] CAT 3, [2001] CompAR 33, [2002] ECC 19, paras 69–70.

[85] Case No 1000/1/1/01 [2002] CAT 1, [2002] CompAR 13, para 101.

[86] [2002] CAT 1, [2002] CompAR 13, paras 105 and 109.

[87] See eg *JJB and Allsports v OFT* [2004] CAT 17, [2005] CompAR 29, paras 195–208; see also Case 1061/1/1/06 *Makers UK Ltd v OFT* [2007] CAT 11, paras 45–52.

[88] OFT decision of 19 February 2003, available at www.oft.gov.uk.

Hasbro Ltd as to the possibility of an infringement of the Chapter I prohibition, have complied with the procedures required by PACE[89]. The OFT has published guidance on the way in which it intends to exercise its powers when investigating a possible commission of the criminal cartel offence: this indicates that, where appropriate, its officers would act in accordance with PACE and the relevant Codes of Practice established thereunder[90].

(G) Offences[91]

There are criminal sanctions for non-compliance with the powers of investigation. Individuals as well as legal persons may commit offences; the penalties in some cases include imprisonment[92]. The relevant offences are set out in sections 42 to 44 of the Competition Act and fall into five main categories:

- failing to comply with a requirement imposed under sections 26, 27, 28, or 28A[93]
- intentionally obstructing an officer investigating without a warrant[94]
- intentionally obstructing an officer investigating with a warrant[95]
- intentionally or recklessly destroying, disposing of, falsifying or concealing documents, or causing or permitting those things to happen[96]
- knowingly or recklessly supplying information which is false or misleading in a material particular either directly to the OFT, or to anyone else, knowing it is for the purpose of providing information to the OFT[97].

The Act allows various defences to these penal provisions. If a person is charged with not producing a document it is a defence to show that he did not have it in his possession or control and it was not reasonably practical for him to get it[98]. A similar statutory defence applies to failure to provide information. In relation to all requirements under sections 26 and 27 (written notice and investigation without a warrant) there is a general defence if the investigator failed to act in accordance with the section[99]. This shows the importance of ensuring that all the procedural steps are properly taken. There is no statutory defence in relation to investigations with a warrant, presumably because the judge asked to issue the warrant would effectively consider them anyway; furthermore it is possible to appeal against the issue of the warrant itself. There are no statutory defences to the charges of knowingly or recklessly destroying documents or providing false or misleading information.

The penalties can be substantial and depend on whether the offence is tried summarily or is serious enough to be taken on indictment to the Crown Court (or the High Court of Justiciary in Scotland)[100]. Usually the penalties are financial but in the case of any obstruction of investigators with a warrant, destruction of documents or provision of false or misleading information imprisonment for up to two years is possible (as well as a fine in some cases)[101].

---

[89]   Ibid, 19 February 2003, para 186.
[90]   Powers for investigating criminal cartels, OFT 515, January 2004, para 4.1.
[91]   Powers of investigation, para 7.   [92]   See below.   [93]   Competition Act 1998, s 42(1).
[94]   Ibid, s 42(5).   [95]   Ibid, s 42(7).   [96]   Ibid, s 43(1).   [97]   Ibid, s 44(1), (2).   [98]   Ibid, s 42(2), (3).
[99]   Ibid, s 42(4).   [100]   Powers of investigation, para 7.5.
[101]   Competition Act 1998, ss 42(6), (7), 43(2), 44(3); *Powers of investigation*, para 7.7 describes the penalties in detail.

As already described the powers of investigation, and the offences, are applicable to 'persons', which can include an undertaking[102]. In addition, under section 72, officers of bodies corporate are liable to punishment if they have consented to or connived at an offence or it is due to neglect on their part[103]. Officer means a director, manager, secretary or other similar officer, or anyone purporting to act as such[104]. There are similar provisions applicable to companies managed by their members (who can be liable) and, in Scotland, to partners and partnerships[105]. The fact that individuals themselves can be personally liable under these provisions of the 1998 Act, and that there is even a possibility of imprisonment, will no doubt concentrate the minds of those responsible for ensuring compliance with the legislation; this point is even more significant now that the Enterprise Act 2002 has established the criminal cartel offence and the power to seek a company director disqualification order[106].

(H) EC investigations

The European Commission has power, under Articles 20 and 21 of the EC Modernisation Regulation, to conduct on-site investigations in relation to possible infringements of Articles 81 and 82 EC, and may seek the assistance of a national competition authority when doing so. Article 22(1) of the Regulation enables the Commission to ask a national authority to conduct an investigation on its behalf, and Article 22(2) gives the same power to the competition authorities of the other Member States of the EU. Sections 61 to 65 of the Competition Act 1998 set out, in considerable detail, the rules that govern inspections by the OFT under the Modernisation Regulation, and the OFT has provided guidance on their application in practice[107].

3. COMPLAINTS AND SUPER-COMPLAINTS

(A) Complaints

Although the Competition Act 1998 does not establish a procedure for complaining to the OFT, complaints are an important source of information about possible infringements. The OFT has issued a Guideline *Involving third parties in Competition Act investigations*[108] which sets out the mandatory and optional information that should be included in a written, reasoned complaint; this may lead to the establishment of 'Formal Complainant' status. A Formal Complainant enjoys defined rights in relation to file closures[109], statements of objections[110], and interim measures applications[111]. The mandatory information includes information about the complainant and the complainee, details of the complaint, factual evidence supporting the complaint, and other information, if available, about matters such as whether the issues in dispute are being litigated anywhere, or whether they are being investigated by another competition authority

---

[102] Competition Act 1998, s 59(1); see *Powers of investigation*, para 4.3.
[103] Competition Act 1998, s 72(2); see *Powers of investigation*, para 7.4.
[104] Competition Act 1998, s 72(3).   [105] Ibid, s 72(4)-(6).
[106] See pp 415–422 (the cartel offence) and pp 422–423 (company director disqualification) below.
[107] Powers of investigation, paras 9 and 10.   [108] OFT 451, April 2006.
[109] Involving third parties, para 2.   [110] Ibid, para 3.   [111] Ibid, para 4.

in the EU or another public body in the UK[112]. The optional information includes the complainant's assessment of the relevant product and geographic markets and the competitive conditions within them and information about the agreements and/or conduct complained about[113].

Complaints raise questions of confidentiality which can be difficult. Where a complainant provides confidential information to the OFT[114] the OFT requires a non-confidential version of such information that can be disclosed to the complainee[115]. Some complainants wish to remain anonymous and this can make it difficult for the OFT to pursue the complaint. The complainant should explain to the OFT why its identity should not be disclosed; if the OFT is satisfied that this is the case it will seek to maintain the anonymity 'to the extent that this is consistent with the OFT's statutory obligations'[116]. Part 9 of the Enterprise Act 2002 contains rules against the disclosure of certain information about individuals or undertakings unless disclosure is permitted by one of the so-called 'gateways' set out in sections 239 to 242 of the Act. These provisions are explained in the OFT's guideline *Modernisation*[117].

The rights of a complainant to appeal against, or seek judicial review of, a rejection of a complaint is considered in section 7 below[118].

(B) Super-complaints

The Enterprise Act 2002 provides a procedure whereby nominated bodies may make a 'super-complaint' to the OFT or to a sectoral regulator: this possibility is dealt with in the chapter on market investigations under that Act[119].

4. NOTIFICATION

(A) Abolition of notification

The Competition Act as originally enacted provided a system of notification of agreements (and conduct) to the OFT for guidance or a decision as to whether the Chapter I or Chapter II prohibitions were being infringed[120]. The abolition of notification under EC law as a result of the adoption of the EC Modernisation Regulation[121] has been mirrored in domestic law: the Amendment Regulations repealed the provisions on notification with effect from 1 May 2004.

(B) Opinions and informal advice

The abolition of notification by the EC Modernisation Regulation led the European Commission to publish a *Notice on informal guidance relating to novel questions*

---

[112] Ibid, Annexe, Part B.   [113] Ibid, Annexe, Part C.

[114] Confidential information for this purpose is defined in Rule 1(1) of the OFT's Rules, SI 2004/2751.

[115] Involving third parties, para 2.14.   [116] Ibid, para 2.15.   [117] OFT 442, December 2004, para 9.

[118] See pp 426–436 below.   [119] See ch 11, pp 442–445.

[120] The relevant provisions were Competition Act ss 12–16 and Schs 5 and 6; they are described at pp 371–376 of the fifth edition of this book.

[121] See ch 4, pp 162–164.

concerning Articles 81 and 82 of the EC Treaty that arise in individual cases (guidance letters)[122] in which it explained the circumstances in which it might issue 'Guidance Letters', in particular where a case gives rise to genuine uncertainty because it presents novel or unresolved questions for the application of Articles 81 or 82 EC. In the same way the OFT, in its Guideline *Modernisation*[123], sets out in part 7 the circumstances in which it might provide an Opinion[124] or give informal advice[125].

(i) Opinions

The OFT will consider a request for an Opinion only where the following three conditions are fulfilled:

- there is no sufficient precedent in EC or UK case law;
- there is a need for a published Opinion, for example because of the economic importance for consumers of the goods or services affected by the agreement or conduct in question or because of the scope of the investment related to the agreement or conduct;
- it is possible to provide an Opinion without the need for substantial further fact-finding[126].

Undertakings that request an Opinion may withdraw their request[127]. Any Opinion given by the OFT will be published on its website[128]. No Opinions had been given under these provisions by 12 March 2008. However a request for one was made to the OFT in 2004 by a group of publishers, distributors and wholesalers concerning the distribution of newspapers and magazines; a draft Opinion was published on 31 May 2006[129].

(ii) Informal advice

The OFT offers confidential informal advice to undertakings on the application of EC and UK competition law on an *ad hoc* basis, but such advice is not binding[130].

5. ENFORCEMENT

This section will explain the various possibilities that exist where the OFT or a sectoral regulator[131] intends to take enforcement action under the Competition Act.

(A) Procedure

Where the OFT suspects an infringement of the Act or of Articles 81 or 82 EC it will first carry out an investigation pursuant to section 25. If, as a result of that investigation, the OFT proposes to adopt a decision that there has been an infringement of the Chapter I and/or Chapter II prohibition or of Articles 81 and/or 82 EC section 31 of the Act requires it to give 'written notice' – better known as a 'statement of objections' – to the person or persons 'likely to be affected'[132] and to give that person (or persons) an

---

[122] OJ [2004] C 101/78.   [123] OFT 442, December 2004.   [124] *Modernisation*, paras 7.5–7.19.
[125] Ibid, para 7.20.   [126] Ibid, para 7.5.   [127] Ibid, para 7.14.   [128] Ibid, para 7.15.
[129] See OFT Press Release 94/06; it, and the draft Opinon, can be accessed at www.oft.gov.uk/shared_oft/reports/comp_policy/oft851.pdf.
[130] *Modernisation*, para 7.20.   [131] As defined in Competition Act 1998, s 54.
[132] Competition Act 1998, s 31(1)(a).

opportunity to make representations[133]. The form of the statement of objections is set out in rules 4 and 5 of the *OFT's Rules*[134]; rule 5 also deals with access to the file[135] and the right to make oral representations[136]. The CAT summarised the principles applicable to the statement of objections in its judgment in *Apex Asphalt and Paving Co Ltd v OFT*[137]; in that case it concluded that a defect in the statement of objections should not lead to the annulment of the decision since the defect had not caused Apex any prejudice[138].

Various possibilities exist following the issue of a statement of objections. One is that the OFT might decide not to proceed with the case: where this happens it may be that a third party complainant will appeal to the CAT that the case-closure decision of the OFT amounted to an appealable decision that the undertakings under investigation had not infringed competition law and that that decision was wrong[139]. A different possibility is that the OFT might accept legally binding 'commitments' that the undertaking(s) will modify their behaviour in order to overcome the competition problems that led to the initiation of the investigation (see section (B) below). Provision is made for the OFT to adopt interim measures (section (C)). Where the OFT finds an infringement it may give directions to bring the infringement to an end (section (D)) and may require an infringing undertaking to pay a penalty (section (E)). Undertakings that 'blow the whistle' on infringements of the Chapter I prohibition or Article 81 EC may be able to claim total immunity from penalties, or at least substantial reductions (section F). Some infringement decisions are adopted following discussions between the OFT and the undertakings concerned that are sometimes referred to as settlements (section (G)). Section H will consider how the provisions on penalties have been applied in practice.

(B) Commitments

Just as Article 9 of the EC Modernisation Regulation introduced a procedure enabling the European Commission to adopt a decision whereby undertakings make legally binding commitments to change their behaviour in order to address its competition concerns, so too the Amendment Regulations introduced sections 31A to 31E into the Competition Act 1998. The OFT, as required by section 31D of the Act, has provided guidance on the commitments procedure in Part 4 of *Enforcement*[140]. Section 31(2) enables the OFT to accept commitments from undertakings to take such action or to refrain from taking such action as the OFT considers appropriate; provision is made for the variation[141], substitution[142], and release[143] of commitments. Schedule 6A of the Act sets out the procedural requirements that are to be followed in commitments cases. Where the OFT accepts commitments its investigation ceases and it cannot make a decision finding an infringement under section 31 or issue a direction under section 35[144]. Where an undertaking fails to adhere to its commitments the OFT may apply to the court for an order to enforce compliance[145].

The OFT has said that it is likely to consider accepting commitments only in cases where the competition concerns are readily identifiable and are fully addressed by

---

[133] Ibid, s 31(1)(b).   [134] SI 2004/2751.   [135] Ibid, rule 5(3).   [136] Ibid, rule 5(4).
[137] Case No 1032/1/1/04 [2005] CAT 4, [2005] CompAR 507, para 100.
[138] Ibid, paras 109–110, relying on the CFI's judgment in Case T-48/00 *Corus UK v Commission* [2004] ECR II-2325, paras 154–158.
[139] See pp 427–431 below.   [140] *Enforcement*, OFT 407, December 2004.
[141] Competition Act 1998, s 31A(3)(a).   [142] Ibid, s 31A(3)(b).   [143] Ibid, s 31A(4).
[144] Ibid, s 31B.   [145] Ibid, s 31E. 'court' for this purpose is defined in s 59 of the Act.

the commitments offered and where the commitments are capable of being implemented effectively and, if necessary, within a short period of time[146]. The OFT would
not, other than in very exceptional cases, accept commitments in the case of hard-core
secret cartels or serious abuses of dominance[147]; however such cases might culminate
in a settlement whereby the undertakings concerned are fined a lesser sum than they
would have been in return for enabling the OFT to reach an infringement decision
more quickly than would otherwise have been the case[148]. Commitments may be both
structural and behavioural[149]. Third parties will be involved in the commitments procedure[150]. Decisions by the OFT not to release commitments when requested by the
parties that offered them to do so can be appealed to the CAT[151], as can decisions where
there are no longer grounds for competition concerns[152]; third parties can appeal to
the CAT against decisions to accept or release commitments or to accept a material
variation[153]. In *Pernod-Ricard SA v OFT*[154] the OFT had closed a case, which pre-
dated the commitments procedure introduced by the Amendment Regulations, on
the basis of 'voluntary assurances' offered by Bacardi-Martini Ltd to change some of
its distribution practices. In its ruling disposing of the proceedings brought by a third
party that had been dissatisfied with the assurances, but where the parties were now
all agreed on remedies, the CAT noted that 'as far as the future is concerned . . . binding
commitments have advantages from the point of view of enforcement over voluntary
assurances, and may well prove to be a weapon in the OFT's armoury that needs
further development'[155].

In practice the OFT has accepted commitments in two cases. In the first, *TV Eye*, the
OFT was concerned that TV Eye, a company owned by four broadcasters, was able to
agree collectively some of the terms and conditions on which it sold airtime to media
agencies, thereby placing them in an unduly weak bargaining position; commitments
were accepted on 24 May 2005[156]. Some of the commitments were released in March
2006[157]. The OFT also accepted commitments in the case of *Associated Newspapers Ltd*
where that company agreed to modify the exclusive contracts that it had entered into
with London Underground Ltd, Network Rail and a number of train operating companies, in order to provide for the distribution at their railway stations of 'free' newspapers that were competitors of Associated Newspapers' 'Metro' newspaper[158]. The Gas
and Electricity Markets Authority accepted commitments in the case of *Manweb*[159] that
Manweb would provide connection services to independent connections providers in a
non-discriminatory manner and within recommended timescales.

[146] *Enforcement*, para 4.3.   [147] Ibid, para 4.4.   [148] See pp 407–408 below.
[149] *Enforcement*, para 4.6.   [150] Competition Act 1998, Sch 6A and *Enforcement*, paras 4.21–4.22.
[151] Competition Act 1998, s 46(3)(g).   [152] Ibid, s 46(3)(h).   [153] Ibid, s 47(1)(c).
[154] Case No. 1017/2/1/03 [2005] CAT 9, [2005] CompAR 894.   [155] Ibid, para 7.
[156] See OFT Press Release 93/05; it is available, along with the OFT decision and the text of the commitments, at www.oft.gov.uk/news/press/2005/93-05.
[157] See OFT Press Release 58/06, available at www.oft.gov.uk/news/press/2006/58-06.
[158] See OFT Press Release of 2 March 2006, available at www.oft.gov.uk/advice_and_resources/
resource_base/ca98/decisions/anl.
[159] See OFGEM Information Note R/42 of 27 October 2005, available at www.ofgem.gov.uk/Media/
PressRel.

(C) Interim measures

If the OFT has begun an investigation under section 25 and has not completed it, it may adopt interim measures if this is necessary as a matter of urgency to prevent serious, irreparable damage to a particular person or category of persons or to protect the public interest[160]; however it cannot adopt interim measures if undertakings are able to show on the balance of probabilities that the criteria in section 9 of the Competition Act or Article 81(3) EC are satisfied[161]. The OFT must give notice to the affected persons before giving directions, thus giving them an opportunity to make representations[162]. Such notice must indicate the nature of the proposed direction and the OFT's reasons[163]. The OFT has indicated that it may be willing, in some cases, to accept informal interim assurances in lieu of adopting formal interim measures decisions[164]; it has accepted informal assurances on a few occasions[165].

The first occasion on which the OFT adopted an interim measures decision was in the case of *London Metal Exchange*[166] where the OFT was concerned that the LME might have been about to abuse its dominant position by extending the hours of trading on its electronic trading platform, LME Select: it was possible that this might amount to predatory conduct. The LME appealed to the CAT against this decision; subsequently the OFT, having received substantial new evidence, withdrew the decision. In a judgment on whether the LME should be awarded costs against the OFT for the time spent on the appeal up to the date of the withdrawal the CAT suggested that, in interim measures cases, the OFT should follow the procedure that the High Court does when a party seeks an interim injunction[167]. The OFT should be circumspect about relying solely on uncorroborated information not contained in response to a section 26 notice[168]. Since the CAT considered that the OFT's investigative process had been superficial and flawed the CAT awarded the costs of the work done on the appeal to the LME[169].

(D) Directions

Section 32(1) of the Competition Act provides that, when the OFT has made a decision that an agreement infringes the Chapter I prohibition or Article 81 EC, it may give to such person or persons as it considers appropriate directions to bring the infringement to an end. Section 32(3) expands on the content of these directions which may require the parties to an agreement to modify it or require them to terminate it. There are corresponding provisions in section 33 for directions in the case of infringements of the Chapter II prohibition or Article 82 EC; in this case section 33(3) provides that the direction may require the person concerned to modify the conduct in question, or require him to cease that conduct. In either case directions may also include other

---

[160] Competition Act 1998, s 35(1) and (2); the OFT guideline *Enforcement*, OFT 407, December 2004, explains the OFT's approach to the interim measures procedure.

[161] Competition Act 1998, s 35(8) and (9). [162] Ibid, s 35(3); see also the OFT's Rules, rule 9.

[163] Competition Act 1998, s 35(4). [164] *Enforcement*, paras 3.17–3.20.

[165] See eg *Robert Wiseman Dairies* OFT Press Release PN 39/01, 14 September 2001; *Oakley (UK) Ltd*, case closure of February 2007, available at www.oft.gov.uk/advice_and_resources/resource_base/ca98/closure.

[166] OFT decision of 27 February 2006.

[167] Case No 1062/1/1/06 *London Metal Exchange v OFT* [2006] CAT 19, [2006] CompAR 781, paras 139–140, citing the *Practice Direction – Interim Injunctions* (CPR Part 25).

[168] Ibid, paras 141–142. [169] Ibid, para 170.

provisions such as positive action and reporting obligations[170]. Recipients of directions must be informed in writing of the facts on which the directions are based and the reasons for them[171]; directions under sections 32 and 33 must be published[172].

(i) Can directions be structural?

It is not clear whether the power to give directions includes the right to impose structural remedies such as the right to require the divestiture of assets or the break-up of an undertaking; Article 7 of the EC Modernisation Regulation explicitly provides that the European Commission can impose structural and behavioural remedies[173]. Where an infringement of the Chapter I or Chapter II prohibitions or of Articles 81 or 82 is itself the consequence of a structural change in the market it would seem, in principle, that a structural remedy to bring the infringement to an end would be justified: for example if undertakings were to establish, contrary to the Chapter I prohibition or Article 81 EC, a joint venture company to act as a joint sales agency the most effective remedy would probably be a structural one, requiring the dissolution of the company. It is less obvious, however, that it is possible to issue a structural remedy, for example, to break up a dominant firm guilty of serial abusive behaviour; such a situation would appear to be more suitable for a market investigation reference under the Enterprise Act 2002, under which legislation a structural remedy is, explicitly, available[174].

(ii) The directions provisions in practice

In some cases the OFT refrains from giving directions since the infringement of the Act has ended by the time of its decision[175]. However in other cases the OFT has issued directions: for example in the case of *Napp Pharmaceutical Holdings Ltd*[176] it ordered Napp to amend its prices for certain morphine medicines to bring its abusive pricing to an end, while in *Lladró Comercial* the OFT required the porcelain producer to modify its distribution agreements to make clear that the practice of resale price maintenance would not continue[177]. Similarly in *Genzyme Ltd*[178] the OFT obliged that company to charge separately for Cerezyme, a drug that it produced, and for the various homecare services it provided; and to offer Cerezyme to competing homecare operators at a price no higher than that charged to the National Health Service[179]. There were protracted proceedings in the CAT as to the correct price to be charged by Genzyme, culminating in a judgment on remedy two and a half years after the OFT's decision[180]. In the course of these proceedings the CAT stated that the primary responsibility for bringing

---

[170] See *Enforcement*, para 2.3.   [171] OFT Rules, rule 8(1).   [172] Ibid, rule 8(3).

[173] See ch 7, p 252.   [174] See ch 11, p 462.

[175] See eg *Price fixing and market sharing in stock check pads*, OFT decision of 31 March 2006, [2007] UKCLR 211, para 235; *Agreement to fix prices and share the market for aluminium double glazing bars*, OFT decision of 28 June 2006, [2006] UKCLR 921, para 535.

[176] *Directions given by the Director General of Fair Trading under section 33 of the Competition Act 1998 to Napp Pharmaceutical Holdings Ltd and its subsidiaries*, 4 May 2001, upheld on appeal Case No 1000/1/1/01 *Napp Pharmaceutical Holdings Ltd v Director General of Fair Trading* [2002] CAT 1, [2002] CompAR 13, [2002] ECC 177, paras 553–562.

[177] OFT decision of 31 March 2003, [2003] UKCLR 652, paras 117–118.

[178] OFT decision of 27 March 2003, substantially upheld on appeal Case No 1016/1/1/03 *Genzyme Ltd v Office of Fair Trading* [2004] CAT 4, [2004] CompAR 358.

[179] Case No 1016/1/1/03 *Genzyme v Office of Fair Trading* [2005] CAT 32, [2006] CompAR 195.

[180] Case No 1013/1/1/03 (IR) *Genzyme Ltd v Office of Fair Trading* [2003] CAT 8.

the abuse to an end in that case rested with Genzyme, rather than with the OFT or the CAT[181].

In the case of *English Welsh & Scottish Railways Ltd*[182] the Office of Rail Regulation found that EW&S was guilty of abusing a dominant position in the market for the carriage by rail of industrial coal to power stations; it gave directions to EW&S requiring it to remove or modify various terms in the coal carriage agreements it had entered into with some of its customers, including the power company E.ON[183]. E.ON appealed against these directions to the CAT, arguing that they were excessive in scope and too uncertain to be valid[184]. In the meantime the High Court held in *English Welsh & Scottish Railway Ltd v E.ON UK plc* that the directions of the ORR meant that the offending clauses had been void from their inception and that, since they could not be severed, the entire coal carriage agreement was void and unenforceable[185]. E.ON appealed against this judgment to the Court of Appeal, but the case was settled out of court; the proceedings in the CAT were therefore terminated.

(iii) Persons who may be the subject of directions

Directions may be given to 'appropriate' persons, who will not necessarily be the parties to the agreement or perpetrators of the conduct. The purpose of this is to enable the OFT to give directions to parents, affiliates or private individuals with the ability to influence or procure actions by the infringing persons[186]. Section 34 of the Act allows the court to order an undertaking or its officers to obey a direction relating to the management of that undertaking if the person subject to the direction has failed to comply.

(iv) Enforcement of compliance with directions

If a person subject to directions (whether interim or final) fails to comply without reasonable excuse the OFT may apply to the court[187] for an order requiring compliance within a specified time or, if the direction concerns the management of an undertaking, ordering another officer to carry it out[188]. Breach of such an order would be contempt of court, punishable by fines or imprisonment, at the court's discretion[189]. There is nothing in section 34 that limits the court's order-making powers to persons within the UK[190].

(E) Penalties

Section 36(1) of the Competition Act provides that a penalty may be imposed for an infringement of the Chapter I prohibition or Article 81 EC; section 36(2) provides correspondingly for an infringement of the Chapter II prohibition or Article 82 EC. As a prerequisite for the imposition of a penalty section 36(3) requires that the OFT must be satisfied that the infringement has been committed intentionally or

---

[181] See the transcript of the hearing of 13 October 2004.
[182] ORR decision of 17 November 2006, [2007] UKCLR 937.   [183] Ibid, paras D2–D5.
[184] Case No 1076/2/5/07 *E.ON UK Plc v Office of Rail Regulation*.
[185] [2007] EWHC 599 (Comm); on the doctrine of severance in the English law of contract see *Chitty on Contracts* (Sweet & Maxwell, 29th ed, 2004) paras 16-188–16-197.
[186] See *Enforcement*, para 2.2.   [187] 'Court' for this purpose is defined in Competition Act 1998, s 59(1).
[188] Ibid, s 34.   [189] *Enforcement*, para 2.9.   [190] On the territorial scope of the Act see ch 12, pp 484–486.

negligently[191]; it is sufficient to decide that the infringement was *either* intentional *or* negligent, without deciding which[192], and the distinction between intention and negligence goes, at most, to mitigation of the fine[193]. Intention may be deduced from internal documents or from deliberate concealment of the agreement or conduct in question[194]. The Competition Act does not specify a limitation period for the imposition or recovery of penalties: this is a matter of general law, as established by the Limitation Act 1980 which prescribes a period of six years. Penalties received by the OFT are paid into the Consolidated Fund[195]: that is to say they go to the Government and not, for example, to the victims of the anti-competitive behaviour. The latter may be able to obtain compensation through recourse to the courts[196]. Where a penalty has not been paid by the date required by the OFT it may be recovered through the courts as a civil debt[197]. An appeal to the CAT postpones the obligation to pay any penalty until the appeal is determined[198]; however the CAT may add interest to any penalty imposed[199].

It should be recalled that, apart from the possibility of undertakings being required to pay penalties for competition law infringements, section 188 of the Enterprise Act 2002 makes it a criminal offence for individuals to engage dishonestly in certain horizontal agreements such as price fixing and market sharing, and that this can lead to a term of imprisonment of up to five years and/or an unlimited fine[200].

(i) Maximum amount of a penalty

Section 36(8) provides that penalties may not exceed 10 per cent of an undertaking's worldwide turnover in the business year preceding the OFT's decision[201].

(ii) The OFT's *Guidance as to the appropriate amount of a penalty*

The OFT has published *Guidance as to the appropriate amount of a penalty*[202] ('the *Guidance on penalties*') pursuant to section 38 of the Act; the *Guidance* has been approved by the Secretary of State, as required by that provision[203]. Section 3 of the *Guidance on penalties* dealing with whistleblowing should be ignored since the OFT has published fresh guidance on this subject (see section (F) below).

---

[191] See *Enforcement*, paras 5.4–5.13.

[192] Case No 1000/1/1/01 *Napp Pharmaceutical Holdings Ltd v Director General of Fair Trading* [2002] CAT 1, [2002] CompAR 13, [2002] ECC 177, para 453; on the meaning of 'intentional' and 'negligent' see paras 456 and 457 of that judgment.

[193] Case No 1009/1/1/02 *Aberdeen Journals Ltd v Office of Fair Trading* [2003] CAT 11, para 484.

[194] *Enforcement*, para 5.11.   [195] Competition Act 1998, s 36(9).

[196] See ch 8, pp 292–309.   [197] Competition Act 1998, s 37.

[198] Ibid, s 46(4); there is no provision for the OFT to ask for security for the penalty (or for the costs of the appeal): it follows that, if an undertaking goes out of business in the meantime, the penalty may be irrecoverable.

[199] See the Competition Appeal Tribunal Rules 2003, SI 2003/1372, r 56; see Case No 1000/1/1/01 *Napp Pharmaceutical Holdings Ltd v Director General of Fair Trading* [2002] CAT 1, [2002] CompAR 13, paras 542–543 and Case No 1009/1/1/02 *Aberdeen Journals Ltd v Office of Fair Trading* [2003] CAT 11, para 500; Case No 1032/1/1/04 *Apex Asphalt and Paving Co Ltd v OFT* [2005] CAT 11, [2005] CompAR 825, para 23.

[200] On the cartel offence see pp 415–422 below.

[201] See the Competition Act 1998 (Determination of Turnover for Penalties) Order 2000, SI 2000/309, as amended by SI 2004/1259.

[202] OFT 423, December 2004; this replaced the earlier *Guidance* of March 2000.

[203] *Guidance on penalties*, para 1.8.

The Court of Appeal has explained that the *Guidance on penalties* is not binding on the OFT, but that it must give reasons for any significant departure from it[204]. The CAT is not bound by the OFT's *Guidance on penalties*[205]. The CAT's practice has been to review the OFT's application of the *Guidance* and then to set out its own views on the seriousness of the infringement and to make its own assessment of the level of the penalty on the basis of a 'broad brush' approach, taking the case as a whole. It then carries out a 'cross check' to see whether the amount it has arrived at would be within the parameters set out in the OFT's *Guidance*. The Court of Appeal has said that it thinks that this is an appropriate approach for the CAT to take[206]. The Court of Appeal has also said that it should hesitate to interfere with the CAT's assessment of penalties given that it is an expert and specialised body[207].

Paragraph 1.4 of the *Guidance on penalties* sets out the OFT's policy objectives in setting the level of penalties: to reflect the seriousness of the infringement and to deter undertakings from engaging in anti-competitive practices. Paragraph 1.15 explains that undertakings found to have infringed both UK and EC competition law will not be fined twice for the same anti-competitive effects; however paragraph 1.16 adds that there might be different levels of penalties for the EC and the domestic infringements, for example if the infringement of EC law pre-dated the entry into force of the Competition Act in March 2000.

(iii) The OFT's five-step approach

In determining the level of the penalty the OFT adopts a five-step approach[208]; the OFT must give reasons for its decision, including setting out the methodology whereby it reaches its conclusion[209]:

- **Step 1: Starting point**[210]. The starting point is to apply a percentage of the 'relevant turnover' of the undertaking to be fined according to the seriousness of the infringement[211]. In determining the seriousness of an infringement the OFT will take a number of factors into consideration including the nature of the infringement and the effect of the anti-competitive behaviour on competitors, third parties and, most importantly, consumers[212]. In cases based on Articles 81 and/or 82 EC, effects in another Member State may be taken into account if that Member State expressly gives its consent[213]. Relevant turnover for this purpose means the turnover in the relevant product and geographic market affected by the infringement in the undertaking's last financial year[214]; the starting point cannot exceed 10 per cent of an undertaking's relevant turnover[215]. Where several undertakings are involved in the same infringement the starting point will be worked out for each of them individually in order to take account of each undertaking's impact on the market[216].

- **Step 2: Adjustment for duration**[217]. Having established the starting point the OFT, at Step 2, may increase or, exceptionally, decrease the penalty to take into account the duration of the infringement. Where the infringement lasts longer than one year the penalty may be increased by not more than the number of years of the infringement; the OFT may treat part of a year as a whole year, although in some cases it has decided to apply a smaller

---

[204] *Argos Ltd and Littlewoods Ltd v OFT* and *JJB Sports plc v OFT* [2006] EWCA Civ 1318, [2006] UKCLR 1135, para 161.
[205] Ibid, para 160. [206] Ibid, para 163. [207] Ibid, para 165. [208] *Guidance on penalties*, para 2.1.
[209] Case No 1061/1/1/06 *Makers UK Ltd v OFT* [2007] CAT 11, [2007] CompAR 699, para 134.
[210] *Guidance on penalties*, paras 2.3–2.9. [211] Ibid, paras 2.3. [212] Ibid, paras 2.4–2.5.
[213] Ibid, para 2.6. [214] Ibid, para 2.7. [215] Ibid, para 2.8. [216] Ibid, para 2.9. [217] Ibid, para 2.10.

multiplier[218]. In *Apex Asphalt Paving Co v OFT*[219] the CAT noted that, in the case of collusive tendering, the fact that a particular tendering process might take place over a short period does not necessarily mean that there should be a reduction of the penalty, since the effect of the unlawful behaviour could have a continuing impact on future tenders and because, once a contract is awarded, it is irreversible in relation to that tender[220].

- **Step 3: Adjustment for other factors**[221]. At Step 3 the OFT will take into account 'adjustments for other factors' in order to achieve the policy objectives set out in paragraph 1.4 of the *Guidance*, in particular the need for deterrence, not only of the undertakings involved in the infringement but of others that might be contemplating anti-competitive behaviour[222]. At this stage the OFT may take into account the gains made by the infringing undertaking from its behaviour[223].

- **Step 4: Adjustment for aggravating and mitigating factors**[224]. At Step 4 the OFT will consider whether there are any aggravating and mitigating factors.

  Aggravating factors include[225]:
  - an undertaking was a leader in, or the instigator of, the infringement
  - directors or senior managers were involved
  - retaliatory or coercive action was taken against other undertakings in order to continue the infringement
  - the infringement was continued after the commencement of an investigation
  - repeated infringements by the same undertaking or undertakings in the same group (recidivism)
  - intentional rather than negligent infringement
  - retaliation against a leniency applicant.

  Mitigating factors include[226]:
  - an undertaking acted under severe duress or pressure
  - genuine uncertainty on the part of an undertaking as to whether its agreement or conduct constituted an infringement
  - adequate steps having been taken with a view to ensuring compliance with competition law
  - termination of the infringement as soon as the OFT intervenes
  - cooperation which enables the OFT's enforcement process to be concluded more effectively and/or speedily.

- **Step 5: Adjustment to prevent the maximum penalty being exceeded and to avoid double jeopardy**[227]. At Step 5 the OFT will make any necessary adjustments to ensure that the statutory maximum penalty of 10 per cent of worldwide turnover is not exceeded[228]. If a fine has been imposed by the European Commission or by a court or competition authority in another Member State this must also be taken into account at Step 5 in order to avoid double jeopardy[229].

---

[218] See eg para 323 of the OFT decision in *Hasbro UK Ltd, Argos Ltd and Littlewoods Ltd* of 19 February 2003, [2003] UKCLR 553, where the OFT applied a multiplier of 1.2, as opposed to 2, where the duration of the infringement was in the region of 14½ months.
[219] Case No 1032/1/1/04, [2005] CAT 4, [2005] CompAR 507. [220] Ibid, para 278.
[221] *Guidance on penalties*, paras 2.11–2.13. [222] Ibid, para 2.11. [223] Ibid.
[224] Ibid, paras 2.14–2.16. [225] Ibid, para 2.15. [226] Ibid, para 2.16. [227] Ibid, paras 2.17–2.20.
[228] As to the maximum penalty see p 401 above; note that, prior to 1 May 2004, the maximum penalty under s 36(8) was calculated by reference to UK turnover rather than worldwide turnover, and that this may, in some cases, require a further adjustment of the penalty: see *Guidance on penalties*, para 2.18.
[229] Ibid, para 2.20.

(iv) Immunity for small agreements and conduct of minor significance

Section 39, in conjunction with section 36(4), of the Competition Act confers immunity from penalties for infringing the Chapter I prohibition in the case of 'small agreements', other than price-fixing agreements[230], where the OFT is satisfied that an undertaking acted on the reasonable assumption that section 39 gave it immunity. A small agreement is one where the combined turnover of the parties in the preceding calendar year was £20 million or less[231]. Provision is made by section 39(3)–(8) for the OFT to withdraw this immunity, subject to the observation of some basic procedures[232]. There is no immunity from penalties for agreements that infringe Article 81 EC, which is why section 39 refers only to 'partial' immunity in its heading.

Section 40 provides similar partial immunity for 'conduct of minor significance'. Conduct is of minor significance where the perpetrator's worldwide turnover in the preceding calendar year was £50 million or less[233]. Section 40(3)–(8) provides power for withdrawal of the immunity. There is no immunity for infringements of Article 82 EC.

As the OFT points out in its guidance on *Enforcement* the immunity provided by sections 39 and 40 does not prevent it from taking other enforcement action, and the immunity does not prevent third parties from bringing damages actions[234]. This point is nicely illustrated by the case of *JJ Burgess v OFT*. In its judgment in this case the CAT found that W Austin Ltd had abused a dominant position by refusing Burgess access to its crematorium[235]. In the course of that judgment the CAT noted that Austin would not be subject to a penalty if found to have infringed the Act since its conduct was of minor significance in the terms of section 40 of the Act[236]. Subsequently, however, Burgess brought a 'follow-on' action for damages before the CAT[237]; the case was settled out of court.

(F) Whistleblowing: the leniency programme

The OFT encourages whistleblowing. Decisions establishing an infringement of the Chapter I prohibition (and Article 81 EC) very often originate from an application for leniency[238]. A parent company may make a leniency application on behalf of a subsidiary[239]. The OFT has published two sets of guidance on its leniency policy; further guidance will be published in due course, probably in the autumn of 2008. The OFT's

---

[230] A price-fixing agreement for this purpose is defined in s 39(9) of the Act.

[231] See the Competition Act 1998 (Small Agreements and Conduct of Minor Significance) Regulations 2000, SI 2000/262, Art 3.

[232] The OFT must give the parties or persons in respect of which the immunity is withdrawn written notice of its decision and must specify a date which gives them time to adjust (ss 39(5), (8), 40(5), (8) Competition Act 1998).

[233] See the Competition Act 1998 (Small Agreements and Conduct of Minor Significance) Regulations 2000, SI 2000/262, Art 4.

[234] *Enforcement*, para 5.20.

[235] Case No1044/2/1/04 *JJ Burgess & Sons v OFT* [2005] CAT 25, [2005] CompAR 1151.

[236] Ibid, paras 117–118.   [237] Case No 1088/5/7/07.

[238] See below.

[239] *Collusive tendering for mastic asphalt flat-roofing contracts in Scotland*, OFT decision of 15 March 2005, [2005] UKCLR 638, para 396.

Guidance as to the appropriate amount of a penalty[240] deals with civil cases under the Competition Act 1998 while *The cartel offence – Guidance on the issue of no-action letters for individuals*[241] deals with criminal cases under the Enterprise Act 2002. In November 2006 the OFT published a draft of *Leniency and no-action – OFT's guidance note on the handling of applications*[242]: this Notice will not replace the earlier documents, but it will provide a comprehensive view of the current position; it will become the suggested starting point for anyone needing guidance on the subject. It is understood that the final version of this Notice may differ in some material respects from the draft of November 2006; it follows that the text below may be superceded by events. A pro-forma corporate leniency agreement and pro-forma no-action letters are included in the Annexes to the draft Guidance note, and it is intended that there will be a 'leniency flow-chart'.

(i) Terminology

Paragraph 1.3 of the draft *Leniency and no-action guidance* sets out the terminology of the subject, including the following:

- 'leniency': this is a 'catch all' term that refers to all the types of immunity and reduced fines that are available under the Guidance

- 'civil immunity': this refers to immunity granted to undertakings from penalties for infringing the Chapter I prohibition or Article 81 EC

- 'criminal immunity': this refers to immunity granted to individuals from prosecution for the cartel offence in the Enterprise Act 2002

- 'Type A immunity': this refers to a situation where an undertaking is granted *automatic* civil immunity and all of its current and former employees and directors are granted automatic criminal immunity for cartel activity; Type A immunity is available where the undertaking was the first to apply and there was no pre-existing civil and/or criminal investigation into such activity

- 'Type B immunity': this refers to a situation where the type of immunity available under Type A is granted on a *discretionary* rather than an automatic basis. Type B immunity is available where the undertaking was the first to apply but there was already a pre-existing civil and/or criminal investigation into the cartel activity

- 'Type B leniency': this refers to a situation where an undertaking is granted a reduction of, but not immunity from, a financial penalty in a cartel case. As in the case of Type B immunity, Type B leniency arises where the undertaking was the first to apply but there was already an investigation under way into the cartel in question

- 'Type C leniency': this refers to a situation in which a reduction in the penalty of up to 50 per cent is granted where the undertaking was not the first to apply and where there may or may not already be an investigation into the cartel.

(ii) Key features of the UK leniency system

Paragraph 1.5 of the draft *Leniency and no-action guidance* sets out the key features of the UK leniency system, including:

- **informal guidance**: the OFT will provide informal guidance on a no-names basis about 'hypothetical' cases when asked

---

[240] OFT 423, December 2004.   [241] OFT 513, April 2003.   [242] OFT 803.

- the 'marker system': markers will be available while the application is perfected (a marker system is also available under the EC leniency system)[243], thereby enabling an undertaking to preserve its position in a queue of leniency applicants
- oral applications: applications do not have to be in writing (oral applications are also available under the EC system)[244]
- guarantees of criminal immunity: criminal immunity is available for all cooperating current and former employees and directors in Type A or Type B immunity cases
- ready availability of Type B immunity: Type B immunity will be the norm, not the exception, where an undertaking is the first to approach the OFT, even if there is a pre-existing investigation into the cartel in question
- a 'high bar': the OFT will impose a high bar as to the circumstances in which an undertaking will be found to be a coercer and therefore ineligible for civil and/or criminal immunity.

(iii) Confidential guidance

Part 2 of the draft *Leniency and no-action guidance* explains that, at the outset, individuals or undertakings may approach the OFT for confidential guidance on any aspect of the OFT's leniency and no-action programme.

(iv) Type A immunity

The draft of the *Leniency and no-action guidance* explains the procedure when applying for Type A immunity, including the information that the undertaking making the application must provide[245]. The applicant's 'marker' becomes operational from the moment that the identity of the applicant is made known to the OFT[246]. Where an undertaking is also making a leniency application to the European Commission a marker will be allowed on a 'no-names' basis while the Commission is considering its position[247].

(v) Type B immunity

The draft of the *Leniency and no-action guidance* also sets out the position in relation to Type B immunity. Although Type B immunity is discretionary, it is expected to be the norm rather than the exception in cases where an undertaking is the first to make an application[248]. Type B applications often arise as a result of the OFT conducting an inspection at an undertaking's premises: it is understood that an application should be made to the OFT's Director of Cartels and his deputies, not to the officials present at the inspection[249]. Paragraphs 2.33 to 2.36 explain how an applicant for Type B immunity should go about perfecting its marker.

(vi) Type B and Type C leniency

The draft of the *Leniency and no-action guidance* discusses Type B and Type C leniency. In determining the amount of any discount available to the applicant the OFT will take into account the overall added value of the material provided by the applicant[250]. A discount of up to 50 per cent might be possible in a Type C case[251].

(vii) The coercer test

Type A and Type B immunity are not available to an undertaking that has coerced another firm or firms into taking part in cartel activity. Part 3 of *Leniency and no-action*

---

[243] See ch 7, pp 277–278. [244] Ibid. [245] *Leniency and no-action* letters, para 2.13.
[246] Ibid, para 2.15. [247] Ibid, paras 2.16–2.20. [248] Ibid, para 2.29.
[249] This point is likely to be included in the final *Guidance*. [250] Ibid, para 2.43. [251] Ibid, para 1.3.

provides guidance on this rule. It does not provide a definition of coercion, but notes that physical violence or threats of physical violence and strong economic pressure such as the organisation of a collective trade boycott of a small firm that might cause it to exit the market might be examples of coercion[252].

(viii) The grant of criminal immunity: no-action letters

This part of the OFT's guidance will be discussed below in the context of the cartel offence under the Enterprise Act 2002[253].

(ix) Other issues in relation to civil leniency and no-action letters

Normally a leniency applicant would be expected to terminate its involvement in the cartel. In rare cases, however, it is possible that the OFT might direct an applicant to continue to participate, for example so that the other members of the cartel will not suspect that it has been in contact with the OFT: this might put them on notice that an inspection is imminent[254]. Paragraphs 5.5 to 5.6 explain the circumstances in which a leniency application might fail due to a failure to cooperate with the OFT, and paragraph 5.10 discusses the idea of bad faith, which can even lead to prosecution of individuals under sections 43 and 44 of the Competition Act and section 201 of the Enterprise Act. The Guidance also discusses the use and transfer to third parties, the Serious Fraud Office and to the European Commission and the national competition authorities of the Member States of information received by the OFT as a result of a leniency application[255].

(x) Leniency plus

Paragraphs 3.16 and 3.17 of the OFT's *Guidance as to the appropriate amount of a penalty*[256] provide for an 'amnesty-plus' or 'two for one' policy: if a firm is already cooperating with an investigation in respect of one cartel, and comes forward with information that entitles it to total immunity in relation to a second cartel, it may receive an additional reduction in the penalty to be applied in relation to the first cartel. Leniency was provided on this basis in *Collusive tendering for mastic asphalt flat-roofing contracts in Scotland*[257].

(xi) Vertical agreements

The OFT's *Guidance as to the appropriate amount of a penalty*[257a] includes (somewhat oddly) in its definition of cartel activity resale price maintenance, and allows for leniency in respect of such cases[257b]. The Guidance on *Leniency and no-action* adds that leniency might be available where vertical behaviour might be said to facilitate horizontal cartel activity[257c].

(G) Settlements and early resolution of cases[258]

One of the mitigating factors mentioned in Step 3 of the OFT's *Guidance on penalties* is cooperation which enables the OFT's enforcement process to be concluded more

[252] Ibid, para 3.5.   [253] See pp 420–421 below.   [254] *Leniency and no-action*, para 5.1.
[255] Ibid, paras 5.7–5.9 and 5.11–5.13.   [256] OFT 423, December 2004.
[257] OFT decision of 15 March 2005, [2005] UKCLR 638, para 410.   [257a] OFT 423, December 2004.
[257b] Ibid, footnote 8; note that the European Commission's *Notice on Leniency* does not apply in the case of vertical agreements: see ch 7, p 276, n 219.
[257c] *Leniency and no-action*, para 6.13.
[258] On settlements under EC law see ch 7, pp 258–261; see also Lawrence and Sansom 'The Increasing Use of Administrative Settlement Procedures in UK and EC Competition Investigations' (2007) Competition Law Journal 163.

effectively and/or speedily. On four occasions the OFT (in *Independent fee paying schools*, *British Airways* and *Dairies*) and the Office of Rail Regulation (in *English Welsh and Scottish Railway Ltd*) have adopted, or are in the process of adopting, decisions in which the penalty was reduced in return for cooperation[259]. In March 2007 the OFT announced that it was looking to 'fast track' its investigation into bid-rigging in the construction industry by making an offer of reduced financial penalties to all firms implicated in the cartel that had not so far applied for leniency but which were willing to cooperate with the OFT in its investigation by admitting their participation[260]. This process is sometimes referred to as one of 'settlement' or 'early resolution'; it should be distinguished from applications for leniency whereby full immunity or a reduced penalty are allowed in return for the provision of information to the OFT that enables it to investigate a case[261]. It is possible that at some point in the future the OFT may, in the light of its own experience and of that of the European Commission, publish guidance on its approach to the early resolution of cases.

(H) The penalty provisions in practice

By 12 March 2008 penalties had been imposed in 21 cases under the Chapter I and II prohibitions and Articles 81 and 82 EC, as shown in the Table of Penalties below.

10.1 Table of Penalties

Decision	Date of the decision	Amount of the penalty (before and after leniency)	Amount of the penalty after appeal to the CAT
Napp Pharmaceutical Holding Ltd	5.4.2001	£3.21 million Infringement of Chapter II prohibition	Reduced to £2.2 million[1]
Market sharing by Arriva plc and First Group plc	5.2.2002	£848,027 (before leniency) £203,632 (after leniency) Infringement of Chapter I prohibition	No appeal
John Bruce Ltd, Fleet Parts Ltd and Truck and Trailer Components	17.5.2002	£33,737 Infringement of Chapter I prohibition	No appeal

---

[259] See the Table of Penalties below.
[260] See OFT Press Release 49/07 of 22 March 2007, available at www.oft.gov.uk.
[261] On whistleblowing and leniency see pp 404–407 above.

Decision	Date of the decision	Amount of the penalty (before and after leniency)	Amount of the penalty after appeal to the CAT
Aberdeen Journals Ltd	16.9.2002	**£1.328 million** Infringement of Chapter II prohibition	Reduced to **£1 million**[2]
Hasbro I	6.12.2002	**£9 million** (before leniency) **£4.95 million** (after leniency) Infringement of Chapter I prohibition	No reduction as appeal was withdrawn[3]
Genzyme Ltd	27.3.2003	**£6.8 million** Infringement of Chapter II prohibition	Reduced to **£3 million**[4]
Replica Football Kits	1.8.2003	**£18.668 million** (before leniency) **£18.627 million** (after leniency) Infringement of Chapter I prohibition	Reduced to **£14.92 million**[5]
Hasbro II	2.12.2003	**£38.25 million** (before leniency) **£22.66 million** (after leniency) Infringement of Chapter I prohibition	Reduced to **£19.50 million**[6]
West Midlands roofing contractors	17.3.2004	**£971,186** (before leniency) **£297,625** (after leniency) Infringement of Chapter I prohibition	Reduced to **£288,625**[7]
UOP Ltd/Ukae Ltd etc (Desiccants)	9.11.2004	**£2.433 million** (before leniency) **£1.707 million** (after leniency)	Reduced to **£1.635 million**[8]

Decision	Date of the decision	Amount of the penalty (before and after leniency)	Amount of the penalty after appeal to the CAT
Collusive tendering for felt and single ply flat-roofing contracts in the North East of England	8.4.2005	£598,223 (before leniency) £471,029 (after leniency) Infringement of Chapter I prohibition	No appeal
Collusive tendering for mastic asphalt flat-roofing contracts in Scotland	8.4.2005	£231,445 (before leniency) £87,353 (after leniency) Infringement of Chapter I prohibition	No appeal
Collusive tendering for felt and single ply roofing contracts in Western Central Scotland	12.7.2005	£238,576 (before leniency) £138,515 (after leniency) Infringement of Chapter I prohibition	No appeal
Collusive tendering for flat roof and car park surfacing contracts in England and Scotland	23.2.2006	£1.852 million (before leniency) £1.557 million (after leniency) Infringement of Chapter I prohibition	No reduction[9]
Stock check pads	4.4.2006	£2.184 million (before leniency) £168,318 (after leniency) Infringement of Chapter I prohibition	No reduction[10]
Aluminium spacer bars	29.6.2006	£1.384 million (before leniency) £898,470 (after leniency) Infringement of Chapter I prohibition	No reduction[11]

Decision	Date of the decision	Amount of the penalty (before and after leniency)	Amount of the penalty after appeal to the CAT
English Welsh and Scottish Railway Ltd (ORR)	17.11.2006	**£4.1 million** Infringement of Chapter II prohibition	No appeal as to penalty (appeal by a third party against the directions given by ORR, subsequently set aside)[12]
Schools: exchange of information on future fees	21.11.2006	**£489,000** (before leniency) **£467,500** (after leniency) Infringement of Chapter I prohibition	No appeal
British Airways[13]	1.8.2007	**£121.5 million** Infringement of Chapter I prohibition	No appeal
Dairy products[13a]	7.12.2007 15.2.2008	Six undertakings agreed to pay fines of £116 million An additional undertaking agreed to pay a fine **Total fines agreed amount to more than £120 million**	
National Grid (OFGEM)	25.2.2008	**Fine of £41.6 million** Infringement of Chapter II prohibition and Article 82	Application for interim relief pending[14] Appeal pending[15]

[1] Case 1001/1/1/01 *Napp Pharmaceutical Holding Ltd v Director General of Fair Trading* [2002] CAT 1.
[2] Case 1009/1/1/02 *Aberdeen Journals Ltd v Office of Fair Trading* [2003] CAT 11.
[3] Case 1010/1/1/03 *Hasbro UK Limited v The Director General of Fair Trading.*
[4] Case 1016/1/1/03 *Genzyme Ltd v OFT* [2004] CAT 4.
[5] Cases 1019/1/1/03 etc *Umbro Holdings Ltd v OFT* [2005] CAT 22.
[6] Cases 1014/1/1/03 and 1015/1/1/03 *Argos Ltd and Littlewoods Ltd v OFT* [2005] CAT 13.
[7] Case 1032/1/1/04 *Apex Asphalt and Paving Co Ltd v OFT* [2005] CAT 4 and Case No 1033/1/1/04 *Richard W Price Ltd v OFT* [2005] CAT 5.
[8] Case 1048/1/1/05 *Double Quick Supplyline Ltd v OFT*, Consent Order of 19 May 2005.
[9] Case 1061/1/1/06 *Makers UK Ltd v OFT* and Case No 1065/1/1/06 *Prater Ltd v OFT* [2006] CAT 11.

[10] Case 1067/1/1/06 *Achilles Paper Group Ltd v OFT* [2006] CAT 24.
[11] Case 1072/1/1/06 *Double Quick Supplyline Ltd and Plastic Building Materials Ltd v OFT* [2007] CAT 13.
[12] Case 1076/2/5/07 *E.ON UK plc v Office of Rail Regulation*.
[13] Note that the OFT's Press Release in this case, 113/07 of 1 August 2007, states that an infringement decision against BA will be taken and published 'in due course'.
[13a] As in the case of British Airways, a formal decision has not yet been adopted in this case.
[14] Case 1097/1/2/08 (IR) *National Grid plc v The Gas and Electricity Markets Authority (Interim Relief)*.
[15] Case 1099/1/2/08 *National Grid plc v The Gas and Electricity Markets Authority*.

(i) Statistical analysis

The total amount of the penalties imposed under the Competition Act (and Articles 81 and 82) by 12 March 2008 was £417,319,194 before reductions for leniency and £391,050,507 after leniency. On appeal to the CAT some of the penalties were reduced: after making allowance for those reductions the figure should be reduced to £336,011,389. Clearly the penalty in the case of British Airways, of £121.5 million, represents a major landmark in the competition policy in the UK since it is considerably higher than in any previous case.

(ii) Cases in which penalties were reduced

The CAT reduced the penalties in the first six cases that it dealt with, but it has not done so in any of the appeals since the *West Midlands* case[262]. In *Napp Pharmaceutical Holdings Ltd*[263] Napp had been found by the OFT to have abused its dominant position both by excessive and by predatory pricing; the CAT reduced the penalty from £3.21 to £2.2 million since the principles upon which a price can be considered to be excessive were unclear, there had been no decided EC case upholding an abuse of excessive pricing, and Napp had been involved in a price regulation scheme[264]. In *Aberdeen Journals Ltd*[265] Aberdeen Journals had been found guilty of predatory pricing; the CAT reduced the penalty from £1.3 million to £1 million, acknowledging that predatory pricing was a 'particularly serious' infringement when practised by an incumbent monopolist against a sole competitor, for which deterrent sanctions were appropriate[266]; the reduction was made due to the short period of the infringement[267]. In *Genzyme Ltd*[268] the OFT imposed a penalty on Genzyme of £6.8 million for infringing the Chapter II prohibition. The CAT reduced the penalty to £3 million for a variety of reasons, including that one of the OFT's findings of abuse was set aside and that the abuse was of shorter duration than the OFT had held[269].

In both *Hasbro II*[270] and *Football Replica Kits*[271] the CAT reduced the penalties imposed by the OFT. In *Hasbro II* the CAT felt that the OFT had miscalculated the

[262] Case Nos 1032/1/1/04–1033/1/1/04 *Apex Asphalt and Paving Co Ltd v OFT* [2005] CAT 4, [2005] CompAR 507.
[263] Case No 1000/1/1/01 [2002] CAT 1, [2002] CompAR 13, [2002] ECC 177.
[264] Ibid, paras 533–534.
[265] OFT Decision *Aberdeen Journals – remitted case*, 16 September 2002, [2002] UKCLR 740, upheld on appeal Case No 1009/1/1/02 *Aberdeen Journals Ltd v Director General Office of Fair Trading* [2003] CAT 11, [2003] CompAR 67.
[266] Case No 1009/1/1/02 *Aberdeen Journals Ltd v Office of Fair Trading* [2003] CAT 11, [2003] CompAR 67, paras 491–492.
[267] Ibid, paras 497–499.   [268] OFT Decision, 27 March 2003, [2003] UKCLR 950.
[269] Case No 1016/1/1/03 *Genzyme Ltd v OFT* [2005] CAT 32, [2006] CompAR 195, paras 700–708.
[270] Case Nos 1014/1/1/03–1015/1/1/03 *Argos Ltd v OFT* [2005] CAT 13, [2005] CompAR 834.
[271] Case Nos 1019/1/1/03–1022/1/1/03 *JJB Sports Plc v OFT* [2005] CAT 22, [2005] CompAR 1060.

'relevant turnover' of Argos and Littlewoods. In *Football Replica Kits* the CAT reduced the fines of JJB and Umbro as some of the findings of infringement were set aside; the CAT also reduced the fine imposed on Manchester United as it had strengthened its competition law compliance programme and accepted responsibility for the infringement[272]. In *Richard W Price (Roofing Contractors) Ltd v OFT*[273] the CAT reduced the penalty on Price from £18,000 to £9,000 because, when comparing the penalty imposed on Price with those of other undertakings in the cartel, it considered that there had been a breach of the principle of equal treatment[274]. The CAT rejected Price's argument that payment of a penalty would jeopardise its solvency[275]. In *Makers UK Ltd v OFT*[276] Makers claimed that it had been the victim of unequal treatment: the OFT had made an arithmetical error in calculating the penalty paid by another undertaking, Coverite, with the result that Coverite's penalty was significantly lower than Makers'. The CAT refused to reduce the penalty imposed on Makers since the error was not one of methodology nor a departure from the OFT's Guidance on penalties, but was simply arithmetical[277]; one member of the CAT dissented on this point, considering that it was simply unfair that Makers should have to pay a significantly higher penalty than Coverite, and that it was irrelevant whether the OFT's error was one of law on the one hand or arithmetic on the other[278].

(iii) Aggravating factors

In *Genzyme Ltd* the OFT considered that the fact that Genzyme had committed a further infringement after the OFT had begun its investigation into Genzyme's pricing practices was an aggravating factor[279]. In the first Hasbro case, *Hasbro UK Ltd*[280], the OFT increased Hasbro's fine by 10 per cent at Step 4 because senior management were aware of the infringement and because the resale price maintenance took place on Hasbro's initiative[281].

(iv) The CAT can increase penalties

The CAT has power to increase as well as to decrease a penalty. In *Football Replica Kits* the CAT increased the penalty on one of the appellants, Allsports Ltd, by £170,000[282]. The OFT had allowed a 5 per cent decrease of the penalty that would otherwise have been imposed on Allsports in recognition of its cooperation. In the proceedings before the CAT it became clear, when witnesses were subjected to cross-examination, that Allsports had been less cooperative than the OFT had thought, and the reduction was therefore revoked.

(v) Decisions in which no penalty was imposed

There have been occasions when the OFT has found an infringement but decided not to impose a penalty. In *Northern Ireland Livestock and Auctioneers' Association*[283] the OFT decided not to impose a penalty on the Association, which had recommended to

---

[272] Ibid, para 266.   [273] Case No 1033/1/1/04 [2005] CAT 5, [2005] CompAR 801.
[274] Ibid, para 63.   [275] Ibid, paras 64–65.
[276] Case No 1061/1/1/06 [2007] CAT 11, [2007] CompAR 699.   [277] Ibid, paras 163 and 167.
[278] Ibid, para 172.   [279] OFT decision of 27 March 2003, [2003] UKCLR 950, para 436.
[280] OFT decision of 28 November 2002, [2003] UKCLR 150.   [281] Ibid, paras 89–92.
[282] Case Nos 1019/1/1/03–1022/1/1/03 *JJB Sports Plc v OFT* [2005] CAT 22, [2005] CompAR 1060, paras 208–235.
[283] OFT decision of 3 February 2003, [2003] UKCLR 433.

its members a standard commission that should be paid by purchasers of livestock at
Northern Ireland cattle marts, since the recommendation was publicised, there was no
attempt to conceal it, and since the beef industry in Northern Ireland had been badly
hit by the unfortunate combination of 'mad cow' disease and foot and mouth disease[284].
In *Lladró Comercial*[285] no penalty was imposed on Lladró, despite a finding that it had
fixed the retail selling price of its merchandise, since the European Commission had
sent a comfort letter to Lladró which it could reasonably have interpreted as suggesting
that its agreements did not infringe the Competition Act[286].

6. THE CARTEL OFFENCE AND COMPANY DIRECTOR DISQUALIFICATION

The Enterprise Act 2002 introduced two provisions designed to encourage individuals
to ensure compliance with competition law. First, Part 6 of the Act established the 'cartel
offence', the commission of which can lead, on indictment, to a term of imprisonment
of up to five years and/or an unlimited fine[287]. Second, the Act introduced the possibility
of company directors being disbarred from office for a period of up to 15 years where
they knew, or ought to have known, that their company was guilty of an infringement of
EC or UK competition law[288]. These important provisions attempt to address the problem that the imposition of fines – even very substantial ones – on undertakings may
not have a sufficiently deterrent effect, especially where the cost of the fines is simply
transferred to customers through higher prices; and that if a fine is so large that it results
in the insolvency and liquidation of an undertaking, this will result in the loss of a competitor from the market, a somewhat perverse achievement for a system of competition
law[289]. The criminal sanction is a very important feature of US law on cartels: there have
been many high-profile cases in recent years in which senior executives of major companies have had to serve terms of imprisonment[290]. At least thirteen Member States of

[284] Ibid, para 72; see similarly Case T-86/95 *Compagnie Générale Maritime v Commission* [2002] ECR
II-1011, [2002] 4 CMLR 1115, para 481, where the CFI decided that no fine should be imposed on a cartel,
among other reasons, because it was not secret but was widely known to exist.
[285] OFT decision of 31 March 2003, [2003] UKCLR 652.   [286] Ibid, paras 124.
[287] Enterprise Act 2002, s 190(1).   [288] Ibid, s 204.
[289] For discussion of criminalisation, both generally and as a matter of UK law, see Hammond and Penrose
'Proposed criminalisation of cartels in the UK' OFT 365, November 2001; Pickford 'The Introduction of
a New Economic Crime' (2002) 1 Competition Law Journal 35; Harding 'Business Cartels as a Criminal
Activity: Reconciling North American and European Models of Regulation' (2002) 9 Maastricht Journal
of European and Comparative Law 393; Harding and Joshua 'Breaking up the Hard Core: Prospects for
the New Cartel Offence' (December 2002) Criminal Law Review 933; Joshua 'A Sherman Act Bridgehead
in Europe or a Ghost Ship in Mid-Atlantic?' (2002) 23 ECLR 231; Green 'The Road to Conviction – the
Criminalisation of Cartel Law' [2003] Fordham Corporate Law Review (ed Hawk), ch 2; Macdonald and
Thompson 'Dishonest agreements' (2003) 2 Competition Law Journal 94; Beard 'The Cartel Criminal
Offence' (2003) 2 Competition Law Journal 156; MacNeil 'Criminal Investigations in Competition Law'
(2003) 24 ECLR 151; Joshua 'The UK's new cartel offence and its implications for EC competition law: a
tangled web' (2003) 28 ELR 620; Dobbin and Peretz 'The Cartel Offence' in Ward and Smith *Competition
Litigation in the UK* (Sweet & Maxwell, 2003), ch 5; Furse and Nash *The Cartel Offence* (Hart Publishing,
2004); Rosochowicz 'The Appropriateness of Criminal Sanctions in the Enforcement of Competition Law'
(2004) 25 ECLR 752; Perrin 'Challenges facing the EU Network of Competition Authorities: insights from
a comparative criminal law perspective' (2006) 31 ELR 540; MacCulloch 'Honesty, Morality and the Cartel
Offence' (2007) 28 ECLR 355.
[290] See ch 13, pp 500–501.

the EU, including the UK, have some form of criminal sanction against individuals for infringements of substantive competition law[291].

As a separate matter the House of Lords has held, in *Ian Norris v Government of the USA*[292], that 'mere' price fixing, without aggravating features, does not amount to conspiracy to defraud, a criminal offence at common law; this matter is discussed in section (C) below[293]. It is at least arguable that some types of cartel activity might infringe section 4 of the Fraud Act 2006[294].

(A) The cartel offence

(i) Definition of the cartel offence

Section 188 of the Enterprise Act 2002 establishes the criminal 'cartel offence'. The cartel offence is quite distinct from Article 81 EC and the Chapter I prohibition in the Competition Act: this means that where a price-fixing agreement is found the possibility exists that the undertakings involved may be the subject of proceedings under Article 81 EC or the Chapter I prohibition, leading to the imposition of fines, and that the individuals responsible for setting up the agreement may be prosecuted criminally under the cartel offence. The criminal prosecution is likely to precede the proceedings against the undertakings[295].

Section 188 of the Enterprise Act provides (in formalistic, indeed tortuous terms) that an individual is guilty of an offence if he or she dishonestly agrees with one or more other persons that undertakings[296] will engage in one or more of the following cartel activities, namely direct and indirect price-fixing[297]; limitation of supply[298] or production[299]; market-sharing[300]; or bid-rigging[301]. The Act specifically provides that, in relation to price fixing and the limitation of supply or production, the parties must have entered into a reciprocal agreement[302]; this is not specified in relation to market-sharing and bid-rigging, since these actions are, by their nature, reciprocal. A key feature of the criminal offence is that there must have been dishonesty on the part of the individuals concerned. In *R v Ghosh*[303] the Court of Appeal established a two-part test for determining dishonesty: the first part asks, as an objective matter, whether the defendant was acting dishonestly according to the standards of reasonable and honest people; the

---

[291] See Bellamy and Child *European Community Law of Competition* (eds Roth and Rose, OUP, 6th ed, 2008), para 14.171.

[292] [2008] UKHL 16, reversing the judgment of the High Court on this point, *Ian Norris v Government of the USA* [2007] EWHC 71 (Admin), [2007] UKCLR 1487.

[293] See p 423–424 below.

[294] See Corker and Smith, arguing against the application of the Fraud Act to price fixing, in 'Cartels: who's liable?' (2007) 157 New Law Journal 1593.

[295] See p 420 below.

[296] The term 'undertaking' has the same meaning for this purpose as it has in the Competition Act 1998: Enterprise Act 2002, s 188(7).

[297] Enterprise Act 2002, s 188(2)(a); indirect price fixing would include, for example, agreements about relative price levels or price ranges, rebates and discounts: see the DTI's *Enterprise Bill: Explanatory Notes*, para 391.

[298] Enterprise Act, s 188(2)(b).   [299] Ibid, s 188(2)(c).   [300] Ibid, s 188(2)(d) and (e).

[301] Ibid, s 188(2)(f): a definition of bid-rigging is provided by s 188(5) of the Act; there is no offence where the person requesting the bids is aware of the bid-rigging arrangements: ibid, s 188(6).

[302] Ibid, s 188(3).   [303] [1982] QB 1053, [1982] 2 All ER 689, CA.

second asks, as a subjective matter, whether the defendant must have realised that what he was doing was dishonest by those standards. The offence applies only in respect of horizontal agreements[304]: vertical agreements, and in particular vertical resale price maintenance, are not covered by the cartel offence. The cartel offence will have been committed irrespective of whether the agreement reached between the individuals is implemented by the undertakings, and irrespective of whether or not they have authority to act on behalf of the undertaking at the time of the agreement[305]. If the agreement is entered into outside the UK, proceedings may be brought only where the agreement has been implemented in whole or in part in the UK[306].

(ii) Powers of investigation and search

The OFT may conduct an investigation if there are reasonable grounds for suspecting that the cartel offence has been committed[307], and the Enterprise Act gives it powers to require information and documents[308] and to enter and search premises under a warrant[309]. The OFT has published guidance on how it intends to exercise the powers conferred upon it for this purpose[310]. There are criminal sanctions for non-compliance with the powers of investigation: for example the intentional destruction of documents could lead to a maximum prison sentence of five years[311]. The OFT may also obtain information about the cartel offence through informal enquiries: it will make clear to individuals and undertakings that there is no compulsion to respond to informal enquiries[312].

(A) Powers to require information and documents The OFT can, by written notice, require a person to answer questions, provide information or produce documents for the purposes of a criminal investigation[313]; the term 'document' includes information recorded in any form and includes information that may be held electronically[314]. The OFT can exercise this power against any person it has reason to believe has relevant information[315], who must provide the information or documents required other than communications protected by professional privilege[316] or confidential information between a bank and its client[317]. In urgent cases the OFT may require immediate compliance with a notice[318]. The OFT can also require, in writing, a person to attend a 'compulsory interview' to answer questions on any matter relevant to the investigation[319]. Section 197 of the Act imposes restrictions on the use of statements obtained under section 193 (and section 194, dealt with below)[320] in order to protect against self-incrimination[321]. There are also restrictions on the disclosure of confidential information[322]. The OFT issued 14 notices under section 193 in the period to which the 2006–2007 Annual Report relates, one to a business and 13 to individuals relating to two separate cases[323].

---

[304] Enterprise Act 2002, ss 188(4) and 189.
[305] *The cartel offence: Guidance on the issue of no-action letters for individuals*, OFT 513, April 2003, para 2.3 and *Powers for investigating criminal cartels*, OFT 515, para 1.1.
[306] Enterprise Act 2002, s 190(3).   [307] Ibid, s 192(1).   [308] Ibid, s 192(2).   [309] Ibid, s 194.
[310] *Powers for investigating criminal cartels*, OFT 515.
[311] Enterprise Act 2002, s 201; see also *Powers for investigating criminal cartels*, paras 7.1–7.4 and Table 7.1.
[312] Ibid, para 2.3.
[313] Enterprise Act 2002, s 193; *Powers for investigating criminal cartels*, paras 3.2–3.5.
[314] Enterprise Act 2002, s 202.   [315] Ibid, s 193(1).   [316] Ibid, s 196(1).   [317] Ibid, s 196(2).
[318] *Powers for investigating criminal cartels*, para 3.4.   [319] Ibid, para 3.2.
[320] Enterprise Act 2002, s 197.   [321] See *Powers for investigating criminal cartels*, paras 6.3–6.5.
[322] Enterprise Act 2002, ss 237–246 and *Powers for investigating criminal cartels*, paras 6.6–6.8.
[323] 2006–2007 Annual Report and Resource Accounts of the Office of Fair Trading Annex C, p 1.

(B) Power to enter premises under a warrant The OFT may apply to the High Court (or in Scotland the procurator fiscal may apply to the sheriff) for a warrant authorising a named officer of the OFT, or any other authorised person such as a forensic IT expert, to enter premises[324]. This power permits forcible entry into and a search of the premises[325]; explanations of documents can be required[326] and the OFT can require that information stored in an electronic form can be taken away in a visible and legible form[327]. The OFT's officers may take away original documents[328]; a copy of documents removed will be provided as soon as is reasonably practicable after the execution of the warrant[329]. Privileged information cannot be insisted upon[330]. A warrant may be issued, first, if there are reasonable grounds for believing that there are documents on any premises that the OFT could require by written notice[331] and, second, if a person has failed to comply with a written notice[332]; or if it is not practicable to serve such a notice[333]; or if the service of such a notice might seriously prejudice the investigation[334].

Entry under a warrant will be conducted in accordance with the requirements of Code B of the Police and Criminal Evidence Act 1984 Codes of Practice[335]. Although the Police and Criminal Evidence Act does not apply in Scotland, the OFT may follow its procedures there[336].

The investigating officer will not wait for a legal adviser to be present before commencing a search, though he will normally ensure that the search is witnessed by a third party[337]. A person under investigation will, however, be entitled to seek legal advice in the event that he or she is required to attend an interview or if the OFT intends to exercise its 'seize and sift' powers[338]. The OFT may exercise seize and sift powers that enable its officers pre-emptively to seize material when it is not reasonably practicable to determine on the premises whether the material is seizeable or not[339].

The exercise of these powers is subject to strict safeguards such as a requirement to give a written notice of what material has been seized[340], and an obligation to return any material which is subject to legal privilege[341]. The OFT visited four business premises under the authority of section 194 criminal search warrants in the period to which the 2006–2007 Annual Report relates, relating to two separate cases[342].

(iii) Powers of surveillance

(A) Enterprise Act: intrusive surveillance and property interference The Enterprise Act gives powers of 'intrusive surveillance' and 'property interference' to the OFT for the purpose of investigating the commission of the cartel offence: these powers are *not* available for investigations under the Competition Act[343]. In certain circumstances the Chairman of

---

[324] Enterprise Act 2002, ss 194 and 195; *Powers for investigating criminal cartels*, paras 3.6–3.14.

[325] Enterprise Act 2002, s 194(2)(a) and (b).   [326] Ibid, s 194(2)(c).   [327] Ibid, s 194(2)(d).

[328] Ibid, s 194(2)(b)(i).   [329] *Powers for investigating criminal cartels*, paras 3.8.

[330] Enterprise Act 2002, s 196.   [331] Ibid, s 194(1)(a).   [332] Ibid, s 194(1)(b)(i).

[333] Ibid, s 194(1)(b)(ii).   [334] Ibid, s 194(1)(b)(iii).

[335] *Powers for investigating criminal cartels*, paras 3.10–3.16.   [336] Ibid, para 3.17.

[337] Ibid, para 3.15.   [338] Ibid, para 3.16.

[339] Enterprise Act 2002, s 194(5) incorporating the statutory powers of seizure under the Criminal Justice and Police Act 2001, s 50; see also *Powers for investigating criminal cartels*, paras 3.13–3.14.

[340] Criminal Justice and Police Act 2001, s 52.   [341] Ibid 2001, s 55.

[342] 2006–2007 Annual Report and Resource Accounts of the Office of Fair Trading Annex C, p 1.

[343] Enterprise Act, 2002, s 199 amending Regulation of Investigatory Powers Act 2000, s 32ff and Enterprise Act 2002, s 200 amending Police Act 1997, ss 93–94.

the OFT, with prior approval from the Office of the Surveillance Commissioners, may issue an authorisation for the presence of an individual or the planting of surveillance devices in residential premises, including hotels, and in private vehicles in order to hear or see what is happening there ('intrusive surveillance')[344]. The criteria for the grant of an authorisation are contained in section 32(3) of the Regulation of Investigatory Powers Act 2000 and include situations in which the use of intrusive surveillance is necessary for the prevention or detection of a serious crime, such as the cartel offence, and where it is necessary to act in the interests of the economic well-being of the UK. The OFT could use these powers, for example, to obtain a recording of a meeting of cartel members in a hotel room following a 'tip-off' from one of their employees or a disaffected member of the cartel. When authorisation is granted the OFT intends to outsource the technical deployment of surveillance devices to those public authorities which themselves have such powers as well as practical experience of exercising them. An authorisation by the Chairman of the OFT under section 93 of the Police Act 1997, as amended by section 200 of the Enterprise Act, allows for the covert installation of a surveillance device: if it were not for this section the installation would involve some element of trespass.

(B) Further powers: directed surveillance, covert human intelligence sources and access to communications data[345] The OFT has been given further powers that are regulated by the Regulation of Investigatory Powers Act 2000. The Regulation of Investigatory Powers (Directed Surveillance and Covert Human Intelligence Sources) Order 2003[346] adds the OFT to the list of public authorities that are able to authorise 'directed surveillance': this would allow it, for example, to carry out covert surveillance of a person's office[347]; the OFT may also use 'covert human intelligence sources', for example by asking informants to attend cartel meetings and to report back to it[348]. The Regulation of Investigatory Powers (Communications Data) Order 2003[349] provides that the OFT may be given access to communications data such as the times, duration and recipients of telephone calls, though not their content. The first two of these powers are available in both civil and criminal investigations: the last only for a criminal case.

(C) OFT Codes of Practice The OFT has published two Codes of Practice explaining how it will exercise the additional powers described in the preceding paragraph, Covert surveillance in cartel investigations[350]and Covert human intelligence sources in cartel investigations[351]. The codes follow closely best practice guidelines issued by the Home Office.

(iv) Prosecution and penalty

The cartel offence is triable on indictment before a jury in the Crown Court, where a term of imprisonment of up to five years may be imposed or an unlimited fine[352], or in a magistrate's court, where the maximum prison sentence would be six months and

---

[344] *Powers for investigating criminal cartels*, paras 5.2–5.3; in situations of urgency, the Chairman of the OFT may authorise the use of intrusive surveillance and give notice to the Surveillance Commissioner, who will be the ultimate arbiter in such cases: ibid, para 5.3.

[345] See *Powers for investigating criminal cartels*, paras 5.4–5.5.   [346] SI 2003/3171.

[347] See Regulation of Investigatory Powers Act 2000, s 28.   [348] Ibid, s 29.

[349] SI 2003/3171.   [350] OFT 738.   [351] OFT 739.   [352] Enterprise Act 2002, s 190(1)(a).

where a fine may also be imposed[353]. Prosecutions may be brought by the Serious Fraud Office (SFO) or the OFT[354]; in practice the SFO will undertake this function in England, Wales and Northern Ireland where serious or complex fraud is involved[355]. The factors that the SFO will take into account in defining a serious or complex fraud case include cases where the value of the alleged fraud exceeds £1 million[356]; cases that are likely to give rise to national publicity and widespread public concern; and cases where legal, accounting and investigative skills need to be brought together[357]. If the SFO agrees to accept a case it may carry out additional enquiries using its powers under section 2 of the Criminal Justice Act 1987, which are broadly the same as the powers of the OFT under the Enterprise Act[358]. The SFO is bound by the Code for Crown Prosecutors[359]. Prosecutions in Scotland are brought by the Lord Advocate[360]. The OFT could decide to prosecute a case itself where it unearths a hard-core cartel that does not amount to a serious fraud for the Serious Fraud Office's purposes. Bid-rigging of the kind found in *West Midlands Roofing Cartel*[361] would not satisfy the £1 million test of seriousness, but might be viewed as such a blatant case that the OFT would decide to proceed itself.

The OFT has agreed a *Memorandum of Understanding* with the SFO which records the basis on which they will cooperate to investigate and/or prosecute individuals in respect of the cartel offence where 'serious or complex fraud' is suspected; a similar *Memorandum* has been agreed with the Head of the International and Financial Crime Unit of the Crown Office in Scotland: both *Memoranda* are available on the OFT's website[362]. Initial enquiries into possible cartel activity will be undertaken by the OFT; if it considers that the SFO's 'acceptance' criteria are satisfied – that is to say that serious or complex fraud may be involved – the OFT will refer the matter to the SFO, the Director of which will endeavour to decide whether to accept the case, or to require the OFT to make further enquiries, within 28 days[363]. Where the SFO accepts an OFT referral the case team will consist of both SFO and OFT staff, under the direction of an SFO case controller[364]. The OFT is responsible for the grant of leniency and the issue of no-action letters, but where this could affect the outcome of an SFO investigation the OFT will consult with it[365]. The SFO would not prosecute a cartel as a conspiracy to defraud or under the Fraud Act 2006 where the OFT has granted immunity under the Enterprise Act.

(v) Parallel OFT criminal and administrative investigations

When the OFT first receives information about alleged cartel activity it may not immediately be clear whether the case will involve a criminal prosecution of individuals, or

---

[353] Ibid, s 190(1)(b).   [354] Ibid, s 190(2)(a).

[355] *The cartel offence: Guidance on the issue of no-action letters for individuals*, OFT Guideline 513, para 2.7.

[356] See the *Background note to the Memorandum of Understanding*, available at www.oft.gov.uk; the value of the fraud presumably relates to the loss caused to the victims or to the profit made by the fraudsters.

[357] *Powers for investigating criminal cartels*, para 3.18.

[358] *Powers for investigating criminal cartels*, paras 3.20–3.23.

[359] Available on the website of the Crown Prosecution Service: www.cps.gov.uk/Home/CodeFor CrownProsecutors.

[360] In Scotland the Lord Advocate exercises the same powers as the SFO under the Criminal Law (Consolidation) (Scotland) Act 1995.

[361] OFT Decision, 17 March 2004, [2004] UKCLR 1119, on appeal Case 1032/1/1/04 *Apex Asphalt and Paving Co Ltd v OFT* [2005] CAT 4, [2005] CompAR 507.

[362] www.oft.gov.uk.   [363] *Memorandum of Understanding*, paras 3 and 4.

[364] Ibid, para 6.   [365] Ibid, para 13.

whether it will 'merely' lead to an administrative procedure against the undertakings concerned under the Chapter I prohibition in the Competition Act and/or Article 81 EC. In order not to compromise any criminal prosecution the OFT will, where appropriate, follow the procedures required by the Police and Criminal Evidence Act 1984 and its associated Code of Practices from the outset; this will include giving individuals the standard criminal caution before being questioned, and allowing the presence of a legal adviser[366]. If the OFT decides to conduct a 'compulsory' interview, the difference between this and a 'voluntary' interview must be explained, as well as the restrictions on the use of information obtained in a voluntary interview[367].

Where there is a possibility of both criminal and administrative proceedings the OFT and the SFO will consult on timing, and the OFT will not institute an administrative procedure without prior consultation with the SFO[368]. Where the OFT and SFO are proceeding simultaneously the two investigating teams will maintain an 'on-going dialogue' in order to ensure that the administrative procedure does not prejudice the parallel criminal investigation[369]. Statements obtained under the Competition Act will usually not be available for the purpose of a criminal prosecution if they have not been obtained according to criminal law standards; it may therefore be necessary to conduct a further interview in accordance with Police and Criminal Evidence Act procedures[370]. It is possible that a civil claim for damages might be stayed until a criminal trial has been held[371].

(vi) No-action letters

Section 190(4) of the Enterprise Act provides for the issue by the OFT of so-called 'no-action letters' whereby individuals who provide information about cartels to the OFT will be granted immunity from prosecution. This is a further example of encouraging whistleblowers to provide information about cartels in return for leniency[372]. The OFT has published two sets of guidance on the issue of no-action letters, *The cartel offence: Guidance on the issue of no-action letters for individuals*[373] and *Leniency and no-action – OFT's guidance note on the handling of applications*[374]. The latter document is the suggested starting point for anyone needing guidance on the subject: pro-forma no-action letters are included in Annexes 2 and 3 of the Guidance note. The OFT cannot offer leniency from prosecution in Scotland since that is a matter for the Lord Advocate; however he will 'take into account' cooperation on the part of individuals when deciding whether to prosecute[375].

Where a person is a principal offender in a dishonest cartel a full admission of their participation in the offence, including that they behaved dishonestly, will usually be required as a condition of gaining a no-action letter[376], although there may be some circumstances in which the OFT would not require an admission of dishonesty[377]. In some cases, for example where an individual is on the 'periphery' of a cartel, the OFT may simply issue a 'comfort letter' to the effect that the individual is not at risk of prosecution[378].

---

[366] *Powers for investigating criminal cartels*, paras 4.1–4.2.   [367] Ibid, para 4.3.
[368] Ibid, para 4.6.   [369] Ibid, para 4.7.   [370] Ibid, para 4.8.
[371] See *Secretary of State for Health v Norton Healthcare Ltd* [2004] EuLR 12, para 40.
[372] On leniency for undertakings see pp 404–407 above.   [373] OFT 513, April 2003.
[374] OFT 803, January 2008.   [375] *The cartel offence*, OFT 513, para 3.1; see also para 3.10.
[376] *Leniency and no-action*, para 7.3.   [377] Ibid, para 7.4.   [378] Ibid, para 7.5.

Where an undertaking is granted Type A immunity[379] all current and former employees and directors will gain automatic criminal immunity[380]; the same is true where Type B immunity is granted[381]: the Guidance refers to this as 'blanket' immunity. Blanket immunity is not available in Type B leniency and Type C leniency cases: in those cases immunity is considered by the OFT on an individual-by-individual basis[382]. Immunity may also be granted to individuals on their own account, that is to say irrespective of any approach to the OFT by an undertaking[383]. There will be automatic criminal immunity where an individual tells the OFT about cartel activity before any other individual or undertaking and where there is no pre-existing criminal or civil investigation[384]. In other cases criminal immunity may be available on a discretionary basis[385]. Guidance is provided on the process of interviewing individuals who apply for criminal immunity[386]. The Guidance also examines the relationship between the cartel offence in the UK and leniency applications to the European Commission[387], in particular in light of the concern that exposure to criminal action in the UK might deter undertakings from applying for leniency to the Commission. One way of addressing this is to allow an undertaking that applies to the Commission also to put down a 'marker' for Type A blanket immunity on a no-names basis with the OFT[388].

(vii) Extradition

Section 191 of the Enterprise Act 2002 makes provision for the extradition of individuals who commit the cartel offence or who conspire to or attempt to commit it[389]. This means that, in so far as another country, such as the US, has a criminal offence that corresponds with the cartel offence under the Enterprise Act, it can apply to the UK for the extradition of an individual or individuals and vice versa. This provision, of course, is not retrospective, so that there is no possibility of anyone being extradited under the Enterprise Act in respect of conduct occurring before that Act entered into force on 20 June 2003.

The process of extradition as between the UK and 'designated territories'[390] is governed by the Extradition Act 2003. The extradition arrangements differ according to whether the partner country is a 'Category 1' or a 'Category 2' country. The US falls into Category 2. The Act provides that where a Category 2 country seeks extradition it does not have to prove a *prima facie* case that extradition should be allowed: indeed section 84(7) of the Act forbids a court from considering the sufficiency of the evidence of the requesting state[391]. Instead the requesting state simply has to prove 'double criminality', that is to say it must show that:

- the conduct complained of occurred in the territory of the requesting state
- the conduct would constitute a criminal offence under UK law punishable by a term of imprisonment of at least 12 months if it had occurred in the UK
- the conduct is subject to the same punishment under the law of the requesting state[392].

---

[379] See p 405 above on the terminology used in this section.   [380] Leniency and no-action, para 7.13.
[381] Ibid, para 7.20.   [382] Ibid, paras 7.24–7.26.   [383] Ibid, paras 7.27–7.28.   [384] Ibid, para 7.29.
[385] Ibid, para 7.30.   [386] Ibid, paras 7.35–7.39.   [387] Ibid, paras 7.40–7.52   [388] Ibid paras 3.15–3.16 and 7.41.
[389] For further explanation of s 191 see the DTI's *Enterprise Bill: Explanatory Notes*, paras 398 and 399.
[390] See the Extradition Act 2003 (Designation of Part 1 Territories) Order 2003, SI 2003/3333 and the Extradition Act 2003 (Designation of Part 2 Territories) Order 2003, SI 2003/3334.
[391] On this point, and on the controversy over a lack of reciprocity over extradition between the US and the UK, see the related case of *R (Norris) v SSHD*, High Court [2006] EWHC 280 (Admin), judgment of 24 February 2006.
[392] Extradition Act 2003, s 64(2) (for part 1 territories) and Extradition Act 2003, s 137(2) (for part 2 territories).

Extradition may be denied where it would be unjust or oppressive by reason of passage of time since the extradition offence occurred[393].

(viii) Relationship between the cartel offence and proceedings against cartels under EC competition law

Where a European Commission cartel investigation involves a potential criminal cartel offence under the Enterprise Act the OFT will cooperate with the Commission to coordinate the progress of the two investigations[394].

(ix) The cartel offence in practice

The first case under section 188 of the Enterprise Act arose from a cartel in the supply of marine hoses[395], and resulted in terms of imprisonment on three individuals between 2 and a half and three years. It is known that the OFT is considering a criminal investigation in relation to an alleged cartel in fuel surcharges in the aviation sector[396].

(B) Company director disqualification

The Enterprise Act 2002 introduces a second provision designed to encourage individuals to ensure compliance with competition law: under section 204, which inserts new sections into the Company Directors Disqualification Act 1986 (the 'CDDA 1986'), company directors can be disqualified for up to fifteen years where their companies are guilty of a competition law infringement: it is important to understand that disqualification of individuals is *not* limited to circumstances in which the cartel offence has been committed, but applies to any infringement of Articles 81 and 82 EC and of the Chapter I and II prohibitions[397]; however the OFT will not seek to disqualify unless the infringement would be likely to lead to a fine[398]. It is for the High Court (or the Court of Session in Scotland) to make a competition disqualification order ('a CDO'), not the OFT or the sectoral regulators[399]: their function is to determine whether to seek such an order, which the CDDA 1986 gives them power to do[400], and whether to accept an undertaking in lieu of an order, for which provision is also made[401]. The OFT has published guidance on these issues[402]. These powers were first exercised in relation to the marine hose cartel, leading to disqualification of directors for periods between five and seven years[402a].

(i) Grounds for disqualification

Under section 9A of the CDDA 1986 the court must make a CDO against a person if a company of which he is a director commits an infringement of EC and/or UK competition law[403] and the court considers that his conduct as a director makes him unfit to be con-

---

[393] Ibid, s 82. [394] *Powers for investigating criminal cartels*, para 4.10.

[395] See OFT Press Release 72/08, 11 June 2008.

[396] See OFT Press Release 113/07, 1 August 2007; British Airways has agreed to pay a penalty of £121.5m for its admitted participation in this cartel: see p 412 above.

[397] CDDA 1986, s 9A(4). [398] *Competition disqualification orders*, OFT 510, para 4.10.

[399] CDDA 1986, s 9E(3).

[400] Ibid, s 9A(10): s 9D provides that the Secretary of State may make regulations as to the concurrent functions of the OFT and the sectoral regulators in relation to CDOs; in the text that follows the term OFT is used to include the powers of the sectoral regulators.

[401] CDDA 1986, s 9B. [402] *Competition disqualification orders*, OFT 510, May 2003.

[402a] OFT Press Release 72/08, 11 June 2008.

[403] CDDA 1986, s 9A(2).

cerned in the management of a company[404]; the OFT considers that the term 'director', for this purpose, includes a *de facto* director[405]. In deciding whether the conduct of a director makes him unfit, the court must have regard to whether his conduct contributed to the breach of competition law; or, where this is not the case, whether he had reasonable grounds to suspect a breach and took no steps to prevent it; or, if he did not know of the breach, he ought to have done[406]. Furthermore the court may have regard to his conduct as a director of a company in connection with any other breach of competition law[407]. The maximum period of disqualification is fifteen years[408], and during that time it is a criminal offence to be a director of a company, to act as a receiver of a company's property, to promote, form or manage a company or to act as an insolvency practitioner[409]. Any person involved in the management of a company in contravention of a CDO is personally liable for the debts of the company[410] and may be placed on a public register maintained by the Secretary of State for Business, Enterprise and Regulatory Reform[411].

(ii) Procedure

The OFT has power to make inquiries and investigations under sections 26 to 30 of the Competition Act for the purpose of deciding whether to apply for a disqualification order[412]. The OFT may accept undertakings in lieu of seeking a CDO[413]. When deciding whether to apply for an order the OFT will adopt the procedure set out in its guidance[414]. It will not seek a CDO in respect of any current director whose company has benefited from leniency in relation to the activities to which the leniency relates[415]; this largesse would not extend to a director who had been removed as a director as a result of his role in the breach of competition law or for opposing the relevant application for leniency. The extent of the director's responsibility for the breach of competition law will be relevant to the decision whether to apply to the court[416]. The guidance sets out various aggravating and mitigating factors[417]. The OFT would not seek a CDO if an individual is being prosecuted under the cartel offence, since the court dealing with that matter would have the right to make a CDO anyway[418]; nor would it proceed against anyone who is the beneficiary of a no-action letter[419]. The OFT must send a notice to anyone in relation to whom it applies for a CDO: the information that will be contained in this notice is set out in the OFT's guidance[420].

(C) Conspiracy to defraud at common law[421]

In *Norris v Government of the United States of America*[422] the US Government was seeking extradition of Mr Norris under the terms of the Extradition Act 2003. The conduct complained of by the US authorities was illegal price fixing contrary to section 1 of

---

[404] Ibid, s 9A(3).

[405] *Competition disqualification orders*, para 2.3.   [406] CDDA 1986, s 9A(5)(a) and (6).

[407] Ibid, s 9A(5)(b).   [408] Ibid, s 9A(9).   [409] Ibid, ss 1(1) and 13.   [410] Ibid, s 15(1)(a).

[411] Ibid, s 18.   [412] Ibid, s 9C, inserted by Enterprise Act 2002, s 204.

[413] CDDA 1986, s 9B; *Competition disqualification orders*, paras 3.1–3.4.

[414] Ibid, paras 4.1–4.27.   [415] Ibid, para 4.12.   [416] Ibid, paras 4.15–4.21.   [417] Ibid, paras 4.22–4.24.

[418] Ibid, paras 4.25–4.26.   [419] Ibid, para 4.27; on no-action letters see pp 420–421 above.

[420] Ibid, paras 5.1–5.2.

[421] See Lever and Pike 'Cartel Agreements, Criminal Conspiracy and the Statutory "Cartel Offence"' (2005) 26 ECLR 90 and (2005) 26 ECLR 164.

[422] [2008] UKHL 16, reversing the judgment of the High Court on this point in *Ian Norris v The Government of the USA* [2007] EWHC 71 (Admin), [2007] UKCLR 1487.

the Sherman Act 1890. Under the Extradition Act the US had to demonstrate 'double criminality', that is to say that price fixing was illegal under US law and that the same conduct, if it had occurred in the UK, would have been punishable there by a term of imprisonment of at least 12 months. At the relevant time the criminal offence under section 188 of the Enterprise Act 2002 did not exist. The Administrative Court had held that price fixing could amount to conspiracy to defraud, a criminal offence at common law pre-dating the Enterprise Act, where there is an agreement 'between two or more persons dishonestly to prejudice or to risk prejudicing another's right, knowing that they have no right to do so'[423]. On appeal the House of Lords held that 'mere' price fixing did not amount to conspiracy to defraud: it followed that there was no double criminality and that Norris could not be extradited on this ground[424]. A price fixing agreement could be actionable at common law only where there were aggravating features: fraud, misrepresentation, violence and intimidation were referred to as examples[425].

7. CONCURRENCY

An interesting feature of the 1998 Act is that concurrent powers are given to the OFT and the sectoral regulators to enforce the Chapter I and Chapter II prohibitions and Articles 81 and 82 EC. In their respective spheres of influence the Office of Communications, the Gas and Electricity Markets Authority, the Water Services Regulation Authority, the Civil Aviation Authority, the Office for the Regulation of Gas and Electricity (Northern Ireland) and the Office of Rail Regulation enjoy concurrent powers. The Postal Services Commission sits as an observer at meetings of the Concurrency Working Party although it does not enjoy concurrent powers. The availability of these competition law powers raises the interesting dilemma for the sectoral regulators of whether they should use competition law when they suspect there to be anti-competitive behaviour or whether they should use the sector-specific regulatory powers available to them under their governing legislation[426].

(i) The Concurrency Regulations and the Concurrency Guideline
As far as the Competition Act itself is concerned provisions have been put in place in order to ensure that concurrency operates in a satisfactory manner; the Act deals with this issue in section 54 and Schedule 10. Acting under section 54 of the Competition Act the Secretary of State has adopted the Competition Act (Concurrency) Regulations 2004[427]. The OFT, in conjunction with the regulators, has published a Guideline on *Concurrent application to regulated industries*[428]. The Guideline provides the best

---

[423] Ibid, para 56.
[424] A possibility remains that Mr Norris may be extradited on the different ground of perverting the course of justice.
[425] [2008] UKHL 16, para 17; see also *R v GG plc* [2008] UKHL 17, a case arising out of the Serious Fraud Office's prosecution of a number of pharmaceutical companies for price fixing prior to the entry into force of the cartel offence in the Enterprise Act 2002.
[426] See ch 23, pp 970ff.   [427] SI 2004/1077.
[428] OFT Guideline 405, December 2004; note that all of the concurrent regulators, with the exception of the CAA, have published guidelines on the application of competition law to their respective sectors: see ch 9, pp 325–326 for a list of all the available guidelines.

picture of the operation of the concurrency provisions. It explains that the regulators have the same powers as the OFT[429], save that only the latter can issue guidance on penalties and make and amend the OFT's Rules[430]. The Guideline describes the purpose of the Concurrency Regulations[431] and explains the role of the Concurrency Working Party ('the CWP'), which is chaired by a representative of the OFT and brings together officials from all the regulators[432]. The CWP discusses, among other things, general principles and information sharing, the guidelines and disagreements over who should exercise jurisdiction in a particular case[433]. The proceedings of the CWP are confidential, and no minute of its meetings is made publicly available. The Guideline considers how cases will be allocated: in the event of a dispute on jurisdiction the matter will be referred to the Secretary of State[434]: this has never occurred, and it can reasonably be assumed that it will happen only exceptionally. Complaints may be made to the OFT or the relevant regulator[435]; the same is true for applications for interim measures[436]. The Guideline also discusses the relationship between the regulators' powers under competition law and their sector-specific powers[437] and explains the law on confidentiality and disclosure of information[438].

(ii) The concurrency arrangements in practice

The only infringement decisions to have been adopted by a sectoral regulator by 12 March 2008 were taken by the Office of Rail Regulation in the case of *English Welsh & Scottish Railway Ltd* in November of 2006[439] and by the Gas and Electricity Market Authority in February 2008[440]. There have been a number of non-infringement decisions[441]; several of the non-infringement decisions of OFCOM and the Water Services Regulation Authority were appealed to the CAT which, in some of its judgments, has shown frustration with both the slowness of the procedure and the substantive outcome[442]. In the case of *Albion Water* the CAT set aside the non-infringement decision of the Water Services Regulation Authority and substituted its own finding that there had been an abusive margin squeeze[443].

(iii) The DTI/HM Treasury report on concurrency

In May 2006 the Department of Trade and Industry (now Business Enterprise and Regulatory Reform) and Her Majesty's Treasury published a report on *Concurrent competition powers in sectoral regulation*[444]. The report concluded that the process for deciding who should deal with a particular complaint appears to work well, but that it might

---

[429] OFT Guideline 405, paras 2.2–2.3.

[430] Ibid, paras 2.4; note also that only the OFT can proceed under Part 6 of the Enterprise Act in relation to the cartel offence.

[431] Ibid, paras 3.1–3.3.   [432] Ibid, para 3.9–3.11.   [433] Ibid, para 3.10.   [434] Ibid, para 3.12–3.19.

[435] Ibid, para 3.20.   [436] Ibid, para 3.23.   [437] Ibid, paras 4.1–4.3.   [438] Ibid, paras 5.1–5.6.

[439] ORR Decision, 16 November 2006, [2007] UKCLR 937.

[440] *National Grid Co*, GEMA decision of 25 February 2008.

[441] See the Table of Competition Act decisions in ch 9, pp 367–381.

[442] See, in particular, the history of the litigation of the *Freeserve, Floe Telecommunications, VIP Communications* and *Albion Water* cases contained in the Table of Competition Act decisions.

[443] Case No 1046/2/4/04 *Albion Water Ltd v OFWAT* [2006] CAT 36, [2007] CompAR 420; the Court of Appeal gave permission to Dŵr Cymru to appeal against the CAT's judgments of 6 October and 18 December 2006: it upheld the CAT's judgment on May 2008, [2008] EWCA Civ 536.

[444] URN 06/1244, May 2006, available at www.berr.gov.uk.

be possible to enhance the existing cooperation between the OFT and the sectoral regulators. In particular the report considered that the CWP should carry out a more detailed analysis of how the approaches of the OFT and the regulators might differ from one another, and that there might be scope for them to share best practice and expertise[445]. The report raised the question of when it would be appropriate for the regulators to withdraw from sector-specific regulation and to rely on competition forces and competition law to ensure the attainment of desired market outcomes[446]. The report noted the lack of infringement decisions on the part of the sectoral regulators, but said that this did not in itself mean that the regime was not working since there could be a number of explanations, including the structure of the markets concerned and high levels of compliance with competition law[447]. The report recommended that the regulators should publish a response to its conclusions within six months[448]: these are available on the OFT's website[449]. The House of Lords Select Committee on Regulators published a report in November 2007 in which it recommended that the concurrency arrangements should be retained[450]. It noted that in some cases the sectoral regulators tend to be so involved in regulating the industry for which they are responsible that they pay insufficient attention to establishing and maintaining effective competition; it therefore suggested that complainants should have the option of taking their case to the OFT rather than to the regulator in question[451]. The Committee was critical of OFWAT, expressing the opinion that it should examine critically whether it could not find a 'more constructive approach' to implementing the findings of the CAT[452]. It endorsed a proposal of the OFT that it should report annually to the Joint Regulators' Group providing an overall view of whether competition law is being applied consistently and pro-actively across all the sectors[453].

8. APPEALS

The Competition Act deals with appeals in sections 46 to 49 and in Schedule 8, as amended by the Enterprise Act 2002. The powers available to the OFT and the sectoral regulators under the Act are considerable. To balance this, and to ensure compliance with the Human Rights Act 1998 which requires that decisions should be made by an independent and impartial tribunal, it was felt that a full right of appeal – not merely the possibility of judicial review – should be available; furthermore that the appellate body should be one with appropriate expertise in matters of competition law and policy. For this reason appeals are taken to the CAT[454]. The Court of Appeal has acknowledged that the CAT, as a specialist tribunal, is better placed to determine complex matters of

---

[445] Ibid, paras 5–6. [446] Ibid, para 10. [447] Ibid, para 11. [448] Ibid, para 14.
[449] See www.oft.gov.uk/advice_and_resources/resource_base/legal/competition-act-1998/Concurrency/ Responses.
[450] *UK Economic Regulators*, available at www.parliament.uk/parliamentary_committees/lordsregulators. cfm.
[451] Ibid, para 6.41. [452] Ibid, paras 7.22–7.23. [453] Ibid, para 7.48.
[454] The establishment and the functions of the CAT are described in ch 2, pp 72–73; appeals to the CAT are governed by Part II of the Competition Appeal Tribunal Rules 2003, SI 2003/1372 as amended by the Competition Appeal Tribunal (Amendment and Communications Act Appeals) Rules 2004, SI 2004/2068 and by the Amendment Regulations.

competition law and economics than the 'ordinary' courts[455]. Once an appeal has been lodged with the CAT it can be withdrawn only with the Tribunal's permission: the CAT deals with cases in the public interest, and improper pressure should not be applied by one litigant upon another to withdraw an appeal[456].

In so far as the Act does not provide for an appeal there remains the possibility that a claim for judicial review may be brought before the Administrative Court of the Queen's Bench Division under Part 54 of the Civil Procedure Rules[457] in relation to perceived procedural irregularities (for example unreasonable delay[458]) or the improper exercise of administrative discretion. It may be that permission would be refused if the Administrative Court were to consider that a particular issue can be addressed within the statutory appeal procedure[459].

(A) 'Appealable decisions'

Section 46[460] of the Competition Act sets out a list of 'appealable decisions' and states that the recipients of such decisions may appeal them to the CAT; appealable decisions include, for example, decisions as to whether the Chapter I and II prohibitions or Articles 81 and 82 EC have been infringed[461], interim measures decisions and decisions as to the imposition of, or the amount of, a penalty[462]. As can be seen from the Table of Competition Act decisions in chapter 9 many of the OFT's infringement decisions have been appealed to the CAT[463], both as to substance and as to the level of the penalty. For the most part the OFT's infringement decisions have been upheld by the CAT: only one such decision has been annulled in its entirety[464]. The penalties imposed by the OFT have been reduced in some cases, as shown in the Table of Penalties earlier in this chapter[465].

Section 47 of the Competition Act, as substituted by section 17 of the Enterprise Act 2002[466], gives third parties with a sufficient interest a right to appeal to the CAT in relation to appealable decisions. The CAT has said that there is no difference in principle between its treatment of an appeal against an infringement decision and an appeal by a third party against a non-infringement decision[467]. There have been several appeals to the CAT by third parties disappointed that either the OFT or a sectoral regulator had

[455] Case No C/2002/0705 *Napp Pharmaceutical Holdings Ltd v Director General of Fair Trading* [2002] EWCA Civ 796, [2002] 4 All ER 376, paras 31 and 34.

[456] Case 1008/2/1/02 *Claymore Dairies Ltd v OFT* [2006] CAT 3, [2006] CompAR 360, paras 82–89.

[457] Available at www.open.gov.uk/lcd/civil/procrules_fin/crulesfr.htm.

[458] See eg *OFCOM v Floe Telecom Ltd (in administration)* [2006] EWCA Civ 768, [2006] ECC 445, para 45.

[459] See *Harley Development Inc v IRC* [1996] 1 WLR 727, 736C (Privy Council); on judicial review where an appeal system is in place see Craig *Administrative Law* (Sweet & Maxwell, 5th ed, 2003), pp 842–844.

[460] As amended by Article 10 of the Competition Act 1998 (Notification of Excluded Agreements and Appealable Decisions) Order 2000, SI 2000/263.

[461] Competition Act 1998, s 46(3)(a) and (b).   [462] Ibid, s 46(3)(i).   [463] See ch 9, pp 367–381.

[464] Case No 1035/1/1/04 *The Racecourse Association and Others v OFT* [2005] CAT 29, [2006] CompAR 99.

[465] See pp 408–411 above.

[466] The new s 47 avoids the cumbersome procedure for third parties in the Competition Act 1998 as originally drafted, of which the CAT was critical in Case No 1006/2/1/01 *BetterCare Group v Director General of Fair Trading* [2002] CAT 6, [2002] Comp AR 226, paras 115–125.

[467] Case No 1046/2/4/04 *Albion Water Limited v Director General of Water Services* [2005] CAT 40, para 243, citing earlier judgments in *Freeserve v Director General of Telecommunications* [2003] CAT 5 and *JJ Burgess & Sons v OFT* [2005] CAT 25.

failed to find an infringement of the Competition Act or of Article 81 or 82 EC. In some cases the OFT or regulator had explicitly decided that there was no infringement, so that there was no doubt that an appealable decision had been adopted; in some other cases, however, the OFT or regulator closed the file without explicitly deciding that there was no infringement: in these cases the CAT has had to decide whether, at least implicitly, a finding of non-infringement had been reached, in which case an appealable decision could be brought before the CAT. If a decision is not an appealable one, a third party cannot appeal on the merits to the CAT; at most it can seek a judicial review in the Administrative Court[468].

(i) Successful appeals against explicit non-infringement decisions

There have been several successful appeals[469] by third parties against explicit non-infringement decisions of the OFT or a sectoral regulator. The first decision of the OFT under the Competition Act, *General Insurance Standards Council*[470], was taken on appeal by third parties to the CAT[471]. The CAT disagreed with the OFT's finding that the rules of GISC, which prevented its insurer members from dealing with insurance intermediaries unless they were themselves members of GISC, did not infringe the Chapter I prohibition in the Competition Act and remitted the case to the OFT for further consideration. As the rule to which the appellants had taken objection was then dropped the OFT was able to adopt a second non-infringement decision[472].

An appeal was brought by a third party against a decision by the OFT that there had been no infringement of the Chapter II prohibition in *Refusal to supply JJ Burgess Ltd with access to Harwood Park Crematorium*[473]. The case concerned a refusal on the part of W Austin, a funeral director, to provide access to a crematorium to a competitor, JJ Burgess. In *JJ Burgess & Sons v OFT*[474] the CAT set aside the OFT's non-infringement decision and made its own finding that there had been an infringement. The CAT was frustrated at the amount of time that the administrative proceedings had taken, and was concerned that a small operator such as JJ Burgess had failed to get redress from the OFT. It is of interest to note that the Consumers' Association (now known as Which?) intervened in this case in support of JJ Burgess, and that the CAT welcomed the intervention. It remains to be seen how the CAT's concern that small operators should be able to obtain redress can be reconciled with the OFT's prioritisation criteria, according to which the OFT will select cases that will have the highest impact and greatest effect[475].

In *Floe Telecom Ltd v OFTEL*[476] the CAT annulled a non-infringement decision of OFTEL (now OFCOM), *Disconnection of Floe Telecom Ltd's Services by Vodafone Ltd*[477].

[468] In the case of Case No 1071/2/1/06 *Cityhook v OFT* Cityhook not only appealed to the CAT but also sought judicial review in the Administrative Court.
[469] For an example of an unsuccessful appeal against an explicit non-infringement decision see Case No 1073/2/1/06 *Terry Brannigan v OFT* [2007] CAT 23.
[470] OFT decision of 26 January 2001, [2001] UKCLR 331.
[471] Case Nos 1002–1004/2/1/01 *Institute of Independent Insurance Brokers v Director General of Fair Trading* [2001] CAT 4, [2001] CompAR 62.
[472] *General Insurance Standards Council*, 13 November 2002, [2003] UKCLR 39.
[473] OFT decision of 12 August 2004, [2004] UKCLR 1586; there had been an earlier decision to the same effect in *Harwood Park Crematorium* OFT decision of 6 August 2002.
[474] Case No 1044/2/1/04 [2005] CAT 25, [2005] CompAR 1151.
[475] See the OFT's *Annual Plan 2007–08*, p 16, available at www.oft.gov.uk.
[476] Case No 1024/2/3/04, [2004] CAT 18, [2005] CompAR 290.
[477] OFTEL decision of 3 November 2003, [2004] UKCLR 313.

OFCOM subsequently adopted a second non-infringement decision which was upheld on appeal to the CAT, albeit on different grounds from those given by OFCOM[478]. The CAT set aside the non-infringement decision of OFWAT in *Albion Water Ltd (Thames Water/Bath House) v Water Services Regulation Authority (formerly the Director General of Water Services)*[479]. It also annulled OFWAT's finding of non-infringement in *Albion Water/Dŵr Cymru*[480] and adopted a decision that Dŵr Cymru had abused its dominant position by imposing a margin squeeze on Albion Water[481].

(ii) Successful appeals against implicit non-infringement decisions[482]

On four occasions the OFT or a regulator, having received a complaint that the Competition Act or that Articles 81 or 82 EC had been infringed, decided to close the file and to inform the complainant accordingly; the complainant then successfully appealed to the CAT that the decision was in fact one of non-infringement. In three of the cases, *BetterCare Group v Director General of Fair Trading*[483], *Freeserve.com plc v Director General of Telecommunications*[484], and *Claymore Dairies Ltd and Express Dairies plc v Director General of Fair Trading*[485], the CAT concluded that the OFT or regulator had adopted an appealable decision that there was no infringement of the Chapter II prohibition, and rejected the argument that the closure of the file was simply an administrative decision not to proceed with the matter: as a consequence the CAT had jurisdiction to deal with the substance of the appeal. In *Pernod-Ricard SA v OFT*[486] the CAT held that the OFT had adopted a non-infringement decision when it closed its file against voluntary assurances offered by Bacardi that it would change its distribution practices in relation to light rum.

In the *Claymore* judgment the CAT summarised the law on the meaning of an appealable decision as follows[487]. First, the question of whether an appealable decision has been taken is primarily a question of fact, to be decided in accordance with the particular circumstances of the case. Second, whether such a decision has been taken is a question of substance, not form, to be determined objectively, taking into account all the circumstances of the case: the test to be applied is whether a decision has been taken on an appealable matter, 'either expressly or by necessary implication'. Third, there is a distinction between the mere exercise of an administrative discretion not to proceed to the adoption of a decision, and the actual adoption of an appealable decision. At paragraph 148 of the *Claymore* judgment the CAT suggested that it would be useful to pose

[478] OFCOM decision of 28 June 2005, [2005] UKCLR 1112, upheld on appeal Case No 1024/2/3/04 *Floe Telecom Ltd v Office of Communications* [2006] CAT 17, [2006] CompAR 637; the Court of Appeal has given permission to OFCOM and to T-Mobile to appeal against the order of the CAT of 18 January 2007.

[479] [2006] CAT 7, [2006] CompAR 451.   [480] OFWAT decision of 26 May 2004, [2004] UKCRL 1317.

[481] Case No 1046/2/4/04 *Albion Water Ltd v OFWAT* [2006] CAT 36, [2007] CompAR 420; the Court of Appeal gave permission to Dŵr Cymru to appeal against the CAT's judgments of 6 October and 18 December 2007, and upheld the CAT's judgment in May 2008: [2008] EWCA Civ 536.

[482] For comment on the issue of appealable decisions see Bailey 'When are decisions appealable under the Competition Act 1998?' (2003) 2 Competition Law Journal 41; Alese 'The Office Burden: Making a Decision Without Making a Decision for a Third Party' (2003) 24 ECLR 616; Rayment 'What is an Appealable Decision under the Competition Act 1998?' (2004) 3 Competition Law Journal 132.

[483] Case No 1006/2/1/01 [2002] CAT 6, [2002] CompAR 226.

[484] Case No 1007/2/3/02 [2002] CAT 8, [2003] CompAR 1.

[485] Case No 1008/2/1/02 [2003] CAT 3, [2004] CompAR 1.   [486] [2004] CAT 10, [2004] CompAR 707.

[487] *Claymore Dairies Ltd and Express Dairies plc v Director General of Fair Trading* [2003] CAT 3, [2004] CompAR 1, para 122.

two questions when deciding whether an appealable decision had been taken: first, did the OFT ask itself whether the Competition Act had been infringed, and second, if so, what answer did it give to that question? At paragraph 151 of *Claymore* the CAT gave examples of various reasons for the closure of a case file that would not amount to an appealable decision: for example where the OFT concludes that, as a matter of priority, other cases have a higher importance[488]; or that a market investigation reference should be made to the Competition Commission under the Enterprise Act 2002[489]; or that another competition authority is investigating the matter[490]; or that the case should not be pursued because it might prejudice a criminal investigation under section 188 of the Enterprise Act 2002[491]. A further example was given in the *Freeserve* judgment, of a complaint that was so badly organised that the OFT might decide not to proceed with it[492]; another one not mentioned by the CAT would presumably arise where the matter complained of was the subject of civil litigation in the 'normal' courts[493].

(iii) Unsuccessful appeals by third party complainants

In five cases, *Aquavitae (UK) Ltd v Director General of Water Services*[494], *Independent Water Company v OFWAT*[495], *Casting Book Ltd v OFT*[496], *Cityhook Ltd v OFT*[497], and *Independent Media Support Ltd v OFCOM*[498], the CAT reached the conclusion that the OFT or the sectoral regulator had not adopted an appealable decision, with the consequence that the appeals were outside the jurisdiction of the CAT and inadmissible. In *Aquavitae* the CAT accepted that the Director General of Water Services had not made an appealable decision that the Chapter II prohibition had not been infringed: rather he had chosen to deal with the problems raised by Aquavitae by introducing a statutory scheme for retail licensing under new regulatory rules to be established by the Water Act 2003. In *Independent Water Company v OFWAT* the CAT concluded that the Water Services Regulation Authority had not adopted an appealable decision under the Competition Act but had instead decided to deal with the terms and prices on which Bristol Water was to supply bulk water under the regulatory provisions of the Water Industry Act 1991. In *Casting Book Ltd v OFT* the CAT was satisfied that the OFT had closed its investigation into an alleged collective boycott for reasons genuinely independent of the merits of the case and without having reached any conclusion on those merits; in doing so it took into account the fact that the evidence-gathering was still at an early stage, the apparent scarcity of resources in the relevant branch at the OFT and that the OFT's resources would be more usefully deployed on higher priority investiga-

---

[488] On this point the CAT specifically referred to the judgment of the CFI in Case T-24/90 *Automec v Commission (No 2)* [1992] ECR II-2223, [1992] 5 CMLR 431.

[489] On market investigations under the Enterprise Act 2002 see ch 11 generally.

[490] Presumably this could refer to a competition authority in another jurisdiction or, in the specific context of UK law, to an authority with concurrent powers to enforce the CA 1998; on concurrency, see pp 424–426 above.

[491] On the criminal cartel offence see pp 415–422 above.

[492] Case No 1007/2/3/02 *Freeserve.com plc v Director General of Telecommunications* [2002] CAT 8, [2003] CompAR 1, para 101.

[493] Note that this was a reason for the Commission's closure of the file in the *Automec* case, n 491 above.

[494] Case No 1012/2/3/03 [2003] CAT 17, [2004] CompAR 117.

[495] Case No 1058/2/4/06 *Independent Water Company Ltd v OFWAT* [2007] CAT 6, [2007] CompAR 614.

[496] Case No 1068/2/1/06 *Casting Book Ltd v OFT* [2006] CAT 35, [2007] CompAR 446.

[497] Case No 1071/2/1/06 *Cityhook Ltd v OFT* [2007] CAT 18, [2007] CompAR 813.

[498] Case No 1087/2/3/07 [2007] CAT 29.

tions. In *Cityhook Ltd v OFT* the CAT concluded that the OFT, when closing its file, had not adopted an appealable decision, but said that it had not found the case an easy one to decide[499]; the CAT also noted the 'incongruous' result that this meant that Cityhook did not have a right to appeal on the merits to the CAT[500]. The former President of the CAT drew attention to the position in the CAT's Annual Report for 2006/2007, saying that the 'invidious' position of complainant's having to choose whether to apply to the CAT or to the Administrative Court for a judicial review, depending on whether a decision was appealable or not, 'should have no place in a modern legal system'[501]. In *Independent Media Support Ltd v OFCOM* the CAT drew attention to the same problem. In that case the CAT was satisfied that, when OFCOM decided to close its file, it had 'genuinely abstained from expressing a firm view, one way or the other, on the question of infringement'[502]; however it considered that the position of the complainant was therefore an unsatisfactory one, but one that could be remedied only by legislation[503].

(B) The Competition Appeal Tribunal Rules 2003

Following a DTI consultation document[504] the Secretary of State adopted the Competition Appeal Tribunal Rules 2003[505]. The CAT has published *A Guide to Proceedings*[506]. The CAT has pointed out that, when a case reaches it, the matter ceases to be an administrative procedure, as it is when the OFT acts as prosecutor and decision-maker, and becomes, instead, a judicial proceeding[507]. The rules of the CAT are based on five main principles[508]:

- first, early disclosure of each party's case, and of the evidence relied on
- second, active case management by the CAT to identify the main issues early on and avoid delays
- third, strict timetables, with straightforward cases to be completed within six months: for example when rejecting an application for an extension of time in which to lodge an appeal in the *Hasbro* case the CAT said that respect for the deadline in commencing proceedings is, in many ways, the 'keystone' of the whole procedure[509]
- fourth, effective procedures to establish contested facts
- fifth the conduct of oral hearings within defined time limits.

---

[499] Ibid, para 296.   [500] Ibid, para 299.   [501] See the CAT's Annual Review and Accounts 2006/2007, p 4.
[502] Ibid, para 42.   [503] Ibid, para 56.   [504] URN 99/1154, October 1999.
[505] SI 2003/1372, repealing and replacing, for cases commenced on or after 20 June 2003, the earlier Competition Commission Appeal Tribunal Rules 2000, SI 2000/261; the 2003 Rules were amended by the Competition Appeal Tribunal (Amendment and Communications Act Appeals) Rules 2004, SI 2004/2068.
[506] October 2005, available at www.catribunal.org.uk; see also Rayment 'Practice and Procedure in the Competition Commission Appeal Tribunal' (2002) 1 Competition Law Journal 23.
[507] Case No 1000/1/1/01 *Napp Pharmaceutical Holdings Ltd v Director General of Fair Trading* [2002] CAT 1, [2001] CompAR 13, para 117.
[508] See Guide to Proceedings, para 3.4.
[509] Case No 1010/1/1/03 *Hasbro UK Ltd v Director General of Fair Trading* [2003] CAT 1, [2003] CompAR 47; in practice some cases before the CAT have been quite protracted: for example OFWAT's decision in the case of *Albion Water/Dŵr Cymru* of 27 May 2004, [2004] UKCLR 1317 was annulled by the CAT on 18 December 2006, Case No 1046/2/4/04 *Albion Water Ltd v Water Services Regulation Authority* [2006] CAT 36, [2007] CompAR 328.

The CAT has pointed out that when a case reaches it what was previously an administrative procedure, with the OFT acting both as prosecutor and decision-maker, becomes a judicial proceeding in which the CAT can decide the case 'on the merits'[510].

(C) Procedure before the CAT[511]

The procedure before the CAT is predominantly written; submissions should be kept as short as possible. Where an expert is asked to produce a report, for example by an applicant to the CAT, that expert's duty is to assist the Tribunal, and this overrides its obligation to the person from whom the instructions were received and from whom payment was received[512]. The oral hearing should be regarded as an opportunity to debate contentious issues rather than to state a case which has already been made in writing. In cases where facts are in dispute between the OFT (or a regulator) and the appellants, such as *Hasbro II*[513] and *Football Replica Kits*[514], the CAT's ability to probe the evidence and to provide for the cross-examination of witnesses has been an important feature of the procedure. To some extent the CAT can act in an inquisitorial capacity where complex issues of fact are involved, and this may provide a better way of discovering the true facts of a case than is the case in purely adversarial proceedings.

As a general proposition new evidence that could have been made available during the OFT's administrative procedure will not be allowed to be submitted to the CAT[515], although the CAT will allow some flexibility[516]. Where third parties appeal against a decision of the OFT or a sectoral regulator the CAT considers that the onus is on the complainant to show that the decision should be set aside: in particular sophisticated complainants with the resources to present a properly supported case should produce evidence rather than relying on unsupported assertion[517]. The CAT has been extremely meticulous in its work, producing lengthy and very detailed judgments, although the Court of Appeal in the *Hasbro II* and *Football Replica Kits* judgment[518] did wonder

---

[510] Case No 1000/1/1/01 *Napp Pharmaceutical Holdings Ltd v Director General of Fair Trading* [2002] CAT 1, [2001] CompAR 13, para 117.

[511] See further Rayment 'Practice and Procedure before the Competition Appeal Tribunal' in Ward and Smith *Competition Litigation in the UK* (Sweet & Maxwell, 2003), ch 4.

[512] Case No 1009/1/1/02 *Aberdeen Journals Ltd v Office of Fair Trading* [2003] CAT 11, para 288; see also Case No 1000/1/1/01 *Napp Pharmaceutical Holdings Ltd v Director General of Fair Trading* [2002] CAT 1, [2001] CompAR 13, para 254; see also (in proceedings in the High Court) *Leeds City Council v Watkins* [2003] UKCLR 467, para 88.

[513] Case Nos. 1014/1/1/03 and 1015/1/1/03 *Argos Ltd and Littlewoods Ltd v Office of Fair Trading* [2004] CAT 24, [2005] CompAR 588.

[514] Case Nos 1021/1/1/03 and 1022/1/1/03 *JJB Sports plc and Allsports Ltd v Office of Fair Trading* [2004] CAT 17, [2005] CompAR 1145.

[515] See Case No 1000/1/1/01 *Napp Pharmaceutical Holdings Ltd v Director General of Fair Trading* [2002] CAT 1, [2001] CompAR 13, para 59.

[516] [2002] CAT 1, [2001] CompAR 13, paras 60ff; see also the final judgment of 22 May 2001 Case No 1000/1/1/01 [2002] CAT 1, [2002] Comp AR 13, [2002] ECC 177, paras 114–126; a strict approach was taken to the issue of fresh evidence by the CAT in Case No 1005/1/1/01 *Aberdeen Journals Ltd v Director General of Fair Trading* [2002] CAT 4, [2002] CompAR 167, paras 162–178.

[517] See Case No 1007/2/3/02 *Freeserve.com plc v Director General of Telecommunications* [2003] CAT 5, paras 114–115.

[518] *Argos Ltd and Littlewoods Ltd v OFT* and *JJB Sports plc v OFT* [2006] EWCA Civ 1318, [2006] UKCLR 1135, para 161.

whether, in the future, the CAT might be able 'to express its findings of facts and its reasoning in more succinct form'[519].

(D) The powers of the CAT

The Competition Act provides for an appeal 'on the merits' and the powers of the CAT are extensive: considerably wider than those of a court exercising judicial review in the UK or the CFI when dealing with cases under Article 230 EC[520]. The CAT's powers are set out in paragraph 3 of Schedule 8 of the Competition Act, and include the power to adopt interim measures[521], to confirm or set aside the decision that is the subject of the appeal, to remit the matter to the OFT or sectoral regulator, to impose or revoke or vary the amount of a penalty[522], to give directions, for example to bring an end to an abuse of a dominant position[523] or to make a decision, for example finding an infringement of the Competition Act or the EC competition rules.

The way in which the CAT exercises its jurisdiction will depend on the particular circumstances of the case. In the *Aberdeen Journals* case[524] the CAT was dissatisfied with the OFT's treatment of market definition in a Chapter II case but remitted the matter to the OFT for further consideration rather than substituting its finding which, as a matter of law, it was at liberty to do. Similarly in the *Freeserve* case[525] the CAT remitted the issue of whether BT was guilty of abusive pricing practices to OFTEL (the predecessor of OFCOM). In each of these cases the CAT was mindful of the need to avoid the risk of converting itself from an appellate tribunal into a court of first instance. However there have been some occasions when the CAT has made its own decisions on substance, as in the *JJ Burgess v OFT* and in *Albion Water Ltd v OFWAT* cases that were discussed above[526]. In *VIP Communications Ltd v OFCOM*[527] the CAT rejected an argument of T-Mobile that it should not make a decision that T-Mobile had abused a dominant position since this would be to confuse the roles of OFCOM as the administrative body charged to make decisions and the CAT as an appellate body: in the CAT's view this would fail to take into account the fact that an appeal to the CAT is a 'full merits'

---

[519] Ibid, paras 5 and 6.
[520] See Case No 1000/1/1/01 *Napp Pharmaceutical Holdings Ltd v Director General of Fair Trading* [2003] CAT 5, para 106.
[521] See Case No 1000/1/1/01 (IR) *Napp Pharmaceuticals Holdings Ltd v Director General of Fair Trading* [2001] CAT 1, [2001] Comp AR 1, [2002] ECC 1, where the President of the CAT followed judgments of the Community Courts, pursuant to s 60 of the Competition Act 1998, in determining the appropriate test for the adoption of interim measures; the CAT also ordered interim measures in Case No 1013/1/1/03 (IR) *Genzyme Ltd v OFT* [2003] CAT 8, [2003] CompAR 290; Case Nos 1034/2/4/04 (IR) and 1046/2/4/04 *Albion Water Ltd v Director General of Water Services* [2005] CAT 19, [2005] CompAR 993; the CAT rejected an application for interim measures in Case No 1074/2/3/06(IR) *VIP Communications Ltd (in administration)* [2007] CAT 12, [2007] CompAR 781, which it considered to be 'manifestly unfounded': ibid, paras 100–103.
[522] The penalty is automatically suspended pending the appeal (CA 1998, s 46(4)), but the CAT may order that interest is payable (ibid, Sch 8, para 10 and the Competition Appeal Tribunal Rules 2003, SI 2003/1372, r 56).
[523] See eg Case No 1016/1/1/03 *Genzyme Ltd v OFT* [2005] CAT 32, [2006] CompAR 195.
[524] Case No 1005/1/1/01 *Aberdeen journals v Director General of Fair Trading* [2002] CAT 4, [2002] CompAR 167.
[525] Case No 1007/2/3/02 *Freeserve.com plc v Director General of Telecommunications* [2003] CAT 5, [2003] CAT 202.
[526] See pp 428–429 above. [527] Case 1027/2/3/04 [2007] CAT 3, [2007] CompAR 666.

jurisdiction[528]. The CAT has on a number of occasions substituted its own finding on the level of penalties[529].

In *Floe Telecom Ltd v OFTEL*[530] the CAT annulled a non-infringement decision of OFTEL (now OFCOM), *Disconnection of Floe Telecom Ltd's Services by Vodafone Ltd*[531]. The CAT was concerned at the amount of time that the proceedings had taken in this case and it imposed a timetable on OFCOM for its reconsideration of the matter. OFCOM appealed to the Court of Appeal on the question of whether the CAT had the power to set a time limit in this way and the Court of Appeal held that the CAT did not have the power to do so[532]. In the opinion of Lloyd LJ:

> The Tribunal, as a statutory body, has the task of deciding such appeals as are brought to it in accordance with the provisions of the 1998 Act and the rules, but it does not have a more general statutory function, of supervising regulators. On that basis it seems to me that the CAT's reasoning is based on a misconception of the relationship between the Tribunal and the regulators. When a decision is set aside and remitted to the relevant regulator, that particular matter is then to be dealt with by that regulator in accordance with its own statutory duties and functions.[533]

While the CAT's concern as to the apparent slowness of proceedings may be understandable, equally the OFT and the sectoral regulators have a real problem in determining how to deploy the limited resources at their disposal. As Lloyd LJ said in the *Floe* case:

> The Tribunal cannot know what are the competing demands on the resources of the particular regulator at the given time. It may well be that it cannot properly be told of this by the regulator because of issues of confidentiality as to current investigations. It cannot, therefore, form any proper view as to the relative priority of one case as compared with others.[534]

(E) Costs[535]

The Competition Appeal Tribunal Rules 2003[536] enable the CAT to make such order as it thinks fit in relation to costs[537].

The CAT does not apply the conventional rule in civil litigation that 'costs follow the event': instead it has repeatedly said that 'the only rule is that there are no rules'[538]. The CAT's determination not to fetter its discretion in relation to costs in the early days of the new regime is sensible: it needs to obtain experience of the full range of matters that might arise before it begins to formulate specific rules. However some trends in its judgments can be discerned.

First, the CAT has not wanted to deter small or medium-sized firms from appealing against cartel decisions of the OFT for fear of having to pay the OFT's costs if unsuccessful: this can be seen in *Apex Asphalt and Paving Co v OFT*[539], although the

---

[528] Ibid, para 45.   [529] See the Table of Penalty Decisions at pp 408–411 above.
[530] Case No 1024/2/3/04, [2004] CAT 18, [2005] CompAR 290.
[531] OFTEL decision of 3 November 2003, [2004] UKCLR 313.
[532] *OFCOM and OFT v Floe Telecom Ltd* [2006] EWCA Civ 768, [2006] ECC 445.   [533] See para 34.
[534] *OFCOM and OFT v Floe Telecom Ltd* [2006] EWCA Civ 768, [2006] ECC 30, para 37.
[535] See *Guide to Proceedings*, October 2005, paras 17.1–17.9.   [536] SI 2003/1372.
[537] SI 2003/1372, r 55(2).
[538] See eg Case No 1062/1/1/06 *The London Metal Exchange v OFT* [2006] CAT 19, [2006] CompAR 781, para 108 and Case Nos 1054/1/1/05–1056/1/1/05 *Mastercard UK Members Forum Ltd* [2006] CAT 15, [2006] CompAR 607, para 46.
[539] Case No 1032/1/1/04 *Apex Asphalt and Paving Co Ltd v OFT* [2005] CAT 11, [2005] CompAR 825.

CAT also noted other factors in that case that contributed to its decision to make no order for costs against the unsuccessful appellant[540]. However in *Sepia Logistics Ltd v OFT*[541] the CAT did award costs to the OFT in a case where the unsuccessful appellant was not a substantial undertaking, but where the appeal did not involve novel points of law. The CAT noted that the appellant had raised a number of points that lacked merit and that this had added significantly to the length and complexity of the case. The CAT had a similar concern of not deterring small or medium-sized firms from bringing an action in the CAT in the case of a follow-on action brought by BCL Old in the *Vitamins* case, where it declined to make an order of security for costs against the applicants[542].

A second point is that the CAT does not have the same anxiety in the case of more substantial firms. In *Aberdeen Journals v OFT*[543] the CAT expressed concern at the significant costs to the public purse involved in competition law appeals, a point repeated in *Genzyme v OFT*[544] and in *Football Replica Kit*[545]. In *Argos and Littlewoods*[546] the OFT and the parties to the appeal reached an agreement on costs. The CAT decided not to interfere with the settlement reached, but noted that it had the power to make an alternative costs order should it think this necessary in order to dispose of the case as justly as possible[547]. Third, the CAT's frustration at the slowness and/or ineffectiveness of the OFT's administrative procedures was reflected in the costs awards against it in *London Metal Exchange*[548] and *MasterCard*[549]. Finally it is clear that the CAT has, on some occasions, felt disquiet at the level of the fees charged by City law firms for their advice; and in particular at the number of hours charged by partners as opposed to associates[550].

(F) Appeals from the CAT to the Court of Appeal

Appeals on points of law lie, with permission, from the CAT to the Court of Appeal[551]. An application for permission to appeal was rejected both by the CAT[552] and by the Court of Appeal in *Napp Pharmaceuticals Holdings Ltd v Director General of Fair*

---

[540] Ibid, para 26.　　[541] Case 1072/1/1/06 [2007] CAT 14, [2007] CompAR 779.

[542] Case No 1028/5/7/04 *BCL Old Co Ltd v Aventis SA* [2005] CAT 2, [2005] CompAR 485.

[543] Case [2002] CAT 21.

[544] Case No 1013/1/1/03 (IR) and Case No 1016/1/1/03 consent order of 14 November 2005 and Case No 1016/1/1/03 consent order of 29 November 2005.

[545] Case Nos 1019/1/1/03 etc *Umbro Holdings Ltd v OFT* [2005] CAT 26, [2005] CompAR 1232.

[546] Case Nos 1014/1/1/03–1015/1/1/03 *Argos Ltd v OFT: Ruling – Observation on Costs* [2005] CAT 15, [2005] CompAR 996.

[547] Ibid, paras 4–5.

[548] Case No 1062/1/1/06 *The London Metal Exchange v OFT* [2006] CAT 19, [2006] CompAR 781.

[549] Case Nos 1054/1/1/05–1056/1/1/05 *Mastercard UK Members Forum Ltd* [2006] CAT 15, [2006] CompAR 607.

[550] See eg Case Nos 1035/1/1/04–1041/2/1/04 *The Racecource Association v OFT* [2006] CAT 1, [2006] CompAR 438, paras 30–35; Case No 1049/4/1/05 *UniChem Ltd v OFT* [2005] CAT 31, [2006] CompAR 172, paras 27–31; and Case No 1062/1/1/06 *The London Metal Exchange v OFT* [2006] CAT 19, [2006] CompAR 781, paras 176–177.

[551] Competition Act 1998, s 49.

[552] Case No 1000/1/1/01 *Napp Pharmaceuticals Holding Ltd v Director General of Fair Trading* [2002] CAT 5.

Trading[553]. There have been several occasions on which the CAT has refused permission to appeal, but the Court of Appeal has subsequently granted it[554].

9. ARTICLE 234 REFERENCES

An important aid to the consistency of application of EC law in Member States is the preliminary ruling procedure of Article 234 EC, which enables the ECJ to rule on questions referred by national courts or tribunals[555]. Two questions arise: first, can an Article 234 reference be made by a court or tribunal when applying the Competition Act, as opposed to Article 81 and/or Article 82 EC; and second, which courts or tribunals in the UK are able to make an Article 234 reference.

(A) Can an Article 234 reference be made where a court or tribunal is applying the Competition Act 1998?

Since the EC Modernisation Regulation the competition authorities and courts in the UK apply Articles 81 and 82 EC themselves when an agreement or conduct has an effect on trade between Member States. However there will be some cases where the effect on trade is purely within the UK and where only the Competition Act is applicable. The question then arises or whether an Article 234 reference can be made where a court or tribunal is purely applying domestic law. The jurisprudence of the ECJ strongly suggests that references under Article 234 will be possible in such cases. The ECJ would not want a position to develop in which national laws based upon Articles 81 and 82 are interpreted in a substantially different way from the meaning given to them by Community institutions. In *Kleinwort Benson Ltd v Glasgow City Council*[556] the ECJ declined to give a ruling on the interpretation of the Civil Jurisdiction and Judgments Act 1982 in so far as it related to the allocation of jurisdiction as between the courts of England and Wales on the one hand and the courts of Scotland on the other. There the ECJ noted that the domestic court in the UK, when applying the so-called 'modified Convention' (dealing with intra-UK matters), had only an obligation 'to have regard to the Court's case law'; there was no obligation to apply 'absolutely and unconditionally' the Court's case law. This sets up the possibility of distinguishing *Kleinwort Benson* since, in the case of section 60(2) of the Competition Act, there is a duty, albeit a qualified one, to maintain consistency with EC jurisprudence[557]. Subsequent judgments have suggested that the ECJ

---

[553] Case No C/2002/0705 *Napp Pharmaceutical Holdings Ltd v Director General of Fair Trading* [2002] EWCA Civ 796, [2002] 4 All ER 376.

[554] See eg *Argos Ltd and Littlewoods Ltd v OFT* and *JJB Sports plc v OFT* [2006] EWCA Civ 1318, [2006] UKCLR 1135; *OFCOM v Floe Telecom Ltd* [2006] EWCA Civ 768, [2006] ECC 30; *Dŵr Cymru v Albion Water Ltd*, [2008] EWCA Civ 536; *OFCOM v Floe Telecom Ltd* and *T-Mobile Ltd v Floe Telecom Ltd*, not yet decided.

[555] It is for the referring court or tribunal to determine the content of the questions to be put to the ECJ, which will not opine on questions raised by the parties to the litigation unless the referring court asks it to: Cases C-376/05 etc *A Brünsteiner GmbH v Bayerische Motorenwerke AG* [2006] ECR I-11383, [2007] 4 CMLR 259, paras 25–29.

[556] Case C-346/93 [1995] ECR 1-615.   [557] See ch 9, pp 362–367.

may indeed be willing to deal with a reference where a ruling on a point of Community law is necessary to enable a proper interpretation to be made of purely internal rules of a Member State: this can be seen, for example, in *Bernd Giloy v Hauptzollamt Frankfurt am Main-Ost*[558] and *Leur-Bloem v Inspecteur der Belastingdienst*[559], citing earlier judgments in *Masam Dzodzi v Belgium*[560] and *Gmurzynska-Bscher Oberfinanzdirektion Köln*[561].

In *Oscar Brönner GmbH v Mediaprint*[562] the Austrian court of first instance in competition matters referred questions to the ECJ asking it to interpret Article 82 in the context of a refusal to provide access to a daily newspaper distribution system. Although the Austrian court was applying its own domestic law to the case, and although this was not written in the same terms as EC law, it nonetheless felt that an interpretation of Article 82 would enable it to reach a decision, as it would not wish to apply its own law inconsistently with EC competition law. The European Commission argued that the reference was inadmissible as the Austrian court was not applying EC law. The ECJ held as follows:

A request from a national court may be rejected only if it is quite obvious that the interpretation of Community law bears no relation to the actual facts of the case or to the subject matter of the main action (paragraph 17).

Later it said that:

the fact that a national court is dealing with a restrictive practices dispute by applying national competition law should not prevent it from making a reference to the Court on the interpretation of Community law on the matter, and in particular on the interpretation of Article [82] of the Treaty in relation to that same situation, when it considers that a conflict between Community law and national law is capable of arising (paragraph 20).

This ruling would appear to establish that references may be made to the ECJ on the interpretation of Articles 81 and 82 when the domestic court or tribunal is considering corresponding issues under Chapters I and II[563].

(B) Which courts or tribunals in the UK can make an Article 234 reference in a case under the Competition Act 1998?

It is obvious that the House of Lords, the Court of Appeal and the High Court can make Article 234 references. It is also assumed that the CAT can do so: provision is made for this in its Rules[564]. What is less clear is whether the OFT or the sectoral regulators could make a reference. It is a matter of Community law to determine who qualifies as courts or tribunals[565]. Lord Simon, in the House of Lords debate on the third reading of the Bill,

---

[558] Case C-130/95 [1997] ECR I-4291.   [559] Cases C-297/88 and C-197/89 [1990] ECR I-3763.
[560] Cases C-297/88 and C-197/89 [1990] ECR I-3763.   [561] Case C-231/89 [1990] ECR I-4003.
[562] Case C-7/97 [1998] ECR I-7791, [1999] 4 CMLR 112.
[563] See similarly Case C-238/05 *Asnef-Equifax, Servicios de Informaci sobre Solvencia y Crédito, SL v Asociación de Usuarios de Servicios Bancarios (Ausbanc)* [2006] ECR I-11125, [2007] 4 CMLR 224, paras 12–25; Case C-217/05 *Confederación Española de Empresarios de Estaciones de Servicio v Compañía Española de Petróleos SA* [2006] ECR I-11987, [2007] 4 CMLR 181, paras 13–24.
[564] The Competition Appeal Tribunal Rules 2003, SI 2003/1372, r 60.
[565] See eg Case C-54/96 *Dorsch Consult Ingenieurgesellschaft mbH v Bundesbaugessellschaft Berlin mbH* [1997] ECR I-4961, [1998] 2 CMLR 237; Case C-178/99 *Re Salzman* [2001] ECR I-4421, [2003] 1 CMLR 918; on this point see Brown and Jacobs *The Court of Justice of the European Communities* (Sweet & Maxwell,

thought that it would be possible for the OFT and/or the sectoral regulators to make a reference[566], although he subsequently resiled from this position[567]. It may be that the point will not arise, since the OFT and the regulators may determine of their own volition not to attempt to make such a reference. In this connection it is of interest to note that, in the *Syfait* case, the ECJ reached the conclusion that the Greek Competition Authority was not a court or tribunal for the purposes of Article 234 EC[568].

5th ed, 2000), pp 223–227; Wyatt and Dashwood's *European Union Law* (Sweet & Maxwell, 5th ed, 2006), pp 508–509.

[566] 25 November 1997, col 963.   [567] Ibid, col 975.

[568] Case C-53/03 *Syfait and Others v GlaxoSmithKline and Others* [2005] ECR I-4609, [2005] 5 CMLR 1.

11

Enterprise Act 2002: market studies and market investigations

CHAPTER CONTENTS

1. INTRODUCTION

Part 4 of the Enterprise Act 2002 provides for the reference of markets to the Competition Commission for investigation. These provisions replace the law on scale and complex monopoly situations contained in the Fair Trading Act 1973[1], which itself had replaced the earlier Monopolies and Restrictive Practices (Inquiry and Control) Act 1948. In July 2001 the Government signalled its intention to overhaul the monopoly provisions in its White Paper *Productivity and Enterprise – A World Class Competition Regime*[2]. In particular the Government proposed that decisions in the new regime for investigating markets should be taken primarily by the Office of Fair Trading ('the OFT')[3] and the Competition Commission ('the CC')[4], and that the Secretary of State should become involved only in cases which raise exceptional public interest issues[5]; the decisions to be adopted by the OFT and CC would be made against a new test based on the prevention, restriction or distortion of competition, as opposed to the public interest test set out in section 84 of the Fair Trading Act. Part 4 of the Enterprise Act 2002 entered into force on 20 June 2003. The relationship between the Enterprise Act 2002, the Competition Act 1998 and the EC Modernisation Regulation is considered further below[6].

---

[1] The provisions in the Fair Trading Act 1973 on general and labour references are also repealed: see s 208 EA 2002.

[2] Cm 5233 (2001), ch 6; see also the Government's Response (December 2001).

[3] On the OFT see ch 2, pp 64–68.   [4] On the CC see ch 2, pp 69–71.

[5] Cm 5233 (2001), paras 6.41–6.45.   [6] See p 455 below.

Section 2 of this chapter will provide an overview of market investigations. Sections 3 and 4 discuss the ways in which the OFT obtains and analyses information about markets, in particular through the receipt and investigation of 'super-complaints' and by conducting market studies. Section 5 describes the market investigation provisions in the Enterprise Act. 'Public interest cases' are briefly referred to in section 6, while sections 7 and 8 deal with the issue of enforcement and other supplementary matters. Section 9 of the chapter considers how the market investigation provisions have been working in practice since the Enterprise Act entered into force. The final section of the chapter briefly refers to the enforcement and review of undertakings and orders still in force under the monopoly provisions in the Fair Trading Act 1973.

2. OVERVIEW OF THE PROVISIONS ON MARKET INVESTIGATION REFERENCES

(A) Part 4 of the Enterprise Act 2002

Part 4 of the Enterprise Act 2002 consists of four chapters; the Government's *Explanatory Notes* to the Bill as introduced into Parliament on 26 March 2002 are a helpful adjunct to the Act itself[7]. Chapter 1 of Part 4 of the Act is entitled 'Market investigation references': it deals both with the making of references and their determination. Chapter 2 of Part 4 of the Act deals with 'public interest cases', which will be rare in practice and are described below in brief outline. Chapter 3 contains rules on enforcement which set out the various undertakings that can be accepted by the OFT and the CC in the course of market investigations and the orders that may be made to remedy any harmful effects on competition. Chapter 4 deals with supplementary matters such as investigatory powers and review by the Competition Appeal Tribunal ('the CAT').

(B) Brief description of the system of market investigation references

The OFT (concurrently with the sectoral regulators such as the Gas and Electricity Markets Authority and the Office of Communications ('OFCOM')) has power to make a reference to the CC where it has reasonable grounds for suspecting that any 'feature or combination of features' of a market prevent, restrict or distort competition in the UK or a part of it; the possibility also exists for the Secretary of State, in limited circumstances, to make a reference. Provision is made for the OFT or a sectoral regulator to accept legally binding undertakings in lieu of a reference. The CC must determine whether there is an adverse effect on competition; if so it must decide on suitable remedies, bearing in mind the need to achieve as comprehensive a solution as is reasonable and practicable to any adverse effects identified. In taking remedial action the CC may also take into account any 'relevant customer benefits', as defined by the Act. A wide array of powers to change markets prospectively is available to the CC following its investigation including, where appropriate, the power to impose a structural remedy;

---

[7] The Explanatory Notes are available at www.opsi.gov.uk/acts/en2002/2002en40.htm.

however the market investigation system does not involve any sanctions for past behaviour. References by the OFT and reports of the CC are required to be published.

(C) Institutional arrangements

As explained above, market investigation references can be made by the OFT and the sectoral regulators; in exceptional cases the Secretary of State can make a reference. Within the OFT the Markets and Projects division is responsible for assessing markets that might be appropriate for reference; the actual decision to refer is taken by the Board of the OFT. The CC decides whether competition is being restricted in the cases referred to it and, if so, what remedies should be adopted; the CC makes the final determination in market investigation references. The OFT has a duty to monitor remedies and to advise on whether they should be varied or revoked. Decisions of the OFT, the Secretary of State and the CC are subject to review by the CAT.

(D) Guidelines, rules of procedure and other relevant publications

In addition to Part 4 of the Enterprise Act, various guidelines, rules and other publications seek to explain the operation of the UK system of market investigations.

(i) OFT publications

The OFT has published *Market investigation references: Guidance about the making of references under Part 4 of the Enterprise Act*[8], replacing earlier *Guidance* published in 2003, which explains how it intends to apply the Act.

(ii) CC publications

Acting under Schedule 7A of the Competition Act, inserted by Schedule 12 of the Enterprise Act 2002, the CC has adopted the *Competition Commission Rules of Procedure 2006*, which superseded the earlier rules of June 2003; they are available on its website[9]. The CC has also published three sets of guidelines of relevance to market investigations:

- *Market Investigation References: Competition Commission Guidelines*[10]
- *General Advice and Information*[11]
- *Statement of Policy on Penalties*[12].

The Chairman of the CC has published three further documents of relevance to market investigations:

- *Guidance to Groups*[13]
- *Disclosure of Information in Merger and Market Inquiries*[14]
- *Disclosure of Information by the Competition Commission to Other Public Authorities*[15].

---

[8] OFT 511, March 2006, available at www.oft.gov.uk.
[9] CC1, March 2006, available at www.competition-commission.org.uk.
[10] CC3, June 2003.   [11] CC4, March 2006.   [12] CC5, June 2003.   [13] CC6, March 2006.
[14] CC7, July 2003.   [15] CC12, April 2006.

(iii) Department of Business Enterprise and Regulatory Reform
(formerly the Department of Trade and Industry)

The Secretary of State has adopted the *Competition Appeal Tribunal Rules*[16] which govern the way in which the CAT will deal with applications for review of decisions of the OFT, the Secretary of State and the CC in relation to market investigations. Statutory instruments have also been adopted in relation to the marking of 'super-complaints'[17].

(iv) CAT

The CAT has published a *Guide to Proceedings*, section 6B of which deals specifically with applications for review under the Enterprise Act 2002[18].

3. SUPER-COMPLAINTS

Section 11 of the Enterprise Act provides for so-called 'super-complaints' to be made to the OFT. Super-complaints are handled within the OFT by the Markets and Projects division. The OFT has published *Super-complaints: Guidance for designated consumer bodies*[19] to assist those wishing to make a super-complaint. The *Guidance* describes the information that should be contained in a super-complaint, how cases will be handled and possible outcomes. Section 205 of the Act enables the Secretary of State to extend the system so that super-complaints can be made to the sectoral regulators; this was effected by statutory instrument in 2003[20]. The *Guidance* explains how these concurrency arrangements will work[21]; the terms of reference of the Concurrency Working Party in relation to super-complaint concurrent duties can be found on the OFT's website[22].

The idea of a super-complaint is that a designated consumer body can make a complaint to the OFT about features of a market for goods or services in the UK which appear to be significantly harming the interests of consumers[23]. This is a way of making the consumer's voice more powerful: individual consumers often lack the knowledge or experience to complain effectively, but a designated consumer body should have the resources and ability to do so. In such a case the OFT must publish a 'fast-track' report on what action, if any, it intends to take within 90 days[24]; the Secretary of State has power to amend the 90-day period[25]. The OFT, when dealing with a super-complaint, can request information under section 5(1) of the Enterprise Act 2002; however it has

---

[16] SI 2003/1372, as amended by the Competition Appeal Tribunal (Amendment and Communications Act Appeals) Rules 2004, SI 2004/2068.

[17] See section 3 below.   [18] Available at www.catribunal.org.uk.

[19] OFT 514, July 2003, available at www.oft.gov.uk.

[20] The Enterprise Act 2002 (Super-complaints to Regulators) Order 2003, SI 2003/1368, as amended by the Enterprise Act 2002 (Water Services Regulation Authority) Order 2006, SI 2006/522.

[21] *Super-complaints: Guidance for designated consumer bodies*, paras 3.1–3.4.

[22] OFT 548, November 2003, available at www.oft.gov.uk/advice_and_resources/publications/guidance/enterprise_act/oft548; the operation of the Concurrency Working Party is explained in ch 10, pp 424–426.

[23] Enterprise Act 2002, s 11(1).   [24] Ibid, s 11(2).   [25] Ibid, s 11(4).

formal powers to demand information under section 174 of the Act only where the prospect of making a market investigation reference arises.

In practice the requirement to investigate and report within 90 days imposes a considerable burden on the OFT to gather evidence, synthesise it, and form a view, which in turn results in a corresponding burden on the parties that are the subject of the super-complaint; the 90-day period leaves little time for the OFT and the parties concerned to consider possible remedies to any problems identified. As will be seen from the *Table of Super-complaints* below, it is quite likely that a super-complaint will lead to an OFT market study or even to a market investigation reference to the CC: in other words a super-complaint may lead to a lengthy period of scrutiny of the market, and the firms that operate on the market, to which the complaint relates. The super-complaint on *Payment Protection Insurance* of September 2005 led to a lengthy market study by the OFT which was followed by a market investigation reference to the CC in February 2007; it is unlikely that the case, including the implementation of any necessary remedies, will be concluded before the spring of 2009.

Consumer bodies are designated by the Secretary of State[26], and the DTI (now BERR) has issued *Guidance for bodies seeking designation as super-complainants* on the designation criteria and on how to apply for designated status[27]. Designations are made once yearly, in October; application must be submitted by 30 April of that year at the latest[28]. The Secretary of State has designated the following bodies as super-complainants:

- The Campaign for Real Ale (CAMRA)
- Which? (formerly known as the Consumers' Association)
- Energywatch (formerly known as The Gas and Electricity Consumer Council)
- The General Consumer Council for Northern Ireland
- Citizens Advice (formerly known as The National Association of Citizens Advice Bureaux)
- The National Consumer Council
- Postwatch (formerly known as The Consumer Council for Postal Services)
- The WaterVoice Council[29].

The Consumers, Estate Agents and Redress Act 2007 brought the National Consumer Council, Energywatch and Postwatch together into a new consumer advocacy body, also known as the National Consumer Council.

A super-complaint can lead to a number of responses, including, though not limited to, competition or consumer law enforcement, referral to a sectoral regulator, the launch of a market study by the OFT or a market investigation reference to the Competition Commission[30].

By 12 March 2008 nine super-complaints had been received by the OFT, as set out in the following table. The first three of these were received on a non-statutory basis prior to the entry into force of section 11 of the Act, but were dealt with as though section 11 was in force.

[26] Ibid, s 11(5) and (6); see also the Electricity Act 2002 (Part 8 Designated Enforcers: Criteria for Designation, Designation of Public Bodies as Designated Enforcers and Transitional Provisions) Order 2003, SI 2003/1399, as amended by SI 2006/522.
[27] URL 06/1710, August 2006, available at www.dti.gov.uk.   [28] Ibid, para 1.3.
[29] See the Enterprise Act 2002 (Bodies Designated to make Super-complaints)(Amendment) Order 2005, SI 2005/2340.
[30] *Super-complaints: Guidance for designated consumer bodies*, para 2.25.

11.1 Table of super-complaints

Title	Date of super-complaint	Super-complainant	Date of announcement of result by OFT	Outcome
Private Dentistry	25 October 2001	Which? (known at the time as the Consumers' Association)	23 January 2002	OFT market study
Doorstep Selling	3 September 2002	National Association of Citizens Advice Bureaux	12 November 2002	OFT market study
Mail Consolidation	17 March 2003	Postwatch	16 April 2003	Following discussions with the Postal Services Commission as to the regulatory position the OFT decided that no further action was necessary
Care Homes	5 December 2003	Which? (known at the time as the Consumers' Association)	3 March 2004	OFT market study
Home Collected Credit	14 June 2004	National Consumer Council	10 September 2004	Market investigation reference to the CC
Northern Ireland Banking	15 November 2004	Which? in conjunction with the General Consumer Council for Northern Ireland	11 February 2005	Market investigation reference to the CC
Payment Protection Insurance	13 September 2005	Citizens Advice	8 December 2005	OFT market study followed by market investigation reference to the CC

Title	Date of super-complaint	Super-complainant	Date of announcement of result by OFT	Outcome
Credit Card Interest Calculation Methods	2 April 2007	Which?	26 June 2007	OFT to carry out a programme of work with the credit card industry and consumer bodies to make the cost of credit cards easier for consumers to understand
Scottish Legal Profession	9 May 2007	Which?	31 July 2007	OFT made recommendations to the Scottish Government and the legal profession to lift restrictions that could be causing harm to consumers

4. OFT MARKET STUDIES

Section 5 of the Enterprise Act provides that one of the general functions of the OFT is to obtain, compile and keep under review information about matters relating to the carrying out of its functions. One of the ways in which the OFT carries out this general function is by conducting 'market studies' of markets which appear not to be working well for consumers but where enforcement action under competition or consumer law does not, at first sight, appear to be the most appropriate response[31]. The general function contained in section 5 is the only legal basis for OFT market studies; there are no further provisions, and therefore no specific legal framework. As when dealing with super-complaints, the OFT can *request* information under section 5(1) of the Enterprise Act 2002; however it has formal powers to *demand* information under section 174 of the Act only where the prospect of making a market investigation reference arises[32]. It follows that undertakings, should they so wish, could decide not to cooperate with an OFT market study.

Market studies are usually carried out by the Markets and Projects division of the OFT; they are intended to enable the OFT to understand as well as possible how markets

[31] The sectoral regulators also conduct market studies: see eg ORR's *Approach to reviewing markets* (April 2006) and *The Leasing of Rolling Stock for Franchised Passenger Services* (November 2006), both available at www.rail-reg.gov.uk; see also the study launched by OFGEM into energy supply markets in February 2008: details can be found at www.ofgem.org.uk.
[32] Ibid, paras 3.14–3.16.

are working and whether the needs of consumers are being met. An important feature of the OFT's market studies is that they are a way of scrutinising the extent to which Governmental behaviour and legislation might have a harmful effect on the way in which markets work. The market studies into, for example, *Pharmacies, Taxi Services, Public Procurement, European State Aid Control* and *Public Subsidies* were all concerned with what might be termed 'public' as opposed to private distortions of competition: several cases ended with the OFT providing advice to the Government, as the Table of Market Studies below shows. The Government has indicated that it will respond to OFT reports on public restrictions within 90 days[33].

There is an obvious similarity between the market studies carried out by the OFT and the sectoral investigations that the European Commission is able to conduct under Article 17 of the EC Modernisation Regulation[34]. The OFT has published *Market Studies: Guidance on the OFT approach*[35] on the procedure that it normally follows when selecting a market for study and when carrying out such a study[36]. In the course of 2008 the OFT conducted a review of the market studies regime: this will lead to the publication of revised *Guidance* which will endeavour to provide greater transparency of the system for interested stakeholders.

Market studies may be triggered in various ways: for example the OFT might commence one on its own initiative, trading standards officers might bring problems to the OFT's attention, or a market study might be prompted by a 'super-complaint' from a designated consumer body[37]; any other interested stakeholders may request the OFT to conduct a market study. Market studies are distinct from market investigation references under Part 4 of the Enterprise Act[38], although it is possible that a market study might lead to a market investigation reference. This occurred, for example, in the cases of *Store Card Credit Services, Payment Protection Insurance* and *Airports*: the possibility that an OFT market study might be followed by a market investigation can lead to a somewhat prolonged scrutiny of some markets[39]. The desirability of avoiding unnecessary duplication of work is a factor that the OFT takes into account when deciding whether to launch a market study. Sometimes the OFT outsources the market study or part of it to an external consultancy: for example OXERA, an economics consultancy, carried out the research for the market study on the Financial Services and Markets Act 2000[40]. An account of the OFT's work in studying markets can be found in its *Annual Report and Resource Accounts*[41], and a section of the OFT's website provides details of its completed and current market studies[42]. Sometimes the OFT conducts a 'short' market study, of three to six months or so, often limited to fact-finding; other market studies may be 'full', and may last a year or even more[43]. A decision to launch a full market study is usually taken by the Board of the OFT. Commencement of a market study is

[33] See the Government's White Paper *Productivity and Enterprise – A World Class Competition Regime* Cm 5233 (2001) paras 4.15 and 6.37.

[34] See ch 7, p 265.   [35] OFT 519, November 2004.

[36] The OFT's guidance on *Market Studies* does not apply to the sectoral regulators.

[37] See pp 442–445 above on super-complaints.

[38] See *Market Studies: Guidance on the OFT Approach*, para 1.12.

[39] On this point see Pickering 'UK Market Investigations: An Economic Perspective' (2006) 5 Competition Law Journal, p 215.

[40] Enterprise Act s 5(3) provides a statutory basis for the OFT to do this.

[41] See eg the *Annual Report 2005–06*, pp 59–61; the *Annual Report 2006–07*, pp 53–58.

[42] See www.oft.gov.uk/advice_and_resources/resource_base/market-studies.

[43] See *Market Studies: Guidance on the OFT approach*, paras 1.13 and 3.1–3.3.

announced by a Press Release[44]. There will follow a period of investigation, culminating in the publication of a report[45].

The OFT welcomes reasoned suggestions of UK markets to be considered for market studies, and has produced an electronic suggestions form which can be accessed on its website[46]. The OFT's *Annual Plan for 2007–08* states that it will publish performance monitoring arrangements for market studies and report on success against the targets in its Annual Report[47].

Various outcomes may follow a market study by the OFT. The following possibilities are set out in the OFT's guidance:

- a clean bill of health for the market in question
- the publication of better information for consumers
- encouraging firms to take voluntary action
- encouraging a consumer code of practice
- making recommendations to the Government or regulators
- investigation or enforcement action under consumer or competition law
- a market investigation reference to the CC under Part 4 of the Enterprise Act[48].

By 12 March 2008 the OFT had completed the following market studies:

11.2 Table of market studies

Completed market studies	Date of OFT report	Outcome of study
Extended Warranties for Electrical Goods	July 2002	Complex monopoly reference made to the Competition Commission under the (now-repealed) Fair Trading Act 1973
Consumer IT Goods and Services	December 2002	Generally the consumer IT market works well for consumers; OFT will continue to monitor the market
Pharmacies	January 2003	Recommendation that the Government should take action to liberalise entry to the community pharmacy market. No action was taken to implement this recommendation
Private Dentistry (note that this followed a super-complaint by Which? (formerly the Consumers' Association)	March 2003	Better information on prices and treatments should be given to consumers, and there should be improvements to the self-regulation of the market. The DTI (precursor to DBERR) published an action plan in June 2003 to implement the OFT's proposals[1]

---

[44] Ibid, para 3.4. [45] Ibid, paras 3.5–3.13.

[46] See www.oft.gov.uk/shared_oft/investigations/marketstudiesideas.doc.

[47] HC 339, p 19, available at www.oft.gov.uk.

[48] *Market Studies: Guidance on the OFT approach*, paras 1.10 and 3.18–3.41.

Completed market studies	Date of OFT report	Outcome of study
Payment Systems	May 2003	OFT to examine the effectiveness of the commitment within the Banking Code to inform consumers about the length of clearing cycles; to complete the investigation of the *MasterCard* notification; to consider whether action is required on access to merchant acquiring and on debit card networks; and to monitor undertakings following the CC's report under the Fair Trading Act 1973 on banking services
Liability Insurance Market	June 2003	Changes recommended to certain practices and the OFT to keep the market under review
Taxi Services	November 2003	Recommendation that elements of the regulatory framework for taxi services should be improved: in particular the removal of *quantity* restrictions, and the encouragement of proportionate *quality* restrictions
		In August 2005 the Department of Transport announced that it would introduce Best Practice Guidance for local authorities when deciding on quality issues in licensing matters[2]
New Car Warranties	December 2003	Manufacturers and dealers should improve their advice to consumers on their servicing options; also they should remove servicing restrictions from their new car warranties: failure to do so could lead to a formal investigation by the OFT under Article 81 EC. Subsequently servicing ties were removed from new car warranties and a voluntary code of conduct was adopted
Debt Consolidation	March 2004	Better financial awareness among consumers and provision of clear, accurate and relevant information by credit providers needed to make the use of debt consolidation fairer and clearer
Store Cards	March 2004	Market investigation reference to the CC

Completed market studies	Date of OFT report	Outcome of study
Estate Agents	March 2004	Recommendation that the Estate Agents Act 1979 should be amended to improve enforcement, that self-regulation should be improved, and that consumers should take further action to protect their own position; key recommendations have been implemented by the Consumers, Estate Agents and Redress Act 2007
Doorstep Selling (note that this followed a super-complaint by the NACAB)	May 2004	Consumers require better information as to their rights in relation to doorstep selling, and existing legislation requires amendment to extend cooling-off periods to all forms of doorstep selling; key recommendations have been implemented by the Consumers, Estate Agents and Redress Act 2007
Public Subsidies	November 2004	First stage of research published; further work to be done on the effect of subsidies in practice
Financial Services and Markets Act 2000	December 2004	No adverse effects on competition found to flow from the Act
Ticket Agents	January 2005	Society of Ticket Agents and Retailers to develop model terms for its members to use in consumer contracts
Classified Directory Advertising Services	April 2005	Market investigation reference to the CC
Care Homes (note that this followed a super-complaint by Which? (formerly the Consumers' Association)	May 2005	The OFT recommended that the Government should establish a central information point or 'one-stop shop' where people can get clear information about care for older people; better access to complaints procedures should be achieved; there is a need for fairer contracts
		The Government announced in August 2005 that it broadly accepted the OFT recommendations[3]
Public Sector Procurement	May 2005	Preliminary research published; further research to be conducted in relation to procurement in the waste management and construction sectors; discussions to take place with the Office of Government

Completed market studies	Date of OFT report	Outcome of study
		Commerce with a view to the OFT publishing guidelines for public sector procurers on how to make the most of competition when procuring construction services
Liability Insurance Market Follow-up Review	June 2005	The OFT identified lower increases in premiums, better communication between insurers and policyholders and a reduction in the number of businesses denied cover as key improvements identified in this follow-up review to its earlier market study
Property Searches	September 2005	Recommendation that central Government should provide clearer guidance to local authorities on how they should set prices for providing property information; also that there should be an agreement as to revised targets with local authorities to ensure that this information is made available quickly and on the same time-scale that they apply to themselves The Government announced in December 2005 that it accepted all of the report's recommendations[4]
European State Aid Control	November 2005	Recommendation that the European Commission should adopt an effects-based approach to the assessment of state aid in its guidelines; most cases would be assessed in a 'Phase I' investigation; cases that do not fall within the Commission's guidelines would be subject to a 'Phase II' assessment. National competition authorities should be allowed to give formal advice as to whether a proposed aid meets the criteria of the Commission's guidelines
Public Subsidies	January 2006	Recommendations by OFT that guidance should be given to providers of subsidies on whether the subsidies are likely to have a significant impact on competition. The OFT recommended that the guidance should be issued as a supplement to the HM Treasury 'Green Book', which requires that

Completed market studies	Date of OFT report	Outcome of study
		all costs and benefits should be taken into account when appraising any Government programme or project
Commercial Use of Public Information	December 2006	Recommendation that public sector information holders, such as the Met Office, The National Archives and the Ordnance Survey, should make as much public sector information available for public use as possible, ensure that businesses have access to such information at the earliest point that it is useful to them, provide such information on a non-discriminatory basis and at a reasonable price and enable better regulation by the Office of Public Sector Information
Payment Protection Insurance (note that this followed a super-complaint by Citizens Advice)	October 2006	Market investigation reference to the CC
UK Airports	December 2006	Market investigation reference to the CC Recommendations also made to the Government in relation to airports in the north of England
Pharmaceutical Price Regulation Scheme	February 2007	Recommendation that the Pharmaceutical Price Regulation Scheme, whereby the Government seeks to control the prices of branded medicines through a mix of profit and price controls, should be reformed in order to make the prices paid by the National Health Service reflect the therapeutic value to patients of the drug in question
Internet Shopping	June 2007	The rapid growth of internet selling has been successful for both consumers and businesses; OFT to conduct further work to improve aspects of internet selling

Completed market studies	Date of OFT report	Outcome of study
Medicines Distribution	December 2007	The introduction of 'direct to pharmacy' ('DTP') distribution systems in the pharmaceutical sector could lead to significantly higher costs for the National Health Service and could adversely affect the standard of services available to pharmacies and patients. The Department of Health should factor the possibility of higher costs arising from DTP into its review of the PPRS; and the Government, if appropriate, should take action in relation to service standards

[1] www.dti.gov.uk/files/file25886.pdf.
[2] See www.dft.gov.uk/consultations/archive/2004/tphvbpg/taxisandprivatehirevehicles.
[3] See www.dti.gov.uk/files/file17611.pdf.
[4] www.dti.gov.uk/files/file25861.pdf.

5. MARKET INVESTIGATION REFERENCES[49]

Chapter 1 of Part 4 of the Enterprise Act establishes the system of market investigation references. Sections 131 to 133 deal with the making of references and sections 134 to 138 with their determination. The OFT's *Market investigation references: Guidance about the making of references under Part 4 of the Enterprise Act* ('the OFT Guidance')[50] and the CC's *Market Investigation References: Competition Commission Guidelines* ('the CC Guidance')[51] provide helpful guidance on market investigation references. The market investigation regime is a notable feature of the UK system of competition law, and recognises that not every market failure can be cured through the application of the 'conventional' tools of competition law, Articles 81 and 82, and their domestic analogues. The market investigation regime focuses on markets rather than on the behaviour of individual firms, and enables the CC to investigate whether features of the market such as economies of scale, network effects, switching costs, and barriers to entry, or market imperfections, such as informational asymmetries, have an adverse effect on competition. A wide range of remedies is available to eliminate, as far as possible, such adverse effects and any detrimental effects on customers that the CC identifies.

[49] See Geroski 'The UK Market Inquiry Regime' [2004] Fordham Corporate Law Institute (ed Hawk), 1, also available at www.competition-commission.org.uk/our_role/speeches/index.htm; see also Geroski 'Market Inquiries and Market Studies: The View from the Clapham Omnibus' and Freeman 'Investigating Markets and Promoting Competition: The Competition Commission's role in UK Competition Enforcement', Beesley Lecture of 18 Ocotber 2007, both available at the same website; see further Freeman 'Market Investigations in the United Kingdom: The Story So Far' in *Economic Law and Justice in Times of Globalisation* (eds Monti et al, Nomos, 2007).
[50] QFT 511, March 2006, available at www.oft.gov.uk.   [51] CC3, June 2003.

(A) The making of references

(i) The power of the OFT to make a reference

The OFT (concurrently with the sectoral regulators)[52] may make a market investigation reference to the CC when it has 'reasonable grounds for suspecting'[53] that one or more 'features' of a market prevent, restrict or distort competition in the supply or acquisition of goods or services in the UK or in a part thereof[54]. A decision to make a market investigation reference is made by the Board of the OFT. The CAT has made clear that the 'reasonable grounds for suspecting' test does not impose a particularly high burden on the OFT: the scheme of the Act is that the full investigation of a market is to be carried out by the CC, not the OFT[55]. At the same time the CAT stressed that the first-stage investigation by the OFT should not be unduly protracted[56], and suggested that it was at least arguable that, if the OFT were to delay unreasonably the making of a decision whether to refer or not, an aggrieved person might be able to seek a review of that fact by virtue of section 179(2) of the Act[57]. Features of a market include the structure of the market concerned or any aspect thereof[58]; the conduct of persons supplying or acquiring goods or services who operate on that market, whether that conduct occurs in the same market or not[59]; and conduct relating to the market concerned of customers of any person who supplies or acquires goods or services[60]. Conduct for these purposes includes a failure to act and need not be intentional[61]. The OFT, when making a reference, is not required to specify whether particular features of a market are a matter of structure on the one hand or of conduct on the other[62].

Section 132 of the Act allows the Secretary of State to make a reference when he is not satisfied with a decision of the OFT not to make a reference under section 131, or when he considers that the OFT will not make such a reference within a reasonable period. Section 132 sits a little oddly with the Government's intention that the Secretary of State should be removed from cases except where exceptional public issues arise, for which special provision is made[63]. The section 132 power had not been exercised by 12 March 2008.

Section 133 specifies what the OFT must include in a market investigation reference; in particular it must provide a description of the goods or services to which the feature or combination of features that are restrictive of competition relate[64]. A reference may be framed so as to require the CC to confine its investigation to goods or services supplied or acquired in a particular place or to or from particular persons[65]. Provision is

---

[52] The sectoral regulators with concurrent powers are listed in para 1.2 of the *OFT Guidance*; on the powers of the sectoral regulators in relation to market investigation references see the Enterprise Act 2002, Sch 9, Part 2 and *OFT Guidance*, paras 3.15–3.16.

[53] Note that the Government resisted a proposed amendment to the Enterprise Bill that would have required the OFT to have reasonable grounds for *believing* rather than for *suspecting* there to be a problem: see Lord Sainsbury of Turville, Hansard, 18 July 2002, Col 1511, available at www.publications.parliament.uk.

[54] Enterprise Act 2002, s 131(1).

[55] Case No 1054/6/1/05 *The Association of Convenience Stores v OFT (Ruling Setting Aside of Decision)* [2005] CAT 36, [2006] CompAR 183, para 7.

[56] Ibid, para 8. [57] Ibid, para 12. [58] Enterprise Act 2002, s 131(2)(a). [59] Ibid, s 131(2)(b).

[60] Ibid, s 131(2)(c). [61] Ibid, s 131(3). [62] *OFT Guidance*, para 1.9.

[63] See pp 459–460 below for the provisions on public interest cases.

[64] Enterprise Act 2002, s 133(1)(c).

[65] Ibid, s 133(2) and (3); this power was exercised in the case of *British Airports Authority*.

454 11 ENTERPRISE ACT 2002

made for the variation of references[66]. This occurred, for example, in the case of *Store Card Credit Services* so that network cards and insurance services such as payment protection insurance could be included in the investigation; the variation was made as a result of a request from the CC[67]. In the case of *Classified Directory Advertising Services* the CC issued a notice clarifying the scope of the reference, although the reference itself was not varied[68].

Section 169 of the Act requires the OFT to consult before making a reference and section 172 requires it to give reasons for its decision; these may be given after the date of the reference[69]. The consultation may be a public one, though not necessarily so. The consultation provisions are important, and the OFT takes great care to ensure that it complies with them since a failure to do so could lead to an application to the CAT for a review. An example of these provisions operating in practice is afforded by the reference of *Airports*: the OFT published its market study and its proposal to send the matter to the CC on 12 December 2006, and called for comments by 8 February 2007: the actual reference to the CC was made on 30 March 2007.

The OFT maintains a close relationship with the CC so that the latter body is aware of cases that might be referred to it; this means that the process of transferring a case from the OFT to the CC can be managed as efficiently as possible.

(ii) The discretion of the OFT whether to make a reference

The OFT has a discretion, as opposed to a duty, to make a market investigation reference when the statutory criteria appear to be met. Paragraph 2.1 of the *OFT Guidance* says that it will make a reference only when the following criteria, in addition to the statutory ones, are met:

- it would not be more appropriate to deal with any competition issues under the Competition Act 1998 or by other means, for example the powers of the sectoral regulators
- it would not be more appropriate to accept undertakings in lieu of a reference[70]
- the scale of the suspected problem, in terms of the adverse effect on competition, is such that a reference would be appropriate
- there is a reasonable chance that appropriate remedies will be available.

The *OFT Guidance* provides further insights into each of these criteria.

(A) Relationship between the Competition Act and market investigations The OFT's policy is to consider first whether a suspected problem can be addressed under the Competition Act 1998; it would consider a market investigation reference only where it has reasonable grounds to believe that market features restrict competition, but not to establish a breach of the Chapter I and/or Chapter II prohibitions (or of Articles 81 and/or 82 EC), or when action under the Competition Act has been or is likely to be ineffective for

---

[66] Ibid, s 135.

[67] See www.competition-commission.org.uk/inquiries/completed/2006/storecard/index.htm and OFT Press Release 41/05 of 3 March 2005; a variation was also made in the case of *Domestic Bulk Liquefied Petroleum Gas*: see www.competition-commission.org.uk/inquiries/current/gas/index.htm and OFT Press Release of 20 October 2004.

[68] See www.competition-commission.org.uk/inquiries/ref2005/classdirec/index.htm.

[69] Enterprise Act 2002, s 172(6). [70] On undertakings in lieu see pp 460–461 below.

dealing with any adverse effect on competition identified[71]. The *OFT Guidance* goes on to explain that a market investigation reference might be appropriate for dealing with tacit coordination in oligopolistic markets[72] or with problems arising from networks of vertical agreements[73]. It adds that the majority of references are likely to involve industry-wide market features or multi-firm conduct, of which tacit coordination and parallel vertical agreements are examples[74]. The OFT will review these criteria in the light of emerging case law on the Chapter II prohibition should it appear that it is inadequate to deal with conduct by a single firm which has an adverse effect on competition[75]; also it may make a reference where there has been an abuse of the Chapter II prohibition and it seems that a structural remedy going beyond what could be achieved under the Competition Act is necessary[76].

(B) Relationship with the EC Modernisation Regulation The *OFT Guidance* discusses the relationship between the EC Modernisation Regulation and the market investigation provisions[77]. That Regulation requires national competition authorities to apply Articles 81 and 82 where agreements or abusive conduct have an effect on inter-state trade; as a general proposition it is not possible to apply stricter national law than Article 81, but this is possible in the case of Article 82[78]. The *OFT Guidance* points out that this does not prevent investigations of agreements and conduct that infringe Articles 81 and 82, but that it does affect the remedies that can be imposed[79]. Where Article 81 is applicable to an agreement or agreements, it is unlikely that the OFT would make a reference[80]. However the OFT notes the possibility that in certain circumstances the benefit of a block exemption can be withdrawn from vertical agreements, and that this could be a recommendation of the CC after a market investigation reference[81]. The *OFT Guidance* also notes that the CC could impose remedies in relation to behaviour which amounted to an infringement of Article 82 EC, in which case the OFT would take those remedies into account in the event of it carrying out its own investigation of the infringement of that provision[82]. In the event that the CC were, during the course of a market investigation reference, to discover an infringement of Article 81 or 82, it would not itself have the power to apply those provisions to the behaviour in question, since it has not been designated as a national competition authority for the purpose of applying the EC competition rules: only the OFT and the sectoral regulators have been so designated[83]. In the case of *Store Card Credit Services* the CC stated at paragraph 10.9 that it was satisfied that its proposed remedies were not in conflict with the provisions of EC law[84].

(C) Scale of the problem The *OFT Guidance* discusses the proposition that a reference would be made only where the scale of a suspected problem, in terms of its effect on competition, is such that a reference would be an appropriate response. It will consider whether the adverse effects on competition of features of a market are likely to have a significant detrimental effect on customers through higher prices, lower quality, less

---

[71] *OFT Guidance*, para 2.3.   [72] Ibid, para 2.5.   [73] Ibid, para 2.6.   [74] Ibid, para 2.7.
[75] Ibid, para 2.8, second indent.
[76] Ibid, para 2.8, third indent; on structural remedies under the Competition Act see ch 10, p 399.
[77] Ibid, paras 2.9–2.18.   [78] See generally ch 2, pp 75–78.   [79] *OFT Guidance*, para 2.12.
[80] Ibid, para 2.14.   [81] Ibid, paras 2.17–2.18.   [82] Ibid, para 2.15.   [83] See ch 2, p 71 n 242.
[84] See www.competition-commission.org.uk/inquiries/completed/2006/storecard/index.htm, para 10.9.

choice or less innovation; where the effect is insignificant the OFT would consider that the burden on business and the cost of a reference to the CC would be disproportionate[85]. The *OFT Guidance* also says that, generally speaking, the OFT would not refer a very small market; a market only a small proportion of which is affected by the features having an adverse effect on competition; or a market where the adverse effects are expected to be short-lived[86]. It adds that a reference might not be made where any adverse effect on competition appears to be offset by customer benefits[87].

(D) Availability of remedies The OFT would not refer a market if it appeared that there were unlikely to be any available remedies to deal with an adverse effect on competition, for example where a market is global and a remedy under UK law would be unlikely to have any discernible effect[88].

(iii) Restrictions on the OFT's ability to make a reference

The OFT cannot make a reference if it has accepted undertakings in lieu of a reference within the preceding 12 months[89]. This limitation does not apply where an undertaking has been breached[90]; nor where it was accepted on the basis of false or misleading information[91].

(iv) The OFT's application of the reference test

The discussion in this section so far has concerned the statutory criteria for making a market investigation reference, the way in which the OFT will exercise its discretion whether to refer, and the restriction on it making a reference where it has accepted undertakings in lieu. This leaves one further important issue, which is the OFT's interpretation of the reference test set out in section 131 of the Act. Part II of the *OFT Guidance* contains a helpful discussion of this. In chapter 4 it discusses the meaning of 'prevention, restriction or distortion of competition'. In chapter 5 it considers structural features of markets, including the concentration level within a market, vertical integration, conditions of entry, exit and expansion, regulations and government policies, informational asymmetries, switching costs and countervailing power. Chapter 6 deals with firms' conduct, in particular the conduct of oligopolies, facilitating practices, custom and practice and networks of vertical agreements. Chapter 7 considers the conduct of customers, which section 131(2)(c) of the Act considers to be a feature of a market, and specifically considers the issue of search costs, that is to say the cost that customers may have to incur in order to make an informed choice. By 12 March 2008 the OFT had made eight market investigation references to the CC, and the Office of Rail Regulation had made one: they are set out in the *Table of Market Investigation References* towards the end of this chapter, with some accompanying commentary[92].

(B) The determination of references

(i) Questions to be decided

Once a reference has been made to the CC it must decide whether any feature, or combination of features, prevents, restricts or distorts competition in the referred market(s)[93].

[85] *OFT Guidance*, para 2.27.   [86] Ibid, para 2.28.   [87] Ibid, para 2.29.   [88] Ibid, paras 2.30–2.32.
[89] Enterprise Act 2002, s 156(1); on undertakings in lieu see pp 460–461 below.   [90] Ibid, s 156(2)(a).
[91] Ibid, s 156(2)(b).   [92] See pp 464–466 below.   [93] Enterprise Act 2002, s 134(1)–(3).

If the CC considers that there is an adverse effect on competition, it must decide three additional questions: first, whether it should take action to remedy the adverse effect on competition or any detrimental effect on customers it has identified[94]: detrimental effects are defined as higher prices, lower quality, less choice of goods or services and less innovation[95]; secondly, whether it should recommend that anyone else should take remedial action[96]; and thirdly, if remedial action should be taken, what that action should be[97]. When considering remedial action, the CC must have regard to the need to achieve as comprehensive a solution as is reasonable and practical to the adverse effect on competition and any detrimental effects on customers[98], and may in particular have regard to the effect of any action on any relevant customer benefits[99]. If the CC finds that there is no anti-competitive outcome, the question of remedial action does not arise.

(ii) Investigations and reports

Section 136(1) of the Act requires the CC to prepare and publish a report; this must be done within two years[100]. The report must contain the decisions of the CC on the questions to be decided under section 134, its reasons for those decisions and such information as the CC considers appropriate for facilitating a proper understanding of those questions and its reasons for its decisions[101]. The CC's report on *Store Card Credit Services* sets out, at paragraphs 24 to 37, a summary of the features of that market that prevent, restrict or distort competition, the detrimental effects on customers, the need for remedial action and the decisions on remedies; these matters are then dealt with in more detail in sections 9 and 10 of the report[102]. The time limit of two years within which the CC is to publish its report may not be extended[103], but the Secretary of State may reduce it by order[104]. Experience of the first few years of the market investigation regime shows that the CC is likely to need the full two years to complete its investigation, although it has stated that it will attempt to do so in the future in a shorter period[105]; and that a further period of time thereafter may be needed to implement any necessary remedies (the *implementation* phase of the CC's procedure falls outside the statutory period within which the investigation must be conducted). It is probably correct to suggest that the parties under investigation (as opposed to the CC) will not be in a great hurry to facilitate a quicker conclusion to cases than this, since, in the event of a finding of an adverse effect on competition, it is likely that they will be called upon to alter their behaviour in some way at the end of the process.

(iii) Duty to remedy adverse effects

When the CC has prepared or published a report under section 136 and concluded that there is an adverse effect on competition, section 138(2) requires it to take such action as it considers to be reasonable and practicable to remedy, mitigate or prevent the adverse effect on competition and any detrimental effects on customers

---

[94] Ibid, s 134(4)(a). [95] Ibid, s 134. [96] Ibid, s 134(4)(b). [97] Ibid, s 134(4)(c). [98] Ibid, s 134(6).
[99] Ibid, s 134(7); on the meaning of relevant customer benefits, see s 134(8). [100] Ibid, s 137(1).
[101] Ibid, s 136(2).
[102] Available at www.competition-commission.org.uk/inquiries/completed/2006/storecard/index.htm.
[103] Enterprise Act 2002, s 137(4). [104] Ibid, s 137(3).
[105] See the CC's *Corporate Plan 2007–2008*, page 19, point 5.3.

that have resulted from, or may result from, the adverse effect on competition[106]. The CC would, where it is possible to do so, prefer to address the root cause of the problem – that is to say the adverse effect on competition – than the consequences of it[107]. When deciding what action to take the CC must be consistent with the decisions in its report on the questions it is required to answer, unless there has been a material change of circumstances since the preparation of the report or the CC has a special reason for deciding differently[108]. In making its decision under section 138(2) the CC shall have regard to the need to achieve as comprehensive a solution as is reasonable and practicable to any adverse effects on competition or detrimental effects on customers[109], having regard to any relevant customer benefits of the market features concerned[110]. The remedies phase of a market investigation reference can be quite protracted[111].

(iv) Procedure before the CC

The procedures of the CC during market investigation references are set out in the CC's *Rules of Procedure*[112] and the *Chairman's Guidance to Groups*[113]. Rule 6 of the *Rules of Procedure* requires the CC to draw up an administrative timetable for its investigation. The major stages of an investigation include the gathering and verification of evidence; providing a statement of issues; notifying provisional findings; notifying and considering possible remedies; the publication of the final report; and deciding on remedies. Each investigation has its own home page on the CC's website, and it is a simple matter to follow the progress of the investigation in this way. This accords with the CC's aim to be open and transparent in its working[114]. The home page sets out the core documents of the inquiry; contains the CC's announcements, for example on its 'emerging thinking', provisional findings and final report; and makes available the submissions and the evidence provided to the CC. The home page may also contain surveys and working papers of relevance to the investigation and an account of roundtable discussions, for example with academic economists, held on particular topics: for example economic roundtables were held on local competition and on buyer power in the course of the groceries investigation[115].

The first completed market investigation was *Store Card Credit Services*, and the home page sets out the core documents which provide a helpful insight into the progress of that case[116]:

- terms of reference (**18 March 2004**)
- members of the inquiry
- administrative timetable
- 'issues statement' (**22 September 2004**)
- the CC's 'emerging thinking' (**11 January 2005**)
- variation of terms of reference

---

[106] Enterprise Act 2002, s 138(2).   [107] *CC Guidance*, para 4.6.   [108] Enterprise Act, s 138(3).
[109] Ibid, s 138(4).   [110] Ibid, s 138(5).   [111] See p 465 below in the case of *LPG*.
[112] CC 1, March 2006.   [113] CC 6, March 2006.
[114] See *Chairman's Guidance on Disclosure of Information in Merger and Market Inquiries* (CC7, July 2003), paras 1.5 and 1.6, available at www.competition-commission.org.uk.
[115] See www.competition-commission.org.uk/inquiries/ref2006/grocery/economic_roundtables.htm.
[116] See www.competition-commission.org.uk/inquiries/completed/2006/storecard/index.htm.

- notice of provisional findings (**14 September 2005**)
- notice of possible remedies
- statement of provisional decisions on remedies
- final report (**7 March 2006**)
- administrative timetable for making of Order
- notice of intention to make an Order
- draft Order
- notice of making Order
- *Store Cards Market Investigation Order* (**27 July 2006**).

(v) The CC's Guidance

The CC has published *Market Investigation References: Competition Commission Guidelines*[117] which explain its approach to market investigation references. They deal in turn with issues of market definition, the assessment of competition and remedial action, and contain an extremely useful guide to the competitive process and various factors that adversely affect competition.

6. PUBLIC INTEREST CASES

Chapter 2 of Part 4 of the Act provides for 'public interest cases'. These will be rare and are discussed here in outline only[118]. The Secretary of State may give an 'intervention notice' to the CC within the first four months of a market investigation reference[119], provided that the reference has yet to be determined[120] and that he believes that one or more public interest considerations are relevant to a market investigation[121]. The Secretary of State may also give an intervention notice to the OFT when it is considering undertakings in lieu of a reference[122]. Section 140(1) specifies the information that an intervention notice must contain. The Enterprise Act specifies national security as a public interest consideration[123]; the Secretary of State can add a new public interest consideration by statutory instrument, but this would require the approval of Parliament[124].

When an intervention notice has been given to the CC it will investigate whether features of the market are having an adverse effect on competition and, if so, consider the question of remedies; however it must prepare one set of remedies on the basis that the Secretary of State might decide the case, and a separate set of remedies in case the matter reverts to it[125]. The CC will then publish its report[126]. The Secretary of State must then decide, within 90 days of receipt of the report, whether any public interest considerations raised by the intervention notice are relevant to the remedial action proposed by the CC[127]; if so, the Secretary of State may take such action as he considers to be reasonable and practicable to remedy the adverse effects on competition identified by the CC

---

[117] CC3, June 2003.
[118] The procedure in public interest cases is described in the *CC Guidance*, paras 5.1–5.11.
[119] Enterprise Act 2002, s 139(1)(a)–(b).   [120] Ibid, s 139(1)(c).   [121] Ibid, s 139(1)(d).   [122] Ibid, s 139(2).
[123] Ibid, s 153(1).   [124] Ibid, s 143(3) and (4).   [125] Ibid, s 141.   [126] Ibid, s 142.   [127] Ibid, s 146.

in the light of the relevant public interest considerations[128]. If, however, the Secretary of State does not make and publish his decision within 90 days of receipt of the report, the matter reverts to the CC which will proceed on the basis of the remedies that it proposed in the eventuality of the matter reverting back to it[129].

Section 150 of the Act gives the Secretary of State power to veto the acceptance by the OFT of an undertaking in lieu of a market investigation reference where any public interest considerations outweigh the considerations that led the OFT to propose accepting the undertaking[130].

The OFT has a function of informing the Secretary of State of cases that might raise public interest considerations[131], and the OFT and CC must bring to his attention any representations about the exercise of his powers as to what constitutes a public interest consideration[132].

7. ENFORCEMENT

Chapter 3 of Part 4 of the Enterprise Act deals with the powers of the OFT and the CC to accept undertakings or to impose orders to ensure compliance with the Act and to monitor and enforce them. It begins with the powers of the OFT to accept undertakings in lieu of a reference to the CC; it then sets out the interim and final powers of the CC. Undertakings and orders are legally binding and enforceable in the courts[133]. The OFT is required to maintain a register of undertakings and orders made under the market investigation provisions in the Enterprise Act; it is accessible on the OFT's website[134].

(A) Undertakings and orders

(i) Undertakings in lieu of a reference to the CC[135]

Section 154(2) of the Act gives power to the OFT to accept an undertaking in lieu of a reference to the CC. It can do this only where it considers that it has the power to make a reference to the CC and otherwise intends to make such a reference[136]. In proceeding under section 154(2) the OFT must have regard to the need to achieve as comprehensive a solution as is reasonable and practicable to the adverse effect on competition concerned and any detrimental effects on customers[137], taking into account any relevant customer benefits[138]. The OFT has said that it considers that undertakings in lieu are unlikely to be common[139]; given that the OFT does not conduct a full investigation of the market – that is the function of the CC – it may not be in possession of sufficient information to know whether undertakings in lieu would be adequate to remedy any perceived detriments to competition. This having been said, it may be that, as the

---

[128] Ibid, s 147.   [129] Ibid, s 148.   [130] Ibid, s 150.   [131] Ibid, s 152.   [132] Ibid, s 152.
[133] Ibid, s 167; as to whether a person injured by breach of an undertaking or order could bring an action for damages, see *MidKent Holdings v General Utilities plc* [1996] 3 All ER 132, [1997] 1 WLR 14, brought under s 93 of the (now-repealed) Fair Trading Act 1973.
[134] Ibid, s 166; the OFT's website is www.oft.gov.uk.   [135] See generally *OFT Guidance*, paras 2.20–2.26.
[136] Enterprise Act 2002, s 154(1).   [137] Ibid, s 154(3).   [138] Ibid, s 154(4).
[139] *OFT Guidance*, paras 2.21 and 2.25.

system develops, more use will be made of them: some firms may decide that it would be preferable to offer undertakings in lieu than to bear the intrusion and cost of a two-year investigation; others, however, may prefer a delay of two years (or more) before eventually having to abandon the behaviour in question. If firms were to offer undertakings in lieu but the OFT were to proceed nevertheless to make a market investigation reference, it is obviously possible that they would apply to the CAT for a review of the decision. It is likely that the OFT (or a sectoral regulator) will find it easier to make use of the undertaking in lieu provisions when there are only a few firms involved (or even just one) than when a large number of firms are under investigation.

Before accepting undertakings in lieu the OFT is obliged to publish details of the proposed undertaking, to allow a period of consultation and to consider any representations received[140]; a further period of consultation is required should the OFT intend to modify the undertakings[141]. If an undertaking in lieu has been accepted it is not possible to make a market investigation reference to the CC within the following 12 months[142], unless there is a breach of the undertaking or unless it was accepted on the basis of false or misleading information[143].

Undertakings in lieu of a reference had been accepted in two cases by 12 March 2008, *Postal Franking Machines*[144], an OFT case, and *BT*[145], a case involving OFCOM. In the case of *Postal Franking Machines* the OFT accepted undertakings from the two leading suppliers of franking machines, Pitney Bowes and Neopost, together with Royal Mail; the undertakings were intended to facilitate greater customer choice and more competition in the market, for example by making better price information available and encouraging the provision of third-party maintenance services. This market had been the subject of an investigation under the now-repealed Fair Trading Act 1973 by the Monopolies and Mergers Commission, as it was then called, in 1988; the OFT decided to review the market since the undertakings given in 1988 appeared not to have been effective. In *BT* OFCOM accepted more than 230 separate undertakings from the Board of BT designed to achieve operational separation between BT's infrastructure, where it benefits from a 'bottleneck monopoly', and those parts of its business where it is subject to competition; the monopoly part of the BT business is now operated by 'Openreach', and 'Chinese walls' are established between it and the rest of the BT business. The intention is that this will prevent BT from discriminating in favour of its own vertically-integrated business units. OFCOM publishes a quarterly report setting out BT's progress in implementing the undertakings, and an annual report looking at their overall impact[146].

(ii) Interim undertakings and orders to prevent pre-emptive action

The CC, after a report has been published, can accept interim undertakings and make interim orders to prevent pre-emptive action which might prejudice any final remedy adopted by the CC[147]. The Secretary of State may exercise these powers in public interest cases[148].

---

[140] Enterprise Act 2002, s 155(1)–(3). [141] Ibid, s 155(4)–(5). [142] Ibid, s 156(1). [143] Ibid, s 156(2).

[144] OFT, 17 June 2005, available at www.oft.gov.uk.

[145] OFCOM, 22 September 2005, available at www.ofcom.org.uk.

[146] Details of OFCOM's ongoing work in relation to BT's undertakings can be found at www.ofcom. org.uk.

[147] Enterprise Act 2002, ss 157 and 158. [148] Ibid, s 157(6)(a).

(iii) Final powers

Sections 159 to 161 of the Enterprise Act deal with the final undertakings and orders that are available to the CC after it has completed its investigation and reached its conclusion on the questions contained in section 134. Section 159 provides for the acceptance of undertakings and section 160 for the making of an order where an undertaking is not being fulfilled or where false or misleading information was given to the OFT or CC prior to the acceptance of the undertaking. Section 161 empowers the CC to make a final order. The orders that can be made are set out in Schedule 8 of the Act; they include orders to restrict certain conduct on the part of firms, and also to prohibit acquisitions or even to provide for the division of a business. The provisions that may be contained in an undertaking are not limited to those permitted by Schedule 8 in the case of orders[149]. The CC has a choice of whether to seek undertakings or to make an order, and will proceed on the basis of practicality such as the number of parties concerned and their willingness to negotiate and agree undertakings in the light of the CC's report[150].

The first order to be made by the CC under these powers was the *Store Cards Market Investigation Order* of 27 July 2006. It made provision for full information to be made available to consumers on store card statements, including a warning as to the annual percentage rate of the interest payable; for a direct debit facility to be made available to users of store cards; and for the provision of payment protection insurance as a separate product from the store card itself[151]. By 12 March 2008 the CC had adopted an order in one other case, the *Home Credit Market Investigation Order* of 13 September 2007. Orders will be made in due course following the investigations of *Domestic Bulk Liquefied Petroleum Gas* and *Northern Ireland Banking*. In the case of *Classified Directory Advertising Services* the CC decided that it would accept undertakings from Yell, the publisher of Yellow Pages, rather than make an order; the final undertakings were accepted on 3 April 2007[152].

(B) Enforcement functions of the OFT

Section 162 of the Act requires the OFT to keep enforcement undertakings and enforcement orders under review[153] and to ensure that they are complied with[154]; it is also required to consider whether, by reason of a change of circumstances, there is a case for release, variation, supersession or revocation[155]. The CC may ask the OFT to assist in the negotiation of undertakings[156]. Section 167 provides that there is a duty to comply with orders and undertakings; this duty is owed to anyone who may be affected by a breach of that duty[157]. Any breach of the duty is actionable if such a person sustains loss or damage[158], unless the subject of the undertaking or order took all reasonable steps and exercised all due diligence to avoid a breach of the order or undertaking[159]. Compliance with an order or undertaking is also enforceable by civil proceedings brought by the OFT[160] or the CC[161] for an injunction.

[149] Ibid, s 164(1).   [150] *CC Guidance*, paras 4.42–4.44.
[151] Available at www.competition-commission.org.uk/inquiries/completed/2006/storecard/index.htm.
[152] See www.competition-commission.org.uk/inquiries/ref2005/classdirec/final_yell_undertakings.pdf.
[153] Enterprise Act 2002, s 162(1).   [154] Ibid, s 162(2)(a).   [155] Ibid, s 162(2)(b)–(c).   [156] Ibid, s 162.
[157] Ibid, s 167(2)–(3).
[158] Ibid, s 167(4); as to whether such a person could bring an action for damages, see n 133 above.
[159] Ibid, s 167(5).   [160] Ibid, s 167(6).   [161] Ibid, s 167(7).

8. SUPPLEMENTARY PROVISIONS

Chapter 4 of Part 4 of the Enterprise Act contains a number of supplementary provisions.

(A) Regulated markets

Section 168 provides that, where the CC or the Secretary of State consider remedies in relation to regulated markets such as telecommunications, gas and electricity, they should take into account the various objectives that the sectoral regulators such as the Gas and Electricity Markets Authority and OFCOM have. These may go beyond preventing adverse effects on competition: for example the Postal Services Commission is required to ensure the maintenance of a universal postal service.

(B) Consultation, information and publicity

Sections 169 to 172 of the Act impose various consultation, information and publication obligations on the OFT, the CC and the Secretary of State.

(C) Powers of investigation

Section 174 gives the OFT powers to require information for the purpose of market investigation references; section 175 creates offences where, for example, a person intentionally and without reasonable excuse fails to comply with a notice under section 174.

Section 176 of the Act gives the CC the same powers to require the attendance of witnesses, the production of documents and the supply of information as it has under the provisions in Part 3 of the Act on merger control. These provisions are described in chapter 22 of this book[162].

(D) Reports

Section 177 of the Act makes provision for excisions of inappropriate matter from reports made under the provisions on public interest cases[163], and section 178 allows a dissenting member of the Commission to publish his reasons for disagreeing with the majority. There has been one dissenting opinion in a market investigation report, in the case of Groceries[163a].

(E) Review of decisions under Part 4 of the Enterprise Act

Section 179 of the Act makes provision for review of decisions under Part 4 of the Act. Section 179(1) provides that any person aggrieved by a decision of the OFT, the Secretary of State or the CC may apply to the CAT for a review of that decision: the aggrieved person could be a third party with sufficient interest. The application must be made within two months of the date on which the applicant was notified of the disputed decision

---

[162] See ch 22, p 937. [163] See pp 459–460 above on public interest cases.
[163a] See para 11.347 of the CC's report.

or of its date of publication, whichever is earlier[164]. When dealing with appeals under section 179(1) the CAT will apply the same principles as would be applied by a court on an application for judicial review[165]. The CAT may dismiss the application or quash the whole or part of the decision to which it relates[166]; and, in the latter situation, it may refer the matter back to the original decision-maker for further consideration[167]. An appeal may be brought before the Court of Appeal, with permission, against the CAT's decision on a point of law[168]. Part 3 of the Competition Appeal Tribunal Rules makes provision for appeals under section 179 of the Act[169].

The only application for review under the market investigation provisions of the Enterprise Act to have been made by 12 March 2008 was in the case of *The Association of Convenience Stores v OFT*, where the Association was dissatisfied with a decision of the OFT not to refer the groceries market to the CC; however the OFT subsequently decided that it would reconsider the matter, with the consequence that the CAT handed down a ruling quashing the OFT's decision not to refer and referring the matter back to the OFT[170]. The OFT subsequently referred the groceries market to the CC in May 2006.

9. THE MARKET INVESTIGATION PROVISIONS IN PRACTICE

By 12 March 2008 the OFT had made eight market investigation references to the CC, three of which had been completed and two of which were at the order-making stage; there had also been one reference from the Office of Rail Regulation. The references to date are set out in the following *Table of Market Investigation References*:

11.3 Table of market investigation references

Title of report	Date of reference	Date of report	Outcome
Store Card Credit Services	18 March 2004	7 March 2006	Adverse effect on competition in relation to the supply of consumer credit through store cards and associated insurance in the UK; in particular most store card holders pay higher prices for their credit than would be expected in a competitive market. The CC estimated the customer detriment to be in the region of £55 million a year since 1999, and possibly significantly more

---

[164] Competition Appeal Tribunal Rules SI 2003/1372, as amended by SI 2004/2068, Rule 27.
[165] Enterprise Act 2002, s 179(4); the fact that the CAT is a specialist competition tribunal does not mean that it should apply different principles from the usual ones in a judicial review: see para 53 of the Vice-Chancellor's judgment and paras 88–106 of Carnwath LJ's judgment in *OFT v IBA Health Ltd* [2004] EWCA Civ 142, [2004] 4 All ER 1103 dealing with the merger control provisions of the Enterprise Act 2002, but which would apply in the same way to the market investigation provisions.
[166] Enterprise Act 2002, s 179(5)(a).   [167] Ibid, s 179(5)(b).   [168] Ibid, s 179(6) and (7).
[169] SI 2003/1372, as amended by SI 2004/2068.
[170] Case 1052/6/1/05 *Ruling Setting Aside of Decision* [2005] CAT 36, [2006] CompAR 183 and Order of the Tribunal of 7 November 2005.

Title of report	Date of reference	Date of report	Outcome
			The *Store Cards Market Investigation Order* of 27 July 2006 requires full information to be made available to store card users, including as to the annual percentage rate of interest; direct debit facilities to be made available to users; and the provision of payment protection insurance as a separate product
Domestic Bulk Liquefied Petroleum Gas (LPG)	5 July 2004	29 June 2006	Adverse effect on competition in relation to the supply of domestic bulk liquefied petroleum gas in the UK; in particular there was very little switching by customers between suppliers for a variety of reasons leading to higher prices for the large majority of customers
			The CC announced its intention to make an Order in July 2007; no Order had been made by 12 March 2008
Home Credit Market (note that this reference followed a super-complaint from the National Consumer Council)	20 December 2004	30 November 2006	Adverse effect on competition in relation to the supply of home credit; in particular the weakness of price competition led to higher prices than could be expected in a competitive market
			The *Home Credit Market Investigation Order* of 13 September 2007 requires home credit lenders to share customer repayment data with other potential lenders; to publish information, in particular price information, about the loans they offer to customers; and to provide, at most every three months, an account statement, free of charge, when any of their borrowers ask for one
Classified Directory Advertising Services	5 April 2005	21 December 2006	Adverse effect on competition in relation to classified directory advertising services; Yell's prices for advertising in Yellow Pages would be higher than in a well-functioning market if it were not for the fact that it was already subject to price control as a result of an earlier monopoly investigation under the Fair Trading Act 1973

Title of report	Date of reference	Date of report	Outcome
			On 3 April 2007 the CC accepted final undertakings from Yell Group plc capping its advertising prices; undertakings were also given in relation to other matters such as tying and bundling and the provision of accounts
Northern Ireland Banking (note that this followed a super-complaint from Which? in conjunction with the General Consumer Council for Northern Ireland)	26 May 2005	15 May 2007	Adverse effect on competition in relation to personal current accounts in Northern Ireland; competition limited by banks' unduly complex charging structures and practices, their failure adequately to explain them and customers' reluctance to switch to another bank The *Northern Ireland PCA Banking Market Investigation Order* of 19 February 2008 requires Northern Irish banks to ensure that certain types of communications with customers are easy to understand and to inform customers that they can switch; the Order also deals with the provision of information to the OFT
Groceries Market	9 May 2006	Ongoing	
Payment Protection Insurance (note that this followed a super-complaint from Citizens Advice)	7 February 2007	Ongoing	
Airports	29 March 2007	Ongoing	
Rolling Stock	26 April 2007	Ongoing	

The market investigation provisions (as well as the OFT's market studies) are an important supplement to the 'conventional' competition law tools of Articles 81 and 82 EC and the Chapter I and II prohibitions of the Competition Act 1998. Not all market failures are caused by illegal cartels and abusive behaviour by dominant firms. It is important that competition authorities should have other tools at their disposal such as the powers afforded by the Enterprise Act.

A number of points can be made about the investigations that the CC has so far completed.

(A) 'Adverse effect on competition'

The CC has had to grapple with the meaning of the terms 'features of the market' and 'adverse effect on competition', which appeared in UK competition legislation for the first time in the Enterprise Act 2002. In doing so it has tried to identify an appropriate 'counter-factual' against which to compare the conditions in the market under consideration. In *Home Credit*[171] the CC said that, when identifying features of the market, it would compare what it had found in the investigation with what it would expect to find in a well-functioning market[172]. It then proceeded to summarise the features that could have an adverse effect on competition[173] before concluding that the detrimental effect on customers which may result from that adverse effect was that they may have to pay higher prices for home credit than in a competitive market[174].

A similar approach can be seen in *Northern Ireland Banking*[175]: the CC considered that the features of the market harming competition were that banks had unduly complex charging structures and practices; that they did not fully or sufficiently explain them; and that customers generally did not actively search for alternative suppliers[176]. The last of these findings is of interest, and that it considers the inertia of customers – their tendency not to switch – to be a feature of the market. In *Classified Directory Advertising Services* Yell's prices were already subject to a system of regulation, following an earlier investigation in 1996; nevertheless the CC concluded that features of the market did have an adverse effect on competition in that Yell's prices would be higher than in a well-functioning market but for the price regulation[177]. In *Home Credit* the CC concluded that the fact that excessive profits were being earned was not in itself an adverse effect on competition, although it was indicative of features of the market, such as an incumbency advantage and a lack of customer switching, that did have an adverse effect on competition.

(B) Findings of adverse effects on competition

The CC has found an adverse effect on competition in each of the investigations so far completed. It is noticeable that in several of these cases the CC was concerned about the lack of information, or the complexity of the information, available to

---

[171] See the Final Report, available at www.competition-commission.org.uk/inquiries/current/homecredit/index.htm.

[172] Ibid, para 8.4.   [173] Ibid, paras 8.5–8.9.   [174] Ibid, para 8.11.

[175] See the Final Report, available at www.competition-commission.org.uk/inquiries/ref2005/banking/index.htm; for criticism of this investigation see Ridyard 'The Competition Commission's Northern Ireland Banking Market Investigation – Some Unanswered Questions on the Role of Market Investigations' (2008) 29 ECLR 173.

[176] Final Report, para 5.9.

[177] See the Final Report, paras 8.25–8,26, available at www.competition-commission.org.uk/inquiries/ref2005/classdirec/index.htm.

customers: this was true, for example, in *Store Card Credit Services*, *Home Credit*, and *Northern Ireland Banking*. Another recurrent theme is problems for consumers in switching between suppliers of goods and services: this was a key feature of the investigation into *Liquified Petroleum Gas* and was a concern of the CC in *Northern Ireland Banking*.

(C) Evaluation of the system

In 2007 the CC published a document on its website in which it estimated that the total cost to consumers of the adverse effects on competition that it had discovered in *LPG*, *Home Credit*, and *Classified Directory Advertising Services* was in the region of £103.5 million.

10. ORDERS AND UNDERTAKINGS UNDER THE FAIR TRADING ACT 1973

As was mentioned at the beginning of this chapter, a system for investigating scale and complex monopoly situations had been in place since 1948: from 1973 onwards the relevant provisions were contained in the Fair Trading Act 1973[178]. The monopoly provisions in that Act were superseded by the market investigation provisions in the Enterprise Act 2002. Over the years the CC (or its predecessors) published a large number of reports dealing with many sectors of the economy and numerous practices. Many of these reports led to the Secretary of State accepting undertakings or, in some cases, making orders designed to remedy any competition problems identified. Despite the repeal of the substantive provisions of the Fair Trading Act some of these undertakings and orders remain in force[179].

The OFT maintains a *Register of orders and undertakings – market investigations and monopolies* containing details of orders and undertakings made under the Fair Trading Act (and the Enterprise Act): the register is accessible on the OFT's website[180]. The OFT has a continuing obligation to keep these orders and undertakings under review and may give advice to the Secretary of State and the Competition Commission as to whether their release, revocation, variation or termination is appropriate; the OFT's Annual Report provides a helpful view of its work in this area[181]. The 'undertakings in lieu' under section 159 of the Enterprise Act 2002 in the case of *Postal Franking Machines*[182] followed a review by the OFT of undertakings originally given under the Fair Trading Act. In October 2006 the OFT recommended that several undertakings given by Prosper de Mulder and William Forest and Son (Paisley) Ltd following the

---

[178]   For an account of these provisions see Halsbury's Laws of England, Vol 47, paras 116–125 (Butterworths, 4th ed reissue, 2001).

[179]   Enterprise Act 2002, Sch 24, paras 14–18.

[180]   www.oft.gov.uk; the contents of the register are available to the public between 10.00 am and 4.00 pm on working days: see the OFT Register of Undertakings and Orders (Available Hours) Order 2003, SI 2003/1373.

[181]   See eg the *Annual Report 2005–06*, p 64; the *Annual Report 2006–07*, p 57.

[182]   See p 461 above.

CC's investigation of *Animal Waste* in 1993 should be released[183]; the CC agreed to this in June 2007. In 2007 the OFT gave advice in relation to banking services for SMEs which led the CC to lift certain price controls on the four largest banks in the UK[184]. The market investigation references of *Classified Directory Advertising Services* and of *Groceries* followed the review of undertakings that had been given following FTA investigations.

[183] Available   at   www.oft.gov.uk/advice_and_resources/resource_base/register-orders-undertakings/advice.

[184] Competition Commission news release 68/07, 21 December 2007.

12

The international dimension
of competition law

CHAPTER CONTENTS

1. INTRODUCTION

This book so far has described the main provisions, other than those dealing with mergers[1], of EC and UK competition law, and the way in which those provisions are enforced. This chapter is concerned with an issue of growing importance: the international dimension of competition law.

Dramatic changes have taken place in the world's economy in a remarkably short period of time. State-controlled economies have been exposed to the principles of the market; legal monopolies have been reduced or entirely eliminated; and domestic markets have been increasingly opened up to foreign trade and investment. The World Trade Organisation performs a central role in promoting international trade. These developments present significant challenges for systems of competition law. The economic effects of cartels and anti-competitive behaviour on the part of firms with market power and of mergers are not constrained by national boundaries. It is perfectly possible for a few producers to operate a cartel that has significant effects throughout the world: the OPEC oil cartel is an obvious example of this, although there are both legal and political constraints that prevent competition authorities from tackling this particular organisation[2]. Many of the cartels investigated in recent years by the Department of

---

[1] On mergers see chs 20–22.

[2] To the extent that the actors in this cartel are sovereign states as opposed to undertakings, the doctrine of sovereign immunity prevents the application of the EC competition rules: see ch 3, pp 82–91 on the meaning of 'undertakings' in Articles 81 and 82; on sovereign immunity in US law see the Foreign Sovereign Immunity Act 1976, 28 USC §§1602–1611 (1988) and the joint Department of Justice and Federal Trade

Justice in the US and the European Commission in Brussels have had a wide geographical reach, the *Lysine* and *Vitamins* cartels being good examples of this[3]; non-US citizens responsible for unlawful cartels now face the possibility of extradition to and imprisonment in the US. Undertakings such as Microsoft produce products, such as its computer operating system, that are truly global: Microsoft has been the subject of competition law investigations in several jurisdictions, including the US and the EC. International mergers, for example between car manufacturers, aluminium producers or telecommunications companies, may produce effects in a multitude of countries, and may be subject to notification to a large number of different competition authorities[4]. It is now common practice for competition authorities to cooperate closely with one another when they are conducting investigations that have an international dimension[5].

Until relatively recently the international component of competition law was predominantly concerned with the question of whether one country could apply its competition rules extraterritorially against an undertaking or undertakings in another country, where the latter behave in an anti-competitive manner having adverse effects in the territory of the former; and whether there should be laws (so-called 'blocking statutes') to prevent the 'excessive' assertion of extraterritorial jurisdiction. These issues are considered in sections 2 to 6 of this chapter. However the international dimension of competition law has undoubtedly evolved beyond these somewhat parochial concerns: for the future the interesting question will be how to develop an international system that can address the competition policy issues that arise from the globalisation of markets. A new competition law architecture is needed to deal with this phenomenon: this will be discussed briefly in section 7 of this chapter.

2. EXTRATERRITORIALITY: THEORY

The limits upon a State's jurisdictional competence – and therefore upon its ability to apply its competition laws to overseas undertakings – are matters of public international law[6]. There are two elements to a State's jurisdictional competence. First, a State has jurisdiction to make laws, that is to say to 'lay down general or individual rules through its legislative, executive or judicial bodies'[7]: this is known variously as a State's

---

Commission *Antitrust Enforcement Guidelines for International Operations* (April 1995), para 3.31: these *Guidelines* can be accessed on the Department of Justice's website at www.usdoj.gov/atr/public/guidelines/internat.htm; note also the position in the US on foreign sovereign compulsion, ibid, para 3.32, and the Act of State doctrine, ibid, para 3.33.

[3] See ch 13, pp 502–504.   [4] See ch 20, pp 801–802.

[5] On international cooperation see pp 490–495 below.

[6] For a general account of the relevant principles of public international law see Brownlie *Principles of Public International Law* (Clarendon Press, 6th ed, 2003), ch XV; see also Mann 'The Doctrine of Jurisdiction in International Law' 111 RDC (1964) 9; Akehurst 'Jurisdiction in International Law' (1972–73) 46 British Yearbook of International Law 145; Mann 'The Doctrine of International Jurisdiction Revisited' 186 RDC (1984) 18; Rosenthal and Knighton *National Laws and International Commerce: the Problem of Extraterritoriality* (1982); Lowe *Extraterritorial Jurisdiction* (1983); Olmstead *Extraterritorial Application of Laws and Responses Thereto* (1984).

[7] Per Advocate General Darmon in Cases 114/85 etc *A Ahlström Oy v Commission* (the *Wood Pulp* case) [1988] ECR 5193, p 5217, [1988] 4 CMLR 901, p 923.

legislative, prescriptive or subject-matter jurisdiction. Secondly, a State has jurisdiction to enforce its laws, that is 'the power of a State to give effect to a general rule or an individual decision by means of substantive implementing measures which may include even coercion by the authorities'[8]: this is known as a State's enforcement jurisdiction. It is not necessarily the case that the limits of subject-matter and enforcement jurisdiction should be the same: they do not have to be coextensive. An assertion of subject-matter jurisdiction by one State over natural or legal persons in another may not lead to a conflict at all, provided that the former does not seek to enforce its law in the territory of another State. However when a State goes further and seeks enforcement – for example by serving a writ on a person located in another State or demanding the production of evidence there – the possibility of conflict is obvious. Most of the controversial conflicts between States in these matters have concerned enforcement rather than subject-matter jurisdiction, and it is essentially against enforcement measures that States have adopted blocking statutes[9]. An issue that has arisen relatively recently in the US is whether it is possible to apply its competition law (or 'antitrust law') extraterritorially as a way of gaining access to foreign markets[10].

(A) Subject-matter jurisdiction

As far as subject-matter jurisdiction is concerned, it is generally accepted in public international law that a State has power to make laws affecting conduct within its territory (the 'territoriality principle') and to regulate the behaviour of its citizens abroad, citizens for this purpose including companies incorporated under its law (the 'nationality principle'). The territoriality principle has been extended in a logical way so that a State is recognised as having jurisdiction not only where acts originate in its territory (known as 'subjective territoriality'), but also where the objectionable conduct originates abroad but is completed within its territory ('objective territoriality'). The classic textbook illustration is of a shot being fired across a national boundary: although part of the conduct happened outside the State, it will have jurisdiction as the harmful event occurred within it. A consequence of this is that more than one State may assert jurisdiction in the same matter where the conduct in question straddles national borders. What is controversial is whether, in the area of economic law, it is legitimate to apply the idea of objective territoriality to the *effects* of an agreement entered into, or an anti-competitive act committed in another State.

For the purpose of subject-matter jurisdiction the territoriality and nationality principles are sufficient to comprehend a great number of infringements of competition law, either because the overseas undertaking will have committed some act – for example taking over a competitor or charging predatory prices – within the territory of the State concerned to apply its law, or because an agreement will have been made between a foreign undertaking and a firm established within the State in question. Alternatively it may be that an act has been committed within that State by a subsidiary company of an overseas parent. In this case the question arises whether it is legitimate to treat the two companies as being in reality one economic entity, so that the conduct of the subsidiary can be considered to be that of the parent. If so the territoriality principle will suffice to establish jurisdiction over the parent company. The economic entity approach is a significant feature of EC law[11].

---

[8] Ibid. [9] See pp 487–489 below. [10] See pp 477–478 below. [11] See pp 478–479 below.

However even the objective territoriality principle and the economic entity theory may not be sufficient to account for all cases in which a State may wish to assume jurisdiction over foreign undertakings. For example if all the producers of widgets in Japan were to agree not to export widgets to the UK, their agreement could obviously produce commercial effects in the UK; however it is hard to see how it can be meaningfully said that there is any conduct there. The controversial public international law question is whether a State may assert subject-matter jurisdiction simply on the basis that foreign undertakings produce commercial effects within its territory, even though they are not present there and have not committed any act there. The traditional principles of public international law are inadequate to deal with these issues, since they were developed with physical rather than economic conduct in mind. As a matter of logic, it does not seem absurd to suggest that harmful economic effects as well as physical ones emanating from another State ought in some cases to establish jurisdiction: it is not difficult to see the analogy between a shot being fired across the border of one State into a neighbouring one and a conspiracy by firms in one State to charge fixed and excessive prices or to boycott customers in another one. However some commentators reject the notion of jurisdiction based on effects alone, and the Government of the UK has consistently objected to the idea[12].

(B) Enforcement jurisdiction

Enforcement jurisdiction tends to give rise to the most acute conflicts between States[13]. It is generally recognised that even if subject-matter jurisdiction exists in relation to the conduct of someone in another State, it is improper to attempt to enforce the law in question within that State's territory without its permission. For these purposes enforcement does not mean only the exaction of penalties and the making of final orders such as perpetual injunctions, but refers to all authoritative acts such as the service of a summons, a demand for information or carrying out an investigation. Gathering information can be a particular problem for competition authorities: as business becomes increasingly global, the likelihood of a national authority requiring information which is located outside its jurisdiction increases correspondingly. A problem is that jurisdictional rules developed in the nineteenth century are not particularly well-suited to the business context or the information technology of the twenty-first century.

Many legal systems contain provisions whereby States assist one another in relation to these matters. For example the Hague Convention on the Taking of Evidence Abroad[14] provides for one State to assist another in the gathering of evidence: this Convention is given effect in UK law by the Evidence (Proceedings in Other Jurisdictions) Act 1975. The recognition and enforcement of foreign judgments is an important part of private international law: most foreign judgments can be enforced in the UK[15], though not where they are penal[16]. However cooperation on evidence and the enforcement of

---

[12] See Jennings 'Extraterritorial Jurisdiction and the United States Antitrust Laws' (1957) 33 British Yearbook of International Law 146; Higgins 'The Legal Bases of Jurisdiction' in Olmstead *Extraterritorial Application of Laws and Responses Thereto* (1984); *Lowe* pp 138–186; on the UK's position, see further p 484 below.

[13] See *Brownlie*, pp 310–312.   [14] Cmnd 3991 (1968).

[15] See Dicey and Morris *The Conflict of Laws* (Sweet & Maxwell, 14th ed, 2006), ch 15.

[16] Treble damage awards in the US are probably penal: *British Airways Board v Laker Airways Ltd* [1984] QB 142 at 16t3 and , in the CA, at 201 see also the Protection of Trading Interests Act 1980, s 5, which introduced a statutory prohibition on the enforcement of awards of multiple damages: pp 487–489 below.

judgments is often not provided by one State to another where the former takes exception to an attempt by the latter to assert its law extraterritorially, and most legal systems contain restrictions on the divulging by competition authorities of confidential information. Negotiations took place between the UK and the US for relaxation of these rules in so far as this might assist the pursuit of cartels; this led to an extension of the scope of the UK/US Mutual Assistance Treaty to criminal infringements of competition law[17]; requests for mutual assistance in criminal matters are the responsibility of the Home Office[18].

Part 9 of the Enterprise Act 2002 consolidates and codifies the powers of the Office of Fair Trading ('the OFT') to disclose information to overseas public authorities for the purpose (*inter alia*) of civil and criminal competition law investigations. Section 237 of the Act imposes a general restriction on the disclosure of information; however section 243 sets out circumstances in which, subject to conditions[19], information can be disclosed to an overseas competition authority. Information gathered by the OFT during a merger or market investigation cannot be disclosed[20], and the Secretary of State has power in certain circumstances to direct that information should not be disclosed[21].

3. THE EXTRATERRITORIAL APPLICATION OF US COMPETITION LAW

(A) The *Alcoa* and *Hartford Fire Insurance* cases

As has been mentioned, it is not clear that public international law permits jurisdiction to be taken on the basis of effects alone. However US law has undoubtedly embraced the 'effects doctrine'. In *United States v Aluminium Co of America*[22] (*Alcoa*) Judge Learned Hand said that:

it is settled law...that any State may impose liabilities, even upon persons not within its allegiance, for conduct outside its borders which has consequences within its borders which the State reprehends; and these liabilities other States will ordinarily recognise[23].

The US courts had not always accepted this view[24]; the statement may not have been necessary to the case[25]; and as formulated the doctrine was extremely wide. However *Alcoa* was of seminal importance and triggered off much controversy between the US and other countries. Section 6a of the Foreign Trade Antitrust Amendment Act 1982

---

[17] See *UK/US Mutual Legal Assistance Treaty* Cm 5375 (2001), accessible at www.fco.gov.uk; the UK is in negotiation with Australia, Canada and New Zealand with a view to signing memoranda of mutual assistance in respect of competition and consumer protection enforcement: see *The overseas disclosure of information*, OFT consultation paper 507, April 2003, para 4.26.

[18] For further information see the *Mutual Legal Assistance Guidelines: Obtaining assistance in the UK and Overseas* (5th ed, 2007), available at www.police.homeoffice.gov.uk/docs/news-and-publications.pdf.

[19] See in particular ss 243(6) and 244 of the Enterprise Act 2002.   [20] Ibid, s 243(3)(d).

[21] Ibid, s 243(4).   [22] 148 F 2d 416 (2nd Cir 1945).   [23] 148 F 2d 416, p 444.

[24] See eg *American Banana Co v United Fruit Co* 213 US 347 (1909) in which the Supreme Court held that the Sherman Act did not apply to activities outside the US.

[25] It is arguable that there was conduct within the US since one of the firms involved in the alleged conspiracy, Aluminium Ltd of Canada, had its effective business headquarters in New York and was in the same group as the Aluminium Company of America.

provides that the Sherman Act shall not apply to conduct involving trade or commerce with foreign nations unless such conduct has a 'direct, substantial and foreseeable effect' on trade or commerce in the US. The most recent Supreme Court judgment on extra-territoriality is *Hartford Fire Insurance Co v California*[26], where the Court repeated that jurisdiction could be taken over 'foreign conduct that was meant to produce and did in fact produce some substantial effect in the United States'. The joint Department of Justice/Federal Trade Commission *Antitrust Enforcement Guidelines for International Operations* ('the DoJ/FTC *International Guidelines*') of 1995[27] explain, by reference to a series of illustrative examples, how those enforcement agencies interpret the jurisdictional scope of US antitrust law in the light of these, and other, judgments.

An issue that has recently been litigated is whether a foreign plaintiff can sue for damages in a US court, even though the harm it suffered occurred outside the US. For plaintiffs this is an attractive prospect, given that, firstly, damages actions in competition law are under-developed in most legal systems of the world whereas, secondly, they are well-established in the US, where damages can be trebled, contingency fees can be negotiated with legal advisers, and unsuccessful plaintiffs do not have to pay the costs of successful defendants[28]. The question of access to US courts reached the Supreme Court in a case arising from the *Vitamins* cartel, *Hoffmann-La Roche v Empagran SA*[29]. The Court had to consider the application of the Foreign Trade Antitrust Amendment Act 1982, and concluded that, as the plaintiffs had suffered harm not in the US but in Ukraine, Panama, Australia and Ecuador, they could not sue in the US; the US Court of Appeals for the District of Columbia subsequently concluded that the foreign plaintiffs could not recover damages in the US[30]. The Court was sensitive to the argument that over-exposure to treble damages claims in the US on the part of non-US plaintiffs might amount to a serious deterrent to members of cartels, for example in Europe or East Asia, making a whistleblowing application to local competition authorities: Germany, Canada and the US enforcement authorities had all submitted *amicus curiae* briefs, pointing out this danger to the Court. However an important feature of the Supreme Court judgment in *Empagran* is to note that it left open the question of whether the foreign plantiffs could sue in the US if the foreign injury that they had suffered was inseparable from the domestic harm caused by the cartel to customers in the US[31].

---

[26] 509 US 764 (1993); for comment on this case see Roth 'Jurisdiction, British Public Policy and the US Supreme Court' (1994) 110 LQR 194; Robertson and Demetriou 'The Extraterritorial Application of US Antitrust Laws in the US Supreme Court' (1994) 43 ICLQ 417; also, by the same authors, 'US Extraterritorial Jurisdiction in Antitrust Matters: Recent Developments' (1995) 16 ECLR 461; Trenor 'Jurisdiction and the Extraterritorial Application of Antitrust Laws after *Hartford Fire*' (1995) 62 University of Chicago Law Review 1582; Waller 'From the Ashes of *Hartford Fire*: The Unanswered Questions of Comity' [1998] Fordham Corporate Law Institute (ed Hawk), ch 3; see also *United States v Nippon Paper* 109 F 3d 1 (1st Cir, 1997), for comment on which see Reynolds, Sicilian and Wellman 'The Extraterritorial Application of the US Antitrust Laws to Criminal Conspiracies' (1998) 19 ECLR 151.

[27] See p 470, n 2 above; for commentary on the Guidelines see Griffin *US International Antitrust Enforcement: A Practical Guide to the Agencies' Guidelines* (Bureau of National Affairs, 1996).

[28] See generally ch 8 on the private enforcement of competition law.

[29] 544 US 155, (2004); for comment see Wurmnest 'Foreign Private Plaintiffs, Global Conspiracies, and the Extraterritorial Application of U.S. Antitrust Law' (2005) 28(2) Hastings International and Comparative Law Review 205.

[30] *Empagran SA v Hoffmann-La Roche Ltd* 417 F.3d 1267 (D.C. Cir., 2005); see similarly *Emerson Electric Co v Le Carbone Lorraine SA* 500 F.Supp. 2d 437 (2007).

[31] For a finding that the domestic and foreign injuries were indivisible, so that a foreign plaintiff could sue in the US, see *In re Monosodium Glutamate antitrust Litigation* [2005] WL 1080790 (D. Minn, 2 May 2005).

(B) Comity

Some US courts, drawing on the principle of judicial comity, have attempted to apply the effects doctrine in a relatively restrictive way, requiring not only that there should be a direct and substantial effect within the US, but also that the respective interests of the United States in asserting jurisdiction and of other States which might be offended by such assertion should be weighed against one another[32]. The origins of this approach can be traced back to Brewster's *Antitrust and American Business Abroad* in 1958 in which he called for a 'jurisdictional rule of reason'. The DoJ/FTC *International Guidelines* set out various factors relevant to comity analysis, including:

- the relative significance to the alleged violation of conduct within the US, as compared to conduct abroad
- the nationality of the persons involved or affected by the conduct; the presence or absence of an intention to affect US consumers, markets or exporters
- the relative significance and foreseeability of the effects on the US compared to the effects abroad
- the existence of reasonable expectations that would be furthered or defeated by the action
- the degree of conflict with foreign law or articulated foreign economic policies
- the extent to which the enforcement activities of another country may be affected
- the effectiveness of foreign as opposed to US enforcement[33].

Dealing with the problem of conflicts of jurisdiction by resort to the criterion of reasonableness has its critics, not least because a court hardly seems an appropriate forum in which to carry out such a delicate balancing process[34]. The principle of comity, however, is an important one which has been recognised by the European Court of First Instance ('the CFI') in *Gencor v Commission*[35] and in the dedicated cooperation agreements that the EU has entered into with the US, Canada and Japan[36].

(C) Extraterritorial application of US antitrust law

The competition authorities in the US have had little compunction about enforcing their antitrust laws against overseas companies and have sometimes demanded, for example, that commercial documents located abroad should be handed over; the courts have even issued final orders requiring that foreign companies should change their commercial practices or restructure their industry[37]. An example of extraterritorial action in the US in relation to a foreign merger arose in the case of *Institut Mérieux*[38], where the Federal

---

[32] See *Timberlane Lumber Co v Bank of America* 549 F 2d 597 (9th Cir, 1976) and *Mannington Mills v Congoleum Corpn* 595 F 2d 1287 (3rd Cir 1979); for an account of this development see Fox 'Reasonableness and Extraterritoriality' [1986] Fordham Corporate Law Institute (ed Hawk), p 49.

[33] See the International Guidelines, para 3.2.

[34] See Judge Wilkey in *Laker Airways Ltd v Sabena* 731 F 2d 909 at 945–952 (DC Cir, 1984), [1984] ECC 485; Rosenthal and Knighton *National Laws and International Commerce: the Problem of Extraterritoriality* (1982); Mann 'The Doctrine of International Jurisdiction Revisited After Twenty Years' 186 RDC (1984) 19.

[35] Case T-102/96 [1999] ECR II-753, [1999] 4 CMLR 971: see pp 483–484 below.

[36] See pp 493–495 below.

[37] See eg *United States v Imperial Chemical Industries Ltd* 105 F Supp 215 (SDNY 1952) where the US court ordered ICI to refrain from relying upon its patent rights under UK law: for the response, and other examples of the extraterritorial assertion of US law, see pp 487–489 below.

[38] 55 Fed Reg 1614 (1990).

Trade Commission took action in respect of the acquisition by Institut Mérieux, a French company, of Connaught BioSciences, a Canadian company, because of perceived detriments to competition in the US in the market for anti-rabies vaccines[39].

The International Antitrust Enforcement Assistance Act 1994[40] is intended to improve the ability of the US enforcement agencies to obtain evidence located abroad by providing for reciprocal agreements to be entered between the US and other countries to facilitate the exchange of information, including confidential information. It is relevant also to note that US law makes certain antitrust offences criminal, and that it is possible for individuals to be sentenced to terms of imprisonment. This explains why the executives of some companies have a policy of not visiting the US at all, and why the same executives earnestly hope that aeroplanes will not be diverted for operational reasons to US airports. There have been recent examples of foreign executives being required to serve terms of imprisonment in the US for violations of the antitrust rules[41].

(D) The extraterritorial application of US competition law to gain access to foreign markets

The antitrust laws in the US are applied not only to extraterritorial behaviour that affects imports into the US. Jurisdiction may also be asserted where US companies are obstructed by anti-competitive behaviour in their attempts to gain access to foreign markets. The so-called 'Structural Impediments Initiative'[42] in the US identified the lax enforcement of the Japanese Anti-Monopoly Act against Japanese undertakings as a contributing factor to the difficulties of US firms in expanding into Japanese markets; the Japanese Large Scale Retail Stores Act was considered to be an additional obstacle to would-be importers. The Department of Justice threatened to apply the US antitrust rules against Japanese restrictive practices having the effect of excluding US exporters from Japanese markets[43]. Subsequently the Japanese Government substantially increased the penalties that can be imposed for infringement of the Japanese legislation[44]. The first case in which the US challenged conduct abroad that denied foreign access was in the case of *United States v Pilkington*[45]: the case was settled through

[39] See Owen and Parisi 'International Mergers and Joint Ventures: a Federal Trade Commission Perspective' in [1990] Fordham Corporate Law Institute (ed Hawk), ch 1 at pp 5–14.
[40] 15 USC §§ 6201–6212 (Supp 1995).   [41] See ch 13, p 501 n 18.
[42] See Anwar 'The Impact of the Structural Impediments Initiative on US–Japan Trade' (1992–93) 16(2) World Competition 53; see also the dispute between Eastman-Kodak and Fuji, which ended up as a complaint by the US to the disputes settlement body of the World Trade Organisation, noted by Furse 'Competition Law and the WTO Report: "Japan – Measures Affecting Consumer Photographic Film and Paper"' (1999) 20 ECLR 9.
[43] See the Department of Justice's *Antitrust Enforcement Policy Regarding Anticompetitive Conduct that Restricts US Exports* 3 April 1992; see also Rill 'International Antitrust Policy – A Justice Department Perspective' in [1991] Fordham Corporate Law Institute (ed Hawk), pp 29–43; Coppel 'A Question of Keiretsu: Extending the Long Arm of US Antitrust' (1992) 13 ECLR 192; Ohara 'The New US Policy on the Extraterritorial Application of Antitrust Laws, and Japan's Response' (1993–94) 17(3) World Competition 49; Davidow 'Application of US Antitrust Laws to *Keiretsu* Practices' (1994–95) 18(1) World Competition 5; Yamane and Seryo 'Restrictive Practices and Market Access in Japan – Has the JFTC been Effective in Eliminating Barriers in Distribution?' (1999) 22(2) World Competition 1.
[44] See Yamada 'Recent Developments of Competition Law and Policy in Japan' [1997] Fordham Corporate Law Institute (ed Hawk), ch 5.
[45] (1994–2) Trade Cases (CCH) ¶ 70,482 (1994); for comment see Byowitz 'The Unilateral Use of US Antitrust Laws to Achieve Foreign Market Access: A Pragmatic Assessment' [1996] Fordham Corporate Law Institute (ed Hawk), ch 3.

a consent decree whereby Pilkington agreed not to enforce certain provisions in tech-nology licences against US undertakings. The enforcement agencies in the US may also take action against foreign cartels that have no effect within the US, but that raise prices in relation to transactions where the US Government contributes more than half the funding[46].

4. THE EXTRATERRITORIAL APPLICATION OF EC COMPETITION LAW[47]

Many non-EC undertakings have been held to have infringed the EC competition rules. The ECJ has not yet ruled specifically whether there is an effects doctrine under EC law, since it has always been possible in cases under Articles 81 and 82 to base jurisdiction on some other ground, such as the economic entity doctrine or the fact that an agreement entered into outside the Community was implemented within it. In both the *Dyestuffs*[48] and *Wood Pulp*[49] cases the question of whether EC law should recognise the effects doctrine was argued at length, but the ECJ was able to avoid a pronouncement upon the issue since jurisdiction could be taken on other bases. The EC Merger Regulation ('the ECMR') has often been applied to mergers outside the Community; the CFI has given an important judgment on the territorial application of the ECMR in *Gencor v Commission*[50], but again without explicitly adopting the effects doctrine[51]. This section will deal with subject-matter and enforcement jurisdiction under Articles 81 and 82, and will then discuss the position under the ECMR.

(A) Subject-matter jurisdiction

Articles 81 and 82 apply only to the extent that an agreement or abuse has an effect upon inter-state trade. However there is no reason in principle why, for example, conduct by a US firm might not satisfy this test, particularly given the liberal way in which it has been applied[52]. In *Javico v Yves St Laurent*[53] the ECJ held that it was possible that an export ban imposed upon distributors in the Ukraine and Russia could infringe Article 81(1).

(i) The economic entity doctrine

In the *Dyestuffs* case[54] the ECJ developed the economic entity doctrine. The Court came to the conclusion that Geigy, Sandoz and ICI, three non-EC undertakings, had participated in illegal price fixing within the EC through the medium of subsidiary

---

[46] See the DOJ's Press Release of 18 August 2000 in relation to a construction cartel in Egypt.

[47] See Allen 'The Development of EC Antitrust Jurisdiction over Alien Undertakings' [1974] 2 LIEI 35; Kuyper 'European Community Law and Extraterritoriality: Some Trends and Recent Developments' (1984) 33 ICLQ 1013; Slot and Grabandt 'Extraterritoriality and Jurisdiction' (1986) 23 CML Rev 544; Brittan 'Jurisdictional Issues in EC Competition Policy' in *Merger Control in the Single European Market* (Grotius Publications, 1991).

[48] Cases 48/69 etc *ICI v Commission* [1972] ECR 619, [1972] CMLR 557.

[49] Cases 114/85 etc *A Ahlström Oy v Commission* [1988] ECR 5193, [1988] 4 CMLR 901.

[50] Case T-102/96 [1999] ECR II-753, [1999] 4 CMLR 971.   [51] See pp 482–484 below.

[52] See ch 3, pp 142–146.   [53] Case C-306/96 [1998] ECR I-1983, [1998] 5 CMLR 172.

[54] See n 48 above.

companies located in the EC but under the control of non-EC parents. The ECJ was willing to go beyond the legal façade of the separate legal personalities of the parent and subsidiary companies, and to say that in reality each parent and subsidiary formed one economic entity. This approach was criticised, not only because of the refusal to respect the independent legal personalities of the companies concerned, but also because the ECJ seemed prepared to hold that a parent controlled its subsidiary on limited evidence[55]; however the economic entity doctrine is now undoubtedly a part of EC competition law. The Community Courts and the Commission have relied on the economic entity approach on a number of subsequent occasions, both in the subject-matter and enforcement jurisdiction contexts[56]. The crucial issue is whether the parent controls the subsidiary, for which purpose the size of the shareholding, the representation on the board of directors of the subsidiary, the ability to influence the latter's affairs and actual evidence of attempts to do so will all be relevant[57]. A consequence of the economic entity doctrine is that a claimant may be able to bring an action in the English courts against a UK subsidiary of a foreign parent that participated in an illegal agreement contrary to Article 81 of the Treaty[58].

(ii) Does EC law recognise the effects doctrine?

Many of the Commission's decisions have involved and been addressed to non-EC undertakings[59], but in every case the non-EC firm, either itself or through a subsidiary company[60], entered into an agreement with an EC undertaking[61] or committed some act within the EC. In other words jurisdiction in these cases did not depend upon the existence in Community law of an effects doctrine, since it could be explained in more orthodox ways. The Commission has quite often asserted that Community law does indeed recognise the effects doctrine[62], and this belief was supported by Advocate General Mayras in the *Dyestuffs* case[63] and by Advocate General Darmon in *Wood Pulp*[64]; other Advocates General have also appeared to support this view[65]. However there has been no definitive statement from the ECJ on this issue.

[55] On *Dyestuffs* see Mann 'The Dyestuffs Case in the Court of Justice of the European Communities' (1973) 22 ICLQ 35; Acevedo 'The EC Dyestuffs Case: Territorial Jurisdiction' (1973) 36 MLR 317.

[56] The doctrine may be used to overcome any perceived difficulty in sending a decision to a company in a non-EC State by serving it instead on the EC subsidiary.

[57] See ch 3, pp 91–95.

[58] See *Provimi Ltd v Aventi Animal Nutrition SA* [2003] EWHC 961 (Comm), [2003] All ER (D) 59 (May).

[59] See eg *Genuine Vegetable Parchments Association* OJ [1978] L 70/54, [1978] 1 CMLR 534; *Zinc Producer Group* OJ [1984] L 220/27, [1985] 2 CMLR 108; *Associated Lead Manufacturers* OJ [1979] L 21/16, [1979] 1 CMLR 464; *Cast Iron and Steel Rolls* OJ [1983] L 317/1, [1984] 1 CMLR 694; in each of these cases a non-EC firm was fined.

[60] See eg *Johnson and Johnson* OJ [1980] L 377/16, [1981] 2 CMLR 287.

[61] See eg *French-Japanese Ballbearings* OJ [1974] L 343/19, [1975] 1 CMLR D8; *Franco-Taiwanese Mushroom Packers* OJ [1975] L 29/26, [1975] 1 CMLR D83.

[62] See eg the Commission's XIth *Report on Competition Policy* (1981), points 34–42; the Commission's decisions in *Wood Pulp* OJ [1985] L 85/1, [1985] 3 CMLR 474 and *Aluminium Products* OJ [1985] L 92/1, [1987] 3 CMLR 813 were explicitly adopted on the basis of the effects doctrine.

[63] Cases 48/69 etc [1972] ECR 619, pp 687–694, [1972] CMLR 557, pp 593–609.

[64] Cases 114/85 etc *A Ahlström Oy v Commission* [1988] ECR 5193, p 5227, [1988] 4 CMLR 901, p 932.

[65] See eg Advocate General Roemer in Case 6/72 *Continental Can v Commission* [1973] ECR 215, [1972] CMLR 690; Advocate General Warner in Cases 6/73, 7/73 *Commercial Solvents v Commission* [1974] ECR 223, [1974] 1 CMLR 309.

(iii) The ECJ's judgment in *Wood Pulp*

Against this background the appeal to the ECJ against the Commission's decision in *Wood Pulp*[66] was eagerly awaited. The Commission, in finding that there was a concerted practice between undertakings in several non-EC countries, had held that jurisdiction could be based on the effects of the concerted practice in the EC. However the ECJ, no doubt keen to avoid the adoption of this controversial doctrine if possible, concluded that the case could be settled by reference to conventional public international law criteria. It held[67] that, on the facts of the case, the agreement had been *implemented* within the EC; it was immaterial for this purpose whether this implementation was effected by subsidiaries, agents, sub-agents or branches within the Community. Since the agreement was implemented within the Community, it was unnecessary to have recourse to the effects doctrine: the universally recognised territoriality principle was sufficient to deal with the matter. The Commission expressly cited the *Wood Pulp* judgment in *Amino Acids*, where it imposed fines on a cartel including US, Japanese and Korean companies[68]. The ECJ in *Wood Pulp* did not comment on what the position would have been if the agreement had been formed *and implemented* outside the EC, but had produced economic effects within it; an example would be a collective boycott by members of a non-EC cartel, whereby they refuse to supply customers within the EC: could one argue in such circumstances that this agreement is 'implemented' within the EC by the refusal to supply there? Linguistically this seems hard to sustain; however there is no doubt in this situation that the *effects* of the agreement would be felt within the EC. This issue is unresolved[69]. However there will be relatively few cases in which the pure effects doctrine is crucial in jurisdictional terms: in most cases the economic entity doctrine or the reasoning of the ECJ in *Wood Pulp* will be sufficient to establish jurisdiction. In its decision on *Gas insulated switchgear*[70] the Commission imposed fines of €750 million on a number of European and Japanese undertakings for bid rigging and related practices in relation to switchgear: in essence, the European undertakings would stay out of the Asian market and the Japanese undertakings would not operate in Europe. The Commission reached the conclusion that Article 81 was infringed without resorting to the effects doctrine.

---

[66] OJ [1985] L 85/1, [1985] 3 CMLR 474.

[67] Cases 114/85 etc *A Ahlström Oy v Commission* [1988] ECR 5193, [1988] 4 CMLR 901, paras 11–23; for comment see Ferry 'Towards Completing the Charm: the *Wood Pulp* Judgment' (1989) 11 EIPR 19; Mann 'The Public International Law of Restrictive Trade Practices in the European Court of Justice' (1989) 38 ICLQ 375; Lowe 'International Law and the Effects Doctrine in the European Court of Justice' (1989) 48 CLJ 9; Christoforou and Rockwell 'EC Law: the Territorial Scope of Application of EC Antitrust Law – the *Wood Pulp* Judgment' (1989) 30 Harvard International Law Journal 195; Lange and Sandage 'The *Wood Pulp* Decision and its Implications for the Scope of EC Competition Law' (1989) 26 CML Rev 137; Van Gerven 'EC Jurisdiction in Antitrust Matters: the *Wood Pulp* Judgment' [1989] Fordham Corporate Law Institute (ed Hawk), ch 21.

[68] OJ [2001] L 152/24, [2001] 5 CMLR 322, para 182.

[69] The Commission's *Guidelines on the effect on trade concept contained in Articles 81 and 82 of the Treaty*, OJ [2004] C 101/7, cite the *Gencor* case, discussed under the ECMR below, as authority for the effects doctrine, but this is a questionable interpretation of that judgment.

[70] Commission decision of 24 January 2007.

(B) Enforcement jurisdiction

(i) Initiating proceedings

Where proceedings are started by the Commission under Articles 81 or 82, Article 2(2) of Regulation 773/2004[71] requires that the undertakings concerned must be informed. If the undertaking cannot be served within the EC, the question arises whether a statement of objections may be sent to it abroad. As suggested above this could be considered to contravene public international law, since it amounts to an enforcement of one State's law in the territory of another[72]. However the ECJ has rejected the notion that service without the consent of the foreign State is invalid and vitiates the proceedings. Provided that the non-EC undertaking has received the statement in circumstances which enabled it to take cognisance of the objections held against it, the service is valid. In *Geigy v Commission*[73] the Commission sent its statement of objections to Geigy's Swiss offices. Geigy returned it, acting on instructions from the Swiss authorities, claiming that the service was unlawful both under internal and public international law. The ECJ rejected this. It is sufficient for Community law purposes, therefore, for the Commission to send a registered letter to the non-EC undertaking concerned.

(ii) Information and investigations

The ECJ has not been called upon to consider the extent to which the Commission may require information from or conduct investigations of undertakings abroad under Articles 18 and 20 respectively of Regulation 1/2003[74]. There would seem to be little objection to the Commission simply asking for information under Article 18(2), there being no compulsion to comply with such a request; in practice the Commission does send Article 18(2) requests to non-EC undertakings. It is less certain whether the Commission can make a demand for information under Article 18(3) of the Regulation, and the better view is that this is not possible. Whether the Commission is entitled to compel an EU subsidiary to produce documents of a legal entity located outside the EU is the subject of an appeal pending before the CFI[75].

It is inconceivable that Article 20 entitles the Commission to carry out an investigation abroad unless it has the authority of the State concerned. However the fact that the Commission intends to investigate a trade association within the EC which represents non-EC undertakings does not entitle that association to refuse to submit to the investigation[76]; and if the Commission carries out an investigation in a new Member State of the EC and discovers information relating to infringements carried out by undertak-

---

[71] OJ [2004] L 123/18.

[72] It is arguable that the *initiation* of proceedings is not an issue of enforcement, as it is not in itself a coercive act.

[73] See Case 52/69 [1972] ECR 787, [1972] CMLR 557 (one of the *Dyestuffs* cases).

[74] OJ [2003] L 1/1, [2003] 4 CMLR 551: on the conduct of investigations see ch 7, pp 264–272; in Case 27/76 *United Brands Continental BV v Commission* [1978] ECR 207, [1978] 1 CMLR 429 the ECJ suggested at one point that the Commission might have obtained some information which it needed from United Brands; however United Brands had subsidiaries within the EC, so that it cannot be deduced from this remark that the ECJ was advocating extraterritorial requests for information under Article 11(3) of Regulation 17, the predecessor of Regulation 1/2003.

[75] Case T-140/7 *Chi Mei Optoelectronics Europe v Commission*, not yet decided.

[76] *Ukwal* OJ [1992] L 121/45 [1993] 5 CMLR 632.

ings prior to that State's accession to the Community, the Commission is entitled to take that information into account[77]. The Commission will not be sympathetic to the argument that a non-EC undertaking is unable to provide it with information because of some constraint imposed upon it by its domestic law[78].

(iii) Final decisions

Two issues arise. First, there is the problem of whether a final decision, for example finding an infringement of the competition rules and imposing penalties, may be served on non-EC undertakings. This is more an act of enforcement than merely serving a statement of objections, and so is more open to objection in terms of public international law. For this reason the Commission will often look to serve the decision on a subsidiary within the EC, as it did in the *Dyestuffs* cases, or seek the assistance of the foreign State concerned[79]. However the ECJ has held that service direct upon the non-EC undertaking is valid provided that, as in the case of a statement of objections, it reaches the undertaking and enables it to take cognisance of it; it is no defence that the undertaking received the decision and sent it back without reading it[80].

The second problem is whether it is possible for the final decision to include orders against and impose penalties upon an overseas undertaking. It is clear that the ECJ does not object to orders being made against foreign undertakings[81], although it is recognised by both the Commission and the Community Courts that it would not be possible actually to enforce the order in the territory of a foreign State. It would however be possible to seize any assets that were present within the EC.

(C) EC Merger Regulation

(i) The jurisdictional criteria in the ECMR

Under Article 1(2) of the ECMR[82] concentrations that have a Community dimension must be pre-notified to the Commission in Brussels. Concentrations have a Community dimension where the combined turnover of the undertakings involved exceeds €5,000 million worldwide, provided that at least two of the undertakings have a turnover within the Community of at least €250 million and that their business is not primarily within one and the same Member State[83]; Article 1(3) of the ECMR contains an alternative set of jurisdictional criteria in an attempt to deal with the problem of multiple

---

[77] Case 97–99/87 *Dow Chemical Ibérica SA v Commission* [1989] ECR 3165, [1991] 4 CMLR 410, paras 61–65.

[78] See *Centraal Stikstof Verkoopkantoor (CSV)* OJ [1976] L 192/27.

[79] In the *Dyestuffs* cases the Commission tried in the first place to serve the final decision on the non-EC undertakings by using diplomatic channels; only when this failed did it serve the EC subsidiaries.

[80] See Case 6/72 *Europemballage and Continental Can v Commission* [1973] ECR 215, [1973] CMLR 199.

[81] See eg Cases 6/73 & 7/73 *Commercial Solvents v Commission* [1974] ECR 223, [1974] 1 CMLR 309 where the ECJ upheld the Commission's order that supplies to Zoja be resumed; this would clearly affect CSC in the US; see also *Warner-Lambert/Gillette* OJ [1993] L 116/21, [1993] 5 CMLR 559, where the Commission ordered the Gillette Company of the US to reassign trade marks in third countries to Eemland Holdings NV in order to remove distortions of competition within the EC; the decision was not appealed to the CFI.

[82] See ch 21 for a general discussion of this Regulation.

[83] The thresholds are considered in detail in ch 21, pp 828–832.

notification to Member States. The jurisdictional criteria in the ECMR clearly mean that concentrations involving undertakings which conduct a substantial proportion of their business outside the EC, or which involve transactions far removed physically from the EC, may, nevertheless, have a Community dimension. Countless numbers of concentrations that have little or no effect within the Community have to be notified because of the way in which the thresholds in the ECMR operate. For example a joint venture between two substantial undertakings that brings about a merger of their widget businesses in Thailand could be notifiable under the ECMR, even though the joint venture will have no presence or effect on the EC market, if the parents exceed the turnover thresholds in Article 1. Cases such as this may, however, benefit from the simplified procedure introduced for the speedy disposal of some notifications under the ECMR in 2000[84].

(ii) *Gencor v Commission*

In *Gencor/Lonrho*[85] the Commission prohibited a merger between two South African undertakings on the basis that it would have created a dominant duopoly (collective dominance) in the platinum and rhodium markets, as a result of which effective competition would be significantly impeded in the common market. Gencor appealed to the CFI, *inter alia* on the ground that the Commission did not have jurisdiction under the ECMR to prohibit activities in South Africa which, furthermore, the Government there had approved. In *Gencor v Commission*[86] the CFI upheld the Commission's decision, and reviewed at some length the jurisdictional position[87]. The Court's findings on jurisdiction were divided into two parts, first an assessment of the territorial scope of the ECMR[88] and second a consideration of the compatibility of the Commission's decision with public international law[89]. As to the former, the CFI noted that the parties to the merger exceeded the turnover thresholds in Article 1(2) of the ECMR. It acknowledged that Recital 11 of the Regulation required that the parties should have substantial operations in the Community, but stated that these operations could as well consist of sales as production. The Court added that the *Wood Pulp* judgment, requiring 'implementation' within the Community, did not contradict the Commission's assertion of jurisdiction in this case: indeed the requirement in Article 1(2) of the ECMR, that the parties should have turnover in excess of €250 million within the Community, was consistent with the *Wood Pulp* judgment, since it meant that they must have acted in some way on the EC market.

On the issue of public international law, the CFI said that application of the ECMR is justified under public international law where it is foreseeable that a proposed concentration will have an immediate and substantial effect in the Community[90]. The Court's view was that these criteria were satisfied, but went on to consider whether the exercise of jurisdiction in this case 'violated a principle of non-interference or the principle

---

[84] See the Commission's *Notice on a simplified procedure for treatment of certain concentrations under Council Regulation (EC) No 139/2004* OJ [2005] C 56/04; this procedure is explained briefly in ch 21, pp 845–846; for discussion generally of the application of the ECMR to non-EC concentrations see Ezrachi 'Limitations on the Extraterritorial Reach of the European Merger Regulation' (2001) 22 ECLR 137.

[85] OJ [1997] L 11/30, [1999] 4 CMLR 1076.

[86] Case T-102/96 [1999] ECR II-753, [1999] 4 CMLR 971; for comment see Fox 'The Merger Regulation and Its Territorial Reach: *Gencor Ltd v Commission*' (1999) 20 ECLR 334.

[87] Case T-102/96 [1999] ECR II-753, [1999] 4 CMLR 971, paras 48–111.   [88] Ibid, paras 78–88.

[89] Ibid, paras 89–111.   [90] ibid, para 90.

of proportionality'[91]: in other words it acknowledged that comity analysis should be undertaken when applying the ECMR. The Court's view was that neither principle was violated, so that there was no jurisdictional objection to the Commission's decision.

Clearly this judgment is of considerable significance. It will be noted that the CFI did not adopt an effects doctrine as a matter of Community law, since it determined the Commission's subject-matter jurisdiction on the basis of the turnover thresholds in the ECMR and equated them to the 'implementation doctrine' in *Wood Pulp*; rather the CFI considered the effects of the merger, and the possible comity objections to jurisdiction, as a matter of public international law. As in the case of the ECJ's judgments in *Dyestuffs* and *Wood Pulp*, the CFI avoided the adoption of the effects doctrine. In practice, of course, the Commission could have great problems in enforcing a prohibition decision against non-EC undertakings which are unwilling to cooperate and which are protected by their national Governments. However the Commission works very closely with the competition authorities in other jurisdictions, and in particular with the Department of Justice and the Federal Trade Commission in the US, in order to try to prevent serious conflicts breaking out[92].

5. THE EXTRATERRITORIAL APPLICATION OF UK COMPETITION LAW

The view has always been taken in the UK that jurisdiction cannot be based simply upon commercial effects, but that the territoriality and nationality principles alone are applicable in this area. This is clearly stated in the Aide-Memoire which the UK Government submitted to the ECJ following the Commission's decision in the *Dyestuffs* litigation[93], and is further illustrated by the Protection of Trading Interests Act 1980 which is considered later in this chapter. The submissions of the UK Government in the *Wood Pulp* case maintained its traditional hostility to the effects doctrine. The competition law statutes themselves do not always deal explicitly with jurisdictional issues, but, even where they do not do so, in practice they are not applied extraterritorially on the basis of effects.

(A) Competition Act 1998

(i) Chapter I prohibition
The Chapter I prohibition in the Competition Act 1998 has been discussed in chapter 9[94]. On the issue of jurisdiction section 2(1), which sets out the Chapter I prohibition, provides

---

[91] Ibid, para 102.   [92] See further pp 493–495 below.

[93] Case 48/69 *ICI Ltd v Commission* [1972] ECR 619, [1972] CMLR 557. The Aide-Memoire is produced in full in *Lowe* pp 144–147; details are given there of various diplomatic exchanges between the US and UK Governments on jurisdictional conflicts and other expressions of the UK's views at pp 147–186; see also the UK Government's Amicus Curiae brief in *Washington Public Power Supply System v Western Nuclear Inc* [1983] ECC 261.

[94] See ch 9, pp 327–353.

that an agreement will be caught only where it may affect trade and competition within the UK. This in itself does not answer the jurisdictional issue of whether the Act is applicable to undertakings that are located outside the UK. The answer to this question is given by section 2(3), which provides that:

Subsection (1) applies only if the agreement, decision or practice is, or is intended to be, implemented in the UK.

Section 2(3) is specifically intended to give legislative effect in the UK to the 'implementation doctrine' espoused by the ECJ in the *Wood Pulp* case[95]. This is a sensible resolution on the part of the Government: as already mentioned, the *Wood Pulp* doctrine falls short of being an 'effects doctrine', with the result that section 2(3) does not amount to a reversal of the traditional attitude of the UK described above. At the same time, the 1998 Act is able to adopt a position in relation to jurisdiction which is consistent with EC law as set out in *Wood Pulp*. It follows that agreements implemented in the UK by non-UK undertakings would be caught by the Chapter I prohibition, provided that they meet all the other requirements. What would be interesting in the future would be a situation in which the ECJ extends the jurisdictional reach of the competition rules to include an effects doctrine. In such a situation the basic rule in section 60 of the Competition Act, that there should be no inconsistency between interpretation of the UK legislation and the principles laid down in the Treaty and by the Community Courts, would suggest that the UK should adopt the effects doctrine. However section 60(1) of the Act specifically provides that consistency must be achieved, 'having regard to any relevant differences between the provisions concerned'[96]. Presumably this would be a situation in which the clear wording of section 2(3) would indicate a relevant difference between the 1998 Act and the new case-law of the ECJ, with the consequence that the UK authorities would not be required under the Act to adopt the effects doctrine. An intriguing twist, following the Modernisation Regulation, would arise if the OFT was investigating a case in which Article 81 (or Article 82) was involved: presumably then it would be required to apply EC law, including the effects doctrine.

The OFT's guidelines are silent on the issue of extraterritoriality, which perhaps is itself indicative of the delicate and complex nature of this issue.

(ii) Chapter II prohibition

The Chapter II prohibition has also been discussed in chapter 9[97]. There is no mention of extraterritorial application in section 18, which sets out the Chapter II prohibition, and in particular there is no equivalent of section 2(3) which limits the ambit of the Chapter I prohibition to agreements that are implemented in the UK. Section 18(3) does require that the dominant position must be within the UK. In the debate during the passage of the Bill Lord Simon explained that this would not be the case if the market in which the dominant position is held was entirely outside the UK; however there could be a case in which the dominant position extends beyond the UK, provided that it includes some part of the UK territory[98].

An interesting question is whether the Chapter II prohibition would apply in a case where the dominant position is (wholly or partly) within the UK but the abuse occurs

---

[95] HL Committee, 13 November 1997, col 261 (Lord Simon of Highbury).
[96] See ch 9, pp 362–367.   [97] See ch 9, pp 353–362.
[98] HL Third Reading, 5 March 1998, col 1336 (Lord Simon of Highbury).

in a related market outside the UK, or its effects are felt entirely outside the UK (for example a refusal by a UK company to supply an overseas customer). Here the requirement that trade must be affected within the UK would come into play and determine whether the prohibition applies.

In *Aberdeen Journals Ltd v Office of Fair Trading*[99] the CAT held that the requirement of an effect on trade within the UK is not subject to a requirement of appreciability[100].

(B) Enterprise Act 2002

(i) Market investigations[101]

As far as subject-matter jurisdiction is concerned, the OFT may make a market investigation reference to the Competition Commission ('the CC') where it has reasonable grounds for suspecting that one or more features of a market in the United Kingdom for goods or services prevent, restrict or distort competition there or in a part of it. Section 131(6) provides that a 'market in the United Kingdom' includes a market which operates there and in another country or territory or in a part of another country or territory ('supra-national markets')[102] and any market which operates only in a part of the United Kingdom ('sub-national markets')[103]. Where the geographical market is wider than the UK, the reference to the CC would be concerned only with the UK part of it[104]. In determining whether to exercise its discretion to make a reference, the OFT will consider whether an effective remedy might be available to cure any competition problems: where the relevant market is global, or at least much wider than the UK, it may be that a remedy that applied only to the UK would have little discernible impact on the competition problem there, in which case a reference would not be made[105].

As far as enforcement jurisdiction is concerned, the OFT has power to obtain information under section 174 of the Enterprise Act 2002, and the CC has power to do so under section 176[106]. The Act is silent on the territorial scope of these provisions, as is the guidance issued by each of these bodies on market investigations[107]. It is thought to be unlikely that either the OFT or the CC would seek to exercise these powers against persons or undertakings with no presence in the UK. As far as remedies are concerned, sections 154 to 161 set out a number of possibilities, ranging from the acceptance by the OFT of undertakings in lieu of a reference to the making by the CC of final orders, using the powers provided by Schedule 8 of the Act. Again, the Act is silent as to the territorial scope of these powers, but it is assumed that they are not available extra-territorially[108].

---

[99] Case No 1009/1/1/02 [2003] CAT 11. [100] [2003] CAT 11, paras 459–461: see ch 9, pp 337–338.
[101] The market investigation provisions of the Enterprise Act 2002 are described in ch 11.
[102] Enterprise Act 2002, s 131(6)(a). [103] Ibid, s 131(6)(b).
[104] *Market investigation references: Guidance about the making of references under Part 4 of the Enterprise Act*, OFT Guideline 511, March 2006, para 4.11.
[105] Ibid, para 2.30. [106] See ch 11, p 463.
[107] *Market investigation references: Guidance about the making of references under Part 4 of the Enterprise Act*, OFT Guideline 511, March 2006; *Market Investigation References: Competition Commission Guidelines*, CC 3, June 2003.
[108] OFT Guideline 511, March 2006, para 2.30, seems to make this assumption.

(ii) Mergers[109]

As far as subject-matter jurisdiction is concerned, sections 22(1) and 33(1) of the Enterprise Act provide that merger references may be made to the CC where a relevant merger situation has been or would be created, and where that situation has resulted or would result in 'a substantial lessening of competition within any market or markets in the United Kingdom for goods or services'. As in the case of market investigations, section 22(6) provides that a 'market in the United Kingdom' includes supra-national[110] and sub-national markets[111]. Further jurisdictional requirements are that the value of the turnover of the enterprise being acquired amounts to more than £70 million in the UK[112] or that the 25 per cent 'share of supply' test is satisfied in the UK or in a substantial part of it[113].

As far as enforcement jurisdiction is concerned, section 31 of the Enterprise Act gives the OFT the power to obtain information and the CC has power to do so under section 109. The Act is silent on the extra-territorial application of these provisions and, as in the case of market investigations, it is thought that they would not be used against persons or undertakings with no presence in the UK. The remedies available in merger cases are set out in sections 71 to 95 of the Act. Section 86(1) of the Act provides that an enforcement order may extend to a person's conduct outside the United Kingdom if (and only if) he is a UK national, a body incorporated under UK law or a person carrying on business within the UK; a similar limitation is found in relation to restrictions on share dealings[114].

(iii) The cartel offence

The cartel offence in section 188 of the Enterprise Act is committed only where the agreement is implemented in the UK[115]. Subject to that, individuals guilty of the cartel offence would be liable to a fine and/or imprisonment, irrespective of their domicile or place of residence. An important additional point is that the Act makes provision for the possibility of extradition from or to the UK[116].

6. RESISTANCE TO EXTRATERRITORIAL APPLICATION OF COMPETITION LAW

(A) Introduction

The *Alcoa*[117] case triggered off a number of battles between the US and other States which objected to the extraterritorial application of US antitrust laws[118]. Apart from diplo-

---

[109] The merger provisions of the Enterprise Act 2002 are described in ch 22.

[110] Enterprise Act 2002, s 22(6)(a).   [111] Ibid, s 22(6)(b).   [112] Ibid, s 23(1).   [113] Ibid, s 23(2)–(4).

[114] Ibid, ss 77(7) and 78(5).   [115] See ch 10, pp 415–422.

[116] Ibid, pp 421–422; note that in *Norris v Government of the USA* [2008] UKHL 16 the House of Lords concluded that 'mere' price fixing did not amount to criminal conspiracy to defraud at common law, with the result that he could not be extradited on that basis (his alleged infringement predated the entry into force of the provisions of the Enterprise Act).

[117] See p 474 above.

[118] See Griffin 'Foreign Governmental Reactions to US Assertions of Extraterritorial Jurisdiction' (1998) 19 ECLR 64, and the references in n 1 thereof.

matic protests, several countries have passed 'blocking statutes', whereby they attempt to thwart excessive assumptions of jurisdiction[119]. There are no provisions in EC law which have this effect: the Commission considers that this is essentially a matter for the Governments of individual Member States. The UK has taken a consistently hostile view of US practice, which culminated in the Protection of Trading Interests Act 1980.

The earliest attempt made by the UK Government to prevent the extraterritorial application of US law came in 1952[120]; thereafter it secured the passage of the Shipping Contracts and Commercial Documents Act 1964, the provisions of which were used on several occasions to prevent disclosure of information to US authorities[121]. The courts in the UK have also objected to US practice. In *British Nylon Spinners v ICI*[122] the Court of Appeal ordered ICI not to comply with a court order in America, requiring it to reassign certain patents to Du Pont; the US court considered that the parties were dividing the market horizontally. In *Rio Tinto Zinc v Westinghouse Electric Corpn*[123] the House of Lords declined to assist in the process of discovery in a US court, investigating an alleged uranium cartel, where it considered that the information so acquired would subsequently be used for an improper assertion of extraterritorial jurisdiction. The UK courts are obliged by the Evidence (Proceedings in Other Jurisdictions) Act 1975 to assist in requests for discovery by foreign courts. However the Act provides exceptions to this obligation, and the House of Lords considered that this case fell within these exceptions for two reasons: first, because the request for information was in reality a 'fishing expedition'; and secondly, because Rio Tinto might incriminate itself under EC competition law by divulging the documents sought.

The 1975 Act did not allow a court to resist a request for information simply because the foreign court was making a claim to extraterritorial jurisdiction; this is now dealt with by section 4 of the Protection of Trading Interests Act 1980 (below). At common law a UK court has discretion to order a litigant to restrain foreign proceedings which are oppressive: in *Midland Bank plc v Laker Airways plc*[124] the Court of Appeal ordered Laker to discontinue proceedings against Midland Bank in the US which would have involved the extraterritorial application of US antitrust law. In *British Airways v Laker Airlines*[125], however, the House of Lords refused British Airway's application for a stay; in this case there was no doubt that BA was carrying on business in the US, so that it was subject to US law on conventional jurisdictional principles. If Laker were deprived of the opportunity to litigate in the US, it would have been unable to sue in the UK since it had no cause of action under UK law. In those circumstances the House of Lords was prepared to allow the US litigation to go ahead.

(B) Protection of Trading Interests Act 1980

The Protection of Trading Interests Act 1980 contains wide-ranging provisions[126]. It is not limited to blocking US enforcement of antitrust laws, but may be invoked in

---

[119] See *Lowe*, pp 79 et seq where he lists the many blocking statutes that have been passed; further blocking statutes have been passed since then.

[120] See *Lowe*, pp 138–139.   [121] Ibid, pp 139–143.

[122] [1955] Ch 37, [1954] 3 All ER 88, CA and [1953] Ch 19, [1952] 2 All ER 780, CA.

[123] [1978] AC 547, [1978] 1 All ER 434, HL.   [124] [1986] QB 689, [1986] 1 All ER 526, CA.

[125] [1985] AC 58, [1984] 3 All ER 39, HL.

[126] See generally on this Act Huntley 'The Protection of Trading Interests Act – Some Jurisdictional Aspects of Enforcement of Antitrust Laws' (1981) 30 ICLQ 213; Lowe 'Blocking Extraterritorial Jurisdiction – The

any case in which US law is being applied in a way which could harm the commercial interests of the UK[127]. Section 1 enables the Secretary of State to make orders requiring UK firms to notify him of, and forbidding them to comply with, measures taken under the law of a foreign country affecting international trade and which threaten to damage the trading interests of the UK. This power has been exercised on three occasions[128]. The first order was not concerned with antitrust laws, but with the saga of the Siberian pipeline[129]. The second was concerned with competition law, but not with the specific issue of extraterritoriality; the objection to the US action in question was that it involved a breach of Treaty obligations concerning air travel between the US and the UK[130]. The third was adopted in response to regulations adopted by the US Government on trade with Cuba.

Section 2 of the Act gives the Secretary of State power to prohibit compliance with a requirement by an overseas authority to submit commercial information to it which is not within its territorial jurisdiction. This provision replaces the Shipping and Commercial Documents Act 1964. Section 3 provides for the imposition of penalties upon anyone who fails to comply with orders under the foregoing provisions, but, consistently with the UK approach to these issues, these may be imposed only in accordance with the UK's conventional interpretation of the international law principles of territoriality and nationality. Section 4 provides that a UK court should not comply with a foreign tribunal's request for assistance in the discovery process where this would infringe UK sovereignty. This is statutory reinforcement of the House of Lords' judgment in *Rio Tinto Zinc v Westinghouse Electric Corpn*[131].

Section 5 provides that foreign multiple damages awards shall not be enforceable in the UK. This means that a claimant in the UK could not enforce a treble damages award obtained in the US[132]. Section 6 goes even further and provides that, where a UK defendant has actually paid US multiple damages, he may bring an action in the UK to 'claw back' the excess of such damages over the amount actually required to compensate the claimant. This provision symbolises the degree of antipathy in the UK towards various aspects of US antitrust practice.

British Protection of Trading Interests Act 1980' (1981) 75 American Journal of International Law 257; Collins 'Blocking and Clawback Statutes: the UK Approach' [1986] JBL 372 and 452.

[127] The Shipping Contracts and Commercial Documents Act 1964 could be invoked only where there was an infringement of UK *jurisdiction*; the 1980 Act is wider, as it applies where there is harm to UK commercial interests, whether there is an infringement of jurisdiction or not.

[128] See the Protection of Trading Interests (US Re-export Control) Order 1982, SI 1982/885; the Protection of Trading Interests (US Antitrust Measures) Order 1983, SI 1983/900; and the Protection of Trading Interests (US Cuban Assets Control Regulations) Order 1992, SI 1992/2449.

[129] See *Lowe* pp 197–219.

[130] The vires of the Order in this case were challenged, unsuccessfully, by the plaintiff in the US antitrust action: see *British Airways Board v Laker Airways Ltd* [1984] QB 142, [1983] 3 All ER 375, CA; on appeal [1985] AC 58, [1984] 3 All ER 39, HL; the House of Lords also reversed the Court of Appeal's decision that Laker should discontinue its US action against British Airways as this would mean there was no forum in which it could sue: see n 125 above.

[131] [1978] AC 547, [1978] 1 All ER 434; see p 488 above.

[132] At common law foreign judgments can normally be enforced in the UK but 'penal' judgments cannot be; note that under s 5 of the Act the whole sum is unenforceable, not just the penal element; one order has been made under s 5, the Protection of Trading Interests Act (Australian Trade Practices) Order 1988, SI 1988/569; section 5 of the Act was considered by the Court of Appeal in *Lewis v Eliades* [2004] 1 All ER 1196.

7. THE INTERNATIONALISATION OF COMPETITION LAW[133]

It is clearly unsatisfactory that there should be acrimonious disputes between States over the extraterritorial application of competition law. Principles of public international law do not provide an adequate answer to the problems that arise when true conflicts occur between competition authorities, and yet the scope for such conflicts could increase as more States adopt their own codes of competition law and as business becomes increasingly international. Transnational mergers pose a particular problem where several competition authorities investigate the same transaction and have different perceptions of whether it should be permitted or not. A different, and more positive, point is that competition authorities have become increasingly aware that, since national systems of competition law are not always adequate to deal with cartels, anti-competitive practices and mergers that transcend national boundaries, international cooperation between them may increase the chances of achieving a successful solution. Many steps have been taken towards greater international cooperation between competition authorities, some of which are considered below.

(A) UNCTAD[134]

The United Nations Conference on Trade and Development ('UNCTAD') has taken an interest in the development of competition policy for many years. In 1980 it adopted a voluntary, non-binding code, *The Set of Multilaterally Agreed Equitable Principles and Rules for the Control of Restrictive Business Practices*, setting out suggested core principles to be adopted in systems of competition law. UNCTAD fulfils an important role in providing technical assistance to developing countries that have adopted, or intend to adopt, a domestic system of competition law.

(B) OECD

The Organisation for Economic Cooperation and Development ('the OECD') is active in matters of competition policy. In 1995 it published a *Revised Recommendation Concerning Cooperation between Member Countries on Restrictive Business Practices Affecting International Trade*[135] which provides for voluntary notification, consultation and cooperation in competition law cases involving the legitimate interests of foreign Governments; this Recommendation replaced an earlier one of 1986. The OECD has published numerous studies on aspects of competition policy, details of which can be found on its website[136].

---

[133] See Dabbah *The Internationalisation of Antitrust Policy* (Cambridge University Press, 2003).

[134] See Brusick 'UNCTAD's Role in Promoting Multilateral Cooperation on Competition Law and Policy' (2001) 24 World Competition 23; Lianos 'The Contribution of the United Nations to the Emergence of Global Antitrust Law' (2007) 15(2) Tulane Journal of International and Comparative Law 145.

[135] OECD Doc C(95) 130 (final), 27 July 1995. [136] Available at www.oecd.org.

(C) WTO

Chapter 5 of the post-war Havana Charter for an International Trade Organisation contained an antitrust code[137]; however this was not incorporated into the General Agreement on Tariffs and Trade of 1947, the organisation from which the WTO developed. The WTO was established on 1 January 1995, and is predominantly concerned with issues of trade, rather than with competition policy. The relationship between trade and competition policy is a major subject in its own right, as is the debate as to the institutional mechanisms needed to deal with the new economic order[138]. The rules of the WTO do not impose obligations on undertakings in relation to competition. A working group has been established to examine the interaction between trade and competition policy; a helpful summary of its work can be found in the Commission's *Annual Report on Competition Policy* for 2002[139]. It seems unlikely at the current stage of its development that the WTO will metamorphose into a global competition authority, although it is possible that its system of dispute settlement could be extended to competition law matters[140].

(D) International Competition Network

An important contribution to the debate on the future of international competition policy was the *Final Report of the International Competition Policy Advisory Committee to the US Attorney General and Assistant Attorney General for Antitrust* (the so-called 'ICPAC Report'), published in February 2000[141]. The Report recommended that the US should explore the scope for collaboration among interested governments and international agencies to create a new venue in which ideas could be exchanged and work undertaken towards common solutions of competition law and policy problems: the Report referred to this as the 'Global Competition Initiative'. The Initiative would foster dialogue in relation to a range of matters, including the multilateralisation and deepening of positive comity; the development of consensus principles on best practice in

---

[137] The Charter is set out in Wilcox *A Charter for World Trade* (The Macmillan Company, 1949), pp 231–327; see also speech by Wood 'The Internationalisation of Antitrust Law: Options for the Future' 3 February 1995, available at www.usdoj.gov/atr/public/speeches/future.txt.

[138] The literature on these matters is vast, and the subject merits a separate book. Many of the issues are captured in an interesting series of essays in the Journal of International Economic Law for 1999, for example by Pitofsky 'Competition Policy in a Global Economy' (1999) 3 JIEL 403 and Roessler 'Should Principles of Competition Policy be Incorporated into WTO Law Through Non-Violation Complaints?' ibid, 413; see also Matsushita 'Reflections on Competition Policy/Law in the Framework of the WTO' [1997] Fordham Corporate Law Institute (ed Hawk), ch 4; *New Dimensions of Market Access in a Globalising World Economy* (OECD 1995), in particular the chapters in Part III on Trade and Competition Policies in the Global Market Place; a series of essays on the relationship between competition and trade policy will be found in [1998] Fordham Corporate Law Institute (ed Hawk), chs 13–19; see also Iacobucci 'The Interdependence of Trade and Competition Policies' (1997–98) 21(2) World Competition 5; Rodgers 'Competition Policy, Liberalism and Globalisation: A European Perspective' (2000) 6 Columbia Journal of European Law 289; Guzman 'Antitrust and International Regulatory Federalism' (2001) 76 NYULR 1142; Davidow and Shapiro 'The Feasibility and Worth of a WTO Competition Agreement' (2003) 37 Journal of World Trade 49.

[139] See points 669–672 of the Report.

[140] See Ehlermann and Ehring 'WTO Dispute Settlement and Competition Law' (2003) 26 Fordham International Law Journal 1505

[141] Copies are available from the US Government Printing Office; see also Janow and Lewis 'International Antitrust and the Global Economy' (2001) 24 World Competition 3.

relation to phenomena such as hard-core cartels; consideration and review of the scope of governmental exemptions and immunities from competition law; rationalisation of systems of merger notification and review; new subjects such as e-commerce; collaborative analysis of issues such as global cartels; and, perhaps, the provision of dispute mediation and technical assistance services. The Report examined three particular issues: multi-jurisdictional mergers, the interface of trade and competition policies and anti-cartel enforcement and international cooperation. The ICPAC Report led, in October 2001, to the establishment of the International Competition Network (the 'ICN') as an international forum for competition law and policy. The ICN is an informal, virtual network that seeks to facilitate cooperation between competition authorities and to promote procedural and substantive convergence of competition laws; a Steering Group oversees the conduct of its business. Membership is open to national and multinational organisations responsible for the enforcement of competition law.

The ICN's work is complementary to that of UNCTAD, the OECD and the WTO. The first annual conference of the ICN was held in September 2002 and brought together representatives from 59 competition authorities and various non-governmental agencies; that number has grown since then: a list of members is available on the ICN website[142]. The ICN has established various working groups over the years of its existence: there are currently four, on mergers, cartels, competition policy implementation and unilateral conduct. The work plans of these groups and their output can be accessed on the ICN's website.

(E) International cooperation agreements[143]

International cooperation between competition authorities has been advanced by the adoption of several bilateral and multilateral agreements. For example the United States has negotiated agreements in relation to competition law enforcement with Germany[144], Australia[145] and Canada[146]. US–Canadian cooperation is also facilitated by the Mutual Legal Assistance Treaty which applies to criminal law enforcement generally, but which can be used in relation to criminal law prosecutions in competition law cases[147]. The Closer Economic Relations Agreement, which entered into force between Australia and New Zealand on 1 January 1983[148], provides for close cooperation between those two countries, even allowing for one country to apply the other's law where it is appropriate to do so. Denmark, Iceland, Norway and Sweden entered into an *Agreement on cooperation in competition law matters* in April 2003[149]. Regional agreements have an important role to play in developing a cooperative approach to competition issues; the EC itself is an example of regional cooperation, and Chapter 15 of the North American Free

[142] www.internationalcompetitionnetwork.org.
[143] A useful summary of such agreements will be found in Parisi 'Enforcement Cooperation Among Antitrust Authorities' (1999) 20 ECLR 133; Zanetti *Cooperation Between Antitrust Agencies at the International Level* (Hart Publishing, 2002).
[144] 4 Trade Reg Rep (CCH) para 13,501.   [145] Ibid, para 13,502.   [146] Ibid, para 13,503.
[147] See Goldman and Kissack 'Current Issues in Cross-Border Criminal Investigations: A Canadian Perspective' [1995] Fordham Corporate Law Institute (ed Hawk), ch 4.
[148] See Brunt 'Australian and New Zealand Competition Law and Policy' [1992] Fordham Corp L Inst (ed Hawk), ch 7.
[149] Available at www.kkv.se.

Trade Agreement contains provisions for consultation, cooperation and coordination between the US, Canada and Mexico in matters of competition policy.

(F) The EU's dedicated cooperation agreements on competition policy

The EU has entered into dedicated cooperation agreements with the US, Canada and Japan[150]. The text that follows will examine the agreements with the US; it will then discuss cooperation in practice. The principles of the agreements with Canada and Japan are the same as those with the US. The Commission has also established a permanent forum for discussions with Korea and has agreed to a structured dialogue with China[151].

(i) The EC/US Cooperation Agreement of 23 September 1991[152]

The first Cooperation Agreement was entered into on 23 September 1991[153]. The French Government successfully challenged the legal basis on which the Commission had proceeded, since the Council of Ministers should have been involved in the adoption of the Agreement[154]. The position was rectified by the adoption of a joint decision of the Council and the Commission of 10 April 1995[155].

The Agreement sets out detailed rules for cooperation on various aspects of the enforcement of EC and US competition law. Article II requires the competent authorities in each jurisdiction to notify each other whenever they become aware that their enforcement activities may affect important interests of the other party. Article II(3) contains special provisions on the timing of notifications in the case of mergers. Article III deals with the exchange of information between the authorities in each jurisdiction, and provides for regular meetings between officials of the EC and the US to discuss matters of mutual interest. Article IV deals with cooperation and coordination in enforcement activities, in relation to which each agency will assist the other. Article V is a novel provision going beyond Article IV, as it embodies the idea of 'positive comity': one agency may ask the other to take action in order to remedy anti-competitive behaviour in the *former's* territory[156]. The idea of positive comity is taken further in the second Cooperation Agreement, discussed below.

Article VI requires the parties to avoid conflicts in enforcement activities, and lays down criteria that should be taken into account when an agency is deciding whether to proceed. These criteria reflect the principle of (negative) comity discussed in the context of the US 'jurisdictional rule of reason'[157]. Article VII of the Agreement requires the

---

[150] www.ec.europa.eu/comm/competition/international/bilateral/index.html.   [151] Ibid.

[152] See Ham 'International Cooperation in the Antitrust Field and in particular the Agreement between the United States and the Commission of the European Communities' (1993) 30 CML Rev 571; Torremans 'Extraterritorial Application of EC and US Competition Law' (1996) 21 EL Rev 280.

[153] [1991] 4 CMLR 823.

[154] Case C-327/91 *France v Commission* [1994] ECR 1–3641, [1994] 5 CMLR 517: see Riley 'Nailing the Jellyfish: the Illegality of the EC/US Government Competition Agreement' (1992) 13 ECLR 101 and again in (1995) 16 ECLR 185.

[155] OJ [1995] L 95/45, corrected by OJ [1995] L 131/38.

[156] See Atwood 'Positive Comity – is it a Positive Step?' [1992] Fordham Corporate Law Institute (ed Hawk), ch 4.

[157] See p 476 above.

parties to consult with one another in relation to the matters dealt with by it. Article VIII provides that neither party to the Agreement can be required to provide information to the other where this is prohibited by the law of the party possessing it or where to do so would be incompatible with important interests of the party possessing it; furthermore each party agrees to keep the information it receives from the other confidential to the fullest extent possible. Article IX provides that neither party can be required to do anything under the Agreement that would be inconsistent with existing laws. The Agreement is terminable on 60 days' notice by either party.

(ii) The Positive Comity Agreement of 4 June 1998

A second EC/US Cooperation Agreement was entered into on 4 June 1998, and develops the principle of positive comity in Article V of the first Agreement. The Council and the Commission gave their approval to the Positive Comity Agreement in a joint Decision of 29 May 1998[158]. Article I provides that the Agreement is to apply where one party can demonstrate to the other that anti-competitive activities are occurring within the latter's territory which are adversely affecting the interests of the former. Article II contains definitions; it is important to note that mergers do not fall within the scope of this Agreement as a result of the definition of 'competition law(s)' in Article II(4). Article III contains the principle of positive comity: the competition authorities of a 'Requesting Party' may request the authorities in the 'Requested Party' to investigate and, if warranted, to remedy anti-competitive activities in accordance with the latter's competition laws. Article IV provides that the Requesting Party may defer or suspend the application of its law while the Requested Party is applying its. Article V deals with confidentiality and the use of information. Article VI provides that the Positive Comity Agreement shall be interpreted consistently with the 1991 Agreement. The Positive Comity Agreement is terminable on 60 days' notice by either party.

(iii) The cooperation agreements in practice

The cooperation agreements have been highly successful in practice. Cooperation between the Commission, the US, Canada and Japan is now a fact of daily life: if anything the degree of cooperation has been greater than could have been imagined in the early 1990s. The Commission's annual *Report on Competition Policy* provides a helpful account of the cooperation agreements in practice; in particular details are given of specific cases in which the authorities worked together[159]. An EU–US merger working group has been established, which led to the adoption in 2002 of guidelines on 'best practices' to be followed where the same transaction is being investigated on both sides of the Atlantic[160].

A great deal of attention, including press coverage, is given to the few cases where there is friction between the EC and the US, as in the cases of *Boeing/McDonnell Douglas*[161]

---

[158] OJ [1998] L 173/26, [1999] 4 CMLR 502; the first case to be initiated on the basis of positive comity was *Sabre*: see the Commission's XXXth *Report on Competition Policy* (2000), point 453.

[159] See eg the *Report on Competition Policy for 2005*, SEC(2006)761 final, pp 187–191.

[160] Available at www.europa.eu.int/comm/competition/mergers/legislation/EU_US.pdf.

[161] Case M.877 OJ [1997] L 336/16; for comment, see Bavasso 'Boeing/McDonnell Douglas: Did the Commission Fly Too High?' (1998) 19 ECLR 243; Banks 'The Development of the Concept of Extraterritoriality under European Merger Law Following the *Boeing/McDonnell Douglas* Decision' (1998)

and *GE/Honeywell*[162]. In the *Boeing* case the FTC in the US reached a majority decision not to oppose the merger, while the European Commission seemed likely, at one
point, to prohibit it in its entirety; in the event commitments to modify the transaction
were offered to the Commission with the result that it was given conditional clearance.
In *GE/Honeywell* a merger had been permitted in the US but was prohibited outright
by the European Commission. However exceptional cases such as *Boeing/McDonnell
Douglas* and *GE/Honeywell* ought not to obscure the fact that a large number of cases,
particularly mergers, are successfully completed without any friction between the two
jurisdictions. No matter how sophisticated the machinery for cooperation between the
EC and the US, there will always be some cases in which there is disagreement as to the
appropriate outcome. The success of the Cooperation Agreements should be assessed on
the basis of how rare these cases are, and on this basis they have been very successful.

19 ECLR 306; Fiebig 'International Law Limits on the Extraterritorial Application of the European Merger
Control Regulation and Suggestions for Reform' (1998) 19 ECLR 323.

[162] Case COMP/M.2220, on appeal Cases T-209/01 and T-210/01 *Honeywell v Commission* [2005] ECR
II-5527, [2006] 4 CMLR 652 and [2005] ECR II-5575, [2006] 4 CMLR 686.

13

Horizontal agreements (1) – cartels

CHAPTER CONTENTS

The previous chapters have described the main principles of EC and UK competition law. The focus of attention in this and the following chapters is different. Instead of looking at the individual provisions of competition law, such as Articles 81 and 82 EC and the Chapter I and II prohibitions in the UK Competition Act 1998, a contextual approach will be adopted and the application of the law to various types of agreements and business practices will be analysed.

There are 11 'contextual' chapters. The first three consider horizontal issues: first, cartels; then the 'problem' of tacit collusion and oligopoly; and lastly horizontal cooperation agreements that competition authorities might be willing to countenance. Chapter 16 deals with vertical agreements. Chapters 17 and 18 analyse practices that might be found to be abusive under Article 82 EC and/or the Chapter II prohibition in the Competition Act 1998; the possible application of the UK Enterprise Act 2002 to such practices will also be considered. Chapter 19 considers the relationship between intellectual property rights and competition law, including technology licensing agreements. Chapters 20 to 22 deal with merger control, and the book concludes with a brief discussion of how competition law impacts upon specific sectors of the economy, in particular so-called utilities such as telecommunications, postal services and energy markets.

The scheme of this chapter is as follows. Section 1 discusses the hardening attitude of competition authorities worldwide towards hard-core cartels, and gives examples of recent decisions in a variety of non-EU jurisdictions in which significant fines and sentences of imprisonment have been imposed. Section 2 looks at the European Commission's enforcement activity in relation to cartels in recent years. The chapter then considers the application of Article 81 to particular types of cartels: price fixing, market sharing, agreements on quotas, and analogous practices. The final section of this chapter reviews the record in the UK in enforcing the prohibition on cartels.

1. THE HARDENING ATTITUDE OF COMPETITION AUTHORITIES WORLDWIDE TOWARDS CARTELS

(A) Introduction

Horizontal agreements between independent undertakings to fix prices, divide markets, to restrict output and to fix the outcome of supposedly competitive tenders are perhaps the most obvious target for any system of competition law; they are prohibited by both EC and UK law and are the subject of ever more draconian penalties[1].

Writing in 1776 Adam Smith famously remarked in *The Wealth of Nations* that:

People of the same trade seldom meet together, even for merriment and diversion, but the conversation ends in a conspiracy against the public, or in some contrivance to raise prices.

Evidence suggests that the tendency of competitors to meet in smoke-filled rooms – or perhaps now in smoke-free internet chat-rooms – is just as strong today as it was in the eighteenth century: cartels appear to be alive and kicking throughout the world. The phenomenon described by Smith was not a new discovery in 1776: cartels were recognised – and prohibited – in the days of the Eastern Roman Empire (Byzantium). The Constitution of Zeno of 483 AD punished price fixing in relation to clothes, fishes, sea urchins and other goods with perpetual exile, usually to Britain[2]. Adam Smith's comment was prescient: cartels have thrived through the subsequent centuries, often with implicit or even explicit support from Governments. Even the adoption of competition laws with tough sanctions has not been sufficient to suppress cartel activity.

The members of cartels go to great lengths to suppress evidence of their illegal activity: for example the Commission's decision in *Gas Insulated Switchgear*[3] says that participants in the cartel used codes to conceal their companies' names and encryption software to protect the secrecy of e-mails and telephone conversations; made use of free

---

[1] For detailed texts on cartels and competition law see Harding and Joshua *Regulating Cartels in Europe: A Study of Legal Control of Corporate Delinquency* (Oxford University Press, 2003); Jephcott and Lübigg *Law of Cartels* (Jordans, 2003); Arbaut and Sakkers in Faull and Nikpay *The EC Law of Competition* (Oxford University Press, 2nd ed, 2007), ch 8; Gerard et al *Cartel Law*, Volume III of *EU Competition Law* (eds Siragusa and Rizza, Claeys and Casteels, 2007); *European Competition Law Annual 2006: Enforcement of Prohibition of Cartels* (eds Ehlermann and Atanasiu, Hart Publishing, 2007); Bellamy and Child *European Community Law of Competition* (Oxford University Press, 6th ed, 2008, eds Roth and Rose), ch 5; Sakkers and Ysewyn *European Cartel Digest* (Wolters Kluwer, 2005); see also the series of contributions on the topic in [2006] Fordham Corporate Law Institute (ed Hawk), chs 1–7.

[2] See Codex Iustinianus, c 4, 59, 2, p 186 (Weidmann, 1954); exile to Rome for commission of the UK criminal cartel offence under the Enterprise Act 2002 is thought unlikely to have a sufficiently deterrent effect and is therefore not an available option.

[3] Commission decision of 24 January 2007, available at www.ec.europa.eu/comm/competition/index_en.html, on appeal Cases T-117/07 *Areva & others v Commission*, not yet decided.

e-mail providers and the anonymous mailboxes made available by them; sent messages as password-protected documents: the passwords were regularly changed; systematically destroyed e-mails; downloaded attachments on to memory sticks rather than on to their computers; and made use of mobile telephones provided by a member of the cartel that contained encryption options[4]. In the case of *Industrial Bags*[5] the Commission discovered a document that said that:

In view of the risk taken in this type of meeting and the documentation passed on, this document and all those relating to VALVEPLAST [the industry's trade association] which indicate figures for allocating markets and prices must be destroyed.

(B) The global agenda

There is a very real sense today among the world's competition authorities that, if competition law is about one thing above all, it is the detection and punishment of hard-core cartels. In the European Union Mario Monti, the former Commissioner for Competition, once described cartels as 'cancers on the open market economy'[6], and the Supreme Court in the US has referred to cartels as 'the supreme evil of antitrust'[7]. At both a moral and a practical level there is not a great deal of difference between price fixing and theft. US law has for many decades treated hard-core cartels as *per se* infringements of the Sherman Act and as criminal offences, punishable not only by fines but also by the imprisonment of individuals. In 2008 the House of Lords, the highest appeal court in the UK, reached the conclusion that some forms of price fixing amount to the crime of conspiracy to defraud at common law: in other words some cartels could lead to the imprisonment of individuals even without the specific criminal cartel offence established by section 188 of the Enterprise Act 2002[8]. A significant consequence of this judgment is that price-fixing agreements may therefore be criminal offences in many countries throughout the world whose legal systems are based on the common law of the UK, irrespective of whether they have adopted their own domestic competition laws or, where they have adopted such laws, of whether they contain specific criminal sanctions.

(C) The position of the OECD in relation to cartels[9]

The OECD has been at the forefront of policy in relation to cartels. This in itself reflects an obvious but important point, that cartels are often international in nature, whereas for the most part systems of competition law are purely national in scope. The rules of the European Union are an important exception, since they apply throughout the 27 Member States as well as the three Contracting States of the European Economic Area. International business phenomena such as cartels necessitate an international response, and the OECD is in an important position to give a lead in this respect.

---

[4] Commission decision of 24 January 2007, paras 170–176.

[5] Commission decision of 30 November 2005.

[6] Speech by Mario Monti of 11 September 2000, available at www.ec.europa.eu/comm/competition/speeches.

[7] See *Verizon Communications Inc. v Law Offices of Curtis V Trinko*, www.supremecourtus.gov/opinions/03pdf/02–682.pdf.

[8] See ch 10, pp 423–424.

[9] The OECD documents referred to in this section can all be found at www.oecd.org.

In 1998 the OECD adopted a *Recommendation of the Council concerning Effective Action Against Hard Core Cartels* in which it called upon its member countries to ensure that their laws 'effectively halt and deter hard-core cartels', and invited non-member countries to associate themselves with the *Recommendation* and to implement it. In particular the *Recommendation* said that countries should provide for effective sanctions of a kind and at a level to deter firms and individuals from participating in such cartels as well as effective enforcement procedures to detect and remedy hard-core cartels. The *Recommendation* defined a hard-core cartel as:

an anti-competitive agreement, anti-competitive concerted practice, or anti-competitive arrangement by competitors to fix prices, make rigged bids (collusive tenders), establish output restrictions or quotas, or share or divide markets by allocating customers, suppliers, territories, or lines of commerce.

Subsequently the OECD has published a number of further documents which are of particular interest to the issue of cartel enforcement. In its 2001 *Report on Leniency Programmes to Fight Hard Core Cartels* the OECD discussed the need to penetrate the cloak of secrecy that surrounds hard-core cartels, and the contribution that the encouragement of whistleblowers can make to this need. It noted that the seriousness of the penalties, including the risk of personal liability, can be a powerful motivating factor in encouraging whistleblowing or leniency applications. It considered the procedures that are required for an effective and fair leniency programme, and noted the need for strong protection against unauthorised disclosure of information provided by leniency applicants. Whistleblowing and leniency applications were discussed in chapters 7 and 10 of this book, and are an important feature of competition authorities' pursuit of cartels[10]. A separate matter is whether competition authorities might decide to introduce rewards or financial incentives for informants: this has been done, for example, in South Korea[11] and the UK[12].

In its 2002 *Report on the Nature and Impact of Hard Core Cartels and Sanctions against Cartels under National Competition Laws* the OECD noted that the worldwide economic harm from cartels is very substantial, though hard to quantify: it was estimated that 16 large cartel cases investigated in the US may have caused harm in excess of $US 55 billion. Firms go to great lengths to keep cartel agreements secret, and are in some cases explicit in their contempt for the competitive process. The principal purpose of sanctions in cartel cases is deterrence. Strong sanctions against enterprises and individuals increase the effectiveness of leniency programmes. The Report also noted that, although there is a move towards the imposition of larger penalties for infringement of anti-cartel legislation, sanctions have yet to reach the optimal level for deterrence.

In *Hard Core Cartels: Recent Progress and Challenges Ahead*, published in 2003, the OECD examined the harm that arises from cartels: whilst acknowledging how difficult it is to quantify such harm, it found that it amounted to billions of dollars world-wide each year. It also reviewed recent progress in the fight against cartels, which it found to be significant: new laws had been passed, sanctions had been increased and most countries were now aggressively prosecuting cartels. However the OECD was of the view that more needed to be done in relation to sanctions which, in its view, were still not severe enough; and it also stressed the need for greater international cooperation in combating cartels which, as noted earlier, often transcend national boundaries.

---

[10] See ch 7, pp 275–278 and ch 10, pp 404–407.   [11] See www.ftc.go.kr/data/hwp/rewardsystem.doc.
[12] OFT press release 31/08, 29 February 2008.

In its 2005 *Third Report on the Implementation of the 1998 Recommendation* the OECD focused on four topics: progress in fighting cartels; public awareness of the harm caused by cartels; effective sanctions, in particular against individuals; and international cooperation in cartel cases. The report again noted that there had been considerable progress, but nevertheless concluded that much remains to be done. In particular more countries should expand their awareness programmes, and should work more extensively with procurement officials in an effort to fight bid rigging. The Report also found that countries should seek opportunities to further increase corporate fines, and that they should consider introducing sanctions against individuals, including criminal sanctions. The Report identified opportunities to enhance international cooperation in cartel investigations, and highlighted in particular the OECD's *Best Practices for the Formal Exchange of Information between Competition Authorities in Hard Core Cartel Investigations*. The increasing levels of cooperation between competition authorities is discussed in chapter 12 of this book[13].

(D) The International Competition Network

The International Competition Network has a cartels working group: it is composed of two sub-groups, one of which looks at the general framework and principles for the fight against cartels and the other at enforcement techniques. The work plan of the working group will be found on the ICN website[14]: current projects are to explore the role that settlements can play in anti-cartel enforcement, the determination of the level of corporate fines in cartel cases and the development of an anti-cartel enforcement manual. The ICN holds an annual (anti-)Cartel Workshop: the 2007 event was held in El Salvador.

(E) Recent cartel cases outside the EU

The European Commission, in recent years, has been extremely active in enforcing the prohibition on cartels, as the statistics in section 2 below show. However it is of interest to note that there has been significant enforcement activity throughout the rest of the world, both in 'mature' systems of competition law and in new jurisdictions, and in all types of economy. A useful source of information about the level of enforcement activity in relation to cartels is UNCTAD's website[15]. In September 2005 UNCTAD published an interesting synthesis of publicly available cartel investigations in a number of jurisdictions[16], from the Argentinian cement cartel which attracted fines totalling US $107 million to the Turkish fine on manufacturers of traffic lights of €6 million. A few further examples of major cartel cases in recent years illustrate how active competition authorities throughout the world have been:

- In the US $730 million in criminal fines have been imposed as a result of the DoJ's investigation into price fixing in the DRAM market[17]; and a bid-rigging conspiracy in the marine hose

[13] See ch 12, pp 490–495.   [14] www.internationalcompetitionnetwork.org.
[15] See www.unctad.org.
[16] Available at www.unctad.org/en/docs; see also the publication *The International Comparative Legal Guide to Cartels & Leniency 2008*, Global Legal Group, 2008.
[17] See DoJ's press release of 21 December 2006 available at www.usdoj.gov.

industry has led so far to five individuals (including some UK citizens) pleading guilty and agreeing to serve prison sentences amounting to 112 months[18]

- In Japan the Japanese Fair Trade Commission imposed fines in December 2007 of approximately €10 million for bid rigging in relation to high and medium-pressure gas pipes[19]

- In South Korea the Korean Fair Trade Commission imposed fines in April 2007 of approximately €4 million on two companies for engaging in a cartel in the synthetic rubber sector[20]

- In Australia the Federal Court of Australia imposed fines in November 2007 of approximately €25 million for price fixing and market sharing in the corrugated fibreboard packaging market[21]

- In South Africa the South African Competition Commission reached a settlement in November 2007 with an undertaking involved in a price fixing cartel in the milling and bread industries. The settlement involved payment of a fine of approximately €15 million, subject to confirmation by the Competition Tribunal[22].

2. THE EUROPEAN COMMISSION'S APPROACH TO CARTELS

(A) Statistics

In the years from 2001 onwards the European Commission has been particularly active in enforcing the prohibition on cartels: there have been numerous decisions and the fines have, in many cases, been enormous. 2001 was a particularly striking year, in which the fines totalled €1.836 billion: by far the largest amount in any one year up until that point. In 2006 the Commission exceeded that figure, the fines that year reaching €1.846 billion for five decisions, *Bleaching Chemicals, Acrylic Glass, Road Bitumen, Copper Fittings,* and *Synthetic Rubber.* However these figures were eclipsed in 2007, when they amounted to €3.334 billion: the Commission adopted eight decisions, *Gas Insulated Switchgear, Elevators and Escalators, Dutch Beer, Fasteners and Attaching Machines, Bitumen, Professional Videotapes, Flat Glass,* and *Chloroprene Rubber.* The fines are paid into the Community budget: to that extent they benefit the treasuries of the Member States, whose contributions are proportionally reduced.

---

[18] See DoJ's Press Releases of 6 November 2007 and 12 December 2007, available at www.usdoj.gov; useful statistics on the enforcement activities of the Antitrust Division of the US Department of Justice in relation to cartels (and to other types of case) are available at www.usdoj.gov/atr/public/workstats.htm: they reveal that in 2006 the fines imposed for infringements of section 1 of the Sherman Act 1890 amounted to $473 million, including fines on individuals in excess of $3 million, and that 28 individuals were sentenced for criminal activity, of whom 19 were sentenced to terms in jail. The Department of Justice in the US has adopted a policy of placing indicted individuals, accused of violating the Sherman Act, on a 'Red Notice' list maintained by INTERPOL, with the result that they might be arrested when attempting to cross a national boundary and extradited to the US for prosecution: see speech by Scott Hammond, Deputy Assistant Attorney General for Criminal Enforcement at the DoJ, 16 November 2005, www.usdoj.gov/atr/public/speeches/213247.htm.

[19] See JFTC's press release of 4 December 2007, available at www.jftc.go.jp/e-page.

[20] See KFTC's press release of 4 April 2007, available at http://www.ftc.go.kr/eng.

[21] See ACCC's press release of 2 November 2007, available at www.accc.gov.au.

[22] See South African Competition Commission's press release of 12 November 2007, available at www.compcom.co.za.

Since 1 June 2005 DG COMP has had a dedicated Cartel Directorate with responsibility for prosecuting cartel cases and, in conjunction with the Directorate for Policy and Strategic Support, for developing policy and coordinating the Commission's contributions to international fora such as the OECD and ICN.

The Commission's statistics on its enforcement activity in relation to cartels are available on its website and are regularly updated[23]. They show the total amounts of fines imposed over a six year period (including adjustments for variations in their level by the Community Courts); the ten highest cartels fines by case; the ten largest by undertaking; the total number of undertakings to have been found to have infringed Article 81 in each year; and the total number of decisions each year. These statistics speak eloquently of the Commission's seriousness of purpose in eradicating cartels. It should be recalled that the fining guidelines introduced in 2006 are likely to lead to higher fines than in the past[24]; and that the introduction of a settlement system will probably lead to more decisions than has been possible to date[25]. Bearing in mind that undertakings that cartelise markets can also be sued for damages[26], and that individuals in some jurisdictions also face the possibility of imprisonment[27], it is hard to believe that the deterrent effect of the law on cartels in the EC is insubstantial[28]; and yet the Commission (and the national competition authorities) continue to discover them in significant numbers and in all kinds of markets[29]. In numerous cases the Commission increases the fine that would otherwise have been paid because an undertaking is a recidivist, that is to say a repeat offender[30]; and it often discovers a series of cartels in the same industry: its press release on the cartel in *Nitrine Butadiene Rubber* noted that this was the fourth decision in the rubber industry in three years[31]. Some of these cartels were of very long duration: for example 29 years in the case of *Sorbates*[32], 20 years or more in *Industrial Bags*[33] and 21 years in one of the cartels in *Fasteners*[34]. It is also noticeable how often in the Commission's decisions cartel meetings were held during or just after trade association meetings, as for example in the case of *Industrial Bags* referred to above and in *Synthetic Rubber*[35].

(B) Some landmark decisions

Some of the cartel cases in recent years are of particular interest. In the *Vitamins* case[36] the Commission imposed fines on eight undertakings totalling €855.23 million

---

[23] www.ec.europa.eu/comm/competition/cartels/statistics/statistics/pdf.   [24] See ch 7, pp 273–275.
[25] Ibid, pp. 258–261   [26] See ch 8 generally.
[27] See eg ch 10, pp 415–422 on the position in the UK.
[28] On the issue of deterrence and cartels generally see Wils *The Optimal Enforcement of EC Antitrust Law Essays in Law and Economics* (Kluwer Law International, 2002), ch 2 and Wils *Efficiency and Justice in European Antitrust Enforcement* (Hart Publishing, 2008), ch 3.
[29] DG COMP's website includes a 'drop-down' menu on cartels which includes a 'What's new' section: it provides details of new cases in which inspections have been carried out or a statement of objections sent.
[30] See eg *Nitrine butadiene rubber,* Commission decision of 23 January 2008, where Bayer's fine was increased by 50 per cent for recidivism; see further ch 7, p 274.
[31] Commission Press Release IP/08/78, 23 January 2008.
[32] Commission decision of 1 October 2003, on appeal Case T-410/03 *Hoechst v Commission,* not yet decided.
[33] Commission decision of 20 November 2005.   [34] Commission decision of 19 September 2007.
[35] Commission decision of 29 November 2006, on appeal Cases T-38/07 *Shell Petroleum and others v Commission,* not yet decided.
[36] OJ [2003] L 6/1, [2003] 4 CMLR 1030.

(reduced to €790.50 million on appeal): of this amount, Roche was fined €462 million for its participation in a number of different vitamin cartels; the next largest fine was on BASF, of €296.16 million[37]; Aventis would have been fined €114.4 million, but it paid only €5.04 million as it had blown the whistle on most of the cartels. This cartel was investigated not only under EC law: the Commission's decision followed fines in the US on the major participants of US $862 million and in Canada of Canadian $84.5 million[38]; fines of Australian $26 million were imposed on Roche, BASF and Aventis Animal Nutrition under the Australian Trade Practices Act 1974 on 28 February 2001[39]. Senior executives of Roche and BASF also served terms of imprisonment in the US for their roles in this cartel[40]. Fines were also imposed in South Korea[41]. There have also been a series of actions for damages arising from the vitamins cartel[43].

Other notable decisions in recent years include, in 2007, *Elevators and Escalators*[44] and *Gas Insulated Switchgear*[45] for the sheer size of the fines, €992.31 million in the case of the former and €750.71 in the latter; *Elevators and Escalators* is also of interest as it included the largest ever fine on an undertaking for a single infringement of Article 81: ThyssenKrupp was fined €479.66. It is also of interest to note that, whereas a few years ago several of the Commission's decisions followed earlier enforcement by the Department of Justice in the US in relation to the same cartel – this was true, as we have already seen, of *Vitamins*, but also happened, for example, in *Graphite Electrodes*[46], *Amino Acids*[47], and *Citric Acid*[48] – in recent years the Commission has prosecuted a number of cases where the cartels were purely European: examples are a series of

[37] BASF's fine was reduced on appeal to €236.84 million, Case T-15/02 *BASF AG v Commission* [2006] ECR II-497, [2006] 5 CMLR 27.

[38] OJ [2003] L 6/1, [2003] 4 CMLR 1030, paras 155–157 and see Canadian Competition Bureau News Release, September 22 1999.

[39] *Australian Competition & Consumer Commission v Roche Vitamins Australia Pty Ltd* [2001] FCA 150; see also ACCC Media Release MR 37/01, 1 March 2001.

[40] Department of Justice Press Release, 5 May 2000, available at www.usdoj.gov/atr/public/press_releases/2000/4684.htm.

[41] Press Release of 25 April 2003, available at www.ftc.go.kr.

[43] See eg in the US *Empagran SA v Hoffmann-La Roche Ltd* 315 F 3d 338 (DC Cir 2003) (see ch 12, p 475); in the UK see *Provimi Ltd v Aventis Animal Nutrition SA* [2003] EWHC 961 (Comm), [2003] All ER (D) 59 (May), Case No 1028/5/7/04 *BCL Old Co Ltd v Aventis* (which was settled out of court), order of the CAT of 7 April 2005 and *Devenish v Sanofi* [2007] EWHC 2394 (Ch D).

[44] Commission decision of 21 February 2007, on appeal Cases T-145/07 etc *OTIS and others v Commission*, not yet decided.

[45] Commission decision of 24 January 2007, on appeal Cases 110/07 etc *Siemens v Commission*, not yet decided.

[46] Commission decision of 18 July 2001, OJ [2002] L 100/1, [2002] 5 CMLR 829, on appeal Cases T-236/01 etc *Tokai Carbon v Commission* [2004] ECR II-1181, [2004] 5 CMLR 1465, on further appeal Cases C-289/04 P *Showa Denko v Commission* [2006] ECR I-5859, [2006] 5 CMLR 840; C-301/04 P *Commission v SGL Carbon AG* [2006] ECR I-5915, [2006] 5 CMLR 877 and C-308/04 P *SGL Carbon AG v Commission* [2006] ECR I-5977, [2006] 5 CMLR 922.

[47] Commission decision of 7 June 2000, OJ [2001] L 152/24, [2001] 5 CMLR 322, on appeal Case T-224/00 *Archer Daniels Midland and Archer Daniels Midland Ingredients v Commission* [2003] ECR II-2597, [2003] 5 CMLR 583, on further appeal Case C-347/03 P *Archer Daniels Midland and Archer Daniels Midland Ingredients v Commission* [2006] ECR I-4429, [2006] 5 CMLR 230.

[48] Commission decision of 5 December 2001, OJ [2002] L 239/18, [2002] 5 CMLR 1070, on appeal Cases T-59/02 etc *Archer Daniels Midland v Commission* [2006] ECR II-3627, [2006] 5 CMLR 1528, on further appeal Case C-511/06 P, not yet decided.

decisions imposing fines on cartels in the beer sector[49], haberdashery products[50] and flat glass[51].

(C) Appeals to the CFI

Undertakings found to have infringed Article 81 have a right of appeal to the CFI, which has an unlimited jurisdiction in relation to the level of fines; this includes the right to increase as well as to decrease them, which may act as a disincentive to appeal in some cases[52]. Some of these cases have run for a very long time; in particular, the litigation arising from the *PVC* decision of 1988 did not end until the ECJ's judgment in 2002[53].

Where the Commission is guilty of factual errors the CFI will, of course, reduce the level of fines; it will also do so, for example, where it considers that one member of a cartel has been treated unequally compared with others in the same cartel. However the CFI is fairly reluctant to interfere with the Commission's margin of appreciation in relation to the level of fines, and the Commission's statistics show that, overall, the level of reductions by the CFI is not great: for example the fines imposed by the Commission in 2003 of €404.78 million were reduced on appeal only to €400.79 million. No doubt many undertakings that are fined substantial sums will feel that it is worthwhile appealing to the CFI in the hope of some reduction; and clearly law firms have an interest in their doing so, since this is lucrative work. However appeals consume public resources – of both the Commission and the Courts themselves. This is one of the reasons why a settlements procedure is attractive: not only can quicker decisions be expected under such a regime, but it is also likely that the number of appeals in the future will be considerably fewer than is currently the case[54].

In some cases points have been won on appeal where the Commission had made a procedural error in its administrative procedure, for example failing to address a statement of objections to the legal entity that was subsequently fined. On two occasions in 2006 the Commission, having lost on appeal before the Community courts on procedural grounds such as these, decided to reopen its administrative procedure in order to correct the error: this happened both in *Alloy Surcharge*[55] and in *Steel Beams*[56]. Clearly

---

[49] *Belgian Beer* Commission decision of 5 December 2001, upheld on appeal to the CFI, Case T-38/02 *Group Danone v Commission* [2005] ECR II-4407, [2006] 4 CMLR 1428 and further upheld on appeal to the ECJ Case C-3/06 P *Group Danone v Commission* [2007] ECR I-1331, [2007] 4 CMLR 701; *Luxembourg Beer* Commission decision 5 December 2001, upheld on appeal to the CFI, joined Cases T-49/02 to T-51/02, *Brasserie Nationale SA and others v Commission* [2005] ECR II-3033, [2006] 4 CMLR 222; *French Beer* Commission decision of 29 September 2004 (not appealed); *Dutch Beer* Commission decision of 18 April 2007, on appeal Cases T-240/07 etc *Heineken Netherland and Heineken v Commission*, not yet decided.

[50] *PO/Needles* Commission decision of 26 October 2004, [2005] 4 CMLR 792, on appeal to the CFI, Cases T-30/05 *Prym and Prym Consumer v Commission* [2007] ECR II-000, further appeal to the ECJ, Case C-534/07 P, not yet decided and T-36/05 *Coats Holdings Ltd v Commission* [2007] ECR II-000, [2008] 4 CMLR 45, further appeal to the ECJ, Case C-468/07 P, not yet decided; *Fasteners* Commission decision of 19 September 2007, on appeal Cases T-454/07 etc *Prym and others v Commission*, not yet decided.

[51] Commission decision of 28 November 2007.

[52] See eg Cases T-101/05 *BASF v Commission* [2007] ECR II-000; ch 7, pp 285–289 on appeals to the CFI.

[53] Cases C-238/99 P etc *Limburgse Vinyl Maatschappij (LVM) v Commission and Others* [2002] ECR I-8375, [2003] 4 CMLR 397.

[54] See ch 7, pp 258–261 for discussion of the Commission's proposal for a settlements procedure.

[55] Commission Press Release of 20 December 2006; the decision is now on appeal to the CFI in Case T-24/07 *ThyssenKrupp Stainless v Commission*, not yet decided.

[56] Commission Press Release of 8 November 2006, on appeal Cases T-405/06 *Arcelor Luxembourg and others v Commission*, not yet decided.

the Commission intends, by adopting decisions such as these, to suggest to the legal and business communities that appeals of a technical nature are unlikely to be successful in the end, since the technicality is something that can, in the long run, be corrected. It will be of interest to see whether the CFI upholds these decisions in the fresh appeals that have been brought[57].

3. HORIZONTAL PRICE FIXING

Horizontal price fixing would be regarded by most people as the most blatant and undesirable of restrictive trade practices.

It is interesting in passing to note that price fixing has not always attracted the opprobrium that it does today. In the UK, for example, it was characteristic of most industries during the first half of the twentieth century that prices were set at an agreed level; this was thought to provide stability, to protect firms against cyclical recession and overseas competition, and to facilitate orderly and rational marketing from which purchasers too would benefit[58]. The introduction of power to inhibit price fixing in the Monopolies and Restrictive Practices (Inquiry and Control) Act 1948 was resented and even now resistance to price competition remains deep-rooted in some parts of the economy.

It might be assumed that in the absence of antitrust laws – or at any rate in the absence of any significant prospect of being detected and punished for breaking them – all competitors would find the urge to cartelise and to maximise profits an irresistible one. However participation in a cartel itself has its price and membership will be more profitable to some firms than others[59]. Costs will be incurred in negotiating to fix the price at which the product is to be sold and these costs will inevitably increase as more firms are brought into the agreement and the range of products to be comprehended by it is extended. Firms may find it difficult both to agree a price and to remain faithful to the level set. It will be to the advantage of more efficient firms to fix a lower price, since output (and so their revenue) will then be greater; the producer of strongly differentiated goods will want a higher price, which will cover the cost of promoting its brand image. Having fixed prices, further expense will have to be incurred in monitoring the agreement. Meetings will be necessary to reappraise matters from time to time, resources will need to be expended in policing it to ensure that individual firms are not cheating by cutting prices secretly, offering discounts and bonuses or altering the quality of the product[60]. To prevent cheating, the agreement may fix quotas and provide for the imposition of fines upon firms that exceed them. Further resources may have to be devoted to arrangements such as collective boycotts, patent pooling and the offer of aggregated rebates in order to prevent new entrants coming on to the market with a

---

[57] Note that the Commission's readoption of a decision in the *PVC* case was upheld on appeal: Cases C-238/99 P *Limburgse Vinyl Maatschappij v Commission* [2002] ECR I-8375, [2003] 4 CMLR 397.

[58] See eg Allen *Monopoly and Restrictive Practices* (George Allen & Unwin, 1968), ch 14.

[59] See Scherer and Ross *Industrial Market Structure and Economic Performance* (Houghton Mifflin, 3rd ed, 1990), chs 7 and 8; Neven, Papandropoulos and Seabright *Trawling for Minnows* (CEPR, 1998), ch 3; Bishop and Walker *The Economics of EC Competition Law* (Sweet & Maxwell, 2nd ed, 2002), paras 5.07–5.31.

[60] It is not uncommon for a cartel agreement to break down, or to run the risk of doing so, because of the extent of cheating indulged in by members: see eg *Zinc Producer Group* OJ [1984] L 220/27, [1985] 2 CMLR 108, paras 23–63.

view to sharing in any supra-competitive profits that are being earned. A system of collective resale price maintenance may have to be established to buttress the stability of the cartel. A trade association may have to be established to reinforce the cartel.

The problems inherent in the cartelisation process itself explain why in some industries price fixing has a tendency to break down in the long term and why the parties may attempt to limit competition in other ways than by direct limitations on pricing strategy. For example, it may be easier to prevent 'cheating' where each firm is given an exclusive geographical market or a particular class of customers with which to deal. Furthermore the fact that price fixing becomes more difficult as the number of participants involved in the agreement increases may be considered to signify that competition authorities ought to expend their enforcement resources on those markets where collusion is most likely to be privately profitable because of the high level of concentration that exists or the homogeneity of the products sold[61].

It should not be assumed from the foregoing comments that price fixing is rare. Even the existence of antitrust laws backed up by severe penalties has not dissuaded some firms from attempts to control the market. Experience shows that some industries are particularly prone to cartelisation: any review of enforcement activity in this area will quickly reveal, for example, that this is true of the cement, chemical and construction sectors. It is also important to appreciate that prices can be fixed in numerous different ways, and that a fully effective competition law must be able to comprehend not only the most blatant forms of the practice but also a whole range of more subtle agreements whose object is to limit price competition. For example, where firms agree to restrict credit to customers, to abstain from offering discounts and rebates, to refrain from advertising prices, to notify one another of the prices they charge to customers or intend to recommend their distributors to charge, or to adopt identical cost accounting methods, the object or effect of the agreement may be to diminish or totally prevent price competition. Indeed, agreements to divide markets or produce fixed quotas can in a sense be seen as covert price-fixing agreements, in that they limit the extent to which firms can compete with one another on price. These and other similar agreements will be dealt with separately later in this chapter.

(A) Article 81(1)

Article 81(1) specifically provides that agreements, decisions and concerted practices which 'directly or indirectly fix purchase or selling prices or any other trading conditions' may be caught. Many aspects of Article 81(1) have been discussed earlier in this book. The expressions 'agreement' and 'concerted practice' are given a wide meaning[62]: specifically, the Commission may find a 'single, overall agreement'[63], may adopt a dual classification of an agreement 'and/or' a concerted practice[64]; and attendance at meetings at which prices are discussed between competitors is highly incriminating[65]. The Community Courts and the Commission regard hard-core price-fixing agreements as having as their *object* the restriction of competition for the purposes of Article 81(1), so that there is no need also to show that they have the effect of doing so[66]. However,

---

[61] See Posner *Antitrust Law* (The University of Chicago Press, 2nd ed, 2002), ch 4.

[62] See ch 3, pp 97ff.   [63] See ch 3, pp 100–102.   [64] Ch 3, pp 99–100.   [65] Ch 3, pp 101–102.

[66] Ch 3, pp 119–120; note that there are some exceptional circumstances in which price fixing has been found not to restrict by object, but to do so by effect: ibid, pp 120–122.

it is necessary to show that an agreement will have an appreciable effect on trade between Member States[67] for there to be an infringement of Article 81(1). Furthermore Article 81(1) is capable of being applied extraterritorially to agreements entered into outside but implemented within the Community[68]. This section examines more closely the application of Article 81(1) to price-fixing agreements.

(i) Price fixing in any form is caught

It is clear from the decisions of the Commission and the judgments of the Community Courts that it is not just blatant price fixing that is caught, but that Article 81(1) will catch any agreement that might directly or indirectly suppress price competition. In *IFTRA Rules on Glass Containers*[69] the Commission condemned rules of a glass manufacturers' association which might reduce price competition by including an obligation not to offer discounts, an open information scheme, the adoption of a common accounting procedure and a term providing for the charging of uniform delivered prices. In this decision the Commission pointed out that in the particular product market the potential for non-price competition was weak, the corollary being that maintenance of price competition was particularly important. An agreement not to discount off published prices was held to infringe Article 81(1) in *FETTCSA*[70], even though the parties had not expressly agreed on the level of their published prices. In *Vimpoltu*[71] an agreement to observe maximum discounts and to offer the same credit terms was caught. In *Italian Flat Glass*[72] the participants in the cartel had agreed not only to fix prices, but also to offer identical discounts and to ensure that these were applied downstream in the market.

Many other decisions have condemned agreements which might directly or indirectly facilitate level pricing. Prior consultation on price lists, with a commitment not to submit quotations before such consultation, is prohibited[73]. A substantial body of material on information agreements now exists[74], restrictions upon advertising may be caught[75], as are agreements on terms and conditions which limit price competition[76], agreements on recommended prices[77], maximum pricing[78], and collective resale price maintenance[79]. Objection has been taken to a scheme whereby members of a cartel at times refused to sell and at others themselves purchased zinc on the London Metal Exchange in order to maintain its price[80]. Where an industry considers that cooperation

---

[67] Ch 3, pp 142–145. [68] See ch 12, pp 478–482.

[69] OJ [1974] L 160/1, [1974] 2 CMLR D50; see similarly *IFTRA Rules for Producers of Aluminium Containers* OJ [1975] L 228/10, [1975] 2 CMLR D20.

[70] OJ [2000] L 268/1, [2000] 5 CMLR 1011, paras 132–139 (citing *IFTRA Rules on Glass Containers* and *IFTRA Rules for Producers of Aluminium Containers*), upheld on appeal Case T-213/00 *CMA CGM v Commission* [2003] ECR II-913, [2003] 5 CMLR 2573 , para 184.

[71] OJ [1983] L 200/44, [1983] 3 CMLR 619.

[72] OJ [1989] L 33/44, [1990] 4 CMLR 535, annulled on appeal Cases T-68/89 etc *Società Italiano Vetro SpA v Commission* [1992] ECR II-1403, [1992] 5 CMLR 302.

[73] *Re Cast Iron Steel Rolls* OJ [1983] L 317/1, [1984] 1 CMLR 694: the parties here had established an 'alarm system' in the event that antitrust authorities should become aware of their cartel, upheld on appeal Cases 29/83 and 30/83 *Compagnie Royale Asturienne des Mines SA and Rheinzink GmbH v Commission* [1984] ECR 1679, [1985] 1 CMLR 688.

[74] See pp 523–532 below. [75] See pp 532–535 below. [76] See pp 521–523 below.

[77] Case 8/72 *Cementhandelaren v Commission* [1972] ECR 977, [1973] CMLR 7.

[78] *European Glass Manufacturers* OJ [1974] L 160/1, [1974] 2 CMLR D50.

[79] Cases 43, 63/82 *VBVB & VBBB v Commission* [1984] ECR 19, [1985] 1 CMLR 27.

[80] *Zinc Producer Group* OJ [1984] L 220/27, [1985] 2 CMLR 108.

is necessary because of the depressed state of the market, this should be negotiated with the Commission: undertakings should not take unilateral action which restricts competition[81].

In the case of *British Sugar*[82] the Commission did not find that the prices for sugar had *actually* been fixed, but that the parties to the agreement/concerted practice could rely on the other participants to pursue a collaborative strategy of higher pricing in 'an atmosphere of mutual certainty'[83]. In *Fenex*[84] the Commission considered that the regular and consistent practice of drawing up and circulating recommended tariffs to members of a trade association infringed Article 81(1)[85]. In *Ferry Operators Currency Surcharges*[86] the Commission considered that an agreement on the amount of surcharges, and the timing of their introduction, to be imposed on freight shipments following the devaluation of the pound infringed Article 81(1). Price fixing as part of a strategy to isolate national markets is caught[87], and agreements between distributors are caught as well as between producers[88]. An agreement the effect of which is to maintain a traditional price differential between two geographical markets will infringe Article 81(1)[89]. Fixing the price of imports into the EC has been caught[90]. In *Milchförderungsfonds*[91] the Commission prohibited the German Milk Promotion Board from financially supporting the promotion of exports of German milk products to other EC countries, as this meant that exporters could charge lower prices than without this benefit, so that competition on the market was distorted. In *Fine Art Auction Houses* the essence of the cartel lay in agreeing an increase in the commission paid by sellers at auctions, although the Commission found that Sotheby's and Christie's had also agreed on other trading conditions[92]. It is no defence that a participant in a cartel sometimes does not respect the agreed price increases: in *Cascades v Commission*[93] the CFI said that:

an undertaking which, despite colluding with its competitors follows a more or less independent policy on the market may simply be trying to exploit the cartel for its own benefit.[94]

(ii) Joint selling agencies

The Commission is wary of joint selling agencies, which it regards as horizontal cartels and generally unlikely to satisfy the criteria of Article 81(3)[95], unless they are

---

[81]   OJ [1984] L 220/27, [1985] 2 CMLR 108.
[82]   OJ [1999] L 76/1, [1999] 4 CMLR 1316, substantially upheld on appeal Cases T-202/98 etc *Tate & Lyle v Commission* [2001] ECR II-2035, [2001] 5 CMLR 859.
[83]   See the Commission's XXVIIIth *Report on Competition Policy* (1998), pp 138–140.
[84]   OJ [1996] L 181/28, [1996] 5 CMLR 332.   [85]   Ibid, paras 45–74.
[86]   OJ [1996] L 26/23, [1997] 4 CMLR 798.
[87]   Case 41/69 *ACF Chemiefarma NV v Commission* [1970] ECR 661, [1970] CMLR 43.
[88]   Cases 100–103/80 *Musique Diffusion Française SA v Commission* [1983] ECR 1825, [1983] 3 CMLR 221.
[89]   *Scottish Salmon Board* OJ [1992] L 246/37, [1993] 5 CMLR 602.
[90]   *Re Franco-Japanese Ballbearings Agreement* OJ [1974] L 343/19, [1975] 1 CMLR D8; *Re French and Taiwanese Mushroom Packers* OJ [1975] L 29/26, [1975] 1 CMLR D83; *Wood Pulp* OJ [1985] L 85/1, [1985] 3 CMLR 474; *Aluminium Imports* OJ [1985] L 92/1, [1987] 3 CMLR 813.
[91]   OJ [1985] L 35/35, [1985] 3 CMLR 101.   [92]   Commission Press Release IP/02/1585, 30 October 2002.
[93]   Case T-308/94 [1998] ECR II-925.   [94]   Ibid, para 230.
[95]   *Re Cimbel* OJ [1972] L 303/24, [1973] CMLR D167; *Re Centraal Stikstof Verkoopkantoor* OJ [1978] L 242/15, [1979] 1 CMLR 11; *Re Floral* OJ [1980] L 39/51, [1980] 2 CMLR 285; *Re Italian Flat Glass* OJ [1981] L 326/32, [1982] 3 CMLR 366; *Ansac* OJ [1991] L 152/54; *Astra* OJ [1993] L 20/23, [1994] 5 CMLR 226; *HOV SVZ/MCN* OJ [1994] L 104/ 34, upheld on appeal Case T-229/94 *Deutsche Bahn AG v Commission* [1997] ECR

established pursuant to some other permissible form of cooperation, such as a research and development agreement or a specialisation agreement[96]. In the case of *Britannia Gas Condensate Field*[97] the Commission said that an agreement between several oil and gas companies participating in the development of the Britannia gas field in the UK North Sea was restrictive of competition; however the Commission considered that Article 81(1) was not applicable since the agreement had no effect on trade between Member States.

The joint selling by sporting associations such as UEFA (a European association of national football associations) may infringe Article 81(1): the Commission will consider both the horizontal effects of joint selling, in so far as it prevents the individual sale of broadcasting rights for example by particular football clubs, as well as any vertical foreclosure effects[98].

(iii) Horizontal price fixing in conjunction with other infringements of Article 81(1)

In many cases undertakings have been found guilty of price fixing in conjunction with other types of horizontal collusion. In *Polypropylene*[99] the Commission found price fixing and market sharing; in *Belgian Roofing Felt*[100] the parties were found guilty of price fixing, establishing production quotas and taking collective action to prevent imports into Belgium; in *Italian Flat Glass*[101] the Commission condemned firms for the apportionment of quotas and agreements to exchange products as well as for fixing prices. In *Pre-Insulated Pipes*[102] the Commission identified infringements of virtually every kind, including market sharing, systematic price fixing, collective tendering, exchanging sensitive sales information and attempts to eliminate the only substantial non-member of the cartel. As the Commissioner responsible for competition policy at the time, Karel Van Miert, said: 'it is difficult to imagine a worse cartel'[103]. In *Amino Acids*[104] the Commission found agreements to fix prices, to determine quotas, and to exchange information. In *Methylglucamine*[105] the Commission imposed a fine on Aventis and Rhone-Poulenc for both price fixing and market sharing, and in *Plasterboard*[106] the Commission found market sharing combined with the exchange of information on future prices and sales volumes. In the case of *Industrial Bags*[107] the Commission

---

II-1689, [1998] 4 CMLR 220 and further on appeal to the ECJ Case C-436/97 P [1999] ECR I - 2387, [1999] 5 CMLR 776; see also the Commission's *Guidelines on Horizontal Cooperation Agreements* OJ [2001] C 3/2, [2001] 4 CMLR 819, paras 144 and 145.

[96] On horizontal cooperation agreements generally see ch 15.

[97] OJ [1997] C 291/10, [1996] 5 CMLR 627; see also the Commission's XXVIIth *Report on Competition Policy* (1997), p 139.

[98] *Joint selling of the media rights of the UEFA Champions League on an exclusive basis* OJ [2002] C 196/3, [2002] 5 CMLR 1153; see also Commission Press Release IP/03/1105, 24 July 2003 on the individual exemption given to UEFA's sale of the media rights to the Champions League.

[99] OJ [1986] L 230/1, [1988] 4 CMLR 347.   [100] OJ [1986] L 232/15, [1991] 4 CMLR 130.

[101] OJ [1989] L 33/44, [1990] 4 CMLR 535.

[102] *Pre-Insulated Pipe Cartel* OJ [1999] L 24/1, [1999] 4 CMLR 402, substantially upheld on appeal Cases T-9/99 etc *HFB Holding v Commission* [2002] ECR II - 1487, [2001] 4 CMLR 1066.

[103] Commission Press Release IP/98/917, 21 October 1998.

[104] OJ [2001] L 154/24, [2001] 5 CMLR 322, substantially upheld on appeal Cases T-220/00 etc *Cheil Jedang v Commission* [2003] ECR II - 2473.

[105] OJ [2004] L 38/18, [2004] 4 CMLR 1062.   [106] OJ [2005] L 166/8.

[107] Commission Press Release IP/05/1508 of 30 November 2005.

imposed fines of €290.71 million on 16 firms for agreeing on prices and sales quotas by geographical area, sharing the orders of large customers, organised collusive bidding, and the exchange of information on sales volumes.

(iv) Price fixing in the services sector

Price fixing in the services sector is also subject to Article 81(1)[108]. For example, in *Eurocheque: Helsinki Agreement*[109] the Commission imposed a fine of €6 million where French banks had agreed between themselves on the commissions they would charge to customers and on their amount[110]; the decision was partially annulled and the fines reduced on appeal[111]. In *Bank Charges for Exchanging Euro-zone Currencies – Germany* the Commission fined five banks a total of €120.8 million for fixing the charges for exchanging currencies in the euro zone[112]; however the decision was annulled on appeal as the CFI considered that the evidence adduced by the commission was insufficient[113]. In *Austrian Banks – 'Lombard Club'* the Commission imposed fines of €124.26 million on eight Austrian banks for their participation in a wide-ranging price cartel[114]; the substance of this decision was upheld on appeal but one of the fines was slightly reduced[115]. A fine of €1 million was imposed in *Distribution of Railway Tickets by Travel Agents*[116] where the Commission found that the International Union of Railways was responsible for price fixing in the sale of railway tickets; the decision was annulled on appeal, as the Commission had proceeded under the wrong procedural regulation[117]. In 1999, in the *Greek Ferries* decision, fines were imposed in the case of price fixing in ferry services between Italy and Greece[118]. The Commission has also been investigating the joint selling of sports rights[119].

The Commission is concerned about restrictions of competition in the professional services sector[120]. In *Belgian Architects*[121] it imposed a fine of €100,000 on the Belgian

---

[108] See eg *Re Nuovo CEGAM* OJ [1984] L 99/29, [1984] 2 CMLR 484 (common tariff system infringed Article 81(1)); *Re Fire Insurance* OJ [1985] L 35/20, [1985] 3 CMLR 246, upheld on appeal Case 45/85 *VdS v Commission* [1987] ECR 405, [1988] 4 CMLR 264 (recommendations on tariffs infringed Article 81(1)).

[109] OJ [1992] L 95/50, [1993] 5 CMLR 323.   [110] Ibid, paras 46–55.

[111] Cases T-39/92 etc *Groupement des Cartes Bancaires v Commission* [1994] ECR II-49, [1995] 5 CMLR 410.

[112] OJ [2003] L 15/1, [2003] 4 CMLR 842; see also Commission Press Release IP/01/1796, 11 December 2001 and Commission's XXXIst *Report on Competition Policy*, p 20.

[113] Cases T-44/02 etc *Dresdner Bank and others v Commission*, judgment of 14 October 2004; note that in this case the Commission failed to lodge a defence to the appeals, and the CFI therefore ruled on the merits of the case purely on the basis of the applications received from the banks: a subsequent application by the Commission to have the CFI's judgments set aside was rejected in September 2006, Cases T-44/02 P etc *Dresdner Bank v Commission* [2006] ECR II-3567, [2007] 4 CMLR 467.

[114] Commission Press Release IP/02/844, 11 June 2002.

[115] Cases T-259/02 etc *Raiffeisen Zentralbank Österreich AG v Commission* [2006] ECR II-5169, [2007] 5 CMLR 1142, on appeal Case C-125/07 P, not yet decided.

[116] OJ [1992] L 366/47.

[117] Case T-14/93 *Union Internationale des Chemin de Fer* [1995] ECR II-1503, [1996] 5 CMLR 40.

[118] OJ [1999] L 109/24, [1999] 5 CMLR 47, on appeal Cases T-56/99 etc *Marlines v Commission* [2003] ECR II-5225, [2005] 5 CMLR 28.

[119] See n 98 above; also the Commission's XXIXth *Report on Competition Policy* (1999), pp 54–55; see Brinckman and Vollebreght 'The Marketing of Sport and its Relation to EC Competition Law' (1998) 19 ECLR 281; Nitsche 'Collective Marketing of Broadcasting by Sports Associations in Europe' (2000) 21 ECLR 208.

[120] See ch 3, pp 89–90.

[121] Commission decision of 24 June 2004; see de Waele 'Liberal professions and recommended prices: the Belgian architects case' *Competition Policy Newsletter*, Autumn 2004, p 44.

Architects' Association for adopting a minimum fee scale for the provision of architectural services in Belgium.

(v) Price fixing in regulated markets

The Commission will examine particularly carefully markets in which price competition is already limited by extraneous factors, in order to ensure that the parties themselves do nothing further to limit competition[122], and its decision will not be affected by the fact that a Government agency has itself sanctioned or extended the effect of a price-fixing agreement[123].

(vi) Buyers' cartels

In two cases in 2004 and 2005 the Commission imposed fines on buyer, rather than seller, cartels, in *Spanish Raw Tobacco*[124] and in *Italian Raw Tobacco*[125]. Tobacco processors were accused by the Commission of colluding on the prices and other trading conditions that they would offer to tobacco growers and other intermediaries; on the allocation of suppliers and quantities; on the exchange of information in order to coordinate their purchasing behaviour; and on the coordination of bids for public auctions. The Commission considered that competition was restricted by object rather than effect[126], even though an agreement to pay *lower* prices than might have been paid in the absence of the agreement might have been expected to lead to lower prices for consumers. In the Commission's view an agreement on purchasing eliminates the autonomy of strategic decision-making and competitive conduct, preventing the undertakings concerned from competing on the merits and enhancing their position vis-à-vis less efficient firms[127].

(B) Article 81(3)

As would be expected the Commission has regularly refused to grant exemption to price-fixing agreements. In its 10th *Report on Competition Policy* it stated at point 115 that a price cartel falls into 'the category of manifest infringements under Article 81(1) which it is almost always impossible to exempt under Article 81(3) because of the total lack of benefit to the consumer'. The same attitude is manifested in Regulation 2658/2000 on

[122] Cases 209/78 etc *Van Landewyck v Commission* [1980] ECR 3125, [1981] 3 CMLR 134; similarly see Case 85/76 *Hoffmann-La Roche v Commission* [1979] ECR 461, [1979] 3 CMLR 211, para 123; *British Sugar plc* OJ [1999] L 76/1, [1999] 4 CMLR 1316, para 87, upheld on appeal Case T-202/98 *Tate & Lyle v Commission* [2001] ECR II - 2035, [2001] 5 CMLR 859.
[123] *AROW v BNIC* OJ [1982] L 379/1, [1983] 2 CMLR 240; *Zinc Producer Group* OJ [1984] L 220/27, [1985] 2 CMLR 108; *Benelux Flat Glass* OJ [1984] L 212/13, [1985] 2 CMLR 350 (where competition was also limited by the similar costs faced by glass producers and the structure of the market); see ch 3, pp 135–136 and ch 6 generally on the relationship of the competition rules with state regulation of economic activity.
[124] OJ [2007] L 102/14, [2006] 4 CMLR 866, on appeal Case T-29/05 *Deltafina SpA v Commission*, not yet decided.
[125] OJ [2006] L 353/45, [2006] 4 CMLR 1766, on appeal Case T-12/06 *Deltafina SpA v Commission*, not yet decided.
[126] See ch 3, pp 116ff on the 'object or effect' distinction in Article 81(3).
[127] See *Italian Raw Tobacco*, para 285.

specialisation agreements[128] and Regulation 2659/2000 on research and development agreements[129]: Article 5 of each provides that block exemption will not be available to agreements containing obvious restrictions of competition, such as the fixing of prices, the limitation of output or the allocation of markets or customers.

However it should be recalled that, as a matter of law, it is always open to the parties to an agreement to argue that the terms of Article 81(3) are satisfied, even if they are highly unlikely to be successful[130]. On a few occasions the Commission has permitted arrangements which could limit price competition. For example in *Uniform Eurocheques*[131] the Commission considered that the criteria of Article 81(3) were satisfied in the case of an agreement whereby commissions for the cashing of Eurocheques were fixed: this meant that consumers using such cheques knew that they would be charged a common amount throughout the Community. In *Insurance Intermediaries*[132] the Commission indicated its intention to authorise agreements between non-life insurers to fix maximum discounts. These and other[133] decisions suggest that the Commission might take a slightly more indulgent approach towards agreements that limit price competition in the services sector than in the goods sector.

In *Reims II*[134] the Commission concluded that the criteria of Article 81(3) were satisfied in the case of an agreement between the major postal operators in the Community relating to 'terminal dues' payable by one post office to another when a letter posted in Member State A has to be delivered to an address in Member State B: the Commission's view was that this case involved price fixing with 'unusual characteristics'[135] and that improvements in efficiency and the elimination of cross-subsidy that would flow from the agreement satisfied the terms of Article 81(3). Similarly, in *Visa International – Multilateral Interchange Fee*[136] the Commission stated that it is not the case that an agreement concerning prices is always to be classified as a cartel and therefore as inherently incapable of satisfying Article 81(3)[137]: in that decision it authorised the multilateral interchange fee ('MIF') agreed upon between 'acquiring' and 'issuing' banks within the Visa system; that authorisation expired on 31 December 2007, after which it is for Visa to conduct a 'self-assessment' of whether the level of its MIF continues to be compliant with Article 81. In *MasterCard*[138] the Commission decided in December 2007 that the MIF imposed in that card system infringed Article 81 because its level raised the cost of accepting payments with MasterCard without increasing efficiencies. Clearly Visa will have to consider carefully the terms of the Commission's decision in *MasterCard*, as well as the outcome of the appeal in that case; in the meantime the level

---

[128]   OJ [2001] L 304/3, [2001] 4 CMLR 800; for commentary on this Regulation, see ch 15, pp 589–592.

[129]   OJ [2001] L 304/7, [2001] 4 CMLR 808; for commentary on this Regulation, see ch 15, pp 583–588.

[130]   Case T-17/93 *Matra Hachette SA v Commission* [1994] ECR II-595; see ch 4, pp 150–151.

[131]   OJ [1985] L 35/43, [1985] 3 CMLR 434.   [132]   OJ [1987] C 120/5.

[133]   See also *Nuovo CEGAM* OJ [1984] L 99/29, [1984] 2 CMLR 484; *P and I Clubs* OJ [1985] L 376/2, [1989] CMLR 178; *Associazione Bancaria Italiana* OJ [1987] L 43/51, [1989] 4 CMLR 238; *Tariff Structures in the Combined Transport of Goods* OJ [1993] L 73/38.

[134]   OJ [1999] L 275/17, [2000] 4 CMLR 704; the Commission indicated its intention to renew this exemption: OJ [2003] C 94/3, [2003] 4 CMLR 1176; see also Commission Press Release IP/03/557, 23 April 2003.

[135]   [2000] 4 CMLR 704, para 65.   [136]   OJ [2002] L 318/17, [2003] 4 CMLR 283.   [137]   Ibid, para 79.

[138]   Commission decision of 19 December 2007, on appeal Case T-111/08 *MasterCard v Commission*, not yet decided; see also the Competition Commissioner's speech on this decision, SPEECH/07/832, 19 December 2007, available at www.ec.europa.eu/comm/competition/speeches/ and the 'frequently asked questions' produced by the Commission, MEMO/07/590, available at www.europa.eu/rapid/pressReleases.

of the MIFs of both Visa and MasterCard are under scrutiny under many other systems of competition law, including in the UK[139].

In *AuA/LH*[140] the Commission considered that a 'lasting alliance' between Austrian Airlines and Lufthansa which entailed joint pricing and market sharing[141] satisfied the criteria of Article 81(3) as the alliance would result in 'important synergistic effects and attractive connections for consumers': the Commission could foresee cost savings, improved network connection, better planning of frequencies, a higher load factor, improved organisation of sales systems and groundhandling services, potential for new sales channels such as e-ticketing and access, on Austrian Airlines's part, to a superior airmiles scheme[142]. In *IFPI 'Simulcasting'*[143] the Commission concluded that an agreement that facilitated the grant of international licences of copyright to 'simulcast' music on the Internet involved price restrictions[144] but that the terms of Article 81(3) were satisfied since it contributed to technical and economic progress in the field of collective management of copyright and neighbouring rights[145].

(C) Collective dominance

The extent to which parallel pricing might amount to an abuse of a collective dominant position is considered in chapter 14[146].

4. HORIZONTAL MARKET SHARING

Competition may be eliminated between independent undertakings in other ways than through direct or indirect price fixing. One way of doing so is for firms to agree to apportion particular markets between themselves. For example, three firms in the UK might agree that each will have exclusivity in a particular geographical area and that none will poach on the others' territories; a similar device is division of the market according to classes of customers, for example that one firm will supply trade customers only, another retailers and another public institutions. Geographical market-sharing agreements may be more effective than price fixing from the cartel's point of view, because the expense and difficulties of fixing common prices are avoided: the agreement means that there will be no price competition anyway. Policing the agreement is also relatively simple, because the mere presence of a competitor's goods on one's own 'patch' reveals cheating. Geographical market sharing is particularly restrictive from the consumer's point of view since it diminishes choice: at least where the parties fix prices a choice of product remains and it is possible that the restriction of price competition will force the parties to compete in other ways. Market-sharing agreements in the EC context may be viewed particularly seriously because, apart from the obviously anti-competitive effects already described, they serve to perpetuate the isolation of geographical markets and to retard the process of single market integration which is a prime aim of the EC Treaty.

---

[139] See p 540 below.

[140] OJ [2002] L 242/25, [2002] 4 CMLR 487; for legal and regulatory reasons these undertakings were unable to merge in the sense of the EC Merger Regulation which is why this case was conducted under Article 81.

[141] Ibid, para 76.   [142] Ibid, paras 87–88.   [143] OJ [2003] L 107/58.   [144] Ibid, paras 61–80.

[145] Ibid, paras 84–123.   [146] See ch 14 pp 565–566.

It is sometimes argued in favour of geographical market-sharing agreements that they should be permitted since they reduce the distribution costs of producers, who are relieved of the need to supply outside their exclusive geographical territories or to categories of customers other than those allotted to them. This is unconvincing, as it does not explain why the benefit claimed is dependent upon the horizontal agreement. If a producer found it profitable to do so, it would want to sell outside its allotted territory or class of customer and in determining the profitability of doing so it would take distribution costs into account. All the agreement does is to foreclose this possibility. Potential competition is removed with the same adverse effect upon consumer welfare that other horizontal restrictions may produce: a reduction in output and an increase in price.

It is not inconceivable that in some cases market sharing might be beneficial: in other words that restrictions accepted might be regarded as ancillary to some legitimate objective. Market sharing might enhance efficiency by enabling firms to compete more effectively with large undertakings. For example, a number of small retailers may decide to combine to promote their own 'house-label' in order to try to match other multiple chains[147]. Individually they may be weak and unable to undertake the enormous costs involved in advertising and promotion, but in combination they may be able to do so. It could be argued that each retailer should be able to claim an exclusive sales territory so that it will be encouraged to take its full part in the campaign in the knowledge that it will reap the benefit in its area. The corollary is that without this incentive it will not promote the brand label so actively and enthusiastically. The argument is similar to that applicable to many vertical restraints[148]. The conclusion ought therefore to be that in some exceptional cases horizontal market sharing should be permitted.

(A) Article 81(1)

There have been many decisions under Article 81 on market sharing, which is specifically mentioned in Article 81(1)(c)[149]. There are two obvious reasons for this. First, geographical market sharing can be achieved relatively easily in the EC context, since there are many ways of segregating national markets from one another. Until a truly single market is established, the factual, legal and economic disparities between national markets will continue to act as an obstacle to inter-state trade. Secondly, the policy of the Commission is to take action to prevent anything which might inhibit market penetration and it therefore has tended to expend much of its resources on dealing with this problem. It can be anticipated that horizontal market sharing will be punished increasingly severely in the future. In *Peroxygen Products*[150] fines totalling €9 million were imposed on five producers which, from 1961 until at least 1980, operated a 'home market' agreement which covered most of the EC. A consequence of this was that prices for consumers varied widely between different geographical markets. In *Soda-ash – Solvay/ICI*[151] the Commission imposed fines on Solvay and ICI for geographical market sharing.

---

[147] See eg Commission's *Guidelines on Horizontal Cooperation Agreements* OJ [2001] C 3/2, [2001] 4 CMLR 819, para 156.

[148] See ch 16, pp 616–618.   [149] See ch 3, p 119.   [150] OJ [1985] L 35/1, [1985] 1 CMLR 481.

[151] OJ [1991] L 152/1, [1994] 4 CMLR 454: this investigation resulted in three other decisions imposing fines on ICI and Solvay for breaches of Article 82: *Soda-ash – Solvay* OJ [1991] L 152/21, *Soda-ash – ICI* OJ [1991] L 152/40, both reported at [1994] 4 CMLR 645 and on Solvay and CFK for market sharing: *Soda ash – Solvay, CFK* OJ [1991] L 152/16, [1994] 4 CMLR 482; the decisions were annulled for procedural

In *Quinine*[152] the ECJ upheld the Commission's decision[153] to fine the members of the quinine cartel who had indulged in price fixing, the allocation of quotas and market division, and there have been many other similar cases since[154]. The infringements in the *Pre-Insulated Pipes*[155] decision were wide-ranging. The Commission accused the parties of dividing national markets and, ultimately, the whole European market amongst themselves; of price fixing; and of taking measures to hinder the one substantial competitor outside the cartel and to drive it out of the market. The fines amounted to €92 million. In some cases there have been elements both of vertical and horizontal market division; distributors must refrain from market division as well as producers[156]. In *Cement*[157] the Commission found that cement producers had agreed on the 'non-transshipment of cement to home markets', which prohibited any export of cement within Europe which could threaten neighbouring markets. In *Seamless Steel Tubes*[158] the Commission found that eight producers of stainless steel tubes had colluded to protect their respective domestic markets; Commissioner Monti stated that this amounted to 'a very serious breach of the principles of competition and calls for a really dissuasive penalty': the fines imposed totalled €99 million[159], reduced on appeal to the CFI to €86 million because the Commission had failed to adduce proof of the entire duration of the infringement[160].

In *Gas Insulated Switchgear*[161] fines of €750 million were imposed on a cartel which, amongst other things, divided the world market for switchgear apparatus with the result that Japanese undertakings did not compete for contracts in Europe and *vice versa*[162]; there was also an agreement among the European participants to respect each other's home market rights[163].

---

reasons in Cases T-30/91 etc *Solvay v Commission* [1995] ECR II-1775, [1996] 5 CMLR 57, and the CFI's judgment was upheld in Cases C-286/95 P etc *Commission v ICI* [2000] ECR I-2341, [2000] 5 CMLR 413 and 454; the Commission readopted the decisions against Solvay and ICI in December 2000: OJ [2003] L 10/1.

[152] Cases 41/69 etc *ACF Chemiefarma NV v Commission* [1970] ECR 661.

[153] *Re Quinine Cartel* JO [1969] L 192/5, [1969] CMLR D41.

[154] Cases 40/73 etc *Coöperatieve Vereniging Suiker Unie UA v Commission* [1975] ECR 1663, [1976] 1 CMLR 295; *Re Van Katwijk NTs Agreement* JO [1970] L 242/18, [1970] CMLR D43; Cases 29/83 and 30/83 *Compagnie Royale Asturienne des Mines SA etc v Commission* [1984] ECR 1679, [1985] 1 CMLR 688; *Zinc Producer Group* OJ [1984] L 220/27, [1985] 2 CMLR 108.

[155] *Pre-Insulated Pipe Cartel* OJ [1999] L 24/1, [1999] 4 CMLR 402, substantially upheld on appeal Cases T-9/99 etc *HFB Holding v Commission* [2002] ECR II-1487, [2001] 4 CMLR 1066.

[156] See eg Cases 100–103/80 *Musique Diffusion Française SA v Commission* [1983] ECR 1825, [1983] 3 CMLR 221 in which the ECJ upheld the Commission's decision (OJ [1980] L 60/21, [1980] 1 CMLR 457) that distributors had engaged in concerted practices *amongst themselves* to isolate the French market.

[157] OJ [1994] L 343/1, [1994] 4 CMLR 327, para 45.

[158] OJ [2003] L 14/1, on appeal Cases T-67/00 etc *JFE Engineering and others v Commission* [2004] ECR II-2501, [2005] 4 CMLR 27 and on further appeal to the ECJ Cases C-403 and 405/04 P *Sumitomo Metal Industries v Commission* [2007] ECR I-729, [2007] 4 CMLR 650.

[159] Commission Press Release IP/99/957, 8 December 1999; see also *SAS/Maersk* OJ [2001] L 265/15, [2001] 5 CMLR 1119: fines of €52.5m for market sharing in the aviation sector.

[160] Cases T-44/00 etc *Mannesmannröhren-Werke v Commission* [2004] ECR II-2223; the CFI's judgment was upheld on appeal to the ECJ, Cases C-411/04 P *Salzgitter Mannesmann GmbH v Commission* judgment of 25 January 2007, [2007] ECR I-959, [2007] 4 CMLR 682.

[161] Commission decision of 24 January 2007, on appeal Cases T-117/07 *Areva & others v Commission*, not yet decided.

[162] Commission decision of 24 January 2007, para 114.   [163] Ibid, para 115.

In *PO/Needles*[164] the Commission imposed fines of €60 million on a 'pure' product and geographic market-sharing agreement between Coats and Prym: the Commission's Press Release in this case[165] stressed how unusual it was for cases of this kind not to include price fixing as well; on appeal the fines were reduced from €60 million to €47 million[166].

An unusual feature of the cartel in *Luxembourg Brewers* is that this case concerned a written cooperation agreement between five brewers. Article 4 of the agreement provided that no brewer would sell beer to any distributor in Luxembourg that was 'guaranteed' to another brewer; this agreement was supplemented by a declaration the purpose of which was to defend the Luxembourg market against imports from other Member States. The Commission considered that the agreement had as its object the restriction of competition. As to Article 4, this went beyond an agreement not to interfere with contractual relationships between a supplier and customer: for example it applied even where there was no actual exclusive supply agreement, and even where the agreement was for some reason void or unenforceable[167]. As to the declaration, this was clearly an attempt to impede the penetration of the Luxembourg market, and therefore contrary to the 'single market imperative'[168]. The Commission concluded that the parties could not avail themselves of the *de minimis* Notice[169], since 'hard-core' horizontal agreements can infringe Article 81(1) even below the thresholds in that Notice[170], and even where a participant is a small or medium-sized undertaking[171]. As Brasserie de Luxembourg had voluntarily blown the whistle and provided the Commission with decisive evidence of the agreement, it was given 100 per cent immunity from the fine of €2.4 million that would otherwise have been imposed[172].

Article 81(1) has also been applied to horizontal agreements involving customer restrictions[173].

(B) Article 81(3)

There is no formal provision to prevent the advancement of efficiency arguments under Article 81(3), but it is unlikely that a horizontal geographical market-sharing agreement would satisfy the criteria of that provision, in view of the overriding goal of achieving single market integration. However in exceptional circumstances the criteria of Article 81(3) might be satisfied where market sharing is indispensable to some legitimate objective[174].

---

[164] Commission decision of 26 October 2004.   [165] IP/04/1313, 26 October 2004.
[166] Cases T-30/05 etc [2007] ECR II-000 and [2007] ECR II-000.
[167] OJ [2002] L 253/21, paras 48–66.
[168] Ibid, paras 67–73; on the single market imperative see ch 1, pp 22–23 and ch 2, pp 51–52.
[169] OJ [1997] C 372/13, [1998] 4 CMLR 192.
[170] Ibid, para 11; the same conclusion would be reached under the current Notice: see OJ [2001] C 368/13, [2002] 4 CMLR 699, para ll(l)(c); on the current Notice see ch 3, pp 138–141.
[171] *Notice on Agreements of Minor Importance* OJ [2001] C 368/13, [2002] 4 CMLR 699, para 3.
[172] OJ [2002] L 253/21, [2002] 5 CMLR 1279, paras 102–108.
[173] See eg *Re William Prym-Werke and Beka Agreement* OJ [1973] L 296/24, [1973] CMLR D250 where the Commission required the deletion of a customer restriction clause; *Atka Al S v BP Kemi A/S* OJ [1979] L 286/32, [1979] 3 CMLR 684 where BP was to supply customers with consumption of at least 100,000 gallons; *Belgian Roofing Felt* OJ [1986] L 232/15, [1991] 4 CMLR 130.
[174] See *Transocean Marine Paint Association* JO [1967] L 163/10, [1967] CMLR D9.

5. QUOTAS AND OTHER RESTRICTIONS ON PRODUCTION

A further way in which a cartel might be able to earn supra-competitive profits is by agreeing to restrict its members' output. If output is reduced, price will rise; the oil cartel operated by OPEC does not fix prices as such, but instead determines how much oil each member country will export. Horizontal agreements to limit production need to be carefully monitored, because over-production by some members of the cartel would result in the market price falling, unless the scheme is run in conjunction with a price-fixing system, as often happens. In the absence of direct price fixing, the cartel members will often agree on a quota system whereby they will each supply a specified proportion of the entire industry output within any given period. As in the case of price fixing there will be costs involved in negotiating these quotas, because some firms will be larger or more efficient or expanding more rapidly than others so that there may have to be hard and protracted bargaining. The quotas having been fixed, some mechanism will have to be established to prevent cheating. This may be done, for example, by requiring detailed information about production and sales to be supplied to a central information-gathering agency. The agreement will also commonly provide a system whereby those that exceed their allocated quotas have to make compensating payments to those who, as a necessary corollary, fail to dispose of theirs. Complicated rules may have to be settled on how such payments are to be made. A firm which 'over-produces' will have to sell its products on the market at a higher price than it would wish if it is to make a profit and make a payment to the other cartel members; the loss to the consumer of such schemes is clear.

Some agreements which involve restrictions of production may be beneficial: specialisation agreements, joint production, research and development agreements, restructuring cartels and standardisation agreements may in some circumstances be considered desirable. This chapter is concerned with 'naked' restrictions on production which limit output without producing any compensating benefits; agreements involving restrictions of production which may be ancillary to some legitimate objective will be discussed in chapter 15.

(A) Article 81(1)

Article 81(1)(b) specifically applies to agreements to 'limit or control production, markets, technical development, or investment' and has been applied to agreements to limit production on many occasions. Straightforward quota systems have often been condemned[175].

In *Peroxygen Products*[176] the Commission found that, as well as sharing markets geographically, members of the cartel had entered into a series of detailed national agreements dividing markets in agreed percentages. In *MELDOC*[177] a quota and compensation

---

[175] See eg *Zinc Producer Group* OJ [1984] L 220/27, [1985] 2 CMLR 108; *Benelux Flat Glass* OJ [1984] L 212/13, [1985] 2 CMLR 350; also the various cement cases decided by the Commission involving quota arrangements: see *Re Cementregeling voor Nederland* JO [1972] L 303/7, [1973] CMLR D149; *Re Cimbel* JO [1972] L 303/24, [1973] CMLR D167; *Re Nederlandse Cement-Handelmaatschappij NV* JO [1972] L 22/16, [1973] CMLR D257; see also *Belgian Roofing Felt* OJ [1986] L 232/15, [1991] 4 CMLR 130; *Welded Steel Mesh* OJ [1989] L 260/1, [1991] 4 CMLR 13.

[176] OJ [1985] L 35/1, [1985] 1 CMLR 481.   [177] OJ [1986] L 348/50, [1989] 4 CMLR 853.

scheme in the dairy sector in the Netherlands was held to infringe Article 81, and the Commission imposed fines totalling €6,565,000. An exacerbating fact in this decision was the fact that the Dutch milk producers also agreed to a coordinated response to the threat posed to their market position by imports from other Member States. An agreement not to expand production without the approval of rival firms infringes Article 81(1)[178] and the Commission will not easily be persuaded that a quota scheme will bring about beneficial specialisation[179]. It is not permissible to establish a joint venture to apportion orders between competitors[180], nor will the Commission allow joint production which simply limits competition without producing any compensating benefits[181]. Not infrequently quota agreements confer on particular undertakings exclusive or priority rights in supplying their own domestic markets: they will certainly not be tolerated[182].

An interesting example of a quota scheme condemned by the Commission is *Associated Lead Manufacturers Ltd (White Lead)*[183]. Firms producing white lead in the UK, Germany and the Netherlands agreed that each would supply one third of the white lead to be exported to non-EC countries. A central office was established which gathered information from them on their deliveries of white lead. The producers supplied this office with details of *all* deliveries, including exports to other EC countries. The Commission held that in practice the quota scheme related to all exports, that is to say to intra-Community as well as extra-Community trade, and that it clearly amounted to an attempt to limit and control markets within the terms of Article 81(1)(b). Furthermore the Commission held that it was irrelevant that the quotas were not always meticulously observed: an agreement did not cease to be anti-competitive because it was temporarily or even repeatedly circumvented by one of the parties to it[184].

In *Compagnie Royale Asturienne des Mines SA and Rheinzink GmbH v Commission*[185] the ECJ held that it was an infringement of Article 81(1) for competitors to supply products to each other on a continuing basis. Whereas this might be acceptable to deal with certain emergencies, it was not permissible for competitors to enter into agreements of indeterminate length and for considerable quantities. The effect of doing so was to institutionalise mutual aid in lieu of competition, producing conditions on the market analogous to those brought about by quota arrangements. In *Soda-ash – Solvay/CFK*[186] the Commission condemned an agreement whereby Solvay agreed to allow CFK a guaranteed minimum sales tonnage and to purchase from it any shortfall in order to compensate it. In *Italian Flat Glass*[187] the Commission condemned an agreement between manufacturers to exchange products and agree quantities sold to particular customers. The CFI overturned this aspect of the decision for lack of evidence[188], but it did not question the principle that such an agreement restricts competition. The first fine for a

---

[178] *Re Cimbel* JO [1972] L 303/24, [1973] CMLR D167.
[179] *Re Italian Cast Glass* OJ [1980] L 383/19, [1982] 2 CMLR 61.
[180] *Air Forge* Commission's XIIth *Report on Competition Policy* (1982), point 85.
[181] *Re WANO Schwarzpulver GmbH* OJ [1978] L 322/26, [1979] 1 CMLR 403.
[182] Case 41/69 *ACF Chemiefarma NV v Commission* [1970] ECR 661.
[183] OJ [1979] L 21/16, [1979] 1 CMLR 464.
[184] Similarly see *Re Cast Iron and Steel Rolls* OJ [1983] L 317/1, [1984] 1 CMLR 694 where the Commission fined various French undertakings which operated a quota scheme in respect of deliveries to the Saarland in Germany.
[185] Cases 29/83 and 30/83 [1984] ECR 1679, [1985] 1 CMLR 688.
[186] OJ [1991] L 152/16, [1994] 4 CMLR 482.   [187] OJ [1989] L 33/44, [1990] 4 CMLR 535.
[188] Cases T-68/89 etc *Società Italiana Vetro SpA v Commission* [1992] ECR II-1403, [1992] 5 CMLR 302.

substantive infringement of Article 81 in the maritime transport sector was imposed in *French-West African Shipowners' Committees*[189] upon shipowners which had agreed to a cargo-sharing system in respect of traffic between France and various west African countries.

An elaborate 'price before tonnage scheme' was found to be anti-competitive by the Commission in *Cartonboard*[190] which involved the 'freezing' of market shares, the constant monitoring and analysis of them, and the coordination of 'machine downtime' in an effort to sustain prices and control supply. In *Europe Asia Trades Agreement*[191] the Commission concluded that an agreement for 'capacity non-utilisation' coupled with the exchange of information in relation to maritime transport infringed Article 81(1); in its view the agreement artificially limited liner shipping capacity, thereby reducing price competition[192]. In *Danish Association of Pharmaceutical Producers and the Danish Ministry for Health*[193] the Commission investigated a quota arrangement aimed at controlling public spending on price subsidies for pharmaceuticals. The Commission was concerned that the scheme infringed Article 81(1) and sought a settlement with the parties that would be less restrictive: the parties agreed not to renew the quota scheme when it terminated on 1 March 2001. In *Zinc Phosphate*[194] the Commission considered that the 'cornerstone' of the cartel was the allocation of sales quotas, although it also found that there was an agreement on the fixing of 'bottom' or recommended prices and some allocation of customers[195].

In *Gas Insulated Switchgear*[196] the Commission found that not only were the members of the cartel dividing the global market along geographical lines, but that they had also agreed worldwide quotas; and that the agreed European quota had itself been divided between the European undertakings in the cartel[197].

(B) Article 81(3)

It is unlikely that the type of agreements discussed in this section would satisfy the criteria of Article 81(3), although agreements on capacity and production volume may be permitted when indispensable to a legitimate specialisation agreement[198].

6. COLLUSIVE TENDERING

Collusive tendering is a practice whereby firms agree amongst themselves to collaborate over their response to invitations to tender. It is particularly likely to be

---

[189] OJ [1992] L 134/1, [1993] 5 CMLR 446.

[190] OJ [1994] L 243/1, [1994] 5 CMLR 547, paras 129–132.   [191] OJ [1999] L 193/23, [1999] 5 CMLR 1380.

[192] Ibid, paras 148–156.

[193] Commission Press Release IP/99/633, 17 August 1999; Commission's XXIXth *Report on Competition Policy* (1999), p 170.

[194] OJ [2003] L 153/1.   [195] Ibid, paras 64–72.

[196] Commission decision of 24 January 2007, on appeal Cases T-117/07 *Areva & others v Commission*, not yet decided.

[197] Commission decision of 24 January 2007, paras 116–120.

[198] See Article 5(2)(a) of Regulation 2658/2000, OJ [2000] L 304/3, [2001] 4 CMLR 800; for commentary on this Regulation, see ch 15, pp 589–592.

encountered in the engineering and construction industries where firms compete for very large contracts; often the tenderee will have a powerful bargaining position and the contractors feel the need to concert their bargaining power. From a contractor's point of view collusion over tendering has other benefits apart from the fact that it can lead to higher prices: it may mean that fewer contractors actually bother to price any particular deal (tendering itself can be a costly business) so that overheads are kept lower; it may mean that a contractor can make a tender which it knows will not be accepted (because it has been agreed that another firm will tender at a lower price) and yet which indicates that it is still interested in doing business, so that it will not be crossed off the tenderee's list; and it may mean that a contractor can retain the business of its established, favoured customers without worrying that they will be poached by its competitors.

Collusive tendering takes many forms. At its simplest, the firms in question simply agree to quote identical prices, the hope being that in the end each will receive its fair share of orders. Level tendering however is extremely suspicious and is likely to attract the attention of the competition authorities, so that more subtle arrangements are normally made. The more complicated these are, the greater will be the cost to the tenderers themselves. One system is to notify intended quotes to each other, or more likely to a central secretariat, which will then cost the order and eliminate those quotes which it considers would result in a loss to some or all of the association's members. Another system is to rotate orders, in which case the firm whose turn it is to receive an order will ensure that its quote is lower than everyone else's. Again it may be that orders are allocated by the relevant trade association which will advise each member how it should proceed.

There is no doubt that collusive tendering is caught by Article 81(1)[199]. The practice was condemned by the Commission in *Re European Sugar Cartel*[200]. In *Building and Construction Industry in the Netherlands*[201] the Commission imposed a fine of €22,500,000 for regulating prices and tendering in the Dutch building and construction industry. Twenty-eight associations of firms had established an organisation, the SPO, which established a system of uniform price-regulating rules which were binding on all members. The rules had the effect of restricting or distorting competition, as members exchanged information with one another prior to tendering, concerted their behaviour in relation to the prices for tenders and operated a system whereby the 'entitled' undertaking could be certain of winning a particular contract. The fact that the Dutch Government approved of the system did not provide a defence under Article 81(1): rather it led to the Commission threatening proceedings against the Netherlands under Article 226 for having encouraged this anti-competitive behaviour. The Commission rejected arguments in favour of exemption under Article 81(3) in this decision[202]. In *Pre-Insulated Pipes*[203] the Commission concluded that the allocation of contracts on

[199] Note that it is also illegal in some countries, for example under a specific law in Germany and under the cartel offence in the UK where the agreement involves dishonesty: on the UK cartel offence see ch 10, pp 415–422.

[200] OJ [1973] L 140/17, [1973] CMLR D65.

[201] OJ [1992] L 92/1, [1993] 5 CMLR 135, upheld on appeal Case T-29/92 *SPO v Commission* [1995] ECR 11-289.

[202] OJ [1992] L 92/1, [1993] 5 CMLR 135, paras 115–131.

[203] OJ [1999] L 24/1, [1999] 4 CMLR 402, substantially upheld on appeal Cases T-9/99 etc *HFB Holding v Commission* [2002] ECR II-1487, [2001] 4 CMLR 1066.

the basis of 'respect for existing "traditional" customer relationships', as well as various measures to support the bid-rigging, amounted to an infringement of Article 81(1)[204].

In *FIEC/CEETB*[205] the Commission published a notice in which it indicated its intention to take no action in respect of an agreement between building contractors and sub-contractors which would standardise tendering procedures; the Commission required various amendments before announcing this indulgence. The agreement as amended would not limit price competition, nor would it prevent people from tendering who wished to do so; the advantage of the scheme was that it would reduce the cost of the tendering procedure.

In 2007 the Commission adopted two very important decisions in which it held that undertakings were guilty of bid-rigging: *Gas Insulated Switchgear*[206] and *Elevators and Escalators*[207]. In the former the Commission imposed fines of €750 million for bid-rigging, price fixing, allocation of projects, market sharing, and information exchanging; ABB was given 100 per cent immunity as it had blown the whistle; the fines of Siemens, Alstom and Areva were increased by 50 per cent for their leadership role as secretary of the cartel; the fine of ABB would have been increased by 50 per cent because it was a repeat offender, but ABB did not have to pay it as it was granted full immunity.

In the *Elevators and Escalators* decision the Commission imposed fines of €992 million – the largest set of fines for one decision in the history of Article 81, or indeed for an infringement of competition law anywhere in the world – on a series of undertakings for bid-rigging, price fixing, allocation of projects, market sharing, and the exchange of information in relation to the installation and maintenance of lifts and escalators in Belgium, Germany, Luxembourg, and the Netherlands[208]. The Commission said that the undertakings concerned informed each other of calls for tender and coordinated their bids according to pre-agreed cartel quotas. Cover bids were sometimes made: that is to say bids that gave the pretence of competition, but that were deliberately set at a higher price than that of the member of the cartel whose turn it was to be awarded a contract. Updated project lists were circulated among the members of the cartel, and there was an understanding that, where a member of the cartel had a long-standing or good relationship with a particular customer, it would get most of its business.

7. AGREEMENTS RELATING TO TERMS AND CONDITIONS

We have seen above that apart from agreements directly fixing prices, supra-competitive profits can also be earned in other ways, for example by limiting production, fixing quotas and dividing markets geographically. Similarly restrictive agreements which limit competition in the terms and conditions offered to customers can have this effect. An

---

[204] OJ [1999] L 24/1, [1999] 4 CMLR 402, para 147. [205] OJ [1988] C 52/2.

[206] Commission Press Release of 24 January 2007, on appeal Cases 110/07 etc *Siemens v Commission*, not yet decided.

[207] Commission Press Release of 21 February 2007, on appeal Cases T-145/07 etc *OTIS and others v Commission*, not yet decided.

[208] Note that fines of €75.4 million have also been imposed by the Austria competition authority in this sector: the press release can be found at www.bwb.gv.at.

agreement not to offer discounts is in effect a price restriction, as would be an agreement not to offer credit; it may well exist to buttress a price-fixing agreement. In some market conditions it might be that non-price competition is particularly significant because of the limited opportunities that exist for price-cutting; for example, in an oligopolistic market one oligopolist might be able to attract custom because it can offer a better after-sales service or guarantees or a free delivery service[209].

Although competition in terms and conditions is an important part of the competitive process, it is also true to say that in some circumstances standardisation of terms and conditions can be beneficial. This might have the effect of enhancing price transparency: that is to say a customer might be able more easily to compare the 'real' cost of goods or services on offer if he or she does not have to make some (possibly intuitive) allowances for the disparity in two sets of terms and conditions on offer. Again a trade association may have the knowledge and expertise (and legal resources) to draft appropriate standard form contracts which suit the needs of individual members whereas, acting individually, they would be unable to negotiate and conclude a set of terms and conditions suitable for their purpose. Competition law monitors the activities of trade associations carefully in order to ensure that they do not act as a medium for the restriction of competition, but will usually tolerate this function. Industry-based codes of practice may fall within the ambit of competition legislation, although they may be desirable and may be encouraged or even required by consumer legislation[210].

Article 81 is capable of catching agreements which limit competition on terms and conditions, and to the extent that this is effected through the medium of trade associations the application of that Article to 'decisions by associations of undertakings' will be particularly apposite. The Commission has condemned agreements only to supply on prescribed general conditions of sale[211] and it has also objected to them where they formed part of wider reciprocal exclusive dealing arrangements[212]. In *Vimpoltu*[213] the Commission condemned an agreement on terms and conditions which limited important 'secondary aspects of competition'. In *Publishers' Association: Net Book Agreements*[214] agreements to impose on resellers standard conditions of sale and measures taken to implement this were condemned, as they deprived retailers of the ability to deviate from fixed retail prices. In *TACA*[215] the Commission concluded that an agreement that prohibited members of a liner conference from entering into individual service contracts at rates negotiated between a shipper and an individual line infringed Article 81(1); under the agreement members were permitted to offer standard service contracts only on the terms negotiated by the TACA secretariat, which constituted a serious fetter on their ability to compete with one another.

The Commission has recognised the advantages for undertakings in having access to suitably drafted standard terms and conditions and has indicated that their use will

[209] On oligopoly generally see ch 14, pp 544–552.

[210] See eg s 8 of the Enterprise Act 2002.

[211] See *European Glass Manufacturers* OJ [1974] L 160/1, [1974] 2 CMLR D50; see similarly *FEDETAB* OJ [1978] L 224/29, [1978] 3 CMLR 524.

[212] See eg *Donck v Central Bureau voor de Rijwielhandel* OJ [1978] L 20/18, [1978] 2 CMLR 194.

[213] OJ [1983] L 200/44, [1983] 3 CMLR 619.

[214] OJ [1989] L 22/12, [1989] 4 CMLR 825.

[215] OJ [1999] L 95/1, [1999] 4 CMLR 1415, paras 379–380, upheld on this point on appeal in Cases T-191/98 etc *Atlantic Container Line AB v Commission* [2003] ECR II-3275; the Commission subsequently authorised a revised version of *TACA* OJ [2003] L 26/53, [2003] 4 CMLR 1001.

not attract the application of Article 81(1) in the absence of tacit agreements to standardise prices, rebates or conditions of sale[216]. Also the Commission granted individual exemption in the fire insurance sector to an agreement whereby insurance companies would be likely (though not obliged) to adopt the standard terms and conditions of Concordato, a non-profit making trade association[217].

8. INFORMATION AGREEMENTS[218]

(A) Introduction

An important competition law issue is whether undertakings run the risk of infringing Article 81 (or analogous provisions) when they exchange information with one another. This is an issue that the Commission has given consideration to over many years, from as early as 1968 in its *Notice on Cooperation Agreements*[219] and in numerous decisions from the 1970s onwards. Judgments of the ECJ, in particular *John Deere v Commission*[220] in 1994 and *Thyssen Stahl AG v Commission*[221] in 2003, shed important light on the issue. Two recent additions to the stock of knowledge on the exchange of information under Article 81 are the ECJ's judgment of 23 November 2006 in *Asnef-Equifax v Ausbanc*[222] and the Commission's draft *Guidelines on the application of Article 81 of the EC Treaty to maritime transport services*[223]. The draft *Guidelines* are likely to be adopted in the course of 2008 in anticipation of the demise of the block exemption that historically has been available for price-fixing agreements in the containerised maritime transport sector[224]; although they are specific to maritime transport, the principles set out in the draft are equally applicable to the exchange of information in other industries.

Two important preliminary points about information agreements will be made in sections (B) and (C) below.

(B) Exchange of information in support of an anti-competitive practice

There have been many cases in which the Commission has held that the exchange of information was unlawful where it was part of a mechanism for monitoring and/or enforcing compliance with some other agreement that was itself unlawful. For

---

[216] *Notice on Cooperation Agreements* 29 July 1968, para 11(2); the Commission's *Guidelines on Horizontal Cooperation Agreements* OJ [2001] C 3/2, [2001] 4 CMLR 819 replaced the 1968 Notice and do not deal with the point in the text; however there is no reason to suppose that the Commission has changed the view expressed in the 1968 Notice.

[217] *Concordato Incendio* OJ [1990] L 15/25, [1991] 4 CMLR 199.

[218] See generally *The Pros and Cons of Information Sharing* (Swedish Competition Authority, 2006) for a series of essays on the law and economics of information sharing; see also Capobianco 'Information exchange under EC competiton law' (2004) 41 Common Market Law Review 1247.

[219] JO [1968] C 75/3, [1968] CMLR D5; this Notice was repealed by the Commission's Notice *Guidelines on the applicability of Article 81 to Horizontal Cooperation Agreements* OJ [2001] C 3/2.

[220] Cases C-7/95 and C-8/95 [1998] ECR I-3111 and 3175, [1998] 5 CMLR 311; see Lenares 'Economic Foundations of EU Legislation Sharing Among Firms' (1997) 18 ECLR 66.

[221] Case C-194/99 [2003] ECR I-10821.   [222] Case C-238/05 [2006] ECR I-11125, [2007] 4 CMLR 224.

[223] OJ [2007] C 215/3.   [224] See ch 23, pp 964–965.

example where undertakings establish a cartel they will invariably put in place mechanisms that enable them to be sure that each participant is complying with the agreed rules, and the exchange of information is an important part of this policing function. Sometimes there will be a simple exchange of information between the members of the cartel; in other situations the collection, processing and dissemination of the information may be achieved through a trade association or some other common agency. If one looks at almost any of the Commission's decisions on hard-core cartels in the last few years, it will be seen that the unlawful agreement(s) in question – for example to fix prices, share out geographical markets, allocate quotas or to restrict competition in some other way – included the exchange of commercially sensitive business information.

Two examples should be sufficient to illustrate the point. In *Gas Insulated Switchgear*[225] the Commission imposed fines of €750 million on a cartel involving European and Japanese firms that divided the market geographically and allocated quotas. A feature of this case was that cartel secretaries were appointed in Europe and Japan whose function was to receive and disseminate among the members information about forthcoming projects in the sector; this led to discussions about who was interested in winning the contract, whether some members of the cartel would make cover bids to give the (false) impression of competition, and to a final report as to who had actually won the contest.[226] In *Fasteners and Attaching Machines*[227] the Commission imposed fines of €328 million on members of four cartels in which price increases were coordinated, minimum prices were fixed, customers were allocated and commercially important and confidential information was exchanged.

This section is not concerned with this type of information exchange. The illegality of information exchanges of this kind is established by virtue of the fact that it is a mechanism for supporting behaviour that is illegal anyway[228]. Just as ancillary restrictions supportive of a legitimate agreement are legal[229], the exchange of information pursuant to an illegal agreement is itself illegal. Rather this section is concerned with the question of whether the exchange of information can be unlawful in and of itself, irrespective of whether the participants in the exchange of information are guilty of cartelising the market through direct means.

(C) Discussions about current and future prices are usually characterised as price-fixing agreements in their own right

A second preliminary point is that the case law of the Community Courts has established that any discussion among competitors about their current and future prices is likely to be regarded as giving rise to an anti-competitive price-fixing agreement, the object of which is to restrict competition. It is not necessary for A and B to have

---

[225] Commission decision of 24 January 2007, on appeal Cases T-117/07 *Areva & others v Commission*, not yet decided.

[226] Commission decision of 24 January 2007, paras 121–123.

[227] Commission decision of 19 September 2007, on appeal Cases T-454/07 etc *Prym and others v Commission*, not yet decided.

[228] Note that para 40 of the Commission's draft *Guidelines on maritime transport* do not address information exchange of this kind: 'Where an exchange of information is ancillary to an anti-competitive practice its assessment must be carried out in combination with the assessment of that practice.'

[229] See ch 3, p 125

explicitly *agreed* that they will increase their prices: the mere fact of providing information to one another about pricing behaviour – or even for one to provide such information to the other – is likely to be sufficient for a finding of an agreement on prices. It is not a defence for an undertaking to argue that it attended a meeting at which prices were discussed, but that it maintained silence throughout the meeting, and gave no indication of its own intentions. Attendance is sufficient to implicate the undertaking in the price-fixing agreement unless it left the meeting and took positive action to 'publicly distance' itself from any unlawful behaviour[230]. In the absence of public distancing, contact with competitors that involves discussion about present or future prices is likely to be regarded as an infringement of Article 81 in its own right. The message could hardly be clearer: do not remain at a meeting at which competitors discuss prices.

(D) When do 'pure' exchanges of information infringe Article 81?[231]

This section will consider when the exchange of information which is not ancillary to some other anti-competitive practice, as described in (B) above, and which is not regarded as a price-fixing agreement in its own right, as in (C), can infringe Article 81 in its own right.

It is important to understand that information – including, therefore, the exchange of information – may be highly beneficial, to competitors, consumers and to the competitive process. Competitors cannot compete in a statistical vacuum: the more information they have about market conditions, the volume of demand, the level of capacity that exists in an industry, and the investment plans of rivals, the easier it is for them to make rational and effective decisions on their production and marketing strategies. Competitors may benefit, without harming their customers, by exchanging information on matters such as methods of accounting, stock control, book-keeping, or the draftsmanship of standard-form contracts. Benchmarking, whereby undertakings measure their performance against 'best practice' in their industry, may enable them to improve their efficiency[232]. Information may also be exchanged about new forms of technology and the results of research and development projects. By spreading technological know-how, information agreements can help to increase the number of firms capable of operating on the market[233]. Consumers too will benefit from an increase in information: the more they know about the products available and their prices, the easier it will be for them to make satisfactory choices. Indeed perfect competition is dependent on consumers having perfect information about the market[234]: market transparency is, in general, to be encouraged. Quite often the reason why a market does

---

[230] See ch 3, pp 101–102.

[231] For a recent discussion of this topic see Grassani 'Oligopolies and "Pure" Information Exchanges in the EU: New Crops are Growing on the Soils Plowed by "*UK Tractors*"' Fordham Corporate Law Institute (ed Hawk), 2007; this article helpfully reviews – and expresses some concerns about – recent decisions by the NCAs of France, Italy, Spain and the UK, where it perceives possible inconsistencies in enforcement activities.

[232] See Henry 'Benchmarking and Antitrust' (1993) 62 Antitrust Law Journal 483; on benchmarking and EC law see Carle and Johnsson 'Benchmarking and EC Competition Law' (1998) 19 ECLR 74; Boulter 'Competition Risks in Benchmarking' (1999) 20 ECLR 434.

[233] See Teece 'Information Sharing, Innovation and Antitrust' (1993) 62 Antitrust Law Journal 465.

[234] See ch 1, pp 7–8.

not work well for consumers is that the information available to them is too sparse or confusing; in some markets there may actually be too much information for consumers to be able to digest. It is noticeable that, in quite a few of the cases referred by the OFT in the UK to the Competition Commission, the latter body has imposed remedies geared to enable consumers to make better-informed choices by giving them access to better information[235].

However there are, of course, dangers to the competitive process if certain types of information are exchanged in certain market conditions. In essence the question is whether the exchange of information could have an adverse effect[236] on competition by providing a platform for undertakings to coordinate their behaviour and to act in a parallel manner without explicitly entering into an agreement or concerted practice to do so[237]. This was explained by the ECJ in *Thyssen Stahl AG v Commission*[238], at paragraphs 82 and 83 of its judgment, when it was discussing the nature of concerted practices under Article 81(1) EC:

The criteria of coordination and cooperation necessary for determining the existence of a concerted practice, far from requiring an actual plan to have been worked out, are to be understood in the light of the concept inherent in the provisions of the EC and ECSC Treaties on competition, according to which each trader must determine independently the policy which he intends to adopt on the common market and the conditions which he intends to offer to his customers (see Case C-7/95 P *John Deere*, paragraph 86, and the case-law cited therein).

While it is true that this right of independence does not deprive traders of the right to adapt themselves intelligently to the existing or anticipated conduct of their competitors, *it does, however, strictly preclude any direct or indirect contact between such traders, the object or effect of which is to create conditions of competition which do not correspond to the normal condition of the market in question*, regard being had to the nature of the products or services offered, the size and number of the undertakings and the volume of the said market (Case 7–95 *John Deere*, paragraph 87, and the case-law cited therein) (emphasis added).

In *Asnef-Equifax v Ausbanc*[239] the ECJ referred to both the *John Deere* and the *Thyssen Stahl* judgments when it said that:

According to the case-law on agreements on the exchange of information, such agreements are incompatible with the rules on competition if they reduce or remove the degree of uncertainty as to the operation of the market in question with the result that competition between undertakings is restricted.[240]

(E) A full market analysis is required

Since the analysis of information agreements of the kind under discussion in this section requires effects analysis – that is to say since such agreements do not restrict competition by object – it follows that a full review of the context in which the exchange of

---

[235] See ch 11, pp 467–468.

[236] Note that information agreements that do not support an agreement that is itself anti-competitive, and that do not concern current and future prices, do not restrict competition by object, but only by effect: see para 48 of the ECJ's judgment in Case C-238/05 *Asnef-Equifax v Ausbanc* [2006] ECR I-11125, [2007] 4 CMLR 224.

[237] Ch 14 discusses the problem of tacit coordination in oligopolistic markets in detail.

[238] Case C-194/99 [2003] ECR I-10821; the ECJ's judgment on this point can be traced back to its 1975 judgment in Cases 40/73 *Suiker Unie v Commission* [1975] ECR 1663, [1976] 1 CMLR 295, paragraphs 173–174.

[239] Case C-238/05 [2006] ECR I-11125, [2007] 4 CMLR 224.   [240] Ibid, para 51.

information is taking place is required[241]. The point is made very clearly in the ECJ's judgment in *Asnef-Equifax*[242]:

[t]he compatibility of an information exchange system...with the Community competition rules cannot be assessed in the abstract. It depends on *the economic conditions on the relevant markets* and on *the specific characteristics of the system* concerned, such as, in particular, its purpose and the conditions of access to it and participation in it, as well as *the type of information exchanged* – be that, for example, public or confidential, aggregated or detailed, historical or current – the periodicity of such information and its importance for the fixing of prices, volumes or conditions of service[243] (emphasis added).

The purpose of this analysis is to determine whether the exchange could 'reduce or remove' uncertainty between undertakings so that competition is restricted. The ECJ in *Asnef-Equifax* focused on three issues, each of which accords with economic theory.

(i) The economic conditions on the relevant markets

In the first place it is important to consider the structure of the market. It is easier for undertakings to behave in a parallel manner in an oligopolistic market where the products are homogeneous. The greater the degree of product differentiation and the more atomistic the structure of competition, the more difficult and expensive it will be to align prices and to prevent other firms from cheating. In the Commission's draft *Guidelines on maritime transport*[244] it says that the level of concentration and the structure of supply and demand on a given market are key issues in considering whether an exchange falls within Article 81(1)[245]. It notes that the Herfindahl-Hirschman Index may assist in determining the concentration level of the market[246], and that parallel behaviour may be easier depending on the transparency of information on the market[247]. The Commission also notes that the structure of supply and demand is an important consideration, notably the number of competing operators and the symmetry and stability of their market shares[248].

The Commission's concern with the economic conditions of the market when considering whether an exchange of information could be caught by Article 81(1) can be seen in its practice over many years. For example in both *International Energy Program*[249] and *Non-ferrous Semi-manufacturers*[250] it specifically referred to the oligopolistic structure of the markets in question. In *UK Agricultural Tractor Registration Exchange*[251] the Commission condemned an information exchange system, placing considerable emphasis on the fact that the UK tractor market was oligopolistic: in particular it took into account that four firms on the UK market had a combined market share of approximately 80 per cent and that in some geographical areas the concentration was higher; that barriers to entry were high, especially as extensive distribution and servicing networks were necessary; that the market was stagnant or in decline and there was considerable brand loyalty; and that there was an absence of significant imports[252]. The Commission published a Press Release after this decision in which it said that the same result would

---

[241] See ch 3, pp 116ff for a discussion of the distinction between object and effect analysis under Article 81.
[242] Case C-238/05 [2006] ECR I-11125, [2007] 4 CMLR 224.
[243] Ibid, para 54. [244] OJ [2007] C 215/3. [245] Ibid, para 47.
[246] Ibid, para 48; see ch 1, pp 41–42 on the 'HHI Index'. [247] OJ [2007] C 215/3, para 48.
[248] Ibid, para 49. [249] OJ [1983] L 376/30, [1984] 2 CMLR 186.
[250] Commission's Vth *Report on Competition Policy* (1975), point 39.
[251] OJ [1992] L 68/19, [1993] 4 CMLR 358. [252] Ibid, para 35.

not necessarily arise in the car market, which is much more competitive[253]. In its decision in *Wirtschaftsvereinigung Stahl*[254], condemning an information agreement under Article 65 ECSC, the Commission stressed at paragraphs 39 and 44 to 46 of its decision that the market in question was concentrated and had high barriers to entry.

In *Eudim*[255] the Commission was more relaxed about the exchange of information between wholesalers of plumbing, heating and sanitary materials. The information related both to the purchasing and the selling activities of members of the association. Even though some of the information was of a kind that would normally be regarded as confidential, the Commission had no concern at all about the purchasing side of the market, which was highly competitive; it considered that, since there was no oligopoly on the selling side, there could be no appreciable effect on competition.

(ii) The specific characteristics of the system

An important consideration is whether the information exchanged is shared with customers or not: the Commission states in the draft *Guidelines on maritime transport* that the more the information is shared with customers, the less likely it is to be problematic[256]. The Commission had noted this concern in *Re VNP and COBELPA*[257], where the information exchanged was concealed from customers[258]. In *UK Agricultural Tractor Registration Exchange*[259] the Commission was influenced in its adverse view of the information exchange by the fact that participants in the system had kept the information confidential amongst themselves; when this decision was upheld by the ECJ it noted that the information exchanged was not available to purchasers, but only to the parties to the agreement[260].

(iii) The type of information exchanged

A very important consideration is the type or quality of information which is exchanged. The crucial question always is whether it could enable undertakings to behave in a parallel manner. The Commission's draft *Guidelines on maritime transport* are particularly useful on this point.

The exchange of information already in the public domain does not infringe Article 81(1)[261]. Information which is not historic and which relates to matters such as price, capacity, and cost is commercially sensitive, and therefore its exchange is more likely to infringe than other information[262]. The exchange of individual data about particular undertakings is more problematic than aggregated data[263]. The age of the data and the period to which it belongs are relevant[264]: the question is whether the information enables undertakings to predict each other's future behaviour, so that historic data are less significant than current ones. The Commission tends to regard information that

---

[253] Commission Press Release IP/92/148, 4 March 1992.

[254] OJ [1998] L 1/10, [1998] 4 CMLR 450; this decision was annulled on appeal Case T-16/98 *Wirtschaftsvereinigung Stahl v Commission* [2000] ECR II-1217, [2001] 5 CMLR 310.

[255] OJ [1996] C 111/8, [1996] 4 CMLR 871.

[256] OJ [2007] C 215/3, para 59.   [257] OJ [1977] L 242/10, [1977] 2 CMLR D28.

[258] See similarly *Genuine Vegetable Parchment Association* OJ [1978] L 70/54, [1978] 1 CMLR 534.

[259] OJ [1992] L 68/19, [1993] 4 CMLR 358.

[260] Cases C-7/95 P and C-8/95 P *John Deere v Commission* [1998] ECR I-3111, [1998] 5 CMLR 311, para 91.

[261] OJ [2007] C 215/3, para 50.   [262] Ibid, para 51.   [263] Ibid, para 52.   [264] Ibid, para 53.

is more than one year old as historic[265]. The frequency of any information exchange is also a relevant factor[266].

Some Commission decisions illustrate its past decisional practice in relation to the type of information exchanged. For obvious reasons it has always been concerned about price information, but other concerns can be seen. In *Re Cimbel*[267] it condemned the obligation upon members of a trade association that they should inform each other of projected increases in industrial capacity: such an obligation could prevent one firm from gaining an advantage over competitors by expanding in time to meet an increase in demand. Similarly it condemned the obligation to inform rivals of investment plans in *Zinc Producer Group*[268]. It has condemned exchanges of information which specifically identify the output and sales figures of individual firms[269] and which might have the effect of rigidifying the operation of a distribution system, particularly if it might facilitate the partitioning of the market[270]. In 1999 the Commission closed its files in relation to a number of cases involving the exchange of information between manufacturers of tractors and agricultural machinery and their trade associations, in the aftermath of its *Tractors* decision[271], after it had ensured that individual data would not be exchanged earlier than one year after the event to which it pertained and that aggregated data would not be exchanged if it could be used to identify individual information about the position of undertakings[272]. In *EATA*[273] the Commission objected to the exchange of information as to capacity, percentage utilisation and forecast capacity in the maritime transport sector, noting, specifically, that the information was not aggregated but clearly stated to which party it related[274].

In *Steel Beams*[275] the Commission found an information exchange on orders and deliveries of beams by individual companies in each Member State to go 'beyond what is admissible'[276], since the figures exchanged showed the deliveries and orders received by each individual company for delivery to their respective markets; this information was updated every week and circulated rapidly among the participants. The Commission added that the exchange was not limited to figures 'of a merely historical value with no possible impact on competition'[277]. The CFI confirmed the Commission's assessment, since the exchange of confidential information undermined the principle that every trader must determine its market strategy independently. In *Wirtschaftsvereinigung Stahl* the Commission decided that an exchange of information on deliveries and market shares in relation to various products infringed Article 65(1) ECSC; on appeal the CFI annulled this decision because the Commission had erred in its findings of fact[278].

---

[265] Ibid.   [266] Ibid, para 54.   [267] OJ [1972] L 303/24, [1973] CMLR D167.

[268] OJ [1984] L 220/27, [1985] 2 CMLR 108.

[269] See *Associated Lead Manufacturers* OJ [1979] L 21/16, [1979] 1 CMLR 464; *Atka A/S v BP Kemi A/S* OJ [1979] L 286/32, [1979] 3 CMLR 684; *Benelux Flat Glass* OJ [1984] L 212/13, [1985] 2 CMLR 350; *UK Agricultural Tractor Registration Exchange* OJ [1992] L 68/19, [1993] 4 CMLR 358.

[270] *Camera Care Ltd v Victor Hasselblad* OJ [1982] L 161/18, [1982] 2 CMLR 233; *UK Agricultural Tractor Registration Exchange* OJ [1992] L 68/19, [1993] 4 CMLR 358, paras 53–56.

[271] OJ [1992] L 68/19, [1993] 4 CMLR 358.

[272] See the Commission's XXIXth *Report on Competition Policy* (1999), pp 156–157.

[273] OJ [1999] L 193/23, [1999] 5 CMLR 1380.   [274] Ibid, paras 153–155.

[275] OJ [1994] L 116/1, [1994] 5 CMLR 353, paras 263–272, upheld on appeal to CFI in Cases T-141/94 etc *Thyssen Stahl AG v Commission* [1999] ECR II-347, [1999] 4 CMLR 810, paras 385–412 and further upheld on appeal to ECJ in Case C-194/99 P [2003] ECR I-10821.

[276] OJ [1994] L 116/1, [1994] 5 CMLR 353, para 267.   [277] OJ [1994] L 116/1, [1994] 5 CMLR 353, para 268.

[278] OJ [1998] L 1/10, [1998] 4 CMLR 450, annulled on appeal Case T-16/98 *Wirtschaftsvereinigung Stahl v Commission* [2001] ECR II-12217, [2001] 5 CMLR 310.

In *CEPI/Cartonboard*[279] the Commission indicated its intention to approve an information exchange agreement once it had been amended so that only historical, aggregated data would be involved.

(F) *Asnef-Equifax*[280]

The *Asnef-Equifax* case provides an interesting illustration of the application of Article 81 to an exchange of information. In that case credit institutions in Spain provided information to a trade association about the creditworthiness of borrowers: the information was compiled by the association and made available to all the participating institutions. The ECJ noted that credit registers such as this exist in numerous countries, and provide credit institutions with information about borrowers that makes it easier for them to foresee the likelihood of repayment (or default)[281]. The exchange of such information did not restrict competition by object[282]. Having explained that the question therefore was whether the credit register could lead to parallel behaviour, the ECJ noted that the market in question was a fragmented one: that is to say that it was not concentrated, which would have been a factor conducive to parallel behaviour[283]; it also noted that it was a condition of the system that no information was made available to credit institutions about the commercial strategy of competitors[284]; it also stated that it was important that the register should be available to any operator on the market on non-discriminatory terms[285]. As the case was an Article 234 reference from the Tribunal Supremo of Spain, it was not for the ECJ to make a decision on the facts of the case; however it would seem fairly clear that its view was that the register in question did not infringe Article 81(1); the Court also appears to have thought that, in the event that Article 81(1) was infringed, Article 81(3) was likely to be satisfied[286].

(G) Agreement to exchange information

To infringe Article 81(1) undertakings must have agreed to exchange information. It is not sufficient simply that they are able to obtain information about each other's behaviour, for example through the press or by discussions with customers; this in itself does not involve the necessary ingredient of an agreement. Where a (genuine) third party collects, compiles and supplies information to customers, Article 81(1) would not be infringed. In *Wood Pulp*[287] the ECJ ruled that the fact that pulp producers announced price rises to users before those rises came into effect was not, in itself, sufficient to constitute an infringement of Article 81(1)[288]. On the other hand, exchanges of information which were not obligatory in a contractual sense could amount to a 'gentleman's agreement' or a concerted practice and so be caught by Article 81(1) where they have

---

[279] OJ [1996] C 310/3, [1996] 5 CMLR 725.   [280] Case C-238/05 [2006] ECR I-11125, [2007] 4 CMLR 224.
[281] Ibid, para 47.   [282] Ibid, para 48.   [283] Ibid, para 58.   [284] Ibid, para 59.   [285] Ibid, para 60.
[286] Ibid, paras 64–71; see ch 4, pp 157–158, on the discussion of 'a fair share for consumers' in this judgment.
[287] Cases C-89/85 etc *A Ahlström Oy v Commission* [1993] ECR I-1307, [1993] 4 CMLR 407.
[288] [1993] ECR I-1307, [1993] 4 CMLR 407, paras 59–65.

the effect of restricting or distorting competition[289]. In *Asnef-Equifax v Ausbanc*[290] the ECJ held that, where credit institutions participated in the creation of a register of information about the solvency of customers, it was not particularly important to decide whether this happened as a result of an agreement, a concerted practice or a decision of an association of undertakings: the aim of Article 81(1) was to catch different forms of coordination and collusion between undertakings[291].

(H) Fines

On one occasion, in *Fatty Acids*[292], the Commission imposed a fine of €50,000 on undertakings which entered into an agreement to exchange information which enabled each to identify the individual business of its two main rivals on a quarterly basis, thereby removing an important element of uncertainty on the part of each as to the activities of the others. It is not clear whether the Commission would today impose a fine in a case such as this: certainly this would be unusual in the case of a restriction by effect rather than object.

(I) Article 81(3)

Under EC law the main question has revolved around the application of Article 81(1) to information agreements, and in *Re VNP and COBELPA*[293] the Commission indicated that an information agreement within Article 81(1) would be unlikely to satisfy the criteria of Article 81(3). In *UK Agricultural Tractor Registration Exchange*[294] the Commission rejected the parties' request for an exemption in terse terms. However in exceptional circumstances an agreement may satisfy the criteria of Article 81(3) because of its beneficial effects. In *International Energy Program*[295] a programme was drawn up between 21 States belonging to the OECD. The purpose of the programme was to establish cooperation between States in the event of disruptions in the supply of oil. The participation of companies was an important element in this programme and they were required *inter alia* to supply important and normally secret information in the event of a disruption. The Commission granted an individual exemption: not surprisingly it felt that the strategic importance of maintaining supplies of oil outweighed the loss of competition occasioned by the exchange of information. In *Asnef-Equifax* the ECJ suggested that the exchange of information in that case might satisfy the criteria of Article 81(3)[296].

---

[289] See eg *IFTRA Free Trade Rules on Glass* OJ [1974] L 160/1, [1974] 2 CMLR D50: the Commission concluded that the exchanges of information that took place were an integral part of the participants' intention to protect national markets.

[290] Case C-238/05, judgment of 23 November 2006, [2006] ECR I-11125, [2007] 4 CMLR 224.

[291] Ibid, paras 30–32.   [292] OJ [1985] L 3/17, [1989] 4 CMLR 445.

[293] OJ [1977] L 242/10, [1977] 2 CMLR D28.   [294] OJ [1992] L 68/19, [1993] 4 CMLR 358.

[295] OJ [1983] L 376/30, [1984] 2 CMLR 186; see Brands 'The International Energy Agency and the EC Competition Rules' [1984(1)] LIEI 49.

[296] See p 530 above.

(H) B2B markets[297]

A specific issue in relation to the exchange of information is whether the establishment of 'B2B' electronic markets may give rise to competition law problems, in particular by facilitating collusion and/or foreclosing access to the market. Clearly competition authorities would not be happy if Internet chat rooms were to become the twenty-first century equivalent of the 'smoke-filled rooms' of the nineteenth and twentieth centuries. In a B2B market undertakings establish an electronic market place where it is possible, for example, to sell and purchase goods and services. Typically electronic market places result in a considerable exchange of information, both between sellers and purchasers but also between competitors themselves, on both the selling and purchasing side of the market. Universal access to the Internet means that this information is instantly accessible to everyone involved in the electronic market.

The Commission has not adopted any formal decisions on B2B markets under Article 81; however it has settled several cases informally. The first occurred in the case of *Covisint*[298]; several more followed[299]. Many other cases have been dealt with under the EC Merger Regulation rather than Article 81[300]. The Commission's approach has been benign: however, certain guidelines should be followed when establishing B2Bs. First, it is important that B2Bs do not allow the exchange of information of the kind discussed above, since that could facilitate collusive behaviour; second, if necessary 'firewalls' should be established to ensure against such an anticompetitive exchange; third, joint purchasing or commercialisation within a B2B should accord with the general principles set out by the Commission in its Horizontal Cooperation Guidelines[301]; fourth, the Commission may not accept rules that require *exclusive* use of a particular B2B; and fifth, the Commission is likely to require that open, non-discriminatory access to the B2B is available to all interested buyers and sellers[302].

9. ADVERTISING RESTRICTIONS

The function of advertising in competition policy raises important and controversial issues which can be dealt with only briefly here[303]. Advertising is an essential part of the

---

[297] See Vollebregt 'E-Hubs, Syndication and Competition Concerns' (2000) 21 ECLR 437; Lancefield 'The Regulatory Hurdles Ahead in B2B' (2001) 22 ECLR 9.

[298] Commission Press Release IP/01/1155, 31 July 2001.

[299] See *Eutilia and Endorsia* Commission Press Release IP/01/1775, 10 December 2001; *Eurex* Commission Press Release IP/02/4, 3 January 2002; *Inreon* Commission Press Release IP/02/ 761, 24 May 2002; *Multibank trading platform* Commission Press Release IP/02/943, 27 June 2002; *Ondeo and Thames Water* Commission Press Release IP/02/956, 28 June 2002.

[300] See eg Case No M.1969 *UTC/Honeywell/i2/MyAircraft.com*; Case No M.2075 *Jupiter/ M&G/Scudder/JV*.

[301] OJ [2001] C 3/2, [2001] 4 CMLR 819: see ch 15, pp 592–594 (joint purchasing) and pp 594–596 (commercialisation).

[302] For a helpful summary of the Commission's practice see Lucking 'B2B e-marketplaces and EC competition law: where do we stand?' Competition Policy Newsletter, October 2001, p 14.

[303] See eg Cowling *Advertising and Economic Behaviour* (1975); Telser 'Advertising and Competition' 72 J Pol Ec 536 (1964); Brozen 'Entry Barriers: Advertising and Product Differentiation' in *Industrial*

competitive process. Unless the consumer knows what goods and services are on offer and what their price is he or she will be unable to choose what to buy and competition between suppliers will be diminished.

Competition is about attracting business and a vital part of the process is to advertise one's products. Therefore competition law should ensure that advertising is not restricted[304]. Indeed it may be thought appropriate to impose upon businesses a duty to advertise prices, terms and conditions or details of quality in order to provide the consumer with the information needed to enable him or her to make a rational choice; however it should be noted that a perverse consequence of forcing undertakings to publicise their prices could be to facilitate tacit collusion between them. A separate point is that the significance of advertising means that steps should be taken to ensure the truth of advertisements and, perhaps, to prevent the appropriation of innovative advertising ideas by competitive rivals; comparative advertising, whereby a competitor's products are unfavourably compared with one's own, might also be objected to[305].

In some circumstances collaboration between independent undertakings in their advertising activities may not be harmful. For example, a group of small producers may decide to sell a product under a common label and agree on the specifications and publicity of the product in question; they will all contribute to the advertising costs of this product. By doing this they may be able to present a strong brand image which will enhance their ability to compete with other firms on the market. Such schemes may be pro-competitive, although it will be necessary to ensure that nothing in the agreement limits competition unnecessarily, such as direct price fixing or market sharing. Again there may be a case for some collaboration on advertising – for example by agreeing to limit the number of industrial exhibitions visited in a year – if this will have the effect of rationalising advertising efforts and reducing advertising costs.

The importance of advertising in competition policy has an important side effect: namely that the advertising media themselves should function efficiently and be free from restrictive trade practices which might reduce the availability of advertising space. Various cases in the US have endeavoured to maintain an open advertising market[306].

Against the above line of reasoning there runs a quite different argument. This is that advertising costs are a serious barrier to entry to new firms wishing to enter a market as well as being a wasteful use of resources[307]. In some markets, such as lager, detergents and breakfast cereals, enormous amounts of money are spent in building up a brand image and it is argued that new entrants would be unable to expend the money on advertising necessary to match this. The problem, it is said, is accentuated by the fact that established firms have the accumulated advantage of past advertising and also that they have the capacity to indulge in 'predatory' advertising, that is short-term expensive campaigns designed to prevent the new entrant establishing a toe-hold in the market. Opinion on the barrier-raising effect of advertising is divided. Bork and other

Concentration: *The New Learning* (1974); Scherer and Ross *Industrial Market Structure and Economic Performance* (Houghton Mifflin, 3rd ed, 1990), pp 436 et seq.

[304] Restrictions on advertising in the US are regarded as an indirect form of price fixing and are accordingly *per se* illegal; cf *California Dental Association v Federal Trade Commission* 526 US 756 (1999).

[305] Note that there is a Community directive on misleading, including comparative, advertising: Directive 97/55/EC OJ [1997 L 290/18.

[306] See eg *United States v Lorain Journal* 342 US 143 (1951).

[307] See eg Turner 'Conglomerate Mergers and s 7 of the Clayton Act' 78 Harv L Rev 1313 (1965).

commentators have argued forcefully that it should not be treated as a barrier and there is empirical evidence which sheds doubt on the argument[308].

A separate objection to advertising comes from a quite different quarter, namely the liberal professions. They have argued that advertising is inimical to their ethical standards and that consumer protection in their spheres of activity is best served by maintaining professional standards through self-regulation, codes of practice and professional ethics.

(A) Article 81(1)

Article 81(1) does apply to agreements to restrict advertising which have anti-competitive effects. In several decisions the Commission has stated that it considers that such restrictions limit an important aspect of competitive behaviour[309]. In the case of trade fairs, it has often held that the rules for participation infringe Article 81(1), although it has gone on to permit exemption subject to conditions (see below). Trade fair rules may affect competition in various ways: participants may be required not to take part in other fairs, thus limiting their competitive opportunities; other organisers of such fairs will lose business as a result of such exclusivity rules; and potential partici-pants might be excluded from a trade fair by its rules, thus limiting their impact on the market. In 1988 the Commission, for the first time in a trade fair case, imposed a fine (of €100,000) on the *British Dental Trade Association*[310] for anti-competitive exclusion of would-be exhibitors.

In a number of decisions[311] the Commission has revealed a benevolence towards advertising restrictions which might promote a particular brand image without ser-iously impairing competition in other ways. However in *Belgian Roofing Felt*[312] the Commission condemned joint advertising of roofing felt under the Belasco trade mark where this led to the uniform image of products in a sector in which individual adver-tising may facilitate differentiation and therefore competition. The Commission's *Guidelines on Horizontal Cooperation Agreements*[313] provide guidance on the applica-tion of Article 81 to so-called 'commercialisation agreements', which may involve joint advertising[314].

Restrictions on comparative advertising by patent agents practising at the European Patent Office in Munich were held to infringe Article 81(1) in *EPI Code of Conduct*[315] but to be exemptable for a short period whilst new rules were adopted[316].

---

[308] See eg Bork *The Antitrust Paradox* (The Free Press, 1993), pp 314–320.

[309] See eg *Re Vimpoltu* OJ [1983] L 200/44, [1983] 3 CMLR 619.

[310] OJ [1988] L 233/15, [1989] 4 CMLR 1021; an exemption was given for the Association's rules as modi-fied to satisfy the Commission.

[311] *Re VVVF* OJ [1969] L 168/22, [1970] CMLR D1; *Re Association pour la Promotion du Tube d'Acier Soude Electriquement* JO [1970] L 153/14, [1970] CMLR D31; *Re Industrieverband Solnhofener Natursteinplatten* OJ [1980] L 318/32.

[312] OJ [1986] L 232/15, [1991] 4 CMLR 130, upheld on appeal Case 246/86 *Belasco v Commission* [1989] ECR 2117, [1991] 4 CMLR 96.

[313] OJ [2001] C 3/2, [2001] 4 CMLR 819.   [314] See ch 15, pp 594–596.

[315] OJ [1999] L 106/14, [1999] 5 CMLR 540, paras 39–45, partially annulled on appeal to the CFI, Case T-144/99 *Institut des Mandataires Agréés v Commission* [2001] ECR II-1087, [2001] 5 CMLR 77; see the Commission's XXIXth *Report on Competition Policy* (1999), pp 53 and 159–160.

[316] OJ [1999] L 106/14, [1999] 5 CMLR 540, paras 46–48.

(B) Article 81(3)

The Commission has accepted that in appropriate circumstances it can be advantageous to rationalise and coordinate advertising efforts. In a series of cases on trade fairs the Commission has authorised agreements which contain rules requiring participants to limit the number of occasions on which they exhibit elsewhere and restricting the extent to which they are allowed to advertise in other ways[317]. The Commission has often applied conditions to such authorisations. For example in *UNIDI*[318] the Commission required the introduction of an arbitration procedure to deal with complaints by exhibitors excluded from an exhibition. In *VIFKA*[319] it required the removal of a provision requiring exhibitors of office equipment not to exhibit elsewhere for a period of two years, as this was too long.

10. ANTI-COMPETITIVE HORIZONTAL RESTRAINTS

The agreements so far considered have been concerned with cartels limiting competition and raising prices to earn supra-competitive profits. It is likely however that, in the absence of barriers to entry, this in itself will attract new entrants into the market. It is because of this that the members of a cartel will frequently take further action designed to fend off the possibility of new competition in just the same way that a monopolist might. For example, a collective reciprocal exclusive dealing arrangement might be negotiated whereby a group of suppliers agree with a group of dealers to deal only with one another. The effect may be to exclude other producers from the market if they cannot find retail outlets for their products. This is not an inevitable result however: to have a serious foreclosing effect there would have to be a lack of alternative retail outlets, for example due to barriers to entry at the retail level. A common pricing system may be supported by an aggregated rebates cartel, whereby purchasers are offered rebates calculated according to their purchases from all the members of the cartel; the disincentive to buy elsewhere is obvious[320]. Again it may be decided to boycott any dealer who handles the products of producers outside the cartel. As one would expect, exclusionary devices such as these which can cause serious harm to the competitive process are *per se* illegal in the US[321], although it has been argued that

[317] *Re CECIMO* OJ [1969] L 69/13, [1969] CMLR Dl, renewed OJ [1979] L 11/16, [1979] 1 CMLR 419 and again OJ [1989] L 37/11; *Re BPICA* OJ [1977] L 299/18, [1977] 2 CMLR D43, renewed OJ [1982] L 156/16, [1983] 2 CMLR 40; *Re Cematex* JO [1971] L 227/26, [1973] CMLR D135, renewed OJ [1983] L 140/27, [1984] 3 CMLR 69; *Re UNIDI* OJ [1975] L 228/14, [1975] 2 CMLR D51, renewed OJ [1984] L 322/10, [1985] 2 CMLR 38; *Re Society of Motor Manufacturers and Traders Ltd* OJ [1983] L 376/1, [1984] 1 CMLR 611; *VIFKA* OJ [1986] L 291/46; *Internationale Dentalscbau* OJ [1987] L 293/58; *Sippa* OJ [1991] L 60/19, [1992] 5 CMLR 529.

[318] OJ [1984] L 322/10, [1985] 2 CMLR 38, challenged unsuccessfully in Case 43/85 *ANCIDES v Commission* [1987] ECR 3131, [1988] 4 CMLR 821.

[319] OJ [1986] L 291/46.

[320] Aggregated rebates cartels are unlikely where prices are *not* fixed, because they would discriminate against those offering lower prices.

[321] See eg *Klors Inc v Broadway – Hale Stores Inc* 359 US 207 (1959): for a review of US case law see Glazer 'Concerted Refusals to Deal under Section 1 of the Sherman Act' (2002) 70 Antitrust Law Journal 1; see also

the breadth of the rule against collective boycotts is inappropriate[322]. The pejorative label given to group boycotts conceals the fact that in some cases independent firms will inevitably decide to refuse to deal with certain people, for example by refusing inadequately trained people entrance to a profession or inefficient dealers access to a branded product. A distinction should be made between naked restraints which are clearly intended to be exclusionary on the one hand and agreements which promote efficiency and which therefore may be permitted.

The Commission and the Community Courts have had to deal with a great number of collective exclusive dealing arrangements and other potentially exclusionary practices. Often such agreements are entered into by a national association which is keen to keep imports out of the domestic market. A more obvious target for the Commission it is hard to imagine and the Community Courts have usually upheld its findings. A scheme designed to keep washing machines out of the Belgian market was found by the ECJ to infringe Article 81(1)[323], as was a marketing system which could prevent imports of fruit into Holland[324]. The ECJ agreed with the Commission that an exclusive purchasing agreement which obliged members of an association to acquire rennet solely from a Dutch cooperative was unlawful[325]. The ECJ also held that practices designed to buttress the collective resale price maintenance of Dutch and Belgian books infringed Article 81[326].

The rigid collective exclusive dealing systems in two cigarette cases, affecting the Belgian and Dutch markets respectively, were both condemned by the ECJ[327]. The Commission has dealt with many other similar situations, always striking such agreements down[328]. In *Hudson's Bay – Dansk Pelsdyravlerforening*[329] the Commission imposed a fine of €500,000 on a Danish trade association for imposing an obligation on its members that they should sell their entire production to a subsidiary of the association, thereby preventing them from selling their products to other Member States. The decision on this point was upheld on appeal to the CFI[330]. In *Dutch Mobile Cranes*[331] the

the UK Competition Appeal Tribunal in Case No 1003/2/1/01 *Institute of Independent Insurance Brokers v Director General of Fair Trading* [2001] CAT 4, [2001] CompAR 62, para 189.

[322] See eg Bork *The Antitrust Paradox* (The Free Press, 1993), ch 17.

[323] Cases 96/82 etc *IAZ International Belgium NV v Commission* [1983] ECR 3369, [1984] 3 CMLR 276; note the additional fine subsequently imposed by the Commission in this case: *Re IPTC Belgium SA* OJ [1983] L 376/7, [1984] 2 CMLR 131.

[324] Case 71/74 *FRUBO v Commission* [1975] ECR 563, [1975] 2 CMLR 123; see similarly *Irish Timber Importers Association XXth Report on Competition Policy* (1990), point 98.

[325] Case 61/80 *Cooperatieve Stremsel-en Kleurselfabriek v Commission* [1981] ECR 851, [1982] 1 CMLR 240.

[326] Cases 43/82 and 63/82 *VBVB & VBBB v Commission* [1984] ECR 19, [1985] 1 CMLR 27.

[327] Cases 209/78 etc *Van Landewyck v Commission* [1980] ECR 3125, [1981] 3 CMLR 134; Cases 240/82 etc *SSI v Commission* [1985] ECR 3831, [1987] 3 CMLR 661 and Case 260/ 82 *NSO v Commission* [1988] 4 CMLR 755.

[328] *Re Gas Water-Heaters* OJ [1973] L 217/34, [1973] CMLR D231; *Re Stoves and Heaters* OJ [1975] L 159/22, [1975] 2 CMLR D1; *Re Bomée Stichting* OJ [1975] L 329/30, [1976] 1 CMLR D1; *Groupement d'Exportation du Leon v Société d'Investissements et de Cooperation Agricoles (Cauliflowers)* OJ [1978] L 21/23, [1978] 1 CMLR D66; *Donck v Centraal Bureau voor de Rijwielbandel* OJ [1978] L 20/18, [1978] 2 CMLR 194; *Re IMA Rules* OJ [1980] L 318/1, [1981] 2 CMLR 498; *Re Italian Flat Glass* OJ [1981] L 326/32, [1982] 3 CMLR 366.

[329] OJ [1988] L 316/43, [1989] 4 CMLR 340.

[330] Case T-61/89 *Dansk Pelsdyravlerforening v Commission* [1992] ECR II-1931.

[331] OJ [1995] L 312/79, [1996] 4 CMLR 565, upheld on appeal Cases T-213/95 and T-18/96 *SCK and FNK v Commission* [1997] ECR II-1739, [1997] 4 CMLR 259.

Commission imposed fines on a trade association found to have operated a price-fixing system whereby its members were obliged to charge 'recommended' rates for the hiring of mobile cranes; it also condemned the rules of a second association that effectively prohibited members from hiring cranes from firms not affiliated to it.

In *Dutch Electrotechnical Equipment*[332] the Commission imposed fines of €4.4 million on FEG and €2.15 million on TU for entering into collective exclusive dealing arrangements intended to prevent supplies to non-members of the associations by directly and indirectly restricting the freedom of members to determine their selling prices independently. The facts of this case resemble many of the decisions of the Commission on collective exclusive dealing from the 1970s and 1980s[333]: the fact that there are still arrangements like this in existence is perhaps a vindication of the Commission's desire to focus its resources on the elimination of practices that one might have assumed had long since been discontinued. In this decision, the Commission reduced the fine it would otherwise have imposed due to the prolonged period of the proceedings, which had begun in 1991, for which it was partly to blame[334].

In *Road Bitumen*[335] the Commission imposed fines of €266.71 million for price fixing on the part of eight suppliers and six purchasers of road bitumen in the Netherlands. An interesting feature of the case is that the large construction companies that were in the cartel were not particularly concerned that the suppliers were fixing prices: road building in the Netherlands is paid for, ultimately, by the tax-payer. The large construction companies were simply concerned to win as many orders as possible, and there were price rebates on offer from the suppliers that discriminated in favour of them, and against smaller competitors: in other words the pricing system in this case operated to exclude third parties from the market.

In *Morgan Stanley Dean Witter/Visa*[336] the Commission imposed a fine of €10.2 million on Visa for refusing to admit Morgan Stanley to the Visa system without objective justification. This is an example of an anti-competitive horizontal restraint in that Visa consists of a number of undertakings that determine who may become a Visa member. There was a rule that said that membership was not available to a bank that issued a card that would compete with the Visa card. The Commission did not object to the rule as such, but as to the way it was applied in relation to Morgan Stanley: first, it did not issue a card that competed with Visa *within the EU*: Morgan Stanley's Discover Card had a presence only in the US; and, second, Visa had, in practice, allowed other banks to join that did have cards in Europe, so that the rules had been applied in a discriminatory manner. In another decision on payment systems, *Groupement des Cartes Bancaires*[337], the Commission decided that the way in which the rules of the 'Cartes Bancaires' systems were applied in France infringed Article 81 because they operated in favour of

---

[332] OJ [2000] L 39/1, [2000] 4 CMLR 1208, on appeal Cases T-5/00 *NAVEG v Commission* [2003] ECR II-5761, [2004] 5 CMLR 969, on further appeal Cases C-105 and 113/04 P [2006] ECR I-8725, [2006] 5 CMLR 1257; see also the Commission's XXIXth *Report on Competition Policy* (1999), p 135.

[333] See n 328 above.

[334] See paras 151–153 of the decision: the Commission was applying the judgment of the ECJ in Case C-185/95 P *Baustahlgewebe v Commission* [1998] ECR I-8417, [1999] 4 CMLR 1203, reducing (very slightly) a fine due to the protracted hearing of the appeal to the CFI.

[335] Commission Press Release of 13 September 2006, on appeal Cases T-343/06 *Shell Petroleum and Others v Commission*, not yet decided; see Nuijten and Van Barlingen 'Commission fines fourteen undertakings...' *Competition Policy Newsletter*, Spring 2007, p 71.　　　　[336] Commission decision of 3 October 2007.

[337] Commission decision of 17 October 2007, on appeal Case T-491/07 *CB v Commission*, not yet decided.

the major banks in France and to the detriment, for example, of banks established by retailers such as Carrefour and Auchan and Internet banks.

11. **UK LAW**[338]

The UK competition authorities share the European Commission's determination to eliminate cartels. The Competition Act 1998 gives to the OFT substantial powers of investigation and enforcement[339], resembling those of the Commission, to enforce Article 81 EC and the Chapter I prohibition. Some introductory points can be made in respect of the OFT's approach to the eradication of cartels in the UK. First, the OFT has published a number of Guidelines on the Competition Act[340]; paragraphs 3.3 to 3.27 of the Guideline on *Agreements and Concerted Practices*[341] provide guidance on a number of types of agreement that might infringe Article 81 or the Chapter I prohibition, including agreements that have as their object or effect:

*   Directly or indirectly fixing prices
*   Fixing trading conditions
*   Sharing markets
*   Limiting or controlling production or investment
*   Collusive tendering
*   Joint purchasing or selling
*   Sharing information
*   Exchanging price information
*   Exchanging non-price information
*   Restricting advertising
*   Setting technical or design standards.

A second introductory point is that the OFT has published a booklet designed to enable purchasers to identify cartel activity and to encourage them to bring their suspicions to the attention of the OFT[342]; it has also published an empirical study into the economic and structural factors that contribute to the formation, maintenance and detection of cartels[343]. Third, the OFT has a branch specifically established to investigate cartels[344]. Fourth, UK policy is to encourage whistleblowers, and the OFT has received a large number of applications for immunity since the Act entered into force[345]. Finally, the Enterprise Act 2002 introduces a criminal 'cartel offence' which can result in the fining or imprisonment of individuals responsible for hard-core cartel activity[346].

The OFT's enforcement activity in relation to cartels was somewhat limited in the early years of the Competition Act. The position began to change from 2004 onwards,

---

[338]   See generally chs 9 and 10 on the substantive and procedural rules of the Competition Act 1998.
[339]   See ch 10, pp 385–393 and 395–414.   [340]   See ch 9, pp 325–326.
[341]   OFT 401, December 2004; see also *Trade Associations, professions and self-regulating bodies*, OFT 408, December 2004.
[342]   *Cartels and the Competition Act 1998: a Guide for Purchasers*, OFT 435, March 2005.
[343]   *Predicting cartels*, OFT 773, March 2005.   [344]   See ch 2, p 65.   [345]   See ch 10, pp 404–407.
[346]   See ch 10, pp 415–422.

as the OFT began to adopt a series of decisions imposing fines for collusive tendering in the construction sector, although the fines imposed in these cases never amounted to more than £2 million[347]. However a significant change occurred in 2007 when, in the case of *British Airways*[348], the OFT announced that British Airways had admitted colluding with Virgin Atlantic over the price of long-haul passenger fuel surcharges between August 2004 and January 2006; BA agreed to pay a fine of £121.5 million. A formal decision against BA recording the decision will be taken in due course. There was no fine on Virgin Atlantic as it had blown the whistle. The OFT is also conducting a criminal investigation under the Enterprise Act 2002 into whether any individuals involved in this case dishonestly fixed the levels of the surcharges[349]. The Department of Justice in the US announced that BA had pleaded guilty under US law to price fixing in relation to both passenger and cargo flights and that it had agreed to pay a fine in the US of $300 million[350].

The OFT gave details in December 2007 of another significant case in which agreement had been reached with undertakings for the payment of fines. In the *Dairies* case[351] six undertakings – Asda, Dairy Crest, Safeway (in relation to conduct prior to its acquisition by Morrisons), Sainsbury's, The Cheese Company, and Wiseman – admitted involvement in price-fixing practices, of both a horizontal and a vertical nature, and agreed to pay fines of £116 million. Three other undertakings, Lactalis McLelland, Morrisons, and Tesco, refrained from participating in the settlement of this case, and administrative proceedings against them were continuing as at 12 March 2008; Lactalis subsequently did settle with the OFT[352].

Two other major cartel cases came into the public domain in the course of 2007. In March 2007 the OFT announced that it was investigating a number of suspected cartels in the construction sector, involving bid rigging in relation to thousands of tenders with a combined estimated value of £3 billion[353]; the OFT offered reduced fines to all undertakings implicated in these cartels that had not already applied for leniency but that were willing to cooperate with the OFT in the conclusion of the investigations. In May 2007 the OFT announced that it was investigating, in conjunction with the Department of Justice in the US and the European Commission, a cartel in the marine hose sector (marine hoses are used to transport oil from oil tankers to storage depots)[354]. On 19 December 2007 the OFT announced that three individuals had been charged with the criminal cartel offence in section 188 of the Enterprise Act, the first time that this has happened under that legislation: they were sentenced to terms of imprisonment of up to three years in June 2008[355]; these same individuals (and others) have also pleaded guilty to committing criminal offences under US antitrust laws and have agreed to serve terms of imprisonment there of up to 30 months[356]. A feature of this case was the substantial cooperation between the various competition authorities involved.

---

[347] See pp 541–542 below.   [348] OFT Press Release 113/07 of 1 August 2007.

[349] See the Press Release referred to in n 348 above.

[350] DoJ Press Release of 1 August 2007, available at www.usdoj.gov/atr/public/press_releases/2007/224928. htm; the same Press Release states that Korean Air Lines had also agreed to pay a fine of $300 million and that there are other ongoing investigations.

[351] OFT Press Release 170/07 of 7 December 2007.   [352] OFT Press Release 22/08, 15 February 2008.

[353] See OFT Press Releases 49/07 and 50/07 of 22 March 2007.

[354] OFT Press Release 70/07 of 3 May 2007.   [355] OFT Press Release 72/08 of 11 June 2008.

[356] DoJ Press Release of 12 December 2007, available at www.usdoj.gov/atr/public/press_releases/2007/228561.htm.

(A) Horizontal price fixing[357]

The *British Airways* and *Dairies* cases have already been referred to above. The OFT's decisions to date in relation to collusive tendering are discussed in section (D) below. The OFT's decisions in *Football Shirts* and *Toys and Games*, which involved horizontal and vertical price fixing, were discussed in detail in chapter 9[358].

The OFT has dealt with price fixing in a few other cases, some of which were settled informally in the early years of the legislation. In a Press Release in January 2001 the OFT warned that allegations of price fixing, even between small businesses such as private cab firms, would be investigated under the Competition Act 1998[359]. In *Northern Ireland Livestock and Auctioneers' Association*[360] the OFT concluded that a recommendation by the Association as to the commission that its members should charge for the purchase of livestock in Northern Ireland cattle marts infringed the Chapter I prohibition, but it decided not to impose a fine, not least because the infringement occurred at a time when the beef sector was suffering as a result of so-called 'mad cow' disease[361]. The OFT closed its investigation into the fee guidance provided by the Royal Institute of British Architects to its members after RIBA varied the guidance so that it could no longer facilitate collusion on prices[362]. In *Stock Check Pads*[363] the OFT imposed fines of £2,184,767, reduced to £168,318 for leniency, on undertakings found to have fixed prices (and shared markets) for stock check pads, used by staff in cafes and restaurants to record customers' orders. In *Aluminium Spacer Bars*[364] fines of £1,384,050, reduced to £898,470 for leniency, were imposed for price fixing, customer allocation and market sharing for aluminium spacer bars used in double glazing.

In *LINK Interchange Network Ltd*[365] the OFT granted individual exemption to the multilateral interchange fee collectively agreed between banks whose customers withdraw cash from cash points. The OFT's decision that MasterCard's interchange fees infringed the Chapter I prohibition was subsequently withdrawn; the OFT continues to investigate MasterCard's current fees[366].

(B) Agreements relating to terms and conditions[367]

Agreements on terms and conditions and codes of practice may be caught by the Chapter I prohibition.

---

[357] See *Agreements and Concerted Practices*, OFT 401, December 2004, paras 3.4–3.8.
[358] See ch 9, pp 331–333.   [359] OFT Press Release, PN 01/01, 10 January 2001.
[360] OFT Decision of 3 February 2003, [2003] UKCLR 433.   [361] Ibid, paras 37–49.
[362] See *Royal Institute of British Architects* Weekly Gazette of the OFT, Competition case closure summaries, 17–23 May 2003; see similarly the case closures in the case of *The Notaries Society*, 30 April 2004 and in the case of *British Chemical Distributors and Traders Association*, 11 May 2004.
[363] OFT Decision of 4 April 2006, [2007] UKCLR 211, upheld on appeal in Case 1067/1/1/06 *Achilles Group Ltd v OFT* [2006] CAT 24, [2007] CompAR 1.
[364] OFT Decision of 29 June 2006, [2006] UKCLR 921, upheld on appeal in Case 1072/1/1/06 *Sepia Logistics Ltd v OFT* [2007] CAT 13, [2007] CompAR 747.
[365] OFT Decision, 16 October 2001, available at www.oft.gov.uk.
[366] OFT Decision of 5 September 2005, [2006] UKCLR 236.
[367] See *Agreements and Concerted Practices*, OFT 401, December 2004, para 3.9.

(C) Horizontal market sharing[368]

The first fine to be imposed under the Competition Act in a cartel case occurred in *Market Sharing by Arriva plc and FirstGroup plc*[369], where those two companies were found to have shared bus routes in the Leeds area. The *Stock Check Pads*[370] decision involved market sharing as well as price fixing, and the *Aluminium Spacer Bars*[371] decision included findings of customer allocation and market sharing.

A market-sharing agreement was terminated following investigation by the OFT in the case of *Suppliers of Laboratory Materials*[372].

(D) Quotas and other restriction on production[373]

The OFT decided to permit an agreement in *Memorandum of Understanding on the supply of oil fuels in an emergency*[374] which would enable the Government to direct supplies of fuel to 'essential users' such as providers of emergency services in the event of a fuel shortage: the OFT's view was that the agreement satisfied the criteria of section 9 of the Competition Act[375].

(E) Collusive tendering[376]

Beginning with *West Midland Roofing Contractors* in 2004 the OFT has adopted a number of decisions involving collusive tendering. The fines imposed (before and after allowances for leniency and appeals) in these cases were as follows:

- *West Midland Roofing Contractors*[377] (£971,186, reduced to £297,625 after leniency and to £288,625 after appeal[378])

- *Mastic Asphalt Flat-roofing Contracts in Scotland*[379] (£231,445, reduced to £87,353 after leniency)

- *Felt and Single Ply Roofing Contracts in Western-Central Scotland*[380] (£238,576, reduced to £138,515 after leniency)

- *Flat Roof and Car Park Surfacing Contracts in England and Scotland*[381] (£1.852 million, reduced to £1.557 million after leniency).

---

[368] See *Agreements and Concerted Practices*, OFT 401, December 2004, paras 3.10–3.11.

[369] OFT Decision of 30 January 2002.

[370] OFT Decision of 4 April 2006, [2007] UKCLR 211, upheld on appeal in Case 1067/1/1/06 *Achilles Group Ltd v OFT* [2006] CAT 24, [2007] CompAR 1.

[371] OFT Decision of 29 June 2006, [2006] UKCLR 921, upheld on appeal in Case 1072/1/1/06 *Sepia Logistics Ltd v OFT* [2007] CAT 13, [2007] CompAR 747.

[372] OFT Press Release 26/04, 12 February 2004.

[373] See *Agreements and Concerted Practices*, OFT 401, December 2004, para s 3.12–3.13.

[374] OFT Decision, 25 October 2001, available at http://www.oft.gov.uk.   [375] Ibid, paras 62–63.

[376] See *Agreements and Concerted Practices*, OFT 401, December 2004, para 3.14.

[377] OFT Decision of 17 March 2004, [2004] UKCLR 1119.

[378] Case No 1032/1/1/04 *Apex Asphalt and Paving Co Ltd v OFT* [2005] CAT 4, [2005] CompAR 507 and Case No 1033/1/1/04 *Richard W Price Ltd v OFT* [2005] CAT 5, [2005] CompAR 801.

[379] OFT Decision of 7 April 2005, [2005] UKCLR 638.

[380] OFT Decision of 11 July 2005, [2005] UKCLR 1015.

[381] OFT Decision of 23 February 2006, [2006] UKCLR 579.

As noted above the OFT is continuing to investigate a significant number of cases of suspected collusive tendering in the construction sector[382]. In January 2007 the OFT, in conjunction with the Office of Government Commerce, published a joint guide for public sector procurers of construction services on achieving value through the competitive process; it also highlights practical steps to avoid falling victim to collusive tendering[383].

The judgment of the Competition Appeal Tribunal in *Apex Asphalt and Paving Co Ltd v OFT*[384] is particularly useful on the legal analysis of collusive tendering. The OFT had concluded that various roofing contractors, including Apex Asphalt, were guilty of colluding in relation to the making of tender bids for flat roofing contracts in the West Midlands. Having set out the principles of relevance to determining whether undertakings are party to an agreement or concerted practice[385], the CAT proceeded to apply them to a tendering process in which some of the participating undertakings make 'cover bids', that is to say that they submit a price for a contract that is not intended to win the contract (the reason for doing this is that it maintains the appearance of competition, and indicates that the person offering the cover bid wishes to continue participating in future invitations to tender). In the CAT's view:

- A tendering process is designed to produce competition in a very structured way
- Bidders are sometimes required to certify that they have not had contact with competitors in the preparation of their bids
- Where the tendering is selective rather than open to all potential bidders the loss of independence through knowledge of the intentions of other selected bidders is particularly likely to distort competition[386].

The CAT was satisfied on the facts of the case that Apex was party to a concerted practice. The CAT applied the same reasoning in *Makers UK Ltd v OFT*[387], an unsuccessful appeal against the OFT's decision in *Flat Roof and Car Park Surfacing Contracts in England and Scotland*.

(F) Information agreements[388]

In *Exchange of Information on Future Fees by Certain Independent Fee-Paying Schools*[389] the participant schools submitted details of their current fee levels, proposed fee increases (expressed as a percentage) and the resulting intended fee levels to the bursar of one of the schools, who then circulated the information to all the other participants in a tabular form. The OFT concluded that this agreement restricted competition by object; it made no finding as to the effect of the agreement[390]. The OFT declined to accept commitments from the schools under section 31A of the Competition Act since the infringement was a serious one[391]. Each school agreed to pay a nominal fine

---

[382] See p 539 above.
[383] *Making competition work for you*, available at www.ogc.gov.uk/documents.
[384] Case 1032/1/1/04 [2005] CAT 4, [2005] CompAR 507.   [385] Ibid, para 206.
[386] Ibid, paras 208–212.   [387] Case 1061/1/1/06 [2007] CAT 11, [2007] CompAR 699, paras 103–110.
[388] See *Agreements and Concerted Practices*, OFT 401, December 2004, paras 3.17–3.23.
[389] OFT Decision of 20 November 2006.
[390] Ibid, paras 1348–1358.
[391] Ibid, paras 31–32; on the section 31A commitments procedure see ch 10, pp 396–397.

of £10,000, and they agreed to make *ex gratia* payments of £3 million into a trust fund to benefit pupils who attended the schools during the period of the information exchange[392].

(G) Advertising restrictions[393]

The OFT accepts that the restriction of advertising may diminish competition; however, attempts to curb misleading advertising, or to ensure that advertising is legal, truthful and decent, are unlikely to have an appreciable effect on competition[394].

(H) Anti-competitive horizontal restraints

Other anti-competitive agreements could also be subject to the Chapter I prohibition. In the *General Insurance Standards Council* decision[395] the OFT concluded that the rules of that association did not appreciably restrict competition. On appeal the Competition Appeal Tribunal was of the view that a rule that meant that intermediaries could not sell the general insurance products of GISC's members unless they (the intermediaries) were also members of GISC amounted to a collective boycott and therefore a restriction of competition contrary to the Chapter I prohibition; in the Tribunal's view, the rules could be upheld, if at all, only by recourse to the 'exemption' criteria in section 9 of the Act[396]. In the event the offending rule was dropped, so that the OFT was able to adopt a fresh decision confirming that there was no infringement of the Act[397].

In the case of *England Rugby* the OFT closed its file on a complaint that the 'Entry and Ongoing Criteria' rules of English Rugby Ltd that determined entry into the English Premiership discriminated against rugby teams playing in the first Division after some amendments had been made to the entry criteria[398]. The rules of the *Glasgow Solicitors Property Centre* were amended following investigation by the OFT to ensure that they were transparent, proportionate, non-discriminatory and based on objective standards[399].

[392] OFT Press Releases 165/06 of 22 November 2006 and 182/06 of 21 December 2006 provide details of the trustees appointed to administer the fund.

[393] See *Agreements and Concerted Practices*, OFT 401, December 2004, para 3.24.

[394] See also *Trade Associations, Professions and Self-Regulating Bodies*, OFT Guideline 408, December 2004, para 3.14.

[395] OFT Decision of 26 January 2001, [2001] UKCLR 331.

[396] Case No 1003/2/1/01 *Institute of Independent Insurance Brokers v Director General of Fair Trading* [2001] CAT 4, [2001] CompAR 62, para 261.

[397] *GISC*, 22 November 2002, available at www.oft.gov.uk.

[398] Case Closure of 6 August 2003, available at www.oft.gov.uk/advice_and_resources/resource_base/ca98/closure.

[399] OFT Press Release 154/03 of 1 December 2003.

14

Horizontal agreements (2) – oligopoly, tacit collusion and collective dominance

CHAPTER CONTENTS

1. INTRODUCTION

This chapter is concerned with the related topics of oligopoly, tacit collusion and collective dominance. Put at its simplest, a problem for competition policy arises in markets in which there are only a few operators who are able, by virtue of the characteristics of the market, to behave in a parallel manner and to derive benefits from their collective market power, without, or without necessarily, entering into an agreement or concerted practice to do so in the sense of Article 81 EC or the Chapter I prohibition of the Competition Act 1998. This phenomenon is known in economics as 'tacit collusion', an expression which jars with lawyers, who associate the notion of collusion with actively conspiratorial behaviour of the kind captured by the expressions 'agreement' and 'concerted practice' in Article 81 and the Chapter I prohibition. The terms 'conscious parallelism', 'tacit coordination' and 'coordinated effects' may be preferable to tacit collusion, in that they connote the idea of parallel behaviour without attaching the opprobrious term 'collusion'[1]. Nevertheless 'tacit collusion' is included in the title of this chapter in deference to the weight of the economics literature which uses it.

The issue for competition policy is to determine, assuming that the problem just described does indeed exist, how to deal with it: is the 'oligopoly problem' one of behaviour, in which case is it possible to deal with it through the application of Articles 81 and 82 and their domestic equivalents; or is it one that arises from the structure of the industry in question, in which case structural solutions, most obviously through the system of merger control but also, in the UK, through the market investigation provisions of the Enterprise Act 2002 ('the EA 2002'), may be needed to address it?

[1] See pp 547–548 below.

This chapter will begin with discussion of oligopolistic interdependence. Section 3 will consider the extent to which Articles 81 and 82 can be used to address it. Section 4 of the chapter discusses UK law and, in particular, the possible use of the market investigation provisions of the Enterprise Act or the system of merger control established by it. The extent to which the problem of coordinated behaviour on the part of oligopolists can be addressed in the investigation of mergers is discussed further in chapters 20 to 22 of this book.

2. THE THEORY OF OLIGOPOLISTIC INTERDEPENDENCE

(A) Outline of the theory

The basic objection to monopoly is that a monopolist is able to restrict output and thereby increase the price of its goods or services. As a result it earns supra-competitive profits and society is deprived of the output it has suppressed. In perfect competition no firm has sufficient power over the market to affect prices by an alteration in its output; each firm 'takes' the price from the market and that price will coincide with the cost of producing the product in question[2]. Competition law typically intervenes to prevent independent undertakings coordinating their marketing behaviour and earning quasi-monopoly profits by reducing their output: Article 81 EC and Chapter I of the Competition Act 1998 prohibit horizontal price-fixing agreements and analogous 'hard-core' cartels and punish them severely[3].

(i) The meaning of oligopoly and a warning about the term

In reality few markets are perfectly competitive and many are oligopolistic; the general trend in recent years has undoubtedly been towards an increase in industrial concentration. There is a vast literature on the 'problem' of oligopoly[4]. Oligopoly is a phenomenon that exists somewhere on the continuum that begins at monopoly and ends at perfect

---

[2] See ch 1, pp 4–6.   [3] See ch 13 generally.

[4] See eg Turner 'The Definition of Agreement under the Sherman Act: Conscious Parallelism and Refusals to Deal' (1962) 75 Harvard Law Review 655; Posner 'Oligopoly and the Antitrust Laws: A Suggested Approach' (1969) 21 Stanford Law Review 1562; Tirole *The Theory of Industrial Organisation* (The MIT Press, 1988), ch 6; Scherer and Ross *Industrial Market Structure and Economic Performance* (Houghton Mifflin, 3rd ed, 1990), chs 6–8; Stevens 'Covert Collusion and Conscious Parallelism in Oligopolistic Markets: A Comparison of EC and US Competition Law' (1995) Oxford Yearbook of European Law 47; Monti 'Oligopoly: Conspiracy? Joint Monopoly? Or Enforceable Competition?' (1996) 19(3) World Competition 59; Lopatka 'Solving the Oligopoly Problem: Turner's Try' (1996) 41 Antitrust Bulletin 843; Lipsey and Chrystal *Principles of Economics* (Oxford University Press, 9th ed, 1999), pp 176–181; National Economic Research Associates *Merger Appraisal in Oligopolistic Markets* (OFT Research Paper 19, 1999); Europe Economics *Study on Assessment Criteria for Distinguishing between Competitive and Dominant Oligopolies in Merger Control* (DG Enterprise, May 2001); Bishop and Walker *The Economics of EC Competition Law* (Sweet & Maxwell, 2nd ed, 2002), paras 2.28–2.42 and paras 7.28–7.60; Ivaldi, Jullien, Rey, Seabright and Tirole 'The Economics of Tacit Collusion' Final Report for DG Competition, March 2003; Werden 'Economic Evidence on the Existence of Collusion: Reconciling Antitrust Law with Oligopoly' (2004) 71 Antitrust Law Journal 719; Brock 'Antitrust Policy and the Oligopoly Problem' (2006) 51 Antitrust Bulletin 227; see also some of the earlier economics literature, eg Hall and Hitch 'Price Theory and Business Behaviour' (1939) 2 Oxford Economic Papers 12–45; Sweezy 'Demand under Conditions of Oligopoly' (1937) 47 J Pol Ec 568–575; Stigler 'The Kinky Oligopoly Demand Curve' (1947) 55 J Pol Ec 431.

competition, or 'polypoly', where 'mono' means one, 'oligo' a few and the first 'poly' in polypoly means many.

The expression oligopoly is not entirely helpful in describing the situation of concern for competition authorities, since there are many markets in which there are only a few sellers and yet which are highly competitive; and there are others in which there may be many economic operators and yet a failure of the competitive market mechanism. Some oligopolies are 'benign' in terms of competition; others may be malign where they are particularly conducive to uncompetitive outcomes. For this reason it is increasingly recognised that to address the problem of 'oligopoly', as if the problem were purely numerical, is to miss the correct target. The expression oligopoly means 'sale by a few sellers', but it is not the fact of 'fewness', in itself, that is the problem. To depict the problem as a matter of numbers does not do full justice to economists' concept of 'power over a market'; it is market power, whether individual or collective, that confers the ability to suppress output and to raise price to the detriment of consumers. It is true that the fewer the number of players in a market, the more likely it is that collective market power will exist; however, the identification of market power is not simply a matter of counting heads. There is, nevertheless, a certain catchiness in talking of 'the oligopoly problem', and there is no harm in using the expression provided that the caveat just entered is kept in mind.

(ii) The oligopoly problem

The main argument against oligopoly is that the structural conditions of the market in which oligopolists operate are such that they will not compete with one another on price and will have little incentive to compete in other ways; furthermore they will be able to earn supra-competitive profits without entering into the type of collusive agreement or concerted practice generally proscribed by competition law. In a perfectly competitive market a firm which cuts its price will have an imperceptible effect on its competitors, so that they will not need to respond. In an oligopoly a reduction in price would swiftly attract the customers of the other two or three rivals, the effect upon whom would be so devastating that they would have to react by matching the cut. Similarly an oligopolist could not increase its price unilaterally, because it would be deserted by its customers if it did so. Thus the theory runs that in an oligopolistic market rivals are interdependent: they have a heightened awareness of each other's presence and are bound to match one another's marketing strategy. The result is that price competition between them will be minimal or non-existent; oligopoly produces non-competitive stability. The literature on so-called 'game theory' and 'the Prisoner's Dilemma', which recognises that firms take into account the likely actions (and reactions) of competitors when deciding how to behave, is supportive of this view of oligopoly[5].

The argument can be taken further. All firms have a will to maximise profits: profits are greater in monopolistic markets in which output is suppressed. Oligopolists recognise

---

[5] See *Tirole* pp 205–208; *Scherer and Ross* pp 208–215; *Bishop & Walker* paras 2.28–2.30; *Lipsey and Chrystal* p 181; Franzosi 'Oligopoly and the Prisoner's Dilemma: Concerted Practices and "As If" Behaviour' (1988) 9 ECLR 385; Carlton and Perloff *Modern Industrial Organisation* (Longman, 3rd ed, 1999); Church and Ware *Industrial Organisation: A Strategic Approach* (McGraw-Hill/Irwin, 2000); Cabral *Introduction to Industrial Organization* (MIT Press, 2000); Van den Bergh and Camesasca *European Competition Law and Economics: A Comparative Perspective* (Sweet & Maxwell, 2006), pp 156–159; Motta *Competition Policy: Theory and Practice* (Cambridge University Press, 2004), ch 8; see generally Philips *Competition Policy: A Game Theoretic Perspective* (Cambridge University Press, 1995).

their interdependence as well as their own self-interest. By matching each other's conduct they will be able to achieve and charge a profit-maximising price which will be set at a supra-competitive level, without actually communicating with one another in any way at all. There does not need to be a collusive agreement: the structure of the market is such that, through interdependence and mutual self-awareness, prices will rise towards the monopolistic level. Also the non-competitive environment in which oligopolists function will enable them to act in an inefficient and wasteful manner.

These theoretical arguments have been buttressed by empirical research which purports to show that there is a direct correlation between industrial structure and profit levels, which are said to increase in line with the concentration ratio of the industry in question[6], although the soundness of much of this evidence has been called into question[7]. The logical conclusion of the case against oligopoly is that, since it is the industrial structure itself which produces the problem, structural measures should be taken to remedy it by deconcentrating the market. Unless this is done, there will be an area of consciously parallel action in pricing strategies which is beyond the reach of conspiracy laws and yet which has serious implications for consumer welfare.

(iii) Terminology: 'tacit collusion'; 'conscious parallelism'; 'tacit coordination'; 'coordinated effects'

There is little doubt that there are markets in which it is possible for economic operators to coordinate their behaviour without entering into an agreement or being party to a concerted practice in the sense of Article 81(1) or the Chapter I prohibition; such behaviour will be to their own self-advantage and to the disadvantage of customers and ultimately consumers. This situation is often described by economists as 'tacit collusion': enjoying the benefits of a particular market structure without actually entering into an agreement to do so. If the firms in question had achieved the same end through explicit collusion, economists would have the same objection – that prices would be higher than they would be without coordination. Economists have no particular interest in whether collusion is 'tacit' or 'explicit': it is the effects of the collusion that matter.

Lawyers, however, are considerably less comfortable with the expression tacit collusion. 'Collusion' is the evil at which Article 81 and the Chapter I prohibition are directed ('any *agreement* or *concerted practice* which has as its object or effect the prevention, restriction or distortion of competition'); in the same way section 1 of the US Sherman Act forbids 'every *contract* in restraint of trade', where the notion of collusiveness is inherent in the idea of contract. For many lawyers, to ask whether tacit collusion could be caught, for example, by the concept of collective dominance under Article 82 or the Chapter II prohibition in the UK is bizarre, since any behaviour that could be called collusive in a legal sense would be caught by Article 81 or the Chapter I prohibition anyway. If behaviour is not collusive under Article 81, lawyers not unnaturally feel uncomfortable at characterising the same behaviour as tacitly collusive under Article 82. An alternative expression for the conduct in question, 'conscious parallelism', may cause lawyers slightly less discomfort, the opprobrious word 'collusive' being avoided; but even 'consciousness' seems to move the enquiry back to a search for something sufficiently conspiratorial that it should really be investigated, if at all, under Article 81. In the interests of finding terminology

---

[6] See eg Bain 'Relation of Profit Rate to Industry Concentration' (1951) 65 Qu J Ec 293–324.

[7] See eg Weiss 'The Concentration and Profits Issue' in *Industrial Concentration: The New Learning* (1974); Brozen 'The Concentration-Collusion Doctrine' (1977) 46 Antitrust Law Journal 826.

which is meaningful and tolerable both to economists and to lawyers when considering the application of Article 82 it might be better to use the expression 'tacit coordination', since this at least eliminates the pejorative word 'collusion' whilst retaining the notion of parallel behaviour which is beneficial to the collectively dominant operators on the market and disadvantageous to customers and consumers. In the context of merger control, competition authorities often ask whether a merger would make it more likely that there would in the future be 'coordinated effects' on the market, which again has the benefit of avoiding reference to the idea of collusion.

(iv) 'Non-collusive oligopoly'

An additional complication is the recognition that certain mergers might give rise to competition problems where they would result in 'non-collusive oligopoly', that is to say a situation in which one or more members of an oligopoly, without being individually dominant, would be able to derive benefits from their market power without being dependent on the coordinated response of the other oligopolists. The existence of this possibility is now broadly accepted, albeit that it is fairly rare, and is something that can be addressed under the EC Merger Regulation ('the ECMR') since the substantive test was reformulated in 2004[8].

(v) The conditions needed for the successful exercise of collective market power

For tacit coordination to occur it is necessary for firms to indulge in a common form of behaviour[9]. Typically this would involve the charging of similar prices; however it might also involve parallel decisions to reduce production or not to expand capacity: such decisions would, through the suppression of output, in themselves have an impact on prices in the industry in question. Tacit coordination also requires that each firm will be able to monitor quickly and easily how the others are behaving on the market: successful parallel behaviour requires that no one should deviate from the common conduct; transparency is therefore vital to each economic operator to enable it to know what the others are doing, both in terms of their prices and their output. Finally it is important that discipline among the firms with collective market power can be maintained. The benefits to the few of tacit coordination will be lost if one or more firms depart from the appropriate behavioural standard; in order to prevent this from happening, it is necessary that some retaliatory mechanism should be in place to impose sanctions on deviant firms. The most obvious sanction would be a sharp price war which would be harmful to everyone, and would send a severe warning that abandonment of tacit coordination will be to everyone's disadvantage[10].

(B) Criticisms of the theory

The theory of oligopolistic interdependence has attracted criticism[11]. Four particular problems have been pointed out.

---

[8] See ch 21, pp 853–856.

[9] The indicia of tacit coordination have been particularly well explained in the European Commission's *Guidelines on the assessment of horizontal mergers* OJ [2004] C 31/3; they are discussed in ch 21, pp 860–862.

[10] As will be seen, the CFI's judgment in *Airtours* (see n 115 below) defines collective dominance under the ECMR consistently with the conditions set out in this paragraph: see p 564 below.

[11] See eg Bork *The Antitrust Paradox* (Free Press, 1993), ch 8.

The first is that the theory overstates the interdependence of oligopolists. Even in a symmetrical three-firm oligopoly one firm might be able to steal a march on its rivals by cutting its price if, for example, there would be a delay before the others discovered what it had done: in the meantime the price-cutter may make sufficient profit to offset the cost of any subsequent price-war. It may also be that the rivals will be unable to expand their capacity in order to meet the increased demand that could be expected to follow a price cut. Anyway, an expansion in output may simply mean that new customers are attracted to the price-cutter, not that existing ones are drawn from its rivals.

A second problem is that the theory of oligopoly presents too simplistic a picture of industrial market structures. In a symmetrical oligopoly where producers produce identical goods at the same costs interdependence may be strong, but in reality market conditions are usually more complex. The oligopolists themselves will almost inevitably have different cost levels; they may be producing differentiated goods and will usually command at least some consumer loyalty; and their market shares will often not be equal. Furthermore there may be a fringe of smaller sellers which exert some competitive pressure upon the oligopolists and other firms not operating on the market may be capable of entering it if and when it becomes clear that supra-competitive profits are available. Many other factors affect the competitive environment in which oligopolists operate. The concentration of the market on the buying side is also important: the more concentrated it is, the less the oligopolists might compete with one another since it will be relatively easy to detect attempts to attract the custom of particular customers. The transparency of price information is significant: the easier it is to conceal the price of goods from competitors, the less will be the interdependence or mutual awareness of the oligopolists. Similarly oligopolists may be able, through rebates and discounts, secretly to charge prices lower than those in their published price lists. These and many other factors mean that oligopolistic markets differ considerably from one another and this in turn makes it difficult to provide a convincing theoretical explanation of how such markets function and how they should be dealt with.

A third problem with the theory of interdependence is that it fails to explain why in some oligopolistic markets competition is intense. Firms quite clearly do compete with one another in some oligopolies. Such competition may take various forms. Open price competition may be limited, although price wars do break out periodically in some oligopolistic markets, for example between supermarkets or petrol companies. Where open price competition is restricted, this does not mean that secret price cutting does not occur. Non-price competition may be particularly strong in oligopolistic markets. This may manifest itself in various ways: offering better quality products and after-sales service; striving for a lead in technical innovation and research and development (sometimes described as the 'grass-roots' of competition in oligopoly); by introducing loyalty schemes of the kinds offered by airlines and supermarkets; and by making large investments in advertising to improve brand image[12]. Whilst expenditure on advertising has been objected to because it is wasteful of resources and amounts to a barrier to entry to new firms wanting to enter the market, it is inconsistent with the theory that oligopolists do not compete with one another[13].

---

[12] This is a particular feature of certain markets such as breakfast cereals, household detergents and alcoholic drinks such as lagers.

[13] See *Scherer and Ross* pp 592–610.

A fourth objection to the theory of oligopolistic interdependence is that it does not explain satisfactorily its central proposition, which is that oligopolists can earn supra-competitive profits without actually colluding. The interdependence theory says they cannot increase price unilaterally because they will lose custom to their rivals and yet, to earn supra-competitive profits, prices must have been increased from time to time: how could this have been achieved without collusion? A possible answer to this is that a pattern of price leadership develops whereby one firm raises its price and this acts as a signal to the others to follow suit. Prices therefore remain parallel without conspiracy amongst the oligopolists, although this is not particularly convincing[14]. Economists have suggested that price leadership may take three forms[15]. Dominant price leadership exists where a dominant firm raises its price and other firms in the industry follow suit because it is in their best interests to do so. *Ex hypothesi* this is not what happens in an oligopoly, where no firm is dominant. Secondly, barometric price leadership occurs where one firm raises its price because increased costs (for example, in wages or raw materials) force it to do so: other firms faced with the same increase in costs then follow suit. It would be unreasonable to condemn parallel increases in price if they are explicable on an objective basis in this way. The third type of price leadership is termed collusive: here there is an understanding that firms in an industry will follow the signal emitted from time to time by the price leader. However in this case it would seem to be perfectly reasonable to brand their action as an agreement or a concerted practice under Article 81 or the Chapter I prohibition.

Besides these criticisms, there are other objections to the theory of interdependence. One is that it concentrates solely on the tendency to non-collusive price fixing without asking other questions such as why a market is oligopolistic in the first place: this might be because of the superior efficiency associated with economies of scale. In this case, it is necessary to consider at what point the advantages arising from these economies are offset by the adverse effects of a loss of price competition. Others would argue that, even if supra-competitive profits are earned in an oligopolistic market over a short period, that would attract new entrants to the market and increase competition in the long run unless there are significant barriers to entry to the market. In this case the 'problem' of oligopoly is ephemeral: the market could be left to heal the problem itself.

(C) Possible ways of dealing with oligopoly

Having considered this theoretical debate, the pertinent question is what, if anything, should be done about oligopoly in competition law, assuming that a problem exists.

(i) A structural approach

If economic theory were to demonstrate convincingly that oligopoly inevitably leads to non-collusive parallelism of price and an absence of non-price competition, and also that there are no redeeming features of oligopolistic markets, this would suggest that the problem should be seen as a structural one and dealt with as such. In this case it would be necessary to establish a system capable of preventing the structure of the

---

[14] See Posner *Antitrust Law* (University of Chicago Press, 1976), p 59.

[15] See Markham 'The Nature and Significance of Price Leadership' (1951) 41 Am Ec Rev 891–905; the classification suggested there was adopted in the former Monopolies and Mergers Commission's report *Parallel Pricing* Cmnd 5330 (1973).

market from becoming conducive to tacit coordination in the first place. As will be seen in chapters 20 to 22, this is a key consideration when mergers are scrutinised under competition law. An important question however is whether further structural powers are needed to deconcentrate industries that become oligopolistic other than through the process of mergers: should competition law include powers to dismantle oligopolistic market structures, or at least to inject competitiveness into a sleepy, uncompetitive, market? Where an infringement of Article 81 or 82 is the consequence of the structural conditions of the market and there is no effective behavioural remedy, Article 7 of the EC Modernisation Regulation provides, at least theoretically, for structural remedies to bring that infringement to an end[16]. UK competition law does not explicitly provide such a power under the Competition Act 1998. However a structural solution to the problem of oligopolistic markets is possible under the market investigation regime of the Enterprise Act[17]. It goes without saying that it would require an exceptional case for these draconian remedies to be used, but it is important to be aware of the fact that the possibility does exist.

(ii) A behavioural approach

An alternative approach is to see the problem as essentially behavioural in nature, in which case control is necessary to prevent oligopolists behaving in a way that is uncompetitive. Some would favour making any parallelism in price between oligopolists illegal. This however would be quite inappropriate: it would be absurd to forbid firms from behaving in a parallel manner if this is an inevitable consequence of the structure of the market. To put the point another way, it would be strange indeed if competition law were to mandate that firms should behave irrationally, by not acting in parallel, in order to avoid being found to have infringed competition law.

Where oligopolists really do collude, for example to fix prices or to share markets, there is no reason why they – like firms in less concentrated markets – should not be subject to the provisions of Article 81 and the Chapter I prohibition of the Competition Act 1998. The term 'concerted practice' catches any situation in which firms abandon the risks of competition and substitute for them practical cooperation. However when this concept is applied to oligopolists a different problem arises: it can be difficult to distinguish conduct which is collusive in the sense of Article 81 and the Chapter I prohibition from parallel conduct which is attributable to the oligopolistic structure of a market. This problem is compounded by the fact that in many cases there is little or no evidence of actual contact between alleged conspirators: firms that really do intend to rig the market are wise enough usually to destroy incriminating evidence. The danger is that a competition authority will too readily reach the conclusion that parallel conduct means that there is collusion; this can be avoided only by thorough economic analysis of the market in question. An understanding of pricing theory and of the nature of oligopoly is vital when trying to decide whether parallel conduct is collusive (in the legal sense) or not[18].

As a separate matter, it may be appropriate in oligopolistic markets to prohibit 'facilitating practices' that lead to parallel behaviour: an obvious example is the exchange of information between oligopolists that makes it easier for them to behave in the same way. As we have seen, the structure of the market is one of the factors taken into account

---

[16] See ch 7, p 252.   [17] See pp 568–569 below and ch 11, p 462.
[18] See further the discussion of 'concerted practices' in ch 3, pp 104–107.

when analysing information agreements under Article 81 and the Chapter I prohibition[19]. The possibility that an agreement might lead to parallel behaviour may also
be taken into account when considering whether an agreement satisfies the criteria of
Article 81(3)[20]. Finally, it may be sensible to prevent anti-competitive abuses of a collective dominant position which have the effect of eliminating actual or potential competitors from oligopolistic markets; as will be seen, there have been a few cases in which
Article 82 has been used to deal with behaviour of this sort.

(iii) A regulatory approach

A different possibility would be to regulate the prices of undertakings that operate in an
oligopolistic environment. This, however, would be a counsel of despair. Competition
authorities should not be price regulators; they should be the guardians of the competitive process. Where markets are oligopolistic and entry is limited, competition
authorities should be concerned with the question of whether there are barriers to entry
and whether the state itself, for example through restrictive licensing rules, regulation
or legislation, is responsible for a lack of competition. Sectoral investigations under
Article 17 of the Modernisation Regulation may enable the Commission to understand
better why a market is not functioning well, and what steps should be taken to improve
the situation. However, as a matter of policy direct regulation should be a remedy of last
resort.

3. ARTICLE 81

(A) Does parallel behaviour amount to a concerted practice under Article 81?

Both the Commission and the Community Courts appreciate that price competition
in an oligopoly may be muted and that oligopolists react to one another's conduct,
so that parallel behaviour does not, in itself, amount to a concerted practice under
Article 81(1)[21]. In *Dyestuffs*[22] the ECJ said at paragraphs 65 and 66 that:

> By its very nature, then, the concerted practice does not have all the elements of a contract but
> may *inter alia* arise out of coordination which becomes apparent from the behaviour of the partici-
> pants. *Although parallel behaviour may not itself be identified with a concerted practice,* it may how-
> ever amount to strong evidence of such a practice if it leads to conditions of competition which do
> not respond to the normal conditions of the market, having regard to the nature of the products,
> the size and number of the undertakings, and the volume of the said market. Such is the case espe-
> cially where the parallel behaviour is such as to permit the parties to seek price equilibrium at a
> different level from that which would have resulted from competition, and to crystallise the status
> quo to the detriment of effective freedom of movement of the products in the Common Market
> and free choice by consumers of their suppliers (emphasis added).

The ECJ added at paragraph 68 that the existence of a concerted practice could be
appraised correctly only:

---

[19]   See ch 13, pp 523–532 and pp 554–555 below.   [20]   See p 556 below.
[21]   On concerted practices generally see ch 3, pp 104–107.
[22]   Case 48/69 [1972] ECR 619, [1972] CMLR 557.

if the evidence upon which the contested decision is based is considered, not in isolation, but as a whole, account being taken of the specific features of the products in question.

In *Dyestuffs* the parties argued that they had acted in a similar manner only because of the oligopolistic market structure. The ECJ rejected this assertion since the market was not a pure oligopoly: rather it was one in which firms could realistically be expected to adopt their own pricing strategies, particularly in view of the compartmentalisation of the markets along national boundaries. The ECJ recognised that there might be situations in which a firm must take into account a rival's likely responses, but said that this did not entitle them actually to coordinate their behaviour:

Although every producer is free to change his prices, taking into account in so doing the present or foreseeable conduct of his competitors, nevertheless it is contrary to the rules on competition contained in the Treaty for a producer to cooperate with his competitors, in any way whatsoever, in order to determine a coordinated course of action relating to a price increase and to ensure its success by prior elimination of all uncertainty as to each other's conduct regarding the essential elements of that action, such as the amount, subject-matter, date and place of the increases[23].

In *Züchner v Bayerische Vereinsbank AG*[24] the ECJ repeated that intelligent responses to a competitor's behaviour would not bring firms within the scope of Article 81(1). In *Zinc Producer Group*[25] the Commission said that it did not intend to condemn parallel action between 1977 and 1979 which might be explicable in terms of 'barometric price leadership'[26], saying that in such circumstances 'parallel pricing behaviour in an oligopoly producing homogeneous goods will not in itself be sufficient evidence of a concerted practice'[27]. In *Peroxygen Products*[28] however the Commission rejected an argument that an agreement between oligopolists fell outside Article 81(1) since, even without the agreement, the structure of the market would have meant that they would have behaved in the same way. In the Commission's view, the very fact that the firms had entered into an agreement at all indicated that the free play of competition might have led to different market behaviour.

In *Wood Pulp*[29] the Commission held that producers of wood pulp were guilty of a concerted practice to fix prices in the EC. There had been parallel conduct on the market from 1975 until 1981, but there was no evidence of explicit agreements to fix prices. However the Commission concluded that there was a concerted practice, basing its finding on two factors. The first was that there had been direct and indirect exchanges of information which had created an artificial transparency of price information on the market. The second was that, in the Commission's view, an economic analysis of the market demonstrated that it was not a narrow oligopoly in which parallel pricing might be expected. On appeal, the ECJ substantially annulled the Commission's findings[30]. The fact that pulp producers announced price rises to users in advance on a quarterly basis did not in itself involve an infringement of Article 81(1): making information available to third parties did not eliminate the producers' uncertainty as to what each

[23] [1972] ECR 619, [1972] CMLR 557, para 118.
[24] Case 172/80 [1981] ECR 2021, [1982] 1 CMLR 313, para 14.
[25] OJ [1984] L 220/27, [1985] 2 CMLR 108. [26] See p 550 above.
[27] OJ [1984] L 220/27, [1985] 2 CMLR 108, paras 75–76.
[28] OJ [1985] L 35/1, [1985] 1 CMLR 481, para 50. [29] OJ [1985] L 85/1, [1985] 3 CMLR 474.
[30] Cases C-89/85 etc *A Ahlström Oy v Commission* [1993] ECR I-1307, [1993] 4 CMLR 407; see Jones 'Wood Pulp: Concerted Practice and/or Conscious Parallelism?' (1993) 14 ECLR 273; Van Gerven and Varano 'The Wood Pulp Case and the Future of Concerted Practices' (1994) 31 CML Rev 575.

other would do[31]. Furthermore, there were alternative explanations for the system of and simultaneity of price announcements, and the parallelism of prices could be explained other than by the existence of a concerted practice. Information was freely available on the market as buyers informed each other of the prices available, some agents acted for a number of different producers and so were well-informed about prices and the trade press was dynamic. As to parallelism, the ECJ's experts considered that the market was more oligopolistic than the Commission had supposed, and that economic problems had discouraged producers from engaging in price cutting which their competitors would inevitably follow; the experts also considered that there was evidence to suggest that there could not have been concertation: for example, market shares had varied from time to time, which would be unlikely if there was a concerted practice; and the alleged cartel members had not tried to establish production quotas, which they could be expected to have done if they wished to control the market[32].

This important judgment demonstrates that the burden is on the Commission to prove the existence of a concerted practice, and in particular to deal with any alternative explanations advanced by the parties of parallel behaviour on the market. The judgment does acknowledge, however, that, in an appropriate case, parallelism could be evidence of a concerted practice where there is no plausible alternative explanation[33].

In *British Sugar*[34] British Sugar deployed the argument that the oligopolistic nature of the market meant that price competition was limited, and that its price leadership should not be regarded as evidence of a concerted practice. The Commission's reply to this was that, where competition in a market is already restricted, it should be particularly vigilant to ensure that the competition which does exist is not restricted[35]; the CFI upheld this finding on appeal[36]. This is consistent with the judgment of the CFI in the appeal against the Commission's decision in *Steel Beams*[37].

(B) Article 81(1), the exchange of information and other facilitating practices

The previous section has discussed the difficulties in determining whether parallel behaviour may be attributable to a concerted practice. A competition authority must avoid reaching a conclusion that parallel behaviour is unlawful if it can be explained by reference to the conditions of the market. However this is not to say that Article 81(1) cannot be deployed in other ways to deal with the problem of parallel behaviour: in particular it can be applied to what are often referred to as 'facilitating practices', that is to say practices that make it easier for firms to achieve the benefits of tacit coordination. The most obvious of these is the exchange of information which increases the

---

[31] [1993] ECR I-1307, [1993] 4 CMLR 407, paras 59–65.   [32] Ibid, paras 66–127.

[33] Ibid, para 71; for an interesting recent judgment in the US dealing with the problem of the evidence needed to support a finding of illegal behaviour under the Sherman Act, see *Re High Fructose Corn Syrup Antitrust Litigation* 295 F 3d 651 (7th Cir 2002); cert denied 123 S Ct 1251 (2003).

[34] OJ [1999] L 76/1, [1999] 4 CMLR 1316; see also *Cartonboard* OJ [1994] L 243/1, [1994] 5 CMLR 547, para 73.

[35] OJ [1999] L 76/1, [1999] 4 CMLR 1316, para 87.

[36] Substantially upheld on appeal Cases T-202/98 etc *Tate & Lyle v Commission* [2001] ECR II-2035, [2001] 5 CMLR 859, para 46.

[37] Case T-141/94 *Thyssen Stahl AG v Commission* [1999] ECR II-347, [1999] 4 CMLR 810, para 302.

transparency of the market and so makes parallel behaviour easier. It is for this reason that the application of Article 81(1) to information agreements focuses, amongst other things, on the structure of the market[38]: it was the oligopolistic structure of the market in *UK Agricultural Tractor Registration Exchange*[39] that led the Commission to conclude that Article 81(1) had been infringed; and the more competitive nature of the cars' market that led it to the opposite conclusion in relation to it[40]. In *Thyssen Stahl AG v Commission*[41] the CFI held that, where the structure of a market is oligopolistic, it is all the more important to ensure the decision-making independence of undertakings and residual competition, and that therefore the exchange of recent data on market shares could infringe Article 81(1)[42].

The Commission will look for other facilitating practices. For example at paragraph 20 of its *Guidelines on Vertical Restraints*[43] it says that it will examine agency agreements, even where the principal bears all the financial and commercial risks, if they could facilitate collusion[44]. This could happen, in the Commission's view, if a number of principals use the same agents whilst collectively preventing others from doing so, or where they use agents to collude on marketing strategy or to exchange sensitive information between themselves. Similar concerns are expressed throughout the *Guidelines* as to the possibility of vertical agreements facilitating collusion[45]. To give just one example, the Commission expresses the concern that in a narrow oligopoly the practice of using or publishing maximum or recommended resale prices may facilitate collusion by reducing the likelihood of lower prices[46].

The Commission's *Guidelines on Horizontal Cooperation Agreements*[47] state that, in assessing horizontal cooperation agreements other than 'hard-core' cartels of the kind that almost always fall within Article 81(1)[48], the concentration of the market will be taken into account[49]: some agreements may be found not to be anticompetitive where the market is reasonably competitive, but to be problematic where it is oligopolistic. The application of these *Guidelines* is considered in some detail in chapter 15[50].

The Commission has applied the *de minimis* rule narrowly in the case of an oligopoly[51] and has taken a strict approach to the appreciability of the effect on inter-state trade of an agreement where the market was oligopolistic[52].

[38] See ch 13, pp 523–532.
[39] OJ [1992] L 68/19, [1993] 4 CMLR 358, para 16, upheld on appeal to the CFI in Cases T-34/92 and T-35/92 *Fiatagri UK Ltd v Commission* [1994] ECR II-905 and 957 and on appeal to the ECJ in Cases C-7/95 and C-8/95 P *John Deere v Commission* [1998] ECR I-3111, and 3175, [1998] 5 CMLR 311.
[40] See ch 13, pp 527–528.   [41] See n 37 above.   [42] [1993] ECR I-1307, [1993] 4 CMLR 407, paras 393–412.
[43] OJ [2000] C 291/1, [2000] 5 CMLR 1176.
[44] As a general principle agency agreements fall outside Article 81(1): see ch 16, pp 609–612.
[45] See eg the following paragraphs in the *Guidelines,* all of which refer to the possibility of the facilitation of collusion: paras 103(ii), 107, 110, 112, 114, 133, 138, 142, 152, 161, 164, 176 (specifically on exclusive dealerships in an oligopolistic market), 178, 185, 188, 191, 192, 226 and 227.
[46] OJ [2000] C 291/1, [2000] 5 CMLR 1176, para 228.   [47] OJ [2001] C 3/2, [2001] 4 CMLR 819.
[48] That is to say those agreements that have as their object the restriction of competition: see ch 3, pp 116–122 and ch 13 generally.
[49] OJ [2001] C 3/2, [2001] 4 CMLR 819, para 29.   [50] See ch 15 generally.
[51] *Floral* OJ [1980] L 39/51, [1980] 2 CMLR 285, on the *de minimis* doctrine see ch 3, pp 137–142.
[52] *Cast Iron and Steel Rolls* OJ [1983] L 317/1, [1984] 1 CMLR 694, upheld on appeal Cases 29/83 and 30/83 *Compagnie Royale Asturienne des Mines SA and Rheinzink GmbH v Commission* [1984] ECR 1679, [1985] 1 CMLR 688.

(C) Article 81(3)

The structure of the market will be relevant to the analysis of agreements under Article 81(3), in particular since that provision requires that there should be no substantial elimination of competition[53]. The fact that the Commission's block exemptions contain market share caps in itself means that firms in an oligopoly will often not be able to avail themselves of these legal instruments[54]. In *P&O Stena Line*[55] the Commission decided that the criteria of Article 81(3) were satisfied in the case of a joint venture for cross-channel ferry services for a limited period of three years; the decision considered at length whether there was a risk that the joint venture would create a duopoly on the 'short sea tourist market', but concluded that the joint venture and Eurotunnel, the operator of the Channel Tunnel, could be expected to compete with each other rather than to act in parallel to raise prices[56].

An agreement might be found to satisfy Article 81(3) where it would have the effect of introducing more competition into an oligopolistic market[57].

4. ARTICLE 82 AND COLLECTIVE DOMINANCE[58]

One of the most complex and controversial issues in Community competition law has been the application – or non-application – of Article 82 EC (and the ECMR) to so-called 'collective dominance'[59]. Discussion of this question in relation to Article 82 can be traced back at least to the early 1970s[60]; an enormous body of literature has developed[61].

---

[53] See ch 4, pp 159–160.   [54] On the market share caps in the block exemptions see ch 4, p167.

[55] OJ [1999] L 163/61, [2000] 5 CMLR 682.   [56] Ibid, para 127.

[57] See eg *Carlsberg* OJ [1984] L 207/26, [1985] 1 CMLR 735.

[58] The text that follows is based, in part, on *Collective Dominance*, the author's contribution to the Liber Amicorum in Honour of Lord Slynn of Hadley *Judicial Review in European Union Law* (Kluwer Law International, 2000, eds O'Keefe and Bavasso), ch 37.

[59] The expressions 'collective dominance', 'joint dominance' and 'oligopolistic dominance' have tended to be used interchangeably. In Cases C-395/96 P etc *Compagnie Maritime Beige NV v Commission* [2000] ECR I-1365, [2000] 4 CMLR 1076 Advocate General Fennelly indicated that he saw no meaningful distinction between these terms, but used the expression 'collective dominance' as this was the one that the Court itself usually employed; in its judgment in the same case, the ECJ used the expression 'collective dominance' throughout: see in particular para 36; and in Case T-342/99 *Airtours v Commission* [2002] ECR II-2585, [2002] 5 CMLR 317 the CFI also used the expression collective dominance throughout its judgment.

[60] See n 73 below.

[61] See eg Whish and Sufrin 'Oligopolistic Markets and EC Competition Law' (1992) 12 Oxford Yearbook of European Law 59; Winkler and Hansen 'Collective Dominance under the EC Merger Control Regulation' (1993) 30 CML Rev 787; Ridyard 'Economic Analysis of Single Firm and Oligopolistic Dominance under the European Merger Regulation' (1994) 15 ECLR 255; Rodger 'Market Integration and the Development of European Competition Policy to Meet New Demands: A Study of Oligopolistic Markets and the Concept of a Collective Dominant Position under Article [82] of the Treaty' [1994(2)] Legal Issues of European Integration 1; Rodger 'Oligopolistic Market Failure: Collective Dominance versus Complex Monopoly' (1995) 16 ECLR 21; Briones 'Oligopolistic Dominance: is there a Common Approach in Different Jurisdictions?' (1995) 16 ECLR 334; Soames 'An Analysis of the Principles of Concerted Practice and Collective Dominance: a Distinction without a Difference' (1996) 17 ECLR 24; Morgan 'The Treatment of Oligopoly under the European Merger Control Regulation' (1996) 41 Antitrust Bulletin 203; Tillotson and MacCulloch 'EC Competition Rules, Collective Dominance and Maritime Transport' (1997) 21(1) World Competition

The law and decisional practice on collective dominance, under both legal instruments, developed considerably in the years from 1998 to 2002; of particular importance are the ECJ's judgments in *France v Commission* (the so-called *Kali und Salz* case)[62], a case decided under the ECMR, and *Compagnie Maritime Belge Transports SA v Commission*[63] and two judgments under the ECMR of the CFI, *Gencor v Commission*[64] and *Airtours v Commission*[65]. This section will consider in particular the development of the law under Article 82; it would appear to be the case that the expression 'collective dominance' has the same meaning under Article 82 as it has under the ECMR.

(A) The linguistic background

There is a linguistic background to the issue of collective dominance under Article 82 and the ECMR. Article 82 applies to '[a]ny abuse *by one or more undertakings* of a dominant position within the common market' (emphasis added). The same wording has been adopted in numerous domestic systems of competition law[66]. The fact that Article 82 is capable of application to dominance held on the part of more than one undertaking clearly envisages the possibility, though not the inevitability, of 'collective' dominance being enjoyed by legally and economically separate undertakings; a narrow reading would be that the reference to more than one undertaking refers to different legal entities within the same corporate group[67]. In contradistinction to Article 82, Article 2(3) of the ECMR as it was originally drafted in 1989[68] provides that a concentration that creates or strengthens a dominant position as a result of which competition would be significantly impeded in the common market or a substantial part of it may be declared incompatible with the common market; however this provision does not refer specifically to a dominant position *enjoyed by one or more undertakings*. Linguistically, therefore, it could be argued – as indeed it was by France, Société Commerciale des Potasses et de l'Azote (SCPA) and Entreprise Minière et Chemique (EMC) in the *Kali und Salz* case[69] – that the ECMR applies only to single firm dominance,

51; Venit 'Two Steps Forward and No Steps Back: Economic Analysis and Oligopolistic Dominance after *Kali und Salz*' (1998) 35 CML Rev 1101; Elliott 'The Gencor Judgment: Collective Dominance, Remedies and Extraterritoriality under the Merger Regulation' (1999) 24 EL Rev 638; Korah '*Gencor v Commission*: Collective Dominance' (1999) 20 ECLR 337; Stroux 'Is EC Oligopoly Control Outgrowing Its Infancy?' (2000) 23(1) World Competition 3; Fernandez 'Increasing Powers and Increasing Uncertainty: Collective Dominance and Pricing Abuses' (2000) 25 EL Rev 645; Stroux, commenting on *CMBT v Commission*, (2000) 37 CML Rev 1249; Etter 'The Assessment of Mergers in the EC under the Concept of Collective Dominance' (2000) 23(3) World Competition 103; Kloosterhuis 'Joint Dominance and the Interaction Between Firms' (2000) ECLR 79; Monti 'The Scope of Collective Dominance under Article 82' (2001) 38 CML Rev 131; Niels 'Collective Dominance – More than Just Oligopolistic Interdependence' (2001) 22 ECLR 168; Temple Lang 'Oligopolies and Joint Dominance in Community Antitrust Law' [2002] Fordham Corporate Law Institute (ed Hawk), ch 12.

[62] Cases C-68/94 and 30/95 [1998] ECR I-1375, [1998] 4 CMLR 829.

[63] Cases C-395/96 and 396/96 P [2000] ECR I-1365, [2000] 4 CMLR 1076.

[64] Case T-102/96 [1999] ECR II-753, [1999] 4 CMLR 971.

[65] Case T-342/99 [2002] ECR II-2585, [2002] 5 CMLR 317 annulling the Commission's prohibition decision in Case IV/M.1524 *Airtours/First Choice* OJ [2000] L 93/1, [2000] 5 CMLR 494.

[66] See eg s 18 of the UK Competition Act 1998.   [67] See p 558 below.

[68] Note that the 'Recast Regulation' of 2004 places emphasis on the question of whether a merger would significantly impede effective competition in the common market, 'in particular as a result of the creation or strengthening of a dominant position'.

[69] See n 62 above.

even if Article 82 is capable of application to collective dominance. It took many years for the Community Courts to determine the proper scope of Article 82 and the ECMR: in each case in favour of the application of the measure in question to collective dominance.

(B) The definition of collective dominance under Article 82

(i) 'One or more undertakings': the narrow view of Article 82

Article 82 prohibits the abuse of a dominant position 'by one or more undertakings'. The 'narrow' view of the reference to more than one undertaking was that it meant that the market power and behaviour of undertakings within the same corporate group could be aggregated and dealt with under Article 82. In several of the cases on Article 82 a dominant position was found to exist among the members of a group. For example in *Continental Can*[70] three different companies in the same group were involved in the Commission's analysis: Continental Can (a US company), SLW (its German subsidiary) which held a dominant position in Germany and Europemballage (also its subsidiary) which acquired a competitor, TDV. It was the overall effect of these companies' position and behaviour which led to a finding of abuse of dominance. Similarly in *Commercial Solvents v Commission*[71] there were two legal entities within the same corporate group, the US parent, Commercial Solvents, and its Italian subsidiary, ICI. It is easy enough to see that the reference in Article 82 to an abuse *by one or more undertakings* might be thought to refer to an abuse that could be attributed to separate legal entities within the same corporate group; it should be added, however, that if those entities are to be regarded as *one* undertaking – which is now the case – the approach set out above fails to explain what is meant by an abuse by more than one undertaking[72].

(ii) 'One or more undertakings': the wide view of Article 82

An alternative approach to the reference in Article 82 to one or more undertakings is that it has a wider meaning, so that legally and economically independent firms might be considered to hold a 'collective dominant position'. It would follow that abusive market behaviour on the part of collectively dominant firms could be controlled under Article 82 (and, after the adoption of the ECMR, that the Commission would have control over a larger number of concentrations if the same approach could be taken in relation to that legal instrument). The Commission dabbled with the idea of collective dominance under Article 82 in the early 1970s[73], but the ECJ appeared to have rejected it in *Hoffmann-La Roche v Commission*[74]. There the Court seemed to suggest

---

[70] JO [1972] L 7/25, [1972] CMLR D11, annulled on appeal Case 6/72 *Europemballage Corpn and Continental Can Co Inc v Commission* [1973] ECR 215, [1973] CMLR 199.

[71] JO [1972] L 299/51, [1973] CMLR D50, upheld on appeal Cases 6/73 etc [1974] ECR 223, [1974] 1 CMLR 309.

[72] See ch 3, pp 91–95 on the single economic entity doctrine.

[73] See eg the *Report on the Behaviour of the Oil Companies during the period from October 1973 to March 1974*: COM (75) 675, 10 December 1975; *Sugar Cartel* OJ [1973] L 140/17, [1973] CMLR D65 where the Commission held that two Dutch producers held a collective dominant position: the ECJ on appeal said nothing about this because it considered there was no abuse by the companies anyway, Cases 40/73 etc *Suiker Unie v Commission* [1975] ECR 1663, [1976] 1 CMLR 295.

[74] Case 85/76 [1979] ECR 461, [1979] 3 CMLR 211.

that problems of tacit coordination could not be controlled under Article 82:

A dominant position must also be distinguished from parallel courses of conduct which are peculiar to oligopolies in that in an oligopoly the courses of conduct interact, whilst in the case of an undertaking occupying a dominant position the conduct of the undertaking which derives profits from that position is to a great extent determined unilaterally[75].

This apparent rejection of Article 82 as a tool for controlling oligopolistic behaviour was understandable. Oligopolists that actively participate in agreements or concerted practices would be caught by Article 81 anyway. The ECJ appears to have taken the view that where oligopolists behave in an identical fashion because of the structure of the market on which they operate, rather than because of active participation in an agreement or concerted practice, they should not be condemned for abusing their position if their conduct is rational – even inevitable – behaviour. An approach to the 'oligopoly problem' which is based on the concept of abuse in Article 82 seemed inappropriate: or to put it another way, where there was no explicit collusion contrary to Article 81, the Court was not prepared to characterise the economist's notion of tacit collusion as abusive under Article 82. After *Hoffmann-La Roche* a period of relative inactivity followed. For example in *Alcatel v NOVASAM*[76] the Commission invited the ECJ to adopt a theory of collective dominance in an Article 234 reference, but the Court declined to comment on the point in its judgment. In the *Magill* case[77] the Commission took objection to the refusal of three television companies to grant licences of copyright in their TV schedules to a third party wishing to produce a TV listings magazine. The Commission could have tried a collective dominance approach to the case, holding that the companies had collectively abused a collective dominant position in the TV schedules market; instead it found three individual dominant positions on the part of each company, and three individual abuses.

(iii) Confirmation of the wide view

Any suggestion that the concept of collective dominance had been laid to rest was subsequently shown to be wrong. In *Italian Flat Glass*[78] the Commission held that three Italian producers of flat glass had a collective dominant position and that they had abused it. As participants in a tight oligopolistic market they enjoyed a degree of independence from competitive pressures that enabled them to impede the maintenance of effective competition, notably by not having to take into account the behaviour of other market participants. The conduct held to fall within Article 82 had already been condemned earlier in the decision as a concerted practice under Article 81. However the decision opened up the possibility that in other situations the conduct of oligopolists, *though not within Article 81*, might be attacked under Article 82. On appeal the CFI overturned the Commission's decision on collective dominance on the ground that the Commission had simply 'recycled' the facts relied on as constituting an infringement of Article 81, instead of properly defining the relevant product and geographic markets

---

[75] [1979] ECR 461, [1979] 3 CMLR 211, para 39; similarly see Case 172/80 *Gerhard Züchner v Bayerische Vereinsbank* [1981] ECR 2021, [1982] 1 CMLR 313, para 10.

[76] Case 247/86 [1988] ECR 5987.

[77] *Magill TV Guide* OJ [1989] L 78/43, [1989] 4 CMLR 757, upheld on appeal Cases T-69/89 etc *RTE v Commission* [1991] ECR II-485, [1991] 4 CMLR 586 and further, on appeal to the ECJ, Case C-241/91 P [1995] ECR I-743, [1995] 4 CMLR 718.

[78] OJ [1989] L 33/44, [1990] 4 CMLR 535.

in order to weigh up the undertakings' economic power, as is necessary in Article 82 cases.

Nevertheless, the CFI confirmed the principle of collective dominance at paragraph 358 of its judgment:

> There is nothing, in principle, to prevent two or more independent economic entities from being, on a specific market, united by such economic links that, by virtue of that fact, together they hold a dominant position vis-à-vis the other operators on the same market. This could be the case, for example, where two or more independent undertakings jointly have, through agreements or licences, a technological lead affording them the power to behave to an appreciable extent independently of their competitors, their customers and ultimately of their consumers (judgment of the Court in *Hoffmann-La Roche,* cited above, paragraphs 38 and 48)[79].

The judgment in *Italian Flat Glass* was exciting and frustrating in equal measure. Collective dominance on the part of 'two or more independent entities' could exist under Article 82, although the Commission had failed to demonstrate that it existed in this particular case. Clearly, the CFI considered that infringements of Articles 81 and 82 were conceptually independent of one another: this is why the Commission was not permitted simply to 'recycle the facts' used to find an infringement of Article 81 in order to determine an abuse of collective dominance[80]. Each Article must be applied according to its own terms. Behaviour that amounts to a concerted practice is not automatically also abusive; and *vice versa*[81]. However, what is frustrating about the judgment is that it did not advance our understanding of what collective dominance consists of. Did the judgment *require* that collectively dominant entities must be economically linked, or did it simply say that links were an example of collective dominance[82]? If 'links' were required, what exactly did this expression mean? Must the link consist of an agreement between the entities in question: the Court had given as examples 'agreements or licences'? If so, would not such agreements be likely to infringe Article 81, in which case what was the purpose of the principle of collective dominance under Article 82? Could cross-shareholdings amount to an economic link? Or interlocking directorships[83]? Or the sharing of a common infrastructure such as an electricity grid or a gas pipeline? More radically, could firms be economically linked simply by being in a market in which the opportunity for tacit coordination existed? Quite apart from these questions, which concern the identification of the legal concept of collective dominance, the judgment did not ask the more fundamental one: what was the function of the doctrine of collective dominance, and what could amount to an abuse of collective dominance?

---

[79] Cases T-68/89 etc *Società Italiano Vetro SpA v Commission* [1992] ECR II-1403, [1992] 5 CMLR 302; note that the reference to *Hoffmann-La Roche* in this paragraph is a reference to the meaning of market power as defined in that judgment, *not* to the meaning of collective dominance which, as mentioned earlier, the Court appeared to reject.

[80] The differences between Articles 81 and 82 are very clearly stated in the judgment of the CFI in Case T-41/96 *Bayer v Commission* [2000] ECR II-3383, [2001] 4 CMLR 126, paras 174–180 and by the ECJ in the appeal to it from that judgment, Case C-2 and 3/01 P *Commission v Bayer* [2004] ECR I-23, [2004] 4 CMLR 653, para 70.

[81] This point is specifically confirmed at paras 43 and 44 of the ECJ's judgment in Cases C-395/96 and C-396/96 P *Compagnie Maritime Belge Transports v Commission* [2000] ECR I-1365, [2000] 4 CMLR 1076: see pp 563–564 below.

[82] Note the sentence in para 358 that begins 'This could be the case, *for example*, where two or more independent undertakings jointly...' (emphasis added).

[83] AG Fennelly thought that each of these matters could give rise to collective dominance: see para 28 of his opinion in the *CMBT* case.

The judgment failed to provide adequate answers to any of these questions. Given that we now have the benefit of the judgments in *Compagnie Maritime Belge Transports v Commission* under Article 82 and *France v Commission*, *Gencor v Commission* and *Airtours v Commission* under the ECMR it is perhaps no longer necessary to spend time in trying to understand what was meant by paragraph 358 of *Italian Flat Glass*. It is sufficient to say that an important landmark had been reached in this judgment, but that later case law has shed much more light on the concept of collective dominance.

(iv) Further judgments and decisions on collective dominance under Article 82

In the years after *Italian Flat Glass* there were several more judgments and decisions in which collective dominance was referred to, but not until *France v Commission* and *Gencor v Commission* under the ECMR and *Compagnie Maritime Belge Transports v Commission* under Article 82 did a true picture begin to emerge of what was meant by the concept. In *Almelo*[84] the ECJ said that:

> 42 However, in order for such a collective dominant position to exist, the undertakings in the group must be linked in such a way that they adopt the same conduct on the market.
> 43 It is for the national court to consider whether there exist between the regional electricity distributors in the Netherlands links which are sufficiently strong for there to be a collective dominant position in a substantial part of the common market.

This formulation referred back to the concept of a link in *Italian Flat Glass*, without further elaborating on what this means. However it introduced the idea that the significance of the link is that it enables the collectively dominant firms to adopt the same conduct on the market; the second part of the sentence in paragraph 42 suggested that the ECJ was looking at what economists would look at: the adoption of the same conduct on the market or, in other words, tacit coordination. This was an improvement on *Italian Flat Glass*, in that it provided an economic rationale for collective dominance, but it still left the mystery of 'links' to be explained. In particular, paragraph 43 of *Almelo* appeared to require a link as an essential component of collective dominance, without shedding much more light on what the link should consist of.

In *Spediporto*[85], *DIP*[86] and *Sodemare*[87] the ECJ repeated the *Almelo* formulation, but did not advance its notion of collective dominance. In the *Bosman case*[88] Advocate General Lenz assumed that football clubs in a professional football league could be 'united by such economic links' as to be regarded as collectively dominant; the ECJ did not address the issue. In the meantime the Commission began to reach findings of collective dominance in a number of decisions, both under Article 82 and under the ECMR. The decisions under Article 82 did not greatly add to the notion of collective dominance, since they involved undertakings which unmistakably were economically linked in some way. For example in three decisions in the maritime transport sector the

---

[84] Case C-393/92 *Almelo v NV Energiebedrijf Ijsselmij* [1994] ECR I-1477.

[85] Case C-96/94 *Centro Servizi Spediporto Srl v Spedizioni Marittime del Golfo Srl* [1995] ECR I-2883, [1996] 4 CMLR 613, para 33.

[86] Cases C-140/94 etc *DIP Spa v Commune di Bassano del Grappa* [1995] ECR I-3257, [1996] 4 CMLR 157, para 26.

[87] Case C-70/95 *Sodemare SA, Anni Azzurri Holding SpA and Anni Azzurri Rezzato Srl v Regione Lombardia* [1997] ECR I-3395, [1998] 4 CMLR 667, para 46.

[88] Case C-415/93 *Union Royale Belge des Societes de Football Association v Bosman* [1995] ECR I-4921, [1996] 1 CMLR 645.

undertakings were members of liner conferences. In *French-West African Shipowners' Committees*[89] the Commission concluded that members of the shipowners' committees had abused a collective dominant position by taking action designed to prevent other shipping lines establishing themselves as competitors on routes between France and 11 west African states[90]. This decision was adopted after the CFI's judgment in the *Italian Flat Glass* case, and the Commission specifically imposed a fine for the infringement of Article 82 as well as the agreements that were caught by Article 81. In its decision on *Cewal*[91] the Commission found collective dominance between shipping lines that were members of a liner conference. The Commission's finding of collective dominance was upheld on appeal to the CFI[92] and to the ECJ: the latter judgment is of major importance on collective dominance under Article 82 and is considered in some detail below[93].

In *TACA*[94] the Commission imposed fines totalling €273 million on the members of a liner conference for abuses of collective dominance. On appeal to the CFI the Commission's finding of collective dominance was upheld[95]; the CFI stated specifically that, although competition between undertakings in a collectively dominant position was necessarily restricted, this did not imply that competition between them should be entirely eliminated[96]. The Commission's finding that members of TACA had abused their collective dominant position by inducing competitors to join their shipping conference, thereby harming the competitive structure of the market, was annulled, as were the fines[97].

The Commission also reached a finding of collective dominance in *Port of Rødby*[98], where it considered that two ferry undertakings that fixed common rates, coordinated timetables and marketed their services jointly were collectively dominant. In *Irish Sugar*[99] the Commission found 'vertical' collective dominance between Irish Sugar and a distributor of sugar, Sugar Distributors Ltd (SDL). Without finding legal or *de facto* control of SDL, the Commission concluded that the combination of Irish Sugar's equity holding, the structure of policymaking of the two companies and the communication process established to facilitate it, led to direct economic ties between them which created a clear parallelism of interest which amounted to collective dominance of the markets for industrial and retail sugar in Ireland[100]. On appeal the CFI upheld this finding of vertical collective dominance, without shedding any particular light on what this concept consists of[101].

These judgments and decisions under Article 82 after the CFI's judgment in *Italian Flat Glass* see the concept of collective dominance being quite regularly applied, and thereby becoming more familiar to officials, courts and practitioners. However, they did relatively little to answer any of the questions raised by that judgment, other than to introduce the idea of the adoption of common conduct on the market as a significant feature of collective dominance. An interesting glimpse of the way in which

[89] OJ [1992] L 134/1, [1993] 5 CMLR 446.   [90] Ibid, paras 52–69.
[91] OJ [1993] L 34/20, [1995] 5 CMLR 198.
[92] Cases T-24/93 etc *Compagnie Maritime Belge Transports SA v Commission* [1996] ECR II-1201, [1997] 4 CMLR 273.
[93] See pp 563–564 below.   [94] OJ [1999] L 95/1, [1999] 4 CMLR 1415.
[95] Cases T-191/98 etc *Atlantic Container Line v Commission* [2003] ECR II-3275, [2005] 4 CMLR 1283, paras 649–657.
[96] Ibid, paras 653–655.   [97] Ibid, paras 1192–1369 and paras 1597–1634.
[98] OJ [1994] L 55/52, [1994] 5 CMLR 457.   [99] OJ [1997] L 258/1, [1997] 5 CMLR 666.
[100] Ibid, paras 111–113.   [101] Case T-228/97 [1999] ECR II-2969, [1999] 5 CMLR 1300, paras 61–64.

the Commission's view of collective dominance was developing was provided by its *Notice on Access Agreements in the Telecommunications Sector*[102]. At paragraph 79 it said that:

79. In addition, for two or more companies to be jointly dominant it is necessary, though not sufficient, for there to be no effective competition between the companies on the relevant market. This lack of competition may in practice be due to the fact that the companies have links such as agreements for cooperation, or interconnection agreements. *The Commission does not, however, consider that either economic theory or Community law implies that such links are legally necessary for a joint dominant position to exist.* It is a sufficient economic link if there is the kind of interdependence which often comes about in oligopolistic situations. *There does not seem to be any reason in law or in economic theory to require any other economic link between jointly dominant companies.* This having been said, in practice such links will often exist in the telecommunications sector where national [Telecommunications Operators] nearly inevitably have links of various kinds with one another (emphasis added).

(v) The judgment of the ECJ in *Compagnie Maritime Belge Transports v Commission*

Important light was shed on the meaning of collective dominance by the judgment of the ECJ in *Compagnie Maritime Belge Transports v Commission*[103], an appeal from the CFI's judgment[104] upholding the Commission's decision in *Cewal*[105] that there had been an infringement of Article 82. The ECJ deals with collective dominance at paragraphs 28 to 59 of its judgment. At paragraph 36 it states that collective dominance implies that a dominant position may be held by two or more economic entities legally independent of each other provided that from an economic point of view 'they present themselves or act together on a particular market as a collective entity'. The Court says that this is how the expression 'collective dominant position' should be understood in the judgment. It will be noted that this definition of collective dominance focuses on the notion of a collective entity, and not on the links between the undertakings in question. The ECJ then states that, in order to establish collective dominance, it is necessary to examine 'the economic links or factors which give rise to a connection between the undertakings concerned'[106], citing as precedents its earlier judgments in *Almelo*[107] under Article 82 and *France v Commission*[108] under the ECMR: the Court does not appear to consider that collective dominance has a different meaning under these two provisions. It continues that 'in particular' it must be asked whether economic links exist which enable them to act independently of their competitors[109]. However it then says that the fact that undertakings have entered into agreements does not in itself mean that they are collectively dominant[110]; but they might be if it caused them to appear as a collective entity[111]. Importantly, the ECJ then says that:

the existence of an agreement or of other links in law is not indispensable to a finding of a collective dominant position; such a finding may be based on other connecting factors and would depend on an economic assessment and, in particular, on an assessment of the structure of the market in question[112].

---

[102] OJ [1998] C 265/2, [1998] 5 CMLR 521.
[103] Case C-396/96 P [2000] ECR I-1365, [2000] 4 CMLR 1076; for commentary on this judgment, see Stroux (2000) 37 CML Rev 1249.
[104] [1996] ECR II-1201, [1997] 4 CMLR 273.   [105] OJ [1993] L 34/20, [1995] 5 CMLR 198.
[106] Ibid, para 41.   [107] [1994] ECR I-1477.   [108] [1998] ECR I-1375, [1998] 4 CMLR 829.
[109] [2000] ECR I-1365, [2000] 4 CMLR 1076, para 42.   [110] Ibid, para 43.   [111] Ibid, para 44.
[112] Ibid, para 45.

This passage is consistent with the ECJ's judgment in *France v Commission* on collective dominance under the ECMR, where it had placed emphasis on 'connecting factors' rather than on economic links in determining whether there was collective dominance[113], and it is explicit that the existence of an agreement or concerted practice is not a pre-requisite to a finding of collective dominance. On the actual facts of the case the ECJ was satisfied that the members of the liner conference in question were collectively dominant[114].

This is clearly a very important judgment on collective dominance under Article 82: specifically, it would appear that the ECJ considers that the test of collective dominance is the same under Article 82 and the ECMR; and the Court specifically states that there is no legal requirement of an agreement or other links in law for there to be a finding of collective dominance. It is therefore possible that firms could be held to be collectively dominant where the oligopolistic nature of the market is such that they behave in a parallel manner, thereby appearing to the market as a collective entity. The judgment of the CFI in *Airtours v Commission*[115] is consistent with this interpretation: the essence of collective dominance is parallel behaviour within an oligopoly, that is to say tacit collusion or tacit coordination, depending on linguistic preference, as described earlier in this chapter[116]. The CFI's judgment in *Laurent Piau v Commission*[117] states that legally independent economic entities may be collectively dominant where 'they present themselves or act together on a particular market as a collective entity'[118]. The CFI went on to say that there were three cumulative conditions for a finding of collective dominance:

- Each member of the dominant oligopoly must have the ability to know how the other members are behaving in order to monitor whether or not they are adopting the common policy

- The situation of tacit coordination must be sustainable over time, meaning that there must be an incentive not to depart from the common policy on the market

- The foreseeable reaction of current and future competitors, as well as of consumers, must not jeopardise the results expected from the common policy[119].

In *Laurent Piau* the CFI concluded that FIFA, national football associations and the football clubs forming them were collectively dominant on the market for the provision of players' agents' services, but that there was no abusive behaviour on their part[120].

One final point is that the ECJ has said that, where a market is highly heterogeneous and characterised by a high degree of internal competition, such as the market for legal services in the Netherlands, collective dominance would not be found in the absence of structural links[121].

---

[113] Cases C-68/94 and 30/95 [1998] ECR I-1375, [1998] 4 CMLR 829.

[114] [2000] ECR I-1365, [2000] 4 CMLR 1076.

[115] Case T-342/99 [2002] ECR II-2585, [2002] 5 CMLR 317.   [116] See pp 547–548 above.

[117] Case T-193/02 [2005] ECR II-209, [2005] 5 CMLR 42; note that paras 43–50 of the Commission's *Discussion Paper on the application of Article 81 of the Treaty to exclusionary abuses* summarises the concept of collective dominance in the same terms.

[118] Case T-193/02 [2005] ECR II-209, [2005] 5 CMLR 42, para 110.   [119] Ibid, para 111.

[120] Ibid, paras 117–121.

[121] Case C-309/99 *Wouters v Algemene Raad van de Nederlandsche Orde van Advocaten* [2002] ECR I-1577, [2002] 4 CMLR 913, para 114.

(C) Abuse of collective dominance under Article 82

Having established that Article 82 is applicable to collective as well as single firm dominance, it is necessary to consider what kind of conduct would constitute an abuse of a collective dominant position under that provision: it is important to recall that it is not unlawful, in itself, under Article 82 to have a dominant position (whether individual or collective); for there to be an infringement of Article 82 there must be conduct which amounts to an abuse[122]. What qualifies as an abuse of collective dominance is under-developed in the case law[123]. The economic theory around which the doctrine of collective dominance has developed under the ECMR is that in certain market conditions firms may be able to derive benefits from tacit coordination; and the very reason why the Commission might prohibit under the ECMR a concentration that would create or strengthen a collective dominant position is that it would make it easier for firms to benefit from this phenomenon[124]. Does it follow from this that tacit coordination, when actually practised, should be condemned as an abuse of a collective dominant position under Article 82? Is price parallelism in itself an abuse? To put the point another way, does symmetry require that, since predicted tacit coordination can be prevented through the prohibition of a concentration under the ECMR, actual coordination should be condemned under Article 82? If the answer to this question is no, what types of behaviour ought to be condemned under Article 82?

(i) Exploitative abuse of a collective dominant position

Textbooks on Article 82 habitually make a distinction between those abuses that are 'exploitative' and those that are 'anti-competitive', whilst recognising that this is not a watertight distinction[125]. It could be argued that tacit coordination by collectively dominant undertakings is exploitative, since prices are charged which are higher than they would be in a competitive market, albeit without the need to enter into an explicit agreement. However the Commission has not attempted to condemn tacit coordination itself under Article 82, and it is submitted that, as a matter of law, it should not be able to do so. As explained earlier in this chapter[126], parallel behaviour *per se* is not caught by Article 81(1) if it does not arise from an agreement or a concerted practice in the sense of that provision. Tacit coordination comes about in certain market conditions, not because of an agreement or concerted practice between the collectively dominant firms in the legal sense of those terms, but because they react rationally according to the conditions of the market on which they operate. To condemn their parallel behaviour as abusive in itself would be a nonsense: if Article 82 were to mandate that firms must behave *irrationally* in order to comply with the law, it would indeed be an odd provision. This explains the position taken by the ECJ as long ago as *Hoffmann-La Roche*: parallel

---

[122] See ch 5, pp 198–199; the point is made specifically in relation to collective dominance by the ECJ in its judgment in *CMBT v Commission* at paras 37–38.

[123] Paragraphs 74–76 of the Commission's *Discussion Paper on the application of Article 81 of the Treaty to exclusionary abuses* has virtually nothing to say about the idea of the abuse of a collective dominant position.

[124] See ch 21, pp 860–862.

[125] See ch 5, p 119; the Commission itself made this distinction in its decision on *P&I Clubs* OJ [1999] L 125/12, [1999] 5 CMLR 646, paras 127–136.

[126] See pp 552–554 above.

behaviour should be condemned where it is attributable to an agreement or concerted practice contrary to Article 81(1); it is not, in itself, abusive under Article 82[127]. It might seem that this shows an inconsistency between the law under Article 82 and the ECMR: how can it be that the prospect of tacit coordination can be condemned under the Merger Regulation and yet the actuality of the same behaviour cannot be condemned under Article 82? The truth is that the difference makes perfect sense: it is precisely because of the difficulty that competition law has in addressing the problem of tacit coordination when it does occur that competition authorities, through their systems of merger control, endeavour to prevent a market structure that will be conducive to this phenomenon from arising in the first place. This explains the emphasis that has been placed upon tacit coordination in merger control in the US[128].

A distinct issue is whether collectively dominant firms could be held to have abused their position by charging *excessively high* prices: here the abuse would lie not in the *parallelism* of the prices, but in their level. Article 82(2)(a) does condemn unfairly high prices, and it is not obvious that collectively dominant firms should enjoy an immunity from this offence which an individually dominant firm would not enjoy. In principle, therefore, it would seem that action could be taken against excessive pricing in an oligopoly. Such actions are likely to be rare, however, since the Commission does not want to establish itself as a price regulator: there have been very few investigations of high prices under Article 82, and those that have been conducted were often motivated by different considerations, for example that the excessive prices amounted to an obstacle to parallel imports[129]. The Commission contemplated a finding of an exploitative abuse of a collective dominant position of a different nature in its *P&I* decision[130]. The P & I clubs were members of the International Group, and were found to be collectively dominant. They had limited the level of insurance cover available to customers: this was considered by the Commission to be contrary to Article 82(2)(b), since it 'left a very substantial share of the demand unsatisfied'; however an alteration in the rules of the Group meant that the Commission did not reach a formal finding to this effect[131].

(ii) Anti-competitive abuse of a collective dominant position

Article 82 has been applied by the Commission to anti-competitive abuses of collective dominance on several occasions. Anti-competitive abuses are considered in some detail in chapters 17 and 18. It seems reasonable in principle that Article 82 should be applicable to the anti-competitive behaviour not only of individually but also of collectively dominant undertakings. Given that tacit coordination arises where a few firms, without explicit collusion, are able to set prices above the competitive level, the 'subversive' effect of new entrants into markets conducive to this phenomenon is likely to be welcomed by competition authorities: their entry may make tacit coordination less easy to achieve. In *Cewal*[132] the Commission held that Article 82 had been infringed where collectively-dominant members of a liner conference were found to have engaged in

---

[127] See pp 558–559 above.
[128] See DoJ's and FTC's *Horizontal Merger Guidelines*, 2.1–2.22, available at www.usdoj.gov/atr/public/guidelines/hmg.htm.
[129] See ch 18, pp 709–718 and 753–755.   [130] OJ [1999] L 125/12, [1999] 5 CMLR 646.
[131] OJ [1999] L 125/12, [1999] 5 CMLR 646, paras 128–132.
[132] OJ [1993] L 34/2, [1995] 5 CMLR 198; anti-competitive abuse was also found in the earlier *French-West African Shipowners' Committees* decision: OJ [1992] L 134/1, [1993] 5 CMLR 446; see also *P&I Clubs* (n 125 above) paras 134–136.

various practices with the intention of eliminating competitors from the market, such as selective price cutting and the grant of loyalty rebates. The findings of abuse were upheld on appeal to the CFI[133] and the ECJ[134], although the fines were annulled by the ECJ since the Commission had not referred to the possibility that they might be imposed in the statements of objections sent to the individual members of the conference[135]. The Commission's findings of abuse in *TACA*[136] – refusal by members of a liner conference to offer individual service contracts to customers and the abusive alteration of the competitive structure of the market by acting to eliminate potential competition – were annulled on appeal to the CFI[137].

It can be anticipated that the Commission will investigate closely allegations of abusive behaviour by collectively dominant firms where the complainants are actual or potential competitors which might be able to subvert tacit coordination on the market.

(iii) Individual abuse of a collective dominant position

The final question under Article 82 is whether a collective dominant position can be abused only by all of the undertakings which hold that position, or whether it is possible for one or some of them to commit an abuse. To put the matter another way, must there be 'collective' abuse of collective dominance; or can there also be 'individual' abuse? This has been clearly answered by the CFI in the *Irish Sugar* appeal[138]: 'undertakings occupying a joint dominant position may engage in joint or individual abusive conduct', although that was a case on vertical, as opposed to horizontal collective dominance, and it would have been helpful if the judgment had explained in more detail how the Court arrived at its conclusion: it does not fit well with the idea that collectively dominant undertakings should present themselves to the market as a single entity, which implies that they are bound to behave collectively rather than individually. However, if one of several collectively dominant undertakings resorts to anti-competitive behaviour in order to foreclose competitors, it could be argued that this is done to protect the oligopoly generally, and not just that one firm; perhaps this could explain why, at least in some cases, it may be possible for there to be an individual abuse of a collective dominant position.

5. UK LAW

(A) Competition Act 1998

The Chapter I and Chapter II prohibitions in the Competition Act 1998 are based on Articles 81 and 82 EC, and section 60 of the Act requires that consistency should be maintained with the jurisprudence of the Community Courts and that account should

---

[133] Cases T-24/93 etc *Compagnie Maritime Belge Transports SA v Commission* [1996] ECR II-1201, [1997] 4 CMLR 273.

[134] See p 563, n 103 above.

[135] See Case C-395/96 P, paras 140–150.

[136] OJ [1999] L 95/1, [1999] 4 CMLR 1415.

[137] Cases T-191/98 etc *Atlantic Container Line v Commission* [2003] ECR II-3275, [2005] 4 CMLR 1283.

[138] Case T-228/97 [1999] ECR II-2969, [1999] 5 CMLR 1300, para 66.

be taken of the decisional practice of the Commission[139]. It follows that the discussion in the earlier part of this chapter of the application of Articles 81 and 82 to tacit coordination and oligopolistic markets is directly relevant under the UK Act. However two additional points should be made about the domestic law of the UK in relation to this issue. First, the market investigation provisions of the Enterprise Act 2002 provide an alternative mechanism whereby oligopolistic markets may be investigated. Secondly, the system of merger control in the UK requires the Competition Commission to determine whether a merger may be expected to result in a substantial lessening of competition. The following two sections will briefly examine the extent to which these provisions could be deployed to deal with the problem of tacit coordination.

(B) Market investigations under the Enterprise Act 2002

The market investigation provisions of the Enterprise Act 2002 have been described in Chapter 11. The OFT has said that it would not make a reference to the Competition Commission if it was more appropriate to proceed under the Competition Act; other factors, such as the scale of any competition problem and the likelihood of appropriate remedies being available, would also influence the exercise of its discretion[140]. However the OFT specifically notes that there could be problems associated with oligopolistic markets that are not capable of being addressed under the Competition Act 1998, not least because of the uncertainty as to what constitutes an abuse of a collective dominant position under Article 82 EC and therefore, by extension, under the Chapter II prohibition[141]. The possibility exists, therefore, of market investigation references, in particular where problems arise that are industry-wide or that involve multi-firm conduct[142].

The OFT's guidance goes on to refer to the possibility that firms in an oligopoly may be able to coordinate their behaviour for mutual advantage or, at least, lack an incentive to compete, and sets out various factors of a market, such as high barriers to entry, the homogeneity of products and the symmetry of firms' market shares that might be conducive to parallel behaviour[143]. It says that many of the markets that the OFT is likely to be interested in will be oligopolistic[144]; in such markets, price competition may be limited, and firms instead may compete through advertising, loyalty-inducing schemes and similar practices: though these practices may be pro-competitive, they could also be harmful to competition where they raise barriers to entry to new competitors[145]. The OFT also notes that tacit coordination can have a severe effect on competition[146]. In such a case the OFT would look at the pattern of price changes over time, price inertia, and the oligopolists' rates of return compared to returns in comparable markets or to the cost of capital[147]. Switching costs and informational inadequacies may be relevant to the state of competition in a market[148], and the OFT will consider whether there are any facilitating practices that make it easier for firms to act in a coordinated manner[149].

---

[139] On s 60 of the Act see ch 9, pp 362–367.
[140] *Market investigation references*, OFT Guideline 511, March 2006, para 2.1, available on the OFT's website at www.oft.gov.uk.
[141] OFT Guideline 511, para 2.5.   [142] Ibid, para 2.7.   [143] Ibid, paras 5.5–5.7.   [144] Ibid, para 6.4.
[145] Ibid, para 6.5.   [146] Ibid, para 6.6.   [147] Ibid, para 6.7.
[148] Ibid, para 6.8; on switching costs see OFT Economic Discussion Paper 5 (OFT 655) *Switching Costs* (National Economic Research Associates, April 2003).
[149] OFT Guideline 511, paras 6.9–6.11.

The Competition Commission's Guidelines also note the same characteristics of oligopolistic markets[150].

The market investigation provisions are an important part of the overall structure of UK competition law. The majority of competition law problems will be addressed under the Competition Act 1998. However, as the discussion in the early part of this chapter has shown, the 'problem' of oligopoly is a complex one, and the tools provided by Articles 81 and 82 and their domestic analogues are not always suitable for this purpose. The possibility of a market investigation by the Competition Commission, as a 'safety net' for those situations in which there is a failure of the competitive market mechanism that cannot be dealt with under the Competition Act, is in principle desirable; this is not to deny, however, that there are some people in business and legal circles who view these powers with a certain scepticism, since a market investigation could be time-consuming, expensive and intrusive.

The operation of the market investigation provisions in practice was discussed in chapter 11, in several of which the Competition Commission was concerned with switching costs and imperfect information for consumers in concentrated markets[151].

A separate point is that there may be some circumstances in which the OFT might find that the lack of competition in an oligopolistic market may be attributable to a 'public' restriction of competition – for example legislation or regulatory rules – in which case it could play an advocacy role in trying to remove the problem[152].

(C) Merger investigations under the Enterprise Act 2002

The Enterprise Act 2002 subjects 'relevant merger situations' to a 'substantial lessening of competition' test[153]. Prior to the entry into force of the Enterprise Act mergers were subject to a public interest test which, for many years, had been applied according to the 'substantial lessening of competition' standard anyway. UK merger law, therefore, has not had to suffer the growing pains of the concept of collective dominance, examined at length earlier in this chapter in the context of EC law. The competition authorities in the UK have for many years been concerned with the possibility of tacit coordination in merger cases[154].

Under the Enterprise Act regime both the OFT and the Competition Commission have given clear guidance as to the way in which they will approach this issue in merger investigations: the economic considerations are, of course, the same as for market investigation references, although a prospective analysis must be carried out in the case of mergers. The OFT's guidance discusses the ways in which a merger may

---

[150] *Market Investigation References: Competition Commission Guidelines* (June 2003, CC 3), paras 3.58–3.71, available at www.competition-commission.org.uk; note that the Commission published various reports on oligopolistic markets under the now-repealed provisions of the Fair Trading Act 1973, including *Parallel Pricing* Cmnd 5330 (1973); *Credit Card Services* Cm 718 (1989); *White Salt* Cmnd 9778 (1986); *The Supply of Petrol* Cm 972 (1990); *Supermarkets* Cm 4842 (2000); and *The Supply of banking services by clearing banks to small and medium-sized enterprises* Cm 5319 (2002).

[151] See ch 11, pp 467–468.   [152] Ibid, pp 445–452.

[153] See ch 22 generally, and on the SLC test specifically pp 921–925 thereof.

[154] See eg *Interbrew SA/Bass plc* Cm 5014 (2001) and *Lloyds TSB Group plc/Abbey National plc* Cm 5208 (2001).

adversely affect competition in an oligopoly: either through 'non-coordinated effects'[155] ('non-collusive oligopoly'), through 'coordinated effects'[156] or through a combination thereof[157]. The guidance explains that a merger giving rise to non-coordinated effects may lead to a market being less competitive than it was, either through higher prices or reduced output or quality, irrespective of the way other competitors behave; some of the factors which may be conducive to such effects are high market concentration, weak competitive constraints, and close substitutability between the merging firms' products[158], though these factors need not be present in every case[159]. On the problem of coordinated effects the OFT adopts the same approach as that taken by the CFI in *Airtours*[160]. The Competition Commission has similarly provided detailed guidance on non-coordinated and coordinated effects[161].

The 'SLC' test is well-suited to the 'problem' of oligopoly, since it asks a straightforward question: will there be substantially less competition in the market after a merger than there was before: a merger that makes a market more conducive to tacit coordination will clearly be less competitive. There have not been a large number of cases on coordinated effects under the Enterprise Act: those that have arisen are discussed in chapter 22[162].

---

[155] *Mergers: substantive assessment guidance*, OFT Guideline 516, May 2003 paras 4.7–4.10, available at www.oft.gov.uk; on the problem of non-coordinated effects or 'non-collusive oligopoly' see p 548 above and ch 21, pp 853–856.

[156] OFT Guideline 516, paras 4.11–4.16.   [157] Ibid, para 4.6.

[158] Ibid, para 4.8.   [159] Ibid, para 4.9.

[160] Ibid, para 4.12 and footnote 24; on the CFI's judgment in *Airtours* see p 564 above.

[161] *Merger References: Competition Commission Guidelines* (June 2003, CC 2), paras 3.28–3.43, available at www.competition-commission.org.uk.

[162] See ch 22, pp 924–925.

15

Horizontal agreements (3) – cooperation agreements

1. INTRODUCTION

The previous two chapters have considered the law on hard-core cartels and the phenomenon of tacit collusion in oligopolistic markets. However it is important to appreciate that there may be circumstances in which firms that operate at the same level of the market enter into cooperation agreements with one another that produce economic benefits for consumers. It follows that competition law cannot simply prohibit all horizontal agreements outright: efficiency gains may follow from cooperation that are sufficient to outweigh any restriction of competition that it might entail. This chapter is concerned with horizontal cooperation agreements which the competition authorities in the EC and the UK may be prepared to countenance. The chapter is predominantly concerned with the treatment of such agreements under Article 81 EC, although the final section considers the position under the UK Competition Act 1998.

2. FULL-FUNCTION JOINT VENTURES

Where firms decide to cooperate with one another, the medium for their collaboration can vary widely from one case to another. For example firms that wish to cooperate in research and development ('R&D') may simply meet on a periodic basis to discuss matters of common interest; they may share out research work and pool the results; they may establish a committee to oversee the R&D programme; or they may go further and establish a joint venture company to conduct their R&D, while maintaining their independence as producers and suppliers to the market. The same range of possibilities exists in relation to other types of cooperation, for example on production and commercialisation. As a matter of competition law the medium chosen for the horizontal cooperation will not normally affect the legal analysis of an agreement, with one very important exception: where the parties to an agreement establish a joint venture company to carry out their objectives, this may amount to a concentration (to use the language of the EC Merger Regulation ('the ECMR')) or a merger (the term used in the UK Enterprise Act 2002); if so, the joint venture will be considered not under Article 81 or the Chapter I prohibition of the Competition Act 1998, but under the ECMR or the relevant domestic merger control provisions of the Member States. It follows that it is necessary in any particular case to begin by considering whether parties intend to create a full-function joint venture amounting to a concentration or a merger: the meaning of a concentration under the ECMR is dealt with in chapter 21[1]; and chapter 22 considers what is meant by a merger in UK law[2]. It may even be the case that contractual integration, without the establishment of a joint venture company, will amount to a full-function joint venture under the ECMR[3]. Only where it is clear that there is no concentration or merger will it be relevant to consider the possible application of Article 81 and the Chapter I prohibition to horizontal cooperation agreements.

3. THE APPLICATION OF ARTICLE 81 TO HORIZONTAL COOPERATION AGREEMENTS AND THE COMMISSION'S *HORIZONTAL GUIDELINES*[4]

(A) Introduction

The general principles involved in the application of Article 81(1) and Article 81(3) have been described in chapters 3 and 4. In chapter 3, the distinction between agreements that have as their object the restriction of competition and those that have the effect of doing so was explained: as a general proposition the agreements considered in this chapter fall into the 'effect' rather than the 'object' box. The important point was made in chapter 3 that not every contractual restriction necessarily restricts

---

[1] See ch 21, pp 823–827.   [2] See ch 22, pp 524.   [3] See ch 21, p 824.
[4] For a helpful analysis of the Commission's approach to the application of Article 81 to horizontal cooperation agreements see González Díaz in Faull and Nikpay *The EC Law of Competition* (Oxford University Press, 2nd ed, 2007), ch 7.

competition, and examples were given to explain this. The application of Article 81(1) to potential as well as actual restrictions of competition was dealt with, and the point made that a realistic approach must be taken to restrictions of potential competition. Reference was made to a greater willingness on the part of the Commission in recent years to conclude that agreements were not restrictive of competition, so that they did not infringe Article 81(1), rather than being caught by Article 81(1) and having to satisfy the criteria of Article 81(3). The *de minimis* doctrine and the meaning of an effect on inter-state trade were considered, and the chapter concluded with a checklist of agreements that would normally fall outside Article 81(1).

In chapter 4 the criteria for the application of Article 81(3) were explained, as was the impact of the Modernisation Regulation. It is no longer possible to notify an agreement and to receive an 'individual exemption' from the Commission. However it is worth making the point that there may be circumstances in which the Commission has concerns about a horizontal agreement which falls short of being a hard-core cartel, but may be prepared to close the case if the parties offer suitable commitments to allay its competition concerns: some cases of horizontal cooperation have been dealt with in this way, and will be noted in the text that follows.

The point was made in chapter 4 that there is no kind of agreement which is, by its nature, incapable of satisfying the criteria of Article 81(3). The system of block exemptions was described, including the adoption of 'new-style' block exemptions of a less formalistic and more economics-oriented nature. This chapter assumes a knowledge of the contents of chapters 3 and 4, and explains the current position in relation to horizontal cooperation agreements under Article 81[5].

(B) The Community Courts and horizontal cooperation agreements

There is very little case law of the Community Courts specifically on the application of Article 81 to horizontal cooperation agreements. A few cases have reached the ECJ under Article 234, such as *Gøttrup-Klim Grovvareforeninger v Dansk Landburgs Grovvareselskab AmbA*[6]. As for Commission decisions, where the parties receive a decision that states that the criteria of Article 81(3) are satisfied, there is usually little incentive for them to appeal against the finding that the agreement infringed Article 81(1). A notable exception to this is the judgment of the CFI in *European Night Services v Commission*[7] where an appeal was successfully launched against the Commission's

---

[5] For discussion of the position in the US see the Department of Justice and Federal Trade Commission *Antitrust Guidelines for Collaborations Among Competitors*, available at www.usdoj.gov/atr/public/guidelines/jointindex.htm; see also Brodley 'Joint Ventures and Antitrust Policy' (1982) 95 Harvard Law Review 1523; McFalls 'The Role and Assessment of Classical Market Power in Joint Venture Analysis' (1997–98) 66 Antitrust Law Journal 651; Werden 'Antitrust Analysis of Joint Ventures: An Overview' ibid, 701; Correia 'Joint Ventures: Issues in Enforcement Policy' ibid, 737; Gutterman *Innovation and Competition Policy: A Comparative Study of the Regulation of Patent Licensing and Collaborative Research & Development in the United States and the European Community* (Kluwer Law International, 1997).

[6] Case 250/92 [1994] ECR I-5641, [1996] 4 CMLR 191; see also Cases C-399/93 etc *HG Oude Luttikhuis v Coberco* [1995] ECR I-4515, [1996] 5 CMLR 178.

[7] Cases T-374/94 etc [1998] ECR II-3141, [1998] 5 CMLR 718: see ch 3, pp 133–134; see similarly Cases T-79/85 and 80/95 *SNCF v Commission* [1996] ECR II-1491, [1997] 4 CMLR 334; the recipients of an individual exemption in *TPS* OJ [1999] L 90/6, [1999] 5 CMLR 168 appealed unsuccessfully to the CFI in Case T-112/99

decision, in which it had attached conditions and obligations to an individual exemption which the parties considered to be unduly onerous. The CFI concluded that the Commission had failed to demonstrate that the agreement would appreciably restrict competition, as a result of which the decision was annulled. Another exception to the proposition that undertakings that are authorised by the Commission to go ahead with a cooperation agreement under Article 81(3) are unlikely to appeal to the CFI is *O2 (Germany) GmbH & Co. OHG v Commission*[8], where O2 was successful in persuading the Court that national roaming agreements in the mobile telephony sector did not restrict competition in the sense of Article 81(1), and therefore did not need authorisation under Article 81(3)[9].

There have been some other cases in which a third party has challenged the Commission's decision that Article 81(3) was satisfied but these have usually been unsuccessful[10]. Significant exceptions to this include *Métropole télévision SA v Commission*[11] and *M6 v Commission*[12], where the CFI upheld two consecutive appeals by a third party that the Commission had erred in law in concluding that the rules of the European Broadcasting Union satisfied Article 81(3)[13].

(C) The Commission's *Guidelines on Horizontal Cooperation Agreements* and *Guidelines on the application of Article 81(3) of the Treaty*

The Commission adopted its *Guidelines on Horizontal Cooperation Agreements* at the end of 2000; they were published in the Official Journal on 6 January 2001[14]. The *Guidelines* consist of seven chapters. In the first, the Commission sets out its position generally in relation to horizontal cooperation agreements and establishes an analytical framework for the most common types of agreement. Chapters then follow on each of the following six types of agreement: R&D[15]; production agreements, including specialisation agreements[16]; purchasing agreements[17]; commercialisation agreements[18]; agreements on standards[19]; and environmental agreements[20]. The *Guidelines* do not deal with other types of agreement, such as the exchange of information and the acquisition of minority shareholdings[21]. This chapter will follow the pattern of the *Guidelines*, considering first the general framework for the analysis of horizontal cooperation agreements and then each of the six types of agreement specified. It will conclude with a discussion of various other cases, such as restructuring agreements, under EC law and with a brief review of the position under UK law.

Métropole v Commission [2001] ECR II-2459, [2001] 5 CMLR 1236; on the *TPS* decision see Nikolinakos 'Strategic Alliances in the Pay TV Market: The *TPS* case' (2000) 21 ECLR 334.

⁸ Case T-328/03 [2006] ECR II-1231, [2006] 5 CMLR 258.

⁹ The case is discussed in ch 3, p 124.

¹⁰ See eg Case 43/85 *ANCIDES v Commission* [1987] ECR 3131, [1988] 4 CMLR 821; Case T-17/93 *Matra Hachette SA v Commission* [1994] ECR II-595.

¹¹ Cases T-528/93 etc [1996] ECR II-649, [1996] 5 CMLR 386.

¹² Cases T-185/00 [2002] ECR II-3805, [2003] 4 CMLR 707.

¹³ See ch 4, p 161.   ¹⁴ OJ [2001] C 3/2, [2001] 4 CMLR 819.   ¹⁵ *Guidelines*, ch 2: paras 39–77.

¹⁶ Ibid, ch 3: paras 78–114.   ¹⁷ Ibid, ch 4: paras 115–138.   ¹⁸ Ibid, ch 5: paras 139–158.

¹⁹ Ibid, ch 6: paras 159–178.   ²⁰ Ibid, ch 7: paras 179–198.

²¹ Ibid, para 10; on information agreements see ch 13 of this book, pp 523–532; on minority shareholdings see ch 21, p 825.

The *Guidelines* should be read in conjunction with the Commission's subsequent *Guidelines on the application of Article 81(3) of the Treaty*[22] which provide important insights into its approach to the application of Article 81(3) and, in particular, to the evidence needed to mount a successful argument based on that provision[23].

4. THE ANALYTICAL FRAMEWORK IN THE COMMISSION'S *GUIDELINES* FOR THE MOST COMMON TYPES OF HORIZONTAL COOPERATION AGREEMENTS UNDER ARTICLE 81

(A) Purpose of the *Guidelines*

The *Guidelines* state that horizontal cooperation agreements may lead to competition problems where the parties agree to the fixing of prices, output or the sharing of markets or where cooperation enables the parties to maintain, gain or increase their market power, thereby causing negative effects with respect to prices, output, innovation or the variety and quality of products[24]. However the *Guidelines* go on to say that substantial economic benefits can flow from horizontal cooperation, in particular given the dynamic nature of markets, globalisation and the speed of technological progress[25]. Cooperation can be a means for firms to share risk, save costs, pool know-how and launch innovation faster; the benefits to small and medium-sized enterprises are specifically noted[26]. The Commission states that, when analysing horizontal cooperation agreements, greater emphasis should be placed on economic criteria[27], for example on market power and on market structure[28]. The *Guidelines* replace the Commission's 1968 *Notice on agreements, decisions and concerted practices in the field of cooperation between enterprises*[29] and the 1993 *Notice concerning the assessment of cooperative joint ventures under Article [81]*[30], and complement the block exemptions on specialisation agreements and R&D agreements[31].

(B) Scope of the *Guidelines*

(i) The *Guidelines* apply to agreements between actual and potential competitors

The *Guidelines* apply to agreements entered into between two or more competitors operating at the same level in the market: the expression 'competitor' is taken to include both actual and potential competitors[32]. Somewhat strangely, the meaning of 'actual' and of 'potential' competitors is relegated to footnotes 8 and 9 of the *Guidelines*.

---

[22] OJ [2004] C 101/8. [23] The *Guidelines on Article 81(3)* are discussed in ch 4, pp 151ff.
[24] *Guidelines*, para 2. [25] See also *IFPI 'Simulcasting'* OJ [2003] L 107/58, paras 84–88.
[26] *Guidelines*, para 3. [27] Ibid, para 6. [28] Ibid, para 7. [29] OJ [1968] C 75/3. [30] OJ [1993] C 43/2.
[31] *Guidelines*, para 8.
[32] Ibid, para 9; on actual and potential competition under Article 81(1) see also ch 3, pp 133–134.

(A) Actual competitors Footnote 8 states that an undertaking is an actual competitor
either if it is active on the same relevant market or if, in the absence of the agreement,
it is able to switch production to the relevant products and market them in the short
term without incurring significant additional costs or risks in response to a small and
permanent increase in relative prices: the Commission refers to this as 'immediate supply-side substitutability', and cross-refers to paragraphs 20 to 23 of its 1997 *Notice on
Market Definition*[33], which explain this phenomenon in greater detail.

(B) Potential competitors Footnote 9 provides that an undertaking is a potential competitor where, in the absence of the agreement, it would be likely to undertake the necessary investments or other switching costs so that it could enter the relevant market in
response to a small and permanent increase in prices; the assessment must be based on
realistic grounds, and a theoretical possibility is not sufficient[34]. In this formulation of
the meaning of potential competition, the Commission refers to a policy statement that
it made at point 55 of its XIIIth *Report on Competition Policy* in 1983[35], and to its decision
in *Elopak/Metal Box-Odin*[36], where it concluded that a joint venture between those two
undertakings to design a new kind of carton did not infringe Article 81(1) since they were
not actual or potential competitors. The Commission could have, but did not, cite other
decisions in which it reached similar conclusions such as *Optical Fibres*[37], *Mitchell Cotts/
Sofiltra*[38], *Konsortium ECR 900*[39], *Iridium*[40], *Cégétel+4*[41] and *P&I Clubs*[42]; a more recent
decision in which it discussed the issue of potential competition is *Société Air France/
Alitalia Linee Aeree Italiane SpA*[43]. It is interesting to compare these decisions with
others in which the Commission concluded that undertakings were potential competitors, such as *British Interactive Broadcasting/Open*[44] and *GEAE/P&W*[45]; a consequence
of this conclusion was that the agreements in question were held to infringe Article 81(1),
but authorised because they satisfied the provisions of Article 81(3): under the procedural regime in place at the time, the Commission attached conditions and obligations to
the authorisations: that system was abolished by the Modernisation Regulation[46].

Further discussion on the distinction between actual and potential competitors will
be found in the Commission's *Guidelines on the application of Article 81 of the EC Treaty
to technology transfer agreements*[47].

(ii) Relationship with the *Guidelines on Vertical Restraints*

Where an agreement is entered into between undertakings that operate at different
levels of the market, it should be considered under the *Guidelines on Vertical Restraints*

[33] OJ [1997] C 372/5, [1998] 4 CMLR 177: see ch 1, pp 26–40.
[34] One of the criticisms of the Commission by the CFI in *European Night Services v Commission* (p 573,
n 7 above) was that it had failed convincingly to demonstrate that the agreement was entered into between
potential competitors: see ch 3, pp 133–134.
[35] See also Faull 'Joint Ventures under the EEC Competition Rules' (1984) 9 EL Rev 358.
[36] OJ [1990] L 209/15, [1991] 4 CMLR 832.   [37] OJ [1986] L 236/30.
[38] OJ [1987] L 41/31, [1988] 4 CMLR 111.   [39] OJ [1990] L 228/31, [1992] 4 CMLR 54.
[40] OJ [1997] L 16/87, [1997] 4 CMLR 1065.
[41] OJ [1999] L 218/14, [2000] 4 CMLR 106; see also a related decision, *Télécom Développement* OJ [1999]
L 218/24, [2000] 4 CMLR 124.
[42] OJ [1999] L 125/12, [1999] 5 CMLR 646.   [43] Commission decision of 7 April 2004, paras 110–126.
[44] OJ [1999] L 312/1, [2000] 4 CMLR 901, paras 141–144.
[45] OJ [2000] L 58/16, [2000] 5 CMLR 49, paras 71–75.   [46] See ch 4, pp 162–164.
[47] OJ [2004] C 101/2.

and Regulation 2790/99, the block exemption for vertical agreements[48]. However, to the extent that a vertical agreement is entered into between competitors, its effects should also be considered under the *Horizontal Guidelines*[49].

(iii) Relationship with the *Guidelines on the application of Article 81 of the EC Treaty to technology transfer agreements*

Where an agreement involves the transfer of technology between horizontal competitors, it should be considered under the *Guidelines on the application of Article 81 of the EC Treaty to technology transfer agreements* and Regulation 772/2004, the block exemption for technology transfer agreements. That Regulation is discussed in chapter 19 on the relationship between competition law and intellectual property rights, but the reader should be aware that it does apply to some horizontal agreements[50].

(iv) The 'centre of gravity' of an agreement

As mentioned above, the *Guidelines* apply to six types of agreements: R&D, production, purchasing, commercialisation, standardisation, and environmental. In any particular case it is therefore necessary to characterise the agreement in order to be able to determine whether it falls into any of these six categories, and if so which one. Not surprisingly, agreements in commercial practice do not divide themselves neatly in this way: for example undertakings that agree to conduct R&D together will often decide to produce and commercialise the product if the R&D is successful, while the parties to a joint production agreement might agree to some joint R&D as a by-product of their cooperation. Paragraph 12 of the *Guidelines* attempts to provide a basis for allocating agreements to the appropriate category by introducing the notion of an agreement's 'centre of gravity'.

The Commission states that account should be taken of two factors: the first is the starting point of the cooperation and the second is the degree of integration of the different functions that are being combined. Two examples are given. In the first, the parties enter into an R&D agreement and envisage the possibility of proceeding, if successful, to joint production: here, the cooperation originates as an R&D agreement and is characterised as such. In the second, the parties agree to integrate their production facilities, but only partially to integrate their R&D: here, the agreement is essentially concerned with production and should be analysed as such. The Commission adds that so-called 'strategic alliances', which are not narrowly focused on one or a few functions but instead involve undertakings agreeing to cooperate with one another in a fairly vague and aspirational sense, do not fall within the *Guidelines* at all. There have been several occasions on which the Commission has taken a favourable view of strategic alliances in the telecommunications and IT industries[51].

---

[48] *Guidelines*, para 11: on the application of Article 81 to vertical agreements generally see ch 16, pp 618ff.

[49] *Guidelines*, para 11; an agreement whereby one party supplies goods or services to another is vertical where, *for the purposes of that agreement*, the parties operate at different levels of the market, irrespective of the fact that, for other purposes, they are actual or potential competitors: see the definition of a vertical agreement in Article 2 of Regulation 2790/99, explained in ch 16, pp 641–645.

[50] See ch 19, pp 771–781.

[51] See eg *BT/MCI* OJ [1994] L 223/36, [1995] 5 CMLR 285 and *Olivetti/Digital* OJ [1994] L 309/24, both discussed in the Commission's XXIVth *Report on Competition Policy* (1994), points 156–162; *Atlas* OJ [1996] L 239/29, [1997] 4 CMLR 89 and *Phoenix/GlobalOne* OJ [1996] L 239/57, [1997] 4 CMLR 147, discussed in the Commission's XXVth *Report on Competition Policy* (1995), point 57 and the XXVIth *Report on Competition*

(v) The *Guidelines* apply to both the goods and services sectors

The *Guidelines* apply to both the goods and the services sectors. Many of the Commission's early decisions concerned horizontal cooperation in the goods sector; however there are plenty of decisions in more recent years that concerned a range of services sectors including banking, telecommunications, broadcasting, IT, the media and postal services. The *Guidelines* do not apply to the extent that sector-specific rules, for example on agreements in the transport and insurance sectors, are in place[52].

(C) Basic principles for the assessment of horizontal cooperation agreements under Article 81

(i) Article 81(1)

The Commission begins by noting that Article 81(1) applies both to agreements that have as their object the restriction of competition and to agreements that have this effect[53]. Some agreements have as their object the restriction of competition – price fixing, output limitation or the sharing of markets or customers – so that it is unnecessary to consider whether they have this effect[54]. However where agreements do not have as their object the restriction of competition, it is necessary to consider their effects. The Commission states that it is not sufficient simply to consider whether competition between the parties is limited; it is further necessary to consider whether an agreement is:

likely to affect competition in the market to such an extent that negative effects as to prices, output, innovation or the variety or quality of goods and services can be expected[55].

This is an illustration of the Commission's acceptance that economic criteria should be taken into account when applying Article 81(1) or, to put the point another way, that Article 81(1) should not be applied in a formalistic manner. In considering whether an agreement is likely to cause negative effects on the market the economic context must be considered, taking into account the nature of the agreement and the parties' market power which, together with other structural factors, determines the likelihood that horizontal cooperation would adversely affect overall competition to a significant extent[56]. The Commission then proceeds to provide guidance on how the nature of the agreement affects its analysis, and on the relevance of the parties' market power and other structural factors.

(A) The nature of the agreement The relevance of the nature of the agreement to its assessment under Article 81(1) is that some forms of cooperation are entered into

---

Policy (1996), point 67; *Global European Network,* discussed in the XXVIIth *Report on Competition Policy* (1997), point 73 and p 128; *Unisource* OJ [1997] L 381/1, [1998] 4 CMLR 105 and *Unisource* OJ [1997] L 381/24, [1998] 4 CMLR 145, discussed in the XXVIIth *Report,* points 71–72 and p 133; note the revised *Unisource* decision at OJ [2001] L 52/30.

  [52] *Guidelines,* para 13; on the block exemptions in the transport sector see ch 23 pp 961–970; on the insurance sector see below, pp 601–602.
  [53] *Guidelines,* para 17.
  [54] *Ibid,* para 18: note the correspondence between the Commission's approach in the *Guidelines* and the commentary on the application of Article 81(1) in ch 3, pp 116ff.
  [55] *Guidelines,* para 19. [56] *Ibid,* para 20.

between undertakings that are unlikely to affect the marketing of goods or services. Cooperation on R&D, standards and environmental matters would not normally have a direct effect on the parties' prices and output when they take their products to the market: the Commission says that in these cases agreements are only likely to have negative effects, if at all, on the degree of innovation and the variety of products that the parties produce; they may also give rise to a foreclosure of third party access to the market[57]. Other agreements, for example on joint production and purchasing, are more likely to lead to coordination of pricing and output decisions, in particular where this leads to a high degree of common costs, for example through joint manufacture.

In paragraphs 24 to 26 of the *Guidelines* the Commission considers respectively those agreements that, by their very nature, would fall outside Article 81(1); those that almost always fall within it; and those that may fall within it because they have restrictive effects. In each of the subsequent chapters of the *Guidelines* the Commission follows the same pattern of analysis.

In the first of these categories, the Commission says that cooperation between non-competitors and agreements between competing companies that cannot independently carry out the project or activity covered by the cooperation would normally fall outside Article 81(1)[58]; the same is said to be true of 'cooperation concerning an activity which does not influence the relevant parameters of competition'[59]. In the case of the agreements described in paragraph 24, the Commission concludes that Article 81(1) could be infringed only if the parties enjoyed significant market power and if there could be a foreclosure effect[60]. In *Eirpage*[61] the Commission considered that a joint venture in Ireland to establish a nationwide paging service between Bord Telecom Eireann, the national postal and telecommunications company, and Motorola, one of the world's leading manufacturers of mobile telecommunications equipment, could have a deterrent effect on potential market entrants and thereby restrict competition[62]; however the Commission considered that the criteria of Article 81(3) were satisfied and, under the old procedure of individual exemptions, authorized the agreement for a period of 11 years[63]. In *Screensport/EBU Members*[64] the Commission considered that a joint venture to establish a transnational satellite sports channel covering most of western Europe infringed Article 81(1) partly because of its foreclosure effects on third parties[65]; it concluded that the agreement did not satisfy Article 81(3)[66].

In the second category fall those agreements that have as their object the restriction of competition, such as price fixing and output limitation; the Commission states that these will almost always be prohibited[67]. However it acknowledges that an exception to this may arise in the case of a production joint venture, where the parents may agree on the output of the joint venture; they may even collaborate on sales, which therefore involves coordination on prices[68].

---

[57] Ibid, para 22.
[58] See eg *Nuclear Insurance Pools* Commission's XXXIst *Report on Competition Policy* (2001), point 203.
[59] *Guidelines*, para 24.
[60] Ibid; the Commission states at footnote 17 that firms may have significant market power even though they are not dominant in the sense of Article 82.
[61] OJ [1991] L 306/22, [1993] 4 CMLR 64, para 12. [62] Ibid, para 12. [63] Ibid, paras 14–24.
[64] Ibid, paras 57–66; see also *Astra* OJ [1993] L 20/23, [1994] 5 CMLR 226, where the Commission concluded that a joint venture to provide a television distribution service by satellite did not satisfy Article 81(3).
[65] OJ [1991] L 63/32, [1992] 5 CMLR 273, paras 57–66. [66] Ibid, paras 70–76. [67] *Guidelines*, para 25.
[68] Ibid, footnote 18; see further pp 588–592 below on joint production.

In other cases – that is to say in cases that might have as their effect the restriction of competition – the Commission states that further analysis is needed to determine whether Article 81(1) is applicable, and in particular it is necessary to consider the market shares of the parties and other structural factors[69].

(B) Market power and market structure Where it is necessary to consider whether an agreement could have the effect of restricting competition, the starting point for the analysis is the position of the parties on the market[70]. This requires a definition of the relevant market, using the methodology of the Commission's *Notice on Market Definition*[71]. The *Guidelines* provide some additional guidance on market definition, for example in relation to innovation and purchasing markets; where appropriate this further guidance will be referred to later in this chapter when particular types of agreement are discussed. Paragraph 28 states that if the parties have a low combined market share, a restrictive effect is unlikely and no further analysis is required; furthermore if one party has a high market share and the other party to a bilateral agreement has only an insignificant market share there would normally be no problem, since there would be little increment to market power. However the paragraph does not lay down a general market share figure for all the types of agreement covered by the *Guidelines*[72]. It is of course the case that the *Notice on Agreements of Minor Importance*[73] lays down a threshold of 10 per cent, below which horizontal agreements normally do not infringe Article 81(1). In so far as the *Guidelines* give further indications as to the significance of market share figures, these will be dealt with in the context of specific types of agreement later in this chapter. The relevance of particular market shares in the assessment of horizontal agreements is summarised in the following table:

Market shares and horizontal agreements	
25%	An agreement between undertakings with a market share of more than 25% will not benefit from the block exemption on R&D agreements
20%	An agreement between undertakings with a market share of more than 20% will not benefit from the block exemption on specialisation agreements or the block exemption on technology transfer agreements
15%	An agreement between undertakings with a market share of less than 15% will find that their purchasing or commercialisation agreements usually fall outside Article 81(1).
10%	An agreement between undertakings with a market share below 10% will usually benefit from the *de minimis* doctrine.

(C) Assessing market concentration Paragraphs 29 and 30 consider the relevance of structural factors when deciding whether an agreement could have the effect of restricting competition. This cannot be determined on the basis of market shares alone: the

---

[69] *Guidelines*, para 26.   [70] Ibid, para 27.   [71] The Notice is discussed in some detail in ch 1, pp 26–40.

[72] Cf the position in the US where there is a general 'safe harbour' for agreements entered into by firms with less than 20 per cent on each relevant market: see the Department of Justice and Federal Trade Commission *Guidelines for Collaboration Among Competitors* April 2000, para 4.2, available at www.usdoj.gov/atr.

[73] OJ [2001] C 368/13, [2002] 4 CMLR 699; see ch 3, pp 137–142.

concentration of the market is relevant, as are other factors. The Commission suggests two ways of determining how concentrated a market is[74]. The first is to use the so-called 'Herfindahl-Hirschman Index' ('the HHI'). The HHI has been explained in chapter 1.

The Commission also suggests, in paragraph 29 of the *Guidelines*, that, in determining the concentration level of the market, another possible indicator is the leading firm concentration ratio. For example the three-firm concentration ratio is the sum of the market shares of the leading three competitors in a market, and is depicted as 'CR3'; 'CR4' would indicate the outcome of the same exercise in relation to the leading four firms[75].

(D) Other structural factors Paragraph 30 of the *Guidelines* suggests that other factors, such as the stability of market shares over time, entry barriers and the countervailing power of suppliers and buyers should also be taken into account in determining the position of the parties to a horizontal cooperation agreement and their ability to produce negative effects on the market.

(ii) Article 81(3)

Where an agreement is caught by Article 81(1) it remains possible for the parties to argue that it satisfies the terms of Article 81(3). This provision has been discussed at length in chapter 4[76], and the Commission discusses the position briefly in paragraphs 31 to 36 of the *Guidelines*. Under the EC Modernisation Regulation the Commission shares the competence to enforce Articles 81(3) with the national competition authorities of the Member States and national courts, and the system of notification for individual exemption from the Commission has been abolished; however the system of block exemptions is maintained[77]. As noted earlier, the Commission has published *Guidelines on the application of Article 81(3) of the Treaty*[78], and these should be consulted in any case in which undertakings wish to invoke that provision.

5. RESEARCH AND DEVELOPMENT AGREEMENTS[79]

Chapter 2 of the *Guidelines*[80] deals with agreements that have as their centre of gravity R&D, other than concentrations falling within the ECMR[81]. The *Guidelines* point out the benefits of R&D[82] and specifically refer to the benefits for small and medium-sized undertakings of cooperation at this level[83]. Paragraphs 43 to 54 deal with market definition in R&D cases, first in relation to existing markets and then in relation to markets for innovation.

Where an agreement concerns improvements to existing products, they and their close substitutes form the relevant market[84]. This is not the case where there will be a significant change to an existing product, or the development of an entirely new one, although in this situation the possibility exists that cooperation in the new market

---

[74] *Guidelines*, para 29.   [75] *Guidelines*, para 29, footnote 23.   [76] See ch 4 generally.
[77] See ch 4, pp 162–164.   [78] OJ [2004] C 101/8.
[79] For a useful discussion of research and development agreements see *Faull and Nikpay*, paras 7.107–7.212.
[80] *Guidelines*, paras 39–77.   [81] Ibid, para 39.   [82] Ibid, para 40.   [83] Ibid, para 41.   [84] Ibid, para 44.

could lead to coordination in the old one[85]. Where the parties cooperate in relation to components, it is possible that the market for the final products in which the components will be incorporated will be relevant, where the component is a key element in the final product and the parties are important competitors in that market[86]. In some cases the market may be one for technology rather than products, and paragraphs 47 to 49 explain how the market should be defined and market share calculated in those circumstances.

Where the parties conduct R&D in relation to entirely new products the position is more complex[87]. In paragraph 51 the Commission says that it may be possible to identify competing 'poles' of R&D, in which case it is necessary to consider whether, if two competing undertakings were to enter into a horizontal cooperation agreement, there will be a 'sufficient number of R&D poles left'. No guidance is given as to what would qualify as 'sufficient' for this purpose. The credibility of an R&D pole is assessed according to the nature, scope and size of other R&D efforts, their access to financial and human resources, know-how, patents and other specialised assets and their capability to exploit the results[88]. Where it is not possible to identify R&D poles, the Commission would limit its assessment to related product and/or technology markets[89].

Further discussion of technology markets will be found in the Commission's *Guidelines on the application of Article 81 of the EC Treaty to technology transfer agreements*[90], in particular as to methodologies for defining technology markets[91].

(A) The application of Article 81(1) to R&D agreements

(i) Agreements that normally fall outside Article 81(1)

The Commission considers that R&D agreements 'at a rather theoretical level, far removed from the exploitation of the results', fall outside Article 81(1)[92]. So too would agreements between non-competitors[93], unless there is a possibility of a foreclosure effect and one of the parties has significant market power with respect to key technology[94]. The outsourcing of R&D to research institutes and academic bodies which are not active in the exploitation of the results is not caught by Article 81(1)[95]; and 'pure' R&D agreements, that do not extend to joint exploitation of the results, would rarely do so: they would do so only where they significantly reduce effective competition in innovation[96].

(ii) Agreements that almost always fall within Article 81(1)

The Commission says that if the true object of an agreement is not R&D but the creation of a disguised cartel Article 81(1) would apply; however it adds that an R&D agreement which includes the joint exploitation of future results is not necessarily restrictive of competition[97].

---

[85] Ibid, para 45.   [86] Ibid, para 46.
[87] For discussion on competition in innovation see Jorde and Teece 'Innovation and Cooperation: Implications for Competition and Antitrust' (1990) 4 Journal of Economic Perspectives 75; OFT Economic Discussion Paper 3 (OFT 377) *Innovation and Competition Policy* (Charles River Associates, 2002).
[88] *Guidelines,* para 51.   [89] Ibid, para 52.   [90] OJ [2004] C 101/2.   [91] Ibid, paras 19–25.
[92] *Guidelines,* para 55.   [93] Ibid, para 56.   [94] Ibid, footnote 30.   [95] Ibid, para 57.   [96] Ibid, para 58.
[97] Ibid, para 59.

(iii) Agreements that may fall within Article 81(1)

Paragraphs 60 to 67 of the *Guidelines* deal with R&D agreements that may have the effect of restricting competition. They must be analysed in their economic context where the cooperation is 'close to the market launch' and is between competitors on existing product or technology markets or on innovation markets[98]. Three possible anti-competitive effects are noted: a restriction in innovation, coordination in existing markets and foreclosure; however the Commission acknowledges that these are unlikely in the absence of significant market power[99]. No market share figure is given for the application of Article 81(1) to R&D agreements, although the Commission points out that a safe haven is provided by Article 4 of Regulation 2659/00, the block exemption for R&D agreements, where the parties' market share is below 25 per cent[100]. The *Guidelines* say that where the parties have a market share of more than 25 per cent it does not automatically follow that Article 81(1) is infringed, but they continue by saying that an infringement becomes more likely as the parties' position on the market becomes stronger[101]. The *Guidelines* then provide guidance on R&D agreements in relation to existing products[102], entirely new products (acknowledging that cooperation in relation to new products is, in general, pro-competitive)[103] and agreements in between these two situations[104].

(B) The application of Article 81(3) to R&D agreements[105]

Paragraphs 68 to 74 discuss the assessment of R&D agreements under Article 81(3). Paragraph 70 states that the hard-core restrictions that are listed in Article 5 of Regulation 2659/00, and which prevent the application of the block exemption, would be unlikely to be regarded as indispensable in the case of the individual assessment of an agreement under Article 81(3). Paragraphs 73 and 74 deal with the likely permitted duration of cooperation, both under the block exemption and to satisfy Article 81(3) on a case-by-case basis. Where R&D leads to the launch and marketing of a new product, a period of cooperation of seven years beyond the R&D phase will be permitted, even though the market shares of the parties at this stage may be high: the Commission acknowledges that a strong market position is likely due to the 'first mover advantage' that is a consequence of successful R&D. The Commission further acknowledges that a period of more than seven years might be appropriate where the parties can demonstrate that this is necessary to guarantee an adequate return on the investment involved[106].

(C) The block exemption for research and development agreements: Regulation 2659/00

Acting under powers conferred upon it by Council Regulation 2821/71[107] the Commission adopted a block exemption for R&D agreements on 29 November 2000[108]. The Regulation entered into force on 1 January 2001 and will expire on 31

---

[98] Ibid, para 60.   [99] Ibid, para 61.   [100] Ibid, para 62; on the block exemption see below.

[101] *Guidelines*, para 63.   [102] Ibid, para 64.   [103] Ibid, para 65.   [104] Ibid, para 66.

[105] For examples of R&D agreements that the Commission considered satisfied the criteria of Article 81(3) see *Asahi/St Gobain* OJ [1994] L 354/87; *Philips/Osram* OJ [1994] L 378/34, [1996] 4 CMLR 48.

[106] *Guidelines*, para 73, final sentence.   [107] OJ [1971] L 285/46.

[108] OJ [2000] L 304/7, [2001] 4 CMLR 808.

December 2010[109]. The new Regulation replaced Regulation 418/85[110]. Article 8 provides transitional relief for agreements which were in force on 31 December 2000 and which satisfied the conditions for exemption in the old Regulation: they were exempt until 30 June 2002. The new Regulation is without prejudice to Article 82[111].

The Regulation consists of 23 Recitals and 9 Articles. Recital 2 refers specifically to Article 163(2) of the Treaty, which calls upon the Community to encourage undertakings, including small and medium-sized undertakings, in their R&D activities and to support efforts on their part to cooperate with one another. Article 1 confers block exemption upon certain R&D agreements. Article 2 defines key terms such as 'research and development', 'exploitation of the results' and 'competing undertaking'. Article 3 sets out conditions for application of the block exemption. Article 4 imposes a market share cap and deals with the duration of the exemption. Article 5 deals with agreements that are not covered by the block exemption because they contain 'hard-core' restrictions. Article 6 contains provisions on the application of the market share threshold. Article 7 provides for withdrawal of the block exemption. Articles 8 and 9 deal respectively with transitional matters and the period of validity of the Regulation. Regulation 2659/2000, like Regulation 2658/2000[112] and Regulation 2790/99[113], is a 'new-style' block exemption; it does not contain a detailed 'white list' of permitted restrictions, but instead confers block exemption upon a range of agreements up to a certain level of market power and specifies restrictions and clauses that must not be included[114].

(i) Article 1: scope of the block exemption

Article 1(1) confers block exemption, pursuant to Article 81(3) of the Treaty, on three types of R&D agreements in relation to goods or services[115]:

(a) joint research and development of products or processes and joint exploitation of the results of that research and development;

(b) joint exploitation of the results of research and development of products or processes jointly carried out pursuant to a prior agreement between the same parties; or

(c) joint research and development of products or processes excluding joint exploitation of the results.

To benefit from the block exemption the agreement must satisfy the conditions set out in Article 3[116]. Recital 3 of the Regulation states that agreements of the kind described in (c) would not normally fall within the scope of Article 81(1) at all; in case they do however, and for the avoidance of doubt, they are included within the scope of the block exemption. Most agreements exempted by the Regulation will involve joint exploitation of the R&D. Recital 11 of the Regulation states that joint exploitation can be considered as the natural consequence of joint R&D, and can take various forms including manufacture, the exploitation of intellectual property rights or the marketing

---

[109] Regulation 2659/2000, Article 9.

[110] OJ [1985] L 53/5, amended by Regulation 151/93 OJ [1993] L 21/8 and extended in force until 31 December 2001 by Regulation 2236/97 OJ [1997] L 306/12.

[111] Regulation 2659/2000, Recital 20.   [112] See pp 589–592 below.   [113] See ch 16, pp 640–662.

[114] Regulation 2659/2000, Recital 7.

[115] Article 1 refers to research and development of 'products or processes'; products are defined in Article 2(5) to include 'a good and/or a service, including both intermediary goods and/or services and final goods and/or services'; processes are defined in Article 2(6) to mean 'a technology or process arising out of the joint research and development'.

[116] See pp 585–586 below.

of newproducts. Definitions of 'research and development', 'exploitation of the results' and of what is meant by 'joint' exploitation are provided in Article 2. In particular, exploitation means the 'production or distribution of the contract products or the application of the contract processes or the assignment or licensing of intellectual property rights or the communication of know-how required for such manufacture or application'[117]; and R&D and exploitation are 'joint' where the work is carried out by a joint team, organisation or undertaking, is jointly entrusted to a third party or is allocated between the parties by way of specialisation in research, development, production or distribution[118].

Article 1(2) provides that the block exemption also applies to provisions in R&D agreements:

which do not constitute the primary object of such agreements, but are directly related to and necessary for their implementation, such as an obligation not to carry out, independently or together with third parties, research and development in the field to which the agreement relates or in a closely connected field during the execution of the agreement.

However Article 1(2) would not apply to provisions that have the same object as the hard-core restrictions set out in Article 5(1)[119].

(ii) Article 2: definitions

Article 2 contains a series of definitions of expressions used in the Regulation including, as well as those already mentioned, terms such as 'contract process', 'contract product' and 'relevant market for the contract products'.

(iii) Article 3: conditions for exemption

Article 3(1) provides that block exemption is available subject to the conditions set out in paragraphs 2 to 5 thereof; Article 3 should be read in conjunction with Recital 14. It should be stressed that these conditions are applicable only where an agreement infringes Article 81(1) so that the parties wish to avail themselves of the block exemption. If an agreement is not restrictive in the sense of Article 81(1), for example because it is not entered into between competitors, because it involves the outsourcing of R&D to a third party, or because it relates to 'pure' R&D, there is no need to comply with Article 3 of the Regulation.

Article 3(2) provides that all the parties must have access to the results of the joint R&D for the purposes of further research or exploitation[120]. However, the second sentence specifically provides that research institutes, academic bodies or undertakings which supply R&D as a commercial service but are not normally active in exploitation of the results, may agree to confine their use of the results to conducting further research. This means, for example, that a pharmaceutical company that enters into an R&D agreement with a research institute or a university can require its partner not to exploit the results commercially but to limit itself only to further research; if this restriction were not possible, the pharmaceutical company might refrain from beneficial joint

---

[117] Regulation 2659/2000, Article 2(8). [118] Ibid, Article 2(11). [119] Ibid, Article 1(2), second paragraph.
[120] 'Access' is not defined in the Regulation; it must mean more than merely a right to view the results of the R&D, since it is to be granted 'for the purposes of further research or exploitation'; Recital 14 refers to the idea that each party to the agreement should have 'the opportunity of exploiting any results that interest it'.

R&D with the undertaking in question for fear that it would extend its activities beyond research into commercialisation.

Article 3(3) provides that, where an agreement provides only for joint R&D, each party must be free independently to exploit the results of it and of any preexisting know-how necessary for the purposes of such exploitation. The second sentence of Article 3(3) provides that, where the parties were not competing undertakings at the time the agreement was entered into, the exploitation can be limited to one or more technical fields of development[121]. Article 3(3) will presumably apply only rarely, since most of the cases envisaged in this provision would not involve infringements of Article 81(1) anyway.

Article 3(4) provides that joint exploitation is permissible only where it relates to results of cooperation in R&D which are protected by intellectual property rights or are protected by know-how, which substantially contribute to technical or economic progress and where the results are decisive for the manufacture of the contract products or the application of the contract processes. The reason for this condition is that cooperation at the level of exploitation should be limited to those cases in which joint R&D has led to economic benefits; where this is not the case, the rationale for granting block exemption to joint exploitation is not satisfied.

Article 3(5) provides that undertakings charged with manufacture by way of specialisation in production must be required to fulfil orders for supplies from all the parties, except where the R&D also provides for joint distribution. The explanation for this is that where, for example, one party agrees to produce widgets and the other blodgets, each should have access to the products produced by the other and be able to compete in the relevant market; this is not necessary, however, where the parties carry out their distribution jointly.

(iv) Article 4: the market share threshold and duration of exemption

Article 4 deals with the market share threshold and the duration of the exemption. Article 4(1) provides that, where the participating undertakings[122] are not competing undertakings[123], the exemption shall apply for the duration of the R&D and, where the results are jointly exploited, for seven years from the time the contract products are first put on the market within the common market; this is the case irrespective of the parties' market share, while the position stabilises and in order to guarantee a minimum period of return on the investments involved[124]. Article 4(3) provides that, at the end of the seven-year period, the exemption can continue as long as the parties' combined market share does not exceed 25%.

Article 4(2) deals with the position where the participating undertakings are competing undertakings. In that case the block exemption applies only if, at the time the parties entered into the agreement, their share of the market for the products capable of being improved or replaced by the contract products does not exceed 25%. Article 6 contains rules on how to apply the market share threshold; it contains specific rules to deal with the situation where the undertakings outgrow the market share cap[125].

---

[121] Competing undertakings are defined in Article 2(12) to include both an 'actual competitor' that is active on the relevant market and a 'potential competitor' that could realistically enter the market in response to a small and permanent increase in relative prices: on the so-called 'SSNIP test' see ch 1, pp 26–40.

[122] The expression 'participating undertakings' is defined in Article 2(2), and includes 'connected undertakings', defined in Article 2(3).

[123] See n 121 above.   [124] Regulation 2659/2000, Recital 16.   [125] Ibid, Article 6(2)–(4).

(v) Article 5: agreements not covered by the exemption

Article 5(1) prevents the block exemption from applying where agreements contain 'severe anti-competitive restraints'[126] which 'directly or indirectly, in isolation or in combination with other factors under the control of the parties, have as their object' any of the following:

(a) a limitation on the freedom of the parties to carry out R&D in a field unconnected to the agreement;

(b) certain prohibitions on the right to challenge intellectual property rights;

(c) a limitation on output or sales;

(d) the fixing of prices when selling the contract products to third parties;

(e) a restriction of the customers that can be served after a period of seven years from the time when the contract products are first put on the market within the common market;

(f) a prohibition on passive sales in territories reserved for the other parties;

(g) a prohibition on active sales in territories reserved for other parties after the end of seven years from the time when the contract products are first put on the market within the common market;

(h) a requirement not to grant licences to third parties where at least one of the parties is not allowed to or does not in fact exploit the results of the joint R&D;

(i) a requirement to refuse to meet demand from users or resellers in their respective territories who would market them in other territories within the common market;

(j) a requirement to make it difficult for users or resellers to obtain the contract products from other resellers within the common market.

The inclusion of any of these provisions excludes the entire agreement, not just the offensive provisions, from the block exemption[127]. However Article 5(2)(a) provides that the setting of production targets where the exploitation of the results includes joint production of the contract products is not caught by Article 5(1); while Article 5(2)(b) provides that sales targets and the fixing of prices to immediate customers are not caught where the exploitation includes the joint distribution of the contract products.

(vi) Article 6: application of the market share threshold

Article 6 was referred to above in the context of the market share cap in Article 4[128].

(vii) Article 7: withdrawal of the block exemption by the Commission

Article 7 enables the Commission to withdraw the benefit of the block exemption from those R&D agreements which have effects which are incompatible with Article 81(3). The Commission has indicated that it would consider withdrawing the block exemption where the existence of the R&D agreement restricts the scope for third parties to carry out R&D because of the limited research capacity elsewhere[129]; where, because of the structure of supply, the existence of the R&D agreement substantially restricts the access of third parties to the market for the contract products[130]; where, without any objectively valid reason, the parties do not exploit the results of the R&D[131]; where the contract

---

[126] Ibid, Recital 17.   [127] *Guidelines*, para 37.   [128] See p 586 above.
[129] Regulation 2659/2000, Article 7(a).   [130] Ibid, Article 7(b).   [131] Ibid, Article 7(c).

products are not subject to effective competition[132]; or where the existence of the R&D agreement would eliminate effective competition in R&D on a particular market[133].

(viii) Article 8: transitional period
The transitional relief for agreements that benefited from the exemption provided for in Regulation 418/85 was explained above[134].

(ix) Article 9: period of validity
The Regulation entered into force on 1 January 2001 and will expire on 31 December 2010.

6. PRODUCTION AGREEMENTS, INCLUDING SPECIALISATION AGREEMENTS[135]

Chapter 3 of the *Guidelines*[136] deals with production agreements, including specialisation agreements. It notes that broadly speaking production agreements fall into three types: joint production, specialisation and sub-contracting agreements. Sub-contracting agreements between competitors are dealt with by the *Guidelines*[137]; sub-contracting agreements between non-competitors involving the transfer of know-how are dealt with by the Commission's *Notice on Subcontracting Agreements*[138]. In determining whether Article 81(1) applies to production agreements, the relevant product and geographic markets must be defined; it may also be necessary to consider the possibility that there may be a 'spillover effect' in an upstream, downstream or neighbouring market, but only if cooperation in one market necessarily results in the coordination of competitive behaviour in a connected market and if the parties are in a strong position in the spillover market[139].

(A) The application of Article 81(1) to production agreements

(i) Agreements that normally fall outside Article 81(1)
Agreements between non-competitors are normally outside Article 81(1)[140], unless the agreement could have a foreclosure effect, for example because one party has a strong market position on an upstream market for a key component which could raise the costs of competitors in a downstream market[141]. Cooperation between firms that compete on markets closely related to the market directly concerned by the cooperation will not infringe Article 81(1) if cooperation is the only commercially possible way of entering a new market, to launch new product or service or to carry out a specific project[142]. Article 81(1) is unlikely to be infringed where the cooperation does not lead to a high degree of commonality of costs; for example if the parties jointly produce an

---

[132] Ibid, Article 7(d).   [133] Ibid, Article 7(e).   [134] See p 584 above.
[135] See further *Faull and Nikpay*, paras 7.213–7.251.   [136] *Guidelines*, paras 78–114.
[137] Ibids, paras 81 and 100.   [138] OJ [1979] C 1/2; see ch 16, pp 666–667.
[139] *Guidelines*, para 82.   [140] Ibid, para 86.   [141] Ibid, para 85.   [142] Ibid, para 87.

intermediate product which accounts for only a small proportion of the cost of the final product, competition is unlikely to be affected to a material extent[143].

(ii) Agreements that almost always fall within Article 81(1)

Agreements to fix prices, limit output or to share markets or customer groups would be caught; but the parties can agree, for example, on the level of output of a joint venture and on the prices it will charge[144].

(iii) Agreements that may fall within Article 81(1)

Paragraphs 91 to 101 deal with production agreements that may have the effect of restricting competition. As envisaged by the 'analytical framework' set out earlier in the *Guidelines*[145], both the market power of the parties and the structure of the market must be analysed. No market share figure is given for the application of Article 81(1), but the Commission points out that there is a safe haven in the block exemption for unilateral and bilateral specialisation where the parties' market share does not exceed 20 per cent[146]. Where the parties have a market share in excess of 20 per cent, the market concentration should also be considered[147]: the Commission refers at this point to HHI analysis, which was explained earlier[148]. The fact that parties to an agreement might have links with other competitors may be relevant to the competition analysis[149]; and in some cases cooperation between strong *potential* competitors may be caught[150]. Cooperation in an upstream market could be caught if it could give rise to a foreclosure or to a spillover effect[151]. Subcontracting agreements between competitors could be caught for the same reason[152]. Reciprocal specialisation agreements where the parties have a market share of more than 20 per cent, the market share cap for application of the block exemption, would almost always fall within Article 81(1) and would have to be analysed carefully because of the risk of market partitioning before they could be exempted on an individual basis[153].

(B) The application of Article 81(3) to production agreements

Paragraphs 102 to 105 discuss, but do not provide any particular guidance on, the criteria in Article 81(3) and their application to production agreements[154].

(C) The block exemption for specialisation agreements: Regulation 2658/00

Acting under powers conferred upon it by Council Regulation 2821/71[155] the Commission adopted a new block exemption for specialisation agreements on 29 November

---

[143] Ibid, para 88.   [144] Ibid, para 90.   [145] See pp 575–578 above.
[146] *Guidelines*, para 93; on the block exemption see pp 000–000 below.
[147] *Ibid*, para 96.   [148] See p 581 above.   [149] *Guidelines*, para 97.   [150] Ibid, para 98.
[151] Ibid, para 99.   [152] Ibid, para 100.   [153] Ibid, para 101.
[154] For examples of individual exemptions granted to production agreements see eg *Fiat/Hitachi* OJ [1993] L 20/10, [1994] 4 CMLR 571; *Ford/Volkswagen* OJ [1993] L 20/14, [1993] 5 CMLR 617; *Exxon/Mobil* OJ [1994] L 144/20: see Commission's XXIVth *Report on Competition Policy* (1994), pp 169–171; *Fujitsu/AMD* OJ [1994] L 341/66.
[155] OJ [1971] L 285/46.

2000[156]. The Regulation entered into force on 1 January 2001 and will expire on 31 December 2010[157]. The new Regulation replaces Regulation 417/85[158]. Article 8 provides transitional relief for agreements which were in force on 31 December 2000 and which satisfied the conditions for exemption in the old Regulation: they were exempt until 30 June 2002. The new Regulation is without prejudice to Article 82[159].

The Regulation consists of 19 Recitals and 9 Articles. Article 1 confers block exemption upon certain specialisation agreements. Article 2 defines key terms such as 'competing undertaking', 'exclusive supply obligation' and 'exclusive purchase obligation'. Article 3 extends the block exemption to certain purchasing and marketing arrangements. Article 4 imposes a market share cap of 20%. Article 5 deals with agreements that are not covered by the block exemption because they contain 'hard-core' restrictions. Article 6 contains provisions on the application of the market share threshold. Article 7 provides the Commission with the power to withdraw the benefit of the block exemption in certain circumstances. Articles 8 and 9 deal respectively with transitional matters and the period of validity of the Regulation. Regulation 2658/2000, like Regulation 2659/2000[160] and Regulation 2790/99[161], is a 'new-style' block exemption; it does not contain a detailed 'white list' of permitted restrictions, but instead confers block exemption upon a range of agreements up to a certain level of market power and specifies restrictions and clauses that must not be included[162].

(i) Article 1: scope of the block exemption

Article 1(1) confers block exemption, pursuant to Article 81(3) of the Treaty, on three types of specialisation agreements in relation to goods or services[163]:

(a) unilateral specialisation agreements, by virtue of which one party agrees to cease production of certain products or to refrain from producing those products and to purchase them from a competing undertaking, while the competing undertaking agrees to produce and supply those products; or

(b) reciprocal specialisation agreements, by virtue of which two or more parties on a reciprocal basis agree to cease or refrain from producing certain but different products and to purchase these products from the other parties, who agree to supply them; or

(c) joint production agreements, by virtue of which two or more parties agree to produce certain products jointly.

Unilateral specialisation agreements are exempted only where the party that ceases or refrains from production agrees to purchase the products from a competing undertaking[164]. An agreement between non-competitors would be vertical, and could therefore benefit from Regulation 2790/99 on Vertical Agreements, subject to the 30 per cent market share cap and the other terms of that Regulation[165]. This is why the

---

[156] OJ [2000] L 304/3, [2001] 4 CMLR 800.   [157] Regulation 2658/2000, Article 9.

[158] OJ [1985] L 53/1, amended by Regulation 151/93 OJ [1993] L 21/8 and extended in force until 31 December 2001 by Regulation 2236/97 OJ [1997] L 306/12.

[159] Regulation 2658/2000, Recital 18.   [160] See pp 583–588 above.   [161] See ch 16, pp 640–662.

[162] Regulation 2658/2000, Recital 5.

[163] Article 1 refers to specialisation in 'products', which are defined in Article 2(4) to include 'a good and/or a service, including both intermediary goods and/or services and final goods and/or services, with the exception of distribution and rental services'.

[164] Competing undertakings are defined in Article 2(7) to include both an 'actual competitor' that is active on the relevant market and a 'potential competitor' that could realistically enter the market in response to a small and permanent increase in relative prices: on the so-called 'SSNIP test' see generally ch 1, pp 26–40.

[165] See ch 16, pp 641–645.

block exemption in Regulation 2658/2000 is limited to agreements between competing undertakings[166]. In the case of both unilateral and reciprocal specialisation agreements, the party or parties that cease or refrain from production must agree to purchase the products from the other undertaking(s), who in turn must agree to supply them, so that there will continue to be competition in the market downstream from production: these supply and purchase obligations may, but do not have to be, exclusive[167]; if they are exclusive, they will benefit from block exemption under Article 3[168].

Article 1(2) provides that the block exemption also applies to provisions in specialisation agreements:

which do not constitute the primary object of such agreements, but are directly related to and necessary for their implementation, such as those concerning the assignment or use of intellectual property rights.

However Article 1(2) would not apply to provisions that have the same object as the hard-core restrictions set out in Article 5(1)[169].

(ii) Article 2: definitions

Article 2 contains a series of definitions of expressions used in the Regulation, including 'products'[170], 'competing undertaking'[171] and 'exclusive supply obligation' and 'exclusive purchase obligation'[172].

(iii) Article 3: block exemption for purchasing and marketing arrangements

Article 3 confers block exemption on two types of purchasing and marketing arrangements. Article 3(a) exempts exclusive supply and/or purchase obligations contained in any of the agreements exempted in Article 1. An exclusive supply obligation means an obligation not to supply a competing undertaking other than a party to the agreement with the product to which the specialisation agreement relates[173]. An exclusive purchase obligation means an obligation to purchase the product to which the specialisation relates only from the party which agrees to supply it[174]. Where the parties enter into a joint production agreement of the kind exempted by Article 1(1)(c) and do not themselves sell the products which are the subject of the specialisation independently, Article 3(b) exempts joint distribution, or the appointment, on an exclusive or non-exclusive basis, of a third party distributor, provided that it is not a competing undertaking.

(iv) Article 4: the market share threshold

Article 4 provides that the block exemption applies on condition that the combined market share cap of the participating undertakings does not exceed 20 per cent. The expression 'participating undertakings' is defined in Article 2(2), and includes 'connected undertakings', defined in Article 2(3). Article 6 contains rules on how to apply the market share threshold; it contains specific rules to deal with the situation where the undertakings outgrow the market share cap[175].

---

[166] Regulation 2658/2000, Recital 10.   [167] Ibid, Recital 12.   [168] See below.
[169] Regulation 2658/2000, Article 1(2), second paragraph.   [170] See n 163 above.
[171] See n 164 above.   [172] See below.
[173] Regulation 2658/2000, Article 2(8).   [174] Ibid, Article 2(9).
[175] Ibid, Article 6(2)–(4).

(v) Article 5: agreements not covered by the exemption

Article 5(1) prevents the block exemption from applying where agreements contain the following 'severe anti-competitive restraints'[176], that is to say agreements which:

directly or indirectly, in isolation or in combination with other factors under the control of the parties, have as their object:

  (a) the fixing of prices when selling the products to third parties;
  (b) the limitation of output or sales; or
  (c) the allocation of markets or customers.

The inclusion of any of these provisions excludes the entire agreement, not just the offensive provisions, from the block exemption[177]. However Article 5(2)(a) provides that provisions on the amount of products to be produced under a specialisation agreement are not caught by Article 5(1); while Article 5(2)(b) provides that sales targets given to a production joint venture, and the fixing of its prices to its immediate customers, are not caught.

(vi) Article 6: application of the market share threshold

Article 6 was referred to above in the context of the market share cap in Article 4[178].

(vii) Article 7: withdrawal of the block exemption by the Commission

Article 7 enables the Commission to withdraw the benefit of the block exemption, in particular where the agreement is not yielding significant results in terms of rationalisation[179], or where the products which are the subject of the specialisation are not subject to effective competition[180].

(viii) Article 8: transitional period

The transitional relief for agreements that benefit from the exemption provided for in Regulation 417/85 was explained above[181].

(ix) Article 9: period of validity

The Regulation entered into force on 1 January 2001 and will expire on 31 December 2010.

7. PURCHASING AGREEMENTS[182]

Chapter 4 of the *Guidelines*[183] deals with joint purchasing agreements. Surprisingly the *Guidelines* do not refer to the judgment of the ECJ on joint purchasing organisations in *Gøttrup-Klim Grovvareforeninger v Dansk Landburgs Grovvareselskab AmbA*[184]. The

---

    [176] Ibid, Recital 14.   [177] *Guidelines*, para 37.   [178] See above.
    [179] Regulation 2658/2000, Article 7(a).   [180] Ibid, Article 7(b).   [181] See p 590 above.
    [182] See further *Faull and Nikpay*, paras 7.301–7.354; see also OFT Economic Discussion Paper *The competitive effect of buyer groups* (RBB Economics, OFT 863, January 2007).
    [183] *Guidelines*, paras 115–138.
    [184] Case C-250/92 [1994] ECR 1-5641, [1996] 4 CMLR 191; see also Cases C-399/93 etc *HG Oude Luttikhuis v Coberco* [1995] ECR 1-4515, [1996] 5 CMLR 178; on the position in the US see eg *US v Topco Associates Inc* 405 US 596 (1972).

Guidelines point out that joint purchasing is often concluded by small and medium-sized undertakings to enable them to purchase in larger volumes and to obtain larger discounts similar to their bigger competitors[185]. The *Guidelines* consider the horizontal relationship between the members of the group purchasing organisation; the vertical relationships, between it and its suppliers and between it and its members, fall to be considered under the rules on vertical agreements[186]. Joint purchasing must be considered in the context of the relevant procurement market[187]; in some cases it may also be necessary to look at the selling market, if the parties to the joint purchasing agreement also actively compete in that market and if, for example, they jointly purchase a significant amount of what they sell[188].

(A) Application of Article 81(1) to joint purchasing agreements

(i) Agreements that normally fall outside Article 81(1)

Where competing purchasers are not active on the same relevant market further downstream, Article 81(1) is unlikely to be infringed: an example given is where retailers purchase products jointly, but themselves operate in different geographic markets from each other[189].

(ii) Agreements that almost always fall within Article 81(1)

Purchasing agreements would be unlikely to have as their object the restriction of competition, unless they amounted to a disguised cartel[190].

(iii) Agreements that may fall within Article 81(1)

In determining whether joint purchasing could have the effect of restricting competition, the starting point is to determine the parties' buying power[191]. The *Guidelines* note that buying power is not always pro-competitive and may even, under certain circumstances, cause severe negative effects on competition[192]. This could be the case where the purchasers together have power on the selling market, since it would be unlikely in that case that lower costs would be passed on to consumers[193]; or where significant buyer power is used to foreclose competitors or to raise rivals' costs[194]. At paragraph 130, however, the Commission says that, in most cases, it is unlikely that market power exists if the parties to the agreement have a combined market share of less than 15 per cent on each of the purchasing and the selling markets. Other factors, such as the level of market concentration and the countervailing power of strong suppliers, would have to be considered where the market shares exceed 15 per cent[195].

---

[185] *Guidelines*, para 116.

[186] *Guidelines*, paras 117–118; see ch 16, pp 645–646, on the application of Article 2(2) of Regulation 2790/99, the block exemption for vertical agreements, to agreements between associations of retailers and their suppliers and their members.

[187] *Guidelines*, para 120; on procurement markets see ch 1, p 36.   [188] *Guidelines*, para 122.

[189] Ibid, para 123.   [190] Ibid, para 124.   [191] Ibid, para 126.   [192] Ibid, para 127.   [193] Ibid, para 128.

[194] Ibid, para 129.   [195] Ibid, para 131.

The application of Article 81 to 'B2B' joint purchasing, that is to say joint procurement through an electronic market place, was considered by the Commission in the case of *Covisint*, leading to the closure of the file by comfort letter[196].

(B) Application of Article 81(3) to joint purchasing agreements[197]

Paragraphs 132 to 134 of the *Guidelines* discuss Article 81(3) and joint purchasing agreements. Paragraph 133 notes that an obligation to purchase exclusively through the joint purchasing organisation may be regarded as indispensable to achieve the necessary volume for the realisation of economies of scale, but says that this must be assessed in the context of each case. In *Rennet*[198] the Commission considered that an exclusive purchasing requirement that members of a cooperative should purchase all their rennet from the cooperative was a restriction of competition and that it did not satisfy the criteria of Article 81(3). Article 81(3) would not apply to an agreement which would substantially eliminate competition. Paragraph 134 of the *Guidelines* states that, where the joint purchasing agreement could lead to dominance on either the buying or selling side of the market, the terms of Article 81(3) would, in principle, not be satisfied; however this statement is too extreme, and paragraph 106 of the Commission's *Guidelines on the application of Article 81(3) of the Treaty* adopts a more nuanced approach to this issue[199].

8. COMMERCIALISATION AGREEMENTS[200]

Chapter 5 of the *Guidelines*[201] deals with commercialisation agreements, that is to say cooperation between competitors in the selling, distribution or promotion of their products[202]. Distribution agreements generally are covered by the regime for vertical agreements[203]; however where competitors distribute one another's products, horizontal issues arise as well, and they should be analysed in accordance with the *Horizontal Guidelines*[204]. Where joint commercialisation is agreed upon pursuant to some other

---

[196] Commission Press Release IP/01/1155, 31 July 2001; see further Vollebregt 'E-Hubs, Syndication and Competition Concerns' (2000) 10 ECLR 437; ch 13, p 532; Commission's XXXIst *Report on Competition Policy* (2001), pp 58–60.

[197] For examples of joint purchasing agreements that the Commission authorised see *National Sulphuric Acid Association* OJ [1980] L 260/24, [1980] 3 CMLR 429; *National Sulphuric Acid Association (No 2)* OJ [1989] L 190/22, [1991] 4 CMLR 612; *ARD/MGM* OJ [1989] L 284/36, [1991] 4 CMLR 841; *European Broadcasting Union* OJ [1993] L 179/23, [1995] 4 CMLR 56, annulled on appeal Cases T-528/93 etc *Métropole télévision SA v Commission* [1996] ECR II-649, [1996] 5 CMLR 386 and readopted as *Eurovision* OJ [2000] L 151/18, [2000] 5 CMLR 650, annulled on appeal Cases T-185/00 etc *Métropole télévision SA v Commission* [2002] ECR II-3805, [2003] 4 CMLR 707; the Commission decided that Article 81(3) did not apply in the case of *Rennet* OJ [1980] L 51/19, [1980] 2 CMLR 402, upheld on appeal Case 61/80 *Coöperatieve Stremsel-en Kleurselfabriek v Commission* [1981] ECR 851, [1982] 1 CMLR 240, and *Screensport/EBU Members* OJ [1991] L 63/32, [1992] 5 CMLR 273.

[198] See n 197 above.   [199] OJ [2004] C 101/97.   [200] See further *Faull and Nikpay*, paras 7.252–7.300.

[201] *Guidelines*, paras 139–158.

[202] Ibid, para 139; on joint brand advertising see Vollebregt 'Joint Brand Advertising: Is It Allowed?' (1997) 18 ECLR 242.

[203] See ch 16, pp 640–662.   [204] *Guidelines*, para 140.

cooperation, for example on R&D or joint production, the agreement should be ana-lysed under the corresponding chapter of the *Guidelines*[205].

(A) The application of Article 81(1) to commercialisation agreements

(i) Agreements that normally fall outside Article 81(1)

Commercialisation agreements between non-competitors do not create competition problems of a horizontal nature and will therefore not be caught by Article 81(1); this would include a consortium agreement between non-competing firms that jointly ten-der for a project that none of them could carry out individually[206].

(ii) Agreements that almost always fall within Article 81(1)

The commercialisation agreements most likely to give rise to concern under Article 81(1) are those that give rise to price fixing. The Commission says that joint selling is likely to have as its object and effect the coordination of the pricing policy of competing manu-facturers[207]. This may not be the case where the market power of the parties is particu-larly weak[208]; however there have been several examples of the Commission finding that joint sales agencies infringed Article 81(1)[209]. In some of these cases the Commission found the conditions of Article 81(3) were fulfilled[210].

(iii) Agreements that may fall within Article 81(1)

Where joint commercialisation falls short of joint selling, the Commission expresses two possible concerns that might lead to a restrictive effect on competition: one is the exchange of commercially sensitive information, particularly on marketing strategy and pricing; the other is a possible high commonality of costs, which might affect the extent to which the parties can compete on price when they take their products to the market[211]. In the case of distribution agreements between competitors, the Commission is particularly concerned at the possibility of market partitioning[212]. Commercialisation agreements which do not extend to price fixing are unlikely to infringe Article 81(1) where the parties' market shares are below 15 per cent; and would be likely to satisfy the terms of Article 81(3) even if they were caught by Article 81(1)[213]. Where the parties' market share exceeds 15%, market concentration would also have to be considered[214].

(B) The application of Article 81(3) to commercialisation agreements

Paragraphs 151 to 155 discuss Article 81(3). Paragraph 151 states that price fixing can generally not be justified 'unless it is indispensable for the integration of other

---

[205] Ibid, para 141.   [206] Ibid, para 143.
[207] *Guidelines*, paras 144–145; on joint selling see *Faull and Nikpay*, paras 6.259–6.292.
[208] See *SAFCO* OJ [1972] L 13/44.
[209] See eg *Floral* OJ [1980] L 39/51, [1980] 2 CMLR 285; *UIP* OJ [1989] L 226/25, [1990] 4 CMLR 749; *Cekanan* OJ [1990] L 299/64, [1992] 4 CMLR 406; *Ansae* OJ [1991] L 152/ 54.
[210] See below.   [211] *Guidelines*, para 146.   [212] Ibid, para 147.   [213] Ibid, para 149.
[214] Ibid, para 150; see ch 1, pp 41–42 on the HHI.

marketing functions, and this integration will generate substantial efficiencies'. Any efficiencies must result from the integration of economic activities[215], and must be clearly demonstrated[216]. The Commission gives two examples of commercialisation agreements that would satisfy Article 81(3). The first is an agreement between five small food producers, with a total market share of 10 per cent, to combine their distribution facilities, to market under a common brand name and to sell products at a common price; their customers are large retail chains, and substantial multinational food groups dominate the market[217]. The second is where two producers of soft drinks are active on neighbouring markets, each having 20 per cent of its home market; they agree on reciprocal distribution of each other's products, and in each market there is a dominant undertaking having a market share of 50 per cent: the agreement would be exemptable[218].

The Commission has, on a few occasions, concluded that joint selling arrangements satisfied the criteria of Article 81(3). In *Cekanan*[219] the Commission authorised a joint venture that would enable the parties, based in Sweden and Germany, to enter new markets in the European Community with new types of packaging. In the case of *UIP*[220] the Commission decided that a joint venture for the distribution and licensing of the films of Paramount, Universal Studios and MGM satisfied Article 81(3). An issue of particular interest in recent years has been the collective selling of broadcasting rights to sporting events[221]. The Commission authorised the rules of UEFA for selling such rights[222]; and it accepted commitments under Article 9 of the Modernisation Regulation in the case of the German Bundesliga and the English Premier League[223].

9. AGREEMENTS ON STANDARDS[224]

Chapter 6 of the *Guidelines*[225] deals with agreements that have as their primary objective the definition of technical or quality requirements with which current or future products, production processes or methods may comply[226]. The *Guidelines* do not apply to professional rules[227]. Standardisation agreements may have effects in three markets, in the market for the product itself, in the service market for the setting of standards, and in the market for testing and certification[228].

---

[215] *Guidelines*, para 152.   [216] Ibid, para 153.   [217] Ibid, para 156.   [218] Ibid, para 158.
[219] OJ [1990] L 299/64, [1992] 4 CMLR 406.
[220] OJ [1989] L 226/25, [1990] 4 CMLR 749, renewed by comfort letter OJ [1999] C 205/6, [1999] 5 CMLR 732; see XXIXth *Report on Competition Policy* (1999), pp 148–149.
[221] See eg Brinckman and Vollebregt 'The Marketing of Sport and its Relation to EC Competition Law' (1998) 19 ECLR 281; Fleming 'Exclusive Rights to Broadcast Sporting Events in Europe' (1999) 20 ECLR 143; Bishop and Oldale 'Sports Rights: the UK Premier League Football Case' (2000) 21 ECLR 185; Nitsche 'Collective Marketing of Broadcasting by Sports Associations in Europe' (2000) 21 ECLR 208; Commission's XXXIst *Report on Competition Policy* (2001), point 166.
[222] Commission Press Release IP/03/1105, 24 July 2003.
[223] See ch 7, pp 253–257 discussing the Article 9 commitments procedure and providing details of these two cases.
[224] See further *Faull and Nikpay*, paras 7.385–7.402.   [225] Ibid, paras 159–178.   [226] Ibid, para 159.
[227] Ibid, para 160.   [228] Ibid, para 161.

(A) The application of Article 81(1) to standardisation agreements

(i) Agreements that normally fall outside Article 81(1)

Where participation in the setting of standards is unrestricted and transparent, standardisation agreements do not restrict competition. Standards adopted by recognised standards bodies based on non-discriminatory, open and transparent procedures would not be caught[229]. Nor would agreements having no appreciable effect on the market[230].

(ii) Agreements that almost always fall within Article 81(1)

Standardisation agreements aimed at excluding actual or potential competitors from the market would normally be caught, for example where a national association of manufacturers sets a standard and puts pressure on third parties not to market products that do not comply with the standard[231].

(iii) Agreements that may fall within Article 81(1)

Standardisation agreements may have the effect of restricting competition where they impinge upon the parties' freedom to develop alternative standards or products[232]. Standards that are not accessible to third parties may discriminate or foreclose the market, with the result that it is necessary to consider on a case-by-case basis the extent to which such barriers to entry are likely to be overcome[233]. In the specific context of the telecommunications market, the Commission investigated arrangements proposed by the European Telecommunications Standards Institute ('ETSI') to ensure that undertakings would not be unable to make use of a given standard because of the unavailability of necessary intellectual property rights: the Commission indicated that it no longer had competition concerns after ETSI had introduced procedures intended to minimise this risk[234].

(B) The application of Article 81(3) to standardisation agreements

Paragraphs 169 to 175 deal with the application of Article 81(3). The Commission states at paragraph 169 that it generally takes a positive approach towards agreements that promote economic interpenetration in the internal market or encourage the development of new markets and improved supply conditions. For the benefits of standardisation agreements to be realised, the necessary information to apply the standard must be available to those wishing to enter the market and an appreciable proportion of the industry must be involved in the setting of the standard in a transparent manner[235]. Standards must not limit innovation[236]. All competitors in the markets affected should have the possibility of being involved in discussions on the standards, unless it can be shown this would give rise to important inefficiencies or unless there are recognised procedures for the collective representation of interests, as happens in the case of formal standards bodies[237]. As a general rule there should be a clear distinction between

---

[229] Ibid, para 163. [230] Ibid, para 164. [231] Ibid, para 165. [232] Ibid, para 167. [233] Ibid, para 168.
[234] See OJ [1995] C 76/6, [1995] 5 CMLR 352; Commission's XXVth *Report on Competition Policy* (1995), pp 131–132.
[235] Ibid, para 169. [236] Ibid, para 170. [237] Ibid, para 172.

the setting of the standard and the parties' actual behaviour on the market[238]. Where the result of a standardisation agreement is the establishment of a *de facto* industry standard, access to the standard must be possible for third parties on fair, reasonable and non-discriminatory terms[239]; foreclosure of third parties must be avoided[240].

(C) Article 82 and standards

The Commission may proceed under Article 82 where it believes that a dominant firm may be guilty of abusing a standard-setting procedure, for example through 'patent ambushing'[241].

10. ENVIRONMENTAL AGREEMENTS[242]

Chapter 7 of the *Guidelines*[243] deals with environmental agreements, which means agreements whereby the parties undertake to achieve pollution abatement or environmental objectives, in particular those set out in Article 174 EC[244]. Environmental agreements may, for example, set out standards for environmental performance, or provide for recycling, emission reductions or the improvement of energy efficiency[245]. The *Guidelines* do not deal with the position of Member States' obligations under the Treaty, for example where they require or encourage environmental agreements[246], but only with the application of Article 81 to the agreements themselves[247].

(A) Application of Article 81(1) to environmental agreements

(i) Agreements that normally fall outside Article 81(1)

Agreements that do not impose precise obligations on the parties but which loosely commit them to achieving environmental targets are unlikely to infringe Article 81(1)[248]; the same is true of agreements that have little effect on product diversity or on purchasing decisions[249]. Agreements that are innovative, for example by introducing new recycling arrangements, would not be caught[250].

(ii) Agreements that almost always fall within Article 81(1)

An environmental agreement that is really a disguised cartel would have as its object the restriction of competition and would therefore be caught by Article 81(1)[251].

---

[238] Ibid, para 173.   [239] Ibid, para 174.

[240] Ibid, para 175; see eg *Canon/Kodak* Commission's XXVIIIth *Report on Competition Policy* (1998), p 147; *TÜV/Cenelec, Guidelines*, p 159.

[241] See ch 19, pp 793–795.

[242] See further *Faull and Nikpay*, paras 7.403–7.413; see further the Commission's XXVIIIth *Report on Competition Policy* (1998), points 129–134 and pp 150–153 on *EUCAR, ACEA, EACEM and Valpak*; XXIXth *Report on Competition Policy* (1999), p 160 on *JAMA*.

[243] *Guidelines*, paras 179–198.   [244] Ibid, para 179.   [245] Ibid, para 180.

[246] On the position of Member States in relation to agreements entered into between undertakings see ch 6, pp 214–220.

[247] *Guidelines*, para 183.   [248] Ibid, para 185.   [249] Ibid, para 186.   [250] Ibid, para 187.

[251] Ibid, para 188.

(iii) Agreements that may fall within Article 81(1)

Other environmental agreements may have the effect of restricting competition, for example where they limit the parties' ability to decide what to produce or how to produce it [252]; this could happen where the parties allocate pollution quotas [253], or where they appoint an undertaking as exclusive provider of collection and/or recycling services [254].

(B) Application of Article 81(3) to environmental agreements

Paragraphs 192 to 197 of the *Guidelines* discuss Article 81(3); it should be noted that the Commission's later *Guidelines on the application of Article 81(3) of the Treaty* state very clearly that it is economic efficiency that is promoted by Article 81(3), and that other goals – including therefore environmental protection – can be taken into account under that provision only when they can be subsumed within its four conditions [255]. The Commission states specifically that it takes a positive stance on the use of environmental agreements as a policy instrument to achieve the goals enshrined in Article 2 and Article 174 of the Treaty and in Community environmental action plans [256]. The benefits of an environmental agreement may be both individual and collective, but must outweigh its costs [257]. Cost-effectiveness will have to be proven [258]. In its decision in *CECED* [259] the Commission considered that the criteria in Article 81(3) were satisfied in the case of an agreement between manufacturers and importers of washing-machines that would result in the phasing-out of old models that were inefficient in terms of the use of water, detergent and electricity; the Commission was satisfied that both individual and collective benefits would result: cheaper fuel bills for individuals and less pollution for the community at large. In *DSD* [260] the Commission authorised exclusive service agreements which would facilitate the collection and disposal of waste packaging materials, thereby promoting a high level of environmental protection [261]; a challenge by DSD to the Commission's finding that the agreements infringed Article 81(1) failed in *Duales Stsyem Deutschland v Commission* [262].

---

[252] Ibid, para 189. [253] Ibid, para 190.

[254] Ibid, para 191; see eg *Eco-Emballages* OJ [2001] L 319/1, [2002] 4 CMLR 405.

[255] *Guidelines on the application of Article 81(3) of the Treaty*, OJ [2004] C 101/97, para 42; see further ch 4, pp 151ff.

[256] *Guidelines*, para 192. [257] Ibid, para 193. [258] Ibid, para 196.

[259] OJ [2000] L 187/47, [2000] 5 CMLR 635; see also *CEMEP*, Commission Press Release IP/ 00/58, 23 May 2000: clearance of agreement to reduce sales of motors with low energy efficiency; *Dishwashers and Water Heaters*, Commission Press Release IP/01/1659, 26 November 2001: Article 81(3) comfort letters sent in relation to further agreements notified by CECED; see also Martínez-López in the Commission's *Competition Policy Newsletter*, February 2002, p 50.

[260] OJ [2001] L 319/1, [2002] 4 CMLR 405.

[261] Ibid, paras 142–146; the Commission decided that a waste disposal scheme in France did not infringe Article 81(1) in *Eco-Emballages* OJ [2001] L 233/37, [2001] 5 CMLR 1096; see Gremminger Commission's *Competition Policy Newsletter*, October 2001, p 29; speech by Pons 'Europe on competition policy for the recycling markets' 20 September 2001, available at www.europa.eu.int/comm/competition/speeches; see also *ARA, ARGEV, ARO* OJ [2004] L 75/59.

[262] Case T-289/01 *Duales System Deutschland v Commission* [2007] ECR II-000, [2007] 5 CMLR 356.

11. OTHER CASES OF PERMISSIBLE HORIZONTAL COOPERATION

As the CFI stated in *Matra Hachette v Commission*[263], there is no type of agreement which, by its nature, is ineligible for exemption. For example, in the case of *REIMS II*[264] the Commission considered that the criteria of Article 81(3) were satisfied in the case of a price-fixing agreement 'with unusual characteristics' in the postal services sector. The fact that a horizontal cooperation agreement does not fit into one of the categories discussed in the *Guidelines* does not mean that it cannot satisfy the terms of Article 81(3). In each case, the question is whether the parties can demonstrate either that there is no restriction of competition or that the agreement will bring about efficiencies of the type envisaged in Article 81(3).

(A) Restructuring agreements

There may be circumstances in which an industry faces severe problems − perhaps because of recession or because of over-capacity within it − where the competition authorities may be prepared to countenance some degree of cooperation to overcome this. As a general proposition, each operator on the market should make its own independent decision as to what and how much to produce. However making rational decisions about how to 'slim down' production in some economic sectors, perhaps where capital investment is high or where there is extensive vertical integration, may be difficult in the absence of an intelligent understanding of what competitors are going to do. There is a danger that each competitor may slim down so much that the market goes from a position of over-capacity to under-capacity; it may be difficult to put the process into reverse. A different consideration is that the restructuring of industry has a social cost involving loss of employment and harm to the fabric of local communities; there is therefore a political component as well as an economic one to this issue[265].

Restructuring agreements, whereby undertakings agree on their respective levels of output, are likely to infringe Article 81(1): output limitation has as its object the restriction of competition[266]. The fact that an industry faces a crisis does not mean that undertakings can enter into agreements that restrict competition and claim immunity from Article 81(1); the fact that an industry is in crisis may help to mitigate the fine[267]. Where a restructuring agreement is entered into pursuant to state aid authorised by the Commission, it may not infringe Article 81(1) where it is so indissolubly linked to the purpose of the aid that it cannot be separately evaluated[268].

The Commission has on a few occasions allowed restructuring agreements under Article 81(3). It first did so in 1984, having indicated in its Annual Reports that it might

---

[263]   Case T-17/93 [1994] ECR II-595.

[264]   OJ [1999] L 275/17, [2000] 4 CMLR 704; the Commission indicated its intention to renew this exemption: OJ [2003] C 94/3, [2003] 4 CMLR 1176; see also Commission Press Release IP/03/557, 23 April 2003.

[265]   See ch 4, pp 151–157 for a discussion of the issues which can legitimately be taken into account under Article 81(3).

[266]   See ch 3, p 119.

[267]   See eg Case T-145/89 *Baustahlgewebe v Commission* [1995] ECR II-987, para 122.

[268]   Case T-197/97 *Weyl Beef Products v Commission* [2001] ECR II-303, [2001] 2 CMLR 459, para 83.

be inclined to do so[269]. In *Synthetic Fibres*[270] the Commission permitted an agreement which was to last for three years and which would involve the closure of 18 per cent of production capacity. The parties agreed to supply information to each other about their reductions of capacity, to consult one another in the event of important changes in the market, not to increase capacity and to compensate each other if they failed to implement the reductions. The Commission held that this agreement would lead to improved production which would be slimmed down in a socially acceptable way; consumers would get a fair share of the resulting benefit as in due course they would be able to purchase from a healthier industry.

The Commission has permitted several restructuring agreements in the petrochemical and thermoplastics sectors. In *BPCL/ICI*[271] it allowed an agreement achieved by specialisation and the reciprocal sale of plant, assets and goodwill. A similar 'swap' deal was granted exemption in *ENI/Montedison*[272] and again in *Enichem/ICI*[273]. The decision in *BPCL/ICI* was followed by *Bayer/BP Chemicals*[274] in the same sector. Formal comfort letters were sent by the Commission in *Shell/AKZO*[275] and *EMC/DSM (LVM)*[276]. In *Stichting Baksteen*[277] the Commission granted individual exemption to plans for restructuring the Dutch brick industry, which involved agreed action to close plants and to cut capacity.

(B) Insurance sector[278]

In the case of insurance the Commission has authorised a number of horizontal cooperation agreements, for example in *Nuovo CEGAM*[279], *Concordato Incendio*[280], *Teko*[281], *P & I Clubs*[282], *Assurpool*[283] and again in *P & I Clubs*[284].

Council Regulation 1534/91 granted to the Commission the power to adopt a block exemption in the insurance sector[285]; in February 2003 the Commission adopted Regulation 358/2003[286], which replaced Regulation 3932/92[287]. Article 1 of Regulation 358/2003[288], which entered into force on 1 April 2003, grants exemption to agreements

---

[269] See eg the Commission's XIIth *Report on Competition Policy* (1982), points 38–41; XIIIth *Report on Competition Policy* (1983), points 56–61; see also XXIIIth *Report on Competition Policy* (1993), points 82–89.

[270] OJ [1984] L 207/17, [1985] 1 CMLR 787.   [271] OJ [1984] L 212/1, [1985] 2 CMLR 330.

[272] OJ [1987] L 5/13, [1988] 4 CMLR 444.   [273] OJ [1988] L 50/18, [1989] 4 CMLR 54.

[274] OJ [1988] L 150/35, [1989] 4 CMLR 24; see subsequently *Bayer/BP Chemicals* OJ [1994] L 174/34.

[275] Commission's XIVth *Report on Competition Policy* (1984), point 85.   [276] OJ [1988] C 18/3.

[277] OJ [1994] L 131/15, [1995] 4 CMLR 646; see XXIVth *Report on Competition Policy* (1994), pp 178–180.

[278] See further *Faull and Nikpay*, paras 11.92–11.133; Bellamy and Child *European Community Law of Competition* (Sweet & Maxwell, 6th ed, 2007, eds Roth and Rose), paras 12.169–12.179; Roth 'European Competition Policy for the Insurance Market' (2000) 21 ECLR 107.

[279] OJ [1984] L 99/29, [1984] 2 CMLR 484.   [280] OJ [1990] L 15/25, [1991] 4 CMLR 199.

[281] OJ [1990] L 13/34, [1990] 4 CMLR 957.   [282] OJ [1985] L 376/2, [1989] 4 CMLR 178.

[283] OJ [1992] L 37/16, [1993] 4 CMLR 338.

[284] OJ [1999] L 125/12, [1999] 5 CMLR 646; some other cases have been settled informally: see eg Commission's XXVIth *Report on Competition Policy* (1996), pp 131–132; XXVIIIth *Report on Competition Policy* (1998), points 111–115.

[285] OJ [1991] L 143/1.

[286] OJ [2003] L 53/8, [2003] 4 CMLR 734; see Commission Press Release IP/03/291, 27 February 2003; Ryan 'The new block exemption Regulation: a modernised framework for insurance industry and consumers, following extensive consultation' *Competition Policy Newletter*, Summer 2003, 51.

[287] OJ [1992] L 398/7.

[288] OJ [1992] L 398/7, [1993] 4 CMLR 90; see Commission's XXIInd *Report on Competition Policy* (1992), points 274–288.

in the insurance sector which seek cooperation with respect to:

(a) the establishment of common risk-premium tariffs based on collectively ascertained statistics or on the number of claims;

(b) the establishment of non-binding standard policy conditions;

(c) the common coverage of certain types of risks;

(d) the establishment of common rules on the testing and acceptance of security devices.

Each of these four paragraphs is the subject of detailed rules in Titles II–V of the Regulation. Title VI contains miscellaneous provisions, including in Article 11 transitional provisions. The Regulation will apply until 31 March 2010; the Commission has launched a public consultation on its operation in practice[288a].

(C) Banking sector[289]

The Commission has dealt with many horizontal cooperation agreements in the banking sector. Such agreements might be found not to affect trade between Member States, as the ECJ concluded in *Bagnasco*[290] and the Commission in *Dutch Banks*[291]. The Commission has published a *Notice on Cross-border Credit Transfers*[292] on the extent to which cooperation between banks is permissible under the competition rules in order to improve cross-border credit transfers. In its decision in *Uniform Eurocheques*[293] the Commission permitted an agreement which fixed standard terms and conditions in relation to the cashing of Eurocheques. The Commission also permitted a second agreement relating to the production and finishing of the actual Eurocheques and cheque cards[294]. A cooperation agreement was authorised for 10 years in *Banque Nationale de Paris/ Dresdner Bank*[295] between two major banks operating in neighbouring Member States.

The Commission decided in *Visa International – Multilateral Interchange Fee* that Visa International's 'multilateral interchange fee' agreed upon between banks participating within the Visa system satisfied the criteria of Article 81(3)[296]. However in *MasterCard*[297], a decision taken in December 2007, the Commission concluded that the interchange fee did not do so. The *MasterCard* decision is on appeal to the CFI[298]. In the meantime the authorisation granted under the old procedure of notification and individual exemption given to Visa International expired at the end of 2007; it must therefore decide whether its current and future interchange fees are lawful, taking into account the Commission's findings in the MasterCard case, and any future judgments of the Community Courts. Many national competition authorities are investigating the same issue.

[288a] Commission Press Release IP/08/596 of 17 April 2008.

[289] See *Faull and Nikpay*, paras 11.0911.64.

[290] Cases C-215/96 and 216/96 [1999] ECR I-135, [1999] 4 CMLR 624.

[291] OJ [1999] L 271/28, [2000] 4 CMLR 137.

[292] OJ [1995] C 251/3; see Commission's XXVth *Report on Competition Policy* (1995), points 45–48; XXVIth *Report on Competition Policy* (1996), point 109 and pp 128–130.

[293] OJ [1985] L 35/43, [1985] 3 CMLR 434.

[294] OJ [1989] L 36/16; most of this agreement was cleared under Article 81(1) rather than exempted under Article 81(3); for other exemptions on banking see *Belgian Banks* OJ [1986] L 7/27, [1989] 4 CMLR 141; *Associazione Bancaria Italiana* OJ [1986] L 43/51, [1989] 4 CMLR 238.

[295] OJ [1996] L 188/37, [1996] 5 CMLR 582; Commission's XXVIth *Report on Competition Policy* (1996), point 108.

[296] OJ [2002] L 318/17, [2003] 4 CMLR 283.   [297] Commission decision of 19 December 2007.

[298] Case T-111/08 *MasterCard v Commission*, not yet decided.

(D) Transport

Several horizontal cooperation agreements have been allowed in the transport sector. Some of these are discussed in chapter 23[299].

12. THE APPLICATION OF THE CHAPTER I PROHIBITION IN THE UK COMPETITION ACT 1998 TO HORIZONTAL COOPERATION AGREEMENTS

(A) Introduction

The general principles involved in the application of the Chapter I prohibition in the Competition Act 1998 have been described in chapter 9[300]; the procedural aspects of Chapter I were dealt with in chapter 10[301]. Agreements that benefit from block exemption under EC law, or that would do so if they were to affect trade between Member States, enjoy parallel exemption under UK law; it follows, for example, that research and development agreements, horizontal technology transfer agreements, and specialisation agreements might benefit from this facility[302].

(B) Decisions under the Competition Act

There have been few decisions and little case law on horizontal cooperation agreements in the UK since the Competition Act entered into force. The OFT has examined – and in some cases authorised – horizontal cooperation agreements in a few cases, such as *LINK Interchange Network Ltd*[303], *Memorandum of Understanding on the Supply of Oil Fuels in an Emergency*[304] and *Pool Reinsurance Company Ltd*[305]. They have already been discussed in chapter 9, in the context of the exemption criteria in section 9 of the Competition Act, and the reader is referred to those pages[306].

(C) Block exemption for ticketing agreements

The Secretary of State has adopted a block exemption for public transport ticketing schemes: it is discussed in chapter 9[307].

---

[299] See ch 23, pp 961–970.   [300] See ch 9, pp 327–353.   [301] See ch 10 generally.
[302] Competition Act 1998, s 10; on parallel exemptions see ch 9, p 353.
[303] OFT Decision, 16 October 2001, [2002] UKCLR 59.
[304] OFT Decision, 25 October 2001, [2002] UKCLR 74.
[305] OFT decision of 15 April 2004, [2004] UKCLR 893.   [306] See ch 9, pp 351–352.
[307] Ibid, pp 352–353.

16

Vertical agreements[1]

CHAPTER CONTENTS

1. INTRODUCTION

The previous three chapters have been concerned with horizontal relationships between undertakings. This chapter deals with the application of Article 81 EC and Chapter 1 of the Competition Act 1998 to vertical agreements. The law on vertical agreements was fundamentally reformed as a result of the adoption by the European Commission of Regulation 2790/99 which entered into force on 1 June 2000[2]; the Regulation should be read in conjunction with the accompanying *Guidelines on Vertical Restraints*[3] ('the *Vertical guidelines*' or 'the *Guidelines*'). Regulation 2790/99 will expire in May 2010, and the Commission has begun to give thought as to how, if at all, it might wish to amend the law thereafter[4].

---

[1] For further reading on Article 81 and vertical agreements see Wijckmans, Tuytschaever and Venderelst *Vertical Agreements in EC Competition Law* (Oxford University Press, 2006); Faull and Nikpay *The EC Law of Competition* (2nd ed, 2007), ch 9; Bellamy and Child *European Community Law of Competition* (eds Roth and Rose, Oxford University Press, 6th ed, 2008), ch 6.

[2] OJ [1999] L 336/21, [2000] 4 CMLR 398; see pp 640–642 below for detailed commentary on this Regulation.

[3] OJ [2000] C 291/1, [2000] 5 CMLR 1074.   [4] See p 662 below.

In the UK vertical agreements, with the exception of agreements for the maintenance of minimum and fixed resale prices, were at one time excluded from the Chapter I prohibition of the Competition Act 1998: however this exclusion was repealed in 2004 in order to achieve consistency in the application of EC and domestic law: the position in the UK will be considered in the final section of this chapter[5]. To the extent that vertical agreements might result in the abuse of a dominant position, contrary to Article 82 EC and the Chapter II prohibition in the Competition Act 1998, they are dealt with in chapters 17 and 18.

2. THE DISTRIBUTION CHAIN

A producer of goods or a supplier of services will either require them for its own consumption or will want to supply them to the market. A firm wishing to sell its products must decide how to do so. There are various possibilities: it may carry out both the production and the sales and distribution functions itself: this may be referred to as vertical integration; it may use the services of a commercial agent to find customers; or it may supply its products to a distributor whose function is to resell them to other persons, who may or may not be the final consumer. This chapter will consider how the law impacts upon each of these three situations, that is to say vertical integration, agency agreements and vertical agreements with third parties; it will also consider how the law applies to vertical sub-contracting agreements.

For many products it is possible to depict a fairly simple distribution chain: for example a producer may sell goods to a retailer, who deals with the final consumer:

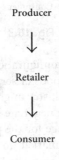

Producer

↓

Retailer

↓

Consumer

Fig. 16.1

In other markets a wholesaler may carry out an important intermediate function, standing between the producer and the retailer:

---

[5] See pp 667–671 below.

Fig. 16.2

A vertically-integrated producer might deal directly with the consumer, for example by mail order, by establishing its own retail outlets or by selling through the Internet. An example of vertical integration in the 'new' electronic economy occurs where, for example, Apple supplies music from its 'iTunes' music website direct to the consumer[6]:

Fig. 16.3

There can, of course, be many other configurations, in which quite different relationships are involved in the delivery of goods or services to their ultimate consumer. For example a brand owner in the food industry might sub-contract manufacture to a sub-contractor; the brand owner may then negotiate sales directly with supermarkets, and engage a transport company to arrange for the physical distribution of the products from the sub-contractor to the supermarket, in which case the diagram would look quite different:

---

[6] See pp 607–608 below.

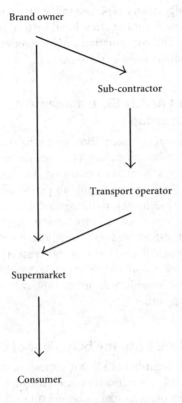

Fig. 16.4

It will be appreciated that many other vertical relationships are possible in the manufacture and supply of goods and services. This chapter will provide some guidance on how these vertical relationships are analysed in EC and UK law.

3. VERTICAL INTEGRATION

One option available for firms is vertical integration. This can be achieved internally by setting up retail outlets in the High Street or by establishing subsidiary companies to which the task of distribution is entrusted. Some firms may be able to sell their products through the Internet, thereby eliminating the need to appoint distributors: this process is known as disintermediation. Alternatively vertical integration may be achieved through external growth, by taking over distribution networks downstream in the market. Various considerations will influence a producer in its decision whether or not to integrate vertically[7]. On the one hand it may be costly to set up or take over one's own distribution channels; also it may be more efficient to appoint an independent

---

[7] See Coase 'The Nature of the Firm' 4 Economica 386 (1937); Williamson 'The Vertical Integration of Production; Market Failure Considerations' 61 Am Ec Rev 112 (1971); Lever and Neubauer 'Vertical Restraints, Their Motivation and Justification' (2000) 21 ECLR 7.

undertaking with knowledge of and expertise in the distributive trade than to attempt to break into this area oneself. On the other hand vertical integration may mean that a high degree of efficiency and coordination can be achieved in a way that would not occur where products are distributed by third parties.

(A) Non-application of Article 81 to agreements within a corporate group

One reason for achieving vertical integration might be that this will result in some immunity from competition law, since in general the internal affairs of companies or groups of companies are not subject to competition law. The ECJ confirmed in *Viho v Commission*[8] that Article 81(1) does not apply to parent–subsidiary agreements: this means that an intra-group agreement forbidding a subsidiary from exporting or selling at less than a certain price would not infringe Article 81(1)[9]. Vertical growth may not be the most efficient use of resources in terms of allocative efficiency and yet it may be the logical defensive response of firms fearful of anti-trust attack[10]. Agreements entered into between members of the group and third parties would themselves be capable of infringing Article 81(1), and would therefore be subject to the law on vertical agreements in the same way as any other.

(B) Application of Article 82 to the behaviour of the group

Vertical integration may be regarded as a factor indicating dominance for the purpose of deciding whether a firm is in a dominant position within the meaning of Article 82[11], and the group may be guilty of an abuse of a dominant position in the way in which it behaves on the market[12].

(C) Application of the EC Merger Regulation to vertical integration

Vertical mergers are notifiable to the Commission under the EC Merger Regulation where the Community dimension thresholds are satisfied[13]. As a general proposition vertical integration is likely to lead to economic efficiency, a fact that is explicitly recognised in the Commission's *Guidelines on non-horizontal mergers*[14]. However there have been occasions on which the Commission has required modifications to, or even the abandonment of, vertical mergers[15]. An obvious example of this is *Time-Warner/AOL*[16], which required the approval of the Commission: this was granted subject to a severance of the structural links between AOL and Bertelsmann, a competitor of Time-Warner.

---

[8] Case C-73/95 P [1996] ECR I-5457, [1997] 4 CMLR 419.   [9] See ch 3, pp 91–95.
[10] Advocate General Warner's Opinion warned of this danger in Case 30/78 *Distillers v Commission* [1980] ECR 2229, [1980] 3 CMLR 121.
[11] See ch 5, p 181.
[12] See *Interbrew* Commission's XXVIth *Report on Competition Policy* (1996), point 53 and pp 139–140.
[13] See ch 21, pp 828–832 on these thresholds.   [14] See ch 21, pp 864–868.
[15] See ch 21, pp 867–868.   [16] Case COMP/M 1845 OJ [2001] L 268/28, [2002] 4 CMLR 454.

4. COMMERCIAL AGENTS

Some producers choose to sell through commercial agents. The function of a sales agent is to negotiate business and to enter into contracts on the producer's behalf[17]. In this case the agent may be paid a commission for the business it transacts or it may be paid a salary. The essential point about its position is that it does not bear any risk itself; no property passes to it under the agreement; and it does not directly share in the profits (or losses) of its principal's business. The agent's position is analogous to that of an employee.

(A) Non-application of Article 81 to agency agreements

Where an agent is appointed which simply negotiates on behalf of a principal it is treated by EC competition law as forming part of the business organisation of the principal, so that the agreement between the parties is an internal matter of that economic entity rather than an agreement between undertakings. The consequence is that the agreement will normally fall outside Article 81(1). Commercial agency is a more common feature of distribution in continental Europe than in the UK. The Council of Ministers has adopted a Directive on the treatment of commercial agents[18], which provides them with protection against wrongful dismissal and with compensation where this occurs.

(B) The application of the Commission's *Vertical guidelines* to agency agreements

As early as 1962 the Commission published a Notice on agency agreements[19] stating that they were not subject to Article 81(1). It became necessary to amend this Notice, in particular since subsequent case law of the ECJ, for example in *Suiker Unie v Commission*[20] and *Vlaamse Reisbureaus*[21], made clear that it was not entirely reliable. The 1962 Notice was replaced by Section II (paragraphs 12 to 20) of the Commission's *Vertical guidelines*[22]; paragraph 12 of the *Guidelines* specifically states that they replace the 1962 Notice. The *Vertical guidelines* should be read subject to subsequent judgments of the CFI and ECJ, in particular *DaimlerChrysler AG v Commission*[23] and *Confederación Española de Empresarios de Staciones de Servicio v Compañía de Petróleos SA*[24], which are discussed in the text that follows.

---

[17] Agents are sometimes appointed simply to canvass potential customers or to introduce them to the producer rather than to negotiate contracts.

[18] Council Directive on the Coordination of the Laws of Member States relating to Self-Employed Commercial Agents 86/653 OJ [1986] L 382/17; the Directive was implemented in the UK by the Commercial Agents (Council Directive) Regulations 1993, SI 1993/3053.

[19] *Notice on exclusive dealing contracts with commercial agents of 1962* OJ 139, 24.12.1962, p 2921.

[20] Cases 40/73 etc [1975] ECR 1663, [1976] 1 CMLR 295.

[21] Case 311/85 *Vereniging van Vlaamse Reisbureaus v Sociale Dienst van de Plaatselijke en Gewestelijke Overheidsdiensten* [1987] ECR 3801, [1989] 4 CMLR 213.

[22] OJ [2000] C 291/1, [2000] 5 CMLR 1074.

[23] Case T-325/01 [2005] ECR II-3319, [2007] 4 CMLR 559; the CFI upheld a finding of agency in Case T-66/99 *Minoan Lines v Commission* [2003] ECR II-5515, [2005] 5 CMLR 1597, paras 121–130.

[24] Case C-217/05 [2006] ECR I-11997, [2007] 4 CMLR 181.

Paragraph 12 of the *Vertical guidelines* defines agency agreements as those that cover a situation where one person negotiates and/or concludes contracts on behalf of another for the purchase or sale of goods or services, by or from the principal. Paragraph 13 states that, in the case of 'genuine' agency agreements, Article 81(1) does not apply to the obligations imposed on the agent; 'non-genuine' agency agreements may be caught: they must be analysed under the later sections of the *Vertical guidelines* and the block exemption. Paragraph 13 provides that the determining factor in assessing whether Article 81(1) is applicable is 'the financial or commercial risk borne by the agent in relation to the activities for which he has been appointed as an agent by the principal'; paragraph 13 states that it is immaterial whether the agent acts for one or several principals, a view that is difficult to reconcile with the judgment of the ECJ in the *Vlaamse Reisbureaus* case[25]. Paragraphs 14 to 18 examine the meaning of risk for this purpose and the obligations that fall outside Article 81(1). Paragraphs 19 and 20 examine two circumstances in which provisions in a genuine agency agreement could infringe Article 81(1).

(i) The criterion of risk

(A) Paragraphs 14 to 18 of the Vertical guidelines Paragraph 14 states that there are two types of financial or commercial risk that are relevant in determining 'genuine' agency: first, those that are directly related to the contracts concluded and/or negotiated by the agent on behalf of the principal, such as the financing of stocks; second, those risks that are related to 'market-specific investments', meaning risks that the agent undertakes in order to be appointed. Paragraph 15 states that, where the agent bears no or only insignificant risks in relation to either of these matters, the agency agreement falls outside Article 81(1): in such a case the selling or purchasing function forms an integral part of the principal's activities, despite the fact that the agent is, as a matter of law, a separate legal entity. Where the agent accepts risk which is more than insignificant it is treated as an independent dealer, and the agreement with it is capable of infringing Article 81(1).

Paragraph 16 states that the question of risk must be assessed on a case-by-case basis and with regard to economic reality rather than legal form. However, for the purpose of guidance, paragraph 16 continues by stating that Article 81(1) would not normally be applicable where the title to the goods does not vest in the agent; nor where the agent does not supply services itself and where the agent:

- Does not contribute to the costs relating to the supply/purchase of the contract goods or services, including the cost of transport
- Is not obliged to invest in sales promotion
- Does not maintain at its own cost or risk stocks of the contracts goods
- Does not create and/or operate an after-sales service, repair service or a warranty service unless it is fully reimbursed by the principal
- Does not make market-specific investments in equipment, premises or training of personnel
- Does not undertake responsibility towards third parties for damage caused by the products sold
- Does not take responsibility for customers' non-performance of the contract.

[25] See n 21 above; on this point see Korah and O'Sullivan *Distribution Agreements under the EC Competition Rules* (Hart Publishing, 2002), pp 101–103.

Paragraph 17 provides that the list in paragraph 16 is not exhaustive and that, where the agent does incur one or more of the costs or risks listed, Article 81(1) may apply as it would do to any other vertical agreement.

Paragraph 18 of the *Vertical guidelines* provides that, where an agency agreement does not fall within Article 81(1), all obligations on the agent will fall outside that provision, including limitations on the territory in which or the customers to which the agent may sell the goods or services and the prices and conditions at which the goods or services will be sold or purchased.

(B) Judgments and decisional practice The application of the *Vertical guidelines* has been considered on several occasions in recent years. In *DaimlerChrysler*[26] the Commission decided that the dealers distributing Mercedes-Benz cars in Germany were responsible for and bore the risk of a wide range of activities, including the acquisition of demonstration vehicles and the provision of after-sales services and that therefore the agreements under consideration were subject to Article 81(1)[27]. A fine was imposed on DaimlerChrysler since the German dealers were subject to export bans. On appeal the CFI disagreed with the Commission's analysis and the fine for this infringement was annulled[28]. After reviewing the case law of the Community Courts on agency agreements[29] the CFI reviewed the terms of the standard-form agreements that Mercedes-Benz entered into with its dealers. The Court noted that the German dealers did not buy vehicles for resale; nor were they required to hold a stock of new vehicles. The dealers were not required to forgo part of their commission in order to sell cars in stock. The sales price of cars was determined entirely by Mercedes-Benz which, in the CFI's view, bore the principal risk[30]. Nor was the CFI satisfied that the dealers were required to bear other risks such as the cost of transport[31] or the cost of acquiring demonstration vehicles and carrying out repair work under the manufacturer's guarantee[32].

In *Souris/Topps*[33] the Commission rejected an argument that agreements between Topps, the producer of Pokémon products, and Rautakirja and NMPP were genuine agency agreements; it considered that each of them did accept some risk, for example in relation to the loss or destruction of the contract goods in the case of Rautakirja and in relation to the distribution of the products in the case of NMPP[34]. The Commission went further and said that, even if these were genuine agency agreements, the obligations in question went beyond the types of provision that fell outside Article 81(1) since they related not to the agency relationship itself: instead they were part of an attempt to exclude third party parallel importers from the market[35].

In *Confederación Española de Empresarios de Staciones de Servicio v Compañía de Petróleos SA*[36] the question arose of whether the operators of service-stations in Spain selling motor fuel did so as agents or as independent dealers. As this was an Article 234 EC reference the ECJ did not make a finding on the facts of the case[37]. However it did set out the criteria that would be relevant to an assessment of whether the station operators were acting as agents including, first, the risks linked to the sale of the goods and,

[26] OJ [2002] L 257/1, [2003] 4 CMLR 95.   [27] Ibid, paras 153–168.
[28] Case T-325/01 *DaimlerChrysler AG v Commission* [2005] ECR II-3319, [2007] 4 CMLR 559.
[29] Ibid, paras 83–87.   [30] Ibid, paras 96–103.   [31] Ibid, paras 105–106.   [32] Ibid, paras 107–113.
[33] [2006] 4 CMLR 1713.   [34] Ibid, paras 97–104.   [35] Ibid, para 103.
[36] Case C-217/05 [2006] ECR I-11997, [2007] 4 CMLR 181; for comment see Dieny 'The Relationship Between a Principal and its Agent in Light of Article 81(1): How Many Criteria?' (2008) 29 ECLR 5.
[37] Ibid, para 49.

second, the risks linked to investments specific to the market[38]. The ECJ summed up the position by saying that the risks should be assessed:

on the basis of criteria such as ownership of the goods, the contribution of the costs linked to their distribution, their safe-keeping, liability for any damage caused to the goods or by the goods to third parties, and the making of investments specific to the sale of those goods[39].

The ECJ added that, even if the agent were to accept some risk, Article 81(1) would still not be applicable if that risk was negligible[40].

(ii) Provisions in genuine agency agreements that may infringe Article 81(1)

The *Vertical guidelines* indicate, in paragraphs 19 and 20, two situations in which there could be an infringement of Article 81(1) in the case of a genuine agency agreement. The first is where the agreement contains exclusive agency or non-compete provisions. Since exclusive agency provisions concern only intra-brand competition[41], paragraph 19 says that they do not in general produce anti-competitive effects. However non-compete provisions may affect inter-brand competition in the provision of agency services[42] and could infringe Article 81(1) if they lead to foreclosure of the market: the Commission refers to the later provisions of the *Guidelines* in section VI.2.1 (paragraphs 138 to 160) on this. The idea that non-compete provisions in an agency agreement could infringe Article 81 was noted with approval by the ECJ in the *CEPSA* case[43].

Paragraph 20 deals with the second situation in which Article 81(1) might be infringed, which is where the agency agreement facilitates an anti-competitive agreement or concerted practice: this could occur where a number of principals use the same agents whilst collectively excluding others from using these agents; or where they use agents for collusion on marketing strategy or to exchange sensitive market information between the principals.

5. VERTICAL AGREEMENTS: COMPETITION POLICY CONSIDERATIONS

(A) Introduction

In this section the competition policy considerations raised by vertical agreements will be examined, using the taxonomy adopted by the Commission in its *Vertical guidelines*. Section 5 of this chapter will consider the application of Article 81(1) to vertical agreements in the light of the jurisprudence of the Community Courts and the Commission's *Guidelines*. Sections 6 and 7 will examine the path to reform of the

---

[38] Ibid, paras 50–59.   [39] Ibid, para 60.   [40] Ibid, para 61.

[41] This expression is explained at p 613 below.

[42] See the Opinion of AG Kokott in Case C-217/05 *Confederación Española de Empresarios de Estaciones de Servicio v Compañía de Petróleos SA* [2006] ECR I-11997, [2007] 4 CMLR 181, paras 44–45.

[43] Case C-217/05 *Confederación Española de Empresarios de Estaciones de Servicio v Compañía de Petróleos SA* [2006] ECR I-11997, [2007] 4 CMLR 181, para 62; see also the Commission's Notice under Article 27(4) of the Modernisation Regulation in the case of *Repsol CPP SA*, OJ [2004] C 258/7, paras 21–24 identifying a possible foreclosure effect which was addressed by Repsol offering commitments under Article 9 of that Regulation.

old EC block exemptions for exclusive distribution, exclusive purchasing and franchising agreements and the very different treatment of vertical agreements under Regulation 2790/99. Section 8 will consider the possibility that a vertical agreement that falls outside the block exemption might nevertheless satisfy the criteria of Article 81(3). Regulation 1400/2002 on the distribution of motor cars will be considered in section 9.

(B) Vertical agreements: possible detriments to competition[44]

(i) Inter-brand and intra-brand competition

The application of Article 81 to vertical agreements has long been controversial. It is fairly obvious that horizontal agreements, for example to fix prices or to limit output, should be prohibited: in this situation firms combine their market power to their own advantage[45]; vertical agreements do not involve a *combination* of market power[46]. Vertical agreements are likely to have an effect on competition only where the firm imposing a vertical restraint already has market power. Where this is the case competition with other firms' products – 'inter-brand competition' – may be limited; as a result it may be desirable to ensure that there is competition between distributors and retailers in relation to the products of the firm with market power – so-called 'intra-brand competition'[47].

Suppose that A is the brand owner of Wonder Widgets and B is the brand owner of Beautiful Blodgets.

A requires its retailers to purchase Wonder Widgets only from it and not to buy the competing products of M, N, and O – a so-called 'single branding agreement'[48]. The diagonal line means that the retailers and M, N, and O have no access to each other.

A   M, N, O

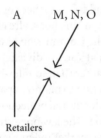

Retailers

Fig. 16.5

The question in this case would be whether the single branding agreement has an effect on inter-brand competition, that is to say on competition between the brands of A and those of its competitors, M, N and O; this will depend on how much market power A has.

Suppose now that B requires its retailers X, Y, and Z not to sell Beautiful Blodgets at less than the recommended price of €100, and not to sell to customers who live in an area allotted to one of the other retailers.

---

[44] For further discussion of the arguments in favour of and against vertical agreements see Bishop and Walker *The Economics of EC Competition Law* (Sweet & Maxwell, 2nd ed, 2002), paras 5.32–5.56; Van den Bergh and Camesasca *European Competition Law and Economics: A Comparative Perspective* (Sweet & Maxwell, 2006), ch 6.

[45] *Vertical guidelines*, para 100.   [46] Ibid, para 100.   [47] Ibid, para 6.   [48] See p 615 below.

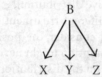

Fig. 16.6

The question in this case is whether the agreements have a significant effect on intra-brand competition between the three retailers X, Y and Z. They do not restrict competition between B and its competitors; however the extent of inter-brand competition in the relevant market will determine the extent to which intra-brand competition is a cause for concern.

(ii) *Consten* and *Grundig v Commission*

It was argued in *Consten and Grundig v Commission*[49] that Article 81(1) should not apply to vertical agreements at all as that provision was simply concerned with horizontal arrangements between undertakings. The ECJ rejected this argument[50] and concluded that the exclusive agreement in that case which conferred absolute territorial protection upon a distributor was caught by Article 81(1) and did not satisfy the criteria of Article 81(3)[51].

(iii) The single market imperative and intra-brand competition

As a general proposition competition law has less concern with restrictions of intra-brand competition than with restrictions of inter-brand competition: a restriction of intra-brand competition is likely to raise concerns only where inter-brand competition is weak. However to this must be added a further concern of EC competition law, which has been mentioned several times in this book already: the integrity of the single market. The Community Courts and the Commission have, from the earliest days, been concerned about vertical agreements that lead to a division of national markets, even where the restrictions relate to intra-brand rather than to inter-brand competition. The strict treatment of export bans, the determination to maintain parallel imports and the reluctance to allow distributors to enjoy absolute territorial protection are all issues affecting intra-brand rather than inter-brand competition. The law on vertical agreements in the Community therefore has a component – single market integration – that will not be found in other (domestic) systems of competition law[52]. It remains to be seen whether the ECJ, in the case of *Glaxo v Commission*, will decide that, at least in relation to pharmaceutical products, a more relaxed approach should be adopted towards this issue in the future[53].

(iv) The commentary in the *Vertical guidelines* on the negative effects of vertical restraints

Paragraph 107 of the Commission's *Vertical guidelines* notes four possible negative effects arising from vertical restraints which EC competition law aims at preventing:

[49] Cases 56/64 and 58/64 [1966] ECR 299, [1966] CMLR 418.   [50] Ibid, p 470; see further ch 3, p 000.

[51] Absolute territorial protection may be permitted in exceptional circumstances, as in Case 262/81 *Coditel II* [1982] ECR 3381, [1983] 1 CMLR 49: see ch 3, p 125.

[52] See the *Vertical guidelines*, para 7.   [53] See ch 3, p 121–122.

- Foreclosure of other suppliers or buyers by raising barriers to entry
- Reduction of inter-brand competition, including the facilitation of both explicit and tacit collusion[54]
- Reduction of intra-brand competition between distributors of the same brand
- The creation of obstacles to market integration.

There are many types of vertical agreement. The Commission, at paragraph 104 of the *Vertical guidelines,* suggests that they can be grouped into four categories:

- A single branding group
- A limited distribution group
- A resale price maintenance group
- A market partitioning group.

Each group, and the negative effects that may follow from agreements in that group, is discussed in the subsequent paragraphs of the *Guidelines.* It is important to become familiar with the terminology introduced in this part of the *Guidelines* in order to understand the law of vertical agreements.

(A) Single branding group[55] The single branding group consists of agreements that have as their main element that the buyer is induced to concentrate its orders for a particular product on one supplier. An agreement not to purchase competing products, agreements which force or induce customers to purchase all or most of their products from one supplier and tie-in transactions fall within this group[56]. In the Commission's view agreements in the single branding group may foreclose access to the market, facilitate collusion, restrict inter-brand competition within retail shops and, in the case of tying, force the buyer to pay a higher price for tied products than would otherwise be the case. Each of these negative effects may lead to a reduction in inter-brand competition[57].

(B) Limited distribution group[58] The limited distribution group consists of agreements which have as their main element that the manufacturer sells to only one or a limited number of buyers. Exclusive distribution, exclusive customer allocation and selective distribution agreements fall within this group. In the Commission's view agreements in the limited distribution group may lead to foreclosure at the buyer's level of the market, facilitate collusion and lead to a reduction, or even a total elimination of, intra-brand competition[59].

(C) Resale price maintenance group[60] This group consists of agreements which impose minimum, fixed, maximum or recommended resale prices[61]. The main negative effects are a reduction in intra-brand competition and increased transparency of prices, which may facilitate collusion between manufacturers and or between distributors[62].

---

[54] On practices, including vertical agreements, that facilitate tacit collusion see ch 14, p 554–555.
[55] *Vertical guidelines,* paras 106–108; on the application of Article 81(1) to such agreements see pp 627–628 and p 658 below.
[56] Ibid, para 106.   [57] Ibid, para 107.
[58] Ibid, paras 109–110; on the application of Article 81(1) to such agreements see pp 628–630 below.
[59] Ibid, para 110.
[60] Ibid, paras 111–112; on the application of Article 81(1) to such agreements see pp 653–654 below.
[61] Ibid, para 111.   [62] Ibid, para 112.

(D) Market partitioning group[63] This group consists of agreements the main element of which is that the buyer is restricted as to where it buys or resells a particular product[64]. The main negative effect is a reduction of intra-brand competition and a partitioning of the market, thereby hindering market integration; such agreements may also facilitate collusion[65].

(C) Vertical agreements: possible benefits to competition

Having set out the Commission's views as to the possible detriments to competition arising from vertical agreements, it is important to stress that there are also significant arguments in their favour. Some theorists argue that vertical restraints are not a suitable target for competition authorities at all[66]; a more realistic view is that they should be investigated only where a producer possesses power over the market[67]. Paragraph 115 of the Commission's *Vertical guidelines* states that vertical restraints often have positive effects, in particular by promoting non-price competition and improved quality of service. Paragraph 116 sets out eight situations in which vertical restraints may help to realise efficiencies and the development of new markets; the Commission says that it does not claim that the list is complete or exhaustive[68].

(i) The free-rider problem

One distributor may take a free ride on the investment of another. For example a retailer may invest in a particular brand and create a demand for it: it has an obvious interest in preventing another retailer from making sales in circumstances where it made no contribution to the creation of that demand. The Commission states that free-riding between buyers can occur only on pre-sales services and not on after-sales services; it adds that free-riding is usually only a problem where the product is relatively new or complex and of reasonably high value. Exclusive distribution agreements may be used to prevent the problem of free-riding: for example if A appoints B as the exclusive distributor for France, this will provide some degree of immunity from intra-brand competition. The *Vertical guidelines* do not say, but it is the case, that absolute territorial protection will not usually be countenanced in vertical agreements, because of the overriding goal of preventing the compartmentalisation of the single market. Community law permits exclusivity, but only a qualified exclusivity, in that parallel imports into the exclusive territory must be possible[69]. A free-rider issue can arise where a supplier invests in promotion at a retailer's premises which a competing supplier takes advantage of: a non-compete provision may be justified to prevent this type of free-riding.

---

[63] Ibid, paras 113–114; on the treatment of direct and indirect export bans under Article 81(1) see pp 622–626 below.

[64] Ibid, para 113.   [65] Ibid, para 114.

[66] See eg Bork *The Antitrust Paradox* (The Free Press, 1993), chs 14 and 15.

[67] See eg White 'Vertical Restraints in Antitrust law – a Coherent Model' (1981) 26 Antitrust Bulletin 327; Easterbrook 'Vertical Arrangements and the Rule of Reason' (1984) 53 Antitrust Law Journal 135; Bock 'An Economist Appraises Vertical Restraints' (1985) 30 Antitrust Bulletin 117; for criticism of the permissive view of vertical restraints adopted by many commentators see Comanor 'Vertical Price Fixing, Vertical Market Restrictions and the New Antitrust Policy' (1985) 98 Harv L Rev 983.

[68] See further *Vertical guidelines*, paras 117–118.   [69] See further p 614 above and pp 654–656 below.

(ii) Opening up and entering new markets

The second situation described in paragraph 116 is a 'special case of the free-rider problem'. This is where a manufacturer wants to enter a new geographic market and this requires its distributor to make 'first time investments'. It may be necessary to protect the distributor from competition so that it can recoup its investment by temporarily charging a higher price; this may mean that distributors in other markets should be restrained for a limited period from selling in the new market.

(iii) The certification free-rider issue

The third situation discussed in paragraph 116 is that, in some sectors, certain retailers have a reputation for stocking only 'quality' products. In such a case a manufacturer must limit its sales to such retailers, since otherwise its products may be delisted. Restrictions from the 'limited distribution' group may be justified in these circumstances.

(iv) The hold-up problem

This refers to a situation in which a supplier or buyer needs to make client-specific investments, and will not commit to these until supply agreements have been concluded. It may be that an undertaking making an investment will require a long-term supply agreement, so that it knows that it will recoup its costs. Where the supplier makes the investment, it may wish the buyer to agree to a non-compete, or to an analogous, provision; a buyer may seek the benefit of an exclusive distribution, customer allocation or exclusive supply provision[70].

(v) The hold-up problem where know-how is transferred

Where know-how is supplied by one firm to another it may be necessary to impose a non-compete provision on the recipient of the know-how to ensure that it is not used by competitors of the owner of it.

(vi) Economies of scale in distribution[71]

Economies of scale on the part of distributors may lead to lower retail prices. Various vertical agreements might contribute to this, including exclusive distribution and exclusive purchasing.

(vii) Capital market imperfections

In some cases banks may be unwilling to provide sufficient capital for the needs of the business of a supplier or a buyer. In such cases the supplier may lend to the buyer or *vice versa*. An obvious example is a brewer which makes a loan available to the operator of a public house or a café. A supplier in such a case may wish to impose a non-compete, or an analogous, provision; and a buyer may insist, for example, on exclusive supply.

---

[70] For an example of the 'hold-up problem' under UK law see OFT decision *Lucite International (UK) Ltd and BASF plc*, 29 November 2002, [2003] UKCLR 176, paras 44–46, available at www.oft.gov.uk.

[71] On economies of scale see ch 1 pp 10–11.

(viii) Uniformity and quality standardisation

Vertical restraints may help to promote the brand image of a product and increase its attractiveness to consumers by bringing about uniformity and quality standardisation. This is typical of selective distribution and franchising systems.

6. VERTICAL AGREEMENTS: ARTICLE 81(1)[72]

(A) Introduction

This section will consider the application of Article 81(1) to vertical agreements. Given the breadth of the new block exemption for vertical agreements, in many cases it is not necessary, in practical terms, to decide whether an agreement infringes Article 81(1) in the first place: if an agreement is within the 'safe haven' of Regulation 2790/99 and therefore satisfies the criteria of Article 81(3) the parties may have little interest in arguing, or even knowing, that the agreement did not infringe Article 81(1) in the first place. Paragraph 120 of the Commission's *Vertical guidelines* suggests, at indents (1) and (2), that there is no need to consider the application of Article 81(1) to agreements that are within the safe haven of the block exemption. This is a sensible and pragmatic point. However it would be intellectually incorrect to conclude that, *because* an agreement benefits from block exemption, it *therefore* infringes Article 81(1); and in some cases an agreement may not benefit from the block exemption, for example because the supplier's market share exceeds 30 per cent[73], in which case the parties may wish to argue that Article 81(1) is not infringed. This is exemplified by the Commission's finding that Interbrew's agreements, which imposed a single branding provision on cafés and bars in Belgium, did not infringe Article 81(1), once they had been modified to its satisfaction[74].

(B) The *de minimis* doctrine

Paragraphs 8 to 11 of the Commission's *Vertical guidelines* point out that agreements of minor importance usually fall outside Article 81(1) altogether. These paragraphs refer to the Commission's 1997 *Notice on Agreements of Minor Importance*[75] which has since been replaced by the 2001 Notice[76]; it is described in chapter 3 of this book[77]. Vertical agreements entered into by undertakings with a market share of less than 15 per cent are usually regarded as *de minimis,* although a 'hard-core' restriction such as an export ban might infringe Article 81(1) even below this threshold[78].

---

[72] For more detailed discussion of this topic readers are referred to Filipponi, Peeperkorn and Woods in Faull and Nikpay *The EC Law of Competition* (Oxford University Press, 2nd ed, 2007), ch 9.

[73] Occasionally it is the buyer's market share that is relevant: see p 651 below.

[74] See Commission Press Release IP/03/545, 15 April 2003.

[75] OJ [1997] C 372/13, [1998] 4 CMLR 192.   [76] OJ [2001] C 368/13, [2002] 4 CMLR 699.

[77] See ch 3, pp 137–142.   [78] See ch 3, p 139 and the *Vertical guidelines*, para 10.

(C) The combined effect of the *de minimis* doctrine and the block exemption

The combined effect of the *de minimis* doctrine and the block exemption is that most vertical agreements where the market share of each of the parties is below 15 per cent fall outside Article 81(1) altogether; and that most vertical agreements, even if they are caught by Article 81(1), will be block exempted under Regulation 2790/99, provided that the supplier's market share is below 30 per cent and that the agreement does not contain any of the 'hard-core' black-listed provisions in Article 4 of that Regulation[79]. As a consequence a very large number of vertical agreements will enjoy the benefit of one of these two 'safe havens'. Individual examination of vertical agreements will be necessary only where none of the safe havens is available, for example because the supplier's market share exceeds 30 per cent or because the parties wish to include a black-listed provision in their agreement. Where the supplier's market share exceeds 30 per cent it may be that it has a dominant position, in which case restrictions in its vertical agreements may amount to an abuse of a dominant position contrary to Article 82 EC: firms have been found to be dominant where they had a market share in the region of 40 per cent, and they are presumed to be dominant at 50 per cent[80]. However in the case of Interbrew's single branding agreements the Commission concluded that, even though Interbrew had a market share of around 56 per cent, the agreements did not appreciably restrict competition once the extent of the exclusivity had been reduced[81]. Agreements containing black-listed provisions are unlikely to satisfy the criteria of Article 81(3), since these are hard-core restrictions to which the Commission generally takes exception. It follows that individual examination of vertical agreements under Article 81(1) and Article 81(3) is likely to be relatively rare: it is most likely to be necessary where the supplier has a market share in excess of 30 per cent but does not have a dominant position in the sense of Article 82.

Market shares and vertical agreements	
50%	An undertaking with a market share of more than 50% is presumed to be dominant
40%	An undertaking with a market share of more than 40% may be dominant
30%	An undertaking with a market share of more than 30% will not benefit from the block exemption. If an agreement is caught by Article 81(1) it will benefit from block exemption if the supplier's (or occasionally the buyer's) market share is below 30% and the agreement does not contain Article 4 hard-core restrictions
15%	An agreement will benefit from the *de minimis* doctrine where the market share of each of the parties is below 15% and the agreement does not contain any Article 4 hard-core restrictions

---

[79] On the black list in Article 4 see pp 652–657 below.   [80] See ch 5, pp 175–178.   [81] See n 74 above.

(D) The case law of the Community Courts on vertical agreements

The Community Courts have repeatedly made clear that, except in those cases where the *object*[82] of an agreement is plainly anti-competitive, for example because of the imposition of an export ban, the application of Article 81(1) to an agreement cannot be ascertained simply by taking into account its formal terms; rather it has to be assessed in its economic context in order to determine whether it could have an effect on competition in the relevant market. This case law is discussed in chapter 3 of this book[83]. Of particular importance in the context of vertical agreements are the judgments in *Société Technique Minière v Maschinenbau Ulm*[84], *Brasserie de Haecht v Wilkin*[85], *Pronuptia de Paris v Schillgalis*[86] and *Delimitis v Henninger Bräu*[87], each of which makes clear that, in 'effect' rather than 'object' cases under Article 81(1), a detailed examination of all the relevant facts is required before a conclusion can be reached as to whether competition is restricted by a vertical agreement.

Notwithstanding these important precedents there was a tendency on the part of the Commission over many years to adopt a formalistic approach to the application of Article 81(1) to vertical agreements, and a reluctance to follow the lead suggested by the Community Courts; the result was that large numbers of vertical agreements required exemption under Article 81(3) and, in particular, under the block exemptions adopted by the Commission. However it is clear from the *Vertical guidelines* that the Commission is now more willing than it was in the past to adopt a flexible and economics-oriented approach to the application of Article 81(1): this is an important part of the Commission's modernisation of its approach to the competition rules in the Treaty, and is a very welcome development. Paragraphs 120 to 133 of the *Vertical guidelines* establish the methodology of analysis for determining whether vertical agreements infringe Article 81(1) and whether they might satisfy the terms of Article 81(3); there is little reference to the jurisprudence of the Community Courts in the *Guidelines*, but of course they must be read subject to the Courts' case law rather than the other way around.

(E) The methodology for the analysis of vertical agreements in the Commission's *Vertical guidelines*

(i) The four steps involved in assessing vertical agreements under Article 81

Paragraph 120 of the *Vertical guidelines* suggests that four steps should be taken when assessing vertical agreements under Article 81. First, the relevant market should be defined in order to determine the supplier's or the buyer's market share, depending on the type of vertical restraint involved; second, where the market share is below 30 per cent the block exemption will usually be applicable, provided that there are no hard-core restrictions contrary to Article 4 of Regulation 2790/99[88]; the third step is that, where

---

[82] See ch 3, pp 116–117. [83] See ch 3, pp 116–134. [84] Case 56/65 [1966] ECR 235, [1966] CMLR 357.
[85] Case 23/67 [1967] ECR 407, [1968] CMLR 26. [86] Case 161/84 [1986] ECR 353, [1986] 1 CMLR 414.
[87] Case C-234/89 [1991] ECR I-935, [1992] 5 CMLR 210. [88] On Article 4 see pp 652–657 below.

the market share of 30 per cent is exceeded, it will be necessary to consider whether the agreement falls within Article 81(1); lastly, where Article 81(1) is infringed, it will be necessary to consider whether the agreement satisfies the terms of Article 81(3).

(ii) Relevant factors for the assessment under Article 81(1)

Paragraphs 121 to 133 set out the factors that are relevant to the analysis of agreements under Article 81(1). Paragraph 121 refers to eight particular factors that are relevant to this assessment:

- the market position of the supplier
- the market position of competitors
- the position of the buyer
- entry barriers
- the maturity of the market
- the level of trade affected by the agreement
- the nature of the product
- 'other factors'.

Each of these factors is expanded upon in the succeeding paragraphs. Paragraphs 126 to 129 are interesting on the issue of entry barriers; specific reference is made in paragraph 128 to the significance of sunk costs in determining how high the entry barriers are in a particular industry. Paragraph 133 deals with 'other factors' that may be relevant to the analysis: these include whether there is a 'cumulative effect' within the market of similar vertical agreements leading to a restriction of competition, the regulatory environment and the possibility of collusive behaviour arising from the operation of vertical agreements.

(iii) Relevant factors for the assessment under Article 81(3)

Paragraphs 134 to 136 discuss the application of Article 81(3) to vertical agreements. They should now be read in conjunction with the Commission's *Guidelines on the application of Article 81(3) of the Treaty*[89]. Paragraph 135 states that, where an undertaking is dominant or becoming dominant as a consequence of the vertical agreement, a vertical restraint that has appreciable anti-competitive effects, in principle, cannot satisfy Article 81(3); this is a somewhat extreme statement, from which the Commission has retreated somewhat in the *Guidelines on Article 81(3)*[90] . Paragraph 136 says that, where there is no dominance, three questions arise: these correspond to the first three requirements of Article 81(3) itself. The first is whether the agreement will lead to efficiencies of the kind discussed in paragraphs 115 to 118 of the *Vertical guidelines*[91]; speculative claims will not be accepted[92]. The second is whether any benefits accrue to

---

[89] OJ [2004] C 101/8; for discussion of the *Guidelines on Article 81(3)* see ch 4, pp 151ff.

[90] See the *Guidelines on Article 81(3)*, para 106 and footnote 92; for discussion of this issue see Bishop and Ridyard 'EC Vertical Restraints Guidelines: Effects-based or *Per Se* Policy' (2002) 23 ECLR 35 and Peeperkorn 'EC Vertical Restraints Guidelines: Effects-based or *Per Se* Policy – A Reply' (2002) 23 ECLR 38.

[91] See pp 616–618 above.

[92] On the type of evidence required in support of an efficiency claim under Article 81(3) see the *Guidelines on the application of Article 81(3) of the Treaty*, OJ [2004] C 101/8, paras 51–58, discussed in ch 4, pp 155–157.

age of consumers rather than the parties to the agreement: in general this
' on the intensity of competition in the market. The third is whether the
n the agreement are disproportionate: the least anti-competitive restraint
⌐ɪosen to obtain the efficiency in question.

(iv) Application of the methodology to particular types of agreement

Having set out this methodology the Commission's *Vertical guidelines* proceed to consider the application of Article 81 to a series of particular types of vertical agreement,
such as single branding and exclusive distribution: these are considered in section (G)
below[93]. The *Vertical guidelines* do not contain a specific section dealing with the application of Article 81(1) to direct and indirect export bans, other than the commentary
on Article 4(b) of the block exemption[94]. However there is a wealth of precedent on this
subject and, as has been stressed throughout this book, the single market imperative is
a dominant feature of Community competition law. For this reason section (F) below
will consider the approach of the Community Courts and the Commission to direct
and indirect export bans before the discussion in the *Vertical guidelines* of other types
of vertical agreement is considered in section (G).

(F) Direct and indirect export bans

(i) Direct export bans

Export bans in vertical agreements will be held to infringe Article 81(1), and will not
be permitted under Article 81(3) except in exceptional circumstances. Such agreements
will be found to have as their object the restriction of competition; anti-competitive
effects do not need to be demonstrated. In *General Motors BV v Commission*[95] the ECJ
held that this was so even if an agreement does not have the restriction of competition as
its sole aim but also pursues other legitimate objectives[96], adding that the same was true
if the restriction of exports happened as a result of indirect rather than direct measures[97]. The judgment of the CFI in *GlaxoSmithKline Services v Commission*[98] somewhat obscures the clarity of the law in this area, since there the Court decided that
contractual measures designed to prevent parallel trade did not, owing to the specific
features of the pharmaceuticals sector, have as their object the restriction of competition, although it proceeded to conclude that they did restrict competition by effect[99].
Both the Commission and Glaxo have appealed this case to the ECJ, and the judgment
of that Court is eagerly awaited[100].

Export bans are black-listed by Article 4(b) of Regulation 2790/99, and their inclusion prevents the application of the block exemption to the agreement in question[101].
Examples of export bans which the Commission has objected to are legion, and the

---

[93] See pp 626–638 below.   [94] See pp 654–656 below.
[95] Case C-551/03 P [2006] ECR I-3173, [2006] 5 CMLR 9.   [96] Ibid, para 64.   [97] Ibid, para 68.
[98] Case T-168/01 [2006] ECR II-2969, [2006] 5 CMLR 29.   [99] See ch 3, pp 121–122.
[100] Case C-501/06 etc *GlaxoSmithKline Services v Commission* and C-513/06 *Commission v GlaxoSmithKline*, not yet decided.
[101] See pp 654–656 below.

Community Courts have been equally opposed to them[102]. It is highly likely that the Commission will impose a fine where it discovers an export ban, although reluctant distributors which accepted the ban under duress may not themselves be fined[103]; alternatively it may be that the fine on unwilling participants will be reduced[104]. In a serious case the fine for imposing export bans could be very substantial: in *VW*[105] the fine on Volkswagen amounted to €102 million, at the time one of the largest penalties to have been imposed by the Commission on one undertaking for infringing the competition rules; the fine was reduced to €90 million on appeal[106].

It is perhaps surprising that, even though the law on export bans has been clearly established for many years, the Commission is still able to unearth new cases. For example in 2000 it imposed a fine of €43 million on *Opel* for pursuing a strategy aimed at limiting sales of Opel cars from the Netherlands to other Member States[107]; a fine of €60,000 on *Nathan-Bricolux* for restricting parallel sales of educational materials within and outside distributors' exclusive territories and for fixing resale prices[108];

---

[102] See eg Case 19/77 *Miller International Schallplatten GmbH v Commission* [1978] ECR 131, [1978] 2 CMLR 334 (export ban regarded by ECJ as a restriction of competition by object under Article 81); *William Teacher* OJ [1978] L 235/20, [1978] 3 CMLR 290; *Arthur Bell* OJ [1978] L 235/15, [1978] 3 CMLR 298; Cases 32/78 etc *BMW Belgium SA v Commission* [1979] ECR 2435, [1980] 1 CMLR 370 (subsidiary of BMW attempted to prevent exports into Germany, despite advice from the parent company not to do so); *Kawasaki* OJ [1979] L 16/9, [1979] 1 CMLR 448; *National Panasonic (UK) Ltd* OJ [1982] L 354/28, [1983] 1 CMLR 497; *Johnson and Johnson* OJ [1980] L 377/16, [1981] 2 CMLR 287 (formal ban dropped, but continued in practice); *Moët et Chandon (London) Ltd* OJ [1982] L 94/7, [1982] 2 CMLR 166 (circulating a price list for sales in UK held tantamount to an export ban); *Polistil SpA* OJ [1984] L 136/9, [1984] 2 CMLR 594; *John Deere* OJ [1985] L 35/58, [1985] 2 CMLR 554; *Tipp-ex* OJ [1987] L 222/1, [1989] 4 CMLR 425, upheld on appeal Case C-279/87 *Tipp-ex GmbH v Commission* [1990] ECR I-261; *Sandoz* OJ [1987] L 222/28, [1989] 4 CMLR 628, upheld on appeal Case 277/87 *Sandoz Prodotti Farmaceutici SpA v Commission* [1990] ECR I-45; *Fisher-Price/Quaker Oats Ltd-Toyco* OJ [1988] L 49/19, [1989] 4 CMLR 553; *Konica* OJ [1988] L 78/34, [1988] 4 CMLR 848; *Viho/Toshiba* OJ [1991] L 287/39, [1992] 5 CMLR 180 (see para 20: export ban a restriction by object under Article 81(1)); *Newitt/Dunlop Slazenger International* OJ [1992] L 131/32, [1993] 5 CMLR 352, paras 48–50, upheld on appeal Case T-43/92 *Dunlop Slazenger International v Commission* [1994] ECR II-441: the fine on one of the addressees of the Commission's decision was annulled in Case T-38/92 *All Weather Sports Benelux BV v Commission* [1994] ECR II-211, [1995] 4 CMLR 43; *Viho/Parker Pen* OJ [1992] L 233/27, [1993] 5 CMLR 382, paras 16–19, upheld on appeal Cases T-66/92 and T-77/92 *Herlitz v Commission* and *Parker Pen v Commission* [1994] ECR II-531, [1995] 5 CMLR 458 and [1994] ECR II-549, [1995] 5 CMLR 435 (fine reduced); *Ford Agricultural* OJ [1993] L 20/1, [1995] 5 CMLR 89, para 12; *Tretorn* OJ [1994] L 378/45, [1997] 4 CMLR 860, upheld on appeal Case T-49/95 *Van Megen Sports Group NV v Commission* [1996] ECR II-1799, [1997] 4 CMLR 843; *BASF Lacke+Farben AG and Accinauto SA* OJ [1995] L 272/16, [1996] 4 CMLR 811, upheld on appeal Cases T-175/95 and T-176/95 *BASF v Commission* [1999] ECR II-1581, [2000] 4 CMLR 33 and 67; *Organon* Commission's XXVth *Report on Competition Policy* (1995), points 37–38 and pp 142–143; *Novalliance/Systemform* OJ [1997] L 47/11, [1997] 4 CMLR 876; *Lee Cooper* Commission's XXIXth *Report on Competition Policy* (1999) p 138.

[103] See eg *Kawasaki* OJ [1979] L 16/9, [1979] 1 CMLR 448; *Johnson and Johnson* OJ [1980] L 377/16, [1981] 2 CMLR 287; *John Deere* OJ [1985] L 35/58, [1985] 2 CMLR 554.

[104] See eg *BMW Belgium* OJ [1978] L 46/33, [1978] 2 CMLR 126; *Hasselblad* OJ [1982] L 161/18, [1982] 2 CMLR 233.

[105] OJ [1998] L 124/60, [1998] 5 CMLR 33.

[106] Case T-62/98 *Volkswagen AG v Commission* [2000] ECR II-2707, [2000] 5 CMLR 853, upheld on appeal to the ECJ in Case C-338/00 *Volkswagen AG v Commission* [2003] ECR I-9189, [2004] 4 CMLR 351.

[107] OJ [2001] L 59/1, [2001] 4 CMLR 1441, upheld in part on appeal Case T-368/00 *Opel Nederland BV v Commission* [2003] ECR II-4491 [2004] 4 CMLR 1302 and on appeal to the ECJ in Case C-551/03 P *General Motors BV v Commission* [2006] ECR I-3173, [2006] 5 CMLR 9.

[108] OJ [2001] L 54/1, [2001] 4 CMLR 1122.

and a fine of €39.6 million on *JC Bamford Group*[109] for restrictions on sales outside allotted territories and associated practices. In *DaimlerChrysler* fines were imposed on DaimlerChrysler, among other reasons, because it was considered to have attempted to inhibit parallel trade in Mercedes-Benz cars; the fines were significantly reduced on appeal, in particular because, on the German market, DaimlerChrysler was found by the CFI to have acted through genuine agents rather than through independent distributors: this meant that Article 81 was not applicable to those arrangements[110]. In *Nintendo Distribution*[111] the Commission took objection to the prevention of parallel trade in video games and their consoles and imposed a fine of €167.8 million on the manufacturer and its distributors; this was the largest fine so far imposed for an unlawful vertical agreement. In *Yamaha* the Commission condemned several practices designed to partition the single market for musical instruments and imposed a fine of €2.56 million[112]. In *Souris/Topps*[113] the Commission imposed a fine of €1.59 million for restricting parallel trade between Member States in relation to Pokémon stickers and cards. No fines were imposed in the case of *OMV/Gazprom* where gas supply contracts prevented OMV from reselling the gas outside Austria: however the offending provisions were dropped, and OMV agreed to increase capacity in the gas pipeline that transports Russian gas through Austria[114].

An important point to bear in mind is that the Commission will take a wide view of the term 'agreement' for the purpose of establishing whether an export ban infringes Article 81(1) and, in particular, that conduct that may appear to be unilateral may be characterised as sufficiently consensual to be caught by that provision[115]; however the Commission's decision to this effect in *Bayer AG/Adalat*[116] was annulled on appeal by the CFI[117], and the CFI's judgment was upheld on appeal to the ECJ[118]. A further point is that it may be relatively easy to establish a concerted practice between a supplier and its distributors to divide up the common market[119].

(ii) Indirect export bans

The Commission and the Community Courts will condemn indirect measures that might have the same effect as an export ban. Indirect export bans are black-listed by Article 4(b) of Regulation 2790/99, and their inclusion in an agreement would prevent

---

[109] JCB OJ [2002] L 69/1, [2002] 4 CMLR 1458, upheld in part on appeal Case T-67/01 *JCB Service v Commission* [2004] ECR II-49, [2004] 4 CMLR 1346 and on appeal to the ECJ in Case C-167/04 P *JCB Service v Commission* [2006] ECR I-8935, [2006] 5 CMLR 1337.

[110] OJ [2002] L 257/1, [2003] 4 CMLR 95, upheld in part on appeal Case T-325/01 *DaimlerChrysler AG v Commission* [2005] ECR II-3319, [2007] 4 CMLR 559; on the agency point see p 611 above.

[111] OJ [2003] L 255/33, [2004] 4 CMLR 421, on appeal Case T-13/03 *Nintendo v Commission*, not yet decided.

[112] Commission Press Release IP/03/1028, 16 July 2003.   [113] [2006] 4 CMLR 1713.

[114] See Commission Press Release IP/05/195, 17 February 2005: Gazprom's commitment to give a right of first refusal to OMV for supplies of gas in Austria was also dropped as part of this settlement; see similarly *E.ON Ruhrgas/Gazprom*, Commission Press Release IP/05/710, 10 June 2005 where territorial restrictions and most-favoured customer clauses were dropped.

[115] See ch 3, pp 107–113.   [116] OJ [1996] L 201/1, [1996] 5 CMLR 416.

[117] Case T-41/96 *Bayer v Commission* [2000] ECR II-3383, [2001] 4 CMLR 126 .

[118] Case C-2/01 P *Bundesverband der Arzneimittel Importeure eV v Bayer AG* [2004] ECR I-23, [2004] 4 CMLR 653; for discussion of this case see ch 3, pp 110–111.

[119] See in particular Cases 100–103/80 *Musique Diffusion Française SA v Commission* [1983] ECR 1825, [1983] 3 CMLR 221.

the application of the block exemption[120]. An example of an indirect export ban would arise if a producer provides that its guarantees are available to consumers in a particular Member State only if they buy the product from a distributor in that state; this obviously acts as a strong disincentive to purchase elsewhere. In *Zanussi*[121] the Commission condemned such an arrangement, and it has taken similar action on several occasions since[122]. As a general proposition customer guarantees should be available for products no matter where they are marketed in the single market. The Commission's approach was endorsed by the ECJ in *ETA Fabriques d'Ebauches v DK Investments SA*[123], in which it held that the partitioning of national markets by denying the benefit of guarantees to imported goods infringed Article 81(1). However it may be legitimate to provide that the guarantee should extend only to services that a local representative is bound to provide in accordance with local safety and technical standards[124], and it is permissible to withhold the guarantee from products sold by a dealer who is not an authorised member of a selective distribution system[125]. A requirement that a distributor that exports goods into the territory of another distributor should pay a service fee to the latter as compensation for the after-sales service that it is required to provide may be treated as an export ban where the fee does not relate to the value of the service to be provided; so may the provision to distributors of financial support conditional on products supplied being used only within a distributor's allotted territory[126].

Another way of indirectly affecting exports is through the use of monitoring clauses in contracts, whereby a producer requires information as to the destination of its products, and by the imposition on products of serial numbers which enable their movement from one territory to another to be traced. While these practices are not objectionable in themselves, they will be condemned where they are used by a producer in order to prevent or control parallel importing[127].

Exports may be impeded in numerous other ways. Price discrimination devised to prevent exports would be caught[128]; the withdrawal of discounts previously granted to a French dealer in so far as it exported the products in question to Italy attracted

---

[120] See pp 654–656 below.   [121] OJ [1978] L 322/26, [1979] 1 CMLR 81.

[122] See *Matsushita Electrical Trading Company* Commission's XIIth *Report on Competition Policy* (1982), point 77; *Ford Garantie Deutschland* XIIIth *Report on Competition Policy* (1983), points 104–106; *Fiat* XIVth *Report on Competition Policy* (1984), point 70; XVIth *Report on Competition Policy* (1986), point 56; *Sony* XVIIth *Report on Competition Policy* (1987), point 67; *Saeco* Commission's *Competition Policy Newsletter*, October 2000, p 48.

[123] Case 31/85 [1985] ECR 3933, [1986] 2 CMLR 674.   [124] See *Zanussi* (n 121 above, para 14).

[125] Case C-376/92 *Metro v Cartier* [1994] ECR I-15, [1994] 5 CMLR 331, paras 32–34.

[126] *JCB* OJ [2002] L 69/1, [2002] 4 CMLR 1458, paras 155–167.

[127] See eg *Victor Hasselblad AB* OJ [1982] L 161/18, [1982] 2 CMLR 233: its cameras had serial numbers on them and the Commission considered that this afforded an opportunity to Hasselblad to discover whether there had been any parallel importing; *Sperry New Holland* OJ [1985] L 376/21, [1988] 4 CMLR 306; *Newitt/Dunlop Slazenger International* OJ [1992] L 131/32, [1993] 5 CMLR 352, paras 59–60.

[128] See eg *Pittsburgh Corning Europe* JO [1972] L 272/35, [1973] CMLR D2; *Kodak* JO [1970] L 147/24, [1970] CMLR D19; Case 30/78 *Distillers v Commission* [1980] ECR 2229, [1980] 3 CMLR 121; the Commission declined to grant individual exemption to a dual pricing policy in *Glaxo SmithKline* OJ [2001] L 302/1, [2002] 4 CMLR 335; this case is on appeal to the ECJ following the CFI's judgment in Case T-168/01 *GlaxoSmithKline Services v Commission* [2006] ECR II-2969, [2006] 5 CMLR 29; see ch 3, pp 121–122.

fines in *Gosmé/Martell*[129]. In *Konica*[130] Konica's policy of buying up supplies of its film imported from the UK into Germany in order to protect its German distributors from cheap imports was condemned under Article 81(1): this did not prevent parallel imports in itself, but it did deprive consumers in Germany of the possibility of buying cheaper film. Restrictions on cross-supplies between distributors would be caught, as they may prevent parallel imports between Member States[131]. A requirement that coffee beans be resold only in a roasted form could affect exports: the Commission required agreements to be amended so that the beans could also be sold in their raw form[132]. Reducing supplies to a distributor in a particular territory so that there are none available for export could be caught, provided that this is done by agreement[133]. In *Bayo-n-ox*[134] the supply of a product for a customer's own use was held to entail an export ban contrary to Article 81(1) and in *Bayer Dental*[135] the Commission condemned a clause forbidding the resale of Bayer's dental products in a repackaged form since it regarded this as an indirect ban on exports.

In *Zera/Montedison*[136] the Commission concluded that an agreement to differentiate agrochemical products between one national market and another, with the consequence that a German distributor enjoyed absolute territorial protection, infringed Article 81(1)[137]. In *DaimlerChrysler*[138] the Commission considered that the requirement that only foreign customers should pay a 15 per cent deposit for a new vehicle unjustifiably hindered cross-border car sales[139].

(G) Application of Article 81(1) to other types of vertical agreements

Paragraphs 137 to 228 of the *Guidelines* provide guidance on the application of Article 81 to eight types of vertical agreements: single branding, exclusive distribution, exclusive customer allocation, selective distribution, franchising, exclusive supply, tying and recommended and maximum resale prices. Each of these categories will be examined in this section; relevant cross-references to Regulation 2790/99 will be provided.

---

[129] OJ [1991] L 185/23, [1992] 5 CMLR 586; see similarly *Newitt/Dunlop Slazenger International* OJ [1992] L 131/32, [1993] 5 CMLR 352, paras 54–57; *Ford Agricultural* OJ [1993] L 20/1, [1995] 5 CMLR 89, paras 13–14 (discounts dependent on non-export and penalties for exporting infringed Article 81(1)).

[130] OJ [1988] L 78/34, [1988] 4 CMLR 848; see similarly *Newitt/Dunlop Slazenger International* OJ [1992] L 131/32, [1993] 5 CMLR 352, para 58.

[131] *German Spectacle Frames* [1985] 1 CMLR 574; *JCB* OJ [2002] L 69/1, [2002] 4 CMLR 1458, paras 174–178.

[132] *Colombian Coffee* OJ [1982] L 360/31, [1983] 1 CMLR 703; see similarly the 'green banana' clause in Case 27/76 *United Brands Co v Commission* [1978] ECR 207, [1978] 1 CMLR 429.

[133] *Sandoz* OJ [1987] L 222/28, [1989] 4 CMLR 628, para 30, upheld on appeal Case C-277/87 *Sandoz Prodotti Farmaceutici SpA v Commission* [1990] ECR I-45; the Commission's decision in *Bayer AG/ADALAT* (p 624 n 116 above) was annulled since the CFI disagreed with the Commission's view that the reduction of supplies to Bayer's wholesalers in France and Spain was effected pursuant to an agreement; see also *Chanelle Veterinary Ltd v Pfizer Ltd (No 2)* [1999] Eu LR 723 (Irish Supreme Court): delisting not attributable to an agreement.

[134] OJ [1990] L 21/71, [1990] 4 CMLR 930, upheld on appeal to the CFI Case T-12/90 [1991] ECR II-219, [1993] 4 CMLR 30, and to the ECJ Case C-195/91 P *Bayer v Commission* [1994] ECR I-5619.

[135] OJ [1990] L 351/46, [1992] 4 CMLR 61.   [136] OJ [1993] L 272/28, [1995] 5 CMLR 320.

[137] Ibid, paras 96–126.   [138] OJ [2002] L 257/1, [2003] 4 CMLR 95.

[139] [2003] 4 CMLR 95, paras 173–175, upheld in part on appeal Case T-325/01 *DaimlerChrysler AG v Commission* [2005] ECR II-3319, [2007] 4 CMLR 559.

(i) Single branding agreements[140]

(A) Possible detriments to inter-brand competition The Commission's concern, expressed in paragraphs 106 to 108 of the *Vertical guidelines*[141] and repeated at paragraph 138, is that single branding agreements, which cause a buyer to purchase all or most of its requirements of products on a particular market from one supplier, may restrict inter-brand competition; this could happen by foreclosing access on the part of other suppliers to the market, by facilitating collusion and by limiting in-store inter-brand competition. The Commission often refers to such agreements in the *Guidelines* as non-compete obligations, since they require or have the effect of reducing competition between the supplier and its competitors by preventing customers from buying competing products.

(B) Application of the block exemption to single branding agreements The block exemption for vertical agreements will apply to single branding agreements, provided that the supplier's market share is less than 30 per cent[142] and provided that the duration of the non-compete obligation is limited to five years or less[143]. Where the block exemption applies, it will not be necessary to consider further whether Article 81(1) is infringed or whether the requirements of Article 81(3) are satisfied; however the *Guidelines* provide guidance for those cases in which individual assessment of agreements is necessary because the block exemption is not applicable[144].

(C) Factors to be considered in determining whether single branding agreements infringe Article 81(1) The Commission sets out the factors that are to be considered in determining whether Article 81(1) is infringed in paragraphs 140 to 152 of the *Vertical guidelines*. The approach taken by the Commission is an economic one, and is consistent with the many judgments of the Community Courts (not referred to in the *Guidelines*) which have held that such agreements must be assessed in their economic context in order to determine whether they have an anti-competitive effect: agreements in the single branding group do not have the *object* of restricting competition. Judgments of particular note on this issue include *Brasserie de Haecht v Wilkin*[145], *Delimitis v Henninger Bräu*[146], *BPB Industries plc v Commission*[147], and *Neste Markkinointi Oy v Yötuuli*[148]. Decisions in which the Commission has concluded that single branding agreements infringed Article 81(1) and did not satisfy Article 81(3) include *Spices*[149], *Bloemenveilingen Aalsmeer*[150] and *Langnese/Schöller*[151].

---

[140] *Vertical guidelines*, paras 138–160.   [141] See p 615 above.
[142] See pp 650–652 below.   [143] See p 658 below on Article 5(a) of Regulation 2790/99.
[144] *Vertical guidelines*, para 139.   [145] Case 23/67 [1967] ECR 407, [1968] CMLR 26.
[146] Case C-234/89 [1991] ECR I-935, [1992] 5 CMLR 210; see Lasok 'Assessing the Economic Consequences of Restrictive Agreements: A Comment on the Delimitis Case' (1991) 12 ECLR 194; Korah 'The Judgment in *Delimitis* – A Milestone Towards a Realistic Assessment of the Effects of an Agreement – or a Damp Squib' (1993) 8 Tulane European and Civil Law Forum 17; a shorter version is to be found at (1992) 5 EIPR 167.
[147] Case T-65/89 [1993] ECR II-389, [1993] 5 CMLR 32, para 66.
[148] Case C-214/99 [2000] ECR I-11121, [2001] 4 CMLR 993.   [149] OJ [1978] L 53/20, [1978] 2 CMLR 116.
[150] OJ [1988] L 262/27, [1989] 4 CMLR 500.
[151] OJ [1993] L 183/19, [1994] 4 CMLR 51, substantially upheld on appeal Cases T-7/93 and T-9/93 *Langnese-Iglo GmbH etc v Commission* [1995] ECR II-1533, [1995] 5 CMLR 602 and [1995] ECR II-1611, [1995] 5 CMLR 659 and Case C-279/95 P [1998] ECR I-5609, [1998] 5 CMLR 933; see also the Commission's decision on Article 81 in *Van den Bergh Foods Ltd* OJ [1998] L 246/1, [1998] 5 CMLR 530, upheld on appeal

As far as Article 81(1) is concerned the market position of the supplier must be considered[152], as must the duration of the agreement[153]. The higher the market share and the longer the duration, the more likely it is that there will be a significant foreclosure of the market[154]. In *DSD*[155] the Commission held that long-term exclusivity obligations in the service agreements of DSD, the largest undertaking in Germany in the market for the collection and sorting of household packaging, infringed Article 81(1)[156], although they fulfilled the criteria of Article 81(3)[157]. Paragraph 141 of the *Vertical guidelines* states that agreements on the part of non-dominant undertakings of less than a year are unlikely to infringe Article 81(l)[158]; between one and five years they may do; and agreements of more than five years would normally be caught. Dominant undertakings would have to adduce an objective justification for any agreement that imposes a non-compete obligation on customers.

Where there are parallel networks of single branding agreements, their cumulative effect may be to foreclose access to the market[159]; this would be unlikely where the largest supplier in the market has a market share of less than 30 per cent and the market share of the five largest suppliers is below 50 per cent[160]. Other relevant factors are the level of entry barriers[161], countervailing power[162] and the level of trade affected[163].

(D) The application of Article 81(3) Article 81(3) issues are discussed in paragraphs 153 to 158 of the *Vertical guidelines*: this is considered below[164].

(ii) Exclusive distribution agreements[165]

(A) Possible detriments to intra-brand competition and to market integration A supplier will often grant exclusive distribution rights to a distributor for a particular territory: for example it might appoint X as the exclusive distributor for France and Y as the exclusive distributor for Germany. The supplier may also agree that it will not sell its products directly into the territories granted to X and Y. The Commission's main concern in relation to exclusive distribution agreements, expressed in paragraphs 109 and 110 of the *Vertical guidelines* and repeated at paragraph 161, is that intra-brand competition will be reduced and that the market will be partitioned. The Commission also notes that, when most or all suppliers in a particular market adopt exclusive distribution systems, this may facilitate collusion, both at the suppliers' and the distributors' level of the market; this would entail harm to inter-brand competition.

Case T-65/98 *Van den Bergh Foods Ltd v Commission* [2003] ECR II-4653, [2004] 4 CMLR 14: the same dispute was the subject of an Article 234 reference to the ECJ in Case C-344/98 *Masterfoods Ltd v HB Ice Cream Ltd* [2000] ECR I-11369, [2001] 4 CMLR 449.

[152] *Vertical guidelines*, para 140.   [153] Ibid, para 141.   [154] Ibid.
[155] OJ [2001] L 319/1, [2002] 4 CMLR 405.   [156] Ibid, paras 121–140.   [157] See pp 662–663 below.
[158] See Case C-214/99 *Neste Markkinointi Oy v Yötuuli* [2000] ECR I-11121, [2000] 4 CMLR 993, where the ECJ concluded that exclusive purchasing agreements for petrol of not more than one year's duration did not infringe Article 81(1); see also Case E-7/01 *Hegelstad Eiendomsselskap Arvid B Hegelstad v Hydro Texaco AS* [2003] 4 CMLR 236, where the EFTA Court held that a 15-year fixed term exclusive purchasing agreement for petrol was permissible where it only made an insignificant contribution to the foreclosure of the market.
[159] *Vertical guidelines*, para 142.   [160] Ibid, para 143.   [161] Ibid, para 144.   [162] Ibid, para 145.
[163] Ibid, paras 146–149.   [164] See pp 662–663 below.   [165] *Vertical guidelines*, paras 161–177.

(B) Application of the block exemption to exclusive distribution agreements The block exemption for vertical agreements will apply to exclusive distribution agreements, provided that the supplier's market share is less than 30 per cent and that there are no 'hard-core' restrictions contrary to Article 4[166]. In particular there should be no restrictions on passive sales (sales in response to unsolicited orders)[167] to other territories; where there is a combination of exclusive distribution and selective distribution, there must be no restrictions even of active sales by retailers to end-users[168], and there must be no restrictions on sales between authorised distributors[169]. The *Guidelines* provide guidance for those cases in which individual assessment of agreements is necessary because the block exemption is not applicable[170].

(C) Factors to be considered in determining whether exclusive distribution agreements infringe Article 81(1) The Commission sets out the factors that are to be considered in determining whether Article 81(1) is infringed in paragraphs 163 to 170 of the *Vertical guidelines*. There is no reference to the judgment of the ECJ in *Société Technique Minière v Maschinenbau Ulm*[171], where the Court held that an exclusive distribution agreement does not have as its object the restriction of competition, but must be considered in its market context to determine whether it has this effect. The reason that the ECJ took a stricter line in *Consten and Grundig v Commission*[172] was that in that case the distributor, Consten, was given absolute territorial protection against parallel imports[173]: because of the single market imperative in Community competition law, absolute territorial protection almost always infringes Article 81(1) and only rarely would benefit from Article 81(3)[174]. It is important however to bear in mind that an exclusive distribution agreement may not infringe Article 81(1) at all where there is not the additional element of absolute territorial protection.

As far as Article 81(1) is concerned the Commission states that the market position of the supplier and its competitors is of major importance, since the loss of intra-brand competition is problematic only if inter-brand competition is limited[175]. Where there are strong competitors, the restriction of intra-brand competition will be outweighed by inter-brand competition[176], although there may be a risk of collusion where the number of competitors is 'rather small'[177]. The *Guidelines* also discuss the possibility of exclusive distribution agreements having a foreclosure effect, which is considered unlikely unless the exclusive distributor has buyer power in the downstream market[178]; the *Guidelines* also discuss the relevance of the maturity of the market[179] and of the level of trade affected[180].

(D) The application of Article 81(3) Article 81(3) issues are discussed in paragraphs 171 to 174 of the *Vertical guidelines*; this is considered below[181].

---

[166] On Article 4 of Regulation 2790/99 see pp 652–657 below. [167] Regulation 2790/99, Article 4(b).
[168] Ibid, Article 4(c). [169] Ibid, Article 4(d).
[170] *Vertical guidelines*, para 162. [171] Case 56/65 [1966] ECR 235, [1966] CMLR 357.
[172] Cases 56/64 and 58/64 [1966] ECR 299, [1966] CMLR 418.
[173] See ch 3, pp 124–125; see also the discussion of the two US cases, *Schwinn* and *Sylvania* at p 122, n 365.
[174] See ch 3, pp 124–125. [175] *Vertical guidelines*, para 163. [176] Ibid, para 164.
[177] Ibid, para 164. [178] Ibid, paras 165 and 166. [179] Ibid, para 168. [180] Ibid, paras 169 and 170.
[181] See pp 662–663 below.

(iii) Exclusive customer allocation agreements[182]

Exclusive customer allocation, whereby a supplier agrees to sell its products to a distributor who will resell only to a particular class of customers, is discussed in paragraphs 178 to 183 of the *Vertical guidelines*. Exclusive customer allocation is treated in much the same way as exclusive distribution, although the Commission makes a few specific comments on this particular type of vertical restraint[183]; in particular it says that the criteria of Article 81(3) are unlikely to be met where the market share of 30 per cent is exceeded[184].

(iv) Selective distribution agreements[185]

Selective distribution agreements are often deployed by producers of branded products. The producer establishes a system in which the products can be bought and resold only by officially appointed distributors and retailers. Non-appointed dealers will not be able to obtain the products, and the appointed dealers will be told that they can resell only to other members of the system or to the final consumer[186]. The *Vertical guidelines* state that selective distribution systems may restrict intra-brand competition, may foreclose access to the market and may facilitate collusion between suppliers and buyers[187]. In determining the application of Article 81 to selective distribution agreements, a distinction must be made between a 'purely qualitative' system and a 'quantitative' system; a purely qualitative selective distribution system will not infringe Article 81(1) at all even though, by its very nature, it may involve the restrictions just mentioned.

(A) Purely qualitative selective distribution systems[188] The ECJ held in *Metro v Commission*[189] that:

the Commission was justified in recognising that selective distribution systems constituted, together with others, an aspect of competition which accords with Article 81(1), provided that resellers are chosen on the basis of objective criteria of a qualitative nature relating to the technical qualifications of the reseller and its staff and the suitability of its trading premises and that such conditions are laid down uniformly for all potential resellers and are not applied in a discriminatory fashion. It is true that in such systems of distribution price competition is not generally emphasised either as an exclusive or indeed as a principal factor ... However, although price competition is so important that it can never be eliminated it does not constitute the only effective form of competition or that to which absolute priority must in all circumstances be afforded[190].

The judgment of the ECJ in *Metro* confirmed that the Commission's approach in earlier decisions had been correct[191] and provided the basis for subsequent cases. The ECJ has

---

[182] *Vertical guidelines*, paras 178–183.   [183] Ibid, paras 179–182.   [184] Ibid, para 180.

[185] Ibid, paras 184–198.   [186] Ibid, para 184.   [187] Ibid, para 185.   [188] Ibid, para 185.

[189] Case 26/16 [1977] ECR 1875, [1978] 2 CMLR 44.

[190] [1977] ECR 1875, [1978] 2 CMLR 44, para 21.

[191] The Commission had granted negative clearance to various aspects of the selective distribution networks in *Kodak* JO [1970] L 147/24, [1970] CMLR D19 and *Omega Watches* JO [1970] L 242/22, [1970] CMLR D49; individual exemption was given to other terms.

itself repeated the *Metro* test on several occasions[192], as has the CFI[193]; the Commission has relied on the *Metro* doctrine on various occasions[194]. Three criteria must be satisfied for a system to be treated as purely qualitative and therefore outside Article 81(1).

First, the product in question must be of a type that necessitates selective distribution. It is only in the case of such goods that the suppression of price competition – inherent in selective distribution – in favour of non-price competition is objectively justifiable. It is not only complex equipment such as cars and electronic equipment that has benefited from the *Metro* doctrine. From the judgments of the Community Courts and the decisions of the Commission it is possible to identify three categories of goods that may come within it, although it should be pointed out that this is not a formal classification that they themselves have adopted. The most obvious category consists of products that are technically complex, so that specialist sales staff and a suitable after-sales service are needed. In this category may be placed cars[195], cameras[196], electronic equipment such as hi-fis[197], consumer durables[198], clocks and watches[199], and computers[200]. The second category consists of products the brand image of which is particularly important, such as perfumes and luxury cosmetic products[201], ceramic tableware[202],

---

[192] See eg Case 99/79 *Lancôme SA v Etos BV* [1980] ECR 2511, [1981] 2 CMLR 164, paras 20–26; Case 31/80 *L'Oréal NV v de Nieuwe AMCK* [1980] ECR 3775, [1981] 2 CMLR 235, paras 15–21; Case 126/80 *Maria Salonia v Giorgio Poidomani* [1981] ECR 1563, [1982] 1 CMLR 64; Case 210/81 *Demo-Studio Schmidt v Commission* [1983] ECR 3045, [1984] 1 CMLR 63; Case 107/82 *AEG-Telefunken v Commission* [1983] ECR 3151, [1984] 2 CMLR 325; Case 75/84 *Metro v Commission (No 2)* [1986] ECR 3021, [1987] 1 CMLR 118.

[193] Case T-19/91 *Vichy v Commission* [1992] ECR II-415; Case T-19/92 *Groupement d'Achat Édouard Leclerc v Commission* [1996] ECR II-1851, [1997] 4 CMLR 995; Case T-88/92 *Groupement d'Achat Édouard Leclerc v Commission* [1996] ECR II-1961, [1997] 4 CMLR 995.

[194] *Junghans* OJ [1977] L 30/10, [1977] 1 CMLR D82; *Murat* OJ [1983] L 348/20, [1984] 1 CMLR 219; *SABA (No 2)* OJ [1983] L 376/41, [1984] 1 CMLR 676; *IBM Personal Computers* OJ [1984] L 118/24, [1984] 2 CMLR 342; *Villeroy Boch* OJ [1985] L 376/15, [1988] 4 CMLR 461; *Grundig* OJ [1985] L 233/1, [1988] 4 CMLR 865; *Yves Saint Laurent Parfums SA* OJ [1992] L 12/24, [1993] 4 CMLR 120, mostly upheld on appeal Case T-19/92 *Groupement d'Achat Édouard Leclerc v Commission* [1996] ECR II-1851, [1997] 4 CMLR 995, and given further approval in 2001, Commission Press Release IP/01/713, 17 May 2001; *Parfums Givenchy System of Selective Distribution* OJ [1992] L 236/11, [1993] 5 CMLR 579, mostly upheld on appeal Case T-88/92 *Groupement d'Achat Édouard Leclerc v Commission* [1996] ECR II-1961, [1997] 4 CMLR 995: an application by Kruidvat challenging the Commission's decision in this case was found to be inadmissible in Case T-87/92 *BVBA Kruidvat v Commission* [1996] ECR II-1931, [1997] 4 CMLR 1046, upheld on appeal Case C-70/97 P *Kruidvat v Commission* [1998] ECR I-7183, [1999] 4 CMLR 68; *Kenwood Electronics Deutschland GmbH* OJ [1993] C 67/9, [1993] 4 CMLR 389; *Schott-Zwiesel-Glaswerke* OJ [1993] C 111/4, [1993] 5 CMLR 85; *Grundig* OJ [1994] L 20/15, [1995] 4 CMLR 658; *Sony España SA* OJ [1993] C 275/3, [1994] 4 CMLR 581.

[195] *BMW* OJ [1975] L 29/1, [1975] 1 CMLR D44; note that there is a specific block exemption for the distribution of cars, Regulation 1400/2002: see pp 663–666 below.

[196] *Kodak* JO [1970] L 147/24, [1970] CMLR D19.

[197] *Grundig* OJ [1985] L 223/1, [1988] 4 CMLR 865 and again OJ [1994] L 20/15, [1995] 4 CMLR 658.

[198] Case 107/82 *AEG-Telefunken v Commission* [1983] ECR 3151, [1984] 3 CMLR 325; it was only when AEG's system was applied in a discriminatory way that it came within Article 81(1).

[199] *Omega Watches* JO [1970] L 242/22, [1970] CMLR D49; *Junghans* OJ [1977] L 30/10, [1977] 1 CMLR D82; note however that the ECJ in Case 31/85 *ETA Fabriques d'Ebauches SA v DK Investment SA* [1985] ECR 3933, [1986] 2 CMLR 674 doubted that mass-produced Swatch watches would qualify for selective distribution under the *Metro* doctrine: ibid, para 16.

[200] *IBM Personal Computers* OJ [1984] L 118/24, [1984] 2 CMLR 342.

[201] Case 99/79 *Lancôme SA etc v Etos BV* [1980] ECR 2511, [1981] 2 CMLR 164; Case T-19/92 *Groupement d'Achat Édouard Leclerc v Commission* [1996] ECR II-1851, [1997] 4 CMLR 995, paras 113–123; Case T-88/92 *Groupement d'Achat Édouard Leclerc v Commission* [1996] ECR II-1961, [1997] 4 CMLR 995, paras 105–117.

[202] *Villeroy Boch* OJ [1985] L 376/15, [1988] 4 CMLR 461.

and gold and silver jewellery[203]. A third category is newspapers, the special characteristic of which is their extremely short shelf-life which necessitates particularly careful distribution[204]. The Commission has doubted whether plumbing fittings qualify for such treatment[205].

The second requirement for the *Metro* doctrine to apply is that the criteria by which a producer may limit the retail outlets through which its products are resold must be purely qualitative in nature, laid down uniformly for all potential resellers and applied in a non-discriminatory manner[206]. Where this is the case, any dealer that can satisfy the qualitative criteria should be able to obtain the products in question: there is no direct, quantitative, restriction on the number of dealers in the system. A producer may require that its goods be sold only to retail outlets which employ suitably trained staff, have suitable premises in an appropriate area, use a suitable shop name consistent with the status of the brand, and provide a proper after-sales service; also a restriction on sales to non-authorised distributors and retailers is permitted, as is a restriction not to advertise products at 'cash-and-carry prices'. A problem is that it is not always obvious whether a particular requirement is 'qualitative' or not. Criteria that do not relate to the technical proficiency of outlets but extend to such matters as the holding of minimum stocks, stocking the complete range of products, the achievement of a minimum turnover or a minimum percentage of turnover[207] in the products in question and the promotion of products have sometimes been treated as quantitative, although they have often been found to satisfy the criteria of Article 81(3)[208].

In *Vichy*[209] the Commission decided that a restriction on the sale of Vichy products except to officially appointed pharmacists was quantitative rather than qualitative, thus bringing the selective distribution system within Article 81(1). In *Yves Saint Laurent*[210] the Commission concluded that provisions on admission to the producer's network, a minimum annual purchase figure and obligations on the carrying of stocks, stock rotation and cooperation in advertising and promotion infringed Article 81(1). The Commission is more comfortable with selective distribution systems which contain

---

[203] *Murat* OJ [1983] L 348/20, [1984] 1 CMLR 219.

[204] See eg Case 126/80 *Maria Salonia v Giorgio Poidomani* [1981] ECR 1563, [1982] 1 CMLR 64; Case 243/83 *Binon v Agence et Messageries de la Presse* [1985] ECR 2015, [1985] 3 CMLR 800; Commission's Notice *Agence et Messageries de la Presse* OJ [1987] C 164/2; Commission's XXIXth *Report on Competition Policy* (1999) pp 161–162.

[205] *Grohe* OJ [1985] L 19/17, [1988] 4 CMLR 612; *Ideal Standard* OJ [1985] L 20/38, [1988] 4 CMLR 627.

[206] For an example of the discriminatory application of a purely qualitative selective distribution system see Case 107/82 *AEG-Telefunken v Commission* [1983] ECR 3151, [1984] 3 CMLR 325, in particular at para 39; where a producer refuses to supply to certain distributors or retailers, the problem arises of whether this refusal is attributable to an agreement or concerted practice, or whether it is a unilateral act and therefore outside Article 81(1): see ch 3, pp 107–113.

[207] Case T-19/92 *Groupement d'Achat Édouard Leclerc v Commission* [1996] ECR II-1851, [1997] 4 CMLR 995, paras 148–155; Case T-88/92 *Groupement d'Achat Édouard Leclerc v Commission* [1996] ECR II-1961, [1997] 4 CMLR 995, paras 141–148.

[208] See eg *Parfums Givenchy* OJ [1992] L 236/11, [1993] 5 CMLR 579; *Grundig* OJ [1994] L 20/15, [1995] 4 CMLR 658.

[209] OJ [1991] L 75/57, upheld on appeal Case T-19/91 [1992] ECR II-415.

[210] OJ [1992] L 12/24, [1993] 4 CMLR 120, mostly upheld on appeal Case T-19/92 *Groupement d'Achat Édouard Leclerc v Commission* [1996] ECR II-1851, [1997] 4 CMLR 995; see also Commission Press Release IP/01/713, 17 May 2001, confirming that Yves Saint Laurent's selective distribution system fell within the block exemption.

a formal procedure for determining whether a particular undertaking qualifies for admission[211].

Selective distribution systems that are within Article 81(1), for example because they contain quantitative as well as qualitative elements, may benefit from the block exemption provided by Regulation 2790/99 provided that its conditions are satisfied[212].

The third requirement of the *Metro* doctrine is that any restrictions that are imposed on appointed distributors and retailers must go no further than is objectively necessary to protect the quality of the product in question: this is a manifestation of the doctrine of proportionality. In *Hasselblad*[213] objection was taken by the Commission to provisions which enabled the producer to exercise supervision of the advertising of its distributors and retailers, as this would mean that control could be exercised over advertisements indicating cuts in prices. In *AEG-Telefunken v Commission*[214] the ECJ made clear that restrictions would not be permitted simply in order to guarantee dealers a minimum profit margin. In *Grohe*[215] and *Ideal Standard*[216] restrictions were imposed on plumbing wholesalers not to resell to anyone but plumbing contractors. Sale and installation of plumbing fittings are separate functions and the laws of Member States require major plumbing work to be done by official plumbers. The Commission decided that this provision did involve a restriction of competition for the purposes of Article 81(1) as it was not necessary for producers to control the quality of plumbing work; the Commission also concluded that the agreements did not satisfy the criteria of Article 81(3).

(B) Selective distribution systems that are not purely qualitative Where a selective distribution system is not purely qualitative in the sense of the *Metro* doctrine it may be caught by Article 81(1), although it may also benefit from the block exemption conferred by Regulation 2790/99[217] or satisfy Article 81(3) on an individual basis[218]. In determining whether Article 81(1) is infringed the Commission will look at the market position of the supplier and its competitors, since the loss of intra-brand competition is problematic only where inter-brand competition is weak[219]. A further issue is whether, in a particular market, there is a number of selective distribution systems in operation: where this is the case the Commission is anxious that there may be a lack of intra-brand competition, a foreclosure of certain types of distributors and retailers and that collusion may be facilitated[220]. In *Metro v Commission (No 2)*[221] the ECJ had warned that where, in a particular market, the existence of a number of selective distribution systems leaves no room for other methods of distribution or results in a rigidity in price structure which is not balanced by other types of competition, Article 81(1) may apply after all[222].

---

[211] See eg *Sony Pan-European Dealer Agreement (PEDA)*, Commission's XXVth *Report on Competition Policy* (1995), pp 135–136.

[212] See pp 634–635 and 656–657 below.   [213] OJ [1982] L 161/18, [1982] 2 CMLR 233.

[214] Case 107/82 [1983] ECR 3151, [1984] 3 CMLR 325, para 42.

[215] OJ [1985] L 19/17, [1988] 4 CMLR 612.   [216] OJ [1985] L 20/38, [1988] 4 CMLR 627.

[217] See pp 640–642 below.   [218] See pp 662–663 below.   [219] *Vertical guidelines*, para 187.

[220] Ibid, para 188.   [221] Case 75/84 [1986] ECR 3021, [1987] 1 CMLR 118.

[222] [1986] ECR 3021, [1987] 1 CMLR 118, paras 41 and 42; a similar argument was considered, but rejected, in Case T-19/92 *Groupement d'Achat Édouard Leclerc v Commission* [1996] ECR II-1851, [1997] 4 CMLR 995, paras 178–192 and in Case T-88/92 *Groupement d'Achat Édouard Leclerc v Commission* [1996] ECR II-1961, [1997] 4 CMLR 995, paras 170–184.

(C) Application of the block exemption to selective distribution systems Selective distribution agreements may benefit from the block exemption conferred by Regulation 2790/99. To do so the producer's market share must be below 30 per cent[223], and the requirements of Articles 4(a), 4(c), 4(d), and 5(c)[224] must be respected. Where a selective distribution system benefits from the block exemption, but there are minimal efficiency-enhancing effects, for example because the product is not suitable for this form of distribution, the Commission may withdraw the block exemption[225]. The Commission has indicated that it would consider withdrawing the benefit of the block exemption from selective distribution systems where there is a cumulative effect problem; however it says that such a problem is unlikely to arise when the share of the market covered by selective distribution is below 50 per cent, or where this figure is exceeded but the aggregate market share of the five largest suppliers is below 50 per cent[226]. An individual supplier with a market share of less than 5 per cent is unlikely to be considered as making a contribution to the cumulative effect[227].

In its decision in *Yamaha*[228] the Commission imposed a fine of €2.56 million on Yamaha for operating a selective distribution system in a way that led to the partitioning of the single market and to the fixing of resale prices. The Commission objected to a series of restrictions imposed on its dealers[229], including:

- obligations on official distributors to sell only to final customers, since this amounted to a restriction on cross-supplies within the network

- obligations on official distributors to purchase exclusively from the Yamaha national subsidiary, as this could inhibit cross-border trade

- obligations on official distributors to supply solely to distributors authorised by the national subsidiary of Yamaha, for the same reason

- obligations on official distributors to contact Yamaha before exporting via the Internet, in relation to which sales there should have been no restriction

- territorial protection concerning the manufacturer's guarantees

- restrictions of parallel trade in Iceland

- the fixing of resale prices.

The selective distribution system in Yamaha failed to benefit from the block exemption partly because in several markets Yamaha's market share exceeded 30 per cent[230] and partly because there were violations of Articles 4(a), (b) and (d)[231].

In some systems of domestic law a selective distribution system is binding on unauthorised third parties, who can be sued for unfair competition if they obtain and attempt to sell the products; in German law there is a requirement on the producer which uses such a system to ensure that it is 'impervious', that is to say that its products are kept

---

[223] See pp 650–652 below.

[224] See *Vertical guidelines*, para 192; these provisions are explained at pp 652–657 below.

[225] Ibid, para 186.   [226] Ibid, para 189.

[227] Ibid, para 189, final sentence; see also the Commission's *Notice on Agreements of Minor Importance* OJ [2001] C 368/13, [2002] 4 CMLR 699, para 8.

[228] Commission decision of 16 July 2003.

[229] Ibid, para 88; each of the offending restrictions is analysed in the paragraphs following paragraph 88.

[230] Ibid, para 168.   [231] Ibid, paras 169–174.

within the system; however the imperviousness ('lückenlosigkeit') of the system is not a requirement for its validity under EC law[232].

(v) Franchising agreements[233]

(A) Pronuptia v Schillgalis The application to franchising agreements of Article 81 was explored by the ECJ in *Pronuptia de Paris v Schillgalis*[234]. Mrs Schillgalis, the franchisee for Hamburg, Oldenburg, and Hanover, was in dispute with Pronuptia, the franchisor, over her royalty payments and in the course of litigation pleaded that the agreement was void as it contravened Article 81. The ECJ identified the crux of a franchise system: that it enables a franchisee to operate as an independent business whilst using the name and know-how of the franchisor. The transfer of intellectual property rights from the franchisor to the franchisee is the feature of franchises that distinguishes them from more conventional distribution systems. In a franchise, the franchisee pays a fee to the franchisor for the right to use the know-how, trade marks, designs, logos and other intellectual property rights of the franchisor. In order for the franchise system to work effectively it is essential that each franchisee should conform with the uniform commercial methods laid down by the franchisor: from the public's point of view, it is important that all franchised outlets should achieve the same standard. Therefore it is essential that the franchisor should be able to impose common standards on all franchisees. Also, as the transfer of intellectual property rights is vital to the whole exercise, it is legitimate for the franchisor to impose terms on the franchisee to protect these rights. The ECJ concluded that restrictions in these two categories, that is to maintain common standards and to protect intellectual property rights, were not within Article 81(1) at all. However restrictions that could divide the market territorially or which imposed resale price maintenance would be within Article 81(1); the former might be granted exemption under Article 81(3), though not the latter.

(B) The position of the commission after Pronuptia The Commission published several individual decisions after this judgment in which it was able to expand upon the main principles laid down by the ECJ. These decisions granted individual exemption to territorial restrictions, and culminated in the publication of a block exemption for franchise agreements in 1988[235]. In *Pronuptia*[236] and *Yves Rocher*[237] the franchisor selected or manufactured the goods sold by the franchisee. In *Computerland*[238] the franchisee was free to acquire microcomputers wherever it wished: the subject-matter of the franchise was the distribution method supplied by Computerland. In *ServiceMaster*[239] the Commission reached a decision on a service franchise for the supply of housekeeping, cleaning and maintenance services to both commercial and domestic customers.

---

[232] Case C-376/92 *Metro-SB-Großmärkte GmbH v Cartier* [1994] ECR I-15, [1994] 5 CMLR 331, para 28; see also Case C-41/96 *VAG-Händlerbeirat eV v SYD-Consult* [1997] ECR I-3123, [1997] 5 CMLR 537.

[233] *Vertical guidelines*, paras 199–201.

[234] Case 161/84 [1986] ECR 353, [1986] 1 CMLR 414; see Dubois 'Franchising Under EC Competition Law: Implications of the *Pronuptia* Judgment and the Proposed Block Exemption' [1986] Fordham Corporate Law Institute ch 6; Waelbroeck 'The *Pronuptia* Judgment – A Critical Appraisal' [1986] Fordham Corporate Law Institute ch 9; Venit '*Pronuptia*: Ancillary Restraints or Unholy Alliances' (1986) 11 EL Rev 213.

[235] Regulation 4087/88, OJ [1988] L 359/46.   [236] OJ [1987] L 13/39, [1989] 4 CMLR 355.

[237] OJ [1987] L 8/49, [1988] 4 CMLR 592.   [238] OJ [1987] L 222/12, [1989] 4 CMLR 259.

[239] OJ [1988] L 332/38, [1989] 4 CMLR 581.

It considered that there were strong similarities between a service franchise and the franchises relating to the distribution of goods dealt with in earlier decisions[240] and granted an individual exemption. In *Charles Jourdan*[241] the Commission granted individual exemption to a franchise system for the sale of medium and top quality shoes.

(C) The commission's guidelines on franchising The *Vertical guidelines* discuss franchising at paragraphs 199 to 201. Paragraph 199 describes what franchising systems typically consist of and how they work. Paragraph 200 refers to paragraphs 23 to 45, which deal specifically with the meaning of vertical agreements in the block exemption and the extent to which the licensing of intellectual property rights, including franchise agreements, are covered by it[242]. Examples of franchise agreements are given in paragraph 201.

(vi) Exclusive supply agreements[243]

An exclusive supply agreement, as defined in Article 1(c) of the block exemption[244], is one that causes a supplier to sell its products only to one buyer within the European Community for the purposes of a specific use or resale. As such it is an 'extreme form of limited distribution' agreement[245]. Exclusive supply agreements may benefit from the block exemption, but in such cases it is the market share of the buyer rather than the seller that must be looked at when applying the 30 per cent market share cap[246]. Paragraphs 204 to 210 discuss the application of Article 81(1) to exclusive supply agreements that are not covered by the block exemption; paragraphs 211 and 212 consider the application of Article 81(3)[247]. In considering whether Article 81(1) applies to such agreements the buyer's market share in its downstream market will be of particular importance: the greater its market share there, the more likely there is to be an anticompetitive effect[248]; the duration of the supply obligation will also be of relevance[249]. Other matters, such as entry barriers[250], the countervailing power of suppliers[251] and the level of trade affected[252], are also discussed.

(vii) Tying agreements[253]

A tying agreement arises where a supplier makes the supply of one product (the 'tying product') conditional upon the buyer also buying a separate product (the 'tied product'). Tying may infringe Article 82 where the supplier has a dominant position[254]; however, a vertical agreement imposing a tie may also infringe Article 81(1) where it has a 'single branding' effect in relation to the tied product[255]. Tying agreements benefit from the block exemption when the market share of the supplier on the markets both for the tying and for the tied products is below the 30 per cent cap in Article 3(1) of Regulation 2790/99[256]. Where the market share threshold is exceeded paragraphs 219 to 221 discuss the application of Article 81 (1) to tying agreements: the market position of the supplier is the most important issue[257]; the position of its competitors and the

---

[240] OJ [1988] L 332/38, [1989] 4 CMLR 581, para 6.
[241] OJ [1989] L 35/31, [1989] 4 CMLR 591.
[242] On Article 2(3) of Regulation 2790/99 see pp 646–648 below.
[243] *Vertical guidelines*, paras 202–214.   [244] See p 641 below.   [245] *Vertical guidelines*, para 202.
[246] On Article 3(2) of Regulation 2790/99 see p 651 below and the *Vertical guidelines*, para 203.
[247] See pp 662–663 below.   [248] *Vertical guidelines*, para 204.   [249] Ibid, para 205.   [250] Ibid, para 207.
[251] Ibid, para 208.   [252] Ibid, para 209.   [253] Ibid, paras 215–224.   [254] See ch 17, pp 679–687.
[255] *Vertical guidelines*, para 215.   [256] Ibid, para 218.   [257] Ibid, para 219.

height of the entry barriers to the market for the tying product must also be considered[258]. Tying is less likely to be problematic where customers possess buyer power[259]. Paragraphs 222 to 224 consider the possibility of tying practices benefiting from the provisions in Article 81(3)[260].

(viii) Recommended and maximum resale prices[261]

(A) Minimum and fixed resale prices infringe Article 81(1) The imposition upon distributors and retailers of minimum or fixed resale prices will be held to infringe Article 81(1): such agreements are considered to have as their object the restriction of competition[262]. Furthermore this practice amounts to a hard-core restriction contrary to Article 4(a) of the block exemption[263]; paragraph 47 of the *Guidelines* considers a range of practices that might be considered as having as their 'direct or indirect object', to use the words of Article 4, the imposition of minimum or fixed resale prices[264].

(B) Could minimum and fixed prices satisfy Article 81(3)? An interesting question is whether minimum or fixed resale price maintenance could ever satisfy the criteria of Article 81(3). On one occasion the Commission appeared to be sympathetic to the idea that a newspaper publisher should be allowed to impose a cover price on newspapers[265], although it never revealed publicly what conclusion it reached on the matter. In recent years there has been a growing body of opinion sympathetic to the possibility that, in some cases, there may be efficiency arguments in favour of resale price maintenance[266]. It should be recalled that the CFI in *Matra Hachette v Commission*[267] has ruled that the parties to any kind of agreement are entitled to defend it under Article 81(3)[268], and that the Commission has set out, in its *Guidelines on Article 81(3)*[269], the type of evidence that is required in support of a defence. In principle there is no reason to believe that a defence of resale price maintenance under Article 81(3) could never succeed. The US Supreme Court judgment in *Leegin* points to the same conclusion.[269a]

---

[258] Ibid, para 220.   [259] Ibid, para 221.   [260] See pp 662–663 below.

[261] *Vertical guidelines*, paras 225–228.

[262] See ch 3, p 119; minimum and fixed resale prices will also infringe the Chapter I prohibition in the UK Competition Act 1998: see pp 667–670 below; in the US the maintenance of minimum resale prices was for many years illegal *per se* as a result of the Supreme Court decision in *Dr Miles Medical Co v John D Park & Sons Co* 220 US 373 (1911); however in *Leegin Creative Leather Products, Inc v PSKS, Inc* 551 US § (2007), the Supreme Court explicitly overruled *Dr Miles*, holding that resale price maintenance should be subject to a rule of reason standard henceforth; for discussion of *per se* rules and the rule of reason in US law see ch 3, pp 131–132.

[263] See pp 653–654 below; see generally Iacobucci 'The Case for Prohibiting Resale Price Maintenance' (1995) 19(2) World Competition 71.

[264] See p 654 below on para 47 of the *Vertical guidelines*.

[265] See the Commission's XXIXth *Report on Competition Policy* (1999) pp 161–162; the Commission's Notice in *Agence et Messageries de la Presse* OJ [1987] C 164/2 had suggested that it might countenance resale price maintenance for newspapers and periodicals; see also Case 243/85 *Binon & Cie v SA Agence et Messageries de la Presse* [1985] ECR 2015, [1985] 3 CMLR 800, para 46.

[266] See eg Van den Bergh and Camesasca *European Competition Law and Economics: A Comparative Perspective* (Sweet & Maxwell, 2006), pp 208–214.

[267] Case T-17/93 [1994] ECR II-595.   [268] See ch 4, pp 150–151.

[269] OJ [2004] C 101/97.   [269a] See n 262 above.

(C) Judgments and decisional practice on resale price maintenance The Commission has condemned resale price maintenance on various occasions[270]. In *Pronuptia de Paris v Schillgalis*[271] the ECJ held that resale price maintenance in the context of a franchising network infringed Article 81(1) and did not satisfy Article 81(3); however the Court did not object to recommended prices. The Commission's decision in *Volkswagen*[272] imposing a fine of €30.96 million for retail price maintenance in Germany was annulled on appeal to the CFI on the ground that the Commission had failed to demonstrate that there was an agreement or concerted practice between Volkswagen and its dealers[273].

(D) Recommended and maximum resale prices Paragraphs 225 to 228 of the *Vertical guidelines* consider the extent to which it is lawful to recommend a resale price to a distributor or retailer or to impose a *maximum* rather than a minimum price[274]. Article 4(a) of the block exemption provides that these practices are not 'hard-core' restrictions, 'provided that they do not amount to a fixed or minimum sale price as a result of pressure from, or incentives offered by, any of the parties'. Agreements containing recommendations or maximum prices would therefore be exempt, provided that the market share cap of 30 per cent is not exceeded[275]. Where the block exemption is not applicable the Commission states at paragraph 226 of the *Guidelines* that it will consider whether recommended or maximum prices might work 'as a focal point for the resellers and might be followed by most or all of them'[276]; it will also examine whether these practices could facilitate collusion between suppliers[277]. The market power of the supplier is the most important factor to be taken into consideration[278]; the next most important issue will be the structure of the market: in particular the Commission considers that, if it is oligopolistic, there is a greater likelihood of collusion[279]. In its Notice in the Official Journal in the case of *Repsol CPP SA* the Commission said that it had no concern about maximum price clauses in agreements between Repsol and service stations selling its fuels[280].

---

[270] See eg *Deutsche Phillips* OJ [1973] L 293/40, [1973] CMLR D241; *Gerofabriek* OJ [1977] L 16/8, [1977] 1 CMLR D35; *Hennessey/Henkel* OJ [1980] L 383/11, [1981] 1 CMLR 601 where the Commission rejected the argument that setting resale prices was justified for the protection of the product's brand image; *Novalliance/Systemform* OJ [1997] L 47/11, [1997] 4 CMLR 876; *Nathan-Bricolux* OJ [2001] L 54/1, [2001] 4 CMLR 1122, paras 86–90; *JCB* OJ [2002] L 69/1, [2002] 4 CMLR 1458, paras 168–173; *CD prices* Commission Press Release IP/01/1212, 17 August 2001; *Yamaha*, Commission Press Release IP/03/1028, 16 July 2003.

[271] Case 161/84, [1986] ECR 353, [1986] 1 CMLR 414.   [272] OJ [2001] L 262/14, [2001] 5 CMLR 1309.

[273] Case T-208/01 *Volkswagen v Commission* [2003] ECR II-5141, [2004] 4 CMLR 727; on appeal to the ECJ the ECJ agreed that the Commission's decision should be annulled, but on different grounds from those of the CFI: Case C-74/04 P *Commission v Volkswagen AG* [2006] ECR I-6585; for discussion see ch 3, p 112.

[274] In *Albrecht v Herald Co* 390 US 145 (1968) the US Supreme Court condemned *per se* the imposition of maximum resale prices; however it overruled itself in *State Oil v Khan*, substituting a rule of reason approach to this particular phenomenon: 522 US 3 (1997); see Steuer '*Khan* and the Issue of Dealer Power – Overview' (1997–98) 66 Antitrust Law Journal 531; Blair and Lopatka '*Albrecht* Overruled – At Last' ibid, 537; Gimes 'Making Sense of *State Oil Co v Khan*: Vertical Maximum Price Fixing under a Rule of Reason' ibid, 567.

[275] *Vertical guidelines*, para 225.   [276] Ibid, para 226.   [277] Ibid, para 226.   [278] Ibid, para 227.

[279] Ibid, para 228.   [280] OJ [2004] C 258/9, paras 18–20.

7. THE PATH TO REFORM OF THE BLOCK EXEMPTIONS[281]

It was explained above that the Commission over many years tended to adopt a formalistic approach to the application of Article 81(1); as a result it was necessary for
many agreements to be brought within the 'safe haven' of one of the Commission's block
exemptions. It adopted Regulation 1983/83 for exclusive distribution agreements[282],
Regulation 1984/83 for exclusive purchasing agreements[283] and Regulation 4087/88 for
franchise agreements[284]. However these Regulations were themselves too formalistic
(insufficiently economics-oriented) in their approach; and many vertical agreements
were not covered at all. Criticism of the decisional practice of the Commission in relation to vertical agreements increased throughout the 1980s and 1990s, both as to its
over-application of Article 81(1) and the content of the block exemptions. The drum-
beat of the calls for reform became ever louder. An important contribution was made
at the Fordham Corporate Law Institute in 1995 when a senior economist within DG
COMP, David Deacon, acknowledged that it was necessary to rethink the application
of Article 81 to vertical agreements[285]. Professor Barry Hawk wrote an article in which
he described a systemic failure in the treatment of vertical agreements under Article 81
necessitating radical reform[286]. The Commission responded, first with its *Green Paper
on Vertical Restraints in EC Competition Policy*[287] suggesting a range of possible options
for reform. More concrete proposals were set out in the Commission's *Follow-up to
the Green Paper on Vertical Restraints*[288]. In this document the Commission concluded
that a more economics-based approach to vertical agreements was required. One broad
'umbrella' block exemption would be adopted for all vertical agreements in both the
goods and services sector (with the exception of the distribution of motor cars). A market-share test would be adopted; and there would be only a 'black-list' approach, to say
what agreements were not block exempted, without a corresponding 'white-list' stating
what could be block exempted: this would avoid the 'strait-jacketing' effect of the old
Regulations and simplify the rules.

---

[281] Part of the text that follows is based on the author's article 'Regulation 2790/99: the Commission's
"New Style" Block Exemption for Vertical Agreements' (2000) 37 CML Rev 887; see also Schaub 'Vertical
Restraints: Key Points and Issues under the New EC Block Exemption Regulation' [2000] Fordham
Corporate Law Institute (ed Hawk), p 201; Subiotto and Amato 'Preliminary Analysis of the Commission's
Reform Concerning Vertical Restraints' (2000) 23(2) World Competition 5; Taylor 'The Vertical Agreements
Regulation – A Critical Appraisal' (2000) 3 Cambridge Yearbook of European Legal Studies 525; Subiotto
and Amato 'The Reform of the European Competition Policy concerning Vertical Restraints' (2001–02)
69 Antitrust Law Journal 147; Korah and O'Sullivan *Distribution Agreements under the EC Competition
Rules* (Hart Publishing, 2002); Verouden 'Vertical Agreements and Article 81(1) EC: The Evolving Role of
Economic Analysis' (2003) 71 Antitrust Law Journal 525; Goyder *EU Distribution Law* (Hart Publishing,
4th ed, 2004); Robertson *Distribution Agreements Under EC Competition Law: An Analytical Review* (in
press, 2008).

[282] OJ [1983] L 173/1.　[283] OJ [1983] L 173/5.　[284] OJ [1988] L 359/46.

[285] Deacon 'Vertical Restraints under EU Competition Law: New Directions' [1995] Fordham Corporate
Law Institute (ed Hawk), p 307.

[286] 'System Failure: Vertical Restraints and EC Competition Law' (1995) 32 CML Rev 973.

[287] COM(96) 721 final, [1997] 4 CMLR 519; see the Commission's XXVIth *Report on Competition Policy*
(1996), points 46–50.

[288] OJ [1998] C 365/3, [1999] 4 CMLR 281; see the Commission's XXVIIIth *Report on Competition Policy*
(1998), points 34–53.

8. VERTICAL AGREEMENTS: REGULATION 2790/99

The Commission adopted the block exemption on Vertical Agreements and Concerted Practices on 22 December 1999[289]. The Regulation entered fully into force on 1 June 2000[290]. The existing block exemptions for exclusive distribution, exclusive purchasing and franchising agreements were prolonged until 31 May 2000 by virtue of Article 12(1) of the new Regulation: Article 12(1) was made effective from 1 January 2000[291]. Article 12(2) provided transitional relief for existing agreements which were in force on 31 May 2000 and which satisfied one of the three existing regulations but not the new one: they were exempt until 31 December 2001. The new Regulation is without prejudice to the application of Article 82[292]. The *Vertical guidelines* were approved by the Commission on 24 May 2000 and were published in the Official Journal in October[293]. The Commission's Press Release issued at the time of the approval of the *Guidelines* stated that they would be revised after a period of four years[294], though this has not happened; instead the Commission is now considering what changes, if any, should be made when Regulation 2790/99 expires in 2010[295].

The Regulation consists of 17 Recitals and 13 Articles. Article 1 defines certain key terms such as 'competing undertakings', 'non-compete obligation' and 'exclusive supply obligation'. The most important terms of all in the Regulation – 'vertical agreements' and 'vertical restraints' – are defined in Article 2. Article 2 is the provision that actually confers block exemption upon certain vertical agreements pursuant to Article 81(3) of the Treaty; Article 3 imposes a market share cap of 30 per cent. Article 4 sets out the 'black list' of provisions that will prevent the block exemption from applying to an agreement. Article 5 sets out a list of obligations that will not be exempt if they are contained in an agreement: it is important to note however that the inclusion of Article 5 obligations does not prevent the block exemption from applying to the remainder of the agreement.

Articles 6 and 7 provide respectively for the possibility of the Commission or the competent authority of a Member State to withdraw the benefit of the block exemption in certain circumstances. Article 8 gives the power to the Commission by regulation to disapply the block exemption to vertical agreements containing specific restraints in a relevant market more than 50 per cent of which is covered by parallel networks of similar vertical restraints. Articles 9 and 10 contain provisions on the calculation of market share and turnover. Article 11 brings 'connected undertakings' into account when applying the Regulation. Articles 12 and 13, as already noted, deal with entry into force of the Regulation and transitional matters.

(A) Article 1: definitions

Article 1 contains important definitions. These will be explained below, in the specific context in which they are used in the Regulation. Two particular definitions merit a brief explanation at this stage. First, the term 'non-compete obligation'. It is important when applying Article 5, which limits the permissible maximum duration of such

---

[289] Regulation 2790/99 OJ [1999] L 336/21, [2000] 4 CMLR 398; see the Commission's XXIXth *Report on Competition Policy* (1999), points 8–19.

[290] Regulation 2790/99, Article 13.   [291] Article 13, proviso to the second indent.

[292] See Recital 16; on the relationship between Article 81(3) exemption and Article 82 abuse see ch 4, p 159.

[293] OJ [2000] C 291/1, [2000] 5 CMLR 1074.   [294] IP/00/520, 24 May 2000.   [295] See p 662 below.

provisions[296]. Article 1(b) provides that 'non-compete obligation' means an obligation not to manufacture, purchase, sell or resell goods or services which compete with the contract goods or services: this is what most people would understand by this expression. However Article 1(b) goes on to provide that the term also includes any obligation on the buyer to purchase from the supplier or from an undertaking designated by the supplier more than 80 per cent[297] of the buyer's total purchases of the contract goods or services and their substitutes on the relevant market, calculated on the basis of the value of its purchases in the preceding year. The Commission's concern is not just that a 100 per cent requirements contract could foreclose access to the market, but that lesser commitments of 'more than 80 per cent' also might do so.

The second definition meriting a brief mention is 'exclusive supply obligation' in Article 1(c). This term is important when applying Article 3(2), which establishes a market share cap for application of the block exemption[298]. Normally the market share of the *supplier* is the measure to be used; however, where there is an exclusive supply obligation in the sense of Article 1(c), the market share is that of the buyer[299].

(B) Article 2: scope of the block exemption

(i) Article 2(1): block exemption for vertical agreements[300]

Article 2(1) confers block exemption on certain vertical agreements pursuant to Article 81(3) of the Treaty. It provides that, subject to the provisions of the Regulation, Article 81(1) shall not apply:

to agreements or concerted practices entered into between two or more undertakings each of which operates, for the purposes of the agreement, at a different level of the production or distribution chain, and relating to the conditions under which the parties may purchase, sell or resell certain goods or services ('vertical agreements').

This exemption shall apply to the extent that such agreements contain restrictions of competition falling within the scope of Article 81(1) ('vertical restraints').

Several points should be noted about Article 2(1).

(ii) Many vertical agreements do not infringe Article 81(1)

It is worth repeating that many vertical agreements do not infringe Article 81(1)[301]; where an agreement does not infringe Article 81(1) it follows that, no matter how generous and flexible the new Regulation is, it will not be necessary to bring the agreement in question within its terms. Despite this, however, many advisers will endeavour to satisfy the block exemption, which provides a 'safe haven' for many vertical agreements: as explained earlier, most firms will have no interest in knowing whether their agreement infringes Article 81(1) if they know that they benefit from exemption under Article 81(3) anyway[302]. The Commission itself, at paragraph 62 of the *Vertical guidelines*, states that

---

[296] See pp 657–659 below.

[297] A literal interpretation would mean that an obligation to purchase 80 per cent of the buyer's total purchases would not amount to a non-compete obligation, but that an obligation to purchase 81 per cent would, since only the latter applies to 'more than 80 per cent'.

[298] See p 651 below.

[299] The term 'buyer' is itself defined in Article 1(g) to include an undertaking which, under an agreement falling within Article 81(1), sells goods or services on behalf of another undertaking.

[300] *Vertical guidelines*, paras 23–25.   [301] See pp 618ff above.   [302] See p 618 above.

vertical agreements falling outside the block exemption will not be presumed to be illegal but may need individual examination, and that in such cases the burden would be on the Commission to show that the agreement violates Article 81(1); in the case of such a violation, the parties could argue that the conditions of Article 81(3) are satisfied[303]. An example of a vertical agreement not infringing Article 81(1) would be a selective distribution system that satisfies the *Metro* doctrine[304]; only to the extent that it does not satisfy that doctrine – for example because the product is not of the type to which the doctrine applies[305] or because quantitative as well as qualitative criteria are applied[306] – is it necessary to have resort to the block exemption.

(iii) If it is not forbidden, it is permitted

A second point to stress about the Regulation is that, in relation to a vertical agreement as defined in Article 2, if the Regulation does not prohibit something, it is permitted. This is the consequence of not having a 'white list', stating what must be included, but only a 'black list', stating what must not be in it, and is an essential feature of the 'new style' block exemption. For example Regulation 1983/83 applied only to an agreement 'whereby one party agrees with the other to supply certain goods for resale within the whole or a defined area of the common market only to that other'[307]. Block exemption is available under the Regulation 2790/99 to all vertical agreements, as defined, subject to Articles 2(2), 2(4) and (5) on agreements made by associations of retailers, agreements between competing undertakings and agreements subject to other block exemptions, Article 3 on market share, and to Articles 4 and 5 which deal with particular vertical restraints that the Commission has concerns about.

(iv) The definition of a vertical agreement is taken from Regulation 1215/99

The definition of a vertical agreement is identical to Council Regulation 1215/99[308], which broadened the *vires* of the Commission in order to enable it to adopt the new Regulation, and specifically to enable agreements concerning intermediate (non-finished) goods and services to be included. Subject to Articles 2(2), 2(4) and (5), 3, 4 and 5, block exemption is conferred on all vertical agreements, whether or not they relate to the supply of goods or services, and irrespective of whether goods are supplied for resale or for use. This means that countless numbers of agreements that would never have been eligible for block exemption under the old Regulations can now benefit.

(v) The exempted agreement may be multilateral

Article 2(1) confers block exemption on agreements between two *or more* undertakings: the old Regulations applied only to bilateral agreements. The position in Article 2(1) of Regulation 2790/99 is possible as a result of the extension of the Commission's *vires* by Council Regulation 1215/99. However the Regulation applies only where each of the

---

[303] On the burden of proof in this situation see Article 2 of the EC Modernisation Regulation and ch 4, pp 149–150.

[304] See pp 630–635 above.

[305] See eg *Grohe* OJ [1985] L 19/17, [1988] 4 CMLR 612; note that, where it *is* necessary to apply the Regulation to a selective distribution system, the definition of this term in Article 1(d) does not bring into account the nature of the product; this consideration is relevant only to the question of whether the system falls outside Article 81(1) altogether.

[306] See p 633 above.   [307] Regulation 1983/83, Article 1.   [308] OJ [1999] L 148/1.

undertakings operates, for the purposes of the agreement, at a different level of the market. Some illustrations may help:

Agreement 1

Supplier

Exclusive wholesaler in UK   Exclusive wholesaler in France

Fig. 16.7

(a) The agreement is trilateral

(b) The supplier supplies goods to each wholesaler

(c) It is agreed that neither wholesaler will sell into the other's territory

The agreement is not vertical since there are two parties, the wholesalers, at the same level of the production and distribution chain.

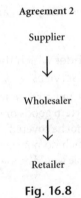

Agreement 2

Supplier

Wholesaler

Retailer

Fig. 16.8

(a) The agreement is trilateral

(b) The agreement sets out the mutual rights and obligations of each party

The agreement is vertical since each party operates at a different level of the production and distribution chain.

Where the agreement is in the form of Agreement 2, both the supplier's and the wholesaler's market share would have to be considered for the purpose of the market share cap in Article 3(1)[309].

---

[309] *Vertical guidelines*, para 93.

(vi) 'For the purposes of the agreement'

The definition of a vertical agreement refers to undertakings which operate, '*for the purposes of the agreement*, at a different level of the production or distribution chain' (emphasis added). It follows that the fact that two firms that are both manufacturers enter into an agreement does not in itself mean that the agreement is horizontal rather than vertical. If a manufacturer of a chemical were to supply the chemical to another chemical manufacturer, the relationship would still be vertical since, for the purposes of that agreement, each undertaking would be operating at a different level of the market. The expression 'for the purposes of the agreement' is essential to this analysis since, without it, it would not be possible to say that the two chemical companies operate 'at a different level of the production or distribution chain'. However Article 2(4) of the Regulation guards against the risk that vertical agreements as defined could be used as a cloak for horizontal restrictions by denying block exemption to certain agreements between actually or potentially competing undertakings[310].

(vii) Agreements with final consumers would not normally be vertical agreements

Agreements entered into with final consumers would not normally be vertical agreements, since they would not be entered into 'between two or more undertakings': a final consumer in the sense of a member of the public buying goods or services would not be carrying on an economic activity[311]. For the same reason, however, such agreements would not infringe Article 81(1) in the first place, and therefore would not need to be exempted.

(viii) 'Relating to the conditions under which the parties may purchase, sell or resell certain goods or services'

To qualify as a vertical agreement it must relate to the conditions under which the parties may purchase, sell or resell certain goods or services. It appears, therefore, that rental and leasing agreements would not be covered[312]; nor would bartering agreements. Provisions in vertical agreements which do not themselves relate to purchase, sale or resale would not be covered: an example would be a covenant not to compete in research and development[313].

(ix) Interconnection agreements

In many industries undertakings require access to an infrastructure owned by someone else in order to be able to operate on the market: for example in the telecommunications sector service providers may need access to the wires and cables of the main telecommunications company; in electricity access will be needed to the national grid. Where access is provided there will be an 'interconnection agreement' between the owner of the infrastructure and the service provider. It would seem that such an agreement would be

---

[310] See p 649 below.

[311] *Vertical guidelines*, para 24: on the meaning of the term 'undertaking' see ch 3, pp 82–91; however the supplier would be an undertaking, and would infringe Article 82 if it held a dominant position and acted in an abusive manner and the other terms of that provision were satisfied: on Article 82 generally see ch 5.

[312] *Vertical guidelines*, para 25.   [313] Ibid, para 20.

vertical in the sense of Article 2(1), since it would relate to the 'conditions under which the parties may purchase, sell or resell...services'[314]. However in many (most?) such cases the owner of the infrastructure would have a market share in excess of 30 per cent, so that Article 3(1) of the Regulation would prevent the application of the block exemption[315].

(x) Agency

Many agency agreements fall outside Article 81(1); paragraphs 12 to 20 of the *Vertical guidelines* deal with this[316]. However those paragraphs suggest that some agency agreements could fall within Article 81(1) if they are 'non-genuine', if they could foreclose access to the market or if they might facilitate explicit or tacit collusion. It is necessary to consider whether an agency agreement that does fall within Article 81(1) would be eligible for block exemption. In such a situation the agent is operating at a different level of the market from the principal in the sense of Article 2(1) of the Regulation. Therefore, to the extent that the agreement relates to the conditions under which the principal or the agent may purchase, sell or resell goods or services, the Regulation would apply. Paragraph 13 of the *Guidelines* specifically states that the Regulation is capable of application to 'non-genuine' agency agreements. In such cases it will be necessary to avoid the hard-core restrictions listed in Article 4[317]; paragraph 48 of the *Guidelines* states that an obligation on a non-genuine agent preventing it from sharing its commission with its customers would be a 'hard-core' restriction under Article 4(a). Also it will be necessary to avoid non-compete provisions of the kind set out in Article 5[318].

(xi) Article 2(2): associations of retailers[319]

A common business phenomenon is that small retailers establish an association for the purchase of goods, which they then resell to final consumers[320]. This is necessary to enable the retailers to achieve some bargaining power in their dealings with large manufacturers and/or intermediaries. Consumers will benefit if the retailers are enabled to obtain lower prices which are transmitted on to them. Article 2(2) provides that *vertical* agreements entered into between such an association and (a) its suppliers or (b) its members[321] can benefit from block exemption, provided that all its members are retailers of goods and provided that no individual member of the association, together with its connected undertakings[322], has a total turnover in excess of €50 million[323]. The Regulation does not define the term retailer, but paragraph 28 of the *Vertical guidelines*

---

[314] Note however that the agreement would not be vertical in so far as it is a rental or leasing arrangement: see above.

[315] Where the infrastructure is an essential facility Article 82 may be applicable to issues of access and pricing: see ch 17, pp 690–699.

[316] See pp 609–612 above.   [317] On Article 4 generally see pp 652–657 below.

[318] On Article 5 generally see pp 657–659 below.

[319] *Vertical guidelines*, paras 28 and 29.   [320] See ch 15, pp 592–594.

[321] In the case of an agreement between an association and its members it is the association's market share that is relevant for the purpose of Article 3(1): *Vertical guidelines*, para 89.

[322] Articles 10 and 11 deal with the calculation of turnover and with connected undertakings.

[323] The final sentence of para 28 of the *Guidelines* states that where only a limited number of the members of the association have a turnover not significantly exceeding €50 million, 'this will not normally change the assessment under Article 81'; the meaning of this is opaque: if this is intended to mean that the block exemption would still be applicable, it does not provide any legal justification for this view.

says that '[r]etailers are distributors reselling goods to final consumers'[324]. The concluding words of Article 2(2) provide that the block exemption for such vertical agreements
is without prejudice to the application of Article 81(1) to the horizontal agreement
between the members of the association and to any recommendations of the trade association itself[325]. Paragraph 29 of the *Guidelines* states that it becomes relevant to assess
the vertical agreements only if the assessment of the horizontal agreement is 'positive'
(meaning presumably that it does not infringe Article 81(1)). There is no legal basis for
this view in Article 2(2) of the Regulation.

(xii) Article 2(3): ancillary provisions in relation to intellectual property rights[326]

Article 2(3) deals with the important question of the extent to which vertical agreements
which contain provisions on intellectual property rights can benefit from Regulation
2790/99. The first sentence of Article 2(3) provides that the exemption shall apply to
vertical agreements:

containing provisions which relate to the assignment to the buyer or use by the buyer of intellectual property rights[327], provided that those provisions do not constitute the primary object of such
agreements and are directly related to the use, sale or resale of goods or services by the buyer or
its customers.

Essentially the policy is that Regulation 2790/99 will apply where any provisions relating to intellectual property rights are ancillary to the main purpose of the vertical
agreement[328]; although the Regulation itself does not use the term, it is helpful to call
such provisions 'IPR provisions'. The policy of Article 2(3) is simple to state; however
the actual application of Article 2(3) is not without its difficulties. A number of points
should be noted: the five headings (xiii–xvii) used below are based upon paragraph 30
of the Commission's *Guidelines*.

(xiii) Article 2(3) is applicable only where there is a vertical agreement

First, for Article 2(3) to apply to the IPR provisions – that is to say if they are to benefit
from block exemption – there must be a vertical agreement; Article 2(1) defines this as
an agreement relating to the conditions under which the parties may purchase, sell or
resell goods or services. It follows that 'pure' licences – for example of know-how or of a
trade mark – would not be covered, since they would not relate to the conditions under
which the parties purchase, sell or resell goods or services: rather, they would authorise
the use of the know-how or of the trade mark. Pure know-how licences, however, would
be able to benefit from Regulation 772/2004[329] on technology transfer agreements[330].
Paragraph 32 of the *Guidelines* gives five examples of agreements that would not benefit
from block exemption:

---

[324] It presumably follows that if the association purchases for its own use, as for example a group of
National Health hospitals in the UK, Article 2(2) would not be applicable since the group does not purchase
in order to *sell* to final consumers.

[325] On such agreements see ch 15, pp 592–594.   [326] *Vertical guidelines*, paras 30–44.

[327] Intellectual property rights are defined in Article 1(e) to include 'industrial property rights, copyright
and neighbouring rights'.

[328] Although the term 'ancillary' does not feature in Article 2(3) itself, recital 3 states that the Regulation
'includes vertical agreements containing ancillary provisions on the assignment of intellectual property
rights'.

[329] OJ [2004] L 123/11.   [330] See ch 19, pp 771–781.

- the provision of a recipe for the production of a drink under licence
- the production and distribution of copies from a mould or master copy
- a pure licence of a trade mark or sign for the purposes of merchandising
- sponsorship contracts[331]
- copyright licensing such as broadcasting contracts concerning the right to record and/or the right to broadcast an event[332].

(xiv) The IPR provisions must be for the use of the buyer

Second, Article 2(3) applies only where the supplier supplies IPRs to the buyer; it does not apply where the buyer supplies IPRs to the supplier. It follows that a sub-contracting agreement, whereby one undertaking asks another to manufacture goods on its behalf, often with the use of its IPRs, would not be covered by the block exemption[333], since the IPRs are supplied by the buyer to the supplier, rather than the other way around. However many sub-contracting agreements do not infringe Article 81(1) at all, so that block exemption is unnecessary[334]; and the *Vertical guidelines* state that, where the buyer simply provides specifications to the supplier as to the goods or services to be supplied, the block exemption remains applicable[335]: in that case there are no IPR provisions, and Article 2(3) is irrelevant.

(xv) The IPR provisions must not be the object of the agreement

Third, for Article 2(3) to apply the IPR provisions must not be the 'primary' object of the agreement: in the language of the *Guidelines*, '[t]he primary object must be the purchase or distribution of goods or services and the IPR provisions must serve the implementation of the vertical agreement'[336].

(xvi) The IPR provisions must be directly related to the use, sale or resale of goods or services by the buyer or its customers

A trade mark licence to a distributor is generally necessary for and ancillary to the distribution of goods or services, so that an exclusive licence would benefit from the block exemption, provided that it satisfies the other rules in the Regulation[337]. A sale of hard copies of software, where the reseller does not acquire a licence to any rights over the software, is regarded as an agreement for the supply of goods for resale[338]. Paragraphs 42 to 44 of the *Vertical guidelines* examine the application of the Regulation to franchise agreements. These were formerly afforded block exemption by Regulation 4087/88[339],

---

[331] On sponsorship contracts see *Danish Tennis Federation Commission* OJ [1996] C 138/6, [1996] 4 CMLR 885, Commission's XXVIIIth *Report on Competition Policy* (1998) p 160 (comfort letter issued).

[332] See *Telenor/Canal+/Canal Digital* Commission decision of 29 December 2003, a case concerning the licensing of premium content channels, protected by copyright, to a pay-TV platform, where the Commission decided that Regulation 2790/99 was not applicable: see in particular paragraph 196 of the Commission's decision.

[333] *Vertical guidelines*, para 33.

[334] See the Commission's *Notice on Subcontracting Agreements* OJ [1979] C 1/2, discussed at pp 665–667 below.

[335] *Vertical guidelines*, para 33.   [336] Ibid, para 34.   [337] Ibid, para 38.

[338] Ibid, para 40; this would cover the sale of software subject to a 'shrink-wrap' licence, the conditions in which the end user accepts by opening the package.

[339] OJ [1988] L 359/46.

but they are no longer subject to a separate regime: instead they are subject to the same rules as other vertical agreements. The Commission's view is that Regulation 2790/99 is capable in principle of application to franchise agreements, other than industrial franchise agreements: the latter would be subject, if at all, to Regulation 772/2004 on technology transfer agreements[340]. Paragraph 43 of the *Guidelines* states that most franchise agreements would be covered by Article 2(3), since the IPR provisions in them are directly related to the use, sale or resale of goods or services by the franchisee. It adds that, where a franchise agreement 'only or primarily concerns licensing of IPRs', it would not be covered by the block exemption, but 'it will be treated in a similar way'. This presumably means that the Commission's analysis would follow the principles of the block exemption, and that the agreement would satisfy Article 81(3) where the franchisor's market share is less than 30 per cent[341], provided that the agreement does not contain any 'black-listed' provisions as set out in Article 4.

Where the franchisor franchises a business method, it is the market share on the market where the business method is to be exploited that must be determined for the purpose of the market share cap in Article 3[342].

Paragraph 44 of the *Vertical guidelines* sets out a series of typical IPR-related obligations that are found in franchise agreements and which, if restrictive of competition, would be regarded as ancillary and therefore would benefit from block exemption. These are obligations on the franchisee:

(a) not to engage, directly or indirectly, in any similar business

(b) not to acquire financial interests in competing undertakings

(c) not to disclose secret know-how to third parties

(d) to grant a non-exclusive licence to the franchisor of know-how obtained from exploitation of the franchise

(e) to assist the franchisor in action to protect the IPRs

(f) only to use the franchisor's know-how for the purpose of the franchise

(g) not to assign the rights and obligations under the franchise agreement without the consent of the franchisor.

(xvii) The IPR provisions must not have an illegitimate object or effect[343]

The final sentence of Article 2(3) provides that the IPR provisions will be exempt only in so far as they 'do not contain restrictions of competition having the same object or effect as vertical restraints which are not exempted under this Regulation'. Thus it is not possible to avoid the provisions of Articles 4 and 5 of the Regulation (see below) by attaching the vertical restraints which they seek to prevent to the IPR provisions rather than to the vertical agreement itself.

Article 2(3) should also be understood in conjunction with Article 2(5), which prevents the application of the new Regulation where another block exemption is applicable (below).

---

[340] The Commission notes the difference between industrial franchise and non-industrial franchise agreements at para 42 of the *Vertical guidelines*, Regulation 772/2004 is dealt with in ch 19, pp 771–781.

[341] See pp 650–652 below on the market share cap in Article 3.

[342] *Vertical guidelines*, para 95.   [343] Ibid, para 36.

(xviii) Article 2(4): agreements between competing undertakings[344]

Article 2(4) provides that the block exemption does not apply to vertical agreements entered into between competing undertakings; this applies to agreements at any level of the market: for example the undertakings may be competing as manufacturers, wholesalers or as retailers.

The definition of competing undertakings refers to 'actual or potential suppliers in the same product market'. Paragraph 26 of the *Vertical guidelines* states that the definition applies irrespective of whether the undertakings are competitors on the same geographic market. The same paragraph goes on to consider what is meant by 'potential suppliers'. This refers to undertakings that could and would be likely to respond to a small and permanent increase in relative prices: such undertakings 'would be able and likely to undertake the necessary additional investments within one year' and so could enter the market. The Commission adds that this assessment must be 'realistic', not 'theoretical'[345]. The *Guidelines* do *not* state that the potential suppliers' response must have been triggered by a price rise by 'competing undertakings', but presumably this is what the spirit of Article 1(a) is envisaging.

Non-reciprocal vertical agreements between competing undertakings are permitted subject to conditions. Article 2(4) allows a non-reciprocal vertical agreement between competing undertakings where:

- the buyer has a total annual turnover not exceeding €100 million[346]; or
- the supplier is a manufacturer and a distributor of goods, whilst the buyer is a distributor not manufacturing goods competing with the contract goods[347]. In this case the manufacturer conducts its own distribution, but also appoints other distributors which are, according to the definition in Article 1(a), 'competing undertakings'. Paragraph 27 of the *Guidelines* describes this phenomenon as 'dual distribution'. There is no turnover restriction in this situation; or
- the supplier is a provider of services at several levels of trade, whilst the buyer does not provide competing services at the level of trade where it purchases the contract services. This is the analogue of the previous situation, adjusted for the purposes of an agreement in the services sector. Again there is no turnover restriction.

(xix) Article 2(5): agreements within the scope of another block exemption[348]

Article 2(5) of the Regulation provides that 'This Regulation shall not apply to vertical agreements *the subject matter of which* falls within the scope of any other block exemption regulation' (emphasis added). The italicised words are important: Article 2(5) does not say that the Regulation shall not apply to an agreement which is exempt under another regulation; rather, it says that it does not apply to agreements which, generically, are of a kind covered by another regulation. It follows that car distribution agreements will be block exempted, if at all, by virtue of Regulation 1400/02[349]; technology

---

[344] Ibid, paras 26–27.

[345] The Commission also refers in the *Vertical guidelines* to paras 20–24 of its *Notice on Market Definition* OJ [1997] C 372/5, [1998] 4 CMLR 177, to point 55 of its XIIIth *Report on Competition Policy* (1983) and to its decision in *Elopak/Metal Box-Odin* OJ [1990] L 209/15, [1991] 4 CMLR 832; see further ch 3, pp 133–134 and ch 15, pp 575–576.

[346] See Articles 10 and 11 on the calculation of turnover and on connected undertakings.

[347] At para 27 of the *Vertical guidelines* the Commission states that an 'own-brand' retailer would not be treated as a manufacturer for this purpose.

[348] *Vertical guidelines*, para 45. [349] OJ [2002] L 203/30; see pp 663–666 below.

transfer agreements by Regulation 772/2004[350]; and both the horizontal and vertical aspects of specialisation and R&D agreements by Regulations 2658/00[351] and 2659/00[352] respectively. If an agreement fails to satisfy the criteria for exemption in any of these Regulations, Article 2(5) prevents the agreement from being exempted by Regulation 2790/99. Article 2(5) would also prevent Regulation 2790/99 from applying to any agreement within the scope of any future block exemption[353].

(C) Article 3: the market share cap[354]

(i) Why a market share test?

One of the key features of Regulation 2790/99 is the inclusion of a market share cap: a manifestation of the 'economics-oriented approach' that the Commission wished to adopt in the new regime. There are various explanations for this. First, the revolt against the over-application of Article 81(1) to vertical agreements stems from the proposition that such agreements are detrimental to competition only if the parties to them possess market power. If market power is at the heart of sensible analysis of such agreements (whether under Article 81(1) or 81(3)), the Commission can hardly be criticised for using a principled, economics-based approach in order to escape from the discredited and formalistic Regulations of the past. Secondly, understanding of market definition on the part of advisors and their clients has developed enormously in recent years[355]. The market share cap is now part of competition law, and it is inconceivable that it will be jettisoned in the foreseeable future.

Recitals 8 and 9 of the Regulation discuss market share. Recital 8 says that it can be presumed that where the market share of the supplier or buyer[356] is below 30 per cent an improvement in production of distribution will follow from which consumers will derive a fair share of the benefit, unless the agreement contains a severe anti-competitive restraint, in which case Article 4 would prevent the agreement from being block exempted; however Recital 9 states that the same presumption cannot be made where the market share exceeds 30 per cent.

(ii) What market share?

Of course it is possible to argue about what the market share cap should be. At one point the Commission suggested that certain restraints might be permitted where the market share was 40 per cent or less, but that others, which could give rise to greater concern, only where the market share was below 20 per cent. This proposal, which would have given rise to unnecessary complexity, was dropped in favour of a compromise market share cap of 30 per cent. A market share cap of 40 per cent would have come close to saying that only vertical restraints, other than the hard-core restrictions set out in Article 4, imposed by dominant undertakings are problematic: perhaps it is not

---

[350] OJ [2004] L 123/11; see ch 19, pp 771–781.
[351] OJ [2000] L 304/3, [2001] 4 CMLR 800; see ch 15, pp 589–592.
[352] OJ [2000] L 304/7, [2001] 4 CMLR 803: see ch 15, pp 583–588.
[353] The Commission specifically says this in para 45 of the *Vertical guidelines*.
[354] Section V of the *Vertical guidelines* deals with market definition and market share calculation issues.
[355] On market definition generally see ch 1, pp 26–40.
[356] See below on the relevance of the buyer's market share.

surprising that the Commission was unwilling to diminish the role of Article 81 to this extent. However it remains to be seen whether the Commission, as part of its review of Regulation 2790/99, might now be prepared to consider a higher market share cap[357].

The inclusion of a market share cap in the new Regulation means that many undertakings which benefited from block exemption under the old Regulations, and whose share of particular markets exceeds 30 per cent, will be ineligible for block exemption under the new Regulation. In *JCB* the Commission held that block exemption was unavailable to JCB's distribution agreements since its market share was in the region of 40 per cent to 45 per cent[358]. In the case of Interbrew's single-branding agreements for bars and cafés in Belgium the Commission concluded that, notwithstanding Interbrew's market share of around 56 per cent, the agreements did not appreciably restrict competition once the extent of the exclusivity had been limited only to pils lager[359]. The 30 per cent rule prevented the application of the block exemption in *Telenor/Canal+/Canal Digital*[360].

(iii) Whose market share?

Article 3(1) provides that it is the market share of the supplier that is to be taken into account in determining whether an agreement benefits from block exemption. Article 3(2) provides the only exception to this: in the case of an exclusive supply obligation, as defined in Article 1(c) of the Regulation, it is the buyer's market share that is relevant. The term 'exclusive supply' has been discussed above[361]: it covers only the situation where there is 'one supplier inside the Community for the purposes of a specific use or resale'. Therefore where a US company appoints one distributor for the UK and Ireland and another for the rest of the Community, there is not an exclusive supply obligation, so that it is the US supplier's market share that is relevant. Where the supplier appoints one undertaking for the entire Community, it is the latter's. In that case the market is determined from the buyer's perspective: that is to say, it is its share of the *purchase* market (goods or services purchased from suppliers) that is calculated; not the buyer's share of the market on which it sells[362].

(iv) The *Vertical guidelines*

Paragraph 21 of the *Vertical guidelines* rehearses the provisions of Article 3. Paragraph 22 goes on to note that an agreement between a supplier and a buyer could have an effect on markets downstream of the buyer; however the Commission says that this is unlikely where the market share of the supplier or buyer is less than 30 per cent, and adds that the block exemption looks only at the market shares of the parties to the agreement itself: to look further downstream in the market would introduce a complexity into the Regulation which should be avoided. Paragraph 22 concludes by noting that, in the event that a vertical agreement causes problems in related markets, there

[357] See p 662 below.
[358] OJ [2002] L 69/1, [2002] 4 CMLR 1458, para 198; the Commission also considered that block exemption was unavailable as a result of the presence of hard-core restrictions in the agreements: ibid, para 199; on hard-core restrictions see pp 652–567 below.
[359] Commission Press Release IP/03/545, 15 April 2003.
[360] Commission decision of 29 December 2003, para 196. [361] See p 641.
[362] *Vertical guidelines*, para 82, following eg the Commission's decision under the EC Merger Regulation in Case No IV/M1221 *Rewe/Meinl* OJ [1999] L 274/1, [2000] 5 CMLR 256.

is the possibility of withdrawing the benefit of the block exemption under Article 6[363]. Paragraphs 68 and 69 of the *Guidelines* deal with the situation where a supplier supplies a portfolio of products, in relation to some of which the market share cap is exceeded and others it is not: the Commission states that the block exemption will not apply to the former but will apply to the latter; in relation to the former there is no presumption of illegality, and the Commission will consider whether any infringement of Article 81(1) could be resolved by alterations to the existing distribution system. If not, some other form of distribution will have to be adopted.

Section V of the *Guidelines* (paragraphs 88 to 99) discusses various issues concerning market share in more detail. Paragraph 91 examines questions concerning the supplier's market share and paragraph 92 the buyer's; paragraph 93 deals with the position where there are more than two parties to the agreement[364]. Paragraph 94 discusses the position of OEM suppliers; and paragraph 95 deals with market shares in the context of franchising agreements. Paragraph 96 considers market definition in the case of individual assessment of agreements rather than the application of the block exemption; and paragraphs 97 to 99 deal specifically with the calculation of market share under the Regulation.

(v) Article 8

It is worth noting in passing that the Regulation has a further market share test in Article 8, albeit one that will have only rare application. This provides that the Commission may withdraw the benefit of block exemption where 50 per cent of a relevant market is covered by a network of similar vertical agreements. This is dealt with below[365].

(D) Article 4: hard-core restrictions[366]

Recital 10 of the Regulation states that vertical agreements 'containing certain types of severely anti-competitive restrictions such as minimum and fixed resale prices, as well as certain types of territorial protection, should be excluded from the benefit of the block exemption'. Even hard-core restrictions might, as a matter of law, fall outside Article 81(1) where they could not have an appreciable effect on competition or on interstate trade[367]. However the Commission's *Notice on Agreements of Minor Importance*[368] provides that, even below the 15 per cent threshold, it cannot be ruled out that vertical agreements that have as their object or effect to fix resale prices or to confer territorial protection on the undertakings or third undertakings might infringe Article 81(1): the point is repeated in paragraph 10 of the *Vertical guidelines*.

Article 4 contains the list of 'hard-core' restrictions which lead to the exclusion of the entire vertical agreement – not just the provision in question – from the block exemption. The Commission states specifically at paragraph 66 of the *Guidelines* that there is no severability for hard-core restrictions. Paragraph 46 of the *Guidelines* adds that it is unlikely that vertical agreements containing such restrictions would satisfy

---

[363] See pp 659–660 below.   [364] See pp 642–643 above.   [365] See p 661.
[366] See *Vertical guidelines*, paras 46–56.
[367] Case 5/69 *Völk v Vervaecke* [1969] ECR 295, [1969] CMLR 273; Case C-306/96 *Javico v Yves Saint Laurent* [1998] ECR I-1983, [1998] 5 CMLR 172; see ch 3, pp 137–146.
[368] OJ [2001] C 368/13, [2002] 4 CMLR 699, para 11.

Article 81(3) on an individual basis[369]. Article 4 is to be contrasted with Article 5, which denies block exemption to certain specific obligations, but which does not deprive the rest of the agreement of the benefit of the block exemption[370]. Each of the hard-core restrictions in Article 4 relates to a restriction of intra-brand competition, although the Commission's view is that in some cases restrictions of intra-brand competition can affect inter-brand competition by facilitating explicit or tacit collusion[371]. Restrictions of inter-brand competition, or situations in which inter-brand competition is weak, are specifically dealt with in other parts of the Regulation, for example Article 2(4) (agreements between competing undertakings); Article 3 (market share cap); Article 5 (specific treatment of non-compete provisions); and Articles 6, 7 and 8 (withdrawal of the block exemption).

Article 4 provides that block exemption will not be available to agreements which 'directly or indirectly, in isolation or in combination with other factors under the control of the parties, have as their object' the matters dealt with below, such as resale price maintenance and excessive territorial protection. It is worth dwelling for a few moments on these opening words of Article 4 before looking at the specific hard-core restrictions themselves. Article 4 denies block exemption to agreements that have as their *object* one of the prohibited provisions: it might have said agreements that have as their object *or effect*, reflecting the wording of Article 81(1) of the Treaty, but it does not do so. The word 'object' in Article 4 of the Regulation, and in Article 81(1) of the Treaty, does not refer to the subjective intention of the parties; rather to the aim of the agreement judged by objective standards[372]. The *Vertical guidelines* are silent on this point. Notwithstanding that Article 4 applies only according to the object, and not the effect, of an agreement, it will prevent the block exemption from applying where the agreement 'directly or indirectly, in isolation or in combination with other factors', has one of the prohibited objects: in other words, even without the use of the word 'effect', the scope of the exclusion of the block exemption is quite extensive.

(i) Article 4(a): resale price maintenance[373]

Block exemption will not be available where the object of the agreement is:

(a) the restriction of the buyer's ability to determine its sale price, without prejudice to the possibility of the supplier's imposing a maximum sale price or recommending a sale price, provided that they do not amount to a fixed or minimum sale price as a result of pressure from, or incentives offered by, any of the parties.

This formulation explicitly recognises that the imposition of maximum[374] sale prices and the recommendation[375] of prices is permitted; this, however, is subject to the

---

[369] See however the comments on p 637 above in relation to resale price maintenance and Article 81(3).

[370] See pp 657–659 below.

[371] For an example of a case where the Commission was concerned that 'most-favoured nation' clauses might be causing price parallelism see its investigation of six Hollywood studios, Commission Press Release IP/04/1314, 26 October 2004.

[372] See ch 3, p 116.

[373] See *Guidelines*, paras 47 and 48 and pp 637–638 above.

[374] The ECJ has never ruled on the imposition of maximum prices; for the position in the US see *State Oil v Khan* 118 US 275 (1997), p 638, n 274 above.

[375] The ECJ held in Case 161/84 *Pronuptia de Paris v Pronuptia de Paris Irmgard Schillgalis* [1986] ECR 353, [1986] 1 CMLR 414 that the recommendation of prices would not, in itself, infringe Article 81(1): see para 25.

proviso that follows, which itself must be read in conjunction with the words 'directly or indirectly' in the opening part of Article 4. Paragraph 47 of the *Vertical guidelines* picks up on the idea that the agreement may have the direct *or indirect* object of resale price maintenance. A contractual restriction establishing a minimum price would be a simple example of an agreement the *direct* object of which is to fix prices. Paragraph 47 gives examples of price maintenance through indirect means:

fixing the distribution margin, fixing the maximum level of discount the distributor can grant from a prescribed price level, making the grant of rebates or reimbursement of promotional costs by the supplier subject to the observance of a given price level, linking the prescribed resale price to the resale prices of competitors, threats, intimidation, warnings, penalties, delay or suspension of deliveries or contract terminations in relation to the observance of a certain price level.

Measures taken to identify price-cutting distributors might also amount to 'indirect pressure' to fix prices; paragraph 47 suggests that printing a recommended resale price or an obligation to apply a most favoured customer clause would reduce the incentive to cut price and so could be within the mischief of Article 4. The paragraph acknowledges that the recommendation of prices is not, in itself, a hard-core restriction.

In the case of genuine agency agreements Article 81(1) would normally not be applicable[376]. However where an agency agreement does fall within Article 81(1), paragraph 48 of the *Guidelines* states that a restriction on the agent preventing or restricting the sharing of commission with its customers, whether fixed or variable, would amount to a hard-core restriction. The agent should be left free to lower the effective price paid by the customer without reducing the income for the principal[377].

(ii) Article 4(b): territorial and customer restrictions[378]

This important provision deals with the extent to which it is possible to grant territorial or customer exclusivity. To some extent it reflects Article 2(2)(c) of the previous block exemption, Regulation 1983/83, which permitted a restriction on a reseller not to pursue an active sales policy outside its territory, but which did not permit a ban on passive sales. However Article 4(b) is more complex than Article 2(2)(c), and the *Vertical guidelines* on it are quite detailed; among other matters they deal with the active/passive sales distinction in the case of e-commerce.

The opening words of Article 4(b) provide that the block exemption will not be available where the object of the agreement is:

the restriction of the territory into which, or of the customers to whom, the buyer may sell the contract goods or services.

Paragraph 49 of the *Guidelines* picks up on the 'direct/indirect object' dichotomy in the opening words of Article 4. Indirect measures to restrict the buyer could include:

refusal or reduction of bonuses or discounts, refusal to supply, reduction of supplied volumes or limitation of supplied volumes to the demand within the allocated territory or customer group, threat of contract termination or profit pass-over obligations.

---

[376] See pp 609–612 above.
[377] See Case 311/85 *Vereniging van Vlaamse Reisbureaus v Sociale Dienst van de Plaatselijke en Gewestelijke Overheidsdiensten* [1987] ECR 3801, [1989] 4 CMLR 213, para 24.
[378] *Vertical guidelines*, paras 49–52.

The withholding of a guarantee service could also amount to indirect means. These practices would be more likely to be considered indirect measures to restrict the buyer's freedom when operated in conjunction with a monitoring system for detecting parallel imports and exports. Clearly this paragraph is based on the Commission's experience, upheld by the Community Courts, in a series of decisions over many years[379].

Paragraph 49 of the *Guidelines* concludes by explaining two restrictions on buyers that would *not* be regarded as hard-core under Article 4(b): a prohibition on resale except to certain end users for which there is an objective justification, for example, on grounds of health or safety[380], and an obligation on the reseller relating to the display of the supplier's brand names[381].

Four exceptions to the basic prohibition in Article 4(b) are set out; the first is particularly important, since it deals with the distinction between active and passive sales.

Exception 1: it is permissible to have a restriction:

of active sales into the exclusive territory or to an exclusive customer group reserved to the supplier or allocated by the supplier to another buyer, where such a restriction does not limit sales by the customers of the buyer.

The first point to note here is that a restriction of active sales to another group of customers is permitted: this was not exempted under Regulation 1983/83[382]. The second point is that, although a restriction of active sales to other territories or customers is permitted, there must remain the possibility of passive sales to them. This is not stated specifically in the Regulation; it is stated explicitly, however, in paragraph 50 of the *Vertical guidelines*. Thirdly, the restriction must be on active sales into the territory or customer group 'reserved to the supplier or allocated by the supplier to another buyer'. It seems, therefore, that the supplier *must* exclusively reserve a territory or customer group to itself or allocate it to another buyer in order to be able to impose an active sales ban: one can expect a reservation to the supplier or an allocation to another buyer to become a standard form clause for all distribution agreements. It is apparently not possible to restrict active sales into an area reserved to a licensee of know-how or of a patent, although no explanation is given of why this should be so.

Paragraph 50 of the *Guidelines* deals with the distinction between active and passive sales. Active selling includes establishing a warehouse or distribution outlet in another's exclusive territory. As to passive selling, paragraph 50 says that 'General advertising or promotion in media or on the Internet' but which is a reasonable way to reach customers in other territories or customer groups would normally be regarded as passive rather than active selling. Paragraph 51 deals specifically with the Internet[383]. It begins by stating that every distributor must be free to use the Internet to advertise or to sell products, and that in general Internet selling is not regarded as active selling, since it is a reasonable way to reach every customer. The paragraph specifically states

---

[379] See pp 622–626 above.   [380] See eg *Kathon/Biocide* OJ [1984] C 59/6, [1984] 1 CMLR 476.

[381] This is presumably based on Case 161/84 *Pronuptia de Paris v Pronuptia de Paris Irmgard Schillgalis* [1986] ECR 353, [1986] 1 CMLR 414.

[382] Article 1 of Regulation 1983/83 exempted only agreements conferring exclusive territories, not customer groups.

[383] See further on Internet sales *Yves Saint Laurent* Commission Press Release IP/01/713, 17 May 2001; *Sammelrevers* Commission Press Releases IP/01/1035, 19 July 2001 and IP/02/ 461, 22 March 2002; and the Commission's *Competition Policy Newsletter* June 2002, pp 35–37.

that the language used on the website would not normally affect the view that sales made as a result of advertising on the Internet are passive sales. An English producer advertising on its website in the German language is not regarded as actively seeking the business of German customers in Germany: intuition might suggest the opposite. The sending of unsolicited e-mails would be regarded as active selling. The supplier is allowed to impose quality standards on the reseller as to the content of the Internet site itself. Paragraph 51 concludes by stating that an outright ban on Internet selling would be possible only if there is an objective justification (no examples are given), and that the supplier cannot reserve to itself sales and/or advertising over the Internet. In *Yamaha*[384] the Commission considered that a restriction on internet selling infringed Article 81(1)[385] and was not covered by the block exemption[386].

Exception 2: it is permissible to have a restriction of sales – both active and passive – to end users by a buyer operating at the wholesale level of trade.

Exception 3: it is permissible to have a restriction on sales – both active and passive – to unauthorised distributors by members of a selective distribution system. This term is defined in Article 1(d) to mean a system where the supplier agrees to supply the contract goods or services only to distributors selected on the basis of specified criteria and those distributors agree not to sell to unauthorised distributors. It should be noted that this definition of a selective distribution system in the Regulation is not limited by reference to the nature of the goods or services in question; nor does it specify that the criteria should be qualitative rather than quantitative.

Exception 4: it is possible to restrict the buyer of components for use from selling them – both actively and passively – to a customer who would use them to manufacture goods that would compete with those of the supplier.

In *Souris-Topps*[387] the Commission concluded that Topps's distribution arrangements for its Pokémon stickers and cards failed to benefit from the block exemption since they violated Article 4(b)[388].

(iii) Article 4(c): the restriction of active or passive sales to end users by members of a selective distribution system operating at the retail level of trade[389]

As noted above, the third exception of Article 4(b) permits the restriction of sales by members of a selective distribution system to unauthorised distributors. However Article 4(c) prevents the application of the block exception when there are restrictions on active or passive sales by selected distributors at the retail level of trade to end users. Paragraph 53 of the *Vertical guidelines* says that the end users may be a professional buyer or a final consumer. However there is a proviso to Article 4(c), which is that the distributor may be prohibited from operating out of an unauthorised place of establishment: without this proviso the distributor would not be complying with the 'specified criteria' that make the system selective, and would effectively be operating as an unauthorised distributor[390].

Paragraph 53 of the *Guidelines* makes an important point which is not explicit in the Regulation itself: that selective distribution may be combined with exclusive

---

[384] Commission decision of 16 July 2003.   [385] Ibid, paras 107–110.   [386] Ibid, para 171.
[387] Commission decision of 24 May 2004.   [388] Ibid, paras 136–140.
[389] *Vertical guidelines*, paras 53–54.   [390] On this point see para 54 of the *Vertical guidelines*.

distribution, provided that active or passive selling is not restricted. The supplier can commit to supply only one dealer or certain dealers in a given territory. A selective distribution system that restricts the number of distributors that the supplier sells to, and which limits the authorised distributors by reference to specified criteria, is block exempted provided that:

- the agreement is a vertical agreement (Article 2(1))
- the supplier's market share is 30 per cent or less (Article 3(1))
- resale prices are not fixed (Article 4(a))
- there are no restrictions on active or passive sales to end users (Article 4(c))
- there are no restrictions on cross-supplies between authorised distributors (Article 4(d)) and
- further, Article 5(c) prohibits group boycotts by members of a selective distribution system[391].

(iv) Article 4(d): restrictions on cross-supplies within a selective distribution system[392]

Article 4(d) prevents the application of the block exemption where there is a restriction of cross-supplies between distributors within a selective distribution system, including distributors at different levels of the market. Thus it is not possible to require a selected retailer to purchase solely from one source: it must be able to buy from any approved distributor[393].

(v) Article 4(e): restrictions on the supplier's ability to supply components to third parties[394]

Article 4(e) prevents the application of the block exemption where a restriction is agreed between a supplier and a buyer of components that the supplier will not sell the components as spare parts to end-users or to repairers or service-providers not entrusted by the buyer with the repair or servicing of its goods. End-users and independent service-providers should be free to obtain spare parts; but the buyer can insist that repairers and service-providers within its system should buy the spare-parts only from him[395].

(E) Article 5: obligations in vertical agreements that are not exempt[396]

Recital 11 of the Regulation states that certain conditions are attached to the block exemption in order to ensure 'access to or to prevent collusion on the relevant market'. Where an agreement contains an obligation of the kind set out in Article 5, that obligation does not benefit from block exemption: this is true whether the supplier's market share is above or below the market share cap. However, as paragraph 57 of the *Vertical guidelines* states, the block exemption continues to apply to the remaining parts of the vertical agreement if they are 'severable' from the non-exempted obligation. Neither the Regulation nor the *Guidelines* discuss the notion of 'severability' for the purpose of

---

[391] See p 659 below.   [392] *Vertical guidelines*, para 55.   [393] Ibid.   [394] Ibid, para 56.
[395] Ibid, para 56.   [396] Ibid, paras 57–61.

Article 5[397]. Paragraph 66 repeats that the benefit of the block exemption is lost only in relation to that part of the vertical agreement which does not comply with the conditions set out in Article 5.

Article 5 contains three exclusions.

(i) Article 5(a): non-compete obligations[398]

Article 5(a) excludes from the block exemption:

any direct or indirect non-compete obligation, the duration of which is indefinite or exceeds five years.

The definition of a non-compete obligation was discussed above[399]. An agreement which is 'tacitly renewable' is treated as having an indefinite duration. Paragraph 58 of the *Vertical guidelines* states that an agreement which requires the explicit consent of both parties for renewal beyond five years is permissible; however there must be no obstacles that prevent the buyer from effectively terminating at the end of five years should it so wish. Longer periods are block exempted when the contract goods or services are sold from land and premises owned by the supplier or leased from third parties: paragraph 49 of the *Guidelines* states that 'artificial ownership constructions' to take advantage of this extension will not be permitted. These 'longer periods' mean that beer and petrol agreements in 'tied' houses and garages will be permissible for more than five years[400].

There have been many cases in the English courts in which the validity of beer ties has been considered[401].

(ii) Article 5(b): post-term non-compete obligations[402]

Article 5(b) excludes from the block exemption obligations, after termination of the agreement, not to manufacture, purchase, sell or resell goods or services. However a limited derogation from this provision allows, for a period of not more than one year, a

---

[397] Whether a contractual obligation is 'severable' for the purpose of Article 81(2) is a matter for the applicable law of the contract: see ch 8, pp 312–314.

[398] Ibid, paras 58–59.   [399] See p 641 above.

[400] For individual exemptions granted by the Commission to beer-tie agreements see *Whitbread* OJ [1999] L 88/26, [1999] 5 CMLR 118, upheld on appeal Case T-131/99 *Shaw v Commission* [2002] ECR II-2023, [2002] 5 CMLR 81; *Bass* OJ [1999] L 186/1, [1999] 5 CMLR 782, upheld on appeal Case T-231/99 *Joynson v Commission* [2002] ECR II-2085, [2002] 5 CMLR 123; *Scottish & Newcastle* OJ [1999] L 186/28, [1999] 5 CMLR 831; in *Roberts/Greene King* the Commission concluded that the beer-supply agreements of Greene King did not contribute to the foreclosure of the UK market because of the weak position of Greene King in the market: Commission Press Release IP/98/967, 6 November 1998; the Commission's finding that Article 81(1) was not infringed was upheld in Case T-25/99 *Roberts v Commission* [2001] ECR II-1881, [2001] 5 CMLR 828; for comment on these cases see Bridgeland 'Court of First Instance upholds three Commission decisions relating to beer ties' Commission's *Competition Policy Newsletter*, June 2002, p 45; negative clearance was also given to the standard agreements of The Grand Pub Company in *Inntrepreneur and Spring* OJ [2000] L 195/49, [2000] 5 CMLR 948.

[401] See eg *Holleran v Thwaites* [1989] 2 CMLR 917; *Inntrepreneur Estates (GL) Ltd v Boyes* [1993] 2 EGLR 112; *Little v Courage Ltd* (1994) 70 P & CR 469; *Star Rider Ltd v Inntrepreneur Bub Co* [1998] 1 EGLR 53; *Greenall Management Ltd v Canavan (No 2)* [1998] Eu LR 507; *Gibbs Mew plc v Gemmell* [1998] Eu LR 588; *Trent Taverns Ltd v Sykes* [1998] Eu LR 492; *Passmore v Morland* [1999] Eu LR 501; *Crehan v Courage* [1999] Eu LR 409; the *Crehan* case was referred to the ECJ under Article 234 EC Case C-453/99 [2001] ECR I-6297, [2001] 5 CMLR 1058, as to which see ch 8, pp 293–294.

[402] *Vertical guidelines*, para 60.

post-term ban on sales of competing goods or services from the point of sale at which the buyer operated during the contract period which is necessary to protect know-how transferred from the supplier to the buyer. Know-how for this purpose is defined in Article 1(f) of the Regulation, and must result from 'experience and testing by the supplier'.

(iii) Article 5(c): competing products in a selective distribution system[403]

Article 5(c) excludes from the block exemption an obligation causing the members of a selective distribution system not to sell the brands of particular competing suppliers. It is permissible, subject to Article 5(a), to require a selective distributor not to handle competing brands in general; however Article 5(c) prevents the exemption from applying where there is a boycott of particular competing suppliers. As paragraph 51 of the *Vertical guidelines* explains, this is to prevent the exclusion of 'a specific competitor or certain specific competitors'.

(F) Article 6: withdrawal of the block exemption by the Commission[404]

Recitals 12 and 13 of the Regulation introduce the idea that the Commission may in certain circumstances withdraw the benefit of the block exemption[405]. Recital 12 states that normally the market share cap in conjunction with the other provisions of the Regulation mean that agreements to which it applies would not substantially eliminate competition; Recital 13 however provides that the Commission may withdraw the benefit of the Regulation, in particular where the buyer has significant market power in the relevant market in which it resells the goods or provides the services or where parallel networks of vertical agreements have similar effects which significantly restrict access to a relevant market or competition therein. The Recital notes that these cumulative effects may arise in particular in the case of selective distribution networks and non-compete obligations.

Article 6 provides that the Commission may withdraw the benefit of the block exemption where it finds in any particular case that vertical agreements to which the Regulation applies have effects which are incompatible with the conditions laid down in Article 81(3), 'and in particular where access to the relevant market or competition therein is significantly restricted by the cumulative effect[406] of parallel networks of similar vertical restraints implemented by competing suppliers or buyers'. Paragraph 73 of the *Vertical guidelines* gives a further example of a situation where withdrawal might be considered: where the buyer has significant market power in a downstream market. Article 6 should be distinguished from Article 8 (below), where the block exemption may be withdrawn from all vertical agreements in a particular

---

[403] *Vertical guidelines*, para 61.   [404] *Guidelines*, paras 71–75.

[405] See *Langnese* OJ [1993] L 183/19 where the Commission withdrew the benefit of Regulation 1984/83 from exclusive purchasing agreements in the German market for impulse ice-cream; the Commission's decision was upheld on appeal in Case T-7/93 *Langnese-Iglo v Commission* [1995] ECR II-1533, [1995] 5 CMLR 602; this is understood to be the only occasion on which the Commission has withdrawn the benefit of a block exemption.

[406] Responsibility for such an effect can be attributed only to those undertakings which make an appreciable contribution to it: *Vertical guidelines*, para 63, applying the ECJ's judgment in Case C-234/89 *Delimitis v Henninger Bräu* [1991] ECR I-935, [1992] 5 CMLR 210, para 24; see p 628 above.

relevant market; under Article 6 the block exemption is withdrawn 'in any particular case...' from the agreements having effects incompatible with Article 81(3). Paragraphs 71 to 75 of Part IV of the *Guidelines* deal with the withdrawal procedure under Article 6. Paragraph 71 says that the Commission may withdraw the benefit of the block exemption 'to establish an infringement of Article 81(1)'; at paragraph 81, which deals with the procedure in an Article 8 case, the Commission goes further and says that a withdrawal under Article 6 'implies the adoption of a decision establishing an infringement under Article 81 by an individual company'. Paragraph 72 states that the Commission would have the burden of proving that Article 81(1) is infringed and that the agreement does not fulfil the conditions of Article 81(3). Paragraph 75 states that a withdrawal can have only an *ex nunc* effect, so that exemption will persist until the time of the withdrawal.

(G) Article 7: withdrawal of the block exemption by a Member State[407]

Recital 14 introduces the idea of the competent authorities of the Member States withdrawing the block exemption. Article 7 provides that this may be done where vertical agreements to which the Regulation applies have effects incompatible with the conditions laid down in Article 81(3) 'in the territory of a Member State, or in part thereof, which has all the characteristics of a distinct geographic market'[408]; Article 7 concludes that withdrawal may be made 'under the same conditions as provided in Article 6'[409]. Article 29(2) of the Modernisation Regulation confers power on the national competition authorities of the Member States to withdraw the benefit of Community block exemptions[410]. Paragraph 77 of the *Vertical guidelines* provides that, where the geographic market is wider than a Member State, the Commission has the sole power to withdraw the block exemption. In other cases the power is concurrent, and some cases will 'lend themselves to decentralised enforcement by national competition authorities'. However the Commission concludes the paragraph by saying that it reserves the right to take on cases that display a particular Community interest, for example because they raise a new point of law. National decisions will have effect only within the Member State concerned (paragraph 78) and must not prejudice the uniform application of Community competition law[411].

---

[407] *Vertical guidelines*, paras 76–79.

[408] Note the similarity of this wording to that found in Article 9 of the EC Merger Regulation: see ch 21, p 836.

[409] The words 'under the same conditions' are opaque, and would perhaps be better understood as 'in the same circumstances set out in Article 6'.

[410] For the position in the UK see OFT Guideline *Modernisation*, OFT 442, December 2004, paras 6.1–6.4.

[411] Case 14/68 *Walt Wilhelm v Bundeskartellamt* [1969] ECR 1, point 4; Case C-234/89 *Delimitis v Henninger Bräu* [1991] ECR I-935, [1992] 5 CMLR 210; see also Recital 14 of Regulation 2790/99; para 78 of the *Vertical guidelines*.

(H) Article 8: disapplication of the block exemption by Commission Regulation[412]

Recital 15 of the Regulation introduces the idea of the Commission disapplying the block exemption from agreements in a given market. Article 8(1) provides that the Commission may by regulation declare that, where parallel networks of similar vertical restraints cover more than 50 per cent of a relevant market, the block exemption shall not apply to vertical agreements containing specific restraints in that market. Article 8(2) provides that such a regulation shall not become applicable earlier than six months following its adoption: as paragraph 86 of the *Vertical guidelines* says, time may be needed for the undertakings concerned to adapt their agreements. The Commission discusses the 'disapplication' of the new Regulation in paragraphs 80 to 87 of Part IV of the *Guidelines*. As it explains in paragraph 80, a regulation under Article 8 removes the benefit of the block exemption and restores the full application of Article 81(1) and (3). It would have to decide how to proceed in relation to any individual agreements, and might take a decision in an individual case in order to provide guidance to undertakings in the market generally. The Commission may in some cases have a choice of whether it wishes to proceed under Article 6 (against a particular undertaking or particular agreements) or under Article 8: paragraph 84 of the *Guidelines* says that, in making this choice, the Commission would consider the number of competing undertakings contributing to the cumulative effect or the number of geographic markets within the Community that are affected. Paragraph 84 of the *Guidelines* states that a regulation under Article 8 would not affect the exempted status of the agreements in question prior to its entry into force.

(I) Articles 9 to 11: market share, turnover and connected undertakings

Article 9 deals with the calculation of market share. Article 9(1) provides that market share should be calculated by reference to market sales value; where market sales value data are not available, estimates based on other reliable market information, including sales volumes, may be used. Article 9(2)(a) provides that the market share data should be calculated by reference to the preceding calendar year. Article 9(2)(c) to (e) provide some marginal relief for up to two years where the market share rises above 30 per cent but not beyond 35 per cent.

Article 10 explains how turnover is to be calculated for the purpose of the rules in Article 2(2) and 2(4). Article 11 contains rules extending the expressions 'undertaking', 'supplier' and 'buyer' to include connected undertakings.

(J) Articles 12 and 13: transitional provisions and entry into force

The Regulation entered into force on 1 January 2000 and the block exemption became available to agreements with effect from 1 June 2000. Transitional relief until the end of 2001 was provided for agreements already block exempted under the old Regulations. The new Regulation will expire on 31 May 2010.

[412] *Vertical guidelines*, paras 80–87.

(K) The Commission's review of Regulation 2790/99

Regulation 2790/99 will expire on 31 May 2010 (at the same time as the Regulation on the distribution of motor vehicles[413]). The Commission has begun a review of the operation of Regulation 2790/99 and the *Vertical guidelines* to consider whether it should propose any changes to the current law. It is unlikely that the Commission will propose changes as radical as those that were introduced at the time of Regulation 2790/99. Any changes that are proposed will be the subject of a process of consultation.

In conducting its review the Commission will examine how the regime for vertical agreements has been operating in practice taking into account recent judgments of the Community Courts, its own decisional practice and, through the European Competition Network, the position in the Member States. It can be anticipated that consideration will be given to the market share threshold of 30 per cent, and whether there might be a case for increasing or (less likely) decreasing it. The Commission will wish to ensure that there is a consistency of approach towards vertical issues under Articles 81 and 82. It will also review the list of hard-core restrictions in Article 4 of the Regulation and consider whether it should be amended in any way: of particular interest is the question of whether Article 4(b), which gives expression to the 'single market imperative' by preventing restrictions on passive sales from one territory to another, is still necessary[414].

9. THE APPLICATION OF ARTICLE 81(3) TO AGREEMENTS THAT DO NOT SATISFY THE BLOCK EXEMPTION

Vertical agreements which infringe Article 81(1) and which are ineligible for block exemption under Regulation 2790/99 may nevertheless satisfy the terms of Article 81(3) on an individual basis.

As we have seen Section VI of the *Vertical guidelines* discusses at length the application of Article 81(1) to a series of different types of vertical agreement[415]. Guidance will also be found in Section VI on the application of Article 81(3) to vertical agreements where this is needed in individual cases because the block exemption is inapplicable. Possible efficiencies arising from vertical agreements are described in paragraph 116[416], and some general comments on the application of Article 81(3) will be found at paragraph 134[417]. It is said that it is unlikely that 'hard-core restrictions' of the kind set out in Article 4 of the block exemption would be found to satisfy Article 81(3)[418], although this may be too strict a view in relation to resale price maintenance[419]; individual assessment of agreements is most likely to be necessary where the 30 per cent market share cap is exceeded.

Specific guidance is given on the application of Article 81(3) to single branding agreements at paragraphs 153 to 158. Where a 'client-specific investment' is made, a

---

[413] See pp 663–666 below.
[414] See ch 3, pp 121–122 for a discussion of the single market imperative in the light of the *GlaxoSmithKline* case.
[415] See p 618ff above.   [416] See pp 616–617 above.   [417] See pp 621–622 above.
[418] *Vertical guidelines*, para 46.   [419] See the discussion on pp 637–638 above.

non-compete obligation of more than five years may be allowed under Article 81(3)[420]: this is consistent with the Commission's past practice where, for example, 15-year exclusive purchase agreements have been allowed where an investment is made in the building of new power stations[421]. Where a non-compete clause is included in an exclusive distribution agreement this may be permitted for the duration of the agreement, even where this is for longer than the five years permitted by Article 5(a) of the block exemption[422]. In *DSD*[423] the Commission considered that the criteria of Article 81(3) were satisfied in relation to an agreement whereby DSD, an undertaking in Germany which operated a nationwide system for the collection and recovery of sales packaging, agreed to purchase collection and sorting services exclusively from one collector in each designated district: the exclusivity made it possible for the parties to plan the provision of services on a long-term basis and to organise it reliably, and this gave practical effect to a scheme intended to provide a high level of environmental protection[424].

The possible application of Article 81(3) to exclusive distribution agreements is considered at paragraphs 171 to 174 of the *Vertical guidelines*. The point is repeated that a non-compete obligation of more than five years may be allowed when it is part of an exclusive distribution agreement[425]. The Commission specifically notes that exclusive distribution is most likely to have efficiency-enhancing effects where the products involved are new, complex or have qualities that are difficult to assess prior to consumption[426]. Paragraph 182 of the *Guidelines* considers the possible improvements in efficiency attributable to exclusive customer allocation. Article 81(3) and selective distribution agreements are considered at paragraphs 195 and 196; exclusive supply is dealt with at paragraphs 210 to 212 and tying at paragraphs 222 to 224.

10. REGULATION 1400/2002 ON MOTOR VEHICLE DISTRIBUTION[427]

The single market in the sale and after-sale servicing of motor vehicles has been slow to develop: differing tax regimes and methods of distribution, fluctuating exchange rates, and the fact that certain Member States drive on the 'wrong' side of the road, have meant that this market remains much less integrated than others. The Commission has, for years, monitored price differentials between Member States[428]. Over the years the Commission has had cause to examine a number of anti-competitive practices in the market for motor cars, in particular the partitioning of national markets to prevent sales of vehicles from low- to high-priced Member States, and has adopted numerous

---

[420] *Vertical guidelines*, para 155.
[421] See eg *Isab Energy* [1996] 4 CMLR 889, Commission's XXVIth *Report on Competition Policy* (1996) pp 133–134; *REN/Turbogás* [1996] 4 CMLR 881, XXVIth *Report on Competition Policy* (1996), pp 134–135.
[422] *Vertical guidelines*, para 158.
[423] OJ [2001] L 319/1, [2002] 4 CMLR 405.   [424] Ibid, paras 141–163.   [425] *Vertical guidelines*, para 171.
[426] Ibid, para 174.
[427] For detailed discussion see Faull and Nikpay *The EC Law of Competition* (Oxford University Press, 2nd ed, 2007), ch 15; Gregório 'Driving Competition: The Impact of Regulation 1400/2002 on Motor Vehicle Distribution' (2008) 31(2) World Competition 299.
[428] See eg Commission Press Release IP/03/290, 27 February 2003; DG COMP's website contains useful material on car distribution: www.ec.europa.eu/comm/competition/sectors/motor_vehicles.

decisions finding infringements both of Article 81(1)[429] and, on a few occasions, of Article 82[430]. As far as the system of block exemptions is concerned the distribution of motor vehicles has, since 1985, been subject to a legislative regime separate from that for vertical agreements generally[431]. There have been many cases brought before the Community Courts relating to the special regime for cars[432].

After a lengthy period of review and consultation of the operation of Regulation 1475/95 the Commission concluded that a more economic and flexible approach to motor car distribution was required[433]. Regulation 1400/2002[434], which entered fully into force on 1 October 2002[435], heralds a significant change in the Commission's approach toward the motor car sector. Regulation 1400/2002 follows the same basic structure

[429] See eg BMW Belgium OJ [1978] L 46/33, [1978] 2 CMLR 126, upheld on appeal Case 32/78 BMW v Commission [1979] ECR 2435, [1980] 1 CMLR 370; Ford Werke OJ [1983] L 327/31, [1984] 1 CMLR 596, upheld on appeal Cases 25 and 26/84 Ford Werke AG v Commission [1985] ECR 2725, [1985] 3 CMLR 528; Fiat XIVth Report on Competition Policy (1984), point 70; Alfa Romeo ibid, point 71; Peugeot OJ [1986] L 295/19, [1989] 4 CMLR 371; Citroen Commission Press Release IP(88)778, [1989] 4 CMLR 338; Peugeot OJ [1992] L 66/1, [1993] 4 CMLR 42, upheld on appeal Case T-9/92 Peugeot v Commission [1993] ECR II-493 and on appeal to the ECJ Case C-322/93 P [1994] ECR I-2727; Volkswagen OJ [1998] L 124/60, [1998] 5 CMLR 33, substantially upheld on appeal Case T-62/98 Volkswagen AG v Commission [2000] 5 CMLR 853 and on appeal to the ECJ, Case C-338/00 P Volkswagen AG v Commission [2003] ECR I-9189, [2004] 4 CMLR 351; Opel OJ [2001] L 59/1, [2001] 4 CMLR 1441, substantially upheld on appeal Case T-368/00 General Motors Nederland BV v Commission [2003] ECR II-4491, [2004] 4 CMLR 1302 and on appeal to the ECJ Case C-551/03 P General Motors BV v Commission [2006] ECR I-3173, [2006] 5 CMLR 9; Peugeot, Commission decision of 5 October 2005, on appeal to the CFI Case T-450/05 Automobiles Peugeot v Commission, not yet decided; the Commission's decision in Volkswagen II [2001] L 262/14 was annulled on appeal Case T-208/01 Volkswagen AG v Commission [2003] ECR II-5141, [2004] 4 CMLR 727 and to the ECJ Case C-74/04 P Commission v Volkswagen AG [2006] ECR I-6585; and the Commission's decision in DaimlerChrysler OJ [2002] L 257/1 was partially annulled on appeal Case T-325/01 DaimlerChrysler v Commission [2005] ECR II-3319, [2007] 4 CMLR 559; see also Commission Press Release IP/03/80 of 20 January 2003 announcing that the Commission had reached agreement with Audi that it would continue to deal with approved Audi dealers and repairers on the basis of objective qualitative criteria.

[430] See eg Case 226/84 BL v Commission [1986] ECR 3263, [1987] 1 CMLR 185; Case 26/75 General Motors Continental NV v Commission [1975] ECR 1367, [1976] 1 CMLR 95.

[431] Prior to Regulation 1400/2002 there were two earlier block exemption Regulations for motor vehicle distribution, Regulation 123/85 OJ [1985] L 15/16, which was replaced by Regulation 1475/95 OJ [1995] L 145/25, [1996] 4 CMLR 69.

[432] See, as well as the cases discussed in the text below, Case 10/86 VAG France v Magne [1986] ECR 4071, [1988] 4 CMLR 98; Case C-70/93 BMW v ALD [1995] ECR I-3439, [1996] 4 CMLR 478; Case C-266/93 Bundeskartellamt v Volkswagen AG [1995] ECR I-3477, [1996] 4 CMLR 505; Case C-226/94 Grand Garage Albigeois [1996] ECR I-651, [1996] 4 CMLR 778; Case C-309/94 Nissan France [1996] ECR I-677, [1996] 4 CMLR 778; Case C-128/95 Fontaine [1997] ECR I-967, [1997] 5 CMLR 39; Case C-41/96 VAG-Handlerbeirat eV v SYD-Consult [1997] ECR I-3123, [1997] 5 CMLR 537; Case C-230/96 Cabour SA v Automobiles Peugeot SA [1998] ECR I-2055, [1998] 5 CMLR 679; cf also in the EFTA Court Case E-3/97 Jan and Kristia]ceger AS v Opel Norge AS [1999] 4 CMLR 147 and, in the UK courts, Cound v BMW [1997] Eu LR 277 and Clover Leaf Cars v BMW [1997] Eu LR 535.

[433] See the Commission's Report on the evaluation of Regulation (EC) No 1475/95, 15 November 2000 COM (2000) 743, accessible at www.europa.eu.int/comm/competition/car_sector.

[434] OJ [2002] L 203/30, [2002] 5 CMLR 777; for an overview of Regulation 1400/2002 see the Commission's Competition Policy Newsletter June 2002, pp 31–34 and October 2002, pp 3–6; speech by Monti 'The new legal framework for car distribution' 6 February 2003, available at www.europa.eu.int/comm/competition/speeches; see also Commission's XXXIInd Report on Competition Policy (2002), points 154–185.

[435] A general one-year transitional period to amend pre-existing distribution agreements is provided for under Article 10 and, under Article 12(2), there is a special transitional period of five years relating to the prohibition on location clauses in selective distribution systems under Article 5(2)(b).

as Regulation 2790/99: it applies a market share test[436]; it denies block exemption to agreements containing hard-core restrictions[437]; and it disapplies the block exemption to specific obligations[438]. However Regulation 1400/2002 is stricter than the general regime for vertical agreements in certain important respects: for example Article 1(b) of Regulation 1400/2002 defines a non-compete obligation to include any obligation on the buyer to purchase from the supplier, or from an undertaking designated by the supplier, more than 30 per cent of the buyer's total purchases of the contract goods or services and their substitutes on the relevant market, whereas Article 1(b) of Regulation 2790/99 sets the figure at 80 per cent; and Article 4(2) of Regulation 1400/2002 requires that independent operators must be given access to technical information, diagnostic equipment, tools, including relevant software, and training: this has no counterpart in Regulation 2790/99. The adoption of Regulation 1400/2002 was accompanied by the publication of an *Explanatory Brochure* by DG Competition, which provides valuable guidance on the provisions of the Regulation as well as other issues such as market definition[439].

The new block exemption concerns all levels of motor vehicle distribution: the sale of new motor vehicles, after-sale servicing and the supply of spare parts[440]; it applies both to cars and to commercial vehicles[441]. Unlike Regulation 1475/95 and Regulation 2790/99[442] the new block exemption does not allow the combination of exclusive distribution and selective distribution; car manufacturers must choose one or the other. This rule is meant to develop more effective intra-brand competition in the distribution of motor vehicles[443] and to remove a strait-jacket on the choice of distribution. An important source of increasing competition in the distribution of motor vehicles has emerged from the Internet, in the form of on-line dealers and electronic market-places; Recital 15 of the block exemption says that authorised car dealers should have the right to use the Internet or an Internet referral site.

One of the Commission's key concerns when reviewing the rules on motor vehicle distribution was the independence of car dealers vis-à-vis car manufacturers[444]. This concern manifests itself in several provisions in the block exemption, notably the ability of dealers to sell more than one brand of car in their showroom[445]; the possibility of contracting out after-sales services to a third party[446]; and, within the context of selective distribution, the possibility of active sales[447] and the establishment by distributors of additional outlets[448]. Regulation 1400/2002 also seeks to improve access to and

---

[436] Articles 3(1)–(2).   [437] Article 4.   [438] Article 5.

[439] Available at www.europa.eu.int/comm/competition/car_sector.

[440] Regulation 1400/02, Article 2(1).   [441] Ibid, Article l(n)–(p).

[442] *Vertical guidelines*, paras 162 and 186.

[443] The Commission found that the combination of exclusive distribution with selective distribution under Regulation 1475/95 had failed to prevent agreements having effects incompatible with Article 81(3); see the Commission's *Report on the evaluation of Regulation (EC) No 1475/95* COM (2000) 742 final, 15 November 2000.

[444] COM (2000) 742 final, paras 250–263 and 267–271.

[445] Article 5(1)(a); non-compete obligations are defined in Article 1(b) to include obligations to purchase more than 30 per cent of a buyer's total requirements which is much wider than the definition used in Article 1(b) of Regulation 2790/99: see p 641 above.

[446] Articles 4(1)(g) and 5(1)(b).

[447] Article 4(1)(d); this does not apply to sales of new passenger cars or light commercial vehicles.

[448] Articles 5(2)(b) and Article 12; the black-listed 'location clauses' in selective distribution agreements were subject to special transitional arrangements and only came into force on 1 October 2005; location clauses

competition in the markets for after-sale servicing and spare parts[449]. In March 2006 the Commission announced that it had settled two cases in which complaints had been made against BMW and General Motors that they had raised unjustified obstacles for multi-brand distribution and servicing and had imposed unnecessary restrictions on garages to become members of the authorized networks[450].

Regulation 1400/2002 will remain in force until 31 May 2010, the same date on which Regulation 2790/99 is due to expire; this will allow the Commission to review its assessment of all vertical agreements at the same time. The Commission published a report in May 2008 on the operation of the block exemption[450a].

The transition from Regulation 1475/95 to Regulation 1400/2002 caused car manufacturers to revise their distribution arrangements and, in some cases, to discontinue existing agreements with dealers. This led to a series of references under Article 234 EC from national courts to the ECJ examining the right of the supplier to do so, *VW-Audi Forhandlerforeningen v Skaninavisk Motor Co. A/S*[451], *A.Brünsteiner GmbH v BMW*[452] and *City Motors Groep NV v Citroën Belux NV*[453].

11. SUB-CONTRACTING AGREEMENTS

Sub-contracting agreements are a common feature of the commercial world. A contractor often entrusts another undertaking – the sub-contractor – to manufacture goods, supply services or to perform work under the contractor's instructions. Where the sub-contractor simply supplies goods or services to the contractor, the agreement would be a vertical one and the agreement would be governed by the Commission's *Vertical guidelines* and by the block exemption for vertical agreements[454]. Where a sub-contracting agreement is entered into between competing undertakings it falls to be considered under the Commission's *Guidelines on Horizontal Cooperation Agreements*[455]. However in some cases the contractor transfers know-how to the sub-contractor in order for it to be able to perform the tasks entrusted to it. The Commission has adopted a *Notice on Sub-contracting Agreements* to explain the application of Article 81(1) to this situation[456].

---

are not similarly black-listed for exclusive distribution because, by their very nature, those agreements exclusively allocate territories to one distributor: see Commission Press Release IP/05/1208, 30 September 2005.

[449] See in particular Articles 4(1)(h)–(1), 4(2), 5(1) and 5(3).

[450] Commission MEMO/06/120, 13 March 2006; see also Becker and Hamilton 'Multi-brand distribution and access to repairer networks under Motor Vehicle Block Exemption Regulation 1400/2002: the experience of the BMW and General Motor cases' Commission *Competition Policy Newsletter*, Summer 2006, p 33; for an earlier complaint that Porsche had failed to open its after-sales service to qualified independent repairers see Commission Press Release IP/04/585, 3 May 2004.

[450a] Commission Press Release IP/08/810, 28 May 2008.

[451] Case C-125/05 [2006] ECR I-7037, [2007] 4 CMLR 1071.

[452] Cases C-376/05 and C-377/05 [2006] ECR I-11383, [2007] 4 CMLR 259.

[453] Case C-421/05 [2007] ECR I-653, [2007] 4 CMLR 455.

[454] See the Commission's *Guidelines on Horizontal Cooperation Agreements* OJ [2001] C 3/2, [2001] 4 CMLR 819, para 80.

[455] Ibid, paras 81, 89 and 100; on these *Guidelines* generally see ch 15, pp 588ff.

[456] OJ [1979] C 1/2; for further discussion of sub-contracting see Bellamy and Child *European Community Law of Competition* (Sweet & Maxwell, 6th ed, eds Roth and Rose, 2007), paras 6–189 to 6–195; note also that in some cases an agreement might amount to a licence of intellectual property of the kind that benefits

The Commission's view is that sub-contracting agreements of the kind just described do not infringe Article 81(1). Subject to the proviso explained below, clauses in such agreements which stipulate that any technology or equipment provided by the contractor to the sub-contractor may not be used except for the purpose of the agreement are outside Article 81(1); so too are restrictions on making that technology or equipment available to third parties and a requirement that goods, services or work arising from the use of the technology or equipment will be supplied only to the contractor. The proviso referred to is that the technology or equipment must be necessary to enable the sub-contractor to manufacture the goods, supply the services or carry out the work: where this is the case, the sub-contractor is not regarded as an independent supplier in the market. This proviso is satisfied where the sub-contractor makes use of intellectual property rights or know-how belonging to the contractor. However it would not be satisfied if the sub-contractor could have obtained access to the technology or equipment in question acting on its own.

The Notice sets out other permissible clauses. In particular the contractor can require the sub-contractor to pass on to it on a non-exclusive basis any technical improvements made during the agreement; an exclusive licence may be acceptable where any improvements or inventions on the part of the sub-contractor cannot be made without use of the contractor's intellectual property rights. The sub-contractor must be free, however, to dispose of the results of its own research and development.

12. UK LAW

(A) Vertical integration

It would be theoretically possible to investigate an industry in which the extent of vertical integration was considered to be problematic under the market investigation provisions of the Enterprise Act 2002[457]; in its guidance on these provisions[458] the OFT specifically notes that vertical integration may foreclose competitors and add to entry barriers within an industry[459]. Under the 'complex monopoly' provisions in the now-repealed Fair Trading Act 1973 the Monopolies and Mergers Commission (the predecessor of the Competition Commission) recommended in *The Supply of Beer*[460] that the 'Big Six' brewers should not be permitted to own more than 2,000 retail outlets each: this would require them to divest themselves of 21,900 retail outlets. Radical changes to the UK beer industry were subsequently set in motion by the Supply of Beer (Loan Ties, Licensed Premises and Wholesale Prices) Order 1989[461] and the Supply of Beer (Tied Estate) Order 1989[462]. These orders have since been revoked[463].

from block exemption under Regulation 772/2004 on technology transfer agreements: on this Regulation, see ch 19, pp 771–781.

[457] See ch 11 for a description of the market investigation provisions in the Enterprise Act 2002.

[458] *Market investigation references*, OFT Guideline 511, March 2006, para 5.1, available on the OFT's website at www.oft.gov.uk.

[459] OFT Guideline 511, March 2006, para 5.8.   [460] Cm 651 (1989).

[461] SI 1989/2258.   [462] SI 1989/2390.

[463] See the Supply of Beer (Tied Estate) (Revocation) Order 2002 SI 2002/3204 and the Supply of Beer (Loan Ties, Licensed Premises and Wholesale Prices) (Revocation) Order 2003 SI 2003/52.

It is possible for vertical mergers to be referred to the Competition Commission where the value of the turnover of the enterprise to be acquired is more than £70 million[464].

(B) Commercial agency agreements

There is no specific guidance in the UK on the treatment of commercial agency agreements under the Competition Act 1998. However it can be assumed, as a result of section 60 of the Act, that the OFT, in its application of the Chapter I prohibition, would follow paragraphs 12 to 20 of the European Commission's *Vertical guidelines*[465]. In *Vodafone Ltd*[466] the Director General of Telecommunications did not accept that agreements between Vodafone and its distributors that fixed the retail prices of pre-pay mobile phone vouchers were genuine agency agreements[467]; however it was concluded that Vodafone was not guilty of infringing the Chapter I prohibition since it was acting pursuant to a regulatory obligation[468].

(C) Vertical agreements under the Competition Act 1998

(i) The exclusion of vertical agreements from the Chapter I prohibition until 30 April 2005

Section 50(1) of the Competition Act 1998 gives a power to the Secretary of State to exclude vertical agreements from the Chapter I prohibition. The Competition Act 1998 (Land and Vertical Agreements Exclusion) Order 2000[469] excluded all vertical agreements, with the exception of those imposing minimum or fixed resale prices, from the Chapter I prohibition until 30 April 2005.

(ii) Repeal of the exclusion for vertical agreements

The adoption of the EC Modernisation Regulation meant that there was much to be said for aligning the domestic law on vertical agreements with the position under EC law. It was decided, therefore, that the exclusion from the Chapter I prohibition should be repealed, and that agreements should be dealt with in accordance with EC principles. The statutory instrument was therefore repealed with effect from 1 May 2005 (allowing a period of one year from the entry into force of the Modernisation Regulation during which undertakings could adapt their agreements)[470], since when there has been no special treatment for vertical agreements under UK law. The position is now that vertical agreements that affect trade between Member States are subject to Article 81 including, when applicable, Regulation 2790/99 or Regulation 1400/2002; and that agreements that do not have an effect on trade between Member

---

[464]   Enterprise Act 2002, s 23(1)(b); on vertical mergers under the Act, see ch 22, pp 927–928.

[465]   See pp 609–612 above; on s 60 Competition Act 1998 see ch 9, pp 362–367.

[466]   OFTEL decision of 5 April 2002.   [467]   Ibid, paras 35–37.   [468]   Ibid, para 47.

[469]   SI 2000/310.

[470]   See the Competition Act 1998 (Land Agreements Exclusion and Revocation) Order 2004, SI 2004/1260.

States are subject to the Chapter I prohibition, which will be interpreted consistently with EC law according to the provisions of section 60 of the Competition Act[471], and the EC block exemption by virtue of section 10 of the Act which provides for parallel exemption[472].

(iii) The OFT's guidance on *Vertical agreements*

The OFT has published guidance on *Vertical agreements*[473], Part 2 of which discusses the application of Article 81 EC and the Chapter I prohibition to vertical agreements and Part 3 of which examines Regulation 2790/99, including withdrawal of the block exemption by the OFT[474]. Part 4 discusses the application of Article 81(3) EC and section 9 of the Competition Act in individual cases, and Part 5 deals with the (now repealed) exclusion order. Part 6 briefly looks at the application of Article 82 EC, the Chapter II prohibition and the Enterprise Act to vertical agreements, and Part 7 concludes with some discussion of the competitive assessment of vertical agreements.

(iv) Decisional practice of the OFT

The OFT has investigated a number of vertical agreements under the Competition Act 1998. In *DSG Retail Ltd*[475] the OFT considered that the exclusive distribution agreements between Compaq and Hewlett-Packard, manufacturers of desktop computers, and Dixons did not infringe the Chapter I and II prohibitions; Dixons did not have a dominant position for the purpose of the Chapter II prohibition, and, in the absence of significant market power on Dixons' part, there were insufficient grounds for using the power that existed at that time to withdraw the exclusion from the Chapter I prohibition[476]. In *Lucite International UK Ltd*[477] the OFT concluded that a long-term supply contract for the supply of hydrogen cyanide by BASF to Lucite International was a vertical agreement and therefore, at the time, excluded from the Chapter I prohibition[478]; it further decided that it would not be appropriate to withdraw the exclusion as it was possible that the agreement would have been granted an exemption: it conferred individual and collective benefits on users and consumers by lessening environmental pollution[479]. An investigation into allegations that record companies were taking steps to impede parallel imports of compact discs into the UK was concluded, as the OFT could not find evidence of continuing agreements against which it could take action, though it stated that it would continue to monitor the market in question[480].

On several occasions the OFT has found that vertical agreements involved the imposition of minimum resale prices. In *John Bruce UK Ltd, Fleet Parts Ltd and Truck and Trailer Components*[481] vertical price fixing between John Bruce and Fleet Parts was held to be outside the Exclusion Order and so an infringement of the Chapter I

---

[471] For discussion of section 60 see ch 9, pp 362–367.
[472] For discussion of parallel exemptions see ch 9, p 353.
[473] OFT 419, December 2004.   [474] Ibid, paras 3.30–3.33.   [475] OFT decision of 18 April 2001.
[476] Ibid, paras 97–98 and paras 111 and 118.
[477] OFT decision of 29 November 2002, [2003] UKCLR 176.   [478] Ibid, paras 11–14.
[479] Ibid, paras 39–41.   [480] *Wholesale supply of compact discs*, OFT 391, September 2002.
[481] OFT decision of 17 May 2002, [2002] UKCLR 435.

prohibition[482]: a relatively small fine of £33,737 was imposed in this case, for a combination of horizontal and vertical price fixing. In *Hasbro UK Ltd*[483] a fine of £4.95 million was imposed on Hasbro for imposing minimum resale prices on its distributors[484]. In *Hasbro UK Ltd, Argos Ltd and Littlewoods Ltd*[485] much larger fines, of £17.28 million on Argos and of £5.37 million on Littlewoods, were imposed for a mixture of horizontal and vertical price fixing[486]; Hasbro was given full immunity because of its cooperation with the OFT[487]. On appeal the findings of infringement were upheld by the Competition Appeal Tribunal, although the fines were reduced to £19.50 million[488]. In *Lladró Comercial*[489] the OFT found minimum resale price maintenance provisions in *Lladró's* standard-form documentation, but refrained from imposing a fine since the European Commission had sent to *Lladró* a comfort letter that could be interpreted to mean that this practice did not infringe competition law[490]. In *Replica Football Kit* the OFT imposed fines totalling £18.6 million for a mixture of horizontal price fixing and resale price maintenance in relation to replica football kits[491]. Some of the findings of infringement were annulled on appeal to the Competition Appeal Tribunal[492], and the fines were reduced to £14.92[493]. The OFT has closed its files on several other cases concerning alleged resale price maintenance, often against assurances that the offending behaviour would be terminated[494].

When the OFT received a complaint concerning Audi's authorized repairer standards its intervention caused Audi to make amendments in order to bring them into conformity with the principles of the block exemption for motor vehicle distribution[495].

(E) Enterprise Act 2002

It is possible for vertical agreements to be investigated under the market investigation provisions in the Enterprise Act 2002: these have been described in chapter 11. They will not be used where use of the Competition Act is more appropriate[496]. However the OFT has recognised that in certain circumstances a market investigation reference might be appropriate, for example where vertical agreements are prevalent in a market and have

[482] Ibid, paras 35–37. [483] OFT decision of 28 November 2002, [2003] UKCLR 150.
[484] Ibid, para 47. [485] OFT decision of 19 February 2003, [2003] UKCLR 553.
[486] On the finding of a multilateral agreement in this case see ch 9, pp 331–333.
[487] On leniency under the Competition Act 1998 see ch 10, pp 404–407.
[488] Case Nos 1014/1/1/03 and 1015/1/1/03 *Argos Ltd and Littlewoods Ltd v OFT* [2005] CAT 13, [2005] CompAR 834.
[489] OFT decision of 31 March 2003, [2003] UKCLR 652. [490] Ibid, paras 120–125.
[491] OFT decision of 1 August 2003, [2004] UKCLR 6.
[492] Case Nos. 1021/1/1/03 etc *JJB v OFT* [2004] CAT 17, [2005] CompAR 29.
[493] Case Nos 1019/1/1/03 etc *Umbro Holdings Ltd v OFT* [2005] CAT 22, [2005] CompAR 1060.
[494] See eg OFT Press Release 86/04 of 18 May 2004 in the case of *Swarovski UK Ltd*; case closure summaries of other cases are available at www.oft.gov.uk.
[495] OFT Press Release 97/07, 6 July 2007.
[496] *Market investigation references*, OFT Guideline 511, March 2006, para 2.3; note that the Commission published various reports on vertical agreements under the now-repealed provisions of the Fair Trading Act 1973, including *The Supply of Beer* (above); *Carbonated Soft Drinks* Cm 1625 (1992); *Newspaper and Periodicals* Cmnd 7214 (1978) and Cm 2422 (1993); *Fine Fragrances* Cm 2380 (1993); *Electrical Goods* Cm 3675 and Cm 3676 (1997); *Foreign Packaged Holidays* Cm 3813 (1997); and *New Cars* Cm 4660 (2000).

the effect of preventing the entry of new competitors[497]; it has also said that it might make a reference where a number of firms in a market are vertically integrated and engage in some common form of anti-competitive conduct, for example discrimination against non-integrated competitors[498].

[497] OFT Guideline 511, para 2.6; see also paras 6.15–6.18 and the *Market Investigation References: Competition Commission Guidelines* (June 2003, CC 3), paras 3.41–3.45; 3.76–3.77, available at www.competition-commission.org.uk.

[498] OFT Guideline 511, para 5.9.

17

Abuse of dominance (1): non-pricing practices

CHAPTER CONTENTS

1. INTRODUCTION

The previous four chapters have been concerned with the application of EC and UK competition law to horizontal and vertical agreements between undertakings. The focus of attention in this and the following chapters turns to a different issue: the extent to which the unilateral acts of dominant firms might infringe Article 82 EC and the Chapter II prohibition in the Competition Act 1998.

The main principles underlying Article 82 were discussed in chapter 5; the Chapter II prohibition was explained in chapter 9[1]. It may be helpful to recall that care must be taken in the application of Article 82 and the Chapter II prohibition not to prevent dominant firms from being able to compete 'on the merits'[2]; that Article 82 has been applied to exploitative abuses, to exclusionary practices and to actions that partition the single market[3]; that the dominant position, the abuse and the effects of the abuse may arise on different markets[4]; that a distinction should be drawn between horizontal and vertical foreclosure of the market[5]; and that some limited defences based on the idea of objective justification are available to dominant undertakings accused of abusing a dominant position[6].

This chapter is concerned with non-pricing practices; abusive pricing practices are considered in chapter 18. There is no legal significance in this division of the material: pricing and non-pricing practices can have the same anti-competitive effect. However any analysis of pricing abuses requires an understanding of a number of cost concepts, and these are introduced at the beginning of chapter 18[7]. Abuses that involve the exercise, or non-exercise, of intellectual property rights are considered in chapter 19.

[1] See ch 9, pp 353–362. [2] See ch 5, pp 189–193. [3] See ch 5, pp 199–206.
[4] See ch 5, pp 203–205. [5] See ch 5, pp 202–203. [6] See ch 5, pp 206–209.
[7] See ch 18, pp 707–708.

This chapter will deal in turn with exclusive agreements; with the practice of tying; with refusals to supply, including the so-called 'essential facilities' doctrine; with abusive practices that are harmful to the single market; and with miscellaneous other practices which might infringe Article 82 or the Chapter II prohibition. In each section the application of Article 82 by the European Commission and in the jurisprudence of the Community Courts will be considered first, followed by cases dealt with by the competition authorities in the UK. Reference will be made where appropriate to DG COMP's *Discussion paper on the application of Article 82 of the EC Treaty to exclusionary abuses*[8] ('the *Discussion paper*'), but the reader is reminded that it is not a publication of the Commission, but is rather a staff working paper produced by officials working in DG COMP; and that the *Discussion paper* is not, and should not be read as, draft guidelines, still less as actual guidelines[9].

2. EXCLUSIVE AGREEMENTS[10]

(A) EC case law

The application of Article 81 to vertical agreements was considered in chapter 16, where the Commission's concerns with four groups of agreements – single branding, limited distribution, resale price maintenance and market partitioning – were discussed[11]. Regulation 2790/99 on vertical agreements confers block exemption on such agreements where the supplier has a market share of 30 per cent or less[12], provided that the agreement contains no hard-core restrictions contrary to Article 4[13]; where the agreement is one for exclusive supply, the relevant market share is that of the buyer[14]. Article 5 of the block exemption limits the permissible duration of a non-compete clause to five years[15]. Where the market share exceeds 30 per cent, an individual assessment of a vertical agreement is necessary to determine whether it infringes Article 81(1)[16] and whether it satisfies the terms of Article 81(3)[17]. Paragraph 135 of the Commission's *Guidelines on Vertical Restraints*[18] states that vertical agreements are 'in principle' ineligible for exemption where an undertaking is dominant or becomes dominant as a consequence of a vertical agreement, a contentious point[19] from which the Commission appears to have resiled in paragraph 106 of its *Guidelines on the application of Article 81(3) of the Treaty*[20].

---

[8] Available at www.ec.europa.eu/comm/competition/antitrust/art82/index.html.
[9] See ch 5, pp 210–212.
[10] For further reading on exclusive dealing see section 7 of DG COMP's *Discussion paper on the application of Article 82 of the Treaty to exclusionary abuses*; Motta *Competition Policy: Theory and Practice* (Cambridge University Press, 2004), pp 363–372; O'Donoghue and Padilla *The Law and Economics of Article 82 EC* (Hart Publishing, 2006), pp 352–374.
[11] See ch 16, pp 615–616.   [12] Regulation 2790/99, Article 3(1): see ch 16, p 651.
[13] See ch 16, pp 652–657.   [14] Regulation 2790/99, Article 3(2): see ch 16, p 651.
[15] See ch 16, pp 657–659.   [16] See ch 16, pp 618–638.   [17] See ch 16, pp 662–663.
[18] OJ [2000] C 291/1, [2000] 5 CMLR 1074.
[19] Bishop and Ridyard 'Vertical Restraints Guidelines: Effects based or *Per se* Policy' (2002) 23 ECLR 35; Peeperkorn 'Vertical Restraints Guidelines: Effects based or *Per se* Policy: A Reply' (2002) 23 ECLR 38.
[20] OJ [2004] C 101/97.

A separate issue from the application of Article 81 is whether vertical agreements can infringe Article 82: it is clear that this is possible. In this section consideration will be given to the possibility that exclusive agreements – in particular single branding agreements – might infringe Article 82; the extent to which pricing practices such as the grant of rebates might have the same effect as a single branding agreement is considered in chapter 18[21]. A difference between the application of Article 81 and Article 82 to such agreements is that, where an agreement infringes Article 81, both (or all) of the parties to the agreement will have committed an infringement, since the offence lies in the fact of the agreement. In the case of Article 82, however, it is the dominant firm that infringes the competition rules, since Article 82 applies to a dominant firm's *unilateral* behaviour; the conclusion of an anti-competitive agreement can be an abusive unilateral act, so that the dominant firm can be fined and sued for damages, as well as being unable to enforce the offending provision of the agreement[22].

(i) The application of Article 82 to single-branding agreements

The most obvious vertical agreement that could infringe Article 82 is one whereby a customer is required to purchase a particular brand of goods or services only from a dominant supplier. Various terminology can be used to describe such agreements – 'single branding', 'exclusive purchasing', 'requirements contracts' and 'non-compete obligations'. Each of these terms connotes the same idea: that the purchaser is prevented from purchasing competing products from anyone other than the dominant firm, and that this might lead to horizontal foreclosure of the market by excluding competitors wishing to supply customers served by the dominant firm. The Commission discusses single branding agreements at paragraphs 138 to 160 of the *Guidelines on Vertical Restraints*[23]. As far as Article 82 is concerned, the *Guidelines* state that a dominant firm may not impose a non-compete obligation[24] on buyers unless it can objectively justify such a commercial practice[25]. The *Guidelines* state that Article 82 prevents dominant companies from applying so-called 'English clauses', which require the buyer to report any better offer that it receives and allow it to accept that offer only if the dominant supplier does not match it[26]: clauses such as this enable the dominant firm to exclude competitors, and they heighten the transparency of oligopolistic markets and thereby foster tacit coordination[27]. The *Guidelines* also state that fidelity rebate schemes on the part of dominant firms are prohibited[28]. DG COMP's *Discussion paper* also notes the possible anti-competitive effects of single branding obligations (and rebate systems), although in less emphatic terms than the *Guidelines on Vertical Restraints*[29].

A requirement to purchase all of one's requirements from a dominant firm will be viewed less favourably than an obligation to purchase only a certain percentage: the block exemption for vertical agreements characterises a requirement to purchase more than 80 per cent of one's requirements as a non-compete obligation[30]. The duration of

---

[21] See ch 18, pp 719–727.   [22] On the final point see ch 8, pp 315–316.
[23] OJ [2000] C 291/1, [2000] 5 CMLR 398: see ch 16, pp 627–628.
[24] This term is defined in Article 1(b) of Regulation 2790/99: see ch 16, p 641.
[25] OJ [2000] C 291/1, [2000] 5 CMLR 398, para 141.
[26] [2000] 5 CMLR 398, para 152; this rule is based on Case 85/76 *Hoffmann-La Roche v Commission* [1979] ECR 461, [1979] 3 CMLR 211, paras 102–108.
[27] See ch 14, pp 554–555.
[28] OJ [2000] C 291/1, [2000] 5 CMLR 398, para 152; on loyalty rebates see ch 18, pp 719–727.
[29] See paras 134–150 of the *Discussion paper*.
[30] See Article 1(b) of Regulation 2790/99, discussed in ch 16, p 641.

the agreement will be a critical feature in determining whether it is abusive: the shorter it is, the less likely it is to infringe Article 82: these two factors – the extent and the duration of the exclusive obligation – should always be considered when analysing exclusive agreements under Article 82.

(A) Judgments of the Community Courts There is not a great deal of judicial precedent on the application of Article 82 to single branding agreements; however it is clear that there is a strong possibility that Article 82 will be applied to such agreements when entered into by a firm in a dominant position. Once the ECJ had held in *Suiker Unie v Commission*[31] that it was contrary to Article 82 for a dominant firm to foreclose competition by offering loyalty rebates to customers that purchase only from it, it was inevitable that the same condemnation would apply to a single branding commitment. This was confirmed in *Hoffmann-La Roche v Commission*[32]. The ECJ held that:

An undertaking which is in a dominant position on a market and ties purchasers – even if it does so at their request – by an obligation or promise on their part to obtain all or most of their requirements exclusively from the said undertaking abuses its dominant position within the meaning of Article [82] of the Treaty, whether the obligation in question is stipulated without further qualification or whether it is undertaken in consideration of the grant of a rebate[33].

This language suggests a *per se* approach on the part of the ECJ, that any single branding agreement on the part of a dominant undertaking is abusive. However it is questionable whether it is appropriate to apply *per se* rules under Article 82: a preferable position would be that liability is dependent on plausible evidence that the agreement could foreclose access to the market[34].

In *BPB Industries v Commission*[35] the CFI held that a single branding agreement cannot, as a matter of principle, be considered to infringe Article 81, that is to say that it does not restrict by object: rather it is necessary to examine the effects of such an agreement in its specific context[36]. However the Court went on to say that those considerations:

which apply in a normal competitive market situation, cannot be unreservedly accepted in the case of a market where, precisely because of the dominant position of one of the market operators, competition is already restricted[37].

The CFI did not go so far as to say that there is a *per se* rule against single branding agreements on the part of a dominant firm, but at the very least it suggests a very strict standard.

An important point about the statement by the ECJ in *Hoffmann-La Roche* quoted above is that it is no defence that the customer willingly entered into the agreement, or even that it requested exclusivity: the issue in these cases is not whether the agreement is oppressive to the customer, but whether it could horizontally foreclose competition in the relevant market.

In *Almelo*[38] the ECJ considered that an exclusive purchasing clause in a supply contract for electricity could infringe Article 82 if entered into by a dominant firm, even where the clause was requested by local distributors.

---

[31] Cases 40/73 etc [1975] ECR 1663, [1976] 1 CMLR 295.
[32] Case 85/76 [1979] ECR 461, [1979] 3 CMLR 211; see also Case T-65/89 *BPB Industries plc and British Gypsum v Commission* [1993] ECR II-389, [1993] 5 CMLR 32, paras 65–77, upheld on appeal Case C-310/93 P [1995] ECR I-865, [1997] 4 CMLR 238.
[33] [1979] ECR 461, [1979] 3 CMLR 211, para 89.   [34] See ch 5, pp 195–197.
[35] Case T-65/89 [1993] ECR II-389, [1993] 5 CMLR 32.   [36] Ibid, para 66.   [37] Ibid, para 67.
[38] Case C-393/92 [1994] ECR I-1477.

676 17 ABUSE OF DOMINANCE (1): NON-PRICING PRACTICES

(B) Decisional practice of the Commission In *Istituto/IMC and Angus*[39] the Commission intervened in a case where the dominant supplier of a raw material was refusing to supply a customer except on terms which would have foreclosed competition from its competitors; the Commission persuaded IMC and Angus to offer supply contracts that would last two years with automatic renewal for one year unless terminated by six months' notice. In the *Soda-ash* decisions[40] the Commission fined Solvay €20 million and ICI €10 million for requiring customers to enter into long-term indefinite require-ments contracts and granting fidelity and top-slice rebates designed to exclude competi-tors from the market. The Commission brought an end to exclusive contracts entered into by AC Nielsen for the procurement of data in relation to fast-moving consumer goods in 1997[41]. The Commission took action against Nordiron in respect of exclusive, long-term supply clauses for Molybdenum 99, a base product for radiopharmaceuticals used in nuclear medicine; following the receipt of a statement of objections Nordiron dropped the clauses[42]. The Commission required Frankfurt Airport to abandon long-term contracts covering periods from three to ten years which it had entered into with airlines for the provision of ramp-handling services[43]; the Commission had required the termination of Frankfurt Airport's monopoly of such services and, not surpris-ingly, was unwilling to see this replaced by long-term exclusive terms that would have the same effect in practice of excluding third parties. Agreement was reached with the Commission that the contracts would be for a period of one year only, automatically renewable but terminable on six months' notice[44].

The Commission accepted commitments from The Coca-Cola Company under Article 9 of the Modernisation Regulation[45] that it would refrain from entering into single branding commitments with customers in 2004; the company also agreed not to require customers to purchase a specified minimum percentage of their requirements from it[46]. In the case of *Distrigas* the Commission announced in October 2007 that it had accepted Article 9 commitments from Distrigas, an undertaking that at one time was the only gas supplier on the Belgian wholesale market and that remained dominant on it, that it would limit the duration of future agreements for the supply of gas, and that it would reduce the volume of gas subject to long-term supply commitments[47]. The Commission announced on 11 May 2007 that it had initiated investigations into long-term single-branding agreements for the supply of electricity between Electrabel and its industrial customers in Belgium and between EDF and its customers in France[48].

In the case of *De Beers*[49] the Commission considered that long-term exclusive supply terms for rough diamonds agreed between Alrosa and De Beers could infringe Article 82. Alrosa and De Beers were competitors in the relevant market, and the Commission's concern was that the supply arrangement led to de Beers, *de facto*, acting as an exclusive

---

[39] XVIth *Report on Competition Policy* (1986), point 76.

[40] *Soda-ash/Solvay* OJ [1991] L 152/21 and *Soda-ash/ICI* [1991] L 152/40; these decisions were annulled on procedural grounds by the CFI Cases T-30/91 etc *Solvay SA v Commission* [1995] ECR II-1775, [1996] 5 CMLR 57, confirmed on appeal by the ECJ Cases C-286/95 P [2000] 5 CMLR 413 and 454; however the Commission readopted the decisions in December 2000: OJ [2003] L 10/1.

[41] Commission's XXVIIth *Report on Competition Policy* (1997), pp 144–148.

[42] Commission's XXVIIIth *Report on Competition Policy* (1998), pp 169–170.

[43] *Frankfurt Airport* OJ [1998] L 72/30, [1998] 4 CMLR 779.

[44] Commission Press Release IP/98/794, 8 September 1998.

[45] See ch 7, pp 253–257 on Article 9 of the Modernisation Regulation.

[46] Commission decision of 22 June 2005. [47] Commission Press Release IP/07/1487, 11 October 2007.

[48] Commission MEMO/07/313, 26 July 2007. [49] Commission decision of 22 February 2006.

distributor. De Beers offered commitments to bring the arrangements to an end, which the Commission accepted under Article 9 of the Modernisation Regulation. However Alrosa successfully appealed against the Commission's decision, arguing that the commitments would impact disproportionately on its own business[50].

The Commission condemned exclusivity terms (and other practices such as rebates) in *Prokent-Tomra*[51].

(ii) Article 82 applies to *de facto* as well as to contractual exclusivity

In *Van den Bergh Foods*[52] the Commission concluded that it was an abuse of a dominant position for Van den Bergh to provide freezer cabinets free of charge to retail outlets on condition that they were to be used exclusively for the storage of its ice-cream products[53]. The consequence of this practice was that, *de facto*, Van den Bergh achieved outlet exclusivity, since retailers were unlikely to, and in practice did not, maintain a second freezer in their shops; in effect, therefore, the retailers would purchase ice-cream exclusively from Van den Bergh. This decision, which was upheld on appeal to the CFI[54] and to the ECJ[55], demonstrates that Article 82 can be applied to *de facto* as well as to contractual exclusivity[56].

(iii) Long-term agreements are not necessarily abusive

In some circumstances long-term supply agreements may be justifiable, for example where the supplier has to make a client-specific investment in order to be able to supply[57]. It was noted in chapter 16 that this may result in the terms of Article 81(3) being satisfied in relation to an agreement that infringes Article 81(1); in the case of Article 82, the same reasoning may result in a finding that an agreement is not abusive. In *Gas Natural/Endesa* the Commission required changes to a supply agreement for gas by Gas Natural, the dominant supplier in the Spanish gas market, to Endesa, the leader in electricity there: the agreement would have resulted in Endesa taking all its gas from Gas Natural, but this was changed so that Endesa could purchase a certain proportion of its requirements elsewhere; the duration of the agreement was limited to 12 years[58].

(B) UK case law

The OFT has published a guideline on *Vertical agreements*[59] which sets out its thinking on the application of Article 81 EC and the Chapter I prohibition to vertical agreements[60], but which also sets out some general thoughts on the assessment of

---

[50] See ch 7, p 256.

[51] Commission decision of 29 March 2006; the case is on appeal to the CFI, Case T-155/06 *Tomra Systems and others v Commission*, not yet decided; see Maier-Rigaud and Vaigauskaite 'Prokent/Tomra, a textbook case? Abuse of dominance under perfect competition', Summer 2006 *Competition Policy Newsletter*, 19.

[52] OJ [1998] L 246/1, [1998] 5 CMLR 530.   [53] Ibid, para 265.

[54] Case T-65/98 *Van den Bergh Foods Ltd v Commission* [2003] ECR II-4653, [2004] 4 CMLR 1.

[55] Case C-552/03 P *Unilever Bestfoods (Ireland) v Commission* [2006] ECR I-9091, [2006] 5 CMLR 1460.

[56] See para 94 of the Opinion by Advocate General Cosmas in Case C-344/98 *Masterfoods Ltd v HB Ice Cream Ltd* [2000] ECR I-11369, [2001] 4 CMLR 449.

[57] See the Commission's *Guidelines on Vertical Restraints*, paras 116, sub-para 4 and 155; see also para 138 and paras 172–176 of DG COMP's *Discussion paper*.

[58] Commission Press Release IP/00/297, 27 March 2000.   [59] OFT 419, December 2004.

[60] Ibid, paras 5.1–5.5.

vertical restraints, including efficiencies that may be associated with them[61]. The OFT also published a draft competition law guideline on *Assessment of conduct* in April 2004 which specifically addressed the application of Article 82 EC and the Chapter II prohibition to various types of behaviour[62]. However the OFT decided not to proceed to the publication of a final guideline, given that the European Commission had initiated its own review of Article 82. The draft guideline remains on the website of the OFT[63]. The text that follows will not draw upon it, given that it was simply a draft for consultation; however relevant paragraphs will be cited for readers interested in the embryonic views of the OFT at that time. Specific guidelines have been published on the application of the competition rules, including Article 82 and the Chapter II prohibition, in particular regulated sectors, namely telecommunications[64], water and sewerage[65], energy[66], and railways[67].

The OFT has intervened on a few occasions in relation to exclusive agreements that it considered to be abusive[68]. In *Bacardi* the OFT was concerned that Bacardi's vertical agreements foreclosed the market by requiring pubs and bars to sell exclusively its white rum and thereby infringed the Chapter II prohibition[69]. The case was closed on Bacardi giving (non-binding) assurances that it would not insist on single branding[70], although this was challenged on appeal before the Competition Appeal Tribunal by a third party complainant[71]. This case was eventually settled[72]; it is interesting to note that the CAT suggested that in future a settlement of a case such as this should be made under the statutory procedure now set out in section 31A of the Competition Act 1998, a procedure that was not available at the time that the OFT was dealing with the case[73].

In *Calor Gas Northern Ireland* the OFT investigated five-year single branding agreements entered into in Northern Ireland between Calor Gas and various retailers; it concluded that Calor Gas was dominant and that the effect of its network of agreements was to make entry into or expansion within the market more difficult. A negotiated settlement was achieved whereby Calor Gas agreed to reduce the length of the agreements to two years[74].

In *English Welsh and Scottish Railway Ltd*[75] the Office of Rail Regulation found that EW&S had abused its dominant position in a number of ways, including by entering

---

[61] Ibid, paras 7.1–7.29.   [62] OFT 414a, April 2004.   [63] www.oft.gov.uk.

[64] *The application of the Competition Act in the telecommunications sector*, OFT 417, February 2000.

[65] *The application of the Competition Act in the water and sewerage sectors*, OFT 422, February 2000.

[66] *Application in the energy sector*, OFT 428, January 2005.

[67] *Application to services relating to railways*, OFT 430, October 2005.

[68] The OFT's draft guideline on *Assessment of conduct*, OFT 414a, April 2004, discusses vertical restraints at paras 7.1–7.12.

[69] OFT Press Release PN 38/02, 28 June 2002.   [70] OFT Press Release PN 10/03, 30 January 2003.

[71] Case No 1017/211/03 *Pernod Ricard Sa and Campbell Distillers v Office of Fair Trading* [2004] CAT 10, [2004] CompAR 707.

[72] Case No 1017/211/03 *Pernod Ricard Sa and Campbell Distillers v Office of Fair Trading* [2005] CAT 9, [2005] CompAR 894.

[73] Ibid, para 7; for discussion of s 31A of the Competition Act see ch 10, pp 396–397.

[74] OFT case closure of 30 June 2003, available at www.oft.gov.uk; see also *Calor Gas Ltd v Express Fuels Ltd* [2008] CSOH 13, where the Outer House of the Court of Session in Scotland decided that single branding agreements with a minimum duration of five years infringed Article 81 and were therefore void and unenforceable.

[75] ORR decision of 17 November 2006, [2007] UKCLR 937; the agreements in question were void and unenforceable as a result of the ORR's directions that the exclusive terms should be removed: see *English Welsh & Scottish Railway Ltd v E.ON UK plc* [2007] EWHC 599 (Comm), [2007] UKCLR 1653.

into exclusive agreements for the carriage of coal to various power stations: a fine of £4.1 million was imposed. In *National Grid*[76] the Gas and Electricity Markets Authority concluded that National Grid had abused its dominant position in the market for the provision of domestic gas meters by entering into long-term contracts with gas suppliers that rent meters from National Grid; its view was that the contracts had the effect of preventing gas suppliers from acquiring less expensive and/or more technologically advanced meters from competing operators. National Grid was fined £41.6 million for this infringement[77].

In *Claymore Dairies Ltd v OFT*[78] the Competition Appeal Tribunal was critical of the OFT's investigation into whether Robert Wiseman Dairies had entered into agreements with two customers in Scotland that, *de facto*, resulted in a single branding arrangement[79] and therefore set the decision on this point aside[80]; no further order was made since, by the time of the CAT's judgment, the position in the market had changed.

3. TYING[81]

This section considers the extent to which tying may infringe Article 82 EC or the Chapter II prohibition in the Competition Act 1998.

(A) Terminology and illustrations of tying

Tying is the practice of a supplier of one product, the tying product, requiring a buyer also to buy a second product, the tied product. Tying may take various forms:

- **Contractual tying** The tie may be the consequence of a specific contractual stipulation: for example in the *Hilti* case Hilti required users of its nail guns and nail cartridges to purchase nails exclusively from it[82]

- **Refusal to supply** The effect of a tie may be achieved where a dominant undertaking refuses to supply the tying product unless the customer purchases the tied product

- **Withdrawal or withholding of a guarantee** A dominant supplier may achieve the effect of a tie by withdrawing or withholding the benefit of a guarantee unless a customer uses a supplier's components as opposed to those of a third party[83]

---

[76] OFGEM decision of 21 February 2008.

[77] The case is on appeal to the CAT, Case No 1097/1/2/08 *National Grid Co v the Gas and Electricity Markets Authority*, not yet decided.

[78] Case 1008/2/1/02 [2005] CAT 30, [2006] CompAR 1.   [79] Ibid, paras 287–313.   [80] Ibid, para 318.

[81] For further reading on tying and bundling see section 8 of DG COMP's *Discussion paper on the application of Article 82 of the Treaty to exclusionary abuses*; Bishop and Walker *The Economics of EC Competition Law* (Sweet & Maxwell, 2nd ed, 2002), paras 6.54–6.68; Nalebluff *Bundling, Tying, and Portfolio Effects* (DTI Economics Paper No 1, 2003), available at www.dti.gov.uk/ccp/publications.htm; Motta *Competition Policy: Theory and Practice* (Cambridge University Press, 2004), pp 460–483; O'Donoghue and Padilla *The Law and Economics of Article 82 EC* (Hart Publishing, 2006), ch 9; Van den Bergh and Camesasca *European Competition Law and Economics: A Comparative Perspective* (Sweet & Maxwell, 2nd ed, 2006), pp 264–276.

[82] See p 683 below.

[83] The Commission required an end to this practice in *Novo Nordisk*: XXVIth *Report on Competition Policy* (1996), pp 142–143.

- **Technical tying** This occurs where the tied product is physically integrated into the tying product, so that it is impossible to take one product without the other: this is what happened in the *Microsoft* case, discussed below[84]

- **Bundling** is closely related to the idea of tying. It refers to a situation in which two products are sold as a single package at a single price. Two types of bundling should be noted:
  - **Pure bundling** This occurs where it is only possible to purchase the two products together
  - **Mixed bundling** This occurs where the two products are sold separately; however, when they are sold together they are available at a discount to the price that would be charged if they were purchased separately.

The extent to which bundling might lead to an infringement of Article 82 is discussed in chapter 18 on pricing abuses, since it is necessary to analyse the price of the bundle to determine whether this is the case[85].

(B) Policy considerations: arguments for and against tying

A simplistic objection to tying is that it involves the dominant firm 'leveraging' its position in relation to the tying product to achieve increased sales in the market for the tied product, thereby extending its market power. This would be an example of horizontal foreclosure of the market[86]. So powerful was this argument that, at one time, US law took a strict standard against the practice, holding it to be a *per se* infringement. However this approach was subjected to sustained criticism, in particular by 'the Chicago School'[87]: the central thrust of this criticism was that a monopolist can earn its monopoly profit only once, and that if it has monopoly power over product A, it cannot increase its profit by leveraging its position into product B. The insights of the Chicago School were persuasive, and there is now general recognition that *per se* illegality is inappropriate for tying: it is now subjected in the US to rule of reason analysis[88], requiring a full analysis of the likelihood of competitive harm.

It is not only that tying is no longer thought to be eligible for *per se* illegality. There is now much better understanding that tying is a normal feature of commercial life, and not something that should be regarded as inherently suspicious. Tying involves the integration of components into one product and this can lead to significant economic efficiencies, resulting in lower costs of production and distribution and improvements in quality. Manufacturing activity, by its very nature, involves the bringing together of different components, and it would be perverse to suggest that, when engaged in by a dominant firm, such behaviour should be stigmatised as presumptively unlawful: the presumption should be the other way[89].

A few illustrations of the benefits of tying may assist. Tying may be used to maintain the efficiency of the tying product: for example a piece of equipment may function at

---

[84] See pp 684–685 below.   [85] See ch 18, pp 727–729.   [86] See ch 5, pp 202–203.

[87] See eg Bork *The Antitrust Paradox* (1978, Basic Books), ch 19; Bowman 'Tying Arrangements and the Leverage Problem' (1967) 67 Yale Law Journal 67; Turner 'The Validity of Tying Arrangements under the Antitrust Laws' (1958) 72 Harvard Law Review 73; Ridyard 'Tying and Bundling – Cause of Complaint?' (2005) 26(6) ECLR 316; for a review of the different arguments see Scherer and Ross *Industrial Market Structure and Economic Performance* (Houghton Mifflin, 3rd ed, 1990), pp 565–569.

[88] *US v Microsoft* 253 F. 3d 34 (2001).

[89] For a discussion of efficiency explanations for the practice of tying and bundling see Nalebluff *Bundling, Tying, and Portfolio Effects* (DTI Economics Paper No 1, 2003), part 4.3.

its best only if a particular chemical or material is used which is available solely from the manufacturer, because it has a patent or relevant know-how. Another reason for tying may be to enable economies of scale or scope to be achieved: a manufacturer of a photocopying machine which also supplies ink, paper and spare parts will be able to reduce costs if all these items are delivered to customers at the same time; tying all these products to one another may lead to lower prices. A third reason for tying is to enable a producer to discriminate between its customers: the manufacturer of a photocopying machine may wish to charge high-volume users more than low-volume ones; this it can do by tying photocopying paper: the customer which uses the machine the most will have to pay the most and the tie operates as a substitute for putting a meter onto the machine[90]. A further example of a tying practice that may promote efficiency is where X produces game consoles and computer games that operate only with those consoles: as consumers buy more consoles of a particular type, software writers produce more games that are compatible with it. This, in due course, may lead to higher sales of consoles and, therefore, lower prices overall. In this case the network effect leads to efficiencies to the benefit of consumers[91].

However there may be circumstances in which tying might have a foreclosure effect on the market. Some 'post-Chicago' authors have identified some vitality in the 'leveraging' theory, for example where the firm with dominance over the tying product also has some market power in relation to the tied product and is able to raise barriers to entry in that market[92]. DG COMP's *Discussion paper* suggests that a dominant undertaking might be able to achieve a horizontal foreclosure of the market if it could reduce the number of potential customers available for competitors in the tied market; this might cause existing competitors to be marginalised or to exit from the tied market and act as a barrier to entry for potential new entrants[93]. The *Discussion paper* also suggests that tying might protect the dominant undertaking's position in the tying market, since a would-be entrant might need to produce both the tying and the tied product in order to compete effectively[94].

(C) EC case law

Both Article 81(1)(e) and Article 82(2)(d) specifically state that tie-in agreements may amount to infringements. Although Article 81 may be applicable to such agreements[95], most cases have been brought under Article 82, including the landmark decision in *Microsoft*[96]. Article 82(2)(d) gives as an example of abuse:

making the conclusion of contracts subject to acceptance by the other parties of supplementary obligations which, by their nature or according to commercial usage, have no connection with the nature of such contracts.

The ECJ has established that tying practices may also be caught by Article 82 where they do not fall within the precise terms of Article 82(2)(d): in *Tetra Pak v Commission* the

[90] See Bowman 'Tying Arrangements and the Leverage Problem' (1957) 67 Yale Law Journal 19.
[91] On network effects see ch 1, pp 11–12.
[92] See Whinston 'Tying, Foreclosure and Exclusion' (1980) 80 American Economic Review 837; *Bundling, Tying, and Portfolio Effects* (DTI Economics Paper No 1, 2003), para 4.4.2.
[93] See the *Discussion paper*, para 180.   [94] Ibid, para 181.
[95] See the Commission's *Guidelines on Vertical Restraints* OJ [2000] C 291/1, [2000] 5 CMLR 1074, paras 215, 224.
[96] Case T-201/04 *Microsoft Corpn v Commission* [2007] ECR II-000, [2007] 5 CMLR 846.

Court concluded that there was an unlawful tie even though the products in question were connected by commercial usage, a situation not covered by the express wording of paragraph (d)[97].

Issues of tying (and bundling) have also arisen in cases under the EC Merger Regulation, most noticeably in *Tetra Laval/Sidel*[98] and in *GE/Honeywell*[99]; the Commission's *Guidelines on the assessment of non-horizontal mergers*[100] explain the circumstances in which it might proceed against a merger on the basis of so-called 'conglomerate effects'[101].

In determining whether there is an infringement of Article 82, five issues must be addressed:

- does the accused undertaking have a dominant position?
- is the dominant undertaking guilty of tying two distinct products?
- was the customer coerced to purchase both the tying and the tied products?
- could the tie be detrimental to competition by foreclosing access to the market?
- is there an objective justification for the tie?

Each of these requirements will be considered in turn.

(i) Does the accused undertaking have a dominant position?

Clearly there can be an infringement of Article 82 only if an undertaking has a dominant position, and this would be in the tying market; there is no need for there to be dominance in the tied market. DG COMP's *Discussion paper* suggests, uncontroversially, that a finding of abuse would be more likely where the dominant undertaking is dominant in both markets[102].

(ii) Is the dominant undertaking guilty of tying two distinct products?[103]

(A) The legal test The notion of tying is, at first sight, simple enough; a customer is forced to purchase two distinct products that could have been bought individually. However a moment's reflection reveals that there is a real difficulty in determining when two or more products should be regarded as distinct so that their sale together should be regarded as a tie. A car is sold with wheels and tyres: clearly this does not involve a tie; there will also be a spare wheel: presumably this is not a tie; the car may be fitted with a radio: this perhaps does amount to a tie; if the purchaser is required to insure the car with an insurance company specified by the manufacturer or dealer, this presumably would be a tie. In the same way a pair of shoes would not be regarded as a tie; nor would

---

[97]   Case C-333/94 P [1996] ECR I-5951, [1997] 4 CMLR 662, para 37; the CFI makes the same point at para 861 of its judgment in Case T-201/04 *Microsoft Corpn v Commission* [2007] ECR II-000, [2007] 5 CMLR 846, although it concluded that the abuse in that case fell fully within Article 82(2)(d) anyway: ibid, para 862.

[98]   Case M 2416, decision of 30 October 2001, OJ [2004] L 43/13, on appeal Case C-12/03 P *Commission v Tetra Laval BV* [2005] ECR I-987, [2005] 4 CMLR 573.

[99]   Case M 2220, decision of 3 July 2001, OJ [2004] L 248/1, on appeal Case C-210/01 *General Electric v Commission* [2005] ECR II-5575, [2006] 4 CMLR 686.

[100]   Available at www.ec.europa/comm/competition/mergers.

[101]   Ibid, paras 91–121.   [102]   *Discussion paper*, para 184.

[103]   For an interesting discussion of this issue in the Irish Supreme Court, concluding that a savings protection scheme was an integral part of the service provided by credit unions so that there was no tie, see *The Competition Authority v O'Regan and others* [2007] IESC 22, [2007] ECC 343.

the sale of shoes with laces; but a requirement to purchase a particular brand of polish with the shoes presumably would be. It is necessary to determine at what point a case becomes one of tying: the burden of proving that two products are the subject of a tie is on the competition authority or the plaintiff in proceedings before a national court.

According to the formulation in Article 82(2)(d) products are tied when they have no connection either 'by their nature or according to commercial usage'. This position was somewhat blurred by the ECJ's judgment in the *Tetra Pak* case where it held that, in some cases, two products could be tied even where they were connected by commercial usage[104].

The Commission's *Guidelines on Vertical Restraints* state that, in determining whether two products are distinct, one should look at the demand of buyers and ask whether, from their perspective, in the absence of a tie-in, they would purchase the two products on different markets[105]. DG COMP's *Discussion paper* repeats this idea, adding that it is not necessary for the two products to belong to different product markets for them to regarded as distinct[106]. It also discusses the evidence that may enable a decision on distinctness to be made: direct evidence may be available, that customers, when given a choice, purchase the products separately; so may indirect evidence, for example that undertakings that do not have market power do not sell the products together, or that there are independent undertakings on the market that sell the tied product without selling the tying one[107].

A problem arises when *new* products are developed and sold together: the evidence just described will not exist in such circumstances. This can pose a serious problem where highly complex products – for example in IT and multimedia cases – are introduced to the market. In such cases it may be necessary to concentrate on the effect a tie-in might have on competition and whether an apparent tie-in can be objectively justified rather than on whether it amounts to a tie-in in the first place.

Given that commercial usage is part of the test of what amounts to a tie, it must follow that what was once a tie may cease to be so because of changed consumer perceptions: the *Discussion paper* suggests that a time may come where there would be no independent demand for the tied product[108].

(B) The Hilti *case* In *Eurofix-Bauco v Hilti*[109] the Commission held that the requirement of Hilti that users of its patented nail cartridges should also acquire nails from it exploited customers and harmed competition and was an abuse of a dominant position; a fine of €6 million was imposed for this and other infringements. Hilti appealed[110], *inter alia*, on the ground that the Commission had been wrong to find that the nail guns, the cartridge strips and the nails were three distinct product markets rather than forming one indivisible whole, a 'powder actuated fastening system' comprising the nail guns and their consumables. The CFI held that there were three markets, and that independent producers should be free to manufacture consumables intended for use in equipment manufactured by others unless in so doing they would infringe intellectual property rights[111].

---

[104] See pp 681–682 above.   [105] *Guidelines on Vertical Restraints*, para 216.

[106] *Discussion paper*, para 185.

[107] Ibid, para 186.   [108] Ibid, para 187.   [109] OJ [1988] L 65/19, [1989] 4 CMLR 677.

[110] Case T-30/89 *Hilti AG v Commission* [1990] ECR II-163, [1992] 4 CMLR 16, upheld on appeal Case 53/92 P *Hilti AG v Commission* [1994] ECR I-667, [1994] 4 CMLR 614.

[111] Case T-30/89 *Hilti AG v Commission* [1990] ECR II-163, [1992] 4 CMLR 16, para 68.

(C) The Tetra Pak *case* In the *Tetra Pak II* case[112] Tetra Pak required customers to whom
it supplied liquid packaging machines to purchase cartons from it; it also insisted that
only it should provide the services of repair and maintenance. Tetra Pak argued that it
supplied an integrated distribution system for liquid and semi-liquid foods intended for
human consumption and could not therefore be guilty of an abuse in tying the supply
of its filling machines to the supply of its cartons. The Commission stated at paragraph
119 of its decision that it was not customary to tie cartons to machines. As in *Hilti*, the
Commission held that the consumable cartons formed a separate market upon which
the dominant firm was trying to eliminate competition. A particularly noteworthy feature of the ECJ's judgment is that it stated that:

> even where tied sales of two products are in accordance with commercial usage or there is a
> natural link between the two products in question, such sales may still constitute abuse within the
> meaning of Article [82] unless they are objectively justified[113].

(D) The Microsoft *case* The question of whether two distinct products were the subject
of a tie was a key issue in the *Microsoft* case. The Commission found that Microsoft had
tied its Media Player to its personal computer operating system[114]. In the Commission's
view there was a separate demand for stand-alone media players, distinguishable from
demand for operating systems: there were a number of operators on the market developing and supplying media players on a standalone basis; and Microsoft itself sold versions
of its Media Player separately from its operating system[115]. The Commission considered
that the ubiquity of Microsoft's operating system, including Media Player, meant that
content providers and software developers would tend to rely on Microsoft's technology;
consumers in turn would therefore prefer to use Media Player because of the wide array
of complementary software and content available for that product: a self-reinforcing network effect. The Commission rejected Microsoft's claim that efficiency considerations
justified the inclusion of Media Player in the operating system[116]. The tie in this case
was an example of technical bundling: customers were not forced contractually to take
Media Player; nor were they induced to do so by pricing incentives; rather Microsoft's
operating system included Media Player, whether customers wanted it or not.

On appeal to the CFI the Commission's decision was upheld[117]. The CFI agreed with
the Commission's finding that the operating software system and the media player were

---

[112] OJ [1992] L 72/1, [1992] 4 CMLR 551, upheld on appeal to the CFI Case T-83/91 *Tetra Pak International
SA v Commission* [1994] ECR II-755, [1997] 4 CMLR 726 and on appeal to the ECJ Case C-333/94 P *Tetra
Pak International SA v Commission* [1996] ECR I-5951, [1997] 4 CMLR 662; see Korah 'The Paucity of
Economic Analysis in the EEC Decisions on Competition: Tetra Pak II' (1993) 46 Current Legal Problems
148, pp 156–172.

[113] Case C-333/94 P *Tetra Pak International SA v Commission* [1996] ECR I-5951, [1997] 4 CMLR 662,
para 37.

[114] *Microsoft* Commission decision of 24 March 2004, upheld on appeal Case T-201/04 *Microsoft Corpn
v Commission* [2007] ECR II-000, [2007] 5 CMLR 846; for comment on the finding of a tie in the *Microsoft*
decision see Art and McCurdy 'The European Commission's Media Player Remedy in its Microsoft Decision:
Compulsory Code Removal Despite the Absence of Tying or Foreclosure' (2004) 11 ECLR 694 (the authors of
this article were advisers to Microsoft during the proceedings in this case); see also Banasevic, Huby, Pena,
Castellot, Sitar and Piffaut 'Commission adopts Decision in the Microsoft case' Competition Policy Newsletter,
Summer 2004, pp 46–47 (the authors of this article were officials at DG COMP at the time of the decision).

[115] Commission decision of 24 March 2004, paras 800–813.   [116] Ibid, paras 956–970.

[117] Case T-201/04 *Microsoft Corp v Commission* [2007] ECR II-000, [2007] 5 CMLR 846; for discussion of
the case by Commission officials see Kramler, Buhr and Wyns 'The judgment of the Court of First Instance
in the Microsoft case' *Competition Policy Newsletter* Number 3, 2007, 39.

separate products[118]. The Court noted that the IT and communications industry was in constant and rapid evolution, so that what appear to be separate products may subsequently be regarded as forming a single product[119]; it then pointed out that the CFI's function in this case was to consider whether the operating system and Media Player were separate products *in May 1999* when the conduct complained of was alleged to be harmful, rather than at the time of the judgment (September 2007) when a different answer might be given[120]. The CFI said that the distinctness of the products had to be determined by reference to consumer demand[121]. In the Court's view there was a functional difference between system software (the operating system itself) and applications software (word processing, media player etc)[122]; there were operators on the market that supplied the tied product (a media player) without the tying product (an operating system): the CFI pointed out that case law had established that this was 'serious evidence' of there being separate products[123]; Microsoft supplied Media Player as a separate product to work with its competitors' operating systems[124]; it was possible to download Microsoft's media player independently from its website[125]; Microsoft promoted its media player as a standalone product[126]; it had a separate licence agreement for its media player[127]; and customers did acquire media players from Microsoft's competitors[128].

In January 2008 the Commission announced that it had initiated fresh proceedings against Microsoft in relation to alleged tying[129]. In this case Opera, a producer of a competing browser, complained that Microsoft's inclusion of Internet Explorer amounted to an illegal tie, in particular since Microsoft had introduced proprietary technologies in its browser that would reduce compatibility with open internet standards. Much is at stake in this case: is Microsoft entitled to include new functionalities in its operating system, or should it be required to 'componentise' the products that it offers to the market, so that different applications software should be supplied separately?

(iii) Was the customer coerced to purchase both the tying and the tied products?

The language of Article 82(2)(d) suggests that a component of the abuse of tying is that the customer is coerced into acquiring the tied product: 'making the conclusion of contracts subject to acceptance by the other parties of supplementary obligations'. A contractual stipulation obviously satisfies this test; however in *Microsoft* there was no contractual requirement to take Media Player; rather it was included in the operating software, whether customers wanted it or not: in the parlance of the subject, this was technical bundling. The CFI concluded in *Microsoft* that there was coercion of customers to take Media Player because it was impossible to uninstall it from the operating software system[130]; the Court was unimpressed by the fact that there was no extra charge for the inclusion of Media Player[131].

(iv) Could the tie have a market-foreclosing effect?

The fact that dominance, abuse and the effects of the abuse can be in different markets is particularly significant in analysing tie-ins, where an undertaking will be dominant in one market and impose a tie which has an effect in a neighbouring market[132]. The

---

[118] Ibid, paras 912–944. [119] Ibid, para 913. [120] Ibid, para 914. [121] Ibid, para 917. [122] Ibid, para 926.
[123] Ibid, para 927. [124] Ibid, para 928. [125] Ibid, para 929. [126] Ibid, para 930. [127] Ibid, para 931.
[128] Ibid, para 932. [129] Commission MEMO/08/19, 14 January 2008.
[130] Case T-201/04 *Microsoft Corp v Commission*, para 963. [131] Ibid, para 967–969.
[132] See ch 5, pp 203–205.

Commission has applied Article 82 to several tying transactions because it considered that the practice could have a foreclosure effect. In *IBM*[133] it brought an end to IBM's practices of 'memory bundling' and 'software bundling', accepting an undertaking that IBM would offer its System/370 central processing units without a main memory or with only sufficient memory as was needed for testing.

In *Centre Belge d'Etudes de Marche-Télémarketing v CLT*[134] the ECJ held that it was an abuse of a dominant position for the Luxembourg radio and television station, which had a statutory monopoly, to insist that advertisers should channel their advertising through its advertising manager or an agency appointed by it. This amounted to an extension of its monopoly power from one market into a neighbouring one, a kind of 'tie-in' that prevented other advertising agencies from competing with it and which limited the commercial freedom of users. In *Napier Brown-British Sugar*[135] the Commission applied this principle when condemning British Sugar's refusal to allow customers to collect sugar at ex-factory prices, thereby reserving to itself the distribution function in respect of this product. In *London European-Sabena*[136] the Commission held that an attempt by Sabena to stipulate that access to its computer reservation system on the part of London European should be conditional upon London European using Sabena's ground-handling services was an abuse under Article 82. In *De Post/La Poste*[137] the Commission objected to the Belgian postal operator giving a more favourable tariff for its general letter mail service to those customers who also purchased its new business-to-business mail service.

In its *Microsoft* judgment the CFI agreed with the Commission's finding that the inclusion of Media Player led to a foreclosure of the market[138]. It considered that the inclusion of Media Player had appreciably altered the balance of competition in favour of Microsoft to the detriment of competitors[139]. The Court referred to the ubiquity of the Windows operating system which, in 2002, enjoyed a market share of more than 90 per cent[140]. It also said that users who find that Media Player is pre-installed on their operating system would be less likely to make use of an alternative media player[141]. The Court considered that the inclusion of Media Player created disincentives for manufacturers of computers ('OEMs') to include the media player of a competitor in their computers[142]. The CFI also agreed with the Commission that the ubiquity of Windows was likely to have a strong influence upon content providers and software designers[143]. The Court also noted market surveys that demonstrated a trend towards the use of Media Player to the detriment of other media players[144].

(v) Is there an objective justification for the tie?

A dominant undertaking may be able successfully to argue that tying is objectively justified or enhances efficiency: the burden of proof would be on the dominant firm[145].

---

[133] Commission's XIVth *Report on Competition Policy* (1984), points 94–95; see further on this matter XVIth *Report on Competition Policy* (1986), point 75 and XVIIth *Report on Competition Policy* (1987), point 85.

[134] Case 311/84 [1985] ECR 3261, [1986] 2 CMLR 558.   [135] OJ [1988] L 284/41, [1990] 4 CMLR 196.

[136] OJ [1988] L 317/47, [1989] 4 CMLR 662.   [137] OJ [2002] L 61/32, [2002] 4 CMLR 1426.

[138] Case T-201/04 *Microsoft Corpn v Commission* [2007] ECR II-000, [2007] 5 CMLR 846, paras 1031–1090.

[139] Ibid, para 1034.   [140] Ibid, para 1038.   [141] Ibid, para 1041.   [142] Ibid, para 1043.

[143] Ibid, para 1060.   [144] Ibid, para 1078.

[145] See ch 5, pp 206–209; paras 205 and 206 of the *Discussion paper* discuss possible efficiency defences.

In *Hilti* the Commission's concern was that the practice of tying would prevent produ-cers of nails from supplying users of Hilti nail guns. Hilti argued that its behaviour was objectively justifiable as it was necessary to maintain safety standards, so that operators would not be injured by nail guns. The Commission had rejected this argument on the facts, concluding that Hilti's primary concern was the protection of its commercial position rather than a disinterested wish to protect users of its products. The CFI upheld this finding. It pointed out that in the UK, where the competitors were selling their nails, there were laws about product safety and authorities which enforced them. In those circumstances it was not the task of a dominant undertaking to take steps on its own initiative to eliminate products which, rightly or wrongly, it regarded as dangerous or inferior to its own products.

The CFI concluded in *Microsoft* that Microsoft had failed to show any objective justi-fication for tying Media Player with its operating software[146].

(D) UK case law[147]

As in the case of Article 82(2)(d), section 18(2)(d) of the Competition Act 1998 specifi-cally states that a tie-in agreement may constitute an abuse of a dominant position.

In the case of *Pricing of BT Analyst*[148] OFCOM received a complaint that BT had tied a billing analysis product, BT Analyst, to the provision of business telephony services. OFCOM's conclusion was that the billing product was part of the telephony service, and that therefore there was no tie[149]. On two occasions OFTEL[150] and the OFT[151] have been asked to investigate allegations of tie-in practices, but in each case they concluded that there was one single market over which there was no dominance, rather than a domi-nated primary market and a separate, secondary market[152].

4. REFUSAL TO SUPPLY[153]

There are some circumstances in which a refusal on the part of a dominant firm to sup-ply goods or services can amount to an abuse of a dominant position. Refusal to supply is a difficult and controversial topic in competition law. First, as a general proposition most legal systems in countries with a market economy adopt the view that firms should

---

[146] Case T-201/04 *Microsoft Corpn v Commission* [2007] ECR II-000, [2007] 5 CMLR 846, paras 1144–1167.

[147] The OFT's draft guideline on *Assessment of conduct*, OFT 414a, April 2004, discusses vertical restraints, including tying and bundling, at paras 7.1–7.12; note also the guidelines on the application of the competi-tion rules to telecommunications, water and sewerage, energy and railways, cited in nn 64–67 above.

[148] OFCOM Decision of 27 October 2004, [2005] UKCLR 15.   [149] Ibid, paras 46–53.

[150] *Swan Solutions Ltd/Avaya Ltd*, 6 April 2001.   [151] *ICL/Synstar*, 26 July 2001.

[152] On this point see ch 1, pp 35–36.

[153] For further reading on refusals to supply see section 9 of DG COMP's *Discussion paper on the application of Article 82 of the EC Treaty to exclusionary abuses*; Bishop and Walker *The Economics of EC Competition Law* (Sweet & Maxwell, 2nd ed, 2002), paras 6.104–6.124; Motta *Competition Policy: Theory and Practice* (Cambridge University Press, 2004), pp 66–68; O'Donoghue and Padilla *The Law and Economics of Article 82 EC* (Hart Publishing, 2006), pp ch 8; Van den Bergh and Camesasca *European Competition Law and Economics: A Comparative Perspective* (Sweet & Maxwell, 2nd ed, 2006), pp 276–280.

be allowed to contract with whomsoever they wish; compulsory dealing is not a normal part of the law of contract. Secondly, irrespective of whether the law should sometimes require that a dominant firm should be required to supply, there are many perfectly reasonable explanations for a refusal to do so: for example that a customer is a bad debtor, that there is a shortage of stocks, or that production has been disrupted. Thirdly, forcing a dominant undertaking to supply may not be conducive to economic welfare if it means that 'free riders' can take advantage of investments that have been made by other firms in the market: this will be discussed specifically in the context of the so-called 'essential facilities doctrine' below[154].

When considering the law of refusal to supply it is helpful to keep in mind the distinction suggested in DG COMP's *Discussion paper* between horizontal and vertical foreclosure of the market[155]. Most cases on refusal to supply involve harm to the downstream market, that is to say vertical foreclosure; however there have been some cases that were concerned with horizontal foreclosure, and these are noted towards the end of this section[156]. The point is also made there that discrimination on grounds of nationality is likely to attract attention under Article 82[157]; and that it is unclear whether it is unlawful for a dominant pharmaceutical manufacturer to withhold sales in order to prevent parallel imports to a higher-priced Member State[158].

DG COMP's *Discussion paper* did not provide an exhaustive account of all abusive refusals to supply: rather it examined the law from three perspectives: the termination of an existing supply relationship; refusal to supply a new customer; and refusal to licence intellectual property rights or to provide information needed for interoperability. This is a useful way of presenting the material and will be adopted in the text that follows, with the caveat that the *Discussion paper* should not be read as guidelines[159].

EC case law will be considered first, then that of the UK.

(A) EC case law[160]

(i) Termination of an existing supply relationship[161]

Unilateral[162] refusals to supply are caught, if at all, under Article 82. The term 'refusal' in this context includes a constructive refusal, for example by charging unreasonable prices[163] or by imposing unfair trading conditions for the supply in question or by treating a particular customer in a discriminatory manner; a margin squeeze can also be seen as a constructive refusal to supply[164].

(A) Commercial Solvents v Commission It was established by the ECJ in *Commercial Solvents v Commission*[165] that a refusal to supply could, in some circumstances, amount

---

[154] See pp 690–699 below.   [155] See ch 5, pp 202–203.   [156] See pp 699–700 below.

[157] See p 700 below.   [158] See p 700 below.   [159] See ch 5, pp 210–212.

[160] Note that the Commission has given specific guidance on the application of Article 82, including the rules on refusal to supply, in the postal services and electronic communications sectors: see ch 23, pp 974–975 and pp 978–979.

[161] *Discussion paper*, paras 217–224.

[162] Note the extent to which apparently 'unilateral' action may be held to be attributable to an agreement or concerted practice contrary to Article 81: ch 3, pp 107–113.

[163] See ch 18, pp 709–718 on excessive pricing.

[164] See the *Discussion paper*, para 220; margin squeezing is discussed in ch 18, pp 744–748.

[165] Cases 6/73 & 7/73 [1974] ECR 223, [1974] 1 CMLR 309.

to an abuse of a dominant position. Zoja was an Italian producer of a drug used in the treatment of tuberculosis; it was dependent upon supplies of a raw material, amino-butanol, the dominant supplier of which was Commercial Solvents. When the latter refused to make amino-butanol available to Zoja, the Commission found that it had abused its dominant position and ordered it to resume supplies. The Commission's decision was upheld on appeal by the ECJ. In this case not only was Commercial Solvents a dominant supplier of amino-butanol in the upstream market for the raw material; its refusal to supply Zoja coincided with the emergence of Commercial Solvent's own subsidiary, ICI, onto the downstream market for the anti-TB drug, on which Zoja was operating: the refusal to supply would eliminate Zoja from the downstream market. In the language of DG COMP's *Discussion paper* this was a case of vertical foreclosure. This is an important point, since it means that it was not the 'mere' refusal to supply that infringed Article 82: rather it was a refusal which:

would amount to eliminating one of the principal manufacturers of ethambutol in the common market[166].

More specifically, the ECJ said that:

[a]n undertaking which has a dominant position in the market in raw materials and which, with the object of reserving such raw material for manufacturing its own derivatives, refuses to supply a customer, which is itself a manufacturer of these derivatives, and therefore risks eliminating all competition on the part of this customer, is abusing its dominant position[167].

DG COMP's *Discussion paper* notes that the *Commercial Solvents* judgment requires a finding of competitive harm, but that it does not require the elimination of all competition on the downstream market[168]: as explained above, the ECJ's concern was that CSC's refusal to supply would eliminate '*one* of the principal manufacturers' (emphasis added) on the market. A case-by-case analysis should therefore be undertaken to ascertain whether a particular refusal to supply is likely to have a significant impact upon competition in the downstream market[169].

The fact that the *Commercial Solvents* judgment requires a finding of competitive harm should provide some comfort to dominant firms that are concerned as to whether they are obliged to continue to supply existing customers *ad infinitum*, or that they could only discontinue the relationship on the basis of objective justification, as to which they would bear the burden of proof[170]. It is obviously wise that a dominant firm that intends to cease supplying a customer should give a reasonable period of notice and treat it in a reasonable manner; however, as a general proposition, a competition authority's predominant concern will be with competitive harm and a detriment to consumer welfare, and not with the commercial relationship between the parties to an agreement.

(B) Aftermarkets In *Hugin*[171] the Commission condemned that firm's decision to discontinue the supply of spare parts for Hugin's cash register machines to Liptons, a firm in the UK that serviced cash registers; Hugin's intention was itself to operate on the downstream market for servicing. On appeal[172] the ECJ annulled the Commission's decision because of the failure on its part to show that trade between Member States

---

[166] Ibid, para 25. [167] Ibid. [168] *Discussion paper*, para 222. [169] Ibid, paras 222–223.
[170] On the burden of proof in Article 82 cases see ch 5, p 209.
[171] OJ [1978] L 284/41, [1978] 1 CMLR D19.
[172] Case 22/78 *Hugin Kassaregister v Commission* [1979] ECR 1869, [1979] 3 CMLR 345.

would be affected; the ECJ did not express any opinion upon the Commission's finding of abuse. The most controversial issue in *Hugin* was whether it was correct to define a separate product market for spare parts, or whether the Commission should have widened the market to include the original equipment itself: market definition in such cases is discussed in chapter 1[173]. As far as the abusive refusal is concerned, the Commission's decision was not that the 'mere' refusal to supply on Hugin's part was unlawful, but that this would lead to a vertical foreclosure of the downstream market; in other words the case is consistent with the approach taken in *Commercial Solvents*.

(C) Economic dependency It is important to point out that many Member States have laws that impose obligations on undertakings, *whether dominant or not*, to supply customers which are in a position of economic dependency: examples are Article L420-2, paragraph 2 of the French Commercial Code and section 20 of the German Act against Unfair Restraints of Competition of 1957. A separate examination of this issue must therefore be undertaken both by dominant and non-dominant undertakings: it should be recalled that Article 3(2) of the Modernisation Regulation permits the application of national legal provisions that are stricter than Article 82 to unilateral behaviour[174]. A useful guide to such laws will be found in *Dominance: the regulation of dominant firm conduct in 38 jurisdictions worldwide*[175], which specifically addresses the question, in relation to each jurisdiction, whether there are any rules applying to the unilateral conduct of non-dominant firms.

(ii) Refusal to supply a new customer[176]

The *Commercial Solvents* judgment established that a refusal to supply *an existing customer* could amount to an abuse of a dominant position. An obvious question that then had to be addressed was whether there could be circumstances in which a dominant undertaking could be required to supply goods or services *to a new customer*. It is unprovable, but may be the case, that courts and competition authorities feel that a dominant undertaking owes a responsibility to treat its existing customers in a 'fair' or 'reasonable' manner, and it was noted above that many Member States have laws that protect economically dependent firms from their suppliers, whether dominant or not; furthermore the customer of a dominant firm may have made investments connected to the supply relationship that exists between them, as would have been true of Zoja in the *Commercial Solvents* case[177]. None of these considerations applies where a *new* customer asks a dominant firm to supply it with goods or services.

It has become clear that there are circumstances in which a dominant firm may be under an obligation to deal with a new customer, but that there should be strict limitations upon this duty: a refusal will be unlawful only where the goods or services in question are 'indispensable' for a firm to operate on a downstream market.

The text that follows will begin with discussion of the so-called 'essential facilities' doctrine. Then the ECJ's judgment in the *Oscar Bronner* case will be examined, followed by some other case law of the Community Courts. After some comments on market definition in essential facilities cases the application in practice of Article 82 to refusals

---

[173] See ch 1, pp 35–36.   [174] See ch 2, p 77.
[175] Global Competition Review, 2008, eds Janssens and Wessely.
[176] See DG COMP's *Discussion paper*, paras 225–236.
[177] This point is noted at para 217 of DG COMP's *Discussion paper*.

to supply new customers will be examined, including a review of various facilities to which the doctrine has been applied.

(A) The essential facilities doctrine The expression 'essential facilities' will often be encountered in discussions of refusal to supply new customers: the idea is that there are some facilities that firms must have access to if they are to be able to compete in a downstream market. There is a vast amount of periodical literature on the essential facilities doctrine[178]. It has its antecedents in US antitrust; the first case is considered to have been *United States v Terminal Railroad Association of St. Louis*[179], although the term was not used in that case. Much more recently, in *Verizon Communications Inc v Law Offices of Curtis Trinko*[180], the Supreme Court adopted a notably unenthusiastic approach to the essential facilities doctrine. A case was brought under section 2 of the Sherman Act asserting the right of third parties to have access to Verizon's local tele-communications network. The New York and federal telecommunications regulators had conducted investigations and concluded them; the plaintiff was not satisfied with the outcome, and therefore brought a claim based on competition law. The Supreme Court reviewed the case law on essential facilities, in particular the *Aspen Skiing* case[181], which it regarded as 'at or near the outer boundary of section 2 liability'.

The term 'essential facility' is particularly apt where an undertaking seeks access to a physical infrastructure such as a port, airport, railway network or a pipeline: it is a fairly natural use of language to regard such infrastructures as 'facilities'; however the case law has demonstrated that there might also be an obligation, for example, to license intellectual property rights or to provide proprietary information[182], where the expres-sion 'essential facility' is less appropriate. However the term essential facility will be used in the text that follows in deference to the weight of literature that deploys it.

There is an obvious reason why the issue of access to essential facilities has aroused so much interest. From the 1980s onwards the Commission (and many Member States) developed a policy that favoured the demonopolisation and liberalisation of sectors that for much of the twentieth century were regarded as natural monopolies, or which were considered to be inappropriate for the market mechanism; often these sectors were under state control or in state ownership. Exposing sectors such as telecommunications,

[178] The following articles would capture much of the writing on this subject: Areeda 'Essential Facilities: An Epithet in Need of Limiting Principles' 58 Antitrust Law Journal 841 (1990); Temple Lang 'Defining Legitimate Competition: Companies' Duties to Supply Competitors and Access to Essential Facilities' (1994) 18 Fordham International Law Journal 439; Ridyard 'Essential Facilities and the Obligation to Supply Competitors under UK and EC Competition Law' (1996) 17 ECLR 438; Lipsky and Sidak 'Essential Facilities' (1999) 51 Stanford Law Review 1187; Korah 'Access to Essential Facilities under the Commerce Act in the Light of Experience in Australia, the European Union and the United States' (2000) 31 Victoria University of Wellington Law Review 231; Capobianco 'The Essential Facility Doctrine: Similarities and Differences between the American and European Approaches' (2001) 26 EL Rev 548; Doherty 'Just What are Essential Facilities?' (2001) 38 CML Rev 397; Pitofsky, Patterson and Hooks 'The Essential Facilities Doctrine under US Antitrust Law' (2002) 70 Antitrust Law Journal 443; Bavasso 'Essential Facilities in EC Law: the Rise of an "Epithet" and the Consolidation of a Doctrine in the Communications Sector' [2003] Yearbook of European Law (Oxford University Press, eds Eeckhout and Tridimas), ch 2.
[179] 224 US 383 (1912).
[180] 540 US 398 (2004); for comment see Géradin 'Limiting the Scope of Article 82 EC: What can the EU learn from the US Supreme Court's Judgment in *Trinko* in the wake of *Microsoft*, *IMS*, and *Deutsch Telekom*?' (2004) 41 CML Rev 1519.
[181] *Aspen Skiing Co v Aspen Highlands Skiing Corp* 472 U.S. 585 (1985).   [182] See ch 19, pp 786–792.

energy markets and transport to competition was considered desirable. However competition would be slow to emerge where service providers could compete only if they had access to important infrastructures such as telecommunication wires and cables, the electricity grid, gas and oil pipelines, ports, airports and railway lines owned and operated by dominant undertakings. In such cases control of the infrastructure gives rise to what is often referred to as a 'bottleneck' problem: that competition is impossible where one firm, or a combination of firms, can prevent others from operating on the market by denying access to a facility which is essential and cannot be duplicated.

In many Member States this problem was overcome by the establishment of specific regulatory regimes that mandate access to such infrastructures on reasonable, non-discriminatory terms[183]; and in some systems of competition law there are specific rules requiring undertakings in particular sectors to supply[184]. It may be sensible in principle that situations of natural or persistent monopoly should be dealt with by a system of *ex ante* regulation rather than by competition law: a competition authority is likely to be ill-equipped to deal with the persistent disputes in relation to access, and the appropriate price for access, that arise in relation to essential facilities. However the Commission, proceeding from the ECJ's judgment in *Commercial Solvents*, began to develop its practice under Article 82 in such a way that a refusal to allow access to an essential facility could be found to be an abuse of a dominant position. As a result of this, there are circumstances in which access can be achieved by invoking competition law.

In *Oscar Bronner* Advocate General Jacobs set out the main features of the US doctrine of essential facilities at paragraph 47 of his Opinion, and in the following paragraph referred to two decisions of the Commission concerning Holyhead Harbour. At paragraphs 56 to 58 of his Opinion the Advocate General pointed out very clearly to the ECJ that allowing competitors to demand access to the essential facilities of dominant firms, which might seem to be pro-competitive by enabling claimants to enter the market in the short term, might ultimately be anti-competitive, if the consequence would be to discourage the necessary investment for the creation of the facility in the first place[185]. At paragraph 56 of his Opinion he pointed out that:

the right to choose one's trading partners and freely to dispose of one's property are generally recognised principles in the laws of the Member States

and that:

incursions on those rights require careful justification.

In the following paragraph the Advocate General stated that, in the long term, it is generally pro-competitive to allow an undertaking to retain its facilities for its own use, since granting access to a third party may remove the incentive to invest in the establishment of efficient facilities. At paragraph 58 the Advocate General stressed the

---

[183] See ch 23, pp 970ff.

[184] See para 53 of the Opinion of Advocate General Jacobs in Case C-7/97 *Oscar Bronner GmbH & Co, KG v Mediaprint Zeitungs-und Zeitschriftenverlag GmbH & Co KG* [1998] ECR I-7791, [1999] 4 CMLR 112; see also Part IIIA of the Australian Trade Practices Act 1974, inserted by the Competition Policy Reform Act 1995, and s 8(b) of the South African Competition Act 1998; on the provisions in Australian law see Kench and Pengilley 'Part IIIA: Unleashing a Monster?' in *Trade Practices Act: A Twenty-Five Year Stocktake* (The Federation Press, 2001, eds Hanks and Williams).

[185] See further paras 235 and 236 of DG COMP's *Discussion paper*; it is noted there that fewer qualms may be felt on the need to protect the investment of a dominant firm whose position may be attributable to special or exclusive rights conferred by a Member State.

importance of the fact that the primary purpose of Article 82 is to prevent distortions of competition, and not to protect the position of particular competitors[186]. While accepting that the case law did, in certain circumstances, impose a duty on dominant firms to supply, the Advocate General advised that the duty should be appropriately confined and should be invoked only where a clear detriment to competition would follow from a refusal.

(B) Oscar Bronner v Mediaprint In *Oscar Bronner*[187] Bronner was an Austrian publisher of a daily newspaper, *Der Standard*, and wished to have access to the highly developed home-delivery distribution system of its much larger competitor, Mediaprint; Bronner complained that a refusal to allow such access amounted to an infringement of the Austrian equivalent of Article 82. The Austrian court sought the opinion of the ECJ, under Article 234 EC, whether such a refusal would infringe Article 82. The entire tone of the judgment is sceptical towards Bronner's case.

The ECJ stated that the first task for the national court would be to determine whether there was a separate market for the home-delivery of newspapers in Austria, and whether there was insufficient substitutability between Mediaprint's nationwide system and other, regional, schemes. If the market was the nationwide delivery of newspapers to homes, the national court would be bound to conclude that Mediaprint had a monopoly, and since this extended to the entire territory of Austria, that this monopoly would be held in a substantial part of the common market[188].

The ECJ then moved on to the question of abuse. It pointed out that in *Commercial Solvents* the effect of the refusal to supply the raw material by the dominant firm was likely to eliminate all competition in the downstream market between its own subsidiary and anyone else[189]. The ECJ then referred to the *Magill* case[190], saying that the refusal by the owner of an intellectual property right to licence it to a third party could, in exceptional circumstances, involve an abuse[191]; in the Court's view *Magill* was an exceptional case for four reasons. First, the information sought by Magill was indispensable to the publication of a comprehensive listings guide: without it Magill could not publish a magazine at all; second, there was a demonstrable potential consumer demand for the would-be product; third, there were no objective justifications for the refusal to supply; and fourth, the refusal would eliminate all competition in the secondary market for TV guides[192]. The ECJ said, therefore, that, for there to be an abuse, it would have to be shown that refusal to grant access to the home-delivery service would be likely to eliminate all competition in the daily newspaper market (the downstream market) and that the home-delivery service was indispensable to carrying on business in the newspaper market[193]. In the ECJ's view, use of Mediaprint's home-delivery

---

[186] See also the Order of the President of the CFI in Case T-184/01 R *IMS Health Inc v Commission* [2001] ECR II-3193, [2002] 4 CMLR 58, para 145.

[187] Case C-7/97 *Oscar Bronner GmbH v Mediaprint Zeitungs- und Zeitschriftenverlag GmbH* [1998] ECR I-7791, [1999] 4 CMLR 112; see Treacy 'Essential Facilities – Is the Tide Turning?' (1998) 19 ECLR 501; Bergman 'The *Bronner* Case – A Turning Point for the Essential Facilities Doctrine?' (2000) 21 ECLR 59.

[188] [1998] ECR I-7791, [1999] 4 CMLR 112, paras 32–36.   [189] Ibid, para 38.

[190] Cases C-241/91 P etc *RTE and ITP v Commission* [1995] ECR I-743, [1995] 4 CMLR 718; for an analysis of this case see ch 19, pp 787–788.

[191] Case C-7/97 *Oscar Bronner GmbH v Mediaprint Zeitungs- und Zeitschriftenverlag GmbH* [1998] ECR I-7791, [1999] 4 CMLR 112 , para 39.

[192] Ibid, para 40.   [193] Ibid, para 41.

service was not indispensable, since there were other means of distributing daily news-papers, for example through shops, kiosks, and by post[194]; furthermore there were no technical, legal, or economic obstacles that made it impossible for other publishers of daily newspapers to establish home-delivery systems of their own[195]. Specifically on the question of whether access to the distribution system could be considered indis-pensable the ECJ said that:

45. It should be emphasised in that respect that, in order to demonstrate that the creation of such a system is not a realistic potential alternative and that access to the existing system is there-fore indispensable, it is not enough to argue that it is not economically viable by reason of the small circulation of the daily newspaper or newspapers to be distributed.

46. For such access to be capable of being regarded as indispensable, it would be necessary at the very least to establish, as the Advocate General has pointed out at point 68 of his Opinion, that it is not economically viable to create a second home-delivery scheme for the distribution of daily newspapers with a circulation comparable to that of the daily newspapers distributed by the existing scheme.

In the ECJ's view, the behaviour of Mediaprint did not amount to an abuse of a domi-nant position.

The ECJ's judgment in *Bronner* establishes that the key to the law on refusal to sup-ply to a new customer is indispensability. The 'facility' must be something that is inca-pable of being duplicated, or which could be duplicated only with great difficulty. In some cases duplication may be physically impossible: for example there may be only one point on the coast-line of a country where a deep-sea port can be established; and plan-ning or environmental reasons may make it impossible to build a competing airport, a nationwide system of gas transportation, or a second rail network. The impossibility of duplication may be legal, for example where an undertaking owns intellectual property rights, such as the copyright in *Magill*. It may also be that a facility cannot be duplicated for economic reasons, although the ECJ was careful to point out in Bronner that this should be determined by reference to a competitor in the position of Mediaprint, not Bronner: that is to say that it is not sufficient for a small firm to argue that, because of its smallness, it should be entitled to have access to its larger competitor's infrastruc-ture; rather economic non-duplicability asks whether the market is sufficiently large to sustain a second facility such as Mediaprint's distribution system. The Court repeated this idea in *IMS Health GmbH & Co v NDC Health GmbH & Co*[196]. The requirement of indispensability means that it is not sufficient that it would be convenient or useful to have access: access must be essential. In the Commission's Notice on the Application of the Competition Rules to Access Agreements in the Telecommunications Sector[197] it states that:

It will not be sufficient that the position of the company requesting access would be more advan-tageous if access were granted – but refusal of access must lead to the proposed activities being made either impossible or seriously and unavoidably uneconomic[198].

(C) *Further case law of the Community Courts* In *Tiercé Ladbroke v Commission*[199] (which pre-dated Bronner but is consistent with it) the CFI rejected a claim by an operator of

---

[194] Ibid, para 42.   [195] Ibid, para 44.

[196] Case C-418/01 [2004] ECR I-5039, [2004] 4 CMLR 1543, paras 28–30.

[197] OJ [1998] C 265/2, [1998] 5 CMLR 821, para 91(a).   [198] Ibid.

[199] Case T-504/93 [1997] ECR II-923, [1997] 5 CMLR 309; see Korah The Ladbroke Saga' (1998) 19 ECLR 169.

betting shops in Belgium that French race-course operators were obliged to provide it with sound and television pictures of horse races in France. At paragraph 131 of its judgment the CFI said that a refusal to supply could not fall within the prohibition of Article 82:

unless it concerned a product or service which was either essential for the exercise of the activity in question, in that there was no real or potential substitute, or was a new product whose introduction might be prevented, despite specific, constant and regular potential demand on the part of consumers[200].

On the facts of *Ladbroke* the televised broadcasting of horse races, which would be an additional, indeed desirable, service for punters in Belgium, could not be regarded as indispensable for the exercise of bookmakers' main activity, namely the taking of bets[201]. Furthermore Ladbroke could not rely on the ECJ's judgments in the *Commercial Solvents v Commission* and the *Télémarketing*[202] cases since, in each of them, the dominant firm was present on the downstream market; the société de courses in *Ladbroke* had no presence on the Belgian betting market.

In *European Night Services*[203], which also predated *Bronner* but is consistent with it, the Commission concluded that a joint venture, European Night Services, established by four rail operators to provide overnight rail services between the UK and the Continent through the Channel Tunnel, infringed Article 81(1); however it concluded that the criteria of Article 81(3) were satisfied, subject to a condition that the parents of the joint venture should supply equivalent services – such as train paths, locomotives, and train crews – to third parties to those that it supplied to European Night Services: in doing this the Commission was treating these services as though they were essential facilities. On appeal to the CFI[204] the Court held that the Commission had failed to demonstrate that the agreement restricted competition contrary to Article 81(1), and annulled it for that reason[205]. However the CFI also held that, even if Article 81(1) was infringed, the condition that rail services should be supplied to third parties should be annulled[206]. Applying *Magill* and *Ladbroke* the CFI said that 'a product or service cannot be considered necessary or essential unless there is no real or potential substitute'[207]. In the CFI's view the Commission had failed to prove that this was the case.

(D) Market definition in essential facilities cases As in any investigation under Article 82, it is necessary to define the relevant market in an essential facilities case. The definition of the essential facility in the upstream market will inevitably be influenced by the downstream market: for example in *Sealink/B&I – Holyhead* the Commission noted that there were three 'corridors' for short-sea routes between Great Britain and Ireland: the northern corridor, served, for example, by Stranraer in Scotland; the central corridor, served predominantly by Holyhead; and the southern corridor, served by

---

[200] The second part of this sentence, focussing on the introduction of a new product, is the key consideration in cases in which a licence of an intellectual property right is sought under Article 82: see ch 19, pp 786–792.

[201] Case T-504/93, para 132.

[202] Case 311/84 *Centre Belge d'Etudes de Marche-Télémarketing v CLT* [1985] ECR 3261, [1986] 2 CMLR 558.

[203] OJ [1994] L 259/20, [1995] 5 CMLR 76.

[204] Cases T-374/94 etc *European Night Services v Commission* [1998] ECR II-3141, [1998] 5 CMLR 718.

[205] See ch 3, pp 133–134.   [206] [1998] ECR II-3141, [1998] 5 CMLR 718, paras 205–221.

[207] Ibid, para 208.

Fishguard, Pembroke, and Swansea in south and west Wales. The Commission defined the upstream market as the provision of port facilities for passenger and ferry services on the central corridor route; however, had it considered that the downstream market was all short-sea crossings between Great Britain and Ireland, it could not have defined the upstream market so narrowly; in this case, Holyhead Harbour (or more precisely the services available there) would not have been found to be essential. This demonstrates that essential facility cases require an analysis of the downstream market, since without this it is not possible to define the upstream one.

A further point about market definition in essential facility cases is that the dominant firm may not be operating on a market, in the colloquial sense of that term, in relation to the product it refuses to supply; it may not be in the business of supplying that input to anyone. However this does not mean that, in competition law terms, it cannot have market power over the input in question: the ECJ has said that it is sufficient that there is a potential, or even a hypothetical, market[208].

(E) Practical application of the law on essential facilities There have been a number of Commission decisions on essential facilities. The first occasion on which the Commission actually used the expression was *Sealink/B&I–Holyhead: Interim Measures*[209]. The Commission received a complaint about Sealink, which owned and operated a port – Holyhead, in north Wales – from which it provided a ferry service to and from Ireland. A rival ferry operator, B&I, also used Holyhead, and claimed that Sealink organised the port's sailing schedules in a way that caused maximum disruption to its (B&I's) services and inconvenience to its passengers. The Commission held that there was a *prima facie* case of abuse and ordered interim measures[210]. It stated that:

A dominant undertaking which both owns or controls and itself uses an essential facility, *ie* a facility or infrastructure without access to which competitors cannot provide services to their customers, and which refuses its competitors access to that facility or grants access to competitors only on terms less favourable than those which it gives its own services, thereby placing the competitors at a competitive disadvantage, infringes Article [82], if the other conditions of that Article are met ... The owner of an essential facility which uses its power in one market in order to strengthen its position on another related market, in particular, by granting its competitor access to that related market on less favourable terms than those of its own services, infringes Article [82] where a competitive disadvantage is imposed upon its competitor without objective justification[211].

Sealink was ordered to change its schedules in order to avoid disruption during B&I's loading and unloading operations.

A clear statement of what constitutes an abuse in an essential facilities case can be found in another Commission decision on access to ports, *Port of Rødby*[212]:

[A]n undertaking that owns or manages and uses itself an essential facility, *ie* a facility or infrastructure without which its competitors are unable to offer their services to customers, and refuses to grant them access to such facility is abusing its dominant position[213].

Where a firm controls an essential facility and operates on a downstream market, it may be sensible for it to operate the facility separately from the downstream activity and to

---

[208] See Case C-418/01 *IMS Health GmbH & Co v NDC Health GmbH & Co* [2004] ECR I-5039, [2004] 4 CMLR 1453, para 44; this point is helpfully discussed in Pitofsky, Patterson and Hooks 'The Essential Facilities Doctrine under US Antitrust Law' (2002) 70 Antitrust Law Journal 443, pp 458–461; see also DG COMP's *Discussion paper*, para 227.
[209] See [1992] 5 CMLR 255.   [210] On interim measures see ch 7, p 253.   [211] Ibid, para 41.
[212] OJ [1994] L 55/52, [1994] 5 CMLR 457.   [213] Ibid, para 12.

maintain separate accounts for each business. If it operates the essential facility as an entirely separate business, without regard to its downstream activity, it is less likely to commit an abuse.

The owner of an essential facility will not commit an abuse where it has an objective justification for a denial of access. Obvious justifications would be that the undertaking seeking access is not creditworthy or that it is technically incapable of using the facility in a proper manner. A particular issue that arises in the case of essential facilities is that there may be capacity constraints which make it impossible for access to be provided[214]. For example the owner of a port might already be using it to full capacity, in which case it would not be possible for it to grant access to a third party. If several competitors are already using the facility and are operating in the same downstream market, this would suggest that granting access to another undertaking would not be necessary to maintain competition there. If there is only capacity for one additional user, it might be appropriate to hold an auction and to grant access to the highest bidder. It has never been decided by the Commission or the Community Courts whether the owner of an essential facility can be under a duty to *increase* capacity in order to enable a third party to have access; the Commission is understood to be investigating this issue in a case against ENI of Italy, in which it is concerned that ENI may be hoarding capacity on and strategically under-investing in its gas transmission system as a way of foreclosing competitors in the supply of gas in Italy[215].

(F) Facilities to which the doctrine has been applied It may be helpful to identify a number of facilities to which access has been mandated under Article 82. Most obviously the doctrine has been applied to physical infrastructures:

- **Ports** The *Sealink* and *Port of Rødby* cases were noted above[216]

- **Airports** In *Frankfurt Airport*[217] the Commission required that the airport authority should terminate its monopoly over ground-handling services and that it should grant access to third parties wishing to supply such services there[218]

- **Rail networks** In *GVG/FS*[219] the Commission concluded that Ferrovie dello Stato, the Italian state-owned railway company, had abused its dominant position by preventing Georg Verkehrsorganisation, a small German railway operator, from providing rail transport from Germany to Milan. The abuses consisted of refusal to grant access to the Italian railway infra-structure[220]: the Commission explicitly described this infrastructure as an essential facility, given the unfeasibility of a competitor duplicating FS's long-distance railway network as a result of the cost involved and the impossibility of obtaining the necessary rights of way[221];

---

[214] The Commission rejected the airport authority's arguments on capacity constraints in *Frankfurt Airports* OJ [1998] L 72/30, [1998] 4 CMLR 779, paras 74–88.

[215] Commission MEMO/07/187, 11 May 2007; note that the Italian Competition Authority was crit-ical of ENI's failure to expand capacity in a decision of 12 February 2006 available at www.agcm.it/eng/index.htm.

[216] Note that the Commission's interim measures in the case of *Irish Continental Group v CCI Morlaix*, reported in the Commission's XXVth *Report on Competition Policy* (1995), pp 120–121 and at [1995] 5 CMLR 177, was different from the *Sealink* case in that the port operator in the *Irish Continental* case was not active on the downstream ferry market; see also *Tariffs for Piloting in the Port of Genoa* OJ [1997] L 301/27.

[217] OJ [1998] L 72/30, [1998] 4 CMLR 779; note that Council Directive 96/97/EC, OJ [1997] L 272/36 lib-eralises ground-handling at airports and prevents discriminatory fees.

[218] See p 676 above on the termination of the long-term supply contracts.

[219] OJ [2004] L 11/17, [2004] 4 CMLR 1446.   [220] Ibid, paras 119–131.   [221] Ibid, para 120.

a refusal to supply traction (a locomotive, driver, and ancillary services)[222]; and a refusal to enter into an international grouping of the kind necessary for cross-border rail passenger services[223].

- **Gas pipelines** The Commission has taken action in relation to access to gas pipelines[224]; it initiated two new sets of proceedings in May 2007 concerning the gas infrastructure of RWE in Germany[225] and ENI in Italy[226].

- **Oil storage** The Commission applied the essential facilities doctrine to equipment for storing jet fuel and transferring it to supply points at Milan's Malpensa Airport; this case was brought under Article 81 rather than Article 82, since a number of undertakings owned the infrastructure in question[227].

- **Telecommunications wires and cables** The essential facilities doctrine is capable of application to telecommunications networks[228].

- **Set-top boxes** It may be possible to invoke the essential facilities doctrine to obtain access to set-top boxes which are necessary, for example, for the provision of interactive television services[229].

The doctrine has also been applied to less obviously 'physical' facilities:

- **Computerised airline reservation system**[230] The Commission has ordered that access be made available to a computerised reservation in the air transport sector.

- **Interlining** In *British Midland/Aer Lingus* the Commission required Aer Lingus to provide 'interlining facilities' to a competing airline, so that passengers of the latter would be able, in certain circumstances, to fly on the aeroplanes of the former[231].

- **Cross-border payment systems** The Commission may insist that access be granted to a cross-border payment system[232]. In *Society for Worldwide International Financial Telecommunications* SWIFT controlled the only international network for transferring payment messages; it also operated the only network capable of supplying connections for banking establishments anywhere in the world. The Commission considered that the network

---

[222] Ibid, paras 132–146.   [223] Ibid, paras 147–152.

[224] See eg *Gaz de France and Ruhrgas*, Commission Press Release IP/04/573, 30 April 2004, where those two gas companies agreed to grant the Norwegian subsidiary of US gas producer Marathon access to their gas networks: a comment on the case will be found by Fernández Salas, Klotz and Moonen, *Competition Policy Newsletter*, Summer 2004, 41; see also *Disma* Commission's XXIIIrd *Report on Competition Policy* (1993), pp 141–143 where the doctrine was applied to equipment for storing jet fuel and transferring it to supply points at Milan's Malpensa Airport; this case was brought under Article 81 rather than Article 82, since a number of undertakings owned the infrastructure in question.

[225] Commission MEMO/07/186, 11 May 2007.   [226] Commission MEMO/07/187, 11 May 2007.

[227] *Disma* Commission's XXIIIrd *Report on Competition Policy* (1993), pp 141–143.

[228] Commission *Notice on the Application of the Competition Rules to Access Agreements in the Telecommunications Sector* OJ [1998] C 265/2, [1998] 5 CMLR 821, paras 49–53 and 87–98; see Nikolinakos 'Access Agreements in the Telecommunications Sector – Refusal to Supply and the Essential Facilities Doctrine Under EC Competition Law' (1999) 20 ECLR 399.

[229] See eg Case JV.37 *BSkyB/KirchPayTV* (under the EC Merger Regulation), Commission Press Release IP/00/279, 21 March 2000; *British Interactive Broadcasting* OJ [1999] L 312/ 1, [2000] 4 CMLR 901, paras 173–181 (a case under Article 81).

[230] *London European-Sabena* OJ [1988] L 317/47, [1989] 4 CMLR 662; see also *Lufthansa* Commission Press Release IP/99/542, 20 July 1999, where the Commission imposed a fine of €10,000 under Council Regulation 2299/89 on a code of conduct for computerised reservation systems.

[231] OJ [1992] L 96/34, [1993] 4 CMLR 596.

[232] Commission *Notice on the Application of the Competition Rules to Cross-border Credit Transfers* OJ [1995] C 251/3; see also the Commission's XXVIth *Report on Competition Policy* (1996), point 109, on the ECU Banking Association.

constituted a 'basic infrastructure in its own right, since to refuse any entity access to such a network is tantamount to a *de facto* exclusion from the market for international transfers'[233]. The Commission's view was that it was a manifest abuse of a dominant position to lay down unjustified admission criteria and to apply them in a discriminatory manner[234]. SWIFT agreed to grant access to any entity meeting the criteria laid down by the European Monetary Institute for admission to domestic payment systems[235]. It should be noted that Article 28(1) of Directive 2007/64/EC on *Payment services in the internal market*[236] requires Member States to ensure that rules on access to payment systems shall be objective, non-discriminatory and proportionate, and that they should not inhibit access more than is necessary to safeguard against specific risks such as settlement risk, operational risk, and business risk and to protect the financial and operational stability of the payment system; Article 28(2) of the Directive excludes certain types of payment systems (so-called three party, closed-loop schemes) from its scope.

- **Cross-border securities clearing and settlement services** In *Clearstream (Clearing and Settlement)*[237] the Commission found that Clearstream had abused its dominant position in relation to clearing and settlement services for registered services by refusing to deal with Euroclear Bank.

- **Postal network** The Commission's view is that there can be an obligation to provide access to postal networks[238].

- **Premium TV content** The Commission has regarded premium TV content as an essential input for Pay-TV operators[239].

(iii) Refusal to license intellectual property rights or to supply information needed for interoperability

A point of particular controversy has been whether the law of refusal to supply could be applied to the owner of intellectual property rights or proprietary information that refuses to grant a licence or to make the information available to a third party. This was dealt with in two major cases, one involving IBM in the 1980s and another that led to the Commission's decision in the *Microsoft* case in 2004. It would appear to be the case that the law is stricter – that is to say that it is more difficult to establish an abuse – in such cases; this is discussed in chapter 19, which examines the relationship between competition law and the law of intellectual property[240].

(iv) Horizontal foreclosure

(A) Refusal to supply a distributor as a disciplining measure A refusal to supply may be abusive where a dominant firm does so as a disciplinary measure against a distributor who

---

[233] Commission's XXVIIth *Report on Competition Policy* (1997), point 68.   [234] Ibid.

[235] For details of the settlement see the Commission's XXVIIth *Report on Competition Policy* (1997), pp 143–145.

[236] OJ [2007] L 319/1.

[237] Commission decision of 2 June 2004, [2005] 5 CMLR 1302; see Martínez and Bufton 'The Clearstream decision: the application of Article 82 to securities clearing and settlement' *Competition Policy Newsletter*, Summer 2004, 49.

[238] Commission *Notice on the Application of the Competition Rules to the Postal Sector* OJ [1998] C 39/9, [1998] 5 CMLR 108, paras 2.8–2.9.

[239] For a summary of the Commission's decisional practice see Géradin 'Access to Content by New Media Platforms: A Review of the Competition Law Problems' (2005) 30(1) EL Rev 68.

[240] See ch 19, pp 786–792.

handles competitors' products. This happened in *United Brands v Commission*[241], where United Brands was trying to prevent its distributor, which was not subject to an exclusive purchasing obligation, from taking part in a competitor's advertising campaign. The ECJ held that it was abusive to stop supplying a long-standing customer which abides by normal commercial practice, and that orders should be met which were in no way out of the ordinary. United Brand's objective was to prevent the distributor from selling competitors' products: in other words the practice was intended to achieve single branding. This was not a case in which the refusal to supply was intended to eliminate a competitor in a downstream market, as in the *Commercial Solvents* situation.

(B) Refusal to supply a potential competitor in the supplier's market It may be an abuse to refuse supplies as an exclusionary tactic against a customer trying to enter an upstream market in competition with the supplier. In *BBI Boosey & Hawkes: Interim Measures*[242] the Commission found that Boosey & Hawkes had abused a dominant position by refusing to supply brass band instruments to a distributor which was intending to commence the manufacture of such instruments in competition with it. The Commission said that the dominant firm was entitled to take reasonable steps to protect its commercial interest, but that such measures must be fair and proportional to the threat[243]; in its view it was not reasonable 'to withdraw all supplies immediately or to take reprisals against that customer'[244].

(v) Refusal to supply on the basis of nationality

Discrimination on grounds of nationality is contrary to Article 12 of the Treaty. In *GVL v Commission*[245] the ECJ held that it was abusive for a national copyright collecting society to refuse to admit to membership nationals of other Member States.

(vi) Refusal to supply to prevent parallel imports

In *Syfait v GlaxoSmithKline plc*[246] the ECJ was asked by the Greek Competition Authority whether it could be an abuse of a dominant position for Glaxo to have ceased to supply wholesalers in Greece in order to prevent exports of pharmaceutical products from Greece to higher-priced Member States. Advocate General Jacobs reviewed the law on refusal to supply under Article 82[247]; he did not think that Glaxo's refusal to supply amounted to a *per se* abuse and considered that, given the specific characteristics of the pharmaceuticals market – pervasive and diverse State intervention in the pricing of pharmaceuticals, regulation of distribution, the adverse effect that parallel trade might have on the incentive to innovate, and the fact that end consumers may not themselves benefit from parallel trade – it was not necessarily an abuse for Glaxo to have refused to supply. Frustratingly the ECJ held that, as the Greek Competition Authority was not a court of tribunal for the purpose of Article 234 of the Treaty, the reference was inadmissible; it therefore abstained from expressing an opinion on the extremely important question referred to it. However the same issue was subsequently referred to the ECJ by the Greek Athens Appeal Court[248].

---

[241] Case 27/76 [1978] ECR 207, [1978] 1 CMLR 429.   [242] OJ [1987] L 286/36, [1988] 4 CMLR 67.
[243] Ibid, para 19.   [244] Ibid.   [245] Case 7/82 [1983] ECR 483, [1983] 3 CMLR 645.
[246] Case C-53/03 [2005] ECR I-4609, [2005] 5 CMLR 7.   [247] Opinion of 28 October 2004, paras 53ff.
[248] Cases C-468/06 and C-478/06 *Sot Lélos kai Sia EE and others v GlaxoSmithKline*, not yet decided.

(G) UK case law[249]

In *JJ Burgess & Sons v OFT*[250] the CAT concluded that W Austin & Sons had abused a dominant position by refusing to grant access to Harwood Park Crematorium for the purpose of conducting cremations; in doing so the CAT annulled a decision of the OFT[251] that there had been no abuse. This was the first occasion on which the CAT made its own finding of a substantive infringement of competition law[252]; subsequently JJ Burgess commenced a 'follow-on' action for damages against W Austin: this case was settled between the parties in February 2008[253]. The CAT's judgment surveyed the relevant case law on refusal to supply[254] and formulated three propositions that were sufficient to reach a finding on the facts of that case, while noting that these were not intended to contain an exhaustive statement of the law on refusal to supply[255]:

- an abuse may occur where a dominant undertaking, without objective justification, refuses supplies to an established existing customer who abides by regular commercial practice, at least where the refusal to supply is disproportionate and operates to the detriment of consumers

- such an abuse may occur if the potential result of the refusal to supply is to eliminate a competitor in a downstream market where the dominant undertaking is itself in competition with the undertaking potentially eliminated, at least if the goods or services in question are indispensable for the activities of the latter undertaking, and there is a potential adverse effect on consumers

- it is not an abuse to refuse access to facilities that have been developed for the exclusive use of the undertaking that has developed them, at least in the absence of strong evidence that the facilities are indispensable to the service provided, and there is no realistic possibility of creating a potential alternative[256].

Problems of refusal to supply are sometimes settled informally following investigation by the OFT[257].

In *Disconnection of Floe Telecom Ltd's Services by Vodafone Ltd*[258] Floe complained to OFCOM that Vodafone was abusively refusing to supply it with certain services necessary for it to operate in the market for mobile telephony. OFCOM decided that Vodafone had an objective justification for the refusal, since Floe would have been acting unlawfully on the market. On appeal to the CAT the decision was quashed and remitted to OFCOM[259] which, in a second decision[260], maintained its position that there had not been an unlawful refusal to supply. Floe again appealed against OFCOM's decision; on

---

[249] The OFT's draft guideline on *Assessment of conduct*, OFT 414a, April 2004, discusses refusal to supply at paras 8.1–8.8; note also the guidelines on the application of the competition rules to telecommunications, water and sewerage, energy and railways, cited in nn 64–67 above.

[250] Case No 1044/2/1/04 [2005] CAT 25, [2005] CompAR 1151.

[251] OFT decision of 11 August 2004, [2004] UKCLR 1586.   [252] See ch 10, p 428.

[253] Case No 1088/5/7/07 *ME Burgess, JJ Burgess and SJ Burgess v W Austin and Sons Ltd*, order of the Tribunal of 18 February 2008.

[254] Case No 1044/2/1/04 [2005] CAT 25, [2005] CompAR 1151, paras 291–313.   [255] Ibid, para 312.

[256] Ibid, para 311.

[257] See eg the 2000 *Annual Report of the Director General of Fair Trading*, p 46 (assurances by cement producers to supply bulk cement for resale).

[258] OFCOM decision of 3 November 2003.

[259] Case No 1024/2/3/04 *Floe Telecom Ltd v OFCOM* [2004] CAT 18, [2005] CompAR 290.

[260] OFCOM decision of 30 June 2005.

this occasion the CAT agreed with OFCOM that there had been no infringement, but substituted some reasoning of its own for that of OFCOM[261]. OFCOM and Vodafone were given permission to appeal by the Court of Appeal[262].

There have been a number of cases before the courts concerning refusals to supply by dominant firms that allegedly infringed the Chapter II prohibition; most of these were unsuccessful[263]. In *Network Multimedia Television Ltd v Jobserve Ltd*[264] the defendant operated a website on which IT recruitment agencies advertised job vacancies; it refused to accept advertisements from agencies that had an interest in a competing 'job board'. The court, with which the Court of Appeal agreed, decided that there was a serious issue to be tried, and granted an injunction in the claimant's favour pending the trial of the action. In *Intel Corpn v VIA Technologies* Intel, a manufacturer of computer components, was alleged to have abused its dominant position by refusing to grant a patent licence to one of its competitors. Lawrence Collins J granted summary judgment in favour of Intel on the basis that the mere refusal to grant a license of an intellectual property right was not an abuse[265]. The Court of Appeal disagreed. Having surveyed the relevant EC law it concluded that Intel's refusal to license might fall within the 'exceptional circumstances' found to exist in *Magill*[266] and thereby infringe the Chapter II prohibition. In any event, the Court of Appeal considered that the difficult questions of law and fact raised by the case were not suitable for summary judgment.

In *AAH Pharmaceuticals Ltd v Pfizer Ltd*[267] wholesalers of pharmaceuticals sought an interim injunction to require the defendant to maintain supplies of pharmaceutical products. The OFT had declined a request from the wholesalers for interim measures, and instead launched a market study[268]. The High Court decided that it was not appropriate to grant the relief sought in these circumstances. Interim relief was successfully obtained in a refusal to supply case in *Software Cellular Network Ltd v T-Mobile (UK) Ltd*[269].

5. ABUSES THAT ARE HARMFUL TO THE SINGLE MARKET

As noted in chapter 5, the Commission will condemn abusive practices that are harmful to the single market[270]. In *BL v Commission*[271] the ECJ upheld the decision of the Commission that BL had abused a dominant position by refusing to supply type-approval certificates for Metro cars imported from the Continent; this practice was

---

[261] Case No 1024/2/3/04 *Floe Telecom Ltd v OFCOM* [2006] CAT 17, [2006] CompAR 637.

[262] Note that OFCOM reached similar non-infringement decisions in the case of a complaint by VIP Communications Ltd against T-Mobile in *Disconnection of VIP Communications Ltd's Services by T-Mobile Ltd*, OFCOM decision of 31 December 2003, [2004] UKCLR 637 and *Re-investigation of VIP Communications*, OFCOM decision of 30 June 2005, [2005] UKCLR 914 .

[263] See eg *Claritas (UK) Ltd v Post Office and Postal Preference Ltd* [2001] UKCLR 2; *Land Rover Group Ltd v UPF (UK) Ltd* [2002] All ER (D) 323; *Getmapping plc v Ordnance Survey* [2002] UKCLR 410; *Intel Corpn v VIA Technologies* [2002] UKCLR 576, reversed on appeal [2002] EWCA Civ 1905, [2003] ECC 16.

[264] [2002] UKCLR 184, upheld on appeal [2001] UKCLR 814, CA.   [265] [2002] UKCLR 576, para 173.

[266] *Intel v VIA Technologies* [2002] EWCA Civ 1905, [2003] ECC 16, paras 50–51.

[267] [2007] EWHC 565.   [268] *Medicines Distribution*, 11 December 2007.   [269] Judgment of 17 July 2007.

[270] See ch 5, pp 205–206; see also the Commission's XXVIIth *Report on Competition Policy* (1997) point 63.

[271] Case 226/84 [1986] ECR 3263 [1987] 1 CMLR 185; see also Commission Press Release IP (87) 390 *Re Volvo Italia* [1988] 4 CMLR 423n.

part of a strategy of British Leyland aimed at discouraging parallel imports into the UK. In *United Brands v Commission*[272] one of the abuses committed by United Brands was to impose a restriction on its distributors against exporting green, unripened bananas: in practice this amounted to an export ban, since it would not be possible to export bananas that were already ripe. The Commission's investigation of the ticketing arrangements in *Football World Cup 1998*[273] was prompted by the fact that they discriminated in favour of French residents. In *Amminstrazione Autonoma dei Monopoli dello Stato v Commission*[274] the CFI confirmed the Commission's conclusion that AAMS, which had a dominant position on the Italian market for the wholesale distribution of cigarettes, had abused its dominant position by imposing distribution agreements on foreign producers which contained terms limiting the access of foreign cigarettes to the Italian market; a fine of €6 million was imposed.

6. MISCELLANEOUS CASES[275]

There have been some applications of Article 82 to non-pricing practices that do not fit under any of the headings so far deployed in this chapter. Some are concerned with the exercise (or non-exercise) of intellectual property rights, and are discussed in chapter 19[276]. Some other cases are discussed below.

(i) Harming the competitive structure of the market

It was established in *Continental Can*[277] that Article 82 could be applied to mergers in certain circumstances, and there was one other decision that condemned a merger[278]. However the inadequacy of Article 82 as a tool for controlling EC mergers lay behind the Commission's eagerness for a specific regulation, which finally emerged in 1989 after a gestation period of 16 years[279]. The application of Article 82 to mergers after the ECMR is dealt with in chapter 21.

Even though mergers would now be dealt with under the ECMR, the Commission considers that the *Continental Can* case is authority for the proposition that it can be an abuse to alter the competitive structure of a market where competition on that market is already weakened as a result of the very presence of the dominant undertaking on it. This is demonstrated by *Tetra Pak 1 (BTG Licence)*[280], where the Commission objected to the acquisition, by merger, of an exclusive licence of patents and know-how

---

[272] Case 27/76 [1978] ECR 207, [1978] 1 CMLR 429.

[273] OJ [2000] L 5/55, [2000] 4 CMLR 963; see Weatherill 'Fining the Organisers of the 1998 World Cup' (2000) 21 ECLR 275.

[274] OJ [1998] L 252/47, [1998] 5 CMLR 186 on appeal Case T-139/98 *Amminstrazione Autonoma dei Monopoli dello Stato v Commission* [2001] ECR II-3413, [2002] 4 CMLR 302.

[275] For further reading see O'Donoghue and Padilla *The Law and Economics of Article 82 EC* (Hart Publishing, 2006), ch 10.

[276] See ch 19, pp 786–792.   [277] Case 6/72 [1973] ECR 215, [1973] CMLR 199.

[278] *Warner-Lambert/Gillette* OJ [1993] L 116/21, [1993] 5 CMLR 559.

[279] Council Regulation 4064/89/EEC OJ [1990] L 257/13, as amended by Council Regulation 1310/97/EC OJ [1997] L 180/1.

[280] OJ [1988] L 272/27, [1988] 4 CMLR 881, upheld on appeal Case T-51/89 *Tetra Pak Rausing SA v Commission* [1990] ECR II-309, [1991] 4 CMLR 334.

which would prevent competitors from entering Tetra Pak's market. Another example of harming the structure of the market occurred in *Irish Sugar v Commission*[281], where the CFI upheld the decision of the Commission that it was an abuse of a dominant position for Irish Sugar, the dominant undertaking in the Irish sugar market, to purchase a competitor's sugar from a wholesaler and a retailer and to replace it with its own, a so-called 'product swap'[282].

The Commission's decision in *Trans-Atlantic Conference Agreement*[283] that TACA had abused a dominant position by inducing undertakings to join a liner conference, thereby harming the competitive structure of the market, was annulled on appeal by the CFI[284].

The Commission held in *Decca Navigator System*[285] that it is an abuse for an undertaking in a dominant position to enter into an agreement with an actual or potential competitor with the intention of sharing markets or stunting the efforts of competitors.

(ii) Vexatious litigation

In the course of the *Promedia* case[286] the Commission stated that entering into litigation, which is the expression of the fundamental right of access to a judge, is not an abuse; however it could be abusive if a dominant firm brings an action:

(i) which cannot reasonably be considered as an attempt to establish its rights and can therefore only serve to harass the opposite party, and (ii) which is conceived in the framework of a plan whose goal is to eliminate competition.

The CFI's judgment, in which it upheld the decision of the Commission not to proceed against Belgacom following a complaint from Promedia, appears, at paragraphs 72 and 73, to have confirmed the Commission's view that vexatious litigation could amount to an abuse in the circumstances envisaged by it. The CFI also stated in this judgment that a claim for the performance of a contractual obligation could amount to an abuse where the claim 'exceeds what the parties could reasonably expect under the contract or if the circumstances applicable at the time of the conclusion of the contract have changed in the meantime'[287].

In *Compagnie Maritime Belge Transports SA v Commission*[288] Cewal, a liner conference, had concluded an agreement with the Zairean Maritime Freight Management Office (the so-called 'Ogefrem agreement') granting Cewal exclusive rights to the freight trade between Zaire and northern Europe. When Ogefrem allowed a third party, Grimaldi and Cobelfret, a small amount of the trade in question, Cewal repeatedly insisted that Ogefrem should strictly comply with the terms of the agreement. The ECJ upheld the finding of the Commission that it was abusive of Cewal to insist on its exclusive rights under the Ogefrem agreement in circumstances where the insistence

---

[281]   Case T-228/97 [1999] ECR II-2969, [1999] 5 CMLR 1300.

[282]   [1999] ECR II-2969, [1999] 5 CMLR 1300, paras 226–235.

[283]   OJ [1999] L 95/1, [1999] 4 CMLR 1415.

[284]   Cases T-191/98 etc *Atlantic Container Line AB v Commission* [2003] ECR II-3275, [2005] 4 CMLR 1283.

[285]   OJ [1989] L 43/27, [1990] 4 CMLR 627.

[286]   Case T-111/96 *ITT Promedia v Commission* [1998] ECR II-2937, [1998] 5 CMLR 491; see Preece 'ITT *Promedia v EC Commission*: Establishing an Abuse of Predatory Litigation?' (1999) 20 ECLR 118.

[287]   [1998] ECR II-2937, [1998] 5 CMLR 491, para 140.

[288]   Case C-395/96 P [2000] ECR I-1365, [2000] 4 CMLR 1076.

was intended to remove its only competitor from the market and where Cewal had a discretion under the contract whether to insist on its performance or not[289].

(iii) Other cases

The CFI upheld the Commission's rejection of a complaint that lobbying for the imposition of anti-dumping duties constituted an abuse of a dominant position in *Industrie des Poudres Sphériques v Commission*[290].

[289] Ibid, paras 84–88.   [290] Case T-5/97 [2000] ECR II-3755, [2001] 4 CMLR 1020.

18

Abuse of dominance (2): pricing practices

CHAPTER CONTENTS

1. INTRODUCTION

This chapter will consider abusive pricing practices under Article 82 EC and the Chapter II prohibition in the Competition Act 1998. The chapter will begin with a discussion of various cost concepts used in determining whether a price is abusive. It will then deal in turn with exploitative pricing practices; rebates and other practices that have an effect similar to single branding agreements; bundling; predatory pricing; margin squeezing; price discrimination; and practices that are harmful to the single market. This taxonomy is over-schematic, in that the categories can blur into one another: for example discrimination may be both exploitative and anti-competitive, and an excessively high price may in reality be a way of preventing parallel imports or of excluding a competitor from the market; nevertheless this division may provide helpful insights into the way in which the law is applied in practice. In each section the application of Article 82 by the European Commission and by the Community Courts will be considered first, followed by cases dealt with by the competition authorities in the UK.

The law on abusive pricing practices is complex and controversial. Dominant firms may infringe Article 82 where they raise their prices to unacceptably high levels; they may also be found to have abused their dominant position where they cut their prices, if such cuts can be characterised not as normal, competitive responses, but as strategic behaviour intended to eliminate competitors. Not unnaturally a dominant firm, or one that is anxious that it might be found to be dominant, may feel itself to be on the horns of a dilemma where both a price rise and a price cut might be considered to be abusive; the dilemma might become a trilemma if leaving prices where they are might be considered to be evidence of a concerted practice with the other operators on the market, and if the word trilemma were to exist.

2. COST CONCEPTS

Analysis of whether a dominant undertaking's pricing practices are abusive requires consideration of its costs: a price may infringe Article 82 where the difference between the price charged and the costs incurred is excessive; discrimination may be abusive where it lacks a cost justification; and a price may be unlawful where the price charged is below cost. However it is important to understand at the outset that the apparently simple term 'cost' in fact raises serious problems in practice; it may be helpful therefore to begin this chapter by outlining some of the cost concepts that are deployed in competition analysis[1]. These concepts will be referred to quite often later in this chapter.

(A) Fixed costs and sunk costs

Fixed costs are costs that do not vary with the amount of goods or services that a firm produces; for example a manufacturing firm must buy or rent land on which to build a factory, and will probably incur property taxes as well: these costs are fixed, as they must be paid irrespective of the firm's output.

Sunk costs are a particular type of fixed cost: a sunk cost is one that a firm has already incurred and which cannot be recovered, for example if it were to exit the market. The reason that costs may be sunk is that certain assets cannot be used for more than one purpose, and so have no or very little second-hand value. A typical sunk cost is advertising expenditure (the 'asset' being the advertising campaign) incurred in promoting a new product: if the product fails, the expense involved cannot be recovered. Another example of a sunk cost would be expenditure incurred in designing and/or producing a product for a specific customer, for which no-one else would have any use.

(B) Marginal cost

Marginal cost is the cost incurred by a firm when producing an additional unit of output; it does not include any element of a firm's fixed costs, since fixed costs do not vary with output. Marginal cost usually decreases as the scale of a firm's output expands, but increases as a firm's output reaches total capacity. Marginal cost is a theoretical measure of cost: it is not used in practice[2]. More useful are the concepts of variable costs and avoidable costs, described below.

---

[1] Further definitions of various cost concepts can be found in Black *Oxford Dictionary of Economics* (Oxford University Press, 3rd ed, 2003); the European Commission's *Glossary of Terms used in Competition related matters*, available at europa.eu.int/comm/competition/general_info/glossary_en.html; and in paras 64–65 of DG COMP's *Discussion paper on the application of Article 82 of the Treaty to exclusionary abuses*, available at www.ec.europa.eu/comm/competition/antitrust/art82/index.html.

[2] Marginal cost determines the level of output a firm will produce under conditions of perfect competition; on perfect competition see ch 1, pp 4–6.

(C) Variable costs

Variable costs are costs that vary with the amount of products (rather than each additional unit of output) that a firm produces: for example a firm's expenditure on items such as raw materials, fuel and maintenance will vary according to the amount of its output; variable costs do not include any element of a firm's fixed costs.

(D) Avoidable costs

Avoidable costs refer to those costs which a firm would avoid incurring (or to put the matter another way, the savings it would make) by ceasing a particular activity over a specified period of time; for example where a firm is accused of predatory pricing over an 18-month period, it may be relevant to ask what costs it would have avoided if it had not produced the units that were the subject of the predation. Avoidable costs include some **fixed**, depending on the period of time in question, and **variable** costs, but omit **common costs**, that is to say costs that arise where two or more products are produced together even though they could be produced separately.

(E) Average variable cost ('AVC')

A firm's **average variable cost** is calculated by dividing all its variable costs by the total of its actual output. This calculation indicates the average cost of each extra unit of output.

(F) Average avoidable cost ('AAC')

A firm's **average avoidable cost** is calculated by dividing all its avoidable costs by its output. Because some fixed costs may be included in average avoidable cost, it may be higher than a firm's average variable cost.

(G) Long-run incremental cost ('LRIC')

Long-run incremental cost is the sum of the fixed and variable costs that a firm incurs when deciding to produce a particular product, referred to as 'the increment'. Long-run incremental cost does not include any variable or fixed costs *other* than those of the increment.

(H) Average total cost ('ATC')

A firm's **average total cost** is calculated by dividing both its variable costs and its fixed costs by the total of its output. It will, of course, be higher than its average variable cost.

(I) Stand alone cost

The **stand alone cost** of a firm refers to the cost that it would incur if it were to produce just a single product, so that there would be no common costs as a result of its other activities.

3. EXPLOITATIVE PRICING PRACTICES[3]

Exploitative pricing raises interesting questions for competition law. To the extent that firms form a cartel in order to restrict output, raise prices and take larger profits, EC and UK law both intervene: the price-fixing cartel is the most obvious target for any system of competition law; this has been considered in chapter 13. The position is more complicated where oligopolists indulge in tacit coordination falling short of an agreement or concerted practice; this has been considered in chapter 14. Different problems arise where a monopolist or dominant firm individually exploits its position by charging excessive (that is supra-competitive) prices.

(A) Arguments against direct control

It might seem obvious that competition authorities should take direct steps under Article 82 and analogous provisions to control exploitative pricing[4], but the case for doing so is not as clear-cut as may at first appear. There are persuasive arguments against direct control of prices under competition law.

First, if normal market forces have their way, the fact that a monopolist is able to earn large profits should, in the absence of barriers to expansion and entry, attract new entrants to the market. In this case the extraction of monopoly profits will be self-defeating in the long run and can act as an important economic indicator to potential entrants to enter the market. If one accepts this view of the way that markets operate, one should accept with equanimity periods during which a firm earns a monopoly profit: the market will in due course correct itself, and intervention by the competition authorities will have the effect of undesirably distorting this process.

Second, there are formidable difficulties in telling whether a price really is exploitative: by what standards can this be assessed? To compare a monopolist's price with a hypothetical 'competitive' price is unscientific; alternatively to establish what would be a 'reasonable' price by adding an acceptable profit margin to the actual cost of producing goods or providing services is fraught with difficulties. One is that it is unclear what the relevant 'cost' of producing goods or services is: should one look at the historic costs involved in establishing a production line for goods or the cost that it would take to establish one at today's prices? Another problem is that it is difficult to apportion the common costs of a multi-product firm between its different products in order to determine whether it is making an unreasonable profit in one particular market. Furthermore the fact that a firm is earning a large profit may be attributable to its superior efficiency over its rivals, rather than to its market power.

A third argument against price control is that a monopolist should be permitted to charge a monopoly price so that it will be able to earn sufficiently large profits to be able

---

[3] For further reading on exploitative pricing see Bishop and Walker *The Economics of EC Competition Law* (Sweet & Maxwell, 2nd ed, 2002), paras 6.17–6.22; Evans and Padilla 'Excessive Prices: Using Economics to Define Administrable Legal Rules' (2005) 1 Journal of Competition Law and Economics; O'Donoghue and Padilla *The Law and Economics of Article 82 EC* (Hart Publishing, 2006), ch 12; *The Pros and Cons of High Prices* (Swedish Competition Authority, 2007).

[4] Note that s 2 of the Sherman Act 1890 in the US does *not* apply to exploitative excessive pricing: see Gal 'Monopoly Pricing as an Antitrust Offense in the US and the EC: Two Systems of Belief about Monopoly' (2004) 49 Antitrust Bulletin 343.

to carry out expensive and risky research and development[5]. The Supreme Court of the US stated in its 2004 judgment in *Verizon Communications Inc v Law Offices of Curtis Trinko* that:[6]

The opportunity to charge monopoly prices – at least for a short period – is what attracts 'business acumen' in the first place; it induces risk taking that produces innovation and economic growth.

Another view is that there is no objection to a monopolist increasing its personal wealth at consumers' expense since this involves only a transfer of wealth from one part of the economy to another, rather than a threat to the wealth of society generally. An argument against this view is that, even if one is prepared to tolerate the accretion of wealth by monopolists, there is a welfare loss where output is restricted by a firm with market power[7]; further there may be a loss to consumer welfare if the prospect of making monopoly profits entails a use of resources for that very purpose which might otherwise have been better used elsewhere in the economy[8].

A fourth problem is that even if it is accepted, despite these arguments, that exploitative pricing should be controlled, there is the difficulty of translating this policy into a sufficiently realistic legal test. A legal rule condemning exploitative pricing needs to be cast in sufficiently precise terms to enable a firm to know on which side of legality it stands.

A fifth problem is that, if a competition authority determines that a dominant undertaking is charging an excessive price, it will have to decide what remedial action should be taken: it can impose a fine for past abuse, but what directions should it issue as to future behaviour, and will the issue of such directions require continuous surveillance? Crafting eg pro-competitive remedies to deal with excessive pricing abuses is complex. A final point is that price regulation requires a competition authority to have a considerable amount of information about the market, which it may lack; it is even less easy for courts to determine what the correct level of prices should be, as the UK Court of Appeal found in the *Attheraces* case[9].

Given these problems, it is not surprising that competition authorities tend to prefer to deploy their resources by proceeding against abuses that exclude competitors from the market rather than establishing themselves as price regulators.

Where there are natural monopolies that are not under the direct control of a Government there is much to be said for the establishment of a system of *ex ante* regulation of prices: in the UK sectoral regulators such as the Gas and Electricity Markets Authority and OFWAT have such powers[10]. When the European Commission had concerns about the high cost of tariffs for international mobile roaming services, it dealt with the matter by legislation rather than by intervention under Article 82[11]. In other cases where a competition authority is concerned that prices in a particular market appear to be higher than they would be in competitive conditions it might wish to consider conducting a sectoral review, using powers, if available, such as those in Article 17 of the EC Modernisation Regulation[12], in order to discover what features of the market are causing the high prices. Where 'public' restrictions of competition are responsible, a competition authority may be able to play an advocacy role by suggesting ways in which the market could function more competitively[13].

---

[5] See eg Schumpeter *Capitalism, Socialism and Democracy* (1942) and see ch 1, p 6.
[6] 540 US 398 (2004).   [7] See ch 1, pp 6–7.
[8] See Posner 'The Social Costs of Monopoly and Regulation' (1975) 83 Journal of Political Economy 807.
[9] See p 718 below.   [10] See ch 23, p 971 on these regulatory bodies.
[11] Ibid, p 975.   [12] See ch 7, p 265.   [13] See ch 1, pp 24–25.

These are some of the arguments against the direct control of high prices by com-petition authorites. It is clear that neither the European Commission[14] nor the OFT in the UK have an appetite for investigating high prices under Article 82 or the Chapter II prohibition. However this is not to say that such cases never arise, and, as will be seen in the discussion of EC and UK case law below, there have been investigations of excessive prices in both jurisdictions. One commentator suggested at a conference arranged by the Swedish Competition Authority in November 2007 that perhaps rather more attention should be paid to issues of exploitative abuse than has historically been fashionable[15].

An interesting discussion of the role of a competition authority – as opposed to a price regulator – when faced with a complaint of excessive prices will be found in the reasons of the Competition Tribunal of South Africa in *Harmony Gold Mining Co Ltd v Mittal Steel South Africa Ltd*[16]. There the Tribunal concluded that Mittal was guilty of infringing section 8(a) of the South African Competition Act 1998, which specifi-cally prohibits the charging of an excessive price to the detriment of consumers. The Tribunal was explicit in eschewing the methodologies of price regulation in reaching its conclusion, proceeding instead on the basis of the structure of the market and the practices under review, 'traditional fare in the working life of competition enforcers and adjudicators'[17]. A fine was imposed on Mittal Steel of 691,800,000 South African rand, and other remedies were imposed[18].

(B) EC case law

(i) Determining whether prices are excessive
Article 82(2)(a) gives as an illustration of abuse:

directly or indirectly imposing unfair purchase or selling prices or other unfair trading conditions[19].

A practice which is harmful to consumers can be abusive, notwithstanding that it is not harmful to the structure of competition on the relevant market[20]; furthermore it is not necessary to show that the firm that is guilty of the abuse derives a commercial advantage from it[21].

---

[14] The European Commission has often said that it has no desire to become a price regulator: see eg the Commission's Vth *Report on Competition Policy* (1975), points 3–7 and 76; XXVIIth *Report on Competition Policy* (1997), point 77.

[15] See Lyons 'The Paradox of the Exclusion of Exploitative Abuse' in *The Pros and Cons of High Prices* (Swedish Competition Authority, 2007); this paper is also available on the website of the Centre for Competition Policy, www.ccp.uea.ac.uk.

[16] Case No 13/CR/FEB04 *Harmony Gold Mining Company Ltd v Mittal Steel South Africa* Ltd, judgment of 27 March 2007, paras 70–89.

[17] Ibid, para 89.

[18] Case No 13/CR/FEB04 *Harmony Gold Mining Company Ltd v Mittal Steel South Africa* Ltd, judgment of 6 September 2007.

[19] For examples of the imposition of unfair trading conditions, as opposed to unfair prices, see *1998 Football World Cup* OJ [2000] L 5/55, [2000] 4 CMLR 963; *Amministratzione Autonoma dei Monopoli di Stato* OJ [1998] L 252/47, [1998] 5 CMLR 786, paras 33–46, upheld on appeal Case T-139/98 *AAMS v Commission* [2001] ECR II-3413, [2002] 4 CMLR 302, paras 73–80.

[20] *Football World Cup*, n 19 above, paras 99–100, citing Case 6/72 *Continental Can v Commission* [1973] ECR 215, [1973] CMLR 199, para 26.

[21] *Football World Cup*, paras 101–102.

(A) General Motors *and* United Brands   In *General Motors*[22] the Commission adopted the first decision condemning the excessive pricing of a dominant firm and imposing a fine for that practice. There had been earlier indications from the ECJ, in Article 234 cases concerning the use of intellectual property rights, that such action could be taken under Article 82[23]. On appeal the decision in *General Motors* was quashed by the ECJ[24] because there was insufficient evidence to support it.

In *United Brands*[25] the Commission imposed a fine for excessive pricing, but again its decision was quashed by the ECJ[26] because the Commission had failed to make out a clear case. However the ECJ said that:

charging a price which is excessive because it has no reasonable relation to the economic value of the product supplied is … an abuse[27].

Clearly therefore excessive pricing can amount to an abuse of a dominant position. The difficulty is to know at what point a price is abusive because it bears no relation to the 'economic value' of the product. Various methodologies have used, but none is free from difficulty.

The Commission in *United Brands* inferred that the price of bananas in Germany was too high by looking at the price charged in Ireland: it concluded that, since UBC could charge a low price in Ireland and still make a profit, it must follow that the higher price charged in Germany was excessive. The ECJ annulled the decision on the ground that it was improperly reasoned. In order to establish that a price was excessive the ECJ said, at paragraph 251, that the Commission had at least to:

require UBC to produce particulars of all the constituent elements of its production costs.

The burden was on the Commission to prove that UBC was charging unfair prices. Having undertaken a cost analysis, the ECJ said that the question to be asked is:

whether the difference between the costs actually incurred and the price actually charged is excessive, and, if the answer to this question is in the affirmative, to consider whether a price has been charged which is either unfair in itself or when compared to other competing products[28].

The ECJ accepted that it might be difficult to apportion costs to particular products, but concluded that there were no such difficulties in the case of the market for bananas.

(B) Deutsche Post   In *Deutsche Post AG – Interception of cross-border mail*[29] the Commission considered that Deutsche Post's prices for the onward transmission of cross-border mail were excessive. In doing so the Commission said that, as it could not make a detailed analysis of Deutsche Post's costs, it would have to use an alternative benchmark to determine whether it was guilty of abuse[30]; this it did by comparing Deutsche Post's prices for cross-border mail with its domestic tariff[31], and it decided that there was indeed an abuse. It should perhaps be added that, although cost analysis may be difficult, it

---

[22] OJ [1975] L 29/14, [1975] 1 CMLR D20.
[23] Case 78/70 *Deutsche Grammopbon GmbH v Metro-SB-Grossmärkte GmbH* [1971] ECR 487, [1971] CMLR 631; Case 40/70 *Sirena v Eda* [1971] ECR 69, [1971] CMLR 260.
[24] Case 26/75 *General Motors v Commission* [1975] ECR 1367, [1976] 1 CMLR 95.
[25] OJ [1976] L 95/1, [1976] 1 CMLR D28.
[26] Case 27/76 *United Brands v Commission* [1978] ECR 207, [1978] 1 CMLR 429.
[27] [1978] ECR 207, [1978] 1 CMLR 429, para 250.
[28] Ibid, para 252; see similarly Case 226/84 *BL v Commission* [1986] ECR 3263, [1987] 1 CMLR 185, para 27; Case C-323/93 *Crespelle* [1994] ECR I-5077, para 25.
[29] OJ [2001] L 331/40, [2002] 4 CMLR 598.   [30] Ibid, para 159.   [31] Ibid, paras 160–166.

is certainly not impossible; many reports of the UK Competition Commission have involved complex cost analyses[32].

(C) The Scandlines *case* In *Scandlines Sverige AB v Port of Helsingborg*[33] the Commission, after an extensive investigation, rejected a complaint that port charges at the port of Helsingborg were excessively high. The Commission did not simply look at the costs incurred by the port in order to determine whether the charges were excessive; its view was that a simple 'cost-plus' approach was insufficient to establish that the prices were abusive, since it was necessary also to look at the economic value of the service provided[34]. The Commission looked to see if the charges were unfair, and attempted to compare them with prices charged for other services provided in the same port, and with prices charged to ferry operators in other ports; its conclusion was that, in particular given that the burden of proving an abuse was upon it, there was no infringement of Article 82[35].

(D) Excessive prices in the telecommunications sector In the late 1990s the Commission investigated several cases in which it was concerned about excessive prices in the telecomnications sector; in each case the dominant firm modified its prices as a result of which the proceedings were terminated[36].

(E) Yardstick competition The ECJ suggested in *United Brands* that there are various ways of proving that a price is excessive[37]. In an Article 234 reference from France, *Corinne Bodson v Pompes Funèbres*[38], one question before the ECJ was whether Pompes Funèbres, which had been given an exclusive concession to provide 'external services' for funerals in a particular French town, was guilty of charging excessive prices. The ECJ said that, given that more than 30,000 communes in France had not granted exclusive concessions such as that enjoyed by Pompes Funèbres, but instead had left the service unregulated or operated it themselves, it must be possible to make a comparison between the prices charged by undertakings with concessions and other undertakings:

Such a comparison could provide a basis for assessing whether or not the prices charged by the concession holders are fair[39].

This technique can be described as 'yardstick competition': comparing the performance of one undertaking with that of other ones. The idea in *Bodson* was repeated in *Lucazeau v SACEM*[40], which concerned the level of royalties charged for the playing of recorded music in discotheques; the ECJ again suggested that a comparison should

[32] See eg *The Supply of Banking Services by Clearing Banks to Small and Medium Sized Enterprises* Cm 5319 (2002), paras 2.243–2.431; OFT Economic Discussion Paper 6, OFT 657, *Assessing profitability in competition policy analysis* (NERA, July 2003).

[33] Commission decision of 23 July 2004, [2006] 4 CMLR 1224; a second complaint against the port, by Sundbusserne, was also rejected.

[34] Note that the UK Court of Appeal reached the same conclusion in the *Attheraces* case discussed at p 718 below.

[35] See Lamalle, Lindström-Rossi and Teixeira 'Two important rejection decisions on excessive pricing in the port sector' *Competition Policy Newsletter*, Autumn 2004, 40.

[36] See the Commission's XXVIIth *Report on Competition Policy* (1997) paras 67 and 77 and the XXVIIIth *Report on Competition Policy* (1998) paras 79–81.

[37] Case 27/76 *United Brands v Commission* [1978] ECR 207, [1978] 1 CMLR 429, para 253.

[38] Case 30/87 [1988] ECR 2479, [1989] 4 CMLR 984.   [39] [1988] ECR 2479, [1989] 4 CMLR 984, para 31.

[40] Case 110/88 [1989] ECR 2811, [1991] 4 CMLR 248.

be made with the level of fees charged in other Member States. Yardstick competition is only possible however where a suitable comparator can be found: it would be inappropriate to compare the prices charged in a high-price Member State against those in a low-price one.

(F) Excessive or disproportionate costs should be ignored In *Ministère Public v Tournier*[41], another case concerning the level of royalties charged to discotheques by a French performing rights society, the ECJ said that excessive or disproportionate costs should not be taken into account in determining the reasonableness of prices. The society in question had a *de facto* monopoly and the ECJ suggested that it was the very lack of competition which had led to high administrative costs: the society had no incentive to keep them down.

(ii) Excessive pricing that impedes parallel imports and exports

In the *General Motors* case[42], and subsequently in *BL v Commission*[43], the reason for the Commission's intervention was not that it wished to establish itself as a regulator of the prices charged for the issuance of type-approval certificates for cars, but that the prices that the Commission regarded as excessive were imposed with the intention of impeding parallel imports and exports. The Commission's decision in *Deutsche Post AG – Interception of cross-border mail*[44] is another example of a single market abuse: by charging an excessive amount for the onward transmission of cross-border mail, Deutsche Post was preventing users of the mail system from taking advantage of the developing single market for postal services.

(iii) Excessive pricing that is anti-competitive

Quite apart from excessive prices being exploitative and/or detrimental to the single market, they may also be exclusionary. The most obvious example would be the situation in which the owner of an essential facility charges an excessive (or discriminatory) price for granting access to it: this could be regarded as a constructive refusal to supply, and therefore as an abuse of a dominant position[45]. The Commission specifically states at paragraph 97 of the *Notice on the Application of the Competition Rules to Access Agreements in the Telecommunications Sector*[46] that excessive prices for access to essential facilities can be abusive[47]; the Commission summarises the case law set out above at paragraphs 105 to 109 of this Notice. In practice it is immensely complex to determine what the appropriate price for access to an essential facility should be[48]; a particular problem is that a firm that controls such a facility and makes use of it in a downstream

---

[41] Case 395/87 [1989] ECR 2521, [1991] 4 CMLR 248.   [42] See p 22 above.
[43] Case 226/84 [1986] ECR 3263, [1987] 1 CMLR 185.   [44] OJ [2001] L 331/40, [2002] 4 CMLR 598.
[45] See ch 17, pp 690–699 on the so-called essential facilities doctrine.
[46] OJ [1998] C 265/2, [1998] 5 CMLR 821.   [47] Ibid, para 97.
[48] See Baumol, Ordover and Willig 'Parity Pricing and Its Critics: a Necessary Condition for Efficiency in the Provision of Bottleneck Services to Competition' (1997) Yale Journal of Regulation 14; Armstrong, Doyle and Vickers 'The Access Pricing Problem: A Synthesis' (1996) 44(2) Journal of Industrial Economics 131; OFTEL *The Pricing of Conditional Access and Access Control Services* (May 1999); see also *Telecom Corpn of New Zealand v Clear Communications* [1995] 1 NZLR 385, a case which reached the Privy Council in the UK on appeal from New Zealand, in relation to pricing for access to the telecommunications 'local loop' there: the case is discussed by Tollemache in (1994) 15 ECLR 43, (1994) 15 ECLR 236 and (1995) 16 ECLR 248.

market may not make an internal charge to itself for the service in question; this makes it particularly difficult to determine what price it should charge to a third party for access. For this reason the Commission has required, in the *Access Directive* in the electronic communications industry, that separate accounting should be maintained for activities related to interconnection and for other activities[49].

Given the difficulties involved in access pricing, it is not surprising that the Commission would prefer not to become too involved in what may result in a large amount of detailed regulation: this activity is better carried out by a specific regulatory body, such as OFCOM in the UK in the case of electronic communications. However there have been some occasions on which the Commission has investigated access pricing issues. For example in 1997 it took action against Belgacom for charging excessive and discriminatory prices for access to data on its subscribers for voice telephony services[50]. In February 2008 the Commission imposed a penalty of €899 million on Microsoft for charging unreasonable prices for interoperability information[51].

(iv) Excessive pricing and aftermarkets

The ECJ has held that a car manufacturer may refuse to grant licences to third parties to produce spare parts for its cars; however if it charges excessive prices for the spares which it produces itself, this may amount to an abuse of its dominant position[52]. It may be that the market will solve this problem itself. Although such customers appear to be 'locked in' to the manufacturer's spare parts, the original car will eventually need to be replaced; excessive prices for spare parts may deter buyers of new cars from buying from their existing manufacturer: this in turn may deter the manufacturer from an excessive pricing policy for parts in the first place[53].

(v) Buyer power – excessively low prices

In *CICCE v Commission*[54] the ECJ rejected a complaint that the Commission had refused to condemn unfairly low prices paid by a monopsonist on the buying side of the market, as there was insufficient evidence to support the allegation. The complainant in this case was arguing that French television companies with a statutory monopoly were paying unfairly low fees for showing films. The ECJ agreed with the Commission that the complainant had to show that the price was low in relation to each individual film, and that it could not rely on average or undifferentiated figures. The interest of the case is that it demonstrates that, just as charging an excessively high price can be abusive, so too can the extraction of an unfairly low one demanded by an undertaking in a dominant position on the buying side of the market; on the facts of this case, however, the complainant failed.

[49] *Directive of the European Parliament and of the Council on access to, and interconnection of, electronic communications networks and associated facilities* OJ [2002] L 108/7, Article 11.

[50] See the Commission's XXVIIth *Report on Competition Policy* (1997), point 67: the terms on which the case was settled are set out at pp 152–153 of the Report; see also point 77 of the same Report on the Commission's action against Deutsche Telekom for charging excessive prices for access to its infrastructure, and points 79–86 of the XXVIIIth *Report on Competition Policy* (1998) on further action in relation to excessive and discriminatory prices in the telecommunications sector.

[51] Commission Press Release IP/08/318 of 27 February 2008.

[52] Case 53/87 *CICRA v Renault* [1988] ECR 6039, [1990] 4 CMLR 265; Case 238/87 *AB Volvo v Erik Veng* [1988] ECR 6211, [1989] 4 CMLR 122.

[53] For discussion of this issue see ch 1, pp 35–36.

[54] Case 298/83 [1985] ECR 1105, [1986] 1 CMLR 486.

(C) UK case law

As noted in chapter 17, the OFT published a draft competition law guideline on *Assessment of conduct* in April 2004 which specifically addressed the application of Article 82 EC and the Chapter II prohibition to various types of behaviour[55]; however the OFT decided not to proceed to the publication of a final guideline, given that the European Commission had initiated a review of Article 82. The draft guideline remains on the website of the OFT[56]. The text that follows will not draw upon it, given that it was simply a draft for consultation; however relevant paragraphs will be cited for readers interested in the embryonic views of the OFT at that time. Section 2 of the draft guideline specifically discusses excessive prices. Guidelines have been published on the application of the competition rules, including Article 82 and the Chapter II prohibition, in particular regulated sectors, namely telecommunications[57], water and sewerage[58], energy[59], and railways[60]. An OFT Economic Discussion Paper, issued in July 2003, explores the issue of how to determine profitability in competition cases[61].

(A) Cases on excessively high prices In *Napp Pharmaceutical Holdings Ltd*[62] the OFT concluded that Napp had abused a dominant position contrary to the Chapter II prohibition by operating a discriminatory discount policy, by predatory price cutting, and by charging excessive prices. Napp supplied sustained release morphine (referred to by its trade name of MST) to hospitals and to patients in the community. The prices for sales to the community were typically more than ten times higher than to hospitals. Paragraphs 203 to 234 of the decision deal with excessive pricing. The OFT considered that the margin between Napp's costs and its prices was excessive: it did this by comparing the profit margin Napp earned on community sales of MST and comparing it with the margins it earned on sales of other products and on the sale of MST to other markets. The OFT also considered the actual prices of MST and compared them with what a competitive price for it would be likely to be. On appeal the Competition Appeal Tribunal (the 'CAT') noted the difficulties involved in determining whether a price is excessive, and concluded that the various methods used by the OFT were 'among the approaches that may reasonably be used', adding 'there are, no doubt, other methods'[63]. The CAT upheld the OFT's finding of excessive pricing, but considered that there were certain mitigating factors in favour of Napp, not least the uncertainty of the law on this issue, and it therefore reduced the fine that the OFT had imposed from £3.21 million to £2.2 million[64].

[55] OFT 414a, April 2004. [56] www.oft.gov.uk.
[57] *The application of the Competition Act in the telecommunications sector*, OFT 417, February 2000.
[58] *The application of the Competition Act in the water and sewerage sectors*, OFT 422, February 2000.
[59] *Application in the energy sector*, OFT 428, January 2005.
[60] *Application to services relating to railways*, OFT 430, October 2005.
[61] OFT Economic Discussion Paper 6, OFT 657 *Assessing profitability in competition policy analysis* (NERA, July 2003).
[62] OFT Decision, 30 March 2001, [2001] UKCLR 597; for comment on the finding of excessive pricing in this case see Kon and Turnbull 'Pricing and the Dominant Firm: Implications of the [Competition Appeal Tribunal's] Judgment in the *Napp* Case' (2003) 24 ECLR 70, pp 82–86.
[63] Case No 1000/1/1/01 *Napp Pharmaceutical Holdings Ltd v Director General of Fair Trading* [2002] CAT 1, [2002] CompAR 13, para 392.
[64] Ibid, paras 497–541.

In *Thames Water Utilities Ltd/Bath House and Albion Yard*[65] the Director General of Water Services decided that Thames Water had not abused its dominant position by charging an excessive amount for the carriage of water extracted by Enviro-Logic to the latter's customers.

The complexity of determining access prices in the case of essential facilities is vividly illustrated by *Albion Water Ltd v Water Services Regulation Authority*. The CAT handed down a judgment in October 2006[66] in an appeal against a finding by OFWAT[67] that Dŵr Cymru was not guilty of charging an excessive price for the transportation of water through its water pipelines. The CAT's judgment reviewed the position at great length; it included extensive discussion of relevant cost principles[68] and of the 'efficient component pricing rule' ('the ECPR') advocated by some commentators as a methodology for determining the access price to essential facilities: the ECPR deducts from the retail price of a product the cost that an undertaking would avoid if it did not provide an upstream service such as the carriage of water[69]. The CAT's view was that the ECPR, which has been the subject of much criticism and has actually been banned by legislation in New Zealand following litigation in the telecommunications sector which reached the Privy Council in London[70], should not be accepted by the Tribunal 'without careful scrutiny'[71]. Later in its judgment the CAT decided that the ECPR was not a safe methodology to use in the case before it[72], and concluded that the evidence 'strongly suggested' that the price charged by Dŵr Cymru was excessive[73]. At that stage in the proceedings it had not been established whether Dŵr Cymru was in a dominant position; in a further judgment in December 2006[74] the CAT concluded that Dŵr Cymru was indeed dominant[75]. However the CAT declined to make its own finding that the access price was excessive, preferring instead to remit the matter to OFWAT for further analysis of the costs involved in transporting water through Dŵr Cymru's pipelines, and of the fairness of its prices[76]. OFWAT reported back to the CAT and a further hearing was held in February 2008.

In *SSL International plc: contraceptive sheaths*[77] the OFT concluded that, although it was possible that the prices of SSL's male condoms were high, a substantial amount of time and expense would be needed to reach a view as to whether they were excessive. The OFT's view was that further investigation was unlikely to be a sensible use of resources; in particular the OFT considered that there was evidence of emerging competition and that, if the outcome of the case were to be the imposition of a price cap, this might stifle such entry.

An intervention by the OFT under the Financial Services and Markets Act 2000 led to the London Stock Exchange reducing its issuing fees in 2003[78].

[65] OFT Decision, 31 March 2003, [2003] UKCLR 709.
[66] Case 1046/2/4/04 [2006] CAT 23, [2007] CompAR 22.
[67] OFWAT decision of 26 May 2004, [2004] UKCLR 1317.
[68] Case 1046/2/4/04 [2006] CAT 23, [2007] CompAR 22, in particular paras 448–637.
[69] Ibid, paras 638–836.
[70] *Telecom Corporation of New Zealand v Clear Communications* [1994] 6 TCLR 138.
[71] Case 1046/2/4/04 [2006] CAT 23, [2007] CompAR 22, para 739.   [72] Ibid, para 835.
[73] Ibid, para 637.   [74] Case 1046/2/4/04 [2006] CAT 36, [2007] CompAR 328.
[75] Ibid, paras 183–198.   [76] Ibid, paras 279–281.
[77] OFT case closure of 11 May 2005, available at www.oft.gov.uk.
[78] See *London Stock Exchange issuer fees*, OFT 713, March 2004, available at www.oft.gov.uk.

A particularly interesting case on excessive pricing arose in *Attheraces Ltd v The British Horseracing Board Ltd*[79], a 'standalone' action by Attheraces with no involvement on the part of any competition authority. Attheraces, a broadcaster, required so-called 'pre-race data' about British horse races in the possession of the British Horseracing Board ('the BHB'), the administrator and regulator of British horseracing. Attheraces wanted to make these data available to overseas bookmakers. It complained, and the judge at first instance held[80], that BHB had abused a dominant position by threatening to refuse to supply Attheraces, by charging it unfair prices, and by discriminating against it. The Court of Appeal allowed the appeal by BHB. It is of interest to note that Mummery LJ stated at the outset that the nature of the issues under consideration were ones that might more satisfactorily be solved by arbitration or by a specialist body equipped with appropriate expertise and flexible powers, rather than within the adversarial procedures of an ordinary private action[81]. The Court of Appeal accepted the suggestion in paragraph 250 of the ECJ's judgment in *United Brands v Commission* that a price that significantly exceeds the economic value of the product supplied could be abusive, but pointed out that this formulation 'begs a fundamental question: what constitutes economic value?'[82]. The Court concluded that it was not possible to conclude that a price was abusive simply on the basis of a 'cost plus' approach: that is to say that it is not sufficient merely to show that a price exceeds cost by more than a 'reasonable' amount[83]. In so far as the judge had reached his conclusion on the basis of cost plus a reasonable return he had adopted too narrow an approach: in particular he was wrong to reject BHB's contention that, in considering the economic value of the data, he should consider the value of the data to Attheraces itself[84]. The Court of Appeal specifically noted that the principal object of Article 82 was to protect consumers – in this case the ultimate punters who bet on horse races – and not business competitors such as Attheraces: it said that there was little, if any, evidence of harm to competition in the market[85].

(B) Excessively low prices In *The Association of British Travel Agents and British Airways plc*[86] the OFT concluded that BA was not guilty of paying excessively *low* prices to travel agencies by offering a commission that failed to cover their costs of selling tickets: in the OFT's view it would have been possible for the agents to charge their clients a fee for the service of issuing tickets, and it was not incumbent on BA to pay them an amount that would cover their costs in doing so[87].

(C) Section 13 Competition Act 1980 There is a provision in section 13 of the Competition Act 1980, which remains in force, whereby the Secretary of State may ask the OFT to investigate prices 'of major public concern': only a factual report may be made under this section, which has never been used[88].

---

[79] [2007] EWCA Civ 38, [2007] UKCLR 309, CA.
[80] *Attheraces Ltd v The British Horseracing Board Ltd* [2005] EWHC 3015 (Ch), [2005] UKCLR 757, ChD.
[81] [2007] EWCA Civ 38, [2007] UKCLR 309, CA, para 7.   [82] Ibid, para 204.   [83] Ibid, para 209.
[84] Ibid, para 218.   [85] Ibid, para 215.   [86] OFT Decision, 11 December 2002, [2003] UKCLR 136.
[87] Ibid, paras 28–37.   [88] See 47 *Halsbury's Laws of England*, para 505, n 21.

4. REBATES THAT HAVE EFFECTS SIMILAR TO SINGLE BRANDING AGREEMENTS[89]

In chapter 17 the application of Article 82 to exclusive agreements, and in particular single branding agreements[90], was considered. The basic objection to such agreements is that they may horizontally foreclose competitors of the dominant firm. Article 82 may also apply to pricing practices that have the same effect as single branding agreements. As we shall see, there have been many cases in which 'fidelity' or 'loyalty' rebates[91], 'target' rebates, discounts and bonuses have been found to be abusive. The text that follows will use the expression 'rebates' to include all these practices. It is perhaps worth saying at the outset that this is one of the least satisfactory areas of EC competition law. Three particular inter-connected problems can be identified.

First, the law has developed along formalistic lines, whereas the economics that inform the way in which firms charge for their products are complex: this complexity suggests that form-based rules are not sophisticated enough to deal with the phenomena under scrutiny. A second problem – which restates the first one in the language of competition law – is that some of the case law suggests that loyalty rebates are unlawful *per se*, whereas it is arguable that actual or potential anti-competitive effects ought to be demonstrated before a rebate is condemned as unlawful[92]. A variant of *per se* unlawfulness is that loyalty rebates are presumed to be unlawful unless they can be objectively justified. Although this position is less extreme than outright *per se* unlawfulness, it is also questionable for two reasons. The first argument against this variant is that rebates are often pro-competitive, so that it makes little sense to presume the contrary. The second is that the burden of proving that a rebate is objectively justified would be on the dominant undertaking[93]: if it has to prove a precise cost justification for every rebate this might be impossible to achieve in practice, because some rebates are simply offered to retain customers rather than to reflect savings in costs: it follows that they could not be objectively justified, so that a presumed unlawfulness would increase the likelihood of 'Type II errors'[94].

---

[89] For further reading on single branding agreements and rebates see the OECD report on *Loyalty and Fidelity Discounts and Rebates*, DAFFE/COMP (2002) 21, available at www.oecd.org; section 7 of DG COMP's *Discussion paper on the application of Article 82 of the Treaty to exclusionary abuses*; Bishop and Walker *The Economics of EC Competition Law* (Sweet & Maxwell, 2nd ed, 2002), paras 6.23–6.44; O'Donoghue and Padilla *The Law and Economics of Article 82 EC* (Hart Publishing, 2006), pp 374–406; Van den Bergh and Camesasca *European Competition Law and Economics: A Comparative Perspective* (Sweet & Maxwell, 2nd ed, 2006), pp 254–264; there is also an abundance of periodical literature on this subject: see eg Ridyard 'Exclusionary Pricing and Price Discrimination Abuses Under Article 82 – An Economic Analysis' (2002) 19 ECLR 286; Temple Lang and O'Donoghue 'Defining Legitimate Competiton: How to Clarify Pricing Abuses under Article 82 EC' (2002) 26 Fordham International Law Journal 83; Kallaugher and Sher 'Rebates Revisited: Anti-competitive Effects and Exclusionary Abuse Under Article 82' (2004) 21 ECLR 263; Gyselen 'Rebates, Competition on the Merits or Exclusionary Practice?' in *What is an Abuse of a Dominant position?: European Competition Law Annual* (eds Ehlermann and Atanasiu, Hart Publishing, 2006), 287; Spector 'Loyalty Rebates: An Assessment of Competition Concerns and a Proposed Structured Rule of Reason' (2005) 1(2) Competition Policy International 89; Ahlborn and Bailey 'Discounts, Rebates and Selective Pricing by Dominant Firms: A Trans-Atlantic Comparison' (2006) 2 European Competition Journal 101.

[90] See ch 17, pp 673–679.   [91] These two terms can be used interchangeably.   [92] See ch 5, pp 195–198.
[93] See ch 5, p 209.   [94] See further p 726 below on 'permissible' rebates.

The final problem, which follows from formalism, is that the law on rebates has developed with little or no reference to the cost concepts described at the beginning of this chapter. Later in this chapter we will see that the case law on predation, for example, is built upon the concepts of average variable and average total cost. The case law on rebates, which developed from the rule against dominant firms entering into single branding agreements, does not have an explicit cost component, other than the defence that a rebate has a cost justification[95]. The fact that the case law does not focus on cost means that there has been little attention paid to the question of whether any competitor that might be eliminated by rebating practices is 'as efficient' as the dominant firm[96]. DG COMP's *Discussion paper on the application of Article 82 of the Treaty to exclusionary abuses* introduces cost concepts and 'as efficient competitors' into the discussion, though it struggles to formulate operational rules that it would be possible to apply in practice[97].

(A) EC case law

The case law on rebates began by condemning them where they were explicitly linked to the loyalty of a customer. Subsequently it has been extended to target rebates which, though not explicitly linked to loyalty, have a loyalty-inducing effect. The ECJ has stated that the law that forbids exclusionary rebates is based on Article 82 as a whole: it is not based solely upon the wording of Article 82(2)(b), which refers to practices that limit production, markets or technical development to the prejudice of consumers[98].

(i) Loyalty rebates: *Hoffmann-La Roche v Commission*

The obvious starting point is the ECJ's judgment in *Hoffmann-La Roche v Commission*[99]. The ECJ held that Hoffmann-La Roche had abused its dominant position both by entering into single branding agreements with some of its customers and by offering others loyalty rebates. In relation to the latter the ECJ said that it was unlawful for a dominant firm to tie a customer by a single branding commitment and that:

The same applies if the said undertaking, without tying the purchasers by a formal obligation, applies, either under the terms of the agreements concluded with these purchasers or unilaterally, a system of fidelity rebates, that is to say discounts conditional on the customer's obtaining all or most of its requirements – whether the quantity of its purchases be large or small – from the undertaking in a dominant position[100].

This passage makes clear that the prohibition of loyalty rebates is directly related to the law that prohibits single branding agreements. Behaviour becomes abusive when the inducement caused by the promise of loyalty rebates to a customer to purchase all or most of its requirements from the dominant firm is so great that it has the same effect that a contractual stipulation to purchase exclusively would have done[101].

[95] See p 726 below.   [96] On the 'as efficient competitor' test see ch 5, p 195.

[97] See p 726 below.

[98] Case C-95/04 P *British Airways plc v Commission* [2007] ECR I-2331, [2007] 4 CMLR 982, para 58.

[99] Case 85/76 [1979] ECR 461, [1979] 3 CMLR 211; loyalty rebates were condemned in an earlier case that was predominantly concerned with cartelisation of the sugar market: Cases 43/73 etc *Suiker Unie v Commission* [1975] ECR 1663, [1976] 1 CMLR 295, paras 517–528.

[100] [1979] ECR 461, [1979] 3 CMLR 211, para 89; the ECJ also objected to the 'English clause' requiring the buyer to report any better offer it received to Hoffmann-La Roche and preventing it from accepting the offer unless Roche chose not to match it: ibid para 102–108.

[101] It should be noted that, where a dominant firm offers different rebates to different customers, this may result in an accusation of discrimination contrary to Article 82(2)(c) as well: see pp 748–753 below.

The test set out in paragraph 89 of *Hoffmann-La Roche* (and in subsequent cases) is expressed as a *per se* rule[102]; however, as has been pointed out in chapter 5[103], it is highly questionable whether *per se* illegality is appropriate under Article 82: this is particularly so in the case of rebates. Most rebates are simply manifestations of the competitive process; customers obviously benefit from the lower price that a rebate necessarily results in. Assuming that the rebate does not result in the dominant firm selling at a loss, it is difficult to see why rebates should be *per se* unlawful or even subject to a rebuttable presumption of unlawfulness. In principle it seems appropriate to require that a rebate should be condemned only where it can be shown that it is likely to be detrimental to the competitive process and to lead to harm to consumers.

Paragraph 89 of the judgment in *Hoffmann-La Roche* states that it is abusive to offer rebates 'conditional on the customer's obtaining all or most of its requirements – whether the quantity of its purchases be large or small – from the undertaking in a dominant position'. As has been seen in chapter 16, the block exemption for vertical agreements defines a non-compete obligation as one which requires a customer to obtain 80 per cent or more of its requirements of goods or services from the supplier[104]; it is reasonable to suppose that a similar threshold applies under Article 82 when determining what is meant by 'most' of a customer's requirements.

The stipulation that loyalty rebates are unlawful even where the quantities involved are small imposes a strict standard: where the customer purchases small quantities, the anti-competitive foreclosure effect – if any – is likely to be insignificant; however the ECJ's formulation indicates that there would still be an abuse. DG COMP's *Discussion paper* suggests that any foreclosure should be more than insubstantial[105], and it is questionable whether a competition authority would initiate proceedings today in the absence of a significant detriment to competition.

(ii) Further case law on loyalty rebates under Article 82

There have been several further cases in which rebates that were explicitly based on loyalty were condemned.

In *BPB Industries*[106] the Commission held that British Gypsum Ltd and its parent, BPB Industries plc, had abused their dominant position by offering loyalty payments to builders' merchants in Great Britain who stocked only their plasterboard. This had the effect of excluding new competition from producers in France and Spain. BPB and British Gypsum claimed that the payments were made in order to assist merchants with the cost of promotion and advertising. The Commission held that, even if there was truth in this, the payments were also intended to induce loyalty on the part of merchants and so were abusive. A fine of €3 million was imposed. The Commission's decision was substantially upheld on appeal[107].

In the *Soda-ash* decisions[108] the Commission condemned the exclusionary practices, including loyalty rebates, of Solvay and ICI. One of the abuses was the granting

---

[102] See similarly para 152 of the Commission's *Guidelines on Vertical Restraints*, OJ [2000] C 291/1: 'Article 82 specifically prevents dominant companies from applying...fidelity rebate schemes': this is too strict a proposition and should, it is suggested, be amended in a future iteration of these *Guidelines*.

[103] Ch 5, pp 195–198.   [104] See ch 16, pp 640–641.   [105] *Discussion paper*, para 59.

[106] OJ [1989] L 10/50, [1990] 4 CMLR 464.

[107] Case T-65/89 *BPB Industries plc and British Gypsum v Commission* [1993] ECR II-389, [1993] 5 CMLR 32, upheld on appeal to the ECJ Case C-310/93 P [1995] ECR I-865, [1997] 4 CMLR 238.

[108] *Soda-ash/Solvay* OJ [1991] L 152/21 and *Soda-ash/ICI* OJ [1991] L 152/40.

of 'top-slice' rebates: customers for soda-ash tended to purchase some of their requirements from a source other than the dominant undertaking in their market; this was a
way of reducing dependency on a supplier. The dominant undertaking in these circumstances would offer special rebates on such 'marginal tonnage' in order to secure that
custom. The Commission found that this practice was abusive. In the Solvay decision it
rejected Solvay's argument that the rebates were based on objective and predetermined
thresholds[109]. The decisions were annulled on appeal for procedural reasons[110], but
readopted by the Commission at the end of 2000[111].

The CFI upheld a finding of the Commission that loyalty rebates infringed Article 82
in *Irish Sugar v Commission*[112]. The CFI said that it was necessary to:

appraise all the circumstances, and in particular the criteria and detailed rules for granting rebates,
and determine whether there is any tendency, through an advantage not justified by any economic service, to remove or restrict the buyer's choice as to his sources of supply, to block competitors' access to the market, to apply dissimilar conditions to equivalent transactions with other
trading parties, or to reinforce the dominant position by distorting competition[113].

In *Compagnie Maritime Belge v Commission*[114] the ECJ upheld the decision of the
Commission that the granting of loyalty rebates by members of a liner conference
amounted to an abuse of a collective dominant position[115]; it was irrelevant to the finding of abuse under Article 82 that the rebates may have benefited from block exemption
under Regulation 4056/86 on maritime transport[116].

Loyalty rebates were also found to be abusive in *Deutsche Post*[117]. The Commission
stressed the distinction between quantity rebates exclusively linked to the volume of
purchases from a supplier, fixed objectively and applied without discrimination, and
rebates granted in return for loyalty[118]; it added that a rebate linked to quantity, but
where the quantity was actually calculated by reference to the estimated capacity of
absorption of the customer, would be treated as a loyalty rebate[119]. The policy of granting loyalty rebates was regarded as a serious infringement having as its object or effect
the exclusion of private operators from the German parcel services market[120], and the
Commission imposed a fine of €24 million.

(iii) Individualised target rebates

The cases just discussed were concerned with rebates explicitly granted in return for
loyalty. However it will take only a moment's reflection to recognise that a dominant
firm may be able to achieve 'loyal' purchasing without specifically linking rebates to
loyalty. One obvious method is to set customers a target, and to promise rebates – perhaps very generous ones – if the target is met. It is normal practice for firms – whether
dominant or not – to want to increase sales, and there is nothing sinister in a pricing
policy which is geared to the incentivisation of a customer to purchase more units in the
future than in the past. The question under Article 82 is when such a practice should be

---

[109] OJ [1991] L 152/40, para 54.
[110] Cases T-30/91 etc *Solvay SA v Commission* [1995] ECR II-1775, [1996] 5 CMLR 57, upheld by the ECJ
Cases C-286/95 P etc *Commission v ICI* [2000] ECR I-2341, [2000] 5 CMLR 413.
[111] *Soda-ash/Solvay* OJ [2003] L 10/10 and *Soda-ash/ICI* OJ [2003] L 10/33.
[112] Case T-228/97 [1999] ECR II-2969, [1999] 5 CMLR 1300.
[113] [1999] ECR II-2969, [1999] 5 CMLR 1300, para 197.
[114] Cases C-395/96 P etc [2000] ECR I-1365, [2000] 4 CMLR 1076.   [115] Ibid, paras 129–137.
[116] Ibid, para 130.   [117] OJ [2001] L 125/27, [2001] 5 CMLR 99.
[118] Ibid, para 33; see p 726 below on permissible rebates.   [119] Ibid.   [120] Ibid, para 50.

condemned as abusive? It is important in such cases to distinguish two questions: first, whether a rebate could have a loyalty-inducing effect; and second, whether a loyalty-inducing rebate could have an anti-competitive foreclosure effect. These two effects are different, since a rebate might have the effect of inducing loyalty without necessarily being harmful to competition.

There have been several cases in which target rebates have been condemned because of their loyalty-inducing effects, even though there was no explicit requirement of loyalty: in most cases the targets were individualised for each customer according to its particular procurement needs. In its first *Michelin*[121] decision the Commission condemned rebates payable to customers for replacement tyres in the Netherlands that reached annual sales targets. The targets were set for each customer individually, and were usually higher than for the preceding year. The ECJ upheld the Commission's finding on this point[122], saying that:

any system under which discounts are granted according to the quantities sold during a relatively long reference period has the inherent effect, at the end of that period, of increasing pressure on the buyer to reach the purchase figure needed to obtain the discount or to avoid suffering the loss for the entire period[123].

The case made clear that a lack of transparency in a system of rebates is an exacerbating factor, making a finding of abuse more likely[124]. However the opposite point should also be noted: if a rebate scheme is loyalty-inducing and otherwise abusive, it will not be saved by the fact that it is transparent[125].

In a second decision against Michelin, *PO–Michelin*[126], the Commission condemned various practices in the French (as opposed to the Dutch) replacement tyre market, including individualised annual volume targets. The Commission said that rebates operated by reference to a period of more than three months will always be unlawful[127], a statement that seems clearly to be incorrect. The CFI upheld the Commission's findings of abuse in this case[128]. The CFI said that the loyalty-inducing nature of a system increases in proportion to the length of the reference period: '[t]he longer the reference period, the more loyalty-inducing the quantity rebate system'[129]; however the CFI also said that the ECJ had never held that the reference point could not be for more than three months[130]. On the facts of that case the CFI was satisfied that the scheme in question, which had a reference period of one year, and where the discount was fixed on the basis of total turnover, had a loyalty-inducing effect.

In the case of *Coca-Cola/San Pellegrino* the Commission accepted that rebates awarded on the basis of performance over a period of not more than three months would not be abusive[131].

---

[121] OJ [1981] L 353/33, [1982] 1 CMLR 643.

[122] Case 322/81 *NV Nederlandse Banden-Industrie Michelin v Commission* [1983] ECR 3461, [1985] 1 CMLR 282.

[123] Ibid, para 81.

[124] Ibid, para 83; the Commission announced in April 2004 that it had closed an investigation into Interbrew's practices towards Belgian wholesalers of its beer following changes introduced by Interbrew: one was that its rebate system in future would be entirely transparent: Commission Press Release IP/04/574, 30 April 2004.

[125] Case T-203/01 *Michelin v Commission* [2003] ECR II-4071, [2004] 4 CMLR 923, para 111.

[126] OJ [2002] L 143/1, [2002] 5 CMLR 388; for critical comment see Sher 'Price Discounts and *Michelin 2*: What Goes Around, Comes Around' (2002) 23 ECLR 482.

[127] *Michelin II*, OJ [2002] L 143/1, [2002] 5 CMLR 388, para 216.

[128] Case T-203/01 *Michelin v Commission* [2003] ECR II-4071, [2004] 4 CMLR 923.   [129] Ibid, para 88.

[130] Ibid, para 85.   [131] Commission's XIXth *Report on Competition Policy* (1989), point 50.

In an Article 9 commitments case concluded on 22 June 2005 The Coca-Cola Company gave commitments to the Commission that it would not set target rebates to customers conditional upon them reaching individually-set purchase thresholds during a prescribed reference period, nor upon them achieving purchase thresholds or growth rates calculated by reference to purchases of its products in a previous reference period[132].

In *Prokent-Tomra* the Commission imposed a fine of €24 million on Tomra for entering into exclusivity agreements, quantity commitments and loyalty-inducing rebate schemes on the market for the supply of machines for the collection of used drink containers in return for a deposit[133]. In its decision the Commission noted that, although it was not formally obliged to demonstrate the effect that Tomra's practices would have on competition, nevertheless it had done so[134]: in its view Tomra's stable market shares compared with the weak position of its rivals, and the link between the size of the market subject to Tomra's various practices and Tomra's market share, indicated that it was having an effect on competition[135].

In July 2007 the Commission announced that it had sent a statement of objections to Intel outlining its belief that it had abused a dominant position in the market for computer processing units by offering substantial rebates to original equipment manufacturers conditional upon them purchasing all or the great majority of their CPUs from it; the Commission also considers that Intel may be guilty of targeted payments of an anti-competitive nature and of some acts of predatory pricing[136].

(iv) The *Virgin/British Airways* case

The *Virgin/British Airways* case[137] merits separate discussion for a variety of reasons. The Commission imposed a fine of €6.8 million on British Airways ('BA') for operating a system of commission payments and other incentives with travel agents which it considered had the object or effect of excluding BA's competitors from UK markets for air transport, by rewarding loyalty and by discriminating between travel agents.

The first point to note about this decision is that BA was a *purchaser* of services from travel agents, to which it paid a commission for tickets sold: the 'rebates' in this case refer to the level of commissions paid. A second point is that the level of commission payable increased as a new target was reached, and that increased amount was payable on *all* the tickets sold, not just on the *incremental* sales above the target. This meant that the loyalty-inducing effect was a powerful one. A third point is that the thesis of the Commission was that the incentive system affected the ability of other airlines to compete with BA but there was no convincing evidence that Virgin was being excluded from the aviation market: the CFI's conclusion that the Commission had demonstrated anti-competitive effects is very unconvincing[138]. A fourth point is that the Commission

---

[132] Commission decision of 22 June 2005; see Gasparon and Višnar 'Coca-Cola: Europe-wide Remedies in Fizzy Drinks' (2005) *Competition Policy Newsletter* Autumn 2005, 6.

[133] Commission decision of 29 March 2006; see Maier-Rigaud and Vaigauskaite 'Prokent/Tomra, a textbook case? Abuse of dominance under perfect competition', Summer 2006 *Competition Policy Newsletter*, 19; the case is on appeal to the CFI, Case T-155/06 *Tomra Systems and others v Commission*, not yet decided.

[134] Ibid, paras 331–346.

[135] For some sceptical comments on the Commission's views see RBB Brief 21, February 2007, available at www.rbbecon.com.

[136] Commission MEMO/07/314, 27 July 2007.   [137] OJ [2000] L 30/1, [2000] 4 CMLR 999.

[138] See in particular paras 293–298 of the CFI's judgment.

considered that the reward scheme also led to discriminatory treatment of different travel agents, an independent abuse contrary to Article 82(2)(c)[139].

A criticism of the Commission's decision is that, in an industry such as aviation, where fixed costs are high, any revenue that can be earned and contribute to those costs is desirable; BA's interest was to ensure that its aeroplanes were always full, in order to derive the maximum revenue possible. However the Commission's finding that BA's reward scheme was abusive was upheld on appeal to the CFI[140] and to the ECJ[141]. The ECJ noted that the important precedent was *Michelin* rather than *Hoffmann-La Roche*, since the British Airways reward scheme was not based on loyalty but rather targets[142]. The Court said that, in order to decide whether a scheme such as that of British Airways could be abusive:

it first has to be determined whether those discounts or bonuses can produce an exclusionary effect, that is to say whether they are capable, first, of making market entry very difficult or impossible for competitors of the undertaking in a dominant position and, secondly, of making it more difficult or impossible for its co-contractors to choose between various sources of supply or commercial partners[143].

The Court noted that BA devised bonus schemes on an individualised basis, linked to travel agents' growth in turnover during a given period[144]. The Court referred to the very strong inducement effect that arose from the fact that the bonus was payable not simply by reference to the *growth* in turnover, but to the *whole* of the turnover:

It could therefore be of decisive importance for the commission income of a travel agent as a whole whether or not he sold a few extra BA tickets after achieving a certain turnover[145].

The ECJ rejected the argument that the rebates were objectively justified[146].

The Commission has investigated a number of other incentive schemes operated by other airlines. In 2003 it announced that it had closed its investigation: in some cases because the airline in question was not dominant; in others because the scheme complied with, or was altered to comply with, Article 82; and in one case because a national competition authority had dealt with the matter[147]. It is interesting to note that an appeal court in the US concluded that BA's incentive schemes did not amount to unlawful monopolisation under section 2 of the Sherman Act 1890[148].

---

[139] See p 750 below.
[140] Case T-219/99 *British Airways plc v Commission* [2003] ECR II-5917, CMLR, paras 241–249 and 270–300.
[141] Case C-95/04 P *British Airways plc v Commission* [2007] ECR I-2331, [2007] 4 CMLR 982; on the ECJ judgment see Odudu 'Case C-95/04 P *BA plc v Commission*' (2007) 44 CML Rev 1781; Bacon 'European Court of Justice Upholds Judgment of the European Court of First Instances in the *British Airways/Virgin Saga*' (2007) 3 Competition Policy International 227.
[142] Case C-95/04 P, para 65.   [143] Ibid, para 68.   [144] Ibid, paras 71–72.   [145] Ibid, paras 73–74.
[146] See p 726 below.
[147] See Tomboy and Stehmann 'Commission closes probe into major EU airlines' incentive schemes for travel agents' *Competition Policy Newsletter* Summer 2003, 65.
[148] *Virgin Atlantic Airways Ltd v British Airways plc* 257 F 3d 256, US Court of Appeals for the Second Circuit; the South African Competition Tribunal found that South African Airways' incentive scheme, similar to that of British Airways, infringed the equivalent of Article 82 in South Africa's Competition Act, and imposed a fine upon it of 45 million South African rands, Case No 18/CR/Mar01 *Competition Commission v South African Airways (Pty) Ltd*, judgment of 28 July 2005.

(v) The *Duales System Deutschland* case

In *Duales System Deutschland AG*[149] the Commission condemned a fee structure for the use of a trademark, the effect of which was that users dealt exclusively with DSD to the exclusion of competitors in the market for organising the collection and recycling of sales packaging in Germany[150]. This case was not concerned with rebates. It nevertheless shows that the Commission will be concerned with any pricing practice that could have the effect of excluding competitors by anti-competitive means.

(vii) Permissible rebates

As already noted, rebates and similar practices are a normal part of commercial life. Rebates should be condemned only where they could have a detrimental effect on competition, for example because they operate as a surrogate for a single branding agreement. In *Hoffmann-La Roche v Commission* the ECJ accepted that not all discounts should be treated as abusive: for example it said that quantity discounts linked solely to the volume of purchases, fixed objectively and applicable to all purchasers, would be permissible[151]. Rebates granted for prompt payment would presumably also be regarded as objectively justifiable. Payments for services rendered by a customer, such as participation in a special promotion or for providing shelf-space in a supermarket, should also be permissible, provided that they are not, in fact, loyalty payments for exclusivity. In 1992 the Commission issued four Notices in the Official Journal indicating that it proposed to take a 'favourable view' of various rebating and pricing rebates in the plasterboard and related markets in the case of *British Gypsum*[152]: some of the rebates related to quantities purchased; others to sales promotion.

In *British Airways plc v Commission*[153] the CFI rejected British Airways' argument that its travel reward scheme was objectively justified because of the contribution it made to the recovery of its fixed costs[154].

(viii) DG COMP's *Discussion paper*

Paragraphs 151 to 171 of DG COMP's *Discussion paper* considers the application of Article 82 to rebates. It draws a distinction between conditional and unconditional rebates, and notes the distinction between rebates applicable to all sales as opposed to rebates paid only on incremental sales. The *Discussion paper* makes a valiant attempt to introduce the cost concepts outlined at the start of this chapter to the analysis of rebates; however the discussion becomes so complex that it is difficult to see how it could be translated into clear, administrable, rules.

---

[149] OJ [2001] L 166/1, [2001] 5 CMLR 609, upheld on appeal, Case T-151/01 *Duales System Deutschland v Commission* [2007] ECR II-000; the case is on appeal to the ECJ, Case C-385/07 P *Duales System Deutschland v Commission*, not yet decided.

[150] For comment see Gremminger and Miersch 'Commission acts against Duales System Deutschland AG for the abuse of a dominant position' Commission's *Competition Policy Newsletter,* June 2001, p 27.

[151] Case 85/76 [1979] ECR 461, [1979] 3 CMLR 211, para 90.

[152] OJ [1992] C 321/9-C 321/12, [1993] 4 CMLR 143n.

[153] Case T-219/99 *British Airways plc v Commission* [2003] ECR II-5917, [2004] 4 CMLR 1008; the ECJ dismissed the appeal by British Airways on this point since, in effect, it was questioning the factual assessment of the CFI, which is not possible in appeals to the ECJ: see Case C-95/04 P *British Airways plc v Commission* [2007] ECR I-2331, [2007] 4 CMLR 982, paras 84–91.

[154] Case T-219/99 *British Airways plc v Commission* [2003] ECR II-5917, [2004] 4 CMLR 1008, paras 279-291.

(B) UK case law[155]

In *Napp Pharmaceutical Holdings Ltd*[156] the OFT held that Napp had abused its dominant position in the market for sustained release morphine by offering very large discounts to hospitals while charging excessive prices to patients in the community; more particularly Napp had targeted particular competitors, offering larger discounts to hospitals where it faced or anticipated competition and by granting higher discounts for specific products which were under competitive threat[157]. The OFT considered that Napp's intention was to eliminate competitors, and rejected its argument that it was simply 'meeting competition'; its reaction to its competitors was held to be unreasonable and disproportionate[158]. On appeal the CAT found that Napp's discounts meant that it was selling at less than cost, and that they were therefore predatory[159].

In *English Welsh and Scottish Railway Ltd*[160] the Office of Rail Regulation found that EW&S had abused its dominant position in a number of ways, including by offering discounts having an exclusionary effect in relation to the carriage of coal to various power stations: a fine of £4.1 million was imposed.

The OFT closed two cases concerning discounts and rebates in 2007. In *British Airways*[161] it had been investigating a complaint that BA had offered non-linear discounts to corporate customers, but decided that the case was no longer an administrative priority. In *Walkers Snacks Ltd*[162] the OFT had been investigating practices such as growth rebates and single branding agreements but concluded that, although there might be some foreclosure of the market, this was unlikely to be material and that significant consumer detriment was therefore unlikely.

5. BUNDLING[163]

(A) EC case law

The application of Article 82 to tie-in agreements was considered in chapter 17[164]. It may be possible to achieve the same effect as a tie-in agreement through pricing practices.

---

[155] The OFT's draft guideline on *Assessment of conduct*, OFT 414a, April 2004, discusses discounts at paras 5.1–5.13.

[156] OFT Decision, 30 March 2001, [2001] UKCLR 597.   [157] Ibid, paras 144–202.

[158] Ibid, paras 197–202.

[159] Case No 1000/1/1/01 *Napp Pharmaceutical Holdings Ltd v Director General of Fair Trading* [2002] CAT 1, [2002] CompAR 13, paras 217–352.

[160] ORR decision of 17 November 2006, [2007] UKCLR 937; see Part IIA of the decision.

[161] OFT case closure, 30 April 2007, available at www.oft.gov.uk.

[162] OFT case closure, 3 May 2007, available at www.oft.gov.uk.

[163] For further reading on tying and bundling see section 8 of DG COMP's *Discussion paper on the application of Article 82 of the Treaty to exclusionary abuses*; Bishop and Walker *The Economics of EC Competition Law* (Sweet & Maxwell, 2nd ed, 2002), paras 6.54–6.68; Motta *Competition Policy: Theory and Practice* (Cambridge University Press, 2004), pp 460–483; O'Donoghue and Padilla *The Law and Economics of Article 82 EC* (Hart Publishing, 2006), ch 9; Van den Bergh and Camesasca *European Competition Law and Economics: A Comparative Perspective* (Sweet & Maxwell, 2nd ed, 2006), pp 264–276.

[164] See ch 17, pp 679–687.

(i) Rebates having a tying effect

In *Eurofix-Bauco v Hilti*[165] the Commission held that it was an abuse of a dominant position to reduce discounts to customers for orders of nail cartridges without nails[166]; the Commission's decision was upheld on appeal[167]. In *Tetra Pak II*[168] the Commission held that Tetra Pak had adopted a pricing policy that was a means of persuading customers to use its maintenance services[169]. In its *PO – Michelin*[170] decision the Commission found that Michelin had a bonus scheme that enabled it to leverage its position on the market in new tyres to preserve or improve its position on the neighbouring retreads market[171].

(ii) 'Across-the-board' rebates

In *Hoffmann-La Roche v Commission*[172] the ECJ condemned Hoffmann-La Roche's 'across-the-board' rebates, which were offered to customers which acquired the whole range of its vitamins; these rebates meant that customers were dissuaded from acquiring any particular vitamin from other suppliers[173]. The ECJ noted specifically that such rebates amounted to an unlawful tie-in, contrary to Article 82(2)(d)[174].

(iii) Delivered pricing as a tie-in

In *Napier Brown-British Sugar*[175] the Commission held that British Sugar's delivered pricing system constituted an abuse of a dominant position, although it did not impose a fine in respect of this offence as it was the first decision on this particular practice. Until 1986 British Sugar had refused to allow customers to collect sugar at an ex-factory price. The Commission, relying on the ECJ's judgment in *Centre Belge d'Etudes de Marche Télémarketing v CLT*[176], held that British Sugar had reserved to itself an ancillary market (the delivery of sugar) as part of its activity on a neighbouring but separate market (the sale of sugar). The Commission's view was that there was no objective justification for this conduct on the part of British Sugar.

(iv) Bundling[177]

A firm may sell two or more products together as a bundle and charge more attractive prices for the bundle than for the constituent parts of it. Bundling may have the same effect as a tie-in agreement. In *Digital* the Commission objected to the fact that Digital offered prices which were more attractive when the customer purchased software services in a package with hardware services than when purchasing software services

---

[165] OJ [1988] L 65/19, [1989] 4 CMLR 677.   [166] Ibid, para 75.
[167] Case T-30/89 *Hilti AG v Commission* [1990] ECR II-163, [1992] 4 CMLR 16, upheld on appeal to the ECJ Case 53/92 P *Hilti AG v Commission* [1994] ECR I-667, [1994] 4 CMLR 614.
[168] OJ [1992] L 72/1, [1992] 4 CMLR 551, upheld on appeal to the CFI Case T-83/91 *Tetra Pak International v Commission* [1994] ECR II-755, [1997] 4 CMLR 726 and on appeal to the ECJ Case C-333/94 P *Tetra Pak International v Commission* [1996] ECR I-5951, [1997] 4 CMLR 662.
[169] OJ [1992] L 72/1, [1992] 4 CMLR 551, paras 111–114; see also para 139.
[170] OJ [2002] L 143/1, [2002] 5 CMLR 388.   [171] Ibid, paras 300–311.
[172] Case 85/76 [1979] ECR 461, [1979] 3 CMLR 211.   [173] [1979] ECR 461, [1979] 3 CMLR 211, para 110.
[174] Ibid, para 111; for a similar case under US law see *Le Page's v 3M* 323 F 3d 141 (3rd Cir 2003).
[175] OJ [1988] L 284/41, [1990] 4 CMLR 196.   [176] Case 311/84 [1985] ECR 3261, [1986] 2 CMLR 558.
[177] For a detailed discussion of this topic see DTI Economics Paper No 1 *Bundling, Tying, and Portfolio Effects* (Nalebuff, 2003), available at www.dti.gov.uk/ccp/publications.htm.

alone[178]. In *De Poste-La Poste*[179] the Commission imposed a fine of €2.5 million on the Belgian Post Office for, in effect, offering lower prices to customers in the market for the delivery of letters if they also made use of a separate 'B2B' ('business-to-business') service that it provided.

(B) UK case law

In *BSkyB*[180] the OFT was not satisfied that BSkyB's bundling of sports and film premium channels had produced an anti-competitive effect since competitors had not been foreclosed; it therefore found that the Chapter II prohibition had not been infringed[181]. The OFT reached a similar conclusion in respect of the discounts given by BSkyB on the rates charged to distributors of its premium television channels[182]. The *BSkyB* decision illustrates the point that the behaviour of a dominant firm should be considered abusive only where it actually has an anti-competitive effect or where there is a realistic possibility of such an effect.

OFTEL rejected an allegation of bundling in *Alleged cross-subsidy of BT's discounts*[183].

In *Genzyme Ltd*[184] the OFT imposed a penalty of £6.8 million on that company for two pricing abuses, one of which was to charge a price to the National Health Service for a drug that included the price of home delivery, thereby reserving to itself the ancillary, but separate, activity of providing home care services[185]. This part of the OFT's decision was annulled on appeal to the CAT[186].

6. PREDATORY PRICING[187]

This section considers the extent to which predatory price-cutting – selling at a loss – can amount to an infringement of Article 82 or the Chapter II prohibition in the

---

[178] Commission's XXVIIth *Report on Competition Policy* (1997), pp 153–154; see similarly the Commission's action against AC Nielsen to prevent the charging of bundled prices: XXVIth *Report on Competition Policy* (1996), pp 144–148.

[179] OJ [2002] L 61/32, [2002] 4 CMLR 1426.   [180] OFT Decision, 17 December 2002, [2003] UKCLR 240.

[181] Ibid, paras 548–600.   [182] Ibid, paras 601–646.

[183] OFTEL Decision, 28 May 2003, [2003] UKCLR 816.

[184] OFT Decision, 27 March 2003, [2003] UKCLR 950.

[185] Ibid, paras 294–363; the second practice condemned was a vertical margin squeeze: see pp 746–747 below.

[186] Case No 1016/1/1/03 *Genzyme Ltd v Office of Fair Trading* [2004] CAT 4, [2004] CompAR 358, paras 546–548; interim relief was granted pending the CAT's final judgment Case No 1013/1/1/03 [2003] CAT 8, [2003] CompAR 290.

[187] For further reading on predatory pricing see section 6 of DG COMP's *Discussion paper on the application of Article 82 of the Treaty to exclusionary abuses*; Bishop and Walker *The Economics of EC Competition Law* (Sweet & Maxwell, 2nd ed, 2002), paras 6.69–6.103; Motta *Competition Policy: Theory and Practice* (Cambridge University Press, 2004), pp 412–454; O'Donoghue and Padilla *The Law and Economics of Article 82 EC* (Hart Publishing, 2006), ch 5; Van den Bergh and Camesasca *European Competition Law and Economics: A Comparative Perspective* (Sweet & Maxwell, 2nd ed, 2006), pp 280–298; for literature in leading periodicals see eg Areeda and Turner 'Predatory Pricing and Related Practices under Section 2 of the Sherman Act' (1975) 88 Harvard Law Review 697; Scherer 'Predatory Pricing and the Sherman Act: A Comment' (1976) 89 Harvard Law Review 869; Williamson 'Predatory Pricing: A Strategic and Welfare Analysis' (1977) 87

Competition Act; it also considers the rare circumstances in which selective price-cutting to retain customers may amount to an abuse even though no loss is incurred.

(A) Introduction

The idea of predatory price-cutting is simple enough: that a dominant firm that has been charging for its products supra-competitively reduces prices to a loss-making level when faced with competition from an existing competitor or a new entrant to the market; the existing competitor having been disciplined, or the new entrant having been fended off, the dominant firm then raises its prices again, accumulating further profits until the next wave of attacks. Attempts to eliminate an existing competitor may be more expensive and difficult to achieve than deterring a new one from entry, especially where the existing competitor is committed to remaining in the market. Where a dominant undertaking has a reputation for acting in a predatory manner, this in itself may deter new entrants: not only predatory pricing itself but also the reputation for predation may be a barrier to entry.

It is the essence of competition that firms should compete for custom by reducing prices. It has already been pointed out that rebates and similar practices are an essential component of the competitive process, and that the law should not condemn practices, even on the part of dominant firms, that are pro-competitive; in particular a dominant firm should not be deterred from passing on its efficiency to customers in the form of lower prices. The law on predatory price-cutting has to tread a fine line between not condemning competitive responses on the part of dominant firms on the one hand and prohibiting unreasonable exclusionary conduct on the other: this takes us back to the debate on 'Type I' and 'Type II' errors[188]. It would be perverse if the effect of competition law were to be that dominant firms choose not to compete on price for fear that, by doing so, they would be found guilty of abusing a dominant position[189].

There is some theoretical scepticism as to whether a monopolist would ever benefit from predatory price cutting. For example Bork argues that in practice predation is too expensive for the predator; that the predator will not earn monopoly profits until some distant future time when the new firm has disappeared; and that if it is easy to drive firms out, it will be correspondingly easy for new firms to enter when the predator begins to reap a monopoly profit in the future[190]; if one agrees with this view, competition authorities ought not to concern themselves at all with the issue. However that extreme position now has fairly few advocates. Economists today acknowledge that dominant

Yale Law Journal 284; Baumol 'Quasi-Permanence of Price Reductions: A Policy for Prevention of Predatory Pricing' (1979) 89 Yale Law Journal 1; Brodley and Hay 'Predatory Pricing: Competing Economic Theories and the Evolution of Legal Standards' (1981) 66 Cornell Law Review 738; Williamson *Antitrust Economics* (Blackwell, 1987), pp 328–338; Mastromanolis 'Predatory Pricing Strategies in the European Union: a Case for Legal Reform' (1998) 19 ECLR 211; Edlin 'Stopping Above-cost Predatory Pricing' (2002) 111 Yale Law Journal 941; Elhauge 'Why above-cost price cuts to drive out entrants are not predatory – and the implications for defining costs and market power' (2003) 112 Yale Law Journal 681.

[188] See ch 5, pp 190–191.

[189] See eg the Supreme Court in the US in *Matsushita v Zenith Radio* 475 US 574 (1986): 'mistaken inferences in cases such as this chill the very conduct that antitrust laws are designed to protect'.

[190] See eg Bork *Antitrust Paradox* (Basic Books, 1976), pp 148–155; see also Koller 'The Myth of Predatory Pricing: An Empirical Study' (1971) 4 Antitrust L Ec Rev 105; Easterbrook 'Predatory Strategies and Counterstrategies' (1981) 48 University of Chicago Law Review 263.

firms are able to act in a predatory manner, and game theory can help to demonstrate this[191]. There is no doubt that predatory price cutting can amount to an infringement of Article 82 and the Chapter II prohibition in the Competition Act 1998.

(B) The Areeda and Turner test

Many attempts have been made to frame an economic test of when a price is predatory. Areeda and Turner[192] suggested that a price should be deemed predatory under US law where it was below a firm's average variable cost ('AVC')[193].

The Areeda and Turner test relies exclusively on a cost/price analysis. Some commentators think that the test should be less strict, and that predation should be condemned only where it can also be demonstrated that a predator will be able to recoup any losses it has made through the exercise of its market power in the future: some US courts have required proof of recoupment as a key component of the offence of predation[194]. Others question whether the Areeda and Turner test is strict enough, arguing that pricing above AVC could be predatory in some circumstances, especially where there is evidence of an intention to discipline or deter competitors or where in practice it has this effect. However there are difficulties with a legal rule which requires specific proof of a predator's intention. In the ruthless process of competition any competitor that enters a race wishes to win, so that by necessary implication it must also have 'intended' that its competitors should lose; in this sense a requirement of intention is hardly meaningful. In so far as a requirement of intention means that evidence of a 'smoking gun' should be adduced, for example in the form of written memoranda, minutes of meetings and e-mails documenting a settled policy of eliminating competitors, this may be difficult for a competition authority to find: well-advised companies will be perfectly aware that they should not generate incriminating documents of this kind and that they should destroy those that they do. A rule requiring evidence of intention to eliminate would make more sense where it has an objective quality based in economics, for example that a predator's conduct, by departing from short-term profit maximisation, makes commercial sense only as a way of eliminating a competitor; this variant of intention is very different from proving the subjective intention of the predator, but is extremely difficult to prove as a matter of economic analysis. This discussion demonstrates some of the problems involved in establishing a suitable test for cases on predatory price-cutting.

As we shall see, proving intention is sometimes relevant to the EC law on pricing abuses. The ECJ in *AKZO v Commission*[195] decided that pricing above AVC but below

[191] See eg Philips *Competition Policy: A Game-Theoretic Perspective* (Cambridge University Press, 1995).

[192] See Areeda and Turner 'Predatory Pricing and Related Practices under Section 2 of the Sherman Act' 88 Harvard Law Review 697 (1975).

[193] See pp 707–708 above on the meaning of this and various other cost concepts; for a recent case analysing the cost standard to be applied to a case of predation in the airline industry in the US courts see *US v American Airlines Inc*, 355 F 3d 1109 (10th Cir 2003).

[194] See eg *Matsushita v Zenith Radio*, n 189 above; *AA Poultry Farms Inc v Rose Acre Farms Inc* 881 F 2d 1396 (1989); *Brooke Group Ltd v Brown Williamson Tobacco* 509 US 209 (1993); *Weyerhaeuser Co v Ross-Simmons Hardwood Lumber Co Inc* 549 US § (2007) (applying a requirement of proof of recoupment to predatory bidding as well as to predatory selling cases); on recoupment in US law see Joskow and Klevorick 'A Framework for Analysing Predatory Pricing Policy' (1979) 89 Yale Law Journal 213; Elzinga and Mills 'Testing for Predation: Is Recoupment Feasible?' (1989) 34 Antitrust Bulletin 869; *Edlin* (see n 187 above); on recoupment in EC law see pp 735–736 below; in UK law see p 743 below.

[195] Case C-62/86 *AKZO v Commission* [1991] ECR I-3359, [1993] 5 CMLR 215.

average total cost ('ATC') could be abusive where there was evidence of an intention on the part of the dominant firm to eliminate a competitor[196]. In *Compagnie Maritime Belge v Commission*[197] the ECJ held that a policy of selective price cutting to particular customers carried into effect with the intention of eliminating the dominant undertaking's only competitor was abusive in the particular circumstances of the market for the maritime transport of containerised cargo[198]. These judgments seem to be based on the 'smoking gun' variant of intention[199].

(C) EC case law

(i) The rule in *AKZO v Commission*

In *ECS/AKZO*[200] the Commission imposed a fine of €10 million on AKZO for predatory price-cutting. ECS was a small UK firm producing benzoyl peroxide. Until 1979 it had sold this product to customers requiring it as a bleach in the treatment of flour in the UK and Eire. It then decided also to sell it to users in the polymer industry. AKZO, a Dutch company in a dominant position on the market, informed ECS that unless it withdrew from the polymer market it would reduce its prices, in particular in the flour additives market, in order to harm it. Subsequently AKZO did indeed reduce its prices. In holding that AKZO had abused its dominant position the Commission declined to adopt the Areeda and Turner test of predatory price cutting, according to which pricing above AVC should be presumed lawful[201]. While accepting that cost/price analysis is an element in deciding whether a price is predatory, the Commission considered that it was also relevant whether the dominant firm had adopted a strategy of eliminating competition, what the effects of its conduct would be likely to be, and what a competitor's likely reaction to the conduct of the dominant firm would be. At paragraph 79 of its decision the Commission suggested that even a price above ATC might be predatory when assessed in its particular market context[202].

On appeal[203] the ECJ upheld the Commission's finding of predatory pricing, saying that not all price competition can be considered legitimate[204]. The ECJ held that where prices were below AVC predation had to be presumed, since every sale would generate a loss for the dominant firm[205]. The ECJ did not say that the presumption could never be rebutted, and in principle it would be wrong to have a *per se* rule that selling below AVC is always illegal[206]. For example it is arguable that a dominant firm should sometimes

---

[196] [1991] ECR I-3359, [1993] 5 CMLR 215, para 72 and see p 733 below; on the meaning of average total cost see p 708 above.

[197] Cases C-395/96 P etc [2000] ECR I-1365, [2000] 4 CMLR 1076.   [198] See pp 740–741 below.

[199] For argument against the use of evidence of intention when establishing an abuse under Article 82 see Bavasso 'The role of Intent Under Article 82 EC: From "Flushing the Turkeys" to "Spotting Lionesses in Regent's Park"' (2005) 26 ECLR 616.

[200] OJ [1985] L 374/1, [1986] 3 CMLR 273; see Merkin 'Predatory Pricing or Competitive Pricing: Establishing the Truth in English and EC Law' (1987) 7 Oxford Journal of Legal Studies 182.

[201] See p 731 above.

[202] See also the Commission's comments at point 82 of its XVth *Report on Competition Policy* (1985).

[203] Case C-62/86 *AKZO v Commission* [1991] ECR I-3359, [1993] 5 CMLR 215.

[204] [1991] ECR I-3359, [1993] 5 CMLR 215, para 70.

[205] Ibid, para 71; the ECJ did not discuss the period of time over which the AVC should be calculated.

[206] Cf Case C-333/94 P *Tetra Pak International SA v Commission* [1996] ECR I-5951, [1997] 4 CMLR 662, para 41, where the ECJ considered that prices below AVC must 'always' be considered abusive; however in

be able to sell below cost: sales promotions sometimes involve below-cost selling; and the disposal of old stock at the end of the season at a price below cost would presumably not be unlawful.

The ECJ in *AKZO v Commission* went on to hold that where prices are above AVC but below ATC they will be regarded as abusive if they are part of a plan which is aimed at eliminating a competitor[207]; such a pricing policy might mean that a dominant firm drives from the market undertakings that are as efficient as it but which, because of their smaller financial resources, are incapable of withstanding the competition waged against them. The ECJ therefore upheld the Commission's rejection of the Areeda/Turner test.

The rule in *AKZO v Commission* can be depicted as follows, where the dominant firm's prices range from 0 to 100:

100	Where a dominant firm is charging prices above ATC, it is not guilty of predation under the rule in *AKZO v Commission*; however consideration must be given to the rule on selective price cutting in *Compagnie Maritime Belge v Commission* (see below)
ATC	Where a dominant firm is selling at less than ATC, but above AVC, it is guilty of predation where this is done as part of a plan to eliminate a competitor
AVC	Where a dominant firm is selling at less than AVC, it is presumed to be acting abusively; this presumption may be rebuttable where there is an objective justification for below-cost selling
0	

Fig. 18.1

(ii) *Tetra Pak v Commission*

In *Tetra Pak II*[208] the Commission found Tetra Pak guilty of predatory pricing in relation to its non-asceptic cartons[209]; it considered that Tetra Pak was able to subsidise its losses from its substantial profits on the market for asceptic cartons, where it had virtually no competition. The Commission said that in seven Member States the non-asceptic cartons had been sold at a loss[210]. However the Commission concentrated on the position in Italy, where the cartons had been sold below AVC. The Commission did not merely rely on the *AKZO* presumption of predation where prices are below AVC, but said that it had 'gathered sufficiently clear and unequivocal data to be able to conclude that, in that country at least, sales at a loss were the result of a deliberate policy aimed at eliminating competition'[211]. The Commission continued by saying that, although it was difficult to believe that an efficient multi-national company could have indulged

---

the UK the CAT did not consider that the ECJ's *Tetra Pak* judgment should preclude the possibility, in rare cases, of rebutting the presumption of abuse: see Case No 1009/1/1/02 *Aberdeen Journals Ltd v Office of Fair Trading* [2003] CAT 11, para 357.

[207] Case C-62/86 *AKZO v Commission* [1991] ECR I-3359, [1993] 5 CMLR 215, para 72.
[208] OJ [1992] L 72/1, [1992] 4 CMLR 551.   [209] Ibid, paras 147–153.   [210] Ibid, para 147.
[211] Ibid, para 147.

in behaviour so opposed to the logic of economic profitability through management error, it should be asked whether exceptional circumstances, independent of Tetra Pak's free will, forced it to make losses. The Commission concluded that there were no such circumstances and that the prices were simply part of an 'eviction strategy'[212]. The ECJ upheld the Commission's finding of abuse; the judgment is of interest to the issue of recoupment, which is discussed below[213].

(iii) Wanadoo: on appeal *France Télécom v Commission*

In *Wanadoo*[214] the Commission applied the rule in *AKZO v Commission* and imposed a fine of €10.35 million on the subsidiary of France Télécom for having priced residential broadband internet services at levels that, until August 2001, fell considerably below AVC, and which subsequently were approximately equivalent to variable cost, but were significantly below ATC. In the Commission's view Wanadoo's behaviour 'was designed to take the lion's share of a booming market'[215].

The Commission's decision was upheld on appeal to the CFI in *France Télécom v Commission* (by the time of the appeal France Télécom had succeeded to the rights of Wanadoo)[216]. France Télécom challenged the Commission's finding of abuse on two grounds: first that it had applied the wrong test for calculating the rate at which France Télécom should recover its fixed costs in entering the residential broadband market, and had made errors of calculation when applying that test; and second that it had applied the wrong test of predation.

(A) Errors as to costs The CFI rejected France Télécom's appeal as to costs[217]. It began by noting that the analysis of costs involves a complex economic assessment, and that the Commission 'must be afforded a broad discretion'[218]. The CFI noted that, since the case concerned a new product in an expanding market, the Commission had spread the costs over a period of 48 months when determining whether France Télécom was selling at a loss[219]; this did not amount to a manifest error of assessment[220]. The Court also rejected the argument that there were methodological problems with the actual calculations of the Commission[221].

(B) The test of predation The CFI also rejected France Télécom's argument that the Commission had applied the wrong test of predation[222]. France Télécom ran three arguments: first that it was entitled to align its prices on those of its competitors; second, that there was no plan of predation or reduction of competition; and third that the Commission should be required to prove that France Télécom would be able to recoup its losses.

---

[212] Ibid, para 149.
[213] Case C-333/94 P *Tetra Pak International SA v Commission* [1996] ECR I-5951, [1997] 4 CMLR 662; see Korah 'The Paucity of Economic Analysis in the [EC] Decisions on Competition: Tetra Pak II' (1993) 46 Current Legal Problems 148, pp 172–181; Jones 'Distinguishing Predatory Prices from Competitive Ones' (1995) 17 EIPR 252.
[214] Commission decision of 16 July 2006, [2005] 5 CMLR 120.
[215] Commission Press Release IP/03/1025, 16 July 2003.
[216] Case T-340/03 [2007] ECR II-000; the case is on appeal to the ECJ, Case C-202/07 P *France Télécom v Commission*, not yet decided; for comment on the CFI judgment see Gal 'Below-Cost Price Alignment: Meeting or Beating Competition? The *France Télécom* Case' (2007) 28 ECLR 382.
[217] Case T-340/03 [2007] ECR II-000, paras 122–169.   [218] Ibid, para 129.   [219] Ibid, para 137.
[220] Ibid, para 155.   [221] Ibid, paras 162–169.   [222] Ibid, paras 170–230.

On the question of the alignment the CFI was clear: France Télécom did not have the right to align its prices on those of its competitors where this would mean that it was selling at below cost:

It is...not possible to assert that the rights of a dominant undertaking to align its prices on those of its competitors is absolute[223].

The CFI noted that, although a non-dominant undertaking would be allowed to match the prices of competitors, even by selling at below cost, dominant undertakings do not necessarily have the same right[224].

As to the question of a plan, the CFI noted that the Commission had correctly produced evidence that demonstrated a plan of predation for the period during which France Télécom was selling above AVC but below ATC[225].

The issue of recoupment is discussed in the next section.

(iv) Is it necessary to show the possibility of recoupment?

It was pointed out above that in US law some courts have required that an element of the offence of predatory price-cutting is that it can be shown that the predator has the ability to recoup any losses incurred. Many commentators have argued that a recoupment rule should be adopted under Article 82[226], although some argue to the contrary[227]. It is of interest to note that the Privy Council, a court in the UK that hears appeals from some countries in the British Commonwealth, said in *Carter Holt Harvey Building Products Group Ltd v The Commerce Commission*[228] that:

It is the ability to recoup losses because its price-cutting has removed competition and allows it to charge supra-competitive prices that harms competitors[229].

The Community Courts have not adopted a requirement of recoupment under Article 82; the most recent judgment on the point, that of the CFI in *France Télécom v Commission*, states clearly that there is no such requirement.

In *AKZO v Commission* the Court acknowledged the significance of recoupment in paragraph 71 of its judgment, where it noted that a dominant firm has no interest in applying prices below average variable cost:

except that of eliminating competitors so as to enable it subsequently to raise its prices by taking advantage of its monopolistic position.

However it did not expressly incorporate the need to prove recoupment as part of the offence. In *Tetra Pak II* it was argued before the ECJ that the Commission should have to establish the possibility of recoupment as part of the offence of predation. The ECJ, upholding the finding that Tetra Pak was guilty of predatory pricing, remarked that:

it would not be appropriate, *in the circumstances of the present case,* to require in addition proof that Tetra Pak had a realistic chance of recouping its losses. It must be possible to penalise predatory pricing whenever there is a risk that competitors will be eliminated[230] (emphasis added).

---

[223] Ibid, para 182.   [224] Ibid, para 186.   [225] Ibid, paras 195–218.

[226] See eg see Gal 'Below-Cost Price Alignment: Meeting or Beating Competition? The *France Télécom* Case' (2007) 28 ECLR 382 at p 383.

[227] See eg Ritter 'Does the Law of Predatory Pricing and Cross-subsidisation Need a Radical Rethink?' (2004) 27(4) World Competition 613.

[228] [2004] UKPC 37.   [229] Ibid, para 67.

[230] Case C-333/94 P *Tetra Pak International SA v Commission* [1996] ECR I-5951, [1997] 4 CMLR 662, para 44; at paras 76–78 of his Opinion in this case Advocate General Ruiz-Colomer considered that proof of

The *Tetra Pak* case was one in which the anti-competitive intention of Tetra Pak, manifested in a series of abusive acts contrary to Article 82, was particularly clear; furthermore its market power was considerable, so that the case could be considered as one of 'super-dominance' rather than one of 'mere' dominance[231]. This may explain why the ECJ felt that 'in the circumstances of the present case' it was not necessary to impose on the Commission the additional burden of a requirement to prove recoupment; this clearly leaves open the possibility that in future cases, where the evidence of intention to eliminate competition is less clear-cut and where the predator is not super-dominant, the Court might require proof of the possibility of recoupment[232].

In *France Télécom v Commission*[233] the CFI was invited to introduce a recoupment requirement into the test of predation. The Court cited the *AKZO* and *Tetra Pak* cases[234], and concluded that:

The Commission was therefore right to take the view that proof of recoupment of losses was not a precondition to making a finding of predatory pricing[235].

This case is on appeal to the ECJ, which provides that Court with a further opportunity to consider whether there are any circumstances in which proof of the possibility of recoupment should be required.

(v) Are the standards of AVC and ATC always appropriate?

A complicating factor in applying cost-based rules to determine whether prices are predatory is that it may not always be appropriate to apply the standards of AVC or ATC. In some industries fixed costs are very high but variable costs are low. An obvious example is telecommunications, where it is likely to have been very expensive to establish the original infrastructure of wires and cables; once they have been laid, however, the actual cost of carrying telephone calls is low, and may be as low as zero. A further example of high fixed costs but low variable costs is the laying of oil and gas pipelines. In industries such as this, the AVC of telephone calls or the transmission of oil and gas is so low that there would hardly ever be predatory prices if the AVC standard were to be applied; and the ATC standard would require proof of the predator's intention to eliminate competition, following the rule in *AKZO v Commission*, with the difficulties that this entails.

If the AVC and ATC standards in *AKZO v Commission* are inappropriate to determine whether prices are predatory in industries such as these, an alternative rule is needed. The Commission suggests, in its *Notice on the Application of the Competition Rules to Access Agreements*[236], that the *AKZO* standards are not appropriate in a network industry such as telecommunications[237] and that a standard based on long-run incremental cost ('LRIC') might be preferable[238]. Indeed, even a price above LRIC could be considered predatory, if it does not recover some of the common costs that are incurred where a firm supplies a range of different products: for this reason, a 'combinatorial' approach may be taken towards the assessment of cost, whereby a firm's long-run incremental

---

recoupment was not necessary; yet in Cases C-395/95 and 396/95 P *Compagnie Maritime Belge v Commission* [2000] ECR I-1365, [2000] 4 CMLR 1076, Advocate General Fennelly considered that recoupment should be part of the test for predatory pricing: ibid, para 136.

[231] See ch 5, pp 184–186.
[232] On the view of the UK competition authorities on this issue see p 742 below.
[233] Case T-340/03 [2007] ECR I-000.   [234] Ibid, paras 224–227.   [235] Ibid, para 228.
[236] OJ [1998] C 265/2, [1998] 5 CMLR 821.   [237] Ibid, paras 113–115.
[238] On the meaning of long-run incremental cost see p 708 above.

cost is combined with its 'stand alone cost', that is to say the cost that it would incur if it had no other activities at all[239].

The Commission proceeded, for the first time in a formal decision, on the basis of LRIC in *Deutsche Post*[240]. UPS complained that Deutsche Post was using revenue from its profitable letter-post monopoly to finance a strategy of below-cost selling in the commercial parcels market, which was open to competition. The Commission's view was that Deutsche Post, in the period from 1990 to 1995, had received revenue from this business which did not cover the incremental cost of providing it[241]. By remaining in the market without any foreseeable improvement in revenue, Deutsche Post was considered to have restricted the activities of competitors which were in a position to provide the service at a price that would cover their costs[242]. The Commission therefore concluded that Deutsche Post was guilty of predatory pricing; however it did not impose a fine for this infringement, since this was the first time that it had applied the LRIC standard[243]. As a matter of remedy Deutsche Post agreed to create a separate legal entity ('Newco') for its commercial parcels service. The Commission required that at the end of each accounting year Deutsche Post would submit a statement of Newco's costs and revenue and would provide an itemised statement of the transfer prices for all goods and services procured by Newco from it[244].

(vi) Predatory price cutting and cross-subsidisation[245]

An undertaking such as Deutsche Post, which enjoys a legal monopoly in relation to the basic letter service[246], is able to use the profits it makes there to support low prices in other markets where it faces competition: this was the essence of UPS's complaint[247]. Cross-subsidisation may facilitate abusive pricing practices such as predation and selective price cutting. This raises the interesting question of whether cross-subsidisation is an abuse of a dominant position in itself. There are no decisions of the Commission or judgments of the Community Courts finding that cross-subsidy is, in itself, an abuse of a dominant position, although the Commission in its *Notice on the Application of the Competition Rules to the Postal Sector*[248] suggests, at paragraph 3.3, that there could be circumstances in which it could be an abuse to subsidise activities open to competition by allocating their costs to those services in relation to which the postal operator enjoys a monopoly. Despite this statement, however, in principle it would appear that the existing rules on abusive pricing practices, described in this chapter, are sufficient to control the behaviour of dominant firms; the adoption of a rule forbidding cross-subsidy itself is unnecessary. This was the view of the CFI in *UPS Europe SA v Commission*[249].

---

[239] See p 708 above and *The Competition Act 1998: The application to the telecommunications sector*, OFT Guideline 417, February 2000, para 7.11.

[240] OJ [2001] L 125/27, [2001] 5 CMLR 99.

[241] Ibid, para 36; the Commission sets out the relevant cost concepts at paras 6 and 7 of the decision.

[242] OJ [2001] L 125/27, [2001] 5 CMLR 99.

[243] Ibid, para 47; a fine of €24 million was imposed for the separate abuse of offering loyalty rebates: see p 722 above.

[244] See Article 2 of the decision.

[245] See Hancher and Buendia Sierra 'Cross-subsidisation and EC Law' (1998) 35 CML Rev 901; Abbamonte 'Cross-subsidisation and Community Competition Rules: Efficient Pricing Versus Equity?' (1998) 23 EL Rev 414; on the relationship between these concepts see Case No 1007/2/3/02 *Freeserve.com plc v Director General of Telecommunications* [2003] CAT 5, [2003] CompAR 202, paras 171–225.

[246] On the extent of the permissible monopoly in postal services under Community law see ch 23, pp 977–978.

[247] OJ [2001] L 125/27, [2001] 5 CMLR 99, para 5.   [248] OJ [1998] C 39/2, [1998] 5 CMLR 108.

[249] Case T-175/99 [2002] ECR II-1915, [2002] 5 CMLR 67, para 61.

Where cross-subsidy is a problem there are other ways of dealing with it. In the case of regulated industries, specific rules are often imposed to prevent the practice[250]. Useful remedies that the Commission can deploy in Article 82 cases include a requirement to establish different legal entities, the maintenance of separate accounts and full financial transparency of dominant firms' pricing practices.

(vii) Selective price cutting but not below cost

One of the most contentious issues under Article 82 is whether it can be unlawful for a dominant firm to cut its prices selectively, but not to below cost, to customers that might desert to a competitor, while leaving prices to other customers at a higher level. Such a policy might amount to unlawful discrimination contrary to Article 82(2)(c) where it involves the application of dissimilar conditions to equivalent transactions, thereby placing other trading parties at a competitive disadvantage[251]. The specific issue under consideration in this section is whether selective price cutting could be held to be abusive irrespective of whether it infringes Article 82(2)(c) and, more specifically, where the undertaking harmed is a competitor operating at the same level of the market as the dominant firm rather than a trading party in a downstream market.

The position can be depicted as follows:

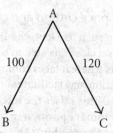

Fig. 18.2 Article 82(2)(c) discrimination

A charges B a price of 100 per widget, but charges C 120; B and C need widgets to manufacture blodgets, a market in which they compete. Clearly the discrimination puts C at a competitive disadvantage in the blodget market as against B. It may be, in a case such as this, that B is a subsidiary of A, or closely associated with it; this may help to explain why A practices discrimination in the first place. The detriment to competition occurs downstream from A's market: that is to say it amounts to vertical foreclosure, or to secondary-line injury, to be contrasted with the horizontal foreclosure, or primary-line injury, in the example that follows[252]:

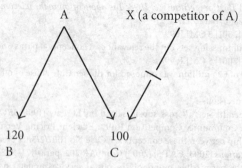

Fig. 18.3 Selective price cutting as an abuse

---

[250] See ch 23, p 970ff.
[251] See pp 000–000 below.   [252] For discussion of this terminology see ch 5, pp 202–203.

In this example A charges B 120 and C 100. B requires widgets for blodgets; C requires them for sprockets. Blodgets and sprockets do not compete, so that there is no harm to competition between B and C in the downstream market. The motivation for A's price cut to C is that A fears that it is going to lose C's business to X; X is able to supply a different input to C from which C could just as easily produce sprockets. The purpose of the selective price cut is to eliminate competition at A's level of the market: the case is one of horizontal foreclosure.

The question of whether selective price-cutting such as this is abusive is controversial[253]. Provided that the dominant firm is not making a loss, it is not guilty of predatory price-cutting; if it has not offered loyalty or target rebates, it has not infringed the rules in *Hoffmann-La Roche* and *Michelin*; and for the reasons just given it may not be infringing Article 82(2)(c). It would appear that, in making selective price cuts, the dominant firm is competing 'on the merits' with X, and that it has not acted abusively. The Community Courts have often stated that dominant firms are allowed to 'meet' competition, which is what A appears to have done[254]; and it is obviously in C's interest, and in the interest of C's customers, that it is the beneficiary of lower prices. Despite this, however, it is possible that selective price cuts of this nature may be held to be abusive, albeit only in narrowly defined circumstances.

(A) Eurofix-Bauco/Hilti In *Eurofix-Bauco/Hilti*[255] the Commission imposed a fine of €6 million on Hilti for abusing its dominant position in a number of ways. Hilti had taken action to prevent customers from purchasing nails from its competitors. Apart from entering into tie-in agreements with some customers[256], Hilti singled out competing firms' main customers and offered them particularly favourable conditions; it removed quantity discounts from long-standing customers who bought from its competitors; and it classified certain customers as 'unsupported', which meant that they qualified for lower quantity discounts than 'supported' firms: it appeared to the Commission that the 'unsupported' firms were ones which had purchased nails and nail cartridges other than from Hilti. Hilti had also given away some products free of charge. The Commission said that the pricing abuses in this case did not hinge on whether the prices were below cost, but on whether Hilti could rely on its dominance to offer discriminatory prices to its competitors' customers with a view to damaging the competitors' business; in other words the Commission proceeded not on the basis of predatory pricing contrary to *AKZO v Commission* nor on the basis of a detriment to competition in a downstream market contrary to Article 82(2)(c). The CFI, upholding the decision of the Commission, stated that Hilti's strategy was not a legitimate mode of competition on the part of an undertaking in a dominant position[257].

---

[253] See eg Elhauge 'Why Above-Cost Price Cuts To Drive Out Entrants Are Not Predatory – and the Implications for Defining Costs and Market Power' (2003) 112 Yale Law Journal 681; some commentators have written in defence of a rule that prohibits above-cost predatory pricing in certain circumstances: see eg Edlin 'Stopping Above-Cost Predatory Pricing' (2002) 111 Yale Law Journal 941; Ritter 'Does the Law of Predatory Pricing and Cross-subsidisation Need a Radical Rethink?' (2004) 27(4) World Competition 613.

[254] See eg the judgment of the CFI in Case T-228/97 *Irish Sugar v Commission* [1999] ECR II-2969, [1999] 5 CMLR 1300, para 112 and the judgments referred to in the footnote to that paragraph; for a general discussion of 'meeting' rather than 'beating' competition see Springer '"Meeting Competition": Justification of Price Discrimination under EC and US Antitrust Law' (1997) 18 ECLR 251.

[255] OJ [1988] L 65/19, [1989] 4 CMLR 677.   [256] See ch 17, p 683.

[257] Case T-30/89 *Hilti AG v Commission* [1990] ECR II-163, [1992] 4 CMLR 16, para 100.

(B) Irish Sugar v Commission The Commission considered that Irish Sugar had abused its dominant position contrary to Article 82 by offering selective price cuts in *Irish Sugar*[258]. The CFI annulled the finding that Irish Sugar had applied selectively low prices to potential customers of a competitor, ASI, on factual grounds[259]; however it upheld the finding that Irish Sugar had been guilty of granting selective rebates to particular customers[260].

(C) Compagnie Maritime Belge v Commission In *Compagnie Maritime Belge v Commission*[261] the Commission investigated the policy of 'fighting ships', whereby members of a liner conference in the maritime transport sector, Cewal, reduced their charges to the level, or to below the level, of their one competitor, Grimaldi and Cobelfret; they also operated the fighting ships on the same route and at the same time as Grimaldi's. The Commission concluded that the policy was one of selective price cutting intended to eliminate the competitor and that Article 82 was infringed. The Commission's decision was upheld by the CFI[262]. The ECJ agreed that there was an infringement of Article 82, although the fines were annulled for technical reasons[263].

Advocate General Fennelly, urging that the application of Article 82 to selective price cutting should be approached with reserve, remarked that:

Price competition is the essence of the free and open competition which it is the objective of Community policy to establish on the internal market. It favours more efficient firms and it is for the benefit of consumers both in the short and the long run. Dominant firms not only have the right but should be encouraged to compete on price[264].

In the Advocate General's view, non-discriminatory price cuts by a dominant undertaking which do not entail below-cost sales should not normally be regarded as being anti-competitive:

In the first place, even if they are only short lived, they benefit consumers and, secondly, if the dominant undertaking's competitors are equally or more efficient, they should be able to compete on the same terms. Community competition law should thus not offer less efficient undertakings a safe haven against vigorous competition even from dominant undertakings. Different considerations may, however, apply where an undertaking which enjoys a position of dominance approaching a monopoly, particularly on a market where price cuts can be implemented with relative autonomy from costs, implements a policy of selective price cutting with the demonstrable aim of eliminating all competition. In those circumstances, to accept that all selling above cost was automatically acceptable could enable the undertaking in question to eliminate all competition by pursuing a selective pricing policy which in the long run would permit it to increase prices and deter potential future entrants for fear of receiving the same targeted treatment[265].

In its judgment the ECJ followed the Advocate General, holding that the selective price-cutting on the facts of this case was abusive[266]. After noting that the scope of the special responsibility of dominant undertakings must be considered in the light of the specific circumstances of each case[267], the ECJ noted that the maritime transport market is 'a very specialised sector'[268]; it declined to establish a general rule for selective

---

[258] OJ [1997] L 258/1, [1997] 5 CMLR 666.

[259] Case T-228/97 [1999] ECR II-2969, [1999] 5 CMLR 1300, paras 117–124. [260] Ibid, paras 215–225.

[261] OJ [1993] L 34/20, [1995] 5 CMLR 198.

[262] Cases T-24/93 etc [1996] ECR II-1201, [1997] 4 CMLR 273.

[263] Cases C-395/95 and 396/95 P *Compagnie Maritime Belge v Commission* [2000] ECR I-1365, [2000] 4 CMLR 1076; for comment see Preece '*Compagnie Maritime Belge*: Missing the Boat?' (2000) 21 ECLR 388.

[264] [2000] ECR I-1365, [2000] 4 CMLR 1076, at para 117 of the Advocate General's Opinion.

[265] Ibid, para 132. [266] See paras 112–121 of the ECJ's judgment. [267] Ibid, para 114.

[268] Ibid, para 115.

price cutting on the part of liner conferences, but, upholding the Commission's finding of abuse, concluded that:

It is sufficient to recall that the conduct at issue here is that of a conference having a share of over 90% of the market in question and only one competitor. The appellants have, moreover, never seriously disputed, and indeed admitted at the hearing, that the purpose of the conduct complained of was to eliminate [Grimaldi & Cobelfret] from the market[269].

As a result of this judgment it is clear that selective price cutting is capable of being abusive in its own right. However it is important to point out a number of features of the *Compagnie Maritime Belge* case that restrict the scope of this precedent and which should therefore limit its application in the future. First, maritime transport is, as the ECJ remarked, an unusual sector in which an incumbent dominant firm is able to target its competitors and eliminate them by strategic behaviour with little regard to cost; second, the conference had 90 per cent or more of the market: it therefore was 'super-dominant', and subject to particularly close scrutiny under Article 82[270]; third, the conference had only one competitor, Grimaldi and Cobelfret; and fourth, there was a 'smoking gun', that is to say evidence of an intention on the part of the conference to eliminate Grimaldi from the market: indeed the smoke was seen by the judges of the ECJ, where the appellants admitted that they had this intention. The ECJ did not say, but may also have been influenced by the fact, that the liner conference itself was the product of a horizontal agreement amongst its members: there was, in effect, a horizontal collective boycott of Grimaldi, which would be a serious offence under Article 81(1)[271]. The case should be read with these special features in mind; this makes it a less menacing precedent than it might otherwise appear to be, with the consequence that other dominant firms, operating in less unusual circumstances, should be free to respond to competition by price cuts that are not contrary to any of the other pricing abuses under Article 82 described in this chapter.

(D) UK case law[272]

In *Freeserve.com plc v Director General of Telecommunications*[273] the CAT explained that, while the concepts of margin squeezing, cross subsidy and predatory pricing may to some extent overlap, they are not identical, and require independent examination[274]. There have been three cases in which predatory pricing has been established by competition authorities in the UK, *Napp*, *Aberdeen Journals* and *EW&S*.

(i) The *Napp Pharmaceutical* case
In *Napp Pharmaceutical Holdings Ltd*[275] the OFT concluded that Napp was guilty of charging predatory prices for sustained release morphine by selling some products to hospitals at less than direct cost, which it considered, on the facts of the case, to be

---

[269] Ibid, para 119.   [270] See ch 5, pp 184–186.   [271] See ch 13, pp 535–538.

[272] The OFT's draft guideline on *Assessment of conduct*, OFT 414a, April 2004, discusses predation at paras 4.1–4.27.

[273] Case No 1007/2/3/02 [2003] CAT 5, [2003] CompAR 202.

[274] Ibid, paras 203 and 219.

[275] OFT Decision, 30 March 2001, [2001] UKCLR 597; for comment on the finding of predatory pricing in this case see Kon and Turnbull 'Pricing and the Dominant Firm: Implications of the [Competition Appeal Tribunal's] Judgment in the *Napp* Case' (2003) 24 ECLR 70, pp 70–82.

742 18 ABUSE OF DOMINANCE (2): PRICING PRACTICES

a proxy for AVC[276]. The OFT rejected Napp's argument that sales below cost to hospitals were objectively justified since Napp would be able to recover the full price from follow-on sales to patients in the community[277]; indeed the very reason that Napp was able to earn high margins on sales to the community was that it had been successful in stifling competition in relation to sales to hospitals[278]. On appeal the CAT held that Napp, as an undertaking which it considered to be 'super-dominant'[279], had abused its dominant position by charging prices below cost to hospitals in order to ward off a competitor[280]. The CAT considered the relevance of intention in the *Napp* case: it held that, as Napp had offered prices below AVC to hospitals, it was not necessary to determine whether it had a plan to eliminate competition[281]; however the CAT found that such a plan existed in any event[282].

(ii) The *Aberdeen Journals* case

In *Aberdeen Journals Ltd*[283] the OFT imposed a penalty of £1,328,040 on Aberdeen Journals for predatory pricing by failing to cover its AVC from 1 March to 29 March 2000. This decision was set aside by the CAT as it was not satisfied by the way in which the OFT had defined the relevant market[284]. The OFT was asked to reconsider the matter, and in September 2002 it adopted a second decision, concluding again that Aberdeen Journals was guilty of predatory pricing[285]. On appeal against the second decision the CAT held that Aberdeen Journals had sold advertising in one of its newspapers at less than AVC contrary to the Chapter II prohibition[286]. This judgment contains several important points on the cost-based rules relating to predatory pricing. First, the CAT emphasised that the rules are not an end in themselves and ought not to be applied mechanistically[287]. Second, the CAT drew attention to the significance of the time period over which costs are to be calculated[288]; the reason for this is that, the longer the timescale, the more likely costs will be assessed as variable rather than fixed, with the result that a failure to cover them will give rise to a presumption of predation[289]. Third, the CAT recognised the possibility that a dominant firm could in certain circumstances objectively justify pricing below cost, though this would be particularly difficult when such pricing occurred in response to a new entrant or as part of a strategy to eliminate a competitor[290]. On the issue of intention the CAT said that, in the absence of exceptional circumstances, the longer a dominant firm prices below total costs, the easier it would be to draw an inference of intention to eliminate competition[291].

---

[276] OFT Decision, 30 March 2001, [2001] UKCLR 597, paras 188–196.   [277] Ibid, paras 192–195.
[278] Ibid, para 195.
[279] Case No 1000/1/1/01 *Napp Pharmaceutical Holdings Ltd v Director General of Fair Trading* [2002] CAT 1, [2002] CompAR 13, paras 219 and 343.
[280] [2002] CAT 1, [2002] CompAR 13, para 352.   [281] Ibid, paras 228 and 307.
[282] Ibid, paras 310 and 333.   [283] OFT Decision, 16 July 2001, [2001] UKCLR 856.
[284] Case No 1005/1/1/01 *Aberdeen Journals Ltd v Director General of Fair Trading* [2002] CAT 4, [2002] CompAR 167, paras 182–186.
[285] *Aberdeen Journals Ltd – remitted case*, 16 September 2002, [2002] UKCLR 740.
[286] Case No 1009/1/1/02 *Aberdeen Journals Ltd v Office of Fair Trading* [2003] CAT 11, [2003] CompAR 67.
[287] Ibid, paras 380 and 411.   [288] Ibid, paras 353–356 and 382–387.
[289] See the discussion of variable and fixed costs at pp 707–708 above.
[290] [2003] CAT 11, [2003] CompAR 67, paras 357–358 and 371.   [291] Ibid, para 356.

(iii) EW&S

In *English Welsh and Scottish Railway Ltd*[292] the Office of Rail Regulation found that EW&S had abused its dominant position in a number of ways, including by predatory pricing[293].

(iv) Is there a need to prove recoupment of losses?

In *Napp*[294] and the second *Aberdeen Journals* case[295] the CAT held that it was a form of recoupment for a dominant firm to engage in predatory pricing in one market so that it could protect its market share or supra-competitive profits in another market and that, in the circumstances of those cases, further evidence of recoupment was unnecessary.

(v) Cases where predatory pricing was not established

There have been some cases in which a complaint of predatory pricing was not upheld. In *The Association of British Travel Agents and British Airways plc*[296] the OFT concluded that BA was not guilty of abusing a dominant position by reducing the commission it paid to travel agents for the sale of tickets for its flights with the consequence that it could sell those same flights at lower fees through its own website: the sale of tickets on-line as opposed to through travel agents was cheaper, and there was an objective justification for this price differential[297].

In *Complaint against BT's pricing of digital cordless phones*[298] OFCOM dealt with a complaint that BT was guilty of charging predatory prices for digital cordless telephones. OFCOM concluded that BT was not dominant[299]. However it also conducted an extensive analysis of whether, if BT was dominant, it would have been guilty of predatory pricing and concluded that this was not so[300].

In *Claymore Dairies Ltd v OFT*[301] the CAT was critical of the OFT's investigation into whether Robert Wiseman Dairies was guilty of predatory pricing in relation to the sale of milk in Scotland: in particular it was not satisfied that the OFT had sufficiently investigated whether Wiseman's prices were above ATC[302], and it therefore set the finding on this point aside[303]. No further order was made since, by the time of the CAT's judgment, market conditions had changed so that the issues were of historical interest only.

The OFT rejected a complaint about predatory prices in *First Edinburgh/Lothian*[304].

---

[292] ORR decision of 17 November 2006, [2007] UKCLR 937. [293] See Part IIC of the decision.
[294] Case No 1000/1/1/01 *Napp Pharmaceutical Holdings Ltd v Director General of Fair Trading* [2002] CAT 1, [2002] CompAR 13, para 261.
[295] Case No 1009/1/1/02 *Aberdeen Journals Ltd v Office of Fair Trading* [2003] CAT 11, [2003] CompAR 67, para 445.
[296] *Association of British Travel Agents and British Airways plc*, 11 December 2002, [2003] UKCLR 136.
[297] Ibid, paras 38–45. [298] OFCOM decision of 1 August 2006, [2007] UKCLR 1.
[299] Ibid, paras 151–429. [300] Ibid, paras 430–662.
[301] Case 1008/2/1/02 [2005] CAT 30, [2006] CompAR 1. [302] Ibid, para 256. [303] Ibid, para 318.
[304] OFT Decision, 9 June 2004, [2004] UKCLR 1554.

7. MARGIN SQUEEZING[305]

(A) The economic phenomenon

A vertical margin squeeze can occur where a firm is dominant in an upstream market and supplies a key input to undertakings that compete with it in a downstream market. In such a situation the dominant firm may have a discretion as to the price it charges for the input, and this could have an effect on the ability of firms to compete with it in the downstream market. Suppose that A supplies widgets, essential for the manufacture of widget dioxide; that B is a subsidiary of A; and that C is an independent downstream competitor.

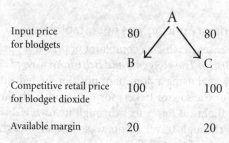

Fig. 18.4 Vertical margin squeeze: example 1

In this example C will be able to compete with B in the downstream market for widget dioxide only if C can transform the widgets into widget dioxide for a price of less than 20: if it cannot do so, it could not charge 100 in the retail market and make a profit. If, on the other hand, A had charged 60 for the widgets, the available margin would be 40, as in the following example:

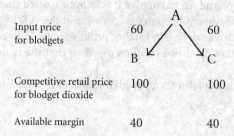

Fig. 18.5 Vertical margin squeeze: example 2

In each situation the total revenue of the integrated undertaking AB amounts to 100, but A has 'squeezed' the margin available to C in example 1 in a way that makes it more

---

[305] For further reading on margin squeezing see O'Donoghue and Padilla *The Law and Economics of Article 82 EC* (Hart Publishing, 2006), ch 6; Kavanagh 'Assessing Margin Squeeze under Competition Law' (2004) 3 Competition Law Journal 187; Crocioni 'Price Squeeze and Imputation Test – Recent Developments' (2005) 10 ECLR 558; Géradin and O'Donoghue 'The Concurrent Application of Competition Law and Regulation: The Case of Margin Squeeze Abuses in the Telecommnications Sector' (2005) 1 Journal of Competition Law and Economics 355.

difficult for C to remain in the market for widget dioxide than in example 2. However, it is a complex matter to determine when a squeeze becomes abusive. For example if, in example 1, B can transform widgets into widget dioxide for, say, 15, whereas C is less efficient and can perform the same task only for 25, there is no reason why C should be able to demand a lower input price: the fact is that it is not as efficient as B, and so does not merit protection from it. However if B's own cost of transformation is 25, and C's is 15, the input price is being manipulated to protect B from a more efficient competitor, C, and so there is an abusive margin squeeze.

There may be other ways of addressing the pricing practices of the vertically-integrated entity AB. One is to enquire whether the input price charged by A to C is excessive; another is to determine whether the output price charged by B is predatory. Both of these issues were explored earlier in this chapter. If A were to charge higher prices to C than it charges to B, there might be a case of discrimination contrary to Article 82(2)(c), which is discussed towards the end of this chapter. However the focus of this section is whether A is guilty of manipulating the relationship of its upstream and downstream prices in order to eliminate its downstream competitor by a margin squeeze. The Commission and the competition authorities in the UK consider this to be an independent abuse in its own right. In a memorandum of 4 July 2007, at the time of its decision in *Telefónica*, the Commission said that a margin squeeze means that the dominant firm leaves an insufficient margin between its upstream and downstream products; and that it is this difference, rather than the specific level of the wholesale or retail prices, that is the essence of the infringement[306]. Whether this is the the correct test of a margin squeeze will be considered by the CFI in the *Telefónica* appeal[307].

(B) EC case law

In *Napier Brown–British Sugar*[308] British Sugar was dominant both in the market for sugar beet and in the market for the derived product, sugar for retail. It reduced the price of retail sugar by more than the cost of transforming the raw material in order to drive sugar merchants such as Napier Brown from the retail level of the market; it also specifically undercut Napier Brown's prices in respect of certain customers. The Commission considered that this practice infringed Article 82. A fine of €3 million was imposed for this (and other) abuses[309].

The CFI upheld the Commission's rejection of a complaint about vertical price squeezing in *Industrie des Poudres Sphériques v Commission*[310].

In *Deustche Telekom* the Commission imposed a fine of €12.6 million on Deutsche Telekom ('DT') for imposing a margin squeeze in relation to access to its local networks[311]. DT had a dominant position in relation to the so-called 'local loop', that is to say the final section of the telecommunications network that connects a customer's premises to the local switching point. DT provided retail services over the local loop to

[306] See MEMO/07/274.
[307] Case T-336/07 *Telefónica and Telefónica España v Commission*, not yet decided.
[308] OJ [1988] L 284/41, [1990] 4 CMLR 196.
[309] See also *National Carbonising* OJ [1976] L 35/6 and the Commission's *Notice on the Application of the Competition Rules to Access Agreements in the Telecommunications Sector* OJ [1998] C 265/2, paras 117–119; for cases under UK law see pp 746–748 below.
[310] Case T-5/97 [2000] ECR II-3755, [2001] 4 CMLR 1020.
[311] Commission decision of 21 May 2003, OJ [2003] L 263/9, [2004] 4 CMLR 790.

its own customers, but also made wholesale capacity available to operators that would themselves like to provide retail services. At one point DT's retail prices were actually less than its wholesale ones: the Commission said that this was a clear case of a margin squeeze, since it left new entrants no margin to compete for downstream subscribers. In the Commission's view the squeeze continued even after DT's prices were raised above its own retail prices, since the difference between the two was still not sufficient to cover DT's own downstream costs. The Commission has monitored DT's wholesale prices since its decision to ensure that any margin squeeze is avoided[312]. The *Deutsch Telekom* decision was upheld on appeal to the CFI[313].

In *Telefónica*[314] the Commission imposed a fine of €151.8 million on Telefónica for engaging in a margin squeeze in relation to residential broadband access in Spain. Commissioner Kroes explained that the fine was so high because the relatively small fines against Deutsche Telekom in 2003 for margin squeezing, and against Wanadoo for predatory pricing, had apparently had an insufficient deterrent effect on Telefónica, whose unlawful behaviour continued until 2006[315].

(C) UK case law[316]

There have been a number of complaints about margin squeezing in the UK, two of which were successful.

(i) Findings of a margin squeeze

In *Genzyme Ltd*[317] the OFT imposed a fine of £6.8 million on that company for abusing its dominant position in two ways, one of which was to have imposed a margin squeeze[318]. The finding of a margin squeeze was upheld on appeal to the CAT[319]; the Tribunal reviewed the law at paragraphs 489 to 493 of its judgment. Genzyme was the producer of a drug, Cerezyme, used in the treatment of Gaucher's disease. Genzyme delivered the drug to patients in their homes; a competitor in the downstream market, Healthcare at Home, provided the same service. Genzyme was found guilty of squeezing the margin available to Healthcare at Home. In September 2005, following protracted but unsuccessful negotiations as to the price that Genzyme should charge for Cerezyme in order to avoid a margin squeeze, the CAT handed down a judgment on remedy[320]. It contained critical comments on Genzyme's approach to the negotiations[321]; noted that it may be the case that there was no longer full vertical integration between Genzyme and the downstream home-provider[322]; but nevertheless concluded that a direction was

---

[312] See eg Commission Press Release IP/05/1033, 3 August 2005.

[313] Case T-271/03 *Deutsche Telecom v Commission*, judgment of 10 April 2008.

[314] Commission decision of 4 July 2007; see Le Meur, Gurpegui and Vierti 'Margin squeeze in the Spanish broadband market: a rational and profitable strategy' (2007) *Competition Policy Newsletter* Number 3, 22; the case is on appeal to the CFI, Case T-336/07 *Telefónica and Telefónica España v Commission*, not yet decided.

[315] See SPEECH/07/460, 4 July 2007.

[316] The OFT's draft guideline on *Assessment of conduct*, OFT 414a, April 2004, discusses margin squeezing at paras 6.1–6.5; see also *The Application of the Competition Act in the Telecommunications Sector*, OFT Guideline 417, February 2000, para 7.26.

[317] OFT Decision, 27 March 2003, [2003] UKCLR 950.   [318] Ibid, paras 364–385.

[319] Case No 1016/1/1/03 *Genzyme Ltd v OFT* [2004] CAT 4, [2004] CompAR 358.

[320] *Genzyme Ltd v OFT* [2005] CAT 32, [2006] CompAR 195.   [321] Ibid, paras 222–223.

[322] Ibid, para 236.

needed to determine a price at which an efficient provider of homecare services would be able to compete in the market[323]. Subsequently Healthcare at Home brought a 'follow-on' action for damages in the CAT[324]: the case was settled without a final judgment, but was notable for the fact that the CAT awarded damages on an interim basis to the claimant[325].

In *Albion Water/Dŵr Cymru* OFWAT rejected a complaint that Dŵr Cymru was guilty of a margin squeeze[326]. Following lengthy proceedings in the CAT the Tribunal held in December 2006 that Dŵr Cymru was indeed guilty of margin squeezing[327]. The CAT suggested two different tests of whether there was an unlawful margin squeeze:

(i) that the dominant company's own downstream operations could not trade profitably on the basis of the upstream price charged to its competitors by the upstream operating arm of the dominant company; or (ii) that a reasonably efficient downstream operator could not earn (at least) a normal profit when paying input prices set by the vertically integrated undertaking[328].

The Court of Appeal gave permission to Dŵr Cymru to appeal, and upheld the CAT's finding on the margin squeeze[329].

(ii) Rejections of complaints about margin squeezes

The OFT concluded that there was no margin squeeze in *Companies House*[330]. In *BSkyB*[331] the OFT investigated complaints by three competitors at the distribution level of the market, NTL, Telewest and ITV Digital, that BSkyB was guilty of a margin squeeze by setting its wholesale prices for the provision of premium channels at a level that would mean that distributors with the same efficiency as BSkyB would have to operate at a loss[332]. Following an extensive economic analysis, the conclusion was reached that there were insufficient grounds for believing that there was an abusive margin squeeze.

OFTEL, and its successor OFCOM, have investigated several cases of margin squeezing, and have always reached the conclusion that there was no abuse. In *BT/UK-SPN*[333] OFTEL found that the prices BT charged for its UK-SPN service indicated a possible margin squeeze[334], but concluded that there was insufficient evidence of either an anticompetitive effect or of an intention to eliminate competition[335]. OFCOM decided that there was no margin squeeze in *Alleged anti-competitive practices by BT in relation to BTOpenworld's consumer broadband products*[336], *Investigation against BT about*

---

[323] Ibid.   [324] Case No 1060/5/7/06 *Healthcare at Home v Genzyme Ltd*.

[325] Case No 1060/5/7/06 *Healthcare at Home v Genzyme Ltd* [2006] CAT 29, [2007] CompAR 474.

[326] OFWAT decision of 27 May 2004, [2004] UKCLR 1317.

[327] Case No 1046/2/4/04 *Albion Water Ltd v Director General of Water Services* [2006] CAT 36, [2007] CompAR 328, paras 896–919; see also the Interim Judgment in this case of 22 December 2005, [2005] CAT 40, [2006] CompAR 269, in which the CAT discusses the issue of margin squeeze at length (paras 385–419) without reaching any conclusions on it.

[328] Ibid, para 898.

[329] *Dŵr Cymru Cyfyngedig v Water Services Regulation Authority*, judgment of 22 May 2008, [2008] EWCA Civ 536.

[330] OFT Decision, 25 October 2002, [2003] UKCLR 24, paras 29–36.

[331] OFT Decision, 17 December 2002, [2003] UKCLR 240, paras 341–547.   [332] Ibid, paras 341–547.

[333] OFT Decision, 22 May 2003, [2003] UKCLR 794, paras 21–53.   [334] Ibid, paras 37–41.

[335] Ibid, para 49.

[336] OFCOM Decision of 20 November 2003, [2004] UKCLR 496, paras 6.1–6.162, on appeal Case No 1026/2/3/04 *Wanadoo UK plc (formerly Freeserve.com plc) v OFCOM*; this appeal is stayed pending further deliberation by OFCOM.

potential anti-competitive behaviour[337], *BT 0845 and 0870 retail price change*[338] and in *Suspected margin squeeze by Vodafone, O2, Orange and T-Mobile*[339]. In these decisions OFCOM has used various methodologies to determine whether there was a margin squeeze. It has repeatedly found that, even if there was a margin squeeze, there was no evidence of an adverse effect in the downstream market; for example in the last of the decisions just listed it concluded that the mobile operators competed effectively with one another and that their corporate customers had buyer power which prevented them having to pay higher prices than in a competitive market. OFCOM again concluded that there was no margin squeeze in *Complaint from Gamma Telecom against BT about reduced rates for Wholesale Calls from 1 December 2004*[340], applying four different tests but concluding that there was no margin squeeze under any of them[341].

8. PRICE DISCRIMINATION[342]

Article 82(2)(c) specifically gives as an example of abuse:

applying dissimilar conditions to equivalent transactions with other trading parties, thereby placing them at a competitive disadvantage.

Clearly therefore price discrimination may infringe Article 82; so too could other types of discrimination, such as refusals to supply and preferential terms and conditions. Price discrimination may be exploitative of customers, for example where higher prices are charged to 'locked-in' customers unable to switch to alternative suppliers; it can also be harmful to the competitive process, where it leads to a distortion of competition in markets downstream of the dominant undertaking.

(A) The meaning of price discrimination

Price discrimination may be defined as the sale or purchase of different units of a good or service at prices not directly corresponding to differences in the cost of supplying them. There can be discrimination both where different, non-cost related prices are charged for the sale or purchase of goods or services of the same description and also where identical prices are charged in circumstances in which a difference in the cost of supplying them would justify their differentiation.

There are many costs involved in supplying goods or services which may result in the charging of differentiated yet non-discriminatory prices. For example, apart from the cost of transporting goods, a manufacturer may incur heavier costs where it has to handle a series of small orders from a particular customer rather than a single, annual one.

---

[337] OFCOM Decision, 12 July 2004, [2004] UKCLR 1695, paras 108–128.

[338] OFCOM Decision, 19 August 2004, [2005] UKCLR 31, paras 3.24–3.100.

[339] OFCOM Decision, 26 May 2004, [2004] UKCLR 1639, paras 148–178.

[340] OFCOM Decision, 16 June 2005, [2005] UKCLR 882, paras 47–120.   [341] Ibid, paras 47–120.

[342] For further reading on price discrimination see Scherer and Ross *Industrial Market Structure and Economic Performance* (Houghton Mifflin, 3rd ed, 1990), ch 13; Bishop and Walker *The Economics of EC Competition Law* (Sweet & Maxwell, 2nd ed, 2002), paras 6.23–6.44; Motta *Competition Policy: Theory and Practice* (Cambridge University Press, 2004), pp 491–511; O'Donoghue and Padilla *The Law and Economics of Article 82 EC* (Hart Publishing, 2006), ch 11; Van den Bergh and Camesasca *European Competition Law and Economics: A Comparative Perspective* (Sweet & Maxwell, 2nd ed, 2006), pp 254–264.

Orders for large quantities of goods may mean that a producer can plan long production runs and achieve economies of scale which lead to lower unit costs. The incidence of different contractual terms and conditions, payment of local taxes and duties, the different costs involved in operating distributorship networks from one area to another, may all explain the charging of different prices. However it can be difficult to determine whether differences in the cost of supplying goods or services justify, objectively, the charging of differentiated prices; and even more difficult to calculate the justifiable differentiation.

It is important to appreciate that price discrimination can be positively beneficial in terms of allocative efficiency, since it may result in an *increase* in output[343]: a theatre might be able to sell 80 per cent of its tickets to the public at £40 each, or alternatively 100 per cent of its tickets by charging 70 per cent of its customers £50 and the remaining 30 per cent £10 each (for example to impoverished students). Through such discrimination more theatre tickets will have been sold than would otherwise have been the case: resources have been more efficiently allocated. A specific example of efficient price discrimination is so-called 'Ramsey pricing'. This occurs where a company supplies different products which share common costs[344]. It may be that customers for product A are highly price sensitive, but that customers for product B are not; if customers for product B are charged high prices and customers for product A low ones – that is to say if prices are marked up in inverse proportion to customers' respective price sensitivities – output will be increased and economic efficiency will therefore be maximised. The principle of Ramsey pricing has been accepted by regulators and competition authorities in some sectors[345], although it was rejected by the UK Competition Commission in its investigation of call-termination charges in the mobile telephony sector[346].

In practice the allocative effects of discrimination will vary from one market situation to another: the question is ultimately an empirical rather than a theoretical one. There is no case for a *per se* prohibition of price discrimination, even on the part of a dominant firm. It may be that preventing discrimination has the effect of redistributing income from poorer consumers to richer ones[347]. This can be illustrated by imagining what might happen if discrimination is prevented. A producer may charge £10 per widget in a prosperous area and £5 per widget in a poorer one. If this discrimination is prevented the producer may sell at a uniform price of, say, £7 in both areas. It is reasonable to assume that as a result fewer people in the poorer area will buy widgets, and that those that do will pay a higher proportion of their income than those in the prosperous one. The net effect therefore is to transfer wealth from poorer consumers with the result that more prosperous ones will be better off.

---

[343] See eg Schmalensee 'Output and Welfare Implications of Third Degree Price Discrimination' (1981) 71 American Economic Review 242.

[344] On the meaning of common costs see p 708 above.

[345] See Pflanz 'What Price is Right? Lessons from the UK Calls-to-Mobile Inquiry' (2000) 21 ECLR 147; the potential efficiency of price discrimination is explicitly recognised in the UK in the OFT's guideline on the domestic equivalent of Article 82(2)(c), *Assessment of Individual Agreements and Conduct* (OFT Guideline 414), paras 3.6–3.10.

[346] See *Mobile phone charges inquiry* (18 February 2003), paras 2.213–2.215, available at www.competition-commission.org.uk; the Commission's report was unsuccessfully challenged on judicial review in *R v Competition Commission, Director General of Telecommunications, ex p T-Mobile (UK) Ltd, Vodafone Ltd, Orange Personal Communication Services Ltd* [2003] EWHC 1555 (Admin Ct).

[347] See Bishop 'Price Discrimination under Article [82]: Political Economy in the European Court' (1981) 44 MLR 282.

(B) EC case law

(i) The Commission's decisional practice under Article 82(2)(c)

The Commission has applied Article 82(2)(c) on a number of occasions, in particular in relation to the operation of airports within the Community[348]. The ECJ upheld findings by the Commission that Article 82(2)(c) had been infringed in *Hoffmann-La Roche v Commission*[349] and in *United Brands v Commission*[350]. The Commission's decision in *Michelin*[351] that there had been an infringement of Article 82(2)(c) was annulled by the ECJ[352]. The ECJ upheld the Commission's finding of an Article 82(2)(c) abuse in *GVL v Commission*[353], where a copyright collecting society in Germany refused to provide its services to non-German residents, thereby placing them at a competitive disadvantage as against German residents.

The decision of the Commission in *Irish Sugar*[354] that there had been an infringement of Article 82(2)(c) was upheld by the CFI[355]. Irish Sugar granted 'sugar export rebates' to industrial customers in Ireland in relation to sugar exported to other Member States, to the disadvantage of customers selling in Ireland[356]. Irish Sugar also practised discrimination against sugar packers in Ireland, a practice which the CFI found to infringe Article 82(2)(c)[357].

In *Virgin/British Airways*[358] the Commission concluded that BA was not only guilty of abuse by offering travel agents loyalty rebates; there was discrimination contrary to Article 82(2)(c), since travel agents in the same circumstances received different levels of rebates[359]. This finding was upheld on appeal to the CFI[360] and to the ECJ[361]. The ECJ noted that BA's reward scheme led to different rates of commission being applied to an identical amount of revenue generated by the sale of BA tickets by two travel agents, and that this distorted the level of remuneration received by them[362]. In the Court's view the Commission was right to hold that BA's reward schemes were abusive:

in that they produced discriminatory effects within the network of travel agents established in the UK, thereby inflicting on some of them a competitive disadvantage within the meaning of subparagraph (c) of the second paragraph of Article 82 EC[363].

In *Deutsche Post AG – Interception of cross-border mail*[364] the Commission found that Deutsche Post was guilty of discrimination under Article 82(2)(c) by treating different types of cross-border mail in different ways: the Commission was concerned about the effect of this discrimination on consumers, and considered that it was not necessary to demonstrate serious harm to competition[365].

---

[348] See pp 751–752 below.   [349] Case 85/76 [1979] ECR 461, [19791 3 CMLR 211.
[350] Case 27/76 [1978] ECR 207, [1978] 1 CMLR 429.   [351] OJ [1981] L 353/33, [1982] 1 CMLR 643.
[352] Case 322/81 [1983] ECR 3461, [1985] 1 CMLR 282.
[353] Case 7/82 [1983] ECR 483, [1983] 3 CMLR 645.   [354] OJ [1997] L 258/1, [1997] 5 CMLR 666.
[355] Case T-228/97 *Irish Sugar plc v Commission* [1999] ECR II-2969, [1999] 5 CMLR 1300.
[356] Ibid, paras 125–149.   [357] Ibid, paras 150–172.   [358] OJ [2000] L 30/1, [2000] 4 CMLR 999.
[359] Ibid, paras 108–111.
[360] Case T-219/99 *British Airways plc v Commission* [2003] ECR II-5917, [2004] 4 CMLR 1008, paras 233–240.
[361] Case C-95/04 P *British Airways plc v Commission* [2007] ECR I-2331, [2007] 4 CMLR 982.
[362] Ibid, paras 235–236.   [363] Ibid, para 240.   [364] OJ [2001] L 331/40, [2002] 4 CMLR 598.
[365] Ibid, paras 121–134.

(ii) The specific application of Article 82(2)(c) to airport operations

Article 82(2)(c) has been applied to discriminatory practices at a number of Community airports. In *Alpha Flight Services/Aéroports de Paris*[366] the Commission found that the operator of the two Paris airports (Orly and Charles de Gaulle) had abused its dominant position by imposing discriminatory commercial fees on suppliers or airlines providing ground-handling or self-handling services such as catering, cleaning and freight-handling. The Commission's decision was upheld on appeal to the CFI[367] and the ECJ[368].

In *Portuguese Airports*[369] the Commission adopted a decision establishing that Portugal was in breach of Article 86 read in conjunction with Article 82 in respect of a system of discounts on landing charges at the airports of Lisbon, Oporto, Faro and the Azores. Discounts were offered to airlines according to the number of flights that landed at Portuguese airports. For example, the second 50 flights would be charged at a discount of 7.2 per cent from the price for the first 50; the third 50 at 14.6 per cent and so on. As a result of this discounting structure TAP and Portugalia (Portuguese airlines) respectively enjoyed discounts of 30 per cent and 22 per cent on the total of their flights; the next beneficiary was Iberian Airlines (of Spain), which earned a discount of 8 per cent. Airlines from beyond the Iberian peninsular received meagre discounts. At paragraph 27 of its decision the Commission cited the CFI's statement in *BPB Industries v Commission*[370] that business practices considered to be normal may constitute an abuse if carried out by an undertaking in a dominant position.

On appeal the ECJ acknowledged that quantity discounts linked solely to the volume of purchases may be permissible, but said that the rules for calculating the discounts must not result in the application of dissimilar conditions to equivalent transactions contrary to Article 82(2)(c)[371]. It went on to say that:

where, as a result of the thresholds of the various discount bands, and the levels of discount offered, discounts (or additional discounts) are enjoyed by only some trading parties, giving them an economic advantage which is not justified by the volume of business they bring or by any economies of scale they allow the supplier to make compared with their competitors, a system of quantity discounts leads to the application of dissimilar conditions to equivalent transactions.

In the absence of any objective justification, having a high threshold in the system which can only be met by a few particularly large partners of the undertaking occupying a dominant position, or the absence of linear progression in the increase of the quantity discounts, may constitute evidence of such discriminatory treatment[372].

The ECJ noted that the highest discount rate was enjoyed only by the two Portuguese airlines, that the discount rate was greatest for the highest band and that the airports concerned enjoyed a natural monopoly; it concluded that in these circumstances the discounts were discriminatory[373].

---

[366] OJ [1998] L 230/10, [2001] 4 CMLR 611.

[367] Case T-128/98 [2000] ECR II-3929, [2001] 4 CMLR 1376.

[368] Case C-82/01 P [2002] ECR I-9297, [2003] 4 CMLR 609.

[369] OJ [1999] L 69/31, [1999] 5 CMLR 103, upheld on appeal, Case C-163/99 *Portugal v Commission* [2001] ECR I-2613, [2002] 4 CMLR 1319.

[370] Case T-65/89 [1993] ECR II-389, [1993] 5 CMLR 32.

[371] Case C-163/99 *Portugal v Commission* [2001] ECR I-2613, [2002] 4 CMLR 1319, para 50.

[372] Ibid, paras 52–53.   [373] Ibid, paras 54–57.

The Commission has adopted decisions under Article 82(2)(c) condemning similar discount schemes in *Zaventem*[374], *Finnish Airports*[375] and *Spanish Airports*[376]. The Commission announced in May 2001 that it had completed its investigation into discriminatory landing fees at Community airports[377].

(iii) The need for competitive disadvantage

The wording of Article 82(2)(c) specifically requires that one component of the abuse is the infliction of 'competitive disadvantage'. In some cases little attention was given to this issue. In *Corsica Ferries*[378] the ECJ said that Article 82(2)(c) applied to 'dissimilar conditions to equivalent transactions with trading partners', without mentioning the requirement of competitive disadvantage at all[379]. In its judgment the Court said that if different tariffs were applied for compulsory piloting, according to whether a maritime transport undertaking was operating between Member States on the one hand or within one and the same Member State on the other, there would be an infringement of Article 82(2)(c); however there would be no competition between these two categories of undertakings, so that the Court seems to have written competitive disadvantage out of Article 82(2)(c) on this occasion.

In the Commission's decisions on Community airports[380] scant attention was given to the need for competitive disadvantage; the same was true in *Deutsche Post AG – Interception of cross-border mail*[381]. It may be that this element of the offence will be applied in a particularly liberal manner where, as in those decisions and as in *Corsica Ferries*, the discrimination is practised on national lines, to the detriment (though not the competitive disadvantage) of undertakings in other Member States.

In *British Airways v Commission*[382] the ECJ gave some consideration to the requirement of competitive disadvantage in Article 82(2)(c)[383]. The ECJ was explicit that it is necessary in a case under this provision to show that competition is distorted: the distortion may be between the suppliers or between the customers of the dominant undertaking[384]. There must be a finding that the discriminatory conduct in question:

tends to distort that competitive relationship, in other words to hinder the competitive position of some of the business partners of that undertaking in relation to others[385].

The ECJ held that it is sufficient that the behaviour 'tends' to distort competition; there is no need to adduce evidence of an actual quantifiable deterioration in the competitive position of the business partners taken individually[386]. The ECJ concludes that the CFI had sufficiently satisfied itself that the test of Article 82(2)(c) was met[387].

---

[374] *Brussels National Airport (Zaventem)* OJ [1995] L 216/8, [1996] 4 CMLR 232.
[375] *Ilmailulaitos/Luftfartsverket* OJ [1999] L 69/24, [1999] 5 CMLR 90.   [376] OJ [2000] L 208/36.
[377] Commission Press Release IP/01/673, 10 May 2001.
[378] Case C-18/93 *Corsica Ferries Italia Srl v Corporazione dei Piloti del Porto di Genoa* [1994] ECR I-1783.
[379] Ibid, para 43.   [380] See pp 751–752 above.   [381] OJ [2001] L 331/40, [2002] 4 CMLR 598.
[382] Case C-95/04 P *British Airways plc v Commission* [2007] ECR I-2331, [2007] 4 CMLR 982.
[383] Ibid, paras 142–148.   [384] Ibid, para 143.   [385] Ibid, para 144.   [386] Ibid, para 145.
[387] Ibid, paras 146–148.

(C) UK case law[388]

In *BT/BSkyB broadband promotion*[389] OFTEL concluded that any discrimination on BT's part in relation to the promotion of its broadband services did not have a material effect on competition, and in *BT TotalCare*[390] OFTEL rejected an allegation by Energis Communications Ltd that BT had been guilty of discrimination towards it in relation to the provision of certain broadband services.

In *English Welsh and Scottish Railway Ltd*[391] the Office of Rail Regulation found that EW&S had abused its dominant position in a number of ways, including by discriminating between customers[392].

9. PRICING PRACTICES THAT ARE HARMFUL TO THE SINGLE MARKET

The Commission will condemn pricing practices on the part of dominant firms that are harmful to the single market. High prices that are charged in order to prevent parallel imports will infringe Article 82.

(A) Excessive pricing that impedes parallel imports and exports

In *BL*[393] the Commission condemned that firm for charging £150 to any importer of BL cars from the continent requiring a type-approval certificate to enable the cars to be driven in the UK. The interest of this case is that the purpose of the excessive pricing was not to exploit a monopoly situation by earning excessive profits, but to impede parallel imports into the UK: the Commission's action was motivated by single-market considerations, and not by a desire to establish itself as a price regulator; the circumstances in the *General Motors* case were the same[394]. The Commission's decision in *BL* was upheld on appeal by the ECJ, which accepted that the price charged by BL was disproportionate to the value of the service provided[395]. The Commission's decision in *Deutsche Post AG – Interception of cross-border mail*[396] is another example of the same point[397].

(B) Geographic price discrimination

In *United Brands v Commission*[398] the ECJ held that UBC had abused its dominant position by charging different prices for its bananas according to the Member State of their destination. It sold bananas to distributors/ripeners at Rotterdam and Bremerhaven,

---

[388] The OFT's draft guideline on *Assessment of conduct*, OFT 414a, April 2004, discusses price discrimination at paras 3.1–3.10.

[389] OFTEL Decision, 19 May 2003.   [390] OFTEL Decision, 10 June 2003.

[391] ORR decision of 17 November 2006, [2007] UKCLR 937.

[392] See Part IIB of the decision.   [393] OJ [1984] L 207/11, [1984] 3 CMLR 92.

[394] OJ [1975] L 29/14, [1975] 1 CMLR D20, annulled on appeal for want of evidence Case 26/75 *General Motors v Commission* [1975] ECR 1367, [1976] 1 CMLR 95.

[395] Case 226/84 [1986] ECR 3263, [1987] 1 CMLR 185.   [396] OJ [2001] L 331/40, [2002] 4 CMLR 598.

[397] See pp 712–713 above.   [398] Case 27/76 [1978] ECR 207, [1978] 1 CMLR 429.

and charged the lowest price for bananas destined for Eire and the highest for those going to West Germany. The different prices were not based on differences in costs: in fact transport to Eire, for which UBC itself paid, cost more than to other countries so that, if anything, prices should have been higher there. UBC was also condemned for including clauses in contracts with distributors which had the effect of preventing parallel imports from one country to another by prohibiting the export of unripened bananas[399].

The decision is curious[400]. UBC claimed that it was being required to achieve a common market by adopting a uniform pricing policy for all Member States and that this was an unreasonable requirement on the part of the Commission. The ECJ retorted that it was permissible for a supplier to charge whatever local conditions of supply and demand dictate, that is to say that there is no obligation to charge a uniform price throughout the EC. However it added that the equation of supply with demand could be taken into account only at the level of the market at which a supplier operates. In *United Brands* this would mean that only a retailer in a given Member State could consider what price the market could bear; UBC could not do so since it did not sell bananas at retail level in Member States: it supplied distributors/ripeners at Rotterdam and Bremerhaven. In the ECJ's view, therefore, it was entitled to take into account local market conditions only 'to a limited extent'. The reasoning has been questioned: supply and demand at retail level would inevitably exert a backward influence on UBC, and anyway it, rather than retailers, employed the staff who carried out market research and monitored the level of demand throughout the EC. A different criticism of the case is that the judgment could have undesirable redistributive effects. The logical response of UBC would be to charge a uniform price higher than that in Eire but lower than that in Germany; it would seem therefore that the judgment would benefit the Germans at the expense of the Irish. It is therefore arguable that the discrimination in *United Brands* should not have been condemned; the practice which was rightly found to be abusive was the prohibition on the export of unripened (green) bananas, since this is what had the effect of harming the single market. In the absence of this practice, bananas could have moved from low- to high-priced parts of the Community.

The Commission also condemned geographical price discrimination in *Tetra Pak II*[401]. The Commission's view was that the relevant geographic market was the Community as a whole, and yet Tetra Pak had charged prices that varied considerably from one Member State to another. The Commission said that the price differences could not be explained in economic terms and lacked objective justification. They were possible because of Tetra Pak's policy of market compartmentalisation which it maintained by virtue of its other abusive practices, thereby enabling it to maximise its profits on the basis of discrimination and the elimination of competitors.

---

[399] See ch 17, p 703.

[400] For criticism see Bishop 'Price Discrimination under Article [82]: Political Economy in the European Court' (1981) 44 MLR 282; Zanon 'Price Discrimination under Article [82] of the [EC] Treaty: the *United Brands* Case' (1982) 31 ICLQ 36.

[401] OJ [1992] L 72/1, [1992] 4 CMLR 551, paras 154, 155 and 160, upheld on appeal Case T-83/91 *Tetra Pak International SA v Commission* [1994] ECR II-755, upheld on appeal to ECJ Case C-333/94 P *Tetra Pak International SA v Commission* [1996] ECR I-5951, [1997] 4 CMLR 662.

(C) Rebates that impede imports and exports

The Commission will condemn rebates and similar practices which have the effect of impeding imports and exports. Pricing practices that were intended to dissuade customers from importing plasterboard from other Member States were held to be abusive in the *Plasterboard*[402] case. The Commission's decision in *Irish Sugar*[403] was prompted by single market considerations. Irish Sugar had a share of the Irish sugar market in excess of 90 per cent and was found to have acted abusively by seeking to restrict competition from other Member States. In particular Irish Sugar was found to have offered selectively low prices to customers of an importer of French sugar and to have offered 'border rebates' to customers close to the border with Northern Ireland and who were therefore in a position to purchase cheaper sugar from the UK. On appeal to the CFI the Court annulled the former finding[404], but agreed that the border rebates were unlawful[405]. The CFI stressed the importance in Community competition law of the competitive influence on one national market from neighbouring markets, 'the very essence of a common market'[406].

---

[402] Case T-65/89 *BPB Industries plc and British Gypsum v Commission* [1993] ECR II-389, [1993] 5 CMLR 32, paras 117–122.

[403] OJ [1997] L 258/1, [1997] 5 CMLR 666.

[404] Case T-228/97 *Irish Sugar v Commission* [1999] ECR II-2969, [1999] 5 CMLR 1300, paras 117–124.

[405] [1999] ECR II-2969, [1999] 5 CMLR 1300, paras 173–193.   [406] Ibid, para 185.

19

The relationship between intellectual property rights and competition law

CHAPTER CONTENTS

This chapter considers the relationship between intellectual property rights and competition law. After a brief introduction, section 2 of the chapter will deal in general terms with the application of Article 81 to licences of intellectual property rights; section 3 will examine the provisions of Regulation 772/2004[1], the block exemption for technology transfer agreements. Section 4 will consider the application of Article 81 to various other agreements concerning intellectual property rights such as technology pools and settlements of litigation. This will be followed by a section on the possible application of Article 82 to the way in which dominant undertakings exercise their intellectual property rights, including an examination of the controversial subject of refusals to license intellectual property rights which are sometimes found to be abusive. Section 6 of this chapter will look at the position in UK law.

1. INTRODUCTION

(A) Definitions

It is not possible to deal with the substantive law of intellectual property here in detail[2]. For present purposes the term 'intellectual property' includes patents, registered and

---

[1] OJ [2004] L 123/11.

[2] For a general account of the law see Torremans and Holyoak *Intellectual Property Law* (Oxford University Press, 4th ed, 2005); Cornish and Llewellyn *Intellectual Property Law* (Sweet & Maxwell, 6th ed, 2007);

unregistered designs, copyrights including computer software, trade marks and analogous rights such as plant breeders' rights. It should also be taken to include know-how, defined for the purpose of the block exemption on technology transfer agreements as 'a package of non-patented practical information, resulting from experience and testing': such information must be secret, substantial and identified in a sufficiently comprehensive manner that it is possible to verify that it is secret and substantial[3]; although not strictly speaking an intellectual property right[4], know-how may be extremely valuable and may be sold or 'licensed' for considerable amounts of money.

(B) Intellectual property rights and the single market

Generally speaking intellectual property rights are the product of, and are protected by, national systems of law, although the growth of international commerce has resulted in an increasing measure of international cooperation[5]. The existence of different national laws on intellectual property presents particular difficulties in the European Union in so far as this may be detrimental to the goal of single market integration. The European Court of Justice developed the 'exhaustion of rights' doctrine to prevent an undertaking that has voluntarily placed goods on the market within the European Union from using a national intellectual property right to prevent the free movement of those goods around the Community[6]; the exhaustion of rights doctrine does not apply to goods placed on the market outside the EU[7]. Various harmonisation measures have been adopted to reduce the differences between different systems of law; an obvious example is the Trade Mark Directive[8], implemented in the UK by the Trade Marks Act 1994. The adoption

Bently and Sherman *Intellectual Property Law* (Oxford University Press, 2nd ed, 2004); for specific discussion of the relationship between intellectual property rights and Community competition law see Rothnie *Parallel Imports* (Sweet & Maxwell, 1993); Tritton *Intellectual Property in Europe* (Sweet & Maxwell, 2nd ed, 2002); Govaere *The Use and Abuse of Intellectual Property Rights in EC Law* (Sweet & Maxwell, 1996); Anderman *EC Competition Law and Intellectual Property Rights: The Regulation of Innovation* (Clarendon Press Oxford, 1998); Maher 'Competition Law and Intellectual Property Rights: Evolving Formalism' in Craig and De Búrca (eds) *The Evolution of EU Law* (Oxford University Press, 1999); Oliver and Jarvis *Free Movement of Goods in the European Community* (Sweet & Maxwell, 4th ed, 2003); Korah *Intellectual Property Rights and the EC Competition Rules* (Hart Publishing, 2006); *European Competition Law Annual: The Interaction between Competition Law and Intellectual Property Law* (eds Ehlermann and Atanasiu, Hart Publishing, 2007); Faull and Nikpay *The EC Law of Competition* (Oxford University Press, 2nd ed, 2007), ch 10; Bellamy and Child *European Community Law of Competition* (eds Roth and Rose, Oxford University Press, 6th ed, 2007), ch 9; Stothers *Parallel Trade in Europe: Intellectual Property, Competition and Regulatory Law* (Hart Publishing, 2007).

[3] Regulation 772/2004, Article 1(1)(i); the Regulation is considered at pp 771–781 below.

[4] Know-how is protected by the law of obligations: see generally on confidential information *Cornish and Llewellyn*, ch 8.

[5] See *Cornish and Llewellyn*, paras 1.29–1.34.

[6] See Coates, Kyølbye and Peeperkorn in Faull and Nikpay *The EC Law of Competition* (Oxford University Press, 2nd ed, 2007), paras 10.36–10.49.

[7] Ibid, paras 10.50–10.54.

[8] Council Directive 89/104, OJ [1989] L 40/1; see also the Directives on computer software, Directive 91/250, OJ [1991] L 122/42; on rental rights, Directive 92/100, OJ [1992] L 346/1; on the duration of copyright, Directive 93/98, OJ [1993] L 290/9; on satellite broadcasting and cable transmissions, Directive 93/83, OJ [1993] L 248/15; on databases, Directive 69/9, OJ [1996] L 77/20; on biotechnology, Directive 98/44, OJ [1998] L 213/3; on designs, Directive 98/71, OJ [1998] L 289/28; and on copyright and related rights, Directive 2001/29/EC of the European Parliament and of the Council on the harmonisation of certain aspects of copyright and related rights in the information society OJ [2001] L 167/10.

of the Community Trade Mark Regulation[9] takes matters a step further, by creating an intellectual property right that is itself a creature of Community rather than national law; there is also a Regulation on designs[10] and there are plans for a Community Patent Regulation[11]. Much of this chapter is concerned with the problem that intellectual property rights may be used in a way that compartmentalises the single market.

(C) Is there an inevitable tension between intellectual property rights and competition law?

The essential characteristic of intellectual property rights is that they confer upon their owners an exclusive right to behave in a particular way. For example the UK Patents Act 1977 grants the owner of a patent the right to prevent others from producing the patented goods or applying the patented process for a period of 20 years; patents may be granted where a product or process is technically innovative[12]. A patent does not necessarily make the patentee a monopolist in an economic sense: there may be other products that compete with the subject-matter of the patent; however the patent does afford a degree of immunity from the activities of rival firms. The owner of a registered trade mark can prevent anyone else applying that name to goods or services where this would be confusing to consumers.

Because intellectual property rights confer exclusive rights upon their owners on the one hand, whereas competition law strives to keep markets open on the other, it is easy to suppose that there is an inherent tension between these two areas of law and policy[13]. However it has increasingly been recognised that this is simplistic and wrong[14]. As paragraph seven of the European Commission's *Guidelines on the application of Article 81 of the EC Treaty to technology transfer agreements*[15] ('the *Technology Transfer Guidelines*') says:

Indeed, both bodies of law share the same basic objective of promoting consumer welfare and an efficient allocation of resources. Innovation constitutes an essential and dynamic component of an open and competitive market economy.

Clear statements to the same effect will be found in an invaluable document issued by the Department of Justice and the Federal Trade Commission in the US in April 2007

---

[9] Regulation 40/94, OJ [1994] L 11/1.   [10] Council Regulation 6/2002/EC OJ [2002] L 3/1.
[11] OJ [2000] C 337 E/278, COM(2000) 412 final, 1 August 2000; the Council has agreed upon a common political approach for the creation of a Community patent: see Commission Press Release, MEMO/03/47, 3 March 2003.
[12] On the law of patents see *Cornish and Llewellyn*, chs 3–7.
[13] For general discussion of the relationship between intellectual property and competition law see the publications cited in n 2 above.
[14] See eg Tom and Newberg 'Antitrust and Intellectual Property: From Separate Spheres to Unified Field' (1997–98) 66 Antitrust Law Journal 167 on the 'marked reduction in antitrust hostility toward intellectual property' in the US in the last 50 years; see also Kobak 'Running the Gauntlet: Antitrust and Intellectual Pitfalls on the Two Sides of the Atlantic' (1995–96) 64 Antitrust Law Journal 341; Commission's *Evaluation Report on the Transfer of Technology Block Exemption Regulation No 240/96*, December 2001, para 29; Report for the European Commission on *Multi-Party Licensing* (Charles River Associates, April 2003), pp 58–59; Kovacic and Reindl 'An Interdiscipinary Approach to Improving Competition Policy and Intellectual Property Policy' (2005) 28 Fordham International Law Journal 1062; Lianos 'Competition Law and Intellectual Property Rights: Is the Property Rights' Approach Right?' Chapter 8 in Cambridge Yearbook of European Legal Studies, eds Bell and Kilpatrick (Oxford: Hart Publishing, 2006).
[15] OJ [2004] C 101/2.

entitled *Antitrust Enforcement and Intellectual Property Rights: Promoting Innovation and Competition*[16]. It begins with the following very clear statement:

> Over the past several decades, antitrust enforcers and the courts have come to recognize that intellectual property laws and antitrust laws share the same fundamental goals of enhancing consumer welfare and promoting innovation. This recognition signaled a significant shift from the view that prevailed earlier in the twentieth century, when the goals of antitrust and intellectual property law were viewed as incompatible: intellectual property law's grant of exclusivity was seen as creating monopolies that were in tension with antitrust law's attack on monopoly power. Such generalizations are relegated to the past. Modern understanding of these two disciplines is that intellectual property and antitrust laws work in tandem to bring new and better technologies, products, and services to consumers at lower prices.

Many of the issues discussed in this chapter are analysed in the DoJ/FTC document, which will be cited at various points in the text that follows. In the same spirit as that document, the current block exemption in force in the EU for technology transfer agreements, Regulation 772/2004[17], and the accompanying *Technology Transfer Guidelines* adopt a much less grudging attitude towards such agreements than used to be the case: indeed recital 5 of the Regulation notes that such agreements 'will usually improve economic efficiency and be pro-competitive'; the same point is made at several points in the *Guidelines*[18]. The complex matter in modern competition policy is to determine at what point, if at all, the exercise of an intellectual property right could be so harmful to consumer welfare that competition law should override the position as it would be on the basis of intellectual property law alone.

2. LICENCES OF INTELLECTUAL PROPERTY RIGHTS: ARTICLE 81

(A) Introduction

A patentee may decide, instead of producing the patented goods or applying the patented process itself, to grant a licence to another firm enabling it to do so. The same may be true of any other intellectual property right. There are many reasons why a firm may choose to grant a licence. A patentee may lack the resources to produce in quantity; it may wish to limit its own production to a particular geographical area and to grant licences for other territories; or it may wish to apply a patented process for one purpose and to allow licensees to use it for others. A patentee may wish to impose various restrictions upon its licensees, for example as to the quantity or quality of goods that may be produced or the price at which they may be sold; these provisions relate to the patentee's own products and so can be restrictive only of intra-technology competition[19].

The argument for controlling restrictions of intra-technology competition in patent licences is weak. Given that a patentee has an exclusive right to produce and sell the patented goods, it is not obvious why it should not be able to impose whatever restrictions it chooses upon its licensees; the ability to do so is a manifestation of the right con-

---

[16] This document can be accessed at www.ftc.gov.   [17] OJ [2004] L 123/11.

[18] See eg paras 8, 9, 17 and 146ff.

[19] For discussion of this expression see the *Technology Transfer Guidelines*, paras 11–12.

ferred by statute. Indeed the grant of a licence can be seen as increasing competition, by introducing a licensee onto the market which, without the licence, would not be there at all; even if the patentee imposes restrictions of intra-technology competition, these are likely to be compensated for by the stimulation of inter-technology competition[20]. However Article 81(1) has been applied to intra-technology restrictions in patent (and other) licences, in particular where they divide the single market: the 'single market imperative' is as influential in this area of EC competition law as it is elsewhere[21].

Some terms in patent licences may affect inter-technology competition: examples are tie-in clauses requiring a licensee to acquire particular technology or products solely from the patentee and non-competition clauses forbidding the licensee to compete or to handle technology or products which compete with the patentee's: provisions such as these may foreclose the opportunities of other producers. Objection might be taken to terms which are perceived to be an attempt to extend a patentee's monopoly power beyond the protection afforded to it by the law and/or which might be considered to be oppressive to a person in a weak bargaining position.

(B) Typical terms in licences of intellectual property rights

It will facilitate an understanding of the law on licensing agreements to have some knowledge of typical clauses that may be found in them. In the absence of legal controls it would be a matter for the parties to the agreement to settle the terms of the licence through the bargaining process. It would be wrong to assume that it is always the patentee that is in the more powerful bargaining position: a patentee may be an individual inventor and his prospective licensee a powerful company, in which case the former's position may be weak.

(i) Territorial exclusivity[22]

In EC law territorial exclusivity is the most critical aspect of licensing agreements because of the overriding determination of the Commission and the Community Courts to prevent the isolation of national markets. A licensee may consider that the risk involved in exploitation of a patent is that the high level of capital investment required is so great that it would not be worth taking a licence at all unless it is given immunity from intra-technology competition from the licensor, other licensees and their customers: these issues have been discussed already in relation to vertical agreements[23]. A licensee will often be taking a greater risk than a 'mere' distributor, since it has to invest in production as well as distribution, and so may require more protection against free riders than a distributor needs. The extent of the exclusivity required will be a calculation for the licensee; the amount actually given, apart from any limiting legal constraints, will be a matter for bargaining between the licensor and licensee.

Often the licensor will grant to the licensee an exclusive right to manufacture and sell the goods in a particular territory and agree to refrain from granting similar rights to anyone else there; in this situation the licensor retains the right to produce the goods in the territory itself: this is known as a 'sole' licence. A sole licence may be distinguished from an 'exclusive' licence, where the licensor also agrees not to produce the goods in the licensee's territory itself; this of course gives the licensee more protection than in

---

[20] Ibid.   [21] See ch 1, pp 22–23 and ch 2, pp 51–52.
[22] See further the *Technology Transfer Guidelines*, paras 161–174.   [23] See ch 16, pp 616–617.

the case of a sole licence. The licensee's position may be further reinforced by the licensor agreeing to impose export bans on its other licensees preventing them, or requiring them to prevent their customers, from selling into the licensed territory. Apart from the imposition of export bans, there are indirect ways of achieving the same end: for example a maximum quantities clause can limit the amount that a licensee can produce to the anticipated level of demand on its domestic market. As we shall see, the mere grant of territorial exclusivity in a licence of an intellectual property right does not necessarily infringe Article 81(1); this will depend on the effect that this would have on the market. However, where a licensor grants a licensee absolute territorial protection against any form of intra-technology competition there will almost certainly be an infringement of Article 81(1) and it is unlikely that the terms of Article 81(3) will be satisfied.

(ii) Royalties[24]

A licensor will usually require the licensee to pay royalties for use of the patent. The licensee may be required to make lump-sum payments, and in some situations the parties may agree upon a profit-sharing scheme. The licensor may ask for a payment 'up-front' before production begins. A licensor may stipulate that the licensee must pay a minimum amount of royalties in a given period in order to encourage it to exploit the patented process.

(iii) Duration

A licensor will specify what the duration of the agreement should be. It may decide to grant only a limited licence which will expire before the patent itself, after which it can reconsider its position. On the other hand it may attempt to tie the licensee even after the patent has expired, for example by requiring it to continue to pay royalties or to take licences of newly discovered technology.

(iv) Field of use restrictions[25]

A common clause is a 'field of use' restriction whereby a licensor limits the licensee's authority to produce goods to a particular purpose: a chemical protected by a patent may be useful both medicinally and industrially and the licensee could be limited to production for one purpose only. Field of use clauses are normally seen as a reasonable exploitation of the patentee's position, although the Commission may object where the restriction appears to be motivated by an intention to divide markets.

(v) Best endeavours and non-competition clauses[26]

To ensure that the licensee does exploit the patent (and that the patentee receives adequate royalties) the licensee may be required to produce minimum quantities or to use its best endeavours to do so. A non-competition clause, whereby the licensee is forbidden to compete by using its own or rival technology, may encourage it to concentrate on producing the patented goods, although the tendency of such a clause to foreclose competitors might alarm the competition authorities.

---

[24] See further the *Technology Transfer Guidelines*, paras 156–160.   [25] Ibid, paras 179–185.
[26] Ibid, paras 196–203.

(vi) No-challenge clauses

The licensor may insist upon a no-challenge clause whereby the licensee agrees not to challenge the validity of the intellectual property right in question. A licensee with intimate knowledge of, say, a patented process may be in the best position to show that it lacks originality, and a licensor may be unwilling to grant a licence at all if it knows that the licensee might undermine its position by successfully applying for the patent to be revoked.

(vii) Improvements

A licensor may be fearful that the licensee will build upon the knowledge that becomes available from using the patent and emerge as a strong competitor; it may therefore require the licensee to grant back to it any know-how or intellectual property rights acquired and not to grant licences to anyone else. Objection may be taken to this practice if the licensor requires the licensee to grant it exclusive access to such know-how, since this deprives the licensee of the opportunity to pass on the technology to third parties.

(viii) Tying and bundling[27]

The licensor may make the licensing of technology conditional upon the licensee taking a licence for another technology or purchasing a product from the licensor or a designated third party; or may bundle two technologies or a technology and a product together. These practices are capable of foreclosing access to the market, but may also lead to economic efficiencies.

(ix) Prices, terms and conditions

The licensor may wish to fix the prices at which the licensee sells or the terms and conditions on which it does so. The Commission, however, takes the view that the licensee should be free to determine its own policy when it brings the patented products to the market.

(C) The application of Article 81(1) to licences of intellectual property rights[28]

(i) The Commission's evolving policy in relation to patent licences in the 1960s and 1970s

In the early 1960s the Commission took the view that most provisions in patent licences did not infringe Article 81(1) at all, since restrictions of intra-brand competition simply

---

[27] Ibid, paras 191–195.
[28] See the *Technology Transfer Guidelines*, paras 10–17 and paras 130ff; on the position in the US see the *Antitrust Guidelines for the Licensing of Intellectual Property* of the Department of Justice and Federal Trade Commission of 6 April 1995, available at www.usdoj.gov/atr/public/guidelines/ipguide.htm; the *Guidelines* state at para 2.0 that there is no presumption that intellectual property creates market power and they also say that licences of intellectual property rights are generally pro-competitive; the approach in the 1995 *Antitrust Guidelines*, which suggests that terms in licences should be subject to a rule of reason standard rather than 'bright line' *per se* legality or illegality, was endorsed by the DoJ/FTC report on *Antitrust Enforcement and Intellectual Property Rights* of April 2007: see in particular chapter 4 of the report.

emanate from the exclusive right of the patentee. The Commission's *Notice on Patent Licensing Agreements*[29] of 1962 reflected this approach. However the Commission's abstentionist view began to alter towards the end of the decade; the change can be traced back to the judgment of the ECJ in *Consten and Grundig v Commission*[30]. There the ECJ established that vertical agreements could fall within Article 81(1) and, of particular importance in this context, that the use of intellectual property rights could contribute to an infringement where it enabled a distributor to enjoy absolute territorial protection in its allotted territory; in *Consten and Grundig* it was the assignment to Consten of the GINT trade mark for France that enabled Consten to repel parallel imports from other Member States[31]. The distinction drawn by the ECJ in this case – between the existence of an intellectual property right on the one hand and its improper exercise on the other – provided the foundation of much of the law in this area including, in particular, the exhaustion of rights doctrine.

In a series of decisions from the early 1970s the Commission applied Article 81(1) to various clauses found in patent licences, and in particular to territorial restrictions, although in some cases it was prepared to grant individual exemption under Article 81(3)[32]. In a series of block exemptions, beginning with Regulation 2349/84 in 1984[33] up until Regulation 240/96 in 1996[34], the Commission maintained a fairly formalistic approach to the application of Article 81(1), applying that provision to a wide variety of contractual restrictions but then exempting them according to the terms of the relevant Regulation. The latest block exemption, Regulation 772/2004, is noticeably less formalistic and, in conjunction with the *Technology Transfer Guidelines*, provides a more benign legal environment for the transfer of technology. The *Technology Transfer Guidelines* explain both the ways in which licences of technology containing restrictive terms may have negative[35] and positive[36] effects on competition.

(ii) Territorial exclusivity and the *Maize Seeds* case

In many of the decisions referred to above the Commission held that manufacturing and sales licences granting territorial exclusivity to the licensee infringed Article 81(1); it also considered that export bans and provisions having similar effects such as maximum quantities clauses were caught. Having concluded that many patent licences were caught by Article 81(1), the Commission proceeded to grant them block exemption.

---

[29] JO [1962] 2922; this Notice was withdrawn in 1984, OJ [1984] C 220/14.

[30] Cases 56/84 and 58/64 [1966] ECR 299, [1966] CMLR 418; for discussion of this case see ch 3, pp 124–125; on the Commission's change of policy see *Anderman*, ch 5.

[31] See ch 3, pp 124–125.

[32] In chronological order the Commission's decisions on patent licences are *Burroughs AG and Deplanque & Fils Agreement* OJ [1972] L 13/50, [1972] CMLR D67; *Burroughs AG and Geha-Werke GmbH Contract* OJ [1972] L 13/53, [1972] CMLR D72; *Davidson Rubber Co Agreements* OJ [1972] L 143/31, [1972] CMLR D52; *Raymond and Nagoya Rubber Ltd Agreement* OJ [1972] L 143/39, [1972] CMLR D45; *Kabelmetal/Luchaire* OJ [1975] L 222/ 34, [1975] 2 CMLR D40; *Zuid-Nederlandsche Bronbemaling en Grondboringen BV v Heidemaatschappij Beheer NV* OJ [1975] L 249/27, [1975] 2 CMLR D67; *AOIP v Beyrard* OJ [1976] L 6/8, [1976] 1 CMLR D14; *Vaessen BV v Moris* OJ [1979] L 19/32, [1979] 1 CMLR 511; *IMA AG Windsurfing International Inc* OJ [1983] L 229/1, [1984] 1 CMLR 1, upheld on appeal Case 193/83 *Windsurfing International Inc v Commission* [1986] ECR 611, [1986] 3 CMLR 489; *Velcro/Aplix* OJ [1985] L 233/22, [1989] 4 CMLR 157; the Commission has reached decisions on other types of licences in which it has applied similar principles: see below.

[33] OJ [1984] L 219/15.   [34] OJ [1996] L 31/2, [1996] 4 CMLR 405.

[35] *Technology transfer agreements*, paras 141–145.   [36] Ibid, paras 146–152.

However, as we have seen in chapter 3, Article 81(1) applies only to agreements 'which have as their object or effect the prevention, restriction or distortion of competition'[37]. It was explained there that the mere grant of exclusive territorial rights does not have as its object the restriction of competition[38]; such cases infringe Article 81(1), there-fore, only where they can be shown to have appreciable effects on competition[39] and on trade between Member States[40]. The reason for the strict treatment of the agreement in *Consten and Grundig v Commission* was that it went beyond the mere grant of exclusive distribution rights in France by conferring upon Consten absolute territorial protection against parallel imports from other Member States. The application of Article 81(1) to territorial exclusivity in licence agreements follows the same contours.

The first case on the licensing of intellectual property rights to come before the ECJ was *Nungesser v Commission*[41] (often referred to as the *Maize Seeds* case). One issue for the ECJ was whether an exclusive licence of plant breeders' rights[42] by its very nature infringed Article 81(1): in other words, whether such agreements had as their object the restriction of competition[43]. The ECJ distinguished between an 'open exclusive licence', whereby a licensor agrees not to license anyone else in the licensee's territory, and not to compete there itself; and an exclusive licence which confers absolute territorial pro-tection, so that all competition from third parties is eliminated[44]. This, of course, is the difference between the facts of *Société Technique Miniere v Maschinenbau Ulm*[45] and *Consten and Grundig v Commission*. As to the open exclusive licence, the ECJ noted that a licensee of new technology might be deterred from accepting the risk of cultivating and marketing a new product unless it knew that it would not encounter competition from other licensees in its territory[46]. It followed that an open licence which does not affect the position of third parties such as parallel importers does not have as its object the restriction of competition; a detailed analysis would be required to determine the effects of the agreement[47]. Absolute territorial protection however would automatically be caught by Article 81(1)[48] and was not eligible for exemption under Article 81(3)[49].

The *Maize Seeds* judgment meant that open exclusivity did not necessarily infringe Article 81(1); in particular where the licensee was accepting risk and marketing a new product the licence would not be caught. However in the years following the *Maize Seeds* judgment the Commission adopted a narrow approach to its application. For example in *Velcro/Aplix*[50] it held that although the doctrine may have applied to the licence in that case in its early years, when the technology in question was novel, this

[37] See ch 3, pp 116 ff.
[38] See ch 3, p 124; see in particular the discussion of Case 56/65 *Société Technique Minière v Maschinenbau Ulm* [1966] ECR 235, [1966] CMLR 357.
[39] On the *de minimis* doctrine see ch 3, pp 137–142.
[40] On the requirement for an appreciable effect on trade between Member States see ch 3, pp 142–146.
[41] Case 258/78 [1982] ECR 2015, [1983] 1 CMLR 278.
[42] Plant breeders' rights are analogous to patents.
[43] See ch 3, pp 119–122 for a discussion of agreements that have as their object the restriction of competition.
[44] Case 258/78 [1982] ECR 2015, [1983] 1 CMLR 278, para 53.
[45] Case 56/65 [1966] ECR 235, [1966] CMLR 357.
[46] Case 258/78 [1982] ECR 2015, [1983] 1 CMLR 278, para 57.   [47] Ibid, para 58.
[48] Ibid, paras 60–63.
[49] Ibid, paras 68–79; note that in the *Coditel* case even absolute territorial protection was found not to infringe Article 81(1) in the case of a performing copyright: see p 765 below.
[50] OJ [1985] L 233/22, [1989] 4 CMLR 157, paras 43, 44 and 60.

was no longer the case by the time of the decision. In *Tetra Pak I (BTG Licence)*[51] the Commission held that the doctrine was not applicable where an undertaking in a dominant position took over important technology: a dominant firm did not bear the same commercial and technical risks as a smaller undertaking and was not subject to strong inter-brand competition which might justify immunity from intra-brand competition. In *Delta Chemie/DDD Ltd*[52], a decision on a licence of know-how rather than a patent, the Commission again concluded that the technology in question did not benefit from the *Maize Seeds* doctrine[53]. This reluctance on the part of the Commission to conclude that territorial exclusivity did not restrict competition was consistent with its formalistic approach at the time towards vertical agreements[54]. The Commission did acknowledge the *Maize Seeds* doctrine in recital 10 of the (now repealed) block exemption on technology transfer agreements, Regulation 240/96, but one suspects with no great enthusiasm; its preferred way of dealing with licences at the time was to exempt under Article 81(3) rather than to grant negative clearance under Article 81(1).

(iii) The case law of the Community Courts on territorial exclusivity after *Maize Seeds*

In chapter 3 we have seen that the ECJ has, in a number of judgments, refrained from concluding too readily that agreements containing contractual restrictions necessarily restrict competition: these two ideas should not be confused with one another[55]. Some agreements – for example to fix prices or to share markets – are so obviously reprehensible that they are considered to have as their object the restriction of competition[56]; other agreements, however, infringe Article 81(1) only where it can be demonstrated that they will produce appreciable anti-competitive effects on the market[57]. In various judgments since *Maize Seeds* the ECJ has concluded that provisions involving territorial exclusivity did not infringe Article 81(1). In *Coditel v Ciné Vog Films*[58] the ECJ acknowledged that, in the special circumstances of a performance copyright, a licensee may need absolute territorial protection from re-transmissions of films from neighbouring Member States. In *Louis Erauw-Jacquery Sprl v La Hesbignonne Société*[59] the ECJ held that a prohibition on the export of so-called 'basic seeds' did not infringe Article 81(1), but rather was a manifestation of Erauw-Jacquery's plant breeders' rights and necessary for their protection[60]. In *Pronuptia de Paris v Schillgalis*[61] the ECJ suggested that the grant of exclusive territorial rights to a franchisee for a particular territory might not infringe Article 81(1) where the business name or symbol of the franchise was not well-known[62].

Collectively these cases demonstrate that it is wrong to assume that all territorial exclusivity in licences of intellectual property rights infringes Article 81(1); a more

[51] OJ [1988] L 272/27, [1990] 4 CMLR 47, upheld on appeal Case T-51/89 *Tetra Pak Rausing SA v Commission* [1990] ECR II-309, [1991] 4 CMLR 334.
[52] OJ [1988] L 309/34, [1989] 4 CMLR 535, para 23.
[53] See also *Knoll/Hille-Form* XIIIth *Report on Competition Policy* (1983), points 142–146.
[54] For criticism of the Commission's historical position towards vertical agreements see ch 16, p 639.
[55] See ch 3, pp 124–126.   [56] See ch 3, pp 119–122.   [57] See ch 3, pp 122 ff.
[58] Case 262/81 [1982] ECR 3381, [1983] 1 CMLR 49.
[59] Case 27/87 [1988] ECR 1919, [1988] 4 CMLR 576.
[60] See p 769 below.   [61] Case 161/84 [1986] ECR 353, [1986] 1 CMLR 414.
[62] [1986] ECR 353, [1986] 1 CMLR 414, para 24.

nuanced approach is required than this, and even absolute territorial protection and export bans may be justified in particular circumstances.

(iv) Non-territorial restrictions caught by Article 81(1)

The Commission's decisions have sometimes applied Article 81(1) to non-territorial restrictions in licences of intellectual property rights, as have some judgments of the Community Courts, in particular the judgment of the ECJ in *Windsurfing International Inc v Commission*[63]. The treatment of non-territorial restrictions will be considered below in the context of Articles 4 and 5 of Regulation 772/2004[64].

(v) Know-how licences

The Commission applied the principles that it had developed in its decisions on patent licences to licences of know-how[65]. This culminated in the adoption of Regulation 556/89[66] granting block exemption to know-how licences. As was noted at the beginning of this chapter, know-how is not an intellectual property right as such: it is protected by the law of obligations. An anxiety for the Commission was that spurious claims to exclusivity might be made for agreements that do not in practice have an enhancing effect on economic efficiency; this is why successive block exemption regulations have stipulated that know-how must be secret and substantial[67]. In practice the licensing of know-how is as important and as common as patent licensing, so that the extension of the protection of block exemption to this category of agreements was important for industry.

(vi) Copyright licences

There is not a great deal of authority specifically on the application of Article 81(1) or Article 81(3) to copyright licences. As we have seen, the ECJ held that absolute territorial protection was not contrary to Article 81(1) in the specific context of a performance copyright in *Coditel v Ciné Vog Films*[68].

The Commission has taken action in relation to copyright licences on a few occasions and in doing so it has applied the principles developed in relation to patent and know-how licences. In *Neilson-Hordell/Reichmark*[69] the Commission gave details of its objections to clauses in a licence of technical drawings and the products they represent; in particular it required the abandonment of a no-challenge clause, a royalties clause extending to products not protected by any copyright of the licensor, a non-competition clause which was to continue after the agreement and an exclusive grant-back to the

---

[63]   Case 193/83 [1986] ECR 611, [1986] 3 CMLR 489.   [64]   See pp 776–780 below.

[65]   In chronological order the Commission's decisions on know-how licences are *Boussois/Interpane* OJ [1987] L 50/30, [1988] 4 CMLR 124; *Mitchell Cotts/Sofiltra* OJ [1987] L 41/ 31, [1988] 4 CMLR 111; *Rich Products/Jus-Rol* OJ [1988] L 69/21, [1988] 4 CMLR 527; *Delta Chemie/DDD Ltd* OJ [1988] L 309/34, [1989] 4 CMLR 535; see also *ICL/Fujitsu* XVIth *Report on Competition Policy* (1986), point 72 (case dealt with by comfort letter).

[66]   Corrected version at OJ [1990] L 257/15; this Regulation was replaced by Regulation 240/96, which in turn has been replaced by Regulation 772/2004: see pp 771–781 below.

[67]   See now Regulation 772/2004, Article 1(1)(i).

[68]   Case 262/81 [1982] ECR 3381, [1983] 1 CMLR 49; see p 765 above.

[69]   Commission's XIIth *Annual Report on Competition Policy* (1982), points 88–89.

licensor of the improvements. In *Ernest Benn Ltd*[70] the Commission took objection to a standard contractual term which prevented the export of books from the UK. In *Knoll/Hille-Form*[71] the Commission intervened in the case of an exclusive licence of a design right relating to furniture and closed its file after the parties agreed to remove export bans and to allow direct sales into each other's territories.

In *Film Purchases by German Television Stations*[72] the Commission investigated exclusive licence agreements entered into between MGM/UA, a major US film production and distribution company, and ARD, an association of public broadcasting organisations in Germany. The agreements granted ARD exclusive television rights to a large number of MGM/UA's feature films, including 14 James Bond films, in most cases for a period of 15 years. The Commission's view was that the agreements restricted competition, in particular because of the large number of the licensed rights and the duration of the exclusivity[73]. However the Commission decided that the criteria of Article 81(3) were satisfied following modifications to the agreements, for example so that ARD would license the films to third parties at certain periods known as 'windows'.

There is no specific block exemption for copyright licences, although it may be possible to take the benefit of Regulation 2790/99 on vertical agreements or of Regulation 772/2004 on technology transfer agreements where the licensing of copyright is ancillary to an agreement covered by one of those Regulations[74].

(vii) Software licences[75]

In the case of *Sega and Nintendo*[76] the Commission required the deletion of clauses in licences of computer software with publishers of video games which, in the Commission's view, enabled Sega and Nintendo to control the market for video games; this intervention followed the Competition Commission's investigation of *Video Games* in the UK[77]. In the *Microsoft Internet Explorer*[78] case the Commission required Microsoft to remove clauses from its software licences providing for minimum distribution volumes for its Internet Explorer browser technology and imposing a prohibition on advertising competitors' browser technology. A minimum quantities clause is normally considered not to be restrictive of competition at all; the Commission's concern here, however, was that the two clauses in question could have a foreclosure effect on competitors. A comfort letter was sent after these amendments had been made; the Commission did not give a

---

[70] Commission's IXth *Report on Competition Policy* (1979), points 118 and 119; see also *The Old Man and the Sea* VIth *Report on Competition Policy* (1976), point 164; *STEMRA* XIth *Report on Competition Policy* (1981), point 98.

[71] Commission's XIIth *Report on Competition Policy* (1983), points 142–146.

[72] OJ [1989] L 284/36, [1990] 4 CMLR 841; the decision is criticised by Rothnie 'Commission Re-runs Same Old Bill' (1990) 12 EIPR 72.

[73] OJ [1989] L 284/36, [1990] 4 CMLR 841, paras 41–46.   [74] See p 772 below.

[75] See Forrester 'Software Licensing in the Light of Current EC Competition Law Considerations' (1992) 13 ECLR 5; Darbyshire 'Computer Programs and Competition Policy: A Block Exemption for Software Licensing?' (1994) 16 EIPR 374.

[76] See the Commission's XXVIIth *Report on Competition Policy* (1997), point 80 and pp 148–149; see also, on the similar *Sony* case, the XXVIIIth *Report on Competition Policy* (1998), pp 159–160.

[77] Cm 2781 (1995).

[78] See the Commission's XXIXth *Report on Competition Policy* (1999), points 55 and 56 and p 162: details of Microsoft's notification in this case can be found at OJ [1998] C 175/3; for a separate investigation of Microsoft's licensing terms, following a complaint by Santa Cruz Operation in relation to the UNIX operating system, see the Commission's XXVIIth *Report on Competition Policy* (1997), point 79 and pp 140–141.

ruling on whether Microsoft's behaviour overall might amount to an abuse of a dominant position[79]. Microsoft's refusal to make interoperability information, assumed to be protected by intellectual property rights, available to third party competitors was found to be an abuse of a dominant position in March 2004[80].

There are some typical clauses in software licences which have no analogies in the general law, for example prohibiting decompilation of a computer programme and restrictions on copying[81]. Software licences are now covered by the *Technology Transfer Regulation*[82].

(viii) Trade mark licences[83]

The Commission has applied Article 81(1) to exclusive trade mark licences but decided that the criteria of Article 81(3) were satisfied by applying principles derived from the block exemptions for vertical agreements. In *Davide CampariMilano SpA Agreement*[84] the Commission considered that Article 81(3) applied in the case of a standard form of agreement whereby firms were licensed to use the Campari trade mark and were given exclusive rights in their own territory to apply that mark and required not to pursue an active sales policy elsewhere.

In *Moosehead/Whitbread*[85] an exclusive licence of a trade mark with associated know-how was investigated by the Commission. The licensee wished to manufacture and to promote the Moosehead brand, a popular Canadian beer, in the UK. The licence prohibited active selling outside the UK. The Commission concluded that the exclusive trade mark and the restriction on active sales infringed Article 81(1), as did a non-competition clause[86]. The know-how was considered by the Commission to be ancillary to the trade mark, so that the block exemption for know-how licensing in force at that time, Regulation 556/89, was not applicable[87]; presumably the same conclusion would be reached under Regulation 772/2004[88]. However the Commission granted an individual exemption as consumers would have the advantage of another beer from which to choose[89]. The agreement contained a no-challenge clause in respect of the trade mark, but the Commission held this to be outside Article 81(1) because the mark was not well-known and its non-availability to competitors was not a barrier to entry[90].

Where a trade mark is ancillary to a vertical agreement or to a technology transfer agreement, it may benefit from the block exemption conferred by Regulation 2790/99 or Regulation 772/2004[91].

---

[79] Commission's XXIXth *Report on Competition Policy* (1999), point 56.   [80] See pp 790–792 below.

[81] It may be arguable that, by analogy from the *Erauw-Jacquery* judgment on the propogation of seeds, a restriction on copying software is outside Article 81(1).

[82] See p 772 below.

[83] See Joliet 'Territorial and Exclusive Trade Mark Licensing under the EC Law of Competition' [1984] IIC 21.

[84] OJ [1978] L 70/69, [1978] 2 CMLR 397; see similarly *Goodyear Italiana SpA's Application* OJ [1975] L 38/10, [1975] 1 CMLR D31.

[85] OJ [1990] L 100/32, [1991] 4 CMLR 391; see Subiotto '*Moosebead/Whitebread*: Industrial Franchises and No-challenge Clauses Relating to Licensed Trade Marks in the EEC (1990) 11 ECLR 226.

[86] OJ [1990] L 100/32, [1991] 4 CMLR 391, para 15(1).

[87] Ibid, para 16(1); a corrected version of Regulation 556/89 will be found at OJ [1990] L 257/15.

[88] See p 772 below.   [89] OJ [1990] L 100/32, [1991] 4 CMLR 391, para 15(2).

[90] Ibid, para 15(4).   [91] See p 772 below.

(ix) Licences of plant breeders' rights

As we have seen in *Nungesser v Commission*[92] the ECJ held that an open exclusive licence to produce maize seeds did not infringe Article 81(1) where exclusivity was required to protect the investment of the licensee; the Court also considered that absolute territorial protection would infringe Article 81(1) and would be ineligible for exemption under Article 81(3). In *Louis Erauw-Jacquery Sprl v La Hesbignonne Société*[93] the ECJ was asked to rule on the application of Article 81(1) to two clauses in a licence for the propagation and sale of certain varieties of cereal seeds. Erauw-Jacquery had licensed La Hesbignonne to propagate 'basic seeds' and to sell seeds reproduced from them ('reproductive seeds'). Clause 2(f) of the licence prohibited the export of basic seeds; clause 2(i) required the licensee not to resell the reproductive seeds below minimum selling prices. The ECJ's view was that the export ban in relation to basic seeds did not infringe Article 81(1): a plant breeder is entitled to reserve the propagation of basic seeds to institutions approved by him and an export ban is objectively justifiable to protect this right[94]. Basic seeds are not intended for sale to farmers for sowing, but are intended solely for the purpose of propagation; it follows that an export ban of this kind arises from the existence of the plant breeders' rights and is not an improper exercise of it[95]. The ECJ concluded that the provision on minimum pricing for reproductive seeds had as its object and effect the restriction of competition[96] but that the national court must decide on the facts whether it had an effect on trade between Member States[97].

In *Sicasov*[98] the Commission applied the ECJ's judgment in the *Erauw-Jacquery* case to the standard licences of Sicasov, a French cooperative of plant breeders. The Commission explains in more detail than the judgment in *Erauw-Jacquery* the distinction between basic seeds, which are intended only for propagation, and 'certified' seeds, intended for sale to farmers for sowing[99]. The breeder is entitled to control the destination of basic seeds by virtue of its plant breeders' rights[100], but cannot control certified seeds that have been put onto the market with its consent[101]. It followed that obligations not to entrust basic seeds to a third party, not to export them and related provisions did not infringe Article 81(1)[102]. However a restriction on the export of certified seeds did infringe Article 81(1)[103] but was found to satisfy the terms of Article 81(3)[104].

In *Roses*[105] the Commission condemned two clauses in a standard licence of plant breeders' rights. The first was an exclusive grant-back clause, which effectively removed the sub-licensee from the market for mutations which it discovered. The second was a no-challenge clause: the fact that plant breeders' rights are conferred only after a

---

[92] Case 258/78 [1982] ECR 2015, [1983] 1 CMLR 278.

[93] Case 27/87 [1988] ECR 1919, [1988] 4 CMLR 576.   [94] Ibid, para 10.

[95] This was the view of Advocate General Mischo in this case, and of the Commission: [1988] ECR 1919, [1988] 4 CMLR 576, para 9.

[96] [1988] ECR 1919, [1988] 4 CMLR 576, para 15.   [97] Ibid, para 19.

[98] OJ [1999] L 4/27, [1999] 4 CMLR 192.   [99] Ibid, paras 21–27.

[100] Ibid, para 50, citing *Erauw-Jacquery*.   [101] Ibid, para 51.   [102] Ibid, paras 53–61.

[103] Ibid, paras 62–64.

[104] Ibid, paras 73–77; note that Regulation 240/96 on technology transfer agreements did not apply since the standard licence did not correspond with any of the provisions listed in Article 1(1) thereof: ibid, para 72.

[105] OJ [1985] L 369/9, [1988] 4 CMLR 193; see Harding 'Commission Decision on Breeders' Rights in Relation to Roses: Hard Line on Breeders' Rights Maintained' (1986) 9 EIPR 284.

national authority's involvement does not mean that there might not have been an error of appreciation that could be challenged by a licensee.

(x) Sub-contracting agreements

Sub-contracting agreements typically involve a licence from the principal to the sub-contractor. Horizontal sub-contracting agreements have been considered in chapter 15 and vertical ones in chapter 16[106].

(D) The application of Article 81(3) to licences of intellectual property rights[107]

Licensing agreements which are not covered by Regulation 772/2004 and which contain provisions which are not ancillary to an agreement covered by that Regulation or by Regulation 2790/99 on vertical agreements[108] may still fulfil the conditions of Article 81(3). With the entry into force of the Modernisation Regulation the system of notifying agreements to the Commission for individual exemption has ceased to exist. Instead, firms must assess the validity of their licences under the competition rules for themselves. When doing so they will derive guidance from the Commission's block exemptions. The Commission has said that the restrictions listed as 'hard core' in Article 4 of the *Technology Transfer Regulation* would be likely to satisfy the criteria of Article 81(3) only in exceptional circumstances[109]; however it also says that there is no presumption that agreements that fall outside the block exemption are caught by Article 81(1) or fail to satisfy the terms of Article 81(3)[110].

In *Telenor/Canal+/Canal Digital*[111] the Commission decided that the criteria of Article 81(3) were satisfied and therefore permitted for five years agreements concerning the distribution of pay-TV premium content channels on the satellite platform of Canal Digital in the Nordic region. The agreements involved in this case concerned the licensing of material protected by artistic copyright, and fell outside the block exemption for vertical agreements because the licences were not ancillary to a vertical agreement in the sense of Article 2(3) of that Regulation[112]. Similarly the licences were not ancillary to a technology transfer agreement, as artistic copyright is not regarded as technological. The interesting issue raised by a case such as this is whether a licence is more analogous to a vertical agreement or to a transfer of technology: this will determine whether the principles of Regulation 2790/99 or Regulation 772/2004 provide better guidance for firms having to conduct a self-assessment under Article 81(3). As a general proposition Regulation 772/2004 permits more restrictions than Regulation 2790/99: for example the former allows (limited) restrictions on passive sales which the latter does not.

---

[106] See ch 15, p 558 and ch 16, pp 666–667.
[107] See the *Technology Transfer Guidelines*, para 18 and paras 130ff.
[108] On ancillary provisions see p 772 below.   [109] *Technology Transfer Guidelines*, para 18.
[110] Ibid, para 37.   [111] Commission decision of 29 December 2003.   [112] See ch 16, p 647.

3. TRANSFER TECHNOLOGY AGREEMENTS: REGULATION 772/2004

Acting under powers conferred on it by Council Regulation 19/65[113] the Commission has adopted Regulation 772/2004[114] conferring block exemption on technology transfer agreements pursuant to Article 81(3) of the Treaty. Regulation 772/2004 replaced Regulation 240/96[115]. The adoption of Regulation 772/2004 followed the publication by the Commission in December 2001 of an *Evaluation Report*[116] on the previous block exemption, which was followed by a public debate which was generally in favour of reform of the law. The Commission recognises in the recitals of Regulation 772/2004 that technology transfer agreements usually improve economic efficiency and are pro-competitive, but notes that this depends on the degree of market power that the parties have or, to put the point another way, the extent to which they face competition from undertakings owning substitute technologies or undertakings producing substitute products[117].

The Commission adopted Regulation 772/2004 on 27 April 2004. It entered into force on 1 May 2004 and will expire on 30 April 2014[118]. Regulation 772/2004, the format of which is similar to Regulation 2790/99 on vertical agreements, consists of 20 recitals and 11 Articles. Article 1 contains a series of definitions. Article 2 confers block exemption on certain technology transfer agreements. Article 3 imposes market share caps, which differ depending on whether an agreement is horizontal or vertical, the former being treated more strictly. Article 4 contains a list of hard-core restrictions, the inclusion of which in an agreement will prevent the block exemption from applying: the list is stricter for horizontal than for vertical agreements. Article 5 sets out certain restrictions that are not block exempted, but which do not prevent the application of the Regulation to the rest of the agreement. Articles 6 and 7 provide for the block exemption to be withdrawn from agreements in certain circumstances. Subsequent provisions deal with matters such as the calculation of market share thresholds and transitional arrangements. Regulation 772/2004 should be read in conjunction with the Commission's *Technology Transfer Guidelines*.

(A) Article 1: definitions

Article 1 of the Regulation contains a series of definitions. Some of these will be explained in the text that follows, in the specific context in which they are used in the

---

[113] JO [1965] 533, OJ Sp Ed [1965–66] 87.

[114] OJ [2004] L 123/11; see the speech of the Commissioner for Competition describing the main features of the new block exemption: SPEECH/04/19, 16 January 2004; for detailed commentary on Regulation 772/2004 see Dolmans and Piilola 'The New Technology Transfer Block Exemption: A Welcome Reform After All' (2003) 27(3) World Competition 351; Anderman and Kallaugher *Technology and the New EU Competition Rules: Intellectual Property Licensing after Modernisation* (Oxford University Press, 2006); Korah *Intellectual Property Rights and the EC Competition Rules* (Hart Publishing, 2006); Coates, Kyølbye and Peeperkorn in Faull and Nikpay *The EC Law of Competition* (Oxford University Press, 2nd ed, 2007), paras 10.58–10.125.

[115] OJ [1996] L 31/2, [1996] 4 CMLR 405.

[116] COM(2001)786 final, available at www.europa.eu.int/comm/competition/antitrust/technology_transfer.

[117] Regulation 772/2004, recitals 5 and 6.   [118] Ibid, Article 11.

Regulation. Of particular importance is Article 1(1)(b), which defines what is meant by a technology transfer agreement. This term includes licences[119] of:

- Patents[120]
- Know-how, meaning a package of non-patented information that is secret, substantial and identified[121]
- Software copyright[122]
- A mixture of patents, know-how and software copyright
- Provisions in a technology agreement that do not constitute the primary objective of such agreements, but are directly related to the application of the licensed technology (sometimes referred to as 'ancillary provisions')[123].

Recital 7 of the Regulation explains that it applies only to agreements whereby a licensor permits a licensee to exploit the licensed technology for the production of goods or services: it therefore does not apply to an agreement that sub-contracts research and development to another party, since in that case the sub-contractor, to whom some technology may be transferred by the principal, will not exploit the technology itself[124]. Recital 7 also explains that the Regulation does not apply to technology pools[125].

Article 1(2) of the Regulation explains that the terms 'undertaking', 'licensor', and 'licensee' include 'connected undertakings', as defined therein.

(B) Article 2: exemption

Article 2 of the Regulation confers block exemption on certain technology transfer agreements pursuant to Article 81(3) of the Treaty. It provides that, subject to the provisions of the Regulation, Article 81(1) shall not apply:

to technology transfer agreements entered into between two undertakings permitting the production of contract products[126].

Several points should be noted about Article 2(1).

---

[119] The Regulation can also apply to assignments where part of the risk associated with the exploitation of the technology remains with the assignor: ibid, Article 1(1)(b); and the Regulation can apply to sub-licensing whereby a licensee, with authority of the licensor, sub-licences to a third party for the exploitation of the technology: *Technology Transfer Guidelines*, para 48; the Regulation does not apply to a 'master licence' where sub-licensing is the primary object of the agreement: ibid, para 42.

[120] The term patents includes numerous rights, including utility models, designs, topographies of semi-conductor products, supplementary protection certificates for medicinal products and plant breeder's rights: ibid, Article 1(1)(h).

[121] Ibid, Article 1(1)(i); see also the *Technology Transfer Guidelines*, para 47.

[122] Note that copyright, other than software copyright, would not be included in this term, although the Commission will as a general rule apply the principles set out in the Regulation to copyright licences: *Technology Transfer Guidelines*, para 51, although not necessarily in the case of *performance* copyright: ibid, para 52; see the Commission's decision in *Telenor/Canal+* discussed at p 770 above.

[123] See further the *Technology Transfer Guidelines*, paras 49–53.

[124] See further the *Technology Transfer Guidelines*, paras 44–45; on horizontal sub-contracting agreements see ch 15, p 588 and on vertical ones see ch 16, pp 666–667.

[125] On pooling agreements see pp 781–785 below.

[126] On the meaning of 'product' and 'contract products' see Article 1(1)(e) and (f) of the Regulation.

(i) Many technology transfer agreements do not infringe Article 81(1)

It is worth recalling that many technology transfer agreements do not infringe Article 81(1) at all, and therefore do not need to be block exempted. It has already been noted that Recital 5 of the Regulation acknowledges that such agreements usually improve economic efficiency and are pro-competitive, a point which is picked up in paragraph 9 of the *Technology Transfer Guidelines*, which states that there is no presumption that licence agreements give rise to competition concerns. Indeed paragraph 17 of the *Guidelines* goes as far as to say that licence agreements 'have substantial pro-competitive potential'; it continues that 'the vast majority of licence agreements are pro-competitive'. Recital 12 of the Regulation states that there is no presumption that agreements above the market-share thresholds in Article 3 infringe Article 81(1), a point repeated in paragraph 37 of the *Technology Transfer Guidelines*. It is almost unthinkable that the Commission would have said such things in, say, the 1970s and 1980s, and this shows how far the Commission has moved in wanting to take a more economics-oriented, less regulatory approach to the application of the competition rules.

(ii) If it is not forbidden, it is permitted

The Commission's less regulatory approach, specifically stated in Recital 4 of the Regulation, is reflected in the removal from the Regulation of a 'white list', stating what must be in a technology transfer agreement[127]; instead there is a market share cap in Article 3, and the 'black list' of what must not be included in Article 4. These two are the Articles of key importance. Provisions in an agreement that are not black-listed in Article 4 are permitted, subject to the 'excluded restrictions' of Article 5 and the possibility of withdrawal of the block exemption by the Commission or a Member State (see below). Other than that the maxim of the verticals regulation, 'If it is not forbidden, it is permitted', is equally applicable under the *Technology Transfer Regulation*[128].

(iii) The exempted agreement must be bilateral

An interesting distinction between the vertical block exemption and the one for technology transfer is that the latter is applicable only in the case of bilateral agreements, whereas the former is capable of application to multilateral ones[129]. Council Regulation 19/65 does not provide a legal basis for block exemption of multilateral technology transfer agreements[130]. However Recital 19 of the Regulation explains that the Regulation can apply to an agreement between a licensor and licensee where the licensor makes stipulations for more than one level of trade. For example the licensor may impose conditions and obligations on the licensee not only in relation to its own production and sales; it may also require the licensee to impose conditions and obligations on its own distributors, for example requiring them to maintain a selective distribution system. The agreement between the licensor and licensee is still a bilateral agreement, and so capable of being covered by the block exemption; however the agreement(s) between the licensee

---

[127] See Recital 8 of the *Technology Transfer Regulation*.
[128] See ch 16, p 642 for the position under the vertical block exemption.
[129] Ibid, pp 642–643.
[130] Specific provision for the block exemption of multilateral vertical agreements was made by Council Regulation 1215/99, OJ [1999] L 148/1.

and any distributor would not be covered by the *Technology Transfer Regulation*, but might satisfy the block exemption for vertical agreements[131].

Where a technology transfer agreement is multilateral, but of the same nature as one covered by the Regulation, the Commission will analyse the agreement by analogy to the principles contained in the Regulation[132].

(iv) Duration

The block exemption will run until 30 April 2014. However Article 2 contains a further relevant provision as to the duration of block exemption in relation to any particular agreement. It provides that the exemption lasts only as long as the intellectual property right in the licensed technology has not expired, lapsed, or been declared invalid; or, in the case of know-how, that the exemption lasts only as long as the know-how remains secret. The block exemption will cease to apply on the date of the last intellectual property right to expire, become invalid or enter the public domain[133].

(v) Relationship with other block exemptions

Paragraphs 56 to 64 of the *Technology Transfer Guidelines* explain how the Technology Transfer Regulation relates to other block exemptions, in particular the regulation for *Specialisation Agreements*[134], for *Research and Developments Agreements*[135] and *Vertical Agreements*[136].

(C) Article 3: the market share cap

The Regulation applies only to technology transfer agreements that do not exceed a market share cap. Recital 12 states that there is no presumption that an agreement above the thresholds infringes Article 81(1) or that it is incapable of satisfying the terms of Article 81(3). Article 3(1) of the Regulation requires that the combined market share of the parties does not exceed 20 per cent of the affected relevant technology and product market for horizontal agreements; Article 3(2) provides that, in the case of vertical agreements, the market share of each of the parties must not exceed 30 per cent.

(i) Horizontal agreements

In order to determine whether an agreement is a horizontal agreement it is necessary to ask whether the parties to an agreement are 'competing undertakings' as defined in Article 1(1)(j) of the Regulation[137]. Undertakings may compete on a technology market or on a product market.

(A) Technology markets Article 1(1)(j)(i) provides that undertakings compete on the relevant technology market where they license out competing technologies without infringing each others' intellectual property rights. The relevant technology market includes technologies which are regarded as interchangeable with or substitutable for the licensed technology, by reason of the technologies' characteristics, their royalties,

---

[131] See further the *Technology Transfer Guidelines*, para 39 and paras 61–64.   [132] Ibid, para 40.
[133] Ibid, para 55.   [134] Regulation 2658/2000: see ch 15, pp 589–592.
[135] Regulation 2659/2000: see ch 15, pp 583–588.   [136] Regulation 2790/99: see ch 16, pp 640–662.
[137] See further the *Technology Transfer Guidelines*, paras 26–33.

and their intended use. This definition captures only *actual* competitors in the technology market: it does not apply to potential competitors[138].

(B) Product markets Article 1(1)(j)(ii) provides that undertakings compete on the relevant product market where, even without a technology transfer agreement, they are both active on the relevant product and geographic markets on which the contract products are sold without infringing each others' intellectual property rights (actual competitors) and where they might realistically be able to enter and compete on the market within 'a period of one to two years'[139] in response to a small but permanent increase in product prices (potential competitors). The relevant product market includes products which are regarded as interchangeable with or substitutable for the contract products by reason of the products' characteristics, their prices, and their intended use.

(ii) Vertical agreements
Where an agreement is not horizontal, because it is not between competing undertakings as defined in Article 1(1)(j), it is vertical, and so the higher market share cap of 30 per cent is applicable. An agreement will not be horizontal where one party can use its intellectual property to prevent the other entering the market, or where both parties need the other's technology to operate on the market: these are referred to as 'one-way' and 'two-way' blocking positions, as to which the Commission will require objective evidence, for example court judgments and the opinions of independent experts[140]. It can be the case that two undertakings compete in relation to existing products, but that a licence by A to B is not between competitors because A's technology is so innovative that B's current products are now obsolete or uncompetitive: such an agreement would be regarded as vertical and therefore subject to the higher market share cap (and the more lenient list of hard-core restrictions)[141].

Where the parties are not competing undertakings at the time of the agreement, but subsequently become so, they will usually continue to be considered to be non-competing: Article 4(3) of the Regulation provides that this means that the less strict list of hard-core restrictions for vertical agreements will continue to apply[142].

(iii) Technology markets
Paragraphs 19 to 25 of the *Technology Transfer Guidelines* discuss market definition for the purpose of analysing technology transfer agreements. In particular they explain that such agreements can have an effect on competition both in the upstream technology market and in the downstream product market[143]. Article 3(3), in conjunction with paragraph 23 of the *Technology Transfer Guidelines*, explains that a licensor's share of a technology market is to be calculated by reference to the value of the licensed technology on the relevant product market; this figure is calculated on the basis of both the licensor's and its licensee's sales[144]. Where a new technology has yet to generate any sales a market share of zero is assigned[145].

---

[138] Ibid, para 66.   [139] Ibid, para 29.   [140] Ibid, para 32.   [141] Ibid, para 33.   [142] See pp 776–779 below.
[143] *Technology Transfer Guidelines*, para 20.
[144] See the final sentence of Article 3(3) of the Regulation and the *Technology Transfer Guidelines*, para 70.
[145] Ibid.

(iv) Product markets

A licensee's market share of a product market is calculated on the basis of its sales of products incorporating the licensor's technology and competing products, that is to say the total sales of the licensee on the product market in question; sales by other licensees are not taken into account[146].

(v) Article 8: calculation of market share and marginal relief

Article 8(1) of the Regulation deals with the calculation of market share, which should be done by reference to market sales value data. Where such data are not available, estimates based on other reliable information, including sales volumes, may be used to establish the market share of the undertaking concerned. Market shares should be calculated on the basis of data relating to the preceding calendar year.

Article 8(2) provides some marginal relief for up to two years where the market share caps of 20 per cent or 30 per cent are subsequently exceeded.

(vi) Examples

The *Technology Transfer Guidelines* provide examples of how the market share figures operate, both in relation to licensing between non-competitors and between competitors[147].

(D) Article 4: hard-core restrictions

Recital 13 of the Regulation states that technology transfer agreements should not enjoy block exemption when they contain 'severely anti-competitive restraints such as the fixing of prices charged to third parties...irrespective of the market shares of the undertakings concerned'. The block exemption ceases to apply to the entire agreement, not just to the offending provisions[148]. The Commission considers that the hard-core restrictions are restrictions by object in the sense of Article 81 EC[149]. The Regulation contains one set of hard-core restrictions for agreements between competing agreements in Article 4(1) and a different set for agreements between non-competing undertakings in Article 4(2). As one would expect the provisions are stricter in the case of agreements between competing undertakings than between non-competing undertakings. Article 4(3) provides that, where the parties were non-competing at the time that they entered into an agreement, Article 4(2) applies to their agreement throughout its lifetime unless the agreement is subsequently amended in any material respect; in other words the agreement does not metamorphose into a horizontal one, and so become subject to the stricter standard of Article 4(1), simply because the firms subsequently become competitors.

(i) Agreements between competing undertakings: horizontal agreements[150]

The concern of the Commission is that a technology transfer agreement between competing agreements might be a cloak for, or have the effect of, a horizontal cartel.

---

[146] Ibid, para 71.   [147] Ibid, para 73.   [148] Ibid, para 75.   [149] Ibid, para 14.
[150] See generally the *Technology Transfer Guidelines*, paras 77–95.

Article 4(1) therefore provides that block exemption is not available for agreements that, directly or indirectly, in isolation or in combination with other factors, have as their object restrictions concerning prices, output, the allocation of markets or customers, and the exploitation by the licensee of its own technology: such restrictions are regarded as hard-core. The provisions on price and output are simple, but those on markets and customers can be complex. In some cases restrictions are treated as hard-core only where an agreement is reciprocal, that is to say where each undertaking grants a licence to the other and where the licences concern competing technologies or can be used for the production of competing products[151]; the same restriction in a non-reciprocal agreement[152] is not regarded as hard-core[153].

(A) Prices Article 4(1)(a) provides that the block exemption is not applicable to an agreement between competing undertakings that restricts a party's ability to determine its prices to third parties. It is immaterial whether the agreement concerns fixed, minimum, maximum, or recommended prices[154]. Where there are cross licences between two undertakings that have no pro-competitive purpose and where the parties agree to pay running royalties to one another the Commission might treat the case as sham and tantamount to a price-fixing agreement[155]. Article 4(1)(a) (and Article 4(1)(d)) may be infringed where royalties are based on the sales of products irrespective of whether the licensed technology was used in the production of those products[156].

(B) Output Article 4(1)(b) provides that the block exemption is not applicable to an agreement between competing undertakings that has as its object the limitation of output, other than a limitation on the output of contract products imposed on the licensee in a non-reciprocal agreement or imposed on only one of the parties in a reciprocal agreement. Non-reciprocal agreements are treated more favourably than reciprocal ones since they are less likely to lead to a restriction of output and they are more likely to lead to an improvement in economic efficiency[157].

(C) The allocation of markets and customers Article 4(1)(c) provides that the block exemption does not apply to an agreement between competing undertakings that allocates markets or customers[158]. However there are seven exceptions to this:

- An obligation on the licensee(s) to produce with the licensed technology only within one or more technical fields of use or one or more product markets. The field of use restriction must not go beyond the scope of the licensed technology[159]. It does not matter whether, in a reciprocal agreement, the field of use restrictions are symmetrical or asymmetrical[160]

- An obligation on the licensor and/or the licensee in a non-reciprocal agreement not to produce with the licensed technology within one or more technical fields of use or one or more product markets or one or more exclusive territories reserved for the other party

---

[151] *Technology Transfer Regulation*, Article 1(1)(c).   [152] Ibid, Article 1(1)(d).
[153] See the *Technology Transfer Guidelines*, para 78.   [154] Ibid, para 79.   [155] Ibid, para 80.
[156] Ibid, para 81; see also paras 156–160.   [157] Ibid, para 82; see also paras 175–178.
[158] The terms 'exclusive territory' and 'exclusive customer group' are defined in Articles 1(1)(l) and 1(1)(m) of the Regulation; for further discussion of exclusive licensing and sales restrictions see the *Technology Transfer Guidelines*, paras 161–174.
[159] *Technology Transfer Guidelines*, para 90; see also paras 179–185.   [160] Ibid, para 91.

- An obligation on the licensor not to license the technology to another licensee in a particular territory

- The restriction in a non-reciprocal agreement of active and/or passive sales by the licensee and/or the licensor into the exclusive territory or to the exclusive customer group reserved for the other party

- The restriction in a non-reciprocal agreement of active sales by the licensee into the exclusive territory or to the exclusive customer group allocated by the licensor to another licensee provided the latter was not a competing undertaking of the licensor at the time of the conclusion of its own licence. An agreement between licensees not to sell, actively or passively, into each others' territories would be regarded as a cartel agreement between them and would fall outside the scope of the block exemption[161]

- An obligation on the licensee to produce the contract products only for its own use provided that the licensee is not restricted in selling the contract products actively and passively as spare parts for its own products: these are known as 'captive use restrictions'[162]

- An obligation on the licensee in a non-reciprocal agreement to produce the contract products only for a particular customer where the licence was granted in order to create an alternative source of supply for that customer.

(D) Exploitation by the licensee   Article 4(1)(d) provides that the block exemption does not apply to an agreement between competing undertakings that restricts the licensee's ability to exploit its own technology or that prevents any of the parties to the agreement from carrying out research and development, unless such a provision is indispensable to prevent the disclosure to a third party of the licensed know-how. Where such a restriction is found in an agreement between non-competing undertakings it is excluded from the block exemption under Article 5, but it is not listed as hard-core for the purpose of Article 4[163].

(ii) Agreements between non-competing agreements: vertical agreements[164]

Article 4(2) of the Regulation provides that block exemption is not available for agreements between non-competing undertakings that, directly or indirectly, in isolation or in combination with other factors, have as their object restrictions concerning prices, territories, and customer groups or sales within a selective distribution system[165].

(A) Prices   Article 4(2)(a) provides that the block exemption does not apply to an agreement between non-competing undertakings that restricts a party's ability to determine its prices when selling products to third parties. However it is permissible to impose a maximum price or to recommend a price provided that this does not amount to a fixed or minimum price as a result of pressure from, or incentives offered by, any of the parties. Paragraph 97 of the *Technology Transfer Guidelines* provides examples of agreements that would be considered to fix prices indirectly, for example fixing a licensee's margin, fixing the maximum level of discounts, and making threats or intimidating a licensee as to a particular price level.

---

[161] Ibid, para 89.   [162] Ibid, para 92; see also paras 186–190.   [163] See pp 779–780 below.
[164] See generally the *Technology Transfer Guidelines*, paras 96–106.
[165] This term is defined in Article 1(1)(k) of the Regulation.

(B) Territories and customer groups[166]   Article 4(2)(b) provides that the block exemption does not apply to an agreement between non-competing undertakings that restricts the territory into which, or the customer group to whom, the licensee may passively sell the contract goods. Paragraph 98 of the *Technology Transfer Guidelines* provide examples of indirect methods of preventing passive sales, such as financial incentives, monitoring mechanisms to identify the final destination of the contract products, and, in some cases, quantity limitations. Article 4(2)(b) provides six exceptions to the prohibition on restrictions on passive sales:

- A restriction of passive sales into an exclusive territory or to an exclusive customer group reserved for the licensor
- A restriction of passive sales into an exclusive territory or to an exclusive customer group allocated by the licensor to another licensee during the first two years that the other licensee is selling the contract products in that territory or to that group
- An obligation to produce the contract goods only for its own use provided that the licensee is not restricted in selling the contract products actively and passively as spare parts for its own products
- An obligation to produce the contract products only for a particular customer where the licence was granted in order to create an alternative source of supply for that customer
- A restriction of sales to end-users by a licensee operating at the wholesale level of trade
- A restriction of sales to unauthorised distributors by the members of a selective distribution system.

It should be noted that Article 4(2)(b) does not prohibit sales restrictions on the licensor; nor restrictions on active sales by the licensee, except in the case of selective distribution systems (see below)[167]. Furthermore there is no restriction on active or passive sales by licensees to territories or customer groups reserved to the licensor[168].

(C) Restrictions in selective distribution systems   Article 4(2)(c) provides that the block exemption does not apply where an agreement between non-competing undertakings restricts active or passive sales to end-users by a licensee which is a member of a selective distribution system and which operates at the retail level, without prejudice to the possibility of prohibiting a member of the system from operating out of an unauthorised place of establishment.

(E) Article 5: excluded restrictions[169]

Recital 14 of the Regulation states that, in order to protect incentives to innovate, certain restrictions should be excluded from the block exemption, in particular exclusive grant back obligations for severable improvements; however the inclusion of an Article 5 restriction does not prevent the application of the block exemption to the remainder of the agreement[170].

Article 5(1) lists three excluded restrictions:

- **Exclusive grant back**: an obligation on the licensee to grant an exclusive licence to the licensor or a third party designated by the licensor in respect of its own severable improvements[171] to or its own improvements of the licensed technology

---

[166] The terms 'exclusive territory' and 'exclusive customer group' are defined in Articles 1(1)(l) and 1(1)(m) of the Regulation.

[167] See the *Technology Transfer Guidelines*, para 99.   [168] Ibid, para 100.   [169] Ibid, paras 107–116.

[170] Ibid, para 107.   [171] This term is defined in Article 1(1)(n) of the Regulation.

- **Assignments back**: an obligation to assign back such technology
- **No-challenge clauses**: an obligation on the licensee not to challenge the validity of intellectual property rights held by the licensor in the common market, without prejudice to the right of the licensor to terminate the licence in the event of such a challenge.

Article 5(2) also excludes a restriction, in an agreement between non-competing undertakings, that imposes an obligation limiting the licensee's ability to exploit its own technology or limiting either of the party's ability to carry out research and development, unless the latter restriction is indispensable to prevent the disclosure of the licensed technology to third parties.

(F) Article 6: withdrawal in individual cases[172]

Recital 16 of the Regulation states that the provisions of Articles 3 to 5 mean that agreements to which the block exemption applies normally will not eliminate competition in respect of a substantial part of the products in question, with the result that the fourth requirement of Article 81(3) EC will be satisfied. However, as a safety net, the possibility exists of either the Commission or the NCAs of the Member States, in certain circumstances, withdrawing the benefit of the block exemption. The authority doing so bears the burden of proving that an agreement falls within the scope of Article 81(1) and that the terms of Article 81(3) are not satisfied[173].

(i) Article 6(1): withdrawal by the Commission in individual cases

Article 6(1) provides that the Commission may withdraw the benefit of the block exemption in an individual case where an agreement has effects that are incompatible with Article 81(3). Recital 16 states that this may happen in particular where incentives to innovate are reduced or where access to markets is hindered, and Article 6(1) suggests this could be so where:

- Access of third parties' technologies to the market is restricted, for example as a result of the cumulative effect of parallel networks of similar restrictive agreements prohibiting licensees from using third parties' technologies
- Access of potential licensees to the market is restricted, for example as a result of the cumulative effect of parallel networks of similar restrictive agreements prohibiting licensors from licensing to other licensees
- The parties do not exploit the licensed technology, and have no objective justification for not doing so.

(ii) Article 6(2): withdrawal by an NCA of a Member State

Article 6(2) provides that an NCA of a Member State may withdraw the benefit of the block exemption under the same circumstances specified in Article 6(1) where a technology transfer agreement has effects incompatible with Article 81(3) in the territory of a Member State or a part thereof that has all the characteristics of a distinct geographic market. Recital 17 states that, in exercising this power, Member States must ensure that they do not prejudice the uniform application of the Community competition rules throughout the common market or the full effect of the measures adopted in implementation of those rules.

---

[172] See generally the *Technology Transfer Guidelines*, paras 117–122.   [173] Ibid, para 119.

(G) Article 7: non-application of the Regulation[174]

Article 7(1) of the Regulation provides that the Commission may by regulation declare that the block exemption does not apply to technology transfer agreements containing specific restraints relating to a market where parallel networks of similar technology transfer agreements cover more than 50 per cent of the relevant market. Article 7(2) adds that a regulation adopted pursuant to Article 7(1) will not become applicable earlier than six months following its adoption. Where the Commission exercises the power conferred on it by Article 7 it may make a decision in an individual case to provide guidance on the application of Article 81 EC to the agreements that will have lost the benefit of the block exemption[175].

(H) Article 8: application of the market-share thresholds

This provision was dealt with in the context of Article 3 above[176].

(I) Articles 9 to 11: repeal, transitional period
and period of validity

Article 9 repealed Regulation 240/96, the previous technology transfer regulation. Article 10 granted transitional relief to agreements that satisfied Regulation 240/96 until 31 March 2006. Article 11 provides that Regulation 772/2004 will expire on 30 April 2014.

4. THE APPLICATION OF ARTICLE 81 TO OTHER AGREEMENTS RELATING TO INTELLECTUAL PROPERTY RIGHTS

The previous two sections of this chapter considered the application of Article 81 to agreements to license intellectual property rights, with particular reference to technology transfer agreements and the block exemption conferred by Regulation 772/2004. In this section the application of Article 81 to other agreements relating to intellectual property rights will be examined.

(A) Technology pools[177]

It is not uncommon for two or more undertakings to 'pool' their technology. The *Technology Transfer Regulation* explicitly states that it does not apply to technology pools, that is to say to:

agreements for the pooling of technologies with the purpose of licensing the created package to third parties[178].

---

[174] See generally the *Technology Transfer Guidelines*, paras 123–129.   [175] Ibid, para 124.

[176] See p 776 above.

[177] See generally the report prepared for the European Commission on *Multi-Party Licensing* (Charles River Associates, April 2003).

[178] *Technology Transfer Regulation*, Recital 7; see also the *Technology Transfer Guidelines*, para 210.

However the licences granted by the pool to a third party may not infringe Article 81(1) at all[179]; or they may be block exempted, provided that the conditions of Regulation 772/2004 are satisfied[180].

Sometimes a pooling arrangement is fairly simple and informal; however it is not unknown for the pool to have an elaborate structure, the management of which may be entrusted to a separate entity. In some cases a technology pool may be linked to an industry standard. Industry standards are sometimes established by law ('*de jure*'); in others they may become a standard as a matter of fact ('*de facto*'). It may be that, in order to comply with a standard, access is needed to intellectual property rights, and these rights might be managed through a technology pool. It follows that, just as agreements to establish standards might sometimes infringe Article 81[181], so too might the creation and operation of a pool where it is the product of an agreement between undertakings and where it could have the effect of foreclosing access to the market[182]. A related point is that undertakings that participate in the setting of a standard may own essential patents, a licence of which is needed by anyone wishing to comply with the standard. A deliberate concealment of this fact during the standard-setting procedure, or a refusal to license the patents on reasonable, non-discriminatory terms, might amount to an infringement of Article 82 EC[183].

It may also be the case that, within a particular industry, there may be more than one technology pool, and that the different pools may compete with one another. There may be considerable benefits for a firm or firms which control a standard or a technology pool if the industry 'tips' towards that standard or technology as the industry norm. Obvious industries in which one witnesses this phenomenon are mobile telephony[184], high-density television, and digital broadcasting, where the 'battle of the standards' may be fierce. The example of the video cassette industry tipping to the VHS standard, away from Betamax, 20 years ago was matched, in 2008, by the market opting for Sony's Blu-Ray technology for the next generation of DVD players rather than Toshiba's HD DVD platform.

Technology pools may have both pro-competitive and anti-competitive effects: they are discussed in chapter 3 of the DoJ/FTC report on *Antitrust Enforcement and Intellectual Property Rights*. The Commission's *Technology Transfer Guidelines* provide guidance on the application of Article 81 to technology pools[185]. The Commission explains that pools may be restrictive of competition in two ways. First, the pooling of technology implies joint selling: if the pooled technologies are substitutes for one another this amounts to a price-fixing cartel[186]. Second, technology pools may, in particular when they support

---

[179] See *Philips/Sony CD Licensing program*, Commission Press Release IP/03/1152, 7 August 2003.

[180] *Technology Transfer Guidelines*, para 212.   [181] See ch 15, pp 596–598.

[182] The Commission condemned a patent pooling scheme in *Video Cassette Recorders Agreements* OJ [1978] L 47/42, [1978] 2 CMLR 160; see also *Concast-Mannesman* Commission's XIth *Report on Competition Policy* (1981), point 93; *IGR Stereo Television* ibid, point 94 and XIVth *Report on Competition Policy* (1984), point 92.

[183] See pp 793–795 below.

[184] See Commission Press Release IP/02/1651, 12 November 2002 dealing with pooling arrangements in relation to third generation ('3G') mobile telephony standards; for discussion see Choumelova 'Competition law analysis of patent licensing arrangements—the particular case of 3G3P' Commission's *Competition Policy Newsletter*, Spring 2003, p 41.

[185] See also Piesiewcz and Schellingerhout on the issue of setting standards in 'Intellectual property rights in standard setting from a competition law perspective' *Competition Policy Newsletter*, Summer 2007, 36.

[186] *Technology Transfer Guidelines*, para 213.

an industry standard or establish a *de facto* industry standard, reduce innovation by foreclosing alternative technologies from obtaining access to the market[187]. However the Commission also notes that technology pools may be pro-competitive; for example firms that need access to the technology in the pool will get the benefit of a 'one-stop shop', dealing only with the pool, instead of having to negotiate individually with a number of different owners; this can lead to a reduction in costs[188]. The Commission authorised a technology pool in the case of *MPEG-2*[189]. MPEG-2 is a technology that improves the quality of video signals; to apply the technology it is necessary to have access to a number of patents. These were pooled by their respective owners, who agreed that access to the pool would be permitted on a non-exclusive and non-discriminatory basis. This meant that the pool, far from foreclosing the market to third parties, would enable them to gain access to the technology with a beneficial effect on technical and economic progress.

The *Technology Transfer Guidelines* examine three issues, the nature of the pooled technologies, the assessment of individual restraints, and the institutional framework governing the pool.

(i) The nature of the pooled technologies

The Commission makes a distinction between the situation where the pooled technologies are substitutes for one another and where they are complements to each other[190].

(A) Substitute technologies Where the pooled technologies are substitutes for one another the Commission's prime concern is that the royalties payable will be higher than they would otherwise be[191] and that this amounts to price fixing between competitors; this would violate Article 81(1) and be unlikely to satisfy the criteria of Article 81(3)[192].

(B) Complementary technologies Where the pooled technologies are complements the arrangement is likely to reduce transaction costs and to lead to lower overall royalties[193]; this means that the creation of the pool is likely to fall outside Article 81, irrespective of the market position of the parties[194]. However the conditions on which any licence is granted may be caught by Article 81[195]. In particular the Commission has a concern where a licensee is required to take a licence of 'non-essential' technology as a condition of gaining access to 'essential' technology[196], as this amounts to a bundling practice, and may have a foreclosure effect depending on the market power of the pool[197]. The Commission will be less concerned about pools where, for example, technologies which, over time, become non-essential are excluded from the pool; where licensors remain free to license their technologies independently of the pool, so that a licensee could put together its own technology package; and where it is possible to take a licence of part only of the pooled technology at a lower royalty rate[198].

[187] Ibid.   [188] Ibid, para 214.
[189] See OJ [1998] C 229/6 and the Commission's XXIXth *Report on Competition* Policy (1999), points 55 and 56 and p 162; see similarly *Philips/Matsushita—D2B* OJ [1991] C 220/2, [1991] 4 CMLR 905; *Philips International—DCC* OJ [1992] C 333/8, [1993] 4 CMLR 286; see also *The European Telecommunications Standards Institute's Intellectual Property Rights Policy* OJ [1994] C 76/5, [1995] 5 CMLR 352.
[190] *Technology Transfer Guidelines*, para 215.   [191] Ibid, para 217.   [192] Ibid, para 219.
[193] Ibid, para 217.   [194] Ibid, para 220.   [195] Ibid.
[196] These expressions are discussed in para 216 of the *Guidelines*.   [197] Ibid, para 221.
[198] Ibid, para 222.

(ii) Assessment of individual restraints

Where a technology pool has a dominant position on the market, the royalties and other licensing terms that it offers should be fair and non-discriminatory and the licences granted should be non-exclusive; this is to ensure that there is no foreclosure effect[199]. However it is permissible to charge different royalty rates for different uses and in different product markets[200]. The Commission is also concerned to ensure that a technology pool does not foreclose third party technologies from the market: licensors and licensees must therefore be free to develop competing products and standards and must be free to grant and obtain licences outside the pool[201]. Any grant-back obligations towards the pool should be non-exclusive and limited to developments that are essential or important to the use of the pooled technology[202]. In the event that a licensee challenges the validity of a patent, the pool's right to terminate the licensee's licence is limited to the patent in question, and cannot apply to the licence of other (non-challenged) technology: this is to prevent the 'shielding' of invalid patents[203].

(iii) The institutional framework governing the pool

The Commission considers that the way in which a pool is created, organised, and operated can reduce the risk of it restricting competition[204]. A restriction of competition is less likely when the process of setting a standard and creating a pool is open to all interested parties representing different interests[205]; and the involvement of independent experts may be a helpful factor, for example where they help to ensure that only essential technologies are included in the pool[206]. The Commission is anxious that the operation of a pool does not lead to the exchange of sensitive commercial information that could lead to parallel behaviour, particularly in oligopolistic markets, and will look to see what safeguards have been put in place to prevent this[207]. The Commission also has a preference for there to be dispute resolution mechanisms that are independent of the pool and its members[208].

(B) Copyright pools

Closely related to technology pools are copyright pools. In *IFPI 'Simulcasting'*[209] the Commission authorised an agreement under Article 81(3) whereby two collecting societies, acting on behalf of record companies, established a 'one-stop shop' whereby an international licence could be granted to radio and television broadcasters wishing to 'simulcast' programmes to the public both by conventional radio and television and also, at the same time, via the Internet. For broadcasters the advantage of the agreement was that they could obtain a single licence from one collecting society which would be effective throughout the EU. The Commission required the deletion of territorial restrictions that would have restricted competition between national collecting societies[210].

---

[199] Ibid, para 226. [200] Ibid, para 227. [201] Ibid. [202] Ibid, para 228. [203] Ibid, para 229.
[204] Ibid, para 230. [205] Ibid, para 231. [206] Ibid, paras 232–233. [207] Ibid, para 234.
[208] Ibid, para 235.
[209] OJ [2003] L 107/58; for comment on this decision see Pereira 'From discothéques to websites, a new approach to music copyright licensing: the *Simulcasting* decision' Commission's *Competition Policy Newsletter*, Spring 2003, p 44.
[210] OJ [2003] L 107/58, para 3 and paras 27–28.

The Commission concluded that the joint fixing by the societies of the simulcasting royalty fee infringed Article 81(1)[211]. However, it considered that the agreement met the requirements of Article 81(3) as it would create a new type of licence: a 'one-stop shop' licence for simulcasting across the EU which would give consumers a wider access to audio and video music programmes through the Internet[212]. The Commission required the parties to charge for their administrative costs separately from the royalties[213], which were the subject of the horizontal agreement: this meant that broadcasters could exercise a competitive choice on the basis of different societies' costs.

(C) Settlements of litigation[214]

The Commission will carefully scrutinise trade mark delimitation agreements whereby owners of independent trade marks accept restrictions on the exercise and use of their respective marks[215]. This means that legal advisers must be careful when advising clients as to the terms on which they should settle a trade mark dispute, since it may be that the settlement itself will contravene Article 81(1)[216]. In *BAT v Commission*[217] the ECJ established that trade mark delimitation agreements are permissible and fall outside Article 81(1) where they serve to avoid confusion or conflict; however there must be a genuine dispute between the parties and the agreement must be no more restrictive than necessary to overcome the problem of confusion. In this case there was not a genuine dispute, the apparent intention of BAT being to prevent a Mr Segers from selling his tobacco on the German market; the trade mark in question had not been exploited in the past and was subject to cancellation under German law.

The Commission's *Technology Transfer Guidelines* discuss licensing as a means of settling disputes. Where the parties to a dispute agree, as part of a settlement, to license, or to cross-license, the terms of the licence(s) may be covered by the *Technology Transfer Regulation* subject, of course, to compliance with its conditions. The Commission makes the point that where the undertakings agree to license one another in circumstances where their technologies do not block one another[218] – in other words where they are actual horizontal competitors – an agreement between them would be a hard-core

---

[211] Ibid, paras 69–80. [212] Ibid, paras 86–87. [213] Ibid, paras 99–107.

[214] On the position in the US see the DoJ/FTC report on *Antitrust Enforcement and Intellectual Property Rights*, pp 88–91; see also Willig and Bigelow 'Antitrust Policy Toward Agreements That Settle Patent Litigation' (2004) XLIX Antitrust Bulletin 655; Robert and Falconi 'Patent Litigation Settlements in the Pharmaceutical Industry: Marrying the Innovation Bride and the Competition Groom' (2006) 27 ECLR 524.

[215] See *Sirdar and Phildar Trade Marks* [1975] 1 CMLR D93; *Re Penney's Trade Mark* OJ [1978] L 60/19, [1978] 2 CMLR 100 (Article 81 inapplicable to a trade mark agreement which was a genuine attempt to settle litigation and not an attempt to partition the market); *Syntex/Syntbelabo* [1990] 4 CMLR 343 (Commission required modification of trade mark agreement that unjustifiably partitioned markets); *Toltecs and Dorcet Trade Marks* OJ [1982] L 379/19, [1983] 1 CMLR 412 (this decision was the subject of the appeal in *BAT v Commission* below); *Hershey/Herschi* XXth *Report on Competition Policy* (1990), point 111; *Chiquita/Fyffes plc* XXIInd *Report on Competition Policy* (1992), points 168–176 (agreement by Fyffes not to use the Fyffes trade mark in continental Europe contrary to Article 81; also an abuse of a dominant position under Article 82); see *Fyffes plc v Chiquita Brands International Inc* [1993] ECC 193 on the litigation in the English High Court in this case.

[216] See generally Singleton 'IP Disputes: Settlement Agreements and Ancillary Licences' (1993) 15 EIPR 48.

[217] Case 35/83 [1985] ECR 363, [1985] 2 CMLR 470; see Alexander (1985) 22 CML Rev 709.

[218] See p 775 above on one-way and two-way blocking positions.

restriction contrary to Article 4(1) of the Regulation[219]. On the other hand if one party had the ability to exclude the other from the market by virtue of its technology, a licence would be likely to be pro-competitive[220]. Cross-licences that impose restrictions on the parties' use of their technologies, including restrictions on licensing to third parties, may infringe Article 81, in particular where the parties have significant market power and where the agreement imposes restrictions that clearly go beyond what is required to give access to the disputed technology[221]. The Commission will be concerned to ensure that any settlement between the parties does not inhibit their future opportunity to innovate and thereby gain a competitive advantage over each other[222]. No-challenge agreements in a settlement would generally be regarded as falling outside Article 81, since this is regarded as an inherent aspect of any such agreement[223].

In *Chiquita/Fyffes plc*[224] the Commission took the view that an agreement between Chiquita and Fyffes whereby Fyffes agreed not to use the Fyffes trade mark in continental Europe for a period of 20 years infringed both Articles 81 and 82. The Article 82 infringement lay in the fact that the inability of Fyffes to use that mark diminished its ability to compete vigorously with Chiquita in Europe. Following the Commission's intervention, Chiquita abandoned the agreement.

5. ARTICLE 82 AND INTELLECTUAL PROPERTY RIGHTS

The law of intellectual property confers exclusive rights; Article 82 prohibits the abuse of a dominant position. The question arises of whether Article 82 can be applied in such a way as to limit the exclusive rights given by intellectual property law[225]. The ECJ has made clear that mere ownership of intellectual property rights cannot be attacked under Article 82; however Article 82 may apply to an improper exercise of the right in question[226]. Article 8(2) of the WTO agreement on Trade-Related Aspects of Intellectual Property Rights (the so-called 'TRIPS Agreement') says much the same:

Appropriate measures, provided that they are consistent with the provisions of this Agreement, may be needed to prevent the abuse of intellectual property rights by holders or the resort to practices which unreasonably restrain trade or adversely affect the international transfer of technology.

(A) Compulsory licences

A question that has been much debated is the extent to which the owner of an intellectual property right can be compelled to grant a licence of it to a third party under

---

[219] *Technology Transfer Guidelines*, para 205.   [220] Ibid, para 206.   [221] Ibid, para 207.

[222] Ibid, para 208.   [223] Ibid, para 209.

[224] Commission's XXIInd *Report on Competition Policy* (1992), points 168–176.

[225] For further discussion of this subject see Tritton *Intellectual Property in Europe* (Sweet & Maxwell, 2nd ed, 2002), ch 11; Govaere *The Use and Abuse of Intellectual Property Rights in EC Law* (Sweet & Maxwell, 1996), ch 5; Anderman *EC Competition Law and Intellectual Property Rights: The Regulation of Innovation* (Clarendon Press Oxford, 1998), chs 10–19; Coates, Kyølbye and Peeperkorn in Faull and Nikpay *The EC Law of Competition* (Oxford University Press, 2nd ed, 2007), paras 10.209–10.255.

[226] See Case 24/67 *Parke, Davis & Co v Probel* [1968] ECR 55, [1968] CMLR 47 where the ECJ said that ownership of a patent is not an abuse in itself although 'the utilisation of the patent could degenerate into an improper exploitation of the protection'; the ownership of intellectual property is a factor to be taken into account in assessing whether a firm has a dominant position: see ch 5, p 180.

Article 82. As a general proposition one would expect the issue of compulsory licensing to be addressed as a matter of intellectual property law, and not as a matter of competition law. The case law about to be discussed exhibits a certain deference to intellectual property law; as we shall see below, it imposes higher standards for a successful claim to a licence of an intellectual property right than to access to an essential facility such as a port or gas pipeline[227].

(i) The *Renault* and *Erik Veng* judgments

In the *Renault* case[228] and in *Volvo v Erik Veng*[229] third parties wished to be granted licences of the car manufacturers' intellectual property rights in order to produce spare parts, and claimed that a refusal to grant such licences was an abuse of a dominant position under Article 82. The ECJ adopted an orthodox approach to the application of Article 82 to compulsory licensing and held that, in the absence of Community harmonisation of laws on designs and models, it was a matter for national law to determine the nature and extent of protection for such matters. In the *Volvo* case the ECJ stated at paragraph 8 that:

the right of the proprietor of a protected design to prevent third parties from manufacturing and selling or importing, without its consent, products incorporating the design constitutes the very subject-matter of its exclusive rights. It follows that an obligation imposed upon the proprietor of a protected design to grant to third parties, even in return for a reasonable royalty, a licence for the supply of products incorporating the design would lead to the proprietor thereof being deprived of the substance of its exclusive right, and that a refusal to grant such a licence cannot in itself constitute an abuse of a dominant position.

The ECJ added, however, that a car manufacturer might be guilty of abusing its dominant position where it refused to supply spare parts to independent repairers in an arbitrary manner, charged unfair prices for spare parts[230], or decided no longer to produce spare parts for models still in circulation.

(ii) The *Magill* case

A less orthodox approach was taken by the Commission in *Magill TV Guide/ITP, BBC and RTE*[231], variously known as the *Magill* case or the *TV Listings* case. Mr Magill wished to publish the listings of three television companies broadcasting in the UK and Ireland in a single weekly publication. At the time there was no publication which contained the details of all three companies' programmes for a week in advance; this information was available only in daily newspapers for the day in question, or on a Saturday for the weekend. There was an obvious public demand for listings magazines,

---

[227] For an interesting discussion of whether the law is unduly deferential to intellectual property see Ritter 'Refusal to Deal and "Essential Facilities": Does Intellectual Property Require Special Deference Compared to Tangible Property' (2005) 28(3) World Competition 281.

[228] Case 53/87 *Consorzio Italiano della Componentistica di Ricambio per Autovericoli and Maxicar v Regie National des Usines Renault* [1988] ECR 6039, [1990] 4 CMLR 265.

[229] Case 238/87 [1988] ECR 6211, [1989] 4 CMLR 122; see Korah 'No Duty to Licence Independent Repairers to Make Spare Parts: the *Renault, Volvo* and *Bayer* Cases' (1988) 12 EIPR 381; Groves 'The Use of Registered Designs to Protect Car Body Panels' (1989) 10 BLR 117.

[230] In Case T-198/98 *Micro Leader Business v Commission* [1999] ECR II-3989, [2000] 4 CMLR 886 the CFI held that the Commission, before rejecting a complaint against Microsoft concerning the exercise of its copyright protection, should have investigated whether its prices were discriminatory contrary to Article 82(2)(c): ibid, paras 49–59.

[231] OJ [1989] L 78/43, [1989] 4 CMLR 757.

which were widely available in continental countries. Copyright protection was available for TV listings under UK and Irish law, which is why Magill required a licence. The Commission concluded that the three television companies had abused their individual dominant positions in relation to their own TV listings by refusing to make them available to Magill and required that advance information be supplied in order to enable comprehensive weekly TV guides to be published. The Commission's decision was appealed to the CFI and the ECJ, each of which upheld it[232]. The ECJ stated that the abuse consisted of the refusal to provide basic information by relying on national copyright provisions, thereby preventing the appearance of a new product, a comprehensive guide to television programmes, which the television companies did not offer and for which there was a potential consumer demand[233]; the Court also noted that there was no objective justification for the refusal[234] and that the result of the refusal was to reserve to the television companies the downstream market for television guides[235].

The case was immensely controversial and led to numerous comments and articles, mainly adverse[236]. It appeared to sit oddly with the earlier judgments of the ECJ in *Renault* and *Volvo v Erik Veng*; it meant that the possibility of compulsory licensing had been introduced under Article 82; and it could be seen to be an application of the so-called 'essential facilities doctrine' to intellectual property rights[237]. A particular anxiety was that the precedent might be applied to intellectual property rights that were the consequence of substantial risk-taking and investment – for example patents and computer software – as opposed to a mere list of television programmes, though this did not happen in practice. There is little doubt that the Commission and the Community Courts were influenced in *Magill* by the fact that information as prosaic as TV listings was entitled to copyright protection: most systems of law in the Member States would not have conferred intellectual property protection at all in such circumstances. However this was not an explicit part of the reasoning in the Commission's decision or the Courts' judgments.

(iii) Oscar Bronner

In *Oscar Bronner v Mediaprint*[238] the ECJ stressed the exceptional circumstances in *Magill*: in paragraph 40 of its judgment it referred to four factors in particular: the information sought by Magill was indispensable to the publication of a comprehensive listings guide; there was a demonstrable potential consumer demand for the would-be product; there were no objective justifications for the refusal to supply; and the refusal would eliminate all competition in the secondary market for TV guides.

---

[232] Cases T-69/89 etc *RTE v Commission* [1991] ECR II-485, [1991] 4 CMLR 586, upheld by the ECJ Cases C-241/91 P etc *RTE and ITP v Commission* [1995] ECR I-743, [1995] 4 CMLR 718.

[233] Cases C-241/91 P etc *RTE and ITP v Commission* [1995] ECR I-743, [1995] 4 CMLR 718, para 54.

[234] [1995] ECR I-743, [1995] 4 CMLR 718, para 55.   [235] Ibid, para 56.

[236] For comment on the ECJ's judgment see eg Pombo 'Intellectual Property and Intra-Community Trade' [1996] Fordham Corporate Law Institute (ed Hawk), 491–505; Crowther 'Compulsory Licensing of Intellectual Property Rights' (1995) 20 EL Rev 521; Anderman *EC Competition Law and Intellectual Property Rights: The Regulation of Innovation* (Clarendon Press Oxford, 1998), paras 14.3.1–14.4.

[237] See ch 17, pp 690–699; see generally Cotter 'Intellectual Property and the Essential Facilities Doctrine' (1999) 44 Antitrust Bulletin 211 on the question of whether intellectual property rights can be regarded as essential facilities.

[238] Case C-7/97 [1998] ECR I-7791, [1999] 4 CMLR 112.

(iv) *IMS Health*

In the next case to deal with this matter, *IMS Health GmbH & Co v NDC Health GmbH & Co*[239], the ECJ repeated the formulation of the Court in *Bronner*. The *IMS* case was an Article 234 reference from a German Court[240]. NDC Health was seeking a licence from IMS, the world leader in data collection on pharmaceutical sales and prescriptions, that would give it access to IMS's copyrighted format for processing regional sales data in Germany, the so-called '1,860 brick structure'. After considering whether the brick structure might be an indispensable requirement for NDC, as required by the *Bronner* judgment[241], the ECJ went on to consider the questions of whether a refusal to license NDC might exclude all competition in a secondary market[242], and whether it might prevent the emergence of a new product[243]. On the latter point the ECJ agreed with Advocate General Tizzano that, in achieving a balance between the need to protect the economic freedom of the owner of an intellectual property right on the one hand and the protection of free competition on the other:

the latter can prevail *only where refusal to grant a licence prevents the development of the secondary market to the detriment of consumers*[244] (emphasis added).

In seeking some limitation to what might be meant by 'exceptional circumstances', this last statement of the ECJ in *IMS* was helpful: even if one acknowledges that there is room for debate as to what is meant by 'the development of the secondary market' – what, for example, is a 'new' product – nevertheless the Court establishes clearly that there is no right to a licence simply to duplicate what the owner of the intellectual property right in question is already doing. In DG COMP's *Discussion paper on the application of Article 82 of the Treaty to exclusionary abuses*[245] the Commission suggests that, in cases on refusal to license, there is a specific requirement to show that the refusal would prevent the licensee from producing new goods or services not offered by the owner of the right and for which there is a potential consumer demand[246].

---

[239] Case C-418/01 [2004] ECR I-5039, [2004] 4 CMLR 1543; for comment see Sufrin 'The IMS Case' (2004) 3 Competition Law Journal 18; Brinker 'Essential Facility Doctrine and Intellectual Property Law: Where does Europe Stand in the Aftermath of the *IMS Health* Case?' [2004] Fordham Corportate Law Institute (ed Hawk), 137; Eilmansberger 'The Essential Facilities Doctrine under Art. 82: What is the State of Affairs after IMS Health and Microsoft?' (2005) 16 King's College Law Journal 329; Fox 'A Tale of Two Jurisdictions and an Orphan Case: Antitrust, Intellectual Property, and Refusals to Deal' (2005) 28 Fordham International Law Journal 952; Ahlborn, Evans and Padilla 'The Logic & Limits of the "Exceptional Circumstances Test" in *Magill* and *IMS Health*' (2005) 28 Fordham International Law Journal 1109.

[240] Note that the Commission had adopted interim measures against IMS in *NDC Health/IMS: (Interim Measures)* OJ [2002] L 59/18, [2002] 4 CMLR 111; for comment see Korah 'The Interface between IP and Antitrust: The European Experience' (2001–02) 69 Antitrust Law Journal 801; Fine 'NDC/IMS: In Response to Professor Korah' (2002) 70 Antitrust Law Journal 247; the Presidents of the CFI and the ECJ suspended the Commission's decision pending the CFI's final judgment; both noted that there was a serious dispute as to whether the circumstances in *IMS* were exceptional: Case T-184/01 R [2001] ECR II-3193, [2002] 4 CMLR 58 (President of CFI Order), upheld on appeal Case C-481/01 P (R) [2002] ECR I-3401, [2002] 5 CMLR 44 (President of ECJ Order); in due course the Commission withdrew the interim measures decision, so that the appeal to the CFI was itself withdrawn: see Commission Press Release IP/03/1159, 13 August 2003.

[241] See ch 17, pp 694–695 on the meaning of indispensability in this context.

[242] Case C-418/01 [2004] ECR I-5039, [2004] 4 CMLR 1543, paras 40–47. [243] Ibid, paras 48–50.

[244] Ibid, para 48.

[245] Available at www.ec.europa.eu/comm/competition/antitrust/art82/index.html.

[246] Ibid, para 239.

(v) The *Microsoft* case

The *Magill* and the *IMS* cases established the possibility of a claim to a licence under Article 82 in exceptional circumstances, in particular where the licensee intended to produce a new product for which there was a potential consumer demand. The potential significance of this doctrine was dramatically revealed in the Commission's decision in the *Microsoft* case of 24 March 2004[247]. The Commission held that Microsoft was dominant in two markets, one for personal computer operating systems and the other for work group server operating systems. The Commission held that Microsoft had abused its dominant position by refusing to supply competitors with interoperability information to enable them to develop and distribute products that would compete with Microsoft's on the market for servers. The Commission also found Microsoft guilty of tying its operating system with its Windows Media Player[248]. For the two abuses Microsoft was fined €497 million. The Commission's findings of abuse, and the fine, were upheld on appeal to the CFI in *Microsoft v Commission*[249]. A number of points should be noted about the abusive refusal to supply.

(A) The Commission and the CFI assumed that Microsoft enjoyed intellectual property protection The first point is that the Commission and the CFI proceeded on the assumption that Microsoft's interoperability information was protected by the law of intellectual property, without actually reaching a conclusion on the point[250]. The CFI noted that, in making this assumption, the Commission had imposed upon itself the strictest legal test, that is to say the one most favourable to Microsoft[251].

(B) The CFI's summary of the applicable law The second point is that the CFI then proceeded to analyse the relevant case law, referring in particular to *Magill*, *Bronner* and *IMS Health*, from which it drew the following conclusion:

332 It follows from the case law cited above that the refusal by an undertaking holding a dominant position to license a third party to use a product covered by an intellectual property right cannot in itself constitute an abuse of a dominant position within the meaning of Article 82 EC. It is only in exceptional circumstances that the exercise of the exclusive right by the owner of the intellectual property right may give rise to such an abuse.

333 It also follows from that case law that the following circumstances, in particular, must be considered to be exceptional:

 – in the first place, the refusal relates to a product or service indispensable to the exercise of a particular activity on a neighbouring market;

---

[247] OJ [2007] L 32/23; see Banasevic, Huby, Pena, Castellot, Sitar and Piffaut 'Commission adopts Decision in the Microsoft case' Competition Policy Newsletter, Summer 2004, pp 44–46; Lévêque 'Innovation, Leveraging and Essential Facilities: Interoperability Licensing in the EU Microsoft Case' (2005) 28(1) World Competition 71; Dolmans, O'Donoghue and Loewenthal 'Are Article 82 and Intellectual Property Interoperable? The State of the Law Pending the Judgment in *Microsoft v Commission*' (2007) 3 Competition Policy International 107.

[248] See ch 17, pp 679–687 for discussion of the tying infringement; see also McMahon 'Interoperability: "Indispensability" and "Special Responsibility" in High Technology Markets' (2007) 9 Tulane Journal of Technology and Intellectual Property 123.

[249] Case T-201/04 [2007] ECR II-000, [2007] 5 CMLR 846; for discussion of the case by Commission officials see Kramler, Buhr and Wyns 'The judgment of the Court of First Instance in the Microsoft case'. *Competition Policy Newsletter* Number 3, 2007, 39; see also Howarth and McMahon '"Windows has Performed an Illegal Operation": The Court of First Instance's Judgment in Microsoft v Commission' (2008) 29 ECLR 117.

[250] Case T-201/04, paras 283–290. [251] Ibid, para 284.

– in the second place, the refusal is of such a kind as to exclude any effective competition on that neighbouring market;
– in the third place, the refusal prevents the appearance of a new product for which there is potential consumer demand.

334 Once it is established that such circumstances are present, the refusal by the holder of a dominant position to grant a licence may infringe Article 82 EC unless the refusal is objectively justified.

335 The Court notes that the circumstance that the refusal prevents the appearance of a new product for which there is potential demand is found only in the case law on the exercise of an intellectual property right.

(C) The CFI's benign application of the 'new product' requirement The CFI concluded that the requirement of indispensability was satisfied[252] and that all competition would be eliminated on a secondary market[253]. A notable feature of the CFI's judgment is its treatment of the 'new product' requirement[254]. The CFI began by noting that this consideration was one that should be understood in the context of Article 82(2)(b) of the Treaty which prohibits abusive conduct which consists of 'limiting production, markets or technical development to the prejudice of consumers'[255]. However the CFI did not make a finding, nor did it require the Commission to have made a finding, that any specific new product – such as the composite TV listings magazine in *Magill* – would have resulted from the provision of interoperability information; rather the CFI said that the new product criterion should be read to include a restriction of technical development[256], and that the Commission's emphasis on this factor was not manifestly incorrect[257]. In the Court's view Microsoft's refusal meant that consumers were increasingly locked into Microsoft's platform at the work group server level[258]; and that competitors were prevented from developing operating systems distinguishable from the Windows systems already on the market[259]. The Court concluded with the rather bizarre statement that Microsoft had 'impaired the effective competitive structure on the work group server operating systems market by acquiring a significant market share on that market'[260]. The CFI rejected Microsoft's claim that its behaviour was objectively justified[261].

The Court seems to have taken a somewhat benign approach to the 'new product' rule in this judgment[262]. It can be anticipated that future cases will have to examine further the scope of the new product rule, both as to the 'newness' of the product and the possibility that a restriction of technical development may suffice.

(D) Remedy An obvious difficulty with a case such as Microsoft is to determine an appropriate remedy, and to ensure that there is proper compliance. Courts in the US are reluctant to make positive orders that require supervision[263]. After the Commission's decision in *Microsoft* in March 2004 there were protracted negotiations between the Commission and Microsoft as to whether the latter was making the necessary interoperability information available to the market on 'RAND' terms (reasonable and non-discriminatory). The Commission appointed a Trustee to provide technical advice on compliance[264], although the CFI subsequently ruled that the Commission lacked the

---

[252] Ibid, paras 369–436.   [253] Ibid, paras 479–620.   [254] Ibid, paras 643–665.   [255] Ibid, para 643.
[256] Ibid, para 647.   [257] Ibid, para 649.   [258] Ibid, paras 650–652.   [259] Ibid, paras 653–659.
[260] Ibid, para 664.   [261] Ibid, paras 688–712.
[262] See Vickers 'A Tale of Two EC Cases: *IBM* and *Microsoft*' (2008) 4 Competition Policy International 3.
[263] See ch 17, p 691 discussing the *Trinko* case.
[264] See eg Commission Press Release IP/05/1215, 5 October 2005.

legal power to have done so[265]. The Commission decided in July 2006 that Microsoft had been guilty of failing to provide interoperability information, as required by its decision, from 16 December 2005 to 20 June 2006, and therefore imposed a daily periodical payment penalty of €1.5 million on Microsoft which totaled €280.5 million[266]. In February 2008 the Commission imposed a further penalty of €899 million for charging unreasonable prices for the information from 21 June 2006 until 21 October 2007[267]. In October 2007 the Commission announced that it had finally reached agreement with Microsoft on compliance with its decision going forward[268].

(B) Provision of proprietary information needed for interoperability

DG COMP's *Discussion paper* suggests that where proprietary information is required for interoperability that is *not* protected by intellectual property law, but is 'merely' a trade secret, it is not necessary to apply 'the same high standards' as those for licences of intellectual property rights[269].

(C) Collecting societies

Article 82 may be applied to the activities of collecting societies, that is to say organisations that manage copyright on behalf of authors and publishers; in particular they collect royalties from the media, nightclubs, and other users on behalf of their members and distribute them in return for a fee. Article 82 has been invoked both by the Commission[270] and in private law actions in domestic courts, several of which have reached the ECJ under Article 234 EC[271].

The ECJ has indicated that there is nothing intrinsically objectionable about the establishment of collecting societies, which may be necessary in order that individual artists can obtain a reasonable return for their endeavours[272]. However the activities of a society may amount to a breach of Article 82 in various ways. Of particular significance in Community Law terms will be the tendency of national societies to discriminate

---

[265] Case T-201/04 *Microsoft Corp v Commission* [2007] ECR II-000, [2007] 5 CMLR 846, paras 1251–1279.
[266] Commission decision of 12 July 2006.   [267] Commission Press Release IP/08/318, 27 February 2008.
[268] Commission Press Release IP/07/1567, 22 October 2007; see also Commission MEMO/08/106, 21 February 2008.
[269] *Discussion paper*, paras 241–242.
[270] *GEMA* JO [1971] L 134/15, [1971] CMLR D35; *Interpar v GVL GmbH* OJ [1981] L 370/ 49, [1982] 1 CMLR 221; *GEMA Statutes* OJ [1982] L 94/12, [1982] 2 CMLR 482; *BIEM-FPI* XIIIth *Report on Competition Policy* (1983), points 147–150; *GEMA* XVth *Report on Competition Policy* (1985), point 81; *GVL* OJ [1981] L 370/49, upheld on appeal to the ECJ Case 7/82 *GVL v Commission* [1983] ECR 483, [1983] 3 CMLR 645; the Commission's decision not to proceed with complaints against SACEM, a French collecting society, was unsuccessfully challenged in Case T-114/92 *BEMIM v Commission* [1995] ECR II-147, [1996] 4 CMLR 305 and in Case T-5/93 *Roger Tremblay v Commission* [1995] ECR II-185, [1996] 4 CMLR 305, on appeal to the ECJ Case C-91/95 P [1996] ECR I-5547, [1997] 4 CMLR 211; for comment see Torremans and Stamatoudi 'Collecting Societies: Sorry, the Community is No Longer Interested!' (1997) 2 EL Rev 352.
[271] Case 127/73 *Belgische Radio en Televisie v SABAM* [1974] ECR 313, [1974] 2 CMLR 238; Case 22/79 *Greenwich Film Production v SACEM* [1979] ECR 3275, [1980] 1 CMLR 629; Case 402/85 *Basset v SACEM* [1987] ECR 1747, [1987] 3 CMLR 173; Case 395/87 *Ministère Public v Tournier* [1989] ECR 2521, [1991] 4 CMLR 248; Case 110/88 *Lucazeau v SACEM* [1989] ECR 2811, [1991] 4 CMLR 248.
[272] See Case 127/73 *BRT v SABAM* [1974] ECR 313, [1974] 2 CMLR 238, paras 8–15.

against undertakings from other Member States[273]. In the case of *CISAC* the Commission negotiated commitments under Article 9 of the Modernisation Regulation from the International Confederation of Composers and Authors and 18 collecting societies that restrictions would be ended that obliged authors to transfer their copyright only to their own national collecting society and that required commercial users to obtain a licence only from their domestic collecting society, limited to the domestic territory; there is no formal decision yet[274].

Other aspects of collecting societies' activities have been condemned, such as clauses in the constitution which unreasonably restrict an author's right to act unilaterally and provisions which are unreasonable vis-à-vis the media or which attempt to extend the protection of copyright to non-copyrighted works[275]. In *Basset v SACEM*[276] the ECJ was asked whether SACEM was entitled to charge a 1.65 per cent 'supplementary mechanical reproduction fee' above its normal royalty for performances at discotheques, on juke-boxes and radios, where the recordings in question were imported from other Member States in which no such fee was payable. The ECJ held that the extra charge was not in principle contrary to Articles 28, 30 and 82, as it amounted to a normal exploitation of copyright and was not an act of arbitrary discrimination nor a disguised restriction on inter-Member State trade.

(D) Miscellaneous cases concerning intellectual property rights

(i) Unlawful acquisition of technology

In *Tetra Pak Rausing v Commission*[277] the CFI upheld the Commission's decision[278] that it was an abuse of Tetra Pak's dominant position in the market for cartons and machines for packaging milk to acquire Liquipak and thereby obtain the benefit of an exclusive licence relating to technology for a new method of sterilising cartons suitable for long-life milk. This finding was despite the fact that the licence complied with the provisions of the block exemption in force at the time on patent licensing agreements.

(ii) Demanding excessive royalties

In *Eurofix-Bauco v Hilti*[279] the Commission held that it was an abuse to demand an 'excessive' royalty with the sole object of blocking, or at any rate unreasonably delaying, a licence of right which was available under UK patent law. This was seen as part of Hilti's strategy of preventing competition in respect of its nail cartridges.

In *Duales System Deutschland*[280] the Commission concluded that it was an abuse of a dominant position for DSD, an undertaking that operated a comprehensive system for

---

[273] *Re GEMA* JO [1971] L 134/15, [1971] CMLR D35; Case 7/82 *GVL v Commission* [1983] ECR 483, [1983] 3 CMLR 645.

[274] Details are available on DG COMP's website.

[275] The most thorough decision on these issues remains the Commission's decision in *Re GEMA* JO [1971] L 134/15, [1971] 1 CMLR D35.

[276] Case 402/85 [1987] ECR 1747, [1987] 3 CMLR 173.

[277] Case T-51/89 [1990] ECR II-309, [1991] 4 CMLR 334.

[278] *Tetra Pak I (BTG Licence)* OJ [1988] L 272/27, [1990] 4 CMLR 47.

[279] OJ [1988] L 65/19, [1989] 4 CMLR 677, para 78, upheld on appeal Case T-30/89 *Hilti AG v Commission* [1991] ECR II-1439, [1992] 4 CMLR 16, para 99.

[280] OJ [2001] L 166/1, [2001] 5 CMLR 609, paras 111–113.

the collection and recycling of waste in Germany, to contain a provision in its trademark agreement that its clients would pay a royalty for sales packaging bearing its 'Green Dot' trade mark, irrespective of whether the client actually used the services of DSD. This could dissuade those clients from using the services of competitors. On appeal to the CFI the Commission's decision was upheld[281].

In August 2007 the Commission sent a statement of objections to Qualcomm Inc of the US, the owner of patents in the European standard for third generation (3G) mobile telephony technology, alleging that it had abused its dominant position by failing to license its technology on FRAND (fair, reasonable, and non-discriminatory) terms[282]. An important issue in this case, if the Commission does decide that Qualcomm is guilty of abusing its dominant position, will be its assessment of how the fairness and reasonableness of licensing is to be determined in circumstances where a standard-setting procedure enhances the value of patents that are essential for compliance with the standard[283].

(iii) Vexatious behaviour and abuse of process

In *BBI/Boosey and Hawkes: Interim Measures*[284] the Commission seems to have regarded it as an aspect of Boosey and Hawkes' abusive behaviour to have brought vexatious litigation against an undertaking for 'slavish imitation' of its products[285]. On one occasion the Commission intimated that it might be an abuse for a firm in a dominant position to register a trade mark knowing that a competitor already uses that mark[286].

In *AstraZeneca*[287] the Commission adopted an important decision in which, for the first time, it held that it can be an abuse of a dominant position to misuse regulatory procedures. AstraZeneca had a patent for a highly successful drug, Losec. When a patent expires, it is normal for so-called 'generic' manufacturers to enter the market and to sell the drugs in question at considerably lower prices than were charged during the period of patent protection. AstraZeneca was found by the Commission to have abused regulatory procedures in two ways. First, it had succeeded in persuading various patent authorities to grant it 'supplementary protection certificates', extending the period of patent protection, on the basis of misleading information. Second, AstraZeneca held a

---

[281]   Case T-151/01 *Duales System Deutschland v Commission* [2007] ECR II-000, [2007] 5 CMLR 300; for comment see Gremminger and Miersch 'The Court of First Instance confirms Duales System Deutschland's abuse of dominance in the packaging recycling system' *Competition Policy Newletter* Number 3, 2007, 47; the case is on appeal to the ECJ, Case C-385/07 *Duales System Deutschland v Commission*, not yet decided.

[282]   See Commission MEMO/07/389, 1 October 2007; see also Piesiewcz and Schellingerhout on the issue of setting standards in 'Intellectual property rights in standard setting from a competition law perspective' *Competition Policy Newsletter* Summer 2007, 36.

[283]   See Swanson and Baumol 'Selection of Compatibility Standards and Control of Market Power Related to Intellectual Property' (2005) 73 Antitrust Law Journal 1; Layne-Farrar, Padilla and Schmalansee 'Pricing Patents for Licensing in Standard-Setting Organisations: Making Sense of FRAND Commitments' (2007) 74 Antitrust Law Journal 671; the issues are discussed in 'Untangling FRAND: what price intellectual property?', available at www.oxera.com.

[284]   OJ [1987] L 286/36, [1988] 4 CMLR 67, para 19.

[285]   On vexatious litigation see further ch 17, pp 704–705.

[286]   *Osram/Airam*, XIth *Report on Competition Policy* (1981), point 97.

[287]   Commission decision of 15 June 2005; see De Souza 'Competition in Pharmaceuticals: the challenges ahead post AstraZeneca' *Competition Policy Newsletter* Srping 2007, 39; Gunther and Breuvart 'Misuse of Patent and Drug Regulatory Approval Systems in the Pharmaceutical Industry: an Analysis of US and EU Converging Approaches' (2005) 26 ECLR 669.

market authorisation that allowed the drug to be sold in a capsule form. AstraZeneca withdrew the capsules from the market, selling them in tablet form instead. This meant that the generics companies could no longer market their capsules. The case is on appeal to the CFI[288].

The Commission's website discloses that it has initiated proceedings against Boehringer, a German pharmaceutical company, alleging that it had infringed Article 82 by 'misuse of the patent system' in order to exclude competitors in the market for chronic obstructive pulmonary disease drugs; however there is no explanation of what this misuse consists of[289]. In January 2008 the Commission announced that it had opened a sector inquiry into the pharmaceuticals sector, which would include an investigation of whether undertakings in the sector were creating artificial barriers to entry through practices such as misuse of patents and vexatious litigation[290].

In August 2007 the Commission sent a statement of objections to Rambus alleging that it had infringed Article 82 by conducting a so-called 'patent ambush'. This refers to the phenomenon of an undertaking participating in the setting of an industry standard, but doing so in a deliberately deceptive manner by not disclosing the existence of patents that would be necessary for anyone making use of the standard. This means that, once the standard is set, the owner of the patents will be able to demand unreasonable royalties from licensees that need access to the technology in question[291]. The Commission's intervention in this case followed an earlier action in the US, where the FTC required Rambus to license its technology for computer memory subject to maximum royalty rates; Rambus was also required to employ a compliance officer to ensure that Rambus's patents and patent applications are disclosed to industry standard-setting bodies in which it participates. The FTC's decision was reversed by a Circuit court and the case is now on appeal: information about this case can be found on the FTC's website[292].

6. UK LAW

(A) Licences of intellectual property rights: the Chapter I prohibition

The Chapter I prohibition in the Competition Act 1998 applies to agreements that have as their object or effect the prevention, restriction or distortion of competition[293]. There

---

[288] Case T-321/05 *AstraZeneca v Commission*, not yet decided.

[289] See www.ec.europa.eu/comm/competition/antitrust/cases/decisions/39246/initiations.pdf.

[290] Commission Press Release IP/08/49, 16 January 2008.

[291] See Commission MEMO/07/330, 23 August 2007.

[292] See www.ftc.gov; see also *Broadcom Corporation v Qualcomm Incorporated*, US Court of Appeals for the Third Circuit, 4 September 2007, 501 F 3d 297 [2007] (3d Cir. 2007); for discussion of issues arising from the adoption of standards and intellectual property rights see Ohana, Hansen and Shah 'Disclosure and Negotiation of Licensing Terms Prior to Adoption of Industry Standards: Preventing Another Patent Ambush?' (2003) 24 ECLR 644; on patent ambushing more generally see Naughton 'The Antitrust Risks of Unilateral Conduct in Standard Setting, in the Light of the FTC's Case Against Rambus' (2004) XLIX Antitrust Bulletin 699; Petritsi 'The Case of Unilateral Patent Ambush Under EC Competition Rules' (2005) 28(1) World Competition 25; Farrell, Hayes, Shapiro and Sullivan 'Standard Setting, Patents and Hold-Up' (2007) 74 Antitrust Law Journal 603.

[293] For a general account of the Chapter I prohibition see ch 9, pp 327–353.

are no specific provisions in the legislation on licences of intellectual property rights, and the OFT has not published a guideline on the subject[294]. As a general proposition it can be anticipated that the Chapter I prohibition will be applied to agreements in the same way as Article 81 EC[295]. The possibility exists that some of the jurisprudence of the Community Courts might not be applied to a purely domestic agreement in so far as that jurisprudence reflects single market considerations that need not be applied within the UK; this is a matter that has yet to be addressed by the UK institutions[296].

Perhaps the most important provision of the Competition Act as far as licences of intellectual property rights are concerned is section 10, which provides for so-called parallel exemption[297]. This section means that any agreement that is exempt under the EC *Technology Transfer Regulation*, or that would be if the agreement in question were to have an effect on trade between Member States, is also exempt from the Chapter I prohibition. This means that many agreements are exempt from both EC and UK law, and that there is no need for the UK to adopt a block exemption of its own for technology transfer agreements.

Section 70 of the Competition Act repealed sections 44 and 45 of the Patents Act 1977[298]; section 44 prohibited certain tie-in and non-competition clauses, while section 45 made it possible to terminate, on three months' notice, patent licences or supply agreements for patented products after the expiry of the original patents. Given the broad ambit of the Competition Act 1998 it was considered that special treatment for these 'tie-in' and 'post-expiry' provisions was no longer necessary.

(B) Other agreements relating to intellectual property rights

It is reasonable to assume that domestic law will, subject to the point about single market considerations, be interpreted consistently with the jurisprudence and decisional practice under Article 81 EC; and that the sections of the Commission's *Technology Transfer Guidelines* on matters such as the settlement of litigation and technology pools will be closely followed[299].

(C) Anti-monopoly control of intellectual property rights: the Chapter II prohibition and market investigations

The Chapter II prohibition could apply to abusive behaviour in relation to intellectual property rights; the decisional practice of the Commission and the judgments of the Community Courts would of course be relevant to the application of this prohibition[300]. The OFT has said that a firm's conduct is not immune from the Chapter II prohibition purely on the basis that its market power stems from the holding of intellectual property rights[301]. In the case of *Capita Business Services Ltd and Bromcom Computers plc*[302]

---

[294] A draft Guideline was published in November 2001, OFT 418, but it was not published in final form.

[295] See pp 762 ff above.

[296] See ch 9, pp 362–367 for discussion on section 60 of the Competition Act 1998.

[297] On parallel exemption see ch 9, p 353.   [298] See Heal 'Loosening the Ties' (1999) 21 EIPR 414.

[299] See pp 781–786 above.   [300] See pp 786–796 above.

[301] *BSkyB* OFT Decision, 17 December 2002, available at www.oft.gov.uk, paras 331–340.

[302] Weekly Gazette of the OFT, Competition case closure summaries, 26 April–2 May 2003, available at www.oft.gov.uk; see also *British Standards Institution agrees to grant online licence*, OFT Press Release PN 94/03, 7 July 2003.

Capita gave the OFT voluntary assurances that it would provide 'interface information' to a third party to enable it to have access to data on Capita's server; the case was therefore closed.

The market investigation provisions of the Enterprise Act 2002 may also be relevant where features of a market are anti-competitive as a result of intellectual property rights. These provisions have been described in chapter 11. The Competition Commission did publish some reports under the now-repealed monopoly provisions of the Fair Trading Act 1973 dealing with intellectual property issues, including *Exhaust Gas Analysers*[303], *Recorded Music*[304], *Historical On-line Database Services*[305], *Video Games*[306] and *Performing Rights*[307].

[303] Cm 2386 (1993).   [304] Cm 2599 (1994).   [305] Cm 2554 (1994).   [306] Cm 2781 (1995).
[307] Cm 3147 (1996).

20

Mergers (1) – introduction

CHAPTER CONTENTS

1. Introduction
2. Terminology
3. Merger Activity
4. The Proliferation of Systems of Merger Control
5. Why Do Firms Merge?
6. What is the Purpose of Merger Control?
7. Designing a System of Merger Control

1. INTRODUCTION

This chapter briefly introduces the subject of merger control. This book so far has been concerned essentially with two issues: anti-competitive agreements and abusive conduct. Merger control is an important third component of most, though not all, systems of competition law. The EC Merger Regulation ('the ECMR') will be described in chapter 21 and the merger provisions in the UK Enterprise Act 2002 in chapter 22. Before doing so it may be useful to make some brief preliminary observations about the subject of mergers generally and about systems of merger control in particular. The issues introduced in this chapter will be discussed in more depth in the two that follow.

2. TERMINOLOGY

(A) The meaning of 'merger' and 'concentration'

A true merger involves two separate undertakings merging entirely into a new entity: a high-profile example of this was the fusion in 1996 of Ciba-Geigy and Sandoz to form the major pharmaceutical and chemical company Novartis[1]; a further example in 2000 was the creation of GlaxoSmithKline as a result of the merger of Glaxo Wellcome and

---

[1] Case M 737, decision of 17 July 1996, OJ [1997] L 201/1 these decisions are available on DG COMP's website at www.ec.europa.eu/comm/competition/mergers/cases.

SmithKline Beecham[2]. However it is important to understand that the expression 'merger' as used in competition policy includes a far broader range of corporate transactions than full mergers of this kind. Where A acquires all, or a majority of, the shares in B, this would be described as a merger if it results in A being able to control the affairs of B; even the acquisition of a minority shareholding may be sufficient, in particular circumstances, to qualify as a merger: under the ECMR the question is whether A will acquire 'the possibility of exercising decisive influence' over B[3]; under the Enterprise Act the question is whether A would at least have 'material influence' over B[4]. The acquisition of assets – for example a well-known brand name – can amount to a merger[5]. Two or more undertakings which merge part of their businesses into a newly-established joint venture company, 'Newco', may be found to be parties to a merger[6]. In each case the essential question is whether previously independent businesses have come or will come under common control with the consequence that, in the future, the market will function less competitively than it did prior to the merger. For the sake of convenience the term 'merger' will be used in this and the following chapters to encompass all these phenomena unless the context requires a different usage. When discussing the EC system an alternative expression, 'concentration', will also sometimes be used, since that is the word used in the ECMR itself.

(B) The horizontal, vertical and conglomerate effects of mergers

Competition law is concerned about the possibility that a merger will lead to the market being less competitive in the future than it currently is. The main concern of competition authorities when assessing a merger is whether it will have adverse *horizontal* effects; there may also be concerns about *vertical* and *conglomerate* effects, but these concerns are much rarer. It is possible that the same case can give rise to horizontal, vertical and conglomerate concerns[7].

(i) Horizontal effects

Horizontal effects occur where a merger takes place between actual or potential competitors in the same product and geographic markets and at the same level of the production or distribution cycle. As a general proposition the horizontal effects of mergers present a much greater danger to competition than vertical (or conglomerate) ones, in the same way that horizontal agreements are treated more strictly than vertical agreements. Horizontal mergers may be scrutinised both for their 'unilateral' or 'non-coordinated' effects and for their 'coordinated' effects[8].

---

[2] Case M 1846, decision of 8 May 2000.   [3] See ch 21, pp 824–825.   [4] See ch 22, pp 909–910.

[5] See eg Case M 890 *Blokker/Toys 'R' Us*, decision of 26 June 1997, OJ [1998] L 316/1.

[6] See in particular ch 21, pp 826–827 on the application of the ECMR to so-called 'full-function' joint ventures.

[7] See eg the European Commission's decision in Case M 2220, decision of 3 July 2001, *General Electric/Honeywell* OJ [2004] L 48/1; on appeal to the CFI the Commission's finding on horizontal effects was upheld but the findings of vertical and conglomerate effects were annulled: see Case T-210/01 *General Electric v Commission* [2005] ECR II-5575, [2006] 4 CMLR 15.

[8] See further pp 807–808 below; on horizontal effects under the ECMR see ch 21, pp 857–864; for their treatment under UK law see ch 22, pp 922–927.

(ii) Vertical effects

Vertical effects may be experienced where a merger occurs between firms that operate at different, but complementary, levels of the market for the same final product: for example A might produce a raw material (an 'upstream' product) for a product produced by B (a 'downstream' product). Often such mergers will enhance, or be neutral, in terms of economic efficiency, but there is a possibility that vertical integration may have a harmful effect on competition, either because it gives rise to a risk of the market becoming foreclosed to third parties or because it could lead to collusion between the merged entity and third parties[9].

(iii) Conglomerate effects

There have been a few occasions on which competition authorities have had concerns about mergers not on the basis of horizontal or vertical effects, but because of possible conglomerate effects: for example that a merger between A and B who are neither horizontal competitors, nor functionally related vertically, might enable the merged entity AB to use its market power in two different but related, or even unrelated, markets to foreclose competitors. Whether conglomerate mergers should be controlled at all is a matter of controversy: US law long ago abandoned any interest in the conglomerate effects of mergers[10]; however the European Commission has expressed concern about the 'portfolio' or 'range' or 'conglomerate' effects of mergers on various occasions, though its adverse findings on conglomeracy in both *Tetra Laval/Sidel*[11] and in *General Electric/Honeywell International*[12] were annulled on appeal by the CFI[13].

3. MERGER ACTIVITY

In the corporate world there are frequent bouts of 'merger mania' when the level of merger activity is very high[14]; enormous fees are earned by financial and legal (including competition law) advisers during these periods. For example there was a very high degree of merger activity in the second half of the 1980s[15], and again in the mid-1990s[16]. From 1998 to 2001 there was a period of frenetic merger activity, although this then declined

---

[9] See further pp 808–810 below; on vertical effects under the ECMR see ch 21, pp 866–867; for their treatment under UK law see ch 22, pp 927–928.

[10] See Scherer and Ross *Industrial Market Structure and Economic Performance* (Houghton Mifflin, 3rd ed, 1990), pp 188–190.

[11] Case M 2416 *Tetra Laval/Sidel*, decision of 30 October 2001, OJ [2004] L 43/13.

[12] See Case M 2220, decision of 3 July 2001, *General Electric/Honeywell* OJ [2004] L 48/1.

[13] Case T-5/02 *Tetra Laval v Commission* [2002] ECR II-4381, [2002] 5 CMLR 1182, upheld on appeal Case C-12/03 P *Commission v Tetra Laval* [2005] ECR I-987, [2005] 4 CMLR 8; Case T-209/01 *Honeywell v Commission* [2005] ECR II-5527, [2006] 4 CMLR 652; Case T-210/01 *General Electric v Commission* [2005] ECR II-5575, [2006] 4 CMLR 686; on conglomerate effects see further pp 809–810 below; on their treatment under the ECMR see ch 21, pp 867–868; for their treatment under UK law see ch 22, p 928.

[14] See Scherer and Ross *Industrial Market Structure and Economic Performance* (Houghton Mifflin, 3rd ed, 1990), pp 153–159.

[15] See eg the 1986 *Annual Report of the Director General of Fair Trading*, pp 27–28.

[16] See eg the 1995 *Annual Report of the Director General of Fair Trading*, p 13.

markedly as the global economy slowed. Another upswing commenced in 2005 and continued through to 2007, not least as private equity firms became involved in ever-larger acquisitions of well-established firms. In a speech in June 2007 Commissioner Kroes spoke of a 'tsunami' of mergers which she welcomed since it involved the cross-border restructuring of markets in many sectors from energy to banking and from air transport to telecommunications[17]. The European Commission's Table of Statistics, reproduced in chapter 21[18], shows clearly the peaks and troughs of merger notifications under the ECMR: from 335 in 2001, to just 211 in 2003, and up to 402 in 2007.

A notable feature of mergers in recent years has been their increasing complexity, size and geographical reach. Very large mergers have taken place in many sectors as companies have sought to restructure and consolidate their place in an increasingly global market. For example in the pharmaceuticals industry Pfizer and Warner-Lambert merged to become the largest pharmaceutical company in the world[19]. Major mergers have taken place in the car industry, for example between Daimler-Benz and Chrysler[20], between Ford and Volvo[21], between Renault and Nissan[22], and between General Motors and Saab[23]. In the oil industry Exxon merged with Mobil to become the largest oil company in the world[24], and BP Amoco merged with Arco[25]. Many other industries have seen a high degree of merger activity, not least the legal profession. Several times in 1999 the Financial Times announced 'the biggest deal in corporate history'. For example the merger of America Online and Time-Warner[26], announced in January 1999, enjoyed 'biggest deal' status until the VodaphoneAirTouch/Mannesmann merger was announced in February[27]; the latter case was also of interest in that it was the first successful hostile bid for a German company.

4. THE PROLIFERATION OF SYSTEMS OF MERGER CONTROL

A particularly noticeable feature of competition policy in the last fifteen years or so has been the proliferation of systems of competition law around the world. More than 100 countries now have competition law, and at least 80 of these laws include merger control[28]. The profusion of systems of merger control has a greater impact on most firms than rules against cartels and abusive behaviour, not because these firms disregard the latter but because their transactions are often subject to mandatory pre-notification under the former. This means that any sizable transaction with an international dimension – of which there are many – may have to be notified to 10, 20 or even more

---

[17] Neelie Kroes speech of 5 June 2007, available at www.ec.europa.eu/comm/competition/speeches.
[18] See ch 21, p 887.   [19] Case M 1878, decision of 22 May 2000.
[20] Case M 1204, decision of 22 July 1998.   [21] Case M 1452, decision of 26 March 1999.
[22] Case M 1519, decision of 12 May 1999.   [23] Case M 1847, decision of 28 February 2000.
[24] Case M 1383, decision of 29 September 1999, OJ [2004] L 103/1.
[25] Case M 1532, decision of 29 September 1999, OJ [2001] L 18/1, [2001] 4 CMLR 774.
[26] Case M 1845, decision of 11 October 2000, OJ [2001] L 268/28, [2002] 4 CMLR 454.
[27] Case M 1795, decision of 12 April 2000.
[28] On-line access to information about countries with competition (including merger) laws can be obtained through the *Competition Law Toolkit* of the Asian Development Bank, available at www.adb.org/Documents/Others/OGC-Toolkits/Competition-Law/default.asp.

competition authorities. Law firms advising on international transactions must be able to obtain access to all the relevant merger laws in order to determine where filings must be made[29]. Many competition lawyers in firms handling such cases will spend a substantial amount of time overseeing and coordinating a number of national filings; the initial enthusiasm of junior competition lawyers for such work often fades when it becomes apparent that the coordination of filings in Australia, Europe and the US entails an 18-hour working day or longer. It is important for lawyers to manage the expectations of clients who may not fully appreciate how long and tortuous the regulatory road may be ahead of them before the transaction is able to proceed.

The problems that multiple notification can cause to the merging firms themselves – for example the cost of multiple filing, the workload involved in generating the data necessary for each filing, the delay involved in obtaining clearances from numerous jurisdictions, the differing procedural and substantive laws from one jurisdiction to another – are obvious. One of the major issues facing the 'world' of competition law – using this term both in its physical sense and to refer to the constituency of interested parties affected by merger control consisting of competition authorities, legal and business advisers, politicians, economists and the merging firms themselves – is to devise a sensible mechanism for investigating and adjudicating upon mergers having an international dimension in a way that minimises the administrative burden on business while at the same time ensuring that mergers do not escape scrutiny which could have detrimental effects upon competition. These issues are under active consideration within various international fora, notably the International Competition Network[30]: the subject of international cooperation has been discussed in chapter 12[31], while attempts in the European Community to avoid multiple filing in the Member States by introducing the idea of the 'one-stop shop' of notifying the European Commission will be discussed in chapter 21[32].

5. WHY DO FIRMS MERGE?[33]

There are many reasons why firms merge, most of which are beneficial to, or at least not harmful to, the economy; there are others that are more problematic.

(A) Economies of scale and scope

An obvious explanation for some mergers is the achievement of economies of scale and scope[34]. A firm will produce goods at the lowest marginal cost where it is able to operate

---

[29] Some helpful sources are White and Case *2003 Survey of Worldwide Antitrust Merger Notification Requirements* which can be ordered on the Internet at www.whitecase.com; Rowley and Baker *Merger Control: International Mergers* (Sweet & Maxwell, 3rd ed, 2000); Dabbah and Lasok *Merger Control Worldwide* (Cambridge University Press, 2005); *Worldwide Competition Filing Requirements* (Howrey, 2006); *Merger Control 2008* (Global Legal Group, 2007); *The Global Merger Notification Handbook* (Cameron May, 7th ed, 2007, eds Laing, Mobley and Gomez); *Merger Control: The International Regulation of Mergers and Joint Ventures* (Global Competition Review, 2008).

[30] The ICN website is www.internationalcompetitionnetwork.org/index.html.

[31] See in particular ch 12, pp 490–495.   [32] See ch 21, pp 832–834.

[33] See further Scherer and Ross *Industrial Market Structure and Economic Performance* (Houghton Mifflin, 3rd ed, 1990), pp 159–167.

[34] These concepts are discussed in ch 1, pp 10–11.

at the minimum efficient scale. If it operates on a smaller scale than this, marginal cost will increase and there will be a consequent loss of allocative efficiency. Economies of scale may be *product-specific*, where they enable a product to be produced more cheaply; *plant-specific*, where they mean that the overall use of a multi-product plant is made more rational; or *firm-specific*, where they result in lower overall costs. The globalisation of markets in recent years, as tariff and other barriers to trade have come down and as astonishingly rapid technological changes have altered the nature and structure of markets, has given opportunities to firms to grow into larger geographical markets. It may be that a firm can achieve economies of scale by internal growth; equally, however, it may be that this can most easily be achieved by external growth, that is by merging with other firms.

Whereas economies of scale arise from carrying on more of the same activity, economies of scope are the economic benefits generated from carrying on related activities; an obvious example would be lowering overall administrative expenditure through the operation of different lines of production.

Whether mergers actually lead to the achievement of the economies of scale and scope expected of them is another matter: some commentators have argued that in practice the gains anticipated tend to prove illusory[35].

(B) Other efficiencies

Apart from economies of scale and scope a merger may lead to efficiencies in other ways. For example it may be cheaper to take over a distributor than to set up a distribution network on a contractual basis; backward integration may guarantee supplies to a firm concerned about the availability of raw materials; a merger might mean that a firm will have improved access to loan and equity capital than it had when operating alone. A merger may result in a firm that is better able to carry out research and development and with access to a greater pool of industrial technology; quite often a merger is motivated by a desire to acquire the patents and know-how of a particular firm. Another possibility is that a merged firm may be able to make better use of the management skills of its constituent parts.

(C) National champions

Firms within one nation state – or within one political grouping such as the European Union – may wish to merge in order to become a 'national champion' (or a 'European champion'). Governments may positively encourage mergers that will create larger domestic firms more capable of competing on international markets, although 'national champions' free from the disciplining effect of competition on their domestic markets may lack the skills necessary to succeed in the wider world[36].

---

[35] See Scherer and Ross *Industrial Market Structure and Economic Performance* (Houghton Mifflin, 3rd ed, 1990), pp 167–174; Meeks *Disappointing Marriage: A Study of the Gains from Merger* (Cambridge University Press, 1977); see also the speech by Monti 'Review of the EC Merger Regulation—Roadmap for the Reform Project' 4 June 2002, available at www.europa.eu.int/comm/competition/speeches, and the empirical studies referred to therein; Röller, Stennek and Verboven 'Efficiency Gains from Mergers, (The Research Institute of Industrial Economics, Working Paper 543 (2000)), available at www.ec.europa.eu/comm/competition/speeches/text/sp2005_013_en.pdf.

[36] The European Commission is resolutely opposed to the creation by Member States of 'national champions': see ch 21, p 894.

(D) Management efficiency and the market for corporate control

An explanation for some mergers is that one firm competes to run another. The threat of a successful takeover bid acts as an important influence upon the existing management of a firm to ensure that it functions as efficiently as possible. Where shareholders are satisfied with the current management's performance they will not sell their shares to another bidder, unless it is overbidding: the new regime would not be capable of generating greater profits than the existing one. If shareholders are dissatisfied, they may prefer to sell at the price offered and to reinvest the proceeds elsewhere; the result is likely to be that the old management will be replaced by the bidder. According to this argument the 'market for corporate control' is a crucial element in the promotion of economic efficiency[37]. It is particularly attractive if one agrees with the view that shareholders' influence over directors through the Annual General Meeting has been seriously diminished; at least the ability to sell to a bidder exercises some influence on the management of the company's affairs. If the threat of takeovers is considered to have this significant role, this has implications for merger policy: an interventionist approach to mergers on the part of a public authority in itself distorts the market for corporate control and thus weakens its disciplining effect on management.

(E) Exiting an industry

Mergers present firms that wish to do so with an opportunity of exiting an industry. In a free market it is important to encourage entrepreneurs to invest their money and skills in setting up new businesses and in entering new markets. Just as it is desirable to prevent the erection of barriers to entry and expansion that prevent new firms from competing on the market, so too it is necessary to avoid barriers to exit that make it difficult to leave the market. The incentive to set up a firm, invest risk capital and develop new products may be diminished if it is not possible to sell the enterprise in question as a valuable going concern. It is quite common, for example, for firms to acquire small undertakings which possess useful know-how or intellectual property rights and, from the perspective of the innovator of such technology, the freedom to sell may be an important element in the reward for the risks taken. A strict approach to mergers could have an undesirable effect if it were to make exit unduly difficult.

(F) Greed, vanity, fear and drugs

Having rehearsed some of the arguments in favour of mergers, and therefore against too strict a system of merger control, some opposing views should be mentioned. A sceptical view is that many mergers cannot be explained in the rational economic terms outlined above, but that instead they are fuelled by the speculative greed of individuals

[37] See eg Manne 'Mergers and the Market for Corporate Control' (1965) 73 Journal of Political Economy 110; Easterbrook and Fischel 'The Proper Role of a Target's Management in Responding to a Tender Offer' (1981) 94 Harvard Law Review 1161; Coffee 'Regulating the Market for Corporate Control: a Critical Assessment of the Tender Offer's Role in Corporate Governance' (1984) 84 Columbia Law Review 1145; Rock 'Antitrust and the Market for Corporate Control' (1989) 77 California Law Review 1367; Bradley 'Corporate Control: Markets and Rules' (1990) 53 MLR 170; Wright, Wong and Thompson 'The Market for Corporate Control: an Economic Perspective' in Miller (ed) *The Monopolies and Mergers Yearbook* (Blackwell Business, 1992), pp 32–42.

or companies or the personal vanity of a particularly swashbuckling senior executive; it will not take a great deal of imagination to think of certain high-profile entrepreneurs that might answer this description. Some mergers seem to be motivated by simple fear: if every other undertaking in a particular sector appears to be involved in mergers, it may be considered important not to be left behind in the process of industry consolidation. For some individuals 'deal-making' has the same stimulating effect as mood-changing drugs, altogether more exciting than the mundane task of managing a firm well. Even if one shares these sceptical explanations of why firms merge, however, it does not follow that merger control is the appropriate tool to deal with the 'problem'.

(G) Increasing market power

Of course it might be that the real reason why firms wish to merge is that this will elim-inate competition between them, increase their market power and give them the ability to restrict output and raise price. It would be very foolish in today's world of vigorous merger control for merging firms to make such a claim for their merger, although it is sometimes surprising what firms do say in press releases, intended to impress share-holders, as to the expected economic benefits of a merger: for example a claim that a merger will 'eliminate wasteful capacity' and return an industry to greater profitability is unlikely to charm a competition authority into submission; even less charming is a press release that announces that 'this merger will create the dominant world player in the market for widgets'[38]. The systems of merger control in place in the EC, the UK and elsewhere presumably inhibit the incidence of cases in which firms nakedly seek to achieve market power, but it is important to bear in mind that, in the absence of a system of merger control, firms would be able to do precisely this.

6. WHAT IS THE PURPOSE OF MERGER CONTROL?

This brings us to the central question: what is the purpose of merger control? There are many reasons why Governments, firms, shareholders, and individuals might object to mergers. A Government may object to a merger on a number of grounds: for example it might disapprove of a foreign firm taking over a native one, or of a merger that does not fit with its own industrial policy, or of a transaction that would lead to production facilities being closed down leading to unemployment. A firm might object to being the target of a hostile bid, or to a merger between two rivals that might give them a competitive edge. Shareholders (whether legal or natural persons) might be concerned that corporate transactions will have an adverse effect on the value or effectiveness of their shares. Company law is concerned with issues such as the oppression of minority shareholders, and complex regulatory systems also exist to protect shareholders gener-ally. Reference should be made to standard works on the laws and regulations that deal with these matters; in particular in the UK the City Code on Takeovers and Mergers provides an important system of protection. An individual might have qualms about foreign ownership of indigenous firms or the possibility that a takeover might lead to redundancy. These are perfectly understandable concerns, but they are not issues with

---

[38] See ch 5, p 183 on the probative value of statements made by an undertaking.

which competition policy is concerned. Competition policy and competition authorities are concerned with maintaining the process of competition in the market place, not as an end in itself, but as a way of maximising consumer welfare[39].

Some systems of merger control do allow broader 'public interest' criteria to be taken into account in the overall assessment of a merger, a matter that will be discussed below. However for the most part competition authorities are concerned with just one issue, namely the assessment of the competitive effects of mergers.

(A) Is merger control necessary?

Competition law forbids the abuse of market power: Article 82 EC is an obvious example of this. It can reasonably be asked, therefore, why there needs to be a power to prevent the creation or strengthening of market power before it occurs ('*ex ante* control') given that there are legal controls to prevent the abuse of market power when it happens ('*ex post* control'). One answer to this is that merger control is not simply about preventing future abuses: it is also about maintaining competitive market structures which lead to better outcomes for consumers[40]. Another is that Article 82 investigations (and their domestic equivalents) are lengthy, complex, and cumbersome, and that competition authorities lack the resources to police every alleged infringement; exclusive reliance on Article 82 would be unlikely to be effective. In the UK both the OFT and the Competition Commission have attempted in recent times to evaluate the gains to consumers from merger control in specific cases[41].

(B) Assessing the competitive effects of mergers

Assessing the competitive effects of mergers is far from simple. A very helpful starting point when considering this issue is the *ICN Merger Guidelines Workbook* produced by a Subgroup of the International Competition Network ('the Workbook')[42]. This was produced as a tool for countries that are new to or in the early years of merger control; however it is commended to anyone interested in the subject. In particular the Workbook contains a series of eight 'Worksheets' on key matters that are of importance when conducting a substantive assessment of mergers, for example market definition, market structure and concentration, unilateral and coordinated effects, and market entry and expansion; these Worksheets set out the economic principles that are relevant to each subject and provide illustrative case studies. Some of the issues dealt with in the Worksheets, such as market definition and market structure, are relevant to all competition analysis, and have been discussed in chapter 1 of this book. Others, such as unilateral and coordinated effects, are specific to merger control and are considered further below.

---

[39] See ch 1, pp 19 ff.

[40] On this point see Case T-102/96 *Gencor v Commission* [1999] ECR II-753, [1999] 4 CMLR 971, para 106.

[41] See ch 22, p 951; see further Nelson and Sun Su 'Consumer Savings from Merger Enforcement: A Review of the Antitrust Agencies' Estimates' (2002) 69 Antitrust Law Journal 921.

[42] The Workbook is available at www.internationalcompetitionnetwork.org; see also OECD *Substantive Criteria used for Assessment of Mergers* 2003.

Three particular features of merger control that make the analysis of cases complex merit consideration. First, the substantive assessment of a merger is necessarily forward-looking: a competition authority is called upon to consider whether a merger will lead to harmful effects on competition in the future[43]. Most mergers must be notified to the competition authority and cleared before they are put into effect, in which case the substantive analysis is entirely forward-looking. Even in those few jurisdictions, such as the UK and Australia, where a merger can be implemented prior to approval by the competition authority, because there is no duty to pre-notify[44], the assessment is still essentially about predicting the future effects of the merger on the market. The predictive nature of merger control is different from the assessment of agreements and conduct under Articles 81 and 82 EC and the Competition Act 1998, where the competition authority will usually be investigating behaviour that has already taken place and trying to verify, for example, whether and when the members of an alleged cartel met or whether the pricing practices of a dominant firm amounted to a margin squeeze.

The fact that merger control is about predicting future behaviour means, necessarily, that it must be in part theoretical: a competition authority that decides to challenge a merger must have a *theory of competitive harm* as to why the market will work less well for consumers in the future than it does at the moment. However it would not be acceptable for the authority to be able to proceed against a merger simply on the basis of theory. There is nothing unlawful about merger activity, and the market for corporate control, in which firms compete for the right to acquire and manage businesses, is an important feature of a free-market economy. Intervention on the part of public authorities should not be permissible on the basis of mere speculation. It follows that the competition authority should be required to produce *evidence* that supports its theory of competitive harm. Furthermore the competition authority should also have to demonstrate that the market, after the merger has been consummated, will work less well than if there had been no merger: in other words the authority will need not only to predict the likely outcome of the merger, but also to consider the *counterfactual*, that is to say the position if the merger were not to occur.

(i) Theories of competitive harm

Most mergers cause no harm to competition. However there may be cases where it can be predicted that the changed structure of the market will provide the merged entity with the incentive and the ability to exercise market power in a way that will be harmful to consumer welfare. A competition authority concerned about a particular merger will need to articulate its theory as to how competition will be harmed. Various theories of competitive harm have been developed.

(A) Unilateral or non-coordinated effects[45] Unilateral effects occur where A merges with B and the merged entity, AB, will be able, as a result of the merger, to exercise market

---

[43] See Case C-12/03 P *Commission v Tetra Laval BV* [2005] ECR I-987, [2005] 4 CMLR 8, at para 42: 'A prospective analysis of the kind necessary in merger control must be carried out with great care since it does not entail the examination of past events...or of current events, but rather a prediction of events which are more or less likely to occur in future if a decision prohibiting the planned concentration or laying down the conditions for it is not adopted.'

[44] On the voluntary nature of pre-notification in UK law see ch 22, pp 912–914.

[45] See the *Workbook*, Worksheet C; unilateral effects are sometimes referred to as non-coordinated effects, in order to differentiate them from the coordinated effects discussed in the next section.

power. The most obvious manifestation of the exercise of market power is the ability to increase price, but there are other possibilities: for example a reduction of output, quality, variety, or innovation. It is helpful to think of the expression 'price increase' as shorthand which includes all these different manifestations of the exercise of market power. The ability to exercise market power is particularly likely if, prior to the merger, an increase in price on the part of A would have been likely to cause a substantial number of customers to divert their purchases to B: post-merger AB would not lose any profits as a result of such a shift, since AB would benefit from the increased sales of B's products.

It may even be that, after the merger, C, a competitor of AB, will also be able to exercise market power because, if AB was to raise its prices, some customers would divert to C, which in turn could raise its own prices. C may be able to do this without coordinating its behaviour with that of AB, in which case C's behaviour can itself be characterised as unilateral or non-coordinated. This is the phenomenon sometimes known as 'non-collusive oligopoly'[46].

(B) Coordinated effects[47]   Coordinated effects occur where A merges with B and this results in a situation where AB will be able, or more able than when A and B were independent, to coordinate their competitive behaviour on the market with other firms, for example with C and D, and thereby exercise collective market power. As the Workbook suggests, three conditions must be met for coordination to be successful[48]. First it must be possible for AB, C and D to coordinate their behaviour in some way, for example by charging the same prices or, perhaps, by aligning their behaviour on output and capacity expansion. Second, it must be costly for those firms to deviate from coordination, for example because 'cheats' will be punished. Third, AB, C and D must be free from competitive constraint from other participants in the market, for example E and F.

(C) Vertical effects[49]   As a general proposition it is unlikely that a merger will produce adverse vertical effects. Indeed a merger between an upstream firm, A, with a downstream firm, B, is likely to be neutral in terms of economic efficiency or even highly beneficial. For example if A and B are independent each will need to earn a margin on its operation – perhaps A as a producer and B as a distributor. The merged AB will need to earn only one margin: the elimination of 'double marginalisation' may lead to lower costs, and therefore to lower prices for the customers of AB. However there may be circumstances in which a vertical merger could produce adverse effects, first, where the possibility of foreclosure of a third party arises and second, where the vertical integration of AB makes it more likely that there will be coordinated effects on the market.

An example of foreclosure could arise where A, a firm in an upstream market, acquires access through a merger with B, a firm in a downstream market, to an important downstream product, for example a distribution system such as a gas pipeline that is difficult to duplicate. The merged entity AB may have the incentive to deny competitors in the upstream market access to the distribution system, thereby foreclosing them from the downstream market. Similarly where B, a firm in a downstream market,

---

[46] On the treatment of non-collusive oligopoly under the ECMR see ch 21, pp 853–856 and under UK law see ch 22, p 923; an example of such a case in the US is *FTC v HJ Heinz Company Company and Milnot Corpn* 246 F 3d 708 (DC Circuit 2001).

[47] See the *Workbook*, Worksheet D.   [48] Ibid, para D.6.   [49] See the *Workbook*, Worksheet H.

merges with A, a firm that has substantial market power in relation to an important raw material or input in an upstream market, the merged entity AB may have the incentive to deny competitors in the downstream market access to that input. The concern here is that competitors in the downstream market will be unable to obtain supplies of the raw material or input, or that they will be able to do so only on discriminatory terms, with the result that they will be unable to compete effectively. These two examples of foreclosure can be depicted diagrammatically as follows, where the diagonal lines represent the foreclosure effect that arises from the merger of A and B:

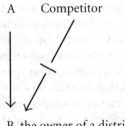

B, the owner of a distribution
system that is hard to duplicate

Fig. 20.1 Foreclosure of access to a downstream distribution system

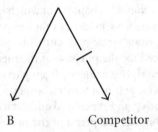

Fig. 20.2 Foreclosure of access to an important input

A merger of vertically-related firms might also increase the possibility of the merged entity, AB, being able to coordinate its behaviour with other competitors if, for example, it will lead to increased price transparency or if it will make it easier to detect firms that deviate from the coordinated behaviour.

In considering whether a merger could give rise to adverse vertical effects a competition authority should not only consider whether the merged entity would have the ability and the incentive to exercise market power; it should also consider carefully whether this would lead to harm to consumers, taking into account in particular the possibility that the merger may give rise to significant economic efficiencies that might be passed on them in lower prices.

(D) Conglomerate effects[50] As a general proposition conglomerate mergers are unlikely to give rise to adverse competitive effects. They do not involve the removal of actual

---

[50] See the *Workbook*, Worksheet H; see also OECD *Portfolio Effects in Conglomerate Mergers* 2002.

or potential competitors from the market as in the case of horizontal mergers; nor do they bring together firms that have a vertical relationship in relation to the same final product, where there may be incentives to foreclose competitors from the upstream or downstream market. Furthermore, as in the case of vertical mergers, conglomerate mergers often result in efficiency gains, for example where the merged entity AB is able to offer complementary products that do not compete with one another to a customer desiring both: if A produces widgets and B blodgets, a 'one-stop shop' may be highly beneficial to a customer that requires both products. The theory of harm in the case of conglomerate effects is particularly speculative – for example that AB might decide to 'tie' the two complementary products together in a way that will foreclose competitors, or to price a bundled package of both of them to similar effect. It is possible that tie-in transactions and bundling practices would violate laws that forbid the abuse of a dominant position or, in the case of US law, monopolization, although the law on this subject is controversial in itself[51]. It is even more controversial that a merger should be prohibited on this ground, and the US authorities do not normally challenge mergers on this basis. Intervention on conglomerate grounds is a possibility in EC and UK law, but would require very convincing evidence in support of the theory of harm[52].

(ii) Evidence

Having identified a theory (or theories) of competitive harm, a competition authority must then search for evidence in support of that theory: its case must be based on empirical facts. The International Competition Network produced, in 2005, a helpful *Investigative Techniques Handbook*[53], chapter 3 of which identifies five types of evidence that may be of use in merger reviews: evidence that was produced before the merger was contemplated, such as corporate strategy documents, planning documents, and sales reports; documents produced for the purpose of the merger, such as surveys, reports, and economic analyses; descriptive evidence from participants in the market, such as customers, suppliers, and competitors; written responses to requests for information from the competition authority; and expert and quantitative evidence, for example from industry experts and economists. Chapter 4 of the *Investigative Techniques Handbook* discusses various types of quantitative analyses, such as the measurement of critical loss[54] and price correlations, that may be helpful when predicting whether a merger might lead to anti-competitive effects. The Worksheets already referred to in the ICN's *Merger Guidelines Workbook* also provide summaries of evidence of value when assessing, for example, whether a merger might lead to adverse unilateral[55] or coordinated[56] effects.

An emerging development, in unilateral effects cases, is the use of so-called 'merger simulation models' which attempt to predict, using a set of quantitative techniques, the effect that a merger will have on the post-merger level of prices[57]. If such an exercise

---

[51] See ch 17, pp 679–687 and ch 18, pp 727–729.

[52] On the position under the ECMR see ch 21, pp 867–868 and under UK law see ch 22, p 928.

[53] The Workbook is available at www.internationalcompetitionnetwork.org.

[54] See also Langenfeld and Li 'Critical loss analysis in evaluating mergers' (2001) 46 Antitrust Bulletin 299.

[55] See *Worksheet C – Unilateral Effects*, para C.10.

[56] See *Worksheet D – Coordinated Effects*, paras D.9–D.16.

[57] A well-known case in the US in which merger simulation was used is the *Staples/Office Depot* case, *FTC v Staples Inc* 970 F Supp 1066, District of Columbia.

could produce entirely reliable evidence the traditional analysis of defining the relevant market, assessing market power and then considering unilateral effects could be considerably abbreviated, perhaps with no need for market definition at all. However the science of merger simulation is not yet sufficiently robust for this, and the technique, at most, can form only part of the overall body of evidence in a particular case[58].

The ECJ has made clear that, where a merger is challenged on conglomerate grounds, the evidence on which the Commission relies must be particularly convincing, given that the chains of cause and effect between the merger and the predicted adverse effects 'are dimly discernible, uncertain and difficult to establish'[59].

An important issue in relation to evidence is to decide what standard of proof a competition authority should have to attain before it can take action to block a merger: should it have to prove its case that a merger would be harmful to competition 'on the balance of probabilities', or should it have to go further and show 'beyond reasonable doubt' that the merger would have detrimental effects? If a competition authority can intervene too easily, on the basis of thin evidence, the possibility exists that 'Type II errors' might arise: that is to say that some innocuous mergers might be blocked; however, if the criteria for intervention are too demanding, or if the standard of proof is set at a very high level, 'Type I errors' might occur: some harmful mergers might be cleared[60]. Being realistic, it is inevitable that some errors of both kinds will be made by competition authorities: it is a matter of public policy to decide which of the two types of error is the more troubling.

(iii) The counterfactual

Merger assessment involves predicting the effect on competition in the market if a particular transaction is consummated. This necessarily involves a comparison between the situation if the merger goes ahead and the position if it did not happen: the competitive situation without the merger is often referred to as the counterfactual[61]. The counterfactual will usually be the prevailing conditions before the merger, although there may be cases in which it is necessary to take into account conditions as they would be in the near future if, for example, it is known that other firms are about to enter or exit the market or to expand capacity; another example would be that one of the merging firms was on the point of failing, so that it would not be present on the market in the future anyway. The Competition Commission in the UK explicitly states the counterfactual in each of its merger enquiry reports[62].

[58] On merger simulation see Werden and Froeb 'Simulation as an Alternative to Structural Policy in Differentiated Products Industries' in *The Economics of the Antitrust Process* (eds Coate and Kleit, Kluwer, 1996); Epstein and Rubinfeld 'Merger Simulation: A Simplified Approach with New Applications' (2002) 69 Antitrust Law Journal 883; Werden, Froeb and Scheffman 'A Daulbert Discipline for Merger Simulation' February 2004, available at www.ftc.gov/be/daubertdiscipline.pdf; Walker 'The Potential for Significant Inaccuracies in Merger Simulation Models' (2005) 1 Journal of Competition Law and Economics 473.
[59] Case C-12/03 P *Commission v Tetra Laval BV* [2005] ECR I-987, [2005] 4 CMLR 8, para 44.
[60] On Type I and Type II errors see Black *Oxford Dictionary of Economics* (Oxford University Press, 3rd ed, 2003) and ch 5, pp 190–191.
[61] See the Workbook, paras 2.9 and 2.10.
[62] See eg *Deutsche Börse AG, Euronext NV and London Stock Exchange plc*, paras 5.125–5.130, available at www.competition-commission.org.uk/rep_pub/reports/2005.

(C) The substantive test: SLC, dominance, SIEC

Any system of merger control must set a substantive test against which to determine whether a particular merger should be modified or prohibited. When the ECMR was in the process of being reformed in the years leading up to 2004 there was an interesting and important debate as to the most appropriate formulation[63]. Many systems, such as the US and the UK, permit the prohibition of a merger which will 'substantially lessen competition'[64]; the original Merger Regulation of 1989 required intervention where a merger would 'create or strengthen a dominant position as a result of which effective competition would be significantly impeded'[65]. Many Member States of the EC use the same formulation; some, for example France and Greece, have both substantial lessening of competition and dominance tests. The test in the ECMR was changed in 2004: the question now to be asked is whether the merger would 'significantly impede effective competition', in particular (but not exclusively) as a result of the creation or strengthening of a dominant position[66].

(D) Guidelines

There are abundant guidelines on the substantive assessment of mergers. Reference has already been made to the ICN's *Merger Guidelines Workbook* and *Investigative Techniques Handbook*[67]. Many competition authorities have also published guidelines on substantive assessment. Of particular importance are the 1992 *Horizontal Merger Guidelines* in the US[68] and the guidelines published in the UK by the Office of Fair Trading[69] and the Competition Commission[70]. The European Commission has published *Guidelines on the assessment of horizontal mergers*[71] and *Guidelines on the assessment of non-horizontal mergers*[72]. A specific problem in systems of merger control is whether a merger which reduces competition but which would lead to gains in efficiency should be permitted: the US Guidelines address this issue specifically in paragraph 4 and do, in very limited circumstances, recognise efficiency arguments[73]. In the UK section 30 of the Enterprise

---

[63] See eg OECD Roundtable 'Substantive Criteria used for the Assessment of Mergers' 11 February 2003, available at www.oecd.org; the European Commission's *Green Paper on the Review of Council Regulation (EEC) No 4064/89* COM (2001) 745/6 final, paras 159–169.

[64] See, eg, s 7 Clayton Act 1914 in the US; s 50 Trade Practices Act 1974 in Australia; s 92 Competition Act 1985 in Canada; s 12A Competition Act 1998 in South Africa.

[65] ECMR, Article 2(2) and 2(3).   [66] For further discussion of this issue see ch 21, pp 851–856.

[67] The ICN has also published 'Recommended Practices' on matters such as remedies, notifications and merger procedures; these are all available at www.internationalcompetitionnetwork.org.

[68] These are available at www.usdoj.gov/atr/public/guidelines/guidelin.htm; some information about the Australian Competition and Consumer Commission's Guidelines can be found at www.accc.gov.au.

[69] *Mergers: Substantive assessment guidance*, OFT 516, May 2003 available at www.oft.gov.uk.

[70] *Merger References: Competition Commission Guidelines*, CC 2, June 2003, available at www.competition-commission.org.uk.

[71] OJ [2004] C 31/5.   [72] Available at www.ec.europa.eu/comm/competition/mergers.

[73] The complexity of allowing efficiencies as a defence in a merger case is vividly illustrated by the *Superior Propane* case in Canada: see *The Commissioner of Competition v Superior Propane Inc* [2003] 3 FC 529, judgment of 31 January 2003 (Federal Court of Appeal), available at www.fca-caf.gc.ca/index_e.shtml; see also the European Commission's *Competition Policy Newsletter*, Summer 2003, pp 43–49; Williamson 'Economies as an Antitrust Defense: The Welfare Trade-off' (1968) 58 American Economic Review 158; Kolasky and Dick 'The Merger Guidelines and the Integration of Efficiencies into Antitrust Review of Horizontal Mergers' (2003) 71 Antitrust Law Journal 207.

Act 2002 allows the OFT and the Competition Commission to take into account 'relevant customer benefits' in certain circumstances[74]; while the European Commission's *Horizontal Guidelines* take efficiencies into account within the overall assessment of a merger[75]. Another issue that sometimes arises is whether a merger should be allowed in order to save a 'failing firm', even though there will be less competition in the market after the merger than before. A failing firm defence does exist in US law[76], has been applied under the ECMR[77], and is recognised in an appropriate case under the guidelines of the UK competition authorities[78].

(E) Remedies

It is quite often the case that most aspects of a particular merger give rise to no competition concerns. However it may be, for example, that there are certain parts of the businesses of A and B that overlap horizontally, in which case a competition authority, rather than prohibiting the entire transaction, may look for a remedy whereby its competition concern is assuaged and the rest of the deal is allowed to proceed. The most obvious remedy is the divestiture of one or other of the overlapping businesses so that there will be no accretion of market power. Some cases may require more complex remedies, for example a right of access to an essential facility or the licensing of technology to competitors on reasonable and non-discriminatory terms. Devising and implementing satisfactory remedies is often a complex matter. The OECD published *Merger Remedies* in 2004 following roundtable discussions in which a number of recommendations as to best practice were made[79]. In 2005 the ICN published a *Merger Remedies Review Project*[80] that provides a practical guide as to the key principles and range of tools available in the establishment of suitable remedies. In 2005 the European Commission published a *Merger Remedies Study*[81] in which it reviewed the effectiveness of 96 remedies accepted in 40 cases in the five-year period from 1996 to 2000. This *Study* had an important bearing on the Commission's draft of a revised *Notice on remedies acceptable under the ECMR*[82] of 2007. In the UK the OFT and the CC have given careful attention to remedies when deciding cases under the Enterprise Act 2002[83].

(F) Merger control and the public interest[84]

As noted at the start of this chapter, numerous arguments may be made against mergers that have nothing to do with the maintenance of competitive markets. It would be

---

[74] See ch 22, p 926; note in particular *Merger References: Competition Commission Guidelines*, CC 2, June 2003, paras 4.34–4.45 and *Mergers: Substantive assessment guidance*, OFT 516, May 2003, paras 4.29–4.35.

[75] See the *Horizontal Guidelines*, paras 76–88; see further ch 21, pp 863–864.

[76] See the *Horizontal Merger Guidelines*, paras 5.0–5.2.

[77] See ch 21, p 864 and the Commission's *Horizontal Guidelines*, paras 76–88.

[78] *Merger References: Competition Commission Guidelines*, CC 2, June 2003, paras 3.61–3.63 and *Mergers: Substantive assessment guidance*, OFT 516, May 2003, paras 4.36–4.39; see ch 22, p 927.

[79] Available at www.oecd.org.   [80] Available at www.internationalcompetitionnetwork.org.

[81] Available at www.ec.europa.eu/comm/competition.

[82] See ch 21, pp 872–877.   [83] See ch 22, pp 916–917 and pp 932–936.

[84] For useful discussion of mergers and the public interest see Chiplin and Wright *The Logic of Mergers* (Hobart Paper 107, 1987); Fairburn and Kay (eds) *Mergers and Mergers Policy* (Oxford University Press, 1989); *Merger & Competition Policy in the European Community* (Blackwell 1990, ed Jacquemain); Neven, Nuttall and Seabright *Mergers in Daylight: The Economics and Politics of European Merger Control* (CEPR, 1993);

possible to devise a system of merger control that allows intervention for non-competition reasons; in so far as it does so the law in question can hardly be called 'competition' law; indeed prohibiting mergers on social grounds or for reasons of industrial policy may be directly antagonistic to the process of competition. Some of the arguments sometimes heard are listed below.

(i) Loss of efficiency and 'short-termism'

Some commentators would argue that mergers, far from promoting economic efficiency, have a disruptive effect upon the management of one or both of the merged firms and may be detrimental to their long-term prospects. This claim is made in particular of contested takeover bids, where it is possible that the management of the target company will either be removed by the new shareholders or will resign rather than stay on in the new conditions. Sceptics of the way in which the market for corporate control functions would argue that it is not inevitable that the decisions of shareholders will produce the best result in the public interest, although it may yield the best financial deal for the shareholders themselves. In particular many would argue that a problem with takeovers is that they are motivated more by short-term profit-taking on the stock exchange than by serious analysis of the long-term prospects of companies. This may be particularly true of institutional investors in the market which are in the habit of regularly turning over their investments in pursuit of short-term gains.

(ii) Concentration of wealth

Mergers may be objected to on the ground that they lead to firms of such size and with such power as to be antithetical to a balanced distribution of wealth. This of course is a socio-political argument, but one which has become more widely accepted as aggregate industrial concentration has increased. In the US the anti-merger laws were strengthened at a time when this problem was a dominant concern[85].

(iii) Unemployment and regional policy

Another objection to mergers is that they may lead to the closure of factories and result in serious unemployment. Mergers that savour of 'asset-stripping' and which appear to have no regard for the social problems that may follow attract particular opprobrium from sceptics of the free market. Opposition to acquisitions by private equity funds in the course of 2007 was partly inspired by this concern. Similarly the market operating in its unfettered form may not attach much weight to the desirability of maintaining a balanced distribution of wealth and job opportunities; the market has no reason to be sentimental about such matters. Governments can choose to adopt a regional policy, however, and it is possible to give expression to this issue in mergers policy as well as in laws on tax, planning and state aids.

Lewis 'The Political Economy of Antitrust' [2001] Fordham Corporate Law Institute, p 617 *et seq*; Bishop and Walker *The Economics of EC Competition Law* (Sweet & Maxwell, 3rd ed, 2007), ch 6; speech by Lewis at the sixth Annual ICN Conference in Moscow, 2006 available at www.internationalcompetitionnetwork. org/index.php/en/library/conference/6.

[85] See eg *Brown Shoe Co v United States* 370 US 294, 344 (1962).

(iv) Overseas control

Mergers may result in the control of indigenous firms passing to overseas companies, in which case any economic advantages of the merger may be thought to be outweighed by the desirability of maintaining the decision-making process and profits at home. Strong opposition was expressed in the US in 2006 when the possibility of sea-ports there coming under the control of Dubai Ports became known. Many UK firms have expanded abroad, in particular into the US, and this makes it somewhat difficult to argue that UK firms should themselves be shielded from hostile foreign takeover bids. However the case for intervention may be more compelling where there is a lack of reciprocity[86] between the laws of the two countries: if the law of country A *prevents* inward investment, whereas country B permits it, there may be a case for blocking a takeover by a firm from A of a firm in B.

(v) Special sectors

Some sectors of the economy – for example the electronic and print media – are especially sensitive and this may mean that concentration of ownership within them requires special consideration. In the UK, as in several other countries, media mergers are subject to special provisions[87] and mergers in industries such as oil, banking and defence may be particularly closely scrutinised; the UK also has a special regime for mergers in the water industry[88] and the Broadcasting Act 1990 contains special provisions on change of control[89]. Article 21(4) of the ECMR specifically recognises that Member States may have a 'legitimate interest' in investigating a merger other than on grounds of harm to competition[90].

7. DESIGNING A SYSTEM OF MERGER CONTROL

Where a country decides, as a matter of policy, to adopt a system of merger control, a number of issues have to be addressed. In chapters 21 and 22 the EC and UK systems will be described; most cases would probably result in the same outcome, irrespective of which of these two laws is applied: the dominant consideration in each jurisdiction is the impact of a merger on competition, and the analysis will be conducted in much the same way in each of them. Despite this, however, it will be seen that the provisions themselves – for example on jurisdiction, notification and substantive analysis – are actually quite different.

The following are some of the issues that must be confronted in designing a system of merger control:

- Which transactions should be characterised as mergers? How should the acquisition of minority shareholdings and of assets be dealt with? Will joint ventures be considered as a matter of merger control or under the legal provisions that prohibit cartels?

---

[86] Or, to put the matter more colloquially, where the 'playing fields' are not even.
[87] See ch 22, pp 951–953.   [88] See ch 22, pp 954–955.   [89] Broadcasting Act 1990, ss 192–194.
[90] See ch 21, pp 839–843.

- How should the jurisdictional test be framed for determining those mergers that can be investigated? Should the test be based on turnover, the value of assets acquired, market share or some other criterion?

- To what extent should a system of merger control apply to transactions consummated outside a country but which have effects within it?

- Should mergers be subject to a system of mandatory pre-notification, or should it be a matter for the parties to decide whether to notify? In the latter case, in what circumstances and for how long after a merger has been completed should a competition authority be allowed to review a case?

- What should be the time period within which a merger investigation must be completed?

- What should be the substantive test for reviewing mergers? Should it be based solely on competition criteria, or should any or all of the other issues discussed above (for example unemployment, regional policy and overseas control) also be taken into account?

- How should the specific issues of (a) efficiency and (b) failing firms be dealt with?

- What mechanism should be put in place for the negotiation of remedies that would overcome any problems identified by the competition authority?

- Who should make decisions in merger cases? A Commission, in which case who should appoint the Commissioners? A court? A Minister in the Government?

- What checks and balances should there be to guarantee due process within merger control? What system of judicial review or appeals should be put in place to test the findings of the decision-maker in merger cases? How quickly will any judicial review or appeal be completed?

These are just some of the many interesting and important issues that arise in relation to the control of mergers. With these preliminary observations in mind, this book will now describe the systems in force in the EC and UK.

21

Mergers (2) – EC law[1]

CHAPTER CONTENTS

1. INTRODUCTION

The EC rules on the control of mergers or, to use an alternative term often used in the parlance of EC law, 'concentrations', are contained in the EC Merger Regulation, Regulation 139/2004[2] ('the ECMR'). The terms 'merger' and 'concentration' are used interchangeably throughout this chapter. The ECMR has been applicable since 1 May 2004; prior to that date Regulation 4064/89[3] had been in effect since 21 September 1990. Regulation 139/2004 amended the rules of merger control in a number of respects, in

---

[1] For further reading on the EC Merger Regulation readers are referred to Levy *European Merger Control Law: A Guide to the Merger Regulation* (LexisNexis, 2003); Cook and Kerse *EC Merger Control* (Sweet & Maxwell, 4th ed, 2005); Navarro, Font, Folguera and Briones *Merger Control in the EU* (Oxford University Press, 2nd ed, 2005); Lindsay *The EC Merger Regulation: Substantive Issues* (Sweet & Maxwell, 2003); Faull and Nikpay *The EC Law of Competition* (2nd ed, 2007), ch 5; Bellamy and Child *European Community Law of Competition* (eds Roth and Rose, Oxford University Press, 6th ed, 2008), ch 8; as to mergers under the EEA Agreement see ch 2, pp 57–58 and Broberg *The European Commission's Jurisdiction to Scrutinise Mergers* (Kluwer International, 3rd ed, 2006), ch 7.

[2] OJ [2004] L 24/1, available at www.ec.europa.eu/comm/competition/mergers/legislation/regulations. html#merger_reg.

[3] OJ [1989] L 395/1, available at www.ec.europa.eu/comm/competition/mergers/legislation/archive. htm; Regulation 4064/89 was repealed by Article 25 of Regulation 139/2004. Note that the EC Treaty does not contain any specific provisions on merger control, and that the legal basis for the ECMR is Article 83 and Article 308 EC. Mergers in the coal and steel sectors that would once have been investigated under Article 66(7) of the ECSC Treaty are now dealt with under the ECMR.

particular by making the allocation of jurisdiction as between Member States and the European Commission more flexible and by amending the substantive test for the analysis of mergers. Attention will be drawn to key changes to the EC system of merger control effected by Regulation 139/2004 in the text that follows. Section 2 of this chapter provides an overview of EC merger control. Section 3 sets out the jurisdictional rules which determine whether a particular merger should be investigated by the European Commission in Brussels or by the national competition authorities ('the NCAs') of the Member States. Section 4 deals with a number of procedural matters such as the mandatory pre-notification to the Commission of mergers that have a Community dimension and the procedural timetable within which the Commission must operate. Section 5 discusses the substantive analysis of mergers under the ECMR and section 6 explains the procedure whereby the Commission may authorise a merger on the basis of commitments, often referred to as remedies, offered by the parties to address its competition concerns. The chapter then contains sections on the Commission's powers of investigation and enforcement, on judicial review of Commission decisions by the Community courts and on international cooperation, both within the Community and with the competition authorities in third countries. Section 10 considers how the merger control provisions work in practice.

2. OVERVIEW OF EC MERGER CONTROL

(A) Brief description of the EC system of merger control

The Commission first proposed that a regulation for the control of mergers should be adopted as early as 1973[4]. The issue was controversial as opinions differed substantially between Member States on the extent to which mergers should be controlled at the Community level as opposed to domestically. It was not until 21 December 1989 that the Council of Ministers finally adopted Regulation 4064/1989; it entered into force on 21 September 1990. Regulation 4064/1989 was amended quite significantly by Regulation 1310/97[5], and was repealed and replaced by the current ECMR in 2004[6].

In essence the EC system of merger control is as follows. Mergers that have a Community dimension must be pre-notified to the Commission; it is an offence to consummate a merger without a prior clearance from the Commission (there are some minor exceptions to this proposition). Whether or not a merger has a Community dimension is determined by reference to the turnover of the undertakings concerned in a transaction. Where a merger has a Community dimension the Commission has sole jurisdiction in relation to it: this is the principle of 'one-stop merger control'. However there are some circumstances in which the Commission might allow jurisdiction (wholly or in part) over a merger having a Community dimension to be ceded to a

---

[4] *Commission Proposal for a Regulation of the Council of Ministers on the Control of Concentrations between Undertakings* OJ [1973] C 92/1; for successive drafts see OJ [1982] C 36/3; OJ [1984] C 51/8; OJ [1986] C 324/5; OJ [1988] C 130/4.

[5] OJ [1997] L 180/1, available at www.ec.europa.eu/comm/competition/mergers/legislation/archive.htm.

[6] For discussion of the changes introduced by Regulation 139/2004 see González Diaz 'The Reform of European Merger Control: *Quid Novi Sub Sole?*' (2004) 27(2) World Competition 177.

Member State; and in certain situations it is obliged to do this. There are also some circumstances in which Member States may transfer jurisdiction to the Commission over mergers that do not have a Community dimension. Once the Commission has jurisdiction it is required, within fixed time limits, to determine whether a merger could significantly impede effective competition in the common market or a substantial part of it; in conducting this assessment the Commission asks, in particular, whether the merger could create or strengthen a dominant position. Most cases are completed within 25 working days of the notification, known as a Phase I investigation. In approximately 5 per cent of cases the Commission finds that, at the end of its Phase I investigation, it has serious doubts as to the compatibility of the merger with the common market and so it proceeds to an in-depth Phase II investigation; this may take an additional 90 working days, and there are provisions for this period to be extended for up to an additional 35 working days.

The Commission has wide-ranging powers under the ECMR, including the power to prohibit a merger in its entirety. This is rare – there have been only 20 prohibitions in the entire lifetime of EC merger control, four of which were overturned by the CFI on appeal[7]. However there have been numerous occasions on which the Commission has authorised a merger only after the parties had offered commitments to remedy the competition concerns of the Commission: this has happened in roughly 6.5 per cent of cases. When the parties offer commitments in this way they become legally binding upon them[8]. The Commission works closely both with the NCAs of the Member States and with competition authorities in other jurisdictions – for example the US, Canada, and Japan – when exercising its powers under the ECMR[9].

(B) Institutional arrangements

The full College of Commissioners takes the most important decisions under the ECMR, for example to prohibit a merger or to clear it subject to commitments at the end of a Phase II investigation. The fact that the full Commission is sometimes involved in decisions of considerable economic and political importance means that there may be a degree of lobbying of individual Commissioners, not just of the Commissioner for competition.

Some powers are delegated by the Commission to the Commissioner for competition. For example decisions at the end of a Phase I investigation can be taken by the Commissioner for competition, who in turn may delegate certain functions to the Director General of the Directorate General for Competition ('DG COMP'). Within DG COMP there is a Deputy Director General with special responsibility for mergers and antitrust. Unit 2 of Directorate A of DG COMP deals with policy and scrutiny in relation to mergers and antitrust. Case-work is handled by merger units within Directorates B to F, each of which has specific sectoral responsibilities[10]. DG COMP has a Chief Competition Economist who reports directly to the Director General to provide independent economic advice on cases and policy[11]. The Commission also has

---

[7] See pp 892–895 below.
[8] On commitments, or 'remedies' as they are often referred to, see pp 872–877 below.
[9] See pp 885–886 below.
[10] See ch 2, p 54.
[11] On the Chief Competition Economist see further www.ec.europa.eu/dgs/competition/cce_en.htm.

two Hearing Officers with a range of functions including overseeing the fairness of the Commission's proceedings and arranging and conducting oral hearings[12].

The Advisory Committee on Concentrations[13] has an important role in EC merger control: it provides the Member States with the opportunity of input into the decision-making process. Appeals against decisions of the Commission are taken to the CFI[14]. Provision has been made for appeals to the CFI in merger cases to be handled under the so-called 'expedited procedure' where appropriate[15].

(C) The Implementing Regulation and the Commission's Notices and Guidelines

In addition to the ECMR anyone interested in EC merger control will require a number of other texts, in particular the so-called Implementing Regulation and a series of Commission Notices and Guidelines, including the Guidelines on Best Practices. The CFI has stated that the Commission is bound by the notices it issues in the area of the supervision of mergers, provided that they do not depart from the rules in the Treaty or from the ECMR[16]. All of the materials set out below can be accessed on DG COMP's website[17].

(i) The Implementing Regulation

Commission Regulation 802/2004 (which replaced earlier legislation) contains rules on notifications to the Commission, time limits, the right to be heard and hearings, access to the file and the treatment of confidential information and remedies[18]. Regulation 802/2004 will be amended by the Commission[19] in order to provide the format for Form RM, a form that will have to be used when undertakings offer commitments to the Commission in order to remedy competition concerns that it may have identified[20].

(ii) Commission Notices and Guidelines

The Commission has published numerous Notices and Guidelines on matters both of procedural and substantive concern, each of which will be referred to where appropriate in the text that follows:

- *Commission Notice on the definition of the relevant market*[21]
- *Guidelines on the assessment of horizontal mergers*[22]
- *Commission Notice on a simplified procedure for treatment of certain concentrations*[23]
- *Commission Notice on restrictions directly related and necessary to concentrations*[24]

---

[12] On the Hearing Officers see further www.ec.europa.eu/comm/competition/hearing_officers/index_en.html.

[13] See pp 885–886 below.

[14] Prior to the Nice Treaty applications by a Member State were made to the ECJ, as in Case C-68/94 *France v Commission* [1998] ECR I-1375, [1998] 4 CMLR 829.

[15] On judicial review under the ECMR and the expedited procedure see pp 879–885 below.

[16] See Case T-282/06 *Sun Chemical Group BV and others v Commission* [2007] ECR II-000, [2007] 5 CMLR 438, para 55 and the judgments referred to therein.

[17] See www.ec.europa.eu/comm/competition/index_en.html.   [18] OJ [2004] L 133/1.

[19] A draft amending regulation is available on DG COMP's website.

[20] See pp 872–877 below.   [21] OJ [1997] C 372/5.   [22] OJ [2004] C 31/5.

[23] OJ [2005] C 56/32.   [24] OJ [2005] C 56/24.

- *Commission Notice on Case Referral in respect of concentrations*[25]
- *Commission Notice on access to the file*[26]
- *Commission Consolidated Jurisdictional Notice*[27]
- *Commission Guidelines on the assessment of non-horizontal mergers*[28]
- *Commission Draft Notice on remedies acceptable under the ECMR*[29]

(iii) Best Practice Guidelines

The Commission has also published Guidelines setting out 'Best Practices' on two aspects of merger control:

- *DG Competition Best Practices on the conduct of EC merger control proceedings*
- *Best Practice Guidelines: the Commission's model texts for divestiture commitments and the trustee mandate*
  - *Commission Model Text for Divestiture Commitments*
  - *Commission Model Text for Trustee Mandate.*

(D) Access to the Commission's decisions

DG COMP's website is an important source of material about the operation of the ECMR. As well as the legislation and guidance just referred to, the website also carries a large amount of information about both completed cases and current investigations; these can be searched for by reference to the case number, a company's name, decision type, or by industry sector. The website also contains interesting statistical information about the ECMR in practice (for example the number of notifications each year and the number of conditional clearances or prohibitions) and some useful studies and reports on matters such as unilateral effects, tacit collusion and the impact of vertical and conglomerate mergers on competition[30].

Each notification received by the Commission is given a case number, which will be prefixed with an 'M' (as in Case M.4600 *TUI/First Choice*). The practice of giving full-function joint ventures a prefix of 'JV' was abandoned in 2002; cases that occurred under the now-repealed European Coal and Steel Community Treaty were prefixed 'ECSC'. When a merger is notified it will appear on DG COMP's website and a provisional deadline for the decision will be given; the website is updated as the investigation progresses.

The Commission's decisions can be accessed in various ways. A press release summarising the Commission's finding in cases other than those for which the simplified procedure is available[31] will usually be published in English, French, German and in the language of the notification. The press release is normally issued at noon on the day following adoption of the decision. It can be obtained on the Rapid database of

---

[25] OJ [2005] C 56/2.   [26] OJ [2005] C 325/7.

[27] Available at www.ec.europa.eu/comm/competition; this Notice replaces four previous Notices adopted by the Commission in 1998 dealing with each of full-function joint ventures (OJ [1998] C 66/1), the concept of a concentration (OJ [1998] C 66/5), undertakings concerned (OJ [1998] C 66/14), and the calculation of turnover (OJ [1998] C 66/25).

[28] Available at www.ec.europa.eu/comm/competition.   [29] See pp 872–877 below.

[30] See www.ec.europa.eu/comm/competition/mergers/studies_reports/studies_reports.html.

[31] On this procedure see pp 845–846 below.

the Commission's website[32]. Phase I decisions – that is to say cases that do not require 'in-depth' investigation – are not themselves published in the Official Journal, other than a brief statement of the outcome. Phase I decisions are published on DG COMP's website, but only in the language in which the parties notified. Decisions following an in-depth, Phase II investigation are more widely available. Summaries of Phase II decisions are published in the 'L' series of the Official Journal together with the final report of the Hearing Officer and the opinion of the Advisory Committee on Concentrations. The non-confidential version of the full decisions are published on the Commission's website; there may be a lengthy delay between the adoption of a decision and its appearance on the website while agreement is reached between the parties and the Commission as to what confidential information should be omitted from the published version.

3. JURISDICTION

This section will deal with the following matters:

(A) **Article 3: meaning of a concentration:** the ECMR applies to mergers or, more precisely, to 'concentrations', a term defined in Article 3 and further explained in the case law of the Community Courts and in the Commission's *Consolidated Jurisdictional Notice*[33] (hereafter 'the *Jurisdictional Notice*').

(B) **Articles 1 and 5:** concentrations having a Community dimension. The ECMR applies to concentrations that have a 'Community dimension'. The meaning of this term is to be found in Article 1, and is further explained in the *Jurisdictional Notice*. It is determined by reference to the turnover of the 'undertakings concerned', including their affiliated undertakings as set out in Article 5.

(C) **One-stop merger control:** as a general proposition concentrations that have a Community dimension should be investigated only by the Commission and not by the Member States; this is the principle of 'one-stop merger control'.

(D) **Article 4(4) and Article 9:** referral of concentrations having a Community dimension to the competent authorities of the Member States. In certain cases Article 4(4) and Article 9 provide a mechanism whereby concentrations that have a Community dimension can be reviewed by the competent authorities of the Member States, either because the undertakings concerned or a Member State make a request to that effect. The Commission's *Notice on Case Referral in respect of concentrations* ('the *Case Referral Notice*') provides important guidance on this topic.

(E) **Article 4(5) and Article 22:** referral of concentrations not having a Community dimension by Member States to the Commission. In certain cases Article 4(5) and Article 22 provide a mechanism whereby concentrations that do not have a Community dimension can be investigated by the Commission, either because the undertakings

---

[32] The website of the Rapid database is www.europa.eu.int/rapid/start/cgi/guesten.ksh.

[33] For an overview of the *Jurisdictional Notice* see Lübking 'Commission adopts Jurisdictional Notice under the Merger Regulation' *Competition Policy Newsletter* (Number 3, 2007) 1.

concerned or a Member State makes a request to that effect. Again the *Case Referral Notice* provides important guidance.

(F) **Article 21(4): legitimate interest clause:** Member States are not allowed to apply their domestic competition law to concentrations that have a Community dimension except in the circumstances in which Article 4(4) or Article 9 are applicable. However provision is made by Article 21(4) of the ECMR for Member States to investigate a concentration having a Community dimension where it threatens to harm some 'legitimate interest' of the State other than the maintenance of competition.

(G) **Defence:** Member States retain jurisdiction to examine the national security aspects of mergers under Article 296 of the EC Treaty.

Each of these propositions will be examined in turn.

(A) Article 3: meaning of a concentration

Part B of the *Jurisdictional Notice* deals with the meaning of a concentration. The footnotes in the *Jurisdictional Notice* contain many references to the decisional practice of the Commission and the judgments of the Community Courts: due to constraints of space they will not be referred to in the text that follows, but the reader should be aware of these useful reference points. Article 3(1) of the ECMR provides that:

A concentration shall be deemed to arise where a change of control on a lasting basis results from:

    (a) the merger of two or more previously independent undertakings or parts of undertakings, or

    (b) the acquisition, by one or more persons already controlling at least one undertaking, or by one or more undertakings, whether by purchase of securities or assets, by contract or by any other means, of direct or indirect control of the whole or parts of one or more other undertakings.

(i) Article 3(1)(a): mergers

Mergers in the sense of Article 3(1)(a) are dealt with in paragraphs 9 and 10 of the *Jurisdictional Notice*, which provides some examples of cases covered by it such as *AstraZeneca/Novartis*[34] and *Chevron/Texaco*[35]. Paragraph 10 explains that there can be factual ('*de facto*') mergers where, in the absence of a legal merger, activities of previously independent entities are combined with the result that a single economic unit is created under a permanent, single economic management; examples given are *Price Waterhouse/Coopers&Lybrand*[36] and *Ernst & Young/Andersen Germany*[37].

(ii) Article 3(1)(b): acquisition of control

In practice most cases are concerned with the acquisition of control in the sense of Article 3(1)(b) of the ECMR, and the *Jurisdictional Notice* deals with this concept from paragraphs 11 to 123. It begins by discussing the concept of control; it then deals in turn with the acquisition of sole control and of joint control.

[34] Case M 1806, decision of 26 July 2000, OJ [2004] L 110/1.
[35] Case M 2208, decision of 26 January 2001.
[36] Case M 1016, decision of 20 May 1998, OJ [1999] L 50/27, [1999] 4 CMLR 665.
[37] Case M 2824, decision of 27 August 2002.

(A) The concept of control Article 3(2) of the ECMR defines control for the purpose of determining whether there is a concentration[38]:

Control shall be constituted by rights, contracts or any other means which, either separately or in combination and having regard to the considerations of fact or law involved, confer the possibility of exercising decisive influence on an undertaking, in particular by:

> (a) ownership or the right to use all or part of the assets of an undertaking;
> (b) rights or contracts which confer decisive influence on the composition, voting or decisions of the organs of an undertaking.

Clearly this is a very broad concept[39], and control can exist on a legal ('*de jure*') or a factual ('*de facto*') basis[40]. The most common means for the acquisition of control is the acquisition of shares, sometimes in conjunction with a shareholders' agreement, in the case of joint control, or the acquisition of assets[41]. However it is also possible for control to be acquired on a contractual basis[42]. A franchise agreement is not normally sufficient to establish control[43]. In exceptional cases a situation of economic dependence resulting from, for example, long-term supply agreements, could give rise to control[44]. It is important to understand that the concept of control as used in the ECMR may be different from the one used in other Community or national laws on matters such as taxation or the media[45]. It should be added that, when deciding under Article 5(4) whether the turnover of affiliated companies should be included within group turnover, a stricter notion of control is applied than in the case of Article 3.

The acquisition of control of assets – for example the transfer of the client base of a business or of intangible assets such as brands, patents or copyrights – will only be considered a concentration if they amount to a business with a market presence to which a market turnover can be clearly attributed[46]. To amount to a concentration the acquisition of control must be on a lasting basis, resulting, as Recital 20 of the ECMR notes, in a change in the structure of the market[47]. Where several undertakings acquire a company, with the intention of dividing up the assets at a later stage, the first acquisition may be regarded as purely transitory with the result that it would not amount to a concentration: the subsequent division of the assets in question would however have to be investigated, and could give rise to more than one concentration[48]. The same analysis could be applied where an operation envisages the joint control of

---

[38] It would seem that the notion of control in Article 3(2) of the ECMR is a weaker one than is used when applying the economic entity doctrine under Article 81 EC: see ch 3, pp 91–95.

[39] Note however that, under the UK Enterprise Act 2002, the concept of 'material influence' is broader than 'the possibility of exercising decisive influence' under Article 3(2) ECMR with the result that some transactions that might not be caught under EC merger control could be under the UK system: see ch 22, pp 908–910. It is possible that the acquisition by A of a shareholding in B, although insufficient to provide the possibility of exercising decisive influence in the sense of Article 3(2) of the ECMR, may give rise to the possibility of coordinated behaviour between A and B and so require consideration under Article 81 EC: see Cases 142/84 and 156/84 *BAT v Commission* [1987] ECR 4487, [1988] 4 CMLR 24, in particular paras 37–39; see also *Warner-Lambert/Gillette* OJ [1993] L 116/21, [1993] 5 CMLR 559, paras 33–39; *BT-MCI* OJ [1994] L 223/36, [1995] 5 CMLR 285; *BiB* OJ [1999] L 312/1, [2000] 4 CMLR 901; see further Struijla 'Minority Share Acquisitions Below the Control Threshold of the EC Merger Regulation: An Economic and Legal Analysis' (2002) 25 World Competition 173; Caronna 'Article 81 as a tool for controlling minority cross-shareholdings between competitors' (2004) 29 ELR 485; Ezrachi and Gilo 'EC Competition Law and the Regulation of Passive Investments Among Competitors' (2006) 26(2) Oxford Journal of Legal Studies 327.

[40] *Jurisdictional Notice*, para 16.   [41] Ibid, para 17.   [42] Ibid, para 18.   [43] Ibid, para 19.
[44] Ibid, para 20.   [45] Ibid, para 23.   [46] Ibid, para 24.   [47] Ibid, para 28.
[48] Ibid, paras 29–33.

a new operation for a start-up period followed by a conversion to sole control: where the joint control does not exceed a year there would not be a concentration during that period[49].

Where an interim buyer, such as a bank, acquires an undertaking on the basis of an agreement in the future to sell it on to an ultimate buyer, the Commission will examine the case as one of acquisition by the ultimate buyer[50]: this is sometimes referred to in practice as a 'warehousing' arrangement. Several transactions may be regarded as a single concentration in the sense of Article 3 where they are unitary in nature, that is to say where they are interdependent in such a way that one transaction would not have been carried out without the other and if they ultimately lead to control by the same undertaking(s)[51]. Article 5(2) of the ECMR establishes a rule that allows the Commission to consider successive transactions occurring within a two-year period to be treated as a single concentration: this is an 'anti-avoidance' rule to ensure that the same persons do not break a transaction down into a series of sales of assets over a period of time with the aim of avoiding the application of the ECMR[52]. The internal restructuring of an undertaking that does not result in a change of control is not covered by the ECMR[53].

(B) Sole control Sole control may be enjoyed on a legal or a factual basis. Legal control is normally acquired where an undertaking acquires a majority of the voting rights of a company, but could also occur, for example, where a minority shareholder owns shares that confer special rights to determine the strategic direction of the company to be acquired[54]. Factual control can occur where a minority shareholder is able to veto the strategic decisions of an undertaking: although it cannot impose decisions, the fact that it can block decisions means that it has the possibility of exercising decisive influence in the sense of Article 3(2) of the ECMR. This is often referred to as negative control[55]. Factual control can also exist where a minority shareholder is likely to be able at shareholders' meetings to achieve a majority: the Commission will look at past voting behaviour to try to predict what the position is likely to be in the future[56]. Depending on the facts of the case, a shareholding of less than 25 per cent can be found to provide the possibility of exercising decisive influence: for example in *CCIE/GTE*[57] CCIE acquired 19 per cent of the voting rights in EDIL and was found to have acquired control, the remaining shares being held by an independent investment bank whose approval was not needed for important commercial decisions.

An option to purchase or convert shares does not in itself confer control unless the option will be exercised in the near future according to legally binding agreements[58].

(C) Joint control Joint control occurs where two or more undertakings have the possibility of exercising decisive influence over another undertaking. Joint control typically arises from the fact that the undertakings in question enjoy negative control, that

---

[49] Ibid, para 34.   [50] Ibid, para 35.   [51] Ibid, paras 36–47.

[52] Ibid, paras 49–50.   [53] Ibid, para 51.   [54] Ibid, paras 56–58.   [55] Ibid, para 54.   [56] Ibid, para 59.

[57] Case M 258, decision of 25 September 1992; similarly in *Mannesmann/Vallourec*, Case M 315, decision of 31 January 1994, OJ [1994] L 102/15, [1994] 4 CMLR 259, a shareholding of 21 per cent was found sufficient to confer sole control; see further ch 22, pp 908–910 on *BSkyB/ITV* where the UK Competition Commission found that BSkyB had 'material influence', the test in the Enterprise Act 2002, over ITV with a shareholding of 17.9 per cent.

[58] *Jurisdictional Notice*, para 60.

is to say the power to reject strategic decisions, which means that they have to act in common in order to determine the joint venture's commercial policy[59]. Joint control can be established both on a legal and a factual basis[60]. The simplest form of joint control arises where there are only two parent companies each with the same number of voting rights[61]. Joint control can also occur where, despite inequality of voting rights, parent companies enjoy veto rights, either by virtue of the statute of the joint venture or a shareholders' agreement between the parents[62]. The veto rights must be related to strategic decisions of the joint venture that go beyond the protection accorded to minority shareholders to protect their investment: examples of veto rights giving rise to joint control would be decisions on issues such as the budget, business plan, major investments or the appointment of senior management[63]. Joint control can also arise even where there are no veto rights if it is likely, in fact or in law, that the parents will act jointly in the exercise of their voting rights, whether as a result of a legally binding agreement[64] or as a matter of fact, because of 'strong common interests'[65].

(iii) Changes in the quality of control

A concentration can occur where there is a change in the quality of control of an undertaking: there may be a change from sole to joint control; a change in the identity of the parent companies so that there is a change in the nature of the joint control; and a change from joint to sole control[66]. However a change from negative to positive control is not regarded as a concentration[67]. A short-form notification may be made in the case of a change from joint to sole control[68].

(iv) Joint ventures – the concept of full-functionality

Article 3(4) of the ECMR provides that:

> The creation of a joint venture performing on a lasting basis all the functions of an autonomous economic entity shall constitute a concentration within the meaning of Article 3(1)(b).

Concentrations in the sense of Article 3(4) are known as 'full-function joint ventures'. It is important to know whether a joint venture is full-function or not since this determines whether the ECMR is capable of application; if the joint venture is not full-function the possibility remains that it might be subject to Article 81 EC. A full-function joint venture having a Community dimension is subject to mandatory pre-notification to the Commission; a partial-function joint venture would not be notifiable under Article 81, the process of notification of agreements under Article 81 having been abolished by the Modernisation Regulation[69].

The *Jurisdictional Notice* provides considerable detail on the concept of full-functionality. It begins by explaining that the requirement of autonomy in Article 3(4) refers to operational autonomy: its parents will be responsible for its strategic decisions, which is precisely why they will be considered to be in joint control in the first place[70]. To be operationally autonomous the joint venture must have sufficient resources to operate independently on a market: this means that it must have a management dedicated to its day-to-day operations and access to sufficient resources including finance, staff and assets to carry

---

[59] Ibid, para 62. [60] Ibid, para 63. [61] Ibid, para 64. [62] Ibid, para 65. [63] Ibid, paras 67–73.
[64] Ibid, para 75. [65] Ibid, paras 76–80. [66] Ibid, paras 83–90. [67] Ibid, para 83.
[68] See Annex II of the Implementing Regulation. [69] See ch 4, pp 162–164.
[70] *Jurisdictional Notice*, para 93.

on the business activities provided for in the joint-venture agreement[71]. A joint venture will not be full-function where it takes over one specific function of its parents' activities, such as R&D or production; similarly a joint sales company would not be full-function[72]. An example of a joint venture found not to be full-function will be found in *Electrabel/ Energia Italia/Interpower*[73]. Such cases would need to be analysed under Article 81.

A joint venture may not be sufficiently autonomous where its parents have a strong presence as suppliers to or purchasers from it; however the Commission recognises that the joint venture might be dependent on sales to or purchases from its parents during its 'start-up' period, which should normally not exceed three years[74]. Where sales are made to the parents on a lasting basis the Commission will consider whether the joint venture is geared to play an active role on the market independently of its parents: the proportion of sales made to the market will be an important considera- tion, and if the joint venture sells more than 50 per cent of its output to the market it would normally be considered to be full-function[75]. The Commission is more sceptical about long-term purchases from the parents, which might mean that the joint venture is closer to being a sales agency[76]; however it recognises that, where the joint venture operates on a 'trade market', it may be full-function even though it purchases from its parents[77]. A trade market is one where undertakings specialise in the selling and dis- tribution of products without being vertically integrated and where different sources of supply are available for the products in question. In such a case a joint venture could be considered to be full-function provided that it has the necessary facilities and is likely to obtain a substantial proportion of its supplies not only from its parents but also from competing sources.

To be full-function a joint venture must be established on a lasting basis; the fact that the parents provide for dissolution of the joint venture, for example in the event of its failure or fundamental disagreement between them, does not mean that it is not estab- lished on a lasting basis[78]. If the joint venture is established for a short, finite period – for example in order to construct a specific project such as a power plant – it would not be considered to be long-lasting[79]. An enlargement of the activities of a full-function joint venture may amount to a new concentration, as will a change from being partial- function to being full-function[80].

As a matter of substantive analysis, agreements between the parents of a full-function joint venture and the joint venture itself may amount to ancillary restraints; or they may require independent assessment under Article 81[81].

(v) Exceptions

Article 3(5) of the ECMR provides that certain operations will not amount to a con- centration: the acquisition of securities by credit or other financial institutions on an investment basis where the voting rights are not exercised other than to protect the investment; the acquisition of control according to the law of a Member State relating to liquidation, winding up and similar matters; and acquisition by financial holding companies in relation to such matters. The *Jurisdictional Notice* explains that these pro- visions are construed narrowly, and they have rarely been applied in practice[82].

---

[71] Ibid, para 94. [72] Ibid, para 95. [73] Case M 3003, decision of 23 December 2002.
[74] *Jurisdictional Notice*, para 97. [75] Ibid, para 98. [76] Ibid, para 101. [77] Ibid, para 102.
[78] Ibid, para 103. [79] Ibid, para 104. [80] Ibid, paras 106–109. [81] See further pp 870–871 below.
[82] Ibid, paras 110–116.

(B) Article 1: concentrations having a Community dimension

Part C of the Commission's *Jurisdictional Notice* deals with the notion of Community dimension. As a general proposition concentrations having a Community dimension are investigated by the Commission; concentrations that do not do so are subject to the merger laws of the Member States[83]. Given that 26 of the 27 Member States have a system of merger control[84], and that one transaction might be subject to investigation under a number of them, there may be significant regulatory advantages in being subject to EC rather than Member State law: this is discussed further below in the context of one-stop merger control[85].

(i) Thresholds

Turnover is used as a proxy for the economic resources that would be combined as a result of a concentration, and it is allocated geographically in order to reflect the geographical distribution of those resources[86]. Turnover thresholds are used in order to provide a relatively simple and objective mechanism for determining the allocation of jurisdiction; they are not intended in any sense to act as a way of predicting the market power of the undertakings concerned: that is a matter of substantive assessment, to be conducted by the competition authority (or authorities) that have jurisdiction[87]. Article 1 of the ECMR sets out the numerical thresholds to establish Community jurisdiction: it should be noted that the ECMR does not require that the undertakings concerned should be domiciled within the EU, nor that the transaction in question should take place there[88]. The method of calculating turnover is set out in Article 5.

Article 1(1) provides that the ECMR shall apply to all concentrations having a Community dimension as defined in Article 1(2) or Article 1(3). The criteria set out in Article 1(2) and 1(3) of the ECMR are *alternative* grounds on which a concentration may have a Community dimension[89].

(A) Article 1(2) Article 1(2) provides that a concentration has a Community dimension where:

(a) the combined aggregate worldwide turnover of all the undertakings concerned is more than €5,000 million; and

(b) the aggregate Community-wide turnover of each of at least two of the undertakings concerned is more than €250 million,

unless each of the undertakings concerned achieves more than two-thirds of its aggregate Community-wide turnover within one and the same Member State.

Article 1(2) is intended to reflect the overall size of the undertakings concerned on a worldwide basis; to establish that there is a minimum level of activities within the EC; and

---

[83] See Case C-170/02 P *Schlüsselverlag J.S. Moser GmbH v Commission* [2003] ECR I-9889, [2004] 4 CMLR 27, at para 34: 'the Community legislature intended to lay down a clear division between the activities of the national authorities and those of the Community authorities, by avoiding successive definitions of positions by those different authorities on the same transaction…'.

[84] Luxembourg is the only Member State that does not have a system of merger control.

[85] See p 832 below.   [86] *Jurisdictional Notice*, para 124.   [87] Ibid, para 127.

[88] On the territorial scope of the ECMR see ch 12, pp 482–484.

[89] Note that the Commission is required by Article 1(4) of the ECMR to report to the Council of Ministers by 1 July 2009 on the operation of the thresholds, and that Article 1(5) enables the Council to revise them in the light of any proposal from the Commission by a qualified majority.

to exclude purely domestic transactions. It is not unusual for very substantial transactions to fall outside the ECMR as a result of the two-thirds rule where two undertakings from the same Member State are involved: this is particular likely to happen in the case, for example, of banks, insurance companies and undertakings in the energy sector that operate predominantly in their domestic market. For example the *Lloyds TSB Group plc/ Abbey National plc* case in 2001 was not subject to the ECMR, since at least two thirds of the turnover of each of those banks arose in the UK; however the case was investigated, and prohibited, under the UK's domestic system of merger control[90]. A controversial case arose in 2005 when Gas Natural, a Spanish company active in the energy sector, notified its intention to make a hostile public bid for Endesa, another Spanish company primarily active in the electricity sector, to the Spanish Competition Authority; Gas Natural claimed that the two-thirds rule was applicable with the consequence that the Commission lacked jurisdiction. Endesa lodged a complaint with the Commission, arguing that the two-thirds rule did not apply. The Commission rejected Endesa's argument[91]; Endesa appealed to the CFI but its appeal was dismissed[92]. As a result of cases such as this the Commission has been considering whether the two-thirds rule should be changed, and has consulted Member States on the issue. Commissioner Kroes has stated, for example in a speech in Brussels in June 2007, that in her own view the two-thirds rule has become outdated[93].

(B) Article 1(3) Article 1(3) provides an alternative basis of jurisdiction to Article 1(2). A concentration that does not meet the Article 1(2) thresholds nevertheless has a Community dimension where:

   (a) the combined aggregate worldwide turnover of all the undertakings concerned is more than €2,500 million; and
   (b) in each of at least three Member States, the combined aggregate turnover of all the undertakings concerned is more than €100 million;
   (c) in each of the three Member States included for the purpose of (b), the aggregate turnover of each of at least two of the undertakings concerned is more than €25 million; and
   (d) the aggregate Community-wide turnover of each of at least two of the undertakings concerned is more than EUR €100 million;

unless each of the undertakings concerned achieves more than two-thirds of its aggregate Community-wide turnover within one and the same Member State.

The purpose of Article 1(3) is to give jurisdiction to the Commission in cases where a concentration does not have a Community dimension in the sense of Article 1(2), but nevertheless could be expected to have a substantial impact in at least three Member States[94]. In practice there has not been a large number of concentrations filed under Article 1(3): only 45 notifications had been made pursuant to Article 1(3) by the end of 1999[95]. Jurisdiction in the *Ryanair/Aer Lingus* case, which the Commission prohibited in 2007, was based on Article 1(3)[96]. What is more common in practice is that parties to

---

[90] Cm 5208 (2001).   [91] See Press Release IP/05/1425 of 15 November 2005.

[92] Case T-417/05 *Endesa v Commission* [2006] ECR II-2533.

[93] Available at www.ec.europa.eu/comm/competition/speeches/index_speeches_by_the_commis-sioner.html; for discussion of the two-thirds rue see Scott 'Last Rites for the Two-Thirds Rule in EC Merger Control?' [2006] Journal of Business Law 619.

[94] *Jurisdictional Notice* para 126.

[95] *Report to the Council on the application of the Merger Regulation thresholds*, COM (2000) 399 final, para 20.

[96] Case M 4439 *Ryanair/Air Lingus*, decision of 27 June 2007, on appeal Case T-342/07 *Ryanair v Commission*, not yet decided.

a concentration that does not have a Community dimension make use of the procedure provided by Article 4(5) of the ECMR to request that their transaction be reviewed by the Commission on a one-stop shop basis[97].

(ii) Notion of undertaking concerned

The first step in determining whether a concentration has a Community dimension is to identify the 'undertakings concerned', an expression that is used in Article 1 of the ECMR. Having done so, turnover is calculated in the manner set out in Article 5; Article 5(4) identifies those other entities that form part of the same group as the undertakings concerned and whose turnover should therefore be included in the calculation. Where the concentration is a merger in the sense of Article 3(1)(a) of the ECMR the undertakings concerned are the merging entities[98]. In cases of the acquisition of control under Article 3(1)(b) it can be a complicated matter to determine who are the undertakings concerned. The *Jurisdictional Notice* gives extensive guidance on this:

- Where A acquires sole control of B, the undertakings concerned will be A and B[99].
- However if A acquires part of B, the undertakings concerned will be A and the part of B to be acquired, in accordance with Article 5(2) of the ECMR: after the concentration has been effected the economic strength of the rest of B would be irrelevant to the position of the merged entity[100].
- Where A and B jointly control C and A acquires B's interest in C, the undertakings concerned are A and C: as in the previous example, once the transaction has been put into effect the position of B is irrelevant to the economic strength of A and C[101].
- Where A and B establish a new entity, C, the undertakings concerned are A and B[102].
- However if A and B acquire joint control of an existing entity, C, each of A, B and C is an undertaking concerned[103].

If a joint venture, C, acquires D, the question arises of whether C, or its parents A and B, should be regarded as the undertakings concerned. The answer to this question may have a decisive effect on jurisdiction: if A and B are undertakings concerned and their group turnover is added into the calculation of turnover, it is more likely that the transaction will be found to have a Community dimension:

- If C is a full-function joint venture and is already operating on the market, it will be regarded as an undertaking concerned, along with D[104].
- If C is a mere vehicle for the acquisition by A and B of D the Commission will consider each of A and B to be undertakings concerned, along with D[105].

(iii) Relevant date for establishing jurisdiction

The relevant date for determining whether a concentration has a Community dimension is the date when a final agreement was concluded or a public bid was announced or a controlling interest was acquired, whichever date is earlier[106].

(iv) Turnover

Article 5(1) of the ECMR defines turnover as the amounts derived by undertakings in the previous years 'from the sale of products and the provision of services falling within the

---

[97] See pp 837–838 below. [98] *Jurisdictional Notice* para 132. [99] Ibid, para 134. [100] Ibid, para 136.
[101] Ibid, para 138. [102] Ibid, para 139. [103] Ibid, para 140. [104] Ibid, para 146. [105] Ibid, para 147.
[106] Ibid, paras 155–156.

undertakings' ordinary activities'. Sales rebates, VAT, and other taxes directly related to turnover (for example taxes on alcoholic drinks and cigarettes) are deducted from any turnover figure, as is internal turnover within a group of companies. Article 5(5)(a) of the ECMR provides that turnover between a joint venture and its parents should be excluded from the calculation of turnover; but Article 5(5)(b) provides that turnover between a joint venture and third parties should be apportioned equally between its parents.

The *Jurisdictional Notice* explains that the Commission will usually base its findings on turnover on the most recent audited accounts of the undertakings concerned; it will rely on management or other provisional accounts only in exceptional circumstances[107]. Where there are major differences between the Community's accounting standards and those of a non-Member State the Commission may consider it necessary to ask for the accounts to be restated according to Community standards[108]. The *Notice* explains the circumstances in which the Commission will accept an adjustment to the figures in the audited accounts, for example where there has since been a divestiture of part of the business of an undertaking concerned[109].

In determining jurisdiction it is necessary not only to take into account the turnover of the undertakings concerned but also that of other undertakings within the same group. This can be problematic where undertakings such as private equity funds do not have consolidated accounts: care must be taken to ensure that all relevant turnover is brought into the calculation. Article 5(4) of the ECMR provides that the aggregate turnover of an undertaking concerned shall be calculated by adding together the respective turnovers of the following:

(a) the undertaking concerned;
(b) those undertakings in which the undertaking concerned directly or indirectly:
    (i) owns more than half the capital or business assets, or
    (ii) has the power to exercise more than half the voting rights, or
    (iii) has the power to appoint more than half the members of the supervisory board, the administrative board or bodies legally representing the undertakings, or
    (iv) has the right to manage the undertaking's affairs;
(c) those undertakings which have in an undertaking concerned the rights or powers listed in (b);
(d) those undertakings in which an undertaking as referred to in (c) has the rights or powers listed in (b);
(e) those undertakings in which two or more undertakings as referred to in (a) to (d) jointly have the rights or powers listed in (b).

The *Jurisdictional Notice* provides fairly extensive guidance on these provisions[110]. An important point is that the criteria in Article 5(4), such as 'the power to exercise more than half the voting rights' or 'the right to manage the undertakings' affairs', are considerably stricter than the concept of 'control' set out in Article 3(2); Article 5(4) provides 'bright-line' criteria for determining which group turnover should be added to that of the individual undertakings concerned in a transaction[111].

(v) Geographic allocation of turnover

It is important to be able to determine where turnover arises, since Article 1(2) and (3) of the ECMR refer to global, Community and Member State turnover. The general

---

[107] Ibid, paras 169–170.   [108] Ibid, para 171.   [109] Ibid, paras 172–174.   [110] Ibid, paras 175–194.
[111] Ibid, para 184.

rule is that turnover should be attributed to the place where the customer is located[112]; the *Jurisdictional Notice* explains how this principle is applied in practice to the sale of goods[113] and the provision of services[114].

(vi) Conversion of turnover into Euros

For the purposes of the ECMR turnover must be calculated in Euros: for many undertakings this will require conversion from another currency. The annual turnover should be converted at the average European Central Bank rate for the twelve months concerned; and this average can be obtained from DG COMP's website[115].

(vii) Provisions for credit and other financial institutions and insurance undertakings

Article 5(3) of the ECMR provides specific rules for the calculation of turnover of credit and other financial institutions. Their operation is explained in the Commission's *Jurisdictional Notice*[116].

(viii) Illustrations

A few examples may help to illustrate how the jurisdictional rules just outlined operate in practice. See Fig. 21.1 on facing page.

(C) Article 21: one-stop merger control

(i) The benefits of one-stop merger control

As a general proposition it is undesirable, both for businesses and for competition authorities, if a particular concentration has to be investigated under two or more systems of law. Multiple investigation leads to administrative inefficiency, duplication, delay, expense, uncertainty and the possibility of conflicting decisions. A central principle of the ECMR is the idea of one-stop merger control: that is to say that concentrations having a Community dimension should be investigated within the EU only by the Commission. This policy is given expression in Article 21 of the ECMR. Article 21(2) provides that, subject to review by the Community Courts, only the Commission may take decisions in respect of concentrations having a Community dimension; Article 21(3) adds that no Member State shall apply its national legislation on competition to such concentrations[117]. However, as explained below, there are some circumstances in

---

[112] Ibid, para 196.   [113] Ibid, paras 197–198.

[114] Ibid, paras 199–202; for an example of a case in which the geographical allocation of turnover was crucial to jurisdiction see Case M 4439 *Ryanair/Air Lingus,* decision of 27 June 2007, on appeal Case T-342/07 *Ryanair v Commission*, not yet decided.

[115] Ibid, para 204; the website is www.ec.europa.eu/comm/competition/mergers/others/exchange_rates. html.

[116] Ibid, paras 206–220.

[117] It is arguable that a national court could apply Articles 81 and 82 to concentrations having a Community dimension, in so far as those provisions are capable of applying to concentrations, on the basis that they are directly effective, though there would appear to be no example of this having happened since the entry into force of the original Merger Regulation in September 1990: for discussion of the point see Cook and Kerse *EC Merger Control* (Sweet & Maxwell, 4th ed, 2005), pp 21–24; Levy *European Merger Control Law: A Guide to the Merger Regulation* (LexisNexis, 2003), ch 21.

Example 1

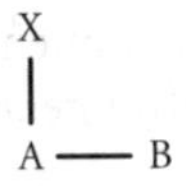

A acquires B: A is the wholly-owned subsidiary of X

Undertakings concerned: A and B (Article 5(1))

Turnover to be taken into account: A and B (undertakings concerned) and X (X's turnover is included as a result of Article 5(4)(c)).

Example 2

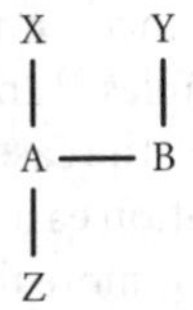

A acquires B, a division of Y; A is a part of X, and has a wholly-owned subsidiary, Z

Undertakings concerned: A and B (Article 5(1))

Turnover to be taken into account: A and B (undertakings concerned: disregard the turnover of Y, as A is acquiring B only, a part of Y: Article 5(2)); X (Article 5(4)(c)) and Z (Article 5(4)(b)).

Example 3

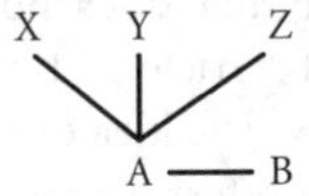

A acquires B. A is jointly controlled by X, Y and Z.

Undertakings concerned: A and B

Turnover to be taken into account: A and B (undertakings concerned); X, Y and Z (this is based on the language of Article 5(4)(c) of the ECMR and is supported by paragraph 182 of the Commission's *Consolidated Jurisdictional Notice*).

Example 4

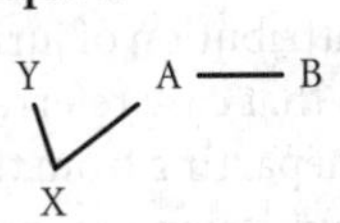

A acquires B; A has joint control of X with Y

Undertakings concerned: A and B

Turnover to be taken into account: A and B (undertakings concerned); but is the turnover of X relevant? The answer to this question could determine whether the concentration has a Community dimension if A and B's combined turnover falls below the Community dimension thresholds. The Commission states at paragraph 187 of its Consolidated Jurisdictional Notice that it would allocate a 50% share of the joint venture's turnover to A in these circumstances.

Fig. 21.1 Illustrative diagram

which cases can be 'reattributed' from and to the Commission. A different point is that Article 21(4) of the ECMR provides that, in defined circumstances, a Member State may be able to apply non-competition legislation to a concentration where this is necessary to protect a 'legitimate interest'; this provision is discussed in section (F) below.

Article 21(1) of the ECMR adds that Regulation 1/2003, the Modernisation Regulation that gives the Commission the power to enforce Articles 81 and 82 EC, shall have no application to concentrations as defined in the ECMR[118]. However Article 21(1) makes clear that the Commission retains the right to use its powers under the Modernisation Regulation in relation to joint ventures that do not have a Community dimension and which have as their object or effect the coordination of the competitive behaviour of undertakings that remain independent.

(ii) The benefits of more flexible jurisdictional rules

Notwithstanding the principle of one-stop merger control the ECMR makes provision for 'case referral', that is to say for the reattribution, in defined circumstances, of cases to and from the Commission. The Commission's *Notice on Case Referral in respect of concentrations* ('the *Case Referral Notice*')[119] provides detailed guidance on the reattribution of jurisdiction under the ECMR, both on the guiding principles[120] and on the mechanics of the system[121]. It also contains some helpful flow charts[122]. The case referral rules have been 'flexibilised' by the 2004 Regulation to make reattribution easier than it had been under the original Merger Regulation; it was felt by 2004 that more flexibility was desirable in order to enable the more appropriate competition authority or competition authorities to conduct the investigation of cases[123].

In certain cases a concentration that has a Community dimension can be referred by the Commission to Member States under the provisions of Article 4(4) and Article 9: this is described in section (D) below; and a concentration that does not have a Community dimension can be referred under Article 4(5) and Article 22 by Member States to the Commission: this is dealt with in section (E) below. The idea of reattribution is consistent with the principle of subsidiarity[124]. The case referral procedures in the ECMR are carried out by the Commission in close and constant liaison with the national competition authorities[125]. A notable feature of the 2004 changes is that the parties themselves can now attempt to precipitate a reallocation of jurisdiction before a formal filing has been made either to the Commission or to the national competition authority or authorities: this is a result of Articles 4(4) and 4(5) of the ECMR, described below. The Commission notes that in applying the rules on reattribution of jurisdiction due account should be taken of the need for legal certainty, so that case referral should normally only be made where there is a compelling reason for departing from the 'original jurisdiction'[126]. Article 4(6) of the ECMR requires the Commission to report to the Council by 1 July 2009 on the operation of Article 4(4) and 4(5) which, on a proposal from the Commission, may revise those provisions by a qualified majority.

---

[118] Theoretically the Commission may be able to proceed under Articles 81 and 82, in so far as they are capable of application to a concentration, under Article 85 EC; at the time of the adoption of the original Merger Regulation the Commission said that it would do so only rarely, and in practice it has never done so; see the Commission's statement entered in the minutes of the Council [1990] 4 CMLR 314; see also Cook and Kerse *EC Merger Control* (Sweet & Maxwell, 4th ed, 2005), pp 24–25; Levy *European Merger Control Law: A Guide to the Merger Regulation* (LexisNexis, 2003), ch 21.

[119] OJ [2005] C 56/2; see also *Joint Statement of the Council and the Commission on the functioning of the network of Competition Authorities* available at www.ec.europa.eu/comm/competition/ecn/documents. html; for discussion of the referral system see Ryan 'The revised system of case referral under the Merger Regulation: experiences to date' *Competition Policy Newsletter*, Autumn 2005, 38.

[120] *Case Referral Notice*, Section II (paras 8–45).   [121] Ibid, Section III (paras 46–82).
[122] Ibid, pp 20–23.   [123] Ibid, paras 4–7.   [124] Ibid, para 8.   [125] Ibid, paras 53–58.
[126] Ibid, paras 13–14.

(D) Article 4(4) and Article 9: referral of concentrations having a Community dimension to the competent authorities of the Member States

The starting point is that concentrations that have a Community dimension benefit from a one-stop shop; the Commission acknowledges that the fragmentation of such cases, that is to say the partial referral of aspects of a concentration having a Community dimension to one or more Member States, is undesirable in principle even though possible as a matter of law[127].

Case referrals of concentrations having a Community dimension may be made following a request from the parties to a concentration prior to a notification having been made ('pre-notification referrals') or following a request from a Member State (or Member States) after a notification ('post-notification referrals'). The Commission's decision to refer a case to a Member State is capable of being challenged by a third party that would prefer the Commission to investigate the case[128].

(i) Pre-notification referrals: Article 4(4)[129]

Article 4(4) was an innovation in the 2004 Regulation. It allows the parties to a transaction to make a 'reasoned submission' to the Commission that a concentration will significantly affect competition in a market within a Member State which presents all the characteristics of a distinct market and therefore that it should be examined, in whole or in part, by that Member State. The parties do not have to demonstrate that the effect on competition is likely to be adverse[130]. The submission must be made in Form RS, the format of which is set out in Annex III of the Implementing Regulation[131].

Having made a request the Commission will transmit it to all Member States without delay. The Member State referred to in the Form RS must express its agreement or disagreement with the request within 15 working days; if it does not do so it is deemed to have agreed. Unless the Member State disagrees with the request the Commission has a discretion to refer whole or part of the case to the Member State in question for it to be investigated under that State's national competition law; this decision must be made within 25 working days of receipt of the Form RS. If the Commission does not take a decision within this period it is deemed to have referred the case. The Commission is most likely to make a referral where the effects of a concentration are likely to be felt within a national market, or a market that is narrower than national, and where the markets are likely to be within one and the same Member State[132]. Where a concentration might affect competition in a number of national markets the Commission might consider it appropriate to retain jurisdiction: this would avoid the need for coordinated investigations by a number of competition authorities and the danger of conflicting outcomes. However referral to a number of Member States might occur, especially where

---

[127] Ibid, paras 11–12.

[128] See Case T-119/02 *Royal Philips Electronics v Commission* [2003] ECR II-1433, [2003] 5 CMLR 2, paras 252–300; Cases T-346/02 and 347/02 *Cabeleuropa SA v Commission* [2003] ECR II-4251, [2004] 5 CMLR 25, paras 100–157.

[129] *Case Referral Notice*, paras 16–23. [130] Ibid, para 17.

[131] Regulation 802/2004, OJ [2004] L 133/1, available at www.ec.europa.eu/comm/competition/mergers/legislation/regulations.html#impl_reg; as to Form RS see the *Case Referral Notice*, paras 59–64.

[132] Ibid, para 20.

competitive conditions vary from one State to another; fragmentation of jurisdiction is less of a concern where the parties themselves have made a request under Article 4(4)[133]. The final paragraph of Article 4(4) provides that, where the whole of the case is referred to a Member State, the duty to notify the case to the Commission ceases to apply.

(ii) Post-notification referrals: Article 9[134]

Article 9 of the ECMR provides a mechanism whereby Member States may make a request that a concentration having a Community dimension should be referred to them. The powers of the OFT in the UK in relation to such cases are set out in a statutory instrument[135]. Article 9(2) establishes two situations in which a Member State may make such a request.

(A) Article 9(2)(a) The first is where a concentration threatens to affect significantly competition in a market within a Member State which presents all the characteristics of a distinct market. Where the Commission considers that these criteria are fulfilled it has a discretion to refer the whole or part of the case to the Member State that made the request[136].

(B) Article 9(2)(b) The second is where a concentration affects competition within a Member State which presents all the characteristics of a distinct market and which does not constitute a substantial part of the common market: the latter expression is likely to refer to a geographical market that is narrow in scope and within a single Member State[137]. Where the Commission considers that these criteria are fulfilled it has an obligation to refer the whole or part of the case relating to the distinct market concerned[138]: the Commission would not be able to take action against a concentration that does not impede competition in a substantial part of the common market anyway[139].

As a general rule the decision to refer must be taken within 35 working days of the receipt of the Member State's request[140]. Once a referral has been made the competent authority of the Member State must decide upon the case 'without undue delay'; within 45 working days of the referral it must inform the undertakings concerned of the preliminary competition assessment and what further action, if any, it proposes to take[141]. Member States may take only the measures strictly necessary to safeguard or restore effective competition on the market concerned[142]. Where the Commission refuses a request a Member State may appeal to the CFI[143].

(iii) Statistics

The statistics on Article 4(4) and Article 9 are of interest[144]. In the years immediately preceding 1 May 2004, when the current ECMR became applicable, Member States were making quite a large number of Article 9 requests – in 2003 the figure was 10. Refusals are very rare: out of a total of 74 Article 9 requests to have been made by 31 January 2008 only four were refused. Since 1 May 2004 the number of Member State requests has

---

[133] Ibid, para 22.   [134] Ibid, paras 33–41.
[135] EEC Merger Control (Distinct Market Investigations) Regulations 1990, SI 1990/1715, as amended by the EC Merger Control (Consequential Amendments) Regulations 2004, SI 2004/1079.
[136] ECMR, Article 9(3).   [137] *Case Referral Notice*, para 40.   [138] ECMR, Article 9(3), final paragraph.
[139] Ibid, Article 2(3).   [140] Ibid, Article 9(4)(a).   [141] Ibid, Article 9(6).   [142] Ibid, Article 9(8).
[143] Ibid, Article 9(9).   [144] See p 887 below for a statistical table of merger notifications.

fallen slightly, but undertakings have made use of the Article 4(4) procedure on quite a number of occasions: 14 Article 4(4) requests were made in 2005, 13 in 2006 and five in 2007: none was refused.

(iv) Article 4(4) and Article 9 in practice

Referrals to a Member State can give rise to problems for the undertakings concerned. In the case of *Interbrew/Bass* the European Commission referred part of the case to the UK[145]. The Competition Commission in the UK recommended that the transaction should be prohibited in its entirety[146], a particularly unfortunate outcome given that the sale agreement had been entered into without a condition that approval from the UK authorities was required. Following a judicial review the transaction was permitted to go ahead in an amended form[147]. In the case of *Tesco/Carrefour*[148] the concentration was approved by the European Commission in December 2005; however the intended acquisitions in Slovakia were prohibited following an Article 9(2)(b) referral of that part of the transaction[149]. In the case of *Foster Yeoman/Aggregate Industries*[150] the UK requested a referral which led to the Office of Fair Trading accepting undertakings in lieu of a reference to the Competition Commission to overcome concerns about both unilateral and coordinated effects that would arise from the transaction there[151]. It is possible for a third party to appeal against a Commission decision to make a referral under Article 9[152].

(E) Article 4(5) and Article 22: referral of concentrations not having a Community dimension by Member States to the Commission

The starting point in the case of concentrations not having a Community dimension is that they are subject to the national systems of merger control of the Member States. With the exception of Luxembourg every Member State has provisions on merger control, and it can happen that one transaction may be reviewable in numerous jurisdictions. As noted already multiple filings can be undesirable both for businesses and for competition authorities. The ECMR makes provision for concentrations not having a Community dimension to be referred to the Commission, in which case they may benefit from the principle of one-stop merger control. As the statistics in the text that follows show these provisions, and in particular Article 4(5), are used quite often.

(i) Pre-notification referrals: Article 4(5)[153]

Article 4(5), like Article 4(4), was an innovation in the 2004 Regulation. Article 4(5) allows the parties to a concentration that is capable of being reviewed under the national competition laws of at least three Member States to make a reasoned submission that it should be examined by the Commission. They must do so on Form RS, and the Commission must transmit the submission to the Member States without delay.

---

[145] Case M 2044, decision of 22 August 2000.   [146] *Interbrew SA/Bass plc* Cm 5014 (2001).
[147] *Interbrew SA and Interbrew UK Holdings Ltd v Competition Commission and Secretary of State for Trade and Industry* [2001] EWHC Admin 367, [2001] UKCLR 954.
[148] Case M 3905, decision of 22 December 2005.
[149] See www.antimon.gov.sk/eng, decision of 17 January 2007.
[150] Case M.4298, decision of 6 September 2006.   [151] OFT decision of 22 December 2006.
[152] See pp 883–884 below.   [153] *Case Referral Notice*, paras 24–32.

Member States competent to examine the concentration must disagree with the request within 15 working days. If one Member State expresses disagreement, the case will not be referred (in other words the case referral process can be vetoed by a single Member State). However if there is no disagreement within the stipulated period the concentration is deemed to have a Community dimension[154] and falls to be dealt with under the provisions of the ECMR; Member States can no longer apply their national competition law to the case, and the case proceeds on the basis of one-stop merger control. In the Commission's view the most appropriate cases for referral under Article 4(5) are those where the potential impact on competition will be felt in markets that are wider than national in geographic scope; the Commission is likely to be in the best position to investigate such cases[155]. It might also be best-placed to investigate where the markets affected are national or narrower, but competition concerns arise in a number of Member States; this may lead to a more coherent and consistent outcome[156]. It might also be appropriate for a referral to the Commission to take place under Article 4(5) even where there are no competition concerns at all, simply to avoid the burden of multiple Member State filings[157].

(ii) Post-notification referrals: Article 22[158]

Article 22 of the ECMR provides a mechanism whereby Member States may refer concentrations that do not have a Community dimension to the Commission for it to investigate: the concentration in question must affect trade between Member States[159] and must threaten to significantly affect competition within the territory of the Member State or States making the request[160]. It is unclear whether a Member State can make an Article 22 request in circumstances where it does not have jurisdiction over the transaction under its own internal law, for example because the merger falls below the relevant turnover thresholds.

When the Commission receives an Article 22 request it must inform the competent authorities of the Member States without delay; other Member States may join the request within 15 working days of being informed of the initial request, and national time limits as to merger control are suspended until the jurisdictional question has been decided[161]. If a Member State decides not to join the request its national time limits revive[162]. That Member State can then apply its own law, even if the Commission accepts the request from other Member States: to put the point another way, the principle of one-stop merger control does not necessarily apply in an Article 22 case, since Member States retain the right to disagree with a request and to apply their own law. The Commission must decide, within a further 10 working days from the end of the period given to Member States to decide whether to join the request, whether to examine the concentration[163]. If the Commission does not take a decision it is deemed to have accepted the request[164]. If the Commission does decide to examine the case it

---

[154] Note that under Article 22 the Commission has a discretion whether to accept a request, whereas under Article 4(5), in the absence of a veto by a Member State, the Commission must accept jurisdiction.

[155] *Case Referral Notice*, para 28.   [156] Ibid, para 29.   [157] Ibid, para 32.   [158] Ibid, paras 42–45.

[159] The Commission's *Notice on the notion of effect on trade concept contained in Articles 81 and 82 of the Treaty*, OJ [2004] C 101/81, may, by analogy, provide helpful guidance on the application of this expression; see the *Case Referral Notice*, footnote 36.

[160] ECMR, Article 22(1).   [161] Ibid, Article 22(2).   [162] Ibid.

[163] For an example of a decision not to examine a concentration following an Article 22 request see *Gas Natural/Endesa*, Commission Press Release IP/05/1356 of 27 October 2005.   [164] ECMR, Article 22(3).

may request the parties to make a formal notification[165]. Once the Commission has taken jurisdiction the case proceeds in accordance with the provisions of the ECMR[166]. The Commission may invite Member States to make a request under Article 22[167].

(iii) Statistics

The statistics on Article 4(5) and Article 22 are of interest, and demonstrate in particular that undertakings have found the Article 4(5) procedure to be a useful provision[168]. In the early years of EC merger control Article 22 requests were rare; three were made by Member States that had no system of merger control at all at the relevant time, and each of them led to an outright prohibition by the Commission[169]. All the Member States now have a system of merger control, with the exception of Luxembourg, so that cases such as these would no longer happen except in relation to that one Member State. More recently Article 22 requests have become a little more common, usually where a number of Member States were willing to transfer jurisdiction to the Commission: four requests were made in 2005 and a further four in 2006 and none was refused. Article 4(5) requests have become common: 28 requests were made in 2005 and 39 in 2006; two were refused. In 2007 there were 51 requests and two refusals.

(iv) Article 4(5) and Article 22 in practice

As already noted, three early Article 22 requests led to outright prohibitions of the concentrations in question. More recently Article 4(5) and Article 22 requests have led to problems for the undertakings concerned. For example an Article 4(5) request in the case of *Metso/Aker Kvaerner* led to a Phase II investigation and was cleared only subject to commitments[170]. Commitments were required following Article 22 requests in *Promatech/Sulzer Textil*[171], *GE/AGFA NDT*[172], *AREVA/Urenco/ETC*[173], and *Omya/J.M.Huber*[174]. The case of *Glatfelter/Crompton Assets*[175] was taken into a Phase II investigation, but was cleared unconditionally.

(F) Article 21(4): legitimate interest clause

The principle of one-stop merger control means that a Member State cannot apply its competition law to a concentration having a Community dimension except where Article 4(4) or Article 9 apply. However there may be circumstances in which a Member

---

[165] Ibid; the parties in an Article 22 case will already have made a notification to the national competition authority or authorities, and it is possible that the Commission will be able to glean the information it requires from those notifications.

[166] Ibid, Article 22(4).   [167] Ibid, Article 22(5).

[168] See p 887 below for a statistical table of merger notifications.

[169] Case M 553 *RTL/Veroncia/Endemol*, decision of 17 July 1996, upheld on appeal Case T-221/95 *Endemol Entertainment Holding BV v Commission* [1999] ECR II-1299, [1999] 5 CMLR 611; Case M 784 *Kesko/Tuko*, decision of 20 November 1996, OJ [1997] L110/53, [1997] 4 CMLR 24, upheld on appeal Case T-22/97 *Kesko Oy v Commission* [1999] ECR II-3775, [2000] 4 CMLR 335; Case M 890 *Blokker/Toys 'R'Us*, decision of 26 June 1997, OJ [1998] L 316/1, [1997] 5 CMLR 148.

[170] Case M 4187, decision of 12 December 2006; see similarly M 4209 *Thule/Schneekten*, subsequently abandoned by the parties.

[171] Case M 2698, decision of 24 July 2002.   [172] Case M 3136, decision of 5 December 2005.

[173] Case M 3099, decision of 6 October 2004.

[174] Case M 3796, decision of 19 July 2006, OJ [2007] L 72/24.

[175] Case M 4215, decision of 20 December 2006, OJ [2007] L 151/41.

State wishes to investigate and perhaps to prohibit a concentration for some other reason: for example because it objects to a domestic undertaking being acquired by a foreign one; because the concentration might lead to unemployment and social disruption; or because the sector in question is a sensitive one in which the Member State wishes to maintain a strong influence which might be undermined by wider participation. Some interventions by a Member State to prevent a concentration involving an undertaking from another Member State might infringe primary provisions of the Treaty, for example Article 43 on the right of establishment or Article 56 on the free movement of capital; in such a situation the Commission may proceed against the Member State in question by bringing proceedings before the ECJ under Article 226 of the Treaty. In other cases the Commission might bring proceedings against a Member State that tries to block a concentration having a Community dimension on the basis that this involves a violation of the ECMR itself since Article 21 confers exclusive competence on the Commission in relation to concentrations having a Community dimension (see below). The Commission made a declaration to the European Parliament in March 2006 stressing its determination to use these legal provisions to ensure that the principles of the single market are upheld[176], and the Commissioner for Competition expressed her strong opposition to national protectionist measures contrary to the principles of the internal market in a speech in St. Gallen in May 2007[177].

Article 21(4) (formerly Article 21(3)) of the ECMR provides that Member States may take appropriate measures to protect legitimate interests other than those taken into consideration by the ECMR that are compatible with the general principles and other provisions of Community law. Public security, plurality of the media and prudential rules – that is to say rules designed to ensure the stability and financial adequacy of banks, insurance companies and similar undertakings – are regarded as legitimate interests for this purpose. Any other legitimate interest must be communicated to the Commission which must inform the Member State in question of its decision within 25 working days of the communication.

(i) Authorised applications of Article 21(4)

Decisions to allow a Member State to proceed on the basis of Article 21(4) are rare: by the end of January 2008 only eight had been granted, although it is interesting to note that two of those were granted in 2006 and one in 2007[178]. As Article 21(4) involves a derogation from the general principles of the ECMR, that concentrations having a Community dimension should be subject to a one-stop shop, the Commission will apply it strictly.

In *Lyonnaise des Eaux SA/Northumbrian Water Group*[179] the Commission accepted that the UK was entitled to investigate the regulatory aspects of a transaction whereby Lyonnaise des Eaux acquired a UK water undertaking, while the Commission considered

---

[176]   Commission Declaration of 15 March 2006, available at www.europarl.europa.eu/news.

[177]   'European competition policy facing a renaissance of protectionism – which strategy for the future?', 11 May 2007, available at www.ec.europa.eu/comm/competition/speeches/index_2007.html; for a more general account of legal provisions intended to inhibit protectionism in the context of mergers see Nourry and Jung 'EU State Measures against Foreign Takeovers: "Economic Patriotism in All But Name"' (2006) 2 Competition Policy International 99.

[178]   See p 887 below for a statistical table of merger notifications.

[179]   Case M 567, decision of 21 December 1995, OJ [1995] C 11/3, [1996] 4 CMLR 145; the Monopolies and Mergers Commission, as it was then called, subsequently published a report *Lyonnaise des Eaux SA and*

the competition issues. The UK also investigated the *Independent Newspaper* case under the (now-repealed) newspaper merger provisions of the Fair Trading Act 1973[180]. In the case of *Sun Alliance/Royal Insurance*[181] the Commission acknowledged in its decision that the UK could consider whether the merger would be in accordance with the Insurance Companies Act 1982, but said that this would be done in close liaison with it. In *Electricité de France/London Electricity*[182] the UK requested a referral under Article 9 of the ECMR and claimed a legitimate interest under Article 21(4); the Commission did not accept either request: the regulatory concerns of the Director General of Electricity Supply were not with the concentration itself but with the conduct of the merged undertakings after it would have taken place, to which the regulatory authority could apply national regulatory provisions. In *Thomson-CSF/Racal* the UK investigated the public security aspects of the proposed transaction under the merger provisions of the now-repealed Fair Trading Act 1973[183]. In *MBDA/SNPE/JV* the European Commission cleared the concentration under the ECMR, and the UK accepted behavioural undertakings in lieu of a reference to the Competition Commission to alleviate public security concerns[184].

(ii) Prohibited applications of Article 21(4)

In *Banco Santander Central Hispano/A Champalimand*[185] a concentration in the financial services sector having a Community dimension was notified to the Commission. The Portuguese Minister of Finance opposed the concentration, claiming to have anxieties about the prudential supervision of Mundial Confianga, an insurance undertaking, and also because he considered that the concentration would interfere with Portuguese national interests; further it would prejudice an integral sector of the Portuguese economy and financial system. The concerns of the Minister were increased by the parties' procedural impropriety in failing to notify the Minister of Finance. The Commission rejected these arguments and required the Minister to suspend his opposition to the transaction[186].

The Commission took a similar view in the case of *Secil/Holderbank/Cimpor*. The Portuguese Minister of Finance objected to the proposed acquisition of a Portuguese cement company, Cimpor, which the Portuguese Government was in the process of privatising. The proposed acquisition had a Community dimension and therefore fell within the Commission's exclusive jurisdiction[187]. The Commission adopted a decision requiring Portugal to withdraw the decisions it had taken opposing the acquisition on the ground

---

Northumbrian Water Group plc Cm 2936 (1995) identifying possible public interest detriments: see 1999 *Annual Report of the DGFT*, p 35.

[180] Case M 423, decision of 14 March 1994, OJ [1994] C 85/0.

[181] Case M 759, decision of 18 June 1996, OJ [1996] C 225/12, [1996] 5 CMLR 136.

[182] See the Commission's XXIXth *Report on Competition Policy* (1999), paras 193 and 197–198.

[183] Commission Press Release IP/00/628, 16 June 2000.

[184] See DTI Press Release P/2002/754, 27 November 2002 and DTI Press Release P/2002/802, 17 December 2002; these press releases can be accessed at www.gnn.gov.uk.

[185] Case M 1616, decision of 3 August 1999, OJ [1999] C 306/37; see Mohamed 'National Interests Limiting EU Cross-border Mergers' (2000) 21 ECLR 248.

[186] Commission decisions of 20 July 1999 and 20 October 2000: see the Commission's XXIXth *Report on Competition Policy* (1999), paras 194–196.

[187] The notification in this case was withdrawn by the parties before the Commission had reached a decision: Case M 2054.

that Portugal had failed to show that it had a legitimate interest in the sense of Article 21(4) of the ECMR[188]. The Government of Portugal challenged the Commission's decision, but in *Portugal v Commission*[189] the ECJ held that the Commission was entitled to adopt an Article 21 decision to preserve the 'effet utile' of that provision; that the Commission can by decision conclude that a decision of a Member State on the public interest is incompatible with Community law even where that interest has not been communicated to it by the Government asserting it; and that the Commission is entitled to require by an Article 21 decision that the state measure in question should be withdrawn.

In the case of *UniCredito/HVB*[190] the Commission cleared the proposed acquisition by UniCredito of Italy of HVB. However Poland required UniCredito to divest itself of shares in a Polish bank, BPH, which was indirectly controlled by HVB; it considered that the retention by UniCredito of these shares would violate the terms of an earlier agreement, in 1999, whereby UniCredito had purchased another bank, Pekao, as part of the process of bank privatization in Poland. The Commission subsequently notified the Polish Government that it considered that the Government had violated both Article 21 of the ECMR[191] and Articles 43 and 56 EC[192], on the right of establishment and the free movement of capital respectively; however these cases were subsequently closed.

In the case of *E.ON/Endesa*[193] the Commission approved the proposed acquisition by E.ON of Germany of a Spanish undertaking in the energy sector, Endesa. Spain took steps to impede the acquisition leading to two decisions of the Commission finding violations of Article 21 of the ECMR[194]. In March 2007 the Commission made a formal request to Spain to comply with these decisions[195]. Spain failed to satisfy the Commission with the result that the Commission referred the matter to the ECJ; the Court ruled in March 2008 that Spain had acted in breach of its obligations under Community law[196]. The Commission also came to a preliminary conclusion that Italy was in breach of Article 21 of the ECMR in relation to the case of *Abertis/Autostrade*[197], a transaction which the Commission cleared[198] but which Italy objected to on the basis that it was concerned that Abertis, of Spain, would not be able to carry out the investment required to maintain and improve the motorway network in Italy. In November 2006 Italy withdrew the obstacles to the merger and offered to cooperate fully with the Commission[199]. In January 2007 Italy made a submission to the Commission fully explaining the public

---

[188] See Commission Press Release IP/00/1338, 22 November 2000; in Case C-367/98 *Commission v Portugal* [2002] ECR I-4731 the ECJ ruled that the law under which the Portuguese Government had proceeded was itself in violation of Article 56 EC.

[189] Case C-42/01 [2004] ECR I-6079, [2004] 5 CMLR 9; see Mäkel 'The Court of Justice rules for the first time on Article 21(3) of the merger regulation in Case C-42/01 *Portuguese Republic v Commission*' *Competition Policy Newsletter*, Spring 2005, 19.

[190] Case M 3894, decision of 18 October 2005; Poland has challenged the Commission's decision to clear the merger: Case T-41/06 *Poland v Commission*, not yet decided.

[191] Commission Press Release IP/06/277, 8 March 2006.

[192] Commission Press Release IP/06/276, 8 March 2006.

[193] Case M 4110, decision of 25 April 2006.

[194] See Commission Press Release IP/06/1265, 26 September 2006 and Commission Press Release IP/06/1853, 20 December 2006.

[195] Commission Press Release IP/07/296, 7 March 2007.

[196] Case C-196/07 *Commission v Kingdom of Spain*, judgment of 6 March 2008; similar proceedings are in contemplation in relation to conditions attached to the proposed acquisition of Endesa by Enel and Acciona: Commission Press Release IP/08/164, 31 January 2008.

[197] See Commission Press Release IP/06/1418, 18 October 2006.

[198] Case M 4249, decision of 22 September 2006.   [199] See MEMO/06/414, 7 November 2006.

interest criteria that were relevant to the case[200]. The Commission, after expressing its frustration for the late reply on the part of Italy, sent a new preliminary assessment again finding Italy in breach of Article 21 of the ECMR[201]. In July 2007 Italy took steps towards addressing the Commission's concerns[202].

(G) Defence

Article 296(1)(b) EC provides that a Member State 'may take such measures as it considers necessary' in matters of security connected with its defence industry; such measures shall not adversely affect the conditions of competition in the common market regarding products which are not intended for specifically military purposes. This means that a Member State may investigate the military aspects of a concentration and the Commission the civilian aspects; this distinction in itself inevitably raises the problem of how to deal with products that have a 'dual-use', that is to say that can be used both for military and for civilian purposes. The UK government successfully invoked Article 296(1)(b) in relation to the proposed takeover of VSEL by British Aerospace[203], where both companies produced military equipment for the British defence forces; it required British Aerospace not to notify the military element of the takeover to the Commission. Subsequent to this the *GEC/Thomson-CSF(II)*[204], *British Aerospace/Lagardère*[205] and *British Aerospace/GEC Marconi*[206] cases all involved the exercise of Article 296 by the UK. In the case of *GEC/Marconi* it was reported that the Competition Commissioner at the time, Karel van Miert, was concerned that the Commission in the past had been too generous in allowing the UK to assert jurisdiction in defence matters: at the least the Commission would wish to look at the civilian aspects of the case and might in future be more sceptical on how 'dual-use' products should be investigated. More recently it seems that the Commission has been taking a stricter view in relation to the application of Article 296; since late 1999 several mergers involving the defence industry in Europe have been fully notified to the Commission[207].

4. NOTIFICATION, SUSPENSION OF CONCENTRATIONS, PROCEDURAL TIMETABLE AND POWERS OF DECISION

This section will deal with the following matters:

(A) **Notification**: concentrations that have a Community dimension are required by Article 4 to be notified on Form CO to the Commission.

(B) **Suspension of concentrations**: Article 7 provides that concentrations that have a Community dimension are automatically suspended until they are declared compatible with the common market; this period may be waived in appropriate cases.

---

[200] See MEMO/07/01, 5 January 2007.
[201] See Commission Press Release IP/07/117, 31 January 2007.
[202] See Commission Press Release IP/07/1119, 18 July 2007.
[203] DTI Press Notice P/94/623 of 19 October 1994, available at www.gnn.gov.uk: see Case M 528, Commission decision of 24 November 1994; see also Case M 529 *VSEL/GEC* decision of 7 December 1994.
[204] Case M 724, decision of 15 May 1996.   [205] Case M 820, decision of 23 September 1996.
[206] Case M 1438, decision of 25 June 1999.
[207] These cases can be accessed at www.ec.europa.eu/comm/competition/mergers/cases/index/by_nace_1_.html#l_75_22.

(C) **Procedural timetables and powers of decision of the Commission**: strict time-limits are imposed on the Commission's decision-making in order to disturb the operation of the market as little as possible: the Community Courts have stressed the importance of speedy procedures under the ECMR on several occasions[208]; the Commission can make a range of decisions when reviewing concentrations.

(A) Notification

Article 4(1) of the ECMR provides that concentrations with a Community dimension must be notified to the Commission following the conclusion of the agreement, the announcement of the public bid, or the acquisition of a controlling interest but prior to their implementation. Notification may also be made where undertakings demonstrate to the Commission a good faith intention to conclude an agreement or to make a public bid: this means that they can begin the investigative procedure, with the benefit of the fixed time-limits, before the formal legalities of the transaction have been completed. The Commission publishes a notice of concentrations having a Community dimension in the Official Journal. Articles 4(4) and 4(5) make provision for the parties to make reasoned submissions for the reallocation of cases to or from the Commission: this has already been discussed in the section on jurisdiction[209]. Fines can be imposed for providing incorrect or misleading information in a notification and for implementing a concentration without prior approval[210].

The Commission may declare a notification to be incomplete – for example because it omits information which ought to have been included – in which case the time-limits for reaching a decision will not have begun to run. Rejection of a notification may have very serious consequences for the undertakings concerned which, for a variety of reasons, may wish to conclude the transaction by a certain date. DG COMP has published *Best Practices on the conduct of EC merger control proceedings*[211] which seek to clarify the day-to-day conduct of proceedings under the ECMR; compliance will make it less likely that a notification is rejected as incomplete. The *Best Practices Guideline* suggests that, even in the simplest of cases, there should be pre-notification contact with DG COMP: the discussions should be commenced at least two weeks prior to notification and will be held in strict confidence[212]. Pre-notification discussions can cover a range of matters from jurisdictional questions and waivers of informational requirements to substantive analysis and possible remedies. The Commission prefers there to be business representatives present at meetings who have knowledge of the relevant markets as well as legal advisers[213]. The *Guideline* goes on to explain that a memorandum should be submitted to DG COMP to facilitate its initial contact with the parties, followed by more detailed submissions or a draft Form CO[214]. The *Guideline* also explains that there may be 'state-of-play' meetings between the notifying parties and officials from DG COMP at key stages of the investigation; DG COMP may also meet with interested third parties, and it may even hold 'triangular meetings' if it would be helpful to

---

[208] See eg Case C-170/02 P *Schülsselverlag J.S. Moser and others v Commission* [2003] I-9889, [2004] 4 CMLR 27, paras 33 and 34; Case C-42/01 *Portuguese Republic v Commission* [2004] ECR I-6079, [2004] 5 CMLR 9, paras 51 and 53.

[209] See pp 835–839 above.   [210] See pp 877–879 below.

[211] Available at www.europa.eu.int/comm/competition/mergers/others.

[212] *Best Practices Guideline*, paras 5–8.   [213] Ibid, para 9.   [214] Ibid, paras 10–23.

hear everyone concerned in a single forum[215]. The *Guideline* also discusses access to the Commission's file following the opening of a Phase II investigation[216], the review of 'key documents' and issues of confidentiality[217]. Officials from DG COMP meet on Mondays to allocate new cases to a particular case team.

The Commission has adopted Regulation 802/2004[218] which sets out the format in which a notification (or a reasoned submission) is to be made.

(i) Notifications

Notifications are made in the format known as Form CO. An original, signed version of the Form CO, on paper, must be submitted to the Commission together with a further five paper copies with annexes and 32 copies of the notification in CD- or DVD-ROM format[219]; the notification is sent to a registry (known as the Greffe) which registers its time of arrival, at which point the merger review timetable begins to run. Form CO requires the notifying firms to provide substantial information: Annex I of Regulation 802/2004 explains the information that must be provided. The pre-notification meetings required by DG COMP's *Best Practices Guideline* provide an opportunity for the parties, their advisers and the officials from DG COMP dealing with the case to satisfy themselves that the Form CO, when it is eventually submitted, contains all the information needed for the Commission to commence its investigation.

In certain circumstances a 'Short Form' notification may be made, relieving the parties from some of the informational burden that they would otherwise bear. The circumstances in which this procedure can be used, and the information required in the short-form notification, are set out in Annex II of Regulation 802/2004. The procedure is available for:

- Joint ventures that have no, or negligible, activities in the EEA
- Concentrations where the parties are not engaged in business activities in the same product and geographical markets or in markets that are vertically related to one another
- Transactions where the parties' combined market shares are below 15 per cent in the case of a horizontal concentration or, in the case of a vertical concentration, where the parties do not have an individual or combined market share in excess of 25 per cent at any level of the market
- Cases where a party is to acquire sole control of an undertaking over which it already has joint control.

When a short-form notification is permitted the Commission will usually adopt a short-form clearance decision within 25 working days from the date of notification: this procedure is described in the Commission's *Notice on a simplified procedure for treatment of certain concentrations under Council Regulation 139/2004*[220]. A significant proportion of cases are dealt with under the simplified procedure. For example of 323 Phase I decisions clearing concentrations unconditionally in 2006, 207 were dealt with under the

---

[215] Ibid, paras 30–39.

[216] See also the Commission's *Notice on access to the file*, OJ [2005] C 325/7.   [217] Ibid, paras 42–47.

[218] OJ [2004] L 133/1; this Regulation replaces the earlier Regulation 447/98, OJ [1998] L 61/1.

[219] See the Commission's *Communication pursuant to Regulation 802/2004* on the format in which notifications should be delivered to the Commission: OJ [2006] C 251/2, updated to take into account the accession of Bulgaria and Romania.

[220] OJ [2005] C 56/32.

simplified procedure; the corresponding figures for 2007 were 368 notifications, 238 of which benefited from the simplified procedure[221]. Cases dealt with under the short-form procedure are still subject to the suspension rule contained in Article 7 of the ECMR, but the undertakings concerned could apply for a derogation under Article 7(3)[222].

(ii) Reasoned submissions

Annex III of Regulation 802/2004 sets out the requirements for a Form RS where the parties seek a reallocation of jurisdiction to or from the Commission.

(B) Suspension of concentrations

Article 7(1) of the ECMR requires automatic suspension of a concentration that the Commission has jurisdiction to investigate before notification and before it has been declared compatible with the common market. Article 7(2) provides that, in the case of a public bid, the bid may be implemented provided that the concentration is notified to the Commission without delay and that the acquirer does not exercise the voting rights attached to the shares in question[223]. Article 14 provides penalties for 'gun-jumping' in breach of Article 7(1): infringement of Article 7 could lead to a fine of as much as 10 per cent of the worldwide turnover of the undertakings concerned[224].

Article 7(3) provides that the Commission may grant a derogation from the provisions on suspension, subject to conditions where appropriate. A request for derogation from the automatic suspension must be reasoned, and the Commission will take into account the effects of the suspension on the undertakings concerned by a concentration or on a third party, and the threat to competition that the concentration poses. A few Article 7(3) derogations are allowed each year, as the *Table of ECMR Statistics* demonstrates[225].

(C) Procedural timetable and powers of decision of the Commission

(i) Phase I investigations

(A) Possible decisions at the end of Phase I The parties having notified a concentration in accordance with the ECMR, the Commission is required by Article 6 to examine it as soon as it is received. The Commission is required to make a decision either that the concentration:

- Is outside the ECMR (Article 6(1)(a)); or
- Is compatible with the common market (Article 6(1)(b)): this finding extends to any restrictions directly related and necessary to the concentration ('ancillary restraints')[226]; or

---

[221] See p 887 below for a statistical table of merger notifications. [222] See below.

[223] This was the position in Case No COMP/M 2283 *Schneider/Legrand*, decision of 10 October 2001, OJ [2004] L 101/1 and Case No COMP/M 2416 *Tetra Laval/Sidel*, decision of 30 October 2001, OJ [2004] L 43/13 where unconditional bids for shares on the Paris Stock Exchange had been made.

[224] See pp 877–879 below; see Modrall and Ciullo 'Gun-Jumping and EU Merger Control' (2003) 24 ECLR 424.

[225] See p 887 below. [226] On ancillary restraints see pp 870–871 below.

- As modified by the parties no longer raises serious doubts and so may be declared compatible with the common market: such a decision may be subject to conditions and obligations ('commitments')[227] (Article 6(1)(b) in conjunction with Article 6(2)); or
- Raises serious doubts as to its compatibility with the common market (Article 6(1)(c)); in this situation the Commission must initiate a Phase II investigation[228].

A decision under Article 6(1)(a) or (b) can be revoked where it is based on incorrect information for which one of the undertakings is responsible or where it has been obtained by deceit[229], where there has been a breach of an obligation attached to a decision[230], or where the decision is illegal in accordance with general principles of Community law[231].

(B) Timetable In general Phase I decisions must, in accordance with Article 10(1) of the ECMR, be made within 25 working days at most of the day following notification; if the notification is incomplete the period begins on the day following receipt of complete information. The Phase I period may, in accordance with the second indent of Article 10(1), be extended to 35 working days where a Member State makes a request for a reference under Article 9, or where the undertakings concerned offer commitments pursuant to Article 6(2).

The Phase I timetable of 25, sometimes extended to 35, working days can place great strain on all the relevant parties – the business people, the professional advisers and the staff at DG COMP – which is why pre-notification meetings are so important. The overwhelming majority of cases are dealt with within the Phase I time limit, a not inconsiderable achievement given the complexity and size of many of the transactions notified.

(ii) Phase II investigations

(A) Possible decisions at the end of Phase II Where a concentration raises serious doubts about compatibility with the common market the Commission will commence proceedings in accordance with Article 6(1)(c) of the ECMR. An Article 6(1)(c) decision inaugurates an in-depth Phase II investigation.

The decisions the Commission may make at the end of Phase II are set out in Article 8. It may decide that the concentration:

- Is compatible with the common market, having regard to the provisions of Article 2(2) and, in some cases, Article 2(4)[232] (Article 8(1)): this finding extends to any ancillary restraints; or

[227] See pp 872–877 below.

[228] An Article 6(1)(c) decision cannot be challenged before the CFI: Case T-48/03 *Schneider Electric v Commission* Order of 31 January 2006; an appeal to the ECJ was dismissed by Order, Case C-188/06 P, [2007] ECR I-35.

[229] ECMR, Article 6(3)(a): see Case M 1397 *Sanofi/Synthélabo*, Commission Press release IP(99)255, 23 April 1999, [1999] 4 CMLR 1178 where the Commission revoked its decision as the notifying parties had failed to produce information about activities in a particular market; the Commission reopened its examination of the case, but allowed a partial exemption from the Article 7(3) suspension that would otherwise have automatically occurred, since the parties were preparing to offer suitable undertakings to overcome any competition concerns and because of the significant prejudice that a delay could have caused to the parties and their shareholders.

[230] Article 6(3)(b): see Case M 1069 *World Com/MCI*, decision of 8 July 1998, OJ [1999] L 116/1, [1999] 5 CMLR 876.

[231] Case T-251/00 *Lagardère SCA and Canal SA v Commission* [2002] ECR II-4825, [2003] 4 CMLR 965, paras 130 and 138–141.

[232] See pp 868–869 below.

- Is compatible with the common market, subject to commitments to ensure compliance with modifications proposed by the parties (Article 8(2)): again this extends to any ancillary restraints; or
- Is incompatible with the common market (Article 8(3)); or
- In so far as it has already been implemented, or implemented in breach of a condition attached to an Article 8(2) decision, must be reversed, or modified in an appropriate way (Article 8(4)).

Further the Commission may order such interim measures as may be appropriate (Article 8(5)) or revoke a decision taken under Article 8(2) where the Commission based its decision of compatibility on incorrect information or where the undertakings concerned have acted in breach of an obligation attached to the Commission's decision (Article 8(6)).

(B) Timetable Article 10 lays down the timetable within which the Commission must reach any of the decisions provided for in Article 8. The basic rule contained in Article 10(3) is that decisions under Article 8(1) to 8(3) must be taken within 90 working days of the date on which proceedings were initiated; the second sentence of Article 10(3) provides that this period may be extended to 105 working days where the undertakings concerned offer commitments pursuant to Article 8(2) provided that they are offered within 55 working days of the commencement of Phase II. The second indent of Article 10(3) makes further provision for an extension of the Phase II time-limit, at the request of the parties, for a period of up to 20 further working days.

Article 10(4) provides that the Phase II time-limits may exceptionally be suspended where the Commission has had to obtain additional information owing to circumstances for which one of the undertakings involved is responsible. This provision is not invoked very often; in the case of *Oracle/PeopleSoft*[233] the Commission did 'stop the clock' pursuant to this provision in circumstances where it may have suited all the parties concerned, given that it meant that the decision under the ECMR could be taken after the proceedings instituted by the Department of Justice in the US had been concluded[234]. However in the case of *Omya/J.M.Huber*[235] the Commission stopped the clock to the annoyance of Omya, which has appealed the matter to the CFI[236].

Where the Commission fails to reach a decision within the prescribed time scale, whether in Phase I or Phase II, the concentration will be deemed to be compatible with the common market[237].

(C) Phase II procedure A Phase II investigation is usually an exhausting and exhaustive exercise for all concerned. The timetables are tight, given that the investigation is 'in depth'. During the 90 working day period there will normally[238] be:

- A detailed market investigation by the Commission, including the sending of questionnaires to the parties, competitors and customers

---

[233] Case M 3216, decision of 26 October 2004, OJ [2005] L 218/6.
[234] *US and Plaintiff States v Oracle Corporation*, available at www.usdoj.gov/atr/cases/oracle.htm.
[235] Case M 3796, decision of 19 July 2006, OJ [2007] L 72/24.
[236] Case T-145/06 *Omya v Commission*, not yet decided.   [237] ECMR, Article 10(6).
[238] It is not inevitable that the full procedure will be followed; for example it may be that the parties offer suitable commitments during the beginning of the Phase II procedure, thereby obviating the need to complete the in-depth investigation; sometimes the parties choose not to have an oral hearing, not least because this can provide an occasion for third parties that object to the transaction to address their concerns orally to the Commission and the national competition authorities that attend the hearing.

- A peer review panel within DG COMP, to test the strength of the case
- A statement of objections sent by the Commission to the undertakings concerned
- A period for them to reply
- Access for the parties to the files of the Commission[239]
- An oral hearing which may last for one or two days
- A meeting (or meetings) of the Advisory Committee on Concentrations
- A period within which commitments can be discussed and an opportunity for interested third parties to comment on any such commitments[240]
- Consultation of other Directorates General
- The preparation of a draft decision for the College of Commissioners to consider the adoption by the full Commission of the final decision.

Achieving all these steps within the Phase II time-limits can be extremely difficult, especially since many of the cases that come to the Commission are immensely complex. The Chief Competition Economist and his team may play an important part in Phase II cases where in-depth economic analysis is called for.

(iii) 'Phase III'

Even when a final decision, whether under Phase I or II, has been made there may be a further period of uncertainty and delay for the undertakings concerned. Where the parties have offered commitments as a condition of clearance it may take a considerable period of time to implement them: practitioners sometimes use the expression 'Phase III' to describe this phase of some merger investigations[241]. Further delay may occur where there are appeals to the Community Courts, either by the undertakings concerned themselves, or by third parties dissatisfied with the outcome of the Commission's investigation[242].

5. SUBSTANTIVE ANALYSIS

Once the Commission has jurisdiction in relation to a concentration its task is to determine whether it is 'compatible with the common market'. The burden of proof is on the Commission which must produce convincing evidence that a merger is incompatible with the common market[243]; there is no presumption in Community law either that a merger is compatible or incompatible with the common market[244].

---

[239] On access to the file see Case T-221/95 *Endemol Entertainment Holding BV v Commission* [1999] ECR II-1299, [1999] 5 CMLR 611, para 68 and Durande and Williams 'The practical impact of the exercise of the right to be heard: A special focus on the effect on Oral Hearings and the role of the Hearing Officers' *Competition Policy Newsletter*, Summer 2005, p 22.

[240] See pp 872–877 below.   [241] On commitments see pp 872–877 below.

[242] On judicial review of Commission decisions see pp 879–885 below.

[243] See eg Case T-342/99 *Airtours v Commission* [2002] ECR II-2585, [2002] 5 CMLR 317, para 63; Case T-5/02 *Tetra Laval v Commission* [2002] ECR II-4381, [2002] 5 CMLR 1182, para 155, on appeal Case C-12/03 P *Commission v Tetra Laval BV* [2005] ECR I-987, [2005] 4 CMLR 573, paras 37–51; Case T-210/01 *General Electric Company v Commission* [2005] ECR II-5575, [2006] 4 CMLR 686, paras 60–64; on the issue of proof in merger cases generally see Bailey 'Standard of Proof in EC Merger Proceedings: A Common Law Perspective' (2003) 40 CML Rev 845.

[244] Case T-210/01 *General Electric Company v Commission* [2005] ECR II-5575, [2006] 4 CMLR 686, para 61.

Article 2(1) sets out certain criteria which the Commission must take into account when making its appraisal: these criteria are described and explained below[245]. Compatibility with the common market turns on the issue of whether the concentration will significantly impede effective competition. Article 2(2) provides that:

A concentration which would not significantly impede effective competition in the common market or in a substantial part of it, in particular as a result of the creation or strengthening of a dominant position, shall be declared compatible with the common market.

Article 2(3) provides that:

A concentration which would significantly impede effective competition in the common market or in a substantial part of it, in particular as a result of the creation or strengthening of a dominant position, shall be declared incompatible with the common market.

The Commission has published three texts of particular importance to the substantive assessment of mergers, the *Notice on the definition of the relevant market*[246], the *Guidelines on the assessment of horizontal mergers*[247] and the *Guidelines on the assessment of non-horizontal mergers*[248].

(A) Market definition

The substantive assessment of mergers under the ECMR begins with a definition of the relevant product and geographic markets. Some commentators believe that too much emphasis is placed on market definition in EC merger control, not least because techniques are being developed that make it possible to predict whether a particular merger would lead to an increase in prices without a formal determination of the relevant market or of market power[249]. Whatever the merits of this opinion may be, current practice assigns an important role to market definition: indeed notifying parties are required to identify any 'affected markets' in their Form CO (see below), and the CFI held in *easyJet v Commission*[250] that it was necessary to define the market when examining whether a merger would create or strengthen a dominant position under the ECMR[251]. Market definition, including the Commission's *Notice on Market Definition*[252], has been discussed in some detail in chapter one to which the reader is referred[253]. A few specific points about market definition under the ECMR follow.

(i) Form CO: 'affected markets'

Sections 6 to 8 of Form CO require the notifying parties to provide information in relation to 'affected markets'. Affected markets are defined to mean, in the case of horizontal relationships, relevant product markets where two or more parties to a concentration have a combined market share of 15 per cent or more at the national or EU level; and, in the case of vertical relationships, where their individual or combined market share is more than 25 per cent at one or more levels of the market. The information required in relation to these affected markets is substantial, including an estimate of the total size of the market, the parties' market shares for each of the last three financial years,

---

[245] See pp 856–857 below.   [246] OJ [1997] C 372/5, [1998] 4 CMLR 177.   [247] OJ [2004] C 31/5.
[248] Available at www.ec.europa.eu/comm./competition.
[249] See ch 20, pp 810–811, on merger simulation.
[250] Case T-177/04 [2006] ECR II-1931, [2006] 5 CMLR 663.   [251] Ibid, para 55.
[252] OJ [1997] C 372/5, [1998] 4 CMLR 177.   [253] See ch 1, pp 26–40.

the HHI before and after the merger[254], the structure of supply and demand and details of barriers to entry. The *quid pro quo* for the supply of such extensive information is that the Commission should be able to make a speedy assessment of the case. As noted earlier the information contained in Form CO must be accurate and complete[255]; if it is not the notification may be declared incomplete, in which case the time within which a decision must be made will not have begun to run. This is why extensive preparation in advance of notification, including contact with DG COMP, is so crucial[256]. It is important to understand that one merger might involve a number of affected markets: multi-product firms may have many overlapping products. For example in the case of *Bayer/Aventis Crop Science*[257] the Commission considered that there were in the region of 130 affected markets for crop protection, professional pest control and animal health products.

(ii) Commission decisions

In the period up to 31 January 2008 the Commission had adopted more than 3,500 decisions under the ECMR, and these contain many useful insights into its likely definition of the relevant market. Practitioners therefore, quite apart from conducting SSNIP (and other) tests to define the relevant market, will have recourse to the decisional practice of the Commission for guidance. How to access these decisions has been described above[258]; of particular interest for the purpose of market definition is that the Commission maintains on its website a classification of merger decisions by industry sector[259]. The point should perhaps be added that in many clearance decisions the Commission does not reach a finding on market definition, since it is clear that to do so would not materially affect its assessment; the Commission will say that, however the market is defined, it is satisfied that the concentration would not be incompatible with the common market.

(iii) Effect of decisions on market definition

In *Coca-Cola Co v Commission*[260] the CFI stated clearly that a market definition in an earlier decision of the Commission could not be binding in the case of a subsequent investigation, either by the Commission itself or a national court or competition authority: each case must turn on the particular facts and circumstances prevailing at the time.

(B) Adoption of the 'significant impediment to effective competition' test

The Commission will declare a merger to be incompatible with the common market where it would significantly impede effective competition, in particular as a result of the creation or strengthening of a dominant position. This formulation is subtly different

---

[254] See pp 858–859 below on the HHI.   [255] See p 844 above.
[256] Ibid.
[257] Case M 2547, decision of 17 April 2002, OJ [2004] L 107/1; see similarly Case M 3465 *Syngenta CP/Advanta*, decision of 17 August 2004.
[258] See pp 821–822 above.
[259] www.europa.eu.int/comm/competition/mergers/cases/index/by_nace.html.
[260] Joined Cases T-125/97 and T-127/97 [2000] ECR II-1733, [2000] 5 CMLR 467.

852 21 MERGERS (2) – EC LAW

from the test in the original Merger Regulation of 1989, which asked whether the merger would create or strengthen a dominant position as a result of which effective competition would be significantly impeded. The change in the substantive test was made in 2004 following a protracted debate which focused, in particular, on the respective merits of a test based on dominance, on the one hand, and on a substantial lessening of competition ('SLC'), on the other; and on the specific question of whether the dominance test left a 'gap' which meant that some mergers that could be harmful to competition could not be challenged under the ECMR. The compromise that emerged from this debate was the significant impediment to effective competition ('SIEC') test.

(i) The dominance/SLC debate

It was not surprising that the original Merger Regulation made use of the concept of a dominant position in the substantive test: this was an expression that was used in Article 82 of the Rome Treaty of 1957; indeed it could also be found in Article 66(7) of the (now expired) Paris Treaty on coal and steel of 1951. By the time that the original Merger Regulation was adopted there was a reasonable amount of jurisprudence on the meaning of dominance under Article 82 EC, in particular in cases such as *Continental Can v Commission*[261] and *United Brands v Commission*[262]; it was obviously attractive to deploy that jurisprudence for the purpose of merger control. In the years that followed the adoption of the Merger Regulation the Commission was able to adapt the dominance test and to apply it successfully to cases on single-firm dominance[263] and to collective dominance[264]; it also prohibited some vertical mergers under the dominance test[265]. For the most part the EC system of merger control developed very successfully. However the Commission's decision in *Airtours/First Choice*[266], in which a proposed hostile acquisition of a UK tour operator was prohibited by the Commission, caused controversy and was annulled on appeal to the CFI[267]. Part of the criticism of the Commission was about its fact-finding and reasoning. However there was also concern that it had tried to stretch the concept of collective dominance beyond its natural limit: whilst there was a reasonable degree of agreement that collective dominance could be applied to 'conscious parallelism' or 'tacit collusion' or, in today's language, 'coordinated effects', it seemed that the Commission in *Airtours* might have been trying to extend collective dominance to what is now referred to as 'non-collusive oligopoly' (see

[261] Case 6/72 *Europemballage and Continental Can v Commission* [1973] ECR 215, [1973] CMLR 199.

[262] Case 27/76 *United Brands Co v Commission* [1978] ECR 207, [1978] 1 CMLR 429.

[263] See eg Case M 53 *Aerospatiale-Alenia/de Havilland*, decision of 2 October 1991, OJ [1991] L 334/42, [1992] 4 CMLR M2: this was the first prohibition decision under the Merger Regulation.

[264] See eg Case M 308 *Kali und Salz* OJ [1994] L 186/38, upheld on appeal Cases C-68/94 and 30/95 *France v Commission* [1998] ECR I-1375, [1998] 4 CMLR 829; Case M.619 *Gencor/Lonrho*, decision of 24 April 1996, OJ [1997] L 11/30, [1999] 4 CMLR 1076, upheld on appeal Case T-102/96 *Gencor v Commission* [1999] ECR II-753, [1999] 4 CMLR 971: this was the first prohibition decision based on collective dominance.

[265] See eg Case M 490 *Nordic Satellite Distribution*, decision of 19 July 1995, OJ [1996] L 53/20, [1995] 5 CMLR 258.

[266] Case M 1524, decision of 22 September 1999, OJ [2000] L 93/1, [2000] 5 CMLR 494.

[267] Case T-342/99 *Airtours plc v Commission* [2002] ECR II-5761, [2002] 5 CMLR 7; for comment on the *Airtours* case see eg O'Donoghue and Feddersen (2002) 39 CML Rev 1171; Stroux 'Collective Dominance under the Merger Regulation: a Serious Evidentiary Reprimand for the Commission' (2002) 27 EL Rev 736; Overd 'After the Airtours Appeal' (2002) 23 ECLR 375; Haupt 'Collective Dominance under Article 82 EC and EC Merger Control in the light of the Airtours judgment' (2002) 23 ECLR 434; Nikpay and Houwen 'Tour de Force or a Little Local Turbulence? A Heretical View on the Airtours Judgment' (2003) 24 ECLR 193.

below). The CFI's judgment in *Airtours* seemed clearly to limit the notion of collective dominance to coordinated effects.

At around the same time as the *Airtours* controversy was raging the review of the Merger Regulation, leading to the adoption of the current ECMR in 2004, began. Not unnaturally, given the uncertainty raised by *Airtours*, some commentators raised the question of whether the dominance test was really an appropriate one to use[268]. Some systems of merger control, in particular in the so-called 'Anglo-Saxon' countries such as the US and Australia, ask whether a merger would lead to an SLC. The UK was in the process of changing its own law at the time that the EC system was under review; the Enterprise Act 2002 abolished the 'public interest' test, that had been used in the UK since 1965, in favour of the SLC test rather than one based on dominance[269]. However many other commentators were far from convinced that a move to an SLC test was necessary or desirable: the dominance test was firmly established, had worked well in practice, and it was unclear that there was a non-collusive oligopoly gap or that dominance could not be adapted to deal with it[270].

(ii) The non-collusive oligopoly gap

The perception that there could be a 'gap' in the coverage of the Merger Regulation arose as a result of the *Airtours/First Choice* decision. Airtours' proposed acquisition of First Choice would reduce the number of major tour operators in the UK from four to three. No firm would be individually dominant after the merger. The Commission prohibited the transaction on the basis that it would create a collective dominant position, but it was not clear whether the Commission's concerns were based on the likelihood of coordinated effects between the three remaining operators or on some other theory of harm. At paragraph 54 of its decision the Commission said:

Furthermore – contrary to the apparent view of Airtours – it is not a necessary condition of collective dominance for the oligopolists always to behave as if there were one or more explicit agreements (eg to fix prices or capacity, or share the market) between them. *It is sufficient that the merger makes it rational for the oligopolists, in adapting themselves to market conditions, to act – individually – in ways which will substantially reduce competition between them, and as a result of which they may act, to an appreciable extent, independently of competitors, customers and consumers (emphasis added).

The Commission talks here of the possibility of the oligopolists exercising their market power *unilaterally* rather than through coordination: in other words the Commission seemed to have applied the concept of collective dominance to address non-coordinated

---

[268] See eg Whish 'Substantive analysis under the EC Merger Regulation: should the dominance test be replaced by "substantial lessening of competition"?' in *EU Competition Law & Policy Developments & Priorities* (Hellenic Competition Commission, 2002), pp 45–62; speech by Whish 'Substantial lessening of competition/creation or strengthening of dominance' 28 September 2002, available at www.internationalcompetitionnetwork.org/conference-speeches.html; speech by Vickers 'How to reform the EC merger test?' 8 November 2002, available at www.oft.gov.uk; Fingleton 'Does Collective Dominance Provide Suitable Housing for All Anti-competitive Oligopolistic Mergers' [2002] Fordham Corporate Law Institute (ed Hawk), pp 181–199; Biro and Parker 'A New EC Merger Test? Dominance v Substantial Lessening of Competition' (2002) 1 Competition Law Journal 157.

[269] See ch 22, pp 897–898.

[270] See eg Böge and Muller 'From the Market Dominance Test to the SLC Test: Are there any reasons for a change?' (2002) 23 ECLR 495; speech by Ulf Böge 'Analytical Framework of Merger Review' 28 September 2002, available at www.internationalcompetitionnetwork.org/conference-speeches.html; Levy 'Dominance vs SLC: A Subtle Distinction' 8 November 2002, available at www.ibanet.org.

rather than coordinated effects[271]. The CFI, on appeal, handed down a judgment that clearly associated collective dominance with coordinated effects and annulled the Commission's decision[272]. It followed that, if the Commission did think that the problem in *Airtours/First Choice* was one of unilateral as opposed to coordinated effects, there appeared to be a gap in the Merger Regulation's coverage. If such a gap did exist it was because of the word 'dominance' which was not applicable in some situations.

A few examples may shed some light on the conundrum. In the following we assume that A, B and C produce high-quality products that are differentiated from one another; in other words the market is not one that is particularly conducive to coordinated behaviour[273]. In each case the proposal is that A will merge with B.

Example 1
Before the merger

A	B	C
50	30	20

After the merger

AB	C
80	20

After the merger AB will probably be individually dominant. The merger can be challenged under the dominance test.

Example 2
Before the merger

A	B	C
20	25	55

After the merger

AB	C
45	55

After the merger AB will certainly not be individually dominant since its market share will be less than C's; if the market is not conducive to coordination AB and C will not be collectively dominant either. The merger cannot be challenged under the dominance test.

Example 3
Before the merger

A	B	C
35	20	45

After the merger

AB	C
55	45

---

[271] See Motta 'Merger Policy and the *Airtours* case' (2000) 21 ECLR 199.
[272] See p 860 below.   [273] See pp 860–862 below.

After the merger AB will be larger than C, but it is unlikely that, with these market shares, it would be found to be individually dominant; as in Example 2 if the market is not conducive to coordination AB and C will not be collectively dominant either. The merger cannot be challenged under the dominance test.

The key question is whether, in Examples 2 and 3, AB and C might be more able, on an individual basis, to exercise market power after the merger than they were before it; if so there is clearly a case for intervention, but intervention is not possible on the basis of individual or collective dominance. Linguistically it is not difficult to see that, after the mergers in Examples 2 and 3, there might be substantially less competition than there was before it, thereby demonstrating the attraction of the SLC test.

(iii) The lack of empirical evidence on the non-collusive oligopoly gap

One of the difficulties at the time of the dominance/SLC debate was that, apart perhaps from *Airtours/First Choice*, there did not appear to be many – or perhaps any – gap cases under the ECMR. If the gap did not exist in practice, or if it was insignificantly small, it could be questioned whether a move from dominance to SLC was really necessary. It was possible that the *Heinz/Beech Nut*[274] case in the US was an example of a gap case; another possibility was the *Lloyds TSB Group plc/Abbey National plc*[275] case in the UK. However little empirical research had been done on the phenomenon of non-collusive oligopoly, with the result that proponents of the SLC test were having to advance their case predominantly on the basis of theory rather than empirical evidence of a gap. Furthermore it might be that some cases that were concerned with non-collusive oligopoly may have been dealt with by 'engineering' the market definition, so that the merged entity would be found to be individually dominant in a narrowly-defined market: however it is extremely difficult to prove in practice that the Commission had done this.

(iv) The solution: 'SIEC'

The actual solution adopted by the Council in the ECMR of 2004 is disarmingly simple: it retains the vocabulary of the old Regulation but rearranges it in a way that retains the existing law of dominance while at the same time endeavouring to close the gap. The wording within each of Articles 2(2) and 2(3) was simply reversed. The test is now whether a merger would lead to an SIEC, in particular by creating or strengthening a dominant position; it used to be whether the merger would create or strengthen a dominant position thereby leading to an SIEC[276]. The revised formulation envisages that most cases will be dealt with under the dominance standard as a result of the inclusion of the words *'in particular'*: this responds to the concern that a repeal of the dominance test would lead to uncertainty and 'undo' thirteen years of know-how and decisional practice of the Commission: recital 26 of the ECMR specifically refers to the desirability of preserving the existing jurisprudence of the Community courts and the decisional practice of the Commission under the old Regulation, as does paragraph 4 of the Commission's *Guidelines on the assessment of horizontal mergers*[277]. However the new

---

[274] *FTC v HJ Heinz Co*, available at www.ftc.gov.   [275] Cm 5208, 2001.

[276] See Schmidt 'The new ECMR: "Significant impediment or significant improvement?"' (2004) 41 Common Market Law Review 1555; Fountokakos and Ryan 'A New Substantive Test for EU Merger Control' (2005) 26 European Competition Law Review 277.

[277] OJ [2004] C 31/3.

test does not make dominance the exclusive test, and would enable the Commission to prohibit or require the modification of a merger that would not create or strengthen a dominant position but would 'significantly impede effective competition'.

Recital 25 of the Regulation makes clear that this formulation is intended to provide jurisdiction to deal with the 'gap', that is to say the problem of non-collusive oligopoly. It notes that in some oligopolistic markets mergers may 'even in the absence of a likelihood of coordination between the members of the oligopoly' result in a significant impediment to competition. It continues by acknowledging that the existing case law of the Community courts does not establish whether this situation is covered by the dominance test, and states that the new test is intended 'in the interests of legal certainty' to make clear that the gap is indeed catered for. Because of the concern that the new test might be too broad, the recital concludes by saying that the notion of 'significant impediment to competition' should be interpreted as extending, beyond the concept of dominance, only to the anti-competitive effects of a concentration resulting from the non-coordinated behaviour of undertakings which would not have a dominant position on the market concerned. The application of the substantive test to cases of non-collusive oligopoly since 2004 will be considered below, in particular the Commission's decision in *T-Mobile/Tele.ring*[278].

(v) The need for a causal link between the concentration and the SIEC

The judgment of the ECJ in *France v Commission*[279] established that there must be a causal link between the concentration and the deterioration of the competitive structure of the market for the ECMR to apply. In that case the ECJ was considering whether a 'failing firm' defence existed under the ECMR[280]. It held that a concentration should not be blocked where the firm would have failed anyway and its market share would have accrued to the acquirer, since the concentration did not cause the harm to competition. In *De Beers/LVMH*[281] the Commission's clearance was specifically based on the absence of any causal link between the creation of the joint venture and the strengthening of De Beer's dominant position in the market for rough diamonds.

(vi) Article 2(1): the appraisal criteria

Article 2(1) of the ECMR sets out a list of 'appraisal criteria' which the Commission must take into account when investigating concentrations. It is important to appreciate that the substantive test for determining whether a concentration is compatible with the common market is contained in Article 2(2) and (3): would the merger lead to an SIEC? The appraisal criteria are a checklist of factors that should guide the Commission towards its conclusion, but they do not in themselves determine the outcome of a case.

Article 2(1) provides that:

In making this appraisal, the Commission shall take into account:-

(a) the need to maintain and develop effective competition within the common market in view of, among other things, the structure of all the markets concerned and the actual or potential competition from undertakings located either within or outwith the Community;

---

[278] See p 860 below.

[279] Cases C-68/94 and C-30/95 [1998] ECR I-1375, [1998] 4 CMLR 829; this case was decided under the original Merger Regulation; there is no reason to suppose that the requirement of a causal link would not apply in the case of the reformulated substantive test.

[280] On the failing firm defence see p 864 below.

[281] Case M 2333, decision of 25 July 2001, paras 112–114; see similarly Case M 2816 *Ernst & Young France/ Andersen France*, decision of 5 September 2002, paras 75 and 90.

(b) the market position of the undertakings concerned and their economic and financial power, the alternatives available to suppliers and users, their access to supplies or markets, any legal or other barriers to entry, supply and demand trends for the relevant goods and services, the interests of the intermediate and ultimate consumers, and the development of technical and economic progress provided that it is to consumers' advantage and does not form an obstacle to competition.

The information required in relation to affected markets by Form CO reflects the appraisal criteria set out in Article 2(1). The list of factors in Article 2(1) is presumably not exhaustive: the Commission must consider all matters relevant to the assessment of a merger. Article 2(1) does not establish a hierarchy, giving greater weight to one assessment factor than another; the impact that the different appraisal criteria have on the Commission's determination will vary from case to case.

(C) Horizontal mergers

The Commission's *Guidelines on the assessment of horizontal mergers*[282] ('the *Horizontal merger guidelines*' or 'the *Guidelines*') provide guidance as to how the Commission assesses concentrations when the undertakings concerned are actual or potential competitors on the same relevant market[283]. The *Guidelines* deal in turn with market shares and concentration thresholds; the likelihood that a merger would have anti-competitive effects; countervailing buyer power; the possibility of entry into the market as a competitive constraint; efficiencies; and failing firms. This sequence will be retained in the text that follows. Paragraph 13 stresses that the *Guidelines* are not to be applied in a mechanical manner in each and every case; rather the competitive analysis in a particular case will be based on an overall assessment of the foreseeable impact of the merger in the light of the relevant factors and conditions. The judgment of the CFI in *Sun Chemical Group BV and others v Commission*[284] endorses this approach by the Commission, noting that the Commission enjoys a discretion enabling it to take into account or not to take into account particular factors[285].

(i) Market shares and concentration levels

The *Horizontal merger guidelines* note that market shares and concentration levels provide useful first indications of the market structure and of the competitive importance of the merging parties and their competitors[286]. The reference to 'useful first indications' is important: market shares and concentration levels are simply a device for conducting a first screening of a merger: they could never be determinative in themselves of the outcome of a case.

(A) Market shares The Commission usually looks at current market shares, although it may adjust them if it is certain that changes are about to occur because of exit, entry

---

[282] OJ [2004] C 31/5; note that prior to the adoption of the *Horizontal merger guidelines* the Commission had published two reports on the topic, *The Economics of Unilateral Effects* and *The Economics of Tacit Collusion*, each prepared by Ivaldi, Julien, Seabright and Tirole: the reports can be accessed on DG COMP's website; for discussion of the *Guidelines* see Voight and Schmidt 'The Commission's guidelines on horizontal mergers: Improvement or deterioration?' (2004) 41 Common Market Law Review 1583.

[283] *Horizontal merger guidelines*, para 5.

[284] Case T-282/06 [2007] ECR II-000, [2007] 5 CMLR 438.

[285] Ibid, para 57.   [286] *Horizontal merger guidelines*, para 14.

or expansion[287]; and in some industries, for example where there are 'large, lumpy' orders – for example irregular purchases of major capital equipment – it may be necessary to look at historical data[288]. Very large market shares of 50 per cent or more may in themselves be evidence of the existence of a dominant position, although they are not conclusive[289]; and the Commission may find a dominant position in the case of market shares between 40 per cent and 50 per cent, and even sometimes of less than 40 per cent, depending on the other factors relevant to the case[290]. The *Horizontal merger guidelines* state that a merger may be presumed to be compatible with the common market where the market share of the undertakings concerned does not exceed 25 per cent[291].

(B) Concentration levels The *Horizontal merger guidelines* state that the overall concentration level in a market may provide useful information about the competitive situation, and that it may use the Herfindahl-Hirschman Index ('HHI') in order to measure it[292]. The Commission is unlikely to be concerned in a market with a post-merger HHI of less than 1,000[293]. The Commission is also unlikely to be concerned where there would be a post-merger HHI between 1,000 and 2,000 and a delta[294] below 250, or a post-merger HHI above 2,000 and a delta below 150, unless there were special circumstances such as:

- The merger involves a potential entrant or a recent entrant with a small market share
- One or more of the parties are important innovators in ways not reflected in market shares
- There are significant cross-shareholdings among the market participants
- One of the merging firms is a maverick firm with a high likelihood of disrupting coordinated conduct
- Indications of past or ongoing coordination or facilitating practices are present
- One or more of the merging parties had a pre-merger market share of 50 per cent or more[295].

The *Horizontal merger guidelines* say that HHI's below the thresholds set out above may be used as an indicator of the absence of competition concerns, but that they do not give rise to a presumption either of the existence or the absence of such concerns[296]. The CFI in *Sun Chemical Group BV and others v Commission*[297] has added, however, that 'the

---

[287] Ibid, para 15; a point not made in the *Horizontal merger guidelines* is that sometimes the Commission will, when investigating one merger, take into account the fact that a subsequent notification has been received in relation to a different merger in the same sector that will have an impact on the future competitive structure of the market: see eg M 938 *Price Waterhouse/Coopers & Lybrand*, decision of 15 October 1997, OJ [1997] L 50/27, [1999] 4 CMLR 665, paras 108–111 and Case M 2389 *Shell/DEA*, decision of 20 December 2001, para 21; see also Schmidt 'Spotting the Elephant in Parallel Mergers: First Past the Post, or Combined Assessment?' (2003) 24 ECLR 183.

[288] *Horizontal merger guidelines*, para 15.

[289] On this point see Case T-282/06 *Cementbouw Handel & Industrie BV v Commission* [2007] ECR II-000, [2007] 5 CMLR 438, para 201.

[290] *Horizontal merger guidelines*, para 17.

[291] Ibid, para 18, referring to recital 32 of the ECMR; note however that this 'safe harbour' does not exist in the case of a collective dominant position involving the undertakings concerned and other third parties.

[292] *Horizontal merger guidelines*, para 16; the Herfindahl-Hirschman Index is explained in ch 1, pp 41–42.

[293] *Horizontal merger guidelines*, para 19.

[294] The delta refers to the change in the HHI as a result of the merger.

[295] Ibid, para 20.   [296] Ibid, para 21.

[297] Case T-282/06 [2007] ECR II-000, [2007] 5 CMLR 438.

greater the margin by which those thresholds are exceeded, the more the HHI values will be indicative of competition concerns'[298].

(ii) Possible anti-competitive effects of horizontal mergers

The *Horizontal merger guidelines* discuss the possible anti-competitive effects of horizontal mergers from paragraphs 22 to 63, dealing in turn with non-coordinated effects[299] and coordinated effects; there is also a brief discussion of mergers with potential competitors. The footnotes in the *Guidelines* contain many references to the case law of the Community Courts and the decisional practice of the Commission: due to constraints of space these judgments and decisions are not reproduced in the text that follows, but the reader should be aware of this useful reference point.

(A) Non-coordinated effects Paragraph 24 of the *Horizontal merger guidelines* explains that a horizontal merger may remove important competitive constraints on one or more firms in the market, thereby enhancing their market power and leading to significant price increases. Paragraph 25 notes that generally this will happen as a result of the creation or strengthening of a dominant position on the part of one firm whose market share, after the merger, will be appreciably larger than its next competitor. However the same paragraph also refers to the possibility of non-collusive oligopoly, that is to say a situation in which the firms remaining in the market after the merger will be able to exercise market power, and therefore increase prices, even though there is little likelihood of coordination among them and even though they are not individually dominant.

Paragraph 26 explains that a number of factors are relevant to a determination of whether non-coordinated effects might occur, but explains that not all of them must be present in a particular case and that the factors set out in the *Guidelines* are not an exhaustive list. The following factors are listed:

- **The merging firms will have large market shares**: the larger the addition of market share, the more likely it is that the merger will produce an SIEC[300]
- **The merging firms are close competitors**: the higher the degree of substitutability between the merging firms' products, the more likely it is that the merger will produce an SIEC[301]
- **Customers of the merging parties will have limited possibilities of switching to other suppliers**[302]
- **Competitors are unlikely to increase supply if prices increase**: in this case the merging parties will have an incentive to reduce output to less than the levels prior to the merger, thereby increasing price[303]
- **The merging firms will be able to hinder expansion by competitors**: for example they may control patents or other types of intellectual property that would make expansion or entry by rivals more difficult[304]

---

[298] Ibid, para 138.

[299] Note that the expression 'unilateral' effects is sometimes used as an alternative for non-coordinated effects: see footnote 27 of the *Horizontal merger guidelines*.

[300] Ibid, para 27.

[301] Ibid, paras 28–30; paragraph 29 discusses various methods of evaluating cross-substitutability eg through customer preference surveys, estimating cross-price elasticities and diversion ratios.

[302] Ibid, para 31.   [303] Ibid, paras 32–35.   [304] Ibid, para 36.

- **The merger would remove an important competitive force**: for example the removal of a particularly innovative firm as a competitor, or a merger between two particularly innovative firms, may change the competitive dynamics of the market considerably[305].

The most common ground for intervention on the part of the Commission is the possibility of non-coordinated effects arising from horizontal mergers. The most recent prohibition decision, *Ryanair/Aer Lingus*[306], was adopted on this basis. The Commission required remedies because of non-coordinated effects in several Phase II cases in 2006 and 2007[307]. The case of *T-Mobile/tele.ring*[308] was of interest since the Commission required a remedy as a result of non-coordinated effects in an oligopolistic market where the number of mobile telephony operators in Austria would be reduced from five to four, and the merging parties would not become the market leader: in other words this was a case of non-collusive oligopoly that the adoption of the SIEC test was designed to address[309].

(B) Coordinated effects   Paragraph 39 of the *Horizontal merger guidelines* explains that in some markets the structure may be such that firms will consider it possible, economically rational, and hence preferable, to adopt on a sustainable basis a course of action aimed at selling at increased prices. Some mergers might lead to an SIEC by increasing the likelihood that firms will be able to behave in a coordinated manner without entering into an agreement or resorting to a concerted practice contrary to Article 81 EC. Such coordination might concern prices, but it could also occur in relation to levels of production, the expansion of capacity, the allocation of markets or contracts in bidding markets[310].

Paragraph 41 says that coordination is more likely to occur where it is fairly simple to reach a common understanding on the terms of coordination. It adds that three further conditions must be satisfied for coordination to be sustainable: these are taken from paragraph 62 of the CFI's judgment in *Airtours v Commission*[311]. First it must be possible for the coordinating firms to monitor whether the terms of coordination are being adhered to; second, there must be some credible deterrent mechanism to maintain the discipline of the coordinating firms and to keep it internally stable; and thirdly there must be no constraint from outsiders that could jeopardise the results expected from coordination and make it externally unstable. Each of these matters is explored further in succeeding paragraphs of the *Guidelines*. They point out that a reduction in the number of firms in the market may be a factor that facilitates coordination; but also that other factors, such as the removal of a 'maverick' firm likely to disrupt an oligopoly, need to be examined[312]. In deciding whether coordination is likely to result from

---

[305] Ibid, paras 37–38.
[306] Case M 4439 *Ryanair/Aer Lingus*, decision of 27 June 2007, on appeal Case T-342/07 *Ryanair v Commission*, not yet decided.
[307] See pp 895–896 below.
[308] Case M 3916, decision of 26 April 2006; see Lübking '*T-Mobile Austria/tele.ring*: Remedying the loss of a maverick' *Competition Policy Newsletter*, Summer 2006, p 46.
[309] See pp 853–856 above; findings of non-collusive oligopoly are rare: one is M 3687 *Johnson & Johnson/ Guidant*, decision of 25 August 2005, paras 312–325 in relation to endovascular stents.
[310] *Horizontal merger guidelines*, para 40.
[311] Case T-342/99 [2002] ECR II-2585, [2002] 5 CMLR 317.
[312] *Horizontal merger guidelines*, para 42.

the merger the Commission will look at evidence of past coordination or evidence of coordination in similar markets[313].

The *Guidelines* discuss the following factors:

- **Reaching terms of coordination**: this is more likely to occur if it is easy to arrive at a common perception as to how the coordination should occur[314]. A number of matters are relevant when determining whether coordination would be easy, though these should not be applied in a mechanistic way[315]:
  - Is the economic environment simple and stable?
  - Are there a few, rather than many, firms in the market?
  - Are the products homogeneous rather than complex?
  - Are price and demand conditions stable rather than constantly changing?
  - Is the market one in which there is little innovation?
  - In the case of coordination by way of market division would it be easy to allocate customers, for example on the basis of geography?
  - Do other factors in the market increase transparency and so make it easier to coordinate prices?
  - Are the firms symmetric in terms of cost structures, market shares, capacity levels and levels of vertical integration?

- **Monitoring deviations**: coordination will work only if the coordinating firms are able to monitor one another to ensure that no-one is cheating, for example by lowering price, expanding output or improving quality. Markets must be sufficiently transparent to prevent this happening[316]. Paragraphs 50 and 51 of the *Guidelines* discuss factors relevant to a determination of transparency: for example transparency is higher where transactions take place on a public exchange than where they are negotiated privately on a bilateral basis.

- **Deterrent mechanisms**: coordination will work only if there is a sufficient threat that there will be retaliation against a firm that deviates[317]. Paragraphs 53 to 55 of the *Guidelines* discuss the credibility of deterrent mechanisms: the coordinating firms must have an economic incentive to retaliate against any firms that deviate; and the deviation does not necessarily have to be in the same market as the coordination.

- **Reactions of outsiders**: coordination will work only if there is no competitive constraint from non-coordinating actual or potential competitors[318].

In *Impala v Commission*[319] the Commission originally had concerns about a merger that it thought might lead to coordinated effects, but, during its Phase II investigation, reached the conclusion that the merger should be cleared unconditionally. A third party successfully challenged the Commission's clearance decision, in particular because the CFI felt that the market was a transparent one in which coordination was possible[320]. On

---

[313] Ibid, para 43; in Case T-464/04 *Impala v Commission* [2006] ECR II-2289, [2006] 5 CMLR 1049 the CFI said that the close alignment of prices over a significant period of time might, together with other factors, be sufficient to prove evidence of past coordination: ibid, paras 252–254.

[314] *Horizontal merger guidelines*, para 44. [315] Ibid, paras 45–48. [316] Ibid, para 49. [317] Ibid, para 52.

[318] Ibid, paras 56–57.

[319] Case T-464/04 [2006] ECR II-2289, [2006] 5 CMLR 1049; for comment see Völcker and O'Daly 'The Court of First Instance's *Impala* Judgment: a Judicial Counter-reformation in EU Merger Control?' (2006) 27 ECLR 589; Brandenburger and Janssens 'The *Impala* Judgment: Does EC Merger Control Need to be Fixed or Fine-Tuned?' (2007) 3(1) Competition Policy International 301; Ysewyn and Tajana 'The *Sony/BMG* Judgment of the Court of First Instance: Its Main Legal Implications and Impact on the Merger Control Process' (2007) 2 European Business Law Journal 233.

[320] Ibid, paras 288–294.

reexamination the Commission again cleared the merger[321], and on this occasion there was no appeal. The Commission was concerned about coordinated effects in *Areva/Urenco/ETC*[322], where it required various commitments, including a cessation of the flow of commercially sensitive information between a joint venture and its parents, as a condition of clearance. Commitments were also required as a condition of clearance in *Linde/BOC*[323], including the divestment of various wholesale supply contracts for helium and the termination of structural links, through a series of Asian joint ventures, between the merged entity and a competitor, Air Liquide. In *Travelport/Worldspan*[324] the Commission concluded, following a Phase II investigation, that a 'four to three' merger in the market for global distribution services would not give rise to coordinated effects since the complexity of the pricing structure and product offerings in that case limited the transparency of the market and therefore the possibility of successfully monitoring coordinated behaviour.

(C) Mergers with a potential competitor Paragraphs 58 to 60 of the *Horizontal merger guidelines* discuss mergers with potential competitors. Such a merger could lead to non-coordinated, or coordinated, effects where the potential competitor significantly constrains the behaviour of the firms active on the market. This is the case if the potential competitor possesses assets that could easily be used to enter the market without incurring significant sunk costs. Paragraph 60 states that for a merger with a potential competitor to give rise to significant anti-competitive effects two conditions must be satisfied: first, the potential competitors must already exert a significant constraining influence; and second, there must be a lack of other potential competitors which could maintain competitive pressure after the merger.

(iii) Countervailing buyer power

Paragraph 64 of the *Horizontal merger guidelines* explains that the competitive pressure on a supplier can come not only from competitors but also from a customer if it has countervailing buyer power, that is to say bargaining strength vis-à-vis a seller due to its size, commercial significance and its ability to switch to alternative suppliers. The Commission will consider to what extent a buyer could immediately switch to other suppliers, credibly threaten to integrate vertically (and therefore self-supply) or sponsor upstream expansion or entry; it is more likely that large and sophisticated customers will have this kind of countervailing buyer power than smaller firms in a fragmented industry[325]. In *Sun Chemical Group BV and others v Commission*[326] the CFI rejected an argument by a third party objecting to the clearance of a merger that the Commission had failed to apply the *Guidelines* on countervailing power correctly[327].

[321] Case M 3333, decision of 3 October 2007; see Lübking, Kijewski, Dupont, Jehanno and Eberl *Competition Policy Newsletter* (Number 3, 2007) 85.

[322] Case M 3099, decision of 6 October 2004.   [323] Case M 4141, decision of 6 June 2006.

[324] Case M 4523, decision of 21 August 2007.   [325] Ibid, para 65.

[326] Case T-282/06 [2007] ECR II-000, [2007] 5 CMLR 438, para 57.

[327] Ibid, paras 209–217; the merger is question was M 4071 *Apollo/Akzo Nobel IAR*, decision of 29 May 2006.

(iv) Entry

Paragraph 68 of the *Horizontal merger guidelines* explains that if entry into a market is sufficiently easy a merger is unlikely to lead to an SIEC: for entry to amount to a sufficient competitive constraint it must be shown to be likely, timely and sufficient:

- **Likelihood of entry**: entry must be sufficiently profitable taking into account the price effects of injecting additional output into the market and the potential responses of the incumbents on the market; the amount of sunk costs will be relevant to the analysis[328]. Barriers to entry include:
  - Legal advantages such as regulatory rules limiting the number of market participants or tariff and non-tariff trade barriers
  - Technical advantages such as access to essential facilities, natural resources, R&D and intellectual property rights
  - Incumbency advantages such as brand loyalty, established relationships with customers and other reputational advantages[329].
- **Timeliness**: entry will be regarded as a competitive constraint only where it would be sufficiently swift and sustained to deter or defeat the exercise of market power; what constitutes an appropriate time period for entry will depend on the characteristics and dynamics of the market, but it should normally occur within two years[330].
- **Sufficiency**: entry must be of sufficient scope and magnitude to deter or defeat the anti-competitive effects of the merger[331].

(v) Efficiencies[332]

Recital 29 of the ECMR says that, when determining the impact of a merger on competition, it is appropriate to take account of any substantiated and likely efficiencies put forward by the undertakings concerned; the Recital adds that the Commission should publish guidance on the conditions under which it may take efficiencies into account. This it has done in paragraphs 76 to 88 of the *Horizontal merger guidelines*. The Commission explains in paragraph 76 that efficiencies brought about by a merger may counteract the effects on competition and the potential harm to consumers that would otherwise have occurred. In making its appraisal of a merger it takes all relevant factors into account including the development of technical and economic progress, as set out in the appraisal criteria in Article 2(1) of the ECMR. It is important to understand that this approach means that there is no 'efficiency defence' – if the merger will lead to an SIEC it cannot be saved by a finding of efficiency: rather the Commission will factor any possible efficiencies into its overall assessment of whether the merger will lead to an SIEC. Paragraph 78 explains that, for efficiencies to be taken into account, they must produce a benefit to consumers, be merger-specific and be verifiable: these

---

[328] *Horizontal merger guidelines*, para 69.   [329] Ibid, para 71.   [330] Ibid, para 74.   [331] Ibid, para 75.

[332] Compare the *Horizontal merger guidelines* on efficiencies with the Commission's *Guidelines on the application of Article 81(3)* OJ [2004] C 101/97, paras 48–72, which are clearly motivated by similar considerations; the *Article 81(3) Guidelines* are discussed in ch 4, pp 151–160; see further Gerard 'Merger control policy: How to give meaningful consideration to efficiency claims?' (2003) 40 Common Market Law Review 1367; Colley 'From "Defence" to "Attack"? Quantifying Efficiency Arguments in Mergers' (2004) 25 ECLR 342; Kocmut 'Efficiency Considerations and Merger Control – Quo Vadis, Commission?' (2006) 27 ECLR 19.

conditions are cumulative:

- **Benefit to consumers**: efficiencies should be substantial and timely and should benefit consumers in the relevant markets where it is likely that competition problems might occur[333]. The efficiency gain might be lower prices, though cost reductions that simply follow from a reduction in output would not qualify[334]; new or improved products or services could also amount to an efficiency gain[335]. Efficiency gains may enable a firm in an oligopolistic market to increase output and reduce prices, thereby reducing the incentive to act in a coordinated manner[336]. There must be an incentive to pass efficiency gains on to consumers, and the Commission will be more sceptical where the merger will lead to a monopoly or a very high degree of market power[337].

- **Merger specificity**: the efficiencies must be a direct result of the notified merger and must not be capable of being achieved by less anti-competitive alternatives; the burden of proof is on the notifying parties[338].

- **Verifiability**: the efficiencies must be verifiable such that the Commission can be reasonably certain that they are likely to materialise, and it is incumbent on the parties to produce the relevant information in due time to demonstrate that the efficiencies are merger-specific and likely to be realised[339].

In *Inco/Falconbridge*[340] the Commission considered, but rejected, arguments that the merger would generate efficiencies; in the Commission's view the parties had failed to demonstrate that the efficiencies were not attainable by less anti-competitive means and that consumers would benefit[341]. The parties were more successful in advancing efficiency arguments in *Korsnäs/Assidomän Cartonboard*[342], albeit in a case which it seems the Commission would have cleared unconditionally anyway.

(vi) The 'failing firm' defence[343]

Paragraph 89 of the *Horizontal merger guidelines* explains that the Commission may decide that an otherwise problematic merger is nevertheless capable of being found compatible with the common market where one of the parties is a failing firm. Three criteria are relevant:

- The allegedly failing firm would in the near future be forced out of the market because of financial difficulties if not taken over by another firm;

- There is no less anti-competitive alternative than the notified merger;

- In the absence of the merger the assets of the failing firm would inevitably exit the market[344].

It is for the notifying parties to provide in due time the relevant information to support a failing firm defence[345].

(D) Non-horizontal mergers

The Commission also investigates whether a merger could have vertical or conglomerate effects: its particular concerns are the possibilities of foreclosure and tacit collusion.

---

[333] *Horizontal merger guidelines*, para 79.   [334] Ibid, para 80.   [335] Ibid, para 81.   [336] Ibid, para 82.
[337] Ibid, para 84.   [338] Ibid, para 85.   [339] Ibid, paras 86–88.   [340] Case M 4000, decision of 4 July 2006.
[341] Ibid, paras 529–550.   [342] Case M 4057, decision of 12 May 2006: see paras 57–64.
[343] See Cases C-68/94 and 30/95 *France v Commission* [1998] ECR I-1375, [1998] 4 CMLR 829; for further discussion see Baccaro 'Failing Firm Defence and Lack of Causality: Doctrine in Europe of Two Closely Related Concepts' (2004) 25 ECLR 11.
[344] *Horizontal merger guidelines*, para 90.   [345] Ibid, para 91.

These concerns were introduced in chapter 20[346]. For many years there was a lack of clarity about the Commission's practice in relation to vertical and conglomerate cases, and its findings in *Tetra Laval/Sidel*[347] and in *GE/Honeywell*[348] were reversed on appeal. In 2003 DG COMP commissioned a report on the competitive effect of vertical and conglomerate mergers which was published on its website in 2005[349]. In 2007 the Commission published *Guidelines on the assessment of non-horizontal mergers*[350] ('the *Non-horizontal guidelines*' or 'the *Guidelines*') which provide valuable guidance as to how the Commission assesses concentrations where the undertakings concerned are active on different relevant markets. The *Guidelines* deal in turn with vertical mergers and with conglomerate mergers[351]. The *Guidelines* draw on the decisional practice of the Commission and the jurisprudence of the Community Courts since the ECMR entered into force in 1990. The text below does not cite this case law, but the reader should be aware that the *Guidelines* contain many useful references to relevant precedents. The *Guidelines* begin with an overview; they then discuss the significance of market shares and concentration levels; thereafter the specific issues arising in relation to vertical and conglomerate mergers are dealt with in turn. This sequence will be retained in the text that follows.

(i) Overview

The *Guidelines* acknowledge that non-horizontal mergers are less likely to significantly impede effective competition than horizontal ones[352]. First, they do not entail the loss of direct competition between the merging firms in the same relevant market[353]. Second, they provide substantial scope for efficiencies, for example by integrating complementary activities which may lead to lower prices and higher output[354] or by enabling a broader portfolio of products to be offered to customers, thereby giving them the benefit of 'one-stop-shopping'[355]. However the *Guidelines* point out that non-horizontal mergers may harm competition where they would alter the ability and incentive of the merged entity and its competitors in a way that could be harmful to consumers[356]. The Commission considers that (as in the case of horizontal mergers) non-horizontal mergers should be scrutinised for possible non-coordinated and possible coordinated

---

[346] See ch 20, pp 808–810.

[347] Case M 2416, decision of 30 October 2001, OJ [2004] L 38/13, on appeal Case T-5/02 *Tetra Laval v Commission* [2002] ECR II-4381, [2002] 5 CMLR 1182, on further appeal Case C-12/03 P *Commission v Tetra Laval BV* [2005] ECR I-987, [2005] 4 CMLR 573.

[348] Case M 2220, decision of 30 October 2001, OJ [2004] L48/1, on appeal Cases T-209/01 *Honeywell International Inc v Commission of the European Communities* [2005] ECR II-5527, [2006] 4 CMLR 652 and T-210/01 *General Electric Company v Commission* [2005] ECR II-5575, [2006] 4 CMLR 686; for comment see Grant and Neven 'The Attempted Merger Between General Electric and Honeywell: A Case Study of Transatlantic Conflict' (2005) 1(3) Journal of Competition Law and Economics 595.

[349] See Church *Impact of Vertical and Conglomerate Mergers* (2004), available at www.europa.eu.int; for discussion see Cooper, Froeb, O'Brien and Vita 'A Critique of Professor Church's Report' (2005) 1(4) Journal of Competition Law and Economics 785; Church 'A Reply to Cooper, Froeb, O'Brien and Vita' (2005) 1(4) Journal of Competition Law and Economics 797.

[350] Available at www.ec.europa.eu; see also *Non-Horizontal Mergers Guidelines: Ten Principles*, a note by the Commission's Economic Advisory Group for Competition Policy of 17 August 2006, available at www.ec.europa.eu/comm/competition/mergers/legislation/non_horizontal_guidelines.pdf.

[351] For a discussion of the differences between horizontal, vertical and conglomerate mergers see ch 20, pp 799–800.

[352] *Non-horizontal guidelines*, para 12.   [353] Ibid, para 12.   [354] Ibid, para 13.   [355] Ibid, para 14.

[356] Ibid, para 15.

effects[357]. Non-coordinated effects could accrue where a merger could lead to foreclosure of competitors[358]; coordinated effects if the merger would make it possible, or make it easier, for firms to act in a coordinated manner[359]. The Commission takes into account possible efficiencies that would arise from a merger as part of its assessment[360].

(ii) Market shares and concentration levels

The *Guidelines* state that the Commission is unlikely to have competition concerns where the market share of the new entity after the merger would be below 30 per cent and where the post-merger HHI would be below 2000[361]. However it does say that there may be some cases where 'special circumstances' might lead it to investigate a merger below these thresholds, for example where a merger involves a company that is likely to expand significantly in the near future, for example because of a recent innovation: in this case its market share would not reflect its likely competitive impact on the market in the future; or where there are factors at play that suggest that the merger could facilitate coordination, for example the removal of a firm 'with a high likelihood of disrupting coordinated conduct' (often referred to as a 'maverick')[362]. There is no presumption *against* a merger above the 30 per cent and 2000 thresholds[363].

(iii) Vertical mergers

(A) Non-coordinated effects: foreclosure The *Guidelines* distinguish two types of foreclosure: **input foreclosure** and **customer foreclosure**.

Input foreclosure occurs where the merged entity would be likely to restrict access to products or services to competitors in a downstream market, thereby raising their costs and making it harder for them to compete in that market. The *Guidelines* say that it is not necessary to show that any competitor would be forced to leave the market, only that the higher input cost would lead to higher prices for consumers[364]. The assessment requires an analysis of whether the merged entity would have:

- the **ability to foreclose** access to inputs, which requires a 'significant degree of market power'[365]
- an **incentive to foreclose**, which requires an analysis of whether the foreclosure would be profitable[366]
- an **overall likely impact on effective competition**, because it would lead to increased prices in the downstream market, for example by raising rivals' costs or raising barriers to entry[367].

Likely efficiencies will be taken into account as part of the assessment[368].

Customer foreclosure occurs where a supplier integrates with an important customer in a downstream market: this may mean that potential rivals in the upstream market no longer have access to a sufficient customer base downstream[369]. As in the case of input foreclosure, the *Guidelines* require an analysis of:

- the **ability to foreclose** access to downstream markets[370]
- whether there is an **incentive to foreclose** access to downstream markets[371]
- whether there is an **overall likely impact on competition**[372].

---

[357] Ibid, para 17.   [358] Ibid, para 18.   [359] Ibid, para 19.   [360] Ibid, para 21.   [361] Ibid, para 25.
[362] Ibid, para 26.   [363] Ibid, para 27.   [364] Ibid, para 31.   [365] Ibid, paras 33–39.   [366] Ibid, paras 40–46.
[367] Ibid, paras 47–51.   [368] Ibid, paras 52–57.   [369] Ibid, para 58.   [370] Ibid, paras 60–67.
[371] Ibid, paras 68–71.   [372] Ibid, paras 72–77.

(B) Other non-coordinated effects The *Guidelines* briefly suggest other possible non-coordinated effects that might be problematic, for example obtaining access to commercially sensitive information about the activities of rivals in upstream or downstream markets leading to less aggressive pricing in the downstream market[373].

(C) Coordinated effects The *Guidelines* discuss the possibility that a non-horizontal merger might lead to a situation in which coordination becomes possible, or more possible, than it previously was: as in the case of horizontal mergers, discussed above, the *Guidelines* explain that it is necessary to consider four issues:

- **reaching terms of coordination**
- **monitoring deviations**
- **deterrent mechanisms**
- **reactions of outsiders**[374].

(iv) Conglomerate mergers[375]

The *Non-horizontal Guidelines* also discuss the possibility that a conglomerate merger could cause competitive harm, although they note that usually there will be no problem[376]; as in the case of vertical mergers they consider first non-coordinated effects and then coordinated effects.

(A) Non-coordinated effects The *Guidelines* explain that the primary concern is that a conglomerate merger could lead to a foreclosure effect, for example by enabling the merged entity to indulge in tying, bundling or other exclusionary practices[377]. As in the case of vertical mergers, the *Guidelines* explain that it is necessary to consider:

- the **ability to foreclose**[378]
- the **incentive to foreclose**[379]
- the **overall likely impact** on prices and choice[380].

(B) Coordinated effects The *Guidelines* also explain that the possibility exists of coordinated effects arising from conglomerate mergers, for example by reducing the number of effective competitors[381].

(v) Recent cases on non-horizontal mergers[382]

In *Thales/Finmeccanica/AAS/Telespazio*[383] the Commission went into a Phase II investigation because of vertical concerns, but concluded that the merged entity would not have the

[373] Ibid, para 78.   [374] Ibid, paras 79–90.
[375] For further reading see Völcker 'Leveraging as a Theory of Competition Harm in EU Merger Control' (2003) 40 Common Market Law Review 581; Koponen 'The Long and Winding Road: The European Commission's Path to a Framework for the Analysis of Conglomerate Mergers' (2007) 1 European Business Law Journal 241; Nalebluff; OECD Roundtable on Portfolio Effects in Conglomerate Mergers.
[376] *Non-horizontal guidelines*, para 92.
[377] Ibid, para 93; on tying and bundling see ch 17, pp 679–687 and ch 18, pp 727–729.
[378] *Non-horizontal guidelines*, paras 95–104.   [379] Ibid, paras 105–110.   [380] Ibid, paras 111–118.
[381] Ibid, paras 119–121.
[382] See also Lahbabi and Moonen 'A closer look at vertical mergers' *Competition Policy Newsletter* (Number 2, 2007) 11.
[383] M 4403, decision of 4 April 2007.

ability or incentive to restrict access to a critical component for the production of telecommunications satellites. In *SFR/Télé 2*[384] the Commission had vertical concerns about a merger that would bring together SFR, part of the Vivendi group that has a strong position in attractive television content, and Télé 2 with a presence in the downstream Pay-TV distribution market. A number of commitments were given, including the provision of access to other Pay-TV operators to the Vivendi group's content on non-discriminatory terms.

(E) Articles 2(4) and 2(5) of the ECMR: full-function joint ventures and 'spillover effects'

Where a full-function joint venture has a Community dimension it falls to be analysed within the procedural framework of the ECMR. In so far as it would bring about a change in the structure of the market it will be investigated in accordance with the provisions of Article 2(1) to (3) that have just been discussed. However there is a further possibility that needs to be considered in relation to full-function joint ventures, which is whether the creation of the joint venture could lead to a coordination of the behaviour of undertakings that remain independent of one another: this is sometimes referred to as a 'spillover effect'. This is tested according to the provisions of Articles 2(4) and 2(5) of the ECMR which are based upon Article 81 of the EC Treaty and the decisional practice of the Commission.

Article 2(4) provides that:

To the extent that the creation of a joint venture constituting a concentration pursuant to Article 3 has as its object or effect the coordination of the competitive behaviour of undertakings that remain independent, such coordination shall be appraised in accordance with the criteria of Article 81(1) and (3) of the Treaty, with a view to establishing whether or not the operation is compatible with the common market.

Article 2(5) provides that:

In making this appraisal, the Commission shall take into account in particular:

- whether two or more parent companies retain, to a significant extent, activities in the same market as the joint venture or in a market which is downstream or upstream from that of the joint venture or in a neighbouring market closely related to this market,
- whether the coordination which is the direct consequence of the creation of the joint venture affords the undertakings concerned the possibility of eliminating competition in respect of a substantial part of the products or services in question.

(i) A practical example

The operation of these provisions is best understood with the benefit of an example.

Example of a full-function joint venture

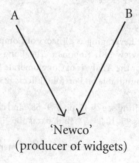

'Newco'
(producer of widgets)

---

[384] M 4504, decision of 18 July 2007.

Suppose that two producers of widgets, A and B, decide to merge their widget production into a joint venture, 'Newco'. Suppose further that both A and B will continue to produce widget dioxide, a raw material essential for the production of widgets, and that they will supply this raw material to Newco. In this case A and B will retain a presence in the 'upstream' market for widget dioxide[385].

The merger of the two widget businesses will be tested according to the criteria in Article 2(1) to (3) of the ECMR and the *Horizontal merger guidelines*:

- What will Newco's market share and market power be?
- Will there be countervailing buyer power?
- Would the merger lead to merger-specific efficiency gains?

However the additional question that has to be asked of this joint venture is whether the participation of A and B in the affairs of Newco will lead to them acting in a coordinated manner in the upstream market, for example because they will get to know about one another's pricing policy or capacity-expansion plans in relation to widget dioxide. This is the question that will be appraised in accordance with the criteria of Articles 2(4) and 2(5) of the ECMR.

(ii) Articles 2(4) and 2(5) in practice

In practice Articles 2(4) and (5) have not given rise to many difficult cases. The first Phase II investigation where possible spillover effects were considered was in the case of a joint venture between the telecommunications operators BT and AT&T[386]. The Commission identified certain 'candidate markets' in which coordination was a possibility and then considered, first, whether that coordination would happen as a result of the joint venture and, secondly, whether any restriction of competition would be appreciable. The joint venture was approved subject to commitments offered by the parties to eliminate the risk of parental coordination, including a divestiture of ACC, a wholly-owned subsidiary of AT&T[387]. In another Phase II investigation, *Areva/Urenco/ETC JV*[388], the Commission was concerned that a joint venture would lead to coordination between Areva and Urenco as a result of the increased scope for the exchange of information through the joint venture in relation to uranium enrichment. Commitments were given to reinforce firewalls between the parties and the joint venture and between the parties themselves[389]. The Commission investigated possible spillover effects in *Sony/BMG* but decided that they were not a concern[390].

---

[385] It is equally possible that the spillover effects might occur in a downstream or a horizontally neighbouring market.

[386] Case JV.15 *BT/AT&T*, decision of 30 March 1999; a Phase II investigation into spillover effects was ended when the concentration in Case JV.27 *Microsoft/Liberty Media/Telewest* was abandoned; the first decision in a Phase I case was Case JV.1 *Schibsted Multimedia AS/Telenor AS/Telia AB*, decision of 27 May 1996, [1999] 4 CMLR 216; commitments have been accepted in some Phase I cases, eg Case M 1327 NC/Canal+/CDPQ/Bank America, decision of 3 December 1998; Case No JV.37 *BSkyB/KirchPay TV*, decision of 21 March 2000.

[387] See the Commission's XXIXth *Report on Competition Policy* (1999), para 185.

[388] Case M 3099, decision of 6 October 2004. [389] Ibid, paras 222–225 and 231–232.

[390] Case M 3333, decision of 19 July 2004, OJ [2005] L 62/30, paras 176–182.

(F) Contractual restrictions directly related to and necessary for a merger: 'ancillary restraints'

(i) Introduction

Recital 21 and Articles 6(1)(b), 8(1) and 8(2) of the ECMR recognise that certain contractual restrictions may be directly related to and necessary for the successful implementation of a merger; a decision that clears a merger is deemed also to clear such restrictions. An obvious example would be where two undertakings merge their widget businesses into a joint venture 'Newco' and agree not to compete with the widget business of Newco since to do so would undermine the very purpose of the transaction. The question is whether clauses of this kind, often referred to for the sake of simplicity as 'ancillary restraints', are cleared at the same time as the merger. The Commission has published a series of notices on this subject, the most recent of which is the 2005 *Notice on restrictions directly related and necessary to concentrations* (the '*Notice on ancillary restraints*')[391]. Although the ECMR provides that a clearance decision will clear any ancillary restraints, it is for the undertakings concerned to conduct a self-assessment of which restrictions are ancillary (as in the case of Article 81 EC generally since the adoption of the Modernisation Regulation). The Commission will not state in a clearance decision which restraints are ancillary: it will provide guidance only in the case of specific novel or unresolved issues giving rise to genuine uncertainty, other disputes having to be resolved before national courts[392]. Where a restriction is not ancillary this is not in itself prejudicial to it: rather it is then subject to independent examination under Articles 81 and 82 EC and national competition law[393].

(ii) General principles

Paragraph 11 of the *Notice* explains that the criteria of direct relation and necessity are objective in nature: it is not sufficient simply that the parties regard them as such. A restriction will be 'necessary' only where, without it, the merger could not be implemented or could be implemented only under considerably more uncertain conditions, at substantially higher cost, over an appreciably longer period or with considerably greater difficulty[394]. Examples given are restrictions necessary to protect the value of the business transferred, to maintain the continuity of supply after the break-up of a former economic entity or enabling the start-up of a new entity, regard being had to the duration, subject-matter and geographical field of application of the restriction in question[395].

(iii) Principles applicable in cases of the acquisition of an undertaking

Paragraph 17 of the *Notice on ancillary restraints* explains that, as a general proposition, it is the acquirer that may need protection, for example to ensure that it acquires the full value of the business it has paid for; greater scepticism is shown to restrictions

---

[391]   OJ [2005] C 56/24, replacing the previous *Notice*, OJ [2001] C 188/5.

[392]   *Notice on ancillary restraints*, paras 2–6; in practice disputes as to whether a restriction is ancillary are quite often dealt with in arbitration proceedings: on the arbitration of competition law see ch 8, pp 317–318.

[393]   Ibid, para 7.   [394]   Ibid, para 13.   [395]   Ibid.

providing protection to the vendor. The *Notice* examines three types of restriction, non-compete clauses, licence agreements and purchase and supply obligations.

- **Non-compete clauses**: these may be necessary to guarantee the transfer to the acquirer of the full value of the assets transferred including both the physical assets and the intangible ones such as goodwill and know-how[396]. Their duration, geographical field of application and subject-matter and personal scope must be limited to what is needed to implement the concentration[397]. As a general proposition a period of up to three years is justifiable where goodwill and know-how are transferred, and two years where only goodwill is included[398]. The geographical scope of the clause should be limited to the area in which the vendor has offered the relevant products or services prior to the transfer[399], and the clause should similarly be limited to the products or services forming the economic activity of the undertaking transferred[400]. Non-solicitation and confidentiality clauses have a comparable effect and are therefore evaluated in the same way[401].

- **Licence agreements**: it may be that the vendor retains intellectual property rights in order to exploit them for activities other than those transferred to the acquirer, but licences them to the acquirer for its purposes. Such licences – for example of patents or know-how – can be ancillary, but territorial limitations on the buyer as to the place of manufacture will not be; nor will restrictions protecting the licensor rather than the licensee[402].

- **Purchase and supply agreements**: these may be needed in order to avoid the disruption of traditional lines of purchase and supply within the business transferred, in favour of both the acquirer and the purchaser, for up to five years; however exclusivity provisions and similar clauses would not be regarded as ancillary[403].

(iv) Principles applicable in cases of full-function joint ventures

Paragraphs 36 to 44 examine the same types of restriction in the case of full-function joint ventures:

- **Non-compete obligations**: in the case of joint ventures an obligation not to compete with the joint venture is necessary to ensure good faith during negotiations, to fully utilize the joint venture's assets and to enable the joint venture to assimilate the know-how and goodwill transferred to it; obligations of this kind can be regarded as ancillary for the entire lifetime of the joint venture, not just for the period of two or three years envisaged in the case of the acquisition of a business from another undertaking[404]. Non-solicitation and confidentiality clauses are evaluated in the same way[405].

- **Licence agreements**: the principles are the same as for the acquisition of an undertaking[406].

- **Purchase and supply obligations**: again the same principles apply as in the case of the acquisition of an undertaking[407].

---

[396] Ibid, para 18.   [397] Ibid, para 19.

[398] Ibid, para 20; longer periods may exceptionally be permitted: see footnote 21 of the *Notice*.

[399] Ibid, para 22.   [400] Ibid, para 23.   [401] Ibid, para 26.

[402] Ibid, paras 27–31; note however that licences that go beyond ancillarity in the terms of the *Notice* may be block exempted under Regulation 772/2004 on technology transfer agreements: see ch 19, pp 771–781.

[403] *Notice on ancillary restraints*, paras 32–35; note however that vertical agreements that go beyond ancillarity in terms of the *Notice* might be block exempted under Regulation 2790/99 on vertical agreements: see ch 16, pp 640–662.

[404] *Notice on ancillary restraints*, para 36.   [405] Ibid, para 41.   [406] Ibid, paras 42–43.

[407] Ibid, para 44.

6. REMEDIES

It is rare for the Commission to prohibit a merger in its entirety: by 12 March 2008 this had only happened in 20 cases, and four of those prohibitions were annulled on appeal. However there have been many cases in which the Commission permitted mergers to go ahead only after the parties had offered commitments to modify notified transactions that addressed competition concerns that it had identified: the Commission refers to such modifications as 'remedies'[408]. By 31 January 2008 the Commission had accepted commitments in 159 Phase I cases and 84 Phase II cases. This means that something in the region of 6.5% of notifications of mergers having a Community dimension required modification before approval was forthcoming from the Commission[409].

The Commission published a draft revised *Notice on remedies* in April 2007[410]; the intention is that the Commission will adopt the new Notice in the course of 2008, replacing an earlier one of 2001[411]. The text that follows proceeds on the basis of the draft of 2007: obviously it is possible that the final Notice may differ from the draft, although it is understood that there are unlikely to be any major changes. The Commission has also published *Best Practice Guidelines: the Commission's model texts for divestiture commitments and the trustee mandate*[412] setting out model texts for divestiture commitments and for the trustee mandate.

(A) The legal basis for commitments

The legal basis for commitments as a way of settling merger cases is provided by Article 6(2) of the ECMR in the case of Phase I investigations and Article 8(2) for Phase II investigations. Each of Articles 6 and 8 provides that the Commission may attach conditions and obligations to a decision to clear a merger; such conditions and obligations are intended to ensure that the undertakings concerned comply with the commitments that they make to the Commission to modify their transaction. Recital 30 states that Phase I commitments are appropriate where the competition problem is easily identifiable and can easily be remedied: it adds that transparency and effective consultation of Member States and interested third parties should be ensured throughout the procedure. Recital 31 explains the various consequences of failure to comply with conditions and obligations. These include:

- The possibility of the Commission ordering that a merger that has already been carried into effect, but in breach of a condition given in Phase II, should be dissolved (Article 8(4))
- The power to take interim measures to restore or maintain conditions of effective competition in the event of a breach of a Phase I or Phase II condition (Article 8(5))
- The power to revoke a decision where undertakings commit a breach of an obligation attached to a decision (Article 8(6)).

---

[408] See para 2 of the *Notice on remedies*, available at www.ec.europa.eu/comm/competition/mergers/legislation/legislation.html.

[409] The statistics in this paragraph can be accessed at www.ec.europa.eu/comm/competition/mergers/statistics.pdf.

[410] The draft is available on the website of DG COMP.   [411] OJ [2001] C 68/3.

[412] Available at www.ec.europa.eu/comm/competition/mergers/legislation/best_practice.html.

Article 14(2) of the ECMR provides for fines of up to 10% of the aggregate turnover of the undertakings concerned to be imposed in the event of failure to comply with a condition or obligation attached to a decision; Article 15(1)(c) provides for periodic penalty payments to be imposed in the event of a failure to comply with an obligation.

(B) The Commission's draft *Notice on remedies*

The Commission will publish the new *Notice on remedies* in the course of 2008. The Commission will also adopt a regulation which will amend the Implementing Regulation in order to provide the format for a new form, Form RM, which undertakings will need to submit to the Commission when offering remedies. There are four reasons for the Commission's revised *Notice on remedies*. The first is that the 2001 *Notice* has become out-dated: it is necessary to take into account changes in the Commission's decisional practice in subsequent years. Secondly the original *Notice* needs to be adapted in the light of the changes to the original Merger Regulation that were effected by Regulation 139/2004, for example to take into account that time limits are now calibrated by reference to working days rather than weeks and months, as well as the adoption of the 2004 Implementing Regulation. Thirdly it is desirable to reflect the insights resulting from the Commission's 2005 *Merger Remedies Study*[413] in which it looked at the design, implementation and effectiveness of 96 remedies that it had accepted in 40 cases under the ECMR from 1996 to 2000. The study concluded that care is needed to define the right scope of a divested business; to ensure its interim preservation until divestiture; to approve adequate purchasers; and to ensure effective monitoring of the implementation of the remedies. Fourthly the revised *Notice* needs to incorporate important jurisprudence from the Community Courts on the subject of remedies in recent years in cases such as *ARD v Commission*[414], *EDP v Commission*[415], *easyJet v Commission*[416] and *CementbouwHandel & Industrie v Commission*[417].

The Commission's draft *Notice* runs to 35 pages and contains detailed guidance on a number of aspects of both the law and practice of remedies. It is considerably more sophisticated than the 2001 *Notice*.

(i) General principles

Section II of the draft *Notice on remedies* discusses the general principles relevant to remedies. Most of the discussion is about the need for remedies to address the possibility that a merger might significantly impede effective competition in the sense of Article 2(3) of the ECMR, but paragraph 4 states that the *Notice* is also relevant to remedies required to address possible spillover effects under Article 2(4). Paragraph 6 of the draft *Notice* acknowledges that the Commission is not in a position to impose unilaterally conditions on the clearance of a merger: it can do so only pursuant to

---

[413] Available at www.ec.europa.eu/comm/competition/mergers/studies_reports/studies_reports.html; see also Davies and Lyons *Mergers and Merger Remedies in the EU* (Edward Elgar, 2008).

[414] Case T-158/00 [2003] ECR II-3825, [2004] 5 CMLR 14.

[415] Case T-87/05 [2005] ECR II-3745, [2005] 5 CMLR 23.

[416] Case T-177/04 [2006] ECR II-1931, [2006] 5 CMLR 11.

[417] Case T-282/02 [2006] ECR II-319, [2006] 4 CMLR 26, upheld on appeal to the ECJ in Case 202/06 P *Cementbouw v Commission* [2007] ECR I-000, judgment of 18 December 2007.

commitments offered by the parties[418]. Paragraph 7 explains the Commission's need to introduce Form RM. Only the parties to a transaction have the relevant information necessary to demonstrate that a remedy would address the Commission's competition concerns: they therefore must provide that information to the Commission so that it can conduct an assessment. However paragraph 8 of the draft *Notice* notes that the Commission retains the burden of proving that the merger, as modified by the commitments proposed, would nevertheless significantly impede effective competition[419].

The draft amended Implementing Regulation will establish a new Annex which sets out the information that must be contained in Form RM. It requires the notifying parties to submit detailed information concerning the commitments offered and, in particular, to provide specific information if the commitments offered consist of the divestiture of a business. The Commission may waive the provision of certain information if it considers that it is not necessary in a particular case. Form RM is divided into five sections dealing respectively with a description of the commitment; its suitability to remove competition concerns; an explanation of any deviation from the Commission's Model Texts; a summary of the commitments; and information on any business to be divested. The last of these five sections requires a considerable amount of information about the nature of the business to be divested including the assets (including IP rights and brands) to be transferred; an organisational chart identifying the personnel currently working for the business concerned; the customers of the business; financial data including turnover for the last two years of the business involved and a prediction for the next two years; and an explanation of why the business will be acquired by a suitable purchaser. The collection and presentation of this information will sometimes be a complex task and yet it will have to be supplied to the Commission within the tight timetables of the ECMR, whether the case is a Phase I or a Phase II one. The parties and their professional advisers will therefore need to begin the process of designing possible remedies and preparing a draft Form RM at quite an early stage of the investigation, very probably at a time when they are still arguing that the case is not one that gives rise to a significant impediment to effective competition or a spillover effect.

The draft *Notice* places considerable emphasis on the need for commitments to be effectively implemented and monitored. Paragraph 14 states that where the parties submit remedies that are extensive and complex it is unlikely that they will be acceptable, citing the cases of *ENI/EDP/GDP*[420] and *Volvo/Scania*[421] as examples. Paragraphs 15 to 17 make clear that there is a strong preference for structural remedies, such as divestitures and granting access to key infrastructure, over behavioural ones, although the use of the latter cannot automatically be ruled out[422]. In the Commission's view a commitment as to future behaviour would be acceptable 'only exceptionally in very specific circumstances'.

---

[418] See Case T-210/01 *General Electric v Commission* [2005] ECR II-5575, [2006] 4 CMLR 15, para 52; Case T-87/05 *EDP v Commission* [2005] ECR II-3745, [2005] 5 CMLR 23, para 105.

[419] See Case T-87/05 *EDP v Commission* [2005] ECR II-3745, [2005] 5 CMLR 23, paras 62ff.

[420] Case M 3440, 9 December 2004, OJ [2005] L 302/69, upheld on appeal Case T-87/05 *EDP V Commission* [2005] ECR II-3745, para 102.

[421] Case M 1672, 15 March 2000, OJ [2001] L 143/74, [2001] 5 CMLR 11.

[422] The possibility of behavioural remedies has been confirmed by the Community Courts in a number of judgments, eg Case C-12/03 P *Commission v Tetra Laval* [2005] ECR I-987, [2005] 4 CMLR 8, paras 85–89; for further discussion see Ezrachi 'Behavioural Remedies in EC Merger Control – Scope and Limitations' (2006) 29(3) World Competition 459.

(ii) Different types of remedies

Section III of the draft *Notice* discusses different types of remedies. Paragraphs 22 to 57 deal with divestiture of a business to a suitable purchaser; paragraphs 58 to 60 discuss the removal of links with competitors; and paragraphs 61 to 69 consider 'other remedies'. The final part of Section III is concerned with review clauses.

(A) Divestiture of a business to a suitable purchaser Paragraph 23 of the draft *Notice* explains that divested activities must consist of a viable business that, if operated by a suitable purchaser, can compete effectively with the merged entity on a lasting basis; the business should be divested as a going concern. Paragraphs 25 to 31 discuss the importance of determining the correct scope of the business to be divested. Paragraph 30 states that the business to be divested must be viable as such, so that the resources of a possible purchaser will not be taken into account at the stage of assessing the remedy. An exception to this is discussed at paragraphs 56 and 57 of the draft *Notice*: where a specific purchaser is identified during the investigation itself and the parties enter into a legally-binding agreement to sell, the Commission will decide in its final decision whether the purchaser is suitable; if it is there will be no need for commitments. The Commission welcomes 'fix it first' remedies of this kind, in particular where the identity of the purchaser is crucial for the effectiveness of the proposed remedy.

Paragraph 32 of the draft *Notice* says that the Commission has a clear preference for the divestiture of a business that can operate on a stand-alone basis, that is to say independently of inputs from or cooperation with the merged entity. Paragraphs 35 and 36 discuss the situation where it is necessary to 'carve-out' a business from the merged entity's other businesses, that is to say to put a set of assets together capable of being divested that did not previously exist as a separate entity[423]; the Commission is not in favour of carve-outs, although it recognises that it would be disproportionate to rule them out altogether. The Commission would be more sympathetic to the sale of a stand-alone business with a 'reverse carve-out' of any business to be retained by the merged entity. Paragraph 37 expresses scepticism about the divestiture of assets such as brands that have not been a uniform and viable business in the past. Paragraph 43 states that, when the parties commit to a divestiture, they would normally be expected to agree not to reacquire influence over the divested business for a period of 10 years. Paragraphs 47 to 57 contain a detailed discussion of the need to transfer the business to a suitable purchaser, that is to say a purchaser who is independent of the parties, who has the financial resources, expertise, incentive and ability to maintain and develop the divested business, and who will be in a position to acquire the business without regulatory problems. The draft *Notice* deals in turn with cases where the Commission requires the business to be divested within a fixed time-limit (paragraph 52), or requires the identification of an 'up-front' buyer before the transaction can be completed (paragraphs 53 to 55), or accepts a 'fix-it-first' solution (see above).

(B) Removal of links with competitors The removal of links with competitors – for example by divesting a minority shareholding in a joint venture or by terminating a distribution agreement – are discussed in paragraphs 58 to 60. Paragraph 59 explains that, in

---

[423] On carve-out remedies see the Commission's 2005 *Merger Remedies Study*, pp 74–80.

exceptional cases, it may be sufficient to agree to waive voting rights attached to shares rather than to actually sell them.

(C) Other remedies Paragraphs 61 to 69 deal with other remedies, in particular commitments to grant access to key infrastructure, networks and key technology such as patents. Remedies of this kind have been accepted in many cases, which are helpfully cited in footnotes to the main text. Considerable emphasis is placed, in paragraph 66, on the need for there to be effective monitoring of remedies of this kind; this may include separation of accounting so that the cost of operating a key infrastructure can be ascertained and a fast-track dispute resolution mechanism to determine disputes about access. Paragraph 69 repeats the point made earlier that behavioural remedies as to future behaviour will only be acceptable in exceptional circumstances.

(D) 'Crown Jewel' commitments In some cases it may be possible to offer alternative commitments consisting of a preferred option but also a second one in case the first is not achieved. Sometimes this is referred to as a 'Crown Jewel' commitment: examples can be found in *Nestlé/Ralston Purina*[424] and *Johnson & Johnson/Guidant*[425].

(E) Review clauses Commitments should normally contain a review clause that allows the Commission to grant an extension of time or to waive, modify or substitute the commitments. This issue is discussed in paragraphs 70 to 75.

(iii) Procedural issues

Section IV of the draft *Notice* is concerned with procedure, dealing in turn with Phase I and Phase II commitments. Article 19(1) of the draft Implementing Regulation requires that Phase I commitments be submitted within 20 working days of the date of receipt of the notification; Article 10(1), second sub-paragraph provides that the deadline for the Commission to make a Phase I decision is extended from 25 to 35 working days where commitments are offered. Paragraph 81 emphasises the need for Phase I commitments to be offered in a timely manner, given the tight timetables involved. Article 19(2) of the Implementing Regulation requires that Phase II commitments be submitted within 65 working days of the date on which the Commission decided to conduct a Phase II investigation; this deadline can be extended by a further 15 working days. Paragraph 86 discusses the 'exceptional circumstances' in which it may be possible to offer commitments after the deadline has expired. Paragraph 89 provides that the same information required in a Phase I case should be provided in a Phase II proceeding.

(iv) Implementation of commitments

Section V of the draft *Notice* discusses the implementation of commitments. It deals in turn with the divestiture process, the approval of purchasers, the obligations of the parties during the interim period, the role of the monitoring and divestiture trustees, and the obligations of the parties following implementation of the divestiture. Paragraph 95 explains that the divestiture process can be divided into two periods. In the 'first divestiture period' the parties look for a suitable purchaser. If they are unsuccessful there follows the 'trustee divestiture period' when a divestiture trustee is appointed to divest

[424] M 2337, decision of 27 July 2001.   [425] M 3687, decision of 25 August 2005.

the business. Paragraph 96 states that the Commission would normally expect the first divestiture period to last around six months and the trustee divestiture period around three months. A further period of three months is foreseen for closing the transaction.

The Commission will require to be satisfied that the purchaser is a suitable one, and if it thinks that this is not the case it will adopt a decision to that effect: such a decision could be challenged before the CFI, for example by a potential purchaser rejected by the Commission[426].

Paragraphs 105 to 114 discuss the obligations of the parties pending the divestiture of the business, dealing in turn with three points: safeguards for the interim preservation of the viability of the business; the necessary steps for a carve-out process if relevant; and the necessary steps to prepare the divestiture of the business. The parties will be required to hold the business separate from its retained business and a 'hold separate manager' will normally be required to be appointed.

Paragraphs 115 to 124 contain a helpful discussion of the respective roles of the monitoring and divestiture trustees. Five main tasks of the monitoring trustee are to ensure that the business to be divested is not degraded during the interim period; in carve-out cases to monitor the splitting of assets and the allocation of personnel between the divested and retained businesses; to oversee the parties' efforts to find a potential purchaser and to transfer the business; to act as a contact point for any requests by third parties; and to report on these issues to the Commission in periodic compliance reports. The divestiture trustee will be given an irrevocable and exclusive mandate to dispose of the business within a specific deadline to a suitable purchaser; a minimum price will not be specified. The monitoring and divestiture trustees may be, but do not have to be, the same person or institution. In the Commission's experience auditing firms and other consulting firms may be particularly well-placed to act as a monitoring trustee; investment banks and large accountancy firms seem to be particularly suitable for the role of divestiture trustee.

Paragraph 125 states that the Commission will wish to be able to monitor compliance with commitments for a period of 10 years after the adoption of its decision and will reserve the right to request information from the parties for that period.

(C) Examples of remedies

Some cases in which the Commission has accepted commitments in recent Phase II cases are discussed in the final section of this chapter[427].

7. POWERS OF INVESTIGATION AND ENFORCEMENT

The Commission is given wide powers of investigation and the ability to impose fines for transgression of the ECMR; these powers are broadly in alignment with the rules

---

[426] See the (unsuccessful) appeal by a potential purchaser in Case T-342/00 *Petrolessence v Commission* [2003] ECR II-1161, [2003] 5 CMLR 9; cf, under UK law, Case 1081/4/1/07 *Cooperative Group Ltd v OFT* [2007] CAT 24: see ch 22, p 917.

[427] See pp 895–896 below.

contained in Regulation 1/2003[428], although there is no power to conduct a 'dawn raid' on the homes of natural persons under the ECMR. To enable the Commission to carry out its functions the ECMR gives it powers to request information (Article 11), to carry out on-the-spot investigations (Article 13)[429] and to impose fines and periodic penalties (Articles 14 and 15) for breach of the Regulation's provisions. Article 11 requests for information are a standard feature of almost all investigations, and may be sent both to the notifying parties and to other undertakings – for example competitors, suppliers and customers – which might be able to supply DG COMP with relevant information. Fines for providing incorrect or misleading information or for breaking seals affixed to premises, books or records during an inspection can be up to 1 per cent of the aggregate group worldwide turnover of the undertakings concerned in the preceding financial year[430]. Fines for implementing a merger without notifying it and without the Commission's authority pursuant to Article 7 of the ECMR, for implementing a merger in breach of an Article 8 decision or for failing to comply with a condition or obligation attached to a decision can attract fines of up to 10 per cent of the aggregate group worldwide turnover in the preceding financial year[431]. In determining the amount of a fine the Commission is required by Article 14(3) to bear in mind the nature and gravity of the infringement. Article 15 provides the Commission with the power to impose periodic penalty payments of up to 5 per cent of average daily turnover where firms continue, for example, to fail to supply correct information or to submit to an inspection. Clearly the possibility of a heavy fine, in association with the power under Article 8(4) to require the reversal of a concentration already effected, means that it is highly unwise to proceed without complying with the requirements of the ECMR. The Community courts are given unlimited jurisdiction by Article 16 to review decisions imposing fines or periodic penalty payments.

By 28 February 2008 there had been eight fines under these provisions. The first fine (of €33,000), for failure to notify and for carrying out an operation without the prior approval of the Commission, was imposed in 1998 in the case of *Samsung*[432]; in the US this phenomenon is often referred to as 'gun-jumping'. In the case of *A P Møller*[433] a larger fine, of €219,000, was imposed for failure to notify and for putting into effect three concentrations which were discovered in the course of an investigation of a notified concentration. In setting the level of the fine the Commission noted that the failure to notify was not intentional but that there had been 'qualified negligence'. A P Møller was a large European undertaking that could be expected to have a good knowledge of the ECMR, and the concentrations had been operated for a considerable time before they were brought to the Commission's attention. A mitigating factor was that there had been no damage to the competitive process. Fines were also imposed for the provision of incorrect information in 1999 in the cases of *Sanofi/Synthélabo*, *KLM/Martinair* and

---

[428] OJ [2003] L 1/1, [2003] 4 CMLR 551.

[429] See M 1157 *Skanska/Scancem*, decision of 19 December 1997, OJ [1999] L 183/1, [2000] 5 CMLR 686, para 11.

[430] ECMR, Article 14(1); under the original Merger Regulation the maximum fine for such infringements was much smaller, €50,000.

[431] ECMR, Article 14(2).

[432] Case M 920, decision of 18 February 1998, OJ [1999] L 225/12, [1998] 4 CMLR 494.

[433] Case M 969, decision of 10 February 1999, OJ [1999] L 183/29, [1999] 4 CMLR 392.

Deutsche Post[434]. In the case of *Mitsubishi*[435] the Commission for the first time imposed a fine on a third party, rather than the parties to the notified concentration; Mitsubishi had failed to provide information in response to requests from the Commission under Article 11 of the ECMR. The fines imposed in this case totalled €950,000. In *BP/ Erdölchemie* the Commission imposed a fine of €35,000 for the provision of misleading information in a Form CO[436]; and a fine of €90,000 in the case of *Tetra Laval/Sidel*[437] for supplying incorrect or misleading information about its technology in the Form CO and for providing incorrect information in reply to a request for information.

8. JUDICIAL REVIEW

Decisions of the Commission under the ECMR are subject to judicial review by the Community courts on the grounds set out in Article 230 EC, that is to say lack of competence, infringement of an essential procedural requirement, infringement of the Treaty or of any rule of law or misuse of powers[438]. Fines and periodic penalty payments are also subject to review, by virtue of Article 229 EC and Article 16 of the ECMR. In the early days of EC merger control appeals were relatively few, although there were some landmark judgments, for example on the meaning of collective dominance[439]. However in the second half of the 1990s anxiety grew that the Commission, acting as prosecutor, judge and jury in merger cases (as in cases under Articles 81 and 82 EC) possessed too much power; or, to put the matter another way, that there was insufficient judicial control of the Commission by the Community Courts. It was during this period that prohibition decisions under the ECMR began to increase in number, culminating in a record number of five prohibitions in 2001[440]. As if in response to this criticism there followed a dramatic series of annulments by the CFI of Commission prohibition decisions in June and October 2002: *Airtours v Commission*[441], *Schneider Electric v Commission*[442] and *Tetra Laval v Commission*[443]. In these judgments the CFI, while acknowledging that the Commission enjoys a considerable margin of appreciation when dealing with complex economic matters, nevertheless demonstrated that it was prepared to look quite deeply into both the Commission's findings on primary facts and into the inferences drawn from them when determining whether its analysis was vitiated by manifest errors of assessment. While each of these three judgments necessarily turned on its own facts,

---

[434] See the Commission's XXIXth *Report on Competition Policy* (1999), Box 9, pp 73–74; the *Deutsche Post* decision will be found at OJ [2001] L 97/1.

[435] Case M 1634, decision of 14 July 2000, OJ [2001] L 4/31; see the Commission's *Competition Policy Newsletter*, October 2000, pp 62–63.

[436] Case M 2624, decision of 19 June 2002, OJ [2004] L 91/40.

[437] Case M 3255, decision of 7 July 2004.   [438] See generally ch 7, pp 285–289.

[439] See Case C-68/94 *France v Commission* [1998] ECR I-1375, [1998] 4 CMLR 829, paras 169–178; Case T-102/96 *Gencor v Commission* [1999] ECR II-753, [1999] 4 CMLR 971, paras 148–158.

[440] See the statistical table of notifications at p 887 below.

[441] Case T-342/99 *Airtours v Commission* [2002] ECR II-2585, [2002] 5 CMLR 317.

[442] Case T-310/01 *Schneider Electric v Commission* [2002] ECR II-4071, [2003] 4 CMLR 768.

[443] Case T-5/02 *Tetra Laval v Commission* [2002] ECR II-4381, [2002] 5 CMLR 1182, upheld on appeal Case C-12/03 P *Commission v Tetra Laval* [2005] ECR I-987, [2005] 4 CMLR 8; for comment on *Schneider* and *Tetra Laval* see Temple Lang 'Two Important Merger Regulation Judgments: The Implications of *Schneider-Legrand* and *Tetra Laval-Sidel*' (2003) 28 EL Rev 259.

collectively they sent a strong signal to the Commission that it needed to be more rigorous in its investigations, and they succeeded in assuaging some of the concerns about the excessive power of the Commission and weak supervision by the CFI.

A different complaint about judicial review has been that, even if the CFI is prepared to exercise effective judicial control over the Commission, the time taken to obtain a judgment from the CFI is so long that the process is essentially without purpose. This has been addressed, to some extent, by the introduction of the so-called 'expedited procedure', discussed below. More radical solutions, such as the introduction of a specialist competition court at a lower level than the CFI[444], or even changing the role of the Commission to that of a prosecutor only, the actual decision to be taken by the CFI, seem, for the time being, to be in abeyance.

Appeals against decisions of the Commission have, in recent years, become more common, both on the part of the parties to the merger under scrutiny and on the part of third parties with objections to the way in which the Commission has handled a case. Advisors therefore need to explain to clients not only the time limits of Phase I and Phase II investigations under the ECMR, but also that a real possibility exists of protracted litigation in the Community courts after the Commission has reached its final decision. The *Sony/Bertelsman* case discussed below is particularly instructive in this respect[445].

(A) Standing

Article 230 EC allows any natural or legal person to institute proceedings against a decision which is addressed to it or which is addressed to another person but which is of direct and individual concern to it.

(i) The parties to the transaction

It is obvious that the parties to the transaction have standing, for example where a merger is prohibited: examples of successful appeals were given above; there have also been several unsuccessful appeals against prohibition decisions[446]. An interesting question is whether parties that offer commitments to the Commission as a condition of being allowed to proceed with a transaction can then appeal to the CFI that the Commission had no right to insist on remedies. On the one hand it can be argued that offering commitments is a voluntary act on the part of the parties, so that they ought not to be able to challenge the Commission[447]; on the other hand the parties can argue that they were effectively 'forced' into offering a commitment in order to save what they could from the transaction, not least because the time limits imposed by the ECMR were soon to be reached. The CFI rejected an appeal of this kind in *Cementbouw Handel Industrie BV v Commission*[448].

---

[444] See ch 2, p 56. [445] See p 882 below.

[446] See eg Case T-102/96 *Gencor Ltd v Commission* [1999] ECR II-753, [1999] 4 CMLR 971; Case T-87/05 *EDP v Commission* [2005] ECR II-3745, [2005] 5 CMLR 23; Case T-210/01 *General Electric v Commission* [2005] ECR II-5575, [2006] 4 CMLR 15.

[447] See the Opinion of AG Kokott in Case C-202/06 P *Cementbouw Handel Industrie BV v Commission*, para 69.

[448] Case T-282/02 [2006] ECR II-319, paras 293–321, upheld on appeal Case 202/06 P [2007] ECR I-000, [2007] 5 CMLR 438; a similar case is pending before the CFI, Case T-275/06 *Omya AG v Commission*.

(ii) Third parties

Third parties also have the right to appeal against merger decisions of the Commission provided that they can demonstrate that the decision is of direct and individual concern to them. Article 18(4) of the ECMR provides that natural or legal persons showing a sufficient interest have a right to be heard during the Commission's administrative procedure, and the CFI has held that such persons have standing to appeal[449]. In some cases third parties that were not involved in the administrative procedure have also been found to have standing to appeal[450]. Many third party appeals have been unsuccessful, but this may be of little comfort to undertakings that have received a clearance from the Commission but then have to undergo a period of further uncertainty while the appeal process plays out. It is arguable that the rules on standing should be somewhat stricter in relation to third parties, at least where the appellant is a competitor of the merging parties whose objection to the transaction has nothing to do with consumer welfare considerations; objections from customers and consumers are likely to be much more meritorious[451]. Further discussion of third party appeals will be found below.

(B) The standard of review[452]

It is well-established that the Commission enjoys a margin of appreciation when assessing mergers and that the Community Courts should not substitute their own views for those of the Commission. The standard of review to be applied was succinctly stated by the CFI in *Sun Chemical Group BV and others v Commission*[453]:

[A]ccording to settled case law, review by the Community judicature of complex economic assessments made by the Commission in the exercise of the power of assessment conferred on it by the Merger Regulation is limited to ascertaining compliance with the rules governing procedure and the statement of reasons, the substantive accuracy of the facts and the absence of manifest errors of assessment or misuse of powers (see Case T-342/00 *Petrolessence and SG2R* v *Commission* [2003] ECR II-1161, paragraph 101; Case T-87/05 *EDP* v *Commission* [2005] ECR II-3745, paragraph 151 and *easyJet* v *Commission*, paragraph 59 above, paragraph 44). In that respect, it should be borne in mind that not only must the Community judicature ascertain whether the evidence relied on is factually accurate, reliable and consistent but also whether that evidence contains all the information which must be taken into account in order to assess a complex situation and whether it is capable of substantiating the conclusions drawn from it (Case C-12/03 P *Commission* v *Tetra Laval* [2005] ECR I-987, paragraph 39).

---

[449] See Case T-2/93 *Air France v Commission* [1994] ECR II-323, paras 42–47; for a case in which the CFI made an order finding that the appellants lacked standing see Case T-350/03 *Wirtschaftskammer Kärnten v Commission*, Order of 18 September 2006.

[450] Case T-342/00 *Petrolessence SA v Commission* [2003] ECR II-1161, [2003] 5 CMLR 9, paras 36–42.

[451] Third parties in the US have standing only where they can show that they would suffer direct antitrust injury: see *Cargill Inc v Monfort of Colorado Inc* 479 US 104 (1986); in a case on state aids the ECJ took a stricter view on the rights of third parties to appeal in Case C-260/05 P *Sniace SA v Commission* [2007] ECR I-000, paras 49–61.

[452] See Bailey 'Standard of Proof in EC Merger Proceedings: a Common Law Perspective' (2003) 40 CMLRev 845; Reeves and Dodoo 'Standards of Proof and Standards of Judicial Review in EC Merger Law' (Fordham Corporate Law Review, 2005, ed Hawk), ch 6; Vesterdorf 'Standard of Proof in Merger Cases: Reflections in the Light of Recent Case law in the Community Courts' (2005) 1(1) European Competition Journal 3.

[453] Case T-282/06 [2007] ECR II-000, [2007] 5 CMLR 438, para 60.

(C) The expedited procedure

The expedited procedure entered into force on 1 February 2001[454]. Under this procedure certain cases can be dealt with by the CFI more quickly than is usual; this is particularly important in the case of a decision prohibiting a merger, since a prolonged appeal may mean that market conditions change so substantially between the Commission's prohibition decision and the CFI's eventual judgment that, even after a successful appeal, it is no longer possible to proceed with the deal. The pleadings in a case under the expedited procedure are simplified and greater emphasis is placed on the oral hearing; this procedure is not suitable for a case involving a substantial number of points of appeal.

By 12 March 2008 the CFI had given judgments in ten merger cases in which the expedited procedure had been used (see Table 21.1 on facing page).

The shortest period between the lodging of an appeal and the judgment in an expedited procedure case was seven months in the case of *EDP v Commission*[455] and the longest was 21 months in the case of *Impala v Commission*[456]. Judgments in cases under the expedited procedure are likely to be shorter than in a 'normal' appeal[457]. In the *Impala* case the CFI was critical of the fact that Impala, having asked for the expedited procedure to be used, was itself responsible for slowing the progress of the case; as a result, although Impala was successful in persuading the CFI to annul the Commission's decision clearing the merger, it was awarded only three quarters of its costs against the Commission[458].

(D) Examples of third party appeals

(i) Appeals against the Commission's refusal to take jurisdiction

In *Schlüsselverlag JS Moser GmbH v Commission*[459] a merger was cleared by the relevant competition authority in Austria. Schlüsselverlag complained to the Commission that the merger in question had a Community dimension, and that therefore the Commission should have investigated it, not the domestic authority in Austria. The ECJ rejected the Commission's argument that it was not obliged to define its position when asked to do so by the appellant: the ECJ considered that it was vital, given that the Commission has sole jurisdiction in relation to concentrations having a Community dimension, that it should be required to take a decision if asked to do so[460]. However the appeal was rejected as the appellant had unduly delayed the making of its complaint to the Commission[461].

---

[454] OJ [2000] L 322/4; on this procedure see Fountoukakos 'Judicial Review and Merger Control: The CFI's Expedited Procedure' Commission's *Competition Policy Newsletter*, October 2002, p 7; Chibnall 'Expedited Treatment of Appeals against EC Competition Decision under the EC Merger Control Regulation' (2002) 1 Competition Law Journal 327.

[455] Case T-87/05 [2005] II-3745, [2005] 5 CMLR 23.   [456] Case T-464/04 [2006] ECR II-2289.

[457] Case T-87/05 *EDP v Commission* [2005] ECR II-3745, [2005] 5 CMLR 23, para 39.

[458] Ibid, paras 544–554.   [459] Case C-170/02 P, [2003] ECR I-9889, [2004] 4 CMLR 27.

[460] Ibid, paras 25–30.   [461] Ibid, paras 31–40.

21.1 Table of Expedited Procedure Cases

Case	Date on which the action was brought	Date on which the judgment was handed down	Time required for the handing down of judgment
Schneider Electric v Commission[1]	13 December 2001	22 October 2002	10 months
Schneider Electric v Commission[2]	18 March 2002	22 October 2002	7 months
Tetra Laval v Commission[3]	15 January 2002	25 October 2002	9 months
Tetra Laval v Commission[4]	19 March 2002	25 October 2002	7 months
BaByliss v Commission[5]	15 April 2002	3 April 2003	1 year
Royal Philips NV v Commission[6]	17 April 2002	3 April 2003	1 year
EDP v Commission[7]	25 February 2005	21 September 2005	7 months
Impala v Commission[8]	3 December 2004	13 July 2006	21 months
Endesa v Commission[9]	29 November 2005	14 July 2006	8 months
Sun Chemical Group v Commission[10]	9 October 2006	9 July 2007	9 months

[1] Case T-310/01 [2002] ECR II-4071.
[2] Case T-77/02 [2002] ECR II-4201.
[3] Case T-5/02 [2002] ECR II4381.
[4] Case T-80/02 [2002] ECR II4519.
[5] Case T-114/02 [2003] ECR II-1279.
[6] Case T-119/02 [2003] ECR II-1433.
[7] Case T-87/05 [2005] ECR II-3745.
[8] Case T-464/04 [2006] ECR II-2289.
[9] Case T-417/05 [2006] ECR II-18.
[10] Case T-282/06 [2007] ECR II-000.

(ii) Appeals against Article 9 references

In *Cableuropa SA v Commission*[462] the CFI held that a third party that objected to the Commission's decision to refer a merger to the Spanish competition authorities under

[462] Cases T-346/02 and T-347/02 [2003] ECR II-4251, [2004] 5 CMLR 25; see similarly Case T-119/02 *Royal Philips Electronics v Commission* [2003] ECR II-1433, [2003] 5 CMLR 2, paras 254–300.

Article 9 of the ECMR had the standing to challenge that decision[463], but upheld the Commission's decision on the merits.

(iii) Appeals against unconditional clearances

There have been several unsuccessful appeals by third parties against unconditional clearance decisions of the Commission[464]. However in one particularly striking case, *Impala v Commission*[465], a third party successfully persuaded the CFI that the Commission had wrongly cleared a merger with the result that the clearance decision in *Sony/Bertelsman* was annulled[466]. This meant that the Commission had to re-investigate the case, leading to a second clearance decision in September 2007, more than three years after the original decision[467].

(iv) Appeals against conditional clearances

There have been several appeals by third parties against conditional clearance decisions, usually unsuccessful[468]. A successful case was *BaByliss v Commission*[469] where the Commission required commitments in relation to certain national markets, for example Germany and Austria, but not in relation to others, for example Spain and Italy, in order to clear a merger[470]. BaByliss appealed to the CFI claiming among other things that the Commission should not have authorised the concentration without commitments in relation to markets with serious competition problems. The CFI accepted the argument and annulled the Commission's decision insofar as it concerned the markets in the countries not covered by the commitments[471]. This led to a second decision again clearing the merger subject to conditions[472].

A different point arose in *Petrolessence SA v Commission*[473] where the Commission required certain assets to be divested as a condition of approving a merger[474]. A potential purchaser of the assets was rejected by the Commission on the basis that it would not be an effective competitor and was therefore an unsuitable purchaser. The CFI held that Petrolessence had standing to appeal[475], but it was unsuccessful on the merits[476].

---

[463] Ibid, paras 47–82.

[464] See eg Case T-2/93 *Air France v Commission* [1994] ECR II-323; Case T-290/94 *Kayserberg v Commission* [1997] ECR II-2137, [1998] 4 CMLR 336; Case T-282/06 *Sun Chemical Group BV and others v Commission* [2007] ECR II-000, [2007] 5 CMLR 438.

[465] Case T-464/04, [2006] ECR II-2289; the case is on appeal to the ECJ Case C-413/06 P *Bertelsmann AG v Commission*, not yet decided.

[466] Case M 3333 *Sony/BMG* decision of 19 July 2004, OJ [2004] L 62/30.

[467] Commission Press Release IP/07/1437, 3 October 2007.

[468] See eg T-119/02 *Royal Philips Electronics BV v Commission* [2003] ECR II-1433, [2003] 5 CMLR 2; Case T-158/00 *ARD v Commission* [2003] ECR II-3825, [2004] 5 CMLR 14; Case T-177/04 *easyJet v Commission* [2006] ECR II-1931, [2006] 5 CMLR 11.

[469] Case T-114/02 *BaByliss v Commission* [2003] ECR II-1279, [2004] 5 CMLR 1.

[470] Case M 2621 *SEB/Moulinex*, decision of 8 January 2002.

[471] Case T-114/02 *BaByliss v Commission* [2003] ECR II-1279, [2004] 5 CMLR 1, paras 308–411.

[472] Case M 2621 *SEB/Moulinex II*, decision of 11 November 2003, *Annual Report on Competition* 2003, paras 259–262.

[473] Case T-342/00, [2003] ECR II-1161, [2003] 5 CMLR 8.

[474] Case M 1628 *TotalFina/Elf*, decision of 9 February 2000, OJ [2001] L 143/1, [2001] 5 CMLR 18.

[475] Case T-342/00, [2003] ECR II-1161, [2003] 5 CMLR 8, paras 36–42.

[476] Ibid, paras 100–123; see similarly in the UK Case No 1081/4/1/07 *Co-Operative Group Ltd v OFT* [2007] CAT 24, discussed in ch 22, p 917.

(E) Damages claims against the Commission[477]

There have been two occasions on which an application for damages has been made to the CFI for harm suffered as a result of a prohibition decision of the Commission which had been annulled on appeal. In *Schneider Electric SA v Commission*[478] Schneider had acquired control of Legrand through the French Stock Exchange. Contrary to the normal rule that requires pre-notification of agreed mergers, Article 7(2) of the ECMR permits the acquisition of control through public bids, provided that the acquisition is notified to the Commission without delay and that the voting rights in the shares are not exercised prior to clearance by the Commission. The Commission prohibited the merger and required the shares to be sold[479]. On appeal to the CFI the prohibition decision was annulled since the Commission had committed procedural errors[480]. Schneider renotified the acquisition of Legrand; the Commission opened a Phase II investigation[481]. Having unsuccessfully tried to negotiate commitments with the Commission, Schneider withdrew its notification and sold Legrand to a third party. It sought damages of €1.66 billion from the Commission, relying on Article 288 EC which deals with the non-contractual liability of the Community.

The CFI held that the Commission was liable for damages where it had manifestly and gravely disregarded the limits on its discretion. The CFI held that the Commission's failure to provide details in its statement of objections of the theory of harm on which it based its prohibition decision was sufficiently serious to found a claim for damages. The damages actually allowed were firstly to cover the cost of the second notification and secondly the difference between the sale price actually obtained and the price that Schneider might otherwise have achieved. As regards the second category of damages the CFI awarded Schneider only two thirds of its loss since, by acquiring the shares in Legrand in the first place, it had assumed the risk that there could subsequently be a prohibition.

In *MyTravel v Commission*[482] MyTravel, formerly Airtours, is suing the Commission for damages arising from its decision in *Airtours/First Choice*[483] which was annulled on appeal by the CFI[484].

9. INTERNATIONAL COOPERATION

(A) Close and constant liaison with Member States

Article 10 of the EC Treaty establishes the principle of cooperation between Member States and the institutions of the EC. In the context of the ECMR Article 19 sets out

---

[477] See generally Bailey 'Damages Actions under the EC Merger Regulation' (2007) 44 CMLRev 101.

[478] Case T-351/03 [2007] ECR II-000, judgment of 11 July 2007; the case is on appeal to the ECJ, Case C-440/07 *Commission v Schneider*, not yet decided; for comment on the CFI judgment see Dawes and Peci '"Sorry, But There's Nothing We Can Do to Help": Schneider II and the Extra-contractual Liability of the European Commission in Merger Cases' (2008) 29 ECLR 151.

[479] Case M 2283 *Schneider/Legrand* decision of 10 October 2001, OJ [2004] L 101/1.

[480] Case T-310/01 *Schneider Electric v Commission* [2002] ECR II-4071, [2003] 4 CMLR 768.

[481] Schneider unsuccessfully challenged the Commission's decision to take the case into Phase II: see Case C-188/06 *Schneider Electric v Commission*, Order of the ECJ of 9 March 2007.

[482] Case T-212/03, not yet decided.

[483] Case M 1524, decision of 22 September 1999, OJ [2000] L 93/1, [2000] 5 CMLR 494.

[484] Case T-342/99 *Airtours v Commission* [2002] ECR II-2585, [2002] 5 CMLR 317.

detailed provisions to establish liaison between the Commission and the Member States. Notifications under the ECMR must be transmitted to the competent authorities of Member States, which must be able to express their views on the Commission's treatment of cases; and the Advisory Committee on Concentrations must be consulted before important decisions – for example at the end of Phase II, or imposing fines – are taken. The Advisory Committee's opinion is not binding on the Commission, but considerable importance is attached to it. The CFI in *Kayserberg SA v Commission*[485] rejected a claim by a third party objecting to the Commission's clearance of the *Procter & Gamble/VP Schickedanz* transaction[486] that the Advisory Committee had not been properly consulted.

The Commission also cooperates with the EFTA Surveillance Authority pursuant to the provisions of the EEA Agreement[487]. This cooperation is provided for by Articles 57 and 58 of the EEA Agreement and Protocol 24.

(B) Relations with non-EC countries

(i) Reciprocity
Article 24 addresses the issue of reciprocity of treatment of mergers by non-EC countries. Some systems of law make it difficult, if not impossible, for foreign firms to take over local ones. Not surprisingly resentment is felt where, for example, a British firm is prevented from taking over a foreign one in circumstances in which, were the roles reversed, there would be no obstacle to the merger under UK law. Article 24(1) of the ECMR requires Member States to inform the Commission of any difficulties encountered by their undertakings in the case of concentrations in non-EC countries. Where it appears that a non-EC country is not affording reciprocal treatment to that granted by a Member State, the Commission may seek a mandate from the Council of Ministers to negotiate comparable treatment.

(ii) The international dimension
It is possible that a transaction might fall within the merger control systems of the EC, the US, Canada and many other countries. The problems associated with the international dimension – the burden on companies of multiple filings, the need for cooperation between competition authorities and the desirability of an expeditious and harmonious outcome – are considerable. These have been discussed in chapter 12, including the territorial reach of the ECMR and cooperation agreements between the EU, the US, Canada and Japan[488].

10. THE ECMR IN PRACTICE

(A) Statistics
From 21 September 1990, when the original ECMR entered into force, until 31 January 2008 the number of notifications received and decisions reached by the Commission were as follows:

[485] Case T-290/94 [1997] ECR II-2137, [1998] 4 CMLR 336, paras 80–97.
[486] Case No IV/M 430 OJ [1994] L 354/32.   [487] See ch 2, pp 57–58.
[488] See ch 12, pp 482–484 and 493–495.

21.2 ECMR Statistics

European Merger Control - Council Regulation 139/2004 - Statistics
21 September 1990 to 31 January 2008

I.) NOTIFICATIONS

	90	91	92	93	94	95	96	97	98	99	00	01	02	03	04	05	06	07	Feb 08	Total
Number of notified cases	11	64	59	59	95	110	131	168	224	276	330	335	277	211	247	313	356	402	64	3732
Cases withdrawn - Phase 1	0	0	3	1	6	4	5	9	5	7	8	8	3	0	3	6	7	5	0	80
Cases withdrawn - Phase 2	0	0	0	1	0	0	1	0	4	5	5	4	1	0	2	3	2	2	0	30

II.) REFERRALS

	90	91	92	93	94	95	96	97	98	99	00	01	02	03	04	05	06	07	Feb 08	Total
Art 4(4) request (Form RS)															2	14	13	5	1	35
Art 4(4) referral to Member State															2	11	13	5	0	31
Art 4(4) partial referral to Member State															0	0	0	1	0	1
Art 4(4) refusal of referral															0	0	0	0	0	0
Art 4(5) request (Form RS)															20	28	38	51	3	140
Art 4(5) referral accepted															16	24	39	50	5	134
Art 4(5) refusal of referral															2	0	0	2	0	4
Art 22 request	0	0	0	1	0	1	1	1	0	0	0	0	2	1	1	4	4	3	0	19
Art 22(3) referral (Art 22.4 taken in conjunction with article 6 or 8 under Reg. 4064/89)	0	0	0	1	0	1	1	1	0	0	0	0	2	1	1	3	3	2	1	17
Art 22(3) refusal of referral																1	1	0	0	2
Art 9 request	0	1	1	1	1	0	3	7	4	9	4	9	8	10	4	7	6	3	1	79
Art 9.3 partial referral to Member State	0	0	1	0	1	0	0	6	3	2	3	6	7	1	1	3	1	1	0	36
Art 9.3 full referral	0	0	0	1	0	0	3	1	1	3	2	1	4	8	2	3	1	1	0	31
Art 9.3 refusal of referral	0	1	0	0	0	0	0	0	0	0	1	0	0	0	1	0	0	0	1	4

III.) FIRST PHASE DECISIONS

	90	91	92	93	94	95	96	97	98	99	00	01	02	03	04	05	06	07	Feb 08	Total
Art 6.1 (a) out of scope Merger Regulation	2	5	9	4	5	9	6	4	4	1	1	1	1	0	0	0	0	0	0	52
Art 6.1 (b) compatible	5	47	43	49	78	90	109	118	196	225	278	299	238	203	220	276	323	368	41	3206
Art 6.1(b) compatible, under simplified procedure (figures included in 6.1(b) above)	0	0	0	0	0	0	0	0	0	0	41	141	103	110	137	167	207	238	26	1170
Art 6.1 (b) in conjunction with Art 6.2 (compatible w. commitments)	0	3	4	0	2	3	0	2	12	16	26	11	10	11	12	15	13	18	1	159

IV.) PHASE II PROCEEDINGS INITIATED

	90	91	92	93	94	95	96	97	98	99	00	01	02	03	04	05	06	07	Feb 08	Total
Art 6.1 (c)	0	6	4	4	6	7	6	11	11	20	18	21	7	9	8	10	13	15	0	176

V.) SECOND PHASE DECISIONS

	90	91	92	93	94	95	96	97	98	99	00	01	02	03	04	05	06	07	Feb 08	Total
Art 8.1 compatible (8.2 under Reg. 4064/89)	0	1	1	1	2	2	1	1	3	0	3	5	2	2	2	2	4	5	2	39
Art 8.2 compatible with commitments	0	3	3	2	2	3	3	7	4	7	12	9	5	6	4	3	6	4	1	84
Art 8.3 prohibition	0	1	0	0	1	2	3	1	2	1	2	5	0	0	1	0	0	1	0	20
Art 8.4 restore effective competition	0	0	0	0	0	0	0	2	0	0	0	0	2	0	0	0	0	0	0	4

VI.) OTHER DECISIONS

	90	91	92	93	94	95	96	97	98	99	00	01	02	03	04	05	06	07	Feb 08	Total
Art 6.3 decision revoked	0	0	0	0	0	0	0	0	0	1	0	0	0	0	0	0	0	0	0	1
Art 8.6 decision revoked	0	0	0	0	0	0	0	0	0	0	0	0	0	0	0	0	0	0	0	0
Art 14 decision imposing fines	0	0	0	0	0	0	0	0	1	4	1	0	1	0	1	0	0	0	0	8
Art 7.3 derogation from suspension (7.4 under Reg. 4064/89)	1	1	2	3	3	2	4	5	13	7	4	7	14	8	10	6	2	3	0	95
Art 21	0	0	0	0	0	1	0	1	0	1	1	0	1	0	0	0	2	1	0	8

http://ec.europa.eu/comm/competition/mergers/statistics.pdf

(B) Table of Phase II investigations

The following Table contains a list of cases in which a Phase II investigation was initiated since the fifth edition of this book was published in 2003 and completed by 12 March 2008[489].

21.3 European community merger regulation: table of Phase II investigations

Name of case	Cleared?	Cleared with commitments?	Prohibited?
Case No COMP/M.3083 *GE/Instrumentarium* 3.9.2003		YES	
Case No COMP/M.3093 *INA/FAG/SNFA* **NB: abandoned by the parties**			
Case No COMP/M.3099 *Areva/Urenco/ETC JV* 6.10.2004		YES	
Case No COMP/M.3178 *Bertelsmann/Springer JV* 3.5.2005	YES		
Case No COMP/M.3216 *Oracle/PeopleSoft* 26.10.2004	YES		
Case No COMP/M.3333 *Sony/Bertelsmann* 19.7.2004 **Annulled on appeal by a third party, Case T-464/04 *Impala v Commission***	YES		
Case No COMP/M.3423 *RWA/AMI/INTER-FERT* **NB: abandoned by the parties**			
Case No COMP/M.3431 *Sonoco/Ahlstrom JV* 6.10.2004		YES	
Case No COMP/M.3436 *Continental/Phoenix* 26.10.2004		YES	

[489] An updated version of this Table will periodically be posted on the OUP website that is linked to this book.

Name of case	Cleared?	Cleared with commitments?	Prohibited?
Case No COMP/M.3440 *ENI/EDP/GDP* 9.12.2004 **Upheld on appeal Case T-87/05** *EDP-Energias de Portugal v* *Commission*			YES
Case No COMP/M.3445 *Microsoft/TimeWarner/* *Contentguard JV* **NB: abandoned by the parties**			
Case No COMP M.3625 *Blackstone/Acetex* 13.7.2005	YES		
Case No COMP/M.3637 *Total/Sasol JV* **NB: abandoned by the parties**			
Case No COMP/M.3653 *Siemens/VA Tech* 13.7.2005		YES	
Case No COMP/M.3687 *Johnson & Johnson/Guidant* *Corporation* 25.8.2005		YES	
Case No COMP/M.3696 *E.ON/MOL* 21.12.2005		YES	
Case No. COMP/M.3796 *Omya/J.M. Huber PCC* 19.7.2006 **On appeal Case T-275/06 *Omya AG*** ***v Commission* (not yet decided)**		YES	
Case No. COMP/M.3848 *Sea-Invest/EMO-EKOM* 18.8.2006	YES		
Case No. COMP/M.3868 *Dong/Elsam/Energie2* 14.3.2006		YES	
Case No. COMP/M.3916 *T-Mobile Austria/tele.ring* 26.04.2006		YES	

Name of case	Cleared?	Cleared with commitments?	Prohibited?
CaseNo. COMP/M.3923 *AMI/Eurotecnica* **NB: abandoned by the parties**			
Case No. COMP/M.3975 *Cargill/Degussa Food Ingredients* 29.03.2006	YES		
Case No. COMP/M.4000 *Inco/Falconbridge* 04.07.2006		YES	
Case No. COMP/M.4009 *China International Marine Containers/Burg Group* **NB: abandoned by the parties**			
Case No. COMP/M.4094 *Ineos/BP Dormagen* 10.08.2006	YES		
Case No. COMP/M.4180 *Gas De France/Suez* 14.11.2006		YES	
Case No. COMP/M.4187 *Metso/Aker Kvaerner* 12.12.2006		YES	
Case No. COMP/M.4209 *Thule/Schneeketten* **NB: abandoned by the parties**			
Case No. COMP/M.4215 *Glatfelter/Crompton Assets* 20.12.2006	YES		
Case No. COMP/M.4381 *JCI/FIAMM* 10.5.2007		YES	
Case No. COMP/M.4397 *CVC/FERD/SIG* **NB: abandoned by the parties**			
Case No. COMP/M.4403 *Thales/Finmeccanica/AAS/Telespazio* 4.4.2007	YES		
Case No. COMP/M.4404 *Universal Music Group/ BMG Music Publishing* 22.5.2007		YES	

Name of case	Cleared?	Cleared with commitments?	Prohibited?
Case No. COMP/M.4439 *Ryanair/AerLingus* On appeal Case T-342/07 *Ryanair v Commission* (judgment pending) and Case T-411/07 *Aer Lingus Group v Commission* (not yet decided)			YES
Case No. COMP/M.3333 *Sony/BMG* 3.10.2007 NB: re-examination of case following annulment of earlier clearance decision on appeal to the CFI	YES		
Case No. COMP/M4498 *HgCapital/Denton* NB: abandoned by the parties			
Case No. COMP/M.4504 *SFR/Télé2* 18.7.2007		YES	
Case No. COMP/M.4523 *Travelport/Worldspan* 21.8.2007	YES		
Case No. COMP/M.4525 *Cronaspam/Constantia* 19.9.2007		YES	
Case No. COMP/M.4647 *AEE/Lentjes GmbH*	YES		
Case No. COMP/M.4662 *Syniverse/BSG*	YES		
Case No. COMP/M.4726 *Thomson Corporation/Reuters Group*		YES	
Case No. COMP/M.4731 *Google/Doubleclick*	YES		
Case No. COMP/M.4734 *INEOS Group Ltd/Kerling*	YES		
Case No. COMP/M.4747 *IBM/Teleologic*	YES		
Case No. COMP/M.4.781 *Norddeutsche Affinerie AG/Cumerio*	YES		

(C) Comment

(i) Outright prohibitions

Outright prohibitions are rare: by 12 March 2008 there had been only 20 examples, of which four were annulled on appeal to the CFI[490]. Since 2001 there have been only two prohibitions[491]. The first concentration to be blocked, in 1991, was *Aerospatiale-Alenia/de Havilland*[492]. Aerospatiale and Alenia intended to purchase the De Havilland division of Boeing. The Commission defined three relevant product markets: regional turbo-prop aircraft, excluding regional jet aircraft and jet aircraft of around 100 seats developed for short-haul and medium-haul flights, with 20 to 39 seats, 40 to 59 seats and 60 seats and over; it defined the geographical market as the world excluding China and Eastern Europe. The Commission concluded that the concentration would create a dominant position in the 40 to 59 seats and the 60-plus seats market, in which its market shares would be 63 per cent or more; also the takeover of de Havilland would remove Aerospatiale/Alenia's most effective competitor and would give the latter complete coverage of the market and significantly broaden its customer base. The Commission also considered that new entry into the market was unlikely and decided to block the concentration. Its decision was not unanimous, and the Advisory Committee on Concentrations was also divided[493]. The Commissioner responsible for Industry disagreed violently over the decision with Sir Leon Brittan, the Competition Commissioner, in particular as industrial policy considerations were not taken on board. However the language of Article 2(3) of the ECMR does not provide for industrial policy to be taken into account, and the decision set an important precedent in demonstrating that the test of the compatibility of a concentration with the common market was its impact on competition[494].

The second concentration to be blocked, in 1994, was *MSG Media Service*[495]. Three companies intended to establish a German pay-television joint venture, MSG. In the Commission's view the joint venture would give MSG a lasting dominant position on the pay-TV market for administrative and technical services; it would give Bertelsmann and Kirch a dominant position on the German-speaking pay-TV market; and it would protect and strengthen the dominant position of Deutsche Telekom for cable infrastructure. It is of interest that this was the first of several concentrations in the media sector to be prohibited outright: the very rapid changes in technology in this sector, and the possibility that concentrations could have serious foreclosure effects on third par-

---

[490]   See pp 894–895 below.

[491]   Case M.3440, *ENI/EDP/GDP*, decision of 9 December 2004, OJ [2005] L 302/69, upheld on appeal Case T-87/05 *EDP v Commission* [2005] ECR II-3745, [2005] 5 CMLR 23; Case M.4439 *Ryanair/Aer Lingus*, decision of 27 June 2007, on appeal Case T-342/07 *Ryanair v Commission*, not yet decided: for comment on the latter case by DG COMP officials see Gadas, Koch, Parplies and Beuve-Méry 'Ryanair/Aer Lingus: Even "low-cost" monopolies can harm consumers' 2007 *Competition Policy Newsletter* 65; DeLa Mano, Pesaresi and Stehman 'Econometric and survey evidence in the competitive assessment of the Ryanair-Aer Lingus merger' 2007 *Competition Policy Newsletter* 73.

[492]   M 53, decision of 2 October 1991, OJ [1991] L 334/42, [1992] 4 CMLR M2.

[493]   See OJ [1991] C 314/7.

[494]   See Fox 'Merger Control in the EEC—towards a European Merger Jurisprudence' [1991] Fordham Corporate Law Institute (ed Hawk), 738–9.

[495]   Case M 469, decision of 9 November 1994, OJ [1994] L 364/1.

ties, particularly through vertical integration, help to explain the Commission's cautious approach[496].

Three of the outright prohibitions – *RTL/Veronica/Endemol*[497], *Kesko/Tuko*[498]and *Blokker/Toys'R'Us*[499] – were requests from Member States under Article 22 of the ECMR. That these requests led to prohibitions is perhaps not surprising: at the time the Member States making the requests (the Netherlands and Finland) had no domestic system of merger control and had obviously concluded that there was a very serious threat to competition, so that the cases were always likely, at the very least, to raise serious doubts.

Of the other outright prohibitions *Gencor/Lonrho*[500] was an important case on the meaning of collective dominance or, to use more modern language, coordinated effects[501]. In *Saint-Gobain/Wacker-Chemie/NOM*[502] the Commission found that the merged entity would enjoy very high market shares in relation to silicon carbide, substantially higher than its competitors, that potential competition and countervailing power were weak, and that the case could not be 'saved' by an efficiency or a failing firm defence. In *Volvo/Scania*[503] the Commission prohibited a merger that would lead to high market shares for buses and tracks in a series of national markets, Sweden, Finland, Denmark, Norway and Ireland: the delimitation of national markets, rather than a European-wide one, was a crucial feature of this case. In the countries where the Commission identified a problem the evidence showed that Volvo and Scania were each other's closest competitors. The concentration in *SCA/Metsä Tissue*[504] was prohibited as it would have led to very high market shares in hygienic tissue products in Scandinavia and Finland. The Commission blocked the concentration in *CVC/Lenzing*[505] as a result of the high market shares that the merged entity would enjoy in the man-made fibre sector and because CVC already controlled Lenzing's main rival.

The prohibition decision in *GE/Honeywell*[506] was particularly controversial. This was an agreed merger between two US undertakings which had been cleared by the US authorities. The Commission prohibited it, predominantly because of its vertical and conglomerate effects, on grounds that were anathema to the Department of Justice in the US. On appeal to the CFI the Commission's reasoning on both vertical and conglomerate effects was severely criticised; nevertheless the GE's appeal was unsuccessful,

---

[496] See also Case M 490 *Nordic Satellite Distribution*, decision of 19 July 1995, OJ [1996] L 53/20; Case M 553 *RTL/Veronica/Endemol*, decision of 17 July 1996, OJ [1996] L 134/32 (this concentration was subsequently cleared in an amended form: OJ [1996] L 294/14); Case M 993 *Bertelsmann/Kirch/Premiere*, decision of 27 May 1998, OJ [1999] L 53/1 [1999] 4 CMLR 700; Case M 1027 *Deutsche Telecom/BetaResearch* OJ [1999] L 53/31.

[497] Case M 553 *RTL/Veronica/Endemol* decision of 17 July 1996, OJ [1996] L 134/32, upheld on appeal Case T-221/95 *Endemol Entertainment Holding BV v Commission* [1999] ECR II-1299, [1999] 5 CMLR 611.

[498] Case M 784 *Kesko/Tuko*, 20 November 1996, OJ [1997] L 174/47, upheld on appeal Case T-22/97 [1999] ECR II-3775, [2000] 4 CMLR 335.

[499] Case M 890 *Blokker/Toys'R'Us*, decision of 26 June 1997 OJ [1998] L 316/1.

[500] Case M 619, decision of 24 April 1996, OJ [1997] L 11/30, [1999] 4 CMLR 1076, upheld on appeal Case T-102/96 *Gencor v Commission* [1999] ECR II-753, [1999] 4 CMLR 971.

[501] See pp 860–862 above.

[502] Case M 774, decision of 4 December 1996, OJ [1997] L 247/1, [1997] 4 CMLR 25.

[503] Case M 1672, decision of 15 March 2000, OJ [2001] L 143/74, [2001] 5 CMLR 11.

[504] Case M 2097, decision of 31 January 2001, OJ [2002] L 57/1, [2002] 4 CMLR 38.

[505] Case M 2187, decision of 17 October 2001, OJ [2004] L82/20.

[506] Case M 2220, decision of 3 July 2001.

because the CFI accepted that there were some horizontal effects that justified the prohibition of the merger[507].

In *ENI/EDP/GDP*[508] the Commission prohibited a proposed acquisition by EDP, the incumbent electricity company in Portugal, of GDP, the incumbent gas company. The Commission was concerned both at the horizontal and vertical implications of the transaction, and resisted suggestions that a Portuguese 'national champion' should be created. An expedited appeal was made to the CFI which upheld the Commission's decision[509]. The CFI held that the Commission's assessment of the competitive conditions in the gas market in Portugal was incorrect. Portugal enjoyed a derogation from the requirement of the Second Gas Directive, that national monopolies should be abolished, until the end of 2007[510]; it followed that, at the time of the Commission's decision (December 2004) GDP had a lawful monopoly – using the term in its literal sense of only one seller – so that it was impossible that a dominant position could be created or strengthened as a result of the proposed transaction[511]. However the CFI considered that the Commission's reasoning in relation to the electricity market in Portugal did not involve a manifest error of assessment[512]. Where some grounds for a decision contain errors, but other grounds are found to be correct, the operative part of the Commission's decision may be upheld, and on this occasion the CFI's conclusion was that EDP's appeal should be dismissed[513]. The CFI rejected an argument that the Commission had been trying to achieve the objective of liberalising the gas and electricity markets in Portugal rather than applying the ECMR[514].

The most recent prohibition occurred in the case of *Ryanair/Aer Lingus*[515] where the Commission was particularly concerned that the merged airline would have accounted for around 80 per cent of intra-European air traffic from and to Dublin airport.

(ii) Prohibition decisions annulled on appeal

Four of the Commission's prohibition decisions were annulled on appeal. In *Airtours/First Choice*[516] the Commission had prohibited the proposed hostile acquisition by Airtours of First Choice on the basis of collective dominance[517]. The CFI, in an excoriating judgment, annulled the decision on the basis of manifest error of assessment: it was particularly critical of the Commission's assessment of the evidence and of its

---

[507]   Case T-210/01 *General Electric Company v Commission* [2005] ECR II-5575, [2006] 4 CMLR 686.
[508]   Case M 3440, *ENI/EDP/GDP*, decision of 9 December 2004, OJ [2005] L 302/69.
[509]   Case T-87/05 *EDP v Commission* [2005] ECR II-3745, [2005] 5 CMLR 23.
[510]   Directive 2003/55/EC of the European Parliament and of the Council of 26 June 2003 concerning common rules for the internal market in natural gas, OJ [2003] L 176/57.
[511]   Case T-87/05 *EDP v Commission* [2005] ECR II-3745, [2005] 5 CMLR 23, paras 113–133; note that the appeal was brought under the substantive test of the original Merger Regulation, which required the creation or strengthening of a dominant position; the current ECMR requires a finding of a significant impediment to competition in the common market, but the CFI's reasoning in relation to the derogation for Portugal in the gas market would presumably lead to the same conclusion under the new substantive test.
[512]   Case T-87/05 *EDP v Commission* [2005] ECR II-3745, [2005] 5 CMLR 23, paras 171–237.
[513]   Ibid, paras 144 and 238–241.   [514]   Ibid, paras 86–98.
[515]   Case M 4439, decision of 27 June 2007; there are two appeals to the CFI in this case, one by Ryanair against the prohibition, Case T-342/07, *Ryanair v Commission*, not yet decided, and the other by Aer Lingus, against the Commission's decision not to require Ryanair to divest itself of all its shares in Aer Lingus, Case T-411/07 *Aer Lingus Group v Commission*, not yet decided.
[516]   Case M 1524 *Airtours/First Choice*, decision of 22 September 1999, OJ [2000] L 93/1, [2000] 5 CMLR 494.
[517]   See pp 852–853 above.

reasoning[518]. The mergers in *Schneider Electric/Legrand*[519] and *Tetra Laval/Sidel*[520] were both prohibited by the Commission, but each decision (together with additional decisions requiring the mergers to be reversed) was annulled on appeal to the CFI[521]; an appeal by the Commission in the case of the *Tetra Laval/Sidel* case was unsuccessful[522]. In the case of *Schneider/Legrand* the CFI subsequently awarded Schneider damages for some of the economic loss it had suffered[523]. The Commission's prohibition decision in *MCI WorldCom/Sprint*[524] was annulled by the CFI in *MCI Inc v Commission*[525] since the parties had terminated their agreement by the time of the Commission's decision; the mere fact that they were continuing to negotiate an agreement in a modified form did not entitle the Commission to adopt a decision.

(iii) Unconditional clearances

It is not inevitable that a case that is taken to a Phase II investigation will lead to a prohibition or require a remedy. Some Phase II cases culminate in an unconditional clearance: indeed the merger in *Sony/Bertlesmann* was cleared by the Commission twice[526]. This contradicts the view sometimes expressed that, by the time a case reaches Phase II, the Commission has already made up its mind about the outcome; it is possible at the 'in-depth' phase of an investigation to demonstrate to the Commission that a merger will not significantly impede effective competition. By the end of January 2008 this had happened in 39 cases out of a total of 143.

(iv) Clearances subject to commitments

A notable feature of the ECMR is that a majority of Phase II decisions have resulted in clearances subject to commitments. This is shown both in the statistical Table and in the Table of Phase II investigations above. The Commission's approach to remedies in merger cases was discussed above, and its preference for structural rather than behavioural commitments was noted[527]. There are several recent examples of structural remedies at the end of Phase II. In *Sonoco/Ahlstrom*[528] the parties agreed to divest themselves of a plant in Norway that manufactured paper core to an 'up-front' buyer. In *Inco/Falconbridge*[529] the parties agreed to the divestment of a nickel refinery in Norway to an up-front buyer; interestingly in this case the Commission required that the merged entity should agree to provide important input materials to the buyer on a long-term

---

[518] Case T-342/99 [2002] ECR II-2585, [2002] 5 CMLR 317.

[519] Case M 2283, decision of 10 October 2001, OJ [2004] L 101/1.

[520] Case M 2416, decision of 30 October 2001, OJ [2004] L 43/13.

[521] Case T-310/01 *Schneider Electric v Commission* [2002] ECR II-4071, [2003] 4 CMLR 768 (annulment of prohibition decision); Case T-77/02 *Schneider Electric v Commission* [2002] ECR II-4201, (annulment of divestiture decision); Case T-5/02 *Tetra Laval v Commission* [2002] ECR II-4381, [2002] 5 CMLR 1182 (annulment of prohibition decision); Case T-80/02 *Tetra Laval v Commission* [2002] ECR II-4519, [2002] 4 CMLR 1271 (annulment of divestiture decision).

[522] Case C-12/03 P *Commission v Tetra Laval* [2005] ECR I-1113, [2005] 4 CMLR 573 (appeal seeking annulment of the CFI's prohibition decision); Case C-13/03 P *Commission v Tetra Laval* [2005] ECR I-987, [2005] CMLR 667 (appeal seeking annulment of the CFI's divestiture decision).

[523] See p 885 above.

[524] Case M 1741, decision of 28 June 2000, OJ [2003] L 300/1, [2004] 4 CMLR 21; see the Commission's XXXth *Report on Competition Policy* (2000), point 249 and Box 6.

[525] Case T-310/00 [2004] ECR II-3253, [2004] 5 CMLR 26.   [526] See pp 861–862 above.

[527] See pp 872–877 above.   [528] Case M 3431, decision of 6 October 2004.

[529] Case M 4000, decision of 21 July 2006.

basis. In *Gaz de France/Suez*[530] the parties agreed to divest various assets in order to overcome the Commission's concerns about horizontal overlaps at both the wholesale and retail levels of the gas and electricity markets in France and Belgium; the remedy included a termination of the link between the operator of gas network infrastructure and the supply of gas, effectively an unbundling remedy, as well as an agreement to invest in enhancing the capacity and functioning of the gas network[531]. In *Kronospan Group/Constantia*[532] the Commission was concerned that Kronospan's acquisition of three companies owned by Constantia that produced raw particle board used in the manufacture of furniture would lead to a significant impediment to effective competition; the simple remedy in this case was that Kronospan would acquire only two of the three companies: the third one, Fundermax of Austria, would remain with Constantia.

There have also been some cases in which behavioural commitments have been accepted. For example in *Deutsche Bahn/English Welsh & Scottish Railway Holdings*[533] (a Phase I case) the Commission accepted commitments by Deutsche Bahn to fulfil EWS's expansion plans for railfreight transport in France by investing in locomotives and personnel and to provide fair and non-discriminatory access to EWS's driver training schools. In *SFR/Télé 2*[534] a series of remedies was offered to ensure that Vivendi, the owner of valuable television content, would not discriminate against competitors in the downstream Pay-TV market; nor that it would weaken competitors in the upstream market for the acquisition of television content.

It is a notable feature of some cases, particularly in the energy and telecommunications sectors, that the package of remedies may be very complex: obvious examples of this are *E.ON/MOL*[535], a merger impacting on the gas sector in Hungary, where the Commission required a divestment on the part of MOL, a release of gas to the wholesale market and access to storage facilities for customers that succeeded in buying the gas; *Gaz de France/Suez*, referred to above; and *T-Mobile/tele.ring*, a case that was discussed in the context of non-collusive oligopoly[536].

(v) Withdrawal of notifications

It is important to note that there have been many cases in which the parties to a merger subject to a Phase II investigation have chosen to withdraw the notification. Out of 46 cases to have gone to a Phase II investigation by the end of February 2008 nine were then withdrawn. It would be reasonable to assume that at least some of these withdrawals were made because it seemed inevitable that the Commission would otherwise have prohibited the merger outright. In this sense the total of 20 prohibitions referred to above may understate the number of cases that might, but for withdrawal, have led to an outright prohibition.

Article 6(1)(c) of the ECMR provides that the Commission shall conclude a Phase II investigation with a decision, unless it is satisfied that the parties have abandoned the merger. The Commission's *Consolidated Jurisdictional Notice* explains, at paragraphs 117 to 121, the procedure to be followed in such circumstances.

---

[530]   Case M 4180, decision of 14 November 2006.
[531]   See Bachour and others '*Gaz de France/Suez*: Keeping energy markets in Belgium and France open and contestable through far-reaching remedies' *Competition Policy Newsletter*, Spring 2007, 83.
[532]   Case M 4525, decision of 19 September 2007.   [533]   Case M 4746, decision of 7 November 2007.
[534]   Case M 4504, decision of 18 July 2007.
[535]   Case M 3696, decision of 21 December 2005, OJ [2006] L 253/20.   [536]   See p 860 above.

22

Mergers (3) – UK law[1]

CHAPTER CONTENTS

1. INTRODUCTION

UK law on the control of mergers is contained in Part 3 of the Enterprise Act 2002, which entered into force on 20 June 2003. This legislation involved a major overhaul of the domestic system of merger control. Merger control was first introduced in the UK by the Monopolies and Mergers Act 1965 which was replaced by the Fair Trading Act 1973. In August 1999 the Secretary of State published a Consultation Document[2] proposing a number of changes to the system of merger control in the UK; a further publication in October 2000 developed these proposals further[3]. The main proposals were included in the Government's White Paper *Productivity and Enterprise – A World Class Competition Regime* of July 2001[4]. A central feature of the Government's proposed reform was that responsibility for making decisions in merger cases should be given to the Office of Fair Trading ('the OFT')[5] and the Competition Commission ('the CC')[6], and that the Secretary of State should become involved only in cases which raise exceptional

---

[1] For more detailed texts on the merger control provisions of the Enterprisse Act 2002 readers are referred to Parr, Finbow and Hughes *UK Merger Control: Law and Practice* (Sweet & Maxwell, 2nd ed, 2005); Bankes and Hadden *UK Merger Control: Law and Practice* (LexisNexis Butterworths, 2006).

[2] *Mergers: A Consultation Document on Proposals for Reform* DTI/Pub 4308.

[3] *Mergers: The Response to the Consultation on Proposals for Reform* URN 00/805, October 2000; see also DTI Press Notice P/2000/705, 26 October 2000.

[4] Cm 5233, ch 5; see also the Government's *Response* (December 2001).

[5] On the OFT see ch 2, pp 64–68.   [6] On the CC see ch 2, pp 69–71.

public interest issues[7]; the decisions to be adopted by the OFT and CC would be made against a 'substantial lessening of competition' test, rather than the public interest test set out in section 84 of the Fair Trading Act. These changes were put into effect by Part 3 of the Enterprise Act 2002, with which this chapter is predominantly concerned. However there are some specific rules for 'public interest cases', for 'other special cases' and for certain mergers between water companies, and these will be briefly described at the end of the chapter. The special regime for newspaper mergers that was contained in the Fair Trading Act was repealed by section 373 of the Communications Act 2003; that Act makes provision for mergers in the newspaper industry that give rise to particular concern in terms of the need for accurate presentation of news, free expression of opinion and plurality to be considered under the 'public interest' provisions of the Enterprise Act[8].

In reading this chapter it should be recalled that, as a general proposition, a merger that has a 'Community dimension' under the EC Merger Regulation (the 'ECMR') cannot be investigated under domestic law[9], although exceptions to this are to be found in Article 4(4)[10], Article 9[11] and in Article 21(4)[12] of that Regulation.

2. OVERVIEW OF UK MERGER CONTROL

(A) Part 3 of the Enterprise Act 2002

Part 3 of the Enterprise Act 2002 consists of five chapters; the Government's *Explanatory Notes* to the Bill as introduced into Parliament on 26 March 2002 are a helpful adjunct to the Act itself; the CAT has noted that they may be used as an aid to ascertaining the intention of Parliament[13]. Chapter 1 of Part 3 of the Act is entitled 'Duty to make references': it deals both with jurisdictional matters, such as the meaning of 'relevant merger situations', and also with the substantive assessment of mergers under the substantial lessening of competition test (hereafter 'the SLC test'). The overwhelming majority of mergers will be considered under Chapter 1. However Chapter 2 contains provisions on 'public interest' cases and Chapter 3 addresses 'other special cases': these provisions will be invoked only rarely, except perhaps in relation to media mergers following amendments made by the Communications Act 2003; the provisions on public interest and other special cases, and on water mergers, are described briefly in section 9 of this chapter[14]. Chapter 4 of Part 3 of the Enterprise Act contains rules on enforcement, which set out the various undertakings that can be accepted by the OFT and the CC in the course of merger investigations and the orders that they may make, as well as certain automatic restrictions on the integration of firms during the currency of an investigation. Chapter 5 deals with numerous supplementary matters, such as merger notices,

---

[7] *Mergers: The Response to the Consultation on Proposals for Reform* URN 00/805, October 2000, paras 4.10–4.12.

[8] See pp 951–955 below.   [9] See ch 21, pp 832–834 on the principle of 'one-stop control' of mergers.

[10] Ibid, pp 835–836.   [11] Ibid, pp 836–837.   [12] Ibid, p 839.

[13] See para 22 of the final judgment in Case 1023/4/1/03 *IBA Health Ltd v OFT* [2003] CAT 27, [2004] CompAR 235; the *Explanatory Notes* are available at www.opsi/gov.uk/acts.

[14] See pp 951–955 below.

investigatory powers, review by the Competition Appeal Tribunal ('the CAT') and the payment of fees.

Section 3 of this chapter explains the procedures of the OFT when determining whether a merger should be referred to the CC and when deciding to accept undertakings in lieu of a reference. Section 4 describes the procedures of the CC and section 5 discusses the way in which the OFT and the CC apply the SLC test in practice. Section 6 explains the enforcement powers in the Act, including the remedies that the CC can impose in merger cases. Various supplementary matters are dealt with in section 7 and section 8 considers how the merger control provisions have been working in practice since the Enterprise Act entered into force. Section 9 contains a brief account of the provisions on public interest cases and mergers in the water industry.

(B) Brief description of the system of merger control in the UK

In essence the system of control for 'ordinary' mergers (as opposed to public interest or other special cases) contained in the Enterprise Act is as follows. The OFT has a duty to refer certain mergers to the CC; in some circumstances it has a discretion not to refer, and some mergers cannot be referred at all. There is no obligation on undertakings to pre-notify mergers to the OFT, although provision is made for them to do so on a voluntary basis either by making an informal submission or by submitting a more formal 'merger notice' for which there is a legislative basis: the difference between the two lies in the timetable that each triggers. In practice many firms voluntarily have pre-merger discussions with the OFT, not least because power exists to refer a merger to the CC after it has been consummated and, where appropriate, to require a merger to be reversed: a highly undesirable outcome for the firms concerned. Provision is made for the OFT to accept legally binding undertakings to modify a merger in lieu of a reference to the CC.

In cases where the OFT is concerned that there is a realistic prospect of an SLC and where it is not possible to agree a remedy, the matter will be referred to the CC: there is an obvious analogy here with the procedure under the ECMR, where cases that raise 'serious doubts' as to the compatibility of a merger with the common market are taken to an in-depth Phase II investigation; however a significant difference is that, in the UK system, Phase II is conducted by a separate body from Phase I. The CC, when conducting an investigation under the Act, must determine whether the merger would lead to an SLC within any market or markets in the UK for goods or services; it must also decide on appropriate remedies, having regard to the need to achieve as comprehensive a solution as is reasonable and practicable to any SLC and any adverse effects resulting from it. In framing remedies, the CC may also take into account any 'relevant customer benefits', as defined in the legislation. The CC has available to it a number of final powers following its investigation including, where necessary, the power to prohibit a merger outright and to require the reversal of a merger that has already been consummated.

(C) Institutional arrangements

An important feature of the merger provisions in the Enterprise Act is that the Secretary of State is not involved at all, unless there is a point of exceptional public interest: such cases are rare. In the overwhelming majority of cases decisions are taken by the OFT[15]; a relatively small number of mergers are referred to the CC, and in those cases the CC will be responsible for the final decision. Decisions of the OFT and the CC are subject to review by the CAT. Sectoral regulators do not have concurrent powers in relation to mergers in the way that they do under the Competition Act 1998 and the market investigation provisions in the Enterprise Act[16]; however they are asked to provide input into the deliberations of the OFT and the CC where appropriate.

Within the OFT the Mergers Group has specific responsibility for mergers. It has a senior director, a director and two deputy directors for casework, and three assistant directors – two for economics and one for law. The Group also has more than 30 case officers to enable the OFT to perform its functions under the Act. The case officers are divided into a number of teams, each of which has responsibility for particular industry sectors; there is also a Head of EC Merger Regulation post which deals with policy and the coordination of OFT input into cases arising from the ECMR. The OFT's website[17] contains a considerable amount of information about mergers under the Enterprise Act such as decisions, case lists and a register of undertakings; it also discusses procedures, facilitates consultation on undertakings in lieu of a reference to the CC and gives details of people to contact and of OFT publications.

The CC has about 50 members. In each case referred to it a group will be appointed to carry out the investigation, usually consisting of four or five members; legal and economics staff as well as accountants and business advisers support the work of the groups.

(D) Guidelines, rules of procedure and other relevant publications

In addition to Part 3 of the Enterprise Act various guidelines, rules and other publications seek to explain the operation of the UK system of merger control: this reflects the Government's intention that the new regime should be as transparent as possible. Section 106 of the Act requires the OFT and the CC to prepare and publish general advice and information about the making of merger references and, in the case of the CC, about the way in which relevant customer benefits may affect the taking of enforcement action. Section 107 of the Act imposes additional publicity requirements on the OFT, the CC and the Secretary of State: for example references, undertakings and orders must all be published.

(i) OFT publications

The OFT has published the following guidance in relation to mergers under the Enterprise Act:

- *Mergers: Substantive assessment guidance*[18]: this should be read in conjunction with a revision explaining the implications of the Court of Appeal judgment in *IBA Health v OFT*[19] and a further revision in relation to *Exception to the duty to refer: markets of insufficient importance*[20]
- *Mergers: Procedural guidance*[21]
- *Merger fees* (explaining how fees are to be paid)[22]

[15] The reference of *BSkyB/ITV plc* was made by the Secretary of State under the public interest provisions in the Enterprise Act: see p 953 below.
[16] On concurrency see ch 10, pp 424–426.   [17] See www.oft.gov.uk.   [18] OFT 516, May 2003.
[19] OFT 516a, October 2004; on the *IBA Health* case see pp 903–904 below.
[20] OFT 516b, November 2007.   [21] OFT 526, May 2003.   [22] February 2006.

- *Merger notice* (providing the format for notices under section 96 of the Enterprise Act)[23]
- *Prior notice of publicly proposed mergers* (explaining the provisions on merger notices)[24]
- *Turnover guidance* (explaining how to calculate turnover for the purposes of Chapter 1 of Part 3 of the Act)[25]
- *Interim arrangements for informal advice and pre-notification contacts*[26]
- The OFT has also published a report, prepared for it, the CC and the DTI, on *Ex post evaluation of mergers*[27].

(ii) CC publications

Acting under Schedule 7A of the Competition Act, inserted by Schedule 12 of the Enterprise Act 2002, the CC has adopted the *Competition Commission Rules of Procedure 2006* which superseded the earlier rules of 20 June 2003; they are available on its website[28]. It has also published *Guidance on the Use of Interim Measures Pending Final Determination of Merger References* under the same provision[29]. The CC has published five sets of guidelines under section 106(3) of the Enterprise Act of relevance to merger investigations[30]:

- *Merger References: Competition Commission Guidelines*[31]
- *General Advice and Information*[32]
- *Statement of Policy on Penalties*[33]
- *Application of Divestiture Remedies in Merger Inquiries: Competition Commission Guidelines*[34]
- *Water Merger References: Competition Commission Guidelines*[35].

The Chairman of the CC has published three further documents of relevance:

- *Guidance to Groups*[36]
- *Disclosure of Information in Merger and Market Inquiries*[37]
- *Disclosure of Information by the Competition Commission to Other Public Authorities*[38].

The CC has also published:

- *Guidance on the use of interim measures pending final determination of merger references*[39].

(iii) Department of Business, Enterprise and Regulatory Reform (formerly the Department of Trade and Industry) delegated legislation[40]

The Secretary of State has made the following orders under the Enterprise Act of relevance to merger investigations:

- The Enterprise Act 2002 (Merger Fees and Determination of Turnover) Order 2003[41]: this establishes how turnover is to be calculated when determining whether a merger qualifies as

---

[23] June 2003.   [24] June 2003.   [25] July 2003.   [26] April 2006.   [27] OFT 767, March 2005.
[28] See www.competition-commission.org.uk.   [29] Ibid.   [30] Ibid.
[31] CC2, June 2003; it is intended that revised guidance will be published by the end of 2008.
[32] CC4, March 2006.   [33] CC5, June 2003.   [34] CC8, December 2004.   [35] CC9, December 2004.
[36] CC6, March 2006.   [37] CC7, July 2003.   [38] CC12, April 2006.
[39] See www.competition-commission.org.uk/rep_pub/corporate_documents/other_guidance_documents.htm.
[40] The documents referred to in the text that follows are available at www.opsi.gov.uk/stat.htm.
[41] SI 2003/1370.

a 'relevant merger situation' for jurisdictional purposes[42] and the amount of any merger fee that may be payable to the OFT[43]. The level of fees was raised by the Enterprise Act (Merger Fees)(Amendment) Order 2005[44]

- The Competition Commission (Penalties) Order 2003[45]: this establishes the maximum levels of penalties that the CC can impose for offences under section 110 of the Act[46]

- The Enterprise Act (Merger Pre-notification) Regulations 2003[47]: this makes provision for the serving of merger notices by parties who pre-notify a merger to the OFT

- The Competition Appeal Tribunal Rules 2003[48]: this governs the way in which the CAT deals with applications for review of decisions of the OFT, the Secretary of State and the CC in relation to mergers

- The OFT Registers of Undertakings and Orders (Available Hours) Order 2003[49]

- The Enterprise Act (Protection of Legitimate Interests) Order 2003[50]: this enables the Secretary of State to issue a European intervention notice and to take appropriate measures to protect legitimate interests which may be adversely affected by a merger

- The Enterprise Act (Supply of Services) Order 2003[51]: this sets out the situations in which permission to use land will be regarded as a supply of services

- The Enterprise Act (Anticipated Mergers) Order 2003[52]: this makes provision for the aggregation of two or more transactions which take place between the same parties within a two-year period

- The Enterprise Act 2002 and Media Mergers (Consequential Amendments) Order 2003[53]

- The EC Merger Control (Consequential Amendments) Regulations 2004[54]

- The Enterprise Act 2002 (Enforcement Undertakings) Order 2006[55]

- The Enterprise Act 2002 (Enforcement Undertakings and Orders) Order 2006[56].

3. THE OFT'S DUTY TO MAKE REFERENCES

Chapter 1 of Part 3 of the Enterprise Act is entitled 'Duty to make references', and is central to the domestic system of merger control. Chapter 1 contains both jurisdictional rules, explaining what is meant by a merger and which mergers can be investigated under the Act, and substantive rules, setting out the test to be applied by the OFT and the CC when investigating mergers. Chapter 1 also defines the respective roles of the OFT and the CC in relation to merger investigations: the OFT conducts the preliminary analysis of mergers, analogous to a Phase I investigation under the ECMR; cases that raise serious competition concerns and that cannot be resolved at the stage of the OFT's investigation are referred to the CC for an in-depth analysis, analogous to a Phase II investigation under the ECMR. The procedures of the OFT and the CC in merger investigations will be explained in the text that follows[57].

---

[42] See pp 908–912 below.   [43] See p 917 below.   [44] SI 2005/3558.   [45] SI 2003/1371.
[46] See p 937 below.   [47] SI 2003/1369.
[48] SI 2003/1372, as amended by the Competition Appeal Tribunal (Amendment and Communications Act Appeals) Rules 2004, SI 2004/2068.
[49] SI 2003/1373.   [50] SI 2003/1592.   [51] SI 2003/1594.   [52] SI 2003/1595.   [53] SI 2003/3180.
[54] SI 2004/1079.   [55] SI 2004/354.   [56] SI 2004/355.
[57] See pp 912–917 (OFT) and pp 918–921 (CC) below.

Sections 22 to 32 of the Enterprise Act deal with the position of the OFT in relation to mergers that have already been consummated ('completed mergers') and sections 33 to 34 set out the relevant provisions in relation to mergers that have yet to be completed ('anticipated mergers'). Unlike the position under the ECMR, there is no duty under UK law to pre-notify mergers to the OFT. In practice many firms bring their transactions to the attention of the OFT on a voluntary basis prior to completion, although in recent years there has been a noticeable increase in the number of completed mergers that have been investigated by the OFT and CC, sometimes leading to the forced divestiture of assets already acquired[58]. There is evidence to suggest that quite a few mergers that might be harmful to competition escape the scrutiny of the competition authorities in the UK[59].

Sections 35 to 41 of the Act are concerned with the determination of references by the CC.

(A) Duty to make references: completed mergers

(i) Duty to refer

Section 22(1) of the Enterprise Act provides that the OFT has a duty to make a reference to the CC if it believes that it is or may be the case that a 'relevant merger situation'[60] has been created and that the creation of that situation has resulted, or may be expected to result, in an SLC within any market or markets in the UK, or a part of the UK, for goods or services[61]. It is important to note that the Act imposes a duty, rather than conferring a discretion, on the OFT to refer mergers of the kind set out in section 22(1): this means that it is possible for a firm that is opposed to a particular merger, for example the victim of a hostile bid, a customer or a competitor, to apply to the CAT for a review of the decision of the OFT not to refer that merger to the CC[62]. The fact that a decision not to refer a merger can be challenged, as well as a decision to refer one, has resource implications for the OFT, which has to take care to ensure that it publishes a decision setting out the primary evidence and the reasoning that led to its decision in a manner which is clear to all interested parties.

(A) The IBA Health *case* The first application by a third party for a review concerned a proposed acquisition by iSOFT Group plc of Torex plc, two direct competitors in the supply of software applications to hospitals; the merger would result in the merged entity having a significant market share. This case led to an important judgment of the Court of Appeal which examined the nature of the duty of the OFT under the Act to make a reference. The OFT decided in November 2003 that it would not refer the iSOFT/Torex merger to the CC. IBA Health, a competitor of the parties, challenged the decision not to make a reference before the CAT; the CAT reached the conclusion that the OFT's decision should be quashed and that the matter should be referred back to

[58] See pp 949–950 below.
[59] See *The deterrent effect on competition enforcement by the OFT: a report prepared for the OFT by Deloitte*, OFT 962, November 2007, paras 4.48–4.61.
[60] This term is defined in s 23 of the Act: see pp 908–912 below.
[61] On the meaning of 'markets in the UK for goods and services' see Enterprise Act 2002, s 22(6).
[62] On the review of decisions under Part 3 of the Enterprise Act 2002, see pp 937–938 below.

it for reconsideration[63]. In reaching this conclusion the CAT considered the scheme of the merger control provisions in the Act and noted that the OFT's role is to act as a 'first screen' in relation to mergers, but not to be a decision-maker: that is the function of the CC. Section 33[64] imposes a duty on the OFT to refer a merger where it believes that 'it is or *may be*' the case that a merger '*may be* expected to result' in an SLC (emphasis added). In the CAT's view this formulation (and in particular the appearance in section 33(1) of the word 'may' in two places (the so-called 'double may')) meant that if the OFT itself did not consider that a merger would result in an SLC, but if it was possible that the CC might credibly have that view, the OFT was obliged to refer:

If there is room for two views, the statutory duty of the OFT is to refer the matter[65].

The CAT considered that, as the OFT had not asked whether there was a significant prospect that the CC might consider that the merger would give rise to an SLC, it had failed to ask itself the correct question and so had erred in law[66]; the CAT also held that the OFT's decision was defective because it was not based on sufficient evidence and was insufficiently reasoned[67]. In the OFT's view the CAT's formulation of the duty upon it would significantly lower the threshold for referring mergers to the CC and might lead to many more mergers being referred: this raised important policy questions, as a result of which the OFT sought, and was given, permission to appeal to the Court of Appeal. The Court of Appeal gave a judgment on 19 February 2004 in which it upheld the decision of the CAT to quash the decision and refer the matter back to the OFT on the facts of the case, but concluded that the CAT's formulation of the duty on the OFT was incorrect[68]. The Vice-Chancellor (as he then was) was of the opinion that the CAT's 'two part' test was wrong and that it would make various provisions in the Act unworkable:

the relevant belief is that the merger may be expected to result in a substantial lessening of competition, not that the Commission may in due course decide that the merger may be expected to result in a substantial lessening of competition. Further, the body which is to hold that belief is OFT not the Commission.[69]

The Vice-Chancellor went on to say that the words in section 33 should be applied in accordance with their ordinary meaning.

(B) The OFT's revised guidance The OFT subsequently amended paragraph 3.2 of its *Mergers: Substantive assessment guidance* in the light of this judgment and of some specific guidance that the Vice-Chancellor provided on the proper application of section 33(1) in paragraphs 44 to 49 of his judgment. The *Revised Guidance*[70] says that the OFT will refer a merger where it has reasonable belief, objectively justified by relevant facts,

---

[63] Case 1023/4/1/03 *IBA Health Ltd v OFT* [2003] CAT 27, [2004] CompAR 235.

[64] Because the *iSOFT/Torex* merger was anticipated rather than completed, the relevant section was s 33(1) rather than s 22(1); the wording under consideration in the case is identical in each section.

[65] Case 1023/4/1/03 *IBA Health Ltd v OFT* [2003] CAT 27, [2004] CompAR 235, para 192.

[66] Ibid, para 232.

[67] When the OFT reconsidered the case it found that there could be an SLC in relation to the supply of laboratory information management systems to NHS hospitals, but did not refer the merger to the CC as iSOFT offered undertakings in lieu: see OFT Press Release 56/04, 24 March 2004; the undertakings can be found at www.oft.gov.uk/advice_and_resources/resource_base/Mergers_home/register/undertakings-in-lieu.

[68] *OFT v IBA Health Ltd* [2004] EWCA Civ 142, [2004] UKCLR 683; for comment see Parr 'Merger Control in the Wake of *IBA Health*' (2007) 6 Competition Law Journal 282.

[69] Ibid, para 38. [70] OFT 516a, October 2004.

that there is a realistic prospect that a merger will lessen competition substantially. The OFT explains that 'realistic prospect' means not only a prospect that has more than a 50 per cent chance of occurring, but also a prospect that is not fanciful but has less than a 50 per cent chance of occurring. It adds that, in the latter situation, it is not possible to give an exact mathematical formulation of the degree of likelihood which is required in order to make a reference; rather the OFT has a wide margin within which to exercise its judgment as to whether it may be the case that the merger would result in an SLC. In *UniChem v OFT*[71] counsel for the OFT argued that the OFT had a wide 'discretion' when deciding whether to refer a merger to the CC. The CAT suggested that the term discretion was the wrong one to use, since it has a connotation of policy; the correct concept is one of a margin of judgment or the evaluation of facts[72].

(C) The UniChem *case* In the *UniChem* case UniChem objected to the fact that the OFT had not referred a proposed acquisition by Phoenix Healthcare Distribution Ltd of East Anglian Pharmaceuticals Ltd to the CC. The CAT considered that much of the OFT's decision was soundly based, but nevertheless referred it back to the OFT since the OFT had made primary findings of fact about UniChem's position on the market on the basis of information provided by the merging parties but without any reference to UniChem itself. In the CAT's view a 'balanced and fair procedure' would have been for the OFT to have checked these important facts with UniChem[73]. On reconsideration of the matter the OFT again cleared the merger without a reference to the CC[74].

(D) The Celesio *case* In *Celesio AG v OFT*[75] Celesio unsuccessfully challenged the decision of the OFT not to refer a proposed acquisition by the Boots Group plc of Alliance UniChem plc; the CAT explicitly rejected a submission by Celesio that the OFT is always under a duty to refer a merger where the prospect of there being an SLC is greater than fanciful[76].

(E) Other points about the duty to refer The OFT may by notice require information from the merging parties for the purpose of deciding whether to make a reference under section 22. However it has no powers to force the parties to provide this information, nor does it have any powers to require information from third parties[77]. The lack of such powers can be a handicap to the OFT, and might even mean that, in some cases, it has to make a reference to the CC since it cannot satisfy itself that a merger would not result in an SLC. It would be a criminal offence for firms to provide the OFT with false or misleading information[78].

Section 5 of this chapter will consider how the OFT (and the CC) apply the SLC test, in particular in the light of the guidance that has been published on this matter[79].

The duty imposed on the OFT by section 22(1) must be read subject to the provisions of section 22(2) and (3), which provide a discretion not to refer certain mergers and which prevent the reference of some others.

---

[71] Case 1049/4/1/05 [2005] CAT 8, [2005] CompAR 907. [72] Ibid, para 172 [73] Ibid, paras 268–269.
[74] www.oft.gov.uk/advice_and_resources/resource_base/Mergers_home/decisions/2005/phoenix-healthcare.
[75] Case 1059/4/1/06 [2006] CAT 9, [2006] CompAR 515. [76] Ibid, para 74.
[77] Enterprise Act 2002, s 31; see further *Mergers: Procedural guidance*, paras 5.2–5.4.
[78] Enterprise Act 2002, s 117. [79] See pp 921ff below.

(ii) Discretion not to refer

Section 22(2) provides the OFT with a discretion not to make a reference in two situations[80].

(A) Markets of insufficient importance The first is where the OFT believes that the market or markets concerned are not of sufficient importance to justify the making of a reference to the CC[81]. The purpose of this provision is to avoid references where the costs involved would be disproportionate to the benefits that could be achieved by a reference: benefits for this purpose are best measured in terms of the consumer harm potentially avoided[82]. The OFT's original guidance on this issue had been taken to suggest that this '*de minimis*' exception would apply only rarely, where the value of the market affected was less than £400,000, and in practice quite a few 'small' mergers were referred to the CC; sometimes this led to the abandonment of the transaction in question, possibly because the parties felt that the expense of an in-depth investigation by the CC could not be justified given the value of the deal. The OFT therefore launched a consultation in June 2007 which led to the publication of revised guidance in November 2007[83]. The revised guidance raises the threshold from £400,000 to £10 million[84]. However there may be some cases in which the OFT would refer a merger below the £10 million threshold, for example where:

- there is very high market concentration and lower prospects of entry
- there is evidence of coordination between competitors
- the case might have an important precedent value
- a high proportion of any detriment would be suffered by vulnerable consumers[85].

In each case the guiding principle is whether the merger could have an adverse effect on consumer welfare. The OFT cleared two mergers arising from the award of rail franchises on *de minimis* grounds in December 2007[86] and another one in January 2008[87]. However in the case of *Dunfermline Press Ltd/Trinity Mirror plc*[88] the OFT announced that, although the case was below the *de minimis* thresholds, it would prefer to address the potential harm to competition that it could foresee in that case on the basis of undertakings in lieu of a reference.

(B) Customer benefits The second situation in which there is a discretion not to make a reference is where any 'relevant customer benefits' in relation to the creation of the merger concerned outweigh the expected SLC and any adverse effects of it[89]. The meaning of relevant customer benefits for this purpose is set out in section 30 of the Act: there must be a benefit for 'relevant customers'[90] in the form of lower prices, higher quality

---

[80] See generally *Mergers: Substantive assessment guidance*, ch 7.

[81] Enterprise Act 2002, s 22(2)(a).

[82] See the OFT's *Consultation on proposed revision to Mergers – Substantive assessment guidance* OFT 933, June 2007, para 2.5.

[83] *Exception to the duty to refer: markets of insufficient importance* OFT 516b.

[84] Ibid, para 7.6.   [85] Ibid, paras 7.7–7.8.   [86] OFT Press Release 180/07, 20 December 2007.

[87] OFT Press Release 16/08, 4 February 2008.   [88] OFT Press Release 15/08, 4 February 2008.

[89] Enterprise Act 2002, s 22(2)(b).

[90] On the meaning of relevant customers see Enterprise Act 2002, s 30(4); the term includes customers in a chain of customers beginning with the immediate customers of the merging parties, and includes future customers.

or greater choice of goods or services in any market in the UK (which need not be the market in which the SLC has occurred or would occur) or greater innovation in relation to such goods or services[91]; and the benefit must have accrued, or be expected to accrue within a reasonable period, as a result of the merger, and be unlikely to have accrued without the merger or a similar lessening of competition[92]. The OFT's guidance states that the parties must adduce detailed and verifiable evidence of anticipated relevant customer benefits[93]. The notion of relevant customer benefits occurs elsewhere in the Act, in particular in relation to the CC's investigations[94]. However, whereas the OFT is asked by section 22 to consider whether any relevant customer benefits would outweigh an SLC, the CC is asked to consider the effect that any remedial action it might take would have on any relevant customer benefits.

The definition of customer benefits is deliberately narrow, to ensure that only demonstrable, merger-specific benefits will be taken into account; however it is important to appreciate that the OFT (and the CC) is asked to consider only whether there will be a *customer* benefit rather than a benefit to consumers generally, which would be a very difficult thing to demonstrate. It would presumably be a matter for the judgment of the OFT (or the CC) to determine how to proceed in circumstances where some customers would benefit from a merger but others would not[95]. A separate point is that there may be cases in which predicted customer benefits would increase the competitive rivalry in a market, in which case this fact could be taken into account as part of the SLC test, rather than as a subsequent counterweight to a possible SLC[96].

(iii) Circumstances in which a reference cannot be made

Section 22(3) sets out various circumstances in which a reference cannot be made: for example where the OFT is considering whether to accept an undertaking in lieu of a reference[97]; where the merger has been, or is being, considered under the provisions on anticipated mergers[98]; in certain public interest cases[99]; and where the European Commission is deciding whether to exercise jurisdiction under the procedures set out in Article 4(5) or Article 22 of the ECMR[100].

(B) Duty to make references: anticipated mergers

In practice most mergers are brought to the attention of the OFT on a voluntary basis prior to their consummation; there is a statutory basis for pre-notification, though its use is not obligatory[101]. Section 33(1) of the Enterprise Act imposes a duty on the OFT to

---

[91] Enterprise Act 2002, s 30(1)(a); see further *Mergers: Substantive assessment guidance*, para 7.8.

[92] Enterprise Act 2002, s 30(2) and (3): note that these sub-sections set out the test for completed mergers and for anticipated mergers respectively.

[93] *Mergers: Substantive assessment guidance*, paras 7.7–7.9.   [94] See p 926 below.

[95] On this point in the context of Article 81(3) EC see Case C-238/05 *Asnef-Equifax v Asociación de Usuarios de Servicios Bancarios (Ausbanc)* [2006] ECR I-11125, [2007] 4 CMLR 224.

[96] *Mergers: Substantive assessment guidance*, paras 4.29–4.35 and 7.10.

[97] Enterprise Act 2002, s 22(3)(b): on undertakings in lieu of a reference, see pp 916–917 below.

[98] Ibid, s 22(3)(c): see below on anticipated mergers.

[99] Ibid, s 22(3)(d): on public interest cases, see pp 951–955 below.

[100] Ibid, ss 22(3)(e) and 22(3)(f): on the Article 4(5) and Article 22 procedure in the ECMR see ch 21, pp 837–839.

[101] See pp 913–914 below.

make a reference of anticipated mergers where it believes that it is or may be the case that arrangements are in progress or in contemplation which, if carried into effect, would result in the creation of a relevant merger situation and the creation of that situation may be expected to result in an SLC within any market or markets in the UK for goods or services[102]. A merger may be 'in contemplation' without there being a binding agreement: in the *London Stock Exchange* case the CC said that there must be 'genuine consideration' on the part of the acquirer to enter into the transaction; its interest in the transaction must be real; there must be an intention to enter into the transaction within a reasonable time; and the acquirer must be capable of bringing the transaction about[103].

As in the case of section 22 for completed mergers the OFT has a duty, rather than a discretion, to refer anticipated mergers. However, as in the case of completed mergers, the OFT has a discretion not to refer markets of insufficient importance or mergers where relevant customer benefits would outweigh the SLC concerned[104]. An additional discretionary ground for non-reference exists for anticipated mergers, where the arrangements are not sufficiently advanced, or are not sufficiently likely to proceed, to justify the making of a reference to the CC[105]. Section 33(3) sets out circumstances in which a reference cannot be made, which mirror the provisions of section 22(3)[106]. Pursuant to section 34, provision has been made for the aggregation of two or more transactions which take place between the same parties within a two-year period[107].

(C) Relevant merger situations

Section 23 of the Enterprise Act defines what is meant by 'relevant merger situations'. Some of the terminology in this and subsequent sections of the Act is taken from the now-repealed merger provisions in the Fair Trading Act 1973, and the decisional practice under that Act will continue to provide useful guidance under the new one. For there to be a relevant merger situation, two or more enterprises must have ceased to be distinct, and the merger must satisfy either the turnover or the share of supply test. It is not unusual for there to be disagreement between the OFT and the parties as to whether a particular transaction involves enterprises ceasing to be distinct or whether the share of supply test is satisfied: this is something that can be addressed during the pre-notification discussions that often take place[108]. In the event of an irreconcilable difference a firm that is dissatisfied with the OFT's analysis could seek a judicial review before the CAT[109].

(i) Enterprises ceasing to be distinct

A merger occurs where two or more enterprises 'have ceased to be distinct'[110]. For this purpose enterprise means the activities, or part of the activities, of a business[111]. There is no requirement that the activities transferred should generate a profit[112]. The transfer of physical assets could amount to an enterprise where this enables a business activity

---

[102] Enterprise Act 2002, s 33(1).

[103] See the Final Report, para 3.26, available at www.competition-commission.org.uk/inquiries/ref2005/lse/index.htm.

[104] Enterprise Act 2002, s 33(2)(a) and (c).   [105] Ibid, s 33(2)(b).   [106] See pp 903–907 above.

[107] The Enterprise Act 2002 (Anticipated Mergers) Order 2003, SI 2003/1595.   [108] See pp 913–915 below.

[109] See pp 937–938 below.   [110] Enterprise Act 2002, s 23(1)(a) and (2)(a).   [111] Ibid, s 129(1).

[112] *Mergers: Substantive assessment guidance*, para 2.7; see *Imperial Cancer Research Fund/Cancer Research Campaign*, 4 June 2002, decided under the FTA 1973 but equally applicable under the Enterprise Act 2002.

to be continued; and intellectual property rights could be considered to be an enterprise where a turnover can be attributed to them that could be transferred to a buyer[113]. In *Arcelor SA/Corus UK Ltd* the CC concluded that the transfer of goodwill, employees, business information and business records constituted the activities of a business or part of a business even though there was no transfer of physical premises or production facilities[114]. The reference to 'part of the activities' of a business means that the sale of a division of a company may be investigated, provided that the other requirements about to be described are satisfied.

Enterprises cease to be distinct if they are brought under common ownership or control[115]. Control for this purpose is defined broadly in section 26 of the Act: it includes legal control[116]; however the definition also covers a situation in which one person is able to control the policy of another, though without having legal control ('*de facto* control'), or has the ability to influence the policy of another ('material influence')[117]. The expression 'material' influence is wider than 'decisive' influence in Article 3(2) of the ECMR, with the result that some transactions that would not amount to mergers under Community law would do under UK law[118]. The effect of the provisions in section 26 of the Enterprise Act is that a person who acquires a shareholding in a company of much less than 51 per cent may have control for the purpose of UK merger control. There can be material influence where the shareholding is less than 25 per cent, and the OFT has said that it will look at any shareholding greater than 15 per cent to determine whether this is the case; even a shareholding of less than 15 per cent might attract scrutiny in exceptional cases[119]. The OFT's guidance states that an assessment of material influence will require a case-by-case analysis and sets out various factors which may be relevant, such as the ownership and distribution of other shareholdings in a company, the pattern of attendance at recent shareholder meetings, the composition of the board of directors and any agreements that may have been made between the shareholders[120].

In *BSkyB plc/ITV plc* the OFT considered that BSkyB's acquisition of a 17.9 per cent stake in ITV gave it the ability materially to influence the policy of ITV and that the test for making a reference to the CC was met[121]; the CC agreed with this finding[122]. The CC noted that BSkyB's holding of 17.9 per cent of the shares in ITV made it the largest shareholder by some margin; the CC also looked at the voting behaviour at past general meetings of ITV, and considered that a holding of 17.9 per cent would have enabled BSkyB to block any special resolutions[123]. The CC also considered that BSkyB's industry knowledge and standing were of relevance and concluded that, in combination with its shareholding of 17.9 per cent, it did have material influence over ITV[124]. This assessment was not countervailed by other considereations, such as the fact that the

---

[113] Enterprise Act 2002, para 2.8; see further, under similar provisions in the Fair Trading Act 1973, *AAH Holdings plc/Medicopharma NV* Cm 1950 (1992) paras 6.101–6.102; *William Cook Acquisitions* Cm 1196 (1990) paras 6.5–6.6; *Stagecoach Holdings plc/Lancaster City Transport Ltd* Cm 2423 (1993) para 6.21.

[114] See the Final Report, para 3.8, available at www.competition-commission.org.uk/rep_pub/reports/2005/498arcelor.htm.

[115] Enterprise Act 2002, s 26(1).   [116] Ibid, s 26(2) and s 129(1) and (2).   [117] Ibid, s 26(3).

[118] On Article 3(2) of the ECMR see ch 21 pp 823–827.

[119] *Mergers: Substantive assessment guidance*, para 2.10.   [120] Ibid.

[121] See the OFT's Report to the Secretary of State for Trade and Industry *Acquisition by British Sky Broadcasting Group plc of a 17.9 per cent stake in ITV plc* of 27 April 2007, available at www.oft.gov.uk.

[122] See the Final Report, paras 3.29–3.67, available at www.competition-commission.org.uk/inquiries/ref2007/itv/index.htm.

[123] Ibid, paras 3.39–3.57.   [124] Ibid, paras 3.58–3.62.

Communications Act 2003 would prevent BSkyB increasing its shareholding to beyond 20 per cent[125]. BSkyB has appealed against this finding to the CAT[126].

The OFT's guidance says that, since a shareholding of 25 per cent or more generally enables the shareholder to block special resolutions, it is likely to be seen as automatically conferring the ability materially to influence policy[127]. It is possible that one person may have the ability materially to influence the policy of a company even though another has a controlling interest[128].

A transition from one level of control to another (for example from material influence to *de facto* control) would itself amount to a merger for the purposes of the Act[129]. As a result, if Company A acquires Company B in stages, this could give rise to several different mergers: first when A acquires material influence over B; secondly when A acquires *de facto* control; and finally when it achieves *de jure* (or legal) control[130]. The OFT has recognised that, in its substantive assessment of a merger, it should not treat the acquisition of material influence in the same way that it would treat *de facto* or *de jure* control[131]. Section 29 of the Act provides that, where a person acquires control in stages within a two-year period, those stages can be regarded as having occurred simultaneously on the date when the last of them occurred.

When deciding whether enterprises have come under common control or ownership, 'associated persons' and any companies which they control will be treated as one person; section 127(4) defines associated persons broadly and includes any individual, their partners, trustees and business partners[132].

The award of a rail franchise under the provisions of the Railways Act 1993 qualifies as the acquisition of control for the purposes of section 23 of the Enterprise Act[133].

(ii) The turnover test

A merger can be investigated under the Enterprise Act only where it satisfies either the turnover test or the share of supply test. Section 23(1)(b) of the Act provides that a relevant merger situation has been created where the value of the turnover in the UK of the enterprise being taken over exceeds £70 million: the requirement that there must be turnover in the UK provides the necessary jurisdictional nexus for the application of the Act. The OFT will keep the turnover threshold under review and advise the Secretary of State from time to time whether it is still appropriate[134]; the Secretary of State has power to amend the figure[135]. Section 28(2) provides that an enterprise's turnover shall be determined in accordance with an order to be made by the Secretary of State: the Enterprise Act 2002 (Merger Fees and Determination of Turnover) Order 2003[136] explains how turnover is to be calculated for the purpose both of the turnover test and the calculation of any merger fees payable[137]. The OFT has published specific

[125] Ibid, paras 3.63–3.65.
[126] Case 1095/4/8/08 *British Sky Broadcasting plc v Competition Commission*, not yet decided.
[127] *Mergers: Substantive assessment guidance*, para 2.10.   [128] Ibid, para 2.12.
[129] Enterprise Act 2002, s 26(4).   [130] *Mergers: Substantive assessment guidance*, para 2.14.
[131] See paras 63 and 64 of the OFT's Report in *Acquisition by British Sky Broadcasting Group plc of a 17.9 per cent stake in ITV plc* of 27 April 2007, available at www.oft.gov.uk.
[132] Enterprise Act 2002, s 127(1); see further *Mergers: Substantive assessment guidance*, paras 2.16–2.17.
[133] See the Final Report in *Firstgroup plc/Scotrail*, para 3.12, available at www.competition-commission.org.uk/inquiries/completed/2004/first/index.htm; several instances of the award of rail franchises have led to CC references: see the *Table of CC Merger Investigations* at pp 939–949 below.
[134] Enterprise Act 2002, s 28(5).   [135] Ibid, s 28(6).   [136] SI 2003/1370.
[137] On merger fees see p 917 below.

guidance on the application of the turnover test[138]. Turnover is defined in the Turnover Order as the amounts derived from the sale of products and the provision of services which an undertaking makes in the ordinary course of its business activities[139], and is calculated by adding together the turnover of the enterprise being taken over and that of any associated enterprises. The period by reference to which turnover is calculated is the business year preceding the date of completion of a merger or, in the case of anticipated mergers, the date of the OFT's decision whether to make a reference to the CC[140].

(iii) The share of supply test

Section 23(2)(b) of the Enterprise Act provides that a relevant merger situation has been created where the merged enterprises supply or acquire 25 per cent or more of a particular description of goods[141] or services[142] in the UK or a substantial part of it; the supply of services includes permitting or making arrangements to permit the use of land for various purposes such as caravan sites or car parks[143]. The share of supply test requires an *increment* in the share of supply, no matter how small that increment may be[144]. The share of supply test enables a merger to be investigated which could give rise to competition problems even though the turnover threshold of £70 million is not achieved: this may be necessary in the case of narrowly-defined product markets or small geographic markets. The OFT (and the CC) has a wide margin of appreciation in determining whether goods or services are of the same description and whether the 25 per cent threshold is achieved[145], in relation to which it can use value, cost, price, quantity, capacity, number of workers or any other criteria considered appropriate[146].

To determine whether the share of supply test is met the OFT will generally use the narrowest reasonable description of a set of goods or services[147], although it will consider broader ones where appropriate. The OFT may also consider different forms of supply, for example the wholesale or resale of goods[148]. When deciding whether the share of supply test is satisfied the OFT is not required to define the relevant product or geographic markets in accordance with the SSNIP test[149]: the share of supply test is jurisdictional, and does not require a full market analysis. The OFT has stated that it does not believe that it is necessary to show a nexus between the area in which an SLC is identified and the area in which the share of supply test is satisfied[150]. A review of the OFT's case lists of merger decisions on its website reveals that there are quite a large number of cases in which the OFT's jurisdiction over a particular merger arises from the parties' share of supply rather than the turnover being acquired[151].

---

[138] *Guidance note on the calculation of turnover for the purposes of Part 3 of the Enterprise Act 2002*, July 2003; see also *Mergers: Substantive assessment guidance*, paras 2.18–2.21.

[139] SI 2003/1370, Sch, para 3.

[140] *Guidance note on the calculation of turnover for the purposes of Part 3 of the Enterprise Act 2002*, July 2003, paras 1.7–1.10; see also *Mergers: Substantive assessment guidance*, para 2.20.

[141] Enterprise Act 2002, s 23(3).   [142] Ibid, s 23(4).

[143] *The Enterprise Act 2002 (Supply of Services) Order 2003*, SI 2003/1594.

[144] *Mergers: Substantive assessment guidance*, para 2.23.   [145] Enterprise Act 2002, s 23(5).

[146] Ibid, s 23(5)–(8).   [147] *Mergers: Substantive assessment guidance*, para 2.24.

[148] Enterprise Act 2002, s 23(6) and (7).   [149] On the SSNIP test see ch 1, pp 26–40.

[150] See the OFT's decision to refer a merger to the CC in *Vue Entertainment Holdings (UK) Ltd/A3 Cinema Ltd*, para 4, available at www.oft.gov.uk/advice_and_resources/resource_base/Mergers_home/decisions/2005/vue.

[151] See eg www.oft.gov.uk/advice_and_resources/resource_base/Mergers_home/2007.

In determining whether the share of supply test is satisfied in relation to a substantial part of the UK the OFT (and the CC) will be guided by the judgment of the House of Lords in *South Yorkshire Transport Ltd v Monopolies and Mergers Commission*[152] which held (under analogous provisions in the Fair Trading Act 1973) that the part must be of such size, character and importance as to make it worth consideration for the purpose of merger control. According to the OFT, among the factors to be taken into account in deciding whether the merger is 'worth' consideration and can therefore be referred are the size of the specified area, its population, its social, political, economic, financial and geographic significance, and whether it has any particular characteristics that might render it special or significant[153]. The CC applied the *South Yorkshire* test in *Archant Ltd/Independent News and Media plc* in determining that the acquisition of some local newspapers, in different localities that were not contiguous, occurred in a substantial part of the UK[154], and in *Arriva plc/Sovereign Bus and Coach Company Ltd*[155] when reaching the same conclusion in relation to bus services in Hertfordshire.

(iv) Time-limits and prior notice

A reference of a completed merger cannot be made if the enterprises ceased to be distinct more than four months prior to the reference to the CC[156] or, if later, more than four months before notice was given to the OFT of the merger or the fact of the merger became publicly known[157]. In certain circumstances these time limits can be extended[158]. Section 27 deals with the question of when enterprises cease to be distinct, in particular where ownership or control is obtained over a period of time. Section 27(2) provides that mergers are treated as having been completed when all the parties to a transaction became contractually bound to proceed: the existence of options or other conditions are irrelevant until the option is exercised or the condition satisfied[159]. Where ownership or control has been acquired incrementally over a period of time through a series of transactions they can be treated as having occurred on the date of the last transaction, subject to a two year cut-off period[160]. In *Archant Ltd/Independent News and Media plc* the CC rejected Archant's argument that the reference had been made outside the four-month statutory period; it also concluded that two successive transactions should be regarded as having occurred on the date of the later of the two[161].

(D) OFT procedure

Having explained the statutory obligations of the OFT in relation to completed and anticipated mergers, it may be helpful to pause at this stage to consider how it exercises

---

[152] [1993] 1 All ER 289, [1993] 1 WLR 23, HL; see also *Stagecoach Holdings v Secretary of State for Trade and Industry* 1997 SLT 940, OH.

[153] *Mergers: Substantive assessment guidance*, para 2.25.

[154] See the Final Report, Appendix C, paras 23–31, available at www.competition-commission.org.uk/inquiries/completed/2004/archant/index.htm.

[155] See the Final Report, paras 3.10–3.14, available at www.competition-commission.org.uk/inquiries/completed/2005/arriva/index.htm.

[156] Enterprise Act 2002, s 24(l)(a). [157] Ibid, s 24(l)(b), (2) and (3). [158] Ibid, s 25. [159] Ibid, s 27(3).

[160] Ibid, s 27(5) and 27(6); on this point see *Tesco plc/Co-operative Group*, OFT 2 February 2004, where the OFT decided not to treat the acquisition of 3 Co-op stores as having occurred on the date of the latest transaction.

[161] See the Final Report, Appendix C, paras 17–22, available at www.competition-commission.org.uk/inquiries/completed/2004/archant/index.htm.

its functions up to the point of making a reference to the CC. There is no statutory duty to pre-notify mergers under UK law, although there is a legal basis in section 96 of the Enterprise Act for making a 'statutory voluntary notification'[162]; alternatively the parties may make an 'informal submission' to the OFT. In practice many firms do approach the OFT prior to a transaction in order to discuss the application of the Act to it. If the parties to a transaction go ahead without discussing the matter with the OFT they run the risk that their completed merger might be detected by the OFT and referred to the CC; this does happen fairly frequently, and on some occasions the CC has required a divestiture of assets that had already been acquired[163]. Useful guidance on the OFT's procedures will be found in its publication *Mergers: Procedural guidance*, but it is important to note that the position in relation to informal advice and confidential guidance has changed since it was issued. The OFT intends to publish revised guidance in the course of 2008; in the meantime interim arrangements are in place for informal advice and pre-notification contacts[164].

(i) Notifying mergers to the OFT

The OFT's *Guidance* explains a number of ways in which the parties might discuss a merger with the OFT.

(A) Informal advice The OFT will provide informal advice only where the parties can demonstrate a good faith intention of proceeding with a transaction: hypothetical advice will not be given; nor will informal advice be given in the case of a transaction that is already in the public domain. Informal advice will be given only where there is a genuine competition issue that could give rise to a reference to the CC: the OFT cannot be used to endorse the advice of professional advisers that a transaction gives rise to no competition problem. Parties seeking informal advice should submit to the OFT a concise briefing paper of no more than five pages. When the OFT provides informal advice in relation to a genuine competition issue it may provide advice on jurisdictional issues as well.

(B) Confidential guidance The OFT's former practice of providing confidential guidance no longer applies.

(C) Pre-notification discussions[165] The OFT encourages pre-notification discussion, which it considers to be beneficial both to the parties and to the OFT. Among the benefits are that the OFT team can be educated where markets are complex and/or unfamiliar; that the discussions can help to identify the information and evidence needed by the OFT; and that they can avoid or minimise burdensome information requests at a later stage.

(D) Statutory voluntary pre-notification[166] Sections 96 to 100 of the Enterprise Act make provision for mergers that qualify for investigation under the Act to be pre-notified to the OFT: the advantage to the parties of a 'statutory voluntary notification' is that the OFT must make a decision whether to refer the case to the CC within 20 working days,

---

[162] See below.   [163] See pp 949–950 below.
[164] See *Interim arrangements*, April 2006, paras 11–17, available at www.oft.gov.uk.
[165] Ibid, paras 18–21.
[166] *Mergers: Procedural Guidance*, paras 3.23–3.25.

with a maximum extension of a further 10 working days if the filing is incomplete or a request for further information is not complied with. There are no statutory time limits where the parties make an 'informal submission': in a case where time is of the essence, therefore, it may be attractive to invoke the statutory procedure. The OFT has to give priority to dealing with cases notified under the statutory procedure because of its obligation to fit in with the fixed time limits: in the case of a statutory notification a merger is cleared if the OFT has not referred it to the CC within the statutory period. The OFT has the power to request a person who gives a merger notice to provide it with information[167]. A fee must be paid in advance when using this procedure, and the clock does not start until this has occurred[168]. Statutory notifications must be made in the prescribed form: a copy can be downloaded from the OFT's website[169]. The Enterprise Act 2002 (Merger Prenotification) Regulations 2003[170] make further provision in relation to the operation of merger notices, and the procedure is explained in Annex A of the OFT's *Guidance* and in an OFT leaflet *Prior notice of publicly proposed mergers*.

(E) Informal submissions[171] Notwithstanding the fact that there is a system of statutory voluntary pre-notification, companies and their professional advisers tend to make so-called informal submissions in relation to transactions that may give rise to competition concerns; unless time is of the essence, there is no particular advantage in the statutory procedure which, in practice, the OFT regards as best suited to straightforward cases. The OFT considers that informal submissions are equally acceptable as statutory ones. Although there is no statutory time limit for dealing with informal submissions, in practice the OFT has an administrative timetable of 40 working days which it meets in about 80 per cent to 90 per cent of cases. In more complex cases the parties prefer the OFT to extend its administrative timetable beyond the 40 day period if this makes it possible to deal with a complex case without a reference to the CC. The OFT will stop the administrative timetable where important information is not provided or is provided late. Where an informal submission is made there is no prescribed form for doing so; however chapter 4 of the OFT's *Guidance* contains advice on the kind of information that should be submitted (see below).

(ii) Content of submissions

Chapter 4 of the OFT's *Guidance* discusses the type of information that an informal submission should contain. This information falls broadly into three categories: general background information; jurisdictional information; and information that is necessary for a substantive assessment of the merger. The OFT may consider whether any contractual restrictions are ancillary to a merger, with the consequence that they would be excluded from the Competition Act 1998[172]: where the parties to a merger require the OFT to give a view on ancillary restrictions, they will have to provide certain information about them as well[173]. The treatment of ancillary restrictions is explained further in Annex B of the OFT's *Procedural Guidance* and in section 11 of its *Substantive Assessment Guidance*[174].

---

[167] Enterprise Act 2002, s 99(2).   [168] See p 917 below on the payment of fees.   [169] See www.oft.gov.uk.
[170] SI 2003/1369.   [171] *Mergers: Procedural Guidance*, para 3.26.
[172] See Competition Act 1998, Sch 1 and ch 9, pp 341–343.
[173] *Mergers: Procedural Guidance*, para 4-25–4.28.   [174] OFT 516, May 2003.

(iii) The assessment process

Chapter 5 of the OFT's *Guidance* explains how it goes about its assessment of mergers. The *Guidance* begins by discussing the gathering of supplementary information and the verification of it, which involves consultation with third parties[175]. A section of the OFT's website lists the cases on which the OFT is inviting third party comments and names the responsible case officer[176]. The *Guidance* goes on to explain that the OFT may consider seeking an initial undertaking or making an order to prevent pre-emptive action that might prejudice a reference to the CC[177]. It then describes the decision-making process[178].

Cases that do not raise serious competition problems are usually decided within the Mergers Group, although a paper is prepared and circulated to other staff of the OFT. In complex or more problematic cases, where a reference might be made to the CC, the parties are sent an 'Issues Letter' setting out the relevant evidence and the core arguments for a reference; the parties are given an opportunity to respond, in writing or at a meeting, and in practice usually do both. Thereafter a case review meeting ('CRM') will take place within the OFT: it is usually chaired by a senior OFT official from outside the Mergers Group or by the Director of Mergers, and always has representatives from the Office of the Chief Economist, the Advisory, Policy and International team and, where appropriate, from individuals with relevant expertise in a particular sector. An individual within the review group will be charged specifically with acting as a 'devil's advocate' at the CRM, to test the soundness of the case-team's assessment and to argue the contrary position. After the CRM there is a separate decision meeting: the person that chaired the CRM will act as a rapporteur when briefing the person responsible for making the final decision: this is usually the Senior Director of Mergers, but, where appropriate, may be the Chief Executive of the OFT. A provisional decision is taken at this meeting; the decision is then drafted, and becomes final when signed by the decision-maker. Notifying parties are contacted one hour before the public announcement of the decision and are informed of the timing and the nature of the decision. The decision is then publicy announced.

If an Issues Letter has been sent, but the OFT then decides not to make a reference to the CC, the Court of Appeal has said that it must be shown that the likelihood of an SLC has been removed and that the material relied on by the OFT can reasonably be regarded as dispelling the uncertainties highlighted by the Issues Letter[179]. This ruling has made the OFT more cautious in sending out Issues Letters.

All decisions on public merger cases must be published; the text of the decision, once any business secrets have been removed, is placed on the OFT's website. The OFT informs the CC of cases that might be referred so that the CC is aware of potential work that is 'in the pipeline' and can prepare accordingly. Once a decision to refer is made the CC receives relevant documentation from the OFT; the staff of the two institutions meet at an early stage to discuss the handing-over of the case. The OFT may then make further information available to the CC.

---

[175] Ibid, paras 5.2–5.11.
[176] See www.oft.gov.uk/advice_and_resources/resource_base/Mergers_home/comment.
[177] *Mergers: Procedural Guidance*, paras 5.12–5,15; on the OFT's enforcement powers see pp 928–932 below.
[178] Ibid, paras 5.16–5.21.
[179] *OFT v IBA Health Ltd* [2004] EWCA Civ 142, [2004] UKCLR 683, paras 73 and 100; see also Case 1049/4/1/05 *UniChem Ltd v OFT* [2005] CAT 8, [2005] CompAR 907, para 201.

(iv) Undertakings in lieu of a reference

Section 73 of the Act gives power to the OFT to accept an undertaking in lieu of making a reference to the CC[180]. In doing so the OFT must have regard to the need to achieve as comprehensive a solution as is reasonable and practicable to the SLC and any adverse effects resulting from it[181], taking into account any relevant customer benefits[182]. The OFT considers that undertakings in lieu of a reference are appropriate only in relatively straightforward cases, when 'the competition concerns raised by the merger and the proposed remedies to address them are clear cut'[183]; structural undertakings are more likely to be acceptable than behavioural ones[184]. In the case of *SvitzerWijsmuller A/S/ Adsteam Marine Ltd* the OFT declined to accept undertakings in lieu where it was not satisfied that a structural remedy that had been offered would restore the pre-merger competition dynamics and where it was difficult to assess, within the OFT's investigation, the precise magnitude of the loss of potential competition that the merger was likely to lead to[185]. Where the OFT considers that undertakings are a suitable remedy there will normally be a period of consultation of at least 15 days; a further period of consultation may take place in the event that the undertakings are modified[186]. If an undertaking in lieu has been accepted it is not possible to make a merger investigation reference to the CC[187], although the position is different if the OFT was not in possession of material facts at the time the undertaking was accepted[188]. The OFT has power to make an order where the undertaking in lieu is not being fulfilled or where false or misleading information was given prior to the acceptance of the undertaking[189]. There is also a power to make a supplementary interim order while the main section 75 order is being prepared; the same power is available to the CC[190].

Undertakings in lieu of a reference have been accepted by the OFT on a number of occasions: details of cases dealt with in this way are available on the OFT's website[191]. In most cases the undertaking was structural, typically to divest assets. Examples of such undertakings can be found in the case of *Capital Radio plc/GWR Radio plc*, where a local radio station in the East Midlands of England had to be divested[192] and *Boots Group plc/Alliance UniChem plc* where an undertaking was given to divest a number of pharmacies[193]. In *Aggregate Industries Ltd/Foster Yeoman Ltd* the OFT accepted undertakings in lieu that were intended to address not only non-coordinated but also coordinated effects, the first case of this kind[194].

---

[180] See *Mergers: Substantive assessment guidance*, paras 8.1–8.10; *Mergers: Procedural Guidance*, paras 7.1–7.9.

[181] Enterprise Act 2002, s 73(3).   [182] Ibid, s 73(4).

[183] *Mergers: Substantive assessment guidance*, para 8.3.   [184] Ibid, para 8.6.

[185] See www.oft.gov.uk/advice_and_resources/resource_base/Mergers_home/decisions/2006/svitzerwij smuller.

[186] *Mergers: Procedural Guidance*, paras 7.7 and 7.8.   [187] Enterprise Act 2002, s 74(I).

[188] Ibid, s 74(2)–(4).   [189] Ibid, s 75(1).   [190] Ibid, s 76.

[191] See www.oft.gov.uk/advice_and_resources/resource_base/Mergers_home/register/undertakings-in-lieu.

[192] See www.oft.gov.uk/advice_and_resources/resource_base/Mergers_home/register/undertakings-in-lieu/capital.

[193] See www.oft.gov.uk/advice_and_resources/resource_base/Mergers_home/register/undertakings-in-lieu/boots; note that the OFT's decision not to refer this case to the CC was the subject of an unsuccessful judicial review before the CAT by a third party in Case 1059/4/1/06 *Celesio AG v OFT* [2006] CAT 9, [2006] CompAR 515.

[194] See www.oft.gov.uk/advice_and_resources/resource_base/Mergers_home/decisions/2006/Aggregate3.

In the case of *Cooperative Group (CWS) Ltd (CGL)/Fairways Group UK Ltd* an undertaking in lieu was given to the OFT by CGL to divest a number of funeral businesses in five local areas of the UK[195]. When the OFT decided that Southern Cooperatives Ltd was an unacceptable purchaser, since the Chief Executive of Southern was a member of the board of CGL, CGL challenged the OFT's decision before the CAT[196]. The CAT rejected the appeal. After setting out the general scheme of section 73 of the Act[197] the CAT said that it was reasonable of the OFT to have sought to restore the market to the '*status quo ante*'[198]; it also noted the broad margin of assessment that the OFT has in merger cases and that, when exercising the power to accept undertakings in lieu of a reference to the CC, it could not be expected to conduct a detailed investigation[199].

There has been one occasion on which the OFT has accepted a quasi-structural remedy: in *Tetra Laval Group/Carlisle Process Systems* an undertaking was given to grant an irrevocable EEA-wide licence of a package of intellectual property rights to a third party, approved 'up-front' by the OFT, that would enable it to compete in the market for equipment used in the industrial manufacture of cheddar cheese[200]. An unusual remedy in an early case under the Enterprise Act was *IVAX International GmbH/3M*, where the OFT accepted a behavioural undertaking to limit the price of asthma inhalers until such time as competitive products emerged onto the market[201].

(v) Fees

Pursuant to section 121 of the Enterprise Act provision is made by the Enterprise Act 2002 (Merger Fees and Determination of Turnover) Order 2003[202] for the payment of fees in connection with the exercise of the functions of the OFT (and, exceptionally, the Secretary of State) in relation to mergers. Article 3 sets out the circumstances in which fees are payable, and Article 4 specifies certain cases in which fees are not payable. The level of fees – from £15,000 to £45,000, depending on the turnover of the enterprise taken over or to be taken over[203] – is set out in Article 5. Article 6 explains who must pay the fee[204], and Article 7 provides an exemption for small- and medium-sized enterprises. Article 8 provides that the fees are payable to the OFT and Article 9 establishes when the fees are payable. Provision is made for the repayment of fees in certain cases. Part 3 of the Order explains how turnover is to be calculated for the purpose of determining the appropriate level of the fee (and for the purpose of establishing whether a relevant merger situation in the sense of section 28(2) of the Act has been created)[205]. Further guidance on merger fees can be found in chapter 6 of the OFT's *Guidance*.

---

[195] See www.oft.gov.uk/advice_and_resources/resource_base/Mergers_home/register/undertakings-in-lieu/cooperative.

[196] Case 1081/4/1/07 *Cooperative Group Ltd v OFT* [2007] CAT 24.   [197] Ibid, para 102.

[198] Ibid, paras 150–151.   [199] Ibid, paras 179–180.

[200] See www.oft.gov.uk/advice_and_resources/resource_base/Mergers_home/register/undertakings-in-lieu/tetra.

[201] See www.oft.gov.uk/advice_and_resources/resource_base/Mergers_home/register/undertakings-in-lieu/ivax.

[202] SI 2003/1370.

[203] Note that the figures in the 2003 Order were increased by the Enterprise Act 2002 (Merger Fees) (Amendment) Order 2005, SI 2005/3558; this change followed a public consultation, as to which see *Government Response to Consultation: Changing the System of Charging for the Costs of Merger Control*, URN 06/629, January 2006.

[204] Note that Article 6(5) of the 2003 Order was repealed by Article 2(8) of the Enterprise Act 2002 (Merger Fees)(Amendment) Order 2005, SI 2005/3558.

[205] See pp 910–911 above.

4. DETERMINATION OF REFERENCES BY THE CC

Once a reference has been made by the OFT to the CC section 35 of the Enterprise Act sets out the questions to be decided in relation to completed mergers and section 36 the questions in relation to anticipated mergers. Sections 38 and 39 deal with the reports of the CC and the time-limits within which they must be produced. Section 41 requires the CC to take action to remedy any loss of competition.

(A) Questions to be decided in relation to completed mergers

Section 35(1) of the Enterprise Act requires the CC to decide, first, whether a merger situation has been created[206] and second, whether, if so, the creation of that situation has resulted, or may be expected to result, in an SLC within any market or markets in the UK for goods or services[207]. The CC will always try to identify how the market would look if the merger were not to happen: in other words it will attempt to establish the 'counter-factual' in order to determine the extent of any SLC[208]. The way in which the CC is likely to apply the SLC test is considered in section 5 below[209]. If the CC considers that there is an 'anti-competitive outcome'[210], it must decide three additional questions: first, whether it should take remedial action[211]; second, whether it should recommend that anyone else should take remedial action[212]; and third, if remedial action should be taken, what that action should be[213]. When considering remedial action the CC must have regard to the need to achieve as comprehensive a solution as is reasonable and practical to the SLC and any adverse effects resulting from it[214], and may in particular have regard to the effect of any action on any relevant customer benefits[215]. If the CC finds that there is no anti-competitive outcome, no question of considering remedies arises.

(B) Questions to be decided in relation to anticipated mergers

Section 36 requires the CC to decide similar questions in relation to anticipated mergers, with the necessary linguistic adjustments to address the fact that such mergers are yet to be completed.

---

[206] Enterprise Act 2002, s 35(1)(a).   [207] Ibid, s 35(1)(b).

[208] See eg *Somerfield plc/Wm Morrison Supermarkets plc*, paras 7.56–7.60, available at www.competition-commission.org.uk/rep_pub/reports/2005/501somerfield.htm; *Deutsche Borse AG, Euronext NV/London Stock Exchange plc*, paras 5.125–5.130, available at www.competition-commission.org.uk/rep_pub/reports/2005/504lse.htm; *Vue Entertainment Holdings (UK) Ltd/A3 Cinema Ltd*, paras 6.20–6.24, available at www.competition-commission.org.uk/rep_pub/reports/2006/508vue.htm; *Stagecoach/Scottish Citylink*, paras 5.1–5.62, available at www.competition-commission.org.uk/rep_pub/reports/2006/516citylink.htm; *Stericycle International LLC/Sterile Technologies Group Ltd*, paras 6.1–6.4, available at www.competition-commission.org.uk/rep_pub/reports/2006/519stericycle.htm; *Hamsard 2786 Ltd/Academy Music Holdings Ltd*, paras 5.64–5.68, available at www.competition-commission.org.uk/rep_pub/reports/2007/522hamsard.htm; *Stonegate Farmers Ltd/Dean Food Group Ltd*, paras 3.1–3.2, available at www.competition-commission.org.uk/rep_pub/reports/2007/524stonegate.htm.

[209] See pp 921–928 below.   [210] This term is defined in Enterprise Act 2002, s 35(2).   [211] Ibid, s 35(3)(a).

[212] Ibid, s 35(3)(b).   [213] Ibid, s 35(3)(c).   [214] Ibid, s 35(4).

[215] Ibid, s 35(5); on relevant customer benefits see pp 906–907 above.

(C) Investigations and reports

Section 37 of the Enterprise Act contains provisions for the cancellation and variation of references by the OFT or the CC, for example where a referred merger has been abandoned: as will be seen from the *Table of CC Merger Investigations* later in this chapter, a significant number of mergers are abandoned following reference to the CC[216]. Section 38(1) of the Act requires the CC to prepare and publish a report within the period permitted by section 39. Section 39(1) requires the CC to do so within 24 weeks of the date of the reference, a longer period than the 90 working days available to the European Commission in a Phase II case under the ECMR[217]. The 24 week period may be shorter where this is necessary to comply with Article 9(6) of the ECMR[218]; and may be extended by no more than eight weeks where there are 'special reasons' for doing so[219], or where there has been a failure to comply with a requirement of a notice under section 109[220]. The CC extended the inquiry period in the case of two bids for the London Stock Exchange in 2005 due to the 'exceptional complexity' of the inquiry[221]. It also extended the period in the case of *Railway Investments Ltd/Marcroft Holdings Ltd*, because a significant amount of new evidence became available after it published its preliminary findings[222], and in *Stonegate Farmers Ltd/Deans Food Group Ltd*, because of the complexity of the possible remedy options in that case[223]. The CC extended the inquiry period in the case of *Tesco plc/Cooperative Group* in order to ensure a consistency of approach with the CC's ongoing inquiry into the supply of groceries in the UK[224].

The time-limits in section 39 may be reduced by the Secretary of State[225]. The report must contain the decisions of the CC on the questions to be decided under sections 35 or 36, its reasons for those decisions and such information as the CC considers appropriate for facilitating a proper understanding of those questions and its reasons for its decisions[226]. In the CAT's view the duty to give reasons has three main purposes: to allow interested persons to know the justification for the decision; to enhance public confidence in the decision-making process; and to concentrate the mind of the decision-maker[227].

The implementation of remedies following the CC's report does not have to be completed within the statutory period for the investigation, and may be quite protracted; the group of CC members conducting an inquiry will be discharged only when the remedies have been finally accepted.

---

[216] See pp 939–949 below.   [217] See ch 21, pp 847–849.

[218] Enterprise Act 2002, s 39(2); on Article 9 ECMR see ch 21, pp 836–837.

[219] Ibid, s 39(3): special reasons might be the illness or incapacity of a member of the group of members investigating the case or an unexpected merger of competitors: *Explanatory Notes*, para 132; only one such extension is possible: s 40(4).

[220] Ibid, s 39(4); on s 109 see p 937 below.

[221] See www.competition-commission.org.uk/inquiries/ref2005/lse.

[222] See www.competition-commission.org.uk/inquiries/ref2006/marcroft/index.htm; see similarly *Greif Inc/Blagden Packaging Group*, available at www.competition-commission.org.uk/inquiries/ref2007/blagden/index.htm#gro.

[223] See www.competition-commission.org.uk/inquiries/ref2006/stonegate/index.htm; see also *Stagecoach/Scottish Citylink*, www.competition-commission.org.uk/inquiries/ref2006/citylink/index.htm.

[224] See www.competition-commission.org.uk/inquiries/ref2007/tesco/index.htm.

[225] Enterprise Act 2002, s 40(8).   [226] Ibid, s 38(2).

[227] Case 1051/4/8/05 *Somerfield plc v Competition Commission* [2006] CAT 4, para 62.

(D) Duty to remedy the anti-competitive effects of completed or anticipated mergers

Where the CC has prepared and published a report under section 38 within the time-limits established by section 39 and has concluded that there is an anti-competitive outcome section 41(2) requires it to take such action as it considers to be reasonable and practicable to remedy, mitigate or prevent the SLC and any adverse effects of it[228]. In doing so the CC must be consistent with the decisions in its report on the questions it is required to answer, unless there has been a material change of circumstances since the preparation of the report or the CC has a special reason for deciding differently[229]. In making its decision under section 41(2) the CC must have regard to the need to achieve as comprehensive a solution as is reasonable and practicable to the SLC and any adverse effects resulting from it[230].

(E) CC procedure

The procedures of the CC during merger references are set out in its *Rules of Procedure*[231] and the *Chairman's Guidance to Groups*[232]. When a reference is made the Chairman will appoint members of the CC to a group, consisting of a minimum of three, though usually four or five, who will carry out the inquiry. Rule 6 of the *Rules of Procedure* requires the CC to draw up an administrative timetable for its investigation. The CC has wide-ranging investigatory powers to enable it to carry out its investigation effectively[233], and can impose penalties for non-compliance[234]. The major stages of an investigation include the gathering and verification of evidence; providing a statement of issues; notifying provisional findings[235]; notifying and considering possible remedies; the publication of the final report; and deciding on remedies. Hearings will be held with third parties and with the main parties to the proceedings; where appropriate there will also be hearings on remedies. Often the CC visits appropriate facilities of the merging parties in order better to understand the context of the merger. Each investigation has its own home page on the CC's website, as explained below in relation to the *Vue Entertainments* case, and it is a simple matter to follow the progress of the investigation in this way. This accords with the CC's aim to be open and transparent in its working[236]. The home page sets out the core documents of the inquiry; contains the CC's announcements, for example on its provisional findings, possible remedies, and its final report; and makes available the parties' responses to the CC's questionnaires, third party submissions, consumer reports, and comments on draft remedies.

The case of *Vue Entertainments Holdings (UK) Ltd/A3 Cinema Ltd* was a reference of a completed acquisition by Vue Entertainments of A3 Cinema. The OFT had accepted an undertaking that the two businesses would be held separate until the conclusion of the case, and the CC adopted this undertaking and maintained it in effect during its

---

[228] Enterprise Act 2002, s 41(2). [229] Ibid, s 41(3). [230] Ibid, s 41(4). [231] CC1, March 2006.

[232] CC6, March 2006. [233] Enterprise Act 2002, s 109. [234] Ibid, s 110.

[235] It can happen that the CC changes its assessment of a merger between its provisional findings report and its final report: see eg its investigation of *British Salt Ltd/New Cheshire Salt Works*, available at www.competition-commission.org.uk/inquiries/ref2005/britishsalt.htm.

[236] See *Chairman's Guidance on Disclosure of Information in Merger and Market Inquiries* (CC7, July 2003), paras 1.5 and 1.6, available at www.competition-commission.org.uk.

investigation. The CC concluded that the merger did involve an SLC in cinema exhibition in the town of Basingstoke and required a divestiture of one of the two cinemas owned by Vue Entertainments there. The home page of the inquiry sets out the core documents which provide a helpful insight into the progress of the case[237]:

- terms of reference (**23 September 2005**)
- members of inquiry
- administrative timetable
- adoption of undertakings (**28 September 2005**)
- issues statement
- notice of provisional findings (**20 December 2005**)
- provisional findings report
- notice of possible remedies
- final report (**24 February 2006**)
- draft undertakings for consultation
- notice of proposal to accept undertakings
- notice of acceptance of undertakings (**18 May 2006**)
- undertakings given to the CC by Vue Entertainment Holdings (UK) Ltd.

5. THE 'SUBSTANTIAL LESSENING OF COMPETITION' TEST

The Enterprise Act subjects mergers to an SLC test. This section considers how the OFT and the CC apply the SLC test in practice.

(A) Publication of merger guidelines

Section 106(1) of the Enterprise Act requires the OFT and the CC to publish general advice and information about the making and assessment of merger references. Pursuant to section 106(1) the OFT has published *Mergers: Substantive assessment guidance*[238] ('the *OFT guidance*') and the CC has published *Merger References: Competition Commission Guidelines*[239] ('the *CC Guidelines*'). These two pieces of guidance are configured differently, although their content is much the same. Their content can be divided into four main categories: market definition; horizontal mergers; vertical mergers; and conglomerate mergers. This section will proceed on this basis.

(B) Market definition

The *OFT guidance* explains that, when assessing the competitive constraints upon firms, a market definition, though not an end in itself, provides a framework for the analysis[240]. It cross-refers to the OFT's guideline under the Competition Act 1998 *Market*

---

[237] See www.competition-commission.org.uk/inquiries/ref2005/vue/index.htm.

[238] OFT 516, May 2003.

[239] CC 2, June 2003; the CC and the OFT have said that they intend to publish revised joint guidance in the course of 2008.

[240] *OFT guidance*, para 3.11.

Definition[241] which explains its methodology for defining markets[242]. The *OFT guidance* says that in defining markets the OFT will have regard to previous decisions of the OFT, the CC and the European Commission; however it will not consider itself bound by them, in particular because markets may change over time[243]. It then refers to the 'SSNIP test'[244] and describes the kind of evidence that may be used in its application, for example information from customers, competitors and suppliers, evidence of switching strategies and relative price histories, details of switching costs and the existence of spare capacity[245].

Part 2 of the *CC Guidelines* explains its approach to market definition. It states that, when applying the SSNIP test, it will usually hypothesise an increase in prices of around 5 per cent[246]: other formulations of the SSNIP test usually hypothesise an increase 'of five to ten percent'[247]. The *CC Guidelines* note the problem of the 'Cellophane Fallacy'[248], and say that, where appropriate, it might apply the SSNIP test to a price other than the one currently prevailing on the market[249]. They proceed to discuss how the CC will assess demand-side substitution[250] and supply-side substitution[251], and specific issues such as chains of substitution[252], different groups within a market[253] and upstream and downstream markets[254].

The CC has published an interesting paper in its 'Topics in competition policy' series explaining its use of customer surveys when defining the relevant market in merger investigations (and when assessing the competitive effects of mergers)[255]. The paper notes the value of such surveys, but points out the need to design the survey carefully in order to be able to have confidence in its results; it also stresses that the results of such surveys can only be part of the evidence on which the CC bases its findings.

(C) Horizontal mergers

Chapter 4 of the *OFT guidance* and Part 3 of the *CC Guidelines* deal with horizontal mergers. The *OFT guidance* presents the issues in the following sequence, which will be adopted here: market structure and concentration; non-coordinated effects; coordinated effects; entry and expansion; countervailing power; efficiencies; and the 'failing firm' defence.

(i) Market structure and concentration

The *OFT guidance* states that the OFT evaluates how the competitive incentives of the merging firms and their competitors will change as a result of a merger. The starting point of its analysis is to look at changes in the market structure arising from the merger[256]. It uses three principle measures for this purpose: market shares; concentration ratios; and the Herfindahl-Hirschman Index ('HHI')[257]. The OFT says that it is likely to find that a market with a post-merger HHI of more than 1,800 is 'highly

---

[241] OFT 403, December 2004. [242] *OFT guidance*, para 3.12. [243] Ibid, para 3.16.
[244] On the SSNIP test see ch 1, pp 26–40. [245] *OFT guidance*, para 3.18. [246] *CC Guidelines*, para 2.7.
[247] See eg the *OFT guidance*, para 3.17. [248] See ch 1, pp 30–31. [249] *CC Guidelines*, paras 2.9–2.10.
[250] Ibid, paras 2.15–2.19. [251] Ibid, paras 2.20–2.23. [252] Ibid, paras 2.30–2.32.
[253] Ibid, paras 2.33–2.34. [254] Ibid, paras 2.35–2.36.
[255] *The relevance of surveys to the 'relevant market'*, available at www.competition-commission.org.uk/our_role/analysis/topics.htm.
[256] *OFT guidance*, para 4.1.
[257] Ibid, para 4.3; for further discussion of the HHI see ch 1, pp 41–42.

concentrated'; a market with a post-merger HHI of more than 1,000 will be regarded as 'concentrated'. Where a market is highly concentrated, a change of more than 50 in the HHI as a result of a merger may give rise to competition concerns; where a market is concentrated, a change of 100 may be problematic[258]. The OFT adds that these measures for looking at changes in the structure of markets do not give rise to a presumption that a merger may be expected to lessen competition substantially: further investigation will always be necessary to determine if this is so[259].

The *CC Guidelines* also discuss market shares and concentration[260]. The CC says that a post-merger market share of more than 25 per cent would normally be sufficient to raise potential competition concerns; market shares of less than 25 per cent are less likely to do so, although this possibility cannot be ruled out[261]. It adds that, where it uses the HHI, the CC will have regard to the thresholds in the *OFT guidance*, but only as one factor in its wider assessment[262]. The *CC Guidelines* also discuss other structural factors such as network effects[263], switching costs[264], and information asymmetries[265].

(ii) Non-coordinated effects

Both the *OFT guidance*[266] and the *CC Guidelines*[267] discuss the problem of non-coordinated effects arising from mergers. The *OFT guidance* says that non-coordinated effects may arise where a merged entity finds it profitable to increase prices (or reduce output or quality) as a result of the loss of competition between the merged parties[268]. It then sets out a series of factors which might make a market conducive to non-coordinated effects, for example high market concentration, restricted customer choice and weak competitive constraints from rivals; further issues of significance are whether one of the merging firms is a 'maverick' – a particularly rivalrous force in the market – or a recent entrant or a strong potential entrant into the market[269]. The OFT stresses that this is not a mechanical check-list[270]. The *OFT guidance* points out that not only the merging parties, but also their rivals, may be able to share the benefit of greater post-merger profitability: this is a reference to the 'problem' of non-collusive oligopoly referred to in chapter 21[271]. The *CC Guidelines* adopt a similar approach to non-coordinated effects[272].

Firms sometimes argue that apparently high post-merger market shares ought not to be indicative of an SLC because they operate in a 'bidding market' in which they compete *for* the market and not *within* the market[273]. The CC and the OFT have both published working papers on bidding markets which point out various fallacies inherent in arguments for the lenient treatment of such markets[274], and rejected bidding market arguments in *Arcelor SA/Corus UK Ltd*[275] and in *Cott Beverages Ltd/Macaw (Holdings) Ltd*[276]. The OFT has also published a discussion paper on the same subject produced by

[258] Ibid, para 4.3.　[259] Ibid, para 4.4.　[260] *CC Guidelines*, paras 3.3–3.10.　[261] Ibid, para 3.4.
[262] Ibid, para 3.10.　[263] Ibid, para 3.13.　[264] Ibid, para 3.14.　[265] Ibid, para 3.15.
[266] *OFT guidance*, paras 4.7–4.10.　[267] *CC Guidelines*, paras 3.28–3.31.　[268] *OFT guidance*, para 4.7.
[269] Ibid, para 4.8.　[270] Ibid, para 4.9.　[271] See ch 21, pp 853–856.　[272] *CC Guidelines*, paras 3.28–3.31.
[273] On bidding markets see ch 1, p 40.
[274] See Klemperer 'Bidding markets', available at www.competition-commission.org.uk/our_role/analysis/working_papers.htm.
[275] See the Final Report, paras 6.48–6.56, available at www.competition-commission.org.uk/inquiries/completed/2005/arcelor/index.htm.
[276] See the Final Report, paras 5.24–5.27, available at www.competition-commission.org.uk/inquiries/ref2005/macaw/index.htm.

an economics consultancy which concluded that bidding processes are unlikely to create significantly different issues to those that may arise in a more traditional market[277].

(iii) Coordinated effects

Both the *OFT guidance*[278] and the *CC Guidelines*[279] discuss the problem of coordinated
effects arising from mergers. The problem of tacit coordination in oligopolistic markets
was discussed in detail in chapter 14, to which the reader is referred. The OFT considers
that there are three necessary conditions for tacit coordination: sufficient market transparency for the firms to be able to align their behaviour; an effective retaliatory mechanism; and ineffective competitive constraints[280]. This formulation is clearly consistent
with the judgment of the Court of First Instance in *Airtours v Commission*[281] and with
the European Commission's *Guidelines on the assessment of horizontal mergers*[282]. The
CC Guidelines adopt a similar approach to coordinated effects; they contain a useful
review of factors that might make a market conducive to tacit coordination, for example
a high degree of product homogeneity, similarity in the size of the firms in the market,
high market transparency, and the stability of market shares over time[283]. The CC has
also published a working paper that discusses a methodology for evaluating coordinated effects in markets for differentiated products[284].

    There have not been many cases under the Enterprise Act in which the OFT and/or the
CC have considered coordinated effects in detail. As already noted, the OFT accepted
undertakings in lieu of a reference to the CC in *Aggregate Industries Ltd/Foster Yeoman
Ltd*, partly because of concerns about coordinated effects[285]; it did so for the same reason in *Lloyds Pharmacy Ltd/Independent Pharmacy Care Centres plc*[286]. The CC was primarily concerned with the possibility that the merger in *DS Smith/LINPAC Containers*
might lead to coordinated effects but concluded that, even though the conditions for
achieving coordination might be present on the market, smaller suppliers would have
the incentive to respond to any increase in the price of corrugated cardboard sheet by
expanding output through existing and new capacity; the CC also rejected the suggestion that the acquisition of LINPAC would remove a maverick from the market[287]. The
CC found in *Napier Brown Foods plc/James Budgett Sugars Ltd* that coordinated effects
probably were occurring in the market for industrial sugar in Great Britain prior to the
merger, but that the merger would not make any coordinated effects more sustainable
or effective[288]. In *Wienerberger Finance Service BV/Baggeridge Brick plc* the OFT was
concerned about a merger in the market for the supply of clay bricks that would reduce
the number of major firms from four to three, but the CC decided that the conditions

---

[277] *Markets with bidding processes*, OFT 923, May 2007.   [278] *OFT guidance*, paras 4.11–4.16.
[279] *CC Guidelines*, paras 3.32–3.43.   [280] *OFT guidance*, para 4.12.
[281] Case T-342/99 [2002] ECR II-2585, [2002] 5 CMLR 317; see ch 21, pp 860–862.
[282] OJ [2004] C 31/5, available at www.ec.europa.eu/comm/competition/mergers/legislation.
[283] *CC Guidelines*, para 3.41.
[284] See Davis 'Coordinated effects merger simulation with linear demands', available at www.competition-
commission.org.uk/our_role/analysis/working_papers.htm.
[285] See www.oft.gov.uk/advice_and_resources/resource_base/Mergers_home/decisions/2006/Aggregate3.
[286] See www.oft.gov.uk/advice_and_resources/resource_base/Mergers_home/2007/lloyds.
[287] See the Final Report, paras 5.50–5.99, available at www.competition-commission.org.uk/inquiries/
completed/2004/linpac/index.htm.
[288] See the Final Report, paras 5.44–5.63, available at www.competition-commission.org.uk/inquiries/
completed/2005/napierbrown/index.htm.

for coordination were not met and that the merger would not make coordination more likely[289]. The OFT was worried about a three to two situation in relation to the wholesale supply of books to independent book retailers in *Woolworths Group plc/Bertram Group Ltd*. The CC decided to give the merger unconditional clearance[290].

(iv) Entry and expansion

Market power is unlikely to exist where there are low barriers to entry into and exit from the market[291]. The *OFT guidance* notes that the question of whether new entry, or the threat thereof, will be a sufficient constraint on the merging parties depends on the satisfaction of three conditions. The first is that new entry would have to be likely to occur in the event that the merging parties were to exercise market power after the merger[292]: such entry would have to be profitable at pre-merger prices; the second is that any new entry would have to be sufficient to constrain any attempt by the parties to exercise their increased market power[293]; the third condition is that any entry must be likely to occur reasonably quickly and to be sustainable[294]. The OFT will also consider the ability of existing competitors to expand their output as a potential counterweight to the power of the merging parties over the market[295]. The *CC Guidelines* deal in similar terms with barriers to entry and expansion[296].

(v) Countervailing buyer power[297]

The *OFT guidance*[298] and the *CC Guidelines*[299] both discuss the issue of countervailing power. The *OFT guidance* points out that a buyer may be able to constrain the power of a supplier by switching, or threatening to switch, to another supplier; by increasing the costs of a supplier, for example by delaying purchases; by treating one supplier's goods less favourably in retail premises than another's; and by threatening to enter the market themselves[300]. The fact that a buyer is big is not, in itself, enough to conclude that it has buyer power[301]. The *CC Guidelines* set out various factors that affect the ability of buyers to constrain suppliers, such as the ease with which the buyer can find and switch to alternative suppliers in the event of a price rise; the extent to which it can credibly threaten to establish its own supply arrangements; and the ability of the buyer to threaten to stop buying other products of the supplier[302]. Even if there is a buyer with sufficient power to constrain suppliers, it is necessary to consider whether smaller buyers might be harmed as a result of price discrimination[303]. The buying power of major retailers of carbonated soft drinks was a significant factor in the CC's clearance of the merger in *Cott Beverages Ltd/Macaw (Holdings) Ltd*[304]. However this argument did not avail the parties to a merger between the UK's two principal suppliers of eggs in *Stonegate Farmers Ltd/*

---

[289] See the Final Report, paras 7.9–7.114, available at www.competition-commission.org.uk/inquiries/ref2006/ wienerberger/index.htm.

[290] See the Final Report, available at www.competition-commission.org.uk/inquiries/ref2007/ woolworths/index.htm.

[291] See further ch 1, pp 40–43. [292] *OFT guidance*, paras 4.20–4.21. [293] Ibid, para 4.22.

[294] Ibid, para 4.23. [295] Ibid, para 4.26. [296] *CC Guidelines*, paras 3.49–3.57.

[297] See further ch 1, p 43. [298] *OFT guidance*, paras 4.27–4.28. [299] *CC Guidelines*, paras 3.58–3.59.

[300] *OFT guidance*, para 4.27. [301] Ibid, para 4.28. [302] *CC Guidelines*, paras 3.58–3.59.

[303] *OFT guidance*, para 4.28.

[304] See the Final Report, paras 5.34–5.46, available at www.competition-commission.org.uk/inquiries/ref2005/macaw/index.htm.

Deans Food Group Ltd[305]; rather, the CC was concerned that the merger would result in an SLC between the merging parties in the procurement of shell eggs[306].

(vi) Efficiencies

Efficiencies may be relevant to merger analysis in two distinct ways: first, as part of the assessment of whether a merger gives rise to an SLC; second, in determining whether a merger generates 'relevant customer benefits' for the purpose of section 30 of the Act sufficient to offset any SLC[307].

The *OFT guidance*[308] and the *CC Guidelines*[309] both discuss efficiencies and relevant customer benefits. For efficiencies to be considered as part of the competitive assessment the OFT says that they must increase rivalry among the remaining firms in the market[310]; the OFT requires the parties to prove, on the basis of compelling evidence, that the efficiencies are demonstrable, merger-specific and likely to benefit consumers[311].

Even where a merger would lead to an SLC it may be permitted where it brings about sufficient relevant customer benefits, as defined in section 30 of the Enterprise Act[312]. The OFT has said that alleged customer benefits must be clear and that cost savings must be quantifiable[313]. The *OFT guidance* goes on to require 'detailed and verifiable evidence' of anticipated benefits and that the parties must persuade the OFT that such benefits will accrue within a reasonable period and would not be possible but for the merger[314]. The OFT will consider the parties' incentive to pass on the alleged benefits of the merger to their customers and whether those benefits are of a sufficient magnitude to outweigh any harmful effects of the merger on competition[315]. The OFT also notes that the benefits need not occur in the same market as the one in which there will be an SLC; however 'clear and compelling evidence' would be required to show that customer benefits in one market outweigh the reduction of competition in another market[316]. The *CC Guidelines* deal, in particular, with the issue of selecting an appropriate remedy where a merger would lead to an SLC and yet also yield relevant customer benefits[317]. The CC rejected arguments that the completed merger under investigation in *Vue Entertainment Holdings (UK) Ltd/A3 Cinema Ltd* would lead to relevant customer benefits[318]; on the other hand it did identify possible benefits in *Stagecoach/Scottish Citylink*, but concluded that they did not offset the greater benefits that result from competition[319].

---

[305] See the Final Report, paras 6.64–6.73, available at www.competition-commission.org.uk/inquiries/ref2006/stonegate/index.htm.

[306] Ibid, paras 6.93–6.102.   [307] See further pp 906–907 above.   [308] *OFT guidance*, paras 4.29–4.35.

[309] *CC Guidelines*, paras 3.26–3.27 and 4.34–4.45.

[310] *OFT guidance*, para 4.32; see similarly *CC Guidelines*, paras 3.26–3.27. The CC concluded in *Ardagh International Holdings Ltd/Redfearn Glass Ltd* that it was unconvinced that the merger would have a sufficiently positive effect on rivalry in the market to offset the loss of a competitor: see the Final Report, paras 8.59–8.63, available at www.competition-commission.org.uk/inquiries/ref2005/ardagh/index.htm.

[311] *OFT guidance*, paras 4.34–4.35.   [312] See pp 906–907 above.   [313] *OFT guidance*, para 7.7.

[314] Ibid, para 7.7.   [315] Ibid, para 7.8.   [316] Ibid, para 7.9.   [317] *CC Guidelines*, para 4.45.

[318] See the Final Report, paras 7.62–7.69, available at www.competition-commission.org.uk/inquiries/ref2005/vue/index.htm.

[319] See the Final Report, paras 8.62–8.67, available at www.competition-commission.org.uk/inquiries/ref2006/citylink/index.htm.

(vii) The 'failing firm' defence

Both the *OFT guidance*[320] and the *CC Guidelines*[321] recognise the so-called 'failing firm defence': if a firm would fail, irrespective of the merger under consideration, that merger would not be the cause of any SLC. Identifying the correct counter-factual is important in failing firm cases, as it is necessary to work out what would happen if the merger does not go ahead. The failing firm defence depends on the satisfaction of three conditions: first, that the firm being acquired would exit the market in the near future were it not for the merger; second, that the firm is unable to reorganise its operations; and third, that there is no less anti-competitive alternative purchase to the merger[322]. Even where the 'defence' does not apply, it is conceivable that the acquisition of a failing firm might be permitted where it yields relevant customer benefits[323].

In *British Salt Ltd/New Cheshire Salt Works* the CC concluded that British Salt's acquisition of New Cheshire Salt Works would not result in an SLC since the latter would have closed in the foreseeable future due to large increases in actual and projected energy prices: an interesting point about this case is that the CC changed its position between its provisional and its final determination[324]. However the CC rejected a failing firm defence in *Stagecoach/Scottish Citylink*[325] and in *Thermo Electron Manufacturing Ltd/GV Instruments Ltd*[326].

(D) Vertical mergers

Chapter 5 of the *OFT guidance* deals with vertical mergers; the *CC Guidelines* also discuss them[327]. The OFT takes the view that vertical mergers generally have beneficial effects on competition, although they may have detrimental effects in certain circumstances. One concern is their potential to foreclose access to either an upstream or downstream market: to see whether this concern is a realistic possibility, the OFT will have regard to the alternatives available to the rivals of the vertically-integrated firm and the ability and incentives of that firm to prevent effective competition at either level of trade[328]. The OFT's other concern is that, in rare cases, a vertical merger might enhance the ability and incentive of the merged parties to coordinate their behaviour, either expressly or tacitly, with other firms in the market[329].

The CC identified possible vertical issues in the case of *Deutsche Börse AG/London Stock Exchange plc*[330] and concluded that the acquisition of LSE by either Deutsche Börse or Euronext may be expected to lead to an SLC in the market for the provision of on-book trading services within the UK because of the ability and incentive to foreclose entry or expansion to other providers of trading services. The CC considered whether there were

---

[320] *OFT guidance*, paras 4.36–4.39.   [321] *CC Guidelines*, paras 3.61–3.63.

[322] *OFT guidance*, para 4.37.   [323] Ibid, para 4.38.

[324] See the Final Report, paras 5.28 and 6.1, available at www.competition-commission.org.uk/inquiries/ref2005/britishsalt.htm.

[325] See the Final Report, paras 5.9–5.56, available at www.competition-commission.org.uk/inquiries/ref2006/citylink.htm.

[326] See the Final Report, paras 6.1–6.25, available at www.competition-commission.org.uk/inquiries/ref2006/thermo/index.htm.

[327] *CC Guidelines*, paras 3.64–3.68.   [328] *OFT guidance*, paras 5.3–5.4.   [329] Ibid, para 5.5.

[330] See the Final Report, paras 5.136–5.170, available at www.competition-commission.org.uk/inquiries/ref2005/lse/index.htm.

any vertical problems in the case of *Hamsard 2786 Ltd/Academy Music Holdings Ltd*, which would involve closer vertical integration between the promoters of live musical events and the owners of important venues in London such as the Hammersmith Apollo and the Astoria, but concluded that there were none[331]. Vertical problems were identified in *Railway Investments Ltd/Marcroft Holdings Ltd* which were remedied by a divestiture of some of Marcroft's freight wagon maintenance business[332].

(E) Conglomerate mergers

Chapter 6 of the *OFT guidance* deals with conglomerate mergers; the *CC Guidelines* also discuss them[333]. The OFT says that such mergers rarely lead to competition concerns, though a small number of cases may do so[334]. The OFT expresses three possible concerns. The first is that the compilation of a portfolio of brands may give rise to 'portfolio power', meaning that the market power derived from the merged range of brands is greater than the sum of its parts[335]. Second, the OFT will look to see whether such a merger could lead to the adoption of anti-competitive behaviour by the merged entity such as tying or predation[336]. The third concern that can arise in a conglomerate case is a possible risk that it might facilitate coordination[337].

Conglomeracy does not appear to have been a significant concern either for the OFT or the CC in cases under the Enterprise Act. The question of whether a merger might lead to behaviour that might be abusive under Article 82 EC and/or the Chapter II prohibition of the Competition Act 1998 is a matter that the CC has had to consider (albeit not in a conglomerate case) on one occasion: it is discussed in section 8 below[338].

6. ENFORCEMENT

Chapter 4 of Part 3 of the Enterprise Act deals with the issue of enforcement. It begins by describing the initial undertakings and orders that the OFT may accept or impose and undertakings in lieu of a reference to the CC; it then sets out certain interim restrictions on dealings during the course of a merger inquiry, and concludes with the powers of the CC. Undertakings and orders are legally binding and enforceable in the courts[339]; section 89 of the Act makes clear that undertakings may contain provisions that go beyond the order-making powers in Schedule 8.

Section 90 of the Act provides that Schedule 10 shall have effect when accepting 'enforcement' undertakings or making orders other than initial and interim orders. Schedule 10 establishes the procedural requirements that the OFT and CC must satisfy

---

[331] See the Final Report, paras 6.47–6.67, available at www.competition-commission.org.uk/inquiries/ref2006/hamsard2786/index.htm; the CC also rejected arguments about possible vertical concerns in the Final Report, paras 8.139–8.149, on *SvitzerWijsmuller A/S/Adsteam Marine Ltd*, available at www.competition-commission.org.uk/inquiries/ref2006/adsteam/index.htm.

[332] See the Final Report paras 7.74–7.133, available at www.competition-commission.org.uk/rep_pub/reports/2006/515marcroft.htm.

[333] *CC Guidelines*, paras 3.69–3.72.   [334] *OFT guidance*, para 6.1.   [335] Ibid, paras 6.2–6.3.

[336] Ibid, paras 6.4–6.5.   [337] Ibid, para 6.6.

[338] See pp 950–951 below on the case of *Railway Investments/Marcroft Engineering Ltd*.

[339] See p 936 below.

when they intend to accept, vary or release an undertaking or, as the case may be, make, vary or revoke an order; paragraphs 1 to 5 of the Schedule deal with the acceptance of undertakings and the making of orders; paragraphs 6 to 8 with their termination. The purpose of Schedule 10 is to require the OFT or the CC to set out clearly what they are proposing to do and the reasons for it: this is to meet the criticism that the 'remedy' phase of merger (and monopoly) inquiries under the Fair Trading Act lacked transparency and put firms in the position of having to discuss possible remedies when they were still unclear of the case against them[340].

The OFT is required to maintain a register of undertakings and orders made under the merger provisions in the Enterprise Act; it is accessible to the public on the OFT's website[341].

(A) Initial undertakings and orders

(i) Initial undertakings and orders to prevent pre-emptive action

Under section 71 of the Act the OFT may accept an initial undertaking from the parties to a completed merger for the purpose of preventing 'pre-emptive action', that is to say action which might prejudice a merger reference or impede the taking of any action which may be justified by the CC's decision on the reference[342]. Such an undertaking can be accepted only where the OFT has reasonable grounds for suspecting that a 'relevant merger situation' has been, or may be, created[343]. There are provisions for such undertakings to cease to be in force[344], and for their variation and release[345]. Provision also exists for the OFT to make an initial enforcement order where it has reasonable grounds for suspecting that a relevant merger situation has been created and that pre-emptive action is in progress or in contemplation[346]. An initial enforcement order may prohibit the doing of things that the OFT considers would constitute pre-emptive action; may impose obligations as to the carrying on of any activities or the safeguarding of assets; may appoint a trustee to conduct or supervise matters; and may require the provision of information[347].

The OFT has accepted undertakings to prevent pre-emptive action on a number of occasions[348]. The *Stericycle* case demonstrated the importance of the OFT (and the CC) preventing such action, and the OFT has been taking earlier and more expansive action since the judgment of the CAT in this case[349].

(ii) Undertakings in lieu of a reference to the CC

The ability of the OFT to accept undertakings in lieu of a reference to the CC has already been discussed[350].

---

[340] See further the CC's *General Advice and Information*, CC 4, March 2006, paras 7.23–7.31.
[341] Enterprise Act 2002, s 91; the OFT's website is www.oft.gov.uk.   [342] Ibid, s 71(8).
[343] Ibid, s 71(3).   [344] Ibid, s 71(5) and (6).   [345] Ibid, s 71(4) and (7).   [346] Ibid, s 72.
[347] Ibid, s 72(2) and para 9 of Sch 18.
[348] See eg *Completed acquisition by Cott Beverages of Macaw (Holding) Ltd*, www.oft.gov.uk/advice_and_resources/resource_base/Mergers_home/register/Initial-undertakings/cott and *Completed merger between Stonegate Farmers Ltf and Deans Food Group Ltd*, www.oft.gov.uk/advice_and_resources/resource_base/Mergers_home/register/Initial-undertakings/stonegate.
[349] See pp 930–932 below.   [350] See pp 916–917 above.

(B) Interim restrictions and powers[351]

(i) Statutory restrictions on dealings

Sections 77 and 78 of the Enterprise Act impose automatic restrictions on certain deal-ings in relation to completed and anticipated mergers when a reference has been made to the CC; these are imposed in order to prevent any further integration of the busi-nesses concerned. Section 77 provides that, when a reference has been made of a com-pleted merger and no undertaking has been given in relation to it, no-one may, without the consent of the CC, complete any outstanding matters in relation to that merger or transfer the ownership or control of any enterprises to which the reference relates[352]; any consent of the CC may be general or special, and may be revoked[353]. Section 78 provides that, when a reference is made of an anticipated merger, no-one may, without the consent of the CC, directly or indirectly acquire an interest in shares in a company if any enterprise to which the reference relates is carried on by or under the control of that company[354]; again any consent of the CC may be general or special, and may be revoked[355]. These provisions are quite technical and section 79 deals with numerous points of interpretation, in particular to make clear what is meant by a share acquisi-tion for the purposes of section 78. The CC gave consent to Heinz for the disposal of its ethnic foods business during the course of its investigation in *Heinz/HP Foods Group* which otherwise would not have been possible due to the statutory restriction on share dealings and due to the subsequent interim undertakings that had been given to the CC under the provisions described in the following paragraph[356].

(ii) Interim undertakings and orders to prevent pre-emptive action

Just as the OFT can accept initial undertakings and make final orders to prevent pre-emptive action, section 80 (dealing with undertakings) and section 81 (dealing with orders) of the Act give the CC the same powers[357]; pre-emptive action means action which might prejudice the reference or impede the taking of any action that the CC might consider to be justified as a result of its decision on the reference[358]. Section 80(3) enables the CC to adopt an undertaking that has already been given to the OFT within seven days of the reference to it; section 80(4) provides that the OFT undertaking may be continued in force, varied, released or superceded by a new undertaking. Section 81(3) provides that the CC may adopt an order of the OFT. It is common practice for the CC to adopt OFT undertakings on the basis of section 80(3), although it may then go on to accept undertakings directly from the parties concerned: an example of this can be found in the case of *Greif Inc/Blagden Packaging Group*[359]. Undertakings and orders may be varied[360]. In *Bucher Industries AG/Johnstone Sweepers Ltd* the CC was concerned that

---

[351] See *Mergers: Procedural guidance*, paras 7.10–7.12.   [352] Enterprise Act 2002, s 77(2).
[353] Ibid, s 77(5).   [354] Ibid, s 78(3).   [355] Ibid, s 78(3).
[356] See the Final Report, paras 3.17–3.21, available at www.competition-commission.org.uk/inquiries/ref2005/heinz/index.htm.
[357] See the CC's *General Advice and Information*, paras 7.1–7.8 and 7.11–7.13.
[358] Enterprise Act 2002, s 80(10).
[359] See www.competition-commission.org.uk/inquiries/ref2007/blagden/index.htm.
[360] See eg the consent given to Deans to process liquid egg on behalf of Stonegate in *Stonegate Farmers Ltd/Deans Food Group Ltd*, available at www.competition-commission.org.uk/inquiries/ref2006/stonegate.index.htm.

Bucher appeared not to be complying with its interim undertaking to prevent the integration of the Bucher and Johnstone businesses pending the completion of the investigation and required both an apology from Bucher and the appointment of a monitoring trustee to ensure compliance with the undertaking[361]. A monitor was also appointed in relation to a completed joint venture in the case of *Stagecoach/Scottish Citylink*[362].

There is no duty to pre-notify mergers to the OFT under UK law, and quite a large percentage of the cases referred by the OFT to the CC are of completed mergers[363]. This gives rise to a concern that the CC might investigate a case in which it considers that there is an SLC, only to find that the merging businesses have become so intermingled that it is very difficult in practice to reverse the process and to restore conditions of effective competition[364]. Obviously it is important for the OFT, which will have reviewed the merger prior to the CC, also to consider what measures should be put in place during its (the OFT's) period of investigation so that the CC's position will not be prejudiced. In 2006 the CC issued *Guidance on the use of interim measures pending final determination of merger references*[365] in which it indicated that it would normally expect to receive interim undertakings from the acquirer in the case of a completed merger to clarify how it would treat the acquired business pending the final determination of the reference; the CC would also expect an assurance that there would be a restriction of the flow of commercially valuable information between the parties pending the outcome. The CC explained that it might find it necessary to appoint a 'hold separate' manager to operate the business separately from that of the acquirer, and that a monitoring trustee might have to be appointed as well[366].

In the case of *Stericycle International Llc/Sterile Technologies Group Ltd* Stericycle had purchased STG's clinical waste management business at auction; no notification had been made to the OFT. The OFT investigated the case and referred it to the CC. The CC was concerned that the process of integrating the STG business into Stericycle's was continuing and tried to secure undertakings to prevent pre-emptive action. When these were not forthcoming the CC made an order under section 81 of the Enterprise Act to prevent any further integration of the two businesses, and issued directions for the appointment of a monitoring trustee; subsequently further directions were issued for the appointment of a hold separate manager[367]. Stericycle challenged the CC before the CAT, arguing either that the CC had no power to make the order or that the order was unreasonable[368]. The CAT upheld the action of the CC, holding that it was 'well within

---

[361] See the Final Report, para 9.3, available at www.competition-commission.org.uk/inquiries/ref2005/bucher/index.htm.

[362] See the Final Report, para 8.56, available at www.competition-commission.org.uk/inquiries/ref2006/citylink/index.htm.

[363] For statistics on this point see pp 949–950 below; see French and Scola 'How Risky is Buying in the UK without Merger Clearance?' (2007) 1 European Business Law Journal 196.

[364] The CC has raised the question of whether pre-notification of mergers should become compulsory: see its *Annual Report and Accounts 2006/2007*, p 6, available at www.competition-commission.org.uk/rep_pub/annual_rev_archive/index.htm.

[365] See www.competition-commission.org.uk/rep_pub/consultations/past/pdf/guidance_on_interim_measures_pending_final_determination.pdf.

[366] Ibid, paras 15 and 16.

[367] The order and directions will be found at www.competition-commission.org.uk/inquiries/ref2006/stericycle/index.htm.

[368] Case 1070/4/8/06 *Stericycle International Llc v Competition Commission* [2006] CAT 21, [2007] CompAR 281; for comment see Freeman 'Stericycle: A Lifeline for the UK's Voluntary Merger Control Regime' (2007) 6 Competition Law Journal 298.

the CC's margin of appreciation to propose the appointment of a [hold separate manager] in this case'[369], and that Stericycle was well aware of the risk it was taking by completing the transaction without prior clearance from the competition authorities[370]. The CC's view was that the fact that substantial integration of the two businesses had already taken place made it more, not less, important to appoint a hold separate manager[371]. The final outcome of this case was that Stericycle was required to sell off part of the business that it had acquired to a suitable purchaser to be approved by the CC[372].

(C) 'Final powers' or 'remedies'[373]

Sections 82 to 84 of the Enterprise Act deal with 'final powers', that is to say the remedial action that the CC may take after it has completed its inquiry and reached its conclusion. Section 82 provides for the acceptance of final undertakings and section 83 for the making of an order where an undertaking is not being fulfilled or where false or misleading information was given to the OFT or CC prior to the acceptance of an undertaking. Section 84 gives the power to the CC to make a final order. As a general rule the CC prefers to proceed by accepting undertakings rather than by making final orders; the CC had not made a final order in a merger (as opposed to a market investigation) reference as at 12 March 2008; however it has pointed out that, in the event of undue delay in obtaining suitable undertakings after the completion of an investigation, it could proceed to the making of an order[374]. Undertakings may contain provisions that go beyond the order-making powers in the Act[375]. Provision is made for the variation of remedies[376].

(i) The CCs approach to remedies

The CCs approach to remedies is described in its *Guidelines*: it intends to publish more specific guidance in due course. In considering the appropriateness of a remedy it is unlikely that the CC would take no action where it finds an SLC; however this might happen, for example, where it finds relevant customer benefits[377]. The CC will bear in mind the cost and proportionality of remedies[378] and the likelihood of their effectiveness: for example structural remedies are more likely to be acceptable than behavioural ones[379], as are remedies that can be expected to show results in a relatively short time-period[380].

[369] Case 1070/4/8/06, para 140.   [370] Ibid, para 137.   [371] Ibid, para 158.

[372] For the final undertakings in this case see www.competition-commission.org.uk/inquiries/ref2006/stericycle/pdf/undertakings_given_to_the_cc.pdf.

[373] See the CC's *General Advice and Information*, paras 7.1–7.8 and 7.14–7.16 and *Merger References: Competition Commission Guidelines*, Part 4.

[374] See *General Advice and Information*, para 7.6 and the Final Report in *Firstgroup plc/Scotrail*, para 14, available at www.competition-commission.org.uk/inquiries/completed/2004/first.

[375] Enterprise Act 2002, s 89.

[376] Ibid, s 82(2)(b) (variation of undertakings) and s 83(5)(c) (variation of orders); for an example of the variation of a remedy see *Firstgroup plc/Scotrail*, www.competition-commission.org.uk/inquiries/completed/2004/first/notice_annex_1.htm.

[377] *Merger References: Competition Commission Guidelines*, paras 4.6–4.7; relevant customer benefits are discussed at paras 4.34–4.45 of the *Guidelines*.

[378] Ibid, paras 4.9–4.12.

[379] On the CC's preference for structural remedies see its discussion in the Final Report in *Railway Investments Ltd/Marcroft Holdings Ltd*, paras 8.11–8.16, available at www.competition-commission.org.uk/inquiries/ref2006/marcroft/index.htm.

[380] *Merger References: Competition Commission Guidelines*, paras 4.13–4.16.

In both *Hamsard 2786 Ltd/Academy Music Holdings Ltd*[381] and *SvitzerWijsmuller A/S/ Adsteam Marine Ltd*[382] the CC was offered behavioural remedies, including price controls, but rejected them in favour of partial divestitures. However behavioural remedies are possible: the CC accepted a retail price cap and other behavioural remedies in *Dräger Medical A&G Co KGaA/Hillebrand Industries Inc*[383] and undertakings on both fares and the level of service, frequency and configuration of bus routes in Scotland, particular in the Glasgow and Edinburgh areas, in *Firstgroup plc/Scotrail*[384]. The CC is unlikely to favour remedy packages that are complex and that would be difficult to monitor: a partial divestiture, or even an outright prohibition, might be preferable, as in the case of *Serviced Dispense Equipment Ltd(SDEL)/Coors Brewers Ltd*[385].

The CC will consider remedies of three types[386]. First, remedies that preserve or restore the *status quo ante* market structure, for example the prohibition of an anticipated merger or the divestment of a completed acquisition[387]. The second type of remedy is one that is intended to increase the competition that will be faced by the merged firm, for example by requiring access to essential inputs/facilities; by licensing know-how or intellectual property rights; by dismantling exclusive distribution arrangements; or by removing non-compete clauses from customer contracts[388]. The third type of remedy would deal with the possibility of the merged firm taking advantage of any increase in market power as a result of the merger, either by acting anti-competitively or by exploiting customers and consumers: a price cap, a commitment to act in a non-discriminatory manner and an increase in price transparency might be suitable for these purposes[389].

The CC will also consider whether it should recommend action by persons other than the merging parties[390]. For example it might suggest to the Government that it should amend legislation or regulations that inhibit entry into a particular market; the Government has given a commitment to give a public response to any such recommendation[391]. In the case of *Dräger Medical A&G Co KGaA/Hillenbrand Industries Inc* the CC made recommendations to the Department of Health and the regional authorities in Scotland, Wales and Northern Ireland that they, and their procurement agencies, should exercise their buyer power when purchasing neo-natal warming therapy products and take steps to facilitate entry into the market by new entrants[392].

The CC has established a Remedies Standing Group whose functions include the adoption of interim undertakings from the OFT in relation to merger investigations; enforcing undertakings and orders; varying or releasing undertakings; and overseeing the implementation of undertakings and orders in relation to divestiture. The Group

[381] See the Final Report, paras 6.47–6.67, available at www.competition-commission.org.uk/ref2006/hamsard2786/index.htm.

[382] See the Final Report, paras 9.13–9.17, available at www.competition-commission.org.uk/inquiries/ref2006/adsteam/index.htm.

[383] See Final Report, paras 10.26–10.40, available at www.competition-commission.org.uk/inquiries/completed/2004/dragair/index.htm.

[384] See the Final Report, paras 6.8–6.36, available at www.competition-commission.org.uk/inquiries/completed/2004/first/index.htm.

[385] See the Final Report, paras 6.42–6.48, available at www.competition-commission.org.uk/inquiries/completed/2005/sdel/index.htm.

[386] *Merger References: Competition Commission Guidelines*, para 4.17.

[387] Ibid, paras 4.24–4.28.   [388] Ibid, paras 4.29–4.30.   [389] Ibid, paras 4.31–4.33.   [390] Ibid, para 4.19.

[391] Ibid, para 4.20.

[392] See the Final Report, paras 10.16–10.25, available at www.competition-commission.org.uk/inquiries/completed/2004/drager/index.htm.

is led by the Chief Business Adviser and Head of Remedies at the CC. Details of the work of the Group and of its membership are available on the website of the CC[393]. The CC has published extensive guidance on *Application of Divestiture Remedies in Merger Inquiries* which explains, in particular, the importance of establishing the correct scope of divestiture packages, the need to find a suitable purchaser, how to manage the divestiture process effectively and the employment of trustees[394]. The CC also has a rolling programme of reviewing past remedies in merger cases in order to capture important learning points and to feed them into current remedies policy and practice[395].

(ii) Schedule 8 of the Enterprise Act

The orders that can be made are set out in Schedule 8 of the Act, and are extensive. They include 'general restrictions on conduct' (paragraphs 2 to 9); 'general obligations to be performed' (paragraphs 10–11); 'acquisitions and divisions' (paragraphs 12 to 14); and 'supply and publication of information' (paragraphs 15 to 19); supplementary provisions as to the making of orders are to be found in paragraphs 21 and 22 of Schedule 8. These provisions are described more fully below. An order may not interfere with conditions in patent licences or licences of registered designs[396]. It is specifically provided that an order may prohibit the performance of an agreement already in existence[397]. An order may provide for the revocation or modification of conditions in the licences of regulated undertakings under legislation such as the Telecommunications Act 1984, the Airports Act 1986 and the Gas Act 1986[398]. Section 87 of the Act allows the person making an order to give directions to an individual or to an office holder in a company or association to take action or to refrain from action for the purpose of carrying out or ensuring compliance with the order; failure to comply with such directions may lead to court action[399]. Section 88 sets out the minimum contents of any final order or order to replace an undertaking in lieu of a reference.

(iii) General restrictions on conduct

Paragraphs 2 to 9 of Schedule 8 provide for orders to impose restrictions on conduct. An order may prohibit the making or performance of an agreement or require the termination of one (paragraph 2)[400]; and may forbid refusals to supply (paragraph 3), tie-ins (paragraph 4), discrimination (paragraph 5), preferential treatment (paragraph 6) and deviation from published price lists (paragraph 7). Price regulation is also a possibility (paragraph 8). An order may prohibit the exercise of voting rights attached to shares, stocks or securities (paragraph 9).

(iv) General obligations to be performed

Paragraph 10 of Schedule 8 provides that an order may require a person to supply goods or services, and it can be specified that they should be of a particular standard or that

---

[393] www.competition-commission.org.uk.

[394] CC8, December 2004, available at www.competition-commission.org.uk.

[395] See *Understanding past merger remedies: report on case study research*, January 2007, www.competition-commission.org.uk/our_role/analysis/understanding_past_merger_remedies.

[396] Enterprise Act 2002, s 86(2).   [397] Ibid, s 86(3).   [398] Ibid, s 86(5) and Sch 9, Part 1.

[399] Ibid, s 87(4)–(8).

[400] Such an order may not deal with terms and conditions in contracts of employment or the physical conditions in which workers work: Enterprise Act 2002, Sch 8, para 2(2).

they should be applied in a particular manner: for example a bus company could be required to maintain a certain frequency of service[401]. Paragraph 11 of the Schedule enables an order to require that certain activities should be carried on separately from other activities.

(v) Acquisitions and divisions

Paragraph 12 of Schedule 8 provides that an order may prohibit or restrict the acquisition of the whole or part of an undertaking or the assets of another person's business. Paragraph 13 provides for the division of any business, whether by sale of any part of an undertaking or assets or otherwise; paragraph 13(3) deals with associated issues such as the transfer or creation of property, rights, liabilities and obligations, the adjustment of contracts, share ownership and other matters. Provision is made for the buyer of a business to be approved by the OFT[402], and for the appointment of a trustee to oversee the divestment of a business[403].

In its report on *Somerfield plc/Wm Morrison* the CC required Somerfield to divest itself of four grocery stores that it had acquired from Morrison[404]. Somerfield appealed to the CAT arguing that the CC's remedy was unreasonable, and that it (Somerfield) should be given the option of selling either the stores that it had acquired or the stores that it already owned: since it was the common ownership of the stores that was responsible for the SLC, the situation could be remedied by divesting either the new or the original stores. The CAT upheld the finding of the CC in *Somerfield plc v Competition Commission*[405]. In the CAT's view it was reasonable for the CC to take as its starting point that the '*status quo ante*' would normally involve reversing the acquisition, which would represent a simple, direct and easily understandable approach; the onus was therefore on Somerfield to show why divestment of its original stores would be an equally effective remedy[406]. The CAT considered that Somerfield had failed to show that this was the case, in particular because the CC had been correct to think that Somerfield's existing stores were less attractive to a potential purchaser than the ones that it had acquired from Morrison, meaning that it was less likely that selling the existing stores would be an effective remedy. The CAT also considered that the CC had been correct to exclude owners of discount stores from the set of suitable purchasers, at least during the initial phase of the divestment period[407].

(vi) Supply and publication of information

Paragraph 15 of Schedule 8 provides that an order may require a person to publish price lists. Paragraph 16 allows a prohibition on the practice of recommending prices to dealers. Paragraph 17 enables an order to require a person to publish accounting information. Paragraph 18 provides that orders can specify the manner in which information

---

[401] See *Explanatory Notes* to the Enterprise Bill, para 225.   [402] Enterprise Act 2002, Sch 8, para 13(3)(k).

[403] Ibid, Sch 8, para 13(1).

[404] See the Final Report, paras 11.9–11.23, available at www.competition-commission.org.uk/inquiries/ref2005/somerfield/index.htm.

[405] Case 1051/4/8/05 [2006] CAT 4, [2006] CompAR 390; for comment see Beale 'The *Somerfield* Decisions of the Competition Commission and Competition Appeal Tribunal and the Economics of Divestment Remedies' (2006) 5 Competition Law Journal 45; Jephcott and Mahtani 'The *Somerfield* Judgment: A Damp Squib?' (2006) 5 Competition Law Journal 56.

[406] Case 1051/4/8/05 [2006] CAT 4, [2006] CompAR 390, para 99–105.   [407] Ibid, paras 166–184.

is to be published. There is a general power in paragraph 19 to require a person to provide the competition authorities with information, and for that information to be published.

(vii) National security and media mergers

Paragraphs 20 and 20A make provision for orders to be made in relation to 'public interest cases' under Chapter 2 of Part 3 of the Act[408].

(D) Enforcement functions of the OFT

The lead role in monitoring OFT and CC undertakings and orders is given to the OFT. Section 92(1) of the Act requires it to keep enforcement undertakings and enforcement orders under review and to ensure compliance with sections 77 and 78, which restrict certain dealings; in particular the OFT must consider whether undertakings or orders are being complied with and whether, by reason of a change of circumstances, there is a case for release, variation or supercession[409]. The CC may ask the OFT to assist in the negotiation of undertakings[410]. The OFT also has a responsibility to keep under review undertakings and orders arising from merger cases conducted under the now-repealed Fair Trading Act 1973[411].

Section 94 of the Enterprise Act provides that orders and undertakings can be enforced through the courts. There is a duty to comply with orders and undertakings, and that duty is owed to anyone who may be affected by a contravention of it[412]; any breach of the duty is actionable if such a person sustains loss or damage[413], though a defence exists if the person in question took all reasonable steps and exercised all due diligence to avoid a contravention of the order or undertaking[414]. The OFT maintains a register of undertakings and orders on its website; it is also open to physical inspection between 10.00 and 16.00 on working days. Compliance with an order or undertaking is also enforceable by civil proceedings brought by the OFT[415] or the CC[416] for an injunction (or interdict in Scotland). Similar provisions apply in relation to breaches of the statutory restrictions on certain dealings provided for in sections 77 and 78[417].

7. SUPPLEMENTARY PROVISIONS

Chapter 5 of Part 3 of the Enterprise Act contains a number of supplementary provisions. Some of these, such as the statutory voluntary pre-notification of mergers and the payment of fees, have already been considered[418]. Two issues of particular importance

---

[408] See pp 951–955 below on public interest cases.   [409] Enterprise Act 2002, s 92(2).   [410] Ibid, s 93.

[411] See the Enterprise Act 2002, Sch 24 and the Enterprise Act 2002 (Enforcement Undertakings) Order 2006, SI 2006/354 and the Enterprise Act 2002 (Enforcement Undertakings and Orders) Order 2006, SI 2006/355.

[412] Enterprise Act 2002, s 94(2) and (3).

[413] Ibid, s 94(4); as to whether a person injured by breach of an undertaking or order could bring an action for damages, see *MidKent Holdings v General Utilities plc* [1996] 3 All ER 132, [1997] 1 WLR 14, brought under s 93 of the (now-repealed) Fair Trading Act 1973.

[414] Enterprise Act 2002, s 94(5).   [415] Ibid, s 94(6).   [416] Ibid, s 94(7).   [417] Ibid, s 95.

[418] See pp 913–914 above.

remain to be considered: the information powers of the CC and its ability to impose penalties, and the review of decisions on mergers by the CAT.

(A) Investigation powers and penalties

Sections 109 to 117 of the Enterprise Act deal with the CC's powers of investigation and with penalties. Section 109 gives the CC powers to require, by notice, the attendance of witnesses[419], the production of documents[420] and the supply of various information[421]. A notice given under this section must explain the consequences of non-compliance[422]. The CC can impose a penalty on a person who, without reasonable excuse, fails to comply with a notice given under section 109[423] or who obstructs or delays a person who is trying to copy documents required to be produced[424]. The maximum amounts that the CC may impose as a penalty under section 110(1) and (3) are specified in the Competition Commission (Penalties) Order 2003[425]. It is a criminal offence for a person intentionally to alter, suppress or destroy any document that he has been required to produce under section 109[426]: a person guilty of this offence could be fined or imprisoned for a maximum of two years[427].

Sections 111 to 116 set out the main procedural requirements which the CC must observe when imposing a monetary penalty; the factors which it will have regard to when determining the amount of a penalty are set out in the CC's *Statement of Policy on Penalties*[428]. There is a full right of appeal to the CAT against decisions of the CC to impose monetary penalties: the CAT may quash the penalty or substitute a different amount or different dates for payment[429]. The CC has used or threatened to use its section 109 powers on a few occasions. On page four of its *Annual Report and Accounts 2005/2006*[430] it stated that it had been reviewing whether it should make more systematic use of these powers due to delays in the provision of information and the tendency of some parties not to exercise proper care to ensure the provision of full and accurate information, adding that it had issued formal notices, carrying penalties for non-compliance, to third parties in several recent cases.

(B) Review of decisions under Part 3 of the Enterprise Act

Section 120 of the Enterprise Act makes provision for review of decisions under Part 3 of the Act. Section 120(1) provides that any person aggrieved by a decision of the OFT, the Secretary of State or the CC may apply to the CAT for a review of that decision: the aggrieved person could be a third party with sufficient interest. The application must be made within four weeks of the date on which the applicant was notified of the disputed decision or of its date of publication, whichever is earlier[431]; the date of publication is the date when the parties receive the reasons for the OFT's decision, rather than an earlier Press Release stating the content of the decision but without its reasoning[432]. The CAT's

---

[419] Enterprise Act 2002, s 109(1).   [420] Ibid, s 109(2).   [421] Ibid, s 109(3).   [422] Ibid, s 109(4).
[423] Ibid, s 110(1).   [424] Ibid, s 110(3).   [425] SI 2003/1371.   [426] Enterprise Act 2002, s 110(5).
[427] Ibid, s 110(7).   [428] CC 5, June 2003, paras 17–21.   [429] Enterprise Act 2002, s 114.
[430] Available at www.competition-commission.org.uk.
[431] Competition Appeal Tribunal Rules 2003, SI 2003/1372, as amended by SI 2004/2068, Rule 26.
[432] See Case 1030/4/1/04 *Federation of Wholesale Distributors v OFT* [2004] CAT 11, [2004] CompAR 764, paras 22–26.

view is that, as a general proposition, a hearing on the merits in merger cases should be held within three months of the report of the CC[433]; the CAT has succeeded in dealing with reviews of merger decisions within a short time period, considerably shorter than the CFI when reviewing decisions under the ECMR.

When dealing with appeals under section 120(1) the CAT will apply the same principles as would be applied by a court on an application for judicial review[434]; the fact that it is a specialist competition tribunal does not mean that it should apply different principles[435]. The CAT may dismiss the application or quash the whole or part of the decision to which it relates[436]; and, in the latter situation, it may refer the matter back to the original decision-maker for further consideration[437]. An appeal may be brought before the Court of Appeal, with permission, against the CAT's decision on a point of law[438]. Part 3 of the Competition Appeal Tribunal Rules[439] makes provision for appeals under section 120 of the Act.

There have been several applications for review to the CAT in relation to merger cases[440]. The challenges by third parties to the OFT's decisions not to refer the *iSOFT/ Torex*, *Phoenix Healthcare/East Anglian Pharmaceuticals* and *Boots/Alliance UniChem* mergers have already been discussed in the context of the OFT's duty to refer mergers to the CC that may be expected to result in an SLC[441]. The OFT's decision in the case of *Cooperative Group/Fairways Group* has been dealt with in the discussion of undertakings in lieu of a reference[442] and the CC's suggested remedy in the case of *Somerfield plc/ William Morrison* was discussed in the section on divestiture remedies[443]. Two further cases, *Federation of Wholesale Distributors v OFT*[444] and *Stericycle International Llc v OFT*[445], did not proceed to final judgment.

When the OFT asked for costs against the unsuccessful applicant in *Celesio v OFT* the OFT suggested that where a horizontal competitor (as opposed, for example, to a customer) brings a challenge to the non-referral of a merger, that applicant should bear the risk of failure in costs; however the CAT declined to accept this suggestion, saying only that each case depends on its own circumstances[446]. In the *Celesio* case itself the CAT did not award costs against the unsuccessful applicant since it had not been able to understand the OFT's decision without the witness statement by the OFT's director of mergers produced for the purposes of the appeal[447].

---

[433] See Case 1075/4/8/07 *Stericycle International llc v Competition Commission: Ruling on application for a stay* [2007] CAT 9, para 7.

[434] Enterprise Act 2002, s 120(4).

[435] See para 52 the Vice-Chancellor's judgment and paras 88–106 of Carnwath LJ's judgment in *OFT v IBA Health Ltd* [2004] EWCA Civ 142, [2004] UKCRL 683; see also paras 55–57 of the CAT's judgment in Case 1051/4/8/05 *Somerfield plc v Competition Commission* [2006] CAT 4, [2006] CompAR 390.

[436] Enterprise Act 2002, s 120(5)(a).   [437] Ibid, s 120(5)(b).   [438] Ibid, s 120(6) and (7).   [439] SI 2003/1372.

[440] For comment see Burrows 'Review of Merger Decisions by the CAT: A Question of Evidence' (2006) 5 Competition Law Journal 169.

[441] See pp 903–905 above.   [442] See pp 916–917 above.   [443] See p 935 above.   [444] Case 1030/4/1/04.

[445] Case 1075/4/8/07.

[446] Case 1059/4/1/06 *Celesio AG v OFT – Judgment: Costs* [2006] CAT 20, [2007] CompAR 269, para 47; in the US the Supreme Court ruled in *Cargill, Inc v Monfort of Colorado, Inc.*, 479 US 104 (1986), that an antitrust plaintiff seeking injunctive relief in a merger case must 'allege and ultimately prove that it would suffer threatened loss or damage constituting an antitrust injury', which is 'injury of the type the antitrust laws were intended to prevent and that flows from that which makes defendants' acts unlawful'.

[447] Case 1059/4/1/06 *Celesio AG v OFT – Judgment: Costs* [2006] CAT 20, [2007] CompAR 269, para 50.

8. THE MERGER PROVISIONS IN PRACTICE

The merger provisions of the Enterprise Act entered into force on 20 June 2003. The Table of CC Merger Investigations contains details of all mergers referred to and decided upon by the CC up until 12 March 2008. A number of interesting points that emerge from the Table will be discussed in the text that follows.

22.1 Table Of CC Merger Investigations

Title	Date of reference	Date of publication	Finding of substantial lessening of competition?	Remedy
Sibelco Minerals & Chemicals Ltd/ Tarmac Central Ltd **NB: abandoned by the parties**	14 August 2003			
Stena AB and The Peninsular and Oriental Steam Navigation Company	22 August 2003	5 February 2004	Yes, in relation to ferry operations for freight in the 'central corridor' between Great Britain and Ireland	Prohibition of the transfer of P&O's Liverpool–Dublin route to Stena: undertakings published 15 May 2004
Unum Ltd/ Employee Benefits Business of Swiss Life (UK) plc **NB: abandoned by the parties**	31 October 2003			
AAH Pharmaceuticals Ltd/East Anglian Pharmaceuticals Ltd **NB: abandoned by the parties**	3 December 2003			

Title	Date of reference	Date of publication	Finding of substantial lessening of competition?	Remedy
Dräger Medical A&G Co KgaA/ Hillebrand Industries Inc	18 December 2003	19 May 2004	Yes, in the markets for closed care incubators, opencare warming beds and transport incubators	Preservation of products and accessories; provision of spare parts, training and servicing; retail price caps: undertakings published 21 June 2004
Carl Zeiss Jena GmbH/Bio-Rad Laboratories Inc	30 December 2003	17 May 2004	No	
FirstGroup plc/ Scotrail Railways Ltd	13 January 2004	28 June 2004	Yes, in relation to certain transport markets in Scotland	Behavioural remedies in relation to fares, frequency of services and provision of information about competitors' services; undertakings agreed 15 October 2004
Convatec Ltd/ Acordis Speciality Fibres Ltd **NB: abandoned by the parties**	12 February 2004			
National Milk Records plc/The Cattle Information Service Ltd **NB: abandoned by the parties**	3 March 2004			

Title	Date of reference	Date of publication	Finding of substantial lessening of competition?	Remedy
Archant Ltd/ Independent News and Media plc **NB: completed merger**	29 April 2004	22 September 2004	No	
DS Smith plc/LINPAC Containers Ltd **NB: completed merger**	20 May 2004	21 October 2004	No	
National Express Group plc/Greater Anglia Franchise **NB: completed merger**	27 May 2004	4 November 2004	No	
Knauf Insulation Ltd/Superglass Insulation Ltd	17 June 2004	29 November 2004	Yes	Prohibition (note: market moving from four to three)
Emap plc/ABI Building Data Ltd **NB: completed merger**	1 July 2004	26 January 2005	Yes	Divestiture required
Taminco NV/ Air Products (Chemicals) Teeside Ltd	16 July 2004	29 November 2004	No (by a majority of three to two)	
Arriva plc/ Sovereign Bus and Coach Company Ltd	3 August 2004	7 January 2005	No	
Arcelor SA/Corus UK Ltd **NB: completed merger**	10 September 2004	10 February 2005	No	
Serviced Dispense Equipment Ltd (SDEL)/Coors Brewers Ltd (Coors)	29 September 2004	11 March 2005	Yes	Prohibition

Title	Date of reference	Date of publication	Finding of substantial lessening of competition?	Remedy
Napier Brown/ James Budgett Sugars Ltd NB: completed merger	12 October 2004	15 March 2005	No	
Bretagne- Angleterre-Irlande/ P&O Ferries NB: abandoned by the parties	8 December 2004			
FirstGroup plc/ InterCity East Coast Franchise NB: abandoned by the parties	21 December 2004			
LINK Interchange Network Ltd/ Transaction Network Services (UK) Ltd NB: abandoned by the parties	27 January 2005			
Francisco Partners LP/G. International NB: completed merger	22 March 2005	2 September 2005	No	
Somerfield plc/ Wm Morrison Supermarkets plc NB: completed merger	23 March 2005		Yes	Divestiture of some stores required NB: appeal to the CAT, Case 1051/4/8/05, *Somerfield plc v Competition Commission*; judgment of 13 February 2006 rejecting the appeal, [2006] CAT 4

Title	Date of reference	Date of publication	Finding of substantial lessening of competition?	Remedy
Deutsche Börse AG/London Stock Exchange plc	29 March 2005	1 November 2005	Yes	Combination of structural and behavioural remedies required. On 15 March 2006 the CC accepted undertakings
Euronext NV/ London Stock Exchange plc	29 March 2005	1 November 2005	Yes	Combination of structural and behavioural remedies required. On 15 March 2006 CC accepted undertakings
Bucher Industries AG/Johnston Sweepers Ltd **NB: completed merger**	6 April 2005	15 September 2005	No	
Future plc/ Highbury House plc **NB: abandoned by the parties**	14 April 2005			
British Salt Ltd/ New Cheshire Salt Works Ltd **NB: completed merger**	26 May 2005	8 November 2005	No (provisional finding had been that there would be an SLC)	
Ardagh International Holdings Ltd/ Redfearn Glass Ltd **NB: completed merger**	1 August 2005	20 December 2005	No	

Title	Date of reference	Date of publication	Finding of substantial lessening of competition?	Remedy
National Express Group plc/ Thameslink/Great Northern Rail Franchise NB: completed merger	3 August 2005	22 December 2005	No	
Vue Entertainment Holdings (UK) Ltd/A3 Cinema Ltd (including its subsidiary, Ster Century (UK) Ltd) NB: completed merger	23 September 2005	20 December 2005	Yes	Divestiture required of cinema in Basingstoke
Greater Western Passenger Rail Franchise NB: three applications for the franchise referred; two of the three references cancelled when franchise awarded to First Group	30 September 2005	8 March 2006	No	
South West Airport Ltd/Exeter and Devon Airport Ltd NB: abandoned by the parties	11 October 2005			
Robert Wiseman Dairies Ltd/ Scottish Milk Dairies Ltd NB: abandoned by the parties	19 October 2005			
Heinz/HP Foods Group NB: completed merger	26 October 2005	24 March 2006	No	

Title	Date of reference	Date of publication	Finding of substantial lessening of competition?	Remedy
Macaw (Holdings) Ltd/Cott Beverages Ltd **NB: completed merger**	28 November 2005	28 April 2006	No	
HMV Group plc/ Waterstones plc/ Ottakar's plc	6 December 2005	12 May 2006	No	
Railway Investments/ Marcroft Engineering Ltd **NB: completed merger**	6 February 2006	12 September 2006	Yes	Divestiture required. Final undertakings accepted 5 January 2007
Stagecoach/ Scottish Citylink **NB: completed merger**	15 March 2006	23 October 2006	Yes	Divestiture required. Final undertakings accepted 29 May 2007
Safenet inc/ nCipher plc **NB: abandoned by the parties**	30 March 2006			
Stericycle International LLC/ Sterile Technologies Group ltd **NB: completed merger**	28 June 2006	12 December 2006	Yes	Divestiture required. Final undertakings accepted 30 January 2007 **NB: appeal to the CAT, Case 1070/4/8/06** *Stericycle International LLC v Competition Commission:* judgment of 19 September 2006 rejecting an application for interim relief, [2006] CAT 21

Title	Date of reference	Date of publication	Finding of substantial lessening of competition?	Remedy
Pan Fish ASA/ Marine Harvest NV	6 July 2006	18 December 2006	No	
Hampden Agencies Ltd/CBS Private Capital **NB: completed merger**	14 July 2006	27 October 2006	No	
IPC Media ltd/ Horse Deals Ltd **NB: abandoned by the parties**	16 August 2006			
Hamsard 2786 Ltd/ Academy Music Holdings ltd	21 August 2006	23 January 2007	Yes	Divestiture required. Final undertakings accepted 22 February 2007
SvitzerWijsmuller/ Adsteam Marine ltd	31 August 2006	9 February 2007	Yes	Divestiture required. Final undertakings accepted 30 April 2007
Stonegate Farmers Ltd/Deans Food Group Ltd **NB: completed merger**	13 September 2006	20 April 2007	Yes	Divestiture required. Final undertakings accepted 8 October 2007
Mid Kent Water and South East Water **NB: completed merger**	16 November 2006	1 May 2007	The merger may be expected to prejudice OFWAT's ability to make comparisons between water enterprises	One-off price reduction to be made. Final undertakings accepted 29 November 2007
Wienerberger Finance Service BV/Baggeridge Brick plc	11 December 2006	10 May 2007	No	

Title	Date of reference	Date of publication	Finding of substantial lessening of competition?	Remedy
Thermo Electron Manufacturing Ltd/GV Instruments Ltd	15 December 2006	30 May 2007	Yes	Divestiture required. Final undertakings accepted 31 July 2007
Kemira GrowHow Ojy and Terra Industries Inc	26 January 2007	11 July 2007	Yes	Divestiture required. Also a behavioural commitment to provide a source of supply to a third party. Final undertakings accepted 11 September 2007
MDA Ltd/Quest Associates **NB: abandoned by the parties**	14 February 2007			
Greif INC/Blagden Packaging Group **NB: completed merger**	20 February 2007	17 August 2007	No	
Woolworths Group Plc/Bertram Group Ltd **NB: completed merger**	3 April 2007	4 September 2007	No	
Tesco plc/Co-op **NB: completed merger**	19 April 2007	28 November 2007	Yes	Divestiture required
Sportech plc/ Vernons Football Pools	3 May 2007	11 October 2007	No	
C4S Cash Services/ Abbotshurst Group **NB: abandoned by the parties**	18 May 2007			

Title	Date of reference	Date of publication	Finding of substantial lessening of competition?	Remedy
BSkyB/ITV NB: completed merger	24 May 2007		Yes, decision of the Secretary of State for Business of 29 January 2008	Divestiture required. On appeal to the CAT, Case 1095/4/8/08 *British Sky Broadcasting plc v Competition Commission*; Case 1096/4/8/08 *Virgin Media Inc v Competition Commission*
Polypipe Building Products Ltd/ Verplas Ltd NB: abandoned by the parties	11 July 2007			
Macquarie UK Broadcast Ventures Ltd/National Grid Wireless Group NB: completed merger	8 August 2007		Yes	Price reductions required, in default of which a divestiture will be required
GAME Group plc/ Game Station Ltd NB: completed merger	9 August 2007	16 January 2008	No	
Killarney Manufacturing Group Ltd/ Balmoral Group Ltd NB: abandoned by the parties	25 October 2007			

Title	Date of reference	Date of publication	Finding of substantial lessening of competition?	Remedy
CineWorld Group plc/Hollywood Green Leisure Park, Wood Green NB: abandoned by the parties				

(A) Basic statistical analysis

Sixty-four mergers had been referred by the OFT to the CC by 12 March 2008. The largest number of references in one complete year was 17 in 2005; the smallest was 12 in 2007.

(B) Abandoned mergers

As the Table above demonstrates, quite a few mergers that are referred to the CC are then abandoned by the parties. This occurred in 18 cases out of the total of 64. There are various possible explanations for this. One is that the parties may consider that it is too expensive, in terms of professional fees, to undergo an in-depth investigation by the CC, especially where the value of the business acquired is fairly small. The concern that too many 'small' mergers could be referred to the CC led to the OFT revising its *de minimis* guidance in November 2007[448].

Another explanation for the abandonment of a merger might be that the parties realise that there is such a strong likelihood that the outcome of the investigation will be substantial remedies, or even an outright prohibition, that it is not worth continuing with the transaction. A third explanation for some abandonments is that an acquisition agreement may have been conditional on the merger not being referred to the CC.

(C) Completed mergers

It is noticeable that a significant percentage of mergers referred to the CC were completed ones: a total of 28 out of 64 or, in percentage terms, 43.75 per cent. The UK system does not require pre-notification of mergers, and the parties are perfectly entitled to complete a transaction without prior clearance, although they need to be aware of the risks of doing so. The OFT and the CC will take care, in the case of a completed merger, to ensure that there is no further intermingling of assets once the matter has come to their attention and become the subject of an investigation[449].

It is important to note that in several cases of completed mergers the CC required substantial remedies, including, in some, the total reversal of a transaction.

(A) Full unscrambling In *Emap/ABI*, *Stonegate/Deans* and *Thermo/GVI* the transactions had to be fully unscrambled.

[448] See p 906 above.   [449] See pp 929–932 above.

(B) Substantial unscrambling In *EWS/Marcroft*, *Stagecoach/Scottish Citylink*, *Somerfield/ Morrisons* and *Stericycle/STG* the CC required significant unscrambling of the transaction.

(C) Slight unscrambling In some cases the remedy required was quite limited: for example in *Vue Entertainment Holdings (UK) Ltd/A3 Cinema Ltd* the CC required Vue Entertainment Holdings to divest itself of one of the two cinemas that it operated in the town of Basingstoke to a cinema operator with the resources, expertise, incentive and business plan to operate it as a multiplex cinema showing mainstream films[450].

(D) The number of findings of an SLC

The CC found an SLC in 21 out of the 64 mergers to have been investigated by the 12 March 2008.

(E) The number of outright prohibitions

There have been some cases in which a merger was prohibited in its entirety. The completed mergers in *Emap/ABI*, *Stonegate/Deans* and *Thermo/GVI* have already been referred to. The first occasion on which the CC prohibited a merger in its entirety was in *Knauf Insulation Ltd/Superglass Insulation Ltd*; the CC rejected various remedies suggested by Knauf to address concerns over its ability, after the merger, to raise prices, including a proposal for a system of price control or for the monitoring of prices by the OFT[451].

In *Hamsard 2786 Ltd/Academy Music Holdings Ltd*[452] the CC contemplated the possibility of forbidding the acquisition of a controlling interest by Hamsard 2786 in Academy Music in its entirety, but decided that this would be disproportionate; instead it required a partial divestiture of two live music venues to an up-front purchaser to be approved by the CC[453].

(F) Relationship with Article 82

In *Railway Investments Ltd/Marcroft Holdings Ltd*[454] the CC was concerned that English Welsh & Scottish Railways, the owner of Railway Investments, would be able either to reduce service quality or raise prices in the market for railfreight haulage services. EW&S argued that the behaviour that the CC feared might occur would entail an infringement of Article 82 EC and/or the Chapter II prohibition of the Competition Act, and that the sanctions associated with those provisions would deter it from behaving in that way. The CC concluded that the deterrent effect of the prohibitions was too uncertain to counteract the incentives to indulge in the behaviour predicted[455].

---

[450] See the Final Report, paras 7.19–7.72, available at www.competition-commission.org.uk/inquiries/ ref2005/vue/index.htm.

[451] See the Final Report, paras 9.1–9.21, www.competition-commission.org.uk/inquiries.completed/ 2004/superglass/index.htm.

[452] See the Final Report, paras 6.47–6.67, available at www.competition-commission.org.uk/inquiries/ ref2006/hamsard2786.htm.

[453] Ibid, paras 7.20–7.51.

[454] See www.competition-commission.org.uk/inquiries2006/marcroft/index.htm.

[455] See www.competition-commission.org.uk/rep_pub/reports/2006/515marcroft.htm, paras 7.114–7.126.

(G) Evaluation of the value of the CC's actions[456]

In July 2006 the CC published a document on its website in which it attempted to estimate the value to UK consumers of its work[457]. The CC reviewed four mergers in which it
had required remedies to address an SLC in the previous year: *SDEL/Coors, Somerfield/
Morrisons, LSE/Euronext/Deutsche Börse,* and *Vue/Ster.* The CC concluded that a reasonable estimate of the total costs to consumers if it had not taken action would have
been in the order of £31.5 million per year; it also assumed that these adverse effects
would have lasted for at least three years. The CC repeated the exercise in 2007, estimating a probable detriment to consumers of £3.8 million per year had it not taken action in
relation to the five merger cases in 2006–2007 in which it found an SLC[458]. The CC noted
that the OFT estimated that, over the same period, it (the OFT) had avoided detriment
to consumers of £33 million by accepting undertakings in lieu of a reference, so that the
merger system as a whole had saved consumers £37 million.

9. 'PUBLIC INTEREST CASES', 'OTHER SPECIAL CASES' AND MERGERS IN THE WATER INDUSTRY

(A) Public interest cases[459]

A key feature of the merger provisions in the Enterprise Act is that the Secretary of State
should not be involved in individual cases, and that decisions should be taken by the
OFT and the CC: competition analysis in normal merger cases should be carried out
by specialist competition authorities[460]. However there may be situations in which the
investigation of a merger may be justifiable on grounds of a wider public interest than its
detrimental effect on competition: Article 21(4) of the ECMR recognises that Member
States may have a 'legitimate interest' in investigating a merger other than for reasons
of competition[461], and the Act makes provision for the issue of a European intervention
notice in such cases. Chapters 2 and 3 of Part 3 of the Enterprise Act provide for the
investigation of mergers in 'public interest cases' and 'other special cases' respectively.
Such cases will be rare, and the provisions are deliberately drafted narrowly; they will
be described here only briefly.

Chapter 2 of Part 3 of the Act consists of sections 42 to 58, which deal with public
interest cases. The Secretary of State may give an 'intervention notice' to the OFT if

[456] See also the OFT's *Consumer savings from merger control*, OFT 917, April 2007.
[457] *Estimated costs to consumers of the mergers against which the CC took action between March 2005
and March 2006*, available at www.competition-commission.org.uk/our_role/analysis/estimated_costs_
to_consumers_of_the_mergers.pdf.
[458] See *Estimated costs to consumers of the mergers and market outcomes against which the CC took action
between March 2006 and April 2007* www.competition-commission.org.uk/our_role/analysis/estimated_
costs_to_consumers_of_the_mergers.pdf.
[459] See further the OFT's *Mergers: Substantive assessment guidance*, ch 10 and *Mergers: Procedural guidance*, ch 8; and the CC's *Merger References: Competition Commission Guidelines*, Part 5.
[460] See DTI White Paper on *Productivity and Enterprise: A World Class Competition Regime* Cm 5233,
(2001), para 5.23.
[461] See ch 21, pp 839–843.

he believes that one or more public interest considerations are relevant to a consideration of a relevant merger situation[462]. Section 58(1) of the Enterprise Act specifies national security as a public interest consideration: it is given the same meaning as in Article 21(4) of the ECMR[463]. Section 375 of the Communications Act 2003[464] adds several additional 'media public interest considerations' to section 58 of the Enterprise Act: the need for accurate presentation of news and free expression of opinion in newspapers[465]; the need for a sufficient plurality of views in newspapers in each market for newspapers in the UK[466]; the need for plurality of media ownership[467]; the need for a wide range of high quality broadcasting, appealing to a wide variety of tastes and interests[468]; and the need for media owners to be committed to the objectives set out in section 319 of the Communications Act. In May 2004 the DTI published a helpful Guidance document, *Enterprise Act 2002, Public Interest Intervention in Media Mergers*[469]. The Secretary of State is given power to add a new public interest consideration to section 58 of the Enterprise Act by statutory instrument, but this would require the approval of Parliament[470].

Where an intervention notice has been given the OFT will give a report to the Secretary of State dealing with both the competition and the public interest considerations; in the case of a media merger OFCOM will also report on the media public interest considerations[471]. The Secretary of State then has power to make a reference to the CC[472]; in exercising this discretion the Secretary of State is bound by the OFT's findings as to competition: his intervention is permitted only on public interest grounds[473].

The CC must decide whether a relevant merger situation has been created[474]; it must also report on any competition issues and on admissible public interest considerations, as well as possible remedies[475]. The CC's report must be given to the Secretary of State[476], and must contain its decisions on the questions it is required to answer together with reasons for those decisions[477]. As a general proposition the CC must report to the Secretary of State within 24 weeks of the reference, although in certain circumstances the period may be shorter or longer[478]. Where a 'new' public interest consideration is raised, requiring the approval of Parliament, there are restrictions on the action that can be taken if the public interest is not 'finalised' within 24 weeks of the serving of the intervention notice[479]. At the end of an investigation of a merger under the public interest provisions section 54 gives the Secretary of State power to make an 'adverse public interest finding'[480] within 30 days of receipt of the report from the CC[481]. The Secretary of State is not entitled to diverge from the finding of the CC on the competition issues[482]. Enforcement powers are conferred upon the Secretary of State to accept

---

[462] Enterprise Act 2002, s 42(2).   [463] Ibid, s 58(1) and (2).

[464] Note that s 373 of the Communications Act repeals the provisions in the Fair Trading Act 1973 that subjected newspaper mergers to a special regime; on the current law see Pryor 'The New Regime for the Regulation of Newspaper Mergers' (2003) 4 Competition Law Journal 63.

[465] Enterprise Act 2002, s 58(2A), as added by s 375 of the Communications Act 2003.

[466] Ibid, s 58(2B).   [467] Ibid, s 58(2C)(a).   [468] Ibid, s 58(2C)(b).   [469] Available at www.dti.gov.uk.

[470] Enterprise Act 2002, s 58(3) and (4).

[471] Ibid, s 44, as amended by ss 376 and 377 Communications Act 2003; OFCOM has published *OFCOM guidance for the public interest test for media mergers*, available at www.ofcom.org.uk/tv/ifi/guidance/pi_test.

[472] Enterprise Act 2002, s 45.   [473] Ibid, s 46(2).   [474] Ibid, s 47(1).

[475] Ibid, s 47(2)–(11).   [476] Ibid, s 50(1).

[477] Ibid, s 50(2).   [478] Ibid, s 51; see also s 52.   [479] Ibid, s 53.   [480] Ibid, s 54(2).   [481] Ibid, s 54(5).

[482] Ibid, s 54(7).

undertakings or to make orders to remedy, mitigate or prevent any of the effects adverse to the public interest which have resulted from, or may result from, the creation of any relevant merger situation. The powers available are set out in Schedule 7 of the Act[483], and include the ability to order anything permitted by Schedule 8[484]; paragraph 20 of Schedule 8 enables action to be taken in the interests of national security, and paragraph 20A, added by section 389 of the Communications Act 2003, enables appropriate action to be taken following investigations of media mergers. Provision is made for cases to revert to the competition authorities where an intervention notice ceases to have effect, either because the Secretary of State decides that a public interest consideration should not be taken into account, or because parliamentary approval for a public interest consideration is not given[485]. The OFT has a function of advising the Secretary of State on mergers that might raise public interest considerations[486], and the OFT and CC must bring to his attention any representations about the exercise of his powers as to what constitutes a public interest consideration[487].

By 12 March 2008 the only intervention notice to have been issued under the public interest provisions (as opposed to the 'special' public interest provisions discussed below) arose in the case of the acquisition by BSkyB of 17.9 per cent of the shares of ITV plc. The Secretary of State issued an intervention notice on 26 February 2007[488]. A reference was made to the CC which considered that the transaction would give rise to an SLC; however it did not consider that the transaction endangered the plurality of the media[489]. The Secretary of State decided in January 2008 that BSkyB should reduce its shareholding in ITV to below 7.5 per cent[490]. The case has been appealed to the CAT both by BSkyB[491] and by Virgin Media, which considers that BSkyB should have been required to divest all of its shares in ITV rather than just some of them; Virgin also contests the CC's conclusion that the transaction was not harmful to plurality[492].

(B) Other special cases

Chapter 3 of Part 3 of the Act consists of sections 59 to 70, which deal with 'other special cases'.

(i) 'Special public interest cases'

Sections 59 to 66 are concerned with an exceptional category of mergers that may be referred for investigation on public interest grounds, even though they do not meet either the turnover or the share of supply thresholds for reference contained in section 23 of the Act[493]. Two types of merger may be considered under the 'special public interest' provisions. The first is mergers involving certain government contractors or sub-contractors who may hold or receive confidential information or material relating to defence; the second type is certain mergers in the newspaper and broadcasting sectors that do not qualify for investigation under the general merger rules because

[483] Ibid, s 55(2).   [484] See p 934 above.   [485] Enterprise Act 2002, s 56.   [486] Ibid, s 57(1).
[487] Ibid, s 57(2).   [488] www.dti.gov.uk/files/file38017.pdf.
[489] See www.competition-commission.org.uk/inquiries/ref2007/itv/index.htm.
[490] See www.berr.gov.uk/files/file44136.pdf.
[491] Case 1095/4/8/08 British Sky Broadcasting plc v Competition Commission, not yet decided.
[492] Case 1096/4/8/08 Virgin Media Inc v Competition Commission, not yet decided
[493] See pp 910–912 above.

they fall below the turnover or share of supply tests[494]. Such cases are not scrutinised on competition grounds, but against public interest considerations only. In such cases the Secretary of State serves a 'special intervention notice'[495]. The OFT will then conduct an initial investigation and give a report to the Secretary of State[496]; in media cases OFCOM will report on the media public interest considerations. The Secretary of State has power to refer the matter to the CC[497], but must accept the OFT's decision as to whether a special merger situation has been created[498]. The CC will then investigate the matter and report to the Secretary of State[499]; he has power to take enforcement action[500], but must accept the view of the CC as to whether a special merger situation has been created or may be expected[501]. The Secretary of State has similar enforcement powers to those in public interest cases[502].

There has been one case under these provisions, *Insys Group Ltd/Lockheed Martin UK Ltd*: a special intervention notice was issued by the Secretary of State on 17 August 2005 and the case was settled on the basis of undertakings offered by Lockheed Martin and accepted by him[503].

(ii) European mergers

Where a merger has been completed or is in contemplation which has a Community dimension under the ECMR but which gives rise to a public interest consideration the Secretary of State may give a 'European intervention notice' to the OFT[504], and has power to make an order to provide for the taking of action to remedy, mitigate or prevent effects adverse to the public interest which have resulted from, or may be expected to result from, the creation of the merger[505]. This provides a legal basis to proceed against mergers in relation to which the UK asserts a 'legitimate interest' under Article 21(4) of the ECMR[506]. Further provision is made in relation to European merger cases by the Enterprise Act (Protection of Legitimate Interests) Order 2003[507].

European intervention notices have been issued on four occasions; each case was settled on the basis of undertakings accepted by the Secretary of State to safeguard UK national security[508].

(C) Mergers in the water industry[509]

The Water Industry Act 1991, as amended by section 70 of the Enterprise Act 2002, contains special rules for mergers between water enterprises in England and Wales. The relevant provisions are sections 32 to 35 of the Water Industry Act, as substituted

---

[494] Sections 378–380 Communications Act 2003, amending ss 59 and 61 of the Enterprise Act 2002.
[495] Enterprise Act 2002, s 59.   [496] Ibid, s 61.   [497] Ibid, s 62.   [498] Ibid, s 62(5).   [499] Ibid, ss 63 and 65.
[500] Ibid, s 66.   [501] Ibid, s 66(4).   [502] Ibid, Sch 7, paras 9 and 11.
[503] See www.dti.gov.uk/files/file32736.pdf.   [504] Enterprise Act 2002, s 67.   [505] Ibid, s 68.
[506] On Article 21(4) of the ECMR, see ch 21, pp 839–843.   [507] SI 2003/1592.
[508] See www.dti.gov.uk/bbf/competition/mergers/public-interest/national-security/index.html; note that the same website contains details of similar undertakings (and variations of undertakings) given under the now-repealed provisions of the Fair Trading Act 1973: see eg *British Aerospace plc/General Electric Company plc* where the undertakings were varied in 2007.
[509] See further Weir 'Comparative Competition and the Regulation of Mergers in the Water Industry of England and Wales' (2000) XLV Antitrust Bulletin 811; Barnes 'Holding Back the Flow: Do the UK Water Merger Control Rules Risk Dampening Investment in the Sector?' (2007) 1 European Business Law Journal, 205.

by section 70 of the Enterprise Act 2002; these provisions must be read in conjunction with Schedule 4ZA of the 1991 Act, as inserted by Schedule 6 to the 2002 Act. The purpose behind this special regime is to ensure that mergers do not adversely affect the ability of the Water Services Regulation Authority (OFWAT) to carry out its regulatory functions effectively by reducing the number of companies whose performances can be compared: OFWAT should be able to make use of 'comparative' or 'yardstick' competition. The provisions inserted by the Enterprise Act align the special arrangements for assessing water mergers with the general mergers regime. Two changes in particular should be noted. First, a turnover test is used to determine whether a reference should be made: the threshold was formerly based on the value of the assets acquired. Second, the role of the Secretary of State in relation to water mergers is ended, with the result that the OFT and the CC are now responsible for water mergers.

Under the Water Industry Act, as amended, mergers between water enterprises in England and Wales are subject to a mandatory reference by the OFT to the CC[510], unless the turnover of one or both of the enterprises is less than £10 million[511]. The CC must determine whether a water merger would prejudice the ability of OFWAT to make comparisons between water enterprises[512]. Part 3 of the Enterprise Act applies to water mergers, subject to any modifications that the Secretary of State might make by regulation: thus the powers that the OFT and the CC have in relation to mergers generally also apply in the case of water mergers[513]. The CC has published *Water Merger References: Competition Commission Guidelines* explaining its approach to mergers subject to these provisions[514].

There had been one reference to the CC of a water merger under these provisions by 12 March 2008, *Mid-Kent Water/South-East Water*[515]. The CC concluded that there was a possibility that OFWAT's ability to carry out comparisons might be prejudiced, but only to a limited degree; and the CC was satisfied in this case that the merger would generate customer benefits[516]. The CC required the merging parties to make a one-off price reduction to their customers totalling £4 million[517].

Where a merger does not involve one water company acquiring another it will be subject to the general merger rules. In such a case the OFT will look to OFWAT for advice on those aspects of the offer which will impact upon its ability to regulate the water undertakings or which might impact upon its wider ability to regulate other licensed providers of water and sewerage services.

---

[510] Water Industry Act 1991, s 32.   [511] Ibid, s 33(1).

[512] Ibid, Sch 4ZA, as inserted by Enterprise Act 2002, Sch 6; these provisions must be read in conjunction with the Water Mergers (Modification of Enactments) Regulations 2004, SI 2004/3202.

[513] Ibid, Sch 4ZA, paras 1, 2 and 4(3).   [514] CC9, December 2004.

[515] See www.competition-commission.org.uk/inquiries/ref2006/water.

[516] See the Final Report, paras 8.108–8.160.

[517] Note that the CC investigated seven mergers under the Water Industry Act 1991 prior to its amendment by the Enterprise Act 2002, three of which were prohibited outright: see *General Utilities plc/Colne Valley Water Company/Rickmansworth Water Co* Cm 1929 (1990); *General Utilities plc/Mid Kent Water Co* Cm 1125 (1990); *Southern Water plc/Mid Sussex Water Co* Cm 1126 (1990); *Wessex Water plc/South West Water* Cm 3430 (1996)(prohibited outright); *Severn Trent plc/South West Water* Cm 3429 (1996)(prohibited outright); *Mid Kent Holdings and General Utilities/SAUR Water Services* Cm 3514 (1997)(prohibited outright); *Vivendi Water UL plc/First Aqua (JVCo) Ltd* Cm 5681 (2002).

23

Particular sectors

CHAPTER CONTENTS

1. INTRODUCTION

The final chapter of this book will deal with three issues. First it will examine those sectors of the economy that are wholly or partly excluded from the competition rules in the EC Treaty, namely nuclear energy, military equipment and agriculture; the special regime for coal and steel products under the ECSC Treaty, now expired, is briefly referred to. Second, it will describe how the EC competition rules apply to the transport sector. Finally the chapter will look at the specific circumstances of so-called 'regulated industries' such as electronic communications, post and energy markets and the way in which EC and UK competition law apply to them. Constraints of space mean that these matters can be described only in outline; references to specialised literature on the application of competition law to particular sectors will be provided where appropriate.

2. NUCLEAR ENERGY[1]

The Euratom Treaty, which was entered into on the same day as the EC Treaty, deals with agreements regulating the supply and price of various nuclear materials. Article 305(2)

---

[1] See further Faull and Nikpay *The EC Law of Competition* (Oxford University Press, 2nd ed, 2007), paras 12.12–12.16; Bellamy and Child *European Community Law of Competition* (Oxford University Press, 6th ed, 2008, eds Roth and Rose), ch 12, Part 3; Cusack 'A Tale of Two Treaties: An Assessment of the Euratom Treaty in Relation to the EC Treaty' (2003) 40 CML Rev 117.

of the EC Treaty provides that nothing in it shall derogate from the provisions of the Euratom Treaty. Articles 81 and 82 are capable of application to agreements and to the abuse of a dominant position to the extent that the Euratom Treaty is not applicable. In its decisions under Article 81(3) the Commission has tended to adopt a sympathetic attitude towards cooperation agreements in the nuclear industry[2].

3. MILITARY EQUIPMENT[3]

Article 296(1)(b) of the EC Treaty provides that a Member State may take such measures as it thinks necessary for the protection of the essential interests of its security which are connected with the production of or trade in arms, ammunitions and war materials; however these measures must not adversely affect the conditions of competition in the common market regarding products which are not intended for specifically military purposes. The Council of Ministers has drawn up a list of the products to which Article 296(1) applies, although it has not been published; Article 296(2) provides that the Council may, acting unanimously on a proposal from the Commission, amend this list. There have been some concentrations in which the Commission's jurisdiction to apply the ECMR was limited as a result of the operation of Article 296[4].

4. AGRICULTURE[5]

Articles 32 to 38 of the EC Treaty subject agriculture to a special regime with its own philosophy[6]. Article 36 provides that 'the rules on competition shall apply to production of and trade in agricultural products only to the extent determined by the Council'.

(A) Council Regulation 1184/2006

Article 1 of Regulation 1184/2006[7], which replaced Regulation 26 of 1962, provides that Articles 81 and 82 shall apply to the production of or trade in the products listed in

---

[2] See eg *United Reprocessors GmbH* OJ [1976] L 51/7, [1976] 2 CMLR Dl; *KEWA* OJ [1976] L 51/15, [1976] 2 CMLR D15; *GEC/Weir* OJ [1977] L 327/26, [1978] 1 CMLR D42; *Amersham International and Buchler GmbH Venture* OJ [1982] L 314/34, [1983] 1 CMLR 619; *Scottish Nuclear, Nuclear Energy Agreement* OJ [1991] L 178/31.

[3] See further Faull and Nikpay *The EC Law of Competition* (Oxford University Press, 2nd ed, 2007), paras 3.05–3.11; Bellamy and Child *European Community Law of Competition* (Oxford University Press, 6th ed, 2008, eds Roth and Rose), paras 11.057–11.059.

[4] See ch 21, p 843.

[5] See further Bellamy and Child *European Community Law of Competition* (Oxford University Press, 6th ed, 2008, eds Roth and Rose), paras 12.194–12.209.

[6] On agricultural policy in the EC see *Agricultural Law of the European Union* (Academy of European Law, Trier and Irish Centre for European Law, Trinity College Dublin, 1999, eds Heusel and Collins); Ackrill *The Common Agricultural Policy* (Sheffield Academic Press, 2000); Usher *EC Agricultural Law* (Oxford University Press, 2nd ed, 2002); Cardwell *The European Model of Agriculture* (Oxford University Press, 2003); McMahon *EU Agricultural Law* (Oxford University Press, 2007).

[7] OJ [2006] L 214/7.

Annex I to the Treaty, subject to the derogations set out in Article 2. Article 2 provides that Article 81(1) shall *not* apply to agreements that form an integral part of a national market organisation or that are necessary for the attainment of the objectives set out in Article 33 of the Treaty[8]. These derogations are strictly construed, and the Commission must give adequate reasons in the event that it allows such a derogation[9]. The derogations provided for in Article 2 of Regulation 1184/2006 relate only to the application of Article 81; the Chapter I prohibition of the UK Competition Act 1998 does not apply where there is a derogation from Article 81 in relation to agricultural products[10]. There is no derogation from the application of Article 82 to the agricultural sector.

The monopoly powers of the Milk Marketing Board in the UK were the subject of various proceedings in the civil courts under Article 82[11]. Subsequently the Monopolies and Mergers Commission (now the Competition Commission) conducted an investigation under the now-repealed monopoly provisions of the Fair Trading Act 1973[12] which led to Milk Marque, a successor to some of the assets of the Milk Marketing Board, being voluntarily split into three separate companies; the Secretary of State asked the Office of Fair Trading to continue to monitor the situation[13]. Following the Commission's report a reference was made by the High Court to the ECJ on the relationship between national competition law and the Community rules on the agricultural sector[14]. The ECJ concluded that the existence of specific Community rules did not deprive national competition authorities of their right to apply national law to a milk producers' cooperative in a powerful position on the market; however they should refrain from any measure which might undermine or create exceptions to the common organisation of the market in milk or compromise the objectives of the common agricultural policy.

(B) Annex I products

If a product is *not* mentioned in Annex I of the Treaty, it cannot benefit from the derogations provided by Article 2 of Regulation 1184/2006. In *Coöperative Stremsel-en Kleurselfabriek v Commission*[15] the ECJ held that, as rennet was not specifically mentioned in Annex I, it was fully subject to the competition rules; the fact that rennet was used in the production of cheese, which is itself listed in the Annex, did not provide it with immunity from the application of Article 81(1). In *Pabst and Ricbarz/BNIA*[16] the Commission applied Article 81 to the French trade association responsible for armagnac, pointing out that, as this product did not appear in Annex I, it was to be treated as

---

[8] On Article 33 see pp 960–961 below. Article 2 contains a sentence dealing with the activities of farmers' associations; this is not a further exception, but rather an embellishment of the policy expressed in that provision: see *Milchförderungsfonds* OJ [1985] L 35/35, [1985] 3 CMLR 101, paras 21–22; *Bloemenveilingen Aalsmeer* OJ [1988] L 262/27, [1989] 4 CMLR 500, paras 150–152.

[9] See Cases T-70/92 and T-71/92 *Florimex v Commission* [1997] ECR II-697, [1997] 5 CMLR 769, upheld on appeal Case C-265/97 P *VBA and Florimex v Commission* [2000] ECR I-2061, [2001] 5 CMLR 1343; see also Case T-77/94 *Vereniging van Groothandelaren v Commission* [1997] ECR II-759, [1997] 5 CMLR 812, upheld on appeal Case C-266/97 P *VBA and Florimex v Commission* [2000] ECR I-2135.

[10] Competition Act 1998, Schedule 3, para 9.

[11] See *Garden Cottage Foods v Milk Marketing Board* [1984] AC 130, [1983] 2 All ER 770, HL; *An Bord Bainne Cooperative Ltd v Milk Marketing Board* [1984] 1 CMLR 519; affd [1984] 2 CMLR 584, CA.

[12] *The Supply in Great Britain of Raw Cow's Milk* Cm 4286 (1999).

[13] DTI Press Release P/99/895, 5 November 1999; see also DTI Press Release P/2000/304, 2 May 2000.

[14] Case C-137/00 *R v Monopolies and Mergers Commission and the Secretary of State for Trade and Industry, ex p Milk Marque Ltd* [2003] ECR I-7975, [2004] 4 CMLR 293.

[15] Case 61/80 [1981] ECR 851, [1982] 1 CMLR 240.   [16] OJ [1976] L 231/24, [1976] 2 CMLR D63.

an industrial product. In *BNIC v Clair*[17] the ECJ held, for the same reason, that cognac was an industrial product and rejected an argument that it should be treated in a special way because of its importance to the economic welfare of a particular region of France.

In *BNIC v Yves Aubert*[18] the ECJ had to deal with the application of the competition rules to a demand by BNIC for a levy claimed against a wine grower for having exceeded a marketing quota. One issue was whether the competition rules could be applied to brandy. The ECJ, having observed that brandies are not listed in Annex I and so are industrial rather than agricultural products, added that the fact that some of the proceeds of levies raised by BNIC were intended for measures on wine and must, which do appear in Annex I, did not affect the application of Article 81(1). In *Dansk Pelsdyravlerforening v Commission*[19] the CFI rejected a claim that animal furs should be treated as an agricultural product; in *Gøttrup-Klim Grovvareforeninger v Dansk Landburgs Grovvareselskab AmbA*[20] the ECJ held that fertiliser and plant protection products were not agricultural products. In *Sicasov* the Commission acknowledged that seeds fell within Annex I, but concluded that neither of the derogations in Regulation 26 (now Regulation 1184/2006) was applicable[21].

(C) The first derogation: national market organisations

Article 2 of Regulation 1184/2006 provides that Article 81 shall not apply to agreements which form an integral part of a national market organisation. The Council of Ministers established common organisations for most agricultural products by 1967, so that the majority of national marketing organisations have ceased to exist. The Commission has construed this derogation from the application of Article 81(1) strictly[22]. In *FRUBO v Commission*[23] the ECJ upheld the Commission's decision[24] that a Dutch fruit marketing organisation did not benefit from the immunity contained in Article 2(1) since it was not a national marketing organisation. In *Scottish Salmon Board*[25] the Commission found that, as there was a common organisation of the market in fishery products[26], the Scottish Salmon Board could not rely on the national market organisation defence.

In *New Potatoes*[27] rules were laid down by seven economic committees in France, acting under a French law of 1962, to organise and regulate the production and marketing of new potatoes. The rules were intended to deal with the problem of a slump in the market at a time of over-production. The Commission was asked to declare that Article 81(1) was not applicable: as there was no common organisation of the market in question, the Commission had to decide whether the system qualified as a national market organisation. It held that this term must be defined in a way that would be consistent with the objectives of a common organisation under the second exception of Article 2

---

[17] Case 123/83 [1985] ECR 391, [1985] 2 CMLR 430.

[18] Case 136/86 [1987] ECR 4789, [1988] 4 CMLR 331. [19] Case T-61/89 [1992] ECR II-1931.

[20] Case C-250/92 [1994] ECR I-5641, [1996] 4 CMLR 191, paras 21–27.

[21] OJ [1999] L 14/27, [1999] 4 CMLR 192, paras 65–69.

[22] As well as the decisions mentioned in the text see *Cauliflowers* OJ [1978] L 21/23, [1978] 1 CMLR D66; *Bloemenveilingen Aalsmeer* OJ [1988] L 262/27, [1989] 4 CMLR 500; *Sugar Beet* OJ [1990] L 31/32, [1991] 4 CMLR 629; *Sicasov* OJ [1999] L 14/27, [1999] 4 CMLR 192; *British Sugar* OJ [1999] L 76/1, [1999] 4 CMLR 1316, paras 185–188.

[23] Case 71/74 [1975] ECR 563, [1975] 2 CMLR 123.

[24] *Geeves and Zonen v FRUBO* OJ [1974] L 237/16, [1974] 2 CMLR D89.

[25] OJ [1992] L 246/37, [1993] 5 CMLR 602, para 22.

[26] See Council Regulation 3796/81 OJ [1981] L 379/1. [27] OJ [1988] L 59/25, [1988] 4 CMLR 790.

960 23 PARTICULAR SECTORS

of Regulation 26: thus the objectives of the common agricultural policy, contained in Article 33 EC and referred to below, were read into the first exception of Article 2. The Commission went on to hold that the decisions and agreements of various producer groups did form an integral part of the national market organisation in question and concluded that Article 81(1) was not infringed.

(D) The second derogation: common market organisations

Article 2 of Regulation 1184/2006 also permits agreements which are necessary for the attainment of the objectives of the common agricultural policy. Article 33 sets out these objectives under five heads:

- to increase agricultural productivity
- to ensure a fair standard of living for the agricultural community
- to stabilise markets
- to ensure the availability of supplies
- to ensure supplies to consumers at reasonable prices.

Article 33(2) provides that, in implementing the common agricultural policy, account shall be taken, *inter alia*, of:

the particular nature of agricultural activity, which results from the social structure of agriculture and from structural and natural disparities between the various agricultural regions.

The aims expressed in Article 33 are not necessarily consistent with the normal forces of competition.

In *FRUBO v Commission*[28] the ECJ rejected a defence based on the second derogation in Article 2. A noticeable feature of the judgment is that, although some of the heads of Article 33 may have been satisfied, not all of them were: to put the matter another way, in order to come within this derogation it is necessary to satisfy all five heads of Article 33. In practice it is likely that the Commission and the Community courts will hold that the objectives of Article 33 are expressly or impliedly advanced by the provisions of any particular regulation establishing a common organisation of an agricultural sector, with the result that there is no remaining latitude for the parties to an agreement to argue that their agreement will have this effect[29].

In *Bloemenveilingen Aalsmeer*[30] the Commission rejected an argument that exclusive dealing agreements between auctioneers and flower traders in respect of live plants and floricultural products could advance the objectives of Article 33. It published a decision to this effect, not only as the rules in question were the subject of litigation in the Dutch courts, but also as similar rules were being applied by other auction houses[31]. In *Scottish Salmon Board*[32] the Commission rejected an argument that the Board's conduct was permissible as the industry was in economic difficulties; the Commission's view was that, if this was so, Community initiatives should be taken to deal with the problem: it was not for the parties themselves to take action which was unlawful under Article 81.

[28] Case 71/74 [1975] ECR 563, [1975] 2 CMLR 123, paras 22–27.
[29] See eg *Cauliflowers* OJ [1978] L 21/23, [1978] 1 CMLR D66; *Milchförderungsfonds* OJ [1985] L 35/35, [1985] 3 CMLR 101.
[30] OJ [1988] L 262/27, [1989] 4 CMLR 500.   [31] Ibid, para 168.
[32] OJ [1992] L 246/37, [1993] 5 CMLR 602, para 22.

In *Sicasov*[33] the Commission held that an agreement for the licensing of seeds was not necessary for the attainment of the objectives in Article 33 EC[34].

The Commission rejected defences based on the second derogation in *French beef*[35], *Raw Tobacco Spain*[36], and *Raw Tobacco Italy*[37].

5. COAL AND STEEL

Coal and steel were originally dealt with by the Treaty of Paris of 1951 establishing the European Coal and Steel Community. The ECSC Treaty contained rules on competition that were similar in many respects to Articles 81 and 82 of the EC Treaty, although there were some material differences. The ECSC Treaty expired on 23 July 2002 which means that the coal and steel sectors are now subject to Articles 81 and 82 of the EC Treaty and the EC Merger Regulation. The Commission has published a Communication explaining the consequences of the expiry of the ECSC Treaty[38].

6. TRANSPORT[39]

The EC Treaty contains special provisions on transport in Articles 70 to 80. Article 80(1) provides that these provisions are applicable to road, rail and inland waterway transport; Article 80(2) provides that the Council of Ministers may decide on appropriate measures for the sea and air transport sectors. Thus the Treaty itself recognises a distinction between these two categories, the difficulty being that the latter are subject to numerous international arrangements and are of particular political sensitivity. Articles 81 and 82 do apply to the transport sector (including air transport[40]), but in 1962 Council Regulation 141[41] provided that Regulation 17, which gave the Commission the necessary powers to implement the competition rules, did not apply to transport. The procedural lacuna left by Regulation 141 was filled in three stages: first, Council Regulation 1017/68[42] adopted specific provisions on the application of the competition rules to transport by road, rail and inland waterway (that is to say inland transport);

---

[33] OJ [1999] L 14/27, [1999] 4 CMLR 192.   [34] OJ [1999] L 14/27, [1999] 4 CMLR 192, para 68.

[35] OJ [2003] L 209/12, [2003] 5 CMLR 891, upheld on appeal Cases T-217/03 and T-245/03 *FNCBV v Commission* [2006] ECR II-4987; this case is on appeal to the ECJ Case C-110/07 P *Coopération De France Bétail et Viande v Commission*, not yet decided.

[36] OJ [2007] L 192/14, [2006] 4 CMLR 866, paras 337–348.

[37] OJ [2006] L 353/45, [2006] 4 CMLR 1766, paras 306–311.

[38] Communication from the Commission concerning certain aspects of the treatment of competition cases resulting from the expiry of the ECSC Treaty OJ [2002] C 152/5, [2002] 5 CMLR 1036, section 2.

[39] See further Ortiz Blanco and Van Houtte *EC Competition Law in the Transport Sector* (Clarendon Press Oxford, 1996); Faull and Nikpay *The EC Law of Competition* (Oxford University Press, 2nd ed, 2007), ch 14; Bellamy and Child *European Community Law of Competition* (Oxford University Press, 6th ed, 2008, eds Roth and Rose), paras 12.004–12.051.

[40] See Cases 209/84 etc *Ministère Public v Asjes* [1986] ECR 1425, [1986] 3 CMLR 173 and Case 66/86 *Ahmed Saeed Flugreisen v Zentrale zur Bekämpfung Unlauteren Wettbewerbs* [1989] ECR 803, [1990] 4 CMLR 102.

[41] OJ (Sp edn, 1959–62) 291.   [42] OJ (Sp edn, 1968) 302.

second, Council Regulation 4056/86[43] provided the Commission with powers in the maritime transport sector; last came Council Regulation 3975/87[44] to deal with air transport. Since 1 May 2004 the procedural rules for the enforcement of Articles 81 and 82 in the transport sector are set out in the Modernisation Regulation[45]; this means that the jurisdictional problem exposed in *Union Internationale des Chemins de Fer v Commission*[46], where the CFI concluded that the Commission had proceeded under the wrong procedural regulation when applying Article 81 to arrangements for the sale of railway tickets by travel agents, would no longer occur.

(A) Inland transport

(i) Legislative regime

Article 3 of Council Regulation 1017/68 provides that certain technical agreements do not infringe Article 81; and Article 4 confers block exemption on certain cooperation agreements.

Several Council Directives were adopted in the first railway package of 1991 with the intention of opening up the rail sector to competition[47], although the development of a single market in rail transport has been slow to develop[48]. A second package was adopted in 2004[49], and a third has been proposed[50]. The rail sector is subject to a complex regulatory regime under UK law, and the Office of Rail Regulation enjoys concurrent powers to apply the provisions of the Competition Act 1998 to this sector[51].

(ii) Practical application of the competition rules to inland transport

The Commission has adopted several decisions in relation to inland transport. In *EATE Levy*[52] it condemned an agreement between French waterway carriers and French

---

[43] OJ [1986] L 378/4, [1989] 4 CMLR 461.   [44] OJ [1987] L 374/1, [1988] 4 CMLR 222.

[45] OJ [2003] L 1/1, [2003] 4 CMLR 551, Articles 36–43, see ch 7, p 282.

[46] Case T-14/93 [1995] ECR II-1503, [1996] 5 CMLR 40; the Commission's appeal against this judgment was rejected in Case C-264/95 P *Commission v Union Internationale des Chemins de Fer* [1997] ECR I-1287, [1997] 5 CMLR 49.

[47] Council Directive 91/440/EEC on *Development of the Community's Railways* OJ [1991] L 237/25, as amended by Directive 2001/12/EC of the European Parliament and of the Council OJ [2001] L 75/1; Council Directive 95/18/EC on *Licensing of Railway Undertakings* OJ [1995] L 143/70, as amended by Directive 2001/13/EC of the European Parliament and of the Council OJ [2001] L 75/26; Council Directive 95/19 EC on *Allocation of Railway Infrastructure Capacity and the Charging of Infrastructure Fees* OJ [1995] L 143/75, as amended by Directive 2001/14/EC of the European Parliament and of the Council OJ [2001] L 75/29.

[48] See the Commission's XXXth *Report on Competition Policy* (2000), points 198–199; see also the Commission's White Paper on *European Transport Policy for 2010: Time to Decide* COM (2001) 370 final, 12 September 2001; Stehmann and Zellhofer 'Dominant Rail Undertakings under European Competition Policy' (2004) 10 European Law Journal 327; Elzinga, Jutten and Niels 'Essential or Nice to Have? A Competition-based Framework for "Rail-related Services"' (2008) 29 ECLR 50.

[49] Council Directive 2004/49/EC of the European Parliament and the Council on *Safety of the Community's railways* OJ [2004] L 164/44; Council Directive 2004/50/EC of the European Parliament and the Council on *Interoperability of the trans-European high-speed rail system* OJ [2004] L 220/40; Council Directive 2004/51/ EC of the European Parliament and the Council on *Development of the Community's Railway* OJ [2004] L 164/164.

[50] Proposal for a Directive on *Development of the Community's railways* COM(2004)0139 final.

[51] On concurrency under the Competition Act 1998 see ch 10, pp 424–426; see also *Competition Act 1998: Application to services relating to railways* OFT Guideline 430, October 2005.

[52] OJ [1985] L 219/35, [1988] 4 CMLR 698.

forwarding agents imposing a levy of 10 per cent on freight charges for boat charters to destinations outside France, as it discriminated in favour of French carriers; the ECJ upheld the Commission on appeal[53]. In *Tariff Structures in the Combined Transport of Goods*[54] the Commission considered that the criteria in Article 81(3) were satisfied in the case of a tariff structure agreement between the rail companies of the EC on the sale of rail haulage in the international combined transport of goods.

In *European Night Services*[55] the Commission concluded that a joint venture established by five rail operators to provide night sleeper services through the Channel Tunnel between a variety of cities in the UK and continental Europe satisfied the criteria of Article 81(3). Under the system of granting individual exemptions then in force, the Commission made its decision subject to conditions and obligations to which the parents of the joint venture objected; the Commission limited the exemption to a period of time, ten years, which the parties considered to be too short, given the level of risk that they were undertaking. On appeal against the decision the CFI held in *European Night Services v Commission*[56] that the Commission had abjectly failed to demonstrate that the agreement between the rail operators had the effect of restricting actual and/or potential competition, with the consequence that its decision should be annulled; the CFI went further, holding that, even if there was an appreciable effect on competition, the Commission had failed to demonstrate that the exemption should be subject to the conditions and obligations imposed or should be granted for such a short period[57]. In another case relating to the Channel Tunnel, *ACI*[58], the Commission authorised, subject to conditions, the creation by British Railways Board, SNCF of France and Intercontainer CV of a joint venture company, Allied Continental Intermodal Services, to market intermodal rail services through the Channel Tunnel.

In *HOV SVZ/MCN*[59] the Commission imposed a fine on Deutsche Bahn of €11 million for imposing discriminatory rail transport tariffs for the inland carriage of sea-borne containers to and from Germany, depending on whether they were shipped through German ports on the one hand or Belgian and Dutch ones on the other. The decision was upheld on appeal to the CFI[60], and the ECJ ruled that Deutsche Bahn's appeal to it was inadmissible[61]. In *GVG/FS* the Commission concluded that the Italian rail operator, Ferrovie dello Stato, had abused a dominant position by refusing to provide access to the Italian rail infrastructure, to enter into negotiations for the formation of an international grouping and to provide traction[62].

---

[53] Case 272/85 *ANTIB v Commission* [1987] ECR 2201, [1988] 4 CMLR 677.   [54] OJ [1993] L 73/38.

[55] OJ [1994] L 259/21, [1995] 5 CMLR 76.

[56] Cases T-374/94 etc [1998] ECR II-3141, [1998] 5 CMLR 718; see similarly the Commission's decision in *Eurotunnel* OJ [1994] L 354/66, [1995] 4 CMLR 801: the Commission had granted exemption to the operating agreement for the Tunnel, but its decision was annulled on appeal by the CFI in Cases T-79/95 and T-80/95 *SNCF v Commission* [1996] ECR II-1491, [1997] 4 CMLR 334 since the Commission had failed to demonstrate that the agreement would be restrictive of competition; for the eventual outcome of this case see the Commission's XXIXth *Report on Competition Policy* (1999), p 163.

[57] For further comment on this case see ch 3, pp 117–118 and 133–134.   [58] OJ [1994] L 224/28.

[59] OJ [1994] L 104/34.

[60] Case T-229/94 *Deutsche Bahn AG v Commission* [1997] ECR II-1689, [1998] 4 CMLR 220.

[61] Case C-436/97 [1999] ECR I-2387, [1999] 5 CMLR 776.

[62] OJ [2004] L 11/17, [2004] 4 CMLR 1446; for comment see Stehmann 'Applying essential facility reasoning to passenger rail services in the EU – the Commission decision in the GVG case' (2004) 25 ECLR 390.

In the UK the Office of Rail Regulation imposed a fine of £4.1 million on a rail freight operator, EW&S Ltd, for abusing its dominant position in the market for the haulage of coal by rail, in particular by acting in a discriminatory and a predatory manner[63].

(B) Maritime transport[64]

(i) Legislative regime

For many years maritime transport was subject to a special procedural and substantive regime of its own, set out in Council Regulation 4056/86[65]. The cumulative effect of the Modernisation Regulation of 2004 and of Council Regulation 1419/2006[66], which entered into force in October 2006, is that the special regime has been terminated and the sector is now subject to the same procedural and substantive rules as the rest of the economy.

(A) Procedural rules Regulation 17[67], which gave the Commission power to enforce Articles 81 and 82 in 1962, did not apply to the maritime transport sector. Council Regulation 4056/86[68] provided the Commission with power to enforce Articles 81 and 82 in relation to international maritime transport services from or to one or more Community ports with effect from 1987. Regulation 1/2003[69], the Modernisation Regulation, repealed the special procedural rules with effect from 1 May 2004, since when maritime transport has been subject to the same procedural regime as the rest of the economy. Regulation 4056/86 did not empower the Commission to enforce the competition rules in the case of so-called 'cabotage', that is to say services between ports within the same Member State; also excluded were international tramp vessel services, that is to say the transport of goods in bulk where freight rates are negotiated on a case-by-case basis[70]. These exclusions were maintained by Article 32 of the Modernisation Regulation until October 2006, when Article 2 of Regulation 1419/2006 repealed the exclusion. The current position, therefore, is that the Commission has the power to apply Articles 81 and 82 to the entire maritime transport sector.

(B) Substantive rules Article 2 of Regulation 4056/86 excluded 'technical agreements' from the scope of Article 81. More controversially, Articles 3 and 4 of Regulation 4056/86 provided block exemption for 'liner conferences', that is to say agreements between carriers concerning the operation of scheduled maritime transport services, allowing them to fix prices and regulate capacity. Following a consultation these substantive rules have been abolished[71]: Regulation 1419/2006 repealed Regulation 4056/86 in its entirety; however Article 1 provides transitional relief until 18 October 2008 for

---

[63] ORR decision of 17 November 2007, [2007] UKCLR 937.

[64] See further Ortiz Blanco *Shipping Conferences under EC Antitrust Law* (Hart Publishing, 2008).

[65] OJ [1986] L 378/4, [1989] 4 CMLR 461.

[66] OJ [2006] L 269/1; see Benini and Bermig 'Milestones in maritime transport: EU ends exemptions' *Competition Policy Newsletter*, Spring 2007, p 20.

[67] JO [1962] 13/204.   [68] OJ [1986] L 378/4, [1989] 4 CMLR 461.   [69] OJ [2003] L 1/1.

[70] See Regulation 4056/86, Article 1(3)(a).

[71] See *Review of Council Regulation 4056/86* and the responses to the Consultation, available at www. ec.europa.eu/comm/competition/antitrust/legislation/maritime; see also a speech by Competition Commissioner Monti 'A time for change? – Maritime competition policy at the crossroads', SPEECH/03/294, 12 June 2003, available at www.europa.eu.int/comm/competition/speeches.

the CFI on the ground that the Commission had failed to give good reasons for their belated imposition[100].

On a less hostile note, in *P&O Stena Line*[101] the Commission authorised, for three years, a joint venture to provide short cross-channel ferry services between the UK and France and Belgium. In 2001 the Commission renewed this authorisation for a period of six years[102]. The Commission was aware that there were some anxieties about price rises, but considered that they were understandable as the market adjusted to more normal competitive conditions following the abolition of duty-free sales on ferry crossings, as new capacity was absorbed and as fuel prices rose.

(C) Air transport

(i) Legislative regime[103]

A number of measures have been adopted in order to liberalise air transport in the Community. In the first liberalisation package of 1987[104] the Council of Ministers adopted a Directive on fares for scheduled air services between Member States[105] and a Decision on the sharing of passenger capacity between Member States[106]. The 1987 package was regarded as a first step towards the completion of the internal market in air transport. In 1990 Regulation 2343/90[107] on access for air carriers to scheduled intra-Community routes was adopted. In 1991 the Council adopted Regulation 249/91[108] on air cargo services between Member States and Regulation 295/91 on compensation to passengers denied boarding ('bumped') in air transport; the latter was replaced by Regulation 261/2004[109].

In 1992 a further liberalisation package was adopted. Regulation 2407/92[110] dealt with the licensing of air carriers. Regulation 2408/92[111] provides that all Community carriers should have access to intra-Community routes (cabotage). Regulation 2409/92[112] provides that Community air carriers shall freely set their own fares. In March 2003 the Commission proposed several revisions in the third liberalisation package[113]. Regulation 95/93[114] establishes common rules for the allocation of slots at Community

[100] Case T-213/00 *CMA CGM v Commission* [2003] ECR II-913, [2003] 5 CMLR 268.

[101] OJ [1999] L 163/61, [1999] 5 CMLR 682; see also the Commission's XXVIth *Report on Competition Policy* (1996), points 84–87; and the XXVIIth *Report on Competition Policy* (1997), points 81–84 and pp 134–138.

[102] Commission Press Release IP/01/806, 7 June 2001 and XXXIst *Report on Competition Policy* (2001), point 160.

[103] See *Guide to European Community legislation in the field of civil aviation*, European Commission, June 2007, available at www.ec.europa.eu/transport/air_portal.

[104] The package is helpfully summarised in the Commission's XVIIth *Report on Competition Policy* (1987), points 43–45.

[105] Council Directive 87/601/EEC OJ [1987] L 374/12.

[106] Council Decision 87/602/EEC OJ [1987] L 374/19.   [107] OJ [1990] L 217/8.

[108] OJ [1991] L 36/1, as amended by Regulation 2408/92 OJ [1992] L 240/8.   [109] OJ [2004] L 46/1

[110] OJ [1992] L 240/1.

[111] OJ [1992] L 240/8; on the application of Regulation 2408/92 see Case T-260/94 *Air Inter v Commission* [1997] ECR II-997, [1997] 5 CMLR 851.

[112] OJ [1992] L 240/15.

[113] Commission *Consultation paper with a view to revision of Regulations No 2407/92, 2408/92 and 2409/92*, available at www.europa.eu.int/comm/transport/air/rules/package_3_en.htm; see also Commission Press Release IP/03/281, 26 February 2003.

[114] OJ [1993] L 14/1, as amended by Regulation 894/2000 OJ [2002] L 142/3.

airports in order to ensure that they are made available on a neutral, transparent, and non-discriminatory basis. Council Regulation 2299/89 established a *Code of Conduct for Computerised Reservation Systems*[115]. The ground-handling sector was liberalised to allow greater access to the market by Directive 96/97[116].

Despite these liberalisation measures there remain impediments to free competition in air transport markets. The lack of slots at premier airports distorts the market, as do bilateral agreements between individual Member States and third countries governing access to air space and which discriminate in favour of national carriers: some of these agreements were successfully challenged by the Commission before the ECJ under Article 43 EC in the so-called '*Open Skies*' judgment[117]. Following that judgment Regulation 847/2004[118] requires Member States to notify the Commission of negotiations with third countries and to ensure that their agreements comply with Community law. An important step forward was the signature of the *Air Transport Agreement* between the US, the EU and the Member States on 30 April 2007[119] which authorises US and EU airlines to fly between any city in the US and any city in the EU.

For many years air transport was subject to a special competition law regime contained in Council Regulation 3975/87[120]. It conferred power on the Commission to enforce the competition rules in the air transport sector to air transport services *between Community airports*; air transport between Community airports and third countries could be investigated only under the procedure provided for in Articles 84 and 85 of the EC Treaty[121]. Special arrangements were put in place in Member States to apply the EC competition rules in relation to flights to and from third countries, such as the *EC Competition Law (Articles 84 and 85) Enforcement Regulations 2001*[122] in the UK. The position is now much simpler: the applicable procedural regime is that of the Modernisation Regulation[123], and Council Regulation 411/2004[124] provides

---

[115] OJ [1989] L 220/1, as amended by Council Regulations 3089/93/EEC OJ [1993] L 278/1 and 323/99/EC OJ [1999] L 40/1; a fine of €10,000 was imposed under this Regulation in the case of *Lufthansa:* Commission Press Release IP/99/542, 20 July 1999.

[116] OJ [1996] L 272/56; see Commission Consultation paper on Issues to be addressed in the review of Council Directive 96/97/EC on access to the ground handling market at Community airports, available at www.europa.eu.int/comm/transport/air/rules/competition2/revision_96_67_en.htm.

[117] See Cases C-466/98 etc *Commission v United Kingdom* [2002] ECR I-9427, [2003] 1 CMLR 143; see Communication from the Commission on the consequences of the Court judgments of 5 November 2002 for European air transport policy COM (2002) 649 final, 19 November 2002; Hefferman and McAuliffe 'External relations in the air transport sector: the Court of Justice and the open skies agreements' (2003) 28 European Law Review 601.

[118] OJ [2004] L 157/7; the Commission has adopted two decisions, C(2006) 3009 of 31 May 2006 and C(2006) 2010 of 20 June 2006 setting out the criteria that it will apply when assessing agreements negotiated by Member States.

[119] OJ [2007] L 134/4; see Gremminger 'New EU–US cooperation agreement in air transport' *Competition Policy Newsletter*, Summer 2007, 27.

[120] OJ [1987] L 374/1, [1988] 4 CMLR 222.

[121] For the use of these provisions specifically in relation to air transport prior to the adoption of Regulation 3975/87 see Cases 209/84 etc *Ministère Public v Asjes* [1986] ECR 1425, [1986] 3 CMLR 173; Case 66/86 *Ahmed Saeed Flugreisen v Zentrale zur Bekämpfung Unlauteren Wettbewerbs* [1989] ECR 803, [1990] 4 CMLR 102.

[122] SI 2001/2916, as amended by the EC Competition Act (Articles 84 and 85) Enforcement (Amendment) Regulations 2002, SI 2002/42; these provisions are now otiose, and were repealed by SI 2007/1846.

[123] OJ [2004] L 1/1.   [124] OJ [2004] L 168/1.

that the Commission's powers under that Regulation apply to *all* routes, not only those within the EU.

Council Regulation 3976/87[125], as subsequently amended, gave the Commission power to publish block exemptions in the air transport sector. For many years there were block exemptions for consultations between carriers on passenger tariffs on routes within the EU and for arrangements on slot allocation and airport scheduling: however these have now lapsed[126].

(ii) Practical application of the competition rules to air transport

The Commission has reviewed several cooperation agreements in the air transport sector under Article 81, for example *Lufthansa/SAS*[127], *Austrian Airlines/Lufthansa*[128], *Société Air France/Alitalia Linee Aeree Italiane SpA*[129] and *Austrian Airlines/SAS*[130]. In cases that arose prior to the Modernisation Regulation the Commission sometimes granted individual exemptions to cooperation agreements, subject to conditions and obligations: that was true of the first three cases cited above. Since the Modernisation Regulation the Commission contemplated closing the *Austrian Airlines/SAS* case on the basis of commitments offered by the parties under Article 9[131]; that case did not reach a final decision. The Commission is considering the possibility of accepting commitments in the case of the *SkyTeam* airline alliance[132].

In some cases an alliance between two airlines may fall to be considered under the EC Merger Regulation rather than Article 81. This happened for example in *Alitalia/ KLM* where the Commission regarded the alliance as a full-function joint venture, even though the parties did not create a corporate vehicle for the cooperation; the Commission cleared the merger after the parties agreed to modify the transaction to address its competition concerns[133]. The Commission cleared a merger subject to conditions in the case of *Air France/KLM*[134]; the clearance was unsuccessfully challenged in the CFI by a third party, easyJet[135]. In the case of *Ryanair/Aer Lingus* the Commission prohibited the proposed acquisition of Aer Lingus by Ryanair outright[136].

In the case of *SAS/Maersk Air*[137] the Commission imposed fines of €39.4 million on SAS and €13.1 million on Maersk for market sharing, in particular with the consequence

---

[125] OJ [1988] L 374/9, [1988] 4 CMLR 235; this Regulation was slightly amended by Regulation 2344/90 OJ [1990] L 217/15.

[126] See Beuve-Méry and Struk 'Commission brings air transport in line with other industries by phasing out the block exemptions that have existed in this sector since 1988' *Competition Policy Newsletter*, Summer 2007, 45.

[127] OJ [1996] L 54/28, [1996] 4 CMLR 845; see Crocioni 'The *Lufthansa/SAS* Case: Did the Commission Get the Economics Right?' (1998) 19 ECLR 116.

[128] OJ [2002] L 242/25, [2003] 4 CMLR 252.   [129] Commission Decision of 7 April 2004.

[130] See the Commission's *Market Test Notice*, OJ [2005] C 233/18 in which it invited comments on commitments offered by the airlines to address the Commission's competition concerns.

[131] See ch 7, pp 253–257 on the Article 9 procedure.

[132] See the Commission's *Market Test Notice*, OJ [2007] C 245/46; see also Commission Press Release IP/07/1558, 19 October 2007.

[133] Case COMP/JV.19, decision of 11 August 1999.

[134] See Case COMP/M.3280, Commission Decision of 11 February 2004.

[135] Case T-177/04 *easyJet Co Ltd v Commission* [2006] ECR II-1931, [2006] 5 CMLR 663.

[136] Case COMP M 4439, Commission Decision of 27 June 2007, on appeal Case T-342/07 *Ryanair v Commission*, not yet decided.

[137] OJ [2001] L 265/15, [2001] 5 CMLR 1119.

that SAS acquired a *de facto* quasi-monopoly on the Stockholm to Copenhagen route. The Commission's decision was upheld on appeal[138].

7. REGULATED INDUSTRIES

(A) Demonopolisation, liberalisation and privatisation

One of the most dramatic economic developments in the final two decades of the twentieth century was the demonopolisation and liberalisation of industries which for many years had been the preserve of state-owned monopolies; in many cases this process was coupled with privatisation or partial privatisation of state-owned undertakings[139]. Obvious examples are the so-called 'utilities' such as telecommunications, gas, electricity, and water. The problems for competition policy that arise where former monopolists are 'released' into the free market are obvious: in so far as there is no effective competition, which is particularly likely to be the case in the early years, they may be able to charge excessive prices; and they may also be able to adopt tactics intended to foreclose new competitors from entering the market. At the same time it is necessary to ensure that former monopolists provide adequate services of an appropriate standard. A complicating factor is that utilities are often subject to a requirement that they comply with a 'universal service obligation', for example a duty to undertake the daily delivery of letters or to maintain an electricity or water supply to business and residential premises. Undertakings that are subject to a universal service obligation of this kind may need some immunity from competition so that they can make sufficient profits to enable them to perform it, which is why, for example, postal operators such as Royal Mail Group plc in the UK (formerly the Post Office) historically enjoyed a legal monopoly over the delivery of letters of less than a certain weight and size[140].

(B) EC law and the liberalisation of markets

In the EC considerable steps have been taken towards the liberalisation of utilities and the development of a single market, albeit with greater success in some sectors than in others. Directives have been adopted in the case of electronic communications, post, and energy markets with a view to creating conditions in which competitive markets develop. At the same time the European Commission has been adapting the principles of competition law and applying them to these sectors; in particular the so-called 'essential facilities doctrine' may play an important role in enabling third parties to gain access to physical infrastructures where this is necessary for the provision of competitive services[141].

---

[138] Case T-241/01 *SAS v Commission* [2005] ECR II-2917, [2005] 5 CMLR 922.

[139] On privatisation see Vickers and Yarrow *Privatisation and Economic Analysis* (MIT Press, 1987); Veljanowski *Selling the State – Privatisation in Britain* (Weidenfeld and Nicolson, 1987); *Privatisation and Competition: A Market Prospectus* (Hobart Paperback 28, 1988, ed Veljanowski); Graham and Prosser *Privatising Public Enterprises* (Oxford University Press, 1991).

[140] On the permitted 'reserved area' for letters under EC law, see pp 977–978 below.

[141] See ch 17, pp 690–699 on the essential facilities doctrine, noting the need, discussed there, to impose constraints upon it; these constraints are not so important where a facility was developed by a state-owned monopolist as opposed to an undertaking operating in the private sector.

(C) Regulatory systems in the UK for utilities

In the UK detailed regulatory regimes were established for the industries that were privatised in the 1980s and 1990s, namely telecommunications, gas, electricity, water, and rail transport; these regimes provide, *inter alia*, for price control where persistent market power means that the normal process of competition will not deliver competitive prices to consumers[142]. The regulators – the Office of Communications, the Gas and Electricity Markets Authority, the Water Services Regulation Authority and the Office of Rail Regulation – act as a surrogate for competition, at least until effective competition develops, by imposing constraints on what the regulated undertakings can do; the regulators are charged with the responsibility of protecting consumers, promoting competition where possible and controlling prices. In a sense, regulators 'hold the fort' until competition arrives. Regulated undertakings operate subject to licences that impose obligations upon them and that attempt to prevent conduct, *inter alia*, that will be anti-competitive, discriminatory, or exploitative. The regulators monitor these licences and have powers to enforce compliance with them; in the event of disputes with regulated undertakings as to the appropriate terms for inclusion in a licence, the regulators can make a so-called 'modification reference' to the Competition Commission which will decide whether the matters referred operate, or may be expected to operate, against the public interest, and, if so, whether the effects adverse to the public interest could be remedied by modifications to the licences[143]. The sectoral regulators also have concurrent powers, with the OFT, to apply Articles 81 and 82 EC and the Chapter I and Chapter II prohibitions in the Competition Act 1998 in the sectors for which they are responsible[144].

(D) Price caps

A particular problem in the regulated industries is the control of prices. A central proposition of competition policy is that price should be determined by the market, and not by the state or an agency of the state. Competition authorities take action against excessive prices only rarely[145]. However where there is monopoly or near-monopoly, in particular in relation to essential services such as voice telephony or the supply of electricity, price control may be necessary; where this is the case, various techniques can be deployed to determine what the price should be. One method of capping prices is to fix an upper limit on the rate of return permissible on the capital invested in an industry: this, however, may encourage regulated bodies to over-invest, in order to expand the base on which profit can be earned; furthermore this technique does nothing to encourage efficiency. In the UK the price control function has therefore been exercised through the 'RPI minus X' formula: regulated undertakings are allowed to increase

---

[142] See generally Armstrong, Cowan and Vickers *Regulatory Reform: Economic Analysis and British Experience* (MIT Press, 1994); *Competition in Regulated Industries* (Oxford University Press, 1998, eds Helm and Jenkinson); Baldwin and Cave *Understanding Regulation: Theory, Strategy and Practice* (Oxford University Press, 1999), in particular chs 14–18.

[143] For examples of modification references see *Cellnet and Vodafone* and *British Telecommunications*, 21 January 1999; *AES and British Energy*, 31 January 2001; *Vodafone, O2, Orange, T-Mobile*, 18 February 2003; summaries of these reports can be found at www.competition-commission.org.uk.

[144] On concurrency under the Competition Act 1998 see ch 10, pp 424–426.

[145] See ch 18, pp 709–718.

their prices only by the increase in the Resale Prices Index, less a particular percentage as fixed by the relevant regulator[146]. Over a period of time this formula leads to a reduction in prices in real terms, thereby benefiting the consumer and forcing the privatised industries to increase efficiency in order to continue in profit. The 'RPI minus X' formula encourages firms to become more efficient since, if they can cut their costs, they will make a higher profit. A further benefit of the 'RPI minus X' formula is that it is relatively simple to apply: the regulator simply sets the figure, after which all that is necessary is to check that the price is not being exceeded. When deciding the value of X for the purpose of 'RPI minus X', the industry regulator is asked, in effect, to determine the extent to which added efficiency is possible within the industry in question.

In the text that follows relevant provisions of EC and UK law will be briefly discussed, so that the reader has an idea of the regulatory environment of the electronic communications, post, energy, and water markets and of the possible application of competition law to them. However the text is intended as a mere introduction to subject-matter that is substantial and complex; references to more detailed literature will be provided where appropriate.

8. ELECTRONIC COMMUNICATIONS[147]

(A) EC law

(i) Legislation

There are two 'streams' of Directives of relevance to the electronic communications sector. The first consists of Directives adopted by the Council of Ministers and the European Parliament under Article 95 EC to bring about harmonisation necessary for the establishment of an internal market. A series of Directives, dating back to 1990, had been adopted under Article 95; in March 2001 the Commission produced a Working Document on a *Proposed New Regulatory Framework for Electronic Communications Networks and Services*[148]: the convergence of the telecommunications, media, and information technology sectors meant it was desirable that a single regulatory framework for electronic communications should cover all transmission networks and services.

---

[146] See generally *Incentive Regulation: Reviewing RPI-X and Promoting Competition* (Centre for the Study of Regulated Industries, 1992); Spring 'An Investigation of RPI-X Price Cap Regulation using British Gas as a Case-study' (CRI 1992); Cave and Mill 'Cost Allocation in Regulated Industries' (CRI 1992).

[147] See further Gillies and Marshall *Telecommunications Law* (Butterworths, 2nd ed, 2003), ch 3; Geradin and Kerf *Controlling Market Power in Telecommunications* (OUP, 2003); Nihoup and Rodford *EU Electronic Communications Law* (Oxford University Press, 2004); Garzaniti *Telecommunications, Broadcasting and the Internet: EU Competition Law and Regulation* (Sweet & Maxwell, 2nd ed, 2003); Nikolinakos *EU Competition Law and Regulation in the Converging Telecommunications, Media and IT Sectors* (Kluwer Law International, 2006); Farr and Oakley *EU Communications Law* (Sweet & Maxwell, 2nd ed, 2006); Faull and Nikpay *The EC Law of Competition* (Oxford University Press, 2nd ed, 2007), ch 13; Bellamy and Child *European Community Law of Competition* (Oxford University Press, 6th ed, 2008, eds Roth and Rose), paras 12.087–12.168.

[148] COM (2001) 175 final, 28 March 2001.

This led to the adoption of a new package of five Directives and one Decision in 2002[149]. Under this regulatory framework national regulatory authorities are required to impose regulatory obligations on undertakings in the electronic communications sector that have significant market power, which for this purpose is given the same meaning as 'dominance' in competition law, in any relevant markets. The Commission published a Recommendation on *Relevant Product and Service Markets* to be regulated in accordance with the rules set out in the package[150]: a new Recommendation was published in November 2007[151]; and in July 2002 the Commission published its guidelines on *Market Analysis and the Calculation of Significant Market Power* to be followed by national authorities in reaching their conclusions[152]. A network of national regulatory authorities has been established to facilitate the successful implementation of the regulatory package[153]. There is also a Council and Parliament Regulation of 2000 on *Unbundled Access to the Local* Loop[154]. The Commission reports each year to the Council, the Parliament, ECOSOC and the Committee of the Regions on progress achieved in implementing the Community's electronic communications policy. The Commission has tabled proposals for the regulatory framework to be revised[155].

The second stream of EC legislation consists of Directives adopted by the Commission pursuant to Article 86(3) EC[156]. The first of these was the *Telecommunications Terminal Equipment Directive* of 1988[157], which required Member States to withdraw special or exclusive rights granted to undertakings with respect to the importation, marketing, connection, and bringing into service of telecommunications terminal equipment and the maintenance of such equipment. The Commission subsequently adopted the *Telecommunications Services Directive* of 1990[158], which began the process of opening

---

[149] See Directive of the European Parliament and of the Council on a common regulatory framework for electronic communications networks and services OJ [2002] L 108/33 (the 'Framework Directive'); Directive of the European Parliament and of the Council on the authorisation of electronic communications networks and services OJ [2002] L 108/22 (the 'Authorisation Directive'); Directive of the European Parliament and of the Council on access to, and interconnection of, electronic communications networks and associated facilities OJ [2002] L 108/7 (the 'Access Directive'); Directive of the European Parliament and of the Council on universal service and users' rights relating to electronic communications networks and services OJ [2002] L 108/51 (the 'Universal Service Directive'); Directive of the European Parliament and of the Council concerning the processing of personal data and the protection of privacy in the electronic communications sector OJ [2002] L 201/37 (the 'Data Protection Directive'); and the Radio Spectrum Decision OJ [2002] L 108/1; see Bavasso 'Electronic Communications: A New Paradigm for European Regulation' (2004) 41 Common Market Law Review 87.

[150] OJ [2003] L 114/45.   [151] Available at www.ec.europa.eu/information_society.

[152] OJ [2002] C 165/6, [2002] 5 CMLR 989; these can be accessed at www.ec.europa.eu/comm/competition/liberalization/others.

[153] See Commission Decision of 29 July 2002 establishing the European Regulators Group for Electronic Communications Networks and Services OJ [2002] L 200/38.

[154] Regulation 2887/2000/EC OJ [2000] L 336/00; on the issue of the local loop see Nikolinakos 'Promoting Competition in the Local Access Network: Local Loop Unbundling' (2001) 22 ECLR 266.

[155] See www.ec.europa.eu/information_society/policy/ecomm/tomorrow/reform.

[156] On the Commission's powers to adopt directives under Article 86(3) see ch 6, pp 239–242.

[157] Commission Directive 88/301/EEC OJ [1988] L 131/73, [1991] 4 CMLR 922; on the (mostly unsuccessful) challenge to this Directive see Case C-202/88 *France v Commission* [1991] ECR I-1223, [1992] 5 CMLR 552, and for comment see Naftel 'The Natural Death of a Natural Monopoly' (1993) 14 ECLR 105; on France's failure to implement the Directive correctly see Case C-91/94 *Tranchant v Telephone Store* [1995] ECR I-3911, [1997] 4 CMLR 74; see also Case C-146/00 *Commission v France* [2001] ECR I-9767.

[158] Commission Directive 90/388/EEC, OJ [1990] L 192/10, [1991] 4 CMLR 932; this Directive was unsuccessfully challenged in Cases C-271/90 etc *Spain, Belgium and Italy v Commission* [1992] ECR I-5833, [1993] 4 CMLR 100.

up telecommunications markets themselves to competition. The Services Directive has been amended several times in order to expand its scope; it was successively extended to apply to the satellite[159], cable[160], and mobile telephony[161] sectors, and ultimately required full competition in telecommunications markets[162]. The Commission has also amended the original *Services Directive* to require that, where a single operator owns both a telecommunications and a cable network, they must be established as separate legal entities[163]. A consolidating Directive, bringing all these pieces of legislation into a single legal instrument, was adopted in September 2002[164].

(ii) Application of EC competition law

The Commission has been active in applying the competition rules to the telecommunications sector for many years. In 1991 it published *Guidelines on the Application of EEC Competition Rules in the Telecommunications Sector*[165], and in 1998 it adopted the *Notice on the Application of the Competition Rules to Access Agreements in the Telecommunications Sector*[166]. The latter of these two instruments is of particular interest. Part I is entitled 'Framework', and discusses the relationship between the competition rules and sector-specific regulation. Part II deals with market definition, and Part III provides detailed analysis of the application of the principles of competition law to access agreements; the most extensive discussion is of the essential facilities doctrine under Article 82, but the Notice also contains useful guidance on issues such as network configuration, tying, excessive pricing, predation, vertical price squeezing, and discrimination.

The Commission has adopted numerous favourable decisions on strategic alliances in the electronic communications sector, such as *BT/MCI*[167], *Atlas*[168], *Iridium*[169], *Phoenix/GlobalOne*[170], *Uniworld*[171], *Unisource*[172], *Cégétel+4*[173], and *Télécom Développement*[174]. It also approved the *GSM MoU Standard International Roaming Agreement*, which enables GSM mobile telephone users in one country to use the network in another country[175].

Acting under Article 82 in conjunction with Article 86 the Commission took action against Italy and Spain as a result of their discriminatory treatment of the second operators of mobile telephony in those countries[176]; however it declined to take similar action against Austria, which had not discriminated in favour of the incumbent operator[177].

---

[159] Commission Directive 94/46/EC OJ [1994] L 268/15.
[160] Commission Directive 95/51/EC OJ [1995] L 256/49.
[161] Commission Directive 92/1/EC OJ [1996] L 20/59.
[162] Commission Directive 96/19/EC OJ [1996] L 74/13.
[163] Commission Directive 99/64/EC OJ [1999] L 175/39.
[164] Commission Directive 2002/77/EC OJ [2002] L 249/21.   [165] OJ [1991] C 233/2, [1991] 4 CMLR 946.
[166] OJ [1998] C 265/2, [1998] 5 CMLR 821.   [167] OJ [1994] L 223/36, [1995] 5 CMLR 285.
[168] OJ [1996] L 239/29, [1997] 4 CMLR 89.   [169] OJ [1997] L 16/87, [1997] 4 CMLR 1065.
[170] OJ [1996] L 239/57, [1997] 4 CMLR 147.   [171] OJ [1997] L 318/24, [1998] 4 CMLR 145.
[172] OJ [1997] L 318/1, [1998] 4 CMLR 105; this decision was subsequently withdrawn due to changes in the market: Commission Press Release IP/01/1, 3 January 2001.
[173] OJ [1999] L 218/14, [2000] 4 CMLR 106.   [174] OJ [1999] L 218/24, [2000] 4 CMLR 124.
[175] See the Commission's XXVIIth *Annual Report on Competition Policy* (1997), point 75 and pp 139–140; see also Commission Press Release IP/03/589, 30 April 2003 on the Commission's exemption for a third generation mobile phone network sharing agreement between T-Mobile and MM02.
[176] See *Second Operator of GSM Radiotelephony in Italy* OJ [1995] L 280/49, [1996] 4 CMLR 700; *Second Operator of GSM Radiotelephony in Spain* OJ [1997] L 76/19.
[177] Case T-54/99 *max.mobil Telekommunikation Service GmbH v Commission* [2002] ECR II-313, [2002] 4 CMLR 1356, on appeal Case C-141/02 P *Commission v max.mobil* [2005] ECR I-1283, [2005] 4 CMLR 735.

In 1998 the Commission initiated action in relation to possible excessive or discriminatory prices for calls to mobile telephones[178], which ended in May 1999 following significant price reductions[179]. In 1999 the Commission launched a sector inquiry into three issues, leased lines, mobile roaming services and the local loop[180]. The leased line investigation ended in December 2002, as a result of substantial price decreases[181]. In September 2007 a Regulation of the Council and European Parliament was adopted with the intention of dealing with the problem of excessive prices for international mobile calls[182].

The Commission has taken action on three occasions against incumbent operators for impeding access to the market for the provision of residential broadband internet access: it concluded that Wanadoo of France[183] was guilty of predatory pricing contrary to Article 82; and that Deutsche Telekom of Germany[184] and Telefónica of Spain[185] were guilty of margin squeezes.

The Commission has investigated many concentrations in the telecommunications sector under the ECMR. Of particular interest was *Telia/Telenor*[186], where the Commission granted conditional clearance, following a Phase II investigation, to a proposed concentration between the public telecommunications operators of Sweden and Norway; having received the clearance, the parties decided not to proceed with the transaction. Subsequently, the Commission gave conditional clearance in *Telia/Sonera*[187], the incumbent operators of Sweden and Finland: this merger was consummated in December 2002. The Commission also granted conditional clearance, following a Phase II investigation, to *WorldCom/MCI*[188]; in 2000, however, it prohibited the proposed concentration in *MCI WorldCom/Sprint*[189] which, in its view, would either have created a dominant position for the merged entity or would have reinforced the dominant position of MCI WorldCom in the provision of 'top-level' or universal interconnectivity on the Internet. In the case of *T.Mobile/tele.ring*[190] the Commission granted conditional clearance to a merger that it considered would significantly impede effective competition in the Austrian mobile telephony sector by leading to non-collusive oligopoly.

---

[178] See the Commission's XXVIIIth *Report on Competition Policy* (1998), points 79–81.

[179] See Commission Press Release IP/99/298, 4 May 1999 and Commission's XXIXth *Annual Report on Competition Policy* (1999), pp 375–380.

[180] See the Commission's XXIXth *Report on Competition Policy* (1999), points 74–76; see further the XXXth Report (2000), points 157–160 and XXXIst Report (2001), points 125–131; speech by Sauter 'The Sector Inquiries into Leased Lines and Mobile Roaming: Findings and follow-up of the competition law investigations' 17 September 2001, available at www.europa.eu.int/comm/competition/speeches.

[181] See Commission Press Release IP/02/1852, 11 December 2002; details of the leased line inquires can be found at www.europa.eu.int/comm/competition/antitrust/others/sector_inquiries/leased_lines.

[182] Regulation 717/2007, OJ [2007] L 171/32.

[183] [2005] 5 CMLR 120, upheld on appeal Case T-339/04 *France Télécom v Commission*, judgment of 8 March 2007, on appeal to the ECJ Case C-202/07 P, not yet decided.

[184] OJ [2003] L 263/9, [2004] 4 CMLR 790, on appeal Case T-271/03 *Deutsche Telekom v Commission*, upheld on appeal, judgment of 10 April 2008.

[185] The case is on appeal to the CFI, Case T-336/07 *Telefónica and Telefónica España v Commission*, not yet decided.

[186] Case M 1439 OJ [2001] L 40/1, [2001] 4 CMLR 1226.   [187] Case No COMP/M 2803 [2002] C 201/19.

[188] Case IV/M 1069, OJ [1999] L 116/1, [1999] 5 CMLR 876.

[189] Case COMP/M 1741, annulled on appeal for technical reasons Case T-310/00 *WorldCom v Commission* [2004] ECR II-3253, [2004] 5 CMLR 1274.

[190] Case M 3916, decision of 26 April 2006; on non-collusive oligopoly see ch 21, pp 853–856.

(B) UK law

The Telecommunications Act 1984 established the office of Director General of Telecommunications and the regulatory framework for the telecommunications sector; the position of the Director General of Telecommunications has now been abolished, and his powers have been transferred to the Office of Communications ('OFCOM')[191]. OFCOM is a single regulator for the media and communications industries and has considerable regulatory powers under the Communications Act. It is also responsible for determining whether undertakings in the UK have significant market power under the EU Framework. There is an appeal against OFCOM's findings on SMP to the Competition Appeal Tribunal.

OFCOM has concurrent powers with the OFT to apply Articles 81 and 82 EC and the Chapter I and Chapter II prohibitions in the Competition Act 1998. A Guideline has been adopted under the Act, *Competition Act 1998: The Application in the Telecommunications Sector*[192]. The *Guideline* is divided into seven parts. After an introduction and an explanation of the major provisions of the Act, the *Guideline* goes on to consider the relationship between the Competition Act and EC law. Part 4 of the *Guideline* discusses the relationship between the Competition Act and the Telecommunications Act[193]. Market definition and the assessment of market power are then considered. The *Guideline* concludes with a detailed discussion of how agreements and conduct in the telecommunications sector will be dealt with under the Competition Act; in particular it explains the approach that will be taken to determining costs in a network industry such as telecommunications[194]. The *Guideline* looks in detail at different pricing practices such as predation, price squeezing, and discrimination[195], and it also deals with other types of abuse such as refusal to supply and bundling[196].

OFCOM has adopted numerous decisions in which it concluded that there had been no infringement of the EC or the UK competition rules: these can be found in the Table of Competition Act Decisions in chapter 9[197]. It has also on some occasions closed its file on a complaint without explicitly deciding that there was, or that there was not, an infringement: on one occasion the Competition Appeal Tribunal held that the case closure amounted to an appealable non-infringement decision[198]: this case is not yet resolved.

---

[191] Office of Communications Act 2002, s 1.   [192] OFT Guideline 417 (2000).

[193] Where behaviour may infringe both the Competition Act 1998 and the Telecommunications Act 1984, OFCOM has made clear that it will first investigate under the Competition Act: see Case No 1007/2/3/02 *Freeserve.com plc v Director General of Telecommunications* [2002] CAT 8, [2003] CompAR 1, paras 76–81.

[194] OFT Guideline 417, paras 7.5–7.12.   [195] Ibid, paras 7.13–7.37.   [196] Ibid, paras 7.38–7.57.

[197] See ch 9, pp 367–381.

[198] Case No 1006/2/1/01 *Freeserve.com plc v Director General of Telecommunications* [2002] CAT 6, [2002] CompAR 226; on the meaning of appealable decision see ch 10, pp 427–431.

9. POST[199]

(A) EC law

(i) Legislation

Development of Community law and policy in the postal sector has come about partly through initiatives of the Council of Ministers and the Commission, and partly as a result of the very important judgment of the ECJ in the *Corbeau* case[200]. The Commission first began to take an interest in the postal sector, and the possibility of applying the competition rules to it, in the late 1980s. This culminated in the adoption of the Commission's Green Paper on *The Development of the Single Market for Postal Services*[201]. It proposed that all postal services, except ordinary internal letter deliveries, should be liberalised. In 1993 the Commission issued a communication setting out *Guidelines for the Development of Community Postal Services*[202]. The Council of Ministers asked the Commission to draft a proposal for a legislative framework; there are now two legislative instruments, the Directive of the European Parliament and of the Council on *Common Rules for the Development of the Internal Market of Community Postal Services and the Improvement of Quality of Service*[203] and the Commission *Notice on the Application of the Competition Rules to the Postal Sector*[204]. The Directive was adopted on 1 December 1997 and entered into force on 10 February 1998[205]. The Notice was adopted by the Commission on 17 December 1997. These two measures should be seen as part of a single package, the Directive intended to liberalise access to certain postal activities in the Community and the Notice to ensure that it is understood how the competition rules impact upon the sector.

The Directive establishes common rules throughout the Community on six matters:

- the provision of a universal service
- the extent of the permissible monopoly and the conditions governing the provision of non-monopolised services
- tariff principles and transparency of accounts for universal service provision
- the setting of quality standards for universal service provision
- the harmonisation of technical standards
- the creation of independent national regulatory authorities.

As regards the first two matters the Directive establishes *minimum* standards as to the universal standards and *maximum* limits to the permissible monopoly. Member States are entitled to confer lesser, but not broader, monopoly rights than those set out in the Directive. Article 7(1) provides essentially that the services 'which may be reserved' (that is which may remain a monopoly) shall be 'the clearance, sorting, transport and

---

[199] See further Bellamy and Child *European Community Law of Competition* (Oxford University Press, 6th ed, 2008, eds Roth and Rose), paras 12.004–12.051.

[200] Case C-320/91 *Corbeau* [1993] ECR I-2533, [1995] 4 CMLR 621: see pp 978–979 below.

[201] COM(91)476, June 1991.   [202] COM (93)247.   [203] Directive 97/67/EC, OJ [1998] L 15/14.

[204] OJ [1998] C 39/2, [1998] 5 CMLR 108.

[205] The Directive was implemented in the UK by the Postal Services Regulations 1999, SI 1999/2107.

delivery of items of domestic correspondence, provided they weigh less than 350 grams'. On 10 June 2002, the European Parliament and the Council adopted Directive 2002/39/EC[206] which amends Directive 97/96 and reduces the monopoly to letters weighing less than 50 grams[207]. The new Directive sets 1 January 2009 as a potential date for the accomplishment of the internal market for postal services; the Commission has made a proposal to this effect[208].

(ii) Application of EC competition law

(A) The Corbeau *case and the universal service obligation*[209] There is general agreement among Member States that there are societal benefits in the maintenance of a universal postal service, that is to say a right of access to a minimum range of postal services, of a specified quality, which must be provided in all Member States at affordable prices for the benefit of all users, irrespective of their geographical location. People living in remote rural areas should have access to these services on no less favourable terms than those living in major conurbations; there is an obvious benefit, in terms of social cohesion, if all members of society can communicate with one another through the postal system, no matter where they live. A complex policy issue is to determine whether, and if so how extensive, a legal monopoly needs to be granted to the undertaking charged with performing this universal service in order to enable it to perform its duties; this question turns in part on how costly the universal service obligation is to the undertaking that has to perform it. Clearly the maintenance of a universal service is likely to be expensive, and the relevant provider will need to be assured of sufficient profits to pay for it; competitors should not be able to 'pick the cherries' or, depending on taste, 'skim the cream' and earn profits from lucrative services, while leaving the unprofitable services to the undertaking charged with the universal service obligation.

These issues came before the ECJ in the *Corbeau case*[210]. Corbeau had been charged with infringing a Belgian criminal law which conferred a monopoly on the Regie des Postes to collect, carry, and distribute post in Belgium. Corbeau offered local courier services, but not a basic postal service. The Belgian court sought the opinion of the ECJ on the compatibility of the monopoly conferred by Belgian law with Articles 82 and 86 of the Treaty. The task for the ECJ was to determine whether Belgium was in breach of Article 86(1) in maintaining in force a measure contrary to Article 82, or whether the rights conferred on Régie des Postes satisfied the terms of Article 86(2). This provision does permit a restriction of competition – or even the elimination of all competition – where this is necessary to enable an undertaking to carry on the task entrusted to it[211]. At paragraph 15 of its judgment the ECJ noted that it could not be disputed that Régie des Postes was entrusted with a service of general economic interest[212]; the question was the extent to which a restriction of competition was necessary to enable it to carry on that function[213]. The Court continued at paragraph 17:

The starting point of such an examination must be the premise that the obligation on the part of the undertaking entrusted with that task to perform its services in conditions of economic equilibrium presupposes that it will be possible to offset less profitable sectors against the profitable

---

[206] OJ [2002] L 176/21.   [207] Directive 2002/39/EC, Article 1, amending Article 7 of Directive 97/67/EC.
[208] Available at www.ec.europa.eu/internal_market/post/legislation_en.htm#proposal.
[209] See also Case C-340/99 *TNT Traco SpA v Poste Italiane SpA* [2001] ECR I-4109.   [210] See n 209 above.
[211] See ch 6, pp 233–239.   [212] *Corbeau*, (n 200 above), para 15.   [213] Ibid, para 16.

sectors and hence justifies a restriction of competition from individual undertakings where the economically profitable sectors are concerned.

In the following paragraph the ECJ notes that, in the absence of a monopoly, it would be possible for individual undertakings 'to concentrate on the economically profitable operations' (in other words, to 'cherry pick'). But the ECJ went on, at paragraph 19:

However, the exclusion of competition is not justified as regards specific services dissociable from the service of general interest which meet special needs of economic operators and which call for certain additional services not offered by the traditional postal service, such as collection from the senders' address, greater speed or reliability of distribution or the possibility of changing the destination in the course of transit in so far as such specific services, by their nature and the conditions in which they are offered, such as the geographical area in which they are provided, do not compromise the economic equilibrium of the service of general economic interest performed by the holder of the exclusive right.

At paragraph 20, the ECJ said that the application of the foregoing tests would be a task for the national court dealing with the case.

The importance of this carefully crafted judgment is clear: postal monopolies may be consistent with Community competition law, but subject to the important tests set out in paragraph 19. That paragraph makes clear that it is possible, as a matter of law, that a Member State may have conferred a monopoly that is wider than is legitimate for the purpose of maintaining the universal service, and that, where this is the case, the monopoly rights in question may be unenforceable. The first package of measures in the postal sector attempts on the one hand, in the Directive, to determine the permissible limits of the legal monopoly and on the other, in the Notice, to explain the circumstances in which a legitimate monopolist might nonetheless be found guilty of infringing the competition rules. The Commission has itself taken action to strike down monopolies that go beyond what is justifiable under the *Corbeau* judgment[214].

(B) *The Commission's* Notice on competition in the postal sector[215] This Notice sets out in some detail how the Commission expects to apply the competition rules in the postal sector. It is divided into nine parts. After a preface and a discussion of terminology, the Notice considers market definition in the postal sector. Part 3 considers the issue of cross-subsidisation in some detail; the position of public undertakings and the freedom to provide services are then looked at, followed by state measures and state aid. Part 8 discusses what are meant by services of general economic interest in Article 86(2) EC, and the Notice concludes with a commitment by the Commission to undertake a review of the application of the competition rules to this sector in due course.

(C) *Cases and decisions*[216] In *Spanish International Courier Services*[217] the Commission held that it was unlawful for Spain to reserve to the Spanish Post Office, which already had a monopoly of the basic postal service, the ancillary activity of international courier services. In practice the Spanish Post Office was unable to meet the demand for international courier services (for example it did not cover the whole territory of Spain, nor did it extend to all countries in the world), so that there was a limitation of supply and

---

[214] On the Commission's infringement proceedings see below.

[215] OJ [1998] C 39/2, [1998] 5 CMLR 108.

[216] See Flynn and Rizza 'Postal Services and Competition Law – A Review and Analysis of the EC Case Law' (2002) 25 World Competition 475.

[217] OJ [1990] L 233/19, [1991] 4 CMLR 560.

technical development in the sense of Article 82(2)(b) EC. A similar decision in *Dutch Express Delivery Services*[218] was annulled on appeal by the ECJ as the Commission had not followed the correct procedure in adopting its decision[219]. In *Deutsche Post AG*[220] the Commission imposed a fine of €24 million on Deutsche Post for offering loyalty rebates to customers of its business parcels service, and it also concluded that it was guilty of predatory pricing[221]. In *New Postal Services with a Guaranteed Day- or Time-Certain Delivery in Italy*[222] the Commission concluded that an Italian Decree excluding competition for a specific type of hybridised electronic mail service was contrary to Article 86(1) in conjunction with Article 82. In *Reims II*[223] the Commission decided that the criteria of Article 81(3) were satisfied in the case of an agreement between the postal operators of the EC as to the amount that one operator would pay to another when a letter posted in the former's country had to be delivered in the territory of the latter, so-called 'terminal dues'. There has been a long-running battle between the Union Francaise de l'Express, La Poste of France, and the Commission, in relation to international express mail[224]. In *De Post/La Poste*[225] the Commission imposed a fine of €2.5 million on the Belgian postal operator for giving a more favourable tariff for its general letter mail service to those customers who also used its new business-to-business mail service. In *UPS v Commission*[226] the CFI upheld the Commission's rejection of a complaint by UPS that Deutsche Post was guilty of an abuse of a dominant position by using income from its reserved letter market to finance the acquisition of a shareholding in the express parcels operator DHL.

A number of concentrations have been notified to the Commission under the ECMR. In the first case, *TNT/Canada Post*[227], the establishment of a joint venture between TNT and five postal administrations for the purpose of offering worldwide international express delivery services was cleared, subject to the offering of commitments by the four European postal administrations concerned that they would not discriminate in favour of the joint venture (the Canadian Post Office was not asked to give such a commitment). Similar commitments have been offered in subsequent cases[228]. The Commission granted conditional clearance to a joint venture in *Post Office/TPG/SPPL*[229].

[218]   OJ [1990] L 10/47, [1990] 4 CMLR 947.

[219]   Cases C-48/90 & 66/90 *Netherlands v Commission* [1992] ECR I-565, [1993] 5 CMLR 316.

[220]   OJ [2001] L 125/27 [2001] 5 CMLR 99; see also *Deutsche Post AG II* OJ [2001] L 331/40 [2002] 4 CMLR 598 imposing a 'symbolic' fine of €1,000 on Deutsche Post for abusing its dominant position in relation to so-called 'A-B-A remail'.

[221]   For discussion of the Commission's approach to predatory pricing in this case see ch 18, p 737.

[222]   OJ [2001] L 63/59.

[223]   OJ [1999] L 275/17, [2000] 4 CMLR 704: the Commission renewed the authorisation it had given in this case: OJ [2004] L 56/76, [2004] 5 CMLR 123; on the REIMS agreement see Reeves 'Terminal Problems in the Postal Sector' (2000) 21 ECLR 283; see also Cases C-147/97 and C-148/97 *Deutsche Post v GZS* [2000] ECR I-825, [2000] 4 CMLR 838, dealing with the right of Deutsche Post to impose charges for cross-border mail prior to the agreement on terminal dues.

[224]   The latest judgments handed down by the CFI in this dispute were in Case T-77/95 *Union Française de l'Express v Commission* [2000] ECR II-2167, [2001] 4 CMLR 1210 and a state aid case: Case T-613/97 *Union Francaise de l'Express and others v Commission* [2000] ECR II-4055, on appeal Cases C-83/01 P etc *Ufex and others v Commission* [2003] ECR I-6993, [2003] 3 CMLR 303.

[225]   OJ [2002] L 61/32, [2002] 4 CMLR 1426.

[226]   Case T-175/99 [2002] ECR II-1915, [2002] 5 CMLR 67.

[227]   Case M 102, decision of 2 December 2001.

[228]   See eg Case M 787 *PTT Post/TNT-GD Net*, decision of 22 July 1996 and Case M 1168 *DHL/Deutsche Post*, decision of 26 June 1998.

[229]   Case M 1915, decision of 13 March 2001.

(B) UK law

The Postal Services Act 2000 established the Postal Services Commission and the regulatory framework for the postal sector. The Commission does not have concurrent powers to apply Articles 81 and 82 EC and the Chapter I and Chapter II prohibitions in the Competition Act; the OFT alone can exercise these powers. A 'Decision Document' has been published containing a Memorandum of Understanding between Postcomm and the OFT as to how they will proceed where they have overlapping powers[230]. In June 2001 the OFT decided that the UK Post Office had not abused its dominant position in the postal services market by refusing to license its Royal Mail trade mark to an operator in the market for consumer lifestyle surveys[231].

10. GAS[232]

(A) EC law

(i) Legislation

The Council of Ministers has adopted four Directives in the gas sector. The first establishes a procedure to improve the transparency of prices for gas in the EC[233]. The second Directive requires Member States to take steps to ensure the possibility of transit of gas between Member States[234]. The third Directive establishes common rules for the storage, transmission and distribution of natural gas[235]. The fourth Directive establishes common rules for the internal market in gas[236].

(ii) Application of EC competition law

The Commission gave its approval in 1995 to a joint venture established by nine gas companies to construct and operate a gas interconnector between the UK and Belgium[237]. In 1996 it approved a long-term take-or-pay agreement for the supply of natural gas from Algeria to Portugal in *Transgás/Turbogás*[238] and the arrangements for use of the gas transport network in the UK in *British Gas Network Code*[239]. In 2000 it closed its investigation of a long-term supply agreement between a Spanish natural gas company and a Spanish electricity generator after the parties modified the terms of the agreement[240].

---

[230] June 2003, available at www.postcomm.gov.uk.

[231] See *Consignia/Postal Preference Service Ltd*, 15 June 2001, available at www.oft.gov.uk; see also the interim High Court judgment in *Claritas v Post Office* [2001] UKCLR 2.

[232] See further Faull and Nikpay *The EC Law of Competition* (Oxford University Press, 2nd ed, 2007), ch 12; *Bellamy and Child*, ch 12, Part 3, paras 12.073–12.083; Cameron *Competition in Energy Markets: Law and Regulation in the European Union* (Oxford University Press, 2nd ed, 2007).

[233] Council Directive 90/377/EEC OJ [1990] L 185/16.

[234] Council Directive 91/296/EEC OJ [1991] L 147/37, as amended by Council Directive 95/49/EC, OJ [1995] L 233/86.

[235] Council Directive 98/30/EC OJ [1998] L 204/1, as amended by Corrigendum OJ [1998] L 245/43.

[236] Council Directive 2003/55/EC OJ [2003] L 176/57.

[237] See the Commission's XXVth *Report on Competition Policy* (1995), point 82.

[238] See the Commission's XXVIth *Report on Competition Policy* (1996), p 135.

[239] See the Commission's XXVIth *Report on Competition Policy* (1996), pp 136–137.

[240] See the Commission's XXXth *Report on Competition Policy* (2000), pp 154–155.

In more recent years the Commission has become more anxious about restrictions of competition in the gas (and electricity) sector. It conducted a sector inquiry under Article 17 of the Modernisation Regulation and concluded that energy markets in Europe were not functioning well: in particular many energy markets are highly concentrated; there is an absence of cross-border integration and cross-border competition; and there is insufficient unbundling of network and supply activities[241]. The Commission subsequently proposed a third package of legislative proposals, including network unbundling, that is to say the separation of the supply and generation of gas and electricity from the operation of the networks that transmit them[242]. The proposals are controversial, and some Member States are strongly opposed to them.

In the meantime the Commission has taken action (or is taking action) in a number of cases involving territorial restrictions and profit-sharing mechanisms in gas supply agreements[243], long-term supply contracts for gas[244], or refusals to grant access to gas pipelines[245].

The Commission has investigated several mergers involving undertakings in the gas sector[246].

(B) UK law[247]

The Gas Act 1986 established a regulatory regime for the gas sector. Section 1 of the Act created the post of Director General of Gas Supply, who headed the former Office of Gas Supply. The powers of the Director General of Gas Supply were transferred to the Gas and Electricity Markets Authority ('GEMA') by the Utilities Act 2000; the Authority is assisted by OFGEM. GEMA has concurrent powers with the OFT to apply Articles 81 and 82 EC and the Chapter I and Chapter II prohibitions in the Competition Act 1998. A *Guideline* has been adopted under the Act, *Competition Act 1998: Application in the Energy Sector*[248]. GEMA has adopted one infringement decision under its concurrent powers, imposing a fine of £46.1 million on National Grid plc for abusing its dominant position in the market for the supply of domestic gas meters[249].

Concerns about energy prices led the GEMA to launch an investigation into the markets in gas and electricity for households and small businesses in February 2008[250].

[241] COM(2006)851 final; see the speech of Commission Kroes on this: SPEECH/07/186, 26 March 2007.

[242] See Commission Press Release IP/07/1361, 19 September 2007; for more detail see www.ec.europa.eu/energy/electricity/package_2007; see also Wäktare, Kovács and Gee 'The Energy Sector Inquiry: conclusions and way forward' *Competition Policy Newsletter*, Spring 2007, 55; Lowe, Pucinskaite, Webster and Lindberg 'Effective unbundling of energy transmission networks: lessons from the Energy Sector Inquiry' *Competition Policy Newsletter*, Spring 2007, 23.

[243] See Wäktare 'Territorial restrictions and profit sharing mechanisms in the gas sector: the Algerian case' *Competition Policy Newsletter*, Number 3, 2007, 19.

[244] See eg *Distrigas* where the Commission accepted commitments to reduce the length of gas supply agreements under Article 9 of the Modernisation Regulation: see ch 17, p 676.

[245] See ch 17, p 698.

[246] See Faull and Nikpay *The EC Law of Competition* (Oxford University Press, 2nd ed, 2007), paras 14.428–12.469.

[247] See Harker and Waddams 'Introducing Competition and Deregulating the British Domestic Energy Markets: a Legal and Economic Discussion' [2007] Journal of Business Law 244.

[248] OFT 428, January 2005.

[249] Decision of 25 February 2008, on appeal Case 1097/1/2/08 *National Grid plc v Gas and Electricity Markets Authority*, not yet decided.

[250] See OFGEM Press Release of 21 February 2008, available at www.ofgem.gov.uk.

11. ELECTRICITY[251]

(A) EC law

(i) Legislation

The Council of Ministers has adopted four Directives in the electricity sector. The first establishes a procedure to improve the transparency of prices for electricity in the EC[252]. The second Directive requires Member States to take steps to ensure the possibility of transit of electricity between Member States[253]. The third Directive establishes common rules for the internal market in electricity[254]. The fourth Directive provides for full liberalisation of electricity markets[255].

(ii) Application of EC competition law

The Commission has investigated a number of agreements in the electricity sector. The privatisation of the electricity industry in Great Britain led to a decision that the criteria of Article 81(3) were satisfied in *Scottish Nuclear, Nuclear Energy Agreement*[256] and to two notices in the Official Journal dealing with numerous agreements that had been notified to the Commission under the system of notification for individual exemption in force at that time[257]. In *Northern Irish Electricity*[258] the Commission proposed to take no action as there was no trade between Northern Ireland and any other Member State of the EC. A joint venture to develop independent generators of electricity was the subject of a favourable notice in the Official Journal in 1992[259]. In *IJsselcentrale*[260] the Commission held that an agreement between all the generators of electricity in the Netherlands and a joint subsidiary that only the latter could import and export electricity to and from that country entailed a restriction of competition that infringed Article 81(1). In *REN/Turbogás*[261] and in *ISAB Energy*[262] the Commission approved long-term agreements for the supply of electricity.

The Commission's sector inquiry, referred to in the section on gas above[263], was also concerned with competitive conditions in the electricity sector. In February 2008 E.ON made a proposal to sell its electricity transmission system to an operator with no interests in the generation or supply of electricity: the Commission welcomed this announcement and said that it was exploring the possibility of accepting commitments from E.ON under Article 9 of the Modernisation Regulation[264].

---

[251] See further Faull and Nikpay *The EC Law of Competition* (Oxford University Press, 2nd ed, 2007), ch 12; *Bellamy and Child*, ch 12, Part 3, paras 12.059–12.072; Cameron *Competition in Energy Markets: Law and Regulation in the European Union* (Oxford University Press, 2nd ed, 2007).

[252] Council Directive 90/377/EEC OJ [1990] L 185/16.

[253] Council Directive 90/547/EEC OJ [1990] L 313/30.

[254] Council Directive 96/92/EC OJ [1997] L 27/20.   [255] Council Directive 2003/54, OJ [2003] L 176/37.

[256] OJ [1991] L 178/31.

[257] See OJ [1990] C 191/9 (dealing with ten notifications) and OJ [1990] C 245/9 (dealing with eight notifications).

[258] OJ [1992] C 92/5.   [259] OJ [1992] C 92/4.

[260] OJ [1991] L 28/32, [1992] 5 CMLR 154; the decision was (eventually) partly annulled on appeal in Case T-16/91 RV *Rendo v Commission* [1996] ECR II-1827, [1997] 4 CMLR 453.

[261] OJ [1996] C 118/7, [1996] 4 CMLR 881.   [262] OJ [1996] C 138/3, [1996] 4 CMLR 889.

[263] See p 982.   [264] Commission MEMO/08/132, 28 February 2008.

The Commission has investigated several mergers involving undertakings in the electricity sector[265].

(B) UK law

The Electricity Act 1989 established a regulatory regime for the electricity sector. The powers of the Director General of Electricity Supply were transferred by the Utilities Act 2000 to the Gas and Electricity Markets Authority, which has concurrent powers to apply the Articles 81 and 82 EC and the Competition Act 1998 with the OFT[266]. There is a *Guideline* on the application of the Act to the energy sector[267], and a *Guideline* on its application to the energy sector in Northern Ireland[268].

12. WATER

The Water Industry Act 1991 provides a regulatory regime for water in the UK: the regulator is the Water Services Regulation Authority (formerly the Director General of Water Services), assisted by OFWAT[269]. The Authority has concurrent powers with the OFT to apply Articles 81 and 82 EC and the Chapter I and Chapter II prohibitions in the Competition Act 1998. A Guideline has been adopted under the Act, *Competition Act 1998: Application in the Water and Sewerage Sectors*[270]. OFWAT regulates prices for the provision of water to households; there is no competition in the UK for the supply of residential customers. Theoretically it is possible for undertakings to compete for large industrial customers that use at least 50 megalitres of water a year, but competition has been slow to emerge[271]. There have been several complaints about exclusionary behaviour by incumbents in the water sector, but the Authority has always concluded either that there was no infringement[272] or that the complaint was not one that it wished to pursue under competition law[273]. One case is particularly striking, *Albion Water Ltd v Water Services Regulation Authority*[274], where the Authority had rejected two complaints against an incumbent water undertaking, Dŵr Cymru. On appeal the Competition Appeal Tribunal concluded that Dŵr Cymru was guilty of a margin squeeze and annulled the Authority's decision to the contrary[275]. The judgment of the CAT was upheld on appeal to the Court of Appeal[276]. The CAT is continuing to

---

[265] See Faull and Nikpay *The EC Law of Competition* (Oxford University Press, 2nd ed, 2007), paras 14.428–12.469.

[266] See p 982 above.   [267] OFT 428, January 2005.   [268] OFT 437, July 2001.

[269] OFWAT's website is www.ofwat.gov.uk.

[270] OFT 422, February 2000; see also Bailey 'The Emerging Co-existence of Regulation and Competition Law in the UK Water Industry' (2002) 25 World Competition 127.

[271] See the 'preliminary observations' of the Competition Appeal Tribunal in Case 1046/2/4/04 *Albion Water Ltd v Director General of Water Services* [2005] CAT 40, paras 248–257.

[272] See the Table of Competition Act Decisions in ch 9, pp 367–381.

[273] See eg Case No 1058/2/4/06 *Independent Water Company v OFWAT* [2007] CAT 6, [2007] UKCLR 614.

[274] Case 1046/2/4/04.

[275] [2006] CAT 36, [2007] UKCLR 328.

[276] *Dŵr Cymru Cy fyngedig v Water Services Regulation Authority*, judgment of 22 May 2008, [2008] EWCA Civ 536.

investigate whether Dŵr Cymru was also guilty of charging Albion Water excessive prices for the transmission of water through its pipelines.

There are special rules requiring certain mergers between water companies to be referred to the Competition Commission; these have been amended, to bring the system more closely into alignment with the law on 'normal' mergers under the Enterprise Act 2002[277].

In May 2008 OFWAT published the second part of its *Review of Competition* in which it recommended that contestable water and sewerage markets should be opened to competition[278].

[277] See ch 22, pp 954–955.
[278] See OFWAT PN 13/08, 16 May 2008.

Bibliography

There is a considerable body of literature on competition law. The following books are particularly recommended.

UK and EC competition law combined

Dabbah *EC and UK Competition Law: Commentary, Cases and Materials* (Cambridge University Press, 2004)

Furse *Competition Law of the UK and EC* (Oxford University Press, 6th ed, 2008)

Jephcott and Lübbig *Law of Cartels* (Jordan Publishing, 2003)

Middleton *UK and EC Competition Documents* (Blackstone's Statutes Series, 5th ed, 2007)

Middleton, Rodger and MacCulloch *Cases and Materials on UK and EC Competition Law* (Oxford University Press, 2003)

Rodger and MacCulloch *Competition Law and Policy* (Cavendish Publishing Ltd, 4th ed, 2008)

Slot and Johnston *An Introduction to Competition Law* (Hart Publishing, 2006)

EC competition law

Albors-Llorens *EC Competition Law and Policy* (Willan Publishing, 2003)

Bavasso *Communications in EU Antitrust Law: Market Power and Public Interest* (Kluwer Law International, 2003)

Bellamy and Child *European Community Law of Competition* (Sweet & Maxwell, 6th ed, 2008, eds Roth and Rose)

Buendia Sierra *Exclusive Rights and State Monopolies under EC Law* (Oxford University Press, 1999)

Competition Cases from the European Union (Sweet & Maxwell, 2007, ed Kokkoris)

Competition Law: European Community Practice and Procedure (Sweet & Maxwell, 2007, eds Hirsch and Montag)

EC Competition Procedure (Oxford University Press, 2nd ed, 2006, ed Ortiz Blanco)

Faull and Nikpay *The EC Law of Competition* (Oxford University Press, 2nd ed, 2007)

Garzaniti *Telecommunications, Broadcasting and the Internet: EU Competition Law and Regulation* (Sweet & Maxwell, 2nd ed, 2003)

Geradin and Kerf *Controlling Market Power in Telecommunications* (Oxford University Press, 2003)

D Goyder *EC Competition Law* (Oxford University Press, 4th ed, 2003)

J Goyder *EU Distribution Law* (Hart Publishing, 4th ed, 2005)

Jones and Sufrin *EC Competition Law: Text, Cases and Materials* (Oxford University Press, 3rd ed, 2008)

Jones and van der Woude *EC Competition Law Handbook* (Sweet & Maxwell, 2007/2008 edition)

Kerse and Khan *EC Antitrust Procedure* (Sweet & Maxwell, 5th ed, 2005)

Komninos *EC Private Antitrust Enforcement: Decentralised Application of EC Competition Law by National Courts* (Hart Publishing, 2008)

Korah *Cases and Materials on EC Competition Law* (Hart Publishing, 3rd ed, 2006)

Korah *An Introductory Guide to EC Competition Law and Practice* (Hart Publishing, 9th ed, 2007)

Korah and O'Sullivan *Distribution Agreements under the EC Competition Rules* (Hart Publishing, 2002)

Monti *EC Competition Law* (Cambridge University Press, 2007)

Nazzini *Concurrent Proceedings in Competition Law* (Oxford University Press, 2004)

O'Donoghue and Padilla *The Law and Economics of Article 82 EC* (Hart Publishing, 2006)

Odudu *The Boundaries of EC Competition Law* (Oxford University Press, 2006)

Ortiz Blanco *Shipping Conferences under EC Antitrust Law* (Hart Publishing, 2007)

Prosser *The Limits of Competition Law: Markets and Public Services* (Oxford University Press, 2005)

Ritter, Braun and Rawlinson *European Competition Law: A Practitioner's Guide* (Kluwer Law International, 3rd ed, 2005)

Robertson *Distribution Agreements Under EC Competition Law: An Analytical Review* (in press, 2008)

Sakkers and Ysewyn *European Cartel Digest* (Wolters Kluwer, 2008)

Szyszczak *The Regulation of the State in Competitive Markets in the EU* (Hart Publishing, 2007)

Van Bael and Bellis *Competition Law of the European Community* (Kluwer Law International, 4th ed, 2005)

Wesseling *The Modernisation of EC Antitrust Law* (Hart Publishing, 2000)

Wils *The Optimal Enforcement of EC Antitrust Law: Essays in Law and Economics* (Kluwer Law International, 2002)

Wils *Principles of European Antitrust Enforcement* (Hart Publishing, 2005)

Wils *Efficiency and Justice in European Antitrust Enforcement* (Hart Publishing, 2008)

UK competition law

Furse and Nash *The Cartel Offence* (Hart Publishing, 2004)

O'Neill and Sanders *UK Competition Procedure* (Oxford University Press, 2007)

Ward and Smith *Competition Litigation in the UK* (Sweet & Maxwell, 2005)

Mergers and concentrations

Bankes and Hadden *UK Merger Control: Law and Practice* (LexisNexis Butterworths, 2006)

Broberg *The European Commission's Jurisdiction to Scrutinise Mergers* (Kluwer Law International, 3rd ed, 2006)

Cook and Kerse *EC Merger Control* (Sweet & Maxwell, 4th ed, 2005)

Davies and Lyons *Mergers and Merger Remedies in the EU* (Edward Elgar, 2008)

Finbow and Parr *UK Merger Control: Law and Practice* (Sweet & Maxwell, 2nd ed, 2005)

Furse *The Law of Merger Control in the EC and the UK* (Hart Publishing, 2007)

Levy *European Merger Control Law: A Guide to the Merger Regulation* (LexisNexis, 2003)

Lindsay *The EC Merger Regulation: Substantive Issues* (Sweet & Maxwell, 2nd ed, 2006)

Navarro, Font, Folguera and Briones *Merger Control in the EU* (Oxford University Press, 2002)

Rowley and Baker *Merger Control: The International Regulation of Mergers and Joint Ventures* (Sweet & Maxwell, 3rd ed, 2000)

Wilson *Globalization and the Limits of National Merger Control Laws* (Kluwer Law International, 2003)

Intellectual property

Anderman *EC Competition Law and Intellectual Property Rights: The Regulation of Innovation* (Clarendon Press Oxford, 1998)

Anderman and Kallaugher *Technology and the New EU Competition Rules: Intellectual Property Licensing after Modernisation* (Oxford University Press, 2006)

Cornish and Llewellyn *Intellectual Property Law* (Sweet & Maxwell, 6th ed, 2007)

Korah *Intellectual Property Rights and the EC Competition Rules* (Hart Publishing, 2006)

Economics

Bishop and Walker *The Economics of EC Competition Law: Concepts, Application and Measurement* (Sweet & Maxwell, 2nd ed, 2003)

Black *Oxford Dictionary of Economics* (Oxford University Press, 3rd ed, 2003)

Carlton and Perloff *Modern Industrial Organisation* (Addison Wesley, 4th ed, 2005)

Hildebrand *The Role of Economics in the EC Competition Rules* (Kluwer, 2nd ed, 2002)

Hylton *Antitrust Law: Economic Theory and Common Law Evolution* (Cambridge University Press, 2003)

Lipsey and Chrystal *Principles of Economics* (Oxford University Press, 11th ed, 2007)

Motta *Competition Policy: Theory and Practice* (Cambridge University Press, 2004)

Scherer and Ross *Industrial Market Structure and Economic Performance* (Houghton Mifflin, 3rd ed, 1990)

Sullivan and Harrison *Understanding Antitrust and Its Economic Implications* (LexisNexis, 4th ed, 2003)

Tirole *The Theory of Industrial Organisation* (MIT Press, 1988)

Van den Bergh and Camesasca *European Competition Law and Economics: A Comparative Perspective* (Sweet & Maxwell, 2006)

Miscellaneous

Alese *Federal Antitrust and EC Competition Law Analysis* (Ashgate, 2008)

Amato *Antitrust and the Bounds of Power: The Dilemma of Liberal Democracy in the History of the Market* (Hart Publishing, 1997)

Bork *The Antitrust Paradox* (The Free Press, 1993)

Elhauge and Geradin *Global Competition Law and Economics* (Hart Publishing, 2007)

Gal *Competition Policy for Small Market Economies* (Harvard University Press, 2003)

Gerber *Law and Competition in Twentieth Century Europe* (Oxford University Press, 1998)

Jones *Private Enforcement of Antitrust Law in the EU, UK and USA* (Oxford University Press, 1999)

Posner *Antitrust Law* (The University of Chicago Press, 2nd ed, 2001)

Yeung *Securing Compliance with Competition Law* (Hart Publishing, 2003)

Statutes, treaties, community regulations etc

Butterworths Competition Law Handbook (Butterworths, 12th ed, 2006)

Middleton *Statutes on Competition Law* (Oxford University Press, 5th ed, 2007)

Important websites

Competition Appeal Tribunal	www.catribunal.org.uk
Competition Commission	www.competition-commission.org.uk
Department for Business, Enterprise and Regulatory Reform	www.berr.gov.uk
European Commission, DG COMP	www.europa.eu.int/comm/competition
European Court of Justice	www.curia.eu.int
International Competition Network	www.internationalcompetitionnetwork.org
Office of Fair Trading	www.oft.gov.uk
Organisation for Economic Cooperation and Development	www.oecd.org
US Department of Justice	www.usdoj.gov
US Federal Trade Commission	www.ftc.gov

Index